Voter Registration Application

Before completing this form, review the General, Application, and State s

Are you a citizen of the United States of America?	☐ Yes	☐ No	This space for office
Will you be 18 years old on or before election day?	☐ Yes	☐ No	D0473109

If you checked "No" in response to either of these questions, do not complete form.
(Please see state-specific instructions for rules regarding eligibility to register prior to age 18.)

1	(Circle one) Mr. Mrs. Miss Ms.	Last Name	First Name	Middle Name(s)	(Circle one) Jr Sr II III IV

2	Home Address	Apt. or Lot #	City/Town	State	Zip Code
3	Address Where You Get Your Mail If Different From Above		City/Town	State	Zip Code

4	Date of Birth ___ / ___ / ___ Month Day Year	5	Telephone Number (optional)	6	ID Number - (See Item 6 in the instructions for your state)
7	Choice of Party (see item 7 in the instructions for your State)	8	Race or Ethnic Group (see item 8 in the instructions for your State)		

9 I have reviewed my state's instructions and I swear/affirm that:

- I am a United States citizen
- I meet the eligibility requirements of my state and subscribe to any oath required.
- The information I have provided is true to the best of my knowledge under penalty of perjury. If I have provided false information, I may be fined, imprisoned, or (if not a U.S. citizen) deported from or refused entry to the United States.

Please sign full name (or put mark)

Date: ___ / ___ / ___
Month Day Year

If you are registering to vote for the first time: please refer to the application instructions for information on submitting copies of valid identification documents with this form.

Please fill out the sections below if they apply to you.

If this application is for a **change of name,** what was your name before you changed it?

A	Mr. Mrs. Miss Ms.	Last Name	First Name	Middle Name(s)	(Circle one) Jr Sr II III IV

If you were **registered before but this is the first time you are registering from the address in Box 2**, what was your address where you were registered before?

B	Street (or route and box number)	Apt. or Lot #	City/Town/County	State	Zip Code

If you live in a rural area but do not have a street number, or if you have no address, please show on the map where you live.

C

- Write in the names of the crossroads (or streets) nearest to where you live.
- Draw an **X** to show where you live.
- Use a dot to show any schools, churches, stores, or other landmarks near where you live, and write the name of the landmark.

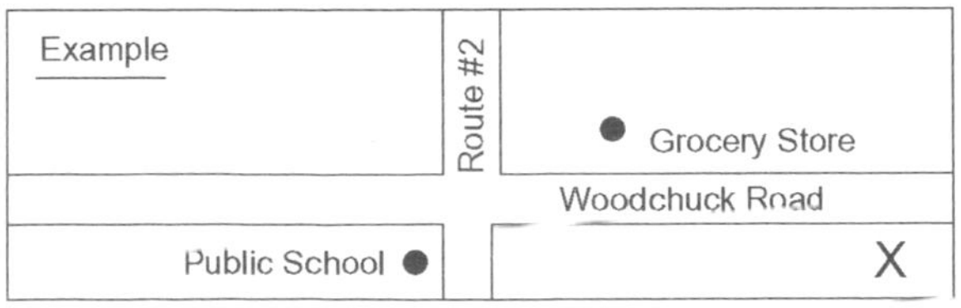

If the applicant is unable to sign, who helped the applicant fill out this application? Give name, address and phone number (phone number optional).

D

Mail this application to the address provided for your State.

Revised 10/29/2003

If you're wondering why you should buy this new edition of *Living Democracy*, here are 10 good reasons!

1. **The 2008 presidential campaigns and elections** are explored throughout the book, including the 2008 primary season, the party conventions, the role of the media, the historic nomination and election of Barack Obama, and voter turnout. Figures and tables have also been updated with complete information on the 2008 elections.

2. With **expanded learning goals, outlines, and review pedagogy** in each chapter, this edition provides clear tools to make studying and learning more effective. **Key Objective Outlines** appear at the beginning of each chapter, with a **Key Question**—modeled after the type of questions often found on tests—tied to each section to help you focus on the most important ideas. **Extended Key Term Definitions** provide more background, with Key Terms defined at the top of the page. An illustrative example of each term appears next to the definition to fully explain the significance of the term in context.

3. **Key Questions** for each main section of the chapter highlight the most crucial information. **Key Objective Review, Apply, and Explore** sections at the end of the chapter include a summary statement about each major section, a list of the Key Terms, Critical Thinking Questions, Internet Resources, and Additional Readings.

4. **"Pathways of Change from Around the World"** offer a comparative perspective by spotlighting stories of political action by young persons in different parts of the world.

5. **"Student Profile"** sections showcase the actions and accomplishments of young persons who have become active in American politics or engaged in making changes in public life.

6. A deep exploration of the **Bush presidency** looks at its effect on the future of presidential powers (Chapter 7), and explores presidential power and global economic change.

7. The ways in which technology is affecting mass communication, the **changing nature of technology** with regard to the use of social networking sites as a tool for campaign communication, and the use of text messaging as a new tool for mass communication are discussed (Chapter 10 and Chapter 12).

8. The **interest groups and political engagement** chapter (Chapter 11) stresses the need for participation and clearly outlines the role of interest in the democratic process. The changing use of technology is discussed, with a focus on new uses of technology in both direct and indirect lobbying.

9. The **current economic situation** is explored, including the subprime mortgage crisis and the Emergency Economic Stabilization Act of 2008, the so-called "Wall Street-Bailout Bill" (Chapter 6) as well as how economic considerations shape the balance of power in our federal system (Chapter 3).

10. **MyPoliSciLab,** Pearson's interactive website offering an array of multimedia activities—videos, simulations, exercises, and online newsfeeds—has been fully integrated with this edition to make learning more effective.

PEARSON

ELECTORAL COLLEGE VOTES IN THE 2008 ELECTION

THE UNITED STATES
A political map showing the number of electoral votes per state

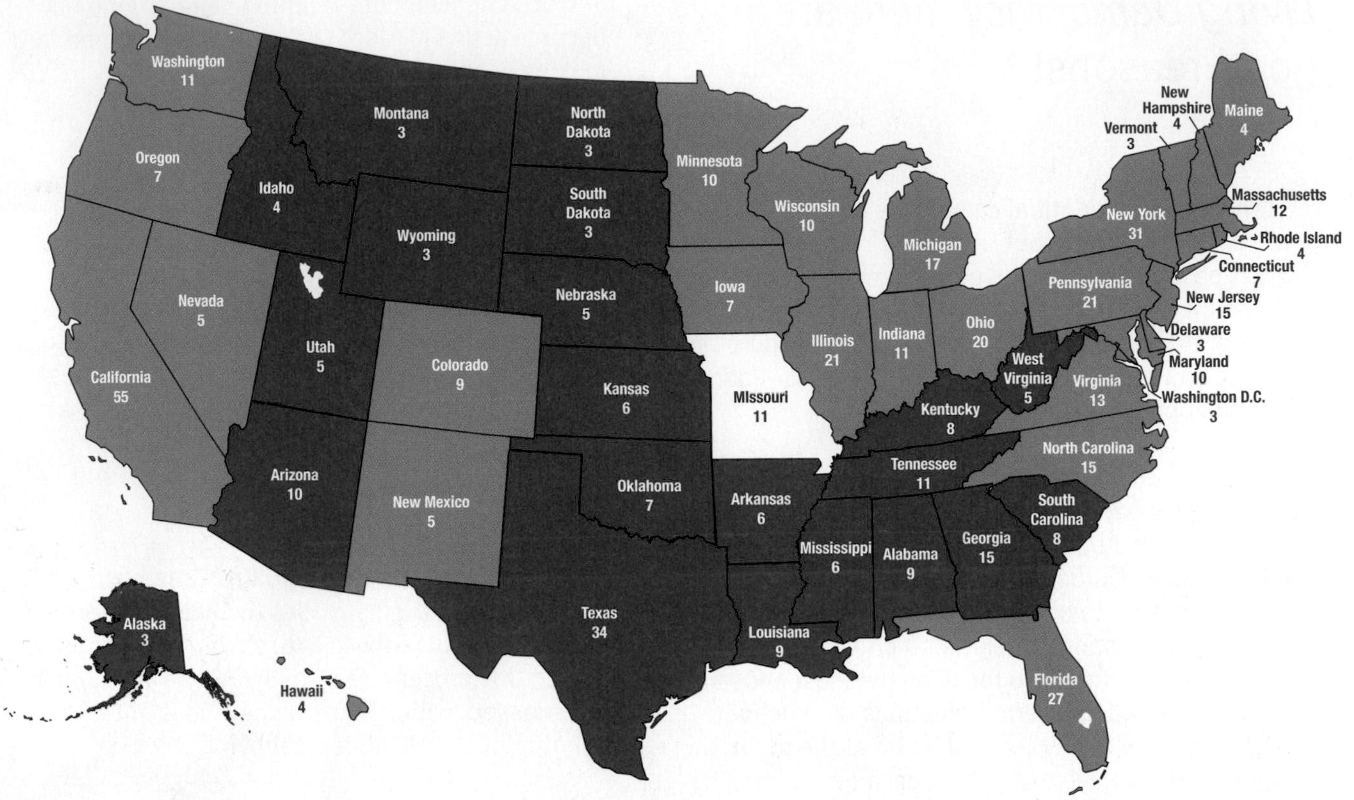

A political map with states drawn in proportion to the number of electoral votes

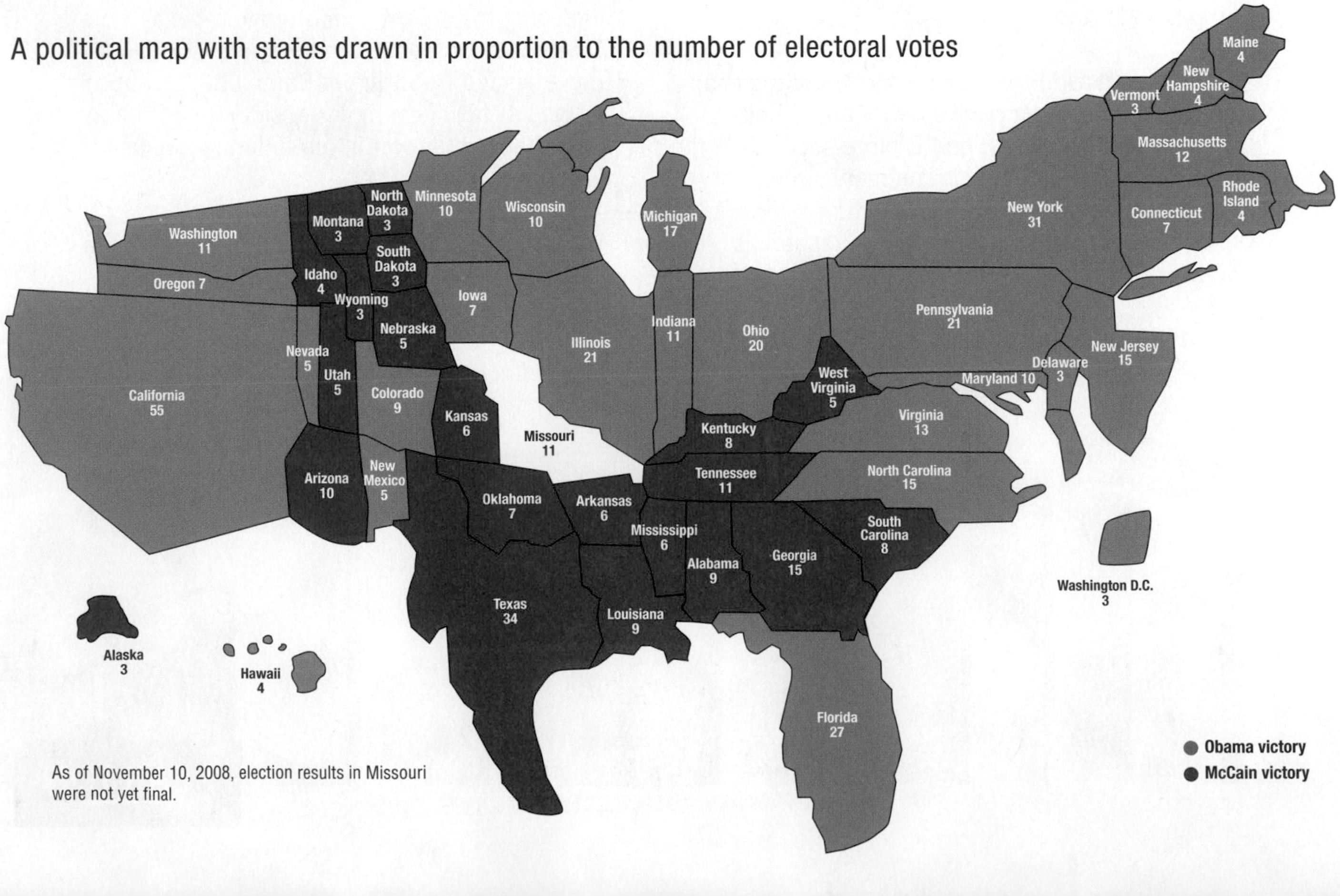

As of November 10, 2008, election results in Missouri were not yet final.

Second Edition

Living DEMOCRACY
BRIEF NATIONAL EDITION

Daniel M. Shea
Allegheny College

Joanne Connor Green
Texas Christian University

Christopher E. Smith
Michigan State University

Longman

New York San Francisco Boston
London Toronto Sydney Tokyo Singapore Madrid
Mexico City Munich Paris Cape Town Hong Kong Montreal

To all the first-time voters and newly active campaign volunteers who helped reinvigorate our democracy by their participation in the 2008 election

Editor-in-Chief: Eric Stano
Assistant Development Manager: David B. Kear
Senior Development Editor: Leah R. Strauss
Associate Development Editor: Donna Garnier
Director of Marketing: Brandy Dawson
Marketing Manager: Lindsey Prudhomme
Production Manager: Eric Jorgensen
Project Coordination, Text Design, Visual Research, and Electronic Page Makeup: GGS Higher Education Resources, a Division of PreMedia Global, Inc.
Cover Design Manager: Wendy Ann Fredericks
Cover Designer: Kay Petronio
Cover Photo: Copyright © Photographer's Choice Photography/Veer
Photo Researcher: Jody Potter
Image Permission Coordination: Ang'John Ferreri
Senior Manufacturing Buyer: Dennis J. Para
Printer and Binder: Courier Kendallville
Cover Printer: Phoenix Color Corporation

For permission to use copyrighted material, grateful acknowledgment is made to the copyright holders on pages C-1—C-2, which are hereby made part of this copyright page.

Library of Congress Cataloging-in-Publication Data

Shea, Daniel M.
Living democracy: brief national edition / Daniel M. Shea, Joanne Connor Green, Christopher E. Smith. — 2nd ed.
p. cm.
ISBN 978-0-13-602735-5
1. United States—Politics and government—Textbooks. I. Green, Joanne Connor. II. Smith, Christopher E. III. Title.
JK276.S34 2009d
320.473—dc22
2008043748

1 2 3 4 5 6 7 8 9 10—CRK—11 10 09 08

Longman is an imprint of

PEARSON

www.pearsonhighered.com

Brief National Edition ISBN-13: 9780136027355
Brief National Edition ISBN-10: 0136027350
Texas Edition ISBN-13: 9780136027898
Texas Edition ISBN-10: 013602789X
California Edition ISBN-13: 9780136027973
California Edition ISBN-10: 0136027970
Alternate Edition ISBN-13: 9780136027669
Alternate Edition ISBN-10: 0136027660

Contents

PART ONE Foundations of American Government

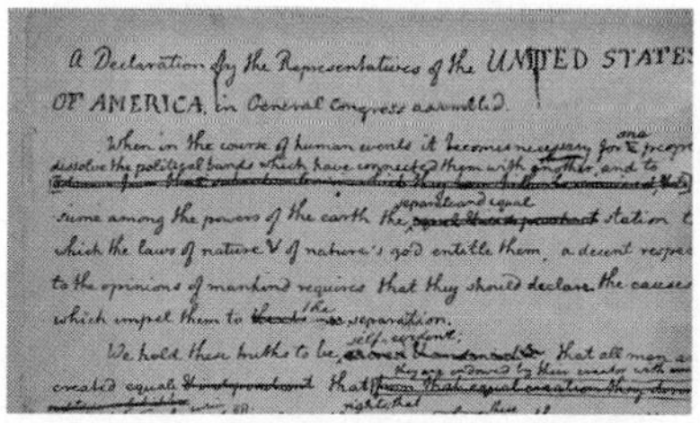
A Declaration by the Representatives of the UNITED STATES OF AMERICA, in General Congress assembled.

PART TWO The Institutions of American Government

CHAPTER 5
Civil Liberties and Civil Rights 139

CHAPTER 6
Congress 211

Chapter 7

Chapter 8

PART THREE The American Public and the Democratic Process

CHAPTER 9

Political Socialization and Public Opinion 321

CHAPTER 10

The Politics of the Media 355

CHAPTER 11

Interest Groups, Social Movements, and Civic Engagement 391

CHAPTER 12

Elections and Participation in America 425

CHAPTER 13
Political Parties 469

PART FOUR Public Policy

CHAPTER 14
The Policy Process 507

Appendices

participate...

Living Democracy, Second Edition, fulfills an important need in today's classroom: It inspires students to want to learn about American government. With a passionate emphasis on political **participation,** the text provides students with a clear, engaging overview of the dynamics of the American political system and with knowledge they can use long after they leave the classroom.

Written with the belief that the American Government course is critically important for students—as well as for the long-term stability of the democratic process—*Living Democracy* helps students draw connections between course topics and current events and find a role for themselves in politics and government. The text's innovative approach to American government presents the dynamic nature of our country's democratic process while offering all the material found in a comprehensive, traditionally organized text.

Now in its second edition, *Living Democracy* is building on its message of participation with new features, such as **Student Profiles** and **Pathways of Change from Around the World,** that showcase the actions and accomplishments of politically active young people and promote students' political participation. The **innovative pedagogical system**—which draws on some theories from cognitive psychology—provides an easy-to-follow chapter organization that breaks content into more manageable and self-contained "chunks." More self-assessment opportunities will help students participate more fully in their own learning process.

Living Democracy is the American government text that engages students, enriches their understanding of government, and inspires them to be active participants in their daily lives.

new to this edition

- **Chapter 1** introduces a clear, concise rationale for engagement in American politics in a more pedagogically focused design format.
- **Chapter 2** has been revised to provide a robust yet more concise exploration of the causes for the American Revolution and the Constitutional Convention as well as a discussion of the election of 1800 and Jacksonian Democracy.
- **Chapter 3** begins with a contemporary analysis of who is responsible for local environmental concerns. Given the current economic situation, the chapter includes updated discussion of how economic considerations shape the balance of power in our federal system.
- **Chapter 4** has been revised to provide a more focused and concise presentation on organization of the court system, and it contains a new graphic display of a case's path to the U.S. Supreme Court.
- **Chapter 5** First Amendment rights have been rearranged to more consistently follow the order of stated rights in the Amendment itself. Coverage of the current Second Amendment controversy over Washington, D.C.'s gun control laws has been added, as well as updated tables on educational attainment and income by race, and median earnings of workers in selected occupational groups by sex.
- **Chapter 6** has been restructured to present a clear review of the key organizing elements of Congress: the committee system, leadership, and legislative norms. It contains a revised section on how a bill becomes law, the results of the 2008 congressional contests, and an updated look at congressional ethics.
- **Chapter 7** presents a deep exploration of the Bush presidency and its effect on the future of presidential powers. This chapter also takes a sharper look at presidential power and global economic change.

- **Chapter 8** presents a more tightly focused explanation of the organization of the federal bureaucracy.

- **Chapter 9** offers an analysis of the power of popular culture on values and behavior with very contemporary examples. This chapter has more streamlined coverage of the controversies surrounding public opinion polling and the manner in which public opinion is measured.

- **Chapter 10** presents greater discussion of the ways in which technology affects mass communication. The changing nature of technology also is discussed with regard to the use of social networking sites as a tool for campaign communication and the use of text messaging as a new tool for mass communication.

- **Chapter 11** begins with a more streamlined discussion of how activism and protest have evolved in the United States. The chapter stresses the need for participation and counters the popular notion that interest groups are solely corrupting entities. The changing use of technology is given attention in this chapter, with a focus on new uses of technology in both direct and indirect lobbying.

- **Chapter 12** offers updated data on levels of political engagement in America, a detailed look at state efforts to alter the effects of the Electoral College, extensive maps and graphics related to the Electoral College, new data on campaign finance, as well as up-to-date turnout figures for several demographic groups.

- **Chapter 13** provides a detailed look at the 2008 presidential nomination process; new data on levels of partisanship, with a keen eye on young voters; and a more concise discussion of parties in American history, especially minor parties.

- **Chapter 14** begins with a condensed introduction about how our government makes policy, then leads into a discussion of how values shape the nature of policies and solutions. In the economic policy section, the role of the Federal Reserve Board is explored in light of the financial crisis that boiled over in the fall of 2008 and the federal government's $700 billion bailout of the credit markets. The factors that shape foreign policy development are discussed, including a new discussion about conflicting evaluations of the Iraq war.

innovative pedagogy...

Informed by cognitive psychology and the learning concept of "chunking," we've designed each chapter of *Living Democracy*, Second Edition, to promote easier retention and recall of information. The design presents the material in an organized way and in discrete, self-contained spreads to help students absorb and process information on each topic. With expanded learning goals, outlines, and review pedagogy for each section of each chapter, this edition provides an excellent and unique set of tools for learning.

Each chapter begins with a **Key Objective Outline** that lists the main concepts and key questions to consider. Each key question is connected to the section of the chapter—with page number—where the answer can be found.

Key Objective Outline
Why is citizen participation so important in a democracy?
It's Your Government! (page 4)
What are the themes of this book?
Themes of This Book (page 8)
What are the various "pathways" of involvement in our political system?
Citizen Participation and Pathways: The Example of Abortion (page 18)
What are the forces of stability in American politics?
Change and Stability in American Government (page 20)
CHANGE WE CAN BELIEVE IN
WWW.BARACKOBAMA.COM

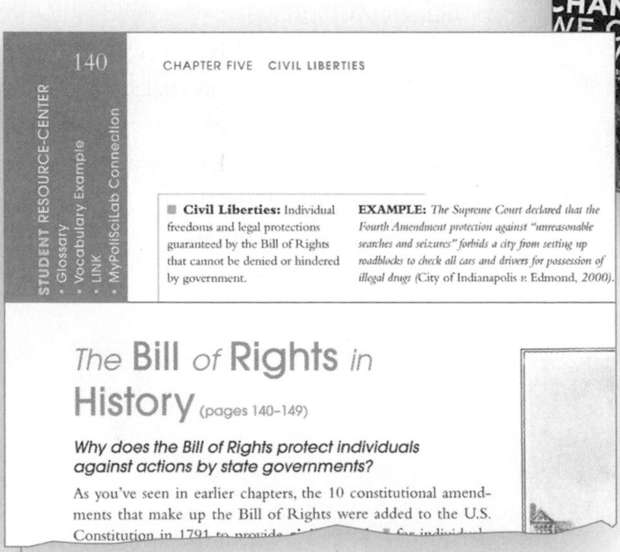

140 CHAPTER FIVE CIVIL LIBERTIES

STUDENT RESOURCE CENTER
• Glossary
• Vocabulary Example
• LINK
• MyPoliSciLab Connection

Civil Liberties: Individual freedoms and legal protections guaranteed by the Bill of Rights that cannot be denied or hindered by government.

EXAMPLE: *The Supreme Court declared that the Fourth Amendment protection against "unreasonable searches and seizures" forbids a city from setting up roadblocks to check all cars and drivers for possession of illegal drugs* (City of Indianapolis v. Edmond, 2000).

The **Bill** *of* **Rights** *in* **History** (pages 140–149)

Why does the Bill of Rights protect individuals against actions by state governments?

As you've seen in earlier chapters, the 10 constitutional amendments that make up the Bill of Rights were added to the U.S. Constitution in 1791 to provide ...

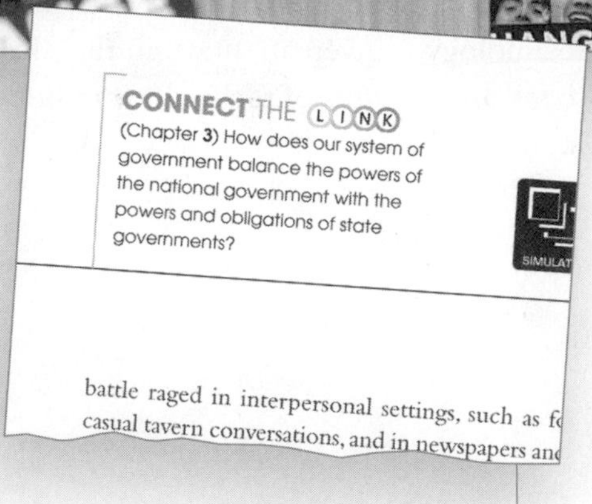

CONNECT THE LINK

(Chapter 3) How does our system of government balance the powers of the national government with the powers and obligations of state governments?

battle raged in interpersonal settings, such as ... casual tavern conversations, and in newspapers an...

Each section of a chapter begins on the top of a new page and includes the **Key Question** to keep in mind as you read the section. Definitions of important **Key Terms** appear in the top margin, along with an illustrative example to fully explain the significance of the term in context.

Connect the LINK features in the top margin help students to make connections about particular topics from one chapter to another.

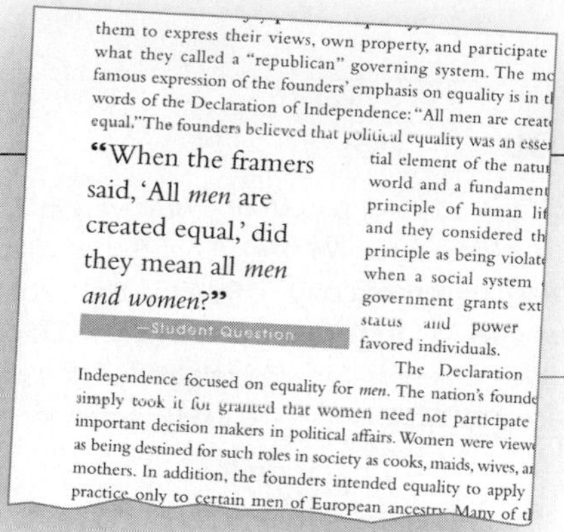

them to express their views, own property, and participate what they called a "republican" governing system. The mo famous expression of the founders' emphasis on equality is in t words of the Declaration of Independence: "All men are create equal." The founders believed that political equality was an esse tial element of the natu world and a fundamen principle of human li and they considered th principle as being violat when a social system government grants ext status and power favored individuals. The Declaration Independence focused on equality for *men*. The nation's founde simply took it for granted that women need not participate important decision makers in political affairs. Women were view as being destined for such roles in society as cooks, maids, wives, a mothers. In addition, the founders intended equality to apply practice only to certain men of European ancestry. Many of t

"When the framers said, 'All *men* are created equal,' did they mean all *men and women?*"

—Student Question

The text features actual student questions that serve as a starting point for class discussion.

Self-assessment tools throughout each chapter help students review material as they work through the text. Each section concludes with a **Practice Quiz, Discussion Questions,** and a **What YOU can do!** exercise.

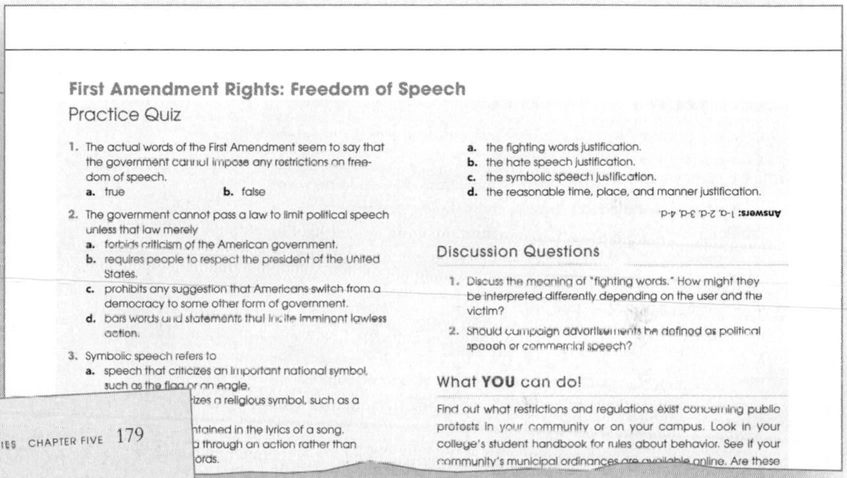

First Amendment Rights: Freedom of Speech

Practice Quiz

1. The actual words of the First Amendment seem to say that the government cannot impose any restrictions on free-dom of speech.
   a. true b. false
2. The government cannot pass a law to limit political speech unless that law merely
   a. forbids criticism of the American government.
   b. requires people to respect the president of the United States.
   c. prohibits any suggestion that Americans switch from a democracy to some other form of government.
   d. bars words and statements that incite imminent lawless action.
3. Symbolic speech refers to
   a. speech that criticizes an important national symbol, such as the flag or an eagle.
   ...izes a religious symbol, such as a
   ...ntained in the lyrics of a song.
   ...a through an action rather than ...ords.

a. the fighting words justification.
b. the hate speech justification.
c. the symbolic speech justification.
d. the reasonable time, place, and manner justification.

Answers: 1-a, 2-d, 3-d, 4-d.

Discussion Questions

1. Discuss the meaning of "fighting words." How might they be interpreted differently depending on the user and the victim?
2. Should campaign advertisements be defined as political speech or commercial speech?

What **YOU** can do!

Find out what restrictions and regulations exist concerning public protests in your community or on your campus. Look in your college's student handbook for rules about behavior. See if your community's municipal ordinances are available online. Are these

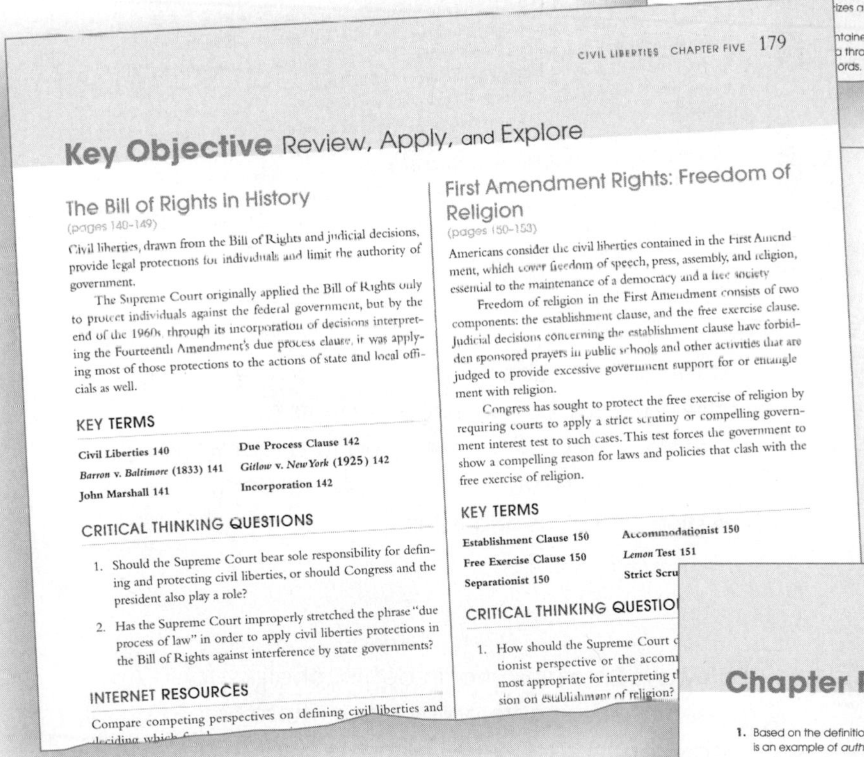

CIVIL LIBERTIES CHAPTER FIVE 179

Key Objective Review, Apply, and Explore

The Bill of Rights in History

(pages 140–149)

Civil liberties, drawn from the Bill of Rights and judicial decisions, provide legal protections for individuals and limit the authority of government.

The Supreme Court originally applied the Bill of Rights only to protect individuals against the federal government, but by the end of the 1960s, through its incorporation of decisions interpreting the Fourteenth Amendment's due process clause, it was applying most of those protections to the actions of state and local officials as well.

KEY TERMS

Civil Liberties 140
Barron v. Baltimore (1833) 141
John Marshall 141
Due Process Clause 142
Gitlow v. New York (1925) 142
Incorporation 142

CRITICAL THINKING QUESTIONS

1. Should the Supreme Court bear sole responsibility for defining and protecting civil liberties, or should Congress and the president also play a role?
2. Has the Supreme Court improperly stretched the phrase "due process of law" in order to apply civil liberties protections in the Bill of Rights against interference by state governments?

INTERNET RESOURCES

Compare competing perspectives on defining civil liberties and deciding which...

First Amendment Rights: Freedom of Religion

(pages 150–153)

Americans consider the civil liberties contained in the First Amendment, which cover freedom of speech, press, assembly, and religion, essential to the maintenance of a democracy and a free society.

Freedom of religion in the First Amendment consists of two components: the establishment clause, and the free exercise clause. Judicial decisions concerning the establishment clause have forbidden sponsored prayers in public schools and other activities that are judged to provide excessive government support for or entangle ment with religion.

Congress has sought to protect the free exercise of religion by requiring courts to apply a strict scrutiny or compelling government interest test to such cases. This test forces the government to show a compelling reason for laws and policies that clash with the free exercise of religion.

KEY TERMS

Establishment Clause 150
Free Exercise Clause 150
Separationist 150
Accommodationist 150
Lemon Test 151
Strict Scru...

CRITICAL THINKING QUESTIO...

1. How should the Supreme Court ... tionist perspective or the accom... most appropriate for interpreting t... sion on establishment of religion?

Each chapter closes with a **Key Objective Review, Apply, and Explore** section that recaps the information in each topic section along with **Key Terms** and **Critical Thinking Questions** (to help students consider the material in a more conceptual way) as well as **Internet Resources** and **Additional Reading.**

In addition to the **Practice Quiz** at the end of each section of the chapter, the **Chapter Review Test** offers multiple-choice questions and answer keys so that students can check their progress.

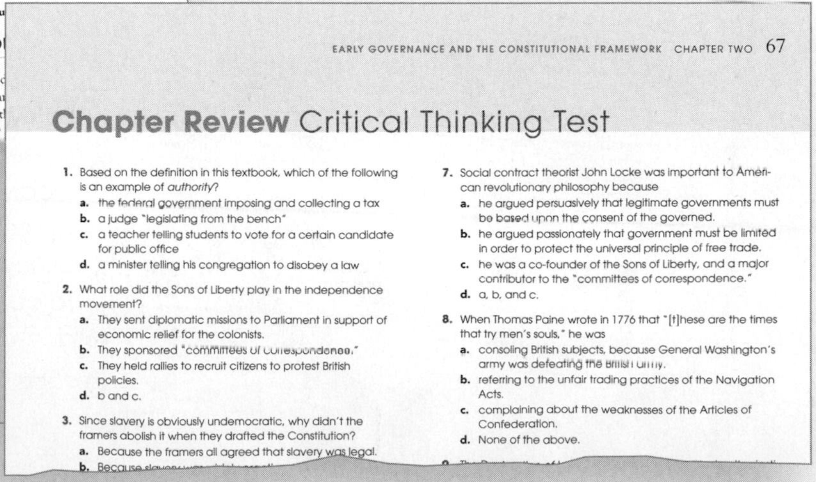

EARLY GOVERNANCE AND THE CONSTITUTIONAL FRAMEWORK CHAPTER TWO 67

Chapter Review Critical Thinking Test

1. Based on the definition in this textbook, which of the following is an example of *authority*?
   a. the federal government imposing and collecting a tax
   b. a judge "legislating from the bench"
   c. a teacher telling students to vote for a certain candidate for public office
   d. a minister telling his congregation to disobey a law
2. What role did the Sons of Liberty play in the independence movement?
   a. They sent diplomatic missions to Parliament in support of economic relief for the colonists.
   b. They sponsored "committees of correspondence."
   c. They held rallies to recruit citizens to protest British policies.
   d. b and c.
3. Since slavery is obviously undemocratic, why didn't the framers abolish it when they drafted the Constitution?
   a. Because the framers all agreed that slavery was legal.
   b. Because slavery...
7. Social contract theorist John Locke was important to American revolutionary philosophy because
   a. he argued persuasively that legitimate governments must be based upon the consent of the governed.
   b. he argued passionately that government must be limited in order to protect the universal principle of free trade.
   c. he was a co-founder of the Sons of Liberty, and a major contributor to the "committees of correspondence."
   d. a, b, and c.
8. When Thomas Paine wrote in 1776 that "[t]hese are the times that try men's souls," he was
   a. consoling British subjects, because General Washington's army was defeating the British army.
   b. referring to the unfair trading practices of the Navigation Acts.
   c. complaining about the weaknesses of the Articles of Confederation.
   d. None of the above.

a theme of participation...

Living Democracy includes a variety of engaging features that foster in-class participation and discussion. Additionally, the book offers activities and features that encourage students to apply key concepts outside the classroom and participate in our political system.

What YOU can do!

Learn about the continuing existence of slavery in various countries. See, for example, the Web site of Anti-Slavery International at **http://www.antislavery.org** and of Free the Slaves at **http://www.freetheslaves.net**. What actions could be taken today to eliminate modern slavery and advance civil rights for victimized people around the world? What role should the United States play?

Stressing the idea that American politics is not a spectator sport, the **What YOU can do!** exercise at the end of each section prompts students to explore politics on a local level, on campus, and in their local governments.

STUDENT | PROFILE

Like most young Americans, Nick Anderson and Ana Slavin spend a lot of time on social network sites. Facebook and MySpace are entertaining, a way to make social connections, but could they also be harnessed to do good work? Young people certainly care about problems in the community and around the world—and they are anxious to roll up their sleeves and make a difference. But how might social network sites be used?

During a trip to South Africa in 2005, Anderson was blown away by the plight of people in the Darfur region of western Sudan. For nearly a decade, Arab militias backed by the Sudanese government had waged a genocidal war on tribes in the region, killing upwards of 300,000 men, women, and children. Anderson wit-

The new **Student Profiles** showcase the actions and accomplishments of young persons who have become active in American politics or engaged in making changes in public life. This feature promotes students' awareness of their potential to be part of the process.

You decide!

In 2007, Columbia University invited Mahmoud Ahmadinejad, the President of Iran, to give a speech on its campus during his visit to New York for meetings at the United Nations. President Ahmadinejad is a highly controversial figure, both for his country's alleged sponsorship of terrorist groups and for his personal statements advocating the destruction of Israel and denying that Hitler's Nazi soldiers murdered hundreds of thousands of Jews in concentration camps during World War II. Imagine that President Ahmadinejad was invited to your campus to give a speech entitled, "Why the Nations of the World Should Unite to Fight Against the United States." Would you feel comfortable listening to such a speech? Should U.S. government officials prevent him from giving such a speech? If so, why? If a friend asked you to help organize a demonstration against President Ahmadinejad that would include sitting in the auditorium and shouting to prevent him from being heard by the rest of the audience, would you agree to participate? Would you be interfering with President Ahmadinejad's freedom of speech or merely exercising your own freedom of speech? Does President Ahmadinejad deserve freedom of speech when he presides over a country where people are sometimes sent to prison for criticizing the Iranian government?

At the end of each chapter, **You decide!** critical thinking activities challenge students to apply the information they've learned to a real-world situation. This feature also provides opportunities to stimulate class discussion.

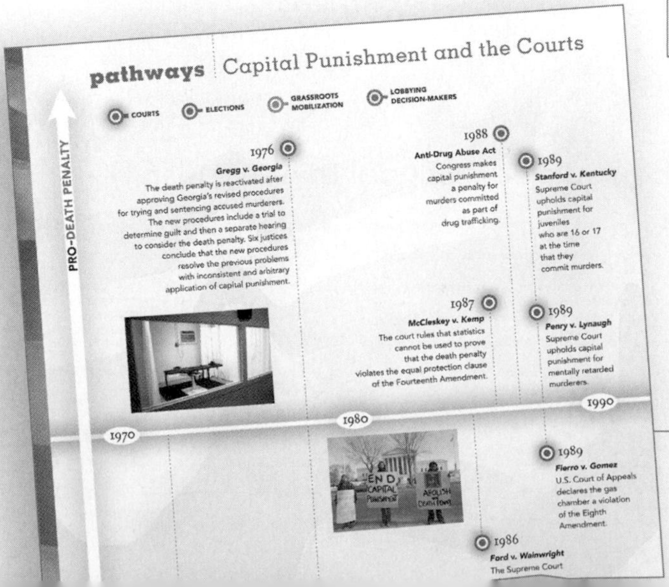

Pathways Timelines offer in-depth, photographic presentations of core policy issues. These timelines, located in the Appendix, combine photographs and text to present a visually rich treatment of a specific, core policy issue. Provocative essay questions prompt students to consider the interrelated forces that affect the democratic process.

Living Democracy provides students with the means—and the inspiration—to participate directly in the political process. Recurring *Pathways* features help students to understand the dynamic nature of the American political system—and their ability to make a difference.

Pathways appear within the narrative rather than being set off in boxes, making it more likely that students will read and benefit from these enriching passages.

PATHWAYS | of change from around the world

What would you do if the independence of the American judiciary was threatened? What if members of Congress sought to impeach a federal judge simply because they disagreed with his or her decision in a criminal case? Would it matter to you? To the country? Would you even notice? In 2007, law students in Pakistan took to the streets with hundreds of lawyers to protest President Pervez Musharraf's effort to suspend and remove from office the chief justice of Pakistan's Supreme Court. These students felt so strongly about the need for judicial independence that they literally risked their lives as armed soldiers tried to stop th...

The new Pathways of Change from Around the World sections offer a comparative perspective by spotlighting stories of political action by young persons in different parts of the world.

PATHWAYS | of action

The Sons of Liberty

During the uneasy and turbulent times of p... America, various resistance groups began to ... secret. Several of these early interest groups b... known as the Sons of Liberty, a name closely li... against Parliamentary rule over the colonies. ... important figures such as John and Samuel Adams, but also enlisting the support of artisans, shopkeepers, and other working people who could be depended on to rebel against abuses like the Tea Tax, the Sons of Liberty organized in one community after another.

They held rallies, sponsored "committees of correspondence" (letter-writing campaigns) ...

Pathways of Action explain how an individual or a group has influenced government. These stories help students to understand how average citizens have affected change—and how they might, too.

PATHWAYS | profile

Ruth Bader Ginsburg

Ruth Bader Ginsburg, the second woman to serve on the U.S. Supreme Court (Sandra Day O'Connor was the first), was born in 1933, graduated from Columbia University's law school, and went on to become a law professor at Rutgers University and Columbia

Pathways Profiles provide detailed information about individuals who have made a difference in American politics.

Living Democracy itself was designed with the participation of students to ensure a visual presentation from which they will enjoy learning.

The trial of Saddam Hussein in Iraq for crimes committed against the people of his country included many features that are familiar in American trials, including arguments by attor-

Comparing Judicial Systems

and criminal cases save ... also benefit the individu... outcome and, in crimin...

Appellate ...

Most states, as well as t... **appellate courts.** The... of appeals," hear appeal... the trial courts. In the ... divided into 11 numbe... Columbia circuit and ... trade cases. The numb... districts in specific sta... Court of Appeals for t... district courts in Texas,

The text features **compelling photos** with many captions that pose questions about important concepts in the text along with many different types of graphs and charts. The presentation of information in a variety of formats helps students to grasp key concepts.

Resources in Print and Online

NAME OF SUPPLEMENT	AVAILABLE IN PRINT	AVAILABLE ONLINE	INSTRUCTOR OR STUDENT SUPPLEMENT	DESCRIPTION
American Government Study Site		✓	Both	Online package of practice tests, Web links, and flashcards organized by major topics and formatted to match this text's table of contents. www.pearsonamericangovernment.com.
Instructor's Manual 0136027903	✓	✓	Instructor	Offers chapter summaries, recent news and pop culture examples, discussion topics, and Web activities.
Test Bank 0136027717	✓	✓	Instructor	Contains over 200 questions per chapter in multiple-choice, true-false, short-answer, and essay format. Questions address all levels of Bloom's taxonomy and have been reviewed and edited for accuracy and effectiveness.
MyTest 0136027709		✓	Instructor	This flexible, online test-generating software includes all questions found in the printed Test Bank.
Study Guide 0136027687	✓		Student	Contains learning objectives, chapter summaries, and practice tests.
PowerPoint Presentation		✓	Instructor	Slides include a lecture outline of the text along with graphics from the book. Available on the Instructor Resource Center.*
Digital Transparency Masters 0136027938		✓	Instructor	These PDF slides contain all maps, figures, and tables found in the text. Available on the Instructor Resource Center.*
Longman Political Science Video Program	✓		Instructor	Qualified college adopters can peruse our list of videos for the American Government classroom.
You Decide! Current Debates in American Politics, 2009 Edition 020568405X	✓		Student	This debate-style reader by John Rourke of the University of Connecticut examines provocative issues in American politics today by presenting various sides of key political topics.
Voices of Dissent: Critical Readings in American Politics, Eighth Edition 0205697976	✓		Student	This collection of critical essays assembled by William Grover of St. Michael's College and Joseph Peschek of Hamline University goes beyond the debate between mainstream liberalism and conservatism to fundamentally challenge the status quo.
Writing in Political Science, Third Edition 0321217357	✓		Student	This guide by Diane Schmidt of California State University—Chico takes students through all aspects of writing in political science step-by-step.
Choices: An American Government Database Reader		✓	Student	This customizable reader allows instructors to choose from a database of over 300 readings to create a reader that exactly matches their course needs. Go to http://www.pearsoncustom.com/database/choices.html for more information.
Ten Things That Every American Government Student Should Read 020528969X	✓		Student	Edited by Karen O'Connor of American University. We asked American Government instructors across the country to vote for the 10 things beyond the text that they believe every student should read and put them in this brief and useful reader. Available at no additional charge when ordered packaged with the text.
American Government: Readings and Cases, Eighteenth Edition 0205697984	✓		Student	Edited by Peter Woll of Brandeis University, this long-time best-selling reader provides a strong, balanced blend of classic readings and cases that illustrate and amplify important concepts in American government along with extremely current selections drawn from today's issues and literature. Available at a discount when ordered packaged with this text.
Diversity in Contemporary American Politics and Government 0205550363	✓		Student	This reader, edited by David Dulio of Oakland University, Erin E. O'Brien of Kent State University, and John Klemanski of Oakland University, explores the significant role that demographic diversity plays in political outcomes and policy processes.
Penguin-Longman Value Bundles	✓		Student	Longman offers 25 Penguin Putnam titles at more than a 60-percent discount when packaged with any Longman text. Go to http://www.pearsonhighered.com/penguin for more information.
Longman State Politics Series	✓		Student	These primers on state and local government and political issues are available at no extra cost when shrink-wrapped with the text. Available for Texas, California, and Georgia.

* Instructor Resource Center located at www.pearsonhighered.com/educator

Improve Results with PEARSON mypoliscilab™

Designed to amplify a traditional course in numerous ways or to administer a course online, **MyPoliSciLab** combines pedagogy and assessment with an array of multimedia activities—videos, simulations, exercises, and online newsfeeds—to make learning more effective for all types of students. Now featuring the combined resources, assets, and activities of both Prentice Hall and Longman Publishers, this new release of **MyPoliSciLab** is visually richer and even more interactive than previous iterations—a quantum leap forward in design with more points of assessment and interconnectivity between concepts.

TEACHING AND LEARNING TOOLS

✓ **Assessment**: Comprehensive online diagnostic tools—learning objectives, study guides, flash cards, and pre- and post-tests—help students gauge and improve their understanding.

✓ **E-book:** Identical in content and design to the printed text, an e-book provides students access to their text wherever and whenever they need it.

✓ ***UPDATED!*** **PoliSci News Review:** A series of weekly articles and video clips—from traditional and non-traditional news sources—recaps the most important political news stories, followed by quizzes that test students' understanding.

✓ ***NEW!*** **ABC News RSS feed:** MyPoliSciLab provides an online feed from ABC News, updated hourly, to keep students current.

✓ **ABC News Video Clips**: Over 60 high-interest 2- to 4-minute clips provide historical snapshots in each chapter of key political issues and offer opportunities to launch discussions.

✓ ***UPDATED!*** **Roundtable and Debate Video Clips**: These video clips feature professors discussing key concepts from ideologically diverse perspectives and debating politically charged issues.

✓ **Student Polling:** Updated weekly with timely, provocative questions, the polling feature lets students voice their opinions in nationwide polls and view how their peers across the country see the same issue.

✓ **Political Podcasts:** Featuring some of Pearson's most respected authors, these video podcasts present short, instructive—and even entertaining—lectures on key topics that students can download and play at their convenience.

✓ ***NEW!*** **Student Podcasts:** The new MyPoliSciLab allows students to record and download their own videos for peer-to-peer learning.

INTERACTIVE ACTIVITIES

✓ **New and Updated Simulations:** Featuring an appealing new graphic interface, these role-playing simulations help students experience political decision-making in a way they never have before—including new "mini activities" that prepare students to make the right decisions.

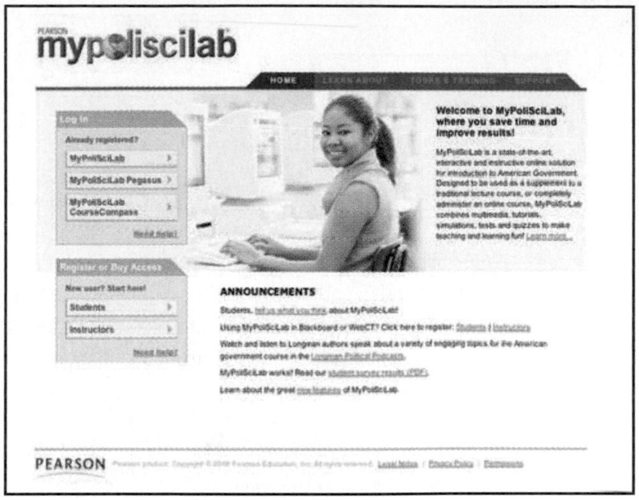

✓ ***NEW!*** **Debate Exercises:** These provocative new exercises present classic and contemporary views on core controversies, ask students to take a position, and then show them the potential consequences of taking that stand.

✓ **More Focused Comparative Exercises:** These exercises have been revised in scope to concentrate on a more specific issue when comparing the US to other political systems, giving students a more concrete foundation on which to analyze key similarities and differences.

✓ **More Interactive Timelines:** With redesigned media and graphics, these timelines let students step through the evolution of some aspect of politics and now include more interactive questions throughout.

✓ **More Dynamic Visual Literacy Exercises:** These revised exercises offer attractive new graphs, charts, and tables and more opportunities to manipulate and interpret political data.

✓ **Expanded Participation Activities:** Reflecting our country's growing political interest, these expanded activities give students ideas and instructions for getting involved in all aspects of politics.

Icons in the top margin of this book direct students to the activities on MyPoliSciLab related to the topics they are studying.

ONLINE ADMINISTRATION

No matter what course management system you use—or if you do not use one at all, but still wish to easily capture your students' grades and track their performance—Pearson has a **MyPoliSciLab** option to suit your needs. Contact one of Pearson's Technology Specialists for more information or assistance.

A **MyPoliSciLab** access code is at no additional cost when packaged with selected Pearson American Government texts. To get started, contact your local Pearson Publisher's Representative at **www.pearsonhighered.com/replocator.**

DEVELOPING Living DEMOCRACY

Living Democracy is the result of an extensive development process involving the contributions of hundreds of instructors and students. More than 300 manuscript reviewers provided invaluable feedback. More than two-dozen focus group participants contributed to decisions about text organization, content coverage, and pedagogical innovation. More than 100 instructors helped shape the design of this second edition. Over 750 students class-tested the manuscript before publication. Student reviewers evaluated the writing style and visual design, helped to select the text's photos, and provided feedback on the in-text assessment tools. We are grateful to all who participated in shaping the manuscript and design of this text.

We would like to thank the following instructors who offered valuable comments during the development of the second edition of *Living Democracy*:

William Adler, *Hunter College*
Victoria Allen, *Queens College*
Bruce Altschuler, *SUNY Oswego*
John Ambacher, *Framingham State College*
Lydia Andrade, *University of the Incarnate Word*
Kwame Antwi-Boasiako, *Stephen F. Austin State University*
Andrew Aoki, *Augsburg College*
Clay Arnold, *University of Central Arkansas*
John Arnold, *Itawamba Community College*
Daniel Aseltine, *Chaffey College*
Yan Bai, *Grand Rapids Community College*
Evelyn Ballard, *Houston Community College*
Robert Ballinger, *South Texas College*
Jodi Balma, *Fullerton College*
Paul Benson, *Tarrant County College*
Demetrius Bereolos, *Tulsa Community College*
Steven Berizzi, *Norwalk Community College*
Rory Berke, *U.S. Naval Academy*
Prosper Bernard, *Baruch College*
David Birch, *Tomball College*
Amy Black, *Wheaton College*
Chris Bonneau, *University of Pittsburgh*
Michael, Bordelon, *Houston Baptist University*
Carol Botsch, *USC Aiken*
Laura Bourland, *University of Alabama*
Phil Branyon, *Gainesville State College*
Ronald Brecke, *Park University*
Mike Bressler, *Long Beach City College*
Claudia Bryant, *Western Carolina University*
Randi Buslik, *Northeastern Illinois University*
Stephen Caliendo, *North Central College*
Jamie Carson, *University of Georgia*
Mark Cichock, *University of Texas at Arlington*
Daniel Coffey, *University of Akron*
Scott Comparato, *Southern Illinois University*
Chris Cooper, *Western Carolina University*
Frank Coppa, *Union County College*
James Corey, *High Point University*
Eric Cox, *Texas Christian University*
Jim Cox, *Georgia Perimeter College*
Gregory Culver, *University of Southern Indiana*
Carlos Cunha, *Dowling College*
William Cunion, *Mount Union College*
Donald Dahlin, *University of South Dakota*
Mark Daniels, *Slippery Rock University*
Kwame Dankwa, *Albany State University*
Kevin Davis, *North Central Texas College*
Paul Davis, *Truckee Meadows Community College*
Robert De Luna, *St. Philip's College*
Michael Deaver, *Sierra College*
Brian Dille, *Mesa Community College*
Agber Dimah, *Chicago State University*
Alesha Doan, *University of Kansas*
Peter Doas, *South Texas College*
John Domino, *Sam Houston State University*
Rick Donohoe, *Napa Valley College*
Douglas Dow, *University of Texas at Dallas*
William Downs, *Georgia State University*
Morris Drumm, *Texas Christian University*
B. M. Dubin, *Oakland Community College–Highland Lakes*
Donna Duncan, *Westwood College*
Keith Eakins, *University of Central Oklahoma*
Jodi Empol, *Montgomery County Community College*
Matthew Eshbaugh-Soha, *University of North Texas*
Henry Esparza, *University of Texas at San Antonio, Northeast Lakeview College*
Karry Evans, *Austin Community College*
Hyacinth Ezeamii, *Albany State University*
Russell Farnen, *University of Connecticut*
John Fielding, *Mount Wachusett Community College*
Terri Fine, *University of Central Florida*
John Fliter, *Kansas State University*
Joseph M. Fonseca, Jr., *St. Mary's University*
Brian Frederick, *Northern Illinois University*
Heather Frederick, *Slippery Rock University*
Rodd Freitag, *University of Wisconsin–Eau Claire*
Scott Frisch, *California State University, Channel Islands*
Joyce Gelb, *City College of New York*
Sandra Gieseler, *Palo Alto College*
Barbara Giles, *Florida Southern College*
Richard Glenn, *Millersville University*
Fran Goldman, *Binghamton University*
Charles Gossett, *California State Polytechnic University, Pomona*
Richard Griffin, *Ferris State University*
Martin Gruberg, *University of Wisconsin–Oshkosh*
Baogang Guo, *Dalton State College*
Hans Hacker, *Stephen F. Austin State University*
Yolanda Hake, *South Texas College*
Willie Hamilton, *Mt. San Jacinto College*
Roger Handberg, *University of Central Florida*
Michael Harkins, *Harper College*
Rebecca Harris, *Washington and Lee University*
Brian Harward, *Southern Illinois University, Edwardsville*
Paul Hathaway, *Idaho State University*
Diane Heith, *St. John's University*
Christopher Henrichsen, *Brigham Young University*
Frank Hernandez, *Glendale Community College*
Marjorie Hershey, *Indiana University*
Bill Hixon, *Lawrence University*
Trey Hood, *University of Georgia*
Jennifer Hora, *Valparaiso University*
Alison Howard, *Dominican University of California*
Charles Jacobs, *Kent State University*
Amy Jasperson, *University of Texas at San Antonio*
Shannon Jenkins, *University of Massachusetts at Dartmouth*
Alana Jeydel, *American River College*
Scott P. Johnson, *Frostburg State University*
Susan Johnson, *University of Wisconsin–Whitewater*
Terri Johnson, *University of Wisconsin–Green Bay*
Frank Jones, *Saint Leo University*
Mark Joslyn, *University of Kansas*
Joseph Jozwiak, *Texas A&M University, Corpus Christi*
Srujana Kanjula, *Community College of Allegheny County, North Campus*
Nina Kasniunas, *Allegheny College*
William Kelly, *Auburn University*
Stephen Kerbow, *Southwest Texas Junior College*
Irina Khmelko, *Georgia Southern University*
Richard Kiefer, *Waubonsee Community College*
Bob King, *Georgia Perimeter College*
Dina Krois, *Lansing Community College*
Michael Kryzanek, *Bridgewater State College*
Ashlyn Kuersten, *Western Michigan University*
Ronald Kuykendall, *Greenville Technical College*
Paul Labedz, *Valencia Community College*

Lisa Langenbach, *Middle Tennessee State University*
Mike Lee, *Western Texas College*
Ron Lee, *Rockford College*
John Linantud, *University of Houston, Downtown*
Robert Locander, *North Harris College*
Brad Lockerbie, *University of Georgia*
Fred Lokken, *Truckee Meadows Community College*
Tim Luther, *California Baptist University*
Gay Lyons, *Pellissippi State Technical Community College*
Gary Malecha, *University of Portland*
Maurice Mangum, *Southern Illinois University, Edwardsville*
David Mann, *College of Charleston*
Michael Margolis, *University of Cincinnati*
Steve Marin, *Victor Valley College*
Nancy Marion, *University of Akron*
Asher J. Matathias, *St. John's University*
Derek Maxfield, *Capital Community College*
Madhavi McCall, *San Diego State University*
Richard Medlar, *Dickinson State University*
Vinette Meikle Harris, *Houston Community College*
Mark Milewicz, *Gordon College*
Eric Miller, *Blinn College*
Rhonda Miller, *Eastfield College*
Richard Millsap, *University of Texas at Arlington*
Ken Moffett, *Southern Illinois University, Edwardsville*
Wyatt Moulds, *Jones County Junior College*
Stacia Munroe, *Lincoln Land Community College*
William Murin, *University of Wisconsin, Parkside*
Martha Musgrove, *Tarrant County College, Southeast Campus*
Jason Mycoff, *University of Delaware*
Carolyn Myers, *Southwestern Illinois College*
Napp Nazworth, *Texas A&M University, Corpus Christi*
Steven Nelson, *Northern Michigan University*
Brian Newman, *Pepperdine University*
James Newman, *Idaho State University*
Adam Newmark, *Appalachian State University*
Peter Ngwafu, *Albany State University*
Laura Olson, *Clemson University*
Richard Pacelle, *Georgia Southern University*
David Penna, *Gallaudet University*
Geoffrey Peterson, *University of Wisconsin–Eau Claire*
J. D. Phaup, *Texas A&M University–Kingsville*
Daniel Ponder, *Drury University*
Greg Rabb, *Jamestown Community College*
Jan Rabin, *Roanoke College*
Lee Rademacher, *Purdue University, Calumet*
Mitzi Ramos, *University of Illinois at Chicago*
Christopher Reaves, *School of Social and Behavioral Sciences*
Deanne Repetto, *Folsom Lake College*
Steven Reti, *College of the Canyons*
James Rhodes, *Luther College*
Laurie Rice, *Southern Illinois University, Edwardsville*
John Roche, *Palomar College*
Bernard Rowan, *Chicago State University*
Donald Roy, *Ferris State University*
Paul Rozycki, *Mott Community College*
Cristina Ruggiero, *Chabot College*
Chris Saladino, *Virginia Commonwealth University*
Erich Saphir, *Pima Community College*
Greg Schaller, *Villanova University*
Calvin Scheidt, *Tidewater Community College*
Adam Schiffer, *Texas Christian University*
Andrew Schlewitz, *Albion College*
Diane Schmidt, *California State University*
Erin Scholnick, *College of San Mateo San Francisco State University*
Ronnee Schreiber, *San Diego State University*
T. M. Sell, *Highline College*
Brett Sharp, *University of Central Oklahoma*
Charles Shipan, *University of Michigan*
Mark Shomaker, *Blinn College, Bryan Campus*
Tom Simpson, *Missouri Southern State University*
Brian Smith, *St. Edward's University*
Candy Smith, *Texarkana College*
Daniel Smith, *Northwest Missouri State University*
Gary Sokolow, *College of the Redwoods*
Robert Speel, *Penn State, Erie*
John Speer, *Houston Community College, Southwest*
Debra St. John, *Collin County Community College District*
Jim Startin, *University of Texas at San Antonio*
Robert Sterken, *University of Texas at Tyler*
Theresia Stewart, *Elizabethtown Community and Technical College*
Adam Stone, *Georgia Perimeter College*
J. Cherie Strachan, *Central Michigan University*
Pamela Stricker, *California State University, San Marcos*
Michael Sullenger, *Texas State Technical College*
Bobby Summers, *Harper College*
Dari Sylvester, *University of the Pacific*
Barry Tadlock, *Ohio University*
Carolyn Taylor, *Rogers State University*
Kenneth Tillett, *Southwestern Oklahoma State University*
Judy Tobler, *Northwest Arkansas Community College*
Charles Turner, *California State University, Chico*
Chris Turner, *Laredo Community College*
Jamilya Ukudeeva, *Cabrillo College*
Richard Unruh, *Fresno Pacific University*
David Uranga, *Pasadena City College*
Laura van Assendelft, *Mary Baldwin College*
Ronald Vardy, *Wharton County Community College*
Dwight Vick, *University of South Dakota*
Adam Warber, *Clemson University*
Eddie Washington, *Rio Hondo College*
Ruth Ann Watry, *Northern Michigan University*
Wendy Watson, *University of North Texas*
Paul Weizer, *Fitchburg State College*
Lois Duke Whitaker, *Georgia Southern University*
James Wilson, *Southern Methodist University*
Robert Wood, *University of North Dakota*
Heather Wyatt-Nichol, *Stephen F. Austin State University*
Ann Wyman, *Missouri Southern State University*
Peter Yacobucci, *Walsh University*
Chunmei Yoe, *Southeastern Oklahoma State University*

We also extend our thanks to the following instructors who offered valuable comments during the development of the first edition of *Living Democracy*:

Danny Adkison, *Oklahoma State University*
William Adler, *Hunter College*
Victor Aikhionbare, *Palm Beach Community College*
Bruce Altschuler, *SUNY Oswego*
John Ambacher, *Framingham State College*
Lydia Andrade, *University of the Incarnate Word*
Kwame Antwi-Boasiako, *Stephen F. Austin State University*
John Arnold, *Itawamba Community College*
Daniel Aseltine, *Chaffey College*
Yan Bai, *Grand Rapids Community College*
Evelyn Ballard, *Houston Community College*
Robert Ballinger, *South Texas College*
Jodi Balma, *Fullerton College*
Joseph A. Barder, *Robert Morris College*
Susan M. Behuniak, *Le Moyne College*
Paul Benson, *Tarrant County College*
Demetrius Bereolos, *Tulsa Community College*
Prosper Bernard, *Baruch College*
David Birch, *Tomball College*
Amy Black, *Wheaton College*
Melanie J. Blumberg, *California University of Pennsylvania*
Michael Bordelon, *Houston Baptist University*
Carol Botsch, *USC Aiken*
Catherine Bottrell, *Tarrant County College*
Phil Branyon, *Gainesville State College*
Ronald Brecke, *Park University*
Martha Burns, *Tidewater Community College*
James Chalmers, *Wayne State University*
Mark Cichock, *University of Texas at Arlington*
Allan Cigler, *University of Kansas*
Scott Comparato, *Southern Illinois University*
Paul Cooke, *Cy-Fair College*
Chris Cooper, *Western Carolina University*
James Corey, *High Point University*
John H. Culver, *California Polytechnic State University*
Carlos Cunha, *Dowling College*
William Cunion, *Mount Union College*
Marian Currinder, *College of Charleston*
Mark Daniels, *Slippery Rock University*
Kwame Dankwa, *Albany State University*
Kevin Davis, *North Central Texas College*
Paul Davis, *Truckee Meadows Community College*
Donald Dahlin, *University of South Dakota*
Michael Deaver, *Sierra College*
Denise DeGarmo, *Southern Illinois University, Edwardsville*
Robert Dewhirst, *Northeast Missouri State University*
Brian Dille, *Mesa Community College*
Agber Dimah, *Chicago State University*
Peter Doas, *South Texas College*
Alesha Doan, *University of Kansas*
Rick Donohoe, *Napa Valley College*
William Downs, *Georgia State University*
Dave Dulio, *Oakland University*
Keith Eakins, *University of Central Oklahoma*
J. Eddy, *Monroe Community College*
Matthew Eshbaugh-Soha, *University of North Texas*
Russell Farnen, *University of Connecticut*
John Fielding, *Mount Wachusett Community College*
Terri Fine, *University of Central Florida*
John Fliter, *Kansas State University*
Brian Frederick, *Northern Illinois University*
Heather Frederick, *Slippery Rock University*
Rodd Freitag, *University of Wisconsin–Eau Claire*
Scott Frisch, *California State University, Channel Islands*
Joyce Gelb, *City College of New York*
Anthony Giarino, *Tarrant County College*
Dana Glencross, *Oklahoma City Community College*
Richard Glenn, *Millersville University*
Dennis Goldford, *Drake University*
Fran Goldman, *Binghamton University*
Charles Gossett, *California State Polytechnic University, Pomona*
John C. Green, *University of Akron*
Nathan Griffith, *Belmont University*
Martin Gruberg, *University of Wisconsin–Oshkosh*
Baogang Guo, *Dalton State College*

Hans Hacker, *Stephen F. Austin State University*
Mel Hailey, *Abilene Christian University*
Angela Halfacre-Hitchcock, *College of Charleston*
Willie Hamilton, *Mt. San Jacinto College*
Roger Handberg, *University of Central Florida*
Rebecca Harris, *Washington and Lee University*
Michael Harkins, *Harper College*
Brian Harward, *Southern Illinois University, Edwardsville*
Paul Hathaway, *Idaho State University*
Diane Heith, *St. John's University*
Frank Hernandez, *Glendale Community College*
Marjorie Hershey, *Indiana University*
Fred R. Hertrich, *Middlesex County College*
Kenneth Hicks, *Rogers State University*
Anne Hildreth, *SUNY Albany*
Trey Hood, *University of Georgia*
Donna Hooper, *North Central Texas College*
Jennifer Hora, *Valparaiso University*
Alison Howard, *Dominican University of California*
Nikki Isemann, *Southeastern Iowa Community College*
Charles Jacobs, *Kent State University*
Amy Jasperson, *University of Texas at San Antonio*
Shannon Jenkins, *University of Massachusetts at Dartmouth*
Alana S. Jeydel, *Oregon State University*
Scott Johnson, *Frostburg State University*
Susan Johnson, *University of Wisconsin–Whitewater*
Terri Johnson, *University of Wisconsin–Green Bay*
Frank Jones, *Del Mar College*
Mark Joslyn, *University of Kansas*
Joseph Jozwiak, *Texas A&M Corpus Christi*
David Keefe, *SUNY Brockport*
William Kelly, *Auburn University*
Stephen Kerbow, *Southwest Texas Junior College*
Beat Kernen, *Southwest Missouri State University*
Richard Kiefer, *Waubonsee Community College*
Dina Krois, *Lansing Community College*
Michael Kryzanek, *Bridgewater State College*
Ashlyn Kuersten, *Western Michigan University*
Ronald Kuykendall, *Greenville Technical College*
Paul Labedz, *Valencia Community College*
Lisa Langenbach, *Middle Tennessee State University*
Christopher Latimer, *SUNY Albany*
John Linantud, *University of Houston, Downtown*
Robert Locander, *North Harris College*
Brad Lockerbie, *University of Georgia*
Robert C. Lowry, *University of Texas at Dallas*
Gay Lyons, *Pellissippi State Technical Community College*
Susan Macfarland, *Gainesville College*
Hamed Madani, *Tarrant County College*
Maurice Mangum, *Southern Illinois University, Edwardsville*
David Mann, *College of Charleston*
Michael Margolis, *University of Cincinnati*
Steve Marin, *Victor Valley College*
Nancy Marion, *University of Akron*
Asher J. Matathias, *St. John's University*
Derek Maxfield, *Capital Community College*
Madhavi McCall, *San Diego State University*
Richard Medlar, *Dickinson State University*
Mark Milewicz, *Gordon College*
Eric Miller, *Blinn College*
Ken Moffett, *Southern Illinois University, Edwardsville*
Matthew Morgan, *Bentley College*
Stacia Munroe, *Lincoln Land Community College*
William Murin, *University of Wisconsin–Parkside*
Martha Musgrove, *Tarrant County College–SE Campus*
Jason Mycoff, *University of Delaware*
Napp Nazworth, *Texas A&M University, Corpus Christi*
Katherine Nelson-Born, *Columbia Southern University*
James Newman, *Idaho State University*
Adam Newmark, *Appalachian State University*
Peter Ngwafu, *Albany State University*
Randy Nobles, *Northeast Texas Community College*
Pat O'Connor, *Oakland Community College*
Laura Olson, *Clemson University*
Richard Pacelle, *Georgia Southern University*
Richard M. Pearlstein, *Southeastern Oklahoma State University*
David Penna, *Gallaudet University*
Clarissa Peterson, *DePauw University*
Geoffrey Peterson, *University of Wisconsin–Eau Claire*
Daniel Ponder, *Drury University*
Greg Rabb, *Jamestown Community College*
Jan Rabin, *Roanoke College*
Lee Rademacher, *Purdue University Calumet*
Mitzi Ramos, *University of Illinois at Chicago*
Kirk Randazzo, *University of Kentucky*
Christopher Reaves, *School of Social and Behavioral Sciences*
Steven Reti, *College of the Canyons*
James Rhodes, *Luther College*
Laurie Rice, *Southern Illinois University, Edwardsville*
Ken Robbins, *U.S. Military Academy at West Point*
John Roche, *Palomar College*
J. Philip Rogers, *San Antonio College*
Bernard Rowan, *Chicago State University*
Donald Roy, *Ferris State University*
Paul Rozycki, *Mott Community College*
Erich Saphir, *Pima Community College*
Chris Saladino, *Virginia Commonwealth University*
Greg Schaller, *Villanova University*
Calvin Scheidt, *Tidewater Community College*
Adam Schiffer, *Christian Texas University*
Diane Schmidt, *California State University*
Ronnee Schreiber, *San Diego State University*
Joseph Scrocca, *U.S. Military Academy at West Point*
T. M. Sell, *Highline College*
Brett Sharp, *University of Central Oklahoma*
James F. Sheffield, Jr., *University of Oklahoma*
Mark Shomaker, *Blinn College/Bryan Campus*
Steve Shupe, *Sonoma State University*
Tom Simpson, *Missouri Southern State University*
Brian Smith, *St. Edward's University*
Karen Smith, *Columbia Southern University*
John Speer, *Houston Community College, Southwest*
Jim Startin, *University of Texas at San Antonio*
Robert Sterken, *University of Texas at Tyler*
Theresia Stewart, *Elizabethtown Community and Technical College*
J. Cherie Strachan, *Central Michigan University*
Pamela Stricker, *Ohio University*
Carolyn Taylor, *Rogers State University*
Jeremy Teigen, *Ramapo College*
Judy Tobler, *Northwest Arkansas Community College*
Charles Turner, *California State University, Chico*
Chris Turner, *Laredo Community College*
Wilson Ugwu, *Concordia University*
Richard Unruh, *Fresno Pacific University*
David Uranga, *Pasadena City College*
James Van Arsdall, *Metropolitan Community College*
Ronald Vardy, *Wharton County Community College*
Dwight Vick, *University of South Dakota*
Adam Warber, *Clemson University*
Eddie Washington, *Rio Hondo College*
Ruth Ann Watry, *Northern Michigan University*
Wendy Watson, *University of North Texas*
Paul Weizer, *Fitchburg State College*
Mike Lee Western, *Texas College*
James Wilson, *Southern Methodist University*
Sean Wilson, *Penn State*
Heather Wyatt-Nichol, *Stephen F. Austin State University*
Peter Yacobucci, *Walsh University*
Chunmei Yoe, *Southeastern Oklahoma State University*

Acknowledgments

We are extremely grateful to the people at Pearson Longman for building on the success of the first edition of *Living Democracy* and helping us find ways to improve it. Although it required the work of numerous people to make this revision possible, several deserve special recognition. Development editor Leah Strauss provided wonderful suggestions at every stage of the project. Senior Production Editor Doug Bell (of GGS Higher Education Resources) deserves thanks for playing an essential role in keeping the authors on track, solving numerous problems, and ensuring the quality and consistency of our presentation. Finally, Editor-in-Chief for Political Science, Eric Stano, was instrumental in shaping the revision, and he deserves our gratitude for his energy and support.

Three scholars were kind enough to make significant contributions to the content of the policy chapters: Richard Barberio of the State University of New York at Oneonta, Paul Benson of Tarrant County College, and James Hastedt of James Madison University. For their contributions to features in this book, we are grateful to Bradley Dyke, Des Moines Area Community College; Laura Moyer, Louisiana State University; and Holley Tankersley, Coastal Carolina University. We are also grateful to Dana Glencross at Okalahoma City Community College for her careful reading of the manuscript. For photo research from a student's perspective, we thank Kaelyn Lowmaster for her assistance.

Joanne would like to thank her students in her American Politics classes, who have solidified her love of the subject. They are a continuing source of inspiration and motivation. A special thanks go to her family, Craig, Emma, and Connor—to whom her efforts are devoted—for their continued patience.

Chris thanks his wife, Charlotte, and children, Alicia and Eric, for their support and encouragement. Dan would like to thank his colleagues in the Department of Political Science and the Center for Political Participation at Allegheny College for their assistance and encouragement. And, as always, he offers a special thanks to his wonderful family—Christine, Abby, Daniel, and Brian—for their love, guidance, and unwavering support.

About the Authors

Daniel M. Shea is a Professor of Political Science and Director of the Center for Political Participation at Allegheny College. He earned his Bachelor of Arts degree in Political Science and American Studies from the State University of New York at Oswego, his Master of Arts degree in Campaign Management from the University of West Florida, and his Ph.D. in Political Science from the State University of New York at Albany. Dan has received numerous awards for his teaching and scholarship and has authored or co-authored several books on the American political process. In the fall of 2002, he founded the Center for Political Participation (CPP) to foster a greater appreciation for political engagement and to develop hands-on programs that bring young people into the civic realm. The CPP develops programs for Allegheny students, for community partners, and for scholars nationwide, and several of their recent initiatives have garnered national media attention.

Joanne Connor Green is an Associate Professor of Political Science, the Director of the Institute on Women and Gender, and the former Director of Women's Studies at Texas Christian University. She earned her Bachelor's degree in Political Science from the University of Buffalo in 1990 and her Ph.D. in American Politics from the University of Florida in 1994. Joanne's research and teaching interests include the role of gender in congressional elections and interest group politics. She has published a number of articles in scholarly journals, including *Women & Politics*, as well as other academic outlets.

Christopher E. Smith is a Professor of Criminal Justice at Michigan State University. He previously taught at the University of Akron and the University of Connecticut at Hartford. He earned his Ph.D. in Political Science at the University of Connecticut at Storrs and also holds degrees from Harvard University, the University of Bristol (U.K.), and the University of Tennessee College of Law. As a specialist on courts and constitutional law, he has written more than 20 books. He has also written more than 100 scholarly articles on law and politics.

Living DEMOCRACY

BRIEF NATIONAL EDITION

Key Objective Outline

Why is citizen participation so important in a democracy?

What are the themes of this book?

What are the various "pathways" of involvement in our political system?

What are the forces of stability in American politics?

CHAPTER 1
AMERICAN GOVERNMENT: DEMOCRACY IN ACTION

Can average citizens play a meaningful role in American politics?

Early in the 2008 race for the presidency, New York Senator Hillary Clinton seemed the inevitable Democratic nominee. She had higher name recognition than any other candidate and had raised more money than everyone else. She was way ahead in the polls, and it certainly did not hurt that her husband, Bill, remained very popular with average Democrats.

Then a first term Senator from Illinois by the name of Barack Obama jumped into the race. He had little experience and paltry name recognition. But young people in particular seemed attracted to his message of change. As the Iowa Caucuses drew near, Obama was getting inexplicably huge crowds—but mostly from young folks at college campuses. Some dismissed his chances, because support from young Americans had proven, time and again, to be more fizzle than bang. All too often young Americans seemed content to sit on the sidelines. Surely Clinton would win.

Hillary Clinton didn't win, however, because young voters didn't stay home. A massive young voter turnout in Iowa gave Obama a stunning victory. Turnout for those younger than 30 quadrupled from 2004 levels. Some 57 percent of this group gave their support to Obama. Young Americans had won the day for the junior senator from Illinois.

And it did not stop there. In one state after another, from one primary and caucus to the next, young voters came out in record numbers. In the California and Maryland primaries, youth turnout grew by 50 percent. In Connecticut, Massachusetts, and Louisiana, it doubled, and in Oklahoma, Texas, Mississippi, Missouri, Georgia, and Florida, it tripled. Not all of these young men and women supported Obama, but the surge of young voters proved to be a critical part of his nomination victory.

In the general election, the level of youth engagement was dramatic. Young activists filled campaign offices, knocked on doors, e-mailed literature, texted friends, raised unprecedented sums of money, and above all, organized. On election day, the percentage of those under 30 who voted mushroomed, with a stunning 68 percent casting their ballot for Obama—likely the highest share of the youth vote obtained by any candidate in American history.

Yes, history was made in 2008. "Our campaign," noted President-elect Obama on the night of his victory, "was not hatched in the halls of Washington—it began in the backyards of Des Moines and the living rooms of Concord and the front porches of Charleston . . . [And] it grew strength from the young people who rejected the myth of their generation's apathy."

STUDENT RESOURCE-CENTER
- Glossary
- Vocabulary Example
- LINK
- MyPoliSciLab Connection

COMPARATIVE **Comparing Political Landscapes**

Politics: The process by which the actions of government are determined.

EXAMPLE: *By appealing to members of the city council to change the new housing ordinance, several students decided to roll up their sleeves and become engaged in local politics.*

It's Your Government!

(pages 4–7)

Why is citizen participation so important in a democracy?

Everyone knows that government affects our lives. We must obey laws created by government. We pay taxes to support the government. We make use of government services, ranging from police protection to student loans. It is easy, however, to see government as a distant entity that imposes its will on us. It provides benefits and protections, such as schools, roads, and fire departments. But it also limits our choices by telling us how fast we can drive and how old we must be to get married, purchase alcoholic beverages, and vote.

Would your view of government and your sense of distance from this source of power change if a new law dramatically affected your choices, plans, or expectations? Imagine that you and your four best friends decide to rent a house together for the next academic year. You find a five-bedroom, furnished house near campus that is owned by a friendly landlord. You sign a lease, put down your deposit, and look forward to the fun that you will have when the fall semester begins. During the summer, however, the landlord sends you a letter informing you that two of your friends will need to find someplace else to live. The city council has passed a new ordinance—the kind of law produced by local governments—declaring that not more than three unrelated people may live in a house together.

Now what would you think about government? Your planned living situation and social life for the upcoming year might change dramatically. After your initial feelings of anger, you might resign yourself to the disappointment of moving back into a dormitory or finding a different apartment. You might also ask yourself an important question: Is there anything that you can do about this new ordinance?

> "What can I do to influence government?"
>
> —Student Question

A distinguishing feature of democracy—the form of government in the United States—is that people have opportunities to influence the decisions of government. A single individual cannot realistically expect to control the government's choice of priorities or the laws that are produced. In fact, individuals may fail in their attempts to change laws. In some circumstances, individuals can participate in activities that ultimately change government and lead to the creation of new laws and regulations. Let us take the example of the housing ordinance and consider what you might do to attempt to change that law:

- You could encourage students to register to vote and help with political campaigns for city council candidates who promise to listen to students' concerns and get rid of the housing ordinance. In some college towns, individual students have become so energized by specific political issues that they have actually run for and been elected to the city council. These activities, *voting* and *elections,* are the most familiar forms of citizen participation in a democracy.
- You could organize your friends to write letters and make phone calls to members of the city council asking them to change the restrictive new law. You could also go to city council meetings and voice your opposition to the law. We often characterize these activities as *lobbying* lawmakers in order to pressure or persuade them to make specific decisions.
- You could talk to the local landlords' association about whether it might file a lawsuit challenging the ordinance on the grounds that it improperly interferes with the landlords' right to decide how to use their private property. You might talk to an attorney yourself about whether, under the laws of your state, a new ordinance can override the rental lease agreement that you and your friends had already signed. If the new ordinance violates other existing laws, then taking the issue to court by filing lawsuits—a process known as *litigation*—may provide the means for an individual's lawyer to persuade a judge to invalidate the city council's action.
- You could write articles in the college newspaper to inform other students about the new ordinance and the effect of the law on their off-campus housing choices. You could publicize and sponsor meetings in order to organize *grassroots activities,* such as marches, sit-ins, or other forms of nonviolent protests. All this will draw news media attention and put pressure on city officials to reconsider their decision.

There is no guarantee that any of these approaches will produce the change that you desire. But each of these courses of action, depending on the circumstances in the community and the number of people who provide support, presents the possibility that the government's decision may be altered.

CONNECT THE LINK (Chapter **2**, pages **32–33**) Is there really a difference between government and politics?

Public Policy: What government decides to do or not do; government laws, rules, or expenditures.

EXAMPLE: *It is public policy that you must be 21 years old to purchase alcohol in Pennsylvania.*

All these approaches are part of **politics**. A more complete discussion of this topic is provided in LINK Chapter 2, pages 32–33, but for now, you should understand that politics concerns the activities that seek to affect the composition, power, and actions of government.

American government should *not* be viewed as "distant," "all-powerful," or "unchangeable." It might be easy to see the government in these terms. When you see a courthouse, a state capitol building, or one of the massive stone buildings that house government agencies in Washington, D.C., it's easy to see these impressive structures as monuments to be revered and admired. Government buildings are often designed to instill a feeling of respect and to convey permanence, stability, and power. In reality, these buildings are much more than awe-inspiring works of architecture. They are *arenas of activity* that determine **public policy**. The laws and policies produced by government in these arenas affect the lives of everyone in the United States—including students just like you, as suggested in Table 1.1. It is essential that you understand laws and

TABLE 1.1 | Government Is All Around Us

Doubt government plays a role in your daily life? Consider the following timeline of a typical day in the life of an average college student and the number of times governmental control comes into play. Keep in mind that this is only the tip of the iceberg.

TIME	EVENT	GOVERNMENT AGENCY
6:22 A.M.	You are awakened by the sounds of a garbage truck outside. Annoyed, you realize that you have forgotten to bring the recyclables to the street last night.	Local department of sanitation; local recycling program
6:49 A.M.	Unable to get back to sleep, you take a shower, thinking about the cost of rent for your apartment and wondering if your next place will have a decent shower.	Local water filtration plant; federal Department of Housing and Urban Development
7:22 A.M.	You read the newspaper, noting that interest rates are going up and the war in Iraq seems to be going better.	Federal Reserve Board; Selective Service; Department of Defense
8:34 A.M.	Driving to class, you notice the airbag—and you don't notice dirty car exhaust. You also note that your inspection sticker is about to expire.	Federal Environmental Protection Agency, state and local environmental agencies; state Motor Vehicle Bureau
8:43 A.M.	You stop at a gas station and wonder why gas prices continue to shoot upward.	Federal government investments in oil exploration and alternative fuels; presidential oversight of the Strategic Oil Reserves; federal trade agreements
9:05 A.M.	You arrive on campus, find a parking space, and walk to class.	State and federal support for higher education; state and federal tuition support and student loan programs
11:00 A.M.	In accounting class, you discuss the CPA exam.	State professional licensing program
12:09 P.M.	At lunch, you discuss the upcoming elections. Your best friend realizes that she won't be able to vote because she missed the registration deadline.	State election commission
3:00 P.M.	You receive a paycheck for your part-time restaurant job. In spite of the low hourly wage you receive, a bunch of money has been deducted for taxes.	Federal and state minimum wage laws; local, state, and federal income tax regulations; federal unemployment program; federal Social Security program
4:15 P.M.	You figure out a customer's bill, carefully adding the sales tax to the total.	Local and state sales taxes
9:47 P.M.	You settle in for some television after studying and are surprised at how much profanity cable stations allow.	Federal Communications Commission
11:49 P.M.	You collapse into bed and slip into a peaceful sleep, taking for granted that you are safe.	Local police department; state militia; U.S. military

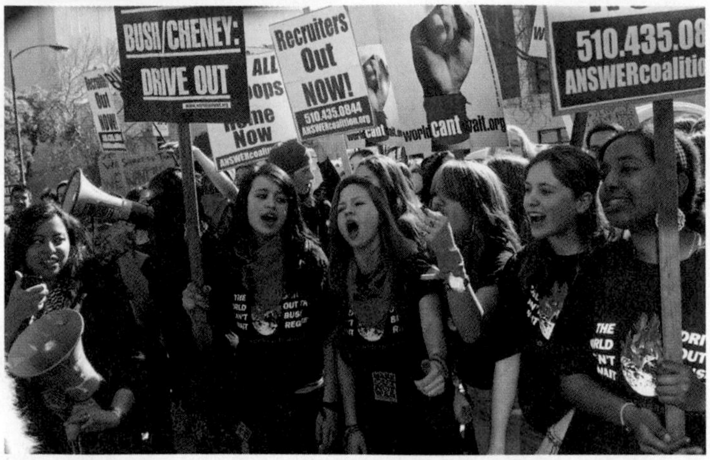

One of the great myths of our day is that young Americans are apathetic, indifferent, and lazy. In truth, many are deeply concerned about public matters and are civically active. Unfortunately, however, many doubt the effectiveness of politics as a viable avenue for change. This book is designed to help students understand their potential in a democratic political system.

COUNTRY	RATING	CLASSIFICATION
Canada	1	Free
France	1	
Netherlands	1	
South Africa	1	
United States	1	
India	2	
Jamaica	2	
Mexico	2	
Bolivia	3	
Kenya	3	
Nigeria	4	Partly Free
Afghanistan	5	
Jordan	5	
Egypt	6	Not Free
Russia	6	
China	7	
North Korea	7	
Saudi Arabia	7	

MAP OF FREEDOM, 2007

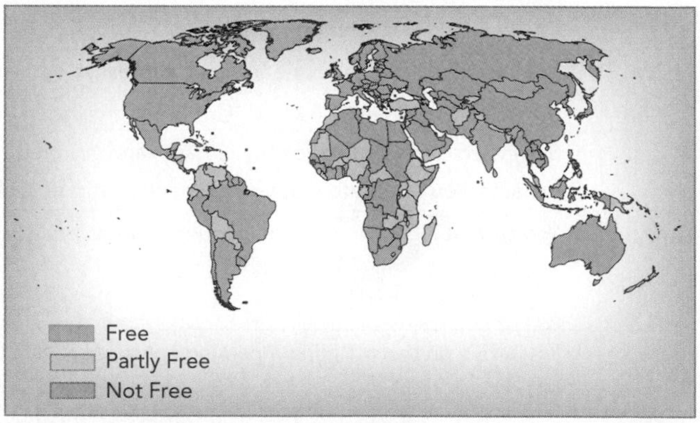

FIGURE 1.1 | **Global Ratings on Political Rights**

Do you find anything in this figure surprising, or are the ratings as you expected?

SOURCE: Reprinted by permission of Freedom House, Inc. www.freedomhouse.org

policies are themselves influenced by the actions of groups and individuals. Citizens just like you can play an important role in the policy process.

Our Unique Political System

The United States is different from other governments in the world; it developed as a result of the specific social conditions, social values, and historical events that shaped this country. Our government and laws reflect this country's history as a group of former British colonies that fought a war for independence, expanded westward across a wilderness through the efforts of pioneers, and survived a bloody civil war that occurred, in large part, over the issue of race-based slavery.

Many aspects of American government, such as elections and the right to a fair trial before being convicted of a crime, can be found in other countries, but the organization of American elections and the rights possessed by criminal defendants in American courts differ from those found elsewhere in the world. There are other aspects of American politics and government that are unique to the United States. Because democracy creates opportunities for citizens to influence government, people can seek to adjust the design and operation of government as well as to affect the laws and policies produced by government.

If we look at countries around the world, we can discover a variety of forms of government. By classifying forms of government according to two factors, citizen participation in governmental

CONNECT THE LINK
(Chapter **2,** pages **34–35**) How does one classify different types of government?

decisions and freedom for individuals, a number of different types of governments emerge. (We'll also say more about this in LINK Chapter 2, pages 34–35.) Freedom House, a nonprofit, nonpartisan organization, makes just such an assessment. Every year, it issues a rating of countries according to the extent of political rights (for example, voting) and individual liberties (for example, freedom of speech) that their citizens have. Countries are rated on a scale from 1 to 7, with 1 meaning the highest level of political rights. Political rights are evaluated based on voters being presented with genuine choices, selection of candidates without government approval, lack of military involvement in elections and government, and related factors. Representative findings are shown in Figure 1.1.

"What is unique about the way Americans practice democracy?"
—Student Question

At the top end of the scale are democracies, including the United States, in which citizens enjoy a large measure of personal freedom and have meaningful opportunities to participate in government through voting, organizing protests against government policies, and other forms of free speech and political action. All democracies are not identical, however. As we will see later in the book, compared to judges in other democracies, American judges possess significant power to invalidate laws and policies created by other government decision makers. Thus Americans have unique opportunities to use litigation as a means to influence government. Democracies also differ in the organization and rules for their governments.

As a knowledgeable student of American government and a citizen whose actions can help shape decisions in a democracy, you should seize the opportunity to think critically about the design and operation of the governing system. Unlike the residents of many other countries throughout the world, you can actually use your knowledge, critical analysis, time, and energy to improve your country's laws and policies. Your efforts might be aimed at decisions by local government, as in the example of the controversial housing ordinance, or you might roll up your sleeves to help an underdog candidate win an election, as some young Americans did for Barack Obama in 2008. There are numerous pathways for your involvement, and you can seek to affect government at the state and national levels. The chapters of this book will help you to see how you can actively participate in processes that influence the decisions and actions of your government.

It's Your Government
Practice Quiz

1. According to the Map of Freedom in Figure 1.1, most of the continent of Asia is labeled
   a. free. **b.** partly free.
   c. not free. **d.** failed states.

2. In the United States, voting is only one of many forms of participation available to citizens.
   a. true **b.** false

Answers: 1-c, 2-a.

Discussion Questions

1. What are some of the distinguishing features of a democracy?
2. What are some aspects of democratic government that are unique to the United States?

What **YOU** can do!

To see state laws concerning crimes, traffic regulations, and other matters that concern you where you live and where you are attending college, you can look up statutes by state on the Internet at **http://www.findlaw.com/11stategov**

Themes *of* This Book

(pages 8–17)

What are the themes of this book?

American government is complex. The functions of government are divided among different institutions and people. Courts handle certain kinds of decisions that are presented to government in the form of lawsuits. Congress and other lawmaking bodies handle other kinds of matters. And the president bears responsibility for additional matters, such as military affairs. In some countries, a national government creates law and public policy to handle all issues and priorities for its people. In the United States, by contrast, there are multiple governments. In addition to the familiar institutions of the national government, including the president, Congress, and the U.S. Supreme Court, there are parallel institutions and actors in all 50 states, plus additional agencies and actors in cities, counties, and townships within each state. Although this book primarily focuses on the national government, you must remain aware of the importance of laws and policies produced by other levels of government.

To illustrate how government works and how you can affect the way it works, this book first shows the opportunities for *citizen participation in democratic government.* Second, the text will identify and analyze the *pathways of action* through which individuals and groups can seek to influence law and public policy in American government. Third, the text will emphasize the importance of American society's *diversity and the effect that has on government and our participation in it.* Let's take a moment to consider these three themes in greater detail.

Rallies, protests, and demonstrations have always been effective modes of political participation in our country. ***—Have you ever taken part in this type of political action?***

Citizen Participation in Democratic Government

As we noted earlier, opportunities for citizens to participate in their government are a distinguishing feature of democracy. In nondemocratic governing systems, people have few ways, if any, to shape law and policy. For example, *totalitarian governments* swiftly arrest and even kill people who express opposition to the central authority. But the near absence of opportunities for citizen participation and input does not mean that citizens can never do anything to influence the government. The only option available to citizens in some countries is an armed revolt—using violence to change the system of government. In today's world, given the firepower that all governments (and especially dictatorial ones) command, such revolts rarely succeed. And when they occur, violent revolts typically impose significant destruction and human suffering, especially on innocent civilians who are caught in the crossfire. When violence is the sole mechanism available to citizens who seek to influence their government, the results of that violence can lead to very unpredictable and tragic results.

In contrast, people in the United States have opportunities to express their viewpoints and take actions to influence the government without resorting to violence. Opportunities for citizen participation can help create and maintain a stable society. The chapters of this book will provide many examples of such opportunities.

These opportunities for citizen participation will not be fully effective, however, unless people actually become engaged in public affairs. If large numbers neglect to vote, fail to keep themselves informed about the government's actions, or passively accept all decisions by lawmakers, governing power may come to rest in the hands of a small number of individuals and groups. The quality and effectiveness of laws and policies may suffer if there is inadequate input from the full range of people who will be affected by them. Without knowledge about the lives of the poor, for example, well-intentioned decisions to address poverty by Congress and the president may be misdirected and fail to get at the actual source of the problem. In the same way, lawmakers might make more effective laws concerning financial aid programs for college students if students provide information and express their viewpoints about the best course of action. In other words, the laws and policies of a democracy can reflect the preferences and viewpoints of a diverse country only if citizens from all segments of society make their voices heard.

Now look at the comparison of voting rates in Figure 1.2. Does this raise any concerns about whether Americans are active enough in shaping their government's decisions? Note that some of the countries with the highest voting rates impose fines on citizens who fail to register to vote and cast their ballots. Would such a law violate Americans' notions of freedom?

To many, it seems ironic that the legal opportunities to participate in the electoral process have expanded greatly during the past 50 years, but a bare majority of Americans seem willing to do so. Numerous measures of political engagement suggest a rather disengaged citizenry in the United States. The American National Election Study at the University of Michigan has been surveying the public every two years since the late 1940s. Scholars will often turn to this data to explore all sorts of political behaviors and trends. It suggests that about 7 percent of Americans attend political meetings, 10 percent give money to political candidates, and only 3 percent work for political parties or candidates. Just one-third of us actually try to influence how others vote (in some years, this figure has been below 20 percent). In many recent presidential elections, as much as 30 percent of Americans had no interest in who wins. Only about one out of five Americans follow public affairs "most of the time."

The Center for Information and Research on Civic Learning and Engagement at Tufts University has also done a good deal of work on measuring trends in political involvement. In 2006, they issued a report called "The 2006 Civic and Political Health of the Nation." It is based on the results of a survey of nearly 2,300 Americans. The report notes improvements, but it also underscores nagging problems—particularly low levels of engagement among young Americans. Figure 1.3 provides the results of several questions from the survey. Overall the picture is of a modestly engaged public.

As noted, active participation by citizens is necessary in order for a democracy's laws and policies to reflect what people want. Yet there will always be disagreements and conflicts among an active citizenry. Democracy can seem inefficient, because debates and competing groups' political strategies can prolong the process of making decisions. Laws and policies in a democracy often represent compromises

FIGURE 1.2 | (a) A Comparative Look at Voting Rates Since 1992; (b) Voter Turnout in Six Democracies

Americans clearly vote less often than citizens in other countries.—***Why do you suppose this is true?*** Not only do Americans vote less often than citizens of other nations, the general trend since the 1960s has been toward less participation.

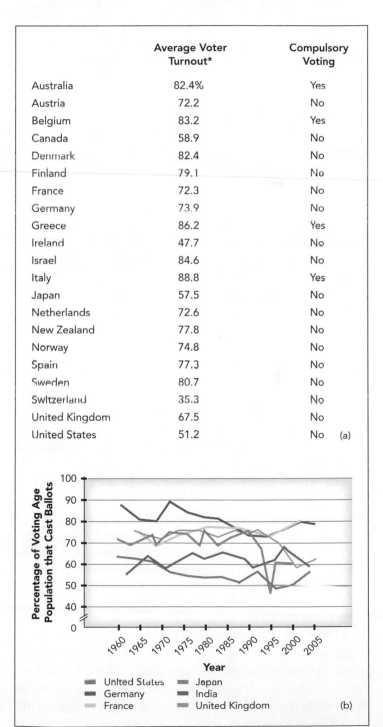

	Average Voter Turnout*	Compulsory Voting
Australia	82.4%	Yes
Austria	72.2	No
Belgium	83.2	Yes
Canada	58.9	No
Denmark	82.4	No
Finland	79.1	No
France	72.3	No
Germany	73.9	No
Greece	86.2	Yes
Ireland	47.7	No
Israel	84.6	No
Italy	88.8	Yes
Japan	57.5	No
Netherlands	72.6	No
New Zealand	77.8	No
Norway	74.8	No
Spain	77.3	No
Sweden	80.7	No
Switzerland	35.3	No
United Kingdom	67.5	No
United States	51.2	No

(a)

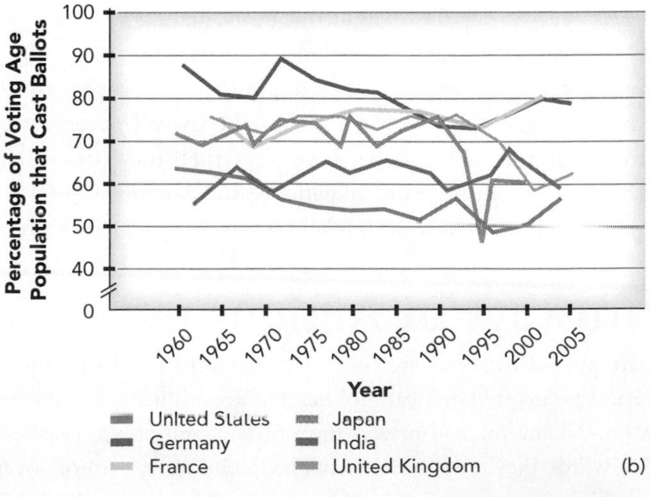

(b)

*Percentage of total voting-age population participating in election for highest-level office (president of the United States, for example).

SOURCE: Reprinted by permission of CIRCLE, School of Public Affairs, University of Maryland. www.idea.int; www.civicyouth.org and Electionworld.org

Pathways of Action: The activities of citizens in American politics that affect the creation, alteration, and preservation of laws and policies.

EXAMPLE: *Average citizens can help change the course of public policy by lobbying legislators.*

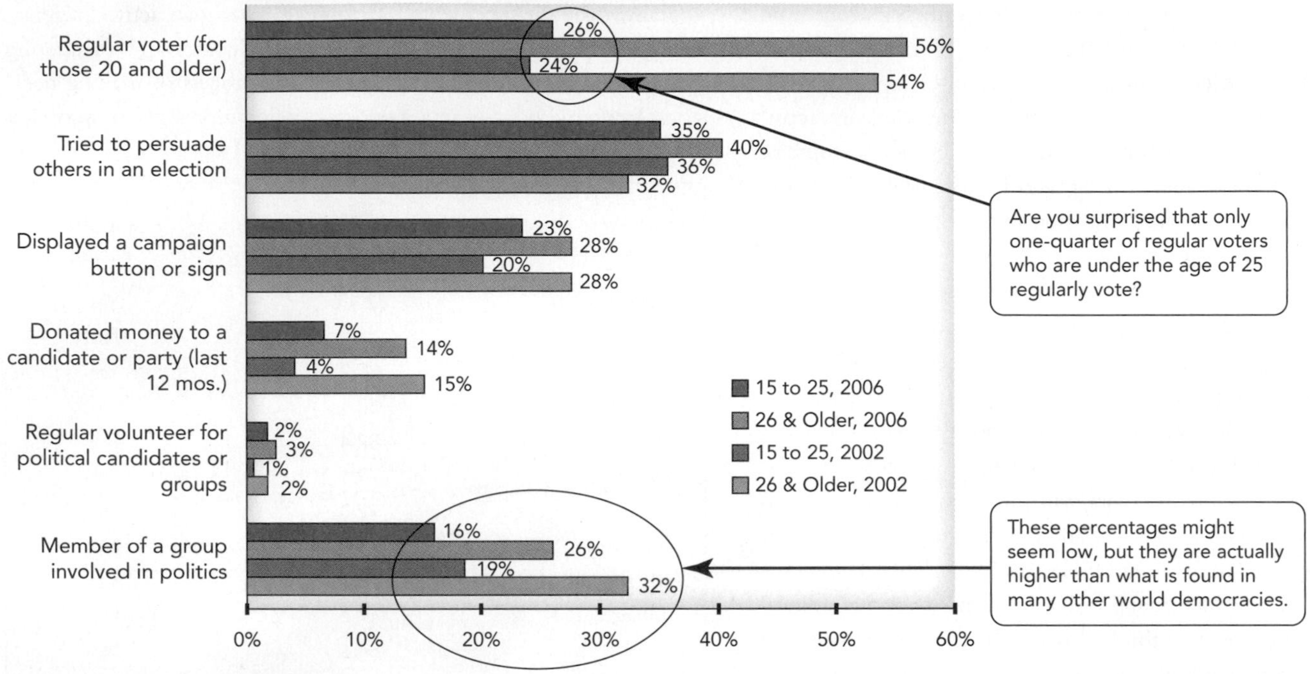

FIGURE 1.3 | **The Political Health of the Nation**

SOURCE: *The 2006 Civic and Political Health of the Nation: A Detailed Look at How Youth Participate in Politics and Communities* (College Park, MD: CIRCLE: Center for Information and Research on Civic Learning and Engagement, October 2006), Figure 8 (p. 16), http://www.civicyouth.org/PopUps/2006_CPHS_Report_update.pdf. Reprinted by permission of CIRCLE.

between the viewpoints and interests of different individuals and groups. On top of this, the framers sought to create a system that would produce slow, moderate change. As discussed in the next chapter, they worried a great deal about sudden shifts in public policy. So active citizen participation does not produce smooth, dramatic policymaking. It simply makes sure that a range of viewpoints and interests is presented before compromises are produced.

As you will see throughout this book, getting what you want out of government requires patience and perseverance. Citizens' actions don't always produce desired results. Some people can work for many years seeking to change a specific law yet never succeed, but that's not a reason to be discouraged. History provides too many lessons about the value of patience and perseverance for us to give up on efforts that seem unlikely to succeed in the near future.

Pathways of Action

Pathways of action are the various activities, institutions, and decision points in American politics and government that affect the creation, alteration, and preservation of laws and public policies. In other words, they are the routes of change in our system of government. Certain pathways are open to individual citizens, who can cast their votes, initiate lawsuits, and organize public demonstrations as a means to influence government. The effectiveness of activities within these pathways may depend on the resources, organizational skills, and knowledge possessed by the people making use of them. For example, people who have a lot of money may be able to use litigation more effectively, because they can hire experienced lawyers and carry their lawsuits through all levels of the court system. Resources and organizational skills can also affect people's efforts to conduct petition drives, advertise community meetings, and stage public rallies. Because resources, knowledge, and skill can enhance the effectiveness of citizen participation, powerful organized groups, such as the National Rifle Association, the Chamber of Commerce, and AARP, are often better positioned than single individuals to achieve their public policy goals through specific pathways.

As you will see, not all pathways of action are equally open to all people. For example, effective lobbying and the use of personal contacts to influence decisions by Congress may require resources and skills possessed only by organized groups and experienced, well-connected individuals. However, because personal freedom in the United States includes opportunities to publicize ideas and form political organizations, highly motivated individuals may be able to gain the resources and contacts necessary for active participation in these less accessible pathways of action. For example, Mothers Against Drunk Driving (MADD) was started in 1980 by a small group of ordinary people with friends or family members who had been killed by drunk drivers. Two decades later, MADD had 3 million members and exerted substantial influence over national, state, and local policies concerning alcohol consumption and traffic enforcement.

The existence of several pathways of action to influence American government does not mean that the United States is always able to resolve conflicts peaceably. The bloody Civil War of 1861–1865, which cost more American lives than any other war, reflected the nation's inability to use democratic processes to resolve the controversial issues of race-based slavery and federal versus state control of public policy. These conflicts ran so deep that they were probably not susceptible to compromise solutions. Timothy McVeigh's politically motivated bombing of a federal office building in Oklahoma City in 1995, which killed 168 people, shows that some individuals and groups reject the give-and-take interactions and compromise results of nonviolent pathways of action in a democratic society. If people have fundamental objections to the nature and existence of the democratic governing system of the United States, they may resort to terrorism. Brief episodes of public disorder and violence also erupt periodically in urban neighborhoods, often triggered by police officers shooting a suspected criminal. These episodes are often attributed to frustration felt by poor people who perceive their opportunities for effective political participation and economic success to be blocked by racial, ethnic, or social-class discrimination. Some participants in these events may simply join a frenzy of theft and property destruction. Others may participate, in part, because they do not believe that pathways of action, such as voting, lobbying, and organized protests, provide realistic opportunities for them to have their viewpoints heard and understood by decision makers in government. Throughout American history, we can identify instances in which people, seeking to express themselves and influence government, used violence instead of the pathways of peaceful action presented in this book. However, the relative stability of American society and the longevity of its governing system are attributable to the existence of nonviolent pathways that provide opportunities for meaningful participation in democratic government.

The chapters of this book are organized to highlight important pathways of action that provide opportunities for citizens' participation in and influence over American government. Let's introduce these pathways of action. As you consider these opportunities for citizen action, think about how you might contribute to or participate in activities within each pathway. Figure 1.4, on pp. 12–13, shows the 10 steps in choosing a pathway of action. As an example, we review the creation of tough drunk driver laws in the past two decades.

ELECTIONS PATHWAY American government is based on representative democracy, in which voters elect leaders and then hold those leaders accountable for the decisions they make about law and public policy. If the voters disagree with the decisions that leaders make, the voters can elect different leaders in the next election. Because government leaders in a democracy are usually concerned about maintaining public support in order to gain reelection, they feel pressured to listen to the public and to please a majority of the voters with their actions. Even officials who do not plan to run for reelection or who have served the maximum number of terms the law permits, such as a president who has been elected to a second four-year term, demonstrate their concern for voters' preferences, because they want to help the election chances of other members of their political party.

A variety of activities, actors, and institutions are involved in the elections pathway. For example, political parties are important actors in this pathway. By organizing like-minded individuals into a group that can plan strategies for winning elections, a political party can raise money and provide public information in ways that will help put into office leaders who share the party's specific values and policy preferences. Activities in the elections pathway include voter registration drives, fundraising, political campaigning, and each individual voter's action in casting a ballot.

LOBBYING DECISION MAKERS PATHWAY Legislatures are the central lawmaking bodies at the national, state, and local levels of government. At the national level, the federal legislature is Congress. States also have their own legislatures, and local legislatures include city councils, county commissions, and village boards. Legislatures are made up of elected representatives who must regularly face the voters in elections. Unlike the elections pathway (the mechanisms by which candidates are chosen to fill offices), the lobbying pathway involves attempting to influence the activities, actors, and institutions of government by supplying information, persuasion, or political pressure. Lobbying activities target legislatures and executive officials, such as presidents and governors, as well as the bureaucrats who staff government agencies.

In the lobbying pathway, individuals and organized groups present information and persuasive arguments to government officials. The aim is to convince these decision makers either to support specific proposed laws or to oppose proposed changes in existing laws and policies. Lobbying occurs in the context of the decision-making processes used by each institution. In the legislature, individuals and organized groups can testify before committee hearings attended by legislators. With the president or a governor, the individual or group representative seeks a direct appointment with the decision maker or presents information and arguments to the executive's top aides. Lobbyists also seek meetings with legislators, often buying them meals or taking them on trips that

Step 1 Historical Context
It is essential that the activist understand the legal context, the history surrounding the issue, past governmental and political developments, and previous actors. It is especially important to understand the successes and failures of similar movements and the pathways that were used. → Drunk driving and related injuries and deaths are rampant in the United States. In 1980, some 25,000 are killed by drunk drivers.

Step 2 The Trigger
Why did you become involved in an issue? What fueled your motivation? Was it a steady development or a sudden event that motivated you to act? → 13-year old Cari Lightner is killed by a drunk driver as she walks down a quiet street. Her grieving mother, Candy, sets her sights on tougher drunk driving laws and in 1980 forms Mothers Against Drunk Driving (MADD).

Step 3 Actors That Will Help
Who might you expect to help your efforts and what are their motivations? Who are your potential supporters and what would trigger their action? → Other grieving parents, those in communities that have seen horrific drunk driving accidents, youth advocacy groups such as Students Against Destructive Decisions (SADD).

Step 4 Actors with the Opposition
Who is likely to oppose your efforts and why? How motivated will they be? → Tavern and restaurant owners, liquor industry, civil libertarian groups such as the Center for Consumer Freedom.

Step 5 Timing
When might you best proceed with your efforts? Will there be particular stages or a singular bold stroke? How long will things take? → As new data is revealed on drunk driving accidents, after a high-profile event stirs public emotions.

FIGURE 1.4 | **The Ten Steps in Choosing a Pathway of Action** ***An Illustration: Toughening Drunk Driving Regulations***

In this case, the pathway selected was grassroots mobilization. MADD began with a massive letter-writing campaign, attracted media attention, and changed public opinion. In the end, decision makers had little choice but to respond.

*Note: It is critical that the activist understand that the selection of a pathway is not fixed, but rather is dependent upon new developments, successes and failures, and the adjustments of the opposition. Yet, all political action begins with a step down a pathway of action. Also, remember that several pathways often exist to pursue your objectives—if you are not successful using one pathway, look to another. History has proven that diligence is often the key to success.

will supposedly educate them about issues. Information and persuasion may well be accompanied by financial contributions to the reelection campaigns of legislators or elected executives. Lobbying, in the form of information and persuasion, can also be directed at permanent employees in government agencies who have the authority to create government regulations, such as rules concerning the environment, business practices, and consumer products. Because agency officials do not run for election, any money offered to them by lobbyists would be an illegal bribe, so individuals and organized groups instead seek to persuade these officials while at the same time lobbying legislators and elected executives to put pressure on the government agencies to advance or block specific policy goals.

Effective lobbying typically requires money, time, and other resources, such as a large organizational membership to flood officials'

Step 6 Your Resources
What resources will you bring to the cause? A partial list includes your time, intelligence, passion, financial resources, networks of like-minded activists, ability to garner sympathetic media attention, expertise and experience in similar endeavors, and much else. → Passion, time, media attention, public sympathy.

Step 7 Your Opposition's Resources
What will your opposition bring to the table? Will their resources be similar or different? If they are similar, how can you take best advantage of your resources and minimize the effectiveness of your opponents' resources? → Lobbyists, money, long-standing access to decisionmakers, campaign resources.

Step 8 Pathway Access
Even though your resources might suggest a particular course of action, not all issues fit each of the pathways. For example, there might be no way to pursue a legal course of action. Along similar lines, decision makers might be more receptive to efforts directed down certain pathways. For instance, judges often express indifference to rallies and protests surrounding an issue. → No clear court pathway point of access, yet the cause is ideal for attracting public attention. Graphic stories and visuals are available.

Step 9 Pathway Selected by the Opposition
What pathway has your opposition used, and has it proven successful? If your efforts are successful, which pathway will the opposition likely take? → Lobbying decision makers; elections.

Step 10 How to Measure Success
How will you measure success? How will you sustain your efforts until success is reached? Establishing incremental goals can allow for celebration as they are achieved to create and sustain momentum. → New laws passed, data shows a shrinking number drive while intoxicated, fewer are injured and killed by drunk drivers.

offices with letters and e-mails, or personal relationships between lobbyists and government officials, as when interest groups hire former members of Congress to represent them in presenting information and arguments. Under the right circumstances, people who lack resources may effectively influence government by getting the attention of key officials. For example, research has shown that letters and phone calls from ordinary citizens are an important source of ideas for new laws and policies.[1]

PATHWAYS | of action

Powershift '07

Nearly 6,000 students at a single conference? Seriously?

In early November of 2007, students from around the nation convened at the University of Maryland for a three-day conference—an event dubbed *Powershift '07*. Sponsored by the Energy Action Coalition, the event became the largest student-centered global warming conference ever held. The goals of the event were to share information about the growing threat of climate change and to help committed young citizens become effective political advocates.

Dozens of organizers, policy experts, and public officials addressed the gathering on the first day, including House Speaker Nancy Pelosi, who called young global warming activists the "magnificent disrupters of our time." Dozens of break out sessions were held the next day, where students learned how to become effective at organizing and lobbying. "Advocating for Green Jobs," "How to Start a Nonprofit," and "Sustainable Farming and Dining on Campus" were just a few of these workshops.

There was also time to hear some participants recount worries about climate change. The dramatic moment came when Cheryl Lockwood, a Yupik Eskimo from Alaska, broke into tears when describing the adverse effects of global warming on her hometown and its residents. "Crops were being ruined, and animals were fleeing north." Brittany R. Cochran, a pharmacy student at Xavier University in New Orleans, spoke of the effect that serious hurricanes, like Katrina, have on low-income coastal communities.

On Monday, the third day, students were asked to put their newly acquired skills to use. Nearly 3,000 of them descended on Capitol Hill. They stormed offices, testified before committees, and held a rally on the West Lawn. "We're like dogs," noted Summer Rayne Oakes, one of the organizers. "We can smell fear, and we have no patience for bullshit."

But was anybody listening? According to Congressman Edward Markey, chair of an important House committee, it was the largest turnout for a hearing he had seen in 31 years. And Samantha Kanofsky, a junior from Pomona College in California, seemed quite excited about her involvement and the prospects of it making a difference: "[Members of Congress] kept telling us how it really does make a difference that we were there, speaking our minds on climate change."

SOURCE: Ben Adler, "Students Demand Environmental Power Shift," *Politico,* November 6, 2007. Kevin Nowland, "Reporter's Notebook: Power Shift Conference," *The Student Life News,* November 9, 2007. Elizabeth Hightower, "The Thrill Is Gone," *Outside,* February 2008. ■

COURT PATHWAY In the United States, judges have broader authority than in other countries to order the government to take specific actions. Because people in the United States are granted specific legal rights, they can use those rights as a basis for filing lawsuits against the government. For example, if a man was charged under an old state law for the crime of shouting profanity in front of women and children, his lawyer could challenge the validity of the law by asking a judge to declare that it violated the man's legal right to freedom of speech. Such a case actually occurred in Michigan in 1998, where judges eventually ruled that the law violated the man's free speech rights because it was too vague to give him guidance about what words were illegal.[2] Individuals can also file lawsuits asking judges to order the government to follow its own laws. This often happens in cases concerning environmental issues or consumer products when people believe that government officials are failing to enforce the law properly.

Litigation is expensive. People who use this pathway must hire an attorney and pay for gathering and presenting evidence to a court. Organized groups interested in the issue may use their resources to help people carry their cases through the courts. For example, the National Rifle Association (NRA) may provide assistance to individuals who sue to invalidate firearms regulations, or the American Civil Liberties Union (ACLU) may supply attorneys to represent people who believe that their rights to freedom of speech have been violated by the government. Many important policies have been shaped by the actions of individuals and groups who successfully used the court-centered pathway. The U.S. Supreme Court's decision in *Brown v. Board of Education of Topeka* (1954), which prohibited state and local governments from engaging in racial discrimination in public schools, is one of the most famous examples of this pathway in action. The origins of the case can be traced to a lawsuit filed by the father of Linda Brown, an African-American girl in Topeka, Kansas, who was not permitted to attend an all-white public school near her home. The Brown family was represented in court by lawyers from an interest group, the National Association for the Advancement of Colored People (NAACP).

PATHWAYS | profile

A. Philip Randolph

In 1925, Asa Philip Randolph organized a labor union, the Brotherhood of Sleeping Car Porters, made up of African-American workers at a time in history when racial discrimination led most labor unions to limit their membership to whites. Before this, Randolph had founded a magazine, *The Messenger,* that published articles and essays advocating equal rights and an end to racial discrimination. These experiences provided the foundation for Randolph's contributions to both cultural change and grassroots mobilization pathways. Randolph organized protest marches against discrimination as early as the 1940s. His most famous march was during the 1963 March on Washington, where Martin Luther King, Jr., delivered his famous "I Have a Dream" speech. The march helped pressure Congress to pass new laws to prohibit racial discrimination in employment, public services, and voting. Randolph also lobbied government officials, and his efforts helped persuade President Franklin Roosevelt to issue executive orders in 1940 that barred racial discrimination in federal government employment and in companies that held government defense contracts. Randolph made use of several pathways of action to influence government policies concerning racial equality. ■

GRASSROOTS MOBILIZATION PATHWAY Highly motivated individuals can seek to attract the attention of government officials and influence the direction of law and policy by mobilizing others to join them in strategic actions. Historically, when members of certain groups in society feel that the government

VISUAL LITERACY **Using the Census to Understand Who Americans Are**

VISUAL LITERACY **What Are American Civic Values?**

is unresponsive to their concerns (as expressed through lobbying and elections activity), they seek other means to educate the public and pressure those officials. Martin Luther King, Jr., became a nationally known civil rights figure in the 1950s as a result of his role in organizing and leading a boycott of the public transit system in Montgomery, Alabama, to protest racial segregation on buses. A **boycott** is a coordinated action by many people who agree not to buy a specific product, use a specific service, or shop at a specific store until a policy is changed. Boycotts were a powerful vehicle of colonial protest against British laws in the period leading up to the American Revolution, and they have been used many times since then. Boycotts can place financial pressure on businesses and governments that rely on daily revenue, such as bus fares or the sale of products, in order to stay in business. Advocates of racial equality, opponents of the Vietnam War, individuals concerned about restrictive immigration policies, and others have organized protest marches as a means to attract public attention and pressure the government to change laws and policies. These actions are seldom instantly successful, but over time, they may draw more and more supporters until elected officials begin to reconsider their prior decisions. Successful grassroots mobilization requires organizational skill, publicity, careful planning, and a solid core of committed activists who are willing to take public actions in support of their cause.

There are many ways to draw attention to political concerns. Here, protestors take on ghostly costumes to underscore their concerns and grief about the war in Iraq and the continued loss of lives.

CULTURAL CHANGE PATHWAY The cultural change pathway is an indirect approach to influencing government. It is a long-term strategy that requires persistence and patience. Through this approach, individuals and organized groups attempt to change the hearts and minds of their fellow citizens. By educating the public about issues and publicizing important events, the dominant values of society may change over time. This can lead to changes in law and policy as newly elected officials bring the new values into government with them.

Until the twentieth century, for example, many Americans—both men and women alike—believed that women should occupy a secondary role in society by devoting themselves to the roles of wife and mother. Federal, state, and local laws reflected this belief, and women were generally not permitted to vote in elections and were formally barred from certain occupations. Over a period of several decades, beginning before the Civil War, activist women and their male supporters used newspaper articles, speeches, and demonstrations to educate the public about women's capabilities and the need to grant them opportunities to live and work as citizens equal to men.

In the late nineteenth and early twentieth centuries, women finally gained the right to vote, first on a state-by-state basis but eventually through passage of the Nineteenth Amendment (1920), which guaranteed the vote to women nationwide. But discriminatory attitudes toward women remained prevalent through the 1960s, requiring decades of continued educational work. Gradually, laws and policies changed to protect women against gender discrimination. Eventually, most Americans accepted the idea of women becoming doctors, lawyers, police officers, and elected officials at all levels of government. By 2006, public opinion polls indicated that a vast majority of Americans would consider voting for a woman for president of the United States. Certainly Hillary Clinton's candidacy in 2008 reflected this change. Law and policy changed through the long-term effort to change the culture and values of American society.

The cultural change pathway can be used for a variety of issues, including abortion, the death penalty, environmental protection, and even privatizing Social Security. For people who seek to change society's values, the ultimate outcome of the cultural change pathway can be quite uncertain. Indeed, for some issues, change may occur only long after the passing of the people who initiated the efforts to alter public opinion and social values. And sometimes change never comes.

Diversity in American Society

This book's third theme is the impact of diversity on American government and on the laws and policies that government produces.

Many of the issues facing American government are products of the country's history, and many policy issues that are debated today have their roots in America's history of race-based slavery. Slavery and its consequences, including blatant discrimination against African Americans, which persisted until the 1970s, are at the heart of such difficult contemporary problems as chronic poverty, decaying urban neighborhoods, disproportionate minority unemployment rates, and lingering racial and ethnic hostility and mistrust. Cultural change eventually created a widespread consensus in American society that it was imperative to eliminate overt racial discrimination. Laws and policies, such as the Civil Rights Act of 1964 and the Voting Rights Act of 1965, were enacted in the second half of the twentieth century to prohibit many forms of discrimination that had been endorsed and enforced by various levels of government. However, there is no consensus on how to address other problems arising out of the legacy of slavery and racial discrimination. There have been attempts to apply specific remedies, such as court-ordered busing to achieve public school desegregation, affirmative action programs to increase minority enrollment in colleges and universities, and programs to diversify government employment and contract opportunities. But they have all caused bitter debate and political conflict.

Other challenging policy controversies also relate to the nation's diversity. Contemporary debates about immigration often focus on undocumented workers arriving from Mexico and other countries in violation of American law. Some Americans want stronger measures to prevent illegal immigration, but many businesses hire these undocumented workers because they work more cheaply than most American citizens. At the same time, Latinos in the United States have grown in numbers. In 2004, Latinos became the nation's largest minority group. As noted in Table 1.2, the Hispanic population in the United States is expected to double in the next few decades. Hispanics have also expanded their political power by becoming a significant voting presence in many cities and winning an increasing number of important offices. Many native-born and naturalized Latino citizens are wary of certain anti-immigration proposals, fearing that they may contribute to ethnic discrimination against U.S. citizens while treating noncitizens unduly harshly.

The recent immigration policy debates show how the diverse ethnic and racial composition of the United States contributes to the nation's political controversies at the same time that it adds complexity to the mix of actors seeking to use various pathways of change. All these pathways—elections, lobbying, courts, grassroots mobilization, and cultural change—have been used by a diverse array of Americans, including women, the disabled, homosexuals, and people of color, who have felt excluded from meaningful participation in American government.

Now that we have highlighted the book's important themes, we'll consider an example that illustrates how citizen participation and pathways for action affect the operations of American government.

PATHWAYS | of change from around the world

Would you risk your future career defending a television station? In May of 2007, Venezuelan President Hugo Chavez moved to shut down one of the country's most popular television stations, Radio Caracas Television International (RCTV). Chavez claimed that

TABLE 1.2 | The Face of a Changing Nation

	PERCENTAGE OF TOTAL POPULATION					
	2000	2010	2020	2030	2040	2050
Total	100.0%	100.0%	100.0%	100.0%	100.0%	100.0%
White not Hispanic	69.4	65.1	61.3	57.5	53.7	50.1
Black not Hispanic	12.7	13.1	13.5	13.9	14.3	14.6
Asian	3.8	4.6	5.4	6.2	7.1	8.0
All other races[1]	2.5	3.0	3.5	4.1	4.7	5.3
Hispanic (of any race)	12.6	15.5	17.8	20.1	22.3	24.4

[1]Includes American Indians and Alaska Natives, Native Hawaiians, other Pacific Islanders, and people who belong to two or more racial designations.
SOURCE: U.S. Census Bureau, International Database, Table 094 http://www.census.gov

the station had played a key role in an effort to overthrow the government. Yet RCTV was Venezuela's most popular station, especially with younger citizens, and many saw the move as an attempt to limit criticism of Chavez and his government.

In response, tens of thousands of Venezuelan students took to the streets. They led massive demonstrations—marches, rallies, sit-ins, and more. For weeks, universities drew to a close. Exams were put off, and classes were rescheduled. Political science major Ana Cristina Garanton, who took part in the protests, said the battle was for more than a television station: "We are fighting for the rights we should have as students so that when I graduate I can pursue any career without being discriminated against for political reasons. Our parents will one day leave the country to us. And it is up to us, the young people, to take the reins of the country."

All the students understood the dangers of their activism, such as being put on a government blacklist, a very real possibility that would mean the prospects of a good job after graduation would be slim. But they protested and spoke out nonetheless. Another active student, Carlos Julio Rojas, put it this way: "At the beginning of the year, the government said that, to impose [its program of] '21st Century Socialism,' it would be necessary to control communications . . . That is undemocratic. We believe in debate, freedom of thought."

SOURCE: Michael Bowman, "Venezuelan Students at Forefront of Campaign for Freedom of Expression," Voice of America, VoANews.com, June 2, 2007. Accessed at: http://www.voanews.com/english/archive/2007-07/2007-07-02-voa1.cfm?CFID=186364115&CFTOKEN=88761349 ■

Themes of This Book

Practice Quiz

1. Changing the hearts and minds of citizens over the long term is an example of which pathway of action?
   a. elections **b.** courts
   c. grassroots mobilization **d.** cultural change
2. What amendment to the Constitution granted women the right to vote in national elections?
   a. 13th **b.** 14th
   c. 18th **d.** 19th
3. George Gallup was a pioneer in the profession of
   a. opinion polling. **b.** medicine.
   c. lobbying. **d.** advertising.
4. While Americans tend to vote less often than citizens in other democracies, they find alternative ways of participating actively and meaningfully in politics.
   a. true **b.** false

Answers: 1-d, 2-d, 3-a, 4-a.

Discussion Questions

1. What are some ways that a college student can influence the decisions of local government?
2. What does the textbook mean by *pathways of action*? Describe some of the pathways featured in American politics.

What **YOU** can do!

Read about voter turnout issues as described by International IDEA at **http://www.idea.int** or the Center for Voting and Democracy at **http://www.fairvote.org/turnout**. Think about arguments to make to your friends or ideas to suggest to government leaders about how to increase voter turnout in the United States.

Citizen Participation *and* Pathways: *the* Example *of* Abortion

(pages 18–19)

What are the various "pathways" of involvement in our political system?

LEFT: **The U.S. Supreme Court building is reflected** in a protester's sunglasses during a demonstration against abortion rights. Americans are free to use many methods of expressing their views to public officials. ***—Have you ever made your views known to decision makers in government? What were the results?***

PHOTO: Carol T. Powers/New York Times

RIGHT: **Planned Parenthood, an interest group** that advocates a right of choice for abortion, prepared signs to mobilize people in opposition to a 2006 South Dakota law intended to drastically limit abortions in that state. ***—Why do activists use various pathways for an issue that was originally defined in the court pathway?***

PHOTO: Carmel Zucker/New York Times

Abortion is a divisive, wrenching issue that continues to generate controversy among Americans nationwide. Several major institutional components of American government, including Congress, the president, the U.S. Supreme Court, and state governments, have been involved in defining and changing abortion laws and policies. Thus the abortion issue helps show how American government operates and how citizens can use pathways of action to influence the results of those operations.

Although women gained the right to vote nationwide in the early twentieth century, advocates using the *lobbying pathway* failed to persuade state legislatures to enact abortion choice laws until the 1960s, and then only in a few states. In the early 1970s, however, two young lawyers in Texas volunteered to help a woman who unsuccessfully sought an abortion after she claimed that she had been raped. The lawyers began a legal case to challenge the Texas law that made it a crime to obtain or perform an abortion. The case worked its way through the levels of the court system until it reached the U.S. Supreme Court. In a landmark decision in *Roe* v. *Wade* (1973), the justices of the Supreme Court voted 7-2 to strike down the Texas law as a violation of women's right to privacy in making personal choices about reproduction. Much more will be said about this case in subsequent chapters. For now, you should understand that the *court pathway* was used to change the law for the entire nation.

Of course, opponents of abortion were anxious to move government in a different direction. In the aftermath of *Roe* v. *Wade,* opponents of abortion mobilized supporters and organized political action groups. They used several pathways in their efforts to reimpose legal prohibitions on abortion. In the *elections pathway,* they sought to recruit and elect candidates who pledged to fight abortion. They used the *lobbying pathway* to pressure and persuade elected officials to pass new laws that would place restrictions on abortion that would be acceptable to the courts. They also used the *grassroots mobilization pathway* to organize protest marches and, especially, demonstrations at abortion clinics intended to discourage women from entering to seek abortions. A few opponents of abortion even rejected democratic processes as a means to seek change, instead engaging in such violent acts as firebombing abortion clinics and assaulting or even killing doctors who performed abortions.

> "What other pathways were used after *Roe* v. *Wade* was passed?"
>
> —Student Question

Abortion opponents who worked within the governing system achieved partial success in many state legislatures and in Congress. New laws were adopted imposing restrictions that could discourage or hinder women's efforts to obtain abortions—for example, blocking the use of government funds to pay for poor women's abortions. Laws also limited the ability of teenagers to obtain abortions without informing their parents or obtaining the permission of a judge. States imposed new requirements for counseling women about abortion procedures and, after the counseling session, making them wait 24 hours before making a second trip to the clinic to have the abortion procedure performed by a doctor.

Throughout the three decades in which abortion opponents used these pathways to seek restrictions on abortion, they also focused on the *elections pathway* in an effort to elect Republican presidents who might appoint new Supreme Court justices willing to overturn *Roe* v. *Wade* and to elect senators who would confirm these justices. As a result, the process of obtaining the U.S. Senate's approval of the president's nominees for the Supreme Court became part of the political battles over abortion. Both opponents and supporters of women's right of choice used the *lobbying pathway* to pressure senators to either endorse or oppose judicial nominees on the basis of their perceived stance on abortion. By 2005, the U.S. Supreme Court was closely divided on the issue of abortion rights, with Justice Sandra Day O'Connor casting decisive votes to uphold *Roe* v. *Wade* in a number of close cases. President George W. Bush's nomination of Judge Samuel

Alito to replace Justice O'Connor on her retirement mobilized both supporters and opponents of abortion rights for what both sides realized might be a crucial battle over the issue. After Senate approval of the nomination in 2006, Justice Alito's earlier role as a government lawyer seeking to limit abortion rights raised expectations that he might tip the balance on the divided Supreme Court and thereby severely restrict or eliminate a woman's right to choose to terminate a pregnancy. Sure enough, in April of 2007, Justice Alito joined a five-member majority in upholding the so-called "partial birth abortion" ban.

The struggle between opponents and defenders of abortion choice moved between *different* pathways. With each legislative success that abortion foes won, advocates of choice returned to the *court pathway* to challenge the new state and federal laws on the grounds that they improperly clashed with the Supreme Court's declaration in *Roe* v. *Wade* that women had a constitutionally protected right to choose to have an abortion. Although the Supreme Court and lower federal courts struck down some state laws as conflicting with *Roe* v. *Wade*, the courts also upheld many laws that imposed regulations while not depriving women of the opportunity to make choices.

In March of 2006, when Justice Alito began to hear his first cases as a member of the Supreme Court, state legislators in South Dakota acted quickly to enact a statute that would virtually abolish abortion in their state. Under the law, abortion would be permitted only to save the life of a pregnant woman. Doctors faced criminal prosecution and prison sentences for performing other abortions, including those performed in the aftermath of rape or incest. The purpose of the statute, in large part, was to generate a legal challenge that might ultimately lead the newly constituted Supreme Court to overturn *Roe* v. *Wade*.

A countermove by pro-choice forces might have been a lawsuit. Realizing that most residents of the state would reject the law as too extreme, however, opponents mapped out a different course. They gathered petition signatures to place the measure on the general election ballot for a statewide vote—a process called a *ballot initiative*, which is possible in 23 states. Their strategy worked: The abortion ban was rejected by 55 percent of South Dakota voters.

The opposing sides in the abortion debate have attempted to shape public opinion through the *cultural change pathway*. Supporters of choice seek to persuade the public that control over "reproductive freedom" is a key component of women's equality in American society. They also raise warnings about the risks to women's health if abortion is banned, referring to the time when abortion was illegal and women turned to abortionists who were not doctors, causing many desperate women to die from bleeding and infections. Opponents insist that abortion is murder and use graphic pictures of both developing and aborted fetuses in their publicity campaigns.

This brief snapshot of the abortion issue illustrates how law and policy develop and change through the complex interaction of the pathways of action and the American government's various institutions. Throughout this continuing battle over abortion, both sides rely on the participation of individual citizens for lobbying, contributing money, campaigning, voting, engaging in public protests, and carrying out the specific activities of each pathway of action.

Citizen Participation and Pathways

Practice Quiz

1. Which Supreme Court justice is regarded as a likely vote to form a majority to overturn the *Roe* v. *Wade* decision?
   a. William Rehnquist **b.** Samuel Alito
   c. John Marshall **d.** Ruth Bader Ginsburg
2. Once the court pathway has been used to change the outcome of a court case, no other pathways can legally be used to make a change.
   a. true **b.** false
3. As a result of *Roe* v. *Wade*, no lower court can make a decision to change any aspect of abortion law.
   a. true **b.** false
4. Pathways of action have been a critical feature of democracy because
   a. they allow different groups of citizens to change government policy.
   b. they promote active participation of citizens from all walks of life.
   c. they prevent discrimination against minorities.
   d. a and b

Answers: 1-b, 2-b, 3-b, 4-d.

Discussion Questions

1. How does the issue of abortion reflect diversity in American society?
2. How do changes in the membership of the Supreme Court affect political and legal changes in our society?

What **YOU** can do!

Depending on your views of abortion, you can learn about and provide support for one of the competing organizations involved in the issue, either the National Right to Life Committee **http://www.nrlc.org** or NARAL Pro-Choice America **http://www.naral.org**

■ **Checks and Balances:** A system in our government where each branch (legislative, executive, judicial) has the power to limit the actions of others.

EXAMPLE: *When President George W. Bush vetoed a measure to begin the withdrawal of troops from Iraq, he was carrying out a powerful check on an act of Congress.*

Change *and* Stability *in* American Government (pages 20–23)

What are the forces of stability in American politics?

As we have seen, the pathways of action provide opportunities for citizens to take nonviolent actions to make their voices heard by decision makers in American government. The existence of these pathways is also important for the preservation of the American governing system. No form of government is automatically stable. No form of government automatically functions smoothly. If disagreements within the population are great enough, or if a segment of the population does not accept the design and operation of the governing system, then even democracies will experience violence, disorder, instability, and collapse. The American Civil War vividly reminds us of what can happen when pathways fail to resolve controversies. In that example, the divisive issues of slavery and the authority of state governments were inflamed rather than resolved through actions in the elections pathway (the election of Lincoln as the antislavery president) and the court-centered pathway (a Supreme Court decision that helped the spread of slavery to western territories—*Dred Scott* v. *Sandford,* 1857).

To understand American government and its ability to endure, we must examine the factors that contribute to stability as well as those that help Americans change what their government is doing. This book focuses on pathways of action as a key element for understanding how American government operates. These pathways help explain why the American system of government continues to exist, even after two centuries that included significant social changes and a bloody civil war.

Every nation experiences periods of transformation. These are eras in which new issues, fundamental changes in social and economic conditions, or major events spur adjustments in society and in the priorities and actions of government decision makers. These transformations can also produce changes in a country's system of government. In the 1990s, the world witnessed the emergence of new governing systems in places such as South Africa and the formerly communist countries of Eastern Europe and Russia. In the United States, we have maintained the same Constitution and general blueprint for government through more than 200 years of significant changes in society, politics, and the economy—topics taken up throughout the book.

"What do you mean by 'stability' in government?"
—Student Question

Sources of Stability

Stability in American government and in the governing systems of other countries cannot be taken for granted. We cannot automatically assume that governing systems will be stable or remain stable for any predictable period. Stability in any political system is the result of three closely related elements:

- A broadly accepted political and economic framework
- A stable, powerful political culture
- A variety of ways for citizens to seek and achieve policy changes

We will discuss each of these elements in turn.

BROADLY ACCEPTED FRAMEWORK: REVERENCE FOR THE CONSTITUTION AND CAPITALISM Early in his political career, Abraham Lincoln delivered a speech in which he urged that our Constitution be the "political religion of the nation."[3] We have taken his advice to heart. Indeed, one of the interesting and somewhat unique aspects of American politics is our reverence for the structure of our governing system. Some would say that we treat the Constitution as our nonreligious "bible"—the written document that Americans deeply respect and obey.

This would be a bit surprising to the authors of the Constitution. They planned to compel the sharing of powers among three branches of government. They designed a form of government that divided powers between the national government and the states. They also initiated an elaborate system of **checks and balances**■ between branches of the government. In their view, however, the Constitution was a collection of compromises, ambiguities, and generalized grants of authority to the national government. They wrote the Constitution to replace an earlier governmental blueprint, the Articles of Confederation. If the Constitution had been rejected by the American public or had failed to work well, they might have been forced to go back to the drawing board to write a third version. In other words, to the originators of the country, the Constitution was a practical plan for creating a government. It was not a set of sacred principles. Yet today, Americans express a shared belief in the special wisdom of the Constitution's authors for creating a system of government that would both endure and embody important principles of democracy.

"What is capitalism? Why is it so important to Americans?"
—Student Question

■ **Capitalism:** An economic system where business and industry are privately owned and there is little governmental interference.

EXAMPLE: *Some have suggested that Hong Kong boasts one of the most open capitalist systems in the world.*

■ **Socialism:** An economic system in which the government owns and controls most factories and much or all of the nation's land.

EXAMPLE: *The Socialist Republic of Vietnam.*

CONNECT THE LINK (Chapter **10,** pages **340–343**) How, exactly, does culture shape the politics and policies of a country?

The reverence of modern Americans for the institutional framework of their country's political system extends to their economic system as well. Indeed, the "American dream" rests mostly on the notion that intelligence, ingenuity, and hard work are sufficient for economic success—and for most Americans, economic success is an important goal. Faith in **capitalism**■ is deeply ingrained in Americans' values and beliefs. Capitalism is the economic system based on free enterprise in which individuals compete with each other for jobs, operate privately owned businesses that may succeed or fail, and focus their efforts on accumulating wealth for themselves and their families. In an alternative economic system, **socialism**■, the government owns and controls key factories and sometimes also the land. It may even use that control to assign individuals to specific jobs. Socialist systems may focus on the ideal of individuals working for the good of society rather than pursuing self-interest. In the United States, by contrast, most people have always believed that society as a whole benefits through the continuous creation of new businesses, new jobs, and increased wealth when all individuals pursue their own interests and have opportunities to use their own private property and businesses to create jobs and generate income.

The American idea that people have ample opportunities to become economically successful through their own hard work is not always fulfilled in practice. Historically, racial and gender discrimination have limited opportunities for many Americans to find good jobs or start their own businesses. The ability of rich people to provide superior education for their children and pass on their wealth to family members provides and perpetuates advantages that most Americans do not share. The significant power wielded by corporations in the United States and vast disparities of individual wealth have led to occasional calls for a change in the American economic system. Various plans for a redistribution of wealth to assist poor people have been proposed—for example, through higher taxes on the rich to fund antipoverty programs. For the most part, however, criticisms are focused on specific aspects of the capitalist system, and in recent decades, people have rarely suggested that the United States switch to a different system. Support for free enterprise and capitalism remains strong even when critics point out that the United States falls short of its ideals of equal economic opportunities for all Americans.

Americans believe strongly in the core elements of our political and economic system. Lincoln's hope that Americans would protect their system through an almost religious reverence has come to pass. James Madison and the other framers of the United States would presumably be pleased—and perhaps surprised—to know that the experimental governing system they designed has survived for more than two centuries. They would be doubly surprised to see how Americans cherish the Constitution—the experimental document full of compromises—as the crown jewel of democracy.

One of the best illustrations of our nation's reverence for the Constitution *and* capitalism is our currency. On one side of the dollar bill we pay tribute to the hero of the Revolution and the first president, and on the other side we find the Great Seal of the United States (front and back). The pyramid symbolizes strength, and its 13 steps represent the original 13 colonies. The unfinished summit on the pyramid implies a "work in progress." ***—Do you think the larger message is that our government's fate is linked to the future of free enterprise in America? Or, as capitalism goes, so goes our system of government?***

Political Culture: The "American Creed"

Scholars have long recognized the powerful influence of a nation's *political culture*. Much more will be said of this concept in LINK Chapter 10, pages 340–343, but for now, simply note that the term refers to the fundamental values and dominant beliefs that are shared throughout society and that shape political behavior and government

■ **Alexis de Tocqueville:** A French scholar who traveled throughout the United States in the early 1830s.

SIGNIFICANCE: His published notes, *Democracy in America,* offers a telling account of our nation's formative years—a book that is still widely read.

Americans have always had a deep sense of patriotism, especially when it comes to honoring those who have defended our country during times of war.
—Is it possible to be truly patriotic while at the same time speaking out against our involvement in a war?

"What is our political culture?"
—Student Question

policies. It is the umbrella under which political activities take place, and it defines the arena where political questions are resolved. Political culture incorporates both citizens' personal values—that is, their ideas about what is right and wrong—and their shared ideas about how they should be governed.[4]

One nation's political culture may be more open and obvious than another's. It springs from a number of sources, including the origins of the nation (sometimes called the nation's "creation myth"), historical struggles in the nation's history, the deeds and thoughts of past leaders, important documents and texts, economic conditions, and distinct subcultures. Religion may also play a role, depending on a nation's history and culture. To some extent, a nation's popular culture, including its entertainment, fashions, and media, also contribute to its political culture. For instance, the counterculture movement in the 1960s (hippie culture) had a direct impact on the political process. And many observers suggest that the portrayal of gay men and women in film and on television in recent years has raised levels of tolerance toward homosexuals throughout society. When some or all of these pieces are missing or are not clearly defined, the nation's political identity becomes less clear. Nations with a strong, clearly defined political culture are generally more stable.[5]

Alexis de Tocqueville■ (uh-lek-see duh TOKE-vil), a French scholar who traveled throughout the United States in the early 1830s, found our nation's emerging political culture to be distinctive and powerful. The essence of American politics, Tocqueville wrote in *Democracy in America,* lies not in the complex maze of political institutions but rather in the shared values of American citizens. In fact, he suggested, along with this powerful political identity comes a downside: "I know of no country in which there is such little independence of mind and real freedom of discussion as in America."[6] The widespread nature of shared values and beliefs among Americans, which was observed by Tocqueville and continues today, has tended to limit the range of discussions about government and public policy. As with the economic system, people tend to focus on fixing specific problems within the current system rather than suggesting that the system itself should be changed.

American political culture, as noted by the Swedish social scientist Gunnar Myrdal (GUN-er MEER-dahl) in 1944, is "the most explicitly expressed system of general ideals" of any country in the West[7]—so much so that he saw fit to call our belief system the "American Creed." At least in the abstract, Americans embrace the concepts of "freedom," "equality," "liberty," "majority will," "religious freedom," and "due process under the law." According to Myrdal, "Schools teach the principles of the Creed; the churches preach them; the courts hand down judgment in their terms."[8] According to one commentator, "Myrdal saw the Creed as the bond that links all Americans, including nonwhite minorities, and as the spur forever goading Americans to live up to their principles."[9] Yale University political scientist Robert Dahl echoed this idea a few decades later when he called our set of beliefs the "democratic creed." He wrote, "The common view seems to be that our system is not only democratic but is perhaps the most perfect expression of democracy that exists anywhere. . . . To reject the democratic creed is in effect to refuse to be American."[10]

There are many things that define the American Creed, many of which will be discussed in later chapters. The important point here is to understand that the United States possesses a powerful political culture that is clearly defined and long-lasting. The historical national consensus on political values and democratic institutions helped create stability during times of profound social change. As waves of change transformed the workplace, home life, leisure patterns, and intellectual fabric of the nation, Americans found strength in the stability of their political system.

NUMEROUS AVENUES OF CHANGE Two necessary conditions for any country's political stability are broad popular acceptance of its government and economic system and a clearly defined political culture. If either element is missing, the likelihood of upheaval and collapse increases. Both elements are necessary components for stability, but they do not guarantee stability. For a democratic system to remain stable, its citizens must believe that they can influence the outcome of government activity. The design and operation of government must permit popular participation. In addition, the political culture and laws must encourage civic involvement and protect activists from being silenced either by the government or by majority opinion. There must also be a variety of ways to achieve desired ends. Severe limitations on citizen participation and influence can lead to frustration, cynicism, and in the end, conflict and potential upheaval if people feel forced to use means outside the governing system, such as violence, to make their voices heard. Stated a bit differently, stability in a democratic regime springs from a system that allows participation, a culture that promotes involvement, and a set of options (or, shall we say, "pathways") to help redirect public policy.

If you have ever doubted the power of committed citizens, even young citizens, to make a real difference, read the *Student Profile* about Nick Anderson and Ana Slavin. Here, they are testifying before a congressional committee about the efforts to send aid to Darfur.

STUDENT | PROFILE

Like most young Americans, Nick Anderson and Ana Slavin spend a lot of time on social network sites. Facebook and MySpace are entertaining, a way to make social connections, but could they also be harnessed to do good work? Young people certainly care about problems in the community and around the world—and they are anxious to roll up their sleeves and make a difference. But how might social network sites be used?

During a trip to South Africa in 2005, Anderson was blown away by the plight of people in the Darfur region of western Sudan. For nearly a decade, Arab militias backed by the Sudanese government had waged a genocidal war on tribes in the region, killing upwards of 300,000 men, women, and children. Anderson witnessed a crisis of humanity, and it tugged at his heartstrings. Slavin learned about the situation during an internship at Wellesley College's Women's Research Center. It, too, set her aback. How could young Americans sit by and do nothing?

Together, Anderson and Slavin created a plan to use MySpace and Facebook to urge their peers to host fundraisers to increase awareness about the violence in Darfur. Eventually they met with the Save Darfur Coalition in Washington, D.C., which agreed to support them. "Things kind of snowballed from there," Anderson said. The Dollars for Darfur National High School Challenge spawned a national movement. Young people show videos about the conflict and collect money to support refugees. The program raised over $300,000 and the awareness of crisis among young Americans. ■

Change and Stability in American Government

Practice Quiz

1. According to this textbook, which of the following are basic features of the U.S. Constitution?
   a. checks and balances
   b. division of power between national and state governments
   c. compromises and ambiguities
   d. a, b, and c

2. In terms of economic prosperity, Americans tend to believe that
   a. the state should place strict limits on the amount of wealth and property any individual may own.
   b. all professions should offer similar pay and benefits.
   c. few governmental restrictions should be placed on individual wealth and ownership of property.
   d. all citizens are entitled to ownership of property, even if the government must help them to pay for it.

3. In America, economic prosperity can be assured by hard work and clean living.
   a. true **b.** false

4. The social scientist who termed America's system of political beliefs the "American Creed" was
   a. Alexis de Tocqueville **b.** Gunnar Myrdal
   c. George Gallup **d.** Robert Dahl

Answers: 1-d, 2-c, 3-b, 4-b.

Discussion Questions

1. Describe American political culture. Which aspects seem to be most dominant?
2. How do democracy and capitalism work together to create a society unique to the United States of America?

What **YOU** can do!

Taking a cue from The Dollars for Darfur National High School Challenge discussed above in the Student Profile, consider using MySpace or Facebook to raise awareness and create a fundraising drive for a political or social issue that's important to you and your community.

Conclusion

A key feature of all democracies is the opportunity for citizens to participate in public affairs in order to influence the decisions of government. The design and operation of American government provide a variety of opportunities for citizens to make their voices heard at the national, state, and local levels. In the United States, citizens can use the different pathways for action to influence government and public policies. These pathways include opportunities to participate in campaigns and elections, to file lawsuits in the courts, to lobby government officials, and to mobilize large groups of citizens to pressure officials or seek to change the culture and values of society.

Citizen participation should not be viewed as just a hobby. It is an essential element for maintaining stability in a democratic society. In the United States, stability also depends on shared beliefs in the political and economic systems as well as the shared values that make up what has been called the American Creed. In many other countries, ethnic conflict and social transformations can lead to profound changes in the form of government or public policies. By contrast, despite significant social changes in our diverse society, the United States has maintained a high degree of stability under a founding document, the Constitution, which was written in the eighteenth century. At one point, profound disagreements in society led to the bloody, four-year Civil War. However, after the North's victory resolved regional disagreements over slavery and states' rights, the United States again became a stable democracy thanks to the opportunities it granted all citizens to participate and share in political and economic values.

In the next chapter, we will examine the design of American government, beginning with the blueprint developed in the Constitution. Subsequent chapters will discuss key elements in government and politics, such as the news media and public opinion, as well as the specific institutions of government, such as Congress and the U.S. Supreme Court. As you learn about these key elements and institutions, think about which pathways of action are most important for each aspect of American government. You should also consider how you can participate as an engaged citizen when you want to assert influence over the decisions and priorities of your government.

As you think about your daily life, are there laws or government policies that you regard as unfair or misguided? Listen to the people around you. Are they debating issues that affect their lives? Many people disagree about whether motorcyclists should be required to wear helmets. Some think it unjust that one can vote at age 18 but can't drink alcohol until age 21. Other people feel deeply about issues such as abortion or American military actions overseas. Some of your classmates may believe that public universities have raised their tuition and fees to a level that is too high for the average citizen to afford. Yet others may feel most strongly about the availability of health insurance for students and other individuals with limited incomes. Throughout the country, Americans debate such issues as gun control and affirmative action. Do you worry about whether Social Security funds will be available when you retire? What should be done about immigration or climate change? Unfortunately, many people, including students, appear to feel helpless, and they act as if there is no point in getting involved in contemporary issues. This may explain, in part, why voter participation rates in the United States are low compared to those in many other democracies. As you evaluate your views about government and society, ask yourself: As a college-educated person, do you really want all laws and policies that affect your life and determine what happens in your country to be decided by other people?

Key Objective Review, Apply, and Explore

It's Your Government!

(pages 4–7)

Many Americans, especially young Americans, believe "government" and "politics" are distant, beyond their immediate world. In reality, government is around us; it shapes our lives in important ways every hour of every day. That is why it is particularly important for citizens in a democracy to become involved. Government matters, and you can make a difference.

KEY TERMS

Politics 5 **Public Policy 5**

CRITICAL THINKING QUESTIONS

1. Why do you suppose many young Americans are indifferent to their political world? Some have suggested that we pay scant attention to politics because we are doing well (we are affluent), but at the same time, some of the most "turned off" citizens are those with the most to gain from government action. Does this make sense?
2. If democracy implies a government "by the people" but many of our fellow citizens do not engage in the political process, do we really have a democracy?

INTERNET RESOURCES

To see comparisons of the United States and other countries in terms of political rights and individual freedom, visit the Freedom House Web site at **http://www.freedomhouse.org**

To see comparisons of the United States and other countries in terms of voter turnout, see the Web site of International IDEA at **http://www.idea.int**

ADDITIONAL READING

Almond, Gabriel A., and Sidney Verba. *Civic Culture: Political Attitudes and Democracy in Five Nations*. Princeton, NJ: Princeton University Press, 1963.

Halperin, Morton, Joseph T. Siegle, and Michael M. Weinstein. *The Democracy Advantage: How Democracies Promote Prosperity and Peace*. New York: Routledge, 2004.

Themes of This Book

(pages 8–17)

In a democracy, it's essential that citizens become participants in not merely spectators of, the political process. While many in the United States believe their options for effective involvement are limited, there are numerous pathways for change. Indeed, throughout American history, different political actors have utilized different pathways to achieve their goals.

KEY TERMS

Pathways of Action 10 **Boycott 15**

CRITICAL THINKING QUESTIONS

1. Why do political activists use different pathways for their involvement? What are the factors that shape the choice of which route to utilize? Which of these factors is most important, in your view?
2. In what ways has diversity shaped the nature of politics in the United States? Do you see additional changes in the years ahead?

INTERNET RESOURCES

To read about one organization's strategies for using various pathways to affect government policy concerning firearms, see the Web site of the National Rifle Association at **http://www.nra.org**

Another good example of a powerful political action organization is the AARP, a massive, nationwide unit that works to protect the interests of older Americans: **http://www.aarp.org/issues/support_advocacy/**

There are numerous youth and student political action organizations. To read about the Student Environmental Action Coalition, see **http://www.seac.org/**

ADDITIONAL READING

Frantzich, Stephen E. *Citizen Democracy: Political Activism in a Cynical Age,* 2nd Ed. Boulder, CO: Rowman and Littlefield, 2004.

Wasserman, Gary. *Politics in Action: Cases in Modern American Government*. New York: Houghton Mifflin, 2006.

Key Objective Review, Apply, and Explore

Citizen Participation and Pathways: The Example of Abortion

(pages 18–19)

This section offers a brief look at political action surrounding one of the most controversial issues of our day: abortion. As one side of the argument begins to achieve its goals, the other side of the issue responds by heading down a different pathway. This tale says a lot about various routes of change in American politics.

CRITICAL THINKING QUESTIONS

1. Why do you suppose early defenders of the right to an abortion used the court-centered pathway to achieve its goals?
2. Which of the pathways would likely lead to a longer-lasting victory when it comes to the issue of abortion?

INTERNET RESOURCES

One of the most prominent, well-organized groups to defend abortion rights is Planned Parenthood: **http://www.plannedparenthood.org/index.htm**

There are many organizations dedicated to ending abortions. One such group is the National Right to Life: **http://www.nrlc.org/**

ADDITIONAL READING

Hendershott Anne. *The Politics of Abortion.* New York: Encounter Books, 2006.

Hull, N.E.H., and Peter Charles Hoffer. Roe *v.* Wade: *The Abortion Rights Controversy in American History.* Lawrence: University Press of Kansas, 2001.

Sanger, Alexander. *Beyond Choice: Reproductive Freedom in the 21st Century.* New York: Public Affaris, 2004.

Change and Stability in American Government

(pages 20–23)

There is no doubt that our nation has undergone significant change in the last three centuries. At the same time, however, core elements of our political system have remained remarkably stable. This is due to reverence for democracy and free market capitalism, to a well-crafted Constitution, and to numerous pathways for average citizens to voice their concerns and redirect the course of public policy.

KEY TERMS

Checks and Balances 20
Capitalism 21
Socialism 21
Alexis de Tocqueville 22

CRITICAL THINKING QUESTIONS

1. Is there a relationship between the likelihood of violence erupting in a society and the opportunities for citizens to change public policy? Put a bit differently, do you think our political process has been relatively peaceful because citizens can affect the outcome of government?
2. How does reverence for our "creation myth" continue to shape American politics? For example, might there be a relationship between how our nation started and our current reluctance to create a publicly funded health care system?

INTERNET RESOURCES

There are numerous sites to explore events in American history. You might enjoy spending some time at **http://www.americanheritage.com/**

ADDITIONAL READING

Tocqueville, Alexis de. *Democracy in America.* New York: Signet Books, 2001. (Originally published 1835–1840.)

Chapter Review Critical Thinking Test

1. This textbook defines activities of government officials and citizens who intend to affect the structure, authority, and actions of government as
- **a.** propaganda.
- **b.** discourse.
- **c.** the public's right to know.
- **d.** politics.

2. The decisions in which governments decide what to do or not do—laws, regulations, etc.—are referred to as
- **a.** public discourse.
- **b.** public policy.
- **c.** public opinion.
- **d.** public awareness.

3. *Pathways of action* refers to
- **a.** the organizational channels of government bureaucracy.
- **b.** the connections among the various branches of government.
- **c.** the activities, institutions, and decision points that affect public policy.
- **d.** the confidential relationships between government officials.

4. The selection of leaders by popular vote, and holding those leaders accountable for their decisions, is an example of which pathway of action?
- **a.** court
- **b.** grassroots mobilization
- **c.** cultural change
- **d.** elections

5. All pathways to action are equally open to all people in the United States.
- **a.** true
- **b.** false

6. Democracy can often seem inefficient, because
- **a.** competition and debate among groups slows down decision making.
- **b.** the framers wanted a system of change that was slow and moderate.
- **c.** only a majority can effect change in our system of government.
- **d.** a and b

7. Which of these resources can help citizens to use the pathways of action?
- **a.** money
- **b.** organizational skills
- **c.** social status and personal connections
- **d.** a, b, and c

8. Which pathway of action involves individuals and groups presenting information and persuasive arguments to government officials in order to implement desired change?
- **a.** lobbying
- **b.** elections
- **c.** cultural change
- **d.** court

9. Which of the following is an example of the grassroots mobilization pathway?
- **a.** e-mailing your state legislators to convince them to vote for your position on an upcoming bill
- **b.** organizing a boycott against dangerous toys
- **c.** carrying a sign with a political slogan
- **d.** using desktop publishing to create a political pamphlet

10. Citizens will be most successful in implementing desired change in government if they focus on a single pathway to action.
- **a.** true
- **b.** false

11. Litigants in the Supreme Court abortion case *Roe* v. *Wade* successfully used which of the following pathways of action?
- **a.** court
- **b.** grassroots mobilization
- **c.** lobbying
- **d.** a, b, and c

12. A broadly accepted political and economic framework, a powerful political culture, and a variety of ways to seek political change are all measures of a government's
- **a.** reliability.
- **b.** elasticity.
- **c.** stability.
- **d.** honesty.

13. The authors of the Constitution intended it to be a practical plan for creating a government, not a set of sacred principles.
- **a.** true
- **b.** false

14. The economic system that features government ownership of property, individuals working for the greater good of society rather than for personal gain, and government control of jobs and wages is
- **a.** capitalism.
- **b.** communism.
- **c.** socialism.
- **d.** corporatism.

15. The economic system based on free enterprise, private ownership of property, open competition, and pursuit of individual wealth is
- **a.** capitalism.
- **b.** communism.
- **c.** socialism.
- **d.** corporatism.

Chapter Review Critical Thinking Test

16. Historically, which of the following factors have placed limits on economic opportunities for many Americans?

a. gender and racial discrimination
b. wealthy persons' access to superior education
c. the power of corporations
d. a, b, and c

17. Political culture refers to

a. the prominence of a core set of religious principles in a society.
b. the fundamental values and dominant beliefs shared in a society.
c. the fundamental principles of fairness and equality in a society.
d. a and b

18. Which of the following are potential sources of a nation's political culture?

a. historical origins
b. important documents and texts
c. presence or absence of civilized leaders
d. a and b

19. Alexis de Tocqueville emphasized which aspect of America's political culture?

a. racial composition of the population
b. active citizenship
c. universal suffrage
d. slavery

20. Disparity of wealth threatens to undermine the popularity of capitalism in our society today.

a. true **b.** false

Answers: 1-d, 2-b, 3-c, 4-d, 5-b, 6-d, 7-d, 8-a, 9-a, 10-b, 11-d, 12-c, 13-a, 14-c, 15-a, 16-d, 17-b, 18-d, 19-b, 20-b.

You decide!

To succeed at influencing government, active citizens often must demonstrate that their ideas and suggestions represent the viewpoints of broad segments of society. Make a list of goals, values, and beliefs that you feel are shared broadly in American society. Check your list against the results of public opinion polls, such as those available from the Pew Research Center at **http://pewresearch.org**. Do you see any differences in goals, values, and beliefs when comparing college-aged students with older Americans? Do you see any evidence that the beliefs of American society as a whole have changed over time? Next, at the Pew Research Center Web site, click on the link for "International Opinion Polls" to see the Pew Global Attitudes Project. Which beliefs, goals, and values are shared worldwide? Which seem unique to the United States? What explanations seem likely for the differences and the similarities you see?

Key Objective Outline

What is the difference between government and politics?

- The Nature of Government and Politics **(page 32)**

How does who is allowed to participate, and how decisions are made, shape the nature of government?

- Types of Governments **(page 34)**

How did early politics set the stage for the American Revolution?

- Early Governance in America **(page 36)**

What were the core principles of the American Revolution?

- The American Revolution **(page 38)**

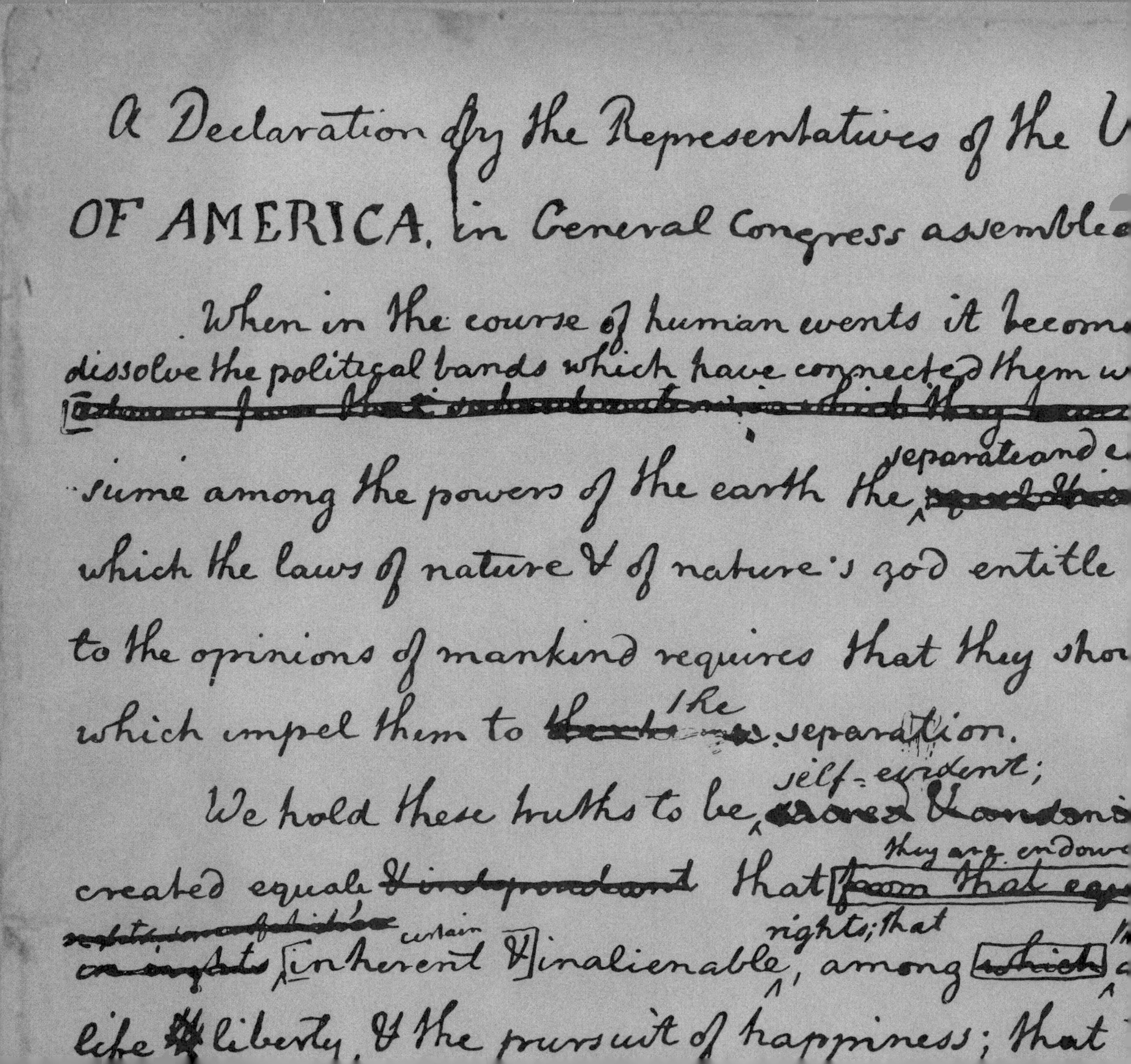
A Declaration by the Representatives of the U
OF AMERICA, in General Congress assemble
When in the course of human events it becom
dissolve the political bands which have connected them w
sume among the powers of the earth the separate and e
which the laws of nature & of nature's god entitle
to the opinions of mankind requires that they shou
which impel them to the separation.
We hold these truths to be self-evident;
created equal, that they are endowe
certain inalienable rights; that among
life, liberty, & the pursuit of happiness; that

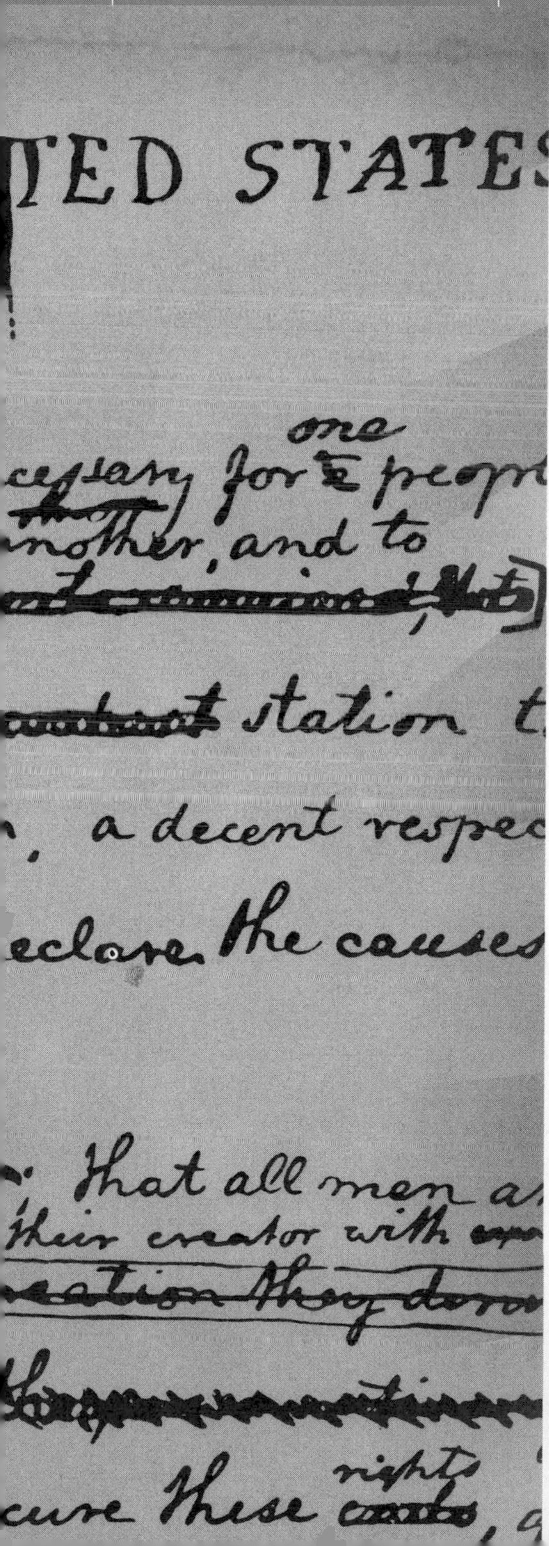

CHAPTER 2

Early Governance and the Constitutional Framework

How does our nation's formative period continue to shape contemporary politics?

The Declaration of Independence is one of the grand documents in world history. As you will soon read, it lays out core democratic principles—notions of liberty, justice, and freedom. When this document was signed, it set to motion the American Revolution, a seven-year struggle to break from England and start an independent, democratic government. What a fine part of our history.

Yet we often skim over the glaring hypocrisy of slavery. Most of the gentleman who signed the document also owned slaves. Thomas Jefferson himself owned hundreds of slaves and probably had several children with one, Sally Hemings. More ironic, early in the war, royal governors and British generals issued proclamations granting slaves their freedom for joining His Majesty's Troops. At least 20,000 took up the offer to fight *against* revolutionary forces. Even more shocking, some southern states promised white men who enlisted in the Continental Army a slave as payment for their services. As noted by historian Ray Raphale, in his book *Founding Myths,* "During the war, Southern white patriots united in opposition to the diabolical designs of the British, who threatened the very roots of their society by offering freedom to slaves."[1]

Is there any way to reconcile these contradictory pieces of our history? One way, perhaps, is to consider that equality and freedom did not arrive with the Revolution, ratification of the Constitution, or any other single event in our nation's history. Maybe our political system is still unfolding. Democracy in America is not a state of being but rather a process of growth. The story of liberty and freedom in America has been the movement toward the realization of an ideal. The Preamble to the Constitution, with its statement that the people are seeking a "more perfect union," implies that perfection is not possible, that the ideal is not achievable. But it also suggests that the challenge is to *strive* toward an open, free, and just system. America is clearly, if somewhat slowly, moving in that direction. Perhaps, also, the story of Barack Obama, touched on in the previous chapter, is testament to that unfolding story.

■ **Civil Law:** A body of law that applies to private rights, such as the ownership of property or the ability to enter into contracts.

EXAMPLE: *When actress Zeta Graff sued Paris Hilton for slander, she sought $10 million in a civil law action.*

■ **Criminal Law:** A body of law that applies to violations against rules and regulations defined by the government.

EXAMPLE: *When someone illegally downloads music from the Internet, they may be violating a criminal law.*

The Nature *of* Government *and* Politics (pages 32–33)

What is the difference between government and politics?

In real ways, *government* is all around us. Government is the formal structures and institutions through which binding decisions are made for citizens of a particular area. We might also say that it is the organization that has formal jurisdiction over a group of people who live in a certain place. Government is *not* the process by which things take place in a political system; rather, it is the "rules of the game" and the structures (the institutions) that make and enforce these rules. In the United States, such institutions include legislatures (city councils, state legislatures, Congress), executives (mayors, governors, the president), the courts, the bureaucracy, and a few independent agencies, such as the Federal Reserve System. It would not include political parties, interest groups, and public opinion, for example; they are key elements of our political system but not formal parts of the governmental structure.

This definition also helps clarify the different types and layers of government. The rules and formal structures of a city government apply to the people living in that city. A school or club government applies only to the students in that school or the members of that club. Occasionally, some people may question their loyalty and obedience to a particular government or feel compelled to change their allegiance from one government to another. On the eve of the Civil War, for example, many southern-born officers, such as General Robert E. Lee of Virginia, felt a sense of duty to the United States, for they had served in the U.S. military and had been trained at West Point. (Lee had been a commandant at West Point, and President Lincoln offered him command of the U.S. Army.) But they felt an even greater responsibility to their home state. Lee considered this loyalty to Virginia more important than his duty to the United States. Indeed, before the Civil War, many Americans felt that they had dual citizenship: first in their state, and second in the federal union. Today most Americans would consider choosing "state citizenship" above federal citizenship rather different.

What does it mean to be "under the rule of the government"? At the most basic level, this suggests that government has the power to enforce its regulations and collect the resources it needs to operate. Rules can be enforced in many ways. One way, called **civil law**■, is for citizens to be required to pay money as a penalty for breaking a rule. **Criminal law**■, by contrast, prescribes that citizens who do not follow regulations pay a monetary penalty (a fine), be removed from society for a period of time or even permanently (through a sentence of death or of life imprisonment without parole), or both. Taxation is the most common way to collect revenue to make the government run.

The words *power* and *authority* are related to government's ability to enforce its rules and collect resources. **Power**■, in the political context, is the ability to get individuals, groups, or institutions to do something. Power determines the outcome of conflicts over governmental decisions; it charts the course of public policy. When the ranks of an interest group grow to the point that governmental decision makers are forced to listen, that group is said to have power. If a handful of corporate elites can persuade public officials to steer public policy their way, they have power. The media would be considered powerful if they were to shift public opinion in favor of one candidate over another or persuade Congress and the president to adopt or change a certain policy.

Authority■ is defined as the *recognized* right of a particular individual, group, or institution to make binding decisions. Most Americans believe that Congress has the authority to make laws, impose taxes, or draft people into military service. We may not like the decisions made in Washington, in our state capital, or at city hall, but we recognize that in our system of government, elected officials have the authority to make those decisions. However, many people balk at the idea of *appointed* bureaucrats making regulations, given that they are not elected, which means that they don't have to answer to the people, only to those who appointed them. Thus bureaucrats have *power* but lack *authority.* We often also hear criticisms of judges "legislating from the bench," meaning that when they make decisions affecting policy matters, they overstep their bounds—that is to say, that they lack authority to make such decisions because they were not elected by the people and do not have to answer to them.

> "Power, authority, legitimacy ... all these terms seem similar. What's the difference?"
>
> —Student Question

Some individuals, groups, and institutions have both power and authority. Again, most Americans believe that Congress has the authority to make laws and that federal law enforcement units have the power to enforce those laws. Most people dread getting a letter from the Internal Revenue Service requiring them to submit to an audit of their tax returns. But as we have pointed out, power and authority are not the same. Perhaps the best contemporary example of when power and authority collide might be education reform. A few years ago, the federal government wrote into law a dramatic effort to improve public education, the No Child Left Behind Act. There is little question that the federal government has the power to enforce this sweeping law. Yet for all of our nation's history, state and local governments have controlled education policy. Many people get angry at the notion of "legislators off in Washington telling us how to run our schools." Many therefore believe that the federal government lacks the authority to regulate education policy.

Power: The ability to exercise control over others and to get individuals, groups, and institutions to comply. **EXAMPLE:** *The National Rifle Associaiton weilds power in American politics because legislators fear the wrath of its large, active membership.*

CONNECT THE LINK (Chapter 1, page 4)

Authority: The recognized right of a particular individual, group, or institution to make binding decisions for society. **EXAMPLE:** *Some might disagree with the Supreme Court's view on school prayer, but they recognize its authority to make binding decisions.*

Baseball

Official Rules (Government)	How the Game is Played (Politics)
1. Pitchers can start from either the windup or the stretch position.	Pitchers grip the ball in different ways to throw fastballs, curveballs, or knuckleballs. Also, pitchers release the ball at different points to change the batter's view of the ball.
2. Batters must keep both feet in the batter's box while hitting.	Batters can "crowd the plate" by standing close to the inside edge of the box.
3. A batter will run to first base after hitting a ball in fair territory.	Batters do not always make a full swing with the bat (for example, bunting).
4. All fielders must be in fair territory when that team's pitcher delivers the ball.	Defense can shift to accommodate for a batter who tends to hit in a certain direction.

American Government

Official Rules (Government)	How the Game is Played (Politics)
Article I, Section 2 The House of Representatives shall choose their speaker and other officers	The majority party uses their power to elect a speaker and other officers from their party, thus enabling them to push their legislative agenda.
First Amendment Freedom of the Press	Corporate conglomerates own media outlets.
Article I, Section 7 Presidential Veto	Presidents can threaten to veto a bill before it passes through Congress in order to influence the legislation.
Article I, Section 3 each Senator shall have one vote	Lobbyists can provide information on issues and influence the way a Senator or Representative votes.
Article I, Section 2 The House of Representatives shall be composed of members chosen every second year by the people of the several States	Candidates raise money and campaign before election day to influence the opinions of the voters.

FIGURE 2.1 | **Government and Politics: What's the Difference?**

It is important that you understand the difference between government and politics. We suggest government is analogous to the official rules of baseball, and politics is similar to how the game is actually played. ***—What is another analogy that might help you and your classmates better understand the difference between governmental institutions and the political process?***

SOURCE: www.usconstitution.net

A final term to consider is *politics*. As noted in LINK Chapter 1, page 4, politics is the *process* by which the character, membership, and actions of a government are determined. It is also the struggle to move government to a preferred course of action. All citizens might agree that a change is needed, but how to reach the desired goal can be hotly disputed. Given that governmental decisions create winners and losers—that is, acts by the government rarely please everyone—politics is a process that causes many to be left frustrated and at times angry. Moreover, politics can prove to be a slow process. The famous German sociologist Max Weber once suggested that politics is the "strong and slow boring of hard boards," and this makes good sense.[2]

The key difference you should keep in mind is that politics is the *process*, whereas government involves the *rules* of the game. An analogy might be helpful: The baseball rulebook is long and complex. It states how runners can arrive at first base safely, how outs are made, and how a team wins. Most rules are clear and have remained the same for generations. But the actual *conduct* of the game is another matter. The rulebook says nothing about split-finger fastballs, change-ups, bunts, intentional walks, double steals, pitching rotations, closers, stoppers, line-up strategy, and other aspects of how the game is played. The rulebook represents government; the way the game is played is politics (see Figure 2.1).

The Nature of Government and Politics

Practice Quiz

1. Our Constitution guarantees both equality and freedom.
   a. true **b.** false
2. Which of the following is an institution of government?
   a. state legislature **b.** governor's office
   c. political parties **d.** a and b.
3. Which of the following best describes "politics"?
   a. the process of influencing government decisions—making public policy
   b. the process by which politicians seek to gain a preferred outcome
   c. the process of determining the character and actions of government
   d. a, b, and c.
4. Which of the following has both power and authority in the United States?
   a. newspaper editors **b.** the president
   c. unelected bureaucrats **d.** affluent lobbyists

Answers: 1-b, 2-d, 3-d, 4-b.

Discussion Questions

1. How does the No Child Left Behind Act illustrate how power can collide with authority?
2. What are some different ways in which politics is practiced by ordinary citizens?

What YOU can do!

Look in today's newspaper or in a weekly news magazine, like *Newsweek* or *U.S. News and World Report*. How often is the word "politics" mentioned compared to "government"? Does one word seem to be used in a more positive light than the other?

■ **Democracy:** A political system in which all citizens have a chance to play a role in shaping government action and are afforded basic rights and liberties.

EXAMPLE: *Since 1994, South Africa has been considered a democracy, because all citizens have the chance to vote and basic political rights are protected.*

■ **Republic:** A system of government in which members of the general public select agents to represent them in political decision-making.

EXAMPLE: *Most campus student organizations can be considered republics, because elections are held to choose student representatives.*

Types *of* Governments

(pages 34–35)

How does who *is allowed to participate, and* how *decisions are made, shape the nature of government?*

Governments come in many forms and modes of operation. Perhaps the best way to think about these differences is to focus on two critical questions: Who is allowed to govern? And how are governmental decisions reached?[3] With regard to *who* is allowed to set the rules and regulations and to enforce them, there are several broad possibilities. **Monarchy** is a system of rule in which one person, such as a king or queen, possesses absolute authority over the government by virtue of being born into a royal family and inheriting the position. Monarchies have been the most common form of rule in world history, and they are still in place in some nations around the globe. For example, Saudi Arabia still relies on a royal family for ultimate authority. (In history, few monarchies were truly "absolute"; kings were normally limited by custom and by the need to consult powerful groups. But in theory, the monarch's authority was unlimited.) Almost all kings and queens today head **constitutional monarchies** in which they perform ceremonial duties but play little or no role in actually governing their country. Examples include the United Kingdom, Spain, Belgium, the Netherlands, and Japan. A **dictator** is also a sole ruler, but often this person arrives at the position of power through a violent overthrow of the previous government. (Sometimes contemporary dictators, such as North Korea's Kim Jong Il or Syria's Bashar Assad, succeed to power like a king or queen on the death of a parent.) Like an absolute king, a dictator theoretically has unlimited control of the government, but again, this power is often limited by the bureaucracy, the military, the ruling party, or even members of the dictator's family.

In some forms of government, a small group, such as military leaders or the economic elite, holds the reins of power. This is known as elitism or **oligarchy** (rule by a few). Decisions in such systems are often made through a council. Some have suggested that Russia has become an oligarchy in recent years due to the growing power of a small group of leaders. **Pluralism** occurs when a number of groups in a system struggle for power. In other words, in a pluralist system, there are multiple centers of power.

Finally, **democracy**■ is a political system in which all citizens have a right to play a role in shaping government action—a mechanism often referred to as *popular sovereignty*. Citizens in a democracy are afforded basic rights and liberties, as well as freedom from government interference with private actions (that is, *liberty*). In a *direct or pure democracy*, all citizens make all decisions. Some tiny Swiss cantons (states) operate in this way, and a small number of communities in the United States are governed through town hall meetings, where everyone in the community has a say in making town policy. A **republic**■ is governed by a small group of elected representatives acting on behalf of the many. If these representatives closely follow the wishes of their constituents (the people they are sent to represent), and if they are elected through a fair and open process in which everyone has the same opportunity to participate, the system is considered a **representative democracy.** The United States is a republic—as are most of the industrialized nations of the world (though some are constitutional monarchies). Whether or not we are a true representative democracy, however, is a point of dispute. Perhaps by the end of the semester, you will be able to make your own assessment on this issue.

The second important question to consider is *how* decisions are reached in a government. In a **totalitarian regime,** leaders have no real limits on how they proceed or what they do. (Formal constitutions might exist in such regimes, seemingly full of formal limits on power, but in practice, such limits are meaningless.) Totalitarian governments control—or at least try to control—almost every aspect of society.[4] The term *totalitarian* was invented in the 1920s by Benito Mussolini in Italy, although in practice, his government exercised less than total control. Nazi Germany, the Soviet Union under Joseph Stalin, China under Mao Zedong, and present-day North Korea are the clearest examples of truly totalitarian dictatorships. Under a dictatorship, there may be an individual ruler, a small group, or even a number of groups, but none of these acknowledges any formal limitations.

In an **authoritarian regime,** government policies are kept in check by informal limits, such as other political forces (maybe political parties), the military, and social institutions (for example, religious groups). Leaders face real limits, but there are no formal or legal restrictions. A good example would be the president of Egypt, Hosni Mubarak. The Egyptian constitution grants the president exceptional powers, and parliament generally agrees to all of Mubarak's wishes. Yet he does face limits from business leaders and religious groups in his country. For instance, Mubarak himself has seemed inclined to maintain a close relationship with the United States but has been forced to demonstrate greater independence due to these influences. When there are both informal and legal limits, the system is a **constitutional government.** In the United States, for example, government action is controlled by strong social and political forces (including religions, interest groups, political parties, and the media) and by what the laws, the courts, and the Constitution allow (see Table 2.1).

TABLE 2.1 | **Types of Government and Economic Systems**

GOVERNMENT SYSTEMS	DEFINITION	EXAMPLES
Who Is Allowed to Participate?		
Monarchy	Individual ruler with hereditary authority holds absolute governmental power	Bhutan, Saudi Arabia, Swaziland
Constitutional Monarchy	Monarch figurehead with limited power, actual governing authority belongs to another body	Denmark, Japan, United Kingdom
Dictatorship	Individual ruler with absolute authority, often comes to power through violent uprising	Hussein's Iraq, North Korea
Oligarchy	A small group of the rich or powerful controls most of the governing decisions	Tunisia, 20th century South Africa, Pakistan
Pluralism	Multiple centers of power vying for authority	Canada, Great Britain, United States
How Are Decisions Reached?		
Pure Democracy	Citizens make all governmental decisions	Some Swiss states, some towns in New England
Representative Democracy	Citizens elect representatives to carry out government functions	United States, Germany, France
Totalitarian Regime	Leaders have no limits on authority	Nazi Germany, 1920s Italy
Authoritarian System	Leaders have no formal legal restraints on authority but are limited by informal forces (i.e. the military, religious forces)	South Korea, Singapore, Taiwan
Constitutional System	Government has both informal and legal restraints on the exercise of power	United States, Germany, France, Mexico

Types of Governments
Practice Quiz

1. A political system in which a number of competing groups struggle for power is termed
   a. pluralism. **b.** direct democracy.
   c. autocracy. **d.** communism.
2. Our textbook defines *liberty* as
   a. freedom from want and freedom from fear.
   b. freedom from government interference with private actions.
   c. freedom with provisions for minorities.
   d. freedom with imposed limitations.
3. One feature that an authoritarian regime has in common with democratic government is that
   a. government policies are enforced primarily by armed force.
   b. political power is concentrated among a small group of national leaders.
   c. government policies are kept in check by informal limits.
   d. the mass media is controlled by governing elites.
4. In a democracy, the right to participate is much more important than the protection of basic civil liberties.
   a. true **b.** false

Answers: 1-a, 2-b, 3-b, 4-b.

Discussion Questions

1. List and discuss at least three ways in which a democratic government is different from a totalitarian government.
2. In what ways does capitalism support representative democracy?

What **YOU** can do!

Sometimes it is easier to understand your own government when you compare it to those of other countries. To get started, compare governments worldwide at **http://www.gksoft.com/govt/en/world.html**

Early Governance *in* America (pages 36–37)

How did early politics set the stage for the American Revolution?

To see how Americans have governed themselves, let's go back to 1620. In that year, a tiny group of English people (41 men and an unknown number of women and children) sailed across the Atlantic to what was called at the time the New World. They were crammed into a leaky old ship called the *Mayflower.* Some members of this band would later be dubbed the **Pilgrims,** because they were coming to America in hopes of finding religious freedom. (Some of the other passengers were not part of this religiously motivated group.) All the *Mayflower* passengers were bound for Virginia, where they expected to join an English colony that had been founded a few years earlier, in 1607. Unfortunately, the place where they landed—New England—was outside the recognized boundaries of Virginia, and the captain of the ship refused to go any farther. Winter was coming, and he did not want to risk any more voyaging. He let the passengers stay on board during the winter, but even so, half of them died. When spring arrived, the captain took his ship back to England, leaving the passengers on the coast of New England.

Recognizing that they were stuck in this bleak place, the Pilgrim leaders insisted that everyone, Pilgrim and non-Pilgrim alike, sign the **Mayflower Compact,** a document legalizing their position as a "civil body politic" under the sovereignty of King James I. Most important for our concerns is that these people, finding themselves in a place outside the jurisdiction of English rule, sought a system where laws, not a small group or a single person, would rule their society.

From the Mayflower Compact until the American Revolution, a mixed system characterized colonial governance. On the one hand, most of the colonies were established through charters from England. There was no question that these settlements would be governed under English rule. Governors were appointed by the Crown to oversee different colonies and were responsible only to the king. On the other hand, the New World was an ocean away. Settling an untamed wilderness created its own set of problems, and ideas favoring self-governance grew in intellectual circles both in America and in Mother England. The compromise came in the form of colonial assemblies. (The first of them was the House of Burgesses, at Jamestown.) Here colonists elected representatives to speak on their behalf and to counsel the governors on the best courses of action. Every colony had an assembly. These bodies had little legal authority, but they carried substantive powers. The royal governors were eager to receive good advice and to win the esteem of the citizens. They did not have to listen to this advice, but very often, it made sense to do so. This mix of appointed rule and self-governance seemed to work, at least at first.

Two developments upset this balance. First, many colonists brought with them the political customs and traditions from their homeland, meaning that the debate over the extent of royal authority in the conduct of government came along as well. As in England, those supporting the Crown were often the wealthiest, having received immense land grants and special privileges from the king. (In eighteenth-century Britain, this group, which dominated Parliament, was often referred to as the Court Party.) Those who were not part of the political in-group were deeply suspicious of the favored elite. Their cynicism ran deep, and their numbers swelled as the years passed. On top of this, if a local governing authority proved oppressive, colonists had the option of simply packing up and moving. This made opposition to royal and elite control easier.

Imagine you have arrived with your family, friends, and a bunch of strangers in a land without any formal rules or regulations.

Second, and more significantly, new financial pressures were thrust on the colonists in the mid-1760s. The **French and Indian War** in North America, which began in 1754 and ended nine years later, pitted Great Britain against France. (The war was part of a larger Anglo-French struggle for global power.) The French and Indian War began over control of the upper Ohio River valley, but the larger issue was which nation would eventually control the continent. Most of the relatively few settlers in this area were British, but the French had entered into trade agreements (and later a military alliance) with many Indian tribes. Through a series of spectacular military engagements over the course of several years, the British defeated the French and took control of North America. Britain won this war with relatively little colonial assistance.

> "If the royal governors were responsive to the concerns of the assemblies, why did the colonists revolt?"
>
> —Student Question

All wars are expensive, but given that this one had been waged an ocean away, the price of protecting Britain's New World empire proved very high. Facing massive debt and grumbling taxpayers, Parliament, with the king's blessing, looked for new ways of raising revenue. Because the war had been fought to protect the colonists, it seemed logical that they should bear much of the responsibility for paying the bill. Thus began a period known as the **Great Squeeze**, in which Parliament passed one measure after another, including the Sugar Act

Great Squeeze: A period prior to the American Revolution when the British Parliament sought to recoup some of the costs associated with the French and Indian War by levying new taxes and fees on colonists.

EXAMPLE: *The Sugar Act and the Stamp Act were measures imposed on the American colonists during the Great Squeeze.*

(1764), the Stamp Act (1765), the Townshend Acts (1767), and the Tea Tax (1773), all designed to wring as much revenue from the colonists as possible. To make matters worse, the Great Squeeze came after more than a generation of what was called "salutary neglect," a policy of casual, loose enforcement of trade laws in the colonies. Parliament had hoped that this freedom would stimulate greater commercial growth, leading to greater profits for British investors. Parliament's decision to raise revenue through a number of taxes after a century of trade freedom proved a bitter pill for the Americans.

In truth, the new taxes were not severe, and colonial Americans were probably among the least taxed people in the Euro-American world at the time. But the colonists were in constant fear of the corruption that, in their eyes, a faraway and arbitrary government could impose on them. ("Corruption" to eighteenth-century Americans meant more than bribery and embezzlement; it also included the distribution of government favors to what we would today call "special interests.") These taxes and other presumed abuses were seen as the opening wedges of creeping corruption and tyranny. It seems, then, that the colonists' obsession about corruption and tyranny and their insistence on guaranteeing limited, accountable government became fundamental to Americans' ideas of just governance. The relationship between the royal governors and the colonial assemblies soured. Because it was the duty of the governors to enforce these unpopular revenue-raising acts, they became the targets of colonial outrage.

PATHWAYS | of action

The Sons of Liberty

During the uneasy and turbulent times of pre-Revolutionary America, various resistance groups began to organize, often in secret. Several of these early interest groups became collectively known as the Sons of Liberty, a name closely linked with protests against Parliamentary rule over the colonies. Led by powerful, important figures such as John and Samuel Adams, but also enlisting the support of artisans, shopkeepers, and other working people who could be depended on to rebel against abuses like the Tea Tax, the Sons of Liberty organized in one community after another.

They held rallies, sponsored "committees of correspondence" (letter-writing campaigns) to spread their views, and recruited community leaders to their cause. They understood the importance of building organizations, rallying individuals in every community, and shaping public opinion. In the end, the Sons of Liberty proved to be one of our nation's first and most influential interest groups, helping set the stage for a revolution and for the creation of a democratic system of government. ■

Early Governance in America

Practice Quiz

1. Before the Revolution, the colonies were governed by a "mixed system." This meant that
   - **a.** some colonies were ruled democratically while others were more autocratic.
   - **b.** some colonies resented British rule while others were content with the system.
   - **c.** most colonies were governed by a local assembly in addition to the authority of the Crown.
   - **d.** the colonies restricted religious freedom, but favored free trade.
2. The "Great Squeeze" was a period in colonial history when
   - **a.** Parliament sought to recover the money spent during the French and Indian War by levying new taxes on American colonies.
   - **b.** colonists were no longer allowed to sell their products to British merchants.
   - **c.** southern colonies threatened to merge and separate themselves from northern colonies.
   - **d.** royal governors were asked to surrender their lands to the control of the colonial assemblies.
3. The taxes imposed during the "Great Squeeze" crippled the colonial economy, leading to widespread disease and starvation.
   - **a.** true
   - **b.** false
4. "Salutary neglect" referred to
   - **a.** the British army's refusal to protect colonial settlements during the French and Indian War.
   - **b.** the Crown's casual enforcement of trade laws, with the expectation of greater economic gains.
   - **c.** the shift in military policy to attack the French and Indians instead of placing garrisons in frontier forts.
   - **d.** Parliament's indifference toward "provincial" affairs in the New World.

Answers: 1-c, 2-a, 3-b, 4-b.

Discussion Questions

1. How did the governing institutions in America change from the time of the Mayflower Compact to the Revolution?
2. How would we describe the Sons of Liberty in modern terms?

What **YOU** can do!

By 1765, Patrick Henry, a lawyer from Hanover County, Virginia, had emerged as a leader in protests against British tyranny. His speech to the Virginia Assembly—demanding "Give me liberty or give me death"—was repeated in taverns, homes, and courtyards throughout the colonies. It is a powerful discourse on the duty of every citizen in a democracy to join the political fray, even when there are risks. You can hear his speech at **http://www.history.org/Almanack/people/bios/biohen.cfm**

■ **Thomas Paine:** An American revolutionary writer and a democratic philosopher whose pamphlet *Common Sense* (1776) argued for complete independence from Britain.

SIGNIFICANCE: *Paine's writings helped inspire colonists to join the Patriot cause and to bolster support for the Continental Army.*

The American Revolution (pages 38–43)

What were the core principles of the American Revolution?

The causes and meanings of the American Revolution are best broken into two broad categories: financial and ideological. With regard to the financial concerns—what you might call Americans' pragmatic issues—the Great Squeeze made life in the colonies harder and the prospects of a profitable future dimmer for most colonists, not only for those in the business class but also for working people in port cities like Boston and Philadelphia. The Stamp and Sugar acts were oppressive, and the backlash against them was fierce. Parliament also passed many measures that placed lands in the western regions under British control. Because land represented profits—from sales of acreage, lumber, or farm products—many colonists saw this move as unbearable. The **Acts for Trade** were an additional series of moves by Parliament to channel money back to the commercial class in Great Britain. King George III (along with Parliament) sought to save money by demanding that each colony pay for the upkeep of the British soldiers occupying its territory. On a practical level, the Revolution was about the money.

> "What about the famous Boston Tea Party . . . wasn't that about taxes?"
>
> —Student Question

At a deeper level was a growing desire among Americans to create a system in which all citizens (at least all white, male, propertied citizens) would have a say in the conduct of government and in which basic freedoms of life and liberty would be protected. Echoing this idea, one of the rallying cries during this period was "No taxation without representation." The essence of self-governance, Americans argued, was the ability to control taxes. After Parliament imposed yet another revenue-raising measure, this time giving the bankrupt but politically powerful East India Company a monopoly on importing tea into the colonies, a band of enraged colonists, disguised as Indians, stormed a merchant ship in Boston harbor in the dark of night and threw the company's tea overboard. For many colonists, the so-called Boston Tea Party was a galvanizing event that rallied patriotic sentiment. It was a public expression of deep and growing animosities between an aristocratic government thousands of miles away and a public yearning for freedom and self-rule. For Parliament and George III, the event reflected growing unrest in the colonies—it was an act of insolence that had to be punished and suppressed. Parliament quickly passed five new measures, which the British called the **Coercive Acts** and the colonists referred to as the **Intolerable Acts**. Of course, these new measures only stoked the flames of rebellion.

Taxation without representation was not the only ideological issue. The old splits over parliamentary prerogatives were transformed into a debate on the exact nature of self-governance. The colonists had grown accustomed to an unprecedented level of freedom. In Great Britain and throughout Europe, laws and customs limited access to trades and professions, controlled land usage, and compelled people to belong to established churches. The Pilgrims had come to the New World in search of religious freedom, and in large measure, they had found it. The following generations began to consider and demand what they saw as their "rights."

During this period, a good deal of attention was paid to the writings of great philosophers on the rights of citizens and the proper conduct of government. The English political theorist **John Locke** (1632–1704), in particular, had written a number of widely read essays on the subject, most notably *Two Treatises of Government,* which first appeared in 1690. Locke argued that all legitimate governing authority is based on the consent of the governed and that all individuals have "natural rights." Later, in the eighteenth century, the Scottish economist **Adam Smith** (1723–1790) wrote about the importance of limiting government in order to protect the economic rights of citizens.

In the colonies, a number of people started to write on liberty, including a young Massachusetts lawyer named **John Adams** (1735–1826). In 1765, he began publishing a series of essays in which he offered a fervent defense of patriotism. "Liberty must at all hazards be supported," he argued.[5] The writings struck an immediate chord, noted one historian.[6] That same year, a group of delegates from the colonies gathered to discuss the new Stamp Act and to consider responses to it. The **Stamp Act Congress** produced the Declaration of Rights and Grievances, a powerful statement on the rights of citizens that was widely circulated. A decade later, when Americans found themselves debating the fateful step of seeking independence, **Thomas Paine**■ (1737–1809) wrote a highly influential and persuasive tract promising freedom, equality, and the prospect of democracy.

Thomas Paine was an important player in the creation of democracy in America. He wrote a number of essays that spelled out, in clear but passionate terms, the power of citizens in just governments—that is, in democracies. These essays also came at a critical juncture, as support for Washington's Continental Army was waning.

PATHWAYS | profile

Thomas Paine and the "Common Sense" of Democracy

"What is the 'common sense' of democracy?"
—Student Question

Immigrating to America in 1775 on the advice of Benjamin Franklin, the English journalist Thomas Paine became known as the "common sense" writer of Revolutionary America. Paine was among the first writers of political pamphlets, his most famous of which, *Common Sense,* strengthened the colonists' will to achieve independence and to demand their rights as citizens. Though not as widely lauded today as George Washington, Thomas Jefferson, and John Adams, Paine was a spirited patriot and a pioneer of grassroots political activism. Perhaps more than anyone else in his day, Paine understood the power of public opinion and how to stir the passions of common men and women. "It is Paine who speaks not only for his own time, the time of change, but for our own, in a language that spans two centuries," wrote a modern scholar.[7] After the American Revolution, Paine returned to England with the intention of building a bridge that he had designed, but with the outbreak of the French Revolution in 1789, he took up the cause of ordinary people in France by writing his equally strong work, *The Rights of Man.* Paine had the bad luck to back the wrong French Revolutionary faction, however, and barely escaped the guillotine. Returning to the United States, he lived the rest of his life in poverty; he was no longer popular among Americans because he had become, like so many of the French revolutionaries, a vocal critic of Christianity. ■

The very nature of life in the New World created a yearning for basic rights, equality, and freedom. All settlers faced the same realities: an untamed wilderness, the approach of winter, and the prospects of disease, starvation, and often hostile natives. In a very real sense, there was simply less opportunity for a rigid class system to emerge in the New World, because all the settlers had to roll up their sleeves and work together. And if colonists felt the yoke of oppression, they could simply move to the next colony. America was not a truly egalitarian society, but realities of life in the New World encouraged thinking about rights, freedoms, and egalitarian societies. And at the very least, the prospects of moving up from the laboring class were somewhat more real here than in Europe, and it was on the mind of every laborer who toiled to make a better life. As John Adams would write, "Let us recollect it was liberty, the hope of liberty, for themselves and us and ours, which conquered all discouragements, dangers, and trials."[8]

Together, financial issues and concerns over the rights of citizens fueled a revolt against British rule. The issue had started to boil over by the mid-1770s. **Edmund Burke,** a member of Great Britain's House of Commons, noted at the time that "the state of America has been kept in continual agitation. Everything administered as remedy to the public complaint, if it did not produce, was at least followed by, an heightening of the distemper." Burke observed that the colonists "owe little or nothing to any care of ours" thanks to "a wise and salutary neglect" from their British overlords.[9] In other words, the stage was set for a dramatic event.

The Declaration of Independence

By September of 1774, in the aftermath of the Coercive Acts and the Boston Tea Party, events seemed to be spinning out of control. Every colony except Georgia sent delegates to the First Continental Congress in Philadelphia. At this point, few openly spoke of breaking ties with Great Britain; most still hoped to find a compromise that would protect the rights of Americans and pull back the harshest tax measures. Still, in the absence of dramatic changes by George III and Parliament, the delegates called on the colonists to boycott all British goods.

"What was the Continental Congress—did it have real powers?"
—Student Question

Matters did not improve. Within a year, the royal governor of Massachusetts, Thomas Gage, ordered his troops to seize what was believed to be a growing supply of arms from the colonists at Concord. Before the 700 red-coated British troops sent from Boston reached Concord, however, 77 militia, called "Minutemen," met them at the small town of Lexington. Shots were fired, and the Minutemen retreated. The Redcoats pressed forward, but by the time they arrived at Concord, the Patriot forces had swelled to more than 300. After another battle, the royal troops had to retreat and were attacked repeatedly as they marched back to Boston. In the end, some 270 British soldiers and 95 colonists were killed. The event sent shockwaves throughout the colonies and across the Atlantic Ocean. The wheels of war had been set in motion.

Although there was still strong sentiment in America for reconciliation with Great Britain, many of the delegates who attended the Second Continental Congress in 1775 considered compromise impossible. They understood that war had, in fact, begun. But they still had to convince others throughout the colonies that armed rebellion was their only remaining chance. Not all Americans were convinced. British oppression had been real, but a war for independence was an altogether different matter. Many of those who had protested British abuses still remained loyal to England, and others were quite unsure of open rebellion. At the very same time that delegates were arriving at Philadelphia, petitions were circulating in towns and villages throughout the colonies calling for reconciliation with Great Britain. Something needed to be done to convince more colonists to rebel, to move with force toward a system of self-governance. Perhaps a statement, a clearly written rationale, would do the trick. A committee of five was formed, and the task of writing a draft was given to a young, rather shy

This famous picture depicts one of the greatest moments in the history of democratic governance—the signing of the Declaration of Independence.***—Did you know that these men all feared they were signing their own death warrants? Indeed, if the British had won the war, it is highly likely that these men would have been hanged as traitors. Would you have put your life on the line for the "cause of liberty?"***

■ **Natural Rights:** Basic rights that no government can deny.

EXAMPLE: *The right to a fair, impartial trial would be considered a natural right.*

■ **Social Contract Theory:** A political theory that holds individuals give up certain rights in return for securing certain freedoms. If the government breaks the social contract, grounds for revolution exist. This notion was at the core of the Declaration of Independence.

SIGNIFICANCE: *This concept reminds us that just governments spring from the will of citizens.*

delegate from Virginia by the name of Thomas Jefferson. He was considered a thoughtful young man and an excellent writer.

Jefferson's Declaration of Independence is today regarded as one of the most lucid statements ever written on the rights of citizens and the proper role of government in a free society. It is one of the world's great democratic documents and has been an inspiration to people yearning for freedom around the globe. As one recent writer noted, even today, "you can still get a rush from those opening paragraphs. 'We hold these truths to be self evident.' The audacity!"[10] The core of the statement can be found in just 83 words:

> We hold these truths to be self-evident, that all men are created equal, that they are endowed by their Creator with certain unalienable Rights, that among these are Life, Liberty and the pursuit of Happiness. That to secure these rights Governments are instituted among Men, deriving their just power from the consent of the governed, That whenever any Form of Government becomes destructive of these ends, it is the Right of the People to alter or abolish it, and to institute new Government. . . .

"Just that first sentence of the Declaration of Independence says a lot, doesn't it?"
—Student Question

Rarely has more been said in so few words. Let us examine this passage in detail. (You might also wish to examine the annotated version of the Declaration in Appendix 1, pages A-1 through A-6.)

First, Jefferson presents a notion of **natural rights**■. That is, individuals possess certain privileges—certain guarantees by virtue of being human. Second, these rights are *not* granted by government but instead by God, whom Jefferson calls the Creator. They cannot be given, nor can they be taken away. Third, Jefferson introduces the **social contract theory**■, drawn in large measure from the writings of John Locke. Humans have the option of living alone in what Locke called "the state of nature." According to this theory, humans originally lived without government or laws, enjoying complete personal freedom. Yet the state of nature meant "a war of all against all," in which—in the words of another philosopher, **Thomas Hobbes**—life was "solitary, poor, nasty, brutish, and short." To end this perpetual conflict and insecurity, people created governments, thereby giving up some of their freedoms in order to protect their lives and their property. Fourth, Jefferson agreed with Locke that governments, having been created by the people to protect their rights, are limited; they get their powers from the will of the people and no one else. (In arguing this, Locke was attacking the traditional claim that kings ruled by the will of God.) Finally, said Jefferson (again following Locke), when a government fails to respect the will of the people—that is, when it appears no longer to be limited—it becomes the right, indeed the obligation, of citizens to change the government. This passage is Jefferson's call for revolution.

It should be restated that Jefferson's assignment was not to create a grand, original statement on the rights of citizens or the proper nature of government. His task was to craft a document that would sum up his fellow patriots' thinking and provide a justification for colonists as they took up arms against British rule. His job was to write a persuasive statement, aimed at public opinion in America, in Britain, and in continental Europe. In fact, he did far more.

Was the Declaration of Independence effective in rallying support behind the Revolutionary cause? We do know that many New Yorkers were so inspired on hearing these words that they toppled a statute of King George and had it melted down to make 42,000 bullets for war.[11] Still, this is a difficult question to answer, because there was no accurate way to measure public opinion in those days. Many did take up arms and rally to the Patriot cause, but many balked at joining the Revolution and even enlisted in the British Army. We also know that public support for the Continental Army, headed by George Washington, lagged considerably throughout the Revolution. Most Americans were deeply suspicious of professional armies, fearing them as a threat to liberty. There were no mechanisms to collect funds to support the Continental Army; state contributions were very stingy (which helps explain the terrible conditions that the troops suffered at Valley Forge in the winter of 1777–1778); and many citizens remained cautious about joining in the bold gamble for independence.

Either way, war had begun between the most powerful nation in the world—Great Britain—and the American colonies. At first, things looked grim for the Patriot cause, and many Americans feared that all would be lost within a matter of weeks. By December of 1776, the end seemed near. But three startling developments seemed to turn the tide.

First, with bold leadership from George Washington, the Continental Army was able to gain a few high-profile victories, which served to assure patriots and foreign governments that the war could, in fact, be won and that their financial contributions to the war effort would not be wasted.

Second, from 1776 to 1783, Thomas Paine espoused the virtues of democracy in his sixteen famous "Crisis" papers. Their tone is apparent in the famous opening of "The American Crisis,

CONNECT THE LINK
(Chapter **1**, page **20**) Why are avenues for involvement so important in a democracy?

ABOVE: **Patriots pulling down a statue of King George III** in New York, after hearing the news of the signing of the Declaration of Independence.

BELOW: **Statue of Saddam Hussein** being pulled down in Bagdad on April 9, 2003. Many assumed that with the toppling of Hussein's regime, a democracy could be created in Iraq. But this goal has proven illusive, and the occupation of Iraq has been vastly more difficult than most had expected. ***—Can you think of some reasons why this is so?***

Number 1," published on December 19, 1776, when Washington's army was on the verge of disintegration:

> These are the times that try men's souls. The summer soldier and the sunshine patriot will, in this crisis, shrink from the service of their country; but he that stands it now, deserves the love and thanks of man and woman. Tyranny, like hell, is not easily conquered; yet we have this consolation with us, that the harder the conflict, the more glorious the triumph.

This was powerful stuff. Washington ordered the pamphlet read to all his troops.[12]

Third, the French government decided to support the Revolutionary forces. This decision came, after a prolonged diplomatic effort spearheaded in Paris by Benjamin Franklin, upon news that the Americans had inflicted a serious defeat on the British Army at Saratoga in October of 1777. Financial support, arms and ammunition, and military assistance from the French government proved immensely helpful—particularly on occasions when the prospects for victory still seemed bleak.

The Colonial Experience and the Pathways of Change

Having some gripes with your government is one thing; deciding to break away and form a new government is quite another. A move of this sort would seem especially momentous given that in 1776 Britain had the world's most powerful army and navy. It has been said that the signers of the Declaration of Independence assumed they were signing their own death warrants. Barbara Ehrenreich writes, "If the rebel American militias were beaten on the battlefield, their ringleaders could expect to be hanged as traitors."[13]

How did things come to this? Ideas of liberty, equality, and self-governance—captured so well by Jefferson's pen—had simmered throughout the colonies for decades. Jefferson's prose captured a sentiment, but he did not bring the idea of democracy to life. Like flowers bursting from the ground after a long winter, liberty and equality were destined to blossom in the American soil. Also, as we noted in LINK Chapter 1, page 20, governments whose citizens yearn for liberty are stable only if those citizens have avenues of change—that is, the means to move public policy in new directions as times and circumstances change. What pathways of change had been available to the colonists? Could they elect a new government or petition the courts for redress? Might average citizens effectively lobby members of Parliament, an ocean away? Protests were tried, such as the Boston Tea Party, but they were met with additional acts of repression. There seemed no option for change. The only recourse was to declare independence and prepare for war. In a very real way, the American Revolution underscores the importance of our pathways concept.

Another interesting issue to ponder is what might be the right course for those who *perceive* no viable pathways of change. If you think that your government is no longer listening to your concerns—the concerns of average citizens—and that there is no way to bring the system back in line, must revolution follow? Is not Jefferson clear that under such circumstances revolution is justified? In 1787, Jefferson claimed that "the tree of liberty must be refreshed from time to time with the blood of patriots and tyrants."[14] And have we seen this process played out in American history since the Revolution? Indeed we have.

The American Revolution

Practice Quiz

1. The call for "no taxation without representation"
   - **a.** implied that taxes were too high and that a new government must be formed to reduce them to reasonable levels.
   - **b.** inspired a new ideological movement to create a government based upon the preferences of the citizens.
   - **c.** did not really inspire citizens to join the revolutionary movement.
   - **d.** a and c.
2. According to Jefferson, people created governments
   - **a.** to end perpetual conflict and insecurity.
   - **b.** to give up some personal freedom to gain protection of their lives and property.
   - **c.** only with the consent of the will of the people.
   - **d.** a, b, and c.
3. According to the Declaration of Independence, "they are endowed by their Creator with certain
   - **a.** provisions and prospects."
   - **b.** universal truths."
   - **c.** unalienable rights."
   - **d.** divine principles and protections."
4. Jefferson suggested that "just" governments should be "limited"; this means that government must
   - **a.** be limited to no more than three branches.
   - **b.** derive their powers from the consent of the governed.
   - **c.** tax citizens only if average citizens are allowed to vote on the issue.
   - **d.** restrict the number of departments and personnel.

Answers: 1-b, 2-d, 3-c, 4-a.

Discussion Questions

1. How would we translate John Locke's views about "the consent of the governed" and "natural rights" in our society today?
2. How would Thomas Paine go about expressing his radical ideas using modern technology and mass media?

What **YOU** can do!

Visit the Thomas Paine National Historical Association of **http://www.thomaspaine.org/contents.html** to read some of Paine's writings, including his pamphlet *Common Sense*. Can you see how he inspired colonists to fight for their independence from Britain?

The Articles *of* Confederation

(pages 44–47)

Why did the Articles of Confederation fail?

Less than a week after the signing of the Declaration of Independence, the Continental Congress set to work drawing up a system of government for the self-declared independent American states. After a year's effort, the model that emerged was called the *Articles of Confederation*. The idea was to draw the 13 states together but, at the same time, to allow each state to remain independent. In this system, the central government could coordinate and recommend policies, but it had no ability to enforce these policies if the states refused. Even so, it took three years for all the states to approve the plan, meaning that during much of the war, no central government existed (although Congress continued to function). The Articles of Confederation were formally adopted on March 1, 1781.

"What kind of government did the colonies adopt during the Revolution?"

—Student Question

The Articles provided for a one-house Congress, in which each state had one vote. The delegates to the Congress were just messengers of the states, appointed to their posts by the state legislature. They were paid by the states and could be removed by the state legislature at any time. (An analogy would be today's United Nations, where each nation has one delegate and one vote and where this person serves at the discretion of the home government.) On paper, at least, this Congress had power to conduct foreign affairs, wage war, create a postal service, appoint military officers, control Indian affairs, borrow money, and determine the value of the coinage.[15] But the Articles did not give the national government the power to force its policies on the states, nor did it allow the levying of taxes to support the federal government (see Table 2.2). It was up to the states to contribute to the federal government's support as they saw fit (just as each member nation of the United Nations contributes what it wishes to the UN budget). And the Articles said nothing about judicial matters.

The fact that the Articles guarded state sovereignty is really not surprising. Given the hardships that the colonists had endured under the government of George III, one can surely understand the desire for something different. In a very real way, our first system of national government was designed to be the opposite of what colonists had experienced under authoritarian, centralized British rule. It was also widely believed at the time that democracy was possible only when government was local. The "will of the people," most Americans thought, was best expressed on a local scale. Would it really make sense to merge the interests of northeastern manufacturing states and those of southern agricultural states? Moreover, if the government were to be a republic, in which representatives speak and act for constituents, then smaller governments would also make better sense, because their representatives would more likely know the interests of their constituents. We should also not be surprised to learn that under the Articles, the governing authority, although weak, rested in the legislature. The Articles did not create an executive office (such as a president). Once again, Americans' fear of creating a system similar to the British model led them in a different direction. Why would they consider crafting a new system of government with a powerful executive, given their recent experience with George III?

TABLE 2.2 | Powers of Congress under the Articles of Confederation

WHAT CONGRESS COULD DO	WHAT CONGRESS COULD NOT DO
Borrow money	Regulate commerce
Request money from states	Collect taxes from citizens
Conduct foreign affairs	Prohibit states from conducting foreign affairs
Maintain army and navy	Establish a national commercial system
Appoint military officers	Force states to comply with laws
Establish courts	Establish a draft
Establish a postal system	Collect money from states for services
Control Indian affairs	

Limitations of the Articles of Confederation

The Articles of Confederation failed for several reasons. First, the national government had no way to collect revenue from the states or from the states' citizens. No government can survive without some means of obtaining the resources it needs to operate. Second, the national government had no way of regulating commerce. For example,

"Why did the Articles of Confederation fail?"

—Student Question

■ **Shays's Rebellion:** An armed uprising in western Massachusetts in 1786 and 1787 by small farmers angered over high debt and tax burdens.

SIGNIFICANCE: *This event helped bring about the Constitutional Convention, as many worried that similar events would happen unless there were changes.*

■ **Constitutional Convention:** A meeting in Philadelphia in 1787 at which delegates from the colonies drew up a new system of government. The finished product was the Constitution of the United States.

SIGNIFICANCE: *A great deal of our current governing system can be traced back to this gathering in the summer of 1787.*

each state could tax the goods imported from other states and coin or print its own money. Imagine the problems that would result today if each of the 50 states issued its own currency! Third, the national government was unable to conduct foreign affairs—that is, to speak to other nations with a unified voice. Fourth, the mechanism to alter the Articles proved too difficult, as any change required the unanimous consent of all 13 states. (In other words, just one state could veto any change.) So even if adjustments, such as giving the national government the power to collect taxes, could have improved matters, the chances of achieving unanimous agreement to do so were slim.

Yet another shortcoming of the Articles was the lack of leadership and accountability within the federal government. There was no one in charge. This was intentional, of course, reflecting the fear that any person or group placed in a position of authority would have the power to abuse that position and become corrupt. This issue of accountability came to a head in 1786 with an event that rocked western Massachusetts. During the mid-1780s, the nation had experienced an economic depression. Particularly hard hit were farmers, who were receiving much less for their crops than in previous years due to a flood of imports. Desperate for relief, a group of farmers led by Daniel Shays, a veteran Patriot militia captain who had fought against the British at Bunker Hill in 1775, gathered to demand changes. Frustrated that their calls for help seemed to fall on deaf ears at the state legislature, Shays's forces grew to nearly 2,500. Soon violence broke out as the group clashed with state militia forces. Shays's men even turned their anger at the national government, threatening to storm an arsenal in Springfield, Massachusetts. The governor and state legislature appealed for assistance in putting down the protest, which they argued had deteriorated into a full-blown riot. Surely this was a matter for the central government to deal with. But there was no person or group outside Massachusetts to take the call for assistance, and no help was available.

Many of the rebels were captured and sentenced to death for treason, but all were later pardoned. Yet **Shays's Rebellion**■ had a profound impact on the future of our nation, because it suggested that liberty and freedom—that is, an open democratic society—carried risks. Many people believed that a truly open system was fertile soil for violence and anarchy. George Washington commented, "There are combustibles in every state which a spark might set fire to. . . . If government cannot check these disorders, what security has a man for life, liberty, or property?"[16] Washington's young wartime aide Alexander Hamilton agreed, noting that the rebellion prompted "the question, whether societies of men are really capable

"What happened to the rebels?"

—Student Question

Shays's Rebellion in 1786 is shown. We often hear that this event shocked the nation and led to the Constitutional Convention a year later. ***—But what did the event signify? What caused Shays and his followers to vent their frustration at the government in Springfield, Massachusetts? Does the answer say anything about the nature of government in Massachusetts in the 1880s?***

or not of establishing good government from reflection and choice, or whether they are forever destined to depend for their political constitutions on accident and force."[17] Many people feared that the answer was the latter. At the very least, the event suggested that the national government was woefully inept.

A few months after the uprising in Massachusetts, a meeting was organized to revise the Articles. This was the **Constitutional Convention**■.

Shays's Rebellion: An Alternative Look

The traditional view of the forces that led to the Constitutional Convention emphasizes the shortcomings of the Articles of Confederation, which we've summarized. The national government was just too weak, says the traditional perspective. It was not able to regulate commerce or conduct foreign policy, and there was no mechanism to deal with emergencies. Shays's Rebellion was simply the straw that broke the camel's back, a focusing event that set the wheels of change in motion.

There is another way to look at this, however, related to how you interpret Shays's uprising. Why would Shays and his 2,500 followers turn to violent protest? Were there no other pathways for change?

Money, especially specie or "hard money" (silver and gold coin), became very scarce throughout the United States in the 1780s, resulting in a severe depression that lasted nearly a decade. But not everyone was affected the same. Hardest hit were working-class citizens and small farmers. Because these people had little or no hard money with which to pay their debts, bank foreclosures skyrocketed. By the mid-1780s, demands for action grew louder. Very much in keeping with the structure of government during this period, people's cries for assistance were directed to the state legislatures. That often worked, and the state legislatures responded with many changes. "Stay laws" were passed to postpone foreclosures, and "tender laws" allowed farmers to use agricultural products (rather than hard money) to help pay loans. Partly as a result, inflation surged, and as paper money became more widespread, it became easier to use this inflated currency to pay off debts, such as the mortgage on a farm. In a very real sense, democracy seemed to be working. There was a call for help, and *most* state legislatures responded.[18]

In one state, the legislature dragged its feet: Massachusetts. What made this state different? For one thing, business interests dominated the state legislature. Instead of helping small farmers, the legislature saw fit to levy heavy taxes in an attempt to pay off the state's wartime debts, with most of the money going to wealthy business owners in Boston. From this vantage point, Shays's Rebellion broke out because the channels of the democratic process were *not* working in Massachusetts. There seemed no other viable pathway for change, and violence erupted.

This perspective also allows us to reconsider the motivations of the delegates to the Constitutional Convention. Today, many historians believe that the aim of that meeting was to fine-tune the democratic process and create a stronger national government. In some ways, this is true. But the policies of the state governments designed to protect farmers and laborers during the depression of the 1780s created hardship for a different group—the economic elite. As noted earlier, there are always winners and losers in politics, and during this period, much that was given to the farmers was taken from business owners and bankers. There were many more farmers and laborers, so you might conclude that the "will of the people" was dictating public policy, a very democratic notion. Perhaps, then, some of the rationale for calling delegates to Philadelphia was to revise the Articles in order to make sure that state governments could not limit the "liberty" of the economic elite. Even James Madison gave a hint at this when, in the *Federalist Papers* (described later in this chapter), he called the "rage for paper money" (inflation) an "improper" and "wicked" project.[19] Would Captain Shays and his followers have thought of inflation and other policies designed to help them keep their homes and livelihoods as wicked? Certainly not. At the very least, perhaps the convention's goal was to check the democratic spirit of the public in the name of stability. This is a controversial perspective but something you might consider.

STUDENT | PROFILE

When most of us think of a soldier in the Revolutionary War, an image comes to mind of a farmer pulling his gun from the mantel, kissing his wife and children goodbye, then jumping in line with other patriots. The story of the "citizen soldier" has some validity, especially in the early years of the conflict. As one historian writes, "At the beginning . . . farmers, artisans, rich and poor, young and old—patriots came forth with uncommon zeal."[20]

But another reality is that the Patriot army soon faded. By late 1776, George Washington wrote to Congress, "The few who act upon principles . . . [are] no more than a drop in the ocean."[21] States resorted to a draft to fill their quotas, but drafts worked differently in those days. A draftee simply had to produce someone, anyone, to fill that position. Those with money often hired a person to fill their spot. Others enlisted because they were without property or jobs. The Continental Army was filled with poor farm boys eager for adventure.

One of these boys was Joseph Plumb Martin. At the age of 15, Martin enlisted as a private in the Connecticut state troops. A year later, in the spring of 1777, he enlisted in Washington's Continental Army—where he served for the duration of the war, seeing action at a number of major battles.

Plumb's experience is recounted in a detailed diary—one of the very few accounts of a teenage soldier in the American Revolution. Of one cold November, Plumb scribbled, "Here I endured hardships sufficient to kill half a dozen horses . . . [W]ithout provisions, without clothing, not a scrap of either shoes or stockings to my feet or legs." Regarding one battle, he wrote, "Our men were cut up like cornstalks. I do not know the exact number of the killed and wounded but can say it was not small." And of a fort after a battle, he noted, "The whole area of the fort was completely ploughed as a field. The buildings of every kind hanging in broken fragments, and the guns all dismounted, and how many of the garrison sent to the world of spirits, I knew not."[22] Several books catalogue Plumb's writings—and what a fascinating tale it is! ■

The Articles of Confederation

Practice Quiz

1. Why did the Articles of Confederation deliberately provide for a weak national government?
   - **a.** The planners made a number of serious mistakes in its construction.
   - **b.** There was residual fear of a strong, centralized government.
   - **c.** There was a widely held belief that democracy could only survive if governments were small and localized.
   - **d.** b and c.
2. Under the Articles of Confederation, each individual state could
   - **a.** conduct its own foreign affairs.
   - **b.** print its own currency.
   - **c.** regulate its own commercial activities.
   - **d.** a, b, and c.
3. Shays's Rebellion was a major event leading to the Constitutional Convention, because
   - **a.** it showed that even one individual could bring down the government.
   - **b.** the federal government proved too weak to respond to the crisis.
   - **c.** state governments were willing to curtail the liberties of individuals if given the opportunity.
   - **d.** Shays was a powerful innovator who was strongly supported by the political elites of the day.
4. One alternative view of Shays's Rebellion is that the framers of the Constitution were powerfully motivated by their own economic interests.
   - **a.** true
   - **b.** false

Answers: 1-d, 2-d, 3-b, 4-a.

Discussion Questions

1. Describe and discuss the backgrounds of the attendees at the Constitutional Convention. How did their backgrounds affect their deliberations?
2. What conditions led to the outbreak of Shays's Rebellion?

What **YOU** can do!

While many people have read at least part of the U.S. Constitution, few have ever read any of the Articles of Confederation. Go to **http://www.earlyamerica.com/earlyamerica/milestones/articles/text.html**, and read the document for yourself. Besides some of the weaknesses described in this chapter, do you see any other shortcomings in this early "blueprint" for a government?

■ **Virginia Plan:** A plan made by delegates to the Constitutional Convention from several of the larger states, calling for a strong national government with a bicameral legislature, a national executive, a national judiciary, and legislative representation based on population.

SIGNIFICANCE: *Much of this plan found its way into the Constitution, shaping the system we live under today.*

COMPARATIVE Comparing Constitutions

The Constitutional Convention (pages 48–51)

How did compromises at the Constitutional Convention shape our political system?

In late May of 1787, some 55 delegates from every state except Rhode Island came together at the Pennsylvania State House in Philadelphia for the purpose of proposing changes to the Articles of Confederation. Congress itself had authorized the meeting, but it did not expect that the Articles would be completely replaced by a new system of government. The delegates were not "average" men but rather included many of America's leading political, economic, and social figures of the time. (Thomas Jefferson, then serving as U.S. minister to France, was not present.) George Washington was selected as the convention's presiding officer, and on May 29, the delegates set to work. Interestingly, and perhaps contrary to what you might think, the convention deliberated in total secrecy—even to the extent of nailing the windows shut!

Opening the convention, Governor Edmund Randolph of Virginia offered a series of resolutions that amounted to an assault on the Articles. Rather than attempting to modify them, Randolph argued, the Articles should be dumped altogether. The delegates agreed; something new and vastly different was needed. Small groups were formed, charged with drawing up plans for a new government. In the end, five plans were submitted for consideration, but the delegates quickly narrowed their consideration to two.

The first was the **Virginia Plan**■, named for the home state of its principal author, James Madison. The delegates from the more populous states favored it. Table 2.3 provides an overview of what the new government would look like under this plan.

"Why did the delegates from large and small states favor different plans at the Constitutional Convention?"

—Student Question

Most delegates agreed with the core idea of the Virginia Plan—that the central government should be strengthened. Yet big differences in population between the states seemed a problem. The most populous states were Virginia, Pennsylvania, North Carolina, Massachusetts, and New York; the smallest states included (besides absent Rhode Island) Georgia, Delaware, Connecticut, and New Jersey. Delegates from the smaller states realized that this scheme would put them at a real disadvantage in the national government—a smaller state's interests would be overwhelmed by those of the larger states. Opposition to the Virginia Plan grew. William Paterson of New Jersey offered an alternative approach. His **New Jersey Plan**■ was designed to stick closer to the Articles of Confederation and would create a system of equal representation among the states: Each state would have the same number of national legislators. Table 2.4 is an overview of this plan.

Although it might seem that both models were similar in terms of the supremacy of the national government, this was really not the case. A national legislature was at the core of both plans, but under the New Jersey Plan, each state would have equal say in the making of public policy. Since a majority of state governors could change the makeup of the executive council, this plan was clearly more state centered. It was much more in keeping with the confederation model that underlay the Articles. In contrast, the Virginia Plan clearly laid out what was called at the time a "consolidated government," one that all but absorbed the states.

TABLE 2.3 | The Virginia Plan

- Three branches of government—a national legislature, an executive, and a judiciary.
- Force each of the branches to rely on the others.
- Grant each branch the ability to keep an eye on the other two so that no one segment of the government would become too powerful.
- Have a legislature with an upper and lower house, with members of the lower house chosen by the people in the various states and the upper chamber made up of legislators chosen by the lower house from a list of nominees put forward by the state legislatures.
- Allow each state a number of seats in the national legislature based on its population (thus the larger states would have more delegates and the smaller states fewer).
- Have an executive, selected by the legislature and serving a single term.
- Have judges who would be appointed to the bench by the legislature for life terms.
- Establish a "council of revision," with members from both the executive branch and the judiciary, which would review all national and state laws; this body would have some control over national legislation and an absolute veto over state legislation.
- Be supreme over the state governments—that is, acts of the new national government would override state law.

■ **New Jersey Plan:** A scheme for government advanced at the Constitutional Convention that was supported by delegates from smaller states. It called for equal representation of states in a unicameral legislature.

EXAMPLE: *Under this approach, each state would have the same say in the national legislature, and the president would have modest powers.*

TABLE 2.4 | The New Jersey Plan

- Have three parts of government—a national legislature, an executive council, and a judiciary.
- Have a legislature consisting of one body, in which each state would have one vote.
- Have a multiperson executive council, chosen by the legislature, with the responsibility of executing national laws; its members could be removed by a vote of a majority of state governors.
- Have a judiciary appointed by the executive council.
- Have a national legislature with the ability to tax the states, proportional to their population.
- Be supreme over the state governments, with the national legislature having the right to override state law.

One of the tragic ironies of our nation's formative period is that while notions of freedom and equality warmed the hearts of patriots, slavery was not eliminated in the Constitution. Indeed, it took two centuries, a bloody civil war, and the courageous acts of untold men and women to advance the cause of racial equality. Here, Rosa Parks, who Congress later called the "mother of the modern-day civil rights movement," refuses to sit in the back of the bus.

The Great Compromise

All the delegates at the convention knew that the legislative branch was critical, but the argument over the allocation of seats in the legislature nearly ended the proceedings. "Delegates conferred, factions maneuvered, and tempers flared."[23] The dispute was serious, because the delegates believed that if the new national government had real powers (as they all hoped), control of the legislative branch was critical. The stakes were high.

> "What was really at stake in the Great Compromise, and why was it so hard to reach agreement?"
>
> —Student Question

The issue also boiled down to different views of representation: a *state-based approach* versus an *individual-based approach*. It should be remembered that at this time most Americans felt loyalty to their state over any sort of national allegiance. At the time, even Thomas Jefferson considered Virginia, not the United States, "my country." As noted earlier, a widespread sense of national citizenship did not emerge until after the Civil War, some 80 years later. So the argument over representation came down to which states would have more sway in the new system, and delegates of the smaller states were not about to join a union that would put their own people at a disadvantage. They argued that states were on an equal par, of course, so all should have the same weight in the new national government. *States* were the units to be represented, not the citizens within each state. But the large states relied on an individual-based notion of representation. The new national government should speak on behalf of *citizens*, not states. If one state had significantly more citizens than another, it was self-evident that the bigger state would have more national representatives.

On June 30, 1787, Roger Sherman of Connecticut presented a compromise plan: The national legislature would have a House of Representatives, based on proportional representation (as under the Virginia Plan), but a second branch, the Senate, would contain an equal number of representatives from each state (as under New Jersey Plan). This **Great Compromise**■, sometimes called the **Connecticut Compromise,** settled the matter (see Table 2.5). Few of the delegates were completely satisfied. Indeed, some walked out of the proceedings, but most agreed that it was the best possible solution. Several of the states had tried this in their own legislatures, with much success. The plan was accepted, and the convention continued.

■ **Great Compromise/Connecticut Compromise:** An agreement at the Constitutional Convention that the new national government would have a House of Representatives, in which the number of members would be based on each state's population, and a Senate, in which each state would have the same number of representatives.

SIGNIFICANCE: *This was a compromise between two competing proposals, the Virginia Plan and the New Jersey Plan, without which the Constitutional Convention would likely have ended without agreement.*

TABLE 2.5 | Differences Between the Virginia Plan, the New Jersey Plan, and the Great Compromise

ISSUE	VIRGINIA PLAN	NEW JERSEY PLAN	COMPROMISE
Source of Legislative Power	Derived from the people and based on popular representation	Derived from the states and based on equal votes for each state	A mix; from the people for one house, from the states for the other
Legislative Structure	Bicameral	Unicameral	Bicameral; one house of equal representation, and another based on population
Executive	Size undetermined; elected and removable by Congress	More than one person; removable by state majority	Single executive; removed by impeachment
Judiciary	Life tenure, able to veto legislation in council of revision	No power over states	Life tenure, judicial review ambiguous
State Laws	Legislature can override	Government can compel obedience to national laws	National supremacy
Ratification	By the people	By the states	Ratification conventions in each state, thus allowing both the people and the states to be involved

The Three-Fifths Compromise

If one of the chambers of the national legislature was to be based on population (the House of Representatives), and if taxation was to be fixed around each state's population, how would the inhabitants of each state be counted? The delegates quickly agreed that a **census** (a complete count) would be conducted every 10 years, and this was written into the Constitution. But *who* might be counted as an inhabitant was a vastly more difficult matter. Here we find one of the most distressing parts of the Constitutional Convention. The issue boiled down to slavery. More than 90 percent of the slaves in North America at that time lived in five American states: Georgia, Maryland, North Carolina, South Carolina, and Virginia.[24] The delegates from these states argued that for the purposes of allocating House seats, slaves should be counted. This was quite a twist, given that slaves were considered property and were not given any rights of citizenship in these states—and the delegates from the northern states retorted as much. Yet given the huge slave populations in the southern states (40 percent or more in some states), not counting them would prove significant. If slaves were not counted, the southern states would have just 41 percent of the seats in the House; if slaves were counted, the South would have 50 percent.

Once again, the convention came to a standstill, delegates threatened to bolt, and a compromise was reached. Population would be used to determine each state's delegation to the House of Representatives, and slaves would be counted as three-fifths of a white person. Put a bit differently, five slaves would equal three white persons in the census. Precisely how the formulation was determined is a bit unclear. We know that a three-fifths figure was used under the Articles of Confederation and was thus ready to hand. Perhaps different offers were sent back and forth until a final figure was accepted. Slaves would not be allowed to vote or to have any of the rights that Jefferson had written about in his Declaration, but they would be counted as inhabitants—or rather as three-fifths of an inhabitant—in order to get both sides to agree to the Constitution. Our history is filled with such tragic ironies.

The Sectional Compromise

Still another deal—what some historians have called the most important compromise—was reached at the Constitutional Convention.[25] Even Madison considered this agreement the most important of all deals at the convention. It dealt with slavery and commerce.

Many Northerners hated slavery and pointed out the irony of celebrating the American Revolution and creating a free nation while preserving the institution of slavery. Southern delegates were not about to join a government that stripped them of their slaves, and even Northerners realized that abolishing slavery would shatter the South's economic base. According to one observer, "The subject haunted the closed-door debates."[26]

Most delegates agreed that the new Congress would have the power to regulate commerce, but many also worried about the potential for abuse. This was a very important power. Southern delegates in particular worried that because the House of Representatives would be based on proportional representation and the power to regulate commerce would reside in the new national government, their states' economic future was at risk. They argued that Congress should require a supermajority (a two-thirds vote, rather than a simple majority) whenever it attempted to regulate commerce. The northern delegates said no, once again worried about giving too much power to less populous states.

This led to another compromise: The Atlantic slave trade would be protected for at least twenty years. Article 1, Section 9, Clause 1 of the Constitution prohibited Congress from stopping the importation of slaves from overseas until 1808. (Slave trading within and among states was not mentioned.) In exchange, it was agreed that a simple majority of both houses of Congress would be needed to regulate commerce. Once again, the convention was able to continue.

The Constitutional Convention

Practice Quiz

1. Which of the following were elements of the Virginia Plan?
   - **a.** a plural executive (an executive branch with several members)
   - **b.** allotting seats in the legislature in proportion to each state's population
   - **c.** lifetime appointment of federal judges
   - **d.** b and c.
2. The "Great Compromise" created
   - **a.** three branches of government.
   - **b.** a bicameral legislature.
   - **c.** a branch of the legislature directly elected by the voters.
   - **d.** b and c.
3. The North-South compromise addressed
   - **a.** the legality of slavery.
   - **b.** the control of commerce by the national government.
   - **c.** the counting of slaves as a portion of each state's voting population.
   - **d.** a and b.
4. What phrase best describes the impact of the Articles of Confederation on the contents of the Constitution?
   - **a.** The Constitution merely revised a few of the principles of the Articles.
   - **b.** The Constitution replaced the Articles with a virtually new document.
   - **c.** The Constitution granted more power to the states and less power to the federal government than the Articles.
   - **d.** a and c.

Answers: 1-d, 2-d, 3-b, 4-b.

Discussion Questions

1. Select one of the issues debated during the Constitutional Convention, and make an argument that it was the most essential item upon which compromise had to be reached.
2. Discuss the rationale behind the three-fifths compromise. Was it worth the effort?

What **YOU** can do!

Walk through an interactive timeline that traces the history and development of the U.S. Constitution at **http://www.constitutioncenter.org/timeline/**. Click on "1787–1790" to see pictures and stories related to the early days of the Constitution.

Sharing of Powers: The U.S. Constitution's granting of specific powers to each branch of government while making each branch also partly dependent on the others for carrying out its duties.

EXAMPLE: *The Supreme Court ruled that "separate but equal" educational systems were unconstitutional in 1954, but the task of actually desegregating schools was left to President Eisenhower.*

Expressed Powers: The powers explicitly granted to the national government in the U.S. Constitution.

EXAMPLE: *Article I, Section 8 of the Constitution grants Congress the power to regulate commerce.*

The U.S. Constitution

(pages 52–55)

What are the core principles of the American Constitution?

On September 17, 1787, after five hot, argumentative months, the delegates to the Constitutional Convention finished their work. After hearing the clerk read the entire document, Ben Franklin rose to the floor to remark that although the form of government they had drafted was not perfect, it was the best that could have been achieved under the circumstances. He then made a motion that each delegate sign the final version. Thirty-nine of the original fifty-five who had begun the convention did so.

Most Americans believe that our Constitution is one of the greatest schemes of government ever devised—due in no small measure to the overarching structural framework that created a vibrant yet controlled government, a system that is both rigid and flexible. Much more will be said of the provisions in the Constitution in subsequent chapters, but some key points are outlined here. (Review the annotated Constitution in the Appendix.)

The Constitution breaks down into seven articles:

Article I: The Legislative Branch (Congress)

Article II: The Executive Branch (President)

Article III: The Judicial Branch (Courts)

Article IV: Guidelines for Relations Between States

Article V: The Amendment Process

Article VI: Federal–State Relations (Supremacy Clause); Oath for Officers

Article VII: How the Constitution Will Be Ratified

Let us consider several core principles embodied in the Constitution:

- **Three Branches of Government.** Understanding both the complexity of governance and the potential for corruption, the framers saw fit to create a system with different branches of government—legislative, executive, and judicial. Simply stated, the legislature would *make* the laws, the president would *enforce* the legislature's will, and the judicial branch would *interpret* the laws and *resolve* disputes according to the law.
- **Separate Institutions Sharing Powers.** One of the greatest challenges the framers faced was creating a system that was neither too weak nor too strong. A weak government would suffer the fate of the Articles of Confederation, but too strong a government might lead to corruption and an excessive concentration of power, minimize the role of the states, infringe on individual rights, and perhaps collapse in civil war. The framers believed that they had found a middle ground through the granting of specific powers for each branch while at the same time making each branch partly dependent on the others for carrying out its powers. This is called the **sharing of powers**.

The Constitutional Convention was one of the great triumphs of our nation's formative years. Facing long odds, a sweltering summer, and a membership that boasted radically diverse interests, these 55 men were somehow able to craft a model for government that has, with only modest adjustments, lasted to this day.

"How did the Constitution provide enough power for the government to act decisively, while preventing it from becoming too powerful?"

—Student Question

We will have a lot to say about the powers and duties of each branch, as well as about the connections between the branches, in the chapters that follow, but a few examples might be helpful here. Although Congress passes laws and appropriates funds, the executive branch enforces these laws and spends the money. The judicial branch can pass judgment on disputes that arise, but it must rely on the executive branch to enforce its rulings. The president can negotiate treaties with other nations, but the Senate must ratify these agreements before they take effect.

Police Powers: The powers reserved to state governments related to the health, safety, and well-being of citizens.	**EXAMPLE:** *Many consider the job of educating children to be the concern of local governments; a police power.*
Bill of Rights: The first 10 amendments to the U.S. Constitution, ratified in 1791, protecting civil liberties.	**EXAMPLE:** *Freedom of speech is one of our core civil liberties, protected in the First Amendment.*

- **Checks and Balances.** Just as each branch shares powers with the others, each branch is limited ("checked") by the other two. That is to say, each branch can review, and in some ways restrict, the acts of the other branches. For instance, Congress passes laws, but the president can veto proposed legislation—and if both houses of Congress can put together a two-thirds vote, they can override a presidential veto. The president can be impeached by the House and, if convicted by a two-thirds vote in the Senate, be removed from office. Federal judges can likewise be removed by impeachment and conviction. The judiciary can invalidate acts of Congress or the president when they are considered "unconstitutional," but Congress and the states can enact amendments to the Constitution that get around judicial decisions (see Figure 2.2).
- **Representative Republicanism.** The framers were anxious to create a republican system, in which leaders speak on behalf of constituents, but they also feared a "runaway" democracy. They wanted to create a limited government, a government "by the people," but they worried that the whims of public opinion would lead to an unstable government and perhaps even mob rule or "anarchy." The government, as Madison would later remark, should "enlarge and refine" the public's will. Representative republicanism proved the solution. The system would not be a direct democracy, where each person has a say on all public matters, but rather a representative republic, in which a small group of elected leaders speak and act on behalf of the many. Members of the House are elected directly by the voters; under the original Constitution, senators were to be selected by the state legislatures (a provision that changed to direct popular election when the Seventeenth Amendment was adopted in 1913); and the president would be chosen by an electoral college—envisioned in 1787 as a gathering of a small group of notable leaders in each state to select the federal chief executive. The Constitution rests firmly on the representative republican principle.
- **Federalism.** None of the framers intended to create a centralized government; instead, they envisioned a system in which a viable national government would undertake certain responsibilities and state governments would handle others. This is known as *federalism*—a system of government in which powers and functions are divided among different layers of the system. The Constitution clearly defines many of the powers of the national government, which are referred to as the **expressed powers**.

  In 1787, the state governments were considered closest to the people and thus best able to look after their health, safety, and well-being. These powers were called **police powers**. The national government, for its part, would focus on commercial matters, foreign affairs, and national security.
- **Reciprocity Among the States.** Although the Constitution permitted each state a degree of independence, delegates to the convention were concerned that citizens should be treated equally in every state. The framers had in mind, for example, that a marriage in one state would be recognized in other states. Two "comity" clauses accomplished this goal. The full faith and credit clause (Article IV, Section 1) said that each state must accept the legal proceedings of the other states, and the privileges and immunities clause (Article IV, Section 2) mandated that out-of-state citizens have the same legal rights as citizens of that state. While on vacation in New York, for instance, you have the same rights as people living there.
- **A Fixed System Open to Change.** The framers had in mind a rather fixed scheme of government, something that would not change with the winds of public opinion or the shifting personnel of government. What good would a constitution be if it could be changed each time new issues emerged or new people took office? At the same time, they recognized that their document was not perfect and that new pressures would arise as the nation grew and society changed. The outcome was to create a difficult but navigable route for change. The Constitution can be amended by a total of four procedures, as noted in Figure 2.3. As you will note, the amendment process entails two steps: proposal and ratification. There are two approaches for each step.

> "Has the Constitution changed much since it was first written? How are changes made?"
>
> —Student Question

Since the Constitution's ratification, there have been thousands of proposals for constitutional amendments, but only 27 have made it through the journey to formal amendment. The first 10 amendments, which make up the **Bill of Rights** (see Table 2.6), were enacted during the very first session of Congress, in large part as a response to criticisms of the original Constitution by its opponents during the ratification process. It would seem that the framers accomplished their goal of creating a fixed structure that could also be changed at critical times. The Bill of Rights and several of the other amendments are discussed in greater detail in subsequent chapters. Also, you will find an annotated discussion of all 27 amendments in Appendix at the end of this book.

The American System of Checks and Balances

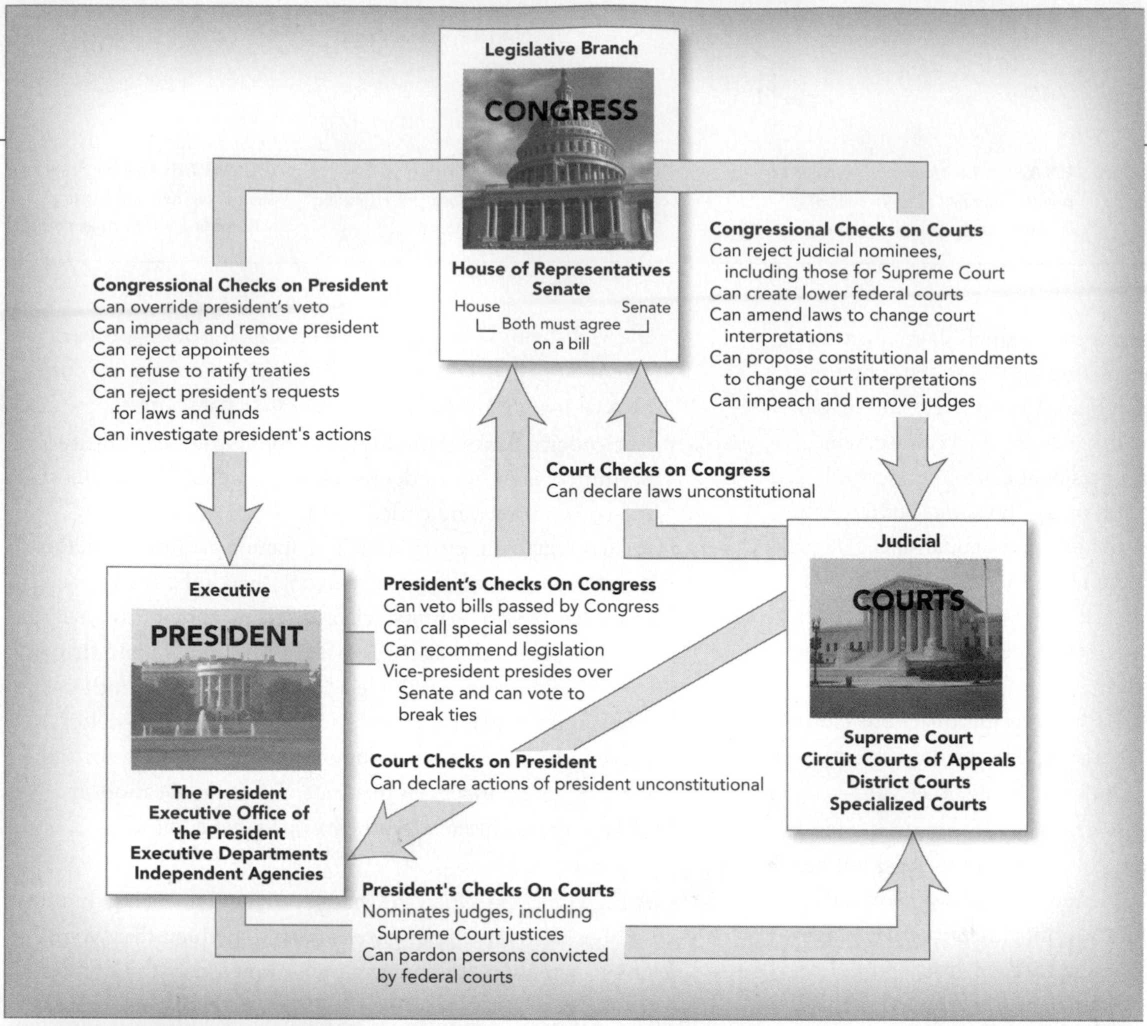
Legislative Branch
CONGRESS
House of Representatives
Senate
House
Senate
Both must agree on a bill
Congressional Checks on President
Can override president's veto
Can impeach and remove president
Can reject appointees
Can refuse to ratify treaties
Can reject president's requests for laws and funds
Can investigate president's actions
Congressional Checks on Courts
Can reject judicial nominees, including those for Supreme Court
Can create lower federal courts
Can amend laws to change court interpretations
Can propose constitutional amendments to change court interpretations
Can impeach and remove judges
Court Checks on Congress
Can declare laws unconstitutional
Executive
PRESIDENT
The President
Executive Office of the President
Executive Departments
Independent Agencies
President's Checks On Congress
Can veto bills passed by Congress
Can call special sessions
Can recommend legislation
Vice-president presides over Senate and can vote to break ties
Court Checks on President
Can declare actions of president unconstitutional
Judicial
COURTS
Supreme Court
Circuit Courts of Appeals
District Courts
Specialized Courts
President's Checks On Courts
Nominates judges, including Supreme Court justices
Can pardon persons convicted by federal courts

FIGURE 2.2 | **Shared Powers, Checks and Balances**

Many applaud this unique system of government in which each branch is somewhat dependent on the others, and each branch is in some ways checked by the others. Our system's longevity would suggest this model works, but others argue that this model makes change difficult—especially when different political parties control other branches of the government. ***—What do you think? Does this system favor pathways for change, or does it stifle the will of the people?***

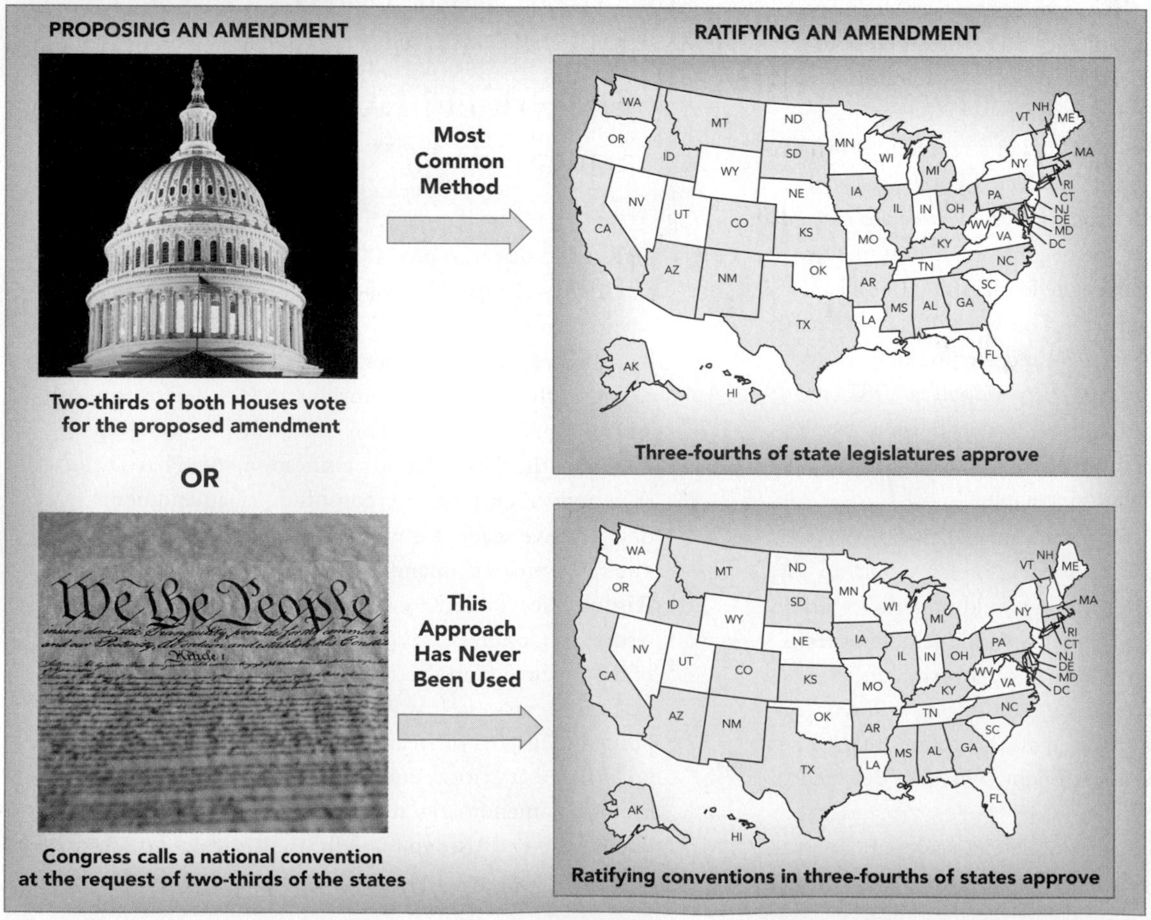
PROPOSING AN AMENDMENT
RATIFYING AN AMENDMENT
Two-thirds of both Houses vote for the proposed amendment
Most Common Method
Three-fourths of state legislatures approve
OR
We the People
Congress calls a national convention at the request of two-thirds of the states
This Approach Has Never Been Used
Ratifying conventions in three-fourths of states approve

FIGURE 2.3 | **How the Constitution Can be Amended**

The framers wanted to create a fixed system, but at the same time allow for some modifications under certain circumstances. ***—With just 27 amendments since 1789, would you say they got things right?***

TIMELINE **The History of Constitutional Amendments**

TABLE 2.6 | The First Ten Amendments to the Constitution (The Bill of Rights)

Safeguards of Personal and Political Freedoms	
1.	Freedom of speech, press, and religion, and right to assemble peaceably and to petition government to redress grievances
2.	Right to keep and bear arms
Outmoded Protection Against British Occupation	
3.	Protection against quartering troops in private homes
Safeguards in the Judicial Process and Against Arbitrary Government Action	
4.	Protection against "unreasonable" searches and seizures by the government
5.	Guarantees of a grand jury for capital crimes, against double jeopardy, against being forced to testify against oneself, against being deprived of life or property without "due process of law," and against the taking of property without just compensation
6.	Guarantees of rights in criminal trials, including right to speedy and public trial, to be informed of the nature of the charges, to confront witnesses, to compel witnesses to appear in one's defense, and to the assistance of counsel
7.	Guarantee of right of trial by a jury of one's peers
8.	Guarantees against excessive bail and the imposition of cruel and unusual punishment
Description of Unenumerated Rights and Reserved Powers	
9.	Assurance that rights not listed for protection against the power of the central government in the Constitution are still retained by the people
10.	Assurance that the powers not delegated to the central government are reserved by the states, or to the people

The U.S. Constitution

Practice Quiz

1. Which of the following is a core principle of the Constitution?
- **a.** Each state has equal representation in the federal government.
- **b.** One branch of government can check the acts of the other branches.
- **c.** Power is divided among the layers of government.
- **d.** b and c.

2. The framers of the Constitution wanted a government by popular consent but also one that would check the "passions of the public."
- **a.** true
- **b.** false

3. Reciprocity among the states implies that
- **a.** citizens must be treated equally in every state.
- **b.** each state must accept the legal proceedings of the other states.
- **c.** states with larger populations should have a greater say in the federal legislature.
- **d.** a and b.

4. What are the constitutional intentions of the three branches of government?
- **a.** The executive will create the laws, the legislature will enforce them, and the courts will administer fines and punishments for violations of the laws.
- **b.** The legislature will create the laws, the executive will enforce them, and the courts will resolve disputes according to the laws.
- **c.** The legislature will pass laws, the president will approve them, and the courts will enforce them.
- **d.** The national government will create laws, the states will cooperate to enforce them, and the courts will resolve disputes according to the laws.

Answers: 1-d, 2-a, 3-d, 4-b.

Discussion Questions

1. How would you describe the purpose of the Bill of Rights in modern terms?

2. What are some of the contradictions inherent to the First Amendment?

What **YOU** can do!

Read the U.S. Constitution at the back of the book, and then go to the Web site of the National Constitution Center at **http://www.constitutioncenter.org/constitution/** to review an interactive version of our constitution. How does this change your own reading of the document?

■ **Federalists:** Supporters of the ratification of the U.S. Constitution.

SIGNIFICANCE: *In the late 1780s, this referred to supporters of ratification of the Constitution. James Madison was one of the leading Federalists during this time. By the late 1790s, it was the name given to one of the first political parties, headed by Alexander Hamilton and John Adams. Many of the* early *Federalists, such as Madison, later joined the Democratic-Republican Party, in opposition to the Federalist Party!*

■ **Anti-Federalists:** Opponents of ratification of the U.S. Constitution in 1787 and 1788.

SIGNIFICANCE: *Those who worried that the new system would give the national government too much power worked against ratification and thus were Anit-Federalists. (Please note that those opposed to the Federalist Party in the late 1790s were not Anti-Federalists but rather Democratic-Republicans.)*

The Struggle *over* Ratification *and* Other Challenges Faced *by the* New Nation (pages 56–61)

How did the struggle over the ratification of the Constitution and other events in the early days help structure the nature of our democracy?

Reaching agreement at the Constitutional Convention on the framework of government was the first step. But the Constitution said that for it to become the law of the land (replacing the Articles of Confederation), it would have to be ratified by 9 of the 13 states. Most contemporaries also understood that if larger states, such as Virginia, Pennsylvania, and Massachusetts, failed to ratify the document, the chances for the long-term success of the new government were slim. The framers said that nine states were needed, but most hoped that ratification would be unanimous. The document was sent to the states, where special ratification conventions would be held.

> "How did the Constitution get ratified by the states?"
>
> —Student Question

It says a lot that state legislatures were bypassed in the ratification process. Most of the framers understood that state governments, fearing the loss of their autonomy, would balk at the formation of the proposed national government. Smaller states also worried about being overpowered by the larger states, and even the larger states were bothered by the supremacy of the national government. The Constitution, with its invocation of "We the People" and the means it prescribed for ratification, implied a system of divided citizenship. A government might be created that included both individual states for local affairs and a federal union for national concerns, such as commerce, foreign affairs, and security. That concept was unknown to the makers of the Articles of Confederation and was a great innovation compared to earlier notions that sovereignty must never be divided. The new Constitution was a radical change—and marked a necessary one for the creation of a true "United States." But this improvement would also lead to difficulties down the road as states sought to exert their sovereignty over federal law. Even today, as you will see in LINK Chapter 3, the battle arising out of divided sovereignty is a key part of American politics—and a critical one for you to understand.

As soon as the ratification process began, two sides emerged. The Constitution's supporters became known as **Federalists**■, and its opponents were called **Anti-Federalists**■. Both sides took their dispute to state capitals, to city halls, to taverns, and to kitchen tables across the nation. It was a critically important issue and was taken very seriously; much was at stake. But the matter was settled peacefully, through logic, persuasion, eloquence, and deliberation. It was the first test of our new take on democracy—and we passed.

> "Who were the Federalists and the Anti-Federalists? Why did they disagree?"
>
> —Student Question

The Federalists believed that a representative republic was possible and desirable—especially if populated by citizens "who possess [the] most wisdom to discern, and [the] most virtue to pursue, the common good of society."[27] The Anti-Federalists countered with the argument that representatives in any government must truly reflect the people, possessing an intimate knowledge of their circumstances and their needs. This could be achieved, they argued, only through small, relatively homogeneous republics, such as the existing states. A prominent Anti-Federalist put it this way: "Is it practicable for a country so large and so numerous [as the whole United States] . . . to elect a representative that will speak their sentiments? . . . It certainly is not."[28]

The Federalist Papers

Persuading citizens that the Constitution should be approved was no simple matter. Today the battle for public opinion would be fought on cable news programs, through television and radio advertisements, in direct mail, and over the Internet. In the late 1780s, the

CONNECT THE LINK
(Chapter **3**) How does our system of government balance the powers of the national government with the powers and obligations of state governments?

SIMULATION **You Are James Madison**

■ ***The Federalist Papers:*** A series of 85 essays in support of ratification of the U.S. Constitution that were written by James Madison, Alexander Hamilton, and John Jay and published under the byline Publius in New York City newspapers between October 27, 1787, and May 28, 1788.

SIGNIFICANCE: *We often turn to* The Federalist Papers *to better understand the intent of the framers.*

battle raged in interpersonal settings, such as formal meetings or casual tavern conversations, and in newspapers and pamphlets, which were often read aloud in group settings or passed from hand to hand. Three leading Federalists—James Madison, Alexander Hamilton, and John Jay—teamed up to write a series of essays, known collectively as ***The Federalist Papers***■, on the virtues of the Constitution. These 85 essays were published in a New York City newspaper, because New York State, where Anti-Federalist sentiment ran high, was a key battleground in the campaign for ratification. The three authors adopted the *nom de plume* Publius (Latin for "public man").

Step by step, *The Federalist Papers* worked their way though the most fought-over provisions in the Constitution, laying out in clear logic and powerful prose why each element was necessary. The essays also explained what the framers had been thinking in Philadelphia while hammering out the document. Indeed, in many places, the Constitution is vague, and if you are interested in understanding what the framers had in mind, *The Federalist Papers* are the best place to look. Constitutional lawyers and Supreme Court justices still cite them.

Some of the essays are particularly important. *Federalist No. 10,* written by James Madison, is at the top of the list (reprinted in the Appendix). The exact purpose of the essay is a bit unclear at first. Madison begins with a detailed discussion of the dangers of "factions," groups that form to pursue the interests of their members at the expense of the national interest. "The friend of popular governments never finds himself so much alarmed for their character and fate, as when he contemplates their propensity to this dangerous vice." In other words, interest groups and political parties have been a problem for all democratic governments—and sooner or later, they all failed. "Measures," Madison notes, "are too often decided, not according to the rules of justice and the rights of the minor party, but by the superior force of an interested and overbearing majority." What can be done about factions? Madison takes the reader through different alternatives, suggesting that suppressing them would be a huge mistake: "Liberty is to faction what air is to fire." Instead, he presents a two-part solution. First, if the faction is less than a majority, then the "republican principle" will solve things, meaning that elected officials, representing the wishes of a majority of constituents, will do the right thing. But if the faction constitutes a majority, which often happens in a community or a state, things are a bit tougher. Here Madison reveals the true purpose of the essay: Extended republics (that is, large countries) make the formation of majority factions less likely. He writes:

> Extend the sphere, and you take in a greater variety of parties and interests; you make it less probable that a majority of the whole will have a common motive to invade the rights of other citizens; or if such a common motive exists, it will be more difficult for all who feel it to discover their own strength, and to act in unison with each other.

Using powerful, direct reasoning, Madison explains why one large nation is preferable to many smaller ones—thus challenging the logic of many political theorists who argued that only small democracies could survive. *Federalist No. 10* is a lucid justification for forming the United States of America, and Madison's insistence on this seeming paradox makes him one of the greatest political philosophers of all time.

Another important essay is *Federalist No. 51,* also written by Madison (and also reprinted in the Appendix). Here he explains the logic behind the sharing of powers and the essence of checks and balances. It is an awkward scheme of government, he admits, but also the best way to give the new government power but not *too much* power. "If men were angels, no government would be necessary," he writes. And "if angels were to govern men, neither external nor internal controls on government would be necessary." Since neither condition prevails, other precautions are needed. Madison proposes that "ambition must be made to counteract ambition"—a truly innovative idea, since all republican thought for 2,000 years had focused on schemes to make citizens more virtuous. In brief, a system of shared powers and of checks and balances would secure the democratic character of the government. Madison also introduces a "double security": Not only will each branch of the national government be dependent on the others, the federal system itself, in which powers are divided between national and state governments, will help secure the rights of the people. Madison's argument is incredibly innovative when viewed from the standpoint of classical political theory. It had always been assumed that virtue (truly good citizens) could ensure the survival of a republic—a view that stretched back to Plato in ancient Greece.

Madison, by arguing that ambition can be harnessed and checked by other ambitions through a layered system of governments, was turning political theory on its head.

The Anti-Federalists' Response

The Anti-Federalists offered clear and thought-provoking counterarguments, many of which also appeared in newspapers. Some of these essays, published under the byline Brutus (the name of the ancient Roman republican leader who had assassinated Julius Caesar to stop him from establishing a monarchy), called attention to the very nature of democracy. Echoing traditional republican ideology, Brutus insisted that large governments could not heed the wishes of average citizens. If we want legislators to speak on behalf of citizens, as democracy demands, these leaders must know the interests of their constituents. When districts are large, as they would have to be in the proposed government, the number of constituents per legislator would be excessive. How could a legislature actually know the wishes of 30,000 residents, the number proposed for House districts? (Today there are more than 650,000 residents per House district!) The Anti-Federalists further argued that the president would inevitably build up too much power and dominate the other branches. Indeed, much of their concern centered on Article II of the Constitution, the office of president. Their worries were slightly eased by the realization that if the Constitution were ratified, George Washington, with his spotless reputation for honesty and patriotism, would be chosen as the first president. (As you will see throughout this book, many of the arguments against ratification of the Constitution continue to be used today against the current political system—including what appears to be the expanding scope of presidential powers.)

Finally, the Anti-Federalists argued that the Constitution did not contain provisions to protect individuals. There were checks on each branch of government but none against the government's infringement on individual rights and liberties. This omission would seem glaring, yet Madison took exception to the criticism, arguing that the national government would be limited exclusively to the powers outlined in the document. It could not infringe on the rights of citizens, because it did not have the power to do so. The absence of such provisions, argued Madison, would be a clear check. But many people found this "protection by omission" worrisome. "Where is the barrier drawn between the government and the rights of citizens?" asked George Mason, a prominent Virginian who had participated in the Convention but refused to sign the Constitution.[29] Concerns over the perceived lack of protection of individual rights threatened to doom ratification efforts.

> "What happened to resolve this issue of individual rights?"
>
> —Student Question

In response to these objections, the Federalists gave in: If the states would ratify the Constitution, they agreed that the first matter of business for the new government would be to amend the Constitution to include a list of individual safeguards—a list of individual protections, which became known as the *Bill of Rights*. With this guarantee, the tide of public opinion shifted, and

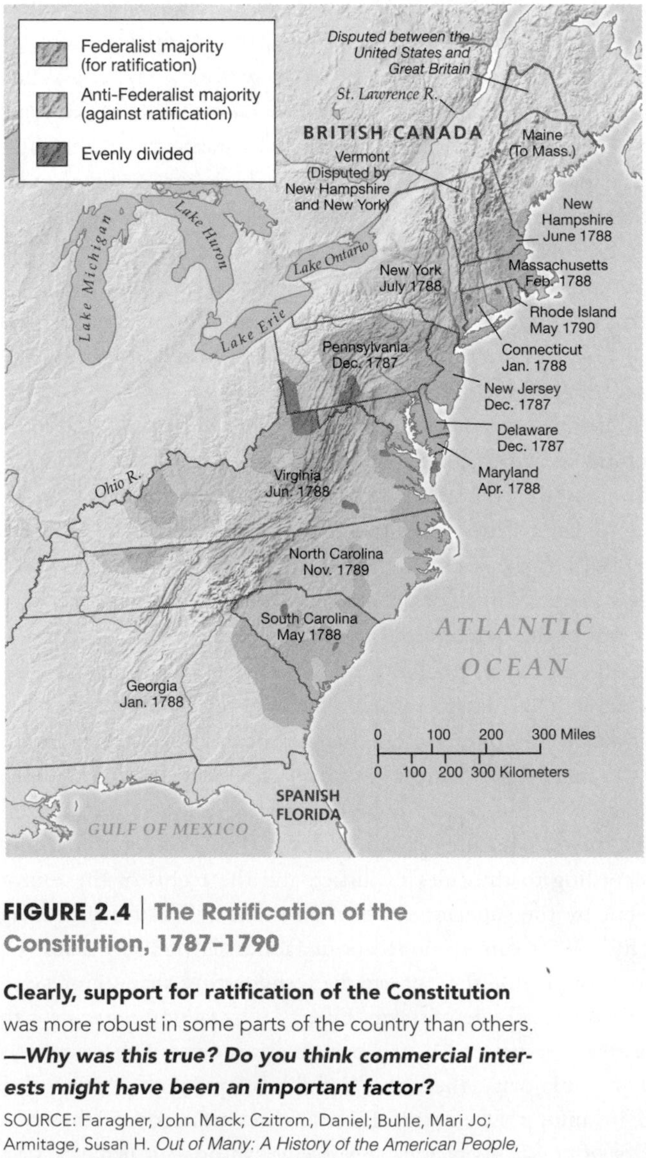

FIGURE 2.4 | The Ratification of the Constitution, 1787–1790

Clearly, support for ratification of the Constitution was more robust in some parts of the country than others. ***—Why was this true? Do you think commercial interests might have been an important factor?***

SOURCE: Faragher, John Mack; Czitrom, Daniel; Buhle, Mari Jo; Armitage, Susan H. *Out of Many: A History of the American People*, combined ed. (Chapters 1-31), 5th. © 2006. Electronically reproduced by permission of Pearson Education, Inc., Upper Saddle River, NJ.

CONNECT THE LINK
(Chapter **15**, page **532**) Why were Hamilton's economic policy proposals so controversial?

by June of 1788, the necessary nine states had ratified the Constitution (see Figure 2.4). In the end, all the states did so. (North Carolina at first rejected the Constitution but then hastily reconvened a ratification convention after the other states had accepted the document. Rhode Island also at first rejected the Constitution and then waited until 1790, when its convention finally voted to join the Union.) The vote in many of the state conventions was quite close. In New York, the margin was 30 to 27; in Massachusetts, 187 to 168; in New Hampshire, 57 to 47; in Virginia, 89 to 79; and (eventually) in Rhode Island, 34 to 32.

The Federalists kept their word and moved to amend the Constitution with the goals of protecting individuals from government infringements. Numerous changes were offered, and eventually 12 amendments were voted on. Ten of these amendments were successful; all passed in 1791. (One additional draft amendment did not receive ratification by three-fourths of all the states until 1992, whereupon it finally became the Twenty-Seventh Amendment. This amendment delays any increase in compensation for members of Congress by at least one election cycle.)

In this cartoon, Thomas Jefferson kneels before the altar of Gallic despotism as God and an American eagle attempt to prevent him from destroying the U.S. Constitution. He is depicted as about to fling a document labeled "Constitution & Independence U.S.A." into a fire fed by the flames of radical writings. Many believe that the character of our democratic system was settled with the ratification of the Constitution, but historians and political scientists understand the importance of the election of 1800.***—Why was this "second revolution" so significant?***

A Second Revolution?

We often assume that the war against the British had a singular focus, even though two names for the conflict are often used interchangeably: the War for Independence, and the Revolutionary War. These names suggest different ways of interpreting the same event. To some observers, the war was about breaking away from British control. A distant government had imposed laws and taxes on Americans without the input of Americans. British citizens had rights and liberties that were for some reason not extended to those citizens living in the new lands. After repeated appeals, it seemed only proper that a new nation be established, the better to protect these liberties. The war was about independence. After victory had been won, there would be a return to the established order, much as before. Liberty and equality were wonderful theoretical constructs, but day-to-day rule should be entrusted to enlightened gentlemen, to whom ordinary people should accord great deference. Those holding this perspective argued that "once the state and national constitutions secured the election of rulers, they warranted obedience, rather than suspicion, from the people."[30]

To others—likely a majority of Americans—the war was not only about independence but also about a dramatic change in the nature of governance. It was about shifting control from a small group of elites to *all* citizens. It was a revolution in governance and in thinking about the proper nature of government and politics. The "Spirit of '76" was about liberty, equality, and the creation of a limited government. "The Revolution had been a social upheaval," this side argued, "a transformation that had won equal rights, liberties, and opportunities for common men by defying domestic aristocrats as well as British rule."[31]

The distinction between these perspectives was very important during the early years, as we began the difficult process of taking our first steps as a sovereign nation. The matter came to a head in the late 1790s as big issues—namely, a series of economic and foreign policy questions—pulled Americans into a debate about the role of average citizens in governance. Alexander Hamilton, Washington's secretary of the treasury, proposed a series of measures that he believed would secure the nation's long-term economic future. But these policies, discussed in greater detail in LINK Chapter 15, page 532,

CONNECT THE LINK
(Chapter **15**, page **532**) How did John Quincy Adams become president when he came in second in the popular vote and second in the Electoral College vote?

seemed to help the business class at the expense of the poor. As for foreign policy, our allegiance in the war between England and France was fiercely debated. Should we help England, our principal trading partner, or France, our ally in the Revolution? The group in power during this period, led by the second president, John Adams, had adopted the name Federalists (inspired by the leaders who had worked to get the Constitution ratified a few years earlier). The other group, led by Thomas Jefferson and James Madison, had begun referring to itself as the Republicans or the Democratic-Republicans, the distant precursor of today's Democratic Party.

The ferocity of the debate and the depth of feelings on each side seemed to threaten the nation in its infancy. Republicans believed that the economic policies of the Federalists and their moves to stifle criticism were an assault on free government. For many people, the issue boiled down to the role of average citizens in society and in the conduct of government. Things came to a head during the election of 1800, which pitted John Adams against Thomas Jefferson. Jefferson narrowly defeated his former friend. Republicans were swept into the Congress and state legislatures across the nation.

Beyond policy changes, the election of 1800 marked three critically important events. First, one administration (led by the Federalists) was removed from power peacefully, being replaced by its political rival. A "Second Revolution" had occurred without violence—a rarity in history. This in itself was a stunning success for the new government. Second, efforts to stifle criticism of government leaders backfired. The

TABLE 2.7 | The Presidential Vote of 1824

Even though Andrew Jackson won more Electoral College and more popular votes than any other candidate, he was denied the presidency in 1824 through a deal between Henry Clay and John Quincy Adams. This election marked the birth of Jacksonian Democracy, the idea that average citizens should play a major role in the electoral process and in government.

CANDIDATE	ELECTORAL VOTE	POPULAR VOTE
Presidential		
John Quincy Adams (MA)	84	115,696
Henry Clay (KY)	37	47,136
Andrew Jackson (TN)	99	152,933
William H. Crawford (GA)	41	46,979
Vice Presidential		
John C. Calhoun (SC)	182	
Nathan Sanford (NY)	30	
Nathaniel Mcaon (NC)	24	
Andrew Jackson (TN)	13	
Martin Van Buren (NY)	9	
Henry Clay (KY)	2	
Votes not cast	1	

During the period known as Jacksonian democracy, political happenings were grand events, where the entire community would come out.—***Would you be willing to give up a full evening, as many as 4 or 5 hours, to hear a politician's speech or watch a debate?***

CONNECT THE LINK (Chapter **14**, pages **484–485**) When was the right to vote extended to non-white men and to women?

■ **Jacksonian Democracy:** A political and social movement that rejected political aristocracy and emphasized the role of the average citizen in public life. It began in 1828 with the election of Andrew Jackson to the presidency and lasted several decades.

SIGNIFICANCE: *By allowing more citizens to participate in the election process, the very nature of our system was changed.*

notion of "legitimate opposition" took hold, meaning that it would be healthy for our system to have an out-of-power group keeping an eye on the in-power group. Third, the election of 1800 seemed to signify that there should be no privileged class in American politics. The process set in motion by the Declaration of Independence was indeed a revolution, not simply a war for independence.

Jacksonian Democracy

Even though Andrew Jackson won more Electoral College and more popular votes than any other candidate in 1824 (see Table 2.7), he was denied the presidency through what many believed was a backroom deal between Henry Clay and John Quincy Adams. (This event is also discussed in LINK Chapter 15, page 532). As rumors of the deal spread, resentment and anger swelled. Once again, elitism had reared its ugly head; the will of the people had been trumped by elites. Jackson, along with a team of skilled operatives, decided to take back the presidency in the next election. They would do so by pulling average citizens into the political process and thus would simply overwhelm the ruling elite. Sure enough, turnout in the 1828 election doubled from that of four years earlier, and Jackson was swept into the White House.

Historians point to this period as the birth of popular democracy, or what has also been dubbed **Jacksonian democracy**■. Indeed, the heyday of electoral participation in America—a time when voting rates were highest and when politics was at the center of daily life for most Americans—was the mid-1800s. We often marvel at the passion of politics during this period and wonder how anyone could listen to political debates for hours. Property requirements for voting were removed, and the turnout of eligible voters during this period often exceeded 80 percent in presidential elections. (Today it rarely exceeds 55 percent.) Of course, it should be noted that "eligible voters" consisted exclusively of white men, a point that we'll take up in greater detail in LINK Chapter 14, pages 484–485). In brief, the widespread notion that average citizens could use elections as a pathway of change was planted into the American psyche during the mid-1800s. Our "craze for elections," which will be discussed at many points to follow, springs from this era.

The Struggle Over Ratification

Practice Quiz

1. The struggle over ratification of the Constitution was
   a. one of the low points of American history due to the violence that broke out during the process.
   b. quite congenial, because the framers were so widely respected and trusted.
   c. especially contentious, because it pitted slaveholding states against abolitionist states.
   d. a high point of American history, because it resolved a contentious issue by logical and peaceful means.

2. The Anti-Federalists opposed ratification of the Constitution primarily because
   a. they believed that too much power would be concentrated in the national government.
   b. they feared that too much power would be granted to the presidency.
   c. they feared that members of Congress would be isolated from their constituents due to the large size of their districts.
   d. a, b, and c.

3. In *Federalist No. 10,* James Madison extolled the virtues of a large national government as opposed to a number of smaller governments.
   a. true **b.** false

4. The "double security" Madison discussed in *Federalist No. 51* refers to
   a. the virtue of checks and balances.
   b. the separate powers of federal and state courts.
   c. the division of power between the national government and the states as well as checks and balances.
   d. the president's veto power and shared powers between the branches.

Answers: 1-d, 2-d, 3-a, 4-c.

Discussion Questions

1. What would be the challenges to public understanding and discussion of *The Federalist Papers* in our society today?
2. How would the process of ratification fare in the modern mass media environment?

What **YOU** can do!

There was a vigorous debate between those who advocated for a stronger national government and those who preferred a larger role for the states. To get a sense of how the Federalists and Anti-Federalists responded to each other and to other events, check out this chronology: **http://www.constitution.org/afp/afpchron.htm**

Conclusion

One of the themes of this book is that the nature and spirit of democracy in America has shifted and changed with the times; it is an evolving *process,* not a state of being. The early period began the journey of liberty and equality in our country, but most observers would agree that we have not yet arrived at a final destination. We might also underscore the interplay of political power, authority, and legitimacy. As noted, even though a government might have the power to compel action by citizens, it may not have the authority; the cry of "no taxation without representation" clearly echoed this notion. But after independence was secured, the tables were turned. On paper, the Articles of Confederation seemed to give Congress an avenue for collecting funds, but the scheme contained few provisions to impose the will of the national government on the states. The central government simply lacked power. And of course, the true challenge of the framers was to find a balance between power and legitimacy.

Another theme springing from these pages is the importance of political participation. Citizens stood up, demanded liberty and freedom, and forged their own system of government. We often hear that the framers were an atypical lot—much wealthier and better educated than average citizens. Although this may be true, we still need to remember the role played by average men and women during this period, not the least of which were the patriots who helped fill the ranks of the Continental Army and local militias and also young citizens like Joseph Plumb Martin. Our democracy would have stumbled—indeed, it would not have taken its first step—were it not for the hard work of citizens fighting for a better life and a better system of government. Widespread political and civic engagement has been one of the many things that has distinguished the American system of government.

Finally, this chapter is also about the importance of pathways of change. As colonists came to believe in individual liberties and their right to participate in the conduct of government, the more frustration they felt over British rule. The Revolution was about creating a limited government—a government that would reflect the concerns of the people. Yet the framers had to fashion a system that was *both* responsive to popular will *and* stable. In some very real ways, the Constitution limits the democratic process and harnesses the will of the people, with the goal of creating a powerful, secure system of government. On its face, you might be hard pressed to label the original Constitution (before the amendments) a plan to enhance democratic principles. But thanks to changes to the original framework (the Bill of Rights in particular) and the toil and sacrifice of countless citizens, numerous pathways have emerged to make the system more democratic.

America has never been a perfect nation (if such a thing is even possible), and many of the wounds from our past linger to this day. But we should also be very proud of our nation's formative years, because it was a very special period in world history.

Key Objective Review Apply, and Explore

The Nature of Government and Politics

(pages 32–33)

Before we begin our exploration of American government, it is important to understand a few basic concepts, such as the difference between government and politics, power and authority, and legitimacy. This section helps set the foundation.

KEY TERMS

Civil Law 32
Criminal Law 32
Power 33
Authority 33

CRITICAL THINKING QUESTIONS

1. Is it possible for the political process to shape the nature of government? If so, can you think of examples in American history when this has occurred?
2. Does the Supreme Court have political power? Does it have authority? Under what conditions does the authority of the Court become threatened?

INTERNET RESOURCES

Many theorists have written about the relationship between power and authority. This Web site offers some thoughts from Montesquieu, an eighteenth-century French philosopher whose writings had a great impact on the framers of our political system: **http://www.lonang.com/exlibris/montesquieu/sol-02.htm**

ADDITIONAL READING

Pious, Richard. *President, the Congress, and the Constitution: Power and Legitimacy in American Politics.* New York; Free Press, 1984.

Types of Governments

(pages 34–35)

There are many types of governments, the foremost distinguishing characteristics being who is allowed to participate and how decisions are made. Using these two dimensions, systems such as monarchies, oligarchies, and totalitarian regimes are more easily understood. Also, terms such as *democracy* and *republic* come into sharper focus.

KEY TERMS

Monarchy 34
Constitutional Monarchy 34
Dictator 34
Oligarchy 34
Pluralism 34
Democracy 34
Republic 34
Representative Democracy 34
Totalitarian Regime 34
Authoritarian Regime 34
Constitutional Government 34

CRITICAL THINKING QUESTIONS

1. What is the difference between a republic and a democracy? Put a bit differently, are all republics also democracies?
2. In January of 2005, Iraqi citizens were given the right to vote, leading some to speculate that democracy was taking hold in that country. But violence continued, and the rule of law seemed elusive. Can elections bring democracy to a country? Is it that simple?

INTERNET RESOURCES

Numerous Web sites chart differences between types of governments around the world. Two of interest include **http://home.earthlink.net/~kingsidebishop/id2.html** and **http://www.twyman-whitney.com/americancitizen/foundations/typesofgovernment.htm**

ADDITIONAL READING

Derbyshire, Denis J. and Ian Derbyshire. *Political Systems of the World.* New York: Palgrave MacMillan, 1996.

Key Objective Review Apply, and Explore

Early Governance in America

(pages 36–37)

During the pre-Revolution period, governance was not exactly democratic. Yet the seeds of a democratic movement were planted. This short section explores those seeds.

KEY TERMS

Pilgrims 36
French and Indian War 36
Mayflower Compact 36
Great Squeeze 36

CRITICAL THINKING QUESTIONS

1. What was so significant about the Mayflower Compact? What did it say about the nature of governance in the New World?
2. This short section touches upon the suspicion of elites in colonial politics. Has this been a recurring theme in American politics?

INTERNET RESOURCES

To learn more about the formative years in American history, visit the Library of Congress's America's Story Web site at **http://www.americaslibrary.gov/cgi-bin/page.cgi**

ADDITIONAL READING

Burns, James MacGregor. *The Vineyard of Liberty.* New York: Knopf, 1982.

Butler, Jon. *Becoming America: The Revolution Before 1776.* Cambridge, MA: Harvard University Press, 2000.

Ellis, Joseph. *Founding Brothers: The Revolutionary Generation.* New York: Vintage Books, 2002.

The American Revolution

(pages 38–43)

When Abraham Lincoln spoke of our nation's birth as "Four score and seven years ago," he was referring to the Revolution and to the signing of the Declaration of Independence. Why didn't he reach back to when the Constitution was ratified, in 1789? This section discusses why Lincoln's view of our nation's birth makes pretty good sense.

KEY TERMS

Acts for Trade 38
Adam Smith 38
Edmund Burke 39
Coercive Acts 38
John Adams 38
Natural Rights 41
Intolerable Acts 38
Stamp Act Congress 38
Social Contract Theory 41
John Locke 38
Thomas Paine 38
Thomas Hobbes 41

CRITICAL THINKING QUESTIONS

1. We often hear about the principles that drove the Patriot cause, such as notions of "No taxation without representation!" A yearning for democracy was surely part of the movement. But is it fair to say that economic issue also compelled action? Was the Revolution really about financial interest—about making and keeping more money?
2. If Thomas Jefferson was right about the duty of citizens to jettison their government when it no longer serves their interests, wouldn't that lead to recurrent revolutions? What would stop "patriots" from starting wars for independence whenever they got really upset with their government?

INTERNET RESOURCES

To better understand some of the developments from the first 100 years of our nation's history, visit From Revolution to Reconstruction: **http://odur.let.rug.nl/~usa**

If you are interested in the writings of some of the leading figures of the formation period, the following may be helpful: *For George Washington:* **http://gwpapers.virginia.edu;** *For Thomas Jefferson:* **http://memory.loc.gov/ammem/mtjhtml/mtjhome.html;** *For James Madison:* **http://www.virginia.edu/pjm/home.html;** *For John Adams:* **http://odur.let.rug.nl/~usa/P/ja2/about/bio/adamsxx.htm;** *For Abigail Adams:* **http://www.whitehouse.gov/history/firstladies/aa2.html;** *For Thomas Paine:* **http://www.ushistory.org/paine**

ADDITIONAL READING

Bailyn, Bernard. *The Ideological Origins of the American Revolution.* Cambridge MA: Harvard University Press, 1967.

Wills, Garry. *Inventing America: Jefferson's Declaration of Independence.* New York: Random House, 1978.

Key Objective Review Apply, and Explore

The Articles of Confederation

(pages 44–47)

Our first stab at self-governance was a flop. But the experience under the Articles of Confederation shaped the motivations of the framers, thus shaping our system of government.

KEY TERMS

Shays's Rebellion 45 **Constitutional Convention 45**

CRITICAL THINKING QUESTIONS

1. The Articles of Confederation had a very weak national government. The system also failed. Why was such a decentralized system created in the first place? Didn't its creators know it would not work?
2. What does the alternative view of Shays's Rebellion say about the core rationale for the Constitutional Convention? Do you agree with this perspective?

INTERNET RESOURCES

For general information on numerous early American documents, try the Avalon Project at Yale University at **http://www.yale.edu/lawweb/avalon/avalon.htm**

ADDITIONAL READING

Jensen, Merrill. *The Articles of Confederation: An Interpretation of the Social-Constitutional History of the Revolution, 1774–1781.* Madison, WI: University of Wisconsin Press, 1959.

Morgan, Edmund S. *The Meaning of Independence: John Adams, Thomas Jefferson, George Washington.* New York: Norton, 1978.

The Constitutional Convention

(pages 48–51)

We often hear that the framers came to the Constitutional Convention eager to create a stronger national government. But the truth is more complex. Numerous motivations drove this historic event, and from these concerns our Constitution was born. The many compromises also speak to the interests of the framers and to the nature of our political system.

KEY TERMS

Virginia Plan 48 **Connecticut Compromise 49**
New Jersey Plan 48 **Census 50**
Great Compromise 49

CRITICAL THINKING QUESTIONS

1. Looking back at the Constitutional Convention, we often shake our heads over the compromises that kept things going. What do you think would have happened if these agreements were not reached? Would there ever have been a "United States" without these agreements?
2. Some have noted that while these compromises kept things going, they also diminished the democratic character of our system. Do you agree?

INTERNET RESOURCES

Visit the Annenberg Learning Center: A Biography of America at **http://www.learner.org/biographyofamerica**

Learn about the periods before, during, and after the Constitutional Convention at the History Place Web site at **http://www.historyplace.com**

ADDITIONAL READING

Wood, Gordon S. *The Radicalism of the American Revolution.* New York: Vintage Books, 1993.

Key Objective Review Apply, and Explore

The U.S. Constitution

(pages 52–55)

The Constitution is made up of both broad principles, such as the sharing of powers and the checks and balances, and specifics, like the enumeration of congressional powers. In order to understand how our government operates, both elements should be acknowledged.

KEY TERMS

Sharing of Powers 52
Expressed Powers 53
Police Powers 53
Bill of Rights 53

CRITICAL THINKING QUESTIONS

1. The U.S. Constitution has been modeled across the globe. Why? What makes our structure of government so special? What is the evidence to suggest our model is so nifty?
2. How would you respond to the argument that the cost of "checks and balances" and "shared powers" is a slow-moving system? (Note that the framers also did not anticipate political parties, which can also slow things down when different parties control different parts of the government.)

INTERNET RESOURCES

To access the Declaration of Independence, the Constitution, and other key documents in our nation's history, see the Library of Congress, Primary Documents in American History at **http://memory.loc.gov/ammem/help/constRedir.html**

ADDITIONAL READING

Bowen, Catherine Drinker. *Miracle at Philadelphia: The Story of the Constitutional Convention May–September 1787.* Boston: Back Bay Books, 1986.

Collier, Christopher. *Decision in Philadelphia: The Constitutional Convention of 1787.* New York: Ballantine Books, 2007.

The Struggle over Ratification and Other Challenges Faced by the New Nation

(pages 56–61)

While Lincoln might have been right to assert that our nation began in 1776, that does not mean that who we are as a people was defined at that period. There have been numerous transformative events in our history, and this short section takes a look at two of them.

KEY TERMS

Federalists 56
Anti-Federalists 56
***The Federalists Papers* 57**
Jacksonian Democracy 61

CRITICAL THINKING QUESTIONS

1. What was so special about the ratification of the U.S. Constitution? Why would some suggest this was a proud moment in our nation's history?
2. How does the Election of 1800 and the period of Jacksonian Democracy continue to shape American politics?

INTERNET RESOURCES

For an online, searchable copy of *The Federalist Papers,* see **http://www.law.ou.edu/hist/federalist**

ADDITIONAL READING

Ketcham, Ralph. *The Anti-Federalist Papers and the Constitutional Convention Delegates.* New York: Signet, 2003.

Smith, Page. *The Shaping of America: A People's History of the Young Republic.* New York: McGraw-Hill, 1979.

Chapter Review Critical Thinking Test

1. Based on the definition in this textbook, which of the following is an example of *authority*?

a. the federal government imposing and collecting a tax

b. a judge "legislating from the bench"

c. a teacher telling students to vote for a certain candidate for public office

d. a minister telling his congregation to disobey a law

2. What role did the Sons of Liberty play in the independence movement?

a. They sent diplomatic missions to Parliament in support of economic relief for the colonists.

b. They sponsored "committees of correspondence."

c. They held rallies to recruit citizens to protest British policies.

d. b and c.

3. Since slavery is obviously undemocratic, why didn't the framers abolish it when they drafted the Constitution?

a. Because the framers all agreed that slavery was legal.

b. Because slavery was widely practiced and tolerated during the eighteenth century.

c. Because it was necessary to compromise with the southern delegations on this sensitive issue.

d. b and c.

4. What drove the colonists toward revolution?

a. their suspicions about the British monarchy

b. the "Big Squeeze"

c. a century of "salutary neglect," which gave colonists a sense of independence from England.

d. a, b, and c.

5. What was the main difference between the Second Continental Congress and the First Continental Congress?

a. The Second spoke glowingly of expanding women's rights.

b. The Second introduced a proposal to outlaw slavery.

c. The Second advocated armed rebellion against the Crown.

d. The Second argued for an open trade policy with all nations, not just those allied with Great Britain.

6. Jefferson passionately suggested that "the tree of liberty must be refreshed . . . with

a. the sweat of the toiling merchants, the backbone of our colonies."

b. the blood of patriots and tyrants."

c. the sweat and blood of our noble citizens, patriots all."

d. the blood, sweat and tears of our citizens, to free us for all posterity."

7. Social contract theorist John Locke was important to American revolutionary philosophy because

a. he argued persuasively that legitimate governments must be based upon the consent of the governed.

b. he argued passionately that government must be limited in order to protect the universal principle of free trade.

c. he was a co-founder of the Sons of Liberty, and a major contributor to the "committees of correspondence."

d. a, b, and c.

8. When Thomas Paine wrote in 1776 that "[t]hese are the times that try men's souls," he was

a. consoling British subjects, because General Washington's army was defeating the British army.

b. referring to the unfair trading practices of the Navigation Acts.

c. complaining about the weaknesses of the Articles of Confederation.

d. None of the above.

9. The Declaration of Independence was supported enthusiastically by the majority of colonists.

a. true **b.** false

10. Oklahoma City terrorist Timothy McVeigh was revolting against what he thought was an oppressive federal government. How did his actions differ from the revolt justified by the Declaration of Independence?

a. McVeigh had more pathways of action open to him than the colonists; therefore, his violent actions were unjustifiable.

b. The Declaration of Independence does not condone violence under any circumstances.

c. The Declaration of Independence does not condone rebellion against one's own country.

d. a and b.

11. The "Great Compromise" at the Constitutional Convention refers to the decision to

a. count a slave as equivalent to three-fifths of a vote in determining the number of representatives allocated to each state in the House.

b. allow congressional representation to both reflect a state's population and represent each state equally (regardless of population).

c. protect the Atlantic slave trade for at least 20 more years.

d. grant strong executive powers to the president but limit his tenure in office to two terms.

12. Among numerous other effects, the ratification of the Constitution created an immediate and widespread sense of national citizenship.

a. true **b.** false

Chapter Review Critical Thinking Test

13. Why is it logical to describe our system of government as both rigid and flexible?
- **a.** It is possible to add amendments to the Constitution, but only through an intricate and challenging process.
- **b.** Power-sharing by way of checks and balances makes it unlikely that any one branch or individual officeholder could seize control of government.
- **c.** Rigidity implies stability; flexibility implies the possibility of major change at any time.
- **d.** a and b.

14. What is the difference between "expressed powers" and "police powers"?
- **a.** Expressed powers are those asserted through speech and written decree; police powers are those that are physically exerted.
- **b.** Expressed powers are the prerogative of the national government; police powers are the prerogative of the states.
- **c.** Expressed powers refer to commercial matters, foreign affairs, and national security; police powers refer to matters of health, safety, and individual well-being.
- **d.** b and c.

15. In order for an amendment to the Constitution to become ratified, it must be passed by three-fifths of the states.
- **a.** true
- **b.** false

16. Why do constitutional lawyers and scholars still make reference to *The Federalist Papers*?
- **a.** because *The Federalist Papers* are so relevant to issues of federal (versus state) power
- **b.** because citing *The Federalist Papers* is a requirement of federal judicial procedure
- **c.** because *The Federalist Papers* offer a comprehensive explanation of Constitutional principles and intentions
- **d.** none of the above

17. James Madison referred to "the vice of faction" in *Federalist No. 10*. But he did not recommend suppressing such factions, because
- **a.** if a faction represents less than a majority, its representatives will be outvoted or overruled by those in the majority.
- **b.** all factions naturally wither over time—"No living thing endures over the long course of human affairs."
- **c.** in the "extended republic" of the nation as a whole, factions would usually never constitute a majority and thus would not direct government policy.
- **d.** b and c.

18. Madison asserted that a divided system of government, with checks and balances, would ensure the longevity of the republic, because
- **a.** such a system would cultivate the virtue of every citizen.
- **b.** such a system would ensure that ambition would counter ambition among competing factions.
- **c.** a and b
- **d.** none of the above

19. The Bill of Rights are
- **a.** a list of individual protections of the rights of all citizens.
- **b.** those amendments to the Constitution passed in the late eighteenth century.
- **c.** one of the key negotiating points that led to unanimous ratification of the Constitution.
- **d.** all of the above

20. Voter turnout in national elections, which began to surge during Jackson's first campaign for the presidency in 1824, has increased steadily ever since.
- **a.** true
- **b.** false

Answers: 1-a, 2-d, 3-d, 4-d, 5-c, 6-b, 7-a, 8-d, 9-b, 10-a, 11-b, 12-b, 13-d, 14-d, 15-b, 16-c, 17-d, 18-c, 19-d, 20-b.

You decide!

Sometimes it can seem as though the development of the American political system was inevitable—it's hard to imagine our government without three branches, for example, or without the balance of power struck by the Great Compromise. But there is an almost infinite number of ways to structure a government.

Turn back to the section in this chapter on the core principles of the U.S. Constitution on pages 52–53. After reviewing these principles, imagine that you have been hired as a consultant for a newly independent country, and your first task is to draw up a draft constitution. The only guidance that you have been given is that the new government may not be divided into three branches (though any other number is acceptable) and that the constitution should be easily amended. How would you structure this government? What rights and liberties would you guarantee? What functions would you require government to perform? Would the economic, religious, and demographic makeup of the population affect your decisions? Why or why not?

Key Objective Outline

What are the advantages and disadvantages of dividing authority between layers of government?

How did the Constitution divide power between national and state governments?

How do economic and social changes impact federalism?

How has federalism changed in recent decades?

CHAPTER 3
FEDERALISM

How has federalism in the United States evolved?

Leadville, Colorado, a city with a rich and interesting history, is thought to be in serious danger. By February of 2008, an estimated 1 billion gallons of water—highly contaminated with heavy metals—were trapped in a drainage tunnel just above the town. This is enough water to fill 1,500 Olympic-sized swimming pools. Due to the large increase in the water pressure, a catastrophic collapse could occur. If the water is released, the town will be devastated, and the contaminated water could flow into the Arkansas River. County commissioners have declared a state of emergency. Many are reminded of the warnings about the vulnerability of the levies in New Orleans and fear that an environmental catastrophe is imminent.

Gold, silver, lead, zinc, copper, and molybdenum, which are used for steel, were all mined in Leadville (founded in 1859). In the years from 1915 until 1999, $4 billion of molybdenum was mined. The U.S. Environmental Protection Agency determined that several former mines were so contaminated that they qualified for federal assistance for environmental cleanup. Water purification plants were making substantial progress, but the Leadville Mine Drainage Tunnel, which was dug by the U.S. Bureau of Mines in 1943, collapsed in 2001, trapping the contaminated water.

Local officials believe that the federal government is not reacting to the threat with sufficient urgency. Many argue that the responsibility of this cleanup should fall to the county and state or private companies, which collectively have earned billions of dollars from the mines. Whose responsibility is this cleanup? Should taxpayers in one state pay for disasters in other states—especially in this instance, where the state, local, and private industry financially benefited from the mines for more than 100 years? Regulation of the environment was traditionally seen as a state and local responsibility, but it is now seen as a national issue. At what point do we hold states and localities liable, and conversely, what responsibility does the federal government have to ensure the safety of its citizens and its natural resources?

■ **Unitary System:** A system of government in which political power and authority is located in one central government that runs the country and that may or may not share power with regional subunits.

EXAMPLE: *Under a unitary system of government, the central government would determine who was eligible to marry whom, at what age, under what conditions, and the process, including the difficulty or ease, by which marriages would be ended.*

COMPARATIVE **Comparing Federal and Unitary Systems**

Dividing Governmental Authority (pages 72–75)

What are the advantages and disadvantages of dividing authority between layers of government?

Governmental authority in the United States has been a source of conflict for more than two centuries. Unlike countries such as the United Kingdom and France, which are governed under a **unitary system**■ (that is, a system where all ruling authority rests in a single national government), in the American model, powers and responsibilities are divided among layers of governments.

There seemed good reasons for dividing power and responsibility when the Constitution was framed: Federalism would create yet another check against the potential abuses of state and local governments, for instance. Yet this unique system has created much uncertainty and many practical management problems. At times in our history, it has even led to violence. Indeed, the greatest crisis in our history, the Civil War, was very much about "states' rights" versus the authority of the national government. We can imagine why foreign policy would fall under the scope of the national government, but what about the general welfare of American citizens? Is crime a problem for a local government, a state government, or the national government? Should the national government be able to control the conduct of doctors and regulate what services they can or cannot provide? How about lawyers, electricians, or hairdressers? Certainly the abortion question is very much entangled with the issue of federalism. So are others: If a state considers the medical use of marijuana permissible, should the federal government be able to step in and ban it? Can the federal government bar gay couples from getting married under one state's laws, or force other states to recognize that marriage?

Then there is the issue of transportation. Just because the Constitution says that Congress shall regulate commerce, does that mean the federal government is responsible for fixing all roads and bridges? Would we want the federal government telling us how many stop signs to put up on a stretch of road? That may seem an extreme example, yet the issue of speed limits has been controversial for decades. In the mid-1970s, when the nation faced a fuel shortage, one of the measures used to save energy was fixing the national speed limit at 55 mph. Many states, especially those in the West, refused to abide by the federal law. In response, Congress threatened to cut off federal highway aid to any state that did not enforce this law. Some states rejected the money and set the speed limits they wanted. Others simply lowered the fines for speeding tickets. The federally mandated 55 mph limit has since been dropped, but some states still abide by it while others allow up to 75 mph. If you exceed the 75 mph limit in Montana, you might get a $40 fine, and in Wyoming, it would be just $25. In many other states, it could cost you more than $300.

In education, law, medicine, transportation, environmental protection, crime, and many other areas of American life, the line between federal and state control has been controversial and fluid. For example, in the not-too-distant past, cleanup from a natural disaster, such as a flood or a hurricane, was entirely the responsibility of state and local governments; today everyone expects the federal government to take the lead. As we saw with the Leadville, Colorado example, the people of Colorado believe that the federal government should be responsible for cleaning up the contaminated water left in abandoned mines previously owned by private mining companies. Indeed, one of the low points in President George W. Bush's administration was the federal government's inept response following Hurricane Katrina in the summer of 2005. Ironically, many of these critics are the same people who argue that the federal government is getting too big and should stay out of the affairs of local governments. You might be tempted to draw a conclusion that things have moved toward more federal control, but even if this is true in some policy areas, in other spheres the states are now being given more control and greater responsibility. Politicians eager to promote local control often suggest that state governments are the "laboratories of democracy," a concept first enunciated by Supreme Court Justice Louis Brandeis in 1932, meaning that difficult challenges are more likely to be resolved when 50 entities are working to find innovative solutions rather than just the federal government. One area where states are being given more authority is welfare reform. During President Bill Clinton's administration, oversight and control of social welfare programs was shifted from the federal government to the states. In short, the pendulum of governmental authority swings both ways.

This chapter will explore the complex, important issue of levels of governmental authority in the United States. As with other elements in our political system, many changes have occurred over the years. Today the relationship between the states and the federal

■ **Federal System:** A system of government in which power and authority is divided between a central government and regional subunits.

EXAMPLE: *Under a federal system of government, state governments would determine the conditions of marriage and divorce to allow local or regional norms to influence public policy. Some states are discussing making divorce more difficult to reflect their political culture's belief in the sanctity of marriage.*

CONNECT THE LINK

(Chapter **2**, pages **52–55**) Why are documents that legalize relationships between people and their government important for stability?

President Clinton addresses the National Governor's Association in Washington in 1993. He promised the governors he would allow states to use federal money for welfare reform experiments, provided they "have the courage to quit" if the initiatives fail. ***—How have the states responded to Clinton's challenge?***

government is vastly different from what it was at the dawn of our nation's history. Rather than being simply a unique, interesting aspect of our government, the debate over governmental authority has been at the center of most of the trying events in our history. This issue also says a great deal about the future directions of American government.

The goal of this chapter is to help you understand that public policy does not spring simply from "government" but rather from different *layers* of government. It would make little sense, for example, to lobby members of Congress to change the zoning laws in a particular municipality or to ask a city council to help lower the cost of prescription drugs. Different governments are responsible for different policies in the United States. This chapter explains why we have such a unique system, examines its advantages and disadvantages, and explores changes over the past 200 years. Politics is not simply about pushing government in a given direction; instead, it is knowing *which* government to push and how.

> "Why is it important to understand how federalism has evolved?"
>
> —Student Question

The federal structure of the United States is not unique: Several other democracies also have federal systems of government, including Canada, Australia, Germany, Switzerland, and India. But most countries, whether or not they are democratic, have unitary systems (see Table 3.1 on page 74). In those countries, there may be viable and active local authorities, but the national government has **sovereignty.** This means that the national government has the ultimate governing authority (and the final say). In the United Kingdom, for example, Parliament can change city and town government boundaries at any time. It may allow certain regions to create their own government, as has been the case with Scotland and Northern Ireland, but at any point, Parliament can abolish these structures and override any of their policies.[1]

Why, then, would the United States choose to create a **federal system**■, in which sovereignty is divided among different levels of government? One explanation is rooted in the history of government in North America. During the period of exploration and discovery, set into motion by Christopher Columbus's voyage in 1492, a number of nations, including England, France, Spain, Portugal, and The Netherlands, sought to establish colonies in the New World. Believing that these lands represented immense economic potential, the race was on to claim different territories. Spain quickly colonized Mexico, Central America, much of South America (except for Portuguese Brazil), as well as what are now Florida and the southwestern parts of the United States. France, spurred on by the rich fur trade, set its sights on what is now Canada, and the Dutch colonized what is now New York State. England eventually planted more than 13 colonies on the North American mainland.[2] As settlers eventually moved to these colonies, they set up their own governments. As we noted in LINK Chapter 2, pages 52–55, before setting foot on American soil in 1620, the Pilgrims drew up the Mayflower Compact, which was essentially an agreement

CONNECT THE LINK
(Chapter **2**, pages **38–43**) How important are the theories presented by these philosophers to contemporary political thought?

TABLE 3.1

Each type of governmental system uses a different means to enact policies. ***—Looking at this table carefully, which system do you think works best? Why?***

Let's consider how each system of government would work to promote water conservation.

FEDERAL	UNITARY	CONFEDERATION
The federal government would pass broad guidelines and provide some financial incentives, but the implementation of the conservation programs would be left to state and local governments.	The central government would pass specific guidelines and ensure that local governments comply with national decrees.	The central government would pass broad guidelines with the hope that state governments agree to comply.
Governmental authority is divided between a national government and state governments.	Ultimate governmental authority comes from the national government.	Ultimate authority comes from the states.
United States under the Constitution (1789–present), Australia, Brazil, Germany, Mexico, Nigeria	France, Spain, Tanzania	United States under the Articles of Confederation (1781–1789), Confederate States of America (1861–1865), Confederation of Independent States (states of the former Soviet Union)

to form a government. In the Virginia colony, a legislative body called the House of Burgesses was established just 12 years after Jamestown, the first permanent British town in the Americas, was settled. Eventually, each colony established its own governing structure. These governments were not sovereign, of course, given that the English Parliament and king could dissolve them at any time (and did so on various occasions), but it is important to understand that as our nation began to take shape, there were many distinct governing entities. Moreover, it is worth noting that there existed a great deal of suspicion and rivalry between the colonies and, after independence, between the early states. One of the greatest hurdles confronted by those anxious to break ties with Great Britain on the eve of the American Revolution was to get people to consider themselves as citizens of an American nation rather than just citizens of their individual colonies. Throughout the Revolutionary War, there was no national government, for the Articles of Confederation were designed to protect state sovereignty while loosely binding the states in ways that might better ensure security and prosperity. After independence had been won, the central point of dispute over the ratification of the Constitution in 1787 and 1788 was the extent to which the new national government might, at some future time, take over the role of state governments. Many Americans agreed that a stronger national government was needed to regulate commerce and deal with foreign nations, but few envisioned that the national government would be fully sovereign.

One explanation for our federal system lies, then, in the historical roots of the United States. Our nation was born through the fusing of independent states—states that would never have agreed to a merger if giving up their independence had been part of the deal. Federalism was a compromise. We might also point to the writings of philosophers who guided the thinking of the framers of our system. As discussed in LINK Chapter 2, pages 38–43, the framers relied heavily on the writings of John Locke, Adam Smith, and Thomas Hobbes. Another very influential philosopher was the Frenchman Baron Montesquieu, who in the early eighteenth century wrote about the virtues of dividing power and authority between different parts of the government. This might be done, he argued, by having different branches of government *and* by creating layers of governmental authority. James Madison echoes Montesquieu's idea in *Federalist No. 51:*

> In the compound republic of America, the power surrendered by the people is first divided between two distinct governments, and then the portion allotted to each subdivided among distinct and separate departments. Hence a double security arises to the right of the people.

In other words, federalism, coupled with the checks and balances and the sharing of powers at the national level, would help guarantee a republican government. Montesquieu also argued that republican institutions were more likely to flourish in a small-scale political system, such as a Swiss canton (state), yet such small states were incapable of defending themselves against attack. The problem could be solved by the creation of a system that would permit a consensus with regard to the domestic affairs among the separate governing units but provide unified action for the common defense.[3]

Still another significant factor behind federalism is the geographic, cultural, and economic diversity of the United States. The distinctiveness of different American regions has been eroding dramatically in recent decades, due in large measure to changes in transportation, entertainment, and the economy. A Wal-Mart in Boise, Idaho, looks exactly the same as a Wal-Mart in Bath, Maine. Kids in Albany, Georgia, watch the same Saturday morning cartoons as kids in Albany, New York. Throughout most of our history, however, culture, language, demographics, economic conditions, and many other aspects of life varied from region to region, from state to state, and even from community to community. And the United States remains one of the most diverse nations in the world, which has contributed to a sense of a localized citizenship.

Finally, federalism has made sense in the American setting for practical reasons. Historians agree that if in 1787 the separate states had not been permitted to have significant powers, the Constitution would never have been ratified. The federal system was also helpful in adding new states to the Union, and it has aided the nation's economic growth. Our system is unique and has some disadvantages, but in many ways, creating a system of layers of governmental authority has made good sense. But that is not to say that things have remained the same since the Constitution was framed.

STUDENT | PROFILE

Even though we have federal laws to protect individuals from discrimination based upon their race and religion, many still feel victimized and misunderstood. These feelings led Harkirat Hansra, a 17-year-old, turban-wearing Sikh in Sacramento, California, to write a book (called *Liberty at Stake*). Growing up in the United States, Hansra did not feel isolated from his community until after the terrorist attacks of September 11, 2001. Following the attacks, he and other members of his Sikh community were the victims of taunts in the streets and belittling comments. He felt compelled to become an activist to teach others about his religion and work to promote racial tolerance. ■

Dividing Governmental Authority

Practice Quiz

1. Federalism, along with the system of separation of power and checks and balances, helps republican governments govern.
   a. true **b.** false
2. The United States is the only country in the world that divides authority between national and subnational governments.
   a. true **b.** false
3. Federalism was a compromise solution to our government's structure, because
   a. it preserved some individual state sovereignty while granting authority to the national government to regulate commerce and conduct foreign policy.
   b. it granted enough individual state sovereignty to coax the states into forming a single, unified national government.
   c. it formed a unitary system of government for the United States.
   d. a and b.
4. The preservation of local authority in American federalism illustrates the fact that
   a. most Americans don't think of themselves in national terms.
   b. most American communities are culturally similar.
   c. most American communities differ in some ways, and local government provides for those differences.
   d. a and c.

Answers: 1-a, 2-b, 3-d, 4-c.

Discussion Questions

1. What are some of the advantages of a federal system of government we experience in today's society?
2. How do speed limits illustrate the way in which government authority is divided in a federal system?

What YOU can do!

Use an Internet search to find examples of an existing unitary government and an existing confederation. Identify possible historical, geographical, cultural, and/or practical reasons that explain why each country chose its particular division of governmental authority.

CONNECT THE LINK
(Chapter **4**, pages **108–113**) Do you think that Marshall would be surprised to see how powerful federal judges have become?

TIMELINE **Federalism and the Supreme Court**

The Evolution of Federalism in the United States (pages 76–85)

How did the Constitution divide power between national and state governments?

During the first few decades after the ratification of the U.S. Constitution, there was great uncertainty about where the lines lay that divided authority and power between the national government and the states. While there seemed strong arguments for such a division of authority and power, the people who wrote and ratified the Constitution did not share a consistent, clear vision of the meaning of American federalism. Fairly broad agreement about the need for a stronger national government had led to the end of the Articles of Confederation and the drafting of the Constitution, but there remained strong disagreements about exactly how much power the states kept under the new governing document. As a result, arguments about federalism played a central role in shaping the country's political system.

Before the Civil War

In the United States, disputes are often resolved through lawsuits that call on federal judges to interpret constitutional provisions defining the extent of federal authority. The judiciary's role in shaping American federalism is not a modern development. Judges have issued rulings on federalism since the first decades after the Constitution's ratification.

PATHWAYS | profile

John Marshall

John Marshall served as chief justice of the United States for 34 years (1801–1835). These were crucial, formative years, when important first decisions had to be made about the powers of national governing institutions. Before his appointment to the Supreme Court by President John Adams, Marshall had served as secretary of state and as a member of Congress and of Virginia's state legislature. As chief justice, Marshall was the leader on the Court, and he wrote many of its most important decisions, defining various aspects of federalism. As we will see in LINK Chapter 4, pages 108–113, Marshall's most famous opinion, *Marbury* v. *Madison* (1803), helped establish the power of federal judges to examine and invalidate actions by other branches of government. In general, Marshall advanced a vision of a strong national government. By leading the Court in interpreting the Constitution to enhance the powers of Congress and the federal courts, Marshall's opinions necessarily diminished the power of states, which would otherwise exercise any authority not granted by the Constitution to the federal government. According to the historian Charles Hobson, Marshall's "constitutional jurisprudence and his political views were decidedly hostile to the doctrine of states' rights."[4] If a different chief justice had led the Supreme Court during the nation's first decades, federalism might have developed in a very different way. ■

In 1816, Congress enacted legislation to charter the Second Bank of the United States. Two years later, the Maryland legislature imposed a tax on all banks within the state that were not chartered by the state legislature. James McCulloch, an official at the Baltimore branch of the federally chartered Bank of the United States, refused to pay the tax. The dispute arrived before the U.S. Supreme Court as the case of ***McCulloch* v. *Maryland*** (1819), and it presented

Chief Justice John Marshall, administering the oath of office to Andrew Jackson in 1829, played a major role in Supreme Court decisions that helped define the power of the federal government in the early nineteenth century.
—How would history have been different if Marshall had not led the Supreme Court to issue decisions strengthening the federal government's authority?

■ **Dual Federalism:** The powers of the federal and state governments are strictly separate, with interaction often marked by tension rather than cooperation.

SIGNIFICANCE: *Under a system of dual federalism, governments have separate spheres of responsibilities and influence and do not cooperate amongst themselves. As our society becomes more and more complex, it is doubtful that dual federalism could be implemented, as the issues our governments often deal with are too complicated and multifaceted to be addressed exclusively by one level of government without the cooperation of the other levels.*

Chief Justice John Marshall with the opportunity to define the respective powers of the state and federal governments.

Marshall's opinion in the case first examined whether the U.S. Constitution granted to Congress the power to charter a bank. Such a power is not explicitly stated anywhere in Article I of the Constitution, which defines the authority of the national legislature. But Marshall focused on the constitutional provision that grants Congress the power to make "all laws which shall be necessary and proper, for carrying into execution the foregoing powers, and all other powers vested by this constitution, in the government of the United States, or in any department thereof." This phrase in the Constitution, known as the **necessary and proper clause,** does not specify what powers, if any, flow from its words. Nevertheless, Marshall relied on the necessary and proper clause to conclude that Congress possessed the power to charter a national bank. The chief justice concluded that the creation of the Bank of the United States was "necessary and proper" as a means to carry out other powers that Article I explicitly granted to Congress, such as the powers to collect taxes, coin money, and regulate commerce. Marshall's opinion rejected Maryland's claim that the word *necessary* granted only powers that were absolutely essential. In this case, Marshall interpreted the Constitution in a way that enhanced the powers of the federal government and empowered Congress to make choices about how it would develop public policy.

After establishing that Congress had properly chartered the bank, Marshall's opinion went on to invalidate Maryland's efforts to impose taxes on the federal government's agencies. "The power to tax," wrote Marshall in a memorable phrase, "is the power to destroy." Realizing that states could use taxation to weaken or destroy federal institutions, the chief justice asserted that the federal government necessarily retained the power to preserve its creations. According to Marshall, the people of the United States grant powers "to a government whose laws, made in pursuance of the constitution, are declared to be supreme. Consequently, the people of a single state cannot confer a sovereignty" on their own government that would extend beyond the borders of the state. By invalidating Maryland's tax on the bank chartered by Congress, Marshall made a strong initial statement about the superior position of the national government in the evolving system of federalism.

Chief Justice Marshall also led the Supreme Court in making other decisions that shaped the law affecting federalism. In *Cohens* v. *Virginia* (1821), for example, brothers who had been convicted under a Virginia law for selling tickets in a lottery approved by Congress appealed to the U.S. Supreme Court. Virginia claimed that the Court had no authority to review decisions by its state courts. Marshall wrote an opinion rejecting that argument and asserting that the U.S. Supreme Court had ultimate authority over judicial matters concerning federal law, whether or not earlier decisions on the matter had been issued by state courts or by lower federal courts. In *Gibbons* v. *Ogden* (1824), Marshall's Court considered a challenge to a New York law that granted specific steamboat operators the exclusive privilege of providing service between New York and New Jersey. The chief justice announced a broad definition of the power granted to Congress by the Constitution to regulate commerce "among the several states." His opinion concluded that Congress possessed exclusive authority over the regulation of interstate commerce, including navigation, and therefore New York and other states had no power to grant such exclusive licenses to steamboat operators. In short, by these and other key decisions, the early U.S. Supreme Court, under Marshall's leadership, shaped federalism by interpreting the Constitution to give the federal government superior powers in certain matters of public policy, thereby imposing limits on the power of the states.

These decisions, however, did not solve all issues or clearly define the respective powers of state and federal governments. The wording of the Constitution raised many questions about the powers of states and the national government. For example, the Tenth Amendment states that "the powers not delegated to the United States by the Constitution, nor prohibited by it to the States, are reserved to the States respectively, or to the people." Many Americans viewed this amendment as embodying a fundamental premise of the Constitution: Governmental powers not explicitly granted to the federal government continue to reside with the states. This viewpoint supported a theory of federal-state relations known as **dual federalism**■. Under dual federalism, state governments and the national government were equally authoritative. The federal government was not superior; it had merely been granted authority over a specific, limited set of responsibilities. In other words, this theory rested on the idea that the national government possessed authority over its powers listed in the Constitution, such as coining money and establishing post offices and military forces, while the Tenth Amendment specifically reserved to the states all other governmental powers not discussed in the Constitution.

In practice, in early nineteenth-century America, dual federalism faced criticism from two directions. Advocates of a strong national government believed that where their spheres of activity overlapped, the powers of the federal government must be superior to those of the states. For example, both the states and the federal government sought to regulate certain aspects of business and commerce, and the Marshall Court had ruled in *Gibbons* v. *Ogden* (1824) that Congress has exclusive authority over "interstate commerce." Others saw the states as the central, sovereign governmental entities

■ **Doctrine of Secession:** Theory that state governments had a right to declare their independence and create their own form of government. Eleven southern states seceded from the Union in 1860–1861, created their own government (the Confederate States of America), and thereby precipitated the Civil War.

EXAMPLE: *The Civil War demonstrated that the doctrine of secession is invalid, but the idea that state governments ought to be very powerful and act in their own self-interest has resurfaced from time to time since the war.*

in the American governing system. These advocates of "states' rights" asserted that the states possessed specific powers superior to those of the national government.

Before the Civil War, southern leaders' **doctrine of nullification** stated that each state had retained its sovereignty upon joining the United States. Therefore, a state could declare any laws or actions of the national government "null and void" if they clashed with that state's interests and goals. In the 1830s, the South Carolina legislature voted to nullify federal tariffs that were believed to help northern manufacturing businesses while hurting southern planters and slave owners. The state later cancelled its action, and no other states acted on the nullification doctrine. The idea, however, was advocated by many who wanted to protect southern agricultural interests and to prevent Congress from interfering with slavery.

The most extreme expression of dual federalism before the Civil War was the **doctrine of secession**■. By asserting that states retained sovereignty and were not subordinate to the national government, advocates of secession claimed that states could choose to withdraw from the United States if they had profound disagreements with laws and policies produced by the national government. When, in 1861, eleven states acted on this theory by leaving the United States and forming the Confederate States of America, a bloody, four-year civil war erupted. The Confederacy's defeat in 1865 ended—presumably forever—the idea that dual sovereignty could be carried to the point of justifying secession.

Competing conceptions of federalism still color historical references to the Civil War because of differences in what Americans learned in school, depending on their home region. Until the second half of the twentieth century, students in many southern states were taught to call the conflict of 1861–1865 the "War Between the States." This label was based on an understanding of the war as reflecting profound disagreements about the rights of states to manage their own affairs without interference from the federal government, and it coincided with efforts by southern whites to defend state-mandated racial segregation. By contrast, elsewhere in the United States, students learned to call the bloody event the "Civil War" and to interpret it as having been fought over North–South disagreements about the institution of slavery and the southern states' unlawful assertion of a right to secede. As the historian James W. Loewen has noted, "History textbooks now admit that slavery was the primary cause of the Civil War."[5] However, the policy issue of slavery was intertwined with disputes about federalism, because the slave states resisted any move by the federal government to outlaw slavery in new territories and states.

"I thought the Civil War was about slavery. What does federalism have to do with the Civil War?"

—Student Question

PATHWAYS | of action

The Civil War and the Failure of American Politics

Throughout this book, we describe the pathways of American politics that produce public policies and shift the balance of power between different political actors and governing institutions. One or more of the pathways can almost always be used to describe and explain activities that shape and change policies. However, the Civil War represents the best example of a policy dispute that was *not* controlled by one of the pathways of American politics. The operation of the pathways depends on the American people's shared democratic values, commitment to the preservation of the constitutional governing system, and willingness to accept individual policy outcomes that are contrary to their personal preferences. In the case of slavery, however, no workable compromise balanced the interests of those who sought to abolish or at least prevent the territorial expansion of slavery and those who wanted to preserve and spread race-based slavery. As a result, people turned to violence to advance their interests. It took many battles and more than a half-million deaths to settle American policy regarding slavery and secession. In this instance, the forces that shaped American policy change resembled the forces that even today use armed conflict to determine policies in unstable countries.

In the post–Civil War American political system, intractable disagreements about public policies need not lead to violent conflicts. Today, for example, there are bitter disagreements over abortion, and some advocates on opposing sides cannot see any workable compromise. However, except for a few extremists who in isolated instances have committed violent acts against abortion clinics or individual abortion providers, activists on both sides of the issue remain committed to the governing system and devote their policy-shaping energies to lobbying, voter mobilization, the courts, and other strategies that use the pathways described in this book. The Civil War demonstrates that not all policy issues have been

ABOVE: **The bloody Civil War** reflected the failure of the pathways of political action to solve disagreements about slavery and federalism. The usual democratic mechanisms of lobbying, elections, and litigation could not forge a compromise resolution. ***—Are there reasons that make another civil war highly improbable in today's United States? What are they?***

BELOW: **Although the Civil War** put to rest the most extreme arguments advocating states' rights, states' rights claims lingered for decades afterward, often as a means to justify discrimination against African Americans. In the 1950s, for example, President Dwight Eisenhower sent federal troops to Little Rock, Arkansas, to protect nine brave African-American students who were attempting to desegregate Central High School. State and local officials in Arkansas were opposed to desegregation. ***—What circumstances today might require the president to use the military in order to force state and local officials to comply with the law?***

settled using the pathways of American politics, yet that war stands as such an unusual example of internal military conflict that it also reminds us about the importance of the pathways for nearly all other policy disputes in American history. ■

The doctrines of nullification and secession were put to rest with the Union victory in the Civil War. The war's outcome did not, however, end all attempts to preserve a "states' rights" conception of federalism. Such arguments remained common, for example, by those southern whites who during the 1950s and 1960s resisted passing and enforcing federal voting rights legislation and other antidiscrimination laws seeking to prevent the victimization of African Americans. The term *states' rights* is seldom used today because of its discredited association with efforts to preserve slavery and, later, to deny civil rights to African Americans.

Federalism After the Civil War

In the aftermath of the Civil War, the Constitution was amended to prevent specific assertions of state authority, particularly with respect to the treatment of newly freed African Americans. The Thirteenth Amendment (1865) banned slavery, thereby eliminating that issue as a source of conflict between states and the national government. The Fourteenth Amendment (1868) sought directly to limit states' authority to interfere with certain rights of individuals. "No State," the Fourteenth Amendment declares, shall deny "due process of law" or "the equal protection of the laws." According to the Fifteenth Amendment (1870), the right to vote shall not be denied "by the United States or by any State on account of race, color, or previous condition of servitude" (that is, slavery). In addition, each of the three post–Civil War amendments contained a statement specifically empowering Congress to enact legislation to enforce them. These amendments specifically limited state authority and enlarged that of the federal government. For nearly a century, federal institutions—courts, Congress, and presidents alike—did not vigorously apply the powers granted by these amendments to protect African Americans from discrimination at the hands of state and local authorities. However, in what was called "nationalizing the Bill of Rights," federal courts, beginning slowly in the 1920s and 1930s and later accelerating the process in the 1960s, often used the Fourteenth Amendment to strike down state laws and state-sanctioned policies that violated the Bill of Rights in such areas as criminal justice,

In the 1980s, President Ronald Reagan sought to reduce the influence of the federal government and increase the power and authority of states to manage their own affairs. ***—What might be some public issues that should be removed from the authority of the federal government and placed under the control of state and local officials?***

freedom of speech, and the separation of church and state. In the 1960s, the Supreme Court revived nineteenth-century federal antidiscrimination statutes affecting contracts, housing, and other matters by declaring that they were appropriate exercises of congressional power under the Thirteenth Amendment. Congress meanwhile relied on the Fifteenth Amendment to enact important voting rights legislation aimed at preventing discrimination in state elections. And as early as the 1940s, presidents issued executive orders designed to ensure the equal treatment of racial minorities, as well as vigorously enforced antidiscriminatory court decisions and congressional legislation.

In the decades following the Civil War, American society was transformed enormously. Many new technologies were developed and refined that helped reshape the economy. The expanded use of railroads, telegraph, and industrial machinery shifted the country's economy from one based primarily on agriculture to one deriving most of its wealth from urban industry. Cities grew with the spread of factories. Industrial demands for energy expanded employment opportunities in coal mines, in shipyards, and on railroads. People left farms and small towns to seek jobs in factories, urban offices, and retail businesses. Increasing numbers of job-seeking immigrants arrived from Europe and East Asia in search of new lives in American cities. In addition, large corporations grew, attempting to consolidate control over entire industries. The changes brought by urbanization and industrialization presented the country with new kinds of economic and social problems. Many government officials believed that new policies were needed to foster economic growth, prevent predatory business practices, protect the interests of workers, and address the growing problems of urban poverty.

In the late nineteenth century, Americans looked first to their states to deal with the effects of industrialization and urbanization. But in most states, corporate interests had significant influence on the state legislatures, which therefore did relatively little to address these issues. Because industries (such as mining companies in West Virginia) could use their substantial resources to influence politics and policy, in only a few states did the legislatures enact economic regulation and social welfare legislation. At the federal level, Congress enacted statutes intended to address specific concerns that affected the entire nation. For example, the Interstate Commerce Act of 1887 established the Interstate Commerce Commission, a regulatory agency responsible for implementing rules for transporting goods by rail and ship. The Sherman Antitrust Act of 1890 sought to prevent individual companies from controlling entire industries and to stop companies from working together to rig prices at artificially high levels. If companies became **monopolies** by gaining control over most or all of a particular industry, those companies could harm the national economy and consumers by raising prices in unjustified ways, because there would be no competing companies to which consumers could turn to obtain similar products. Congress wanted to encourage the existence of a variety of companies in each industry so that market forces, in the form of competition between companies, would keep prices at economically justifiable levels. But such federal legislation did relatively little to curb the excesses of big business. Only in the early twentieth century did some state legislatures and Congress enact additional legislation addressing such issues as working conditions and wages. In 1916, for example, Congress prohibited the transportation across state lines of goods produced using child labor.

Many laws passed in response to changing social conditions and problems were tested through the court pathway. But unlike Marshall's Supreme Court a century earlier, which had consistently sought to strengthen and expand the powers of the federal government, the

Through the first decades of the twentieth century, it was common for American children to work long hours under harsh and dangerous conditions in textile mills, mines, and other industrial settings. Until the late 1930s, the U.S. Supreme Court blocked legislative efforts to enact laws that would protect workers, including children, from danger and exploitation in the workplace. ***—What would labor laws be like today if all regulation was controlled by state governments?***

PHOTO: Lewis Hine (American, 1874–1940) "A Carolina Spinner" 1908. Gelatin Silver Print 4¾ × 7 in. Milwaukee Art Museum, Gift of the Sheldon M. Barnett Family 1973.83.

justices of the Supreme Court of the late nineteenth and early twentieth centuries handed down decisions that generally limited governmental authority to regulate commerce and address issues of social welfare. For example, in 1895, the Supreme Court rejected the government's charge that the American Sugar Refining Company had become an illegal monopoly in violation of the Sherman Antitrust Act, even though the company, by buying up competing sugar businesses, had gained control over 98 percent of the country's sugar-refining capacity (*United States* v. *E. C. Knight Company*). The Court concluded that although the Constitution empowered Congress to regulate interstate commerce, "manufacturing," such as sugar refining, was a separate activity from "commerce." Therefore, the federal government could not regulate the company and other manufacturing enterprises. In *Hammer* v. *Dagenhart* (1918), the Supreme Court struck down the 1916 federal statute barring the interstate transport of goods produced by child labor. The Court said that because the goods themselves were not harmful, the statute had improperly sought to regulate child labor. It ruled that Congress, in exercising its power over "interstate commerce," possessed only the authority to regulate the *transportation* of goods. Decisions like these temporarily limited the expansion of federal governmental authority during decades when Congress sought to become more active in regulating the economy and advancing social welfare goals.

The Supreme Court's actions in limiting federal power did not necessarily mean that the justices intended to shift federalism's balance of power in favor of the states. The Court also struck down similar laws enacted by state legislatures. In 1905, for example, in *Lochner* v. *New York*, the Supreme Court invalidated a New York State statute that sought to limit the working hours of bakery employees to not more than 10 hours per day or 60 hours per week. Although the New York legislature intended to protect the health and well-being of bakers, the Court found that the statute interfered with the workers' liberty to work as many hours as they wished to work. (Of course, workers typically did not toil such long hours because they enjoyed it; they did it because hourly wages were so low that they had no choice.) In effect, the Supreme Court's decisions were not aimed specifically at federalism. Scholars argue that the decisions reflected the justices' views on the limits of legislative power generally, both state and federal.[6] Still, the judicial decisions of this era had the primary effect of preventing the federal government from expanding its authority.

"Why did the Supreme Court reverse directions and stop the federal government from regulating business?"

—Student Question

Federal Power: The Supreme Court and the New Deal

The stock market crash of 1929 signaled the beginning of the Great Depression, which would last through the 1930s. Manufacturing dropped, banks failed, and by early 1933, nearly one-quarter of the American workforce was unemployed. Elected president in 1932,

■ **New Deal:** Programs designed by President Franklin D. Roosevelt to bring economic recovery from the Great Depression by expanding the role of the federal government in providing employment opportunities and social services; advanced social reforms to serve the needs of the people, greatly expanding the budget and activity of the federal government.

SIGNIFICANCE: *The New Deal was a set of initiatives that were designed to stimulate the economy. Their ultimate success helped redefine the very nature of federalism and how Americans viewed their national government.*

CONNECT THE LINK
(Chapter **8**, pages **276–283**) The New Deal dramatically changed the way in which people view the role of the government in solving social and economic problems. Do you think we expect too much from our government?

Franklin D. Roosevelt was inaugurated in early 1933 at the depth of the economic crisis, and he immediately sought to use the federal government's power to spur economic recovery and revive employment. Roosevelt's domestic policy, known as the **New Deal**■, included programs to regulate farm and industrial production; to provide government jobs in construction, environmental conservation, and other public sector projects; and to give relief to people suffering from economic hardships (see also LINK Chapter 8, pages 276–283). It also established the Social Security system. Many of the New Deal programs that Congress enacted collided with the Supreme Court justices' conservative views on the limits of government authority, and the Court initially struck down several important laws that Roosevelt had sponsored. In 1936, for example, the Court decided that Congress lacked the power to impose minimum wage and maximum work hour regulations on coal mines (*Carter* v. *Carter Coal Co.*).

President Roosevelt criticized the Supreme Court for blocking New Deal economic and social welfare laws. In 1937, after he had been elected to a second term, Roosevelt proposed changing the Supreme Court so that the president could appoint a new justice whenever a sitting justice reached the age of 70. The Constitution does not state the size of the Supreme Court, so Congress has the authority to change the number of justices who make up the Court. At the time Roosevelt made his proposal, six justices were older than 70, so under the proposed law, the president would have been able immediately to alter the balance of power on the Court by appointing a half-dozen new justices who would support his New Deal program. This proposal became known as Roosevelt's **court-packing plan**■. Even though Roosevelt had won reelection by an overwhelming popular margin, the public saw in the court-packing plan an attempt to overturn the constitutional system of checks and balances. Reflecting this negative public reaction, Congress rejected the proposal. But many historians believe that the proposal itself may have pushed at least one justice to reconsider his opposition to expanded federal power. The episode is sometimes referred to in jest as "the switch in time that saved nine" (that is, the nine justices on the Court). As the constitutional law scholar Gerald Gunther observed, "While the controversy was raging, the Court handed down a number of decisions sustaining regulatory statutes, and [one justice] retired."[7]

In the late 1930s, after several elderly conservative justices left the bench, Roosevelt was finally able to reshape the Supreme Court by appointing new justices, whom the Senate confirmed. Their views on congressional commerce power and federalism led them to uphold the constitutionality of the New Deal's expansion of federal power. For decades thereafter, the Court permitted Congress to justify nearly any kind of social, economic, and civil rights legislation as an exercise of power under its constitutional authority to regulate interstate commerce. Congress used this power to enact a variety of laws, some which clearly had primary goals other than the regulation of commerce. In the 1960s, for example, people active in several pathways of American politics, including the elections, lobbying, grassroots mobilization, and courts, sought to create laws that would guarantee voting rights and other protections to African Americans, against racial discrimination. Other political actors, especially members of Congress from southern states, opposed these initiatives. In 1964, Congress enacted Title II of the

A boy uses a drinking fountain on the county courthouse lawn in Halifax, North Carolina. The Civil Rights Act of 1964 barred racial discrimination in "public accommodations." ***—What examples of discrimination have you observed in recent years?***

Civil Rights Act of 1964, barring racial discrimination in restaurants, hotels, movie theaters, and other "public accommodations" provided by private businesses. Although it was widely recognized that the statute was created to advance civil rights and combat discrimination, the Supreme Court rejected challenges to the law and accepted the federal government's argument that Title II regulated commerce by attacking a major barrier to interstate travel by African Americans. Before the law's enactment, African Americans often could not find restaurants and motels that would serve them when they traveled. The Court also permitted the law to be applied to businesses that had relatively little contact with interstate commerce, because they sold local products and services to local people (*Heart of Atlanta Motel* v. *United States,* 1964, *Katzenbach* v. *McClung,* 1964). The Court's decisions in these and other cases seemed to indicate that Congress had nearly unlimited authority to make laws under the premise of regulating interstate commerce.

According to the supremacy clause in Article VI of the Constitution, federal laws "shall be the supreme Law of the Land." Acts of Congress were thus to take precedence over state laws. As a result, the expansion of federal lawmaking affected federalism by simultaneously limiting the scope of the states' authority to control their own affairs. State laws still controlled most matters affecting criminal justice, education, property, and many other areas of public policy. Over time, however, the federal government became more active in additional realms of law and policy. In the 1960s and thereafter, Congress defined certain crimes as federal offenses, many of which overlapped with existing state statutes. The federal government became involved in funding—and therefore regulating—various aspects of education. Congress also began to create environmental protection laws that took precedence over state laws and affected individuals' ability to make their own decisions about how to use their property. As the federal government expanded its involvement in public policy, the Supreme Court generally accepted the expansion of federal power at the expense of state authority (see Figure 3.1).

FIGURE 3.1 | **Governmental Powers and Control of Policy Issues**

(a) **Distribution of Powers Between National and State Governments.** The founders of our government created a system that divided power, authority, and responsibility between the federal and state governments. Some powers are exclusive to one entity, but many are shared. Throughout our history, the power of the federal government has grown, but states remain important actors in our political system. Unfortunately, many in our country are overwhelmed with the size of our government and do not correctly understand which level of government is responsible for different issues. ***—How do you think we can better explain to individuals how power is divided and shared?***

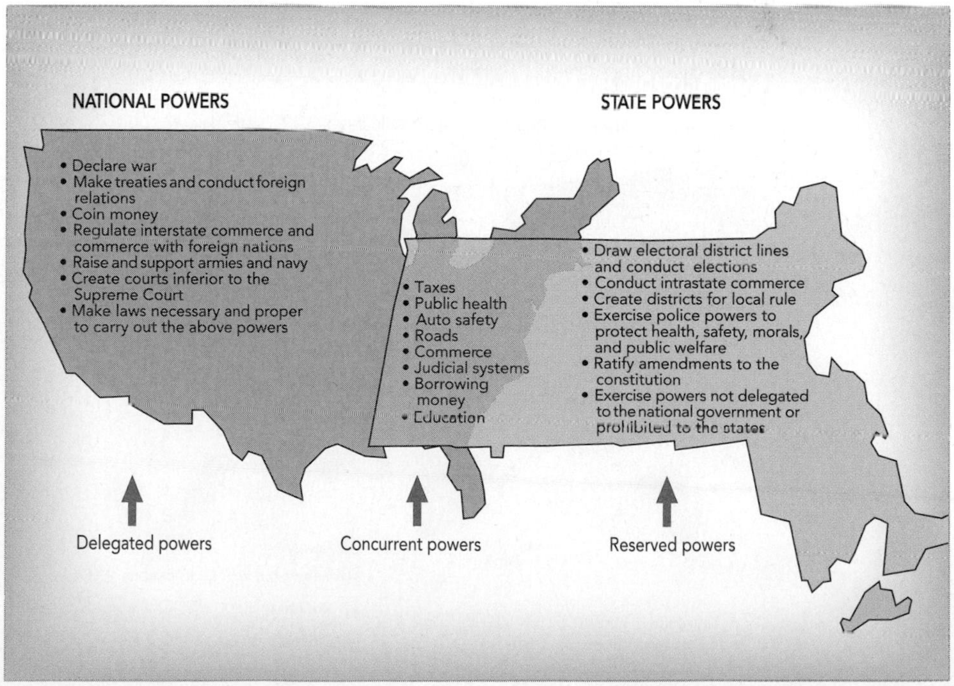

FIGURE 3.1 | **Governmental Powers and Control of Policy Issues *(continued)***

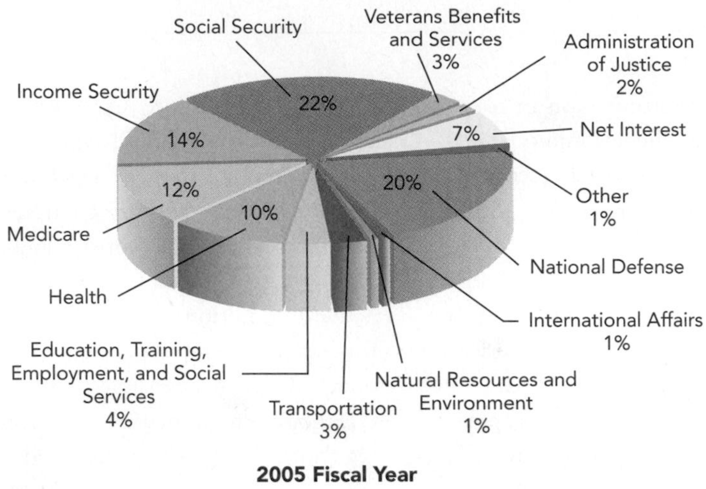

(b) **The Changing Functions of National Grants to States and Localities.** Over the past half-century, the federal government has significantly expanded its involvement in policy issues. As indicated by changes in the percentage of funds devoted to various programs, the federal government now affects a variety of policies that were entirely under the control of states in 1960. A key element of federal involvement for many of these programs has been in providing funding for cities and states. ***—Is the federal government involved in too many policy issues or is its involvement necessary to address the country's problems?***

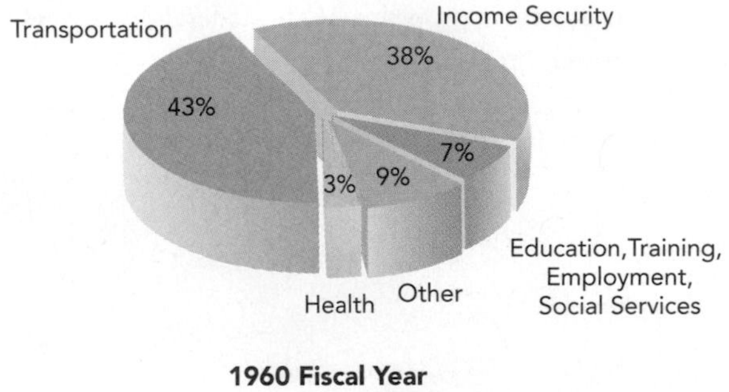

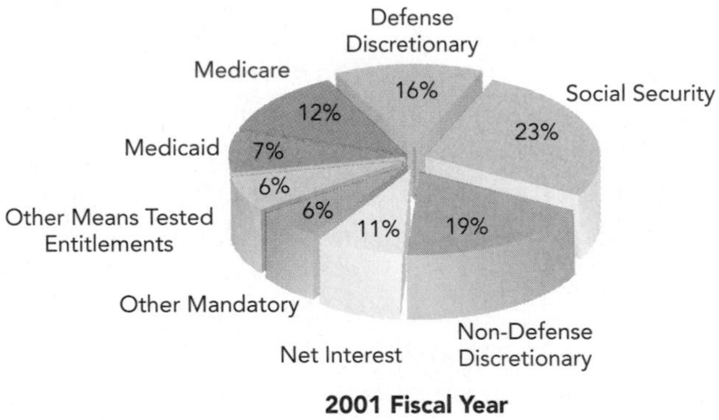

February 12, 2006, New York Times Graphics. Copyright © 2006 by the New York Times Co. Reprinted with permission.

(c) **Ready or Not.** Most states are ready or nearly ready to manage a catastrophic event. However, a number of states are not prepared. ***—Why do you think that states on or near the southern border of our country are more likely to be prepared than those near the northern border? What do you think should be done, and by whom, to ensure that all states are ready for a catastrophic event?***

The Evolution of Federalism in the United States

Practice Quiz

1. In general, Chief Justice John Marshall's opinions regarding federalism tended to
   - **a.** strengthen the power of the national government.
   - **b.** strengthen the power of state governments.
   - **c.** reduce the impact of the federal courts on federalism issues.
   - **d.** b and c.

2. The doctrine of nullification
   - **a.** was never fully exercised by any state.
   - **b.** was a logical extension of Chief Justice Marshall's federalist philosophy.
   - **c.** is implied in the Tenth Amendment.
   - **d.** is now endorsed by most of the states.

3. The Civil War exemplified a policy dispute that followed
   - **a.** the court pathway of American politics.
   - **b.** the cultural change pathway of American politics.
   - **c.** the grassroots activism pathway of American politics.
   - **d.** None of the above.

4. The New Deal
   - **a.** was a collection of antitrust legislation instigated by Theodore Roosevelt.
   - **b.** was a collection of domestic policies instituted by Franklin Roosevelt to help the nation recover from the Great Depression.
   - **c.** was implemented by the introduction of federal programs at the state and local level.
   - **d.** b and c.

Answers: 1-a, 2-a, 3-d, 4-d.

Discussion Questions

1. In what ways could federalism address the problem of our nation's economic recession?
2. What pathway(s) of action could be used to counteract corporate monopolies?

What **YOU** can do!

If you want to see how the Supreme Court is currently shaping the interpretation of national, state, and local governmental authority, search for recent cases and Court opinions involving federalism at **http://www.oyez.org/**

■ **Cooperative Federalism:** The powers of the federal and state government are intertwined and shared. Each level of government shares overlapping power, authority, and responsibility.

EXAMPLE: *We increasingly see cooperative federalism at work in the War on Drugs. Joint operations commonly are conducted between the DEA, ATF, FBI, and local law enforcement agencies to fight the illegal trafficking and selling of illicit drugs.*

VISUAL LITERACY **Federalism and Regulations**

Past Trends *in* Federalism (pages 86–89)

How do economic and social changes impact federalism?

Since the Great Depression, the very nature of federalism has changed dramatically. Perhaps equally as important are the changing views the public has toward the national and state governments.

The New Deal and Cooperative Federalism

Franklin Roosevelt's New Deal programs marked a dramatic shift in our federal system of government. Before the New Deal, many Americans believed that the power of the federal government should be severely limited. However, the Great Depression made it vividly clear that the economic crisis was far too large to be effectively addressed by individual state or local governments or by private charities. As the way in which Americans viewed the responsibilities of the federal government changed, a shift occurred in the nature of federalism itself. President Roosevelt, or FDR, used the power of the presidency and his remarkable personal skills to sell his new vision of federalism to the American people. Under his vision, the power and influence of the federal government changed dramatically, as did the relationship between the national and state governments. Many of FDR's programs involved cooperation between the states and the national government to deal with the complex economic situation. Unprecedented interaction between the different levels of government resulted. Political scientists refer to this changing relationship as **cooperative federalism**■—the belief that state and national governments should work together to solve problems. Programs that involved joint involvement were far-ranging, including public works projects, welfare programs, and unemployment assistance. Many observers believe this marked the beginning of an era of national supremacy, as shown in the dramatic growth of the power, budget, and scope of the federal government. Morton Grozdins, a historian of federalism, aptly contrasted a layer cake and a marble cake in describing the shift from the older, dual federalism to the new, cooperative federalism with its high levels of national–state interaction.[8] As you know, in a marble cake, the two colors are separate, like state and federal governments, but they exist next to each other throughout the cake rather than resting exclusively in separate layers of the cake. The marble cake analogy symbolically portrays state and federal government as coexisting and cooperating in a variety of policy areas.

The New Deal era was critical in reshaping federalism in the United States. Perhaps the most significant change resulting from the New Deal has been in the way Americans think about their problems and the role of the national government in solving them. Issues and problems that at one time had been seen as personal or local are now often seen as national problems needing national solutions. Today Americans take it for granted that issues concerning morality, values, and social policy will be debated at the national level and that Congress and the president will feel pressured to take action. For many years, this has been true of the issue of abortion, but in recent years, it has expanded to other issues traditionally under state control, such as debates about civil unions and legal marriages for gays and lesbians.

The Great Society and Creative Federalism

The nature and role of the federal government and of federalism itself continued to change throughout the twentieth century. The presidency of Lyndon B. Johnson (1963–1969) marked a critical point in the evolution of federalism. Johnson proposed many new social programs to achieve what he called the *Great Society*. Of crucial importance in his vision was the *War on Poverty,* which channeled federal money to states, local governments, and even citizen groups to combat poverty and racial discrimination. Funds were allocated to a variety of social programs for urban renewal, education, and improving the lives of underprivileged children (for example, Head Start). The money was used to advance the agenda of President Johnson and liberal Democrats in Congress, the direct result of which was to bypass governors, state legislatures, and local officials. As we see in Figure 3.2, such federal departments as Agriculture and Commerce, which Democratic leaders did not target, saw only limited growth in the 1960s, while agencies with responsibility for health care, education, and community development saw dramatic growth during Johnson's presidency. These patterns reflected the domestic priorities of Johnson and the liberal wing of the Democratic Party. These priorities are very clear when we examine one aspect of Johnson's Great Society plan: urban development. Figure 3.3 shows the remarkable increases in federal grants for subsidized housing and in urban renewal grants, from $212 million in 1964 to $1.049 billion in 1970.

Under President Johnson, the federal government funneled record amounts of money to states to combat discrimination and

President Lyndon Johnson used various forms of grants from the federal government in order to spur state and local action against such social problems as poverty and racial discrimination. ***—What might be some problems caused by the federal government's use of financial incentives in this way?***

fight poverty. Many states (especially in the South) were blamed for dragging their feet in carrying out social reforms to promote equal rights. If the federal authorities decided that states and local communities were not cooperating, they withheld funds. By using a reward-and-punishment system to allocate resources, the federal government was very successful in getting the states and localities to do its bidding. Liberal members of Congress intentionally bypassed conservative governors, state legislatures, and mayors, giving urban renewal and social welfare grants directly to citizen groups. This put local activists in direct competition with local elected officials, often causing tension. During the Johnson administration, Congress increasingly began to use monetary grants to advance specific agendas—for example, helping the urban poor, combating crime, and protecting

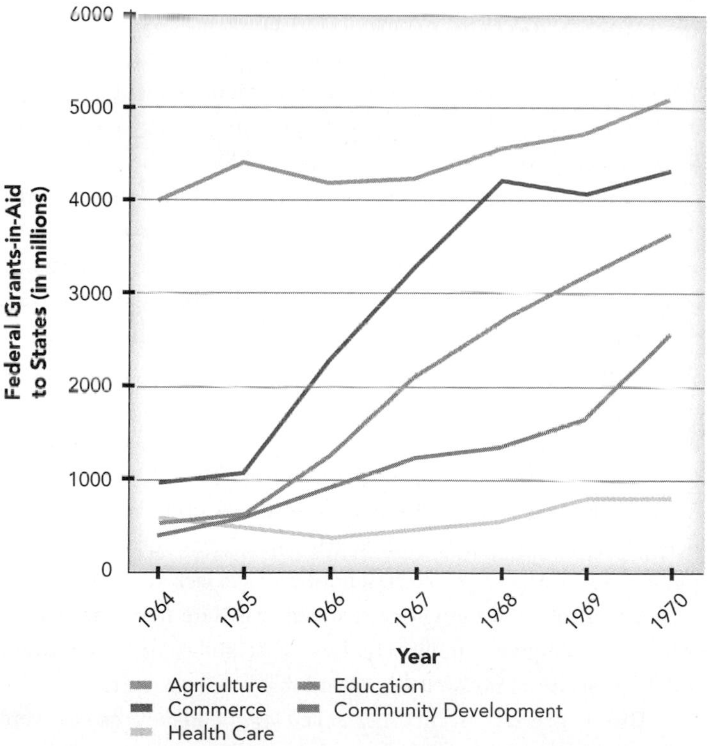

FIGURE 3.2 | **Grants-in-Aid from the Federal Government to States (1964–1970)**

The pattern of distributions of federal grants-in-aid is a good indicator of the priorities of our government and its leaders. During the 1960s, we saw enormous growth in grants for commerce, education, and community development. While there was an increase in grants for agriculture and health care, the rate of growth was substantially less than the other categories, reflecting the policy priorities of Lyndon Johnson and the Democratic leadership in Congress.

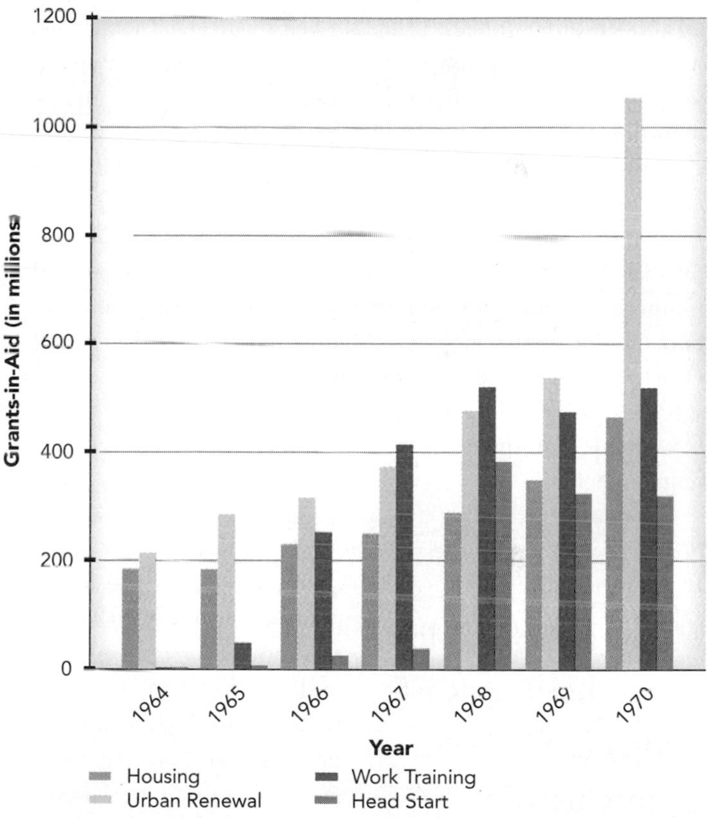

FIGURE 3.3 | **Grants-in-Aid Selected Programs 1964–1970**

Spending on urban renewal increased from around $200 million in 1964 to over $1 billion in 1970. Spending for Head Start and work training increased dramatically over the same time period. During that decade we saw greater demands for minority voting rights and protection from racial and ethnic discrimination. As a larger number of less affluent people got involved in politics, using the grassroots mobilization and elections pathways, the manner in which we allocated federal grants changed. Figures 3.2 and 3.3 provide evidence that our officials respond to our demands for change.

SOURCE: Executive Office of the President, Bureau of the Budget; *Special Analysis of Federal Aid to State and Local Government* derived from The Budget of the United States Government.

Grants-in-Aid: Funds given from one governmental unit to another governmental unit for specific purposes.

SIGNIFICANCE: *Grants-in-aid cover a wide array of programs, from welfare to health care to construction/maintenance of roadways to education. Grants-in-aid help equalize services between states and allow the federal government to influence policymaking at state and local levels.*

Categorical Grants: Grants of money from the federal government to state or local governments for very specific purposes. These grants often require that funds be matched by the receiving entity.

EXAMPLE: *Federal assistance to put more police officers on the street is often in the form of categorical grants (which help localities but usually do not leave much discretion).*

the environment. Often these issues had been low priorities for state and local governments, but given the availability of federal funds to develop new programs, local governments began to restructure their priorities to conform to Washington's wishes. Consequently, as federal aid increased, so did state and local dependence on it.

The Changing Nature of Federal Grants

Grants-in-aid are federal funds given to state and local governments on the condition that the money be spent for specified purposes defined by officials in Washington. They are a means for redistributing income. Under this system, money collected from all citizens by the national government in the form of taxes is then allocated by the federal government for the benefit of certain citizens in specific cities and states. These grants often work to reduce notable inequalities among states, as many are based on economic need. It is important to note, however, that whatever its form, grant money comes with strings attached. Many stipulations are imposed to ensure that the money is used for the purpose for which it was given; other conditions are designed to evaluate how well the grant is working. Both give rise to complex reporting and accounting requirements.

Grants-in-aid go back to our earliest days. The national government gave money to the states to help them pay debts from the Revolutionary War. One of the most important early examples of grants-in-aid was the decision of the national government in the mid-nineteenth century to give the states land grants for educational institutions and to build railroads that promoted westward expansion. (Many of today's leading public universities were founded with the proceeds of these grants.) Cash grants-in-aid were distributed by the federal government early in the nation's history—for example, to pay for state militias—but they did not become common until the twentieth century. Today, however, they are enormously important. It is estimated that in 2006, the federal government spent more than $434 billion in grants-in-aid to state and local governments, benefiting millions of Americans.[9]

"434 billion dollars! For what kinds of projects are these grants used?"

—Student Question

Categorical grants are targeted for specific purposes. Typically, they have strict restrictions, often leaving little room for discretionary spending. Two types of categorical grants exist: formula grants and project grants. Let's consider each in turn.

Formula grants are distributed according to a particular formula, which specifies who is eligible and for how much. For example, the number of school-age children living in families below the poverty line is used to allocate federal funds to each state to subsidize school breakfasts and lunches. The states must spend this money on school meals, according to a very specific formula allowing no flexibility. The money at stake under grants of this type is one reason why the state population figures and other demographic data revealed each decade by the national census are so important—and so controversial. Consider what happens when it is proposed to allocate money to states for homeless shelters based on the number of homeless people in each state. States that are better at finding and counting the homeless would receive more money than states that are less successful or less diligent in accounting for their homeless population—a problem compounded by the irregular lives of many homeless people, who often migrate for a variety of reasons (including the weather).

The second type of categorical federal grants, **project grants,** are awarded on the basis of competitive applications rather than a specified formula. Consider homeless shelters: A community could apply for a project grant to develop a new model of a shelter, one that not only houses the homeless but also involves the efforts of other community organizations to provide education, job training, and substance abuse counseling. The community could receive federal grant money based on the strength of its application and its prospect for innovation.

Typically, state governments must contribute some money of their own, but many times the federal funds support the primary cost of the program. State and local officials have often found these grants frustrating, because they are defined so narrowly and may not fit the needs of the locality. For example, money might be available to hire more public school teachers, but a local school district may actually need money to purchase new textbooks and build new schools. Under most categorical grants, school districts lack discretion: They must either follow Washington's requirements (hire new teachers, for example) or forgo the funds. The lack of flexibility has often meant that local needs are not well served and that money is wasted.

Block grants (sometimes called *revenue-sharing grants*) were developed in 1966 as a response to these problems. Block grants are still earmarked for specific programs, but they are far more flexible. To continue our earlier example, a categorical grant for education might specify that the money be used for teacher salaries, even if that isn't the greatest need in the school district. A block grant would still be available to improve education, but the school district could decide (within specified parameters) how to spend the money—it might choose to buy textbooks rather than hire more teachers. Because block grants allow greater spending flexibility, many observers feel they are a more efficient and more effective form of federal grants.

■ **Block Grants (sometimes called *revenue-sharing grants*):** Grants of money to states, which are given substantial discretion to spend the money with minimal federal restrictions.

EXAMPLE: *State and local governments tend to prefer block grants to other forms of grants-in-aid, as there is more flexibility in how the money is spent.*

Past Trends in Federalism

Practice Quiz

1. Grants-in-aid are federal funds given to state and local governments to
   - **a.** be used for specified purposes defined by federal officials.
   - **b.** reduce economic inequalities.
   - **c.** adjust citizens' tax brackets based on current income levels.
   - **d.** a and b.
2. Block grants
   - **a.** are also known as revenue-sharing grants.
   - **b.** are more flexible than categorical grants.
   - **c.** disburse funds that are allocated at the discretion of state and local managers.
   - **d.** a, b, and c.
3. Congress is the only branch of the federal government that can generate mandates.
   - **a.** true
   - **b.** false
4. Federalism that features national and state government working together to implement procedural changes is termed
   - **a.** collaborative.
   - **b.** combined.
   - **c.** cooperative.
   - **d.** creative.

Answers: 1-d, 2-d, 3-b, 4-c.

Discussion Questions

1. Discuss the relative advantages and disadvantages of categorical grants.
2. In what ways could block grants be abused by their recipients and managers?

What **YOU** can do!

Invite some of your classmates to discuss the proper role of the federal government in funding state and local projects. Should the federal government be paying for local projects, and if so, should it have a say in how the funds are spent and the desired outcomes? What are the benefits of the federal government's role in local policy development? What are the disadvantages?

DEBATE Federalism

Recent Trends *in* Federalism (pages 90–93)

How has federalism changed in recent decades?

The power and influence of the federal government expanded dramatically in the twentieth century. Every president since Richard Nixon (1969–1974) has voiced concern over the size and influence of the federal government. In 1976, Georgia Governor Jimmy Carter successfully ran for the White House as an outsider who opposed federal mandates, which as governor he had disagreed with for a variety of reasons. Although as president Carter did cut back federal grant expenditures, his cuts paled in comparison to those of his successor, Ronald Reagan.

Winning election over Carter in 1980, Reagan pledged to promote a new form of federalism in which more power and responsibility would be returned to the states, including financial responsibility. Reagan and other conservatives strongly disagreed with the diminishing role of state governments in our federal system that had developed over the previous decades. He saw states as vital instruments in our governmental apparatus and vowed to increase their presence. His goals were reflected not only in his rhetoric but also in his budgetary policies. In addition to large income tax cuts, Reagan proposed massive cuts in domestic spending that would roll back and even eliminate many programs created by the Democratic administrations from the New Deal to the Great Society. Reagan successfully pressed Congress not only to reduce the amount of federal grant money that it disbursed but also to shift more money into flexible block grants, which fell into four broad categories—income guarantees, education, transportation, and health. He argued that the states knew best how to serve their citizens and that mandates from Washington were wasteful, failing to meet the needs of the people and also taking away legitimate authority from state and local governments. As you know, this idea of state authority is not new, going back to a view of states as laboratories for public policy experiments. However, this view of states' independence and control over their own affairs had diminished over the course of the twentieth century. By the 1980s, with the power and the budget of the federal government reaching record levels, the idea of strengthening states and curbing the federal government struck a chord with the American public. As is evident in Figure 3.4, Reagan was quite successful in fulfilling his pledge to reduce the role of the federal government in funding state/local government budgets.

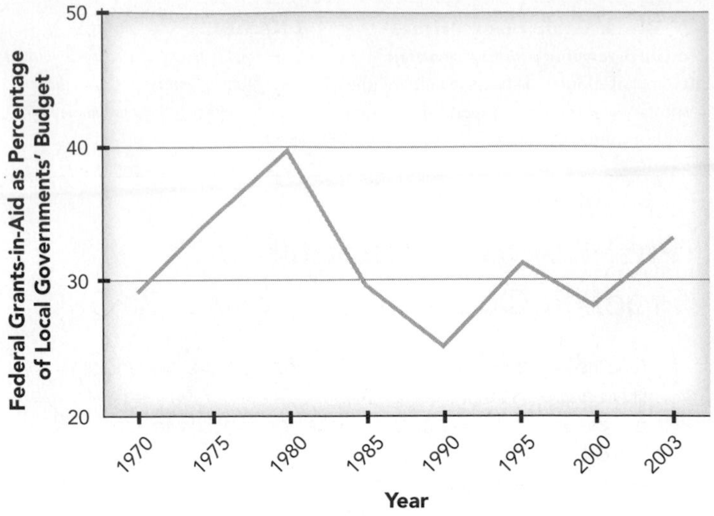

FIGURE 3.4 | **Federal Grants-in-Aid as a Percentage of State and Local Government Budget**

In 1980, 40 percent of local government budgets came from the federal government in the form of grants-in-aid. Ronald Reagan campaigned on a platform that argued that the size, scope, and budget of the federal government needed to be limited. As this graph indicates, he was successful in diminishing the reliance of local governments on federal grants. During Bill Clinton's first term in office, federal grants-in-aid increased, but they began to decrease in the mid-1990s. ***—Why might it be a mistake for local governments to rely on federal grants?***

SOURCE: U.S. Office of Management and Budget based on *Historical Tables and Analytical Perspectives, Budget of the United States Government*, annual.

Dillon's Rule Versus Home Rule

There is a long-standing tradition in the United States of active and powerful local governments. In the earliest days of colonial America, many colonies were actually federations of local governments. In fact, newly independent states often included stipulations in their first constitutions to guarantee that local governments would retain influence over their own affairs. These new arrangements were in striking contrast to English common law, under which local governments had only the powers explicitly assigned to them by the state and hence were very limited in power and influence.

> "Is there some kind of 'federalism' between state and local governments?"
> —Student Question

Some states, however, did hold to the English tradition of weak local governments. A ruling in 1868 by Judge John Dillon of the Iowa Supreme Court held that local governments could rule only in areas explicitly permitted by the state government, providing a legal framework for this view of state-local relationships. His decision became known as **Dillon's rule.** Legally, state governments create and control local governments. Because of this, state governments have great influence on the nature and character of local municipalities. States that

■ **Special Governments:** Local governmental units established for very specific purposes, such as the regulation of water and school districts, airports, and transportation services.

EXAMPLE: *The decisions made by special governments, most notably cities, counties, and school districts, have a very large impact on the daily lives of individuals in many profound ways.*

■ **Devolution:** Transfer of jurisdiction and fiscal responsibility for particular programs from the federal government to state or local governments.

SIGNIFICANCE: *State governments like some components of devolution, most notably having more responsibility over decision-making that impacts their residents; however, the fiscal responsibility that comes with devolution is often difficult for states and localities to bear.*

follow Dillon's rule give local governments very narrow and explicit power to fulfill their responsibilities. Consequently, these state governments are very powerful and have a great deal of influence over municipalities within the state. In contrast are states that follow the theory of **home rule,** which holds that city governments can do anything to serve the needs of their residents that is not prohibited by state law. Although city ordinances must comply with state laws and state legislatures can preempt local laws, home rule states give far more authority to the local governments, which are very important for the administration of many governmental services. As you can see in Figure 3.5, there were 87,525 local governments in 2002, the largest of which were special governments. **Special governments**■ include a wide variety of entities, the most numerous of which are natural resource, fire, housing, and community development districts. It is difficult to imagine life without our local governments.

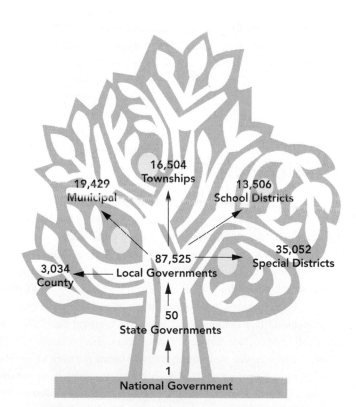

FIGURE 3.5 | **Forms of Local and Special Governments**

There are over 175,000 types of governments in the United States. At the center is the national government, and the branches of government stretch far and wide, giving residents many points of access to governmental officials and leaders. Thus there are numerous pathways that can be used to initiate change or promote the status quo.

Devolution

Concerns about the power and influence of the national government continued to be voiced after President Reagan left the White House. Federal grants-in-aid increased through 1995, leading many advocates of states' authority to be upset with the nature of the federal system in the United States. Republicans once again began to object to the national government asserting such a large role in our federal system. In 1994, the Republican congressional leadership announced its "Contract with America," which called for reducing the size of the federal government and for returning money, responsibility, and power to the states—what has come to be known as **devolution**■, or the transfer of power to political subunits. With Republican majorities elected in the House and Senate in 1994, interest in minimizing the role of the federal government increased. The Republican initiative focused, in part, on returning power to the states, having states complete what had been federal tasks. One prominent example is welfare. Congress passed reforms that returned management of welfare programs to the states. With the aim of moving welfare mothers into the working world, new rules were enacted that limited the number of years women with dependent children could continue receiving public assistance.

Devolution is motivated by a number of factors. One important factor is deeply held ideological beliefs that the federal government is less effective in delivering services and solving problems compared with the states and localities. Many supporters of devolution believe that the state governments are best equipped to solve their own problems and that they only need the power and flexibility to do so. Worry over increasing federal deficits also fuels devolution, with the aim of transferring not only power but also fiscal responsibility to the states. However, many policy advocates are opposed to devolution, fearing a return to the days of great inequality among states and among citizens within states. The weak economies of some states prevent them from keeping pace with other states in education funding, highway construction, and other vital services unless they have financial support from the federal government. In economic hard times, the number of people in need grows dramatically, while the tax revenues required to satisfy these needs shrink. Thus, at a time of great hardship, states often have little ability to meet their citizens' needs adequately. Moreover, most state and local governments are legally prohibited by their own state constitutions from incurring budget deficits, whereas the federal government can freely cover whatever deficits it incurs by selling bonds. So when their tax revenues fall, states have to make the difficult choice between raising taxes and cutting services. Devolution has complicated state and local politics by forcing states to compete for fewer and fewer federal grants. Moreover, during the recession of the early 1990s, many states and cities found themselves in difficult situations because of reduced revenue. In 2003, for instance, New York City had to lay off 3,400 city employees, close 8 firehouses, and cut 3,200 jobs in the Department of Education. In Oregon, police stations often sat vacant at night to save money. Schools had to cut programs, and some districts even had to shave days off the school year. State after state closed schools, faced prison overcrowding, cut Medicaid spending, and raised tuition in public universities.[10] Interestingly, despite these severe experiences, the public generally supports the idea of cutting back on the federal government; thus devolution seems likely to continue in the immediate future.

Although the idea of having more powerful and more independent state governments is popular under today's theory of a new federalism, we have yet to see it reach fruition, and many observers doubt that this vision will ever become a reality. The very issues that brought about a more active federal government—poverty, economic instability, complex relationships at home and with other global powers—still exist. It is therefore difficult to imagine that the federal government might become substantially less active and less involved in the wide array of policy issues. Consider what would happen if one state did not maintain high educational standards. The economy of the entire region could be harmed as the quality of the workforce deteriorated, encouraging employers to relocate their businesses. If the health care system of one state became significantly substandard, neighboring states would experience a crisis as people flocked to them seeking better services. Population shifts can create new burdens for states. When thousands of people left New Orleans and moved to Texas in the aftermath of Hurricane Katrina in 2005, they stretched Texas's resources for education, health care, and housing assistance. With increased globalization and the resultant international competition for scarce resources, the days of big national government are not likely to end.

When Hurricane Katrina devastated New Orleans and the Gulf coast in 2005, the federal government's emergency response agencies were initially slow and ineffective. However, because the federal government possesses many more resources than state and local governments, observers believe that the federal government must maintain a role in responding to major disasters. ***—How can the federal government be more effective and provide better support and coordination with state and local officials when natural disasters occur?***

The Supreme Court's Shift in Perspective

During the 1970s, 1980s, 1990s, and 2000s, Republican presidents selected 13 of the 15 new justices who served on the Court in these decades. Through their judicial opinions, several of these justices expressed concern about a steady lessening of states' authority to manage their own affairs. One of them, Sandra Day O'Connor, had once been a state legislator and seemed especially interested in requiring Congress and federal judges to show greater respect and deference to state governmental authority. By the mid-1990s, the justices who were concerned about striking a new balance of power in American federalism gained a slim 5-4 majority. Beginning in 1995, for the first time since the late 1930s, the Supreme Court issued decisions limiting the power of the federal government and consequently opened the way for states to control a greater number of policy issues. In *United States* v. *Lopez* (1995), the Supreme Court struck down the Gun-Free School Zones Act of 1990, which made it a crime to possess a firearm near a school. The Court's majority concluded that congressional power to regulate interstate commerce did not include the authority to create this particular law. The Court made a similar decision in striking down portions of the Violence Against Women Act of 1994, in which Congress had permitted victims of sexual violence and gender-based attacks to file federal lawsuits against their attackers (*United States* v. *Morrison,* 2000).

"In what direction is federalism headed today?"

—Student Question

The Court also revived the Tenth Amendment, a provision of the Constitution that was generally treated as a powerless slogan by justices from the late 1930s through the mid-1990s. In *Printz* v. *United States* (1997), the Court declared that Congress cannot require state and local officials to conduct background checks on people who seek to buy firearms. The Court's decisions on the Tenth Amendment's protection of state authority and the limits of congressional power to regulate interstate commerce indicated that the Supreme Court would no longer automatically endorse assertions of federal power at the expense of state authority.

By the first years of the twenty-first century, however, the Court has not fundamentally changed the relationship between the federal government and the states. The federal government remains actively involved in a wide array of public policies, including many that do not seem intimately connected with the congressional power to regulate interstate commerce. However, recent decisions indicate that the Supreme Court stands ready to selectively reject specific assertions of federal power that it considers excessive under its new vision of the Constitution's framework for federalism.

PATHWAYS | of change from around the world

Do you think that countrywide youth movements are a thing of the past? Think again—they're alive and well in the former Soviet Union. In 2004, youth-led, pro-Western street protests (called the Orange Revolution) erupted in the Ukraine to protest corruption and electoral fraud surrounding the presidential election. In reaction to these protests, another group, the Nashi youth movement, was created in 2005. The Nashi quickly became very popular, with nearly 120,000 members in its peak in late 2007. Characterized as a highly patriotic, pro-democracy, and anti-Western group, the Nashi is staunchly supportive of former President Vladimir Putin and his United Russia political party. In fact, many have labeled the Nashi as Putin's foot soldiers, because they have the strong backing and financial support of the Kremlin. According to their official stance, they are pro-democracy but believe that a strong president is needed to counter the negative effects of the West. Through their activities, including pickets, protests, and marches, they see themselves as freedom fighters advancing the goals of the Russian society. Not all agree with this characterization, however. In fact, many believe the group is racist and xenophobic and equate it to Hitler Youth. Such comparisons may not be fair but largely stem from the militaristic training that the youth receive in their annual camp, attended by 10,000 participants. With the success of the Putin's United Russia political party in the 2007 parliamentary elections of Putin's hand-picked replacement, Dmitry Medvedev, as president in 2008, many are unsure about the future of the Nashi. Some believe the Kremlin used them as a tool to influence the elections, so they are no longer needed. Others believe the movement will continue to grow and attract more anti-Western youth. Either way, the government of Russia is keenly interested in monitoring the country's youth, as this is the first generation to come to age in the post-Communist Era. ■

New Trends in Federalism

Practice Quiz

1. "New" federalism shifts more power and responsibility
   a. to the executive branch.
   b. to the legislative branch.
   c. back to the states.
   d. back to the federal agencies who started the programs.

2. Reducing the size of the federal bureaucracy while transferring the funds, responsibility, and power to the states is termed
   a. evolution. **b.** devolution.
   c. resolution. **d.** dissolution.

3. What is the best explanation for the difference between Dillon's rule and home rule?
   a. Dillon's rule asserts the national supremacy over the states, while home rule asserts the opposite.
   b. Dillon's rule grants to state governments significant influence over how cities operate, while home rule asserts that local government can do anything not prohibited by state law.
   c. Dillon's rule reflects a states' rights position consistent with current Republican Party ideals, while home rule reflects that position consistent with current Democratic Party ideals.
   d. a and c.

4. Although new federalism ideals remain popular, we have yet to see it reach fruition.
   a. true **b.** false

Answers: 1 c, 2 b, 3-b, 4-a

Discussion Questions

1. What are some of the pitfalls associated with a devolution strategy?
2. If home rule were to be adopted as normal practice, how might it challenge the universal protections of the Bill of Rights?

What **YOU** can do!

Search the Catalog of Federal Domestic Assistance (**http://12.46.245.173/cfda/cfda.html**) for announcements about grants available to state and local governments. Take note of the type of funding (e.g., formula, matching, etc.) and the criteria for judging applications. Does the grant announcement seem to favor a particular type of government (e.g., urban, suburban, etc.)?

SIMULATION You Are a Federal Judge

Conclusion

We have outlined some practical and theoretical reasons for a federal system—why a democracy such as ours might have layers of governmental authority. The foremost original explanation for federalism in the American setting was the need for compromise. Most Americans understood the necessity of a stronger national government given the failures of the Articles of Confederation, but many also worried about a distant, unresponsive, and potentially tyrannical national government. Why not look to one level of government to regulate commerce, conduct foreign policy, and safeguard national security while another level provided basic services and looked after law and order? Dual federalism seemed natural, even logical, during the early years of our republic. Yet determining precisely which layer of government is responsible for certain functions—and, when push comes to shove, which layer is superior—has never been simple. The struggle over appropriate governmental authority has been at the heart of many of the most trying events in our nation's history. One might even say that federalism has been at the core of nearly all critical periods in American history.

Given that there is no clear or universally agreed upon way to allocate responsibilities between layers of our government, the nature of federalism has been shaped by the individuals who happened to be in charge of government, either as elected officials or as judges, during critical periods of our history. In effect, the course of federalism can be like a pendulum that swings between different approaches to allocating national and state authority, depending on the problems faced by the nation and the viewpoints of the individuals in positions of political and judicial power. From FDR's New Deal until the 1980s, for example, the Democrats controlled the federal government most of the time, and with this control came an increase in the power and prerogatives of the national government. Democrats argued that a strong national government offers the best means of helping citizens reach their potential and ridding society of its ills. Their approach called for merging each layer of government into unified action to attack these problems. The use of categorical grants under Lyndon Johnson's Great Society program is a clear example of how officials in Washington have used federal monies to advance their priorities at the state and local levels. The election of Ronald Reagan in 1980 and of a Republican Congress in 1994 produced a shift to less federal intervention—and hence less federal money—at the state level. George W. Bush's recent budget proposals clearly reflect a more constrained view of the federal government's role in many domestic policy areas.

Make no mistake, state and local governments will remain vital in the United States no matter which party controls Congress, the White House, or the federal judiciary. But exactly how much federal help (or interference) states and communities will receive is an open question. One thing is certain: Anyone who is interested in playing a role in politics, in shifting policy to confront areas of concern, should pay close attention to the federalism debate. The pathways of change are not simply about pushing government in a certain direction but rather about pushing the *correct level* of government in a new direction.

Key Objective Review, Apply, and Explore

Dividing Governmental Authority

(Pages 72–75)

Unlike most democracies in the world, which have unitary systems of governance, the United States has a federal system. In this country, power and authority are divided among layers of government. There are many explanations—historical, theoretical, cultural, and pragmatic—for why the United States relies on a federal system. Probably the best explanation is that dividing power between the national government and the state governments was a compromise that kept the Constitutional Convention on track.

KEY TERMS

Unitary System 72
Federal System 73
Sovereignty 73

CRITICAL THINKING QUESTIONS

1. Do you think the people in the United States today would be better governed by a federal system (like we currently have), or would a unitary system be more efficient and appropriate? Why?
2. Do you believe that states are policy "laboratories" and as such are the source of innovation? Or do you think a good deal of resources would be wasted by duplication in the absence of coordination?

INTERNET RESOURCES

Center for the Study of Federalism at Temple University: **http://www.temple.edu/federalism**
The Federalist Society: **http://www.fed-soc.org/**

ADDITIONAL READING

Barbour, Christine, Gerald C. Wright; with Matthew J. Streb, Michael R. Wolf. *Keeping the Republic: Power and Citizenship in American Politics.* 3rd ed., Washington, DC: CQ Press, 2006.

Burgess, Michael. *Comparative Federalism: Theory and Practice.* New York: Routledge, 2006.

Rocher, Francois, and Miriam Catherine Smith. *New Trends in Canadian Federalism.* 2nd ed., Peterborough, Canada: Broadview Press, 2003.

The Evolution of Federalism in the United States

(pages 76–85)

During the early years of our republic, there was much confusion over the division of authority, and this controversy produced crucial Supreme Court cases, such as *McCulloch* v. *Maryland* (1819).

Until the Civil War, dual federalism existed, meaning that neither the state nor the federal government was superior, and each had specific duties and obligations. To a large extent, the Civil War was fought over the issue of supremacy—determining which level of government, state or national, should be supreme.

KEY TERMS

***McCulloch* v. *Maryland* 76**
Necessary and Proper Clause 77
Dual Federalism 77
Doctrine of Nullification 78
Doctrine of Secession 78
Monopolies 80
New Deal 82
Court-Packing Plan 82

CRITICAL THINKING QUESTIONS

1. How did the Civil War change our views of federalism? Which issue—federalism or slavery—do you think was more important in causing the war? Why?
2. How did the Great Depression alter the way in which we expect the federal government to act? Do you think we look too much to the federal government to address societal needs? Should the states and localities be held to higher standards for their failure to problem solve?

INTERNET RESOURCES

The Council of State Governments: **http://www.csg.org/**
The history of U.S. federalism: **http://www.cas.sc.edu/poli/courses/scgov/History_of_Federalism.htm**

ADDITIONAL READING

May, Christopher N., and Allan Ides. *Constitutional Law: National Power and Federalism.* 3rd ed., Gaithersburg, MD: Aspen Publishers, 2006.

Norman, Wayne. *Negotiating Nationalism: Nation-Building, Federalism and Secession in the Multinational State.* Oxford: Oxford University Press, 2006.

Key Objective Review, Apply, and Explore

Past Trends in Federalism

(pages 86–89)

The nature of federalism in the United States changed irrevocably during the Great Depression as Franklin Roosevelt's New Deal thrust the federal government into nearly every realm of domestic governance.

Different ways of providing state and local governments with federal money have shaped the federalism debate since the New Deal.

KEY TERMS

Cooperative Federalism 86
Grants-in-Aid 88
Categorical Grants 88
Formula Grants 88
Project Grants 88
Block Grants 88

CRITICAL THINKING QUESTIONS

1. Do you think that the way in which the federal government uses grant money has a corrupting effect on the relationship between federal, state and local officials?
2. Do you think that the federal government should be able to bypass state officials and deal directly with local governments and private organizations to increase their ability to shape policy making in localities? Why?

INTERNET RESOURCES

National Governors Association: **http://www.nga.org**
United States Conference of Mayors: **http://www.usmayors.org**

ADDITIONAL READING

Nagel, Robert F. *The Implosion of American Federalism*. New York: Oxford University Press, 2001.

Rodden, Jonathan A. *Hamilton's Paradox: The Promise and Peril of Fiscal Federalism*. Cambridge: Cambridge University Press, 2005.

Recent Trends in Federalism

(pages 90–93)

Although it seems that there are fewer and fewer policy areas where the reach of the national government does not extend, a growing concern, especially among conservative politicians, has been to revive local governing authority. *Devolution* is the term used to describe the return of authority from the federal to the state level.

Rather than conceptualize federalism as a static condition, this chapter suggests a "pendulum model," where power and authority continually shift, reflecting the perspective of the people in power, the social and economic conditions, and the outlook of the courts.

KEY TERMS

Dillon's Rule 90
Home Rule 91
Special Governments 91
Devolution 91

CRITICAL THINKING QUESTIONS

1. What aspects of recent trends in federalism do you think are positive? Negative? Overall, do you think the changes are a healthy or harmful evolution of federalism?
2. Do you agree with the recent trend of the Supreme Court to limit some of the authority of the federal government? Why?

INTERNET RESOURCES

The Office of Management and Budget: **http://www.whitehouse.gov/omb/**
The Federalism Project: **http://www.federalismproject.org/**

ADDITIONAL READING

O'Connor, James. *The Fiscal Crisis of the State*. New Brunswick, NJ: Transaction, 2002.

Osborne, David, and Peter Hutchinson. *The Price of Government*. New York: Basic Books, 2004.

Scheberle, Denise. *Federalism and Environmental Policy: Trust and the Politics of Implementation*. 2nd rev. ed., Washington, D.C.: Georgetown University Press, 2004.

Chapter Review Critical Thinking Test

1. In regard to federalism, what is meant by the layers of government?
   a. the legislative, executive, and judicial branches of federal government
   b. federal government officials and all those who work for them
   c. the federal, state, and local governments
   d. the different federal systems that have succeeded each other over time

2. Federalism was developed in response to which of the following factors?
   a. the fusing of independent states
   b. the geographic, cultural, and economic diversity of the nation
   c. significant powers being granted (reserved) to each separate state
   d. a, b, and c.

3. "Laboratories of democracy" refers to
   a. the countries in which different types of democratic government have been introduced.
   b. the innovation of policy by allowing states to tackle social challenges individually.
   c. town hall meetings, which allow for citizen participation.
   d. formative discussions about government structure among the framers of the Constitution.

4. The federal structure of the United States of America is unique among the nations of the world.
   a. true **b.** false

5. The Articles of Confederation reflected widespread agreement on individual state sovereignty.
   a. true **b.** false

6. The Supreme Court case *McCulloch v. Maryland*
   a. made ample use of the Bill of Rights.
   b. found it "necessary and proper" that the state tax all banks within its boundaries, even a branch of the Second Bank of the United States.
   c. found that the federal government's power to charter a national bank was consistent with the "necessary and proper" clause in the Constitution.
   d. a and c.

7. Dual federalism
   a. was a theory of federal–state relations promoted during the 1950s.
   b. asserted that state and federal governments had separate responsibilities; the federal government was not superior to state governments.
   c. asserted that the federal government had responsibility for both national concerns and interstate concerns.
   d. a and c.

8. What is significant about the southern tradition of referring to the Civil War as "The War Between the States"?
   a. The "states' rights" point of view endures in that region.
   b. Southern resistance to the notion that the Civil War was fought primarily over the issue of slavery continues.
   c. The southern conception of federalism was at odds with President Lincoln's.
   d. a, b, and c.

9. To this day, the "states' rights" doctrine is still touted by many politicians, at the national as well as state level.
   a. true **b.** false

10. What statement best summarizes the shared intent of the Thirteenth, Fourteenth, and Fifteenth Amendments?
   a. All forms of racism are contrary to the goals of American democracy.
   b. No state has the authority to deny full citizenship rights to any citizen, even African Americans.
   c. Dual federalism shall apply to all states.
   d. a, b, and c.

11. From the time of their inception, how long did it take for the Fourteenth and Fifteen Amendments to have a genuine and positive affect on the lives of African Americans?
   a. 10 years **b.** 30 years
   c. 50 years **d.** 90 years

12. The Sherman Antitrust Act of 1890
   a. represented a backward step in the expansion of federal authority.
   b. represented a forward step in the expansion of federal authority.
   c. Is an early example of Congress enacting a law that addressed a national problem (corporate monopolies).
   d. b and c.

13. Congressional legislation around the turn of the century was successful in preventing the abuses of corporate power.
   a. true **b.** false

14. Judicial decisions in the late nineteenth century tended to slow the expansion of federal authority.
   a. true **b.** false

15. Following President Franklin D. Roosevelt's appointment of several new justices to the Supreme Court, the Court's decisions
   a. tended to preserve states' rights when they conflicted with federal authority.
   b. upheld the constitutionality of most New Deal legislation.
   c. constituted a reliable check against the president's executive powers.
   d. a and c.

Chapter Review Critical Thinking Test

16. What specific Constitutional authority enhanced the ability of Congress to pass civil rights legislation in the 1960s?
- **a.** the First Amendment
- **b.** the Tenth Amendment
- **c.** the provision to regulate interstate commerce
- **d.** Article IV

17. How does the issue of federal funding impact federalism in modern America?
- **a.** Federal funding may act as another form of interstate commerce.
- **b.** Federal funding may act as a regulatory mechanism at the state and local levels.
- **c.** The federal government simply has more funds available than the states.
- **d.** a, b, and c.

18. "Home rule" refers to the theory that
- **a.** city governments may do anything to serve their residents that is not specifically prohibited by state law.
- **b.** individual private property rights are more significant than the government's right of eminent domain.
- **c.** the rights of parents to administer discipline in their own residence is superior to the government's right to impose its own legal prerogatives.
- **d.** b and c.

19. President Lyndon Johnson's "Great Society" initiatives
- **a.** allocated federal funds to state and local governments to eradicate poverty and racial discrimination.
- **b.** advanced the agenda of southern "Dixiecrats" in Congress.
- **c.** are useful examples of devolution.
- **d.** a and c.

20. Welfare reform in the 1990s demonstrated
- **a.** our nation's preference to have social programs administered by the states.
- **b.** the validity of the "laboratories of democracy" concept.
- **c.** our nation's decreasing support for President Johnson's "War on Poverty."
- **d.** a, b, and c.

Answers: 1-c, 2-d, 3-b, 4-b, 5-b, 6-c, 7-b, 8-d, 9-a, 10-b, 11-d, 12-d, 13-b, 14-a, 15-b, 16-c, 17-b, 18-a, 19-a, 20-d.

You decide!

Many Americans grumble at the "red tape" and inefficiency of government, but they do not realize just how complex policymaking and policy implementation can be in a federal system. Conduct interviews of local public administrators who are responsible for intergovernmental policy implementation. A good place to start might be your local school district (for example, school principals and teachers), hospital (for example, Medicaid administrators), or fire department (for example, emergency first responders). Ask questions about the nature of the relationships among national, state, and local government agencies, and pay special attention to how local service providers are impacted by federal regulations, mandates, budgeting, and so on.

Key Objective Outline

How are American court systems organized?

- Court Structure and Processes **(page 102)**

What makes American judges more powerful than those in other countries?

- The Power of American Judges **(page 108)**

What political processes determine the selection of judges?

- Judicial Selection **(page 114)**

What do we know about how Supreme Court justices really make decisions?

- Judges' Decision-Making **(page 118)**

CHAPTER 4
THE JUDICIARY

How much power should judges have?

When Lindsay Earls first heard the announcement from her high school choir teacher, she thought it was a joke. The local school board in Tecumseh, Oklahoma, had adopted a new policy requiring students to submit to random drug tests in order to participate in after-school clubs. Sixteen-year-old Lindsay, a high-achieving honor student who later attended an Ivy League university, was bothered by the thought of being escorted to a restroom and required to urinate in a cup while a teacher listened. She believed that it was wrong to force students to submit to such an embarrassing act when they had done nothing to raise suspicions about drug use. How would this make you feel?[1]

With help from the American Civil Liberties Union (ACLU), an interest group that uses the courts to protect constitutional rights, Lindsay filed a lawsuit. Despite harsh criticism from many in her small town who believed random tests were necessary to stop drug abuse, Lindsay and her ACLU attorney carried the case through each level of the federal court system until it was heard by the U.S. Supreme Court. Lindsay felt strongly that her school's drug test policy violated her Fourth Amendment right against "unreasonable searches."

The Supreme Court announced its decision in *Board of Education* v. *Earls* on June 27, 2002. By a narrow 5–4 vote, the justices approved the school's drug testing policy. Lindsay lost the case. But the justices left open the question of whether a school could impose drug testing on all students.[2] Similar questions also remain open with respect to college students: Could a college require drug testing as a condition for living in a dorm? Could it require drug testing as a condition for admission and continued enrollment? If such policies emerge, they may be challenged in court by other students who, like Lindsay Earls, feel strongly enough about a matter of constitutional principle to pursue a lengthy lawsuit despite facing public criticism. >> See related **Policy-Shaping Litigation** Figure 4.4 on page 123.

STUDENT RESOURCE-CENTER
• Glossary
• Vocabulary Example
• LINK
• MyPoliSciLab Connection

■ **Adversarial System:** Legal system used by the United States and other countries in which a judge plays a relatively passive role as attorneys battle to protect each side's interests.

EXAMPLE: *When pop star Michael Jackson stood trial on child sex abuse charges in 2005, Jackson's attorneys illustrated the operation of the adversarial system by successfully countering the prosecutor's arguments and persuading the jury to issue a "not guilty" verdict.*

■ **Dual Court System:** Separate systems of state and federal courts throughout the United States, each with responsibilities for its own laws and constitutions.

EXAMPLE: *In 2001, the Georgia Supreme Court used its independent power under the dual court system to rule that use of the electric chair for capital punishment violated the state's constitution.*

Court Structure *and* Processes (pages 102–107)

How are American court systems organized?

The judicial branch is made up of courts that have different responsibilities. As you consider the elements of the judicial branch, remember that there are two types of courts—trial and appellate—and that both types of courts operate in two parallel court systems—state and federal. If you watch television shows such as *Boston Legal* and *Law & Order,* you can become familiar with trial court processes. Such shows emphasize American courts' use of the **adversarial system**■, in which opposing attorneys zealously represent the interest of their clients. By contrast, many other countries use the **inquisitorial system,** in which judges take an active role in investigating cases and questioning witnesses. However, dramatic depictions in television and movies typically show only one type of proceeding (trials) in one type of court (trial courts). They do not adequately convey the idea that most cases in trial courts end in plea bargains or negotiated settlements rather than in trials. Television portrayals also won't educate you about the U.S. Supreme Court and other appellate courts that consider whether errors occurred when a case was decided by a judge or jury in a trial court.

"Why are there two court systems?"

—Student Question

Trial Courts

The United States has a **dual court system**■. In other words, two court systems, state and federal, exist and operate at the same time in the same geographic areas (see Table 4.1 on page 104). Sometimes a state court and a federal court are right next door to each other in a downtown district. In small cities and towns, a courthouse may be run by a single judge. In larger cities, a dozen or more judges may hear cases separately in their own courtrooms within a single courthouse. Both court systems handle **criminal prosecutions,** which involve accusations that one or more individuals violated criminal statutes and therefore should be punished. In addition, in both systems, **civil lawsuits** are presented, in which people or corporations seek compensation from those whom they accuse of violating contracts or causing personal injuries or property damage. Civil lawsuits can also seek orders from judges requiring the government, corporations, or individuals to take specific actions or refrain from behavior that violates the law.

The existence of two court systems within each state reflects American federalism, under which state governments and the federal government both exercise authority over law and public policy. States are free to design their own court systems and to name the different courts within the state. Thus, in some states, trial courts are called "superior courts," while in others, they are known as "district courts," "circuit courts," or "courts of common pleas."

Federal trial courts are called "U.S. district courts." The country is divided into 94 districts. Each state has at least one district court, and larger states have multiple districts. Within each district, there may be multiple judges and courthouses. For example, Wisconsin is divided into the Eastern District of Wisconsin, with courthouses at Milwaukee and Green Bay, and the Western District of Wisconsin, with its courthouse located in Madison. These courts handle cases concerning federal law, such as those based on the U.S. Constitution and statutes enacted by Congress, as well as certain lawsuits between citizens of different states.

Trial courts use specific rules and processes to reach decisions. These courts fit the image of courts portrayed on television, with lawyers presenting arguments to a group of citizen jurors in a **jury trial.** In such a trial, the judge acts as a "referee," who makes sure proper rules are followed and the jurors understand the rules of law that will guide their decision. Some cases use bench trials, in which a single judge rather than a jury is the decision maker. Trial courts are courts of **original jurisdiction,** meaning they receive cases first, consider the available evidence, and make the initial decision. By contrast, appellate courts have **appellate jurisdiction,** meaning they review specific errors that allegedly occurred in trial court processes or in decisions of appellate courts beneath them in the judicial hierarchy. The U.S. Supreme Court is an unusual appellate court in that it also has original jurisdiction in limited categories of cases defined in Article III of the U.S. Constitution, usually lawsuits between the governments of two states.

Although the trial is the final possible stage for these lower-level courts, most cases do not get that far. Trial courts actually process most cases through negotiated resolutions, called **settlements** in civil cases and **plea bargains** in criminal cases. Negotiated resolutions in civil

The trial of Saddam Hussein in Iraq for crimes committed against the people of his country included many features that are familiar in American trials, including arguments by attorneys and rulings by a judge. There were also differences in the Iraqi trial, such as the absence of a jury. ***—Why is so much time and money spent on a lengthy trial when everyone agrees that an individual has committed horrible acts?***

COMPARATIVE **Comparing Judicial Systems**

and criminal cases save time and money for lawyers and courts. They also benefit the individuals involved, because they provide an agreed outcome and, in criminal cases, a less-than-maximum sentence.

Appellate Courts

Most states, as well as the federal court system, have **intermediate appellate courts.** These courts, which are typically called "courts of appeals," hear appeals from judicial decisions and jury verdicts in the trial courts. In the federal system, the U.S. courts of appeals are divided into 11 numbered circuits, and there is also the District of Columbia circuit and a specialized federal circuit for patent and trade cases. The numbered circuits each handle the appeals from districts in specific states (see Figure 4.1). For example, the U.S. Court of Appeals for the Fifth Circuit handles appeals from U.S. district courts in Texas, Louisiana, and Mississippi.[3]

The highest appellate courts in the state and federal systems are **courts of last resort.** In the federal system, the U.S. Supreme Court is the court of last resort. It can also be the court of last resort when issues of federal law, such as questions about civil liberties under the Bill of Rights, arise in cases decided by state supreme

FIGURE 4.1 | **Geographic Jurisdiction of Federal Courts**

The U.S. Courts of Appeals are divided into regional circuits throughout the country. Each numbered circuit handles appeals from federal cases in a specific set of states. ***—In which circuit do you live?***

SOURCE: www.uscourts.gov/courtlinks.cfm

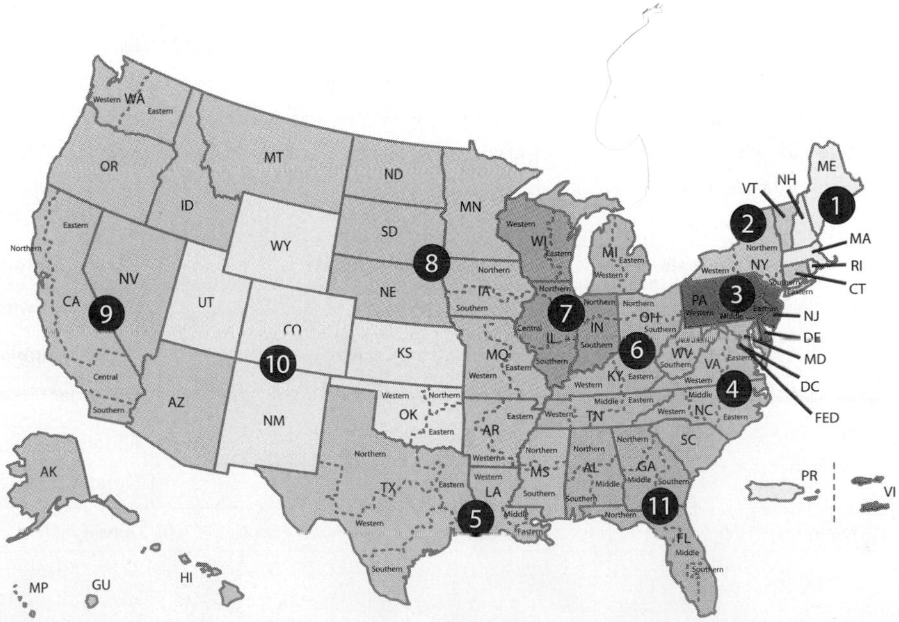

TABLE 4.1a | Structure of American Court System

FEDERAL COURT SYSTEM		STATE COURT SYSTEM
U.S. Supreme Court		**52 State Supreme Courts***
Original jurisdiction in only limited categories of cases that rarely arise: lawsuits between two states and cases involving foreign ambassadors. Appellate jurisdiction in almost all cases that it decides that arrive from U.S. courts of appeals or state supreme courts or Court of Military Appeals.	***courts of last resort***	Appellate jurisdiction for cases concerning state law brought up through their state court systems. There are more than 50 state supreme courts because two states—Texas and Oklahoma—have separate highest courts for civil and criminal cases.
13 U.S. Courts of Appeals		**40 State Courts of Appeals***
No original jurisdiction because no cases are first filed in these courts. These courts handle appeals from cases that were first decided in the U.S. district courts or matters decided by government regulatory commissions.	***intermediate appellate courts***	Appellate jurisdiction over cases from state trial courts. No original jurisdiction. 10 states do not have intermediate appellate courts. Appeals in those states go straight from the trial court to the state supreme court.
94 U.S. District Courts		**State Trial Courts (50 states)**
Original jurisdiction in cases involving: federal criminal and civil law; the federal government; and lawsuits between citizens of different states for amounts over $75,000; bankruptcy; and admiralty (shipping at sea).	***trial courts of general jurisdiction***	Usually called superior courts, district courts, circuit courts, or courts of common pleas. These courts have original jurisdiction and therefore are the first courts to hear cases concerning state law issues for felonies and other serious matters.
(no federal limited jurisdiction trial court)		**Lower-level State Trial Courts**
Federal cases begin in the U.S. district courts.	***trial courts of limited jurisdiction***	Original jurisdiction for minor criminal and civil cases.

TABLE 4.1b | Paths to the U.S. Supreme Court for Criminal and Civil Cases in State and Federal Court Systems

FEDERAL CRIMINAL CASE	FEDERAL CIVIL CASE	STATE CRIMINAL CASE	STATE CIVIL CASE
U.S. Supreme Court	**U.S. Supreme Court**	**U.S. Supreme Court**	**U.S. Supreme Court**
U.S. v. *Gonzalez-Lopez* (2006) Decision: 6th Amendment violation when defendant not allowed to hire attorney of his choice (defendant wins)	*Burlington Northern* v. *White* (2006) Decision: Job reassignment can be improper retaliation under federal employment law (claimant wins)	*Illinois* v. *Cabelles* (2005) Decision: Use of drug-sniffing dog was not an unreasonable search and seizure (defendant loses)	*Kelo* v. *New London* (2005) Decision: No constitutional violation when city used its power to force homeowners to sell home so that a private developer could use the property (claimant loses)
U.S. Court of Appeals	**U.S. Court of Appeals**	**Illinois Supreme Court**	**Connecticut Supreme Court**
Defendant wins	Claimant wins	Defendant wins	Claimant loses
U.S. District Court	**U.S. District Court**	**Illinois Appellate Court**	**Connecticut Superior Court**
Defendant loses	Claimant wins	Defendant loses	Claimant wins
		Illinois Circuit Court	
		Defendant loses	

*A few states use different names for their courts of last resort (e.g., Court of Appeals [NY, MD], Supreme Judicial Court [ME, MA]).

Majority Opinion: Appellate court opinion that explains the reasons for the case outcome as determined by a majority of judges.	**EXAMPLE:** *On behalf of five of the nine justices, Justice Clarence Thomas's majority opinion in Lindsay Earls's case established the new legal rule that public schools can require random drug testing as a condition of participation in all extracurricular activities (*Board of Education *v.* Earls, *2002).*
Dissenting Opinion: Appellate court opinion explaining the views of one or more judges who disagree with the outcome of the case as decided by the majority of judges.	**EXAMPLE:** *Justice Ruth Bader Ginsburg wrote a dissenting opinion that explained her disagreement with the majority opinion and asserted that Lindsay Earls's Fourth Amendment rights were violated by the school's random drug testing policy.*

courts. State supreme courts are courts of last resort for disputes about the meaning of laws created by a state legislature or about provisions of a state constitution.

Appellate courts use different processes than trial courts do. Appeals are heard in multijudge courts. Typically, three judges hear cases in a state or federal intermediate appellate court. State supreme courts generally have five or seven members, while the U.S. Supreme Court is made up of nine justices. There are never juries in appellate courts. These courts do not make decisions about criminal guilt or issue verdicts in civil cases. Instead, they consider narrow issues concerning alleged errors in the investigation and trial process that were not corrected by the trial judge. Instead of listening to witnesses or examining other evidence, appellate courts consider only elaborate written arguments, called **appellate briefs,** submitted by each side's attorneys, as well as oral arguments.

Appellate judges issue detailed written opinions to explain their decisions. The outcome of the case and any announcement of a legal rule are expressed in the **majority opinion**. This opinion represents the views of the majority of judges who heard the case. **Concurring opinions** are written by judges who agree with the outcome favored by the majority but wish to present their own reasons for agreeing with the decision. Appellate decisions are not always unanimous, so judges who disagree with the outcome may write **dissenting opinions** to express their points of disagreement with the views expressed in the majority opinion.[4] Sometimes concurring and dissenting opinions develop ideas that will take hold in later generations and help shape law after new judges are selected for service on appellate courts.

The U.S. Supreme Court

At the top of the American judicial system stands the U.S. Supreme Court. The U.S. Supreme Court has authority over federal court cases and any decision by a state court (including those of a state supreme court) that concerns the U.S. Constitution or federal law. In particular, the U.S. Supreme Court is regularly called on to decide whether state statutes violate the U.S. Constitution or whether decisions and actions by state and local officials collide with federal constitutional principles. The U.S. Supreme Court's decisions shape law and public policy for the entire country. Policy advocates often seek favorable decisions from the Court when they have been unsuccessful in persuading other branches of government to advance their goals. Table 4.2 on pages 106–107 gives the names and backgrounds of the current justices of the Court.

Each case goes through several specific stages in the Supreme Court's decision-making process:

- The justices choose 70 to 80 cases to hear from among more than 8,000 petitions submitted annually.
- Attorneys in the chosen cases submit detailed written arguments, called *appellate briefs,* for the justices to study before the case is argued.
- At oral arguments, each side's attorney can speak for only 30 minutes, and the justices often ask many questions.
- After oral arguments, the nine justices meet privately to discuss and vote on each case. The side that gains the support of five or more justices wins.
- The justices prepare and announce the majority opinion that decides the case as well as additional viewpoints expressed in concurring and dissenting opinions.

Nearly all cases are presented to the Court through a petition for a **writ of certiorari,** a traditional legal order that commands a lower court to send a case forward. Cases are selected for hearing through the Court's "rule of four," meaning that four justices must vote to hear a specific case in order for it to be scheduled for oral arguments.

Thousands of people and corporations ask the Court to hear their cases each year, but very few are accepted for hearing. During the Court's 2006–2007 term, it received 8,857 petitions but granted oral arguments for only 78 of these. However, because some of these cases were later combined or sent back to the lower courts, it produced only 67 full opinions.

The attorneys must be good at thinking quickly on their feet in order to respond, because the justices interrupt and ask questions. The justices also sometimes exchange argumentative comments with each other during oral arguments.

After oral arguments, the justices meet in their weekly conference to present their views on the case to each other. When all the justices have stated a position, the chief justice announces the preliminary vote based on the viewpoints expressed. If the chief justice is in the majority, he designates which justice will write the majority opinion for the Court. If the chief justice is in the minority, then the senior justice in the majority assigns the opinion for the Court. Other justices can decide for themselves whether to write a concurring or dissenting opinion. With the assistance of their law clerks, justices draft preliminary opinions as well as comments on other justices' draft opinions. These draft opinions and comments

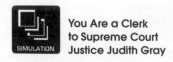

SIMULATION You Are a Clerk to Supreme Court Justice Judith Gray

TABLE 4.2 | Supreme Court Justices

The rate of support for constitutional rights claims is typically used to classify justices as "liberal" (frequent support) or "conservative" (infrequent support).

Name	**John Paul Stevens**	**Ruth Bader Ginsburg**	**David Hackett Souter**	**Stephen G. Breyer**
Support for Constitutional Rights Claims, 2006–2007	65%	65%	57%	52%
Nominated By	Gerald Ford	Bill Clinton	George H. W. Bush	Bill Clinton
Date Confirmed	December 19, 1975	August 10, 1993	October 9, 1990	August 3, 1994
Confirmation Vote Numbers	98–0	96–3	90–9	87–9
Previous Experience	Federal Judge, Private Attorney	Federal Judge, Law Professor	Federal Judge, State Judge	Federal Judge, Law Professor

are circulated to all the justices. They help shape the ultimate reasoning of the final opinions issued in the case and can sometimes persuade wavering justices to change sides.

When the decision of the Court is publicly announced and the opinions for that case are published, the decision becomes final. The legal rule announced in the decision, however, is not necessarily permanent, because the justices can later change their views. If at least five justices agree that the prior decision was wrongly decided, they can use a new case to overrule the Court's earlier opinion and establish a new rule of law on the subject in question. Presidents often focus on this goal when they select new appointees for the Supreme Court, with the hope that the new justices will vote to overrule decisions with which the president disagrees.

PATHWAYS | profile

Ruth Bader Ginsburg

Ruth Bader Ginsburg, the second woman to serve on the U.S. Supreme Court (Sandra Day O'Connor was the first), was born in 1933, graduated from Columbia University's law school, and went on to become a law professor at Rutgers University and Columbia University. Throughout the 1970s, she directed the Women's Rights Project at the American Civil Liberties Union (ACLU). In that capacity, she presented arguments before the Supreme Court in the gender discrimination cases that first successfully turned the high Court's attention to such issues. These cases were not just about discrimination against women. She also presented arguments on behalf of men, such as a case challenging Oklahoma's authority to set a higher minimum drinking age for men than for women (*Craig* v. *Boren*, 1976). In 1980, Ginsburg was appointed by President Jimmy Carter to serve on the U.S. Court of Appeals for the District of Columbia Circuit. President Bill Clinton appointed her to serve as an associate justice on the U.S. Supreme Court in 1993.

During her years as a lawyer, Ginsburg earned a reputation as a strong advocate for equal rights. As a judge, however, she claimed that her job was very different. Rather than advocate for a particular vision of law and policy, she saw herself as carefully interpreting and applying the Constitution and federal statutes. Because her performance on the U.S. Court of Appeals showed her to be a thoughtful judge, the Senate easily confirmed her appointment by a 96–3 vote. As a Supreme Court justice, Ginsburg has supported individuals' claims concerning violations of constitutional rights more frequently than most of her colleagues. ■

Anthony M. Kennedy	**Antonin Scalia**	**John G. Roberts, Jr.**	**Clarence Thomas**	**Samuel Anthony Alito, Jr.**
26%	22%	17%	17%	3%
Ronald Reagan	Ronald Reagan	George W. Bush	George H. W. Bush	George W. Bush
February 18, 1988	September 26, 1986	September 29, 2005	October 23, 1991	January 31, 2005
97–0	98–0	78–22	52–48	58–42
Federal Judge, Law Professor	Federal Judge, Law Professor	Federal Judge, Government Lawyer	Federal Judge, Government Adminstrator	Federal Judge, Government Lawyer

Court Structure and Processes

Practice Quiz

1. Legal processes in which the government seeks to prove that an individual is guilty of a crime and deserving of punishment are called
   a. civil lawsuits. **b.** appellate arguments.
   c. criminal prosecutions. **d.** plea bargains.
2. How are most cases in lower-level courts resolved?
   a. jury or bench trial
   b. settlement or plea bargain
   c. criminal prosecution
   d. referral to a higher court
3. The final outcome and explanation for the decision in an appellate court case is expressed by the judges in a written rationale known as
   a. a majority opinion. **b.** a concurring opinion.
   c. a dissenting opinion. **d.** a case brief.
4. Appellate courts do not examine evidence or hear testimony from witnesses. They determine the outcome based solely on written appellate briefs and lawyers' oral arguments.
   a. true **b.** false

Answers: 1-c, 2-b, 3-a, 4-a.

Discussion Questions

1. Does the adversarial system lead courts to discover the truth, or does the system simply produce victory for whichever side has the best attorney?
2. Does a court system really need appellate courts? Why not just treat the original decision in each case as the final decision?

What **YOU** can do!

Observe a trial or hearing in process at your local courthouse. Also check to see if your community uses specialized courts, such as drug courts or DUI courts, to deal specially with recidivism and substance abuse. Note how what you observe differs from "television court," such as *Law & Order* or *Judge Judy*.

■ **Case Precedent:** A legal rule established by a judicial decision that guides subsequent decisions. The use of case precedent is drawn from the common law system brought from Great Britain to the United States.

EXAMPLE: *In Lindsay Earls's case, the majority opinion relied on the case precedent established in a prior decision,* Vernonia School District v. Acton *(1995), in which a narrow majority of justices approved random drug tests for students who played on school sports teams.*

COMPARATIVE **Comparing Judiciaries**

The Power *of* American Judges (pages 108–113)

What makes American judges more powerful than those in other countries?

The eighteenth-century authors of the U.S. Constitution did not expect the judicial branch to be as powerful as the executive and legislative branches. Although some of the framers wanted to permit judges to evaluate the constitutionality of statutes, they did not generally believe that the courts would be influential policymaking institutions. In *Federalist No. 78,* Alexander Hamilton called the judiciary the "least dangerous" branch of government, because it lacked the power of "purse or sword" that the other branches could use to shape policy and spur people to follow their decisions. Congress could use its "power of the purse" to levy taxes or provide government funds in order to encourage or induce people to comply with government policies. The president, as the nation's commander in chief, could use the "sword" of military action to force people to obey laws. But judges produced only words written on paper and thus appeared to lack the power to enforce their decisions.

Hamilton was not wrong to highlight the inherent weakness of the judiciary's structure and authority. He merely failed to foresee how the Supreme Court and other courts would assert their power and gain acceptance as legitimate policymaking institutions.

To maintain the public's confidence in their fairness, courts portray themselves as the "nonpolitical" institutions of American government. Judges wear black robes and sit on benches elevated above other seats in the courtroom. People are required to rise when judges enter the courtroom and remain standing until given permission to sit down. Such requirements reinforce the status of judges and convey a message that other citizens are subordinate to judicial officers. Many courts operate in majestic buildings with marble columns, purple velvet curtains, fancy woodwork, and other physical embellishments designed to elicit respect for the importance and seriousness of these institutions.

The physical imagery of courts, as well as the dress and language associated with judges, helps convey the message that the judicial branch is different from the other branches of government. In the executive and legislative branches, political battles are open and obvious. Democrats and Republicans criticize one another and portray their opponents' policies as harmful to the nation's best interests.

It is assumed that judges make decisions by following established legal rules—and often this is true. Lower-court judges follow **case precedents**■, which are guiding decisions that higher courts

Alexander Hamilton believed that the judiciary would be the least powerful branch of American government under the U.S. Constitution. ***—Although the judiciary became more powerful than Hamilton predicted, is it more or less powerful than the other branches of government?***

have made in similar cases. By using a system based on *stare decisis*, a Latin term meaning "to stand by prior decisions," judges in the United States convey the impression that they merely follow the law as established by prior judicial decisions and do not rely on their own values. Judges' efforts to portray a nonpolitical image do not, in fact, mean that politics has no role in judicial decision-making. To begin with, political battles determine who will be selected to serve as judges, and judges' personal political values and beliefs can affect their decisions. In addition, the process of interpreting the Constitution and statutes gives judges opportunities to steer many decisions toward their own policy preferences.

There are structural elements and traditions in the American judicial system that make judges in the United States more powerful than their counterparts in many other countries. Let's examine several of these factors. In particular, we will see the importance, first, of judges' authority over constitutional and statutory interpretation;

Statutes: Laws written by state legislatures and by Congress.

EXAMPLE: *The No Child Left Behind Act of 2002 was a statute enacted by Congress with the hope that students' academic performance would improve as a result of the law's requirements for testing schoolchildren.*

Judicial Review: The power of American judges to nullify decisions and actions by other branches of goverment if the judges decide those actions violate the U.S. Constitution or the relevant state constitution.

EXAMPLE: *In 2007, the U.S. Supreme Court used the power of judicial review by declaring aspects of the Bipartisan Campaign Reform Act of 2002 to be unconstitutional for seeking to limit corporations' and other organizations' freedom to broadcast advocacy commercials just prior to elections.*

second, of judicial review; and third, in the federal court system, of judges' protected tenure in office.

Constitutional and Statutory Interpretation

In the United States, although participants in constitutional conventions write constitutions and elected legislators draft statutes, these forms of law still require judges to interpret them. Inevitably, the wording of constitutions and statutes contains ambiguities. Whenever there are disputes about the meaning of the words and phrases in constitutions and statutes, those disputes come to courts in the form of lawsuits, and judges are asked to provide interpretations that will settle those disputes. Therefore judges can provide meaning for law produced by other governmental institutions as well as for case law developed by judges.

For example, the Eighth Amendment to the U.S. Constitution forbids the government to impose "cruel and unusual punishments." Clearly, the provision intends to limit the nature of punishments applied to people who violate criminal laws. The words themselves, however, provide no specific guidance about what kinds of punishments are not allowed. Thus judges have been asked to decide which punishments are "cruel and unusual." Are these words violated when prison officials decline to provide medical care to prisoners? How about when a principal paddles a misbehaving student at a public high school? These are the kinds of cases that confront judges.

Statutes provide similar opportunities for judges to shape the law. Statutes are laws written by elected representatives in legislatures. Statutes for the entire country are produced by Congress, the national legislature. Each state has its own legislature to write laws that apply only within its borders. Judges, when they interpret statutes, are supposed to advance the underlying purposes of the legislature that made the statutes—but those purposes are not always clear. For example, if workers' compensation statutes provide for payments to workers injured "in the course of employment," does that include coverage for a disability resulting from slipping on an icy sidewalk by the employer's business? Inevitably, judges must answer such questions, because legislatures cannot anticipate every possible situation in which issues about a statute's meaning might arise.

As you will see in the later discussion of methods for selecting judges, political battles in state judicial election campaigns and in the nomination processes for federal judges largely arise from the interpretive authority that American judges possess. Political parties, interest groups, and politicians seek to secure judgeships for people who share their values and who, they hope, will apply those values in judicial decision-making.

Judicial Review

One of the most significant powers of American judges is that of judicial review. **Judicial review** permits judges to invalidate actions by other governmental actors, including striking down statutes enacted by Congress, by declaring that those actions violate the Constitution. Judges can also invalidate actions by the president or other executive branch officials by declaring that those actions violate the Constitution (see Table 4.3). Very few countries permit their judges to wield such awesome power over other branches of government.[5] A leading constitutional law expert describes judicial review as "certainly the most controversial and at the same time the most fascinating role of the courts of the United States."[6]

Article III of the Constitution (reprinted in the Appendix) defines the authority of the judiciary, yet there is no mention of the judiciary's power of judicial review. The Constitution declares that there will be "one supreme Court" in Article III, Section 3, but leaves it to Congress to design and establish the other courts of the federal court system. The tenure of federal judges is described as service "during good Behaviour." To protect judges against political pressure, Article III, Section 1 declares that their salaries "shall not be diminished" during their service on the bench. Article III, Section 2 describes the kinds of cases that fall under the authority of federal courts, including cases concerning federal law, disputes between states, and matters involving foreign countries. Article III, Section 3 defines the crime of "treason" and specifies the evidence necessary for conviction. As indicated by this brief description, nothing in Article III directly addresses the power of judicial review.

The framers of the Constitution were aware of the concept of judicial review, yet they made no mention of it in the founding document. Did this mean that the idea had been considered and rejected by the framers? Apparently not—at least not in the eyes of everyone debating the drafting and ratification of the Constitution. In *Federalist No. 78,* Hamilton argued in favor of judicial review, asserting not only that legislative acts violating the Constitution must be invalid but also that federal judges must be the ones who decide whether statutes are unconstitutional. According to Hamilton, limitations on congressional actions "can be preserved in practice no other way than through the medium of the courts of justice, whose duty it must be to declare all acts contrary to the manifest tenor of the constitution void." Other founders, however, worried

■ ***Marbury* v. *Madison* (1803):** Case in which the U.S. Supreme Court asserted the power of judicial review despite the fact that this is not explicitly mentioned in the U.S. Constitution.

EXAMPLE: *Chief Justice John Marshall and other members of the U.S. Supreme Court first used judicial review in* Marbury *v.* Madison *(1803) by declaring that a portion of the Judiciary Act of 1789 was unconstitutional because Congress improperly expanded the kinds of cases that could be filed in the Court.*

TABLE 4.3 | Judicial Review Cases

CASE NAME	DATE	VOTE	AFFECTED INSTITUTION	OVERVIEW OF CASE
Granholm, Governor of Michigan v. *Heald*	May 16, 2005	5–4	State legislatures in Michigan and New York	State laws in Michigan and New York prohibited direct sales of wine to consumers by out-of-state wineries—thus preventing Internet sales and other orders. The U.S. Supreme Court struck down these state laws as violating the Commerce Clause of the U.S. Constitution.
United States v. *Booker*	January 12, 2005	5–4	Congress	Portion of the Sentencing Reform Act of 1984 that makes Federal Sentencing Guidelines mandatory in federal criminal cases found to be unconstitutional as a violation of the Sixth Amendment right to jury trial, because it permits judges to make factual determinations that should be the responsibility of the jury.
Hamdi v. *Rumsfeld*	June 28, 2004	8–1 on the issue in question	President	American citizens detained as terrorism suspects are entitled to appear in court and contest the basis for their detention. The U.S. Supreme Court rejected arguments about the president's power to hold suspects indefinitely without any rights, any contact with attorneys, or any access to the courts.
Ashcroft v. *Free Speech Coalition*	April 16, 2002	6–3	Congress	U.S. Supreme Court invalidated portions of the Child Pornography Prevention Act of 1996 as overly broad and in violation of the First Amendment. Congress cannot ban movies and pictures in which adults portray teenagers engaged in sexual activity.

that it would elevate the power of the judiciary above that of the other governmental branches.

At the beginning of the nineteenth century, the Supreme Court did not rely on any specific provision of the Constitution to justify its exercise of the power of judicial review. Instead, it simply asserted its authority to review the actions of other governmental branches in the case of ***Marbury* v. *Madison* (1803)**■. William Marbury was one of many officials in the administration of Federalist President John Adams who received a last-minute judicial appointment as Adams was leaving office. The appointment of these "midnight judges" was an effort by Adams to place his supporters in positions of judicial influence to counteract the changes in government that would inevitably occur under the administration of the incoming president, Thomas Jefferson. However, in the rush of final activities, the outgoing secretary of state in the Adams administration, John Marshall, never managed to seal and deliver to Marbury his commission as a justice of the peace for the District of Columbia. When Jefferson took office, the incoming secretary of state, James Madison, refused to deliver these commissions to Marbury and several other judicial appointees. Marbury sought his commission by filing a legal action. He followed the requirements of the **Judiciary Act of 1789** by seeking a **writ of mandamus** from the U.S. Supreme Court. A writ of mandamus is a traditional legal order through which a court directs a government official to take a specific action required by law.

Marbury's legal action presented the Supreme Court with a difficult dilemma. Coincidentally, the Court's new chief justice was also a last-minute Adams appointee, just confirmed by the lame-duck, Federalist-dominated Senate. This was John Marshall, the very man whose failure, as Adams's outgoing secretary of state, to seal and deliver Marbury's commission on time had created the legal dispute in the first place. If Marshall and the other justices decided that Marbury was entitled to his commission, it seemed very likely that President Jefferson and Secretary Madison would simply

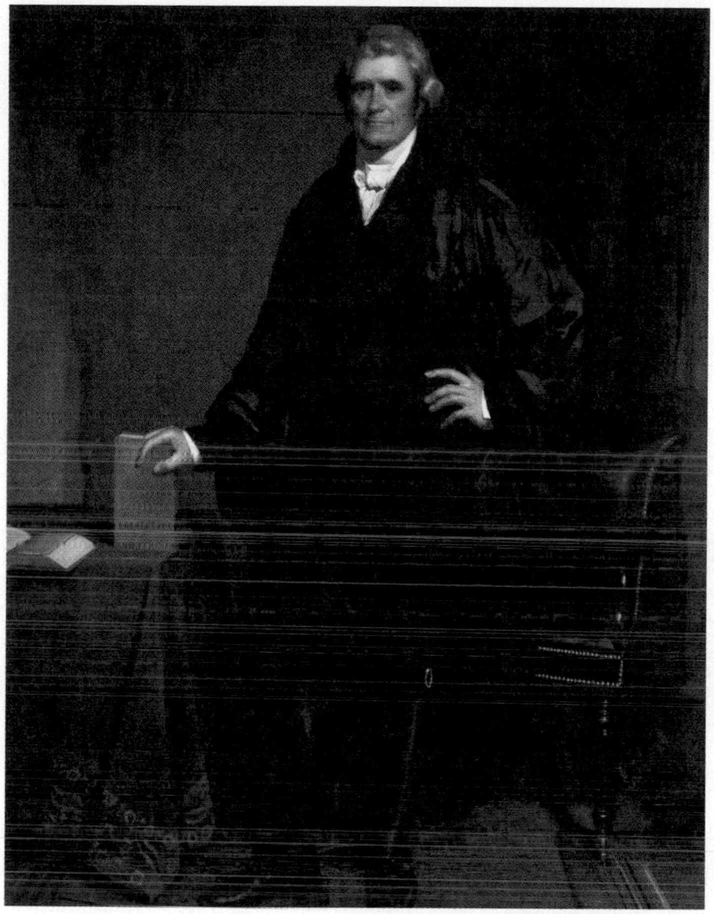

Chief Justice John Marshall's opinion in *Marbury* v. *Madison* helped to establish the concept of judicial review, an important power for American judges. This power was not specifically granted to judges by the U.S. Constitution. ***—Do you think it was implied in that document, or did Marshall act improperly in announcing his opinion?***

PHOTO: John Marshall by Chester Harding (1792–1886). Oil on canvas, 1830. U.R. 106.1830. Collection of the Boston Athenaeum.

disobey the Court by refusing to deliver the commission. Were that to happen, the Court had no practical means to force the president to act. Thus a decision in Marbury's favor carried the risk of the Supreme Court's image and legitimacy being tarnished by revealing that the judiciary has little practical power in the face of resistance by the president and other political actors. Ultimately, the Supreme Court issued a decision that asserted the power of the judiciary without risking any appearance of weakness.

In a unanimous decision written by Chief Justice Marshall, the Court declared that Marbury was indeed entitled to his commission and that the Court possessed the authority to order President Jefferson to have the commission delivered to him. However, the Court declined to issue such an order to the president because—so it declared—a portion of the Judiciary Act of 1789 was unconstitutional. Therefore, it ruled, Marbury had relied on an unconstitutional statute in seeking a writ of mandamus directly from the Supreme Court without first proceeding through the lower courts. According to the Court, statutes, such as the Judiciary Act, cannot define the kinds of cases that may be filed directly in the U.S. Supreme Court without being heard first in the lower courts. Article III of the Constitution specifically lists the kinds of cases in which the Supreme Court has original jurisdiction. Any effort by Congress to expand that list amounts to an improper effort to alter the Constitution by statute rather than by constitutional amendment. In general, the Supreme Court has appellate jurisdiction over cases decided in lower courts that are later brought to the highest court through appeals and other posttrial processes. The Constitution specifies that the Supreme Court will make the first or original decision only in cases concerning states and those involving high officials, such as ambassadors. Marbury's action seeking a writ of mandamus did not fit within these narrow categories of cases specified by the Constitution.

The decision in *Marbury* v. *Madison*—one of the most important Supreme Court decisions in American history—asserted the authority and importance of the Supreme Court without actually testing the Court's power in a confrontation with the president. The Court simply asserted the power of judicial review in striking down a portion of the Judiciary Act without providing any elaborate discussion in its opinion that would raise questions about whether such a power even existed under the Constitution.

The Court did not immediately begin to pass judgment on the propriety of executive and legislative actions. Instead, it waited more than 50 years before again asserting its power of judicial review. In 1857, in its highly controversial decision in *Dred Scott* v. *Sandford,* the Court invalidated the Missouri Compromise—a series of decisions by Congress in 1820 and 1821 that had put limits on the spread of slavery into western territories. By 1900, the power of judicial review came to be used more frequently, and it was used often throughout the twentieth century. Eventually, federal courts struck down hundreds of state statutes and more than 100 acts of Congress. Today judicial review is well entrenched in American governing processes and provides a primary source of judicial power.

■ **Impeachment:** Process in Congress for removal of the president, federal judges, and other high officials.

EXAMPLE: *Congress impeached Judge Harry Claiborne and removed him from office in 1986 after he was convicted of tax evasion and served 17 months in prison.*

Federal Judges' Protected Tenure

As described earlier, Article III of the Constitution specifies that federal judges will serve "during good Behaviour." Effectively, that means lifetime tenure, since these judges typically are removed through **impeachment**■ by Congress only if they commit a crime. The tenure granted to federal judges underscores the emphasis that the Constitution places on ensuring the independence of judicial decision makers. If judges are not afraid of losing their jobs by making unpopular decisions, then presumably they will possess enough protection against political attacks to enable them to do the right thing (see Figure 4.2). This protection may be especially important when judges make decisions that protect the rights of minorities whom large segments of society view unfavorably. For example, many controversial judicial decisions in the mid-twentieth century advancing the equality of African Americans were vigorously criticized, because racial prejudice was widespread among whites. At other times, unpopular court decisions have protected the interests of corporations and the wealthy. For example, in 2005, the U.S. Supreme Court outraged critics by ruling that local governments can force individuals to sell their homes in order to turn the property over to developers who want to advance local economic progress by building office buildings and hotels (*Kelo* v. *City of New London,* 2005).

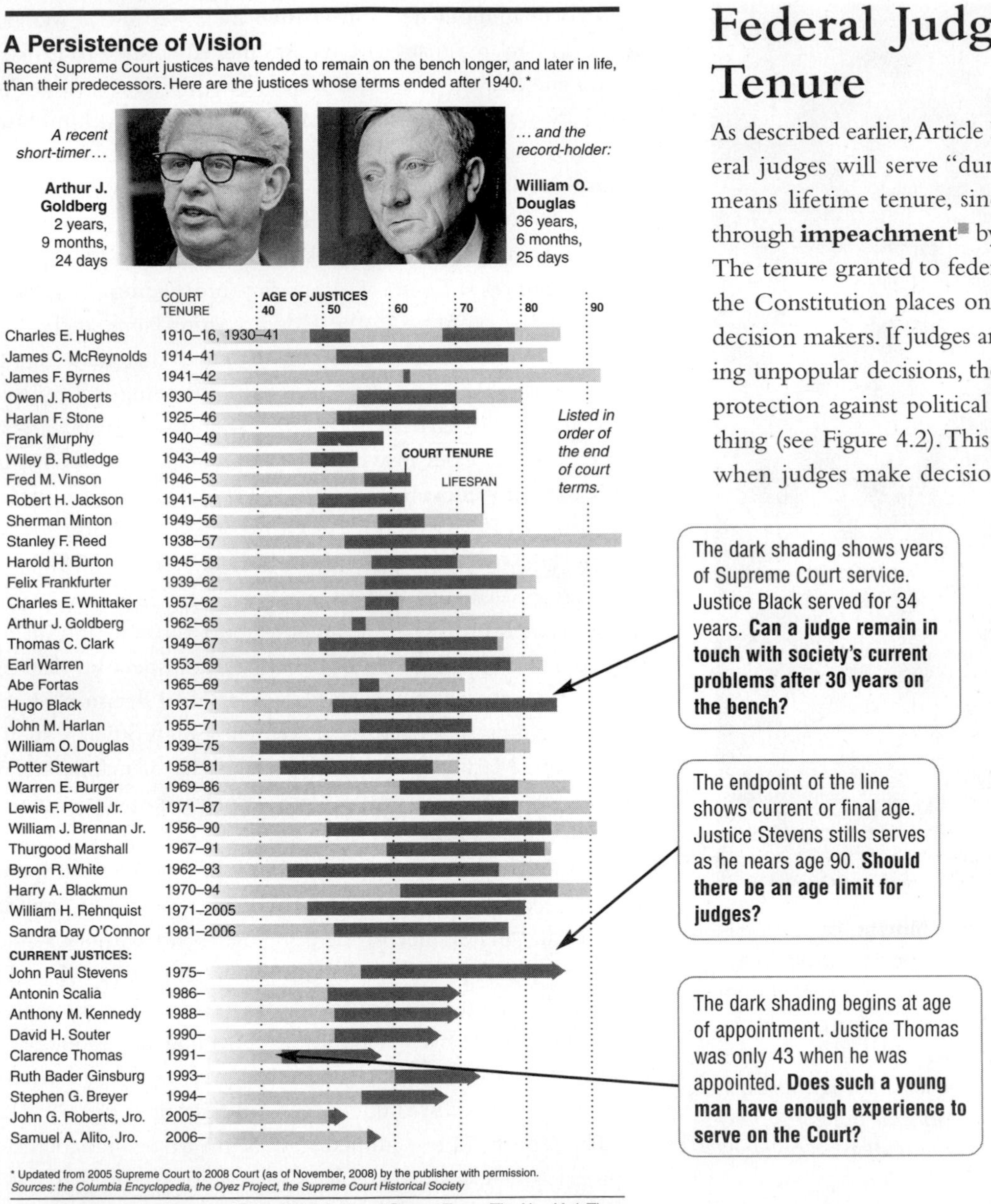

Photographs by Associated Press/© AP (left) and George Tames/The New York Times January 16, 2005, New York Times Graphics. Copyright © 2005 by the New York Times Co. Reprinted with permission. Updated from 2005 Supreme Court to 2008 Court (as of November, 2008) by permission of the publisher.

FIGURE 4.2 | Length of Service of Modern Supreme Court Justices

Some justices have served for several decades and continued to decide cases even after they reached the age of 80. ***—What would be a reason not to limit the term in office for Supreme Court justices?***

"Should we let judges serve for life?"
—Student Question

Because federal judges are exempted from democracy's traditional accountability mechanism—the need to face periodic elections, which often keeps other public officials from making unpopular decisions—judges are better positioned to make decisions that go against society's dominant values and policy preferences (see Figure 4.2). This lack of accountability also creates the possibility that judges' decisions will go "too far" in shaping law and

■ **Court-Packing Plan:** President Franklin D. Roosevelt's unsuccessful proposal in 1937 to permit the appointment of additional justices to the U.S. Supreme Court.

EXAMPLE: *President Roosevelt hoped to make the Supreme Court's composition more supportive of his New Deal policies by proposing that the president appoint an additional justice whenever a sitting justice reached 70 years of age.*

policy in ways that are unpopular and detrimental to society as well as risk a backlash against the entire court system.

A famous example of backlash against the Supreme Court arose in the late 1930s. In 1937, President Franklin D. Roosevelt was frustrated that the life-tenured justices on the Supreme Court were using their power of judicial review to invalidate New Deal legislation that he believed to be necessary to fight the Great Depression. As a result, he proposed restructuring the Supreme Court to permit the president to appoint an additional justice for each serving justice who reached the age of 70. His "**court-packing plan**■," as the press and congressional opponents immediately branded it, would have enabled him to select six new justices immediately and thereby alter the Court's dynamics. Political and public opposition blocked Roosevelt's plan, and he set it aside when elderly justices began to retire, thus permitting him to name replacements who supported his New Deal legislation. Roosevelt's actions demonstrated that decisions by life-tenured judges can stir controversy, especially when those decisions clash with policies preferred by the public and their elected representatives in government. The reaction against packing the Court also demonstrated how much the American public had come to value the judiciary's independence.

The Power of American Judges

Practice Quiz

1. As originally conceived by the framers of the Constitution, the judicial branch of the government was supposed to be
   - **a.** as powerful as the other two branches.
   - **b.** more powerful than the legislative branch but less powerful than the executive branch.
   - **c.** more powerful than the executive branch but less powerful than the legislative branch.
   - **d.** less powerful than the other two branches.
2. The power of judicial review is defined in Article III of the U.S. Constitution.
   - **a.** true
   - **b.** false
3. Why do judges need to interpret constitutions and statutes?
   - **a.** because the legislators who draft these documents are not trained to do this interpretation themselves
   - **b.** because all judges seize every opportunity to expand their own power
   - **c.** because constitutions and statutes frequently contain ambiguities that need to be resolved
   - **d.** because constitutions and statutes are not considered laws unless judges interpret them
4. Why does judicial review make U.S. judges enormously powerful?
   - **a.** because it grants them the authority to invalidate as unconstitutional statutes enacted by Congress and actions taken by the president
   - **b.** because it comes with the trappings of authority: the black robe, the seat on high, the requirement that all in the court must rise when the judge enters
   - **c.** because it means they are appointed for life
   - **d.** because it means they can intervene in any case, ask witnesses and litigants their own questions, and reach verdicts entirely on their own

Answers: 1-d, 2-b, 3-c, 4-a.

Discussion Questions

1. Does the power of judicial review improperly make the judicial branch more powerful than the executive (President) and legislative (Congress) branches of the federal government?
2. Some commentators suggest that federal judges serve only limited terms in office. What impact, if any, would limited terms have on the judicial branch and its role in the governing system?

What **YOU** can do!

Read Justice Ruth Bader Ginsburg's speech on the role of dissenting opinions at **http://www.supremecourtus.gov/publicinfo/speeches/sp_10-21-07.html**. According to Ginsburg, what differences exist between the U.S. Supreme Court and high courts in other countries?

■ **Senatorial Courtesy:** Traditional deference by U.S. senators to the wishes of their colleagues concerning the appointment of individuals to federal judgeships in that state.

EXAMPLE: *Democratic senators were angry at their Republican colleagues during Bill Clinton's presidency for blocking judicial appointments and thereby violating the tradition of senatorial courtesy for controlling the selection of federal judges in their home states.*

CONNECT THE LINK

(Chapter **7**, pages **250–251**) Can a senator really defeat legislation by talking a bill to death?

Judicial Selection

(pages 114–117)

What political processes determine the selection of judges?

Political parties and interest groups regard the judicial selection process as an important means to influence the court pathway. By securing judgeships for individuals who share their political values, these groups can enhance their prospects for success when they subsequently use litigation to shape public policy.

In the American political system, judges are, ideally, placed on the bench for their qualifications of thoughtfulness, knowledge, and experience. In reality, American lawyers do not become judges because they are the wisest, most experienced, or fairest members of the legal profession. Instead, they are selected through political processes that emphasize their affiliations with political parties, their personal relationships with high-ranking officials, and often their ability to raise money for political campaigns. The fact that judges are selected through political processes does not necessarily mean that they are unqualified or incapable of making fair decisions. Individuals who are deeply involved in partisan politics may, upon appointment, prove quite capable of fulfilling a judge's duty to be neutral and open minded. Other judges, however, appear to make decisions that are driven by their preexisting values and policy preferences.

Judicial Selection in the Federal System

The Constitution specifies that federal judges, like ambassadors and cabinet secretaries, must be appointed by the president and confirmed by a majority vote of the U.S. Senate. Thus both the White House and one chamber of Congress are intimately involved in judicial selection.

"What is senatorial courtesy?"

—Student Question

Because there are nearly 850 judgeships in the federal district courts and courts of appeals, the president is never personally knowledgeable about all the pending vacancies. The president does, however, become personally involved in the selection of appointees for the U.S. Supreme Court, because that body is so important and influential in shaping national law and policy. For lower federal court judgeships, the president relies heavily on advice from White House aides, senators, and other officials from his own political party.

Traditionally, senators from the president's political party have effectively controlled the selection of appointees for district court judgeships in their own states. Through a practice known as **senatorial courtesy**■, senators from the president's party have virtual veto power over potential nominees for their home state's district courts. They are also consulted on nominations for the federal court of appeals that covers their state. Because senators are so influential in the selection of federal district court judges, the judges who ultimately get selected are usually acquainted personally with the senators, active in the political campaigns of the senators and other party members, or accomplished in raising campaign funds for the party.

The process begins with the submission of an appointee's name to the Senate Judiciary Committee. The committee typically receives letters of support from individuals and interest groups that endorse the nomination, as well as similar communications from people and groups opposed to giving the appointee a life-tenured, federal judgeship. A few nominees encounter organized opposition and negative publicity campaigns, but this typically happens primarily with nominations to the Supreme Court or the federal courts of appeals. The committee holds hearings on each nomination, including testimony from supporters and opponents.

"What happens if the Senate objects to the president's nominee?"

—Student Question

After the Judiciary Committee completes its hearings, its members vote on a recommendation to the full Senate. Typically, when a nomination reaches the full Senate, that body votes quickly, based on the Judiciary Committee's report and vote. But in controversial cases or when asked to confirm appointments to the Supreme Court, the Senate may spend time debating the nomination. A majority of senators must vote for a candidate in order for that person to be sworn in as a federal judge. However, members of the minority political party in the Senate may block a vote through a **filibuster** (LINK see Chapter 7, pages 250–251), keeping discussion going indefinitely unless three-fifths of the Senate's members—60 senators—vote to end it. Democrats used a filibuster to block several judicial nominations during the first term of President George W. Bush. Eventually, however, senators from both parties negotiated a resolution that permitted Bush's nominees to gain approval.

As in state systems, judicial selection at the federal level is a political process. Presidents seek to please favored constituencies and to advance their policy preferences in choosing appointees. Interest groups find avenues through which they seek to influence

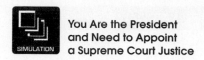

You Are the President and Need to Appoint a Supreme Court Justice

the president's choices as well as the confirmation votes of senators. Judicial selection processes are a primary reason that American courts are political institutions despite their efforts to appear "nonpolitical."

Let's illustrate the politics of judicial selection using the recent, highly publicized maneuvering after Justice Sandra Day O'Connor announced her retirement from the U.S. Supreme Court in 2005. Her retirement was to take effect as soon as a nominee was confirmed by the U.S. Senate to replace her. Justice O'Connor, the first woman ever appointed to the Supreme Court (by President Ronald Reagan in 1981), was a decisive "swing" vote between the Court's liberal and conservative wings on several key issues. President Bush and his political supporters saw O'Connor's retirement as an opportunity to turn the Court in a new direction on issues that closely divided the justices, especially abortion and affirmative action. Liberal and conservative interest groups mobilized their members and prepared significant advertising and lobbying campaigns for the battle over her successor. If she were to be replaced by a more conservative appointee, new decisions by the Supreme Court could potentially rewrite several aspects of constitutional law.

Unexpectedly, President Bush first nominated his long-time personal lawyer, Harriet Miers. Because he was personally acquainted with her, Bush may have felt confident that Miers would make decisions in a manner that would advance his preferred policies. However, she aroused intense public opposition from conservative journalists and interest group leaders as well as some Republican senators, who perceived her as neither professionally distinguished nor sufficiently conservative. Under heavy political pressure, Miers withdrew her name, and President Bush nominated Judge Samuel Alito in her place. No one questioned Alito's outstanding educational credentials and professional experience as an attorney and a judge. But it was widely—and accurately—anticipated that Alito would be more consistently conservative than O'Connor and that his votes could move the Court to the right. A group of Democratic senators attempted to block Alito's confirmation by raising concerns about his judicial decisions involving constitutional rights and questions about his attitudes regarding gender discrimination and other issues. However, he was confirmed in January of 2006 following a largely party-line vote of 58-42, with only one Republican voting against him and only four Democrats supporting him. In his first two terms on the Supreme Court, Justice Alito decided cases in a more consistently conservative manner than Justice O'Connor.[7] Thus President Bush appeared to succeed in his objective of turning the Supreme Court in a more conservative direction.

Judicial Selection in the States

Compare the federal judicial selection process with the various processes used to select judges for state court systems. In general, there are four primary methods that states use for judicial selection: partisan elections, nonpartisan elections, **merit selection,** and gubernatorial or legislative appointment. Table 4.4 shows how judges are selected in each state. Although each of these methods seeks to emphasize different values, they are all closely linked to political processes.

Partisan elections emphasize the importance of popular accountability in a democratic governing system. When judges are elected and must subsequently run for reelection, the voters can hold them accountable if they make decisions that are inconsistent with community values. In selecting candidates to run for judgeships, political parties typically seek individuals with name recognition and the ability to raise campaign funds rather than the lawyer with the most experience. Voters frequently know very little about judicial candidates, so the party label next to the person's name on the ballot can provide important information that distinguishes the candidates in the eyes of the voter. Partisan elections are used to select judges for at least some levels of courts in nine states.

In an effort to reduce the impact of partisan politics, several states began to use nonpartisan elections in the first decades of the twentieth century. In such elections, a judicial candidate's campaign literature does not specify political party affiliation, nor is such affiliation indicated on the ballot. Ideally, voters will simply choose the best judge rather than be influenced by political party labels. In reality, however, political parties remain deeply involved in "nonpartisan" elections. Although technically nonpartisan, in these elections political parties often choose the candidates and provide organizational and financial support for their campaigns. Incumbency can also be a powerful influence in such elections, because the incumbent is the only one whose name sounds familiar to voters.

More than 20 states have sought to reduce the influence of politics and give greater attention to candidates' qualifications when selecting judges. These states have adopted various forms of merit selection systems. The first merit selection process for choosing judges was developed in Missouri in 1949, and many states have used Missouri as a model for developing similar processes. Under the "Missouri plan," the governor appoints a committee to review potential candidates for judgeships. It is presumed that the committee will focus on the individuals' personal qualities and professional qualifications rather than on political party affiliations. The committee

TABLE 4.4 | **Methods of Judicial Selection for State Judges**

PARTISAN ELECTION	NONPARTISAN ELECTION	MERIT SELECTION	LEGISLATIVE (L) OR GUBERNATORIAL (G) APPOINTMENT
Alabama	Arkansas	Alaska	California (appellate) G
Illinois	Arizona (trial)	Arizona (appellate)	Maine G
Indiana (trial)	California (trial)	Colorado	New Hampshire G
Louisiana	Florida (trial)	Connecticut	New Jersey G
New York (trial)	Georgia	Delaware	South Carolina L
Pennsylvania	Idaho	Florida (appellate)	Virginia L
Tennessee (trial)	Kentucky	Hawaii	
Texas	Michigan	Indiana (appellate)	
West Virginia	Minnesota	Iowa	
	Mississippi	Kansas	
	Montana	Maryland	
	Nevada (appellate)	Massachusetts	
	North Carolina	Missouri	
	North Dakota	Nebraska	
	Ohio	Nevada (trial)	
	Oklahoma (trial)	New Mexico	
	Oregon	New York (appellate)	
	South Dakota (trial)	Oklahoma (appellate)	
	Washington	Rhode Island	
	Wisconsin	South Dakota (appellate)	
		Tennessee (appellate)	
		Utah	
		Vermont	
		Wyoming	

SOURCE: American Judicature Society, *Judicial Selection in the States: Appellate and General Jurisdiction Courts* (Des Moines, IA: American Judicature Society, 2004), pp. 1–4. Available at www.ajs.org

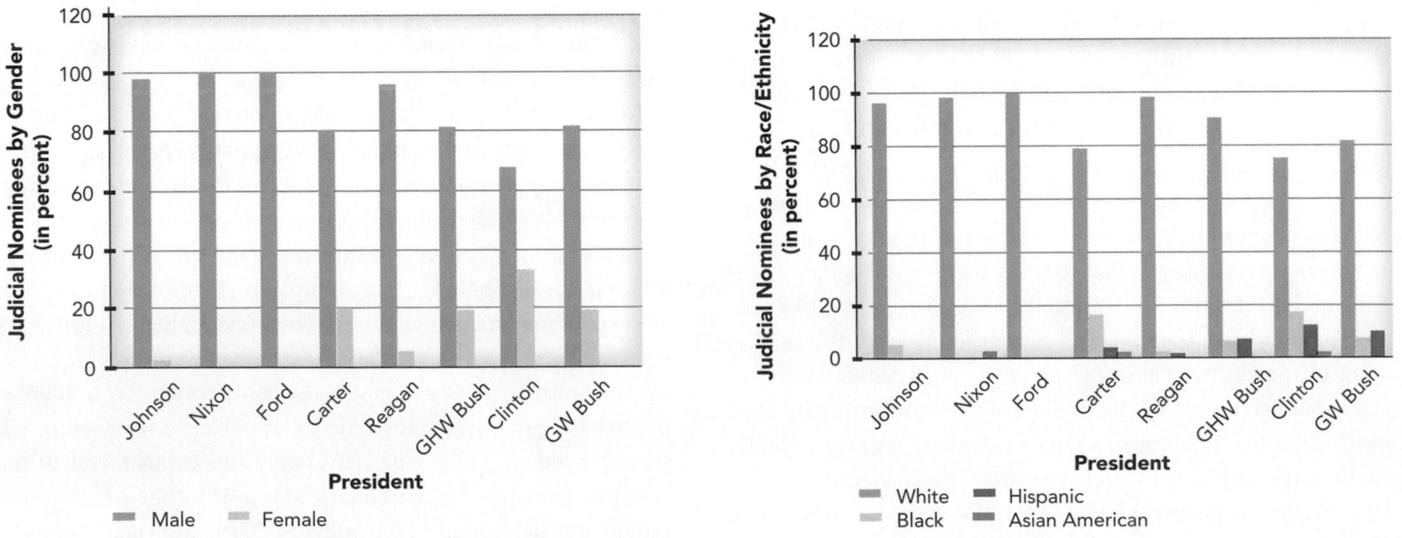

FIGURE 4.3 | **Diversity within the Federal Courts**

Although the percentage of women and minority judges increased in the federal courts over the past three decades, their numbers still do not reflect their composition of American society. ***—Could the credibility or image of the court system be harmed if important decision-making positions remain dominated by white males in an increasingly diverse society?***

SOURCE: www.albany.edu

provides the governor with a short list of recommended candidates. From this list, the governor chooses one candidate and appoints that individual to be the judge. After that, the judge must periodically face the voters in **retention elections.** In a retention election, the judge's name is on the ballot, and voters simply decide whether to give the judge an additional term in office. They don't have a choice of judicial candidates.

One concern voiced by critics about all judicial selection processes is the risk that political connections limit opportunities for women and members of minority groups to be considered for judgeships. Many people believe that a diverse judiciary is necessary to maintain the courts' legitimacy as well as to have decision makers who are knowledgeable about and sensitive to issues that affect all segments of society. If virtually all judges were white and male, would it affect your views about the court system? As indicated by Figure 4.3, relatively few women and members of minority groups were appointed to federal judgeships prior to the Carter administration in the 1970s (1977–1981). Since the 1970s, presidents have shown different levels of commitment to the goal of diversifying the federal courts.

Judicial Selection

Practice Quiz

1. As dictated by the Constitution, federal judges are appointed by the president and are confirmed by
   - **a.** a majority vote in Congress.
   - **b.** a two-thirds vote in the House of Representatives.
   - **c.** a majority vote in the Senate.
   - **d.** a two-thirds vote in the Senate.
2. Why are the characters and political philosophies of nominees for the federal bench scrutinized so carefully?
   - **a.** When judges interpret constitutions and statutes, they inevitably rely on their own values—and their decisions can significantly affect the lives of millions of Americans.
   - **b.** Federal judges are celebrities, and the American public is deeply interested in their private lives.
   - **c.** The Judiciary Act of 1789 requires such scrutiny.
   - **d.** Article II of the Constitution requires such scrutiny, without which judges are subject to impeachment.
3. Senators play a key role in the selection and confirmation of federal judges.
   - **a.** true
   - **b.** false
4. What role do political parties play in the selection of state court judges?
   - **a.** Political parties are only allowed to be involved in partisan judicial elections.
   - **b.** Political parties are often involved in both partisan and nonpartisan judicial elections.
   - **c.** Political parties always determine who will be nominated in the merit selection process.
   - **d.** Political parties have no role in the selection of state judges.

Answers: 1-c, 2-a, 3-a, 4-b.

Discussion Questions

1. What is the best way to select judges?
2. How could you design a merit selection system that would truly select the most qualified individuals for judgeships?

What **YOU** can do!

Visit the American Judicature Society's Web page on judicial selection in the states at **http://www.judicialselection.us/**. Read the voter guides for judicial elections to get a sense about the kinds of issues and positions that appear in these elections as compared to elections of legislative or executive officials. Also at this Web site, look at "History of Reform Efforts" to see both successful and unsuccessful reform efforts in your state as well as opinion polls and surveys on aspects of judicial reform. Which method of judicial selection do you think is the best for states to use? Why?

SIMULATION
You Are a Supreme Court Justice Deciding a Free Speech Case

Judges' Decision-Making (pages 118–121)

Justice Clarence Thomas is very outspoken about his belief that the Constitution should be interpreted strictly according to "original intent." Would interpretation by original intent reduce the recognition of equal rights for women or members of minority groups? ***—If so, should these practical results affect how judges interpret the Constitution?***

What do we know about how Supreme Court justices really make decisions?

The political battles over Supreme Court nominations, as well as over judges at other levels of state and federal court systems, reflect the widespread recognition that judges do not merely "follow the law" in making their decisions. When judges interpret the U.S. Constitution, state constitutions, and statutes, they rely on their own values and judgments. These values and judgments ultimately have a significant effect on public policy affecting many aspects of American life. Hence, in appointing federal judges, the president seeks to name men and women with a politically compatible outlook. Similarly, the involvement of political parties and interest groups in supporting or opposing judicial candidates reflects their interests in securing judgeships for those whom they believe will make decisions that advance their policy preferences. Research by social scientists reinforces this assessment of judges. Studies show, for example, that decisions favoring individuals' claims of rights are more frequently associated with Democratic judges and that decisions favoring business and the prosecution in criminal cases are more frequently associated with Republican judges.

Although judges can apply their values in making many kinds of decisions, they do not enjoy complete freedom to decide cases as they wish. Lower-court judges in particular must be concerned that their decisions will be overturned on appeal to higher courts if they make decisions that conflict with the judgments of justices on courts of last resort. What guides judges to reach conclusions that are not likely to be overturned? They rely on case precedent. Case precedent is the body of prior judicial opinions, especially those from the U.S. Supreme Court and state supreme courts, that establishes the judge-made law that develops from interpretations of the U.S. Constitution, state constitutions, and statutes. When lower-court judges face a particular issue in a case, they do research to determine whether similar issues have already been decided by higher courts. Typically, they will follow the legal principles established by prior cases, no matter what their personal views on the issue. However, if they believe that the precise issue in their case is distinguishable from the issues in prior cases, or if they have new ideas about how such issues should be handled, they can issue an opinion that clashes with established case precedent. Judges make such decisions in the hope that the reasons explained in their opinions will persuade the judges above them to change the prevailing precedent. The law changes through the development of new perspectives and ideas by lawyers and judges that ultimately persuade courts of last resort to move the law in new directions.

For example, when the U.S. Supreme Court decided in 2005 (in *Roper* v. *Simmons*) that the cruel and unusual punishments clause in the Eighth Amendment prohibits the execution of murderers who committed their crimes before the age of 18, it established a new precedent, overturning its previously established precedent permitting execution for murders committed at the ages of 16 and 17 (*Stanford* v. *Kentucky,* 1989). In reaching its conclusion, the nation's highest court upheld a decision by the Missouri Supreme Court that advocated a new interpretation of the Eighth Amendment (*State ex. rel. Simmons* v. *Roper,* 2003).

The U.S. Supreme Court often seeks to follow and preserve its precedents in order to maintain stability in the law. However, it is not bound by its own precedents, and no higher court can overturn the Supreme Court's interpretations of the U.S. Constitution. Thus the justices enjoy significant freedom to shape the law by advancing their own theories of constitutional interpretation and by applying their own attitudes and values concerning appropriate policy outcomes from judicial decisions. State supreme courts enjoy similar freedom when interpreting the constitutions and statutes of their own states. Lower-court judges can also apply their own approaches to constitutional and statutory interpretation, especially when facing issues that have not yet been addressed by any court. Their new approaches may be overturned on appeal, but they may also help establish new law if higher courts agree.

Judicial selection battles in the federal courts, especially those over the nomination of Supreme Court justices, often focus on the nominee's approach to constitutional interpretation. Among the members of the Supreme Court, Justices Clarence Thomas and Antonin Scalia are known for advocating an original intent approach to constitutional interpretation. These justices and their admirers argue that the Constitution must be interpreted in strict accordance with the original meanings intended by the people who wrote and ratified the document. According to Thomas and Scalia, constitutional interpretation must follow original intent in order to avoid "judicial activism," in which judges allegedly exceed their proper sphere of authority by injecting their own viewpoints into constitutional interpretation. That is why the followers of the original intent approach are also known as advocates of "judicial restraint," in which judges defer to the policy judgments of elected officials in the legislative and executive branches of government. Despite their use of "judicial restraint," judges who follow original intent still affect public policy with their decisions. They merely disagree with others about which policies should be influenced by judges.

Critics of original intent argue that there is no way to know exactly what the Constitution's authors intended with respect to each individual word and phrase, or even whether one specific meaning was intended by all of the authors and ratifiers. Moreover, these critics typically argue that the ambiguous nature of many constitutional phrases, such as "cruel and unusual punishments" and "unreasonable searches and seizures," represents one of the document's strengths, because it permits judges to interpret and reinterpret the document in light of the nation's changing social circumstances and technological advances. What would James Madison and the other eighteenth-century founders of the nation have thought about whether the use of wiretaps and other forms of electronic surveillance violates the Fourth Amendment prohibition on "unreasonable searches"? Critics of original intent argue that contemporary judges must give meaning to those words in light of current values and policy problems. Hence the critics of original intent typically want a flexible interpretation that enables judges to draw from the Constitution's underlying principles in addressing contemporary legal issues. Nearly all the Supreme Court justices in the past 50 years have used flexible interpretation, including, among the justices serving in 2008, John Paul Stevens, Ruth Bader

Samuel Alito, shown here at his Senate confirmation hearings, replaced Sandra Day O'Connor on the U.S. Supreme Court in 2006. Because it was widely believed that Alito would tilt the Supreme Court in a more conservative direction, 42 senators opposed his confirmation. ***—How do you think the increased role of partisan politics in the selection and confirmation of Supreme Court nominees affects the quality of the individuals selected?***

PHOTO: Doug Mills/The New York Times

■ **Flexible Interpretation:** An approach to interpreting the U.S. Constitution that permits the meaning of the document to change with evolving values, social conditions, and problems.

EXAMPLE: *When the U.S. Supreme Court decided that the Eighth Amendment's prohibition on "cruel and unusual punishments" forbids the application of the death penalty to mentally retarded offenders* (Atkins *v.* Virginia, *2002*), *the justices used flexible interpretation rather than just the Constitution's specific words.*

CONNECT THE LINK

(Chapter **5**, pages **150–153**) The First Amendment's wording requires judges to interpret the meaning of "an establishment of religion" and the "free exercise" of religion.

Ginsburg, and Anthony Kennedy. However, the justices who use **flexible interpretation**■ frequently disagree with one another about how much flexibility should apply to various provisions in the Constitution.

As you can see, debates about the proper approach to interpreting the Constitution can be central elements in the political battles over the selection of judges. The successful confirmations of Bush appointees John Roberts and Samuel Alito may indicate that Justices Thomas and Scalia have gained new allies in their advocacy of judicial restraint and interpretation by original intent. In their first two terms on the Court, Chief Justice Roberts and Justice Alito were closely aligned with Thomas and Scalia in making decisions on a wide range of issues.

President George W. Bush clearly hoped that his appointees would decide cases in the manner of Justices Thomas and Scalia, but presidents are sometimes disappointed. Presidents cannot accurately predict how a nominee will decide every kind of case, especially because new and unexpected issues emerge each year. Moreover, some Supreme Court justices, as well as judges on lower courts, do change their views over the course of their careers. The views that led the president to select the nominee are not always the views held by nominees at the end of their careers. Justice Harry Blackmun, for example, an appointee of Republican President Richard Nixon, served on the Supreme Court from 1970 to 1994 and became increasingly protective of individuals' rights over the course of his career. Despite the fact that Nixon had envisioned him as a conservative decision maker, he was regarded as one of the Court's most liberal justices at the time of his retirement.

Political Science and Judicial Decision Making

Supreme Court justices present themselves as using particular approaches to constitutional interpretation in making their decisions, and they may honestly believe that these interpretive approaches guide their decisions. Political scientists, however, question whether the justices' decisions can be explained in this way. Through systematic examination of case decisions and close analysis of justices' opinions, researchers have identified patterns and inconsistencies. These examinations of Supreme Court decisions have led to alternative explanations for the primary factors that shape the justices' decisions.

The idea that justices follow specific theories of constitutional interpretation and carefully consider precedents in making decisions is often labeled the **legal model.** Critics argue, however, that the justices regularly ignore, mischaracterize, or change precedents when those case decisions seem to impede the desire of the majority of justices to have a case come out a certain way. As you will see in the discussion of freedom of religion in LINK Chapter 5, pages 150–153, the justices seem to decide cases on the separation of church and state according to a specific test of whether government actions advance a particular religion. In specific cases, however, they ignore the test if it leads to a result that they do not desire. For example, the justices permitted the Nebraska state senate to hire a minister to lead prayers at the start of each legislative session (*Marsh* v. *Chambers,* 1984). If they had applied the usual test, however, they would presumably have been required to prohibit the entanglement of church and state through the use of a Christian minister to deliver prayers in this context.

"What do we know about how Supreme Court justices really make decisions?"

—Student Question

An alternative theory of judicial decision-making, known as the **attitudinal model,** states that Supreme Court justices' opinions are driven by their attitudes and values. Advocates of this model see the justices' discussion of interpretive theories and precedent as merely a means to obscure the actual basis for decisions and to persuade the public that the decisions are, in fact, based on law. Researchers who endorse the attitudinal model do systematic analyses of judicial decisions to identify patterns that indicate the attitudes and values possessed and advanced by individual justices. Put more simply, the attitudinal theorists argue that some justices decide cases as they do because they are conservative and that others decide cases differently because they are liberal.[8]

Other political scientists see judicial decision making as influenced by a **rational choice model.** According to this theory, Supreme Court justices vote strategically in order to advance their preferred goals, even if it means voting contrary to their actual attitudes and values in some cases. For example, a justice may be keenly interested in a specific issue raised by a case presented to the Court. Yet that justice could vote against hearing the case if he or she fears there ultimately would not be enough support among the justices to advance a preferred outcome. By declining to hear the case, the justice helps avoid setting an adverse precedent and can wait for a similar issue to arise again after the Court's composition has changed in a favorable direction. Justices may also vote strategically in order to build relationships with allies in less important cases, with the hope that these relationships will increase the likelihood of persuading those allies to support specific decisions in other cases. These are just two examples of a variety of ways that rational choice strategies may influence Supreme Court decisions.[9]

In recent years, some political scientists have broadened their studies of courts, including judicial decision-making, through an approach commonly labeled new institutionalism. **New institutionalism** emphasizes understanding courts as institutions and seeing the role of courts in the larger political system.[10] The adherents of new institutionalism do not necessarily agree with one another about the causes and implications of judicial action. They do, however, seek to move beyond analyzing judicial decisions solely by looking at the choices of individual Supreme Court justices. Instead, they may focus on the Supreme Court's processes, its reactions to statutes enacted to undercut particular judicial decisions, or its decisions that minimize direct confrontations with other branches of government. Alternatively, the focus could be on judicial inaction, as when the Supreme Court refused to consider lawsuits against President Richard Nixon in the early 1970s for conducting an allegedly "illegal war" in Cambodia during the Vietnam War. In this example, the Supreme Court avoided involvement in issues of presidential war powers that would generate conflicts among the country's governing institutions.

Political scientists continue to debate which model provides the best explanation for judicial decisions. New models are likely to be developed in the future. For students of American government, these models serve as a reminder that you should not automatically accept government officials' explanations for their decisions and behavior. Systematic examination and close analysis of decisions may reveal influences that the government decision makers themselves do not fully recognize.

Judges' Decision-Making

Practice Quiz

1. The "legal model" of judicial decision-making presumes that
   - **a.** judges' decisions are based on their attitudes and values.
   - **b.** judges' decisions are based on their rational strategies.
   - **c.** judges' decisions are based on case precedents.
   - **d.** judges' decisions depend on them persuading each other.
2. Critics who oppose the efforts of Justices Thomas and Scalia to have the Constitution interpreted according to "original intent"
   - **a.** claim that there is no way to know what the authors of the Constitution intended as the meaning of all the document's ambiguous phrases.
   - **b.** claim that the use of original intent always violates the principle of judicial restraint.
   - **c.** do not believe that Supreme Court justices should interpret the Constitution.
3. Usually, the decisions of lower-court judges rely on case precedent, even if their personal views on the issue suggest a different decision.
   - **a.** true
   - **b.** false
4. When political scientists regard Supreme Court justices' decisions as being shaped by concerns about the courts' role in the larger political system, those political scientists believe in
   - **a.** the legal model of judicial decision-making.
   - **b.** the new institutionalism model of judicial decision-making.
   - **c.** the attitudinal model of judicial decision-making.
   - **d.** the rational choice model of judicial decision-making.

Answers: 1-c, 2-a, 3-a, 4-b.

Discussion Questions

1. Should judges be required to follow case precedent, or would it be better for them to make decisions based entirely on their best judgment?
2. Is there any way to prevent judges from using their own values and attitudes in making decisions?

What **YOU** can do!

Think about the Eighth Amendment phrase that prohibits "cruel and unusual punishments." What might the phrase mean under an "original intent" interpretation? Is that meaning different than what your own interpretation would be using a flexible approach? If your definition defined law and policy for the United States, how would that affect sentences imposed on criminal offenders and the treatment of offenders in prisons?

TIMELINE Chief Justices of the Supreme Court

SIMULATION You Are a Young Lawyer

Action *in the* Court Pathway (pages 122–125)

What litigation strategies are employed in the court pathway?

In theory, any individual can make use of the resources of the judicial branch merely by filing a legal action. Such actions may be directed at small issues, such as suing a landlord to recover a security deposit. They may also be directed at significant national issues, including actions aimed at Congress or the president in battles over major public policy issues.

In reality, filing a lawsuit at any level above small-claims courts (where landlord-tenant cases are typically argued) is expensive and requires professional legal assistance. As a result, the courts are not easily accessible to the average American. Typically, this policy-shaping process is used by legal professionals who have technical expertise and financial resources. Nor will courts accept every kind of claim: Claims must be presented in the form of legal cases that embody disputes about rights and obligations under the law. Thus organized interests and wealthy individuals are often best positioned to make effective use of court processes.

For an illustration of the court pathway in the Lindsay Earls case, see Figure 4.4.

The new Chief Justice John Roberts poses for photographs outside the Supreme Court after his swearing-in ceremony in 2005 as his young son rushes to greet him. It has been argued that someone who is barely over 50 years of age lacks the experience and knowledge to lead one of the nation's most powerful policymaking institutions. ***—Do you agree with this argument? Why or why not?***

PHOTO: Stephen Crowley/The New York Times

PATHWAYS | profile

John G. Roberts, Jr.

John Roberts was educated at Harvard College and Harvard Law School. After graduation from law school, he served as a law clerk for a judge on the U.S. Court of Appeals in New York City and then spent a year as a law clerk for U.S. Supreme Court Justice (and future Chief Justice) William Rehnquist. Later, during the presidency of Ronald Reagan, Roberts served as an assistant to the U.S. attorney general and later to the White House counsel. He then entered private practice with a Washington, D.C., law firm. During the presidency of George H. W. Bush (1989–1993), Roberts served as the deputy solicitor general and argued cases in front of the U.S. Supreme Court on behalf of the federal government. Roberts returned to his law firm during Bill Clinton's presidency (1993–2001).

During the first term of President George W. Bush, Roberts was appointed to a seat on the U.S. Court of Appeals for the District of Columbia. Later, upon the death of Chief Justice William Rehnquist in 2005, President Bush nominated Roberts to become chief justice of the United States.

Despite being a newcomer to the Court, as well as its youngest member, Roberts assumed leadership duties as chief justice. This means leading the discussion of cases and designating the specific justices who write opinions on behalf of the Court in cases when the chief justice has voted with the majority. In major cases, the chief justice often assigns the majority opinion to himself.

President Bush selected Roberts for the Supreme Court in the apparent belief that Roberts would move the high court in a conservative direction on such issues as expanded presidential power during the war on terrorism, abortion, and affirmative action. ■

Interest Group Litigation

The court pathway is often attractive to small interest groups, because it is possible to succeed with fewer resources than are required for lobbying or mass mobilization. Larger or resource-rich groups also use litigation, but it tends to be just one among several pathways that they use. To be effective in legislatures, for example, groups need lots of money and large numbers of aroused and vocal members. Lobbyists need to spend money by donating to politicians' campaign funds, wining and dining public officials, and mounting public relations campaigns to sway public opinion. Groups also need to mobilize their membership to flood legislators' offices with phone calls and e-mail messages. By contrast, a small group may be successful using the courts if it has an effective attorney and enough resources to sustain a case through the litigation process. The most important resources for effective litigation are expertise and resources for litigation expenses.[11]

EXPERTISE For effective advocacy in litigation, expertise is essential. This includes thorough knowledge in the areas of law relevant to the case as well as experience in trial preparation or appellate advocacy, depending on which level of the court system is involved in a particular case. Attorneys who have previously dealt with specific issues know the intricate details of relevant prior court decisions and are better able to formulate effective arguments that use those precedents. In addition, attorneys affiliated with large, resource-rich law firms or interest groups have at their disposal teams of attorneys who can handle research and other aspects of investigation and preparation.

LITIGATION RESOURCES Interest groups and individuals who use the court process must have the resources to handle various expenses in addition to the attorneys' fees, which are generally very high unless the lawyers have volunteered to work for little or nothing on a **pro bono** basis. (*Pro bono publico* is a Latin phrase that translates as "for the public good." It means that attorneys and other professionals are waiving their usual fees to work for a cause in which they believe. Some interest groups rely heavily on securing pro bono professional support.)

PATHWAYS | of action

The NAACP and Racial Segregation

Beginning in the 1930s, the National Association for the Advancement of Colored People (NAACP), an important civil rights interest group founded in 1910, filed lawsuits to challenge state laws that segregated African Americans into separate, inferior educational institutions. These lawsuits tested the 1896 U.S. Supreme Court decision (*Plessy* v. *Ferguson*) that had ruled no constitutional violation exists when government gives people

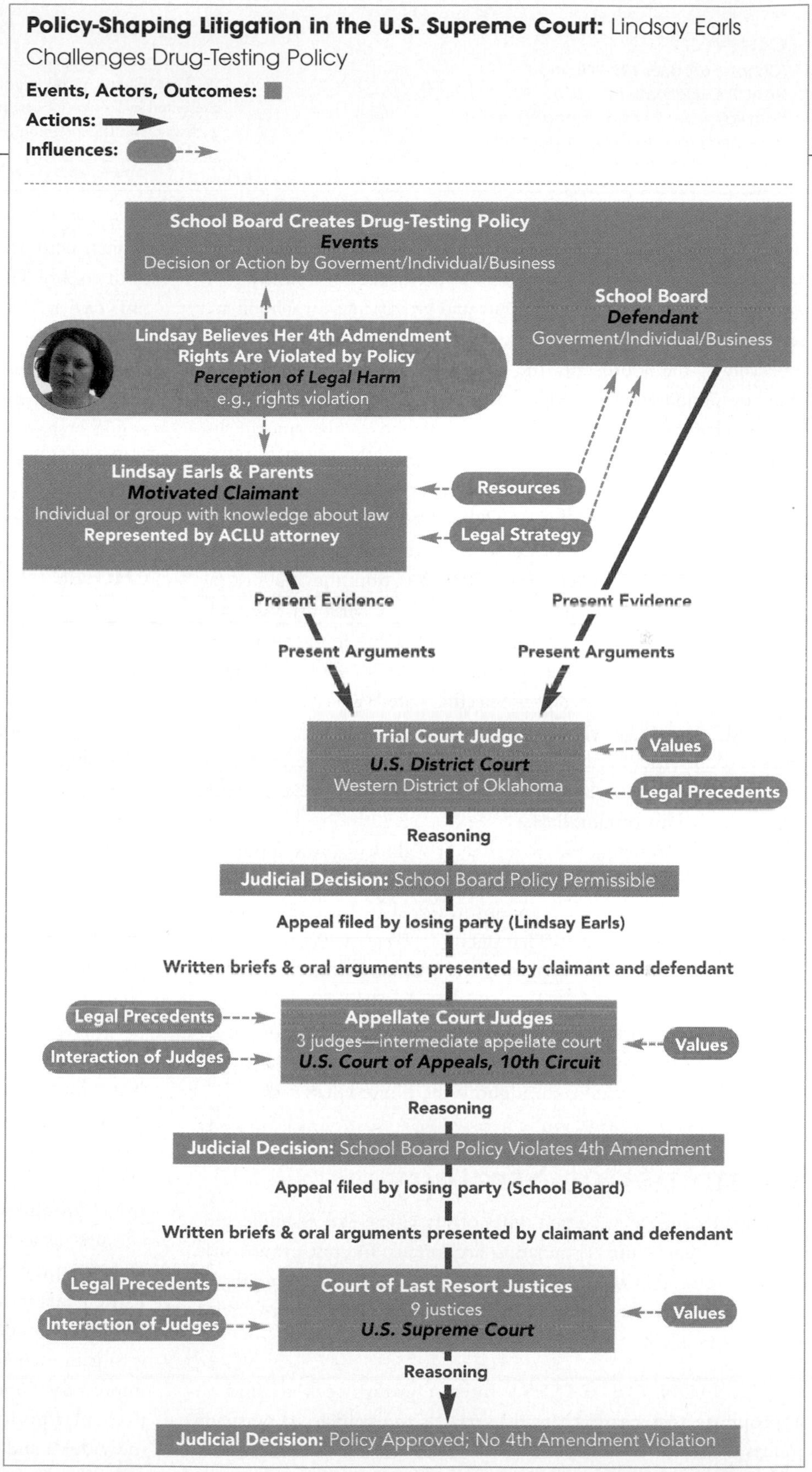

FIGURE 4.4 | Policy-Shaping litigation >> Related to Opening Vignette page 101
Litigation is a long and difficult process. The end result depends on the presistence, resources, and strategy of the competing sides as well as the values and interactions of the judges. ***—Do you have enough knowledge and resources to pursue policy-shaping litigation?***

CONNECT THE LINK
(Chapter **6**, pages **198–200**) The NAACP's litigation in the court pathway was a key factor leading to increased protection of constitutional rights for African Americans.

■ **Test Case:** A case sponsored or presented by an interest group in the court pathway with the intention of influencing public policy.

EXAMPLE: *The ACLU used Lindsay Earls's complaint as a test case to pursue its objective of preventing suspicionless drug tests of high school students.*

from different races "separate but equal" facilities and treatment. Unfortunately, many states used that court decision to justify their existing practice of providing separate and grossly inferior schools and services to African Americans. Rigid racial segregation was imposed, especially in the South, after the end of the post–Civil War Reconstruction period, and it was vigorously enforced for decades afterward.

Led by Thurgood Marshall, an attorney who later became the first African American to serve on the U.S. Supreme Court (1967–1991), the NAACP argued that the separate facilities sanctioned by *Plessy* were not equal and therefore violated the equal protection clause of the Constitution's Fourteenth Amendment. As we will examine in greater detail in LINK Chapter 6, pages 198–200, from the 1930s to the 1950s, the NAACP sued such states as Maryland, Missouri, Texas, and Oklahoma for excluding African-American students from state universities' law schools and graduate programs. By 1950, the U.S. Supreme Court had issued several decisions rejecting states' false claims that they provided "separate but equal" facilities for African Americans in colleges and universities. It was at that point that litigation began, backed by the NAACP, that would lead to public school racial segregation being declared unconstitutional.

After Earl Warren, the governor of California, was appointed chief justice in 1953, the nine justices unanimously declared that school segregation laws are unconstitutional because they violate the equal protection clause. That decision, *Brown* v. *Board of Education of Topeka* (1954), was based on a lawsuit filed by the NAACP on behalf of African-American parents and schoolchildren in Topeka, Kansas. The *Brown* decision established the foundation for subsequent NAACP lawsuits in the 1960s and 1970s seeking to desegregate public school systems throughout the United States. ■

Elements of Strategy

All litigants engage in certain types of strategies—for example, presenting evidence and formulating arguments. Interest groups may benefit from additional opportunities to use specific strategies by choosing which case to pursue or by choosing the court in which a case may be filed.

SELECTION OF CASES Interest groups seek to find an appropriate **test case**■ that will serve as the vehicle to persuade judges to change law and policy. Sometimes they can recruit plaintiffs and then provide legal representation and litigation expenses to carry the case through the court system. In challenging laws that restrict choices about abortion, an interest group would rather bring the case on behalf of a teenage rape victim than pursue the case for a married woman who became pregnant after being insufficiently careful with birth control. The interest group is likely to believe that the rape victim's case will provide more compelling arguments that can generate sympathy from many judges, because this case concerns a young crime victim who became pregnant through no fault of her own.

Interest groups cannot always choose precisely which case would best serve their interests. They may pursue any relevant case available at a given moment, because they cannot afford to watch passively if other cases then working their way through the system may lead to adverse judicial decisions.

CHOICE OF JURISDICTION One important factor in litigation strategies is the choice of courts in which to pursue a legal action. Because of the country's dual court system, there is often a choice to be made about whether state or federal courts are more likely to produce outcomes favorable to a group's interests. In addition to considering whether state or federal law may be more likely to produce a favorable result, litigators may consider whether a specific federal or state judge would be sympathetic to their values and policy preferences.

FRAMING THE ARGUMENTS Litigants must make strategic decisions about how to frame the legal issues and arguments that they present in court. In some cases, they must decide which legal issues to raise. Lawyers must assess the judges before whom the case will be presented and make strategic decisions about which arguments will appeal to the particular decision makers who will consider the case.

When an interest group is not itself involved in a case, it may still seek permission to present written arguments as *amicus curiae* (Latin for "a friend of the court"). For example, it is very common for multiple interest groups to submit **amicus briefs**■, detailed written arguments that seek to persuade the U.S. Supreme Court to endorse a specific outcome or to adopt reasoning that is favorable to the groups' policy preferences. Amicus briefs can be influential, because justices' opinions sometimes draw from these briefs rather than from the arguments presented by the two parties in the case. Participants in a Supreme Court case typically welcome the submission of amicus briefs on behalf of their side. Indeed, one strategy is to gain the endorsement of as many interest groups as possible to impress the Supreme Court with the broad support that exists for a particular position. Over the course of Supreme Court history, individuals and interest groups have increasingly sought to influence the Court's decisions through amicus briefs. From 1946 through 1955, amicus briefs were filed in only 23 percent of Supreme Court cases, but between 1986 and 1995, they were filed in 85 percent of the cases considered.[12]

Amicus Briefs: Written arguments submitted to an appellate court by those who are interested in the issue being examined but are not representing either party in the case; often submitted by interest groups' lawyers to advance a specific policy position.

EXAMPLE: *When Lindsay Earls's case reached the Supreme Court, the Juvenile Law Center submitted written legal arguments known as amicus briefs to support her position while the Washington Legal Foundation submitted amicus briefs in support of the school board.*

PUBLIC RELATIONS AND THE POLITICAL ENVIRONMENT Interest groups have a strong incentive to gain sympathetic coverage from the news media about cases that they are pursuing through the court pathway. Attorneys often develop relationships with reporters in hopes that sympathetic stories will be written about policy-oriented legal cases. Such stories help educate the public and perhaps shape public opinion about an issue. They may also influence judges, because just like other people, they read the newspapers or watch television every day.

STUDENT | PROFILE

What would you do if you believed that your rights were being violated by one of your college's policies? Would you have the courage to speak out? Would you have the persistence and determination to find a lawyer to help take your case through the court system? This is not easy to do.

In 2002, Tyler Deveny, a high school senior in Kanawha County, West Virginia, filed a lawsuit to challenge the school district's policy of permitting prayers to be led at public school graduations. He claimed that such prayers are a form of government-sponsored religious activity in violation of the First Amendment's prohibition on an "establishment" of religion by government. In many towns, when school-sponsored prayers are supported by a majority of citizens, individuals who oppose those practices may be subject to criticism and harassment. However, Tyler stood up for his interpretation of the First Amendment. After the lawsuit was filed with the assistance of the ACLU and another interest group, school officials settled the case by agreeing to change the policy. ■

Action in the Court Pathway
Practice Quiz

1. One advantage in using the court pathway to shape public policy is that
   a. it takes less time than the other pathways.
   b. nearly anyone can do it.
   c. it may require fewer resources than those needed in most other pathways.
   d. it almost always works.
2. When interest groups submit amicus briefs in appellate case, they are
   a. objecting to the appellate court's decision to accept the case for hearing.
   b. presenting elaborate written arguments on behalf of one side in a case, even though they are not directly involved in the case.
   c. informing the judges that they will provide financial campaign contributions and volunteer workers to help the judges win reelection.
   d. announcing that they will monitor the actions of the legislature and executive.
3. When interest groups look for a test case that will help them with their litigation strategy, they seek
   a. a case that will present the issue in a way that will attract the attention and sympathy of the judges.
   b. the first case that they hear about.
   c. a case involving someone rich, who can pay them a great deal of money.
   d. a case that will be easy to resolve through a negotiated settlement.

Answers: 1-c, 2-b, 3-a.

Discussion Questions

1. Why did the NAACP use a litigation strategy instead of lobbying Congress and mobilizing voters to pressure the president to take action against racial segregation?
2. If you wanted to challenge a mandatory drug testing policy imposed by your college, what strategies would you need to use to succeed in the litigation process?

What **YOU** can do!

Pick a controversial issue in the current political arena (for example, immigration, enemy combatants, global warming, abortion, or same-sex marriage), and look at the position of a variety of interest groups on the topic. Possible groups might include the Cato Institute, the American Enterprise Institute, the Family Research Council, the ACLU, or the Center for Constitutional Rights. What strategies, arguments, or approaches are being used by these groups to seek change through the court pathway?

VISUAL LITERACY Case Overload

Implementation *and* Impact (pages 126–127)

What is the image of the courts in the United States?

Court decisions are not automatically implemented or obeyed. Judges have the authority to issue important pronouncements that dictate law and policy, but they have limited ability to ensure that their orders are carried out. To see their declarations of law translated into actual public policy, judges must typically rely on public obedience and on enforcement by the executive branch of government. As you saw earlier in this chapter, this is a primary reason why judges are concerned about preserving the courts' nonpolitical image. If the public came to believe that the courts were no different from branches of government in which partisanship dictates operations and outcomes, the public might be less likely to obey court decisions.

> "Does the executive branch ever refuse to enforce the courts' decisions?"
>
> —Student Question

During the Watergate scandal of the 1970s, in which President Richard Nixon conspired to cover up information about a burglary at Democratic Party offices committed by people working for his reelection campaign, the Supreme Court handed down a decision ordering Nixon to provide a special prosecutor with recordings of secretly taped White House conversations. Years later, Supreme Court Justice Lewis Powell observed that had Nixon refused to comply with the Court's order, "there was no way that we could have enforced it. We had [only] 50 police officers [at the Supreme Court], but Nixon had the [U.S. military at his disposal]."[13] Nixon handed over the tapes, however, and shortly thereafter resigned from office, presumably realizing that public support for his impeachment, already strong, would lead to his conviction by the Senate if he disobeyed a unanimous Court decision that citizens and members of Congress viewed as legitimate.

The weakness of courts has been revealed in a number of cases over the course of American history. In the 1830s, the Cherokee Nation successfully litigated a case against laws that ordered the removal of Cherokees from their lands. The state of Georgia supported removal on behalf of whites who invaded Cherokee lands to search for gold. The U.S. Supreme Court, still led by the aged Chief Justice John Marshall, supported the Cherokees' property rights, but President Andrew Jackson and other officials declined to use their power to enforce the ruling ("John Marshall has made his decision," Jackson is supposed to have said, "now let him enforce it.") Thus, despite using the court pathway in an appropriate manner to protect their property rights, the Cherokees were eventually forced off their land. A few years later, they were marched at gunpoint all the way to an Oklahoma reservation, with an estimated 4,000 dying along the way. The Cherokees' infamous Trail of Tears forced march and loss of land demonstrated that courts cannot automatically ensure that their decisions are enforced and obeyed. Unlike the situation in the 1970s, in which President Nixon felt strong public pressure to obey the Supreme Court or face impeachment, the Cherokees and the Supreme Court of the 1830s did not benefit from public acceptance and political support.

In modern times, analysts have questioned the effectiveness of courts in advancing school desegregation. Although the Supreme Court has earned praise for courageously standing up for equal protection by declaring racial segregation in public schools unconstitutional in *Brown,* the 1954 decision did not desegregate schools. Racial separation continued in public schools throughout the country for years after the Court's decision. In two highly publicized incidents, military force was necessary to enroll African-American students in all-white institutions. In 1957, President Dwight D. Eisenhower sent troops to force Little Rock Central High School to admit a half-dozen black students, and in 1962, President John F. Kennedy dispatched the U.S. Army to the University of Mississippi so that one African-American student could enroll. In both situations, there had been violent resistance to court orders, but the presidents effectively backed up the judicial decisions with a show of force. In other cities, desegregation was achieved piecemeal, over the course of two decades, as individual lawsuits in separate courthouses enforced the *Brown* mandate.

According to Professor Gerald Rosenberg, the actual desegregation of public schools came only after the president and Congress acted in the 1960s to push policy change, using financial incentives and the threat of enforcement actions to overcome segregation. In Rosenberg's view, courts receive too much credit for policy changes that actually only occur when other actors become involved. Courts receive this credit, in part, because of the symbolism attached to their publicized pronouncements.[14]

Similar arguments can be made about other policy issues. For example, the Supreme Court's decision recognizing a woman's right to make choices about abortion (*Roe* v. *Wade,* 1973) does not ensure that doctors and medical facilities will perform such procedures in all locations or that people have the resources to make use of this right.

Other analysts see the courts differently—as important and effective policymaking institutions. They argue that *Brown* and other judicial decisions about segregation were essential elements of social change. Without these judicial decisions initiating, guiding, and providing legitimacy for change, the changes might not have occurred. For example, until the mid-1960s, southern members of Congress who supported segregation were able to block corrective legislation, because the seniority system gave them disproportionate power on congressional committees. In the Senate, they also used the filibuster to prevent consideration of civil rights legislation. Thus they could make sure that proposed bills either died in committee or never came to a vote. In addition, elected officials at all levels of government and in all parts of the country were often too afraid of a backlash from white voters to take strong stands in support of equal protection for African Americans. Analysts point to other court decisions, such as those requiring police officers to inform suspects of their Miranda rights in 1966 and recognizing abortion rights in 1973, to argue that the court pathway has been an important source of policy change.[15] Unelected judges were arguably the only actors positioned to push the country into change.

Implementation and Impact

Practice Quiz

1. A court decision is a declaration of law; once it is formulated by a court, it automatically operates as effective public policy.
   a. true **b.** false
2. It's fair to say that the desegregation of public schools in this country moved forward as a result of
   a. the Supreme Court's decision in *Plessy* v. *Ferguson*.
   b. a series of legislative decisions starting with *Brown* v. *Board of Education*.
   c. the Court's reversal of *Plessy* v. *Ferguson*, lower-level courts' complementary decisions, and enforcing actions by President Eisenhower and President Kennedy.
   d. cultural change that inspired most people in segregated school districts to embrace desegregation.
3. Why might it be appropriate in a democracy that federal judges help formulate public policy?
   a. Federal judges are the elected representatives of the people.
   b. Federal judges can be fired if their decisions too often run contrary to the sentiments of the majority.
   c. Some democratic principles (such as individual rights) can conflict with majority sentiments. Federal judges, appointed for life and insulated from the pressures of popular sentiment, are well positioned to preserve such principles.
   d. Federal judges are appointed by governmental officials who are themselves elected. The votes that elected officials receive represent a level of citizen trust that transcends the changeable sentiments of a majority, making judges appointed by these officials a purer expression of democracy than elected judges would be.

Answers: 1-b, 2-c, 3-c.

Discussion Questions

1. Are courts powerful or weak?
2. How could a president be required to enforce a decision of the U.S. Supreme Court?

What **YOU** can do!

One way to know whether the Supreme Court's decisions make a difference is through measuring public awareness and public opinion. Look at the cases decided during the last term of the Supreme Court at **http://www.supremecourtus.gov/**, and conduct your own informal poll to determine whether your classmates and co-workers are aware of the Court's rulings on particularly high-profile issues. As a comparison, go to the Web site of the Library of Congress at **http://thomas.loc.gov/**, and generate a list of public laws from the last congressional term. Is public awareness of the Supreme Court similar to or different from levels of awareness about the work of Congress?

Judicial Policymaking and Democracy (pages 128–129)

Is it appropriate for judges to shape public policy in a democracy?

Notwithstanding the framers' expectation that the judiciary would be the weakest branch of government, the court pathway presents an avenue for pursuing public policy objectives because American judges possess important powers. But these powers often stir up debates about the role of courts in the constitutional governing system. These controversies are most intense when focused on the actions of appointed, life-tenured, federal judges.[16] In a democratic system, how can unelected, long-serving officials be permitted to make important decisions affecting public policy? This is an important question for Americans and their government.

The power of the judicial branch poses significant potential risks for American society. What if life-tenured judges make decisions that create bad public policy? What if they make decisions that nullify popular policy choices made by the people's elected representatives or that force those elected representatives to impose taxes needed to implement those decisions? Because of these risks, some critics call judicial policymaking undemocratic. They argue that judges should limit their activities to narrow decisions that address disputes between two parties in litigation and avoid any cases that might lead judges to supersede the preferences of the voters' accountable, elected representatives in the legislative and executive branches. These critics want to avoid the risk that a small number of judicial elites, such as the nine justices on the U.S. Supreme Court, will be able to impose their policy choices on the nation's millions of citizens.

Although judicial policymaking by unelected federal judges does not fit conceptions of democracy based on citizens' direct control over policy through elections, advocates of judicial policymaking see it as appropriate. According to their view, the design of the governing system in the U.S. Constitution rests on a vision of democracy that requires active participation and policy influence by federal judges. Under this conception of democracy, the U.S. Constitution does not permit the majority of citizens to dictate every policy decision. The Constitution facilitates citizen participation and accountability through elections, but the need to protect the rights of individuals under the Bill of Rights demonstrates that the majority should not necessarily control every decision and policy. In 1954, for example, racial segregation was strongly supported by many whites in the North and the South. Should majority rule have dictated that rigid racial segregation continue? In essence, the American conception of constitutional democracy relies on citizen participation and majority rule plus the protection of rights for individuals, including members of unpopular political, religious, racial, and other minorities.

After the death of Chief Justice William Rehnquist in 2005, Justice John Paul Stevens leads the other justices down the steps of the Supreme Court building following a ceremony to honor the late chief justice. This small group of unelected officials has significant power to create new law and policy. ***—How do you think this has affected the "separation of powers" set forth in the Constitution?***

PHOTO: Doug Mills/The New York Times

For example, in the aftermath of the September 11, 2001, terrorist attacks on the World Trade Center and the Pentagon, public opinion polls indicated that a majority of Americans favored requiring Arabs, including those who are U.S. citizens, to undergo special searches and extra security checks before boarding airplanes in the United States.[17] Imagine that Congress responded by enacting a law that imposed these requirements based on ancestry without regard to its detrimental impact on U.S. citizens of Arab extraction. Such a policy, if supported by a majority of citizens, would meet many of the requirements for democratic policymaking. However, it would collide with the Fourteenth Amendment's requirement of "equal protection of the laws" for Americans from all races and ethnic groups.

> "Do the Supreme Court justices follow the wishes of the majority? Should they?"
>
> —Student Question

To ensure that majority interests do not trample the

rights of minorities, the Constitution positions federal judges as the decision makers to protect constitutional rights. In this position, because they are appointed, life-tenured officials, federal judges are supposed to have the independence and the insulation from politics necessary to make courageous decisions on behalf of minority group members, no matter how unpopular those minorities may be. In practice, federal judges do not always go against the wishes of the majority, even when the rights of minority group members are threatened or diminished. Such was the case when the Supreme Court endorsed the detention of innocent Japanese Americans in internment camps during World War II (*Korematsu* v. *United States,* 1944). But in other cases, the Supreme Court and other courts can provide a check against the excesses of majority policy preferences. There is broad agreement that judges must uphold the U.S. Constitution, state constitutions, and laws enacted by legislatures through the use of their power of interpretation. Disagreements exist, however, about whether judges have acted properly in interpreting the law, especially when judicial decisions shape public policy. Was it improper for the Supreme Court to recognize a constitutional right of privacy that grants women the opportunity to make choices about abortion (*Roe* v. *Wade,* 1973)? Should the U.S. Supreme Court have prevented the Florida courts from ordering recounts of votes during the closely contested presidential election of 2000 (*Bush* v. *Gore,* 2000)? These and other questions will continue to be debated for decades to come for three primary reasons. First, courts are authoritative institutions that shape law and policy in ways that cannot be directly controlled by the public and other institutions of government. Second, court decisions often address controversial issues that reflect Americans' most significant disagreements about social values and public policies. And third, elected officials may choose to avoid taking action on controversial issues, thereby leaving the court pathway as the sole avenue for government action.

PATHWAYS | of change from around the world

What would you do if the independence of the American judiciary was threatened? What if members of Congress sought to impeach a federal judge simply because they disagreed with his or her decision in a criminal case? Would it matter to you? To the country? Would you even notice? In 2007, law students in Pakistan took to the streets with hundreds of lawyers to protest President Pervez Musharraf's effort to suspend and remove from office the chief justice of Pakistan's Supreme Court. These students felt so strongly about the need for judicial independence that they literally risked their lives as armed soldiers tried to stop the protests. Thankfully, contemporary issues in the United States rarely produce large-scale violence. But the question remains—what would you do under similar circumstances? Write a letter? Call your members of Congress? What could you do if an American president sought to ignore orders of the U.S. Supreme Court or otherwise diminish the power of the judiciary?[18] ■

Judicial Policymaking and Democracy
Practice Quiz

1. The framers of the U.S. Constitution expected that the judiciary would eventually become the most powerful branch of government.
   a. true **b.** false
2. One justification for judicial policymaking in the democratic governing system of the United States relies on
   a. the fact that federal judges are elected by and accountable to the voters.
   b. the provision in Article I of the U.S. Constitution that declares "judges shall have power over public policy."
   c. the need for independent judges to make decisions that protect the constitutional rights of individuals, including members of minority groups.
   d. the UN Declaration on Judicial Power in the Modern World.

Answers: 1-b, 2-c.

Discussion Question

1. Are the principles of American democracy violated when judges make decisions that shape public policy?

What **YOU** can do!

Justice Harry Blackmun was appointed to the U.S. Supreme Court by President Nixon with the expectation that he would vote consistently with Chief Justice Warren Burger, a conservative who had been a childhood friend from Blackmun's days in Minnesota. However, Blackmun's jurisprudence evolved during his time on the court, and he grew more liberal, even authoring the Court's majority opinion in *Roe* v. *Wade* (1973). You can view Blackmun's papers and memos, which are held in the Library of Congress, through this digital archive found at **http://epstein.law.northwestern.edu/research/Blackmun.html**. Since federal judges are appointed for life, is it problematic in a democracy that a judge might change his or her mind about how to decide cases over the course of an often decades-long career?

Lawyers and law students in Pakistan endured beatings and arrests at the hands of police in order to protect against the president's interference with the independence of their country's supreme court. ***—When people display such courage in seeking to protect courts and law, does it give you confidence that democracy will survive and thrive?***

Conclusion

The judicial branch serves important functions under the constitutional governing system of the United States. Judges and juries resolve disputes, determine whether criminal defendants are guilty, impose punishment on those convicted of crimes, and provide individuals with a means to challenge actions by government. These functions are carried out in multilevel court systems, made up of trial courts and appellate courts, that exist in each state as well as in a national system under the federal government. Each system is responsible for its own set of laws, though all must be in accord with the U.S. Constitution, "the supreme law of the land."

The judicial branch provides opportunities for individuals and interest groups to seek to shape law and public policy. Through the litigation process in the court pathway, they can frame arguments to persuade judges as to the best approaches for interpreting the law. Judicial opinions shape many significant public policies for society, including those affecting education, abortion, the environment, and criminal justice. These opinions interpreting constitutions and statutes are written by judges who are selected through political processes, including elections in many states and presidential appointment in the federal system. American judges are exceptionally powerful because of their authority to interpret the U.S. Constitution and their ability to block actions by other branches of government through the power of judicial review. The important impact of federal judges on major public policy issues raises difficult questions about the proper role of unelected officials in shaping the course of a democracy.

Think back to the story that opened the chapter, the Supreme Court's decision in Lindsay Earls's challenge to her school's drug testing policy. In light of what you have learned in this chapter, can you understand why she pursued a litigation strategy instead of just lobbying the school board, the state legislature, or Congress on the issue? Were you surprised or disappointed to learn that cases are determined by human factors beyond merely the words of a law? Do you agree or disagree with the Supreme Court's decision about whether such random, suspicionless drug testing is improper as an "unreasonable search" under the Fourth Amendment? Was it proper for the Supreme Court to decide this issue? Why?

The courts are not easily accessible to citizens, because their use depends on expensive resources, including the patience to sustain extended litigation and the funds to hire expert attorneys and pay for litigation expenses. Because of their resources and expertise, organized interest groups are often better positioned than individual citizens to use the court pathway in pursuing their own policy objectives or in blocking the policy goals of other interest groups. However, the limited ability of judges to implement their own decisions is one factor that leads some observers to debate whether the court pathway provides processes that can consistently and properly develop public policies that are useful and effective.

Key Objective Review, Apply, and Explore

Court Structure and Processes

(pages 102–107)

The United States has a "dual court system," in which each state, as well as the federal government, operates its own multilevel system with trial and appellate courts.

The U.S. Supreme Court carefully selects a limited number of cases each year and then decides important issues of law and policy.

KEY TERMS

Adversarial System 102
Inquisitorial System 102
Dual Court System 102
Criminal Prosecutions 102
Civil Lawsuits 102
Jury Trials 102
Original Jurisdiction 102
Appellate Jurisdiction 102
Settlements 102
Plea Bargains 102
Intermediate Appellate Courts 103
Courts of Last Resort 103
Appellate Briefs 105
Majority Opinion 105
Concurring Opinion 105
Dissenting Opinion 105
Writ of Certiorari 105

CRITICAL THINKING QUESTIONS

1. Does the adversarial system lead courts to discover the truth, or does the system simply produce victory for whichever side has the best attorney?
2. Does a court system really need appellate courts? Why not just treat the original decision in each case as the final decision?

INTERNET RESOURCES

Explore the federal court system: **http://www.uscourts.gov**
Explore the state court system: **http://www.uscourts.gov** and **http://www.uscourts.state.tc.us**

ADDITIONAL READING

Baum, Lawrence. *American Courts: Process and Policy,* 6th ed. Boston: Houghton Mifflin, 2007.

Smith, Christopher E. *Courts, Politics, and the Judicial Process,* 2nd ed. Chicago: Nelson-Hall, 1997.

The Power of American Judges

(pages 108–113)

In contrast with judicial officers in other countries, American judges are especially powerful because of their authority to interpret constitutions and statutes, their power of judicial review, and in the federal system, their protected tenure in office.

KEY TERMS

Case Precedent 108
Statutes 109
Judicial Review 109
***Marbury* v. *Madison* (1803) 110**
Judiciary Act of 1789 110
Writ of Mandamus 110
Impeachment 112
Court-Packing Plan 113

CRITICAL THINKING QUESTIONS

1. Does the power of judicial review improperly make the judicial branch more powerful than the executive (President) and legislative (Congress) branches of the federal governmen?
2. Some commentators suggest that federal judges should serve only limited terms in office. What impact, if any, would limited terms have on the judicial branch and its role in the governing system?

INTERNET RESOURCES

Read judicial opinions from the U.S. Supreme Court and other courts: **http://www.law.cornell.edu** and **http://www.findlaw.com**

ADDITIONAL READING

O'Brien, David. *Storm Center: The Supreme Court in American Politics,* 6th ed. New York, Norton, 2002.

Rehnquist, William H. *The Supreme Court: How It Was, How It Is.* New York: William Morrow, 1987.

Key Objective Review, Apply, and Explore

Judicial Selection
(pages 114–117)

Many states use election systems or merit selection to choose judges, while federal judges must be appointed by the president and confirmed by the Senate.

KEY TERMS

Senatorial Courtesy 114
Merit Selection 115
Filibuster 114
Retention Elections 117

CRITICAL THINKING QUESTIONS

1. What is the best way to select judges?
2. How could you design a merit selection system that would truly select the most qualified individuals for judgeships?

INTERNET RESOURCES

Examine competing perspectives on judicial selection: **http://www.ajs.org** (advocates for merit selection of judges); **http://www.judicialselection.org** (advocates the appointment of politically conservative federal judges); **http://www.allianceforjustice.org** (advocates the appointment of politically liberal justices)

ADDITIONAL READING

Goldman, Sheldon. *Picking Federal Judges: Lower Court Selection from Roosevelt Through Reagan.* New Haven, CT: Yale University Press, 1997.

Yalof, David Alistair. *Pursuit of Justice.* Chicago: University of Chicago Press, 2001.

Judges' Decision-Making
(pages 118–121)

Despite the close connections between the judicial branch and the political system, judges seek to preserve the courts' image as the "nonpolitical" branch of government.

Debates exist about the proper way to interpret the Constitution and statutes, and these debates affect choices about who will be selected to serve as judges.

KEY TERMS

Flexible Interpretation 120
Rational Choice Model 120
Legal Model 120
New Institutionalism 121
Attitudinal Model 120

CRITICAL THINKING QUESTIONS

1. Should judges be required to follow case precedent, or would it be better for them to make decisions based entirely on their best judgment?
2. Is there any way to prevent judges from using their own values and attitudes in making decisions?

INTERNET RESOURCES

Examine the contrasting views on judicial decision-making and constitutional interpretation presented on the Web sites of two prominent organizations for lawyers and law students: the Federalist Society for Law and Public Policy Studies (**http://www.fed-soc.org**) and the American Constitution Society for Law and Policy (**http://www.americanconstitutionsociety.org**).

ADDITIONAL READING

Baum, Lawrence. *The Puzzle of Judicial Behavior.* Ann Arbor, MI: University of Michigan Press, 1997.

Epstein, Lee and Jack Knight. *The Choices Justices Make.* Washington, D.C.: CQ Press, 1998.

Key Objective Review, Apply, and Explore

Action in the Court Pathway

(pages 122–125)

Individuals and interest groups use many strategies in the court pathway, and their likelihood of success will be enhanced if they have expertise, resources, and patience.

KEY TERMS

Pro Bono 123

Amicus Briefs 124

Test Case 124

CRITICAL THINKING QUESTIONS

1. Why did the NAACP use a litigation strategy instead of lobbying Congress and mobilizing voters to pressure the president to take action against racial segregation?
2. If you wanted to challenge a mandatory drug testing policy imposed by your college, what strategies would you need to use to succeed in the litigation process?

INTERNET RESOURCES

Discover interest groups that use the court pathway: Washington Legal Foundation (**http://www.wlf.org**), Pacific Legal Foundation (**http://www.pacificlegal.org**), American Civil Liberties Union (**http://www.aclu.org**), and NAACP Legal Defense Fund (**http://www.naacpldf.org**).

ADDITIONAL READING

Epstein, Lee and Joseph F. Kobylka. *The Supreme Court and Legal Change: Abortion and the Death Penalty*. Chapel Hill: University of North California Press, 1992.

Tushnet, Mark V. *Making Civil Rights Law: Thurgood Marshall and the Supreme Court, 1936–1961*. New York: Oxford University Press, 1994.

Implementation and Impact

(pages 126–127)

Judges cannot always ensure that their decisions are implemented. As a result, their ability to shape public policy may vary from issue to issue.

CRITICAL THINKING QUESTIONS

1. Are courts powerful or weak?
2. How could a president be required to enforce a decision of the U.S. Supreme Court?

INTERNET RESOURCES

Learn about upcoming law and policy controversies that will be addressed by the U.S. Supreme Court on Northwestern University's "On the Docket" Web site: **http://www.journalism.medill.northwestern.edu/docket**

ADDITIONAL READING

Canon, Bradley C. and Charles A. Johnson. *Judicial Policies: Implementation and Impact,* 2nd ed. Washington, D.C.: CQ Press, 1999.

Rosenberg, Gerald N. *The Hollow Hope: Can Courts Bring About Social Change?* Chicago: University of Chicago Press, 1991.

Key Objective Review, Apply, and Explore

Judicial Policymaking and Democracy

(pages 128–129)

Vigorous debates continue to occur about whether it is appropriate for life-tenured, federal judges to create law and public policy in a democracy.

CRITICAL THINKING QUESTION

1. Would judical policymaking be less controversial if we developed ways to hold federal judges accountable for their decisions? Would this be desirable?

INTERNET RESOURCES

Examine information about lawsuits seeking to persuade judges to tell corrections officials how prisons should be run. Consider whether such litigation and resulting judicial policymaking should be considered as proper under the American constitutional governing system: **http://www.middlegroundprisonreform.org/main/**

ADDITIONAL READING

Feeley, Malcolm M. and Edward L. Rubin. *Judicial Policy Making and the Modern State*. New York: Cambridge University Press, 1998.

Sandler, Ross and David Schoenbrod. *Democracy by Decree: What Happens when Courts Run Government*. New Haven, CT: Yale University Press, 2003.

Chapter Review Critical Thinking Test

1. What happens as a result of politicians' recognition that judges' interpretations of the Constitution and statutes are influenced by values and attitudes and not just based on established law?
- **a.** Only the best qualified and most experienced judges receive appointments.
- **b.** Political parties, interest groups, and elected officials want to see judges selected who share their political values.
- **c.** Presidents and governors will fire judges whom they believe to be incompetent.
- **d.** The Senate will only approve judicial nominees who receive top ratings from lawyers' associations.

2. The power of judicial review permits the Supreme Court to invalidate
- **a.** federal statutes and executive actions that the Court deems unconstitutional.
- **b.** the tradition of checks and balances by the other two branches.
- **c.** constitutional amendments that the Court finds to be superfluous or inconsistent with modern jurisprudence.
- **d.** constitutional amendments that the Court finds to be inconsistent with trends in public opinion.

3. All the following statements about the landmark Supreme Court case *Marbury* v. *Madison* are correct EXCEPT:
- **a.** It asserted the Court's authority without directly challenging the powers of the president.
- **b.** It established judicial review by striking down a section of the Judiciary Act of 1789, without elaboration.
- **c.** The power of judicial review established a useful check on the power of the two elective branches of government.
- **d.** The power of judicial review has not been used since *Marbury*, but the power makes Congress careful to enact statutes that comply with the Constitution.

4. Lifetime appointments for federal judges are considered essential, because
- **a.** well-qualified judges are so rare they must be given incentives to serve.
- **b.** they must not have to cater to political preferences or public opinion.
- **c.** they must be discouraged from running for elective office.
- **d.** they require years of experience before they can perform their duties effectively.

5. Regarding presidential selection of Supreme Court nominees, which of the following statements is the most accurate?
- **a.** Justices are selected based upon their reputation for honesty and impartiality.
- **b.** Only candidates with prior experience as lower-court judges can be nominated.
- **c.** Candidates are usually selected based on their presumed political values and policy preferences.
- **d.** All Supreme Court nominees are subject to approval by a majority vote of both chambers of Congress.

6. Most cases heard by the Supreme Court arrive by way of
- **a.** original jurisdiction.
- **b.** appellate jurisdiction.
- **c.** writ of habeas corpus.
- **d.** writ of certiorari.

7. If you are the chief justice on the U.S. Supreme Court, when do you get to decide which justice writes a majority opinion for the Court?
- **a.** in all cases
- **b.** when you are the most senior (longest-serving) justice in the majority
- **c.** when the most senior justice gives you permission to make the assignment
- **d.** when you vote with the majority in a case

8. Which statement accurately describes the Supreme Court's relationship to public policy?
- **a.** Article III of the Constitution says, "The Supreme Court shall have jurisdiction over all public policy matters."
- **b.** The Supreme Court uses its powers of constitutional interpretation and statutory interpretation to shape public policy.
- **c.** The president and Congress recognize that they must always obey and enforce policy-related decisions of the Supreme Court.
- **d.** Article III of the Constitution says, "The Supreme Court can interpret the Constititution, unless its decisions will affect public policy."

9. All of these statements about Supreme Court procedure are correct EXCEPT:
- **a.** Each attorney is limited to 2 hours of uninterrupted time to present a case.
- **b.** Appellate briefs must be submitted prior to oral argument.
- **c.** Four justices must agree to hear a case before it will be accepted.
- **d.** In spite of thousands of petitions, very few are granted a hearing.

10. A traditional legal order requiring a government official to take a specific action is known as a(n)
- **a.** writ of habeas corpus.
- **b.** writ of certiorari.
- **c.** writ of mandamus.
- **d.** obiter dictum.

11. President Franklin D. Roosevelt's plan to appoint additional justices to the Supreme Court in order to challenge the Court's hostility to the New Deal was known as
- **a.** gerrymandering.
- **b.** court-packing.
- **c.** court-bashing.
- **d.** executive privilege.

12. The tactic of using lengthy speeches in the Senate to delay proposed legislation or block the appointment of a federal judge is known as
- **a.** senatorial privilege.
- **b.** gerrymandering.
- **c.** log-rolling.
- **d.** filibuster.

Chapter Review Critical Thinking Test

13. The method of selecting state judges from a list compiled by a committee appointed by the governor, and then permitting voters to decide whether to retain these judges for an additional term, is commonly known as
- **a.** partisan election.
- **b.** the Missouri plan.
- **c.** the renewai cycle.
- **d.** the qualification plan.

14. Regarding the impact of partisan politics on the selection of state judges, which of the following statements is NOT accurate?
- **a.** Listing only the names of judges—not their party affiliations—ensures that the public will choose the most impartial judges.
- **b.** Political parties often choose the judicial candidates and support their campaigns, even in nonpartisan elections.
- **c.** Most voters know little about the candidates and will often vote to retain the incumbent judge.
- **d.** By electing judges, voters can hold judges accountable and remove them from office.

15. A legal rule established by a judicial decision that guides subsequent judicial decisions is known as
- **a.** judicial courtesy.
- **b.** judicial restraint.
- **c.** statutory interpretation.
- **d.** case precedent.

16. Those Supreme Court justices who interpret the Constitution based on the writings and rationales of the founders are following the _________ approach.
- **a.** flexible interpretation
- **b.** preferred freedoms
- **c.** original intent
- **d.** gradual expansionist

17. The political science model suggests justices reach their decisions based upon strategic calculations to achieve their preferred case outcomes is known as
- **a.** the legal model.
- **b.** the attitudinal model.
- **c.** the rational choice model.
- **d.** new institutionalism.

18. Those groups best positioned to make effective use of the court pathway for policy impact are
- **a.** indigent petitioners and minorities.
- **b.** organized interests and wealthy individuals.
- **c.** ideological conservatives.
- **d.** ideological liberals.

19. Regarding enforcement of judicial decisions, which of the following statements is the most accurate?
- **a.** Judges may issue directives but have limited ability to ensure that they are implemented.
- **b.** Courts are designed to obey legislative bureaucracies.
- **c.** The intent of the executive branch will always overcome the intent of the judicial branch.
- **d.** The doctrine of federalism prohibits judges from interpreting the actions of state legislatures.

20. What can be said about federal judges and the protection of rights for members of minority groups?
- **a.** Interest groups effectively used litigation to persuade federal judges to make decisions supporting the concept of equal rights.
- **b.** Interest groups failed in their efforts to persuade federal judges to issue decisions to advance equal rights.
- **c.** Federal judges decided that Congress is solely responsible for protecting the rights of minority groups.
- **d.** Federal judges decided that the president is solely responsible for protecting the rights of minority groups.

Answers: 1-b, 2-a, 3-d, 4-b, 5-c, 6-d, 7-d, 8-b, 9-a, 10-c, 11-b, 12-d, 13-b, 14-a, 15-d, 16-c, 17-c, 18-b, 19-a, 20-a.

You decide!

In the aftermath of the Virginia Tech campus shooting, in which a psychologically troubled student shot and killed more than 30 students and professors in April of 2007, your college has instituted a policy that all students will be frisked and their backpacks and other bags searched by police when entering a university building, including dormitories. A female friend approaches you and describes her anger at having female police officers feel around her body and look inside her purse every time she enters a building. Your friend asks for your advice about how to fight against the policy. (Refer to Student Profile, page 125.) She says, "You have studied about courts and law—is there anything that could be done?" What advice would you give? Would it be possible to challenge this policy in court? What steps would your friend need to take? What resources and strategies would she need?

Key Objective Outline

CHAPTER 5
CIVIL LIBERTIES AND CIVIL RIGHTS

Do Americans have too many or too few civil liberties and civil rights protections?

The crime was so sickening that it seemed like something created by a screenwriter for a frightening crime movie, such as *Silence of the Lambs* or *Psycho*. Seventeen-year-old Christopher Simmons decided to commit a murder. He and another teen abducted a woman, tied her up, and threw her into a river. Simmons confessed to the murder, and after a trial, the judge followed the jury's recommendation that Simmons be sentenced to death.

During the appeal process, attorneys presented information about Simmons's difficult childhood as well as scientific studies about human brain development to show that teenagers do not have the same self-control and understanding of consequences that are characteristic of adults. The death sentence was overturned by the Missouri Supreme Court, and the prosecutor subsequently asked the U.S. Supreme Court to hear the case.

By a 5-4 vote, the U.S. Supreme Court upheld the Missouri Supreme Court's decision (*Roper* v. *Simmons*, 2005). The majority opinion declared that death sentences for juveniles under the age of 18 are inconsistent with contemporary societal values and therefore violate the Eighth Amendment prohibition on "cruel and unusual punishments." The Court's decision provided a new definition of a particular civil liberty and thereby barred all states from imposing capital punishment on juveniles. The decision caused controversy, because many people believe that teenagers should be held fully accountable for their actions.

Judges make decisions that define the civil liberties and civil rights guaranteed by the Bill of Rights. *Civil liberties* are individuals' freedoms and legal protections that cannot be denied by the actions of government. *Civil rights* are legal protections concerning equality and citizens' participation in the country's democratic governing processes. As you saw in Chapter 4, judges use their power of interpretation to ensure the Constitution's protections are available even for individuals whose ideas and actions anger the majority of Americans. The existence of judges' power to interpret the Bill of Rights means that the definitions of civil liberties and civil rights change over time as new judges assume office and as sitting judges' ideas about values and public policy change.

STUDENT RESOURCE-CENTER
• Glossary
• Vocabulary Example
• LINK
• MyPoliSciLab Connection

■ **Civil Liberties:** Individual freedoms and legal protections guaranteed by the Bill of Rights that cannot be denied or hindered by government.

EXAMPLE: *The Supreme Court declared that the Fourth Amendment protection against "unreasonable searches and seizures" forbids a city from setting up roadblocks to check all cars and drivers for possession of illegal drugs (*City of Indianapolis *v.* Edmond, *2000).*

COMPARATIVE **Comparing Civil Liberties**

The Bill *of* Rights *in* History (pages 140–149)

Why does the Bill of Rights protect individuals against actions by state governments?

As you've seen in earlier chapters, the 10 constitutional amendments that make up the Bill of Rights were added to the U.S. Constitution in 1791 to provide **civil liberties**■ for individuals. These amendments were enacted in response to fears that the Constitution had failed to provide enough legal protections for individuals. The experiences of eighteenth-century Americans with British rule gave the founders reason to be concerned that a government might become too powerful and thereby fail to respect individuals' liberty and property. The Bill of Rights spelled out the legal protections that individuals could expect from the federal government. Mere words on paper, however, do not by themselves provide protection against actions by government officials. Those words must be respected by officials, and there must be judges willing to interpret and enforce the underlying meanings.

Early Interpretation of the Bill of Rights

During the first years after ratification of the U.S. Constitution and the Bill of Rights, the tiny federal court system handled relatively few cases. The U.S. Supreme Court's most important cases from this era involved decisions that defined the authority of the various institutions of American government and clarified the respective powers of state and federal governments. The Supreme Court played an important role in interpreting constitutional provisions in ways that created a workable distribution of power among branches of government and defined the relationships between state and federal governments.

The Supreme Court's role as a guardian of civil liberties did not emerge until the 1950s, when the Bill of Rights became a central focus of decisions by federal judges. One reason that the federal

In 1734, British authorities burned copies of John Peter Zenger's *Weekly Journal* in order to stop Zenger from criticizing the colonial governor of New York. Memories of such actions by British authorities remained in the minds of Americans when they later wrote the provisions of the Bill of Rights to protect freedom of the press. ***—How would the United States be different today without the protections for free expression contained in the Bill of Rights?***

CONNECT THE LINK
(Chapter **4**, pages **110–111**) Chief Justice John Marshall was also the author of the famous opinion in *Marbury* v. *Madison* (1803) that established judges' power of judicial review.

Civil Rights: Public policies and legal protections concerning equal status and treatment in American society to advance the goals of equal opportunity, fair and open political participation, and equal treatment under the law without regard to race, gender, disability, and other demographic characteristics.

EXAMPLE: *The U.S. Supreme Court ruled in* Batson v. Kentucky *(1986) that prosecutors cannot use people's race as a basis to systematically exclude them from serving on trial juries.*

"How did the Supreme Court get involved in protecting individual rights?"

—Student Question

courts did not focus much attention on the Bill of Rights was because of the way the Supreme Court first interpreted the legal protections for individuals contained in the Constitution. In the early 1830s, a man named Barron filed a lawsuit against the city of Baltimore claiming that road construction by the city had ruined his wharf in the harbor. Barron believed that the city's action had violated his protections under the Fifth Amendment. Under that amendment, people cannot be "deprived of . . . property, without due process of law; nor shall private property be taken for public use, without just compensation." Barron's lawsuit sought "just compensation" for the loss of his property's value because of the city's road-building activities.

The Supreme Court's opinion in ***Barron* v. *Baltimore* (1833)** was written by Chief Justice **John Marshall,** the crucial figure who, as you saw in LINK Chapter 4, pages 110–111, shaped the Supreme Court's role in the nation during the federal judiciary's formative decades (1801–1835). After examining the arguments in the case, Marshall concluded:

> We are of the opinion that the provision in the Fifth Amendment to the Constitution . . . is intended solely as a limitation on the exercise of power by the Government of the United States, and is not applicable to the legislation of the States.

Marshall's decision reflected the original intent of the Bill of Rights as well as the literal words at the start of the First Amendment, which refer to the federal government: "Congress shall make no law . . ." The effect of Marshall's decision went beyond merely limiting the Fifth Amendment's protections; it also established the fact that all the provisions of the Bill of Rights protected *only* against actions by the *federal* government, not against actions by state and local government.

Think about the implications of the Court's decision. The actual civil liberties enjoyed by citizens could differ dramatically, depending on which state a person happened to inhabit or be visiting. As a result, many states had laws restricting speech, press, assembly, and other aspects of civil liberties, and these laws were unaffected by the existence of the idealistic language of the Bill of Rights.

The Incorporation Process and the Nationalization of Constitutional Rights

Three amendments were added to the Constitution after the Civil War (1861–1865). Members of Congress proposed the amendments primarily to provide protections for African Americans who were newly freed from slavery. They included the Thirteenth Amendment, which prohibits slavery, and the Fifteenth Amendment, which sought to end racial discrimination in voting rights. The other amendment, the Fourteenth, did not merely protect African Americans. Ratification of the Fourteenth Amendment (1868) gave the Constitution language granting legal protections for all individuals against actions by state and local officials. The key language in the first section of the Fourteenth Amendment says:

> No State shall make or enforce any law which shall abridge the privileges or immunities of citizens of the United States; nor shall any State deprive any person of life, liberty, or property, without due process of law; nor deny to any person within its jurisdiction the equal protection of the laws.

The words of the Fourteenth Amendment specified that these constitutional protections were aimed against actions by states, but the precise protections were not clear. It would require interpretations by judges to determine what specific protections, if any, would be provided by the phrases "privileges or immunities of citizens," "due process of law," and "equal protection of the laws." We look to the latter phrase, known as the equal protection clause, as a key provision of the Constitution that is interpreted by judges to protect **civil rights** concerning equal status and treatment by government. One scholar has called the Fourteenth Amendment "probably the most controversial and certainly

■ **Due Process Clause:** A statement of rights in the Fifth Amendment (aimed at the federal government) and the Fourteenth Amendment (aimed at state and local governments) that protects against arbitrary deprivations of life, liberty, or property. The Fourteenth Amendment phrase is also interpreted by the Supreme Court to expand a variety of rights.

EXAMPLE: *In* Roe *v.* Wade *(1973), establishing a right of choice about abortion, the Supreme Court declared that the right to privacy is based on the concept of personal "liberty" embodied in the Fourteenth Amendment due process clause's protection of "liberty" against arbitrary government interference.*

■ **Incorporation:** Process used by the Supreme Court to protect individuals from actions by state and local governments by interpreting the due process clause of the Fourteenth Amendment as containing selected provisions of the Bill of Rights.

EXAMPLE: *In* Klopfer *v.* North Carolina *(1967), the U.S. Supreme Court held that the Sixth Amendment right to a speedy trial is fundamental to the criminal justice process and therefore applies to state criminal trials through the Fourteenth Amendment's due process clause.*

the most litigated of all amendments adopted since the birth of the Republic."[1] The Fifteenth Amendment also protects civil rights by addressing racial discrimination directed at potential voters.

Lawyers used the court pathway to present arguments to the U.S. Supreme Court and to other courts about specific legal protections they believed the Fourteenth Amendment should provide for their clients. In particular, they asked the Court to interpret the **due process clause**■ of the amendment as providing specific civil liberties to protect individuals against actions by state and local officials.

"How did we get our civil liberties protected in the states?"

—Student Question

For several decades, except for one case recognizing property rights protected by the concept of due process (*Chicago, Burlington & Quincy Railroad* v. *Chicago,* 1897), the Supreme Court generally refused to specify the protections provided by the phrase "due process." In 1925, however, the Court began to move in a new direction by declaring that the First Amendment right to free speech is included in the protections of the Fourteenth Amendment due process clause. According to the Court's decision that year in ***Gitlow* v. *New York,*** individuals enjoy the right to freedom of speech against actions and laws by state and local governments. (The state of New York had prosecuted Benjamin Gitlow, a member of the Socialist Party, for distributing publications that advocated overthrowing the U.S. government.)

In subsequent years, the Court began to bring other specific civil liberties under the protection of the Fourteenth Amendment's due process clause. For example, in *Near* v. *Minnesota* (1931), the Court included freedom of the press under the Fourteenth Amendment. The Court added the First Amendment's right to free exercise of religion under the due process clause in 1934 (*Hamilton* v. *Regents of the University of California*) and firmly repeated that conclusion in 1940 (*Cantwell* v. *Connecticut*).

The process through which the Supreme Court examined individual provisions of the Bill of Rights and applied them against state and local officials is called **incorporation**■. The Court *incorporated* specific civil liberties from the Bill of Rights into the meaning of the due process clause of the Fourteenth Amendment.

Benjamin Gitlow (right), shown speaking to a rally of the Workers Party in New York City in 1928, used the court pathway to challenge his criminal conviction for expressing ideas about dramatically altering the American system of government. The U.S. Supreme Court used Gitlow's case in 1925 to begin the incorporation process by declaring that First Amendment protections for freedom of speech also apply against state governments. ***—Are there any statements or ideas that are so dangerous the government should be able to place people in prison for expressing them? If so, what might they be?***

Incorporation gave individuals throughout the nation the same civil liberties protections against actions by state and local governments. This incorporation occurred slowly, over the course of half a century.

On a case-by-case basis through the 1960s, the Court ultimately expanded the meaning of "due process" under the Fourteenth Amendment by selectively incorporating individual civil liberties from the Bill of Rights. By the time of the Supreme Court's decision to apply the right to trial by jury in state courts in 1968 (*Duncan* v. *Louisiana*), most of the provisions in the first eight amendments had been included under the protections of the Fourteenth Amendment's due process clause.

PATHWAYS | of action

Cruel and Unusual Punishments

At first, the Eighth Amendment's prohibition of "cruel and unusual punishments" merely meant that the *federal* government could not impose torturous punishments on offenders who committed *federal* crimes. As individuals pursued their cases through the levels of the court pathway, however, the Supreme Court justices broadened the definition of this Eighth Amendment right. In 1910, the Court expanded the definition to include punishments that are disproportionate to the crime as well as punishments that are similar to torture (*Weems* v. *United States*). The 1910 case concerned a man sentenced to 15 years at hard labor in ankle chains, plus the loss of citizenship rights, for stealing a small amount of money. Later, another individual's case led to incorporation of the Eighth Amendment into the Fourteenth Amendment due process clause for application against the states (*Robinson* v. *California,* 1962). Eventually, additional cases led the Supreme Court to include limited rights for prisoners to receive medical care and food as well as consider issues concerning the administration of the death penalty. In 2005, as you saw in the chapter opening, an appeal on behalf of Christopher Simmons, who confessed to a vicious kidnapping and murder at the age of 17, convinced the Supreme Court to declare that the prohibition on "cruel and unusual punishments" bars the imposition of the death penalty for crimes committed by offenders under the age of 18 (*Roper* v. *Simmons*). By pursuing cases through the court pathway, individual provisions of the Bill of Rights may be interpreted and reinterpreted by judges to either expand or reduce the legal protections provided by the Constitution. During the twentieth century, such interpretations led to an expansion of the protections provided by the Eighth Amendment. The words *cruel and unusual punishments* did not change, but the interpretation and application of those words did as judges applied them to a wider array of actions undertaken by officials at all levels of government. ■

Total incorporation of the Bill of Rights did not occur. A few provisions of the Bill of Rights have never been incorporated and thus still provide protections solely against actions by the federal government. Most notably, these include the Second Amendment's provision linking "a well-regulated Militia" and the right to bear arms; the Third Amendment's provision against housing troops in private homes; the Fifth Amendment's right to a grand jury; the Seventh Amendment's requirement of jury trials in civil cases contesting any amount over $20; and the Eighth Amendment's prohibition of excessive bail (see Figure 5.1a,b on pages 144–148). In 2008, the Supreme Court declared that federal entities, such as the District of Columbia, violate the Second Amendment right to bear arms if they enact laws to prevent law-abiding citizens from keeping handguns in their homes (*District of Columbia* v. *Heller*). In the near future, cases challenging gun laws enacted by cities and states will undoubtedly reveal whether the Supreme Court intends to incorporate the Second Amendment.

The incorporation process served the important function of nationalizing the Bill of Rights (see Figure 5.1b on pages 146–148). As a result, most of its provisions apply everywhere within the borders of the United States to protect individuals against actions by all levels of government. Thus the process of incorporation is also referred to as the "nationalization" of the Bill of Rights.

timeline

1791
Ratification of the Bill of RIghts

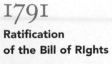

1833
Barron* v. *Baltimore
Bill of Rights apply only against federal government

1868
Ratification of the 14th Amendment, including due process clause

1897
Chicago, Burlington & Quincy Railroad* v. *Chicago
5th Amendment right to just compensation applied against states (property right, not personal civil liberties protection for individuals)

1919
Schenck* v. *United States
1st Amendment right of free speech is subject to a "clear and present danger" test

1925
Gitlow* v. *New York
1st Amendment freedom of speech protection applies against the states through 14th Amendment due process clause

1931
Near* v. *Minnesota
1st Amendment freedom of the press applies against states through the 14th Amendment

1943
West Virginia* v. *Barnette
1st Amendment protection for free exercise of religion permits members of religious minorities to decline to recite the Pledge of Allegiance in public schools

1961
Mapp* v. *Ohio
Exclusionary rule protection of the 4th Amendment applies against states through the 14th Amendment

1963
Gideon* v. *Wainwright
6th Amendment right to counsel for non-petty offenses applies to the states through 14th Amendment

FIGURE 5.1a | **Key Decisions on Civil Liberties**

The Bill of Rights initially protected individuals' civil liberties only against actions by the federal government. The Fourteenth Amendment (1868) added language to the Constitution to prohibit state and local officials from violating the right to "due process." Over the course of several decades, the U.S. Supreme Court interpreted the phrase "due process" in ways that required state and local officials to respect specific civil liberties protections in the Bill of Rights. The Supreme Court also interpreted specific provisions in the Bill of Rights to expand the legal protections enjoyed by individuals.

1969

Brandenburg* v. *Ohio

1st Amendment protection for freedom of speech is broadened to forbid government restraint unless there is a danger of "imminent lawless action" such as a riot or other violence.

1968

Duncan* v. *Louisiana

6th Amendment right to trial by jury applies against the states through the 14th Amendment

1971

Tinker* v. *Des Moines Independent School District

1st Amendment protects the symbolic speech rights of students who wish to wear black armbands in school in order to protest the Vietnam War

New York Times* v. *United States

1st Amendment protection for freedom of the press prevented the government from stopping newspapers' publication of a report on the Vietnam War

Lemon* v. *Kurtzman

1st Amendment test for Establishment Clause violations focuses on the intent of government policies and the entanglement of government with religion

1989

Texas* v. *Johnson

Burning a flag as part of political protest is a protected form of symbolic speech under the 1st Amendment

2003

Lawrence* v. *Texas

The right to privacy prevents states from punishing adults' private, noncommercial sexual conduct, including conduct by gays and lesbians

1966

Miranda* v. *Arizona

5th Amendment protection against compelled self-incrimination requires officers to inform suspects about rights prior to questioning while in custody

1973

Roe* v. *Wade

Right to privacy includes women's right to make choices about abortion in the first 6 months of pregnancy

Miller* v. *California

1st Amendment test for obscene materials focuses on contemporary community standards and patently offensive sexual content

PHOTO: Carol T. Powers/The New York Times

FIGURE 5.1b | **The Selective Incorporation of the Bill of Rights**

AMENDMENT	RIGHT	DATE INCORPORATED	CASE	THE RIGHT IN THE NEWS
First Amendment	Speech	1925	*Gitlow* v. *New York*	 Howard Stern claims that his recent move to Sirius Radio Network was a matter of protecting his First Amendment rights.
	Press	1931	*Near* v. *Minnesota*	*New York Times* reporter Judith Miller was jailed for 12 weeks in 2005 for refusing to reveal her source of information concerning an investigation to discover who revealed the identity of a CIA agent.
	Assembly and Petition	1937	*Dejonge* v. *Oregon*	In response to protesters gathered at military funerals, Congress enacted the Respect Fallen Heroes Act in 2006 to ban protests within 300 feet of national cemeteries during funerals.
	Religion–Exercise	initial 1934	*Hamilton* v. *University of California*	No current issue
	Religion–Exercise	confirmed 1940	*Cantwell* v. *Connecticut*	The U.S. Supreme Court ruled in 2006 that the federal government cannot prevent a small religious sect from using a South American tea containing a regulated hallucinogenic drug as part of its ceremonies.
	Religion–Establishment	1947	*Everson* v. *Board of Education*	 In 2005, a federal judge in Pennsylvania ruled that intelligent design theory cannot be taught as an alternative to evolution in public schools, because intelligent design represents a religious viewpoint that the government (local school board) is imposing on students.
Second Amendment	Bear Arms		Not Incorporated	 In 2008, the U.S. Supreme Court ruled that people possess an individual right to own handguns and to keep them in their homes. This right protects against restrictive gun laws by Congress or federal entities, such as Washington, D.C.
Third Amendment	Quartering Troops		Not Incorporated	No current issue
Fourth Amendment	Search & Seizure	1949	*Wolf* v. *Colorado*	The U.S. Supreme Court announced in 2006 that police cannot enter and conduct a warrantless search of a home with the consent of an occupant when another occupant of the home objects to the search.

AMENDMENT	RIGHT	DATE INCORPORATED	CASE	THE RIGHT IN THE NEWS
	Exclusionary Rule	1961	*Mapp* v. Ohio	The U.S. Supreme Court decided in 2006 that evidence obtained from a search need not be excluded from use in court when officers using a search warrant violate the traditional legal rule requiring them to knock and announce their presence before entering the home to be searched.
Fifth Amendment	Takings and Compensation	1897	*Chicago, B & Q Railroad* v. *Chicago*	 The U.S. Supreme Court ruled in 2005 that a city does not violate the Fifth Amendment provision about taking property for public use when it takes people's homes in order to turn the land over to private developers.
	Self-Incrimination	1964	*Malloy* v. *Hogan*	The Supreme Court of Georgia concluded that Spanish-speaking suspects did not need to be given Miranda warnings by a certified translator (2006).
	Grand Jury		Not Incorporated	No current issue
	Double Jeopardy	1969	*Benton* v. *Maryland*	In 2005, a Salt Lake City man decided to clear his conscience by admitting that he had murdered a toddler in 1991—however, he could not be prosecuted, because he had been tried and found not guilty of the charge 14 years earlier.
Sixth Amendment	Public Trial	1948	*In re Oliver*	A federal appeals court overturned the conviction of a man after the trial judge closed the courtroom and removed spectators while rape victims testified against the defendant (2006).
	Right to Counsel	1963	*Gideon* v. *Wainwright*	In 2008, the U.S. Supreme Court ruled that the right to counsel is triggered early in the criminal case process, when a defendant appears before a judge to hear the charges and face the possibility of being detained in jail before trial.
	Confrontation	1965	*Pointer* v. *Texas*	The U.S. Supreme Court found a violation of the right to confrontation when the prosecution played a tape recording of statements by the defendant's wife, but the wife never testified at the trial (2004).
	Impartial Jury	1966	*Parker* v. *Gladden*	In 2006, the murder trial of a college student accused of killing his father was moved from Albany to a different city in New York, because a judge concluded that extensive publicity about the case in Albany would make it impossible to have an impartial jury in that city's court.

FIGURE 5.1b | **The Selective Incorporation of the Bill of Rights (Continued)**

AMENDMENT	RIGHT	DATE INCORPORATED	CASE	THE RIGHT IN THE NEWS
	Speedy Trial	1967	*Klopfer* v. *North Carolina*	A federal judge found a violation of the right to a speedy trial for a robbery defendant and dismissed all charges after the defendant endured three aborted trials (mistrials) over a 17-month period; however, a court of appeals reversed that decision and ordered yet another trial for the defendant (2006).
	Compulsory Process	1967	*Washington* v. *Texas*	A Wisconsin court of appeals rejected a claim that the right to compulsory process was violated when a defendant was not allowed to call his friend as a witness. The court concluded that the friend's testimony would not have been relevant to the defendant's self-defense claim (2006).
	Jury Trial (criminal)	1968	*Duncan* v. *Louisiana*	The U.S. Supreme Court has struck down sentencing laws that permit judges to enhance sentences based on facts that were never decided upon by the jury (2004).
Seventh Amendment	Jury Trial (civil)		Not Incorporated	Availability of jury trials in civil cases is determined by each state's individual laws.
Eighth Amendment	Cruel and Unusual Punishments	1962	*Robinson* v. *California*	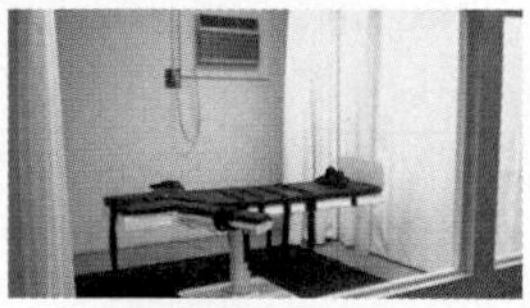 In 2008, the U.S. Supreme Court ruled that lethal injection can continue to be used as a method of execution.
	Excessive Bail		Not Incorporated	 After being convicted in 2006 of conspiracy and fraud charges, former Enron Corporation CEO Kenneth Lay was released on $5 million bail, but died before he was sentenced. PHOTO: Michad Stravato/The New York Times
	Excessive Fines		Not Incorporated	In 2006, a Belgian chemical company was sentenced by a federal court in California to pay a criminal fine of $40.9 million after admitting guilt to violating laws against price fixing.

The Bill of Rights in History

Practice Quiz

1. "Civil liberties" refers to freedoms and legal protections that the federal government can suspend or modify at any given time.
   a. true **b.** false
2. The Supreme Court's role as the guardian of civil liberties
   a. is specified in the Bill of Rights.
   b. is first mentioned in the Declaration of Independence.
   c. did not emerge until the middle of the twentieth century.
   d. emerged during the Court's formative years (1801–1835).
3. Before incorporation (which nationalized citizens' constitutional rights), the Bill of Rights only offered protection
   a. against actions by the federal government.
   b. against infringement of wealthy citizens' rights.
   c. against actions by state governments.
   d. for men who were registered voters.
4. The Fourteenth Amendment was enacted
   a. during the Jefferson administration.
   b. soon after the Civil War.
   c. during Lyndon Johnson's administration.
   d. in the aftermath of the civil rights movement.

Answers: 1-b, 2-c, 3-a, 4-b.

Discussion Questions

1. Instead of using incorporation, should the U.S. Supreme Court have permitted states to use their own constitutions and statutes to define civil liberties protections within their own borders? Why or why not?
2. How would you interpret the right to "due process" in the Fourteenth Amendment? Should that phrase protect any civil liberties beyond those applied by the U.S. Supreme Court through the incorporation process?

What **YOU** can do!

Identify the nonincorporated provisions of the Second, Fifth, and Seventh Amendments. Go to **http://www.uscourts.gov/index.html**, and browse the current dockets for the U.S. District Courts and the U.S. Courts of Appeal. Are there any cases in the federal pipeline that the Supreme Court could eventually use to incorporate the currently nonincorporated provisions? Is incorporation likely? Why or why not?

■ **Establishment Clause:** Clause in the First Amendment guaranteeing freedom from religion by providing a basis for Supreme Court decisions limiting government support for and endorsement of particular religions.

EXAMPLE: *Critics have sought to stop public schools from having children recite the Pledge of Allegiance because they claim that the words "under God" in the Pledge mean that the government is imposing a particular religious concept on children in violation of the establishment clause.*

■ **Free Exercise Clause:** Clause in the First Amendment guaranteeing freedom to practice one's religion without government interference as long as those practices do not harm other individuals or society.

EXAMPLE: *Some people argue that free exercise of religion should prevent the government from using public safety as a justification to prevent individuals from handling poisonous snakes, taking illegal drugs, sacrificing animals, or engaging in other regulated practices as part of religious ceremonies.*

First Amendment Rights: Freedom *of* Religion (pages 150–153)

How are the two dimensions of freedom of religion under the First Amendment different from each other?

Many political scientists believe that the drafters of the Bill of Rights placed special importance on the rights they chose to list first. Indeed, several Supreme Court justices have argued that First Amendment rights should be regarded as "preferred freedoms" that should receive extra attention from judges.[2] The very first rights listed in the First Amendment concern freedom of religion, speech, and press:

> Congress shall make no law respecting an establishment of religion, or prohibiting the free exercise thereof; or abridging the freedom of speech, or of the press; or the right of the people peaceably to assemble, and to petition the Government for redress of grievances.

The importance of these rights to the founders of the United States is quite understandable. Many colonists came to North America from Europe because their membership in minority religious groups led them to seek a land where they could worship as they pleased, without interference by the government. Similarly, the authors of the Bill of Rights were angry that people in the American colonies had been punished for criticizing the British government. Many scholars of government regard freedom of expression as an essential element of any democratic system. If people cannot freely criticize government officials, there is little opportunity to share information and opinions that will shape the voting processes that keep government officials accountable to their constituents.

Religious liberty is the very first right protected by the Constitution's First Amendment: "Congress shall make no law respecting an establishment of religion, or prohibiting the free exercise thereof. . . ." The amendment's first section, called the **establishment clause**■, concerns the connections between government and religion. The establishment clause can be characterized as providing "freedom *from* religion." The second section, the **free exercise clause**■, focuses on people's ability to practice their religion without governmental interference. This clause provides "freedom *of* religion." Individuals and interest groups have used the court pathway to challenge governmental actions as violating both aspects of the First Amendment.

Establishment of Religion

Agreement is widespread that the establishment clause forbids the designation or sponsorship by government of a national religion. Many people describe this clause as mandating "the separation of church and state." However, significant disagreements exist about what connections between religion and government are permitted by the First Amendment. Under a strict **separationist** view, government must avoid contacts with religion, especially those that lead to government support or endorsement of religious activities. This perspective argues that the government cannot provide financial support for religious schools or display religious items in public buildings and parks. Advocates of this viewpoint see such actions as improperly implying governmental favoritism or endorsement of one religion over others—or even of religion itself. By contrast, the **accommodationist** view permits the government to provide support for religion and associated activities. Advocates of this perspective argue that religious displays are permissible on public property and that government can even give financial support to religious schools for the nonreligious aspects of education (for example, reading, math, and science).

During the 1960s, the Supreme Court issued two controversial decisions that tilted toward the strict separationist perspective. In *Engel* v. *Vitale* (1962), the Court found a violation of the establishment clause in the common public school practice of beginning each day with a teacher-led prayer. Although many such prayers used general wording and sought to avoid offending anyone's religion, parents in New York filed lawsuits to challenge the practice. According to Justice Hugo Black's majority opinion, "When the power, prestige, and financial support of government is placed behind a particular religious belief, the indirect coercive pressure upon religious minorities to conform to the prevailing officially approved religion is plain."[3] A second decision barred public schools from reading the Lord's Prayer and Bible verses over their public address systems (*School District of Abington Township, Pennsylvania* v. *Schempp*, 1963). By declaring that long-standing practices provided improper government endorsement and pressure on behalf of religious belief, the Supreme Court generated a storm of controversy that continues today. Although many Americans wonder whether such governmental practices actually cause any harm, the Court has been sensitive to the concern that nonbelievers or members of minority religions, especially children, will feel pressured to participate or will be ostracized by others if they decline to participate.

In the years following these decisions, critics complained that the Supreme Court had "improperly removed God from the schools" and thereby reduced morality and social order in society. Some state legislatures and local officials challenged the Court's decision through

Thomas Jefferson first used the words "separation of church and state" in a letter he wrote in 1802, and this phrase has generated debate ever since. Controversies about the place of religion in American society and government regularly occur in the court pathway. ***Have judges gone too far in separating government from religion?***

Some Christians believe that judges and other public officials discriminate against their religion by banning nativity scenes in public areas and by preventing teacher-led prayers in public schools. ***—Can you think of examples, of favoritism for non-Christian religions?***

various means, such as mandating public display of the Ten Commandments in schools, teaching Bible-based creationism in public school science classes, and conducting student-led school prayers or moments of silence. Such practices were challenged in the court pathway by parents who viewed government-sponsored religious activities as inconsistent with civil liberties under the establishment clause.

In deciding cases concerning establishment clause issues, the Supreme Court has usually instructed judges to follow the so-called ***Lemon* test** (*Lemon* v. *Kurtzman*, 1971). Under this test, a court is to ask three questions about any governmental practice challenged as a violation of the establishment clause (see Table 5.1):

1. Does the law or practice have a secular (nonreligious) purpose?
2. Does the primary intent or effect of the law either advance or inhibit religion?
3. Does the law or practice create an excessive entanglement of government and religion?

If a law or government practice flunks any of the three questions, the law or practice violates the establishment clause and is unconstitutional. The Supreme Court has used the test to invalidate programs that provided public support for religious schools (*Grand Rapids* v. *Ball*, 1985), school-sponsored benediction prayers at public school

TABLE 5.1 | Two Pillars of Religious Freedom

"Congress shall make no law respecting an establishment of religion, or prohibiting the free exercise thereof."

ESTABLISHMENT CLAUSE	FREE EXERCISE CLAUSE
Prohibits:	Protects:
1) the establishment of a national religion by Congress 2) government support for or preference of one religion over another or of religion over non-religious philosophies in general	1) the freedom to believe 2) the freedom to worship and otherwise act in accordance with religious beliefs
Everson v. *Board of Education*, 1947	*Hamilton* v. *University of California*, 1934 *Cantwell* v. *Connecticut*, 1940

In 1962, the Supreme Court decided that teachers could not lead public school students in prayer because such actions violate the First Amendment as an improper "establishment of religion" by government. As a result of the Supreme Court's decision, students in public schools can bow their heads individually in prayer or meet before school for a student-led prayer. However, school officials are not supposed to be involved. ***—Why did this Supreme Court decision generate so much controversy?***

graduation ceremonies (*Lee* v. *Weisman,* 1992), and mandatory instruction in "creation science" as an alternative to evolutionary theory in high school science classes (*Edwards* v. *Aguillard,* 1987).

In the past two decades, several justices on the Supreme Court have harshly criticized the *Lemon* test and sought to replace it with an accommodationist perspective. These critics may have come close to eliminating the test in the case concerning school graduation prayers (*Lee* v. *Weisman,* 1992). The justices originally voted 5-4 to permit such prayers, but during the process of drafting opinions, Justice Anthony Kennedy changed his mind. He provided the decisive fifth vote to declare such prayers unconstitutional because a high school student could have, in his words, "a reasonable perception that she is being forced by the State to pray in a manner her conscience will not allow."[4]

On a single day in 2005, the Court issued two establishment clause decisions that highlighted the difficulties experienced by the justices in attempting to interpret the First Amendment in a clear, consistent manner. In *McCreary County* v. *ACLU* (2005), a majority of justices applied the *Lemon* test to rule that copies of the Ten Commandments could not be posted in Kentucky courthouses. A different combination of justices declared that the *Lemon* test need not apply, however, when those justices formed a majority in *Van Orden* v. *Perry* (2005) to permit Texas to keep a Ten Commandments monument on the state capitol grounds amid a variety of other monuments. The justices regarded the two situations as distinctively different, because the courthouses displayed only the religious documents whereas Texas mixed the religious monument with other cultural and patriotic symbols. These decisions create uncertainty about how the Court will decide individual cases in the future and whether the *Lemon* test will eventually be abandoned as the Court's composition changes.

Free Exercise of Religion

The free exercise clause concerns the right of individuals to engage in religious practices and to follow their beliefs without governmental interference. Several of the important cases that expanded civil liberties in this area were pursued by Jehovah's Witnesses. Just before World War II, the Supreme Court ruled that public schools could punish Jehovah's Witness students for refusing to salute the flag and recite the Pledge of Allegiance, even though the students claimed that being required to salute anything other than God violated their religious beliefs (*Minersville School District* v. *Gobitis,* 1940). Shortly afterward, several justices had second thoughts about the issue, and the Court reversed itself in *West Virginia* v. *Barnette* (1943). Justice Robert Jackson's opinion contained a lofty statement about the importance of freedom of thought and religious belief:

> If there is any fixed star in our constitutional constellation, it is that no official, high or petty, can prescribe what shall be orthodox in politics, nationalism, religion, or other matters of opinion or force citizens to confess by word or act their faith therein.

This does not mean, however, that the free exercise clause provides an absolute right to do anything in the name of religion. For example, if a person believed his religion demanded that he engage in human sacrifice or cannibalism, the Supreme Court would permit legislation to outlaw such practices. In 1990, an opinion written by Justice Antonin Scalia declared that the "right to free exercise of religion does not relieve an individual of the obligation to comply with a 'valid and neutral law of general applicability'" (*Employment Division of Oregon* v. *Smith*).

Many members of Congress want judges to look carefully at which laws will be permitted to override religious practices so that religion does not yield to every law passed by a legislature. In effect, these legislators want judges to apply a kind of analysis called **strict scrutiny** or the compelling government interest test to cases involving free exercise of religion. This analysis places the burden on the government to demonstrate the necessity of a specific law in order to outweigh an individual's desire to engage in a religious practice. The Supreme Court already applies the compelling government interest test to analyze whether other fundamental rights have been violated.

Congress sought to insist that the same protective test cover free exercise of religion by enacting the Religious Freedom Restoration Act. This law, which applies only to protect individuals' free exercise of religion against actions by the federal government, was used by the Supreme Court in 2006 when it found the government did not have a compelling justification to prevent a small religious sect from following its traditional religious practices of ingesting tea containing a hallucinogenic, controlled substance from South America (*Gonzales* v. *O Centro Espirita Beneficente Unaio do Vegetal*). Because the government did not have a compelling reason to prevent the group from consuming the tea in its ceremonies, law enforcement efforts to block the practice were an improper violation of the First Amendment protection for free exercise of religion.

There are often apparent conflicts between civil liberties protected under the establishment clause and those protected under the free exercise clause. For example, some critics argue that the Court's establishment clause decisions barring sponsored prayers in public schools effectively violate the free exercise rights of students who wish to pray. The apparent clash with free exercise of religion, however, is less substantial than it may first appear. Students can pray on their own in school. In addition, the Supreme Court has not ruled against student-organized and student-led prayers in public schools except when those prayers are conducted in a manner that implies sponsorship by school officials, such as a student reading a prayer over the stadium public address system before high school football games (*Santa Fe Independent School District* v. *Doe,* 2000).

First Amendment Rights: Freedom of Religion

Practice Quiz

1. The establishment clause of the First Amendment
   - **a.** limits Americans' freedom of religion.
   - **b.** requires people of all religions to salute the American flag.
   - **c.** guarantees that churches can design their own religious services.
   - **d.** is relevant to prayer cases involving public schools.
2. Teaching creationism in public schools can be construed as a violation of the establishment clause, because
   - **a.** not all parents believe that creationism is a science.
   - **b.** the Supreme Court concluded that teaching creationism advances the beliefs of a particular religious perspective.
   - **c.** creationism is criticized in Article III of the U.S. Constitution.
   - **d.** not enough teachers are certified to teach creationism.
3. As currently interpreted by the Supreme Court, the free exercise clause grants citizens the right to practice any form of religion
   - **a.** provided that such practices do not "offend (current) community standards."
   - **b.** provided that the participants can prove their practices are a "long-standing component of a genuine religious ceremony."
   - **c.** provided that such practices do not violate "a valid and neutral law of general applicability," such as murder or illegal drug use.
   - **d.** provided it is one of the four religions most commonly practiced by people throughout the world.
4. If a law or government policy would create an "excessive entanglement" between government and religion, that policy would violate
   - **a.** the establishment clause.
   - **b.** the free exercise clause.
   - **c.** how easily competing civil liberties can come into conflict.
   - **d.** a, b, and c.

Answers: 1-d, 2-b, 3-c, 4-a.

Discussion Questions

1. Discuss the three components of the *Lemon* test. What issues would likely cause debates and disagreements in interpreting these three components?
2. What kind of justification could the government present that the Supreme Court might accept as a "compelling government interest" that could outweigh an individual's free exercise of religion?

What **YOU** can do!

Survey your classmates to determine whether the high schools they attended set aside time in the morning for quiet reflection or a moment of silence. Were there other religious activities, such as "Meet You at the Pole" or Bible study groups, during nonschool hours? If so, how were these activities discussed by teachers and other students? Were there specific rules and guidelines governing such activities? If so, did the rules and guidelines prevent establishment or promote free exercise of religion?

■ **Clear and Present Danger Test:** A test for permissible speech articulated by Justice Oliver Wendell Holmes in *Schenck* v. *United States* (1919) that allows government regulation of some expressions.

EXAMPLE: *Imagine the injuries that would occur if, as a practical joke, someone yelled "He's got a gun!" in a crowd of hundreds of people waiting in line for a ride at Disney World. Such false statements likely to cause disorder and injuries are a primary focus of the test developed by Justice Holmes.*

First Amendment Rights: Freedom of Speech (pages 154–155)

How "free" is free speech in the United States?

The First Amendment protections for speech and press are expressed in absolute terms: "Congress shall make no law . . . abridging the freedom of speech, or of the press; or the right of the people peaceably to assemble, and to petition the Government for redress of grievances." Although the words of the amendment seem to say that the government cannot impose *any* limitations on your ability to speak, write, or participate in peaceful public demonstrations, you can probably think of several kinds of expressions that are actually limited under American law—for example:

Claiming that you were merely exercising your right to freedom of speech if you telephoned the leaders of Iran and told them how to build nuclear weapons

Claiming that you were merely using freedom of speech and freedom of the press if you filled bottles with tap water and sold them through advertisements calling it "The Amazing Liquid Cure for Cancer"

These examples raise questions about whether freedom of speech is absolute or whether the government can impose limitations. Judges interpret the First Amendment in ways that seek to strike a balance between individual liberty and important societal interests. In the first example, national security interests may outweigh an individual's desire to transmit a specific communication. In the second example, the government can regulate product advertisements and medicines in ways that protect society from harm, even when they limit an individual's speech and written expression. Freedom of expression is important for democracy and liberty in the United States, but these and other limitations are regarded as essential for protecting individuals and society against specific harms. Judges typically demand that governmental regulations concerning speech and the press be supported by strong, persuasive justifications before they can limit individuals' expression of viewpoints.

"How do judges seek to balance individuals' rights with society's interests?"
—Student Question

Justice Oliver Wendell Holmes argued for a **"clear and present danger" test**■ that would permit prosecution only for speeches and publications that actually posed a tangible, immediate threat to American society (*Schenck* v. *United States,* 1919). Holmes illustrated his point with an especially famous descriptive example: "The most stringent protection of free speech would not protect a man in falsely shouting fire in a theater, and causing a panic."

The Ku Klux Klan is an organization founded after the Civil War to use violence to terrorize African Americans. As shown in this photo of a 1998 Klan demonstration in Texas, when the Klan holds protests today, the police must often protect their right to free speech by guarding them against attacks by counter-protesters who object to their philosophy of racial hatred. ***—Do Klan members have the right to express their ideas, or should they be prohibited from using hate speech? What reasons would you give for prohibiting the use of hate speech?***

By the 1960s, the Supreme Court had adopted, expanded, and refined Holmes's suggested test so that political protests, whether by civil rights advocates, antiwar activists, or communists, could express critical viewpoints as long as the nature and context of those expressions did not pose an immediate threat. As stated in *Brandenburg* v. *Ohio* (1969):

> The constitutional guarantees of free speech and free press do not permit a State to forbid or proscribe advocacy of the use of force or of law violation except where such advocacy is directed to inciting or producing imminent lawless action and is likely to incite or produce such action.

Nowadays, it is difficult for people to be prosecuted for **political speech** that expresses their viewpoints about government and public affairs. By contrast, **commercial speech** may be subject to greater regulation because of concerns about protecting the public from misleading advertisements and other harms.

■ **Symbolic Speech:** The expression of an idea or viewpoint through an action, such as wearing an armband or burning an object. Symbolic speech can enjoy First Amendment protections.

EXAMPLE: *The U.S. Supreme Court says that the First Amendment protects people's right to express their opposition to government policies by burning American flags, even though such actions make many Americans very angry (*Texas *v.* Johnson, *1989).*

VISUAL LITERACY **What Speech Is Protected by the Constitution?**

STUDENT | PROFILE

In 2003, Bretton Barber, a senior at Dearborn High School in Michigan, was sent home from school for refusing to remove a T-shirt that was harshly critical of President George W. Bush. Barber filed a lawsuit that led a federal judge to support his right to wear an expressive T-shirt. This decision rested on a Supreme Court decision concerning a courageous Iowa student in the 1960s.

In 1965, Mary Beth Tinker, a 13-year-old student at Harding Junior High School in Des Moines, Iowa, wore a black armband to school to express her opposition to the Vietnam War. She was suspended from school. Despite receiving numerous death threats, Tinker continued to assert her right to peacefully express her views about a matter of public concern through the use of "symbolic speech" (wearing a black armband). **Symbolic speech**■ occurs when people take an action designed to communicate an idea. Tinker's case eventually reached the U.S. Supreme Court. In a 7-2 ruling, the Court decided that the Des Moines school board had violated Tinker's First Amendment rights (*Tinker* v. *Des Moines Independent Community School District,* 1969).

These cases do not demonstrate that judges support every form of expression by students. As a joke, a student in Alaska held up a banner that said "Bong Hits for Jesus" on the sidewalk outside his high school. After he was suspended from school, he took his case to the U.S. Supreme Court. In 2007, a divided Court ruled against him by concluding that the school could prevent expressions that encouraged the use of illegal substances (*Morse* v. *Frederick*). ■

How far has the Supreme Court moved in broadening the concept of freedom of speech? In 1989, a five-justice majority on the U.S. Supreme Court declared that burning the flag is symbolic speech when done during a political protest and therefore is a protected form of expression that falls within the coverage of the First Amendment (*Texas* v. *Johnson,* 1989).

The Court accepts ***reasonable time, place, and manner restrictions*** on political assemblies—restrictions that affect the rights of both speech and assembly. Chaos could harm society if protesters could freely block roadways, jail entrances, hospital parking lots, and other essential public locations. However, the government must demonstrate that important societal interests justify any limited restrictions on expression.

First Amendment Rights: Freedom of Speech

Practice Quiz

1. The actual words of the First Amendment seem to say that the government cannot impose any restrictions on freedom of speech.
   a. true **b.** false

2. The government cannot pass a law to limit political speech unless that law merely
   a. forbids criticism of the American government.
   b. requires people to respect the president of the United States.
   c. prohibits any suggestion that Americans switch from a democracy to some other form of government.
   d. bars words and statements that incite imminent lawless action.

3. Symbolic speech refers to
   a. speech that criticizes an important national symbol, such as the flag or an eagle.
   b. speech that criticizes a religious symbol, such as a cross.
   c. speech that is contained in the lyrics to a song.
   d. expressing an idea through an action rather than through spoken words.

4. The government can prevent protesters from blocking a busy highway through
   a. the fighting words justification.
   b. the hate speech justification.
   c. the symbolic speech justification.
   d. the reasonable time, place, and manner justification.

Answers: 1-a, 2-d, 3-d, 4-d.

Discussion Questions

1. How "free" is freedom of speech in the United States?
2. Should campaign advertisements be defined as political speech or commercial speech?

What **YOU** can do!

Find out what restrictions and regulations exist concerning public protests in your community or on your campus. Look in your college's student handbook for rules about behavior. See if your community's municipal ordinances are available online. Are these regulations too restrictive? If you wanted to organize a public protest, would the regulations prevent you from doing so?

First Amendment Rights: Freedom *of the* Press *and* Obscenity

(pages 156–159)

Is there any justification for government-imposed limitations on written records or artistic and photographic images?

Freedom of the Press

Like free speech, freedom of the press is guaranteed by the First Amendment's absolutist language, and Americans regard this freedom as an essential element of democracy. Voters need free-flowing, accurate information in order to evaluate their elected leaders. They have little hope of using democratic processes to hold their leaders accountable or to elect new legislators and executive officials unless they have access to information. In countries where national leaders closely control the news media, the people seldom have opportunities to use democratic processes to select new leaders.

The Supreme Court issued a strong statement against **prior restraint** of publications that criticize public officials in *Near* v. *Minnesota* (1931). Prior restraint is the government's attempt to prevent certain information or viewpoints from being published (see Figure 5.2). In the *Near* case, the Supreme Court struck down a state law intended to prevent the publication of articles or editorials that used inflammatory language to criticize government officials. As a result, the government generally cannot prevent articles from being published. However, the principle of no prior restraint does *not* prevent authors and publishers from later being sued for the publication of false or misleading information that harms people's reputations. Such civil lawsuits are for **defamation**—false, harmful statements either through spoken words (*slander*) or through written words (*libel*). The Court's decision established the basic presumption that the

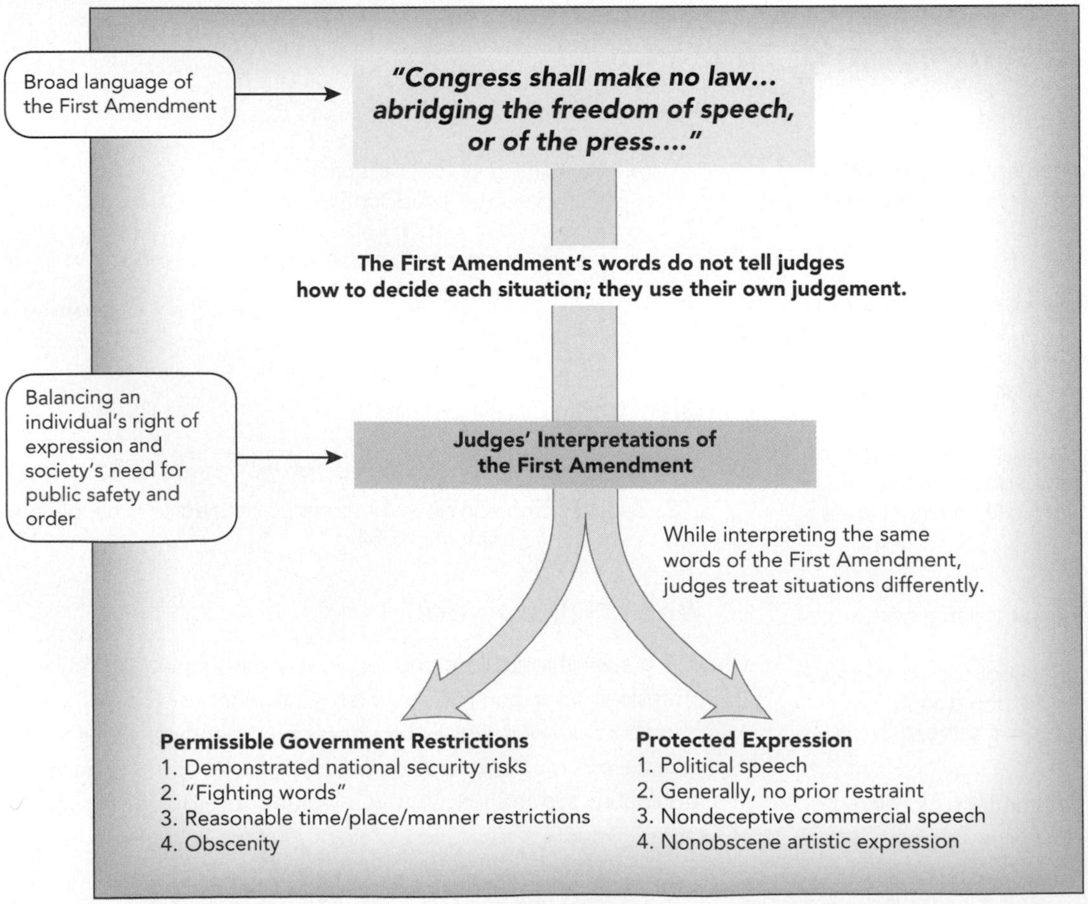

Broad language of the First Amendment
"Congress shall make no law... abridging the freedom of speech, or of the press...."
The First Amendment's words do not tell judges how to decide each situation; they use their own judgement.
Balancing an individual's right of expression and society's need for public safety and order
Judges' Interpretations of the First Amendment
While interpreting the same words of the First Amendment, judges treat situations differently.
Permissible Government Restrictions
1. Demonstrated national security risks
2. "Fighting words"
3. Reasonable time/place/manner restrictions
4. Obscenity
Protected Expression
1. Political speech
2. Generally, no prior restraint
3. Nondeceptive commercial speech
4. Nonobscene artistic expression

FIGURE 5.2 | Freedom of Speech and Press

Civil liberties protections enjoyed by Americans are defined by judges' interpretations of the words in the Bill of Rights. For the First Amendment and several other provisions of the Bill of Rights, judges often seek to strike a balance between protecting the liberty of individuals and acknowledging the need to protect important interests of society. Thus there are limitations on many civil liberties.

Press Shield Law: Statute enacted by a legislature establishing a reporter's privilege to protect the confidentiality of sources.

EXAMPLE: *In 2006, the Connecticut legislature enacted a law to permit reporters to protect the identities of their sources unless overriding societal interests lead judges to order them to provide information sought by prosecutors.*

government will not censor the news media, except perhaps in the most extreme circumstances.

In 1971, the Supreme Court faced a case that raised the issue of prior restraint when the federal government claimed that publication by newspapers of a top-secret, internal Defense Department study concerning the Vietnam War would seriously damage national security. The so-called Pentagon Papers had been given to the *New York Times* and the *Washington Post* by Daniel Ellsberg, a Defense Department analyst who had concluded that the public needed more information about what was really happening in the war—even though he was legally forbidden to make the information available. When the newspapers began to publish this book-length document, under the title *History of the U.S. Decision-Making Process on Vietnam Policy,* the government sought a court order to stop the newspapers. The two newspapers in question, arguably the nation's most prominent at that time, had the money and legal expertise to battle the government on equal terms in the court pathway. The Supreme Court majority declared that the newspapers could continue to publish the report (***New York Times Company* v. *United States,* 1971**). Three justices adopted the absolutist position that the First Amendment bars *all* prior restraint by the government, and three additional justices decided that the government had not adequately proved that publication of the report would actually harm national security.[5] The decision demonstrated that many judges would require exceptionally compelling proof of harm to society before permitting government censorship of publications about public affairs.

The interests of the press can clash with governmental priorities when reporters have information sought by the government and refuse to share it with prosecutors and other officials. Reporters claim that a free press can survive only if they can protect the identities of their sources of inside information. Otherwise, people would not be willing to provide reporters with controversial and even potentially incriminating information about governmental activities and issues of public interest. Government officials argue in response that reporters, like other citizens, should be required to cooperate with criminal investigations to ensure that criminal enterprises are thwarted and that guilty people receive appropriate punishment.

Advocates for the news media feel that the First Amendment should be interpreted to recognize a **reporter's privilege,** which authorizes news agencies to decline to provide information requested by the government. Although some states have enacted **press shield laws** to protect reporters in state justice processes, the federal courts have refused to recognize a constitutional privilege to protect reporters nationwide. Thus reporters are occasionally jailed for contempt of court if they refuse to cooperate with criminal investigations. For example, in 2001, Vanessa Leggett, a freelance writer in Houston who was conducting research for a book on a controversial murder case, spent 168 days in jail for refusing to testify before a federal grand jury about her interviews with criminal suspects. She was released only when the grand jury ended its investigation.[6]

Daniel Ellsberg, shown here speaking to the press outside a courthouse, provided inside information to newspapers about developments that contributed to American involvement in the Vietnam War. The newspapers won a case in the U.S. Supreme Court that permitted them to publish the "Pentagon Papers." The government initially charged Ellsberg with crimes for his actions. ***—Should Ellsberg be regarded as a hero who used the freedom of the press to help inform the American people? Or was he a traitor who knowingly violated the law by releasing secret information about the United States and its war efforts?***

PATHWAYS | of change from around the world

Editors of student newspapers often are visible leaders on university campuses. They shape the content of information made available to students and the public. Because newspapers traditionally present opinionated viewpoints in editorials or arouse controversy by choosing to investigate specific issues, student editors risk severe sanctions when they question and criticize government policies in countries that do not enjoy freedom of expression. During 2006 in Iran, a country in which the government's critics can be threatened and arrested, 47 student publications were closed, and 181 students received letters warning them not to become involved in politics.[7] In March of 2007, two student editors were arrested at Amirkabir University in Iran and accused of publishing articles that insulted Islam. The editors claimed that they were framed and targeted for arrest, because they were known to support student organizations that wanted to reform the government and make it more democratic.[8]

Throughout modern history, there is a tradition of newspaper editors standing up for freedom of expression and democracy. In many times and places, such courageous efforts to advance democratic principles have meant that editors, including editors of student newspapers, endured prison—and worse. Can you picture yourself seeking to write for a newspaper in order to educate and arouse the public on matters of justice, ethics, equality, and other elements of democracy? Would you be willing to assume the visible position of editor—if you knew that authorities might choose to make an example of you? Student editors in the United States face the prospect of losing their positions or perhaps being suspended from school if school or government authorities believe they have gone "too far" in discussing controversial issues. In some other countries, by contrast, student editors find themselves at far greater risk of losing their liberty or lives by standing up for matters of principle. ■

Howard Stern moved his show to satellite radio in 2006 in order to avoid government-imposed fines for broadcasting graphic sexual discussions. By moving his show to satellite radio, Stern now entertains only voluntary, paying customers and thereby moved himself outside the Federal Communication Commission's mandate to protect unsuspecting consumers. The Supreme Court has ruled that obscene material is not protected by the First Amendment and thus can be regulated by the government. ***—What kinds of verbal expression do you think are outside the protections of the First Amendment?***

Obscenity

Judges face challenges in determining if expressions that offend the sensibilities of some community members fall under the protection of the First Amendment. In particular, legislators have regularly sought to prohibit or regulate material with sexual content, such as books, magazines, live performances, films, and Web sites. The Supreme Court has said anything that is "obscene" falls outside the First Amendment and is not considered part of free expression. It has been very difficult, however, for the Court to provide a clear definition of *obscene*. This issue can cause major conflicts, because images and performances that some people consider artistic expression can be regarded by others as harmful to the morals of society.

In the early twentieth century, people were regularly prosecuted in various communities for possessing or selling written materials or pictures with sexual content. James Joyce's novel *Ulysses,* published in France in 1922 and today regarded as one of the great works of modern literature, could not legally be printed, imported, or sold in the United States, because it contained four-letter words and certain sexual allusions. Only in 1933 did a federal judge lift the ban after a leading American publisher brought a lawsuit challenging it.

In the 1950s, the Supreme Court developed a test for obscenity. Its initial efforts focused on whether the work in question was "utterly without redeeming social importance" (*Roth* v. *United States,* 1957). This test was refined as the Court's composition changed over the next two decades.

In an important case challenging the prosecution of a man who mailed brochures that advertised sexually explicit books, the Supreme Court articulated a new test for obscenity. According to Chief Justice Warren Burger's opinion, materials that met a three-part test for obscenity could be prohibited by legislation and lead to prosecutions. The Court's test was stated as follows in ***Miller* v. *California* (1973)**:

> "How do judges decide whether something is obscene?"
> —Student Question

> The basic guidelines for the trier of fact must be: (a) whether the "average person, applying contemporary community standards" would find that the work, taken as a whole, appeals to the prurient interest; (b) whether the work depicts or describes, in a patently offensive way, sexual conduct specifically defined by the applicable state law; and (c) whether the work, taken as whole, lacks serious literary, artistic, political, or scientific value.

The test for obscenity is thus based on "community standards," and those standards change over time. For example, in the 1960s, actors portraying married couples in movies and on television were often shown sleeping in separate single beds so as not to convey any sexual implications by having a double bed on the set. Today, by contrast, scantily clad performers in sexy embraces and dance routines are everyday fare for music videos shown around the clock on cable channels. It seems clear that "community standards" regarding acceptable entertainment have changed over the years. Does this mean that "anything goes" in American entertainment media? No. The Federal Communications Commission (FCC) continues to regulate television and radio broadcasts, and it imposes fines for profanity and sexual content that it believes have gone too far. Broadcasting is subject to stricter government control than newspapers, because the government has the power to regulate use of the public airwaves. The uproar over the momentary exposure of singer Janet Jackson's bare breast on television during the half-time show for the 2004 Super Bowl served as a reminder that there are still limits to expression, especially when that expression is broadcast to the televisions and radios of unwitting consumers who assume that certain standards are in place.

Obviously, a different situation exists for consumers who intentionally seek sexually explicit material in specific magazines or in the back room of their local DVD rental store. Generally, pornographic films and magazines that once would have led to prosecution in most communities are now widely available in the United States, and without legal repercussions as long as the sellers and distributors of such materials take steps to keep such items away from children.

Indeed, except for content standards for broadcasts regulated by the FCC, most regulation of obscenity today focuses on the exposure of children to obscene material or their exploitation in its production. Laws impose prison sentences for the creation, dissemination, and possession of child pornography.

First Amendment Rights: Freedom of the Press and Obscenity

Practice Quiz

1. Freedom of the press is often considered
   - **a.** a form of symbolic speech.
   - **b.** essential for the maintenance of a democracy.
   - **c.** less important than the government's need to keep officials from being criticized.
   - **d.** a right that does not need protection when the nation is at war.

2. The Pentagon Papers case
   - **a.** reinforced the traditional view that the First Amendment generally prohibits prior restraint by the government.
   - **b.** revealed the conservative bias of the Supreme Court's members.
   - **c.** implied that judges need little proof of harm before permitting the government to exercise prior restraint.
   - **d.** led to a new definition for treason.

3. Press shield laws are
   - **a.** laws that shield judges from press scrutiny.
   - **b.** state laws that protect journalists from governmental censorship.
   - **c.** state laws that protect journalists from having to reveal confidential sources.
   - **d.** laws that protect newspapers from being sued when they print false stories about celebrities.

4. The Supreme Court uses current community standards as one of the measures of material defined as obscene.
   - **a.** true **b.** false

Answers: 1-b, 2-a, 3-c, 4-a.

Discussion Questions

1. Under what circumstances, if any, should the government be able to force a journalist to reveal confidential sources?
2. If we think of everyone in the United States as being part of a national "community," what kinds of things would this community regard as obscene?

What **YOU** can do!

Partner with classmates to conduct a "media watch." Pick up a copy of your local newspaper and a national newspaper, watch a national news broadcast, listen to a few morning radio shows, and watch a selection of prime-time television shows, including sitcoms and dramas on network and cable television stations. For each medium, note anything that could arguably be outside the protection of the First Amendment because it is either (1) obscene, (2) communicates false information to harm someone's reputation (slander or libel), or (3) genuinely threatens national security. If you do not see or hear examples, think of two hypothetical examples for each category that you have previously seen or could plausibly see or hear from American news media.

DEBATE **Gun Rights and Gun Control**

Civil Liberties *and* Criminal Justice (pages 160–163)

Why does the Bill of Rights provide protections for criminal suspects?

Several amendments in the Bill of Rights describe protections afforded people who are subject to police investigations, prosecutions, sentencing, and criminal punishment. The protections described in these amendments do not merely safeguard civil liberties for people who have committed crimes. These amendments are designed to protect everyone in the United States, including innocent people, from excessive actions by overzealous law enforcement officials who are seeking to prevent and solve crimes.

The Right to Bear Arms

The Second Amendment contains words about "the right of the people to keep and bear arms." Although this amendment is not always regarded as concerning criminal justice, many Americans see a connection between firearm ownership and criminal justice in two ways. First, people can be prosecuted and sentenced to prison for possessing, carrying, or selling firearms in violation of local, state, or federal laws. Second, advocates of a right to bear arms argue that strong Second Amendment rights are necessary for citizens to protect themselves against criminals.

The Second Amendment is a source of controversy. People interpret its words in quite different ways. Before 2008, the U.S. Supreme Court spent decades avoiding cases that would require it to make a definitive statement about the amendment's precise meaning. The words of the amendment are problematic, because in a single sentence, without separable, free-standing clauses, it mentions "a well-regulated Militia" and "the right of the people to keep and bear arms." The amendment says, "*A well-regulated Militia, being necessary for the security of a free State, the right of the people to keep and bear Arms, shall not be infringed.*" Most scholars interpreted the amendment as guaranteeing the ability of states to arm their militias, known today as the National Guard.

By a narrow 5-4 vote in *District of Columbia* v. *Heller* (2008), the Supreme Court struck down Washington, D.C.'s law that banned the possession of handguns by anyone except retired police officers. Justice Antonin Scalia's majority opinion declared that the Second Amendment guarantees law-abiding individuals' right to own handguns for the protection of their homes. The decision applied to restrictive laws enacted by federal entities, such as the

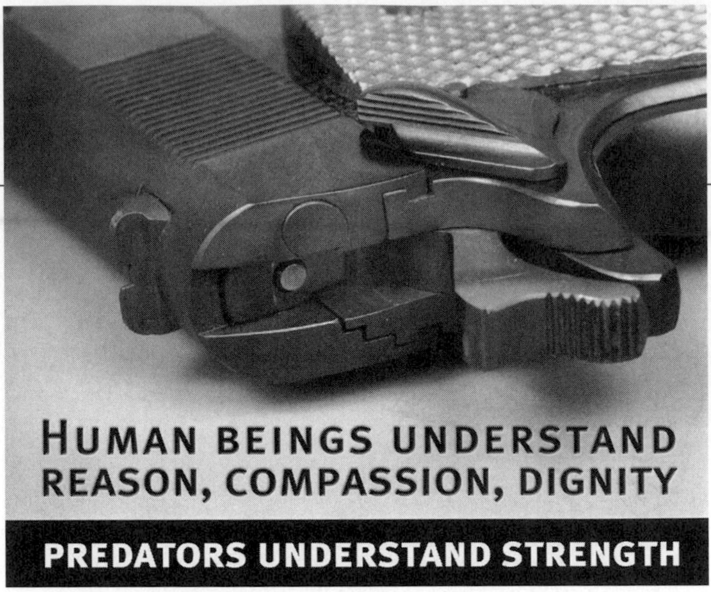
HUMAN BEINGS UNDERSTAND
REASON, COMPASSION, DIGNITY
PREDATORS UNDERSTAND STRENGTH

Interest groups use advertising to persuade the public to support their interpretations of the Second Amendment. Those who see the Amendment as guaranteeing a right for individuals to own firearms design advertisements to emphasize that good citizens are vulnerable to victimization by criminals. The opposing side emphasizes the risks from freely available guns falling into the wrong hands. ***—If you were on the Supreme Court, how would you interpret the words of the Second Amendment?***

District of Columbia. It remains to be seen whether the Court will incorporate the Second Amendment and strike down restrictive laws enacted by states and non-federal cities.

Although the Supreme Court's decision constituted a major legal victory for gun-rights advocates, Justice Scalia's opinion explicitly permitted the continuation of various regulations affecting gun ownership and possession. In Scalia's words,

> [N]othing in our opinion should be taken to cast doubt on longstanding prohibitions on the possession of firearms by felons and the mentally ill, or laws forbidding the carrying of firearms in sensitive places such as schools and government buildings, or laws imposing conditions and qualifications on the commercial sale of arms.

Search and Seizure

The Fourth Amendment is focused on protecting people against improper searches and seizures. In the words of the amendment:

> The right of the people to be secure in their persons, houses, papers, and effects, against unreasonable searches and seizures, shall not be violated, and no Warrants shall issue, but upon probable cause, supported by Oath or affirmation, and particularly describing the place to be searched, and the persons or things to be seized.

Exclusionary Rule: General principle that evidence obtained illegally, including through the violation of Fourth Amendment rights, cannot be used against a defendant in a criminal prosecution. The Supreme Court has allowed certain exceptions to the rule that permit the use of improperly obtained evidence in particular circumstances.

Example: *The Supreme Court ruled that prosecutors could not use blood test results showing traces of cocaine when the blood tests were supplied by a hospital without the consent of the patients and without a warrant issued by a judge. Such use of blood tests in criminal cases violates the Fourth Amendment protection against "unreasonable searches" and thus must be excluded from use in prosecuting any criminal case.*

FIGURE 5.3 | **Gun Laws in the United States**

The Second Amendment is about "the right of the people to keep and bear arms." But because the Supreme Court has never incorporated the Second Amendment, the amendment does not prevent cities and states from enacting their own gun laws. The result can be seen on this map, which shows the many different restrictions and requirements set by states for the purchase, ownership, and right to carry handguns, rifles, and shotguns.

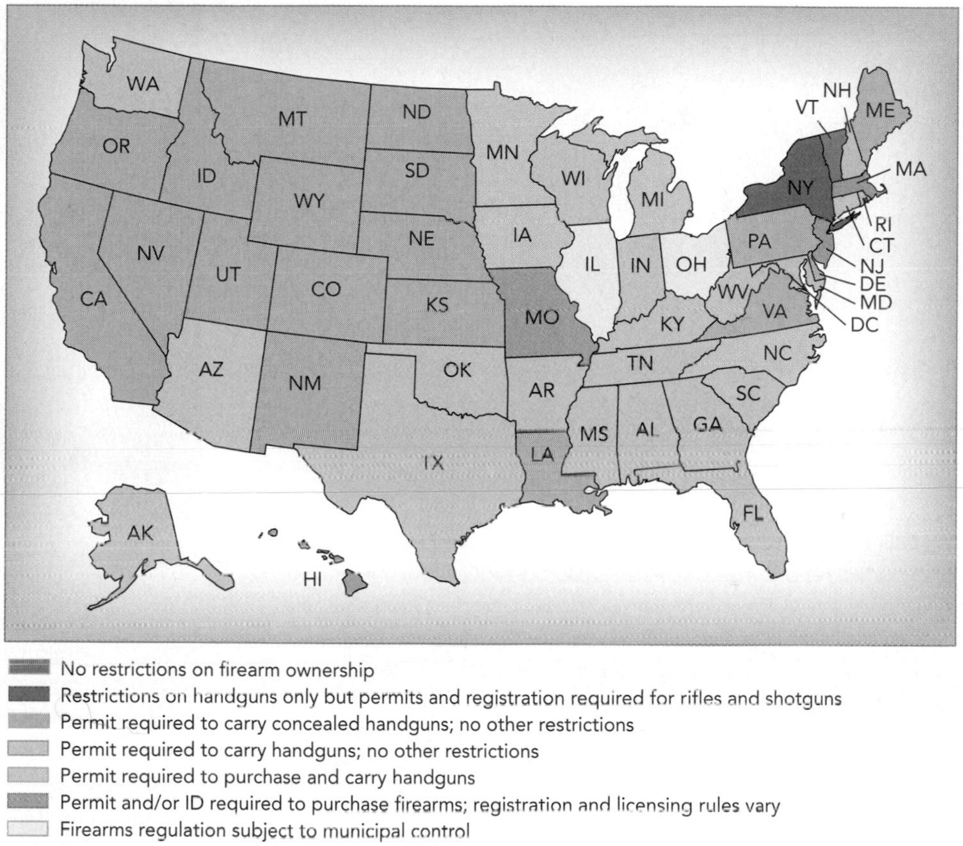

"Why do we have rules that make it harder for police to catch criminals?"

—Student Question

The two key parts of the amendment are the prohibition on "unreasonable searches and seizures" and the requirements for obtaining search and arrest warrants. Like other provisions of the Constitution, the Fourth Amendment contains inherently ambiguous language that must be interpreted by judges. The word *seizure,* for example, includes arrests when people are taken into police custody (that is, seizures of people) as well as situations in which officers seize property that may be evidence of criminal wrongdoing. But how do you know whether a search or seizure is "unreasonable"? Clearly, such a determination is a matter of judgment, and all people will not agree about whether specific actions are "searches" or whether they are "unreasonable."

The U.S. Supreme Court endorsed application of the **exclusionary rule** in *Weeks* v. *United States* (1914). Under this rule, evidence obtained improperly by the police cannot be used to prosecute someone accused of a crime. The intent of the rule is to stop police from undertaking illegal searches or improperly questioning suspects and to remedy the violation of suspects' civil liberties. At first, the rule applied only against federal law enforcement officials, such as FBI agents, but the Supreme Court, in the famous case of ***Mapp* v. *Ohio* (1961),** subsequently applied it to all police officers throughout the country.

As Republican presidents appointed new justices in the 1970s and 1980s who interpreted civil liberties under the Bill of Rights in a narrower manner, Chief Justice Warren Burger (1969–1986) was able to lead the changing Court toward creating limitations on and exceptions to the exclusionary rule. The rule went from being a broad, clear restriction on police after *Mapp* v. *Ohio* (1961) to one with many situational exceptions.

Chief Justice Burger never succeeded in eliminating the exclusionary rule. The rule still applies in many situations, but law enforcement officers now have greater leeway to make errors in conducting searches and questioning suspects without automatically facing the exclusion of evidence.

With respect to a **warrant**, which is an order from a judge authorizing a search or an arrest, the Fourth Amendment specifically requires the police and prosecutor to show the judge sufficient reliable information to establish "probable cause" about the location of evidence or a person's

■ **Warrant:** A judicial order authorizing a search or an arrest. Under the Fourth Amendment, police and prosecutors must present sufficient evidence to constitute "probable cause" in order to obtain a warrant from a judge.

EXAMPLE: *Upon presentation of evidence to show strong suspicion of criminal activity, a judge issued a search warrant in 2007 to permit law enforcement officials to search a home owned by NFL football star Michael Vick, who was suspected—and eventually convicted—of involvement in an illegal dogfighting operation.*

DEBATE **Privacy and Government Surveillance Powers**

In 2005, the New York City police increasingly searched the bags and packages of subway riders in order to reduce the threat of a terrorist attack. In the court pathway, the Supreme Court has interpreted the Fourth Amendment to require a balance between protecting the individual's right against unreasonable searches and the need for government officials to maintain safety and security. ***—When your bag is searched at an airport, concert, or stadium, do you feel that your privacy rights under the Fourth Amendment have been violated?***

> "Do the police have the power to stop and search you or your car if they don't have a warrant?"
> —Student Question

criminal behavior. Other searches conducted without warrants are governed only by the prohibition on "unreasonable searches and seizures." The Supreme Court has identified specific situations in which warrants are not required, because these searches are considered reasonable. Permissible warrantless searches include:

- "Stop and frisk" searches of a suspect's outer clothing on the streets when officers have a reasonable basis to suspect that person is involved in criminal behavior and potentially poses a danger to the public (*Terry* v. *Ohio,* 1968)
- "Exigent circumstances" in which an immediate, warrantless search must be undertaken because of danger to the public or the possible loss of evidence (*Cupp* v. *Murphy,* 1973)
- Searches based on "special needs" beyond the normal purposes of law enforcement, such as luggage searches at airports.

The creation of these categories of warrantless searches demonstrates how judges' decisions in the court pathway define rights and clarify the authority of law enforcement officials. As the United States continues to develop homeland security policies in response to the terrorist attacks of September 11, 2001, new cases will arise that test the government's authority to conduct searches and surveillance, including warrantless monitoring of telephone calls, a practice expanded under the administration of President George W. Bush.

News reports in 2006 revealed that the federal government undertook secret monitoring of Americans' telephone calls and financial transactions without judicial authorization as part of its anti-terrorism efforts. At Senate hearings on the issue, senators grilled then-Attorney General Alberto Gonzales on the legality of such actions. The hearings showed that the elections and lobbying pathways can also provide a basis for action in response to civil liberties controversies. ***—In what ways might the government's war against terrorism be leading to an erosion of Americans' civil liberties?***

Self-Incrimination

The Fifth Amendment describes several rights related to criminal justice, including the concept of **double jeopardy,** which refers to the protection against being tried twice for the same crime. Many controversial cases arise concerning another protection: the privilege against **compelled self-incrimination.** In the words of the amendment, no person may be "compelled in any criminal case to be a witness against himself."

If the individual is not free to walk away from police questioning, the police must make it clear that the person has a right to remain silent and to have an attorney present during questioning. The latter requirement emerged from the Supreme Court's famous

■ ***Miranda* v. *Arizona* (1966):** U.S. Supreme Court decision that requires police officers, before questioning a suspect in custody, to inform that suspect about the right to remain silent and the right to have a lawyer present during custodial questioning.

EXAMPLE: *If a police officer arrested you, the officer is not supposed to ask you any questions about what you did until you have been informed of your right to remain silent and your other Miranda rights. These warnings are intended to protect you from incriminating yourself without being aware of your rights.*

SIMULATION **You Are a Police Officer**

and controversial decision in ***Miranda* v. *Arizona* (1966)**■. Television programs with crime themes regularly show police officers reading people their "*Miranda* rights":

> You have the right to remain silent. Anything that you say can and will be used against you in a court of law. You have the right to have an attorney present during questioning. If you cannot afford an attorney, one will be appointed to represent you.

When police question people on the street or when people come to the police station voluntarily, the police do not have to inform them of their rights. The primary exception to this rule concerns motorists stopped for traffic violations who are not free to drive away; the police can ask them questions without informing them about their *Miranda* rights.

Civil Liberties and Criminal Justice

Practice Quiz

1. The amendments in the Bill of Rights concerning criminal justice are meant to protect both the accused and ordinary citizens from excesses by law enforcement officials.
   - **a.** true
   - **b.** false
2. The U.S. Supreme Court's decision in *District of Columbia* v. *Heller* (2008) will prevent
   - **a.** Congress from prohibiting people to keep handguns in their homes.
   - **b.** state legislatures from prohibiting people to keep handguns in their homes.
   - **c.** Detroit's city council from prohibiting people to keep handguns in their homes.
   - **d.** all governments from prohibiting people to keep handguns in their homes.
3. When prosecutors are not permitted to present evidence in court because the police obtained that evidence through an illegal search, we say this evidence has been subjected to
   - **a.** the warrantless search exception.
   - **b.** the probable cause doctrine.
   - **c.** the exclusionary rule.
   - **d.** the good faith exception.
4. *Miranda* rights are intended to protect a person's
   - **a.** Fourth Amendment warrant requirement.
   - **b.** Fourth Amendment right against unreasonable searches.
   - **c.** Fifth Amendment right against double jeopardy.
   - **d.** Fifth Amendment privilege against compelled self-incrimination.

Answers: 1-a, 2-a, 3-c, 4-d.

Discussion Questions

1. What would be the consequences of a U.S. Supreme Court decision that abolishes the exclusionary rule?
2. Why might suspects provide incriminating information about themselves even after they have been given *Miranda* warnings?

What **YOU** can do!

Visit the American Civil Liberties Union (ACLU) Web site (**http://www.aclu.org/police/gen/14528res20040730.html**) to view their famous "Bust Card." Match up each part of the Bust Card with the appropriate provision in the Fourth, Fifth, Sixth, and Eighth Amendments.

■ **Trial by Jury:** A right contained in the Sixth Amendment to have criminal guilt decided by a body of citizens drawn from the community.

EXAMPLE: *In 2008, movie star Wesley Snipes went to trial in Ocala, Florida, on charges of failing to pay federal income tax. After questioning 60 citizens drawn from the community about their knowledge of the case, the judge and the attorneys selected 12 jurors and 4 alternate jurors to hear the case.*

Trial Rights *and* Capital Punishment (pages 164–167)

Does the Bill of Rights provide enough legal protections to make sure that only guilty people receive criminal punishment?

Trial Rights

The Sixth Amendment contains a variety of legal protections for people who face a criminal trial:

> In all criminal prosecutions, the accused shall enjoy the right to a speedy and public trial, by an impartial jury of the State and district wherein the crime shall have been committed, which district shall have been previously ascertained by law, and to be informed of the nature and cause of the accusation; to be confronted with the witnesses against him; to have compulsory process for obtaining witnesses in his favor; and to have the Assistance of Counsel for his defence.

The right to a **speedy and public trial** provides important protections for criminal defendants. Without a right to a public trial, it would be possible for the government to hold secret proceedings that prevent citizens from knowing whether evidence actually existed to prove a defendant's guilt. Under a system that permits secret trials, people can be convicted and sentenced without the government demonstrating that it is properly exercising its awesome powers to deprive people of their liberty through incarceration. The right to a speedy trial prevents the government from ruining a person's life by holding charges over his or her head for an indefinite period of time.

"Why is it important for a defendant to have a speedy trial?"
—Student Question

Initially, the right to **trial by jury**■ applied only to federal cases. The Supreme Court incorporated the right in 1968 and applied it to state proceedings (*Duncan* v. *Louisiana*).

Although dramatic scenes from jury trials are a central feature of television shows like *Law & Order,* in reality only about 10 percent of criminal convictions result from trials, and only half of those are the result of jury trials.[9] The other trials are **bench trials,** in which the verdict is determined by a judge without a jury. Defendants may request bench trials because they are afraid that jurors may be biased and emotional, especially if there are controversial charges involving sex offenses, guns, or drugs. The other 90 percent of criminal convictions are obtained through **plea bargaining,** a process approved by the Supreme Court in which prosecutors and defense attorneys negotiate a guilty plea in exchange for a less-than-maximum number of charges or a less severe sentence. Plea bargaining has become an essential way to dispose of the vast number of cases that otherwise would overwhelm the resources of the criminal justice system if they all proceeded to trial.

The Sixth Amendment's exact words—"In all criminal prosecutions, the accused shall enjoy the right to . . . an impartial jury"—have

Hurricane Katrina wrecked the courthouses in New Orleans in 2005. Here, evidence for pending criminal cases was severely damaged by flood waters that reached the courthouse. Poor defendants who could not afford to obtain release on bail were trapped in flooded jail cells for several days. They remained in jail for extended time periods because their cases were delayed due to a lack of available attorneys and courtrooms. ***—How could we reform our justice system to ensure that poor defendants receive proper representation by defense attorneys and the complete benefits of constitutional rights?***

VISUAL LITERACY **Race and the Death Penalty**

Capital Punishment: A criminal punishment, otherwise known as the *death penalty*, in which a person is subject to execution after conviction. It is reserved for the most serious offenses.

EXAMPLE: *In 2001, Timothy McVeigh was executed by lethal injection after being convicted for killing 168 people when he used a truck bomb to destroy the Murrah Federal Office Building in Oklahoma City in 1995.*

not been enforced by the Supreme Court. According to the Court, the right to a trial by jury applies only in cases concerning "serious offenses" that are punishable by 6 months or more in jail or prison (*Lewis* v. *United States,* 1996). For lesser crimes, the accused can be forced to accept a bench trial. Because jury trials are expensive and time-consuming, it appears that the Court's interpretation is designed to reduce the costs and administrative burdens that courts otherwise would face.

The right to counsel is an especially important part of the Sixth Amendment. As early as 1932 the Supreme Court, in *Powell* v. *Alabama,* recognized the value of this legal protection by requiring Alabama to provide attorneys for nine African-American youths who had previously been convicted and sentenced to death. Their brief, attorneyless proceeding was based on rape accusations from two white women, one of whom later admitted that her charges were false.

Later, the Supreme Court required that the government provide attorneys for all indigent defendants facing serious criminal charges in federal court (*Johnson* v. *Zerbst,* 1938) and state courts (*Gideon* v. *Wainwright,* 1963). Indigent defendants are people who do not have enough money to hire their own attorneys. The right to counsel for indigents was expanded to all cases in which the potential punishment involves incarceration, even a short stay in jail (*Argersinger* v. *Hamlin,* 1972), as well as initial appeals (*Ross* v. *Moffitt,* 1974). If people have sufficient funds, they are expected to hire an attorney, and the Sixth Amendment right merely means that the government cannot prevent them from seeking legal advice.

Capital Punishment

The Constitution also provides rights for people who have been convicted of crimes—including those who have committed the very worst crimes, such as multiple murders. The Constitution does not require people to forfeit all of their rights if they violate society's rules. The words of the Eighth Amendment include a prohibition of "cruel and unusual punishments." This clearly implies some limitation on the government's ability to punish. Criminal sanctions must not violate this provision, either by being similar to torture or by being disproportionate to the underlying crime. To illustrate the point, burning an offender at the stake, in the manner that offenders were punished in Europe centuries ago, would today be considered torture. And sentencing someone to death for having a parking ticket would certainly be disproportionate for the offense. In its practical application, the Eighth Amendment applies to a variety of contemporary contexts, such as the denial of medical care for prisoners or the administration of beatings to people serving short sentences in jail. The Supreme Court has said that the phrase "cruel and unusual punishments" must be defined according to society's contemporary standards, so the meaning of the phrase changes as society's values change (*Trop* v. *Dulles,* 1958).

An important battleground for the meaning of the Eighth Amendment has been cases concerning **capital punishment** that are appealed through the court pathway.[10] In 1972, the Supreme

For nearly all executions in the United States, the condemned prisoner is strapped down and lethal chemicals are injected into the offender's veins as news reporters and family members watch through a glass window. Interest groups opposed to the death penalty used the court pathway to claim that lethal injection violates the Eighth Amendment prohibition on cruel and unusual punishments. The U.S. Supreme Court ruled in 2008 that lethal injections can continue to be used as a method of execution. ***—Are there any other legal arguments that opponents of the death penalty might use to seek an end to capital punishment? Are these arguments likely to be effective with today's Supreme Court?***

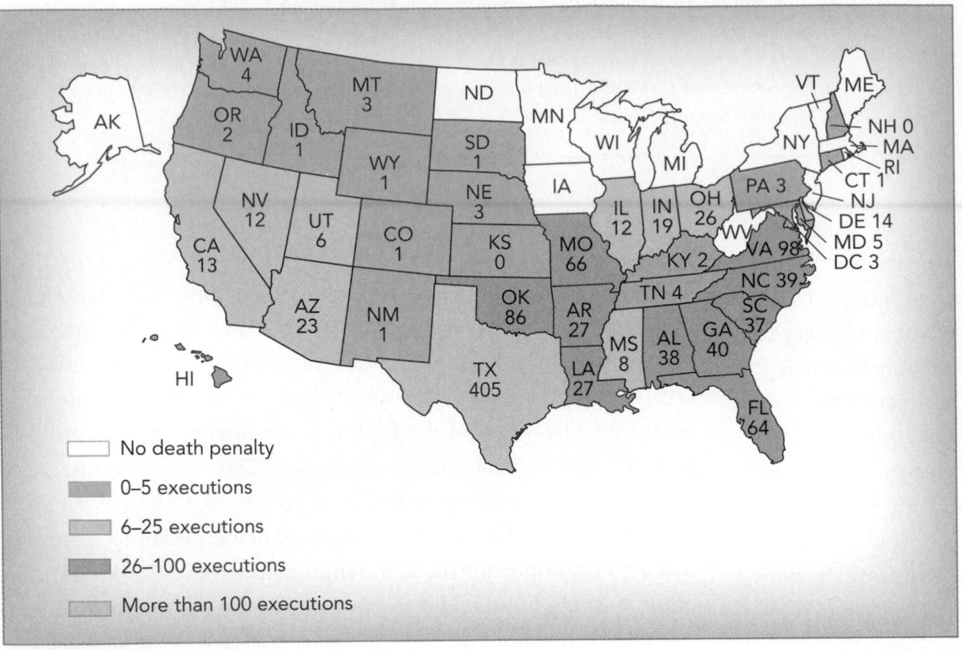

FIGURE 5.4 | **Executions by State**

The number of executions carried out in a state does not depend on the number of people murdered or the murder rate in the state. The frequency of executions is determined by the political culture in that state and the values and beliefs of politicians and the public. Thus the cultural change pathway may ultimately play an important role in determining whether the use of capital punishment expands or shrinks. ***—How might political values explain the relatively large number of executions in Southern states and the small number of executions in California, a large state with many murders?***

SOURCE: www.deathpenaltyinfo.org

Court ruled that the death penalty was unconstitutional as it was then being administered (*Furman* v. *Georgia*). Some justices thought that the death penalty was unconstitutional because it should be regarded as "cruel and unusual" according to the values of contemporary civilization. Other justices believed that the punishment was applied too inconsistently and unfairly and thus violated the Fourteenth Amendment right to due process. The death penalty was reinstated in 1976 after the latter group of justices became persuaded that states had adopted fairer procedures for administering capital punishment cases (*Gregg* v. *Georgia*) (see Figure 5.4). The special procedures for death penalty cases include *bifurcated proceedings* (separate trials to determine guilt and to decide on the appropriate sentence). In addition, judges and juries look specifically for *aggravating factors* that make a particular crime or offender worse than others, such as a murder by a repeat offender or a killing in the course of committing another felony. They also weigh *mitigating factors*, such as the offender's age or mental problems, that might make an offender less deserving of the death penalty.

The death penalty raises important policy issues concerning the appropriate punishments for people who commit murders, acts of terrorism, and other crimes that society considers the most harmful. The weight of scholarly evidence suggests that the death penalty does not deter crime.[11] The prospect of possible execution does not scare people away from committing serious criminal acts, in part because many people are not thinking rationally when they commit murders and also because murderers usually do not believe they will be caught. Advocates of the death penalty argue that only the ultimate punishment can satisfy victims and survivors and show how strongly society disapproves of the worst crimes. Many states have discovered significant problems with the accuracy of their legal proceedings, however. Between 1973 and 2008, a total of 129 people condemned to death in the United States were later released from prison when it was discovered they were actually innocent.[12] Some of these people were exonerated through the use of DNA testing, which showed that physical evidence related to the crime had not been adequately analyzed. Most innocent people were convicted because they had incompetent defense attorneys, because jailhouse informants provided false testimony, or because of other reasons that cannot always be accurately identified and corrected. We do not know how many other innocent people may be on death row, and debates therefore continue about whether the American legal system is capable of imposing capital punishment both accurately and fairly.

Because the Supreme Court has addressed so many issues concerning capital punishment, the court pathway has significantly shaped public policy. For example, the justices have forbidden states from executing mentally retarded murderers (*Atkins* v. *Virginia,* 2002) and, as described in the opening of this chapter, individuals who committed serious crimes before having reached the age of 18 (*Roper* v. *Simmons,* 2005). A majority of justices on the Court views such executions as violating the prohibition on cruel and unusual punishments by being out of step with contemporary values. The Court refused, however, to recognize statistical evidence showing that racial discrimination affects decisions about which offenders will be sentenced to death (*McCleskey* v. *Kemp,* 1987). Through studying more than 2,000 cases in Georgia, social scientists found that people accused of killing whites are much more likely to be sentenced to death than are people accused of killing members of minority groups, especially if the accused killers are African Americans.

New Jersey's legislature voted to abolish that state's death penalty in December of 2007. In addition, several states, including Georgia, Arkansas, Ohio, and Nevada, postponed executions scheduled for 2007 while they awaited the Supreme Court's decision on the constitutionality of lethal injection, the method currently used

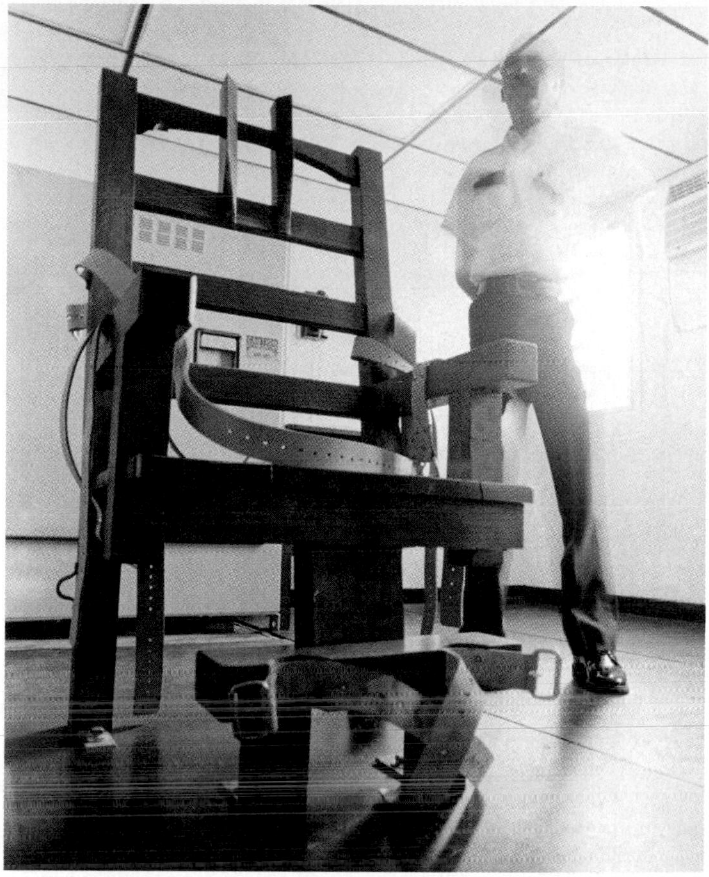

The electric chair was commonly used as a means of execution during most of the twentieth century. Its use declined as courts in various states ruled that the pain and burning inflicted by the chair constituted improper "cruel and unusual punishment." These court decisions did not stop capital punishment, but they did change the nature of the death penalty. ***—How would you judge the use of the electric chair under an original intent approach to constitutional interpretation? What if you interpreted the Constitution in a flexible manner?***

for executions in nearly all capital punishment states. In *Baze* v. *Rees* (2008), the justices, by a 7–2 vote, refused to declare that execution by lethal injection is unconstitutional. Several states immediately began scheduling executions again after the Court's decision. The second major capital punishment case in 2008 produced a 5-4 decision that barred imposition of a death sentence for the rape of a child (*Kennedy* v. *Louisiana*). The Court previously banned capital punishment for the rape of adults (*Coker* v. *Georgia,* 1977) so that states have only executed murderers since the 1970s.

Trial Rights and Capital Punishment
Practice Quiz

1. Most criminal convictions are produced as a result of
   a. plea bargaining. **b.** jury trials.
2. Defendants have a right to a jury trial
   a. in all criminal cases.
   b. only in criminal cases involving "serious offenses" punishable by 6 months or more of incarceration.
   c. only in cases involving federal crimes.
   d. only when the prosecutor agrees that a jury trial is appropriate.
3. According to the Eighth Amendment prohibition of cruel and unusual punishment, prisoners
   a. cannot be tortured.
   b. must receive a punishment proportional to the crime.
   c. must receive punishment that meets society's current moral standards.
   d. a, b, and c
4. The Supreme Court has declared that the use of lethal injections violates the Eighth Amendment prohibition on cruel and unusual punishments because mistakes during some executions have caused the condemned offender to suffer prolonged and severe pain.
   a. true **b.** false

Answers: 1-a, 2-b, 3-d, 4-b.

Discussion Questions

1. Discuss the pros and cons of a trial by jury. Are there circumstances in which a defendant would *not* want a jury trial?
2. How has technology potentially changed the meaning of "cruel and unusual punishments"?

What **YOU** can do!

Visit a local courthouse to observe the processing of criminal cases. As you watch preliminary hearings, pleas, trials, or sentencing, can you see evidence that rights contained in the Bill of Rights affect how cases are processed in court? The next time you watch a TV show in which the police and prosecutors try to bring criminals to justice, keep an eye out for how the guarantees of due process in the Bill of Rights are being observed—or not observed.

■ **Right to Privacy:** A constitutional right created and expanded in U.S. Supreme Court decisions concerning access to contraceptives, abortion, private sexual behavior, and other matters, even though the word *privacy* does not appear in the Constitution.

EXAMPLE: *Although some Americans believe that laws should forbid sexual behavior between same-sex couples (gays and lesbians), the U.S. Supreme Court has declared that consenting adults have a right to privacy that protects their ability to control their own noncommercial sexual activities inside their own homes (*Lawrence *v.* Texas*, 2003).*

■ ***Roe* v. *Wade* (1973):** Controversial U.S. Supreme Court decision that declared women have a constitutional right to choose to terminate a pregnancy in the first 6 months following conception.

EXAMPLE: *Because the American public is divided on the issue of whether abortion should be illegal, politicians supporting each side of the debate have sought to influence the selection of new Supreme Court justices in the hope of either maintaining or reversing the* Roe *decision. Thus the Supreme Court continues to address cases concerning abortion, and the possibility exists that the original* Roe *decision may eventually be overturned.*

Privacy (pages 168–171)

Why is the right to privacy controversial?

The word *privacy* does not appear in the Constitution. The Supreme Court has nevertheless used its interpretive powers to recognize a **right to privacy**■ that protects people from government interference in a number of contexts. The justices first explicitly recognized a right to privacy in 1965. In this case, Connecticut had a statute that made it a crime to sell, possess, use, or counsel the use of contraceptives. After the law was challenged in the court pathway, the Supreme Court struck it down (*Griswold* v. *Connecticut*, 1965). The majority opinion by Justice William O. Douglas concluded that a right to privacy exists as an unstated element of several rights in the Bill of Rights: the First Amendment right to freedom of association, the Third Amendment protection against the government housing troops in private homes, the Fourth Amendment protection against unreasonable searches, and the Fifth Amendment privilege against compelled self-incrimination. Douglas wrote:

> "Where in the Constitution do you find the right to privacy?"
> —Student Question

> The present case . . . concerns a relationship lying within the zone of privacy created by several fundamental constitutional guarantees. . . . Would we allow the police to search the sacred precincts of marital bedrooms for telltale signs of the use of contraceptives? The very idea is repulsive to the notions of privacy surrounding the marriage relationship.

Critics complained that the Court's decision created a new constitutional right that was not grounded in the Bill of Rights. In the words of Justice Hugo Black's dissenting opinion, "I like my privacy as well as the next [person], but I am nevertheless compelled to admit that government has a right to invade it unless prohibited by some specific constitutional provision." Critics feared from this that a five-member majority on the Supreme Court could invent any new rights that the justices wanted to impose on society. By contrast, defenders of the flexible approach to constitutional interpretation claimed that the Court is obligated to adjust the Constitution's meaning to make sure that it remains consistent with the changing values and needs of American society. In subsequent cases, the Court's flexible approach to constitutional interpretation led to the application of a right to privacy to new situations.

Justice William O. Douglas (1898–1980) served on the U.S. Supreme Court for 36 years (1939–1975), a longer period than any other justice in history. His most controversial opinion came in *Griswold* v. *Connecticut* (1965), in which he explained the Supreme Court's recognition of a constitutional right to privacy,even though the word "privacy" does not appear in the Bill of Rights. The Supreme Court still faces privacy issues in the court pathway. ***—Should a right of choice concerning abortion be considered as a part of a constitutional right to privacy? Why or why not?***

Abortion

In 1969, two young lawyers in Texas, Linda Coffee and Sarah Weddington, met a woman who claimed that she had become pregnant as the result of being raped. Because Texas, like other states, made abortion a crime, the woman could not legally terminate the pregnancy (see Figure 5.5). Although the woman gave birth to the baby, she wanted to use her case to challenge the Texas statute through the court pathway. The lawyers took the case, ***Roe* v. *Wade***■, all the way to the U.S. Supreme Court. ("Jane Roe" was not the woman's

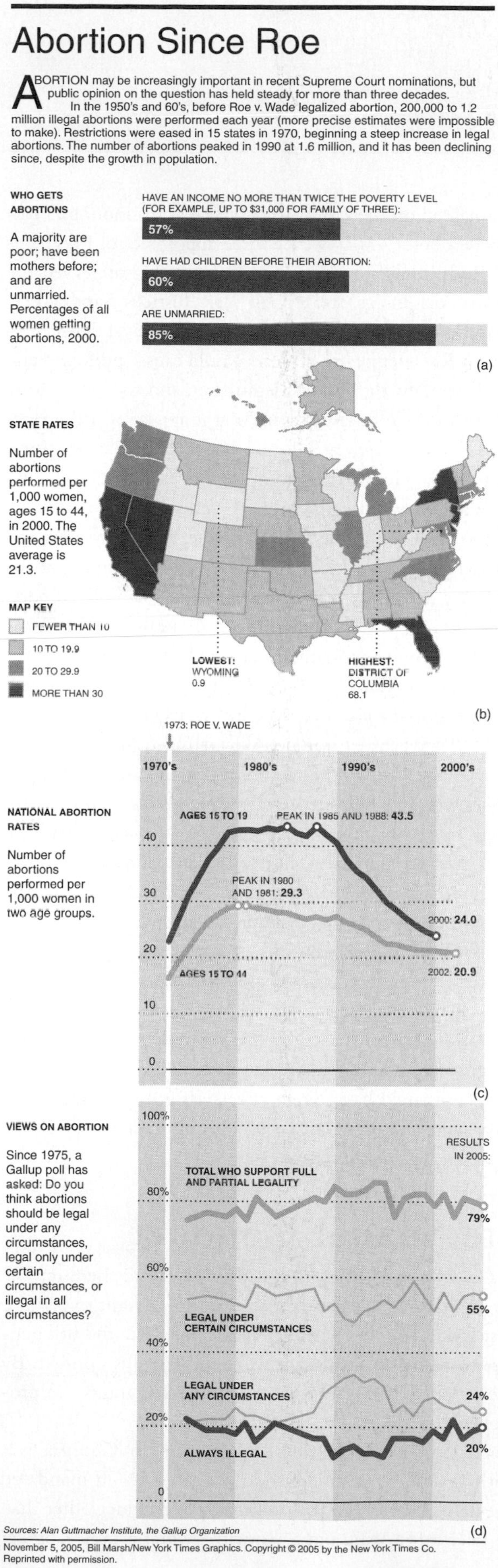

Abortion Since Roe
ABORTION may be increasingly important in recent Supreme Court nominations, but public opinion on the question has held steady for more than three decades.
In the 1950's and 60's, before Roe v. Wade legalized abortion, 200,000 to 1.2 million illegal abortions were performed each year (more precise estimates were impossible to make). Restrictions were eased in 15 states in 1970, beginning a steep increase in legal abortions. The number of abortions peaked in 1990 at 1.6 million, and it has been declining since, despite the growth in population.
WHO GETS ABORTIONS
A majority are poor; have been mothers before; and are unmarried. Percentages of all women getting abortions, 2000.
HAVE AN INCOME NO MORE THAN TWICE THE POVERTY LEVEL (FOR EXAMPLE, UP TO $31,000 FOR FAMILY OF THREE):
57%
HAVE HAD CHILDREN BEFORE THEIR ABORTION:
60%
ARE UNMARRIED:
85%
(a)
STATE RATES
Number of abortions performed per 1,000 women, ages 15 to 44, in 2000. The United States average is 21.3.
MAP KEY
FEWER THAN 10
10 TO 19.9
20 TO 29.9
MORE THAN 30
LOWEST: WYOMING 0.9
HIGHEST: DISTRICT OF COLUMBIA 68.1
(b)
1973: ROE V. WADE
1970's
1980's
1990's
2000's
NATIONAL ABORTION RATES
Number of abortions performed per 1,000 women in two age groups.
AGES 15 TO 19
PEAK IN 1985 AND 1988: 43.5
PEAK IN 1980 AND 1981: 29.3
2000: 24.0
AGES 15 TO 44
2002: 20.9
40
30
20
10
0
(c)
VIEWS ON ABORTION
Since 1975, a Gallup poll has asked: Do you think abortions should be legal under any circumstances, legal only under certain circumstances, or illegal in all circumstances?
100%
80%
60%
40%
20%
0
RESULTS IN 2005:
TOTAL WHO SUPPORT FULL AND PARTIAL LEGALITY
79%
LEGAL UNDER CERTAIN CIRCUMSTANCES
55%
LEGAL UNDER ANY CIRCUMSTANCES
24%
ALWAYS ILLEGAL
20%
(d)
Sources: Alan Guttmacher Institute, the Gallup Organization

FIGURE 5.5 | **Data on Abortion**

Some aspects of abortion have changed since *Roe* v. *Wade* in 1973, but public opinion on the question has held steady for 30 years.

real name; it was used in the case to protect her privacy.) Her lawyers argued that the Texas statute violated the woman's right to make choices about abortion. In 1973, after the Supreme Court heard arguments from lawyers on both sides of the issue, the justices voted 7-2 that the Texas statute violated the Constitution. According to Justice Harry Blackmun's majority opinion:

> The Court has recognized that a right of personal privacy, or a guarantee of certain areas or zones of privacy, does exist under the Constitution. . . . This right of privacy, whether it be founded in the Fourteenth Amendment's concept of personal liberty and restrictions upon state action, as we feel it is, or as the District Court determined, in the Ninth Amendment's reservation of rights to the people, is broad enough to encompass a woman's decision whether or not to terminate her pregnancy.

Congress and several state legislatures sought to counteract the Court's decision by enacting statutes that made it more difficult to obtain abortions by limiting public funding and specifying expensive medical procedures. Initially, the Court struck down several of these restrictive laws. Later, however, as new justices were appointed, the Court became more flexible about accepting regulations. The Court's decisions were based on an "undue burden test" that accepts government regulations as long as they do not impose an undue burden on women's choices about abortion during the first six months of pregnancy.

Abortion became a central consideration in the appointment of newcomers to the Supreme Court as justices retired from the bench. Interest groups representing abortion opponents lobbied presidents and senators and sought to arouse public opinion in support of their position; so did pro-choice groups. Advocates on both sides sought to influence the composition of the nation's highest court. Presidents Ronald Reagan (1981–1989) and George H. W. Bush (1989–1993) vowed to use their appointment powers to put new justices on the Court who would work to overturn the right of choice established in *Roe* v. *Wade*. Thus the stage seemed set for a reconsideration of *Roe* v. *Wade* when the case known as *Planned Parenthood* v. *Casey* (1992) reached the Court.

Pennsylvania had enacted statutes requiring that doctors provide women seeking abortions with detailed information about fetal development, mandating a 24-hour waiting period before a woman could proceed with an abortion, and specifying that minors obtain parental consent and married women notify their spouses before obtaining an abortion. These regulations were challenged as interfering with women's right to make choices about their own health care. In 1992, only one member of *Roe*'s seven-member majority, Justice

ABOVE: **Thousands of anti-abortion protesters** gathered in Washington, D.C., in 2006 to mark the 33rd anniversary of *Roe* v. *Wade* (1973), the Supreme Court's decision that established a constitutional right of choice for abortion. They displayed piles of plastic fetuses to graphically convey their view that abortion kills people.

BELOW: **Both opponents and supporters** of abortion rights use the grassroots mobilization, elections, and lobbying decision makers pathways as well as the court pathway. ***—If you chose to become involved in actions to influence the abortion issue, which pathway would you recommend for your allies to use?***

Blackmun, remained on the Court to defend that decision. In a ruling that surprised observers, however, three appointees of Presidents Reagan and Bush joined in writing an opinion that preserved the right of choice originally created by *Roe*. Justices Sandra Day O'Connor, Anthony Kennedy, and David Souter believed that a decision to overturn *Roe* after nearly 20 years would cause "profound and unnecessary damage to the Court's legitimacy, and to the Nation's commitment to the rule of law" by making it appear as if the right of choice disappeared merely because the Court's composition changed. Justice Blackmun, an appointee of President Nixon, and Justice John Paul Stevens, an appointee of President Ford, also voted to keep the *Roe* precedent. Thus, by a 5–4 vote, the Court approved most of Pennsylvania's regulations but preserved the essence of the right of choice by declining to overturn *Roe*. The majority supporting the preservation of *Roe* later increased to six justices when President Bill Clinton appointed Ruth Bader Ginsburg upon the retirement of Justice Byron White in 1993. Many observers believe that the *Roe* supporters on the Court were subsequently reduced from six to five, however, when Justice Samuel Alito replaced Justice O'Connor in 2006. In the future, President Barack Obama is likely to appoint justices who will help to preserve *Roe* v. *Wade*.

Although some people erroneously hope—or fear—that legal abortion will disappear if *Roe* is eliminated, in reality the Court's decision merely tells states what laws they *cannot* create. Overturning *Roe* would permit states to prohibit or severely restrict abortion. Some are likely to do so, but others are likely to preserve the opportunity for women to terminate their pregnancies legally. Thus abortion is likely to remain legal in some places in the United States even if it is no longer recognized by the Supreme Court as a constitutional right. As a result, the debates and political battles about abortion may ultimately have direct effects on only two groups of women: those who are too poor or too young to travel to a state where abortion is legal and available.[13]

Private Sexual Conduct

Griswold v. *Connecticut* (1965), the case that produced the Supreme Court's first explicit recognition of a constitutional right to privacy, concerned married couples' personal lives. The public did not generally object to recognizing a right to privacy in this context. By contrast, the private sexual conduct of nonmarried adults can produce controversy.

In *Bowers* v. *Hardwick* (1986), a gay man in Georgia was charged with violating the state's sodomy law—which mandated sentences of up to 20 years in prison for sexual conduct other than intercourse between a man and a woman—when a police officer entered his home and found him in a bedroom having sex with another man. The Supreme Court was deeply divided on the question of whether the right to privacy should protect the private sexual behavior of gays and lesbians. The five-member majority of the Court treated the case as if it only concerned, in Justice Byron White's words, "whether the Federal Constitution confers a fundamental right upon homosexuals to engage in sodomy." To that question, the majority answered no. By contrast, the four dissenters, who argued that the law was unconstitutional, viewed the Georgia law as making a general attack on privacy. According to Justice Harry Blackmun's dissenting opinion:

> This case is about "the most comprehensive of rights and the right most valued by civilized men," namely "the right to be let alone." The statute at issue denies individuals the right to decide for themselves whether to engage in particular forms of private, consensual sexual activity.

Seventeen years later, the Supreme Court revisited the issue in ***Lawrence* v. *Texas* (2003),** a case challenging the constitutionality of a Texas statute that criminalized sexual conduct between persons of the same gender. This time, however, the majority on the Supreme Court overruled *Bowers* v. *Hardwick* and declared that the right to privacy protects the private, noncommercial sexual conduct of adults, including gays and lesbians. In the words of Justice Anthony Kennedy's majority opinion:

> The petitioners are entitled to respect for their private lives. The State cannot demean their existence or control their destiny by making their private sexual conduct a crime. Their right to liberty under the Due Process Clause gives them the full right to engage in their conduct without intervention by the government.

Do you believe the Supreme Court has gone too far in identifying and defining the right to privacy? Some people are concerned that judges will do whatever they want to do in creating new rights and affecting public policy. Because of new technology as well as increased governmental surveillance efforts related to computer crime, Internet child pornography, and antiterrorism efforts, additional privacy issues are likely to emerge concerning government intrusion into e-mail, computer systems, and wireless communications. It remains to be seen whether or how the Court will define privacy protections in these contexts.

Privacy
Practice Quiz

1. Although the Supreme Court has established a "zone of privacy," no such right is spelled out in the Constitution.
   a. true **b.** false
2. The Supreme Court majority opinion in *Roe* v. *Wade* (1973)
   a. applied only to federal laws restricting abortion.
   b. found abortion to be "a criminal act in its violation of society's contemporary moral standards."
   c. declared that states could decide for themselves whether to make abortion legal.
   d. used the right to privacy to establish women's opportunity to make choices about abortion.
3. The Supreme Court case *Griswold* v. *Connecticut* (1965)
   a. concerned the personal lives of a gay couple.
   b. generated the Court's first explicit recognition of a right to privacy.
   c. was based solely on the First Amendment.
   d. concerned the issue of abortion.
4. The Supreme Court's decision in *Lawrence* v. *Texas* (2003)
   a. established a privacy right for consenting adults to determine their own noncommercial sexual behavior in private settings.
   b. established a privacy right that legalized prostitution.
   c. limited the right to privacy by endorsing new regulations on abortion.
   d. had no long-term impact because it was reversed by an act of Congress.

Answers: 1-a, 2-d, 3-b, 4-a.

Discussion Questions

1. What would be the political results of the Supreme Court overturning *Roe* v. *Wade*?
2. How do changes in the Supreme Court's membership affect the Court's decisions?

What **YOU** can do!

Since September 11, 2001, the tensions between civil liberties and domestic security policies established as part of the War on Terror have been hot topics of discussion. Research this tension by investigating warrantless wiretapping, military tribunals for detainees, and racial profiling. What parts of the U.S. Constitution serve as the foundation for these policies? Are there historical instances of similar tensions?

■ **Equality of Condition:** Conception of equality that exists in some countries that value equal economic status as well as equal access to housing, health care, education, and government services.

EXAMPLE: *Governments that provide health care, generous unemployment benefits, and government-financed opportunities to attend universities for all citizens are advancing equality of condition.*

The Ideal of Equality

(pages 172–175)

What conception of equality is most appropriate as the goal of the governing system of the United States?

The concept of **civil rights** concerns legal protections for equality and participation in the country's governing processes. As we've discussed in earlier chapters, the founders of the United States wanted to enjoy **political equality,** which would allow them to express their views, own property, and participate in what they called a "republican" governing system. The most famous expression of the founders' emphasis on equality is in the words of the Declaration of Independence: "All men are created equal." The founders believed that political equality was an essential element of the natural world and a fundamental principle of human life, and they considered that principle as being violated when a social system or government grants extra status and power to favored individuals.

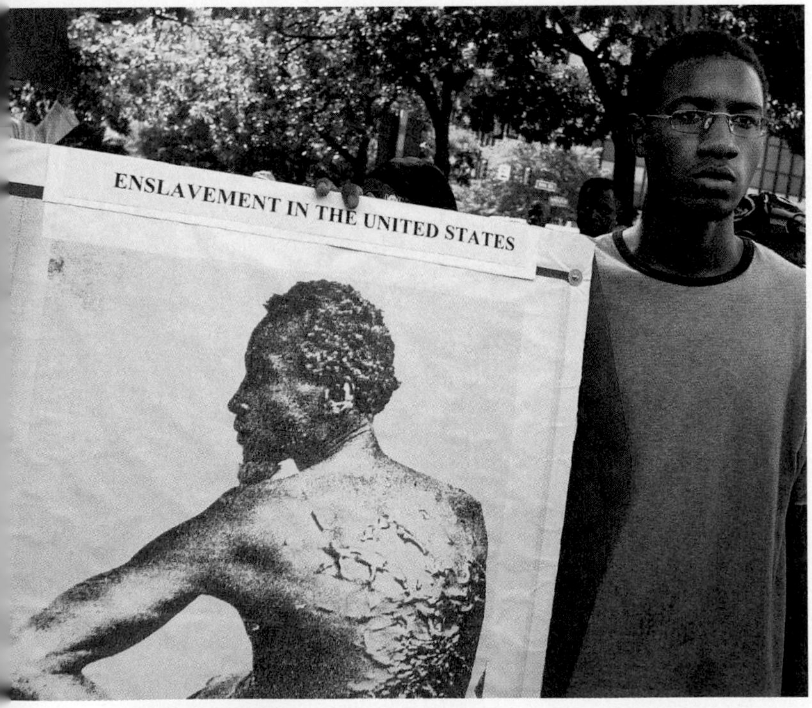

Civil rights protesters use graphic examples to remind the American public of our country's history of violence and unequal treatment aimed at members of racial minority groups. ***—Are such reminders just an attempt to generate guilt, or does this history still have relevance for the problems that we face today?***

"When the framers said, 'All *men* are created equal,' did they mean all *men and women?*"

—Student Question

The Declaration of Independence focused on equality for *men*. The nation's founders simply took it for granted that women need not participate as important decision makers in political affairs. Women were viewed as being destined for such roles in society as cooks, maids, wives, and mothers. In addition, the founders intended equality to apply in practice only to certain men of European ancestry. Many of the founders of the United States were slave owners, and even some who did not own slaves viewed African Americans as less-than-equal beings. Nor did the founders view Native Americans as equal to whites. From the mid-seventeenth century through the late nineteenth century, Native Americans were pushed from their lands, often through military force and other violence.

In practice, the founders did not even view all white men as completely equal for purposes of political participation and influence over public policy. Thus many laws at first restricted voting rights to white men who owned land. Men without property, it was feared, would be too easily controlled by their employers or creditors to act independently.

Despite this, the statement that "all men are created equal" has served as a beacon of inspiration for Americans. Instead of accepting the founders' original limited conception of equality, people have focused on the underlying ideal and asked themselves and their fellow Americans, "Shouldn't I be included in that statement?" Women, African Americans, Latinos, the disabled, and gays and lesbians, among others, have worked through various pathways to broaden the Declaration's original ideal of equality.

Over the course of American history, several factors have contributed to widespread acceptance of a redefinition of political equality that extends beyond white males. These factors include grassroots mobilization, legislative action, legal cases, and even the bloody Civil War of the 1860s. Political activity and social changes over many decades produced new—and now widely accepted—conceptions of equality that embrace women and members of racial and other minority groups (see Table 5.2).

The founders' ideal of equality focused on political participation and civil liberties. By contrast, it would be possible to have a governing system that emphasizes **equality of condition**■. Some governing systems use policy decisions rather than constitutional rights as the means to advance equality of condition. For example, the system of taxation and government benefits in some European countries

Equality of Opportunity: Conception of equality that seeks to provide all citizens with opportunities for participation in the economic system and public life but accepts unequal results in income, political power, and property ownership.

EXAMPLE: *In the United States, there are laws against employment discrimination, but health care is not provided by the government to all citizens. Moreover, stricter eligibility requirements have been imposed in recent decades for the modest government assistance provided to poor people.*

seeks to lift low-income people into the middle class. A fundamental objective of governing systems that pursue such policies is to ensure that everyone has access to important goods and services, such as education, medical care, housing, and at least a modest income.

The American system seeks to advance **equality of opportunity**. This goal has expanded beyond the founders' original concept of political equality to also include the elimination of *some* discriminatory barriers to education, employment, and public accommodation. As we will see, some forms of discrimination are perfectly legal in the United States, while the law bans others. The system does not claim to seek the *elimination* of all differences and disparities or to provide goods and services to everyone. The American political ideology and our free-enterprise economic system emphasize individual achievement and the acquisition of wealth through hard work. People are expected to be self-reliant and to earn enough money to buy their own goods and services. If the government chooses to provide a service, such as public schools or health care for the elderly, it cannot discriminate by race, gender, or ethnicity in serving members of the public. However, the U.S. Constitution does not require the government to provide those services.

TABLE 5.2 | Rights, Pathways, and Results in Advancing Equality of Opportunity

Various groups used specific pathways in order to seek the promise of equality outlined in the Declaration of Independence and the equal protection clause of the Fourteenth Amendment. Multiple pathways were employed, and each group did not use the same strategies.

GROUP	MINORITY RIGHT	PATHWAY	OUTCOME
African Americans	Basic Civil Rights, Prohibit Discrimination, Voting Rights	Equal Access to Education: Court pathway Prohibit Discrimination: Grassroots Mobilization, Elections, and Court pathways Voting Rights: Grassroots Mobilization pathway	*Brown v. Board of Education* (1954) [school desegregation]; Civil Rights Act of 1964 [no discrimination in employment and public accommodations]; Voting Rights Act of 1965
Women	Voting Rights, Prohibit Discrimination	Voting Rights: Grassroots Mobilization and Elections pathways; Prohibit Discrimination: Elections, Court, and Cultural Change pathways	Nineteenth Amendment (1920) [women's right to vote]; Equal Pay Act of 1963; *Reed* v. *Reed* (1971) [no discrimination in inheritance laws]
Japanese Americans	Compensation for Deprivation of Rights During World War II	Compensation for Rights Deprivation: Elections pathways	American Japanese Claims Act of 1948; Civil Liberties Act of 1988
Disabled	Prohibit Discrimination	Prohibit Discrimination: Elections and Grassroots Mobilization pathways	Section 504 of the Rehabilitation Act of 1973 [no discrimination in federally funded programs]; Americans with Disabilities Act of 1990 [no discrimination in employment and public accommodations]
Older Workers	Prohibit Discrimination in Employment	Prohibit Discrimination Employment: Elections pathway	Age Discrimination in Employment Act of 1967 [no discrimination against workers age 40 and over]
Latinos	Basic Civil Rights, Prohibit Discrimination	Basic Civil Rights and Prohibit Discrimination: Grassroots Mobilization and Elections pathways	Agricultural Labor Relations Act of 1975 (California state law) [right of farmworkers to unionize]; Voting Rights Act of 1975 [no discrimination against language minority groups]
Gays and Lesbians	Basic Civil Rights, Prohibit Discrimination	Basic Civil Rights and Prohibit Discrimination: Court and Elections pathways	State court decisions on civil unions and marriage; *Romer* v. *Evans* (1996) [protection against legislation targeted at gays and lesbians]; state and local antidiscrimination laws
Native Americans	Basic Civil Rights, Prohibit Discrimination, Economic Development	Basic Civil Rights, Prohibit Discrimination, Economic Development: Elections pathway	Covered by federal antidiscrimination laws concerning race and ethnicity that were primarily spurred by African Americans; economic development, including gambling enterprises, through state laws

These fists raised in protest before the Lincoln Memorial, in Washington, D.C. symbolize the aspiration—and demand—for equality asserted by members of minority groups in the second half of the twentieth century. Over the course of history, many people have become increasingly frustrated by what they see as the gap between the ideal of equality presented in American law and the reality of widespread inequalities in American society. ***—Have you ever experienced discrimination or had other reasons to feel angry about inequality?***

PHOTO: Doug Mills/The New York Times

The drive for civil rights in the twentieth century focused on two areas: equal access to voting and the prohibition of certain forms of "categorical discrimination," which meant exclusion, by reason of race, gender, or disability, from public education, employment, housing, and public accommodations (restaurants, hotels, and stores). The advancement of these opportunities does not, however, mean that the American governing system is committed to complete equality of opportunity. Belief in the values of individualism and self-reliance in American ideology leads people to benefit from social networks, contacts, and the achievements of their friends and relatives. Many people, for example, get jobs through referrals from family members and friends. (As a college student, you may very well have seen such preferences in action.) Some people inherit money from wealthy relatives and use that money to start businesses. People with wealth and social contacts typically have many more educational and employment opportunities than poor people. This disparity is an accepted aspect of the American free-enterprise system and its emphasis on individualism. As a result, the equality of opportunity advanced by civil rights is limited to specific contexts and does not reflect a comprehensive goal that is vigorously pursued by the American governing system.

In both World Wars, American military units were segregated and African American troops were often commanded by white officers. President Harry Truman's Executive Order in 1948 desegregated the armed forces, but other segments of society remained thoroughly segregated at this time. ***—Could Truman have ordered desegregation throughout American society? What would have happened if he had attempted such a bold move?***

The Ideal of Equality

Practice Quiz

1. Unlike civil liberties, civil rights concern
   - **a.** the individual freedoms that the Bill of Rights protects.
   - **b.** guaranteed education and health care.
   - **c.** equal status and treatment for different groups of people.
   - **d.** social issues addressed exclusively at the federal level.
2. What form of equality is advanced by the American governing system?
   - **a.** equality of condition
   - **b.** equality of opportunity
   - **c.** economic equality
   - **d.** equal access to resources and services
3. Even today, some forms of discrimination are legal in this country.
   - **a.** true
   - **b.** false
4. Categorical discrimination refers to unfair treatment of people because of their
   - **a.** race, gender, or disability.
   - **b.** beliefs and ideas.
   - **c.** national origin.
   - **d.** consumer practices.

Answers: 1-c, 2-b, 3-a, 4-a.

Discussion Questions

1. What would need to be done to achieve political equality for all citizens?
2. Should the United States seek equality of condition instead of equality of opportunity? How would the country be different if we had that goal?

What **YOU** can do!

Our understanding of equality is shaped by the way it is defined in the U.S. Constitution. Other countries and governmental entities think about civil rights and equality in somewhat different terms. Look up the proposed constitution of the European Union (EU) at **http://www.unizar.es/euroconstitucion/Treaties/Treaty_Const.htm**. Go to Part II, the Charter of Fundamental Rights, and read through the sections on "Equality" and "Citizens Rights." Identify provisions that emphasize equality of opportunity and those that emphasize equality of condition. How does the EU's conception of "civil rights" compare to an American understanding? Are there any civil rights identified by the EU that you wish the United States would adopt?

Equal Protection of the Law (page 176–181)

How have the developments of American history led us to where we currently stand with respect to civil rights and equality?

From the 1600s, people who were abducted and brought by force from Africa, and their descendants, worked as slaves in North America. Slavery existed in all 13 American colonies. In the North, it was merely less extensive and abolished years earlier—within several decades of the American Revolution—than in the South. State laws mandating the gradual emancipation of slaves in New York and Connecticut, for example, meant that there were still small numbers of slaves in those states as late as 1827. Slavery was a brutal life, with dehumanizing effects for the African Americans subjected to violence and oppressive controls as well as for the whites, who absorbed an ideology of racial superiority and animosity to justify their mistreatment of dark-skinned people.

"How does our history of slavery affect the current debate on inequality in the United States?"

—Student Question

Slaves worked from sunup to sundown under harsh conditions. They were forced to live in circumstances of limited nutrition, housing, medical care, and clothing, and they had few opportunities to use their creativity, intelligence, and effort to improve the quality of their lives. Slaves were beaten and whipped. Families were forcibly divided, as husbands, wives, and children were separated from their loved ones to be sold at auction and never seen again.[14] Race-based slavery and the subsequent decades of racial discrimination laid the foundation for today's racial gaps in wealth, education, housing patterns, and employment opportunities.[15] These enduring disadvantages for Americans of African ancestry have often proven extremely difficult to undo or overcome (see Table 5.3).

In 1986, Dolly Green stands outside the South Carolina plantation where her grandparents had worked as slaves more than 120 years earlier. Slavery ended many decades ago, yet its legacy, including the century of harsh racial discrimination that followed, has contributed to continuing inequality in American society. ***—What suggestions would you make for reducing the continuing issue of racial inequality?***

TABLE 5.3 | Educational Attainment and Income by Race, 2006 (percentage of adults)

Differences in educational attainment and poverty rates are evident among major ethnic groups in the United States. Over time, some of these disparities have become less stark than in the past. However, these issues that affect millions of Americans have not changed easily or swiftly.

ETHNIC GROUP	HIGH SCHOOL OR HIGHER	FOUR OR MORE YEARS OF COLLEGE	MEDIAN HOUSEHOLD INCOME	LIVING IN POVERTY
White, not Hispanic	86.1%	28.4%	$52,375	9.3%
African American	80.7%	18.5%	$32,372	25.3%
Hispanic	59.3%	12.4%	$38,747	21.5%

SOURCE: Bruce H. Webster, Jr., and Alemayehu Bishaw, *Income, Earnings, and Poverty Data from the 2006 American Community Survey* (Washington, D.C.: U.S. Census Bureau, 2007), pp. 3, 20.

The descendants of whites could enjoy the benefits of education, business contacts, and employment opportunities through social networks. Throughout the United States, freed slaves and their descendants faced the problem of starting from scratch without accumulated or inherited assets. To succeed in the economic system, they needed to seek access to education, employment, political participation, bank loans, land leases, and business contracts—all sectors of society dominated by whites until the late twentieth century. Yet the visibility of their skin color made African Americans easy to exclude by whites who wished to use discrimination to preserve their superior status and to monopolize educational, political, and business opportunities. To varying degrees, women, Latinos, and members of other minority groups have faced parallel problems of exclusion and discrimination.

One central question continues to be debated by individuals and groups who seek to shape American civil rights law and policy: How much should government do to make up for the nation's history of discrimination and its continuing effects? There are significant disagreements about which governmental actions appropriately advance Americans' limited concept of equality of opportunity.

As indicated by this nineteenth-century poster concerning state government in South Carolina, for a brief period in the aftermath of the Civil War, African Americans were elected to Congress and state legislatures. The end of Reconstruction led to many decades in which racial minorities were seldom elected to high offices. In 2006, we saw the first African American elected as governor of Massachusetts as well as African-American candidates for the U.S. Senate and governorships in other states. The next national election in 2008 produced the first widely popular African-American presidential candidate, Barack Obama. ***—Do these recent developments indicate we are reaching a time when people of all races have an equal opportunity to win elections?***

The Fourteenth Amendment and Reconstruction

Immediately after the Civil War, between 1865 and early 1867, President Andrew Johnson—who had succeeded Abraham Lincoln after his assassination—permitted southern whites to determine how the South would reconstruct itself. Not surprisingly, they created laws that sought to maintain white superiority and power. As described by the historian Eric Foner:

> Southern state governments enforced [their] view of black freedom by enacting the notorious Black Codes, which denied blacks equality before the law and political rights, and imposed on them mandatory year-long labor contracts, coercive apprenticeship regulations, and criminal penalties for breach of contract. Through these laws, the South's white leadership sought to ensure that plantation agriculture survived emancipation.[16]

Northerners in Congress reacted by passing the Reconstruction Act of 1867, which required the southern states to establish new state governments based on the granting of voting rights to all men, both white and African American.[17] With the southern states still under Union occupation in the years following the Civil War, military commanders repealed many elements of the Black Codes, and African Americans enjoyed their first opportunities to vote—and to run—for political office. African Americans were elected to high political offices, and 18 served as members of Congress.[18] Events in the late 1870s, however, ended this brief period of political participation by African Americans and eventually led to the reintroduction of severe forms of racial discrimination.

CONNECT THE LINK
(Chapter **5**, pages **141–142**) The creation of the Fourteenth Amendment and its later interpretation by the Supreme Court applied many protections in the Bill of Rights against actions by state and local government officials.

■ **Jim Crow Laws:** Laws enacted by southern state legislatures after the Civil War that mandated rigid racial segregation. The laws were named after a minstrel song that ridiculed African Americans.

EXAMPLE: *Laws mandating the separation of African Americans from whites were so thorough they not only required separate bank teller windows and elevators but also separate Bibles for swearing in African-American witnesses in court.*

Members of Congress from the North also led the effort to create three constitutional amendments after the Civil War to provide important protections for African Americans. However, they could not transform society and create equality merely by adding new words to the Constitution. According to the historian David Kyvig:

> Each of the three Civil War amendments represented an effort to define the rights of free slaves and to give those rights constitutional protection. Each provided less protection than intended, whether as a result of sloppy draftsmanship, deliberate compromises that produced ambiguous perceptions, or determined resistance.[19]

The Thirteenth Amendment (1865) abolished slavery. The Fourteenth Amendment (1868) extended to former slaves the rights of full citizenship, including the equal protection of the laws and the right to due process under the law. The Fifteenth Amendment (1870) sought to guarantee that men would not be denied the right to vote because of their race. Women had not yet gained the right to vote and were deliberately excluded from the purview of the Fifteenth Amendment—over the bitter opposition of women's rights crusaders, who had also been abolitionists.

The language and intended meaning of the Thirteenth and Fifteenth Amendments were relatively straightforward, although as we will discuss later in this chapter, it took additional legislation and court decisions to fulfill the Fifteenth Amendment's goal of ensuring voting rights without racial discrimination. In contrast, the words of the Fourteenth Amendment were ambiguous and required extensive judicial interpretation. Its meaning was refined and adjusted over many decades. These interpretations have had a great impact on the definition of civil rights for all Americans, because the Fourteenth Amendment contains the equal protection clause that victims of discrimination rely on when they go to court to seek judicial protection against unequal treatment by government. Unlike the Bill of Rights—which, as we saw in LINK Chapter 5, pages 141–142, was originally intended to protect individuals against actions by the federal government and only during the twentieth century came to be applied against state and local governments—the Fourteenth Amendment was aimed directly at actions by state governments. The amendment says that "no State shall" deprive people of specific rights. According to one historian, "It was the Fourteenth Amendment, approved by Congress in 1866 and ratified two years later, that for the first time enshrined in the Constitution the ideas of birthright citizenship and equal rights for all Americans."[20]

The Rise and Persistence of Racial Oppression

The disputed outcome of the presidential election of 1876 between Republican Rutherford B. Hayes and Democrat Samuel Tilden affected the fates of African Americans. Election returns from several southern states were in dispute, preventing either Hayes or Tilden from claiming an Electoral College victory. After a special commission (consisting of members of Congress and the Supreme Court) awarded Hayes all the disputed electoral votes, Hayes became president—and promptly withdrew the federal occupation troops from the South. Ending federal occupation permitted those states greater freedom in developing their own laws and policies.[21]

The absence of federal troops unleashed the Ku Klux Klan and other violent secret societies that terrorized African Americans—through beatings, house burnings, and murders—to prevent them from voting or otherwise asserting political and social equality. After 1876, in one southern state after another, self-styled "conservative," white-dominated governments came to power and did everything possible to raise legal barriers to black political participation. These laws could not simply say "black people cannot vote," because such wording would clash with the Fifteenth Amendment's prohibition on racial discrimination in voting. Instead, the new laws did such things as impose literacy tests and "government knowledge" tests as a condition of voter registration. These could also be used to exclude poor whites from voting. In some places, white county clerks administered the tests in a discriminatory fashion to fail all African-American applicants while permitting whites to pass. Intimidation and violence were also used by police to prevent African Americans from voting. As a result, between the 1870s and the 1890s, the number of African-American men who were registered to vote in southern states dropped from tens of thousands to only a handful.

The white-dominated, conservative state governments also began enacting **Jim Crow laws**■, labeled after a minstrel song that ridiculed African Americans. These laws mandated rigid racial segregation throughout southern society. State and local governments required that African Americans attend separate schools and use separate public facilities. By the early twentieth century, this policy had evolved into designating separate and inferior waiting areas in bus stations, public restrooms, and even public drinking fountains. Often, no attempt at all was even made to provide separate public facilities; public swimming pools and parks, for example, were set aside for the use of whites only.

TIMELINE **The Struggle for Equal Protection**

■ ***Plessy* v. *Ferguson* (1896):** U.S. Supreme Court decision that endorsed the legality of racial segregation laws by permitting "separate but equal" services and facilities for African Americans even though the services and facilities were actually inferior.

EXAMPLE: *As a result of the U.S. Supreme Court's decision in* Plessy, *school districts throughout the United States were able to require African Americans and whites to attend separate schools until the Court forbade such forms of racial segregation in* Brown *v.* Board of Education *(1954).*

From the introduction of slavery through the first five decades of the twentieth century, African Americans were victimized by horrific violence and enjoyed little protection from the legal system. White mobs lynched African Americans—hanged and often mutilated innocent people—based on rumors of criminal acts or even for violating white people's expectations that they show deference and obedience. ***—Which pathway had the greatest impact in moving the United States from these gutwrenching scenes to where we are today: court pathway, elections pathway, grassroots mobilization pathway, lobbying decision makers pathway or cultural change pathway?***

> "What did the Court mean by 'separate but equal'?"
>
> —Student Question

With the rise of state-enforced racial discrimination, life for many African Americans was little better than slavery. They were generally stuck in slave-like positions as poorly paid agricultural workers and other laborers. They were virtually unprotected by the law. If whites committed crimes against African Americans, including such horrific acts as rape and murder, there was little likelihood that any arrest would be made.

In the 1890s, a light-skinned African-American man named Homer Plessy, described in court papers as "7/8ths white," worked with lawyers from the North in planning a legal challenge to the rigid segregation of Jim Crow laws. Plessy illegally sat in a "whites only" railroad car and refused to move when asked. As he and his lawyers had planned, Plessy was arrested for violating the law when he disobeyed the racial separation mandated by Louisiana's state law. When the case reached the Supreme Court, Plessy's lawyers argued that racial segregation laws violated the equal protection clause of the Fourteenth Amendment. In an 8-1 decision, however, the Supreme Court decided there was no violation of the constitutional right to equal protection when states had "separate but equal" facilities and services for people of different races (***Plessy* v. *Ferguson*, 1896**).■ The Court's decision effectively endorsed racial discrimination by government, because the separate facilities provided for African Americans, including railroad cars, public restrooms, and schools, were always inferior to those provided for whites. The majority of the justices did not examine whether the

White students at southern universities mounted their own protests against integration in the 1960s. They had been taught to support the idea of white superiority and the policy of racial segregation. ***—As these individuals look back at their actions in the 1960s in light of what has happened since that time, how do you suppose they feel about what they did?***

ABOVE: **The "separate but equal" doctrine** led to strict racial separation in many aspects of American life, especially in southern states. Although some whites argued that separation affected both races equally, the inferiority of services and facilities provided for African Americans made it very clear that the policy targeted one particular group for victimization. ***—Did your parents or other relatives observe or experience aspects of racial segregation? If so, what effect did those experiences have on them?***

BELOW: **The ideology of white superiority** developed as a justification for slavery and then was taught to generations of white children by their parents. Such beliefs motivated individuals to threaten and attack civil rights activists in the 1950s and 1960s. News coverage of such attacks helped to make northern whites sympathetic to African Americans' struggle for equality. ***—How have your views about equality been shaped by news stories, books, or historical events?***

separate facilities were ever equal. It was merely assumed that they were, and the Court turned aside African Americans' hopes for civil rights protection under the Fourteenth Amendment.

The lone dissenter in the *Plessy* case, Justice John Marshall Harlan, who grew up in a Kentucky family that had previously owned slaves, wrote one of the Court's most famous opinions. "Our Constitution is color-blind," he said. As if looking in a crystal ball, he accurately predicted that "the destinies of the two races in this country [whites and African Americans] are indissolubly linked together." The Court's decision endorsing the infliction of harm on one race would, he foresaw, lead to long-term consequences that would adversely affect the entire nation. In Harlan's words, "The common government of all [should] not permit the seeds of race hate to be planted under the sanction of law."

In the southern states, rigid segregation and exclusion of African Americans from political participation continued through the 1960s. Black people continued to be intimidated by violence, including lynching, and remained unprotected by the law. Southern whites maintained their superior status and economic benefits. After 1900, many African Americans began leaving the South and seeking employment in the industrial centers of the North, where they also faced racial discrimination. The South practiced **de jure segregation,** in which state and local laws mandated discrimination and separation. Northern cities used less formal means, often labeled **de facto segregation.** Patterns of segregated housing in the North were usually justified by a presumption that African Americans preferred to live together in the poorest section of each city. In reality, with the help of government home-financing programs, many private decision makers, especially real estate agents and mortgage bankers, steered African Americans into ghettos by refusing to show them houses or finance their attempts to purchase homes in white neighborhoods. In turn, northern school boards used these discriminatory housing patterns as a way to keep African Americans segregated into a school district's worst, most crowded schools. Other school boards redrew school boundaries and transported students to new locations in order to keep African Americans from attending schools with white students. In the same way, African Americans were victimized by other decision makers' racial discrimination, including employers' hiring decisions and police officers' discretionary decisions about whom to stop, search, and arrest.

Other groups faced discrimination during this era as well. For example, immigrants from China began to come to the United States before the Civil War, but they were invariably forced into difficult, low-paying jobs with little opportunity for advancement. At various times, Congress actually banned further immigration from China, and Chinese who lived in the United States always faced severe prejudice and discrimination.[22] In 1927, the U.S. Supreme Court upheld a Mississippi law that barred Chinese-American children from white schools and required them to attend inferior, segregated schools for African Americans (*Gong Lum* v. *Rice*). People of Japanese heritage were victimized by similar treatment in California and other West Coast states where most of them settled. In short, unequal treatment and racial discrimination were pervasive aspects of American life throughout the United States for most of the century following the Civil War, in spite of the post–Civil War amendments that prohibited slavery and promised "equal protection of the laws."

Equal Protection of the Law
Practice Quiz

1. During Reconstruction (1865–1877), the political experience for African Americans in the South can best be described as
- **a.** just as oppressive as during slavery.
- **b.** very promising, with some African Americans getting elected to high offices.
- **c.** without much hope because of the rise of the Ku Klux Klan.
- **d.** better than the political experience of African Americans today.

2. The equal protection clause, so important to the civil rights activism in the court pathway, is included in which amendment to the Constitution?
- **a.** Thirteenth
- **b.** Fourteenth
- **c.** Fifteenth
- **d.** First

3. The notorious "separate but equal" phrase, which endorsed nationwide segregation, was the result of what Supreme Court case?
- **a.** *Marbury* v. *Madison* (1803)
- **b.** *McCulloch* v. *Maryland* (1819)
- **c.** *Plessy* v. *Ferguson* (1896)
- **d.** *Hamdi* v. *Rumsfeld* (2004)

4. De facto segregation of African Americans was routine in the North, even during the twentieth century.
- **a.** true
- **b.** false

Answers: 1-d, 2-b, 3-c, 4-a.

Discussion Questions

1. Why did racial discrimination continue to exist after the Civil War?

2. What is the importance of the U.S. Supreme Court case *Plessy* v. *Ferguson*?

What **YOU** can do!

Learn about the continuing existence of slavery in various countries. See, for example, the Web sites of Anti-Slavery International at **http://www.antislavery.org** and of Free the Slaves at **http://www.freetheslaves.net**. What actions could be taken today to eliminate modern slavery and advance civil rights for victimized people around the world? What role should the United States play?

■ ***Brown* v. *Board of Education of Topeka* (1954):** Supreme Court decision that overturned *Plessy* v. *Ferguson* (1896) and declared that government-mandated racial segregation in schools and other facilities and programs violates the equal protection clause of the Fourteenth Amendment.

EXAMPLE: *Chief Justice Earl Warren's majority opinion in the* Brown *case declared that "... in the field of public education the doctrine of 'separate but equal' has no place. Separate educational facilities are inherently unequal." Thus the Supreme Court highlighted and rejected* Plessy's *assumption that separate facilities for African Americans were equal to those of whites.*

Litigation Strategies

(pages 182–185)

Why have litigation strategies been successful in challenging discrimination during some moments in history but not others?

The **National Association for the Advancement of Colored People (NAACP),** a civil rights advocacy group founded by African Americans and their white supporters in 1909, sought to use the court pathway as the means to attack the forms of segregation and discrimination endorsed by the Supreme Court's decision in *Plessy* v. *Ferguson* (1896). The group originated during a period historians regard as one of the worst for African Americans. In the first three decades of the twentieth century, the Ku Klux Klan grew to more than a million members (many of them outside the South) and was so accepted that President Warren G. Harding reportedly was inducted into membership in a White House ceremony.[23] Racial attacks on African Americans, often called "race riots," broke out in dozens of northern and southern cities, sometimes over nothing more than an African American crossing an invisible dividing line at a segregated beach. In these riots, whites typically roamed the streets assaulting and murdering African Americans and destroying homes and businesses. Modern historians have publicized the large-scale racial assaults on African American communities in Chicago (1919) and Tulsa (1921), and there were similar attacks in many other places. Lynchings continued in the South as well as the North, with individual African Americans who had been accused of some crime or other transgression being brutally mutilated and murdered by white mobs who didn't have to fear that authorities would punish them.[24] Thus the NAACP began its strategic actions for civil rights at a moment when African Americans faced their greatest hostility from American society.

Instead of directly attacking the "separate but equal" *Plessy* rule, the NAACP's lawyers initiated a series of cases that helped to demonstrate how, in practice, the rule had plenty of "separate" but virtually no "equal." In the 1930s, the organization represented an African-American resident of Maryland who was denied admission to the law school at the University of Maryland despite being an outstanding graduate of the prestigious Amherst College in Massachusetts. Although the state of Maryland sought to defend against the lawsuit by saying the state would create a law school just for African Americans or pay for the man to attend an out-of-state school, Maryland's Supreme Court ruled that the admissions policy violated the right to equal protection and ordered that the man be admitted. The court recognized (*Murray* v. *Maryland,* 1936) that the alternatives offered by Maryland would not be equal for the purposes of someone who planned to practice law in Maryland. Over the years, the NAACP pursued similar lawsuits and eventually won cases in the U.S. Supreme Court that banned specific discriminatory graduate school admissions practices at universities in Missouri, Texas, and Oklahoma.

> "How 'equal' were the separate facilities and services for whites and African Americans?"
>
> —Student Question

During the 1940s and early 1950s, it became clear that the Supreme Court recognized segregation in law schools and graduate schools did not fulfill the "separate but equal" requirement. This was especially clear when states undertook such tricks as setting up a one-room law school without a library or other necessary facilities simply to claim that a law school existed for African Americans that was equal to the one provided for whites at the state's main university.

Having won a series of court victories in cases demonstrating the lack of equality caused by racial segregation in law and graduate schools, the NAACP took the next step: pursuing a similar claim with respect to the public education provided for school-age children. This step was very risky. It was widely—and correctly—assumed that whites would have an easier time accepting the presence of small numbers of college-educated African Americans in graduate schools than they would the prospect of their children attending grade school and high school with large numbers of students of a race that many of them feared and despised.

In 1953, the Supreme Court heard the case ***Brown* v. *Board of Education of Topeka* (1954)**■, concerning racial segregation in the public schools of Topeka, Kansas. NAACP attorney Thurgood Marshall, who later became the first African American appointed to serve as a Supreme Court justice, presented the case and argued that the *Plessy* rule of "separate but equal" was inherently unequal. Several justices were reluctant to endorse Marshall's arguments, fearing that a decision striking down racial segregation would lead to violence against African Americans in the South. Other justices believed that the Court needed to be unanimous in such an important decision in order to show the nation that the high court was united in its conclusion. The Court's new chief justice, former California governor **Earl Warren**■, felt strongly that racial segregation violated the equal protection clause. Using his leadership skills and effective persuasion, he convinced his reluctant colleagues to join a strong opinion condemning racial segregation and overturning the

■ **Earl Warren (1891–1974):** Chief Justice of the Supreme Court (1953–1969) who led the Court to its unanimous decision in *Brown* v. *Board of Education of Topeka* (1954) and also took a leading role in many decisions expanding civil liberties and promoting civil rights.

EXAMPLE: *Earl Warren played a key role in important civil liberties decisions, including writing the majority opinion requiring* Miranda *warnings to inform criminal suspects of their rights before questioning in police custody.*

President Dwight D. Eisenhower sent U.S. Army troops to protect nine African-American students who faced violence and harassment when they enrolled at the previously all-white Little Rock Central High School in Arkansas. The effectiveness of pathways of change also depends on the actions of individuals who carry out new laws and policies. This may include physical courage, as illustrated by the Little Rock Nine, and the political courage of leaders such as Eisenhower. ***—Can you think of other examples of courage—physical or political—that helped carry out changes in public policy?***

"Why did it take so long to end school segregation after the *Brown* decision?"

—Student Question

"separate but equal" doctrine of *Plessy* v. *Ferguson*.[25] When the Court finally announced its ruling in 1954, the decision was a controversial blockbuster. Suddenly, it was clear that an important branch of government, the federal judiciary, had endorsed a new concept of equality in which state and local governments were forbidden to provide separate services and facilities for people of different races.

The *Brown* decision did not immediately end racial segregation. A second Supreme Court decision concerning the *Brown* case (*Brown* v. *Board of Education,* 1955-known as "*Brown* II") left it to individual lower court judges and school districts to design and implement desegregation plans "with all deliberate speed." Ultimately, it took two decades of individual lawsuits against school systems and other government institutions throughout the country, both in the South and in the North, to produce the hundreds of court orders that chipped away at racial segregation. Some observers contend that the Supreme Court has been given too much credit for advancing civil rights through its famous first decision in *Brown* because it was actually the long, slow process of many lawsuits and court decisions after *Brown* II that finally broke down the barriers of official segregation. Still, there is broad agreement that the Supreme Court's first *Brown* ruling was a bold and necessary step in the process of increasing civil rights protections for African Americans by withdrawing the judiciary's earlier endorsement of racial segregation.

Additional lawsuits also challenged racial restrictions imposed by government in other aspects of American life. One of the final breakthroughs occurred in 1967, when the Supreme Court struck down state laws that prohibited people from marrying individuals of a different race (*Loving* v. *Virginia*). Today, many people are surprised to realize that only four decades ago, it was a crime in several American states for people of different races to marry.

Why did the NAACP use the court pathway instead of other pathways? Official, legal racial segregation was firmly entrenched in the states of the South, where the majority of African Americans lived. An ideology of white superiority and racial separation was widespread among whites, who controlled dominant institutions, including government. Because African Americans were blocked from voting in southern states, they could not elect their own candidates for public office who would seek to eliminate discriminatory laws through the legislative process. When members of Congress from northern states proposed federal legislation to counteract racial discrimination, congressional committees dominated by seniority-protected southern senators and representatives blocked these proposals, which could seldom reach the point of even being considered for a vote. Delaying tactics by southern senators had the same effect.

Presidents and others in the executive branch of the federal government had little authority over the local and state laws that required segregation and other forms of discrimination. President Truman issued an executive order that led to the desegregation of the armed forces. President Eisenhower sent troops to help enforce a judicial order to desegregate Little Rock Central High School in 1957, and President Kennedy took similar actions in 1962 and 1963 to help enroll the first African-American students at the University of Mississippi and the University of Alabama. In addition, presidents

In 1998, President Bill Clinton honored Fred Korematsu with the Presidential Medal of Freedom, the nation's highest honor for civilians. ***—What does it say about cultural change in the United States when a former wartime detainee who broke the law is later given a high honor at a White House ceremony?***

could propose and endorse federal civil rights legislation. However, they could not make sure that Congress passed such laws, nor could they do anything to change the laws and policies set by state legislatures, city councils, and school districts. State and local laws and policies are not under the control of the federal government. As a result of the unresponsiveness and lack of effectiveness of elected officials, the NAACP saw courts as the only institutions through which to advance the principles of equal protection.

Although judicial action barred governments from continuing the practice of formal racial segregation, the courts did not make sure that schools were integrated and equal in quality. The Supreme Court limited the ability of lower courts to issue desegregation orders by requiring that all orders only affect students within the boundaries of a single school system (*Milliken* v. *Bradley,* 1974). Racial separation remains very common when the composition of city schools is compared to the composition of suburban schools that may be only a few blocks away. Today, racial separation is created by housing patterns reflecting boundaries of cities and suburbs and the inability of poorer people to afford housing in affluent school districts. Judicial decisions prevent racial segregation created by law, but they do not prevent the sort of racial separation that exists in many metropolitan areas.

The foregoing discussion does not mean that the court process was the only pathway of action on civil rights. As we shall see later in this chapter, the grassroots mobilization pathway was important, too, as ordinary people sought to expand civil rights through protest marches, voter registration drives, and other forms of citizen activism.

During World War II, Japanese Americans were removed from the West Coast and held in detention camps without any proof of wrongdoing. The detainees lost homes and businesses as a result of the government's actions. Forty years later, the government paid $20,000 in reparations to each surviving detainee. ***—If you had been among those detainees, how would you have reacted to this payment?***

PATHWAYS | profile

Fred Korematsu

In the aftermath of Japan's surprise attack on the U.S. naval base at Pearl Harbor, Hawaii, on December 7, 1941, government officials were worried about the loyalty of Japanese Americans in the United States. There were fears that they might seek ways to help Japan in the war. In early 1942, Fred Korematsu, an American of Japanese ancestry who had been born in California, was a 22-year-old welder working in the San Francisco shipyard when President Franklin D. Roosevelt issued an executive order requiring that West Coast Japanese Americans be placed in detention camps. Without any proof or even hint of wrongdoing, Japanese Americans were forced to give up their homes and businesses and submit to detention at desert camps in places such as Utah and Arizona merely

CONNECT THE **LINK**

(Chapter **4**, page **101**) The American Civil Liberties Union continues to defend members of minority groups in court, including Arab Americans and African Americans who feel targeted by airport security officials or police officers.

because the government feared that they might spy or provide other assistance for Japan.

Korematsu refused to report for detention. He was arrested and charged with a crime. With the assistance of the American Civil Liberties Union of Northern California, the civil liberties interest group discussed in LINK Chapter 4, page 101, he filed a legal challenge to the president's order by asserting that it was a form of racial discrimination. In 1944, the U.S. Supreme Court ruled against him in *Korematsu* v. *United States.* Many historians regard that decision as one of the most obvious errors made by the Court in the twentieth century. One group of people lost their liberty without any charges or hearings, simply because they or their ancestors came many years earlier from a country that later attacked the United States. Nearly 40 years later, Congress enacted a law apologizing for the mass detentions based only on the detainees' ethnicity and authorizing financial compensation for surviving detainees. In 1998, President Bill Clinton bestowed on Korematsu the Presidential Medal of Freedom to honor his courageous stand. Through the use of the court pathway, Korematsu raised awareness about equal protection of the laws.

SOURCE: "Of Civil Wrongs and Rights: The Fred Korematsu Story," July 2003. Accessed at http://www.pbs.gov/pov on August 24, 2008. ■

Litigation Strategies

Practice Quiz

1. The detention of Japanese Americans during World War II
   - **a.** was deemed a violation of the equal protection clause by the Supreme Court in 1944.
   - **b.** was never considered by the Supreme Court.
   - **c.** did not prompt any protests at the time.
   - **d.** later led to an apology from Congress.
2. When the NAACP was formed in the early twentieth century, its first lawsuit sought to end segregation in American elementary schools.
   - **a.** true
   - **a.** false
3. The Supreme Court's decision in *Brown* v. *Board of Education of Topeka* (1954) was so important for the advancement of civil rights in this country because
   - **a.** it signaled the federal judiciary's condemnation of racial discrimination and made state-mandated segregation illegal.
   - **b.** it immediately brought an end to segregation nationwide.
   - **c.** it confirmed that racial segregation could not be examined by courts.
   - **d.** it instantly created racial harmony in both the North and the South.
4. In many areas of this country, public schools still reflect racial separation and unequal conditions because
   - **a.** the Supreme Court's decision in *Brown* v. *Board of Education* has not been enforced.
   - **b.** subsequent court cases have reversed certain portions of the *Brown* decision.
   - **c.** a disproportionate number of African Americans are still too poor to live in school districts with top-notch facilities and programs.
   - **d.** laws by legislatures in some states have removed their schools from the coverage of the *Brown* decision.

Answers: 1-d, 2-b, 3-a, 4-c.

Discussion Questions

1. Why did the NAACP focus its attention on the court pathway before the 1960s?
2. What is the racial composition of the student body at your school? What are the reasons for that racial composition? If someone wanted to create more diversity at your school, what pathways of action could be used to advance that goal?

What **YOU** can do!

Read some of the Supreme Court's opinion in *Korematsu* v. *United States* (1944) by going to **http://www.oyez.org** and searching for the case name. Do the justices' arguments about civil rights during wartime apply to the detainees held at Guantanamo Bay today? Why or why not? Should judges be able to cite *Korematsu* as a precedent for their decisions today?

Clarifying *the* Coverage *of the* Equal Protection Clause (pages 186–189)

Has the U.S. Supreme Court interpreted the equal protection clause too broadly, too narrowly, or in an appropriate way?

On several occasions, advocates of gender equality pursued cases with the hope that the Supreme Court would interpret the equal protection clause to prohibit discrimination against women. However, the Supreme Court's 1873 decision in *Bradwell* v. *Illinois,* established an unfair, long-standing precedent that provided judicial endorsement of laws that discriminated against women because of their gender—much as the 1896 *Plessy* case did with respect to African Americans. In *Bradwell,* the Court upheld an Illinois statute that prohibited women from becoming licensed attorneys in that state. Justice Joseph P. Bradley's now-discredited opinion relied on prevailing social values and nineteenth-century assumptions about women's "natural destiny" to work solely in the roles of wives and mothers:

"What about civil rights for women?"
—Student Question

> The natural and proper timidity and delicacy which belongs to the female sex evidently unfits it for many of the occupations of civil life. The constitution of the family organization, which is founded in the divine ordinance, as well as in the nature of things, indicates the domestic sphere as that which properly belongs to the domain and functions of womanhood.

The attitudes evident in the *Bradwell* opinion continued for many decades and help to explain why women did not obtain the right to vote nationally until ratification of the Nineteenth Amendment in 1920. In later decades, additional cases tested whether the Court would alter its interpretation of the equal protection clause to advance civil rights for women. In *Goesaert* v. *Cleary* (1948), for example, the Court upheld a Michigan statute that prohibited women from working in establishments that served alcoholic beverages unless they were the wives or daughters of the owner. Like many other statutes that mandated unequal treatment by gender, this law was justified by the state's stated desire to protect women. Such attitudes still dominated the thinking of legislatures and courts in the 1960s, as shown by the Supreme Court's endorsement of a Florida law that automatically excluded women from jury duty unless they asked to serve (*Hoyt* v. *Florida*, 1961). This law led to an overrepresentation of men on juries—and even to many all-male juries—yet the justices endorsed the law by noting that a "woman is still considered as the center of home and family life." The Court concluded that states could enact protective laws that sought to avoid interfering with women's "special responsibilities" as wives and mothers.

During the 1970s, the Women's Rights Project of the American Civil Liberties Union (ACLU) tried to copy the approach of the NAACP by using the court pathway to argue for application of the equal protection clause to gender discrimination. The Supreme Court first struck down a gender-based law as discriminatory in *Reed* v. *Reed* (1971), a case concerning Idaho's inheritance statute that mandated preferences for men. Led by law professor Ruth Bader Ginsburg, who in 1993 would be appointed the second woman justice on the U.S. Supreme Court, the ACLU hoped to persuade the justices in other cases that the equal protection clause should protect against gender discrimination in the same manner that the courts used the clause to prohibit racial discrimination by government (see Table 5.4). As part of the ACLU's litigation strategy, Ginsburg sought to illuminate the issue of gender discrimination for the then-all-male Supreme Court by demonstrating that many discriminatory laws

TABLE 5.4 | Median Earnings of Workers in Selected Occupational Groups by Sex, 2006

Median earnings are the wages earned by workers at the midpoint of the salary scale for this occupation group

OCCUPATIONAL GROUP	MEN	WOMEN
Full-time, year-round civilian workers (age 16 and over)	$42,359	$32,769
Management occupations	$69,669	$50,953
Business and financial occupations	$61,785	$45,315
Computer- and mathematics-related occupations	$70,423	$61,081
Sales and related occupations	$46,650	$30,213
Production occupations	$35,490	$23,940

Disparities could result from discrimination in educational opportunities or job promotions as well as from different pay rates for men and women

SOURCE: Bruce H. Webster, Jr., and Alemayehu Bishaw, *Income, Earnings, and Poverty Data from the 2006 American Community Survey,* (Washington, D.C.: U.S. Census Bureau, 2007), p. 17.

CONNECT THE LINK
(Chapter **5**, pages **152–153**)
Members of Congress have pushed the U.S. Supreme Court to apply the strict scrutiny standard in cases alleging violations of the First Amendment right to free exercise of religion.

treated men in an unequal fashion. In *Craig* v. *Boren* (1976), a key case in which Ginsburg submitted written arguments as an amicus brief, a majority of justices struck down an Oklahoma law that mandated a higher drinking age for men than for women. In making this decision, the Court clarified how lower-court judges should apply the equal protection clause to gender discrimination claims.

The Supreme Court analyzes equal protection cases through three different tests, depending on the nature of the discrimination alleged in the case (see Table 5.5). In cases alleging discrimination by race or national origin, the Court directs judges to provide the greatest level of protection for individuals. In such cases, the courts apply *strict scrutiny,* a concept discussed in LINK Chapter 5, pages 152–153, with respect to alleged violations of fundamental rights. For these cases, the courts require the government to show a compelling justification for any laws, policies, or practices that result in racial discrimination (or the denial of fundamental rights).

TABLE 5.5 | Three Tests for the Equal Protection Clause

TYPES OF RIGHTS AND DISCRIMINATION CLAIMS	TYPES OF TESTS: STRICT SCRUTINY TEST	CONTINUING CONTROVERSIES
Fundamental freedoms: religion, assembly, press, privacy. Discrimination based on race, alienage (foreign citizenship), ethnicity: called suspect classifications " (i.e., such bases for discrimination are especially suspicious in the eyes of judges)	Does the government have a compelling reason for the law, policy, or program that clashes with a fundamental freedom or treats people differently by "suspect" demographic characteristics (i.e., race, alienage, ethnicity)? If there is a compelling justification for the government's objective, is this the least restrictive way to attain that objective? Example: *Loving* v. *Virginia* (1967). Virginia has no compelling justification for prohibiting marriages between whites and people from other races.	*Grutter* v. *Bollinger* (2003). A slim, five-member majority of the Supreme Court approved race-conscious affirmative action programs in admissions decisions at public universities by concluding that the advancement of diversity is a compelling government interest.
	INTERMEDIATE SCRUTINY TEST	
Gender discrimination	Is gender discrimination from a law, policy, or government practice substantially related to the advancement of an important government interest? Example: *Mississippi University for Women* v. *Hogan* (1982) The preservation of a public university as a single-sex institution is not an important government interest that can justify excluding men from a graduate nursing program.	*Rostker* v. *Goldberg* (1981). Despite the service of and casualties suffered by female military personnel in the war zone of Iraq, the Supreme Court has said that the government is advancing an important interest in military preparedness by limiting mandatory Selective Service registration to males, because women are theoretically not eligible for combat roles.
	RATIONAL BASIS TEST	
Other bases of discrimination, including age, wealth, and other classifications not covered by strict scrutiny or heightened scrutiny	Is the government's law, policy, or practice a rational way to advance a legitimate government interest? Example: *San Antonio Independent School District* v. *Rodriguez* (1973) Despite the extra money generated for children in wealthy school districts and the reduced funding for children in poor districts, the use of a property tax system for financing public schools was rational and acceptable.	In *Bush* v. *Gore* (2000), the Supreme Court terminated the Florida vote recount that might have affected the outcome of the contested presidential election by asserting that the recount procedures would violate the equal protection rights of individual voters. The Court's decision did not directly answer whether this case signaled the Court's willingness to thereafter look at voters as claimants deserving of higher levels of scrutiny for equal protection claims.

"How does the Supreme Court decide whether a specific law or policy violates the equal protection clause?"

—Student Question

By contrast, the Supreme Court applies *intermediate scrutiny* to claims of gender discrimination. In such cases, the government need only show a substantial justification, rather than a compelling reason, to explain the different treatment of men and women. This lower level of protection against gender discrimination explains, for example, why the courts accept differential treatment of men and women in military matters, such as the requirement that only men must register with Selective Service (for draft eligibility) when they reach the age of 18.

A third level of scrutiny, called the *rational basis test,* applies for other kinds of equal protection claims. In these cases, the government can justify different treatment by merely providing a rational reason for using a particular policy or practice that advances legitimate governmental goals. For example, the government can have policies and programs that adversely affect the poor. The Supreme Court made this point clear in approving methods of financing public schools, such as property tax systems, that give advantages to residents in wealthy school districts (*San Antonio Independent School District* v. *Rodriguez,* 1973). Similar issues would arise if people sought to use the equal protection clause to raise claims in court concerning discrimination based on age, disability, and other characteristics.

PATHWAYS | of action

Restrictive Covenants

The Shelley family, African Americans who had moved from Mississippi to St. Louis, Missouri, saved their money to buy a home outside of the poor, predominantly African-American neighborhood in which they first lived. After they purchased a house in 1945, their white neighbors filed a legal action against them based on a **restrictive covenant** that was included in the deed to each house, forbidding the sale of any house in the neighborhood to African Americans. Such restrictive covenants were a common technique used in real estate to force minority group members to live in ghetto neighborhoods. In some parts of the country, these restrictive covenants also prevented real estate sales to Jews, Asian Americans, and other religious or ethnic minorities. With assistance from the NAACP, the Shelleys' attorney fought the case all the way to the U.S. Supreme Court, where legal briefs supporting the Shelleys were submitted by a variety of civil rights groups representing Asian Americans, Native Americans, Jews, and labor organizations.[26]

The legal issue was a potential problem, because this form of discrimination involved a contract between private property owners and therefore appeared to fall outside the coverage of the equal protection clause, which is aimed at "state action" (discrimination by government). In an important victory for the civil rights of minority group members, the Supreme Court struck down the enforcement of such restrictive covenants. Even though covenants were a form of private discrimination, the Court ruled that any enforcement of these provisions by government institutions, including courts, constituted state action and therefore violated the equal protection clause. The decision prohibited people from using race-based restrictive covenants to prevent their neighbors from selling homes to members of minority groups. It did not, however, prevent homeowners from racially discriminating when selling their own property. This form of private discrimination was not barred by legislation until the 1960s. The case of *Shelley* v. *Kraemer* (1948) thus demonstrated how individuals can use the court pathway to advance equality and civil rights, but it also showed that court decisions alone cannot block all forms of discrimination. ■

The Supreme Court's decisions have made it clear that the equal protection clause is available only to prohibit specific kinds of discrimination by government, especially race and gender discrimination. It does *not* require the government to treat all people in an equal fashion. As a result, the court pathway does not provide all groups with an equally promising means of advancing civil rights issues by relying on the equal protection clause. The disabled, the elderly, and other groups can use the court pathway to enforce legislatively created *statutes,* such as the Age Discrimination in Employment Act, that protect them from specific kinds of discrimination. It is much more difficult for them to use the equal protection clause, because nearly all government policies and practices can be justified under the rational basis test even if they adversely affect the disabled, the elderly, children, or members of other groups not protected by the strict scrutiny (race and national origin) or intermediate scrutiny (gender) test.

STUDENT | PROFILE

People can only litigate civil rights claims that they have enough knowledge to recognize that unlawful discrimination has occurred. They also need knowledge about how to obtain a lawyer or how to

TIMELINE **The Civil Rights Movement**

pursue other avenues to vindicate their rights. In addition, people who might violate the civil rights of others need knowledge and awareness about equal protection and what actions are permissible under American law. Thus the court pathway for addressing civil rights issues is interconnected with other means of action, including public action and, as we will see in the next section, grassroots mobilization. Students can play a role in both forms of activity. For example, in October of 2007, Bryon Williams, the president of the Black Student Union (BSU) at Kansas State University, helped organize a silent demonstration, rally, and public panel discussion, all intended to raise awareness on his campus about the problem of hate crimes and the role of the media in publicizing—or ignoring—such problems. Members of the BSU were concerned about the limited news coverage of several incidents in which racially motivated actions were directed at African Americans. They distributed pamphlets about hate crimes and then invited several faculty members and students to participate in a panel discussion to illuminate such issues.

Will the actions of the Kansas State University BSU ultimately lead to litigation or concrete change? It is very difficult to predict or even measure the consequences of a specific day of political activism. It is clear, however, that when students initiate programs and actions to educate their fellow students and the general public, they help create new possibilities. A future victim may be more aware of what actions to take. A current or future university administrator may recognize more quickly the need for programs and procedures to address such issues on campus. And future news reporters and voters may learn to pay more attention to such issues, even if those issues do not directly touch their own lives.[27] ■

Clarifying the Coverage of the Equal Protection Clause

Practice Quiz

1. The Supreme Court's 1873 decision in *Bradwell* v. *Illinois*
   - **a.** represented the first court victory on behalf of women's right to equality.
   - **b.** reinforced culturally dominant views of women as naturally domestic and unfit for professional lives.
   - **c.** delayed progress in women's rights but defined the approach to interpreting the equal protection clause that still exists today.
   - **d.** opened the door for women to become medical doctors.
2. Many years before she became the second woman to serve on the Supreme Court, Ruth Bader Ginsburg
   - **a.** was a legal secretary with a law degree.
   - **b.** was a Freedom Rider in the South.
   - **c.** led the ACLU's successful attempt to persuade the Supreme Court to use the equal protection clause to protect women's rights through the intermediate scrutiny test.
   - **d.** led the ACLU's successful attempt to use the incorporation concept under the due process clause, rather than the equal protection clause, to protect women's rights.
3. In cases involving alleged gender discrimination, the Supreme Court uses which test to guide its thinking?
   - **a.** strict scrutiny **b.** intermediate scrutiny
   - **c.** rational basis **d.** conditional basis
4. What are restrictive covenants?
   - **a.** clauses in deeds that prohibit owners from selling their property to racial or ethnic minorities
   - **b.** legal agreements established by communities that make racial integration mandatory
   - **c.** state laws that allow politicians to redraw the boundaries of congressional districts every 10 years
   - **d.** clauses in the charters of private clubs that make it legal for them to discriminate in their admission policies

Answers: 1-b, 2-c, 3-b, 4-a.

Discussion Questions

1. How can discrimination be challenged in court using the equal protection clause?
2. Should the strict scrutiny test be applied to all allegations of discrimination? What effect would such an application of this test have on government and society?

What **YOU** can do!

Identify issues of discrimination and inequality that are of concern to you. Use the Internet to find Web sites of organizations that share your concerns. For example, look at the Disability Rights, Education, and Defense Fund **http://www.dredf.org** or the Native American Rights Fund **http://www.narf.org**. Do these organizations provide opportunities for citizens to contribute to or participate in their activities?

■ **Martin Luther King, Jr. (1929–1968):** Civil rights leader who emerged from the Montgomery bus boycott to become a national leader of the civil rights movement and a recipient of the Nobel Peace Prize.

EXAMPLE: *The Rev. Dr. Martin Luther King, Jr., was a central figure in many of the most important events in the civil rights movement, including the Montgomery bus boycott and the 1963 March on Washington. When he was assassinated by a sniper in 1968, an outpouring of anger and grief by people throughout the country led to civil disorder in several cities.*

Grassroots Mobilization *and* Civil Rights (pages 190–193)

What factors influenced the development and impact of civil rights grassroots mobilization?

Protest marches and other forms of grassroots mobilization were used by various groups before the civil rights movement of the 1950s. American labor unions, veterans' groups, and other organizations had long attempted to mobilize support for their goals. Later, African Americans and their supporters became famous for their courage, their visibility, and their success in changing both laws and societal attitudes.

A major problem for the mobilization of African Americans, especially in the South, was the fact that whites controlled the region's entire criminal justice system, including the police and the prosecutors.[28] Any African American who challenged the status quo by complaining about discrimination and inequality ran the risk of being arrested on phony charges, beaten by the police, or even killed by whites who knew that they would not be convicted for their crimes. Thus the grassroots mobilization of African Americans required great courage in the face of violent responses by whites dedicated to preserving the privileges that a segregated society gave them.

"Why was the Montgomery bus boycott so important?"

—Student Question

One instance of grassroots mobilization was especially important for drawing national attention to racial discrimination and for helping to develop southern organizations for civil rights activism. In December of 1955, African Americans in Montgomery, Alabama, began a boycott of the city bus system in protest against a Jim Crow ordinance that forced them either to sit in the back of the bus or to stand whenever a white person needed a seat. The local chapter of the NAACP had been thinking about initiating a boycott like the ones that had been attempted in other cities. One of the organization's active members, Rosa Parks, refused to surrender her seat to a white man. She was arrested and convicted of violating segregation laws. In response, the NAACP and ministers of local African American churches organized a boycott.[29] In selecting a leader for the boycott organization, the Montgomery Improvement Association (MIA), the civil rights advocates turned to **Martin Luther King, Jr.**■, a 26-year-old minister who had only recently arrived in town to lead a local Baptist church. King proved to be a thoughtful and charismatic leader whose powerful speeches and advocacy for nonviolent methods of protest carried him to the forefront of the national civil rights movement.

The Rev. Dr. Martin Luther King, Jr., sits in a jail cell after one of his many arrests for leading non-violent civil rights protests. ***—What would have happened in the African Americans' struggle for equality if no one had organized mass mobilization, or if civil rights advocates had emphasized the use of violence as a means to seek social change?***

The Montgomery bus boycott lasted 13 months. Eventually, the prosecutor in Montgomery charged King and dozens of other leaders with violating a state law against boycotts. King's trial and conviction brought national news media attention to the boycott, and he was invited to give speeches throughout the country about racial discrimination and civil rights.[30] King's prominence as a civil rights leader enabled him to advocate the benefits of nonviolent, mass mobilization as a means for policy change.

As grassroots protests against racial discrimination continued in many cities, other events contributed to move public opinion as well as the federal government's political power away from acceptance of segregation. For example, the national news media gave great attention to the Little Rock Nine, a group of African-American students who attempted to enroll at all-white Little Rock Central

"Why did President Eisenhower send troops to a high school in Little Rock, Arkansas?"

—Student Question

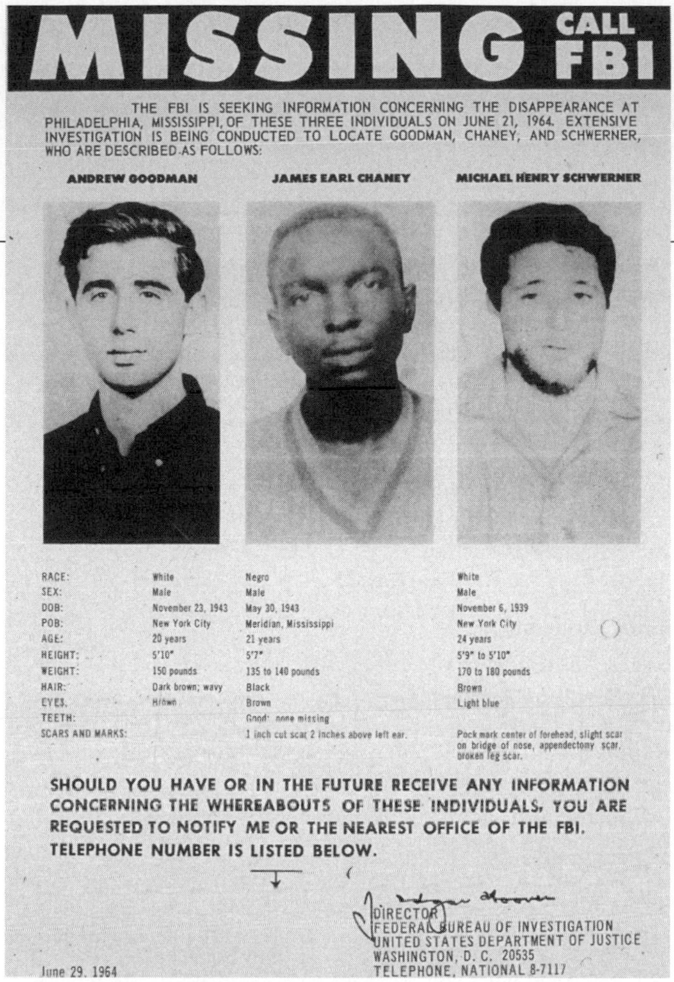
MISSING
CALL FBI
THE FBI IS SEEKING INFORMATION CONCERNING THE DISAPPEARANCE AT PHILADELPHIA, MISSISSIPPI, OF THESE THREE INDIVIDUALS ON JUNE 21, 1964. EXTENSIVE INVESTIGATION IS BEING CONDUCTED TO LOCATE GOODMAN, CHANEY, AND SCHWERNER, WHO ARE DESCRIBED AS FOLLOWS:
ANDREW GOODMAN
JAMES EARL CHANEY
MICHAEL HENRY SCHWERNER
RACE: White / Negro / White
SEX: Male / Male / Male
DOB: November 23, 1943 / May 30, 1943 / November 6, 1939
POB: New York City / Meridian, Mississippi / New York City
AGE: 20 years / 21 years / 24 years
HEIGHT: 5'10" / 5'7" / 5'9" to 5'10"
WEIGHT: 150 pounds / 135 to 140 pounds / 170 to 180 pounds
HAIR: Dark brown; wavy / Black / Brown
EYES: Brown / Brown / Light blue
TEETH: Good: none missing
SCARS AND MARKS: 1 inch cut scar 2 inches above left ear. / Pock mark center of forehead, slight scar on bridge of nose, appendectomy scar, broken leg scar.
SHOULD YOU HAVE OR IN THE FUTURE RECEIVE ANY INFORMATION CONCERNING THE WHEREABOUTS OF THESE INDIVIDUALS, YOU ARE REQUESTED TO NOTIFY ME OR THE NEAREST OFFICE OF THE FBI. TELEPHONE NUMBER IS LISTED BELOW.
DIRECTOR
FEDERAL BUREAU OF INVESTIGATION
UNITED STATES DEPARTMENT OF JUSTICE
WASHINGTON, D. C. 20535
TELEPHONE, NATIONAL 8-7117
June 29, 1964

Poster of civil rights workers who were missing for more than a month before Ku Klux Klan informers helped the FBI solve the case and locate their buried bodies. These murders, carried out by local law enforcement officers and members of the Klan, outraged whites in the North and helped to shift public opinion in favor of African Americans' efforts to gain voting rights and political equality. —***How do shifts in public opinion help to change public policy?***

■ **Civil Rights Act of 1964:** Federal statute that prohibited racial discrimination in public accommodations (hotels, restaurants, theaters), employment, and programs receiving federal funding.

EXAMPLE: *The Civil Rights Act of 1964 barred racial discrimination in a number of aspects of American life. It provided a legal basis for prohibiting racial discrimination by one private citizen against another when such discrimination was undertaken by employers in hiring and promotion and by businesses providing services to customers.*

High School in Arkansas after a successful court case in 1957. President Dwight D. Eisenhower sent hundreds of troops from the U.S. Army's 101st Airborne Division to escort the students into the school and provide protection for them after they were barred from the school and subjected to harassment, threats, and violence.[31]

Acts of violence against African Americans and white civil rights activists continued to capture headlines and produced gripping television footage. In 1962, whites rioted at the University of Mississippi leading to two deaths and hundreds of injuries, as they attempted to prevent one man, Air Force veteran James Meredith, from enrolling as the university's first African-American student. After dozens of federal marshals were injured, President John F. Kennedy sent soldiers to restore order. In 1963, television showed the vicious use by city police of fire hoses, tear gas, and attack dogs to subdue peaceful protesters in Birmingham, Alabama. The bombing of a Birmingham church that year, which took the lives of four young African-American girls attending a Bible study class, shocked the nation. "Revulsion at the church bombing," wrote one historian, "spread swiftly around the world."[32]

In 1964, two young white men from the North, Michael Schwerner and Andrew Goodman, and an African-American civil rights worker from Mississippi, James Chaney, were abducted and murdered in Philadelphia, Mississippi, as they sought to register African-American voters. The vehemence and violence of white resistance to desegregation helped move national public opinion in favor of the African Americans' cause, and it pushed the federal government to take long-overdue action in support of civil rights.

People came from around the country to participate in the 1963 March on Washington to express support for legislation to combat discrimination and enforce civil rights. The quarter of a million participants included tens of thousands of whites.[33] Among the many leaders who spoke to the crowd from the steps of the Lincoln Memorial was the keynote speaker, Martin Luther King, Jr., who delivered what later came to be known as his "I Have a Dream" speech, one of the most famous public addresses in American history (see Figure 5.6 on page 192). News coverage showed a nationwide television audience the huge throng of people, both African American and white, who peacefully rallied for the cause of civil rights. A few months later, President Kennedy was assassinated, and the new president Lyndon Johnson, was able to use public sentiment aroused by the martyred president's death as well as growing concerns about racial discrimination to push the **Civil Rights Act of 1964**■ through Congress.

In 1965, national attention was drawn to Selma, Alabama, where protests focused on registering African-American voters. Many locales across the South used rigged literacy tests in which African Americans were flunked by officials no matter how accurate their responses and thus denied the opportunity to vote. A protest march, planned to proceed from Selma to the state capital, Montgomery, was stopped by dozens of Alabama state police, who attacked the peaceful marchers and beat them with clubs. The brutality of the police attack received significant coverage in newspapers and on television.[34] Public reactions to the violence directed at civil rights protesters helped push Congress into enacting the **Voting Rights Act of 1965**■, the long-sought federal legislation that finally facilitated the participation of African Americans through voting and campaigning for elective office.

Civil Rights Legislation

As attitudes about racial equality changed, people pressured legislators to create new civil rights laws. Many of these new laws were directed at discrimination practiced by private individuals and

■ **Voting Rights Act of 1965:** Federal statute that effectively attacked literacy tests and other techniques used to prevent African Americans from voting.

EXAMPLE: *The Voting Rights Act of 1965 gave the U.S. Department of Justice enforcement powers to oversee voter registration and election procedures carried out by state and local governments, and the federal government used these powers to scrutinize closely any racially motivated efforts to change voting districts or use procedures that might interfere with any citizen's right to vote.*

The 1963 March on Washington showed a national television audience that tens of thousands of African Americans and whites were working together to advance the cause of civil rights. Martin Luther King, Jr.'s "I Have a Dream" speech on the steps of the Lincoln Memorial is considered by many observers to be one of the most inspirational moments in American political history. ***—How might such memorable events contribute to cultural change?***

businesses—discrimination that was beyond the reach of the equal protection clause. Title II of the Civil Rights Act of 1964, for example, forbids discrimination by race, color, religion, or national origin in "public accommodations," which include hotels, restaurants, gas stations, movie theaters, and sports stadiums.

The Voting Rights Act of 1965 was not the first congressional legislation that sought to prevent the racial discrimination that limited African Americans' access to the ballot—discrimination that the Fifteenth Amendment had sought to outlaw back in 1870. The Civil Rights Acts of 1957, 1960, and 1964 all contained provisions aimed at barriers to voting. However, because they relied on litigation for enforcement, they all proved ineffective, as states frequently found new ways to discriminate.[35] The Voting Rights Act of 1965 (and its subsequent extensions in 1970 and later years) barred use of the literacy tests that had been used to keep African Americans away from the polls. Table 5.6 shows the impact of the Voting Rights Act in increasing the registration of African-American voters. The act was also more powerful and effective because of its "preclearance" provision, which required officials in designated districts, primarily in southern states, to obtain the permission of the attorney general before making any changes in elections and voting procedures. The lawsuits filed under the Voting Rights Act provided the basis for judges to stop efforts in several states to create new voting districts that would dilute the voting power of black voters and thereby reduce the potential for African Americans to be elected to public office or to elect candidates favorable to their interests.

A Dream Deferred

In his memorable "I have a dream" speech at the Lincoln Memorial on Aug. 28,1963, Dr. Martin Luther King Jr. looked forward to a time when blacks would live equally with other Americans. While considerable economic progress has been made, blacks still lag well behind. Black Americans own homes at a lower rate than the overall population; a greater percentage live below the poverty line; and a smaller percentage have college degrees.

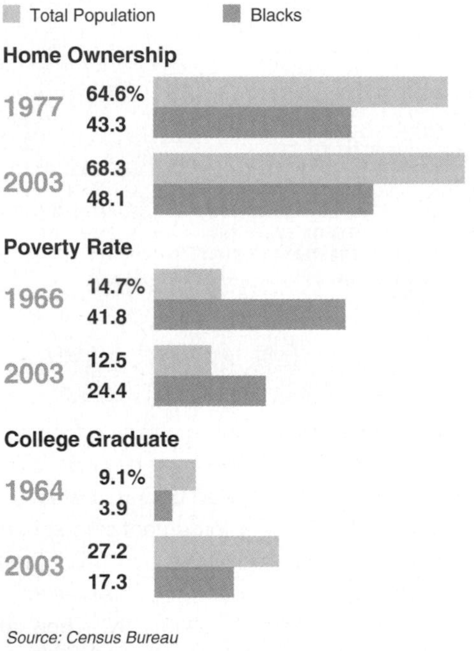

FIGURE 5.6 | A Dream Deferred

Although the measures displayed in this figure show progress, this occurred very slowly over the span of two decades, and significant gaps still remain. ***—What actions can the government take to speed up the process of attaining equality in these measures? Should the government take such actions?***

TABLE 5.6 | Percentage of Eligible Citizens Registered to Vote

Voter registration rates for African Americans in southern states increased dramatically after the Voting Rights Act of 1965 helped to eliminate discriminatory barriers.

	MARCH 1965			NOVEMBER 1988		
STATE	AFRICAN AMERICAN	WHITE	GAP	AFRICAN AMERICAN	WHITE	GAP
Alabama	19.3	69.2	49.9	68.4	75.0	6.6
Georgia	27.4	62.6	35.2	56.8	63.9	7.1
Louisiana	31.6	80.5	48.9	77.1	75.1	-2.0
Mississippi	6.7	69.9	63.2	74.2	80.5	6.3
North Carolina	46.8	96.8	50.0	58.2	65.6	7.4
South Carolina	37.3	75.7	38.4	56.7	61.8	5.1
Virginia	38.3	61.1	22.8	63.8	68.5	4.7

SOURCE: Data from Bernard Grofman, Lisa Handley, and Richard G. Niemi, *Minority Representation and the Quest for Voting Equality* (New York: Cambridge University Press, 1992), pp. 23–24.

Another result of the civil rights movement was the creation of new government agencies to monitor compliance with and enforcement of antidiscrimination laws. The **U.S. Commission on Civil Rights,** created in 1957, was given the task of investigating and reporting to Congress about discrimination and the deprivation of civil rights. The **U.S. Equal Employment Opportunity Commission,** created in 1964, was charged with investigating complaints about illegal employment discrimination. Subsequently, states and cities created their own agencies to investigate and enforce their own civil rights laws. These agencies are typically called "civil rights commissions" (for example, the Iowa Civil Rights Commission), "human rights commissions" (for example, the San Francisco Human Rights Commission), or "equal opportunity commissions" (for example, the Nebraska Equal Opportunity Commission).

Grassroots Mobilization and Civil Rights
Practice Quiz

1. For the most part, court decisions that rely on the U.S. Constitution in order to address civil rights issues
   - **a.** deal with an individual's right to self-expression.
   - **b.** authorize the government to take certain actions to protect the civil rights of minorities.
   - **c.** limit what the government can do to enforce certain forms of discrimination.
   - **d.** avoid using the equal protection clause.
2. What was the first effect of the Montgomery bus boycott?
   - **a.** the prosecution of local African Americans for violating state laws
   - **b.** a revision of the city's Jim Crow busing policy, allowing African Americans to sit "in any open seats"
   - **c.** the celebrity of Rosa Parks
   - **d.** the demise of the Montgomery Improvement Association
3. The March on Washington, the Civil Rights Act, the Voting Rights Act, and the Montgomery bus boycott came in what order chronologically?
   - **a.** march, boycott, Voting Rights Act, Civil Rights Act
   - **b.** boycott, march, Civil Rights Act, Voting Rights Act
   - **c.** Civil Rights Act, boycott, march, Voting Rights Act
   - **d.** Voting Rights Act, boycott, Civil Rights Act, march
4. The use of violence by whites against civil rights activists, such as the murders of Chaney, Goodman, and Schwerner, served to
   - **a.** frighten people away from advocating civil rights.
   - **b.** lead to violent counterattacks against civil rights opponents.
   - **c.** encourage the Supreme Court to intervene.
   - **d.** mobilize northern whites and members of Congress to support civil rights laws.

Answers: 1-c, 2-a, 3-b, 4-d.

Discussion Questions

1. Why was nonviolence ultimately a successful strategy for African Americans in their struggle for civil rights?
2. Are current laws, such as the Civil Rights Act of 1964, sufficient to prevent all forms of discrimination? If not, what further legislation is needed?

What **YOU** can do!

States have their own laws to protect civil rights. Often these laws include different protections from those in federal laws. Find out what civil rights laws exist in your state, either at the library or using Internet sources, such as **http://www.findlaw.com**.

Universal Suffrage: The right to vote for all adult citizens.

EXAMPLE: *As indicated in Figure 5.7, women gained the right to vote in various countries at different points in time from 1893 to 2005. Some countries still do not have universal suffrage, however, because in those countries, women do not yet have the right to vote.*

Women, Latinos, *and* Civil Rights (pages 194–197)

How have the civil rights struggles of women and Latinos differed from those of African Americans?

Women and Civil Rights

Beginning with public meetings and speeches in the first half of the nineteenth century, grassroots mobilization played a crucial role in obtaining the right to vote for women. After the Civil War, the Fifteenth Amendment sought to give African-American men the right to vote. Although advocates for women's civil rights were disappointed that the amendment did not help women get the vote, they took action to mobilize supporters in favor of **universal suffrage**—the right to vote for all adult citizens. One of the most prominent organizations, the National Woman Suffrage Association, was founded and led by Susan B. Anthony and Elizabeth Cady Stanton.[36]

> "When were women first allowed to vote in the United States?"
> —Student Question

Women were able to vote in several northeastern states after the Declaration of Independence in 1776. By 1807, however, all of these states had revoked women's right to vote. It was not until the late nineteenth century that women in various states gradually began to return to polling places as voters.

The first American jurisdiction to grant women the permanent right to vote was the Territory of Wyoming in 1869, followed by the Territory of Utah in 1870. When Wyoming became a state in 1890, its admission effectively permitted its female residents to be the first women in the country to vote in presidential and congressional elections. Colorado and Idaho followed later in the decade. Activists continued to press for suffrage throughout the rest of the country. Over the years, in addition to lobbying legislators and educating the public through publications and speeches, advocates of suffrage organized protest marches and other public demonstrations. Anthony and other activists intentionally faced arrest and prosecution by attempting to vote on election day. Women went to jail for picketing at the White House, and while incarcerated, they went on hunger strikes to draw public attention their harsh treatment and their cause.[37]

Another important strategy was seeking to place the question of women's suffrage on statewide ballots as often as possible. As

Advocates of voting rights for women went to great lengths over the course of many decades to educate the public about the need for universal suffrage. The ratification of the Nineteenth Amendment, which established women's right to vote, represented a major change in the American political system. ***—How would politics and public policy in the United States be different if women were not permitted to participate in the elections pathway?***

FIGURE 5.7 | **Women Gain Votes**

Women's suffrage has been intertwined with other struggles. Canadian women won the right to vote in 1917, but First Nations peoples (those who would be referred to as Native Americans in the United States) were denied the vote until 1960. Likewise, Australia gave most women the vote in 1902, but its aboriginal population had to wait six more decades. New Zealand led the way with universal suffrage in 1893. Here is a timeline showing when some countries—from democracies to dictatorships—granted women the vote, and some others that have yet to do so.

Women Gain Votes

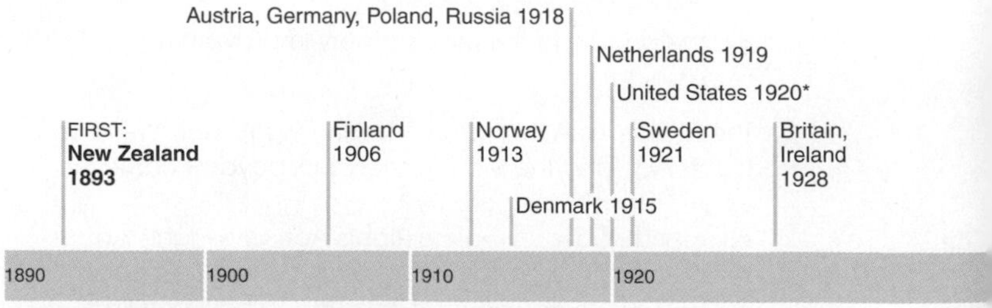

Sources: Interparliamentary Union, United Nations Development Program, CIA World Factbook

*Voting rights for all Americans were not fully guaranteed until passage of the Voting Rights Act in 1965.

TIMELINE Women's Struggle for Equality

TIMELINE The Mexican-American Civil Rights Movement

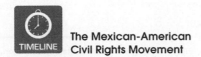

described by one historian, "From 1870 to 1910, there were 480 campaigns in thirty-three states, just to get the issue submitted to the voters, of which only seventeen resulted in actual referendum votes."[38] In the early twentieth century, the suffrage movement gained momentum after winning successful ballot-issue campaigns in Washington (1910), California (1911), Arizona (1912), Kansas (1912), and Oregon (1912). In 1917, several state legislatures gave women the right to vote for specific elections, such as the presidential election or primary elections.[39] Finally, in 1918, the women's suffrage amendment received sufficient support to pass through Congress and be sent to the states for approval. It was ratified as the Nineteenth Amendment and added to the Constitution in 1920.

The right to vote came through organized political action over the course of eight decades. Figure 5.7 illustrates the universal struggle for women's suffrage in the United States and other countries. The mobilization of supporters alone did not lead to women's suffrage. At the same time, American society gradually changed as women gained opportunities to enter the workforce, obtain education, and enter professions that had previously excluded them. All this contributed to the societal changes necessary for women to be viewed as legitimate participants in political processes.

Ratification of the Nineteenth Amendment did not ensure that women would enjoy equal rights. Large segments of the public continued to see women as properly destined for subservient roles as wives and housekeepers or in a few "helping professions," such as nursing, teaching, and secretarial services. Women frequently could not gain consideration for other jobs. After graduating near the top of her class in Stanford Law School in the 1950s, even Sandra Day O'Connor, who eventually became the first woman appointed to the U.S. Supreme Court, received offers to work only as a legal secretary, not as a lawyer. It took decades for women to be elected to public office in appreciable numbers. Even in the twenty-first century, despite the increasing frequency with which women win elections for Congress, governorships, and state judgeships, they remain underrepresented.

Legislatures took little action to initiate laws that would protect women from discrimination until a new grassroots women's movement emerged in the 1960s and 1970s. By then, larger numbers of women were attending college, entering the workforce, participating in campaigns and elections, and challenging traditional expectations about women's subordinate status in society.

By contrast, men and women between the ages of 18 and 21 gained the right to vote during the Vietnam War era through a relatively quick process driven by political elites, especially in Congress, rather than through grassroots mobilization. Previously, the voting age had been 21. Because men younger than 21 were sent to fight and die for their country, however, the issue of lowering the voting age arose. The Twenty-Sixth Amendment was ratified by the necessary 38 states just three-and-a-half months after it was approved by Congress in 1971. This speed can be explained in part because members of Congress and state legislators sought to establish one national voting age through the constitutional amendment process. They wanted to prevent the risk of an inconsistent policy of individual states creating their own separate voting ages.

Latinos and Civil Rights

Latinos, who are frequently also referred to as Hispanics, share a Spanish-speaking heritage, but ethnically and racially, they are highly diverse. Their ancestors may have come from Mexico, Puerto Rico, Cuba, El Salvador, or some other part of Central or South America. They have long faced discrimination in the United States. Some

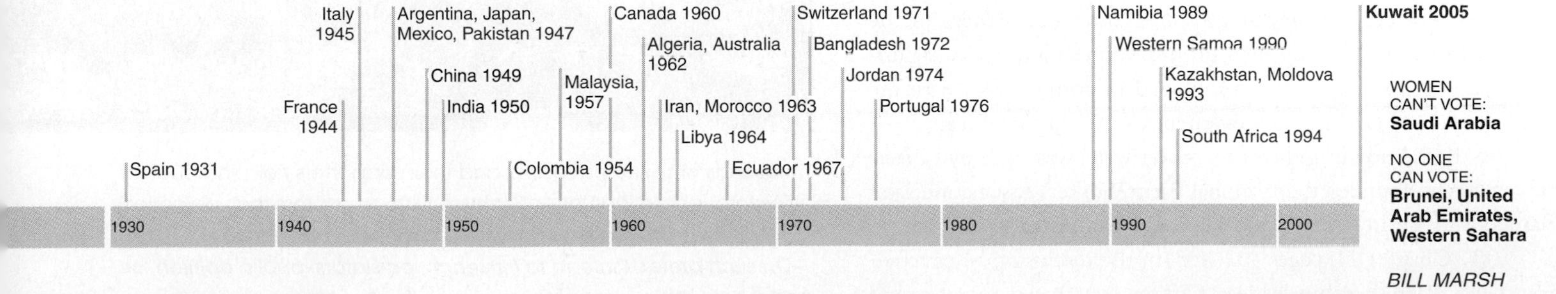

César Chávez (1927–1993): Latino civil rights leader who founded the United Farm Workers and used nonviolent, grassroots mobilization to seek civil rights for Latinos and improved working conditions for agricultural workers.

EXAMPLE: *During the 1960s, Chavez led a national boycott of table grapes that led growers to sign a contract with the United Farm Workers union that improved California farm laborers' wages and working conditions and, later, contributed to passage of California's Agricultural Labor Relations Act.*

Americans perceive Latinos to be recent arrivals who may have entered the country without proper permission from immigration authorities. In reality, many Latinos are descended from people who lived in the territory that became the United States even before whites became the numerically dominant group. For centuries, Latino people lived in parts of what are today California, Texas, New Mexico, and Arizona—all states whose territory originally belonged to Mexico, which the United States annexed in the 1840s after the Mexican War. Latinos from Puerto Rico and Cuba began moving to New York and Florida in the late 1800s. The United States gained control of both islands after the Spanish–American War (1898). Cuba later became an independent country, but Puerto Rico remains under American sovereignty, as an "associated commonwealth." Its people can travel freely to the mainland to live and work. When the Mexican Revolution broke out in the early twentieth century, thousands of Mexicans came north in search of safety and employment. Many American businesses actively recruited workers from Mexico and elsewhere in Latin America.[40] The recruitment and hiring of these workers, including undocumented workers who entered the United States in violation of immigration laws, continued throughout the twentieth century.

Latinos in the United States often received less pay than white workers while being assigned the most difficult and burdensome tasks. Migrant farm workers, who are typically of Mexican or Central American origin, traveled throughout the country harvesting crops, receiving very low pay, and facing difficult living conditions. Latinos suffered discrimination and segregation in housing, employment, public accommodations, and education—and often harsh treatment from police officers and other government officials.[41]

"What are the main civil rights issues affecting Latinos in the United States?"
—Student Question

Latinos formed labor unions and civil rights organizations in the early twentieth century at the same time that others in the United States were forming such groups. Other civil rights organizations emerged when Latinos mobilized in conjunction with the highly publicized civil rights movement of African Americans.

The best-known grassroots movement was led by **César Chávez,** who founded the National Farm Workers Association, later renamed the United Farm Workers (UFW). As you will see in LINK Chapter 11, pages 402–403, in the discussion of effective, charismatic interest group leaders, Chávez led protest marches and organized a national boycott of grapes harvested by nonunion workers

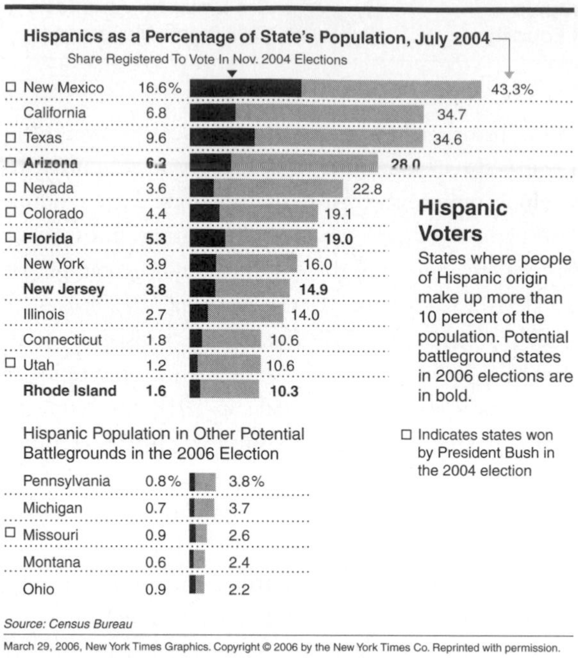

FIGURE 5.8 | Hispanics' Voting Power

Because of trends in population growth, Hispanics will become an increasingly important segment of the American electorate. Political strategists from both the Republican and Democratic parties are already hard at work on plans for persuading Hispanic voters to favor their political party.

Thousands of Latino protesters and their supporters held marches in cities throughout the United States in 2006 to express their objections to restrictive immigration legislation proposed in Congress.
—Do such protests intend to influence legislators, public opinion, or both? How did you react to news reports about these protests?
PHOTO: Monica Almeida/The New York Times

CONNECT THE LINK
(Chapter **11**, pages **402–403**) The work of César Chávez and various Latino organizations provide excellent illustrations of the strategies and effectiveness of interest groups in policy-shaping processes.

during the 1960s. He also went on hunger strikes to protest poor pay and working conditions for farm workers as well as other issues, such as their exposure to dangerous pesticides.[42] He worked on voter registration drives to encourage more Latinos to vote (see Figure 5.8). His efforts brought public attention to the issues of poor working conditions for agricultural workers as well as discrimination against Hispanics. As a result, his struggle contributed to the enactment of new statutes to provide protection for farm workers.

The issue of civil rights and equal treatment for Latinos continues in the twenty-first century, especially because Latinos are now the largest minority group in the United States, surpassing the number of African Americans in 2003 and continuing to grow at a faster rate than most other demographic groups. Latino activists continue to be concerned about such issues as unequal treatment in employment, housing, and the criminal justice system.

In 2006, Congress considered legislation to address immigration issues. Latinos, including U.S. citizens, permanent legal residents, and workers who entered the country illegally, turned out for demonstrations in many cities to support proposed laws to create opportunities to gain citizenship for people who have resided here without authorization for several years. The demonstrators opposed other proposed bills, such as those that sought to impose harsher criminal penalties on people who entered the country illegally and on those who provide assistance to them. President Bush supported a program to permit foreigners to stay in the United States as "guest workers" for a limited number of years. Critics of President Bush's proposal feared that a "guest worker" program would create a permanent underclass of low-paid workers handling difficult, undesirable jobs and that these workers would never have an opportunity to earn citizenship and participate in the government processes that rule their lives through laws enacted by legislatures. In the eyes of some observers, debates about the status and treatment of long-time residents of the United States who entered the country in violation of immigration laws constitute the country's newest civil rights issue.

Women, Latinos, and Civil Rights

Practice Quiz

1. What is the definition of universal suffrage?
   - **a.** It refers simply to the right of all adult citizens to vote.
   - **b.** Suffrage refers to other legal entitlements, such as property rights, along with the right to vote.
   - **c.** Suffrage incorporates social entitlements, such as education, along with the right to vote.
   - **d.** Suffrage means the right to vote in a representational democracy; it does not mean the right to vote in a direct democracy.

2. What amendment to the Constitution granted women the right to vote, and when was the amendment ratified?
   - **a.** Eighteenth Amendment; ratified in 1919
   - **b.** Nineteenth Amendment; ratified in 1920
   - **c.** Seventeenth Amendment; ratified in 1918
   - **d.** Nineteenth Amendment; ratified in 1919

3. Today, thanks to the grassroots mobilization efforts of Susan B. Anthony, Elizabeth Cady Stanton, and thousands of their political descendants, women have achieved equal status, representation, and treatment in all aspects of American life.
   - **a.** true **a.** false

4. César Chávez brought national attention to the plight of Latinos by
   - **a.** organizing lawsuits that exposed the infringement of Latinos' civil rights.
   - **b.** organizing protests against restrictive covenants.
   - **c.** becoming the first Hispanic to run for public office.
   - **d.** exposing the exploitation and dangerous conditions of migrant workers.

Answers: 1-a, 2-b, 3-b, 4-d.

Discussion Questions

1. What issues of equality do women still confront in the workplace and society? How should they be addressed?
2. Should the status of illegal immigrants be considered a civil rights issue? Why or why not?

What **YOU** can do!

While discrimination based on gender and discrimination based on race are often discussed as separate issues, women of color may experience discrimination different from that faced by white women and by men of color. Activists have increasingly pressured women's groups to address the challenges of "intersectionality" (that is, the intersection of multiple characteristics). For one example of a civil rights group's response to this criticism, go to the Web site of the National Organization for Women (**http://www.now.org**), look under "Issues," and click on "Promoting Diversity and Ending Racism."

■ **Affirmative Action:** Measures taken in hiring, recruitment, employment, and education to remedy past and present discrimination against members of specific groups.

EXAMPLE: *Affirmative action efforts can range from advertising employment and educational opportunities in publications with primarily minority readers to giving extra preferences in university admissions processes to members of underrepresented groups, including racial minorities, poor people, women, and the disabled.*

COMPARATIVE **Comparing Civil Rights**

Contemporary Civil Rights Issues (pages 198–199)

Why are there continued debates, lawsuits, and protests about civil rights in the twenty-first century United States?

Some people believe that equality of opportunity has been created through the enactment of laws that forbid discrimination by race and gender. Others believe that more policy actions are necessary to achieve equality for members of groups that have been held back by discrimination. For example, the Supreme Court has examined university admissions policies that employ the use of **affirmative action**■ by giving preferences to members of racial minority groups in order to advance the goal of equal opportunity. People disagree about whether preferential admissions policies are an essential tool to counteract the country's history of discrimination and enable all students to learn within an environment that reflects an increasingly diverse country.

Emerging Groups

The visibility and success of litigation strategies by African Americans and women and of grassroots mobilization strategies of those groups and Latinos provided examples for plans and action by other individuals and groups who saw themselves as victims of discrimination. For example, beginning in the 1970s, people with disabilities lobbied legislators and held public demonstrations in order to gain laws against discrimination in employment and public accommodations.

Advocates of civil rights protections for gays and lesbians use legislative lobbying, litigation, and grassroots mobilization to seek legal protections comparable to those provided for African Americans and women. Gay and lesbian couples used litigation in the court pathway in California, Vermont, and Massachusetts, to gain legal recognition of their committed relationships in civil unions and marriages. Through the lobbying pathway, the Connecticut legislature enacted a law that legalized civil unions. Some states and cities have laws to protect gays and lesbians against discrimination in housing and public accommodations.

Issues of equal treatment under the law have long been a matter of concern for Native Americans as well. They have suffered from overt discrimination, nonexistent economic opportunities, and widespread poverty. Because of their relatively small numbers and isolated locations, Native Americans have not enjoyed success through the grassroots mobilization strategies. In recent years, however, they have advanced their cause through the court pathway. At the end of the twentieth century, some Native American groups became more capable of exerting pressure through the lobbying pathway. Several Native-American groups used their reservations' status as self-governing, sovereign territories as a means to open casinos that would otherwise not be permitted by the states in which the reservations were located. They used revenue from these casinos to increase their efforts to hire lobbyists and make campaign contributions as a means to gain favorable influence and support among members of Congress.

"What other groups in the United States have sought civil rights protection?"

—Student Question

Disabled protesters crawled up the steps of the U.S. Supreme Court in 2004 as the Court prepared to hear a case about the accessibility of courthouses for people who must use wheelchairs. ***—Which pathways of action seem most likely to advance disabled people's goals for new laws and policies to advance their interests?***

PHOTO: Stephen Crowley/The New York Times

SIMULATION

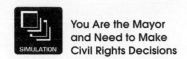

You Are the Mayor and Need to Make Civil Rights Decisions

PATHWAYS | of change from around the world

In December of 2006, students carrying signs protested outside of the Sri Lanka Legal Aid Commission offices in Columbo, Sri Lanka, the island nation off the coast of India. The students claimed that Tamils, members of an ethnic and religious minority, experienced discrimination in admissions decisions at the Law College. Reportedly, only one or two Tamil students were admitted to study law even though Tamils comprised nearly 30 percent of the 10,000 applicants who took the admissions test. The protesters claimed that the admissions committee made numerous errors in translating questions between English and Tamil and that a number of Tamil students were excluded from admission despite obtaining higher scores than admitted students.

Although the protest's impact, if any, can only be judged by the admission of future classes to the country's Law College, the students' effort to make a nonviolent statement against discrimination in a country that is torn with ethnic conflict demonstrated their recognition that any hope for a peaceful democracy rests, in part, on the development of a legal system that is open to participation from all the country's people.[43] ■

Contemporary Civil Rights Issues
Practice Quiz

1. Contemporary kinds of discrimination based on discretionary decisions are
   a. no longer a problem.
   b. based on factors other than race.
   c. always corrected in the court pathways.
   d. a problem only in the South.

2. No court has yet ruled in favor of any protections for gays and lesbians.
   a. true **b.** false

3. Native Americans' ability to use the lobbying pathway has
   a. decreased throughout the country due to poverty.
   b. decreased throughout the country due to discrimination.
   c. increased for Native American groups due to widespread access to college education.
   d. increased for some Native American groups whose revenues from casinos enable them to hire lobbyists and make political contributions.

4. Laws prohibit certain forms of discrimination against people with disabilities.
   a. true **b.** false

Answers: 1-b, 2-b, 3-d, 4-a.

Discussion Questions

1. What other civil rights issues are unresolved in today's society? Which pathway(s) to action would be most useful in seeking resolution?
2. Why are civil rights disputes in today's society seemingly more complex?

What **YOU** can do!

Read about the Native-American plaintiffs who are suing the U.S. Department of the Interior (DOI) in *Cobell* v. *Kempthorne* (**http://www.indiantrust.com/**), and then review the DOI's statements on the litigation at (**http://www.doi.gov/ost/cobell/index.html**). How do you think the federal government should address the civil rights claims raised in this case?

Conclusion

Civil liberties are an especially important part of the governing system in the United States. They reflect the high value that the U.S. Constitution accords to personal liberty, individualism, and limited government. The Bill of Rights, as well as other provisions in the Constitution and in state constitutions, defines legal protections for individuals and imposes limitations on what government can do to individuals. The precise extent of these legal protections changes as judges interpret each constitutional provision.

The United States has a long history of unequal treatment of women and members of various minorities within its society. Although the founders of the United States did not advocate equality for all people, their lofty ideal of equality for most white men provided inspiration for others in American society to share in the benefits of that vision. Hence, there have been efforts throughout American history to gain political equality for women, African Americans, various immigrant groups, and others who were initially excluded from full acceptance and participation in the nation's governing and economic systems.

The court and grassroots mobilization pathways have been especially important for the advancement of civil rights. Judicial enforcement of the constitutional provisions and statutes facilitated significant changes in American society and created opportunities for upward mobility and respectful treatment that would have been nearly unimaginable to African Americans and women a generation earlier.

Civil rights advocates did not invent grassroots action, but they have employed it in an especially successful manner. Ever since the mid-nineteenth century, women's rights advocates have used meetings and protests to educate the public in their struggle to gain the right to vote. The African-American civil rights movement of the 1950s and 1960s had an exceptionally powerful impact on the attitudes of ordinary citizens and eventually convinced the government to create and enforce antidiscrimination laws. Seeing the effectiveness of African Americans' protests, other groups emulated these tactics, although these protesters rarely faced the kinds of violent opposition inflicted on African Americans.

Political equality is an important component of democracy. Without efforts to advance the ideal of equality, the American governing system would fall well short of its professed aspiration to be a democracy that sets an example for other countries around the world.

Key Objective Review, Apply, and Explore

The Bill of Rights in History

(pages 140–149)

Civil liberties, drawn from the Bill of Rights and judicial decisions, provide legal protections for individuals and limit the authority of government.

The Supreme Court originally applied the Bill of Rights only to protect individuals against the federal government, but by the end of the 1960s, through its incorporation of decisions interpreting the Fourteenth Amendment's due process clause, it was applying most of those protections to the actions of state and local officials as well.

KEY TERMS

Civil Liberties 140
***Barron* v. *Baltimore* (1833) 141**
John Marshall 141
Civil Rights 141
Due Process Clause 142
***Gitlow* v. *New York* (1925) 142**
Incorporation 142

CRITICAL THINKING QUESTIONS

1. Should the Supreme Court bear sole responsibility for defining and protecting civil liberties, or should Congress and the president also play a role?
2. Has the Supreme Court improperly stretched the phrase "due process of law" in order to apply civil liberties protections in the Bill of Rights against interference by state governments?

INTERNET RESOURCES

Compare competing perspectives on defining civil liberties and deciding which freedoms are most important for Americans by examining the Web sites of interest groups: **http://www.aclu.org** (American Civil Liberties Union), **http://www.wlf.org** (Washington Legal Foundation), and **http://www.pacificlegal.org** (Pacific Legal Foundation).

ADDITIONAL READING

Abraham, Henry J., and Barbara Perry. *Freedom and the Court: Civil Rights and Liberties in the United States,* 8th ed. Lawrence: University Press of Kansas, 2003.

Curtis, Michael Kent. *No State Shall Abridge: The Fourteenth Amendment and the Bill of Rights*. Durham, NC: Duke University Press, 1986.

First Amendment Rights: Freedom of Religion

(pages 150–153)

Americans consider the civil liberties contained in the First Amendment, which cover freedom of speech, press, assembly, and religion, essential to the maintenance of a democracy and a free society.

Freedom of religion in the First Amendment consists of two components: the establishment clause, and the free exercise clause. Judicial decisions concerning the establishment clause have forbidden sponsored prayers in public schools and other activities that are judged to provide excessive government support for or entanglement with religion.

Congress has sought to protect the free exercise of religion by requiring courts to apply a strict scrutiny or compelling government interest test to such cases. This test forces the government to show a compelling reason for laws and policies that clash with the free exercise of religion.

KEY TERMS

Establishment Clause 150
Free Exercise Clause 150
Separationist 150
Accommodationist 150
***Lemon* Test 151**
Strict Scrutiny 152

CRITICAL THINKING QUESTIONS

1. How should the Supreme Court decide whether the separationist perspective or the accommodationist perspective is most appropriate for interpreting the First Amendment provision on establishment of religion?
2. Should the government ever be able to interfere with an American's free exercise of religion? If so, when and why?

INTERNET RESOURCES

Examine the Web sites of organizations focused on issues of religious liberty: **http://www.becketfund.org** (Becket Fund for Religious Liberty), **http://www.rluipa.com** (issues focused on the Religious Land Use and Institutionalized Persons Act), and **http://www.aclu.org** (American Civil Liberties Union).

ADDITIONAL READING

Levy, Leonard W. *The Establishment Clause: Religion and the First Amendment.* Chapel Hill: University of North Carolina Press, 1994.

Swanson, Wayne R. *The Christ Child Goes to Court*. Philadelphia: Temple University Press, 1992.

Key Objective Review, Apply, and Explore

First Amendment Rights: Freedom of Speech

(pages 154–155)

The actual protections for freedom of speech are less absolute than implied by the words of the First Amendment, because the Supreme Court has accepted time, place, and manner restrictions as well as other limitations that serve society's interests regarding safety, order, and the protection of national security, intellectual property, and personal reputations.

KEY TERMS

"Clear and Present Danger" Test 154
Political Speech 154
Commercial Speech 154
Symbolic Speech 155
Reasonable Time, Place, and Manner Restrictions 155

CRITICAL THINKING QUESTIONS

1. Because the First Amendment's words seem to prevent any government interference with free speech ("Congress shall make no law . . . abridging the freedom of speech"), is it proper for the Supreme Court to identify situations in which the government can limit speech?
2. Should symbolic actions be protected as "free speech" under the First Amendment?

INTERNET RESOURCES

Many contemporary free speech issues are discussed at the Web site of the First Amendment Center: **http://www.firstamendmentcenter.org**

ADDITIONAL READING

Bollinger, Lee, and Geoffrey Stone (eds.). *Eternally Vigilant: Free Speech in the Modern Era*. Chicago: University of Chicago Press, 2003.

Lewis, Anthony. *Freedom for the Thought that We Hate: A Biography of the First Amendment*. New York: Basic Books, 2008.

First Amendment Rights: Freedom of the Press and Obscenity

(pages 155–159)

Courts generally rule against government efforts to impose prior restraints on the press.

Freedom of the press claims by reporters can clash with other priorities, such as the government's need to gather evidence about witnesses and suspects in criminal cases.

The First Amendment does not protect obscenity, but the Supreme Court has struggled to develop a workable definition of what materials are "obscene." As a result, governmental prosecution of obscene material focuses primarily on child pornography, a subject for which a broader consensus about the harm from published materials exists.

KEY TERMS

Prior Restraint 156
Defamation 156
***New York Times Company* v. *United States* (1971) 157**
Reporter's Privilege 157
Press Shield Laws 157
***Miller* v. *California* (1973) 158**

CRITICAL THINKING QUESTIONS

1. Are press shield laws essential to democracy, or do they harm our ability to investigate criminal cases?
2. How would you define obscenity in deciding what kinds of expressions and images could be prohibited by the government?

INTERNET RESOURCES

Examine the Federal Communication Commission's presentation on its duty to prevent obscene and indecent materials over the regulated airwaves on television and radio: **http://www.fcc.gov/eb/oip/Welcome.html**

ADDITIONAL READING

Epps, Garrett (ed.). *Freedom of the Press*. New York: Prometheus Books, 2008.

Friendly, Fred W. *Minnesota Rag: Corruption, Yellow Journalism, and the Case that Saved Freedom of the Press*. Minneapolis: University of Minnesota Press, 2003.

Key Objective Review, Apply, and Explore

Civil Liberties and Criminal Justice

(pages 160–163)

The Fourth Amendment protection against unreasonable searches and seizures requires significant interpretation by courts, especially because so many different situations arise in which the government examines people and their property for evidence of crimes.

The Supreme Court has approved a list of situations in which no warrant is required for searches, because these searches are regarded as "reasonable." Individuals subjected to unreasonable searches may gain protection from prosecution through the exclusionary rule, but the Supreme Court has created exceptions to this rule that permit the use of improperly obtained evidence in some situations.

The Supreme Court's requirement of *Miranda* warnings before the questioning of suspects in custody serves as a central component of the Fifth Amendment privilege against compelled self-incrimination.

KEY TERMS

Exclusionary Rule 161
***Mapp* v. *Ohio* (1961) 161**
Warrant 161
Double Jeopardy 162
Compelled Self-incrimination 162
***Miranda* v. *Arizona* (1966) 163**

CRITICAL THINKING QUESTIONS

1. Does the exclusionary rule advance the interests of justice as evidence of a criminal's guilt may be tossed out due to a police officer's error?
2. Why should criminal suspects be protected against incriminating themselves during questioning?

INTERNET RESOURCES

Examine the U.S. Supreme Court's decisions on the exclusionary rule and *Miranda* warnings: **http://www.law.cornell.edu**

ADDITIONAL READING

Smith, Christopher E. *Constitutional Rights: Myths & Realities.* Belmont, CA: Thomson-Wadsworth, 2004.

White, Welsh S. *Miranda's Waning Protections.* Ann Arbor: University of Michigan Press, 2003.

Trial Rights and Capital Punishment

(pages 164–167)

The Sixth Amendment contains trial rights, including the right to a speedy and public trial and the right to trial by jury. The right to trial by jury applies only for "serious" charges, and the right to counsel applies only for specific stages of the criminal process, from custodial questioning through criminal trials and the first appeal.

Capital punishment is a controversial issue that has divided the Supreme Court's justices over questions about whether it is "cruel and unusual" and therefore in violation of the Eighth Amendment. The Supreme Court's decisions have created rules and restrictions for the use of capital punishment.

KEY TERMS

Speedy and Public Trial 164
Trial by Jury 164
Bench Trials 164
Plea Bargaining 164
Capital Punishment 165

CRITICAL THINKING QUESTIONS

1. Which Sixth Amendment rights are most important for ensuring that criminal defendants receive a fair trial? Why?
2. How would you determine whether capital punishment in general or certain aspects of capital punishment in particular violate the Eighth Amendment prohibition on "cruel and unusual punishments"?

INTERNET RESOURCES

Compare the competing perspectives on capital punishment presented by the Criminal Justice Legal Foundation (**http://www.cjlf.org**) and the Death Penalty Information Center (**http://www.deathpenaltyinfo.org**).

ADDITIONAL READING

Bodenhamer, David J. *Fair Trial: Rights of the Accused in American History.* New York: Oxford University Press, 1992.

Costanzo, Mark. *Just Revenge: Costs and Consequences of the Death Penalty.* New York: St. Martin's Press, 1997.

Key Objective Review, Apply, and Explore

Privacy

(pages 168–171)

The Supreme Court used its interpretive powers to identify and develop a right to privacy that has been applied to give individuals rights related to choices about abortion, contraceptives, and private, noncommercial sexual conduct by adults.

Flexible approaches to constitutional interpretation have triggered debates about whether judges have gone too far in shaping law and public policy and have led to a general politicization of the process of appointing and confirming members of the federal judiciary, especially with respect to the Supreme Court.

KEY TERMS

Right to Privacy 168

***Roe* v. *Wade* (1973) 168**

***Lawrence* v. *Texas* (2003) 171**

CRITICAL THINKING QUESTIONS

1. What, if anything, prevents the Supreme Court's justices from defining the right to privacy as broadly or as narrowly as they personally want it to be?
2. Should the government be able to regulate or ban any aspect of the noncommercial (i.e., no money changes hands) sexual behavior of consenting adults in the privacy of their own homes? Why or why not?

INTERNET RESOURCES

Comparing the competing perspectives on abortion presented by the National Right to Life Committee (**http://www.nrlc.org**) and NARAL Pro-Choice America (**http://www.prochoiceamerica.org**).

ADDITIONAL READING

Craig, Barbara Hinkson, and David M. O'Brien. *Abortion and American Politics*. Chatham, NJ: Chatham House, 1993.

Hull, N. E. H., and Peter Charles Hoffer. *Roe v. Wade: The Abortion Rights Controversy in American History*. Lawrence: University Press of Kansas, 2001.

The Ideal of Equality

(pages 172–175)

"Civil rights" concern issues of equality and involve the development of laws and policies that prevent discrimination, especially forms of discrimination that exclude members of selected groups from full participation in the economic and governing systems.

The founders of the United States advocated an ideal of equality for white men that became a source of inspiration for women, African Americans, Latinos, and others who sought full inclusion in society.

Equality in the United States and laws that advance the American vision of equality focus on equality of opportunity, not on equality of condition.

KEY TERMS

Civil Rights 172

Political Equality 172

Equality of Condition 172

Equality of Opportunity 173

CRITICAL THINKING QUESTIONS

1. How are civil rights different from civil liberties?
2. Why does the United States emphasize equality of opportunity more than equality of condition?

INTERNET RESOURCES

Read about the social welfare system in Sweden, which emphasizes equality of condition, rather than just equality of opportunity, in many aspects of society: **http://www.swedenabroad.com/**

ADDITIONAL READING

Ackerman, Bruce. *We the People: Foundations*. Cambridge, MA: Belknap/Harvard, 1991.

Foner, Eric. *The Story of American Freedom*. New York: W. W. Norton, 1998.

Key Objective Review, Apply, and Explore

Equal Protection and the Law

(pages 176–181)

The United States has a long history of discrimination against women, African Americans, Latinos, and others that inspired the development of civil rights action.

The Fourteenth Amendment's equal protection clause has been an especially important focus of litigation to combat discrimination by government.

Formal racial segregation and discrimination, often enforced by violence against African Americans, became entrenched in American society for nearly a century after the Civil War.

KEY TERMS

Jim Crow Laws 178

***Plessy* v. *Ferguson* (1896) 179**

De Jure Segregation 180

De Facto Segregation 180

CRITICAL THINKING QUESTIONS

1. What aspects of the country's history of racial discrimination may have influenced current issues of inequality?
2. How might the United States be different today if the Fourteenth Amendment had not been ratified and added to the Constitution?

INTERNET RESOURCES

The Web site of the Public Broadcasting System (PBS) presents maps, photos, and other materials about the post–Civil War Reconstruction period: **http://www.pbs.org/wgbh/amex/reconstruction/**

For a detailed discussion of discrimination under Jim Crow laws: **http://www.jimcrowhistory.org**

ADDITIONAL READING

Litwack, Leon F. *Trouble in Mind: Black Southerners in the Age of Jim Crow.* New York: Alfred A. Knopf, 1998.

Takaki, Ronald. *A Different Mirror: A History of Multicultural America.* Boston: Little, Brown, 1993.

Litigation Strategies

(pages 182–185)

The Supreme Court originally endorsed racial segregation in *Plessy* v. *Ferguson* (1896), but after a three-decade court litigation strategy practiced by Thurgood Marshall and the NAACP, the Court became the first major governing institution to firmly reject segregation laws as violating the equal protection clause (*Brown* v. *Board of Education of Topeka,* 1954).

KEY TERMS

National Association for the Advancement of Colored People (NAACP) 182

***Brown* v. *Board of Education of Topeka* (1954) 182**

Earl Warren 182

CRITICAL THINKING QUESTIONS

1. What factors contributed to the NAACP's success in winning the *Brown* case at the Supreme Court?
2. What would have happened if the NAACP had devoted itself to seeking change through a policy pathway other than litigation?

INTERNET RESOURCES

Examine the Web sites of the NAACP and the NAACP Legal Defense and Educational Fund to see these organizations' goals and current activities: **http://www.naacp.org** and **http://www.naacpldf.org**

ADDITIONAL READING

Kluger, Richard. *Simple Justice: The History of Brown v. Board of Education.* New York: Random House, 1977.

Tushnet, Mark V. *Making Civil Rights Law: Thurgood Marshall and the Supreme Court, 1936–1961.* New York: Oxford University Press, 1994.

Key Objective Review, Apply, and Explore

Clarifying the Coverage of the Equal Protection Clause

(pages 186–189)

The Supreme Court's interpretation of the equal protection clause provides protection against racial and gender discrimination by government but little protection against wealth discrimination and some other forms of unequal treatment by government.

KEY TERM

Restrictive Covenant 188

CRITICAL THINKING QUESTIONS

1. Was it appropriate for the Supreme Court to expand the coverage of the equal protection clause to gender discrimination but apply a lesser standard of scrutiny to such claims?
2. What would happen if the Supreme Court applied the strict scrutiny standard to all forms of discrimination by government?

INTERNET RESOURCES

Examine the Web sites of two organizations focused on women's issues to see how they define and pursue their markedly different goals: National Organization for Women (**http://www.now.org**) and Eagle Forum (**http://www.eagleforum.org**).

ADDITIONAL READING

Baer, Judith, and Leslie Friedman Goldstein. *The Constitutional and Legal Rights of Women*. New York: Oxford University Press, 2006.

Hirsch, H. N. *A Theory of Liberty: The Constitution and Minorities*. New York: Routledge, 1992.

Grassroots Mobilization and Civil Rights

(pages 190–193)

African Americans' civil rights movement, led by Martin Luther King, Jr., emerged in the 1950s and 1960s. Whites' violent response to African Americans' nonviolent demonstrations helped dramatize the need for civil rights protections by changing public opinion and spurring the federal government to take action.

The civil rights movement pushed Congress and state legislatures to enact a variety of statutes aimed at preventing discrimination by private actors as well as by government entities.

KEY TERMS

Martin Luther King, Jr. 190
Civil Rights Act of 1964 191
Voting Rights Act of 1965 191
U.S. Commission on Civil Rights 193
U.S. Equal Employment Opportunity Commission 193

CRITICAL THINKING QUESTIONS

1. How does grassroots mobilization make policy change occur?
2. Without the leadership of Martin Luther King, Jr., and Lyndon Johnson, would the same changes in society and public policy ultimately have occurred anyway? If so, how?

INTERNET RESOURCES

Learn about the programs at the King Center, established by the family of Martin Luther King, Jr., to continue his work and legacy; **http://www.thekingcenter.org/**

The Web site of the U.S. Commission on Civil Rights describes its work; **http://www.usccr.gov/**

ADDITIONAL READING

Branch, Taylor. *Parting the Waters: America in the King Years, 1954–1963*. New York: Simon & Schuster, 1988.

Branch, Taylor. *Pillar of Fire: America in the King Years, 1963–1965*. New York: Simon & Schuster, 1998.

Key Objective Review, Apply, and Explore

Women, Latinos, and Civil Rights

(pages 194–197)

Women organized meetings and protests as early as the mid-nineteenth century in a grassroots effort to obtain the right to vote, a goal finally achieved in 1920.

Latinos have used grassroots mobilization to seek civil rights and equal treatment, especially through the farm workers' movement led by César Chávez.

KEY TERMS

Universal Suffrage 194

César Chávez 196

CRITICAL THINKING QUESTIONS

1. What factors may have made women's struggle for universal suffrage different from African Americans' struggle for civil rights, including voting rights?
2. Why might many Latinos and other Americans see today's immigration issues as "civil rights" issues? Do you agree with such a characterization of immigration issues?

INTERNET RESOURCES

The Web site of the Susan B. Anthony Center for Women's Leadership at the University of Rochester provides historical information about women's efforts to obtain the right to vote: **http://www.rochester.edu/SBA/suffragehistory.html**

Learn about contemporary issues affecting farm workers, especially Latino farm workers, at the Web site of the United Farm Workers union, which was founded by César Chávez: **http://www.ufw.org/**

ADDITIONAL READING

Flexner, Eleanor, and Ellen Fitzpatrick. *Century of Struggle: The Women's Rights Movement in the United States*. Cambridge, MA: Belknap/Harvard, 1996.

Gutierrez, David G. *The Columbia History of Latinos in the United States Since 1960*. New York: Columbia University Press, 2006.

Contemporary Civil Rights Issues

(pages 198–199)

Additional groups have emerged to seek civil rights protection through the court and grassroots mobilization pathways. These groups include the disabled and Native Americans as well as gays and lesbians. Although disabled people have been successful in pushing for laws to guard against discrimination in employment and public accommodations, gays and lesbians have been successful in just a few states.

KEY TERM

Affirmative Action 198

CRITICAL THINKING QUESTIONS

1. In light of the complexity of many contemporary issues concerning equality, are there specific policies that could help advance equality and civil rights?
2. Which emerging groups that currently seek civil rights and equality are likely to have the most difficulty advancing their goals? Why?

INTERNET RESOURCES

Read about competing perspectives on affirmative action at the Web sites of the National Leadership Network of Black Conservatives (**http://www.nationalcenter.org/AA.html**) and the American Association for Affirmative Action, (**http://www.affirmativeaction.org/**).

ADDITIONAL READING

Carter, Stephen L. *Reflections of an Affirmative Action Baby*. New York: Basic Books, 1991.

Hensley, Thomas R., Christopher E. Smith, and Joyce A. Baugh. *The Changing Supreme Court: Civil Rights and Liberties*. St. Paul, MN: West, 1997.

Chapter Review Critical Thinking Test

1. If you made a speech advocating a total change in our form of government in today's society,
   - **a.** you could never be prosecuted under any circumstances.
   - **b.** you could not be prosecuted because the Sixth Amendment's right to confrontation permits you to confront the government.
   - **c.** you could be prosecuted for treason.
   - **d.** you could only be prosecuted if your words created the danger of immediate incitement of imminent lawless action.
2. The Eighth Amendment's prohibition against "cruel and unusual punishments"
   - **a.** has had no impact on imposition of the death penalty.
   - **b.** has helped opponents of the death penalty limit the forms and applications of capital punishment.
   - **c.** has offered a clear, unchanging standard for death penalty sentences.
   - **d.** only applies to death by torture.
3. According to strict separationists, the establishment clause prohibits financial support or endorsement of any religion. This means that the government cannot give any aid to parochial schools or permit religious displays on public property.
   - **a.** true **b.** false
4. The accommodationist approach to the establishment clause
   - **a.** often violates the Eighth Amendment.
   - **b.** is always supported by the *Lemon* test.
   - **c.** is universally opposed by all Americans.
   - **d.** is reflected in state laws that attempt to provide money, transportation, and other resources for religious schools.
5. The Supreme Court's development of the exclusionary rule as part of the law governing the Fourth Amendment
   - **a.** means that prosecutors cannot exclude evidence from a trial, even if such evidence undermines their case.
   - **b.** means that evidence improperly obtained by law enforcement officials may be used to prosecute an alleged criminal.
   - **c.** can never be used to prevent the imposition of deserved punishment on someone who committed a crime.
   - **d.** can frustrate police and prosecutors because it may interfere with their preparation of evidence against a defendant.
6. "*Miranda* rights"
   - **a.** must be administered to suspects who appear voluntarily for questioning.
   - **b.** mean that most guilty criminals go free because the police cannot obtain confessions.
   - **c.** are intented to prevent suspects from feeling compelled to say anything that may incriminate them in court.
   - **d.** are likely to be declared unconstitutional as a violation of due process.
7. About half of criminal prosecutions in the United States never reach a trial and are resolved through plea bargaining.
   - **a.** true **b.** false
8. The following arguments have been presented to the Supreme Court concerning the death penalty. Which one persuaded the justices to create a limitation on capital punishment?
   - **a.** Execution by lethal injection is cruel and unusual punishment.
   - **b.** Execution of juvenile offenders is cruel and unusual punishment.
   - **c.** Statistical evidence shows that racial discrimination exists in capital punishment and therefore the death penalty should be banned for violating the equal protection clause.
   - **d.** The selection of jurors for death penalty cases leads to bias against the defendant and therefore causes cruel and unusual punishment.
9. Controversial Supreme Court decisions such as *Roe* v. *Wade* reflect a judicial philosophy that
   - **a.** rigidly follows the exact language of the Constitution and ignores modern social problems.
   - **b.** permits legislatures to decide all important policy issues.
   - **c.** exercises a flexible approach to constitutional interpretation and adjusts the definition of rights as society changes.
   - **d.** rejects the concept of incorporation that has long guided the Supreme Court's decisions
10. Because of the development of DNA testing and other investigative techniques,
    - **a.** American courts no longer ever convict innocent people of crimes that they did not commit.
    - **b.** there is no longer a need for the exclusionary rule.
    - **c.** more than 120 death row inmates have been released when it was discovered that they are actually innocent.
    - **d.** there is no longer a need to question suspects and provide them with *Miranda* warnings.
11. The American system of government promotes equality of opportunity for all citizens, meaning that it
    - **a.** helps guarantee access to essential goods and services to all Americans.
    - **b.** helps ensure individual self-reliance by outlawing *some* discriminatory barriers to education, employment, and public accommodation.
    - **c.** works to reduce economic disadvantages so that all citizens have access to essential goods and services.
    - **d.** assumes that everyone will pursue the American Dream based on their own efforts.
12. Why did the disadvantages of slavery continue to burden African Americans a century after emancipation?
    - **a.** Because economic disadvantage, like economic advantage, accumulates: Poor people cannot afford expensive college educations for their children, which makes those children less likely to get high-paying jobs, which makes them less likely to send their children to expensive colleges, and so on.
    - **b.** Because descendants of slaves are barred from certain occupations.
    - **c.** Because there have been no leaders to inspire changes in our laws and culture.

Chapter Review Critical Thinking Test

d. because the Supreme Court has refused to make any decisions that might reduce the effects of racial discrimination.

13. The equal protection clause protects citizens from being deprived of their rights if those rights are being infringed upon by

a. other individuals.
b. the federal government.
c. a state government.
d. local clubs or associations.

14. Why should every student of American civil rights know about the Supreme Court case *Plessy* v. *Ferguson*?

a. It was the first time the Court applied the equal protection clause to individual acts of discrimination.
b. It started to turn the tide against Jim Crow legislation at the state level.
c. It changed how interstate railroads conducted business.
d. It justified legal segregation across the nation, a backward step in civil rights law that would not be remedied until the middle of the twentieth century.

15. What are the principles of strict scrutiny, intermediate scrutiny, and rational basis?

a. They are those levels of citizen participation in national politics as theorized in *The Federalist Papers.*
b. They are the three tests by which the Supreme Court evaluates cases under the Civil Rights Act of 1964.
c. They are the three tests by which the Supreme Court evaluates cases about the equal protection clause.
d. They are the three levels of discrimination that prosecutors can charge in civil rights cases.

16. Because restrictive covenants are a form of *private* discrimination, the Supreme Court ruled that enforcement of these covenants by government agencies and courts was permissible.

a. true **b.** false

17. The Nineteenth Amendment, granting women the right to vote in national elections,

a. was accomplished without the assistance of any grassroots mobilization.
b. catapulted women into positions of authority equal to men.
c. resulted in part from a positive shift in cultural assumptions about women's capabilities.
d. was mandated by what the Fifteenth Amendment implied.

18. Antidiscrimination activism on behalf of Latinos will probably continue in the years to come, because

a. Latinos are now the largest minority group in the country.
b. television news encourages people to stage protests.
c. a majority of legislators in Texas and California are now Latinos.
d. President George W. Bush devoted his presidency to encouraging people to become involved in civil rights issues.

19. Our society is full of examples of unequal outcomes; some people have always been treated less fairly than others. Our antidiscrimination laws cannot do much to remedy this situation, however, because

a. people never obey laws with which they disagree.
b. laws are directed at only specific kinds of discrimination in limited contexts, such as race discrimination in employment.
c. each individual state has complete control over the antidiscrimination laws that apply within its boundaries.
d. people are poor due to their own desire to be poor.

20. Martin Luther King, Jr. and César Chávez are most closely associated with which pathway of action on civil rights issues?

a. court **b.** lobbying
c. elections **d.** grassroots mobilization

Answers: 1-d, 2-b, 3-a, 4-d, 5-d, 6-c, 7-b, 8-b, 9-c, 10-c, 11-b, 12-a, 13-c, 14-d, 15-c, 16-b, 17-c, 18-a, 19-b, 20-d.

You decide!

In 2007, Columbia University invited Mahmoud Ahmadinejad, the President of Iran, to give a speech on its campus during his visit to New York for meetings at the United Nations. President Ahmadinejad is a highly controversial figure, both for his country's alleged sponsorship of terrorist groups and for his personal statements advocating the destruction of Israel and denying that Hitler's Nazi soldiers murdered hundreds of thousands of Jews in concentration camps during World War II. Imagine that President Ahmadinejad was invited to your campus to give a speech entitled,"Why the Nations of the World Should Unite to Fight Against the United States. "Would you feel comfortable listening to such a speech? Should U.S. government officials prevent him from giving such a speech? If so, why? If a friend asked you to help organize a demonstration against President Ahmadinejad that would include sitting in the auditorium and shouting to prevent him from being heard by the rest of the audience, would you agree to participate? Would you be interfering with President Ahmadinejad's freedom of speech or merely exercising your own freedom of speech? Does President Ahmadinejad deserve freedom of speech when he presides over a country where people are sometimes sent to prison for criticizing the Iranian government?

Key Objective Outline

How should legislators approach their job as a representative of the people?

- The Nature and Style of Representation **(page 212)**

How does the Constitution define the role of the national legislature in American politics?

- Congress and the Constitution **(page 216)**

How do congressional committees help structure the legislative process?

- Organizing Congress: Committees **(page 224)**

How do political parties and legislative leaders help manage the process while at the same time advancing their own initiatives?

- Organizing Congress: Political Parties and Leadership **(page 228)**

CHAPTER 6
CONGRESS

How does the national legislature turn public concerns into public policy?

Can you imagine being tied up, placed on your back in an inclined position, your face tightly covered with fabric or even cellophane, and then water being poured over your nose and mouth? Unlike having your head thrust under water, this process elicits a powerful, immediate gag reflex. You would feel as though you were drowning, and your fright would be overwhelming.

Waterboarding, as this process is called, was widely used in police interrogations during the nineteenth century and was especially popular in the early part of the twentieth century when courts began to deny the admission of coerced confessions. It left no marks, no apparent signs of torture, and thus became the "confession incentive" of choice. The practice began to fade after World War II.

To the surprise of many, waterboarding resurfaced in 2004 when several news reports documented its use by U.S. intelligence officials against terrorist suspects. A heated public debate ensued, with one side claiming that "torture" tactics of this sort violate our nation's norms of civility and the prohibition against cruel and unusual punishment. The other side argued that "aggressive confession" tactics are necessary to protect the country from future terrorist attacks. In July of 2007, President George W. Bush signed an executive order banning torture during investigations, but the issue of waterboarding was not addressed, leaving some to believe it would remain an option.

Responding to public pressure and mounting polling data, in February of 2008. Congress passed a measure to limit interrogation techniques to those spelled out in the Army Field Manual, which does not include waterboarding. "Torture is a black mark against the United States," noted Dianne Feinstein, Democratic Senator for California. The victory was short-lived, however, as President Bush quickly vetoed the bill. "I cannot sign into law a bill that would prevent me, and future presidents, from authorizing the CIA to conduct a separate, lawful intelligence program, and from taking all lawful actions necessary to protect Americans from attack," he said in a statement. Efforts to override the veto failed, leaving the legality of waterboarding an unresolved issue.

The outcry over waterboarding compelled the national legislature to take action. Congress, long dubbed the "People's Branch," is designed to be responsive to the interests of average citizens, so it is not surprising that it moved quickly on this high-profile issue. However, this tale points to a core reality in our government: While Congress is a powerful, responsive institution, changing the course of government often requires the cooperation of other branches.

STUDENT RESOURCE-CENTER
- Glossary
- Vocabulary Example
- LINK
- MyPoliSciLab Connection

■ **Delegate Model of Representation:** The philosophy that legislators should adhere to the will of their constituents.

SIGNIFICANCE: *This approach places a great deal of emphasis on the perspective of average citizens.*

■ **Trustee Model of Representation:** The philosophy that legislators should consider the will of the people but act in ways they believe best for the long-term interests of the nation.

SIGNIFICANCE: *This model underscores the deliberative powers of the legislator and the long-term interests of the nation.*

The Nature *and* Style *of* Representation

(pages 212–215)

How should legislators approach their job as a representative of the people?

There are a number of important questions that we can ask about the precise job of members of Congress. Whom do they represent, and what do they seek to accomplish? At the core, the job of any representative is to speak and act on behalf of others. As we saw in LINK Chapter 2, page 34, except in the smallest of settings—such as a small New England town or a tiny Swiss canton—direct democracy is either impossible or impractical. And even if direct democracy became possible—say, if a tamper-proof computer system were installed in our homes to allow every citizen to vote directly on every proposed law—would we really want such a system? A republic is a democracy in which representatives speak and act on behalf of the citizens. This concept implies a direct extension of popular will. Thomas Paine, the revolutionary propagandist and political thinker, suggested in his famous 1776 pamphlet *Common Sense* that legislators must "act in the same manner as the whole body would act, were they present." This perspective has been called the **delegate model of representation**■ (see Figure 6.1). Here, the legislator does his or her best to discern the will of the people and then acts accordingly.

A very different approach is called the **trustee model of representation**■. This was the outlook favored by most of the delegates at the Constitutional Convention. It holds that the legislator should consider the will of the people but then do what he or she thinks is best for the nation as a whole and in the long term. Edmund Burke, a famous eighteenth-century British politician and political theorist who was very sympathetic to the protests of the American colonists, forcefully articulated this perspective. Legislators, he reasoned, should focus their efforts on protecting the "general whole" rather than simply obeying the wishes of local interests. They are to think of the entire nation and of future generations, not just of a particular district in the here and now. Burke further argued that legislators owe their constituents their reason, expertise, and knowledge; simply following the whims of public opinion is a disservice to their nation and a sin in the eyes of God.

Which model is correct? This is a difficult question, and there is no right or wrong answer. It does seem clear, however, that one or the other of the models has held more sway at different points in our history. As noted, in the early years of the Republic, most legislators held tight to the trustee perspective. Many observers suggest that several changes in the past few decades have made the delegate model more popular today. For example, the number of people wishing to be a legislator for a career has shot up in recent decades. Losing an election often short-circuits such plans, so legislators seem eager to appease the public. "Public opinion" is also much easier to discern these days given the accuracy and frequency of polls. Finally, a growing number of citizens seem concerned that members of Congress do not listen to average folks, thus making the trustee model a dangerous position. Few legislators these days seem willing to vote against their "informed judgment." (Burke got into trouble with *his* constituents by trying to do this!) "The core dictate of this new breed of politician, as we might expect, is to win reelection each year," conclude two contemporary American political scientists. "This means keeping your votes in line with the wishes of those in the district."[1]

> "What kinds of issues should legislators focus on, big topics or constituent needs?"
> —Student Question

Of course, there are middle-ground perspectives, too. The **politico model of representation**■ holds that legislators should feel free to follow their own judgment on matters where the public remains silent. In other words, legislators should be trustees and vote how they see fit until the public gets involved, at which point they should return to the delegate mode. Another perspective is called the **conscience model of representation**■, or what we might call the "pillow test." On most matters, representatives heed the wishes of constituents, but if this position really disturbs representatives to the point that they can't sleep at night, they vote the other way. They are delegates most of the time, but if an issue keeps their head off the pillow, they turn into trustees.

CONNECT THE LINK
Chapter **2**, page **34**) How does a republic differ from a direct democracy?

■ **Politico Model of Representation:** The philosophy that legislators should follow their own judgment (that is, act like a trustee) until the public becomes vocal about a particular matter, at which point they should follow the dictates of constituents.

EXAMPLE: *If a legislator noted "I vote the way I think is best—until the message from folks back home is loud and clear!" she would be acting like a politico.*

Delegate Model

The job of a legislator is to stick to the will of the people

"To say the sovereignty rests in the people, and that they have not a right to instruct and control their representatives, is absurd to the last degree."
—**Representative Elbridge Gerry** (1744–1814) of Massachusetts during a debate over the ratification of the First Amendment

Politico Model

A legislator might follow his or her own sense of what is right until the public becomes involved in the issue, at which point he or she should heed their wishes

"The average legislator early in his career discovers that there are certain interests or prejudices of his constituents which are dangerous to trifle with."
Senator J. William Fulbright (1905–1995) of Arkansas

Conscience Model

A legislator follows the will of the people in most instances until conscience pulls him or her in a different direction

Former House member **Sherwood Boehlert** (1936–) of New York called this the "pillow test." He argued that the job of a legislator is to follow the will of constituents until doing so keeps the legislator awake at night.

Trustee Model

The job of a legislator is to use information and the powers of deliberation to arrive at his or her own assessment; to "enlarge and refine the public's will"

"Have the people of this country snatched the power of deliberation from this body? Are we a body of agents and not a deliberate one?"
—**John C. Calhoun** (1782–1850) of South Carolina, vice president and member of the House and Senate during a debate over a bill fixing compensation for members of Congress

FIGURE 6.1 | **Representing the Will of the People**

There are different approaches to representation, as this figure suggests. ***—Should legislators act as their constituents would if they were present, or should they work to "enlarge and refine" the public will? Are there acceptable intermediate positions? Does it depend on the issue at hand? Which perspective would you hold if you were an elected official? Also, are there contemporary forces pushing legislators toward one perspective?***

Conscience Model of Representation: The philosophy that legislators should follow the will of the people (that is, act like a delegate) until they truly believe it is in the best interests of the nation to act differently.

EXAMPLE: *If a legislator noted "I usually back what the folks back home want—until that choice keeps me up at night!" he would be following this approach.*

Constituent Service: A legislator's responsiveness to the questions and concerns of the people he or she represents.

EXAMPLE: *West Virginia Senator Robert Byrd has spent a great deal of time helping his state receive federal grants.*

When members of Congress take the oath of office to preserve and protect the Constitution, as we see in this picture, it is also assumed that they will work hard to represent the wishes of constituents. ***—But what, exactly, does this concept mean?***

There is also the issue of whether legislators should spend their time working on broad-based policy initiatives or on direct constituency needs. We might call this a question of *representational style*. Some legislators focus on major policy matters, such as health care reform, foreign policy, national defense, international trade, and immigration; others concentrate on helping constituents get their share from the federal government. **Constituent service** (also called *casework*) makes up a great deal of what legislators and their staff do on a daily basis. Letters, telephone calls, e-mails, faxes, and walk-ins every day bring pleas for assistance. These requests are on a variety of issues, including information about pending legislation, finding government jobs, obtaining veterans' benefits, getting help with Social Security, inquiring into military matters, and much else. Although some legislators tackle constituent service with more gusto than others, all agree that it is an important part of representation.

Finally, there is the issue of **symbolic representation.** There is a story about President Calvin Coolidge and his response to criticism that he had appointed a less-than-able businessman to one of his cabinet posts: "But Mr. President," an aide objected, "that fellow is an idiot." "Well," responded Coolidge in his usual dry way, "don't you think they ought to be represented, too?"[2] Humorous as this might seem, many analysts have argued that an important facet of the legislators' job is to speak on behalf of the groups they belong to—especially their demographic group. Regardless of party affiliation, district, or state, many theorists suggest that female legislators should look after the interests of women throughout America. The same might be said about Latino or African-American legislators. As a prominent scholar of the legislative process recently noted, "When a member of an ethnic or racial group goes to Congress, it is a badge of legitimacy for the entire grouping. . . . Moreover, there can be tangible gains in the quality of representation."[3] More will be said of symbolic representation when we discuss redistricting.

The Nature and Style of Representation

Practice Quiz

1. At the most basic level, the job of a member of Congress is to
   - **a.** interpret the Constitution.
   - **b.** uphold the laws of the land.
   - **c.** speak and act on behalf of others.
   - **d.** formulate new policies.

2. What is the difference between the delegate model and the trustee model of representation?
   - **a.** Representatives following the delegate model find out the will of their constituents and act on their behalf; representatives following the trustee model simply do what they think is best for the nation.
   - **b.** Representatives following the delegate model delegate their responsibilities to staff members; representatives following the trustee model carry out those responsibilities themselves.
   - **c.** Representatives following the delegate model simply do what they think is best for the nation; representatives following the trustee model find out the will of their constituents and act on their behalf.
   - **d.** Representatives following the delegate model find out the will of their constituents and act on their behalf; representatives following the trustee model consider the will of their constituents but then do what they think is best for the nation in the long run.

3. If a legislator supported a measure letting factories be built on a river in her home district but then reversed his decision when he worried about pollution being sent downstream, what model of representation would he be following?
   - **a.** hypocritical model
   - **b.** politico model
   - **c.** trustee model
   - **d.** conscience model

4. Which of the following would be an example of constituent service performed by a representative?
   - **a.** drafting a bill that would bring federal assistance to the representative's home district
   - **b.** helping parents in the home district find out where their son is stationed overseas
   - **c.** voting to raise veterans' benefits, and announcing that vote to people in the home district
   - **d.** campaigning for reelection by marching in a local parade

Answers: 1-c, 2-d, 3-d, 4-b.

Discussion Questions

1. In regard to constituent service, is there one constituency or many within a legislator's district? How does this affect constituent service?
2. What are some reasons a legislator would incline toward the trustee model of representation rather than the delegate model?

What **YOU** can do!

To gain a better understanding of styles of representation, identify a handful of faculty members at your university who are members of the faculty's governing body (e.g., Faculty Senate, Faculty Legislature). Survey them about their approach to representation. Do they act as delegates, trustees, politicos, or conscience voters? Why do they take such an approach?

Bicameral Legislature: A legislature composed of two houses.

EXAMPLE: *Congress is a bicameral legislature because it has two chambers, the House of Representatives and the Senate.*

CONNECT THE LINK
(Chapter **2**, pages **52–55**) How are the national government's powers divided among the three branches?

SIMULATION **You Are a Member of Congress**

Congress *and the* Constitution (pages 216–223)

How does the Constitution define the role of the national legislature in American politics?

In LINK Chapter 2, pages 52–55, we discussed three compromises that in 1787 kept the Philadelphia Constitutional Convention on track: the Great Compromise, which created a bicameral legislature; the Three-Fifths Compromise, which settled how slaves would be counted for purposes of representation; and the Sectional Compromise, which gave Congress the power to regulate commerce with a simple majority vote in exchange for permitting the Atlantic slave trade for at least 20 more years. Here, we will take the additional step of outlining the numerous provisions in the Constitution that define the powers, duties, and obligations of Congress.

It is no accident that the framers decided to fill Article I with many details about the legislative branch. They were trying to send the message that Congress would be the heart of the new government, the most important element of the complex, new system. (The Constitution, with numerous annotations, is found in Appendix 2.) Let's look more closely at a few of the most significant elements in this article.

TABLE 6.1 | Key Differences Between the House and the Senate

How do these differences shape the way members of each chamber approach their job of representing the "will of the people?"

HOUSE OF REPRESENTATIVES	SENATE
435 members (apportionment based on state population)	100 members (2 from each state)
2-year terms	6-year terms
Less flexible rules	More flexible rules
Limited debate	Virtually unlimited debate
Policy specialists with an emphasis on taxes and revenues	Policy generalists with an emphasis on foreign policy
Less media coverage	More media coverage
Centralized power (with committee leaders)	Equal distribution of power
More partisan	Somewhat less partisan
High turnover rate	Moderate turnover rate

A Bicameral Legislature

Article I, Section 1, established a two-chamber or **bicameral legislature** (see Table 6.1). The House of Representatives, with its legislators directly elected by the people to relatively short terms of office, seemed to stick closely to the spirit of 1776. That is to say, the House reflected the idea that average citizens should select leaders who would follow their wishes rather closely. Yet the other chamber of the legislature, the Senate, seemed at first glance to move in another direction. By allowing state legislatures to pick senators, and by granting them six-year terms, the Constitution seemed to check the democratic impulses of the day. On closer inspection, however, we see that by giving each state equal representation, the Senate also reflects the spirit of 1776. The Continental Congress gave each state equal weight—a principle that the Articles of Confederation had continued. We might say, then, that the battle of the Virginia Plan against the New Jersey Plan in the Philadelphia Convention had involved two conflicting Revolutionary Era visions of representation: sovereign people versus sovereign states. This balancing act would be revisited throughout much of our history. Before the Civil War, for example, John C. Calhoun, a representative and, later, a senator from South Carolina, as well as vice president under Andrew Jackson, advocated a theory of "nullification." Calhoun's idea was that within their own borders, states had the right to nullify—to declare null and void—acts of Congress. Roughly 100 years later, southern lawmakers again argued that "states' rights" and "state sovereignty" granted them the right to ignore desegregation mandates from the federal courts. More recently, similar battles may be heating up over controversial issues such as doctor-assisted suicide, medical marijuana, and same-sex marriage.

Who Can Serve in Congress?

Article I, Section 2, sets the length of terms for House members (2 years) and specifies the basic qualifications for service. House members must be 25 years of age, a citizen of the United States for at least 7 years, and a resident of the state where they are elected. Notice, however, that the Constitution does *not* say that House members must reside in the district they represent. Throughout our history, on a number of occasions, politicians have been elected to represent districts in which they did not live. Nor does the

■ **Seventeenth Amendment:** Change to the U.S. Constitution, ratified in 1913, that provides for the direct election of senators.

SIGNIFICANCE: *Average citizens are now allowed to vote for Senators instead of relying upon state legislators to make the choice.*

■ **Rotation:** The staggering of senatorial terms such that one-third of the Senate comes up for election every 2 years.

SIGNIFICANCE: *No more than 34 Senators are up for election in a given year, making it more difficult to dramatically change the composition of the Senate.*

"What are the qualifications to serve in Congress?"

—Student Question

Constitution put any limit on the number of terms a representative may serve. In the early 1990s, a number of states tried to limit the terms of members of Congress—both in the House and in the Senate. The Supreme Court, however, in *Term Limits, Inc.* v. *Thornton* (1995), found such restrictions unconstitutional. It seems, then, that the only way to limit the number of terms for members of Congress would be a constitutional amendment.

Article I, Section 3, dealing with the Senate, begins with how a senator is selected. Originally, the Constitution stated that each state legislature would select its two U.S. senators. This changed with ratification of the **Seventeenth Amendment**■ in 1913, and senators are now elected directly by the voters of their state. The next clause deals with the length of senatorial terms (6 years) and makes a special provision called **rotation**■. Rather than have all senators come up for election every 6 years, the Constitution divides the Senate into three "classes," each of which must stand for election every 2 years. While at first this might seem unimportant, the idea was to ensure that the Senate's membership could never be changed all at once just because the public had become outraged over some issue. That gives the Senate greater stability than the House—exactly what the framers intended.

A senator must be 30 years old, a citizen of the United States for at least 9 years, and a resident of the state he or she represents. The Constitution, however, does not stipulate *how long* the person has to be a resident of that state before serving in the Senate. Occasionally, politicians are elected to represent a state where they had not previously lived. The most recent example is the election to the Senate in 2000 of Hillary Rodham Clinton, a native of Illinois and a resident of Arkansas (where her husband had been governor before becoming president), to represent the state of New York.

Aaron Schock was elected to the Peoria, Illinois, school board at the age of 19 and to the state legislature at 23. In this picture, Schock acknowledges applause from supporters after winning—at 27 years of age—the 18th Congressional District Republican primary race in Peoria on February 5, 2008.

Congressional Elections

Article I, Section 4, outlines the congressional election process. Each state can decide the time, place, and manner of elections to the national legislature—so long as Congress remains silent on the matter. For the most part, Congress has left the regulation of congressional elections to the states, but it has stepped in at important and controversial times. Poll taxes, literacy tests, and excessive residency requirements were used, particularly in many southern states, to keep African Americans from voting (in defiance of the Fifteenth Amendment). Congress responded with the Voting Rights Act of 1965. Later, in 1993, hoping to get more Americans to the polls, Congress passed the National Voter Registration Act (also known as the "Motor Voter Law"), which mandates that all states allow citizens to register to vote at certain frequently used public facilities, including motor vehicle offices. Recently, Congress moved to standardize the manner of voting after the Florida recount fiasco during the presidential election in 2000. As you may recall, the election remained undecided for several weeks, because the outcome in Florida was extremely close and election officials were forced to manually count millions of ballots in key counties. This painstaking process dragged on and on, and the public became aware of the many problems of paper and punch-card ballots and of the dangers

■ **Pocket Veto:** The president's killing of a bill that has been passed by both houses of Congress, simply by not signing it; occurs only if Congress has adjourned within 10 days of the bill's passage.

SIGNIFICANCE: *Presidents have used this approach when they wanted to quietly kill a bill, but these days, it is rarely employed.*

■ **Elastic Clause/Necessary and Proper Clause:** A statement in Article I, Section 8, of the U.S. Constitution that grants Congress the power to pass all laws "necessary and proper" for carrying out the list of expressed powers.

SIGNIFICANCE: *This clause has been interpreted in ways that grant Congress very broad policymaking powers.*

of idiosyncratic voting methods. The Help America Vote Act of 2002 mandates election machinery updates (mostly to get rid of fault-prone punch cards, which had caused so much trouble in Florida) and provided some funds to pay for these changes.

Article I, Section 5, deals with a number of procedural matters, such as that each house may determine its own rules and set forth what constitutes a quorum. It stipulates that each chamber keep a journal of its proceedings. Section 6 spells out how members of Congress will be paid (out of the U.S Treasury, not from state governments), and it stipulates that members cannot be arrested while they are attending a session of Congress—except for "Treason, Felony, and Breach of Peace." It further notes that members of the national legislature cannot hold any other federal position.

Lawmaking

Article I, Section 7, addresses how a bill becomes law and also specifies the checks and balances between the two houses of the legislature and between the other branches of the government. The same piece of legislation must be approved by a majority of each house of the legislature before it goes to the president for signature into law. If the president signs the bill, it becomes law. Should the president fail to act on the bill for 10 days (not counting Sundays), it becomes law anyway—unless Congress has adjourned in the meantime, in which case it is known as a **pocket veto**■. If the president vetoes the bill, however, a two-thirds vote in both houses is necessary to override the veto. (See also LINK Chapter 7, page 270.)

Article I, Section 8, is very important, as it lists the powers of the legislative branch (see Table 6.2). This list was controversial for two reasons: First, although the framers thought it important to define Congress' powers, there was still widespread public resistance to giving excessive power to the national government. Second, even though the framers were willing to give the national government broad powers, listing them carried a risk of leaving something out—something that might later prove significant. Inclusion of the last clause of Section 8 seemed to provide a solution. This provision, often called the **elastic clause** or the **necessary and proper clause**■, states that Congress has the power to make all laws "necessary and proper" to implement any of the other powers mentioned in the section. This clause suggested that many of Congress' powers were *implied* rather than spelled out in detail.

The issue of implied versus spelled-out powers came up early in the new republic, when in 1790 Secretary of the Treasury Alexander Hamilton pushed through Congress a bill to charter a national bank, the Bank of the United States. Nowhere did the Constitution directly state that Congress had the power to do this, and Thomas Jefferson and James Madison insisted that Hamilton's proposal went too far. They asked President Washington to veto the bill. Hamilton fought back by citing the "necessary and proper" clause: A national bank, he said, was necessary to ensure that the nation's credit and currency were sound. Washington considered the arguments of both sides before

TABLE 6.2 | Powers of Congress under the U.S. Constitution

One of the dangers of listing an organization's powers is that all circumstances may not be covered. The framers of the Constitution understood this and added the final element to deal with unforseen circumstances. Yet, the "elastic clause" has proven controversial because the Supreme Court has interpreted it in broad terms, thus granting Congress sweeping powers. Do you think the national legislature should have these expansive powers?

CLAUSE	POWER GRANTED IN ARTICLE I, SECTION 8
1	Levy and collect taxes and duties and provide for the common defense
2	Borrow money on credit
3	Regulate commerce with foreign nations and between the states
4	Establish rules on naturalization and bankruptcy
5	Coin money
6	Create punishments for counterfeiting
7	Establish post offices
8	Promote the progress of science and the arts
9	Constitute tribunals below the Supreme Court
10	Punish crimes on the high seas
11	Declare war
12	Raise and support the army
13	Provide and maintain a navy
14	Make rules for the use of armed forces
15	Call out the militia
16	Organize, arm, and discipline the militia
17	Exercise exclusive legislation over the district of the seat of the federal government
18	Make all laws deemed necessary an d proper" for implementing these powers

"What are implied powers? How do we know what they include?"

—Student Question

CONNECT THE LINK
(Chapter **7**, page **270**) How often do presidents veto legislation?

At-Large Districts: Districts encompassing an entire state, or large parts of a state, in which House members are elected to represent the entire area.

EXAMPLE: *Because North Dakota is allotted only one House seat, the entire state is an at-large district.*

accepting Hamilton's position and signing the bill, thus setting an important precedent for interpreting the Constitution's grant of powers broadly rather than narrowly.

By 1819, the Supreme Court had put the argument for implied powers on a stronger foundation. In his majority opinion in the very important case of *McCulloch* v. *Maryland,* Chief Justice John Marshall made it clear that Congress did, indeed, have "implied powers." The case concerned a branch of the federally chartered Bank of the United States located in the state of Maryland. Banks being profitable institutions, the state of Maryland had chartered its own bank, but the Maryland bank was losing money because of competition with the national bank. To recover some of these losses, the Maryland legislature decided to levy a tax on the Bank of the United States. Can a state government tax an institution created by the national government? And—resurrecting the question that Jefferson and Madison had asked back in 1790—where does the Constitution give Congress the power to create a national bank?

As to the first question, Marshall wrote, "The power to tax involves the power to destroy." That would suggest some sort of supremacy. Yet the Constitution is clear that the national government is supreme, so the tax (which could, if heavy enough, put the national bank out of business) was unconstitutional. As to the broader question—the power to charter a bank—Marshall used the same argument Hamilton had advanced:

> Let the end be legitimate, let it be within the scope of the constitution, and all means which are appropriate, which are plainly adapted to that end, which are not prohibited, but consistent with the letter and spirit of the constitution, are constitutional.

In one clean sweep, Marshall's ruling greatly expanded the scope of the national government's power.

Redistricting

The Great Compromise stipulated that Congress be divided into two houses, one with an identical number of legislators from each state (the Senate) and the other based on population (the House of Representatives). But how would we know the number of citizens in each state? The Constitution also stipulates that a census be conducted every 10 years and that seats be allocated to each state based on this count. However, if a state gets more than one seat (and most states do), who then is responsible for drawing the boundaries of legislative districts—or should there even *be* legislative districts? Why not elect all the state's representatives on an at-large basis? The Constitution left these questions to the states to decide, and they have caused considerable controversy ever since.

In the earliest days of the Republic, some states did use **at-large districts**. If they were granted three seats in the House, they would simply elect three members from the entire state. Those states had no districts. Most states, however, chose to divide their territory into a number of congressional districts equal to the number of seats they were allocated in the House of Representatives. A state with five seats would create five congressional districts. The idea of changing legislative districts in response to population shifts stems from the American idea of **geographic representation**. That is, our representatives should be directly responsible to a group of people living in a specific geographic location. Today, drawing the boundaries for congressional districts has become a tricky and controversial process. In all states except very small ones that have only a single representative, the process must be undertaken every 10 years to reflect changes in the state's overall population relative to the rest of the country as well as to respond to population shifts within the state. This process of redrawing the boundaries of legislative districts is called **redistricting**. The Constitution gives state legislatures the redistricting power. Because these bodies have nearly always been partisan (controlled by a majority of members from one party), you probably won't be surprised to hear that the process causes a lot of partisan wrangling.

Gerrymandering is the drawing of legislative districts for partisan advantage. The word immortalizes one Elbridge Gerry, who as governor of Massachusetts around 1800 persuaded his followers in the state legislature to draw an odd-shaped district, wiggling across the state, designed to elect a political ally. Looking at the map, someone said that the new district looked like a salamander, to which someone else replied that it wasn't a salamander but "a Gerrymander" (see Figure 6.2 on page 220).[4] The name stuck. Gerrymandering means the creation of oddly shaped districts as a means of shaping the results of future elections in those districts. This has been done in a number of ways, but mostly through either *packing* or *cracking.* Packing is lumping as many opposition voters as possible into one district. For instance, if the state has five districts, the idea is to fill one of these districts overwhelmingly with supporters of the other party. The party in power—the politicians drawing the lines—would give up that one seat, but the other four districts would be shaped to nearly guarantee that candidates of their party would win. Cracking involves splitting up groups of voters thought to favor the opposition so that they do not make up a majority in any district and thus cannot win in any district.

As you might guess, the redistricting process has also been used to minimize the representation of African Americans and

Geographic Representation: The idea that a legislator should represent the interests of the people living in a specific geographic location.

EXAMPLE: *The cities of Erie, Sharron, Meadville and Butler are located in Pennsylvania's 3rd Congressional District.*

Redistricting: The process of redrawing legislative district boundaries within a state to reflect population changes.

SIGNIFICANCE: *The exact boundaries of a district can determine the partisan leanings of the electorate, thus aiding particular types of candidates.*

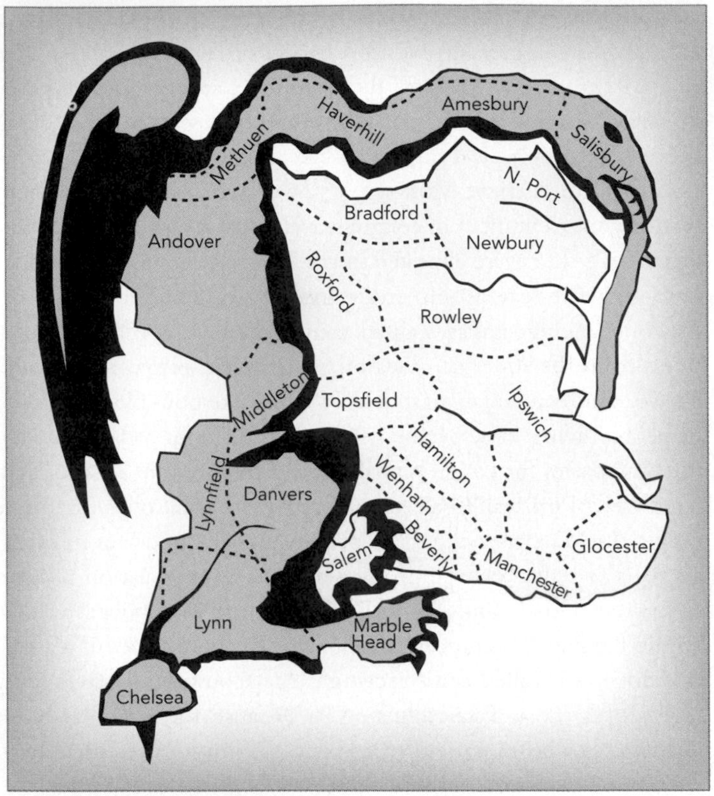

FIGURE 6.2 | **That's not a salamander, its a Gerrymander!**

As Governor of Massachusetts in 1812, Elbridge Gerry prompted his fellow Republicans in the state legislature to draw congressional district lines that favored their party. As the story goes, a reporter looked at one of these new districts and commented that it looked like a salamander. Another noted, "That's not a salamander, that's a Gerrymander!" Partisan-based redistricting is an age-old problem. ***—Should legislatures allow nonpartisan groups to draw new district lines?***

other minority groups. Thirty percent of a state's population, for example, might be black, but through cracking, it could be fixed so that these voters would never be able to elect an African-American legislator without the help of white voters. Or, through packing, most of the black population might be concentrated in one virtually all-black district, enabling whites to elect representatives from the other districts. The tendency of African-American voters to support Democratic candidates could therefore be exploited by a Republican-majority state legislature to minimize the election of Democrats and of African Americans to represent the state in the House.

PATHWAYS | of action

The Texas Redistricting Battle

The quarrelsome nature of redistricting is evident after every census is announced—and it has repercussions in most state legislatures. In 2003, all eyes turned to the struggle over a plan to redraw congressional district lines in Texas. In a somewhat unprecedented move, the former Republican Texas congressman and House majority leader, Tom DeLay, inserted himself into the process. The outcome of his efforts with state legislative leaders, also Republican, was a redistricting plan that many Democrats saw as overwhelmingly partisan. According to the Democrats, the scheme would make at least 22 of the state's 32 congressional districts unshakably Republican, up from the current 15 "safe" Republican seats. Moreover, Democrats argued that the plan would deprive millions of minority people of their voting rights. Republicans responded by arguing that previous redistricting plans had given the Democrats an artificial advantage and that their plan better matched demographic shifts throughout the state.

To stop the state legislature from adopting the plan, many Democrats in both the state house and state senate refused to attend legislative sessions to vote on the measure, denying the Republicans a **quorum** (the minimum number of members who by law must be present in order to transact official business). Fearing that the Republican governor would send state troopers to bring them by force to the legislature and compel a vote, 53 Democrats left the state and holed up in a hotel in Ardmore, Oklahoma, in May of 2003. Without a quorum in the state legislature, the plan stalled, but how long could these legislators stay away from their homes and families? The nation watched and waited. By midsummer, two Democrats broke ranks and, returning to Austin, gave the Republicans a quorum. Then the others returned, and the measure passed during a special legislative session. The scheme seemed to work. In 2002, there had been 15 Republicans in the Texas delegation to the U.S. House. After November 2004, there were 21.[5] In the 2006 election, Republicans won 19 seats.

> "These tactics for redistricting don't seem very democratic. Are they legal?"
> —Student Question

Gerrymandering: Drawing legislative district boundaries in such a way as to gain political advantage.

SIGNIFICANCE: *The majority party in the state legislature will often try to draw new district lines that give candidates in their party a better chance of victory.*

VISUAL LITERACY **Congressional Redistricting**

SIMULATION **You Are Redrawing the Districts in Your State**

The question of whether the Texas redistricting was legal went to the Supreme Court in the spring of 2006. A fractured Court said that states are generally free to draw lines as they want, essentially blessing DeLay's scheme. In fact, the Court noted that the Constitution does not bar states from redrawing lines when one party senses an advantage—nor is there a prohibition against mid-decade redistricting. Yet they also provided Democrats with a partial victory by saying that when excessive political considerations result in the disenfranchisement of groups of voters, the result may be unconstitutional. One of the districts, the 23rd, fell into this category. ■

Some states are moving toward using nonpartisan organizations to draw district lines. Iowa has taken this trend furthest, using a complex computer program administered by a nonpartisan commission to draw geographically compact and equal districts. The state legislature then votes these districts up or down, but it cannot amend them. This process has spared Iowa from court challenges and has produced competitive congressional races. For example, in the 2006 election, three out of five of Iowa's U.S. House races were considered competitive, compared to only 1 out of 10 in the rest of the nation.[6] Several other states are considering similar moves, including New York and Virginia.

In 2003, Texas was the site of an important test case in the evolving story of congressional redistricting. ***—Should state legislatures be allowed to draw district lines in ways that appear to support candidates of one party over the other? If not, should the federal courts step in and correct things? Should the public push state governments to create nonpartisan redistricting commissions?***

For the most part, redistricting has been a tricky issue for the courts. On a number of occasions, they have refused to get involved in the controversy, arguing that the issue was a "political question" and therefore "not *justiciable*."[7] In other words, the courts have concluded that the issue is inappropriate for them to resolve and that another branch of the government must decide. The courts have signaled a greater willingness to hear such cases in recent decades, but the complexity of the reapportionment process makes judicial intervention difficult. Some public anger about uncompetitive elections is now brewing. Perhaps it is noteworthy, however, that in 2005, voters in both Ohio and California rejected referendum proposals to reform the system—and in both states after the party that benefits from congressional gerrymandering (Republicans in the former and Democrats in the latter) argued that the proposed reforms would hurt them! The whole issue remains tangled up in partisanship and is far from settled.

POSITIVE GERRYMANDERING Amendments to the Voting Rights Act of 1965, which were passed in 1982, approached the racial gerrymandering issue from an entirely different direction. If the redistricting process has been used in the past to limit minority representation, could it not be used to *increase* minority representation? Perhaps census data could be used to construct districts that would better ensure the election of minority legislators. After the 1990 census, 24 **majority-minority districts** were created in different states—districts in which a minority group made up a majority of the population. Fifteen of these districts had majorities of African-American voters, and nine had a majority of Hispanic voters. The scheme seemed to work: In each of these districts, the voters chose a minority legislator. Nevertheless, two issues came up. First, the resulting districts were often exceptionally oddly shaped. In North Carolina's 12th Congressional District, for example, a roughly 100-mile strip of Interstate 85, on which almost no one lived, connected black communities in Durham and Charlotte. Second, the overt consideration of race in drawing highly irregularly districts was challenged in the courts as an affront to the equal protection clause of the Fourteenth Amendment. Although the U.S. Supreme Court had tended to stay out of redistricting disputes, this time it did not. In a series of decisions, the Court generally supported plans that improved the likelihood of minority representation, but it also seemed reluctant to allow highly irregularly shaped districts (*Shaw* v. *Reno,* 1993) or to approve schemes that use race as the primary criterion for drawing district lines (*Miller* v. *Johnson,* 1995).

"Does every district have the same number of residents?"

—Student Question

■ ***Baker* v. *Carr* (1961):** Supreme Court case that set the standard that House districts must contain equal numbers of constituents, thus establishing the principle of "one person, one vote."

SIGNIFICANCE: *Every citizen has the same "weight" in the legislative process. However, in order to get the same number of residents in each district, the boundaries are often oddly shaped, and diverse communities are sometimes lumped together.*

■ **Reapportionment:** The process by which seats in the House of Representatives are reassigned among the states to reflect population changes following the census (every 10 years).

SIGNIFICANCE: *Because some states grow in population while others either grow at a slower pace or lose residents, every 10 years each state's allocation of House members is adjusted. Each state is guaranteed at least one House member.*

NUMBER OF RESIDENTS PER DISTRICT Related to the difficult issue of drawing district lines is the question of the number of residents per district. Oddly enough, the Constitution is silent on this matter, and for most of our history, many states did not try to ensure the same number of constituents in every district. Questionable motivations were at work in some instances. On the other hand, precise equality between districts often did not seem logical. Imagine, for example, a state that was allotted three representatives. There were two urban areas, in opposite corners of the state, and one agricultural region in the middle. Wouldn't it seem logical to group constituents with similar interests, producing two urban districts and one rural one, even if they weren't quite equal in numerical size? However, because most Americans believe that each voter should have the same political weight—that all men and women are politically equal—districts with such an imbalance appear to violate this ideal, and others also suggest that it violates the spirit of the Constitution. (Interestingly, few people seem interested in challenging the legitimacy of the U.S. Senate, where the least populous state, Wyoming, and the most populous state, California, each have the same number of seats: two.)

The issue of malapportionment came to a head in the mid-twentieth century when a group of Tennessee residents claimed that the state legislature had denied them equal protection under the law by refusing to draw districts with the same population. In 1961, the Supreme Court decided that the Tennessee districts were so out of proportion that they did violate the plaintiffs' constitutional rights. This case, ***Baker* v. *Carr*** ■, wrote the "one person, one vote" principle into federal law.[8] It also sparked a revolution in the way legislative districts were drawn. In the post-*Baker* era, geographic concerns took a back seat to ensuring equal population in all districts. These later cases also mandated that redistricting happen every 10 years even if the size of the state's congressional delegation remained unchanged, because the new census meant the old districts likely no longer had equal populations, given population shifts over a decade. Perhaps most important, *Baker* v. *Carr* inserted the federal courts into the redistricting process, thereby leaving any plan open to a court challenge. Along with the mandate under the Voting Rights Act of 1965 to prevent racial discrimination in voting, *Baker* v. *Carr* has made redistricting a tedious process of moving district lines block by block until the population balance is correct while constantly facing the threat that a federal court would find the entire scheme unconstitutional.[9]

REAPPORTIONMENT Finally, the redistricting process has been argued about because the allotment of seats per state shifts with each new census (see Figure 6.3). The process of shifting the number of seats allotted to each state is called **reapportionment**■. Originally, the Constitution set the ratio of residents per House member at 1 to 30,000, meaning there were 65 House members in the First Congress. As the nation's population grew, so did the

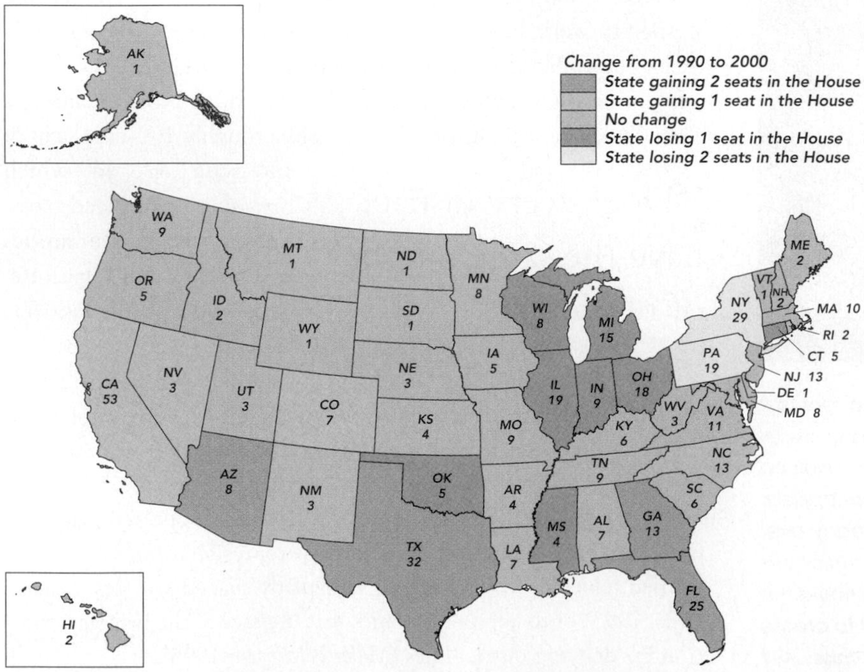

FIGURE 6.3 | Distribution of Congressional Power

The framers understood that our nation would grow. They were wise enough to mandate that a census be taken every 10 years and that the allocation of House seats to each state be reapportioned accordingly. This map shows the changes after the most recent Census (in 2000). ***—What are some of the patterns that emerge? What might be the root of these changes? Also, what will be some of the political implications of population changes in the decades to come?***

SOURCE: U.S. Census Bureau.

VISUAL LITERACY **Why Is It So Hard to Defeat an Incumbent?**

number of representatives in the House. The membership of the House jumped from 141 in 1800 to 240 in 1830. By 1910, the House had grown to 435 members. That seemed large enough, so its membership was capped by Congress. Since then, the ratio has gotten smaller and smaller. Today, there are roughly 670,000 residents for each House district. (If today's House districts still had the 30,000 residents that the Constitution prescribed for the First Congress, there would be 22,333 representatives in the House!)

Reapportionment implies that the fastest-growing states gain seats after each census and that seats are taken from the slower-growing states. (In recent years, several states—such as Michigan, Rhode Island, Ohio, and North Dakota—have experienced a loss or no growth in population.) After the 2000 census, for example, New York and Pennsylvania each lost two House seats. The winners have been southern and southwestern states. These trends, of course, reflect the shift of the U.S. population toward the Sun Belt and away from the old industrial and farming states.

Losing seats in the national legislature can be devastating for a state, because much of federal government's domestic spending is proportionate to a state's population. Having fewer residents means getting fewer federal dollars. And of course, when states lose seats, it often forces some of the state's incumbent representatives to run against one another for the seats that remain. There is nothing an incumbent hates more than to run against a fellow incumbent!

An interesting argument has also emerged over the actual population of each state. Some, mostly Democrats, charge that many citizens are missed in the counting process of the census. They argue that statistical models for estimating populations would actually yield more accurate results than trying to physically count everyone. Others, mostly Republicans, point out that the Constitution stipulates a full *person-by-person* count; until the Constitution is changed, they say, there is no alternative. It is a partisan battle because most analysts agree that the chance of citizens being missed is greatest in the northeastern urban states, which lean Democratic. The argument is likely to simmer for a long time and to climax every 10 years, when a new census is conducted, but for now, the Republicans seem to have the courts on their side.

Congress and the Constitution

Practice Quiz

1. The framers of the Constitution thought that members of Congress should not merely represent the will of their constituents but should "enlarge and refine the public's will."
   - **a.** true
   - **b.** false
2. What is the primary difference between the Senate as it was designed by the Constitutional Convention and how it operates now?
   - **a.** Senators were originally limited to two 4-year terms.
   - **b.** Senators could serve an unlimited number of terms, but each was only 2 years long.
   - **c.** Each state was granted a number of senators proportional to its population.
   - **d.** Each state legislature picked its U.S. senators; they were not chosen through popular election.
3. What inspired national reapportionment so that each member of the House represents roughly the same number of constituents?
   - **a.** the desire to have each state receive as much federal money as any other
   - **b.** the democratic principle that all voters are to be granted the same political weight in Congress
   - **c.** the idea that no state or district should be paying higher taxes than any other
   - **d.** the recognition that "separate" is never "equal"
4. What provision in the Constitution states that Congress has the power to make all the laws needed to implement the other powers specified in the Constitution?
   - **a.** the sufficient and provisional clause
   - **b.** the necessary and proper clause
   - **c.** the *McCulloch* v. *Maryland* clause
   - **d.** the congressional sovereignty clause

Answers: 1-a, 2-d, 3-b, 4-b.

Discussion Questions

1. What are the advantages of a bicameral legislature? What are the inconveniences?
2. Describe and discuss the tactics that have been used to minimize the voting impact of minority groups through legislative redistricting (gerrymandering). Why is it important to know about these tactics in current politics?

What **YOU** can do!

Visit **http://nationalatlas.gov/printable/congress.html** to view the map of congressional districts for your home state. Identify any districts that look as though they may be gerrymandered. Find demographic information for any suspicious districts at **http://www.census.gov** to determine if the district is "packed" or "cracked."

■ **Subcommittees:** Specialized groups within standing committees.

EXAMPLE: *The House Subcommittee on Horticulture and Organic Agriculture is relatively new.*

Organizing Congress: Committees (pages 224–227)

How do congressional committees help structure the legislative process?

The Constitution says very little about how the two legislative chambers should be structured, but how the legislature is organized is as important as its precise powers and responsibilities. Furthermore, this issue is very important when considering how change might be accomplished through the legislative process and how individual citizens might make a difference. Each of the organizing elements that we will discuss here gives citizens points of access into the policy development process. For instance, understanding the importance of committees allows an activist to focus attention on this stage of the process, where real decisions are made. You can no more learn your potential to change the course of government by reading only Article I of the Constitution than you could learn how to succeed as a major league football coach just by reading the NFL rulebook. The next three sections look at the key organizing forces within the legislative process, the nonconstitutional components that help hundreds of individual legislators merge into a lawmaking, appropriating, and oversight body. We begin with the workhorses of the legislature: committees.

Standing Committees

Standing committees are the permanent structures that perform the detailed work of a legislature, such as drafting bills for consideration. There are many advantages to the standing committee system, which was first set up in the House in 1810 and in the Senate shortly thereafter.

First, members of each committee become experts in that policy area so that they can better determine the importance and implications of proposals. To accomplish this, each committee acquires a staff of experts who help legislators make informed decisions. As issues become more and more complex, the "expertise function" becomes even more important.

Second, by dividing the legislature's work between dozens of committees, or "minilegislatures," a vast number of measures can be considered simultaneously. As two leading congressional scholars have noted, "Without committees, a legislative body consisting of 100 senators and [435] House members could not handle roughly 10,000 bills and nearly 100,000 nominations biennially, a national budget over $2 trillion, and a limitless array of controversial issues."[10]

Third, this system enhances the representation process by allowing legislators to sit on committees that deal with issues of interest to their constituents. For example, many legislators from the midwestern Farm Belt might best serve their constituents by sitting on an agriculture committee. Most often, however, constituent interests are varied, making the fit with a particular committee impossible. Even so, many legislators seek committee assignments that allow them to serve their constituents better.

Fourth, committees have taken on a "safety valve" function by becoming the forum for public debate and controversy. They give average citizens a place to vent concerns and frustrations, and they can absorb conflict and resolve the strains of a democratic system. (Of course, by blocking action on measures that some citizens and interest groups ardently support, legislative committees can also promote conflict and increase tensions.)

Finally, and much related to the pathways of change, committees offer citizens many points of access into the legislative process. It might be too much to expect a citizen or a small group of like-minded citizens to persuade an entire chamber, but shifting the course of committee decisions may be more manageable. Given that very few measures are considered by the full legislature without first being passed at the committee level, and given that committee votes are often won or lost by a few votes, swinging a couple of legislators to your point of view can sometimes change the fate of a piece of legislation. This heightens the power of citizens in the policy process.

The number of standing committees has varied over the years. Different subject areas have been more important in some periods than in others. Today, there are 20 standing committees in the House and 16 in the Senate (see Table 6.3). The size of each committee varies as well, but generally speaking, House committees consist of about 50 members, and Senate standing committees have roughly 20 members. As we'll see later in this chapter, the balance of power between the parties in each chamber is reflected in each committee.

Although standing committees are clearly the most important, there are three other types of legislative committees. Nearly all standing committees have one or more **subcommittees**■ under their jurisdiction. Much the same rationale for apportioning legislative work to committees also applies to subcommittees, whose members and staffers specialize, thus breaking down a broad policy area into more manageable parts. Today, any piece of legislation that comes before a committee usually is quickly referred to the appropriate subcommittee. Most of the day-to-day lawmaking and oversight of Congress occur at the subcommittee level.[11]

Congress also uses three other kinds of committee. Today, both chambers establish **select committees** to deal with a particular issue or problem. They are temporary, so they disappear either when the

■ **Conference Committee:** A committee of members of the House and Senate that irons out differences in similar measures that have passed both houses to create a single bill.

SIGNIFICANCE: *If the conference committee cannot arrive at one version of a bill, the measure fails.*

TABLE 6.3 | Standing Committees of the 110th Congress

COMMITTEES OF THE SENATE	COMMITTEES OF THE HOUSE
Agriculture, Nutrition, and Forestry (20 members)	**Agriculture** (46 members)
Appropriations (28 members)	**Appropriations** (66 members)
Armed Services (24 members)	**Armed Services** (66 members)
Banking, Housing, and Urban Affairs (20 members)	**Budget** (39 members)
Budget (22 members)	**Education and Labor** (49 members)
Commerce, Science, and Transportation (22 members)	**Energy and Commerce** (58 members)
Energy and Natural Resources (22 members)	**Financial Services** (72 members)
Environment and Public Works (18 members)	**Foreign Affairs** (41 members)
Finance (20 members)	**Homeland Security** (34 members)
Foreign Relations (18 members)	**House Administration** (9 members)
Health, Education, Labor, and Pensions (20 members)	**Judiciary** (40 members)
Homeland Security and Governmental Affairs (16 members)	**Natural Resources** (52 members)
Indian Affairs (15 members)	**Oversight and Government Reform** (41 members)
Judiciary (10 members)	**Rules** (13 members)
Rules and Administration (18 members)	**Science and Technology** (44 members)
Small Business and Entrepreneurship (18 members)	**Small Business** (36 members)
Veterans' Affairs (14 members)	**Standards of Official Conduct** (10 members)
Senate Special or Select Committees:	**Transportation and Infrastructure** (75 members)
Aging (19 members)	**Veterans' Affairs** (28 members)
Ethics (6 members)	**Ways and Means** (41 members)
Intelligence (15 members)	

problem is resolved or, more likely, when the congressional session ends. They serve primarily in an investigative role and cannot approve legislation or move it forward. Of much more significance is the **conference committee**■. For legislation to become law, both branches of the legislature must first pass exactly the same bill. When each chamber passes similar but not identical legislation, a conference committee is assembled to work out the differences and reach a compromise. Some conference committees are small, consisting of the chairs of corresponding House and Senate committees and a few members; others, dealing with higher-profile matters, can have hundreds of members. In some ways, these conference committees actually write legislation—the version that emerges from conference often contains vital details that differ from what either house originally passed and may deal with entirely unrelated matters. So important are conference committees that some have dubbed them "the third house of Congress." Finally, **joint committees** are composed of members selected from each chamber. The work of these committees generally involves investigation, research, and oversight of agencies closely related to Congress. Permanent joint committees, created by statute, are sometimes called **standing joint committees**.

What Committees Do

Committees are critical to the lawmaking process, and while they do present a few drawbacks, it is impossible to imagine a modern legislature functioning without committees. But what, exactly, do committees do? Let's take a closer look.

REFERRAL AND JURISDICTION The Legislative Reorganization Act of 1946 stated that every piece of legislation introduced for consideration must first be referred to a committee. This may seem rather mechanical, simply matching the topic of the bill with an appropriate committee. The process is much more complex, however, and at times can be quite contentious. For one thing, the topic of the proposed legislation could fall within the jurisdiction or policy area of several committees. In the House, for instance, proposed legislation dealing with an energy issue might be referred to the Energy and Commerce

"How are bills assigned to committees, and who does it?"

—Student Question

Hearings: Committee sessions for taking testimony from witnesses and for collecting information on legislation under consideration or for the development of new legislation.

EXAMPLE: *The House Committee on Oversight and Government Reforms held hearings on steroid use in baseball during the spring of 2008.*

Oversight: Congress's responsibility to keep an eye on agencies in the federal bureaucracy to ensure that their behavior conforms to its wishes.

SIGNIFICANCE: *Oversight is a powerful congressional check on the power of the executive branch.*

Committee, but it could also go to the Natural Resources, Science and Technology, or Transportation and Infrastructure Committee.

The job of referral is given to the speaker of the House or, in the Senate, to the majority leader. During most of our nation's history, bills were referred to just one committee, which caused much turf warfare. Sometimes which committee a bill got referred to depended less on jurisdictional fit than on the impact, positive or negative, that the chair of that committee might have on its fate. Referral to one particular committee over another would often either seal a proposed measure's doom or give it a good chance of enactment. This helped ensure that the committee process was closed and undemocratic. By the early 1970s, the House adopted a process of **multiple referrals**. Now, instead of assigning a new bill to just one committee, it is possible to send the measure to several committees at the same time. Although the process has changed somewhat over the years, it has become customary to designate a "primary committee" that considers a bill but also to assign the bill to other committees as well.

HEARINGS AND INVESTIGATIONS The vast majority of bills that are introduced in the House or Senate, then assigned to a committee, and then often assigned to a subcommittee wind up being never acted on. That is, most bills are deemed unworthy of consideration and are killed. If a measure is not moved out of the committee considering it, that measure dies at the end of the legislative term. Roughly 90 percent of all measures stall in committee and thus die a slow death.

For measures that have a modest chance of committee approval, **hearings** are often the first step. These are fact-finding, informational events that usually first take place in a subcommittee. Experts are asked to testify at hearings. These experts can include the sponsor of the bill, state and federal officials, interest group leaders, private officials, and (if arranged for by the bill's sponsor, by its opponents, or by advocacy groups) even ordinary citizens making highly emotional pleas, largely for the benefit of the media. Occasionally, on high-visibility issues, celebrities get to testify, too. Although a celebrity might not be an expert in the area, the main reason for allowing him or her to speak is publicity. "Quite candidly, when Hollywood speaks, the world listens," Pennsylvania Senator Arlen Specter once commented. "Sometimes when Washington speaks, the world snoozes."[12]

Similar to hearings, both the House and the Senate investigate dramatic issues or ongoing matters of great concern. Many times a special committee will be assembled to deal with a specific issue. In the spring of 2008, for example, there were congressional investigations into the use of steroids in professional baseball.

MARKUP If the measure is still considered important after hearings have been held, the next step in the process is called **markup**. Here, the actual language of the bill is hammered out. The member responsible for crafting the language is called the *prime sponsor*. Often, but not always, the prime sponsor is the subcommittee chair. Markup can be a critical step in the process: The language of the bill must address the concerns of the sponsor, but it also must win the approval of the committee and then the full chamber. Many a good idea has languished in the legislature because its language failed to gather enough support. And sometimes, the language becomes so complex that no one is quite sure what it means.

REPORTS For the fraction of measures that win committee approval, the next step is to send the bill to the floor for consideration. At this point, the staff of the committee prepares a report on the legislation. This report summarizes the bill's provisions and the rationale behind them. It is, in essence, a summary of the committee's deliberations and an argument for why the full chamber should approve the measure. This, too, is a critical step in the process.

"Why is the House Rules Committee considered so powerful?"

—Student Question

THE RULES REPORT There is another stop—and a critically important one—before a bill is sent to the floor. Every bill in the House must pass through a Rules Committee. On the surface, the rationale behind this committee seems logical—namely, to establish rules regarding the consideration of the legislation, which helps streamline the process and make things fair. How long might the House deliberate on a particular bill? Should amendments be allowed? If amendments are permitted, in what order should they be voted on? Among much else, the House Rules Committee states whether the process of consideration will be *open* (meaning that it may be amended), *closed* (so that changes to the bill are prohibited), or *modified* (making certain amendments possible).

BUREAUCRATIC OVERSIGHT Our discussion of committee action thus far has centered on policymaking, the process of creating or changing federal law. This is a key aspect of committee work, but it is not the only aspect. Another critical committee function is **oversight**—that is, the responsibility of Congress to keep a close eye on the federal bureaucracy's implementation of federal law. The Constitution does not spell out a congressional oversight role. Neither does it prohibit such work, however, and congressional oversight has become increasingly important. Senator Trent Lott, a Republican from Mississippi and a former Senate majority leader, has said, "I have always felt that one-third of the role of Congress should be oversight."[13] Oversight is especially time-consuming and contentious in times of divided government (when the president is of one party and the opposition party controls at least one house of Congress).

THE IMPORTANCE OF COMMITTEE STAFF Finally, you cannot accurately understand the process and powers of congressional committees without sharply focusing on staff. Given the hectic schedules of members of Congress and the ever-growing complexity of policy alternatives, it should come as no surprise to learn that staffers do most of the committees' work. "Committee staff spend a lot of their time on policymaking activities," the political scientist David Vogler has noted. "They research issues and generate information relevant to administrative oversight; draft bills; prepare speeches, statements, and reports; organize and help run committee hearings; and sometimes engage directly in legislative bargaining."[14] Furthermore, the size of the committee staff—what some observers have termed the "unelected representatives"[15]—grew tremendously in the late twentieth century. In 1967, there were roughly 600 committee staffers at work on Capitol Hill, but by 1994, their number had jumped to more than 3,000.[16] When the Republicans took control in 1995, moves were made to reduce the overall number of staffers, but the concern remains: A good deal of policymaking is done by staff, without much involvement of the elected representatives.

> "So the image we have of Congress debating the great issues of the day is all wrong? All the real decisions are made in committees?"
>
> —Student Question

Let's summarize. Much of the work of the legislature gets done in congressional committees. Ordinary citizens often believe that floor debates are dramatic events, where opinions are formed through lively discourse, point and counterpoint. Some people think that decisions about tough policy choices are made on the floor and that if you want to influence the policy process, you should focus on this final step. That's wrong. Although occasionally the outcome of a floor vote may be uncertain down to the last minute, the great majority of congressional decisions are made far earlier—usually at the committee level. It is here that information gets collected through hearings and investigations, that the actual writing of bills is done, that negotiations are carried on, and that members are persuaded to support or oppose a measure. Once again, understanding how committees work and grasping their importance are critical for anyone interested in shaping government outputs through an internal, mostly behind-the-scenes lobbying approach. For individuals and interest groups with a stake in the outcome, it is essential to get involved at those early stages. Committees are not only a hub of activity but also the principal decision-making structure of the legislative process.

Organizing Congress: Committees

Practice Quiz

1. The structure of standing committees in Congress is spelled out in Article I of the Constitution.
   a. true **b.** false
2. Most of the work of lawmaking and oversight in Congress happens
   a. on the House floor.
   b. at the committee level.
   c. at the subcommittee level.
   d. in congressional staff meetings.
3. Which of the following takes place when a bill is *first* introduced into the House of Representatives?
   a. The bill is referred to a particular member, who is in charge of overseeing the bill's journey through Congress.
   b. The bill is referred to a standing committee for consideration.
   c. An exact version of the bill is also introduced in the Senate.
   d. All of the above.
4. Committee hearings and investigations are used to
   a. discern the best wording for a new piece of legislation.
   b. explore possible conflicts of interest when all measures are introduced.
   c. collect information on new issues of concern.
   d. determine the fiscal impact of new legislation.

Answers: 1-b, 2-b, 3-b, 4-c.

Discussion Questions

1. What makes the markup session in legislative business so crucial?
2. What biases are evident in the structure of the House Rules Committee? How could they impact the passage of legislation?

What **YOU** can do!

Explore the complexity of congressional committee jurisdiction. Choose a policy issue that interests you, and then make a list of every House and Senate committee and subcommittee that has jurisdiction in that policy area. Use the House and Senate Web sites (**http://www.house.gov** and **http://www.senate.gov**) for guidance.

■ **Voting Cues:** Summaries encapsulating the informed judgment of others in the legislature; members of Congress rely on these to streamline the decision-making process.

SIGNIFICANCE: *Legislators often rely on their party's leadership to provide direction on how they should vote. This becomes a rational short-cut for most busy legislators.*

■ **Speaker:** The presiding officer of the House of Representatives, who is also the leader of the majority party in the House.

EXAMPLE: *The speaker of the 110th Congress was Nanci Pelosi, Democrat from California.*

Organizing Congress: Political Parties *and* Leadership (pages 228-231)

How do political parties and legislative leaders help manage the process while at the same time advancing their own initiatives?

Two other critically important organizing elements are political parties and legislative leaders. Let's begin with political parties.

Parties in the Legislatures

For one thing, parties in the legislature serve an **orientation function**. The job of legislating has always been difficult, but during the past few decades, it has become exceedingly complex. Being a good legislator requires a great deal of time and effort, and few prior positions can prepare anyone for a job as a member of Congress. Both parties conduct extensive orientation sessions for incoming members of Congress. These events often last several days and cover a range of topics. "Beyond the briefings on everything from setting up the office, ethics, legislative customs, and rules," note two scholars of the legislative process, "these orientations help break new representatives into the social fabric of the capital. Scores of receptions and dinners help newcomers feel welcome and at the same time socialize the new representative to the ways of the legislative world."[17]

Second, parties in the legislature set the agenda for the coming session and establish priorities. Each legislator comes to Washington with an agenda, a list of issues that he or she would like to address and in some way resolve. These issues originate with constituents, interest groups, and other elected officials, and they also reflect the convictions of the legislators themselves. Combined, this would make a long, dizzying array of topics. Parties allow rank-and-file members to express their concerns to the leadership, where they are prioritized into an agenda for the session. This process not only narrows the list but also focuses members' efforts on priority items. No longer, for example, are there 200 different members of the same party independently fighting for some type of prescription drug program but rather (or so the party leaders hope) 200 legislators working in a unified, synchronized effort toward a common goal.

Third, parties give their members an important time-saving tool when it comes to committee service and floor voting. Thousands of complex measures are introduced and considered each term. Expecting legislators to be fully informed on all, or even most, of these measures is simply impossible. Parties help legislators cut though the complex maze of initiatives by providing briefs and, more important, **voting cues**■. Party leaders will often take positions on issues, thereby "suggesting" to other members of their party that they do the same. Members of Congress do not have to follow this cue from leadership, and occasionally, they do not—but quite often, they do.

Finally, parties organize the committee appointment process. We noted earlier that legislators try to sit on committees that cover topics of most importance to their constituents. This does not mean, however, that every committee assignment is equally desirable. Some committees, such as those dealing with the raising and distribution of money (Budget, Appropriations, Finance, and Ways and Means), are in more demand than others. There is an important pecking order. Party leaders handle the difficult and sometimes contentious chore of committee appointments—and being a "regular" who goes along with the leadership certainly helps a member get a choice assignment.

THE IMPORTANCE OF MAJORITY STATUS Beyond these organizing functions, another issue to consider when thinking about the importance of parties in the legislative process is status. In each branch, there is a majority party and a minority party, determined by the number of legislators in each party. The majority party has many significant advantages. For one, as you've already seen, the majority of members on all committees belong to the majority party. The majority party sets the ratio of party representation on each committee, which reflects the size of the majority it enjoys in that chamber, and it names the chair of each committee and subcommittee. And as we have discussed, the majority also manages the critically important Rules Committee in the House, thus controlling the flow of legislation to the floor.

Given the importance of this stage of the process, this advantage alone underscores how crucial it is whether a party is in the majority or the minority. The majority party selects the leaders in each chamber. The House elects a **speaker**■, who has a number of advantages, including, as noted, the power of referral. These votes to "organize" the House, which are conducted as soon as each session of Congress convenes, are always along party lines, inevitably leading to the victory of someone from the majority party. Similarly, the Senate chooses a **majority leader**■, who has many of the same advantages (although not quite as many, for Senate tradition dictates that individual members have more leeway than House members to do what they please). Finally, given the advantages of majority status, external players—interest groups and the media, for example—are much more interested in their interactions with the majority party's members.

Partisan control of the legislature is critically important. That's why shock waves went through Washington in 2006 when Connecticut Senator Joseph Lieberman lost his state's Democratic primary but won the general election as an Independent. ***—Would Lieberman side with the Democrats or with the Republicans? Should a legislator's party label really matter?***

CONNECT THE LINK (Chapter **13**, page **474**) Have party unity scores in Congress gone up?

■ **Majority Leader:** The head of the majority party in the Senate; the second-highest-ranking member of the majority party in the House.

SIGNIFICANCE: *The majority leader in both the House and Senate wields a great deal of power.*

LEGISLATIVE PARTIES AND CHANGE Obviously, then, when you consider the possible ways of bringing about change using the congressional pathway, another factor to remember is the far-reaching role of political parties in Congress. Political parties are very much alive and well in Congress as we will see in LINK Chapter 13, page 474. Other things being equal, an activist would surely find it more profitable to lobby and work with members of the majority party than with members of the minority party. In fact, most seasoned political activists consider it so important whether the party with which they are dealing is the majority or minority party that the first step of their lobbying strategy is to focus on elections. If, as an activist, your concerns match one of the party's platforms or philosophy better than the other, then helping that party either win or retain control of the legislature is critical to everything you want to accomplish. Hence the enormous amounts of money and member effort that organizations such as the National Rifle Association (NRA), the National Education Association (NEA), the American Medical Association (AMA), the United Auto Workers (UAW), and the National Beer Wholesalers Association (NBWA), National Organization for Women (NOW), the NAACP, the labor unions, and the Christian Coalition give to the benefit of one party or the other.

Legislative Leadership

As noted, the framers of the constitution believed that giving one legislator, or a group of legislators, more power in the system would upset what should be an enlightened, deliberative process. The Constitution states that each chamber will have "leaders": in the House, a speaker (the title *speaker* was used in the British House of Commons and in the colonial assemblies), and in the Senate, a president. In the framers' minds, these posts were meant to aid organization; each was to be a mere parliamentarian who structured debate, made sure that rules of order were followed, guaranteed equal access, and so forth. Leaders were to be impartial. And this is precisely what occurred for the first few decades; legislative leaders simply helped create an orderly process. It was rare, in fact, for leaders of either chamber to even cast a vote.

All that changed in the 1820s. First, the election of 1824, leading to the so-called Corrupt Bargain, reinvigorated party spirit in the United States, and partisanship soon intensified in both houses of Congress. Second, Henry Clay of Kentucky had been elected speaker in 1823. An affable, whiskey-drinking, card-playing master of politicking in the Washington boardinghouses where members lived during sessions of Congress, Clay was also aggressive, outspoken, ambitious, and highly partisan. And he was not about to use his position merely to aid debate. As speaker, he cast votes on nearly every measure, began the practice of referral, and used his office to fill the majority of committee posts with his supporters. Speaker of the House Clay, in fact, contributed enormously to building what eventually became the Whig Party, and the role of speaker as moderator faded into the history books.[18] In the Senate, the move to aggressive leadership was a bit slower, given the smaller size of the chamber and most senators' insistence on their greater political independence, but within two decades, it also developed aggressive, partisan leadership. (Clay eventually moved from the House to the Senate, and there, too, he was always one of the top Whig leaders.)

At the beginning of each legislative term—that is, at each 2-year interval—every member of the House casts a vote for a speaker. Since the 1820s, the winner of these internal elections has always been a member of the majority party. It has become customary for the members of each party to decide on their choice for speaker in advance and to expect every member to vote for that person. Because deviations from this party line vote never occur, the majority party's candidate always prevails.

Rather than having one leader, a hierarchy of leadership now exists for both parties in both chambers. In the House, the most powerful person after the speaker is the majority leader, followed by the majority **whip**■. In brief, majority leaders work with the speaker to coordinate strategy and to advance the party's policy goals. The whip is

■ **Whips:** Assistants to House and Senate leaders, responsible for drumming up support for legislation and for keeping count of how members plan to vote on different pieces of legislation.

SIGNIFICANCE: *Whips help party leaders keep track of the preferences of other members and push those members to stick with the party when their vote is needed.*

■ **Minority Leader:** The leading spokesperson and legislative strategist for the minority party in the House or the Senate.

EXAMPLE: *In the 110th Congress, Democrats controlled both the House and the Senate. As such, the minority leaders in both chambers were Republicans.*

responsible for garnering support for the party's agenda and for making sure that the party leadership has an accurate count of the votes both for and against different pieces of legislation. If members of the party are inclined to vote against a measure deemed important to the leadership, it is the whip's job to help those legislators think otherwise—that is, to "whip" them into line. They also have the added responsibility of passing information along to other members and of working to ensure that members of their party show up for important floor votes.

The Constitution stipulates that the vice president of the United States shall be president of the Senate. Under the Constitution, however, the vice president can vote only to break a tie. The first vice president, John Adams, came into office expecting that even if he did not vote, he would also be able to take a leading role in Senate deliberations—and he was bitterly disappointed and offended when the senators told him that all he could do was preside, in silence. "The most insignificant office that the mind of man ever devised" was Adams's sour verdict on the vice presidency.

When the vice president is not present—which is usually the case except on solemn occasions or when a tie vote is expected—the Senate is formally led by its elected **president pro tempore** (*pro tempore* is a Latin phrase meaning "for the time being" and is usually abbreviated to *pro tem*). Through tradition, this position has become purely ceremonial and is always bestowed on the most senior member of the majority party. The real job of moderating debate in the Senate usually falls to a junior member of the majority party, chosen for that assignment on a rotating basis. The job confers little real power. Much more power in the Senate rests with the majority leader. In some ways similar to the speaker in the House, the majority leader of the Senate is elected and is the head of his or her party. Correspondingly, the Senate **minority leader**■ is the top dog of the minority party. Each has an assistant leader and a whip, charged with much the same responsibilities as those in the House. There are also conference chairs for both parties in the Senate.

Incoming Speaker of the House Nancy Pelosi (D-CA) holds up the speaker's gavel before being confirmed as the first woman speaker of the house on January 4, 2007. She is flanked by her grandchildren.

PATHWAYS | profile

Congresswoman Nancy Pelosi Makes History

Few people would be surprised to hear that the number of women who have served in Congress has been small, but it may be dismaying for some to hear that no woman ever led a party in either branch of Congress until the fall of 2002. Nancy Pelosi, a Democrat from San Francisco, waited until her children were grown to begin her political career even though she comes from a political family: Both her grandfather and her father, who had the same name, Thomas D'Alessandro, had been mayors of Baltimore, Maryland. Pelosi was first elected to the House of Representatives in 1986 and has been reelected easily ever since. Known as a smart, aggressive, and congenial legislator, Pelosi quickly gained the respect of colleagues in both parties. She also worked hard to raise funds for Democratic congressional and presidential candidates. So when the sitting House minority leader stepped down in the summer of 2002, it seemed only natural that her caucus would turn to Pelosi. She was overwhelmingly elected in November of 2006, becoming the first woman speaker of the House of Representatives. Many would agree that since her start, she has matured into the job of House leader. As Michele Cottle, a senior editor the *New Republic,* noted: "Chronic underestimation, say those close to her, has chafed but has also helped Pelosi fuel her rise with a blend of political cunning, hard work, and raw will. . . . Pelosi is a savvy institutionalist who amassed power in part because of her intimate understanding of the House's rules, quirks, and mores."[19] ■

TIMELINE **The Power of the Speaker of the House**

LEADERSHIP POWERS What makes legislative leaders powerful? The answer is a mix of formal and informal powers. Let's begin with the formal powers: Speakers of the House refer legislation to committee, preside over floor proceedings, appoint members to conference and other joint committees, and set the rules of how legislation will be debated and how long such debates might last. They establish the floor agenda, meaning that they decide which bills will—and will not—be scheduled for consideration on the floor. These are weighty formal advantages, but they are just the beginning. The speaker can also use the force of personality and prestige to persuade other members of the legislature to go along with his or her wishes. Great speakers have been able to merge their formal and informal powers. The ability of the speaker to attract national press attention has become another powerful tool. Few speakers were more adept at seizing national press coverage, and thus enhancing their power base, than Georgia Republican Newt Gingrich in his first term (1995–1997).

> "Why is the Speaker of the House considered the most powerful person in Congress?"
> —Student Question

Great as the powers of the speaker may be, however, they are not absolute. On a number of occasions, a speaker has seemed to go too far and was humbled by his fellow legislators. Although Gingrich was clearly a powerful speaker at first, many members of his own party soon thought him too heavy-handed. He also lost favor with the public because of his confrontational ways and his advocacy of heavy cuts in popular government programs. When challenged for the post after the 1998 midterm election, in which the Republicans lost seats, Gingrich resigned from the House.

In the Senate, the majority leader's powers are broad but clearly not as extensive as the speaker's. Majority leaders have great influence on committee assignments, on the scheduling of floor debate, on the selection of conference committee members, and in picking their own conference's leaders. Yet majority leaders have less sway in the Senate for several reasons: first, because of that institution's somewhat different internal rules; second, because of the long-standing notion that the Senate is the "upper chamber," filled with more experienced and higher-status politicians; and third, because Senate norms dictate a more egalitarian process. In other words, Senate rules protect each member's right to participate far more than House rules do.

Organizing Congress: Political Parties and Leadership

Practice Quiz

1. Parties in Congress perform an important orientation function. This implies helping new members
   a. understand expected norms and behaviors.
   b. understand the official law-making process.
   c. work with colleagues on a range of topics.
   d. all of the above.

2. Political parties perform all of the following functions in Congress except
   a. offering judicial nominations for federal judgeships.
   b. setting the agenda for the upcoming legislative session.
   c. conducting orientation sessions for new members.
   d. providing members with briefs and voting cues on important issues.

3. In order to preserve the spirit of bipartisanship, the majority party shares responsibilities for electing committee chairs with the minority party.
   a. true b. false

4. Garnering support for the party's legislative agenda and keeping an accurate record of votes is the responsibility of the party's
   a. speaker b. majority leader
   c. minority leader d. whip

Answers: 1-d, 2-a, 3-b, 4-d.

Discussion Questions

1. What tactics can the minority party use to confound the legislative agenda of the majority party?
2. Compare and contrast the powers of the speaker of the House of Representatives with those of the president.

What **YOU** can do!

Examine the voting records of a sample of House and Senate members; you should choose an equal number of Republicans and Democrats for each chamber. Identify the number of times that each member voted with their congressional leadership. Be sure to note where members deviated from their leadership. Are members more likely to vote against party leadership on certain types of policy issues?

■ **Filibuster:** Process in the U.S. Senate used to block or delay voting on proposed legislation or on an appointment of a judge or other official by talking continuously. Sixty senators must vote to end a filibuster.

SIGNIFICANCE: *This important Senate rule helps promote incremental policy changes.*

Organizing Congress: Rules *and* Norms

(pages 232–235)

How do rules and norms of behavior help ensure a more orderly, efficient legislative process?

The final organizing elements in any legislative body are its formal and informal rules of behavior. Let's begin with the formal regulations. The Constitution states that each house establishes its own rules. Not surprisingly, given the different sizes of the two chambers, the House has a longer set of rules than the Senate. It is difficult to list all the regulations that structure proceedings in the House, but a few of the most significant deal with how measures proceed from committee to floor consideration and with the actions that might be taken to modify a measure once it reaches the floor. Scheduling refers to floor (full-house) consideration of committee-approved measures. All bills approved at the committee level must be scheduled for consideration on the floor. This might seem a straightforward matter, but many issues come into play with this process, including when—if ever—the bill will be considered. If a measure finds itself on a floor calendar, the rules regarding amendments become important, as noted earlier.

The longest speech in the history of the U.S. Senate was made by Strom Thurmond of South Carolina. Thurmond, a Democrat who later became a Republican, spoke for 24 hours and 18 minutes during a filibuster against passage of the Civil Rights Act of 1957.

The Filibuster

The Senate is somewhat less bound by formal rules than the House, but this does not mean that anything goes. Three formal rules stand out as most significant. First, leaders of both parties in the Senate quite often will informally negotiate the terms for debate and amendment of a bill scheduled to be sent to the floor. This is called **unanimous consent,** because all senators must be in agreement. The idea is to try to establish some limits and control in order to expedite floor actions and to impose some predictability. To block legislation or confirmation votes, Senate minorities may resort to use of the **filibuster**■, or unlimited debate, in which one senator or a group of senators keeps talking without interruption unless three-fifths of the chamber (60 senators) votes to end the discussion.

> "Can a senator really defeat legislation by talking a bill to death?"
>
> —Student Question

Conservative southern Democrats were particularly known for filibustering civil rights bills in the second half of the twentieth century. The longest filibustering speech in American history occurred in 1957, when Senator Strom Thurmond of South Carolina (a Democrat who later became a Republican) held the floor for more than 24 hours in an effort to block a vote on what became the Civil Rights Act of 1957. More recently, Republicans have used filibusters in an attempt to derail campaign finance legislation, and Democrats have threatened to use them to block the appointment of several of President George W. Bush's judicial nominations.

To some observers, use of the filibuster is a clear violation of majority rule. However, where you stand on the strategic use of the filibuster is most likely a function of the issue under consideration. Recently, liberal Democrats argued that it was a fair and common procedural move to block "extreme" conservatives from joining the courts, but in the past, as when it was used to block civil rights legislation, they argued that filibusters thwarted the majority will.

Without a unanimous-consent agreement, extended debates can become a problem. A filibuster can be used, but another delay variant is to switch control of floor discussion from one member to

■ **Cloture:** Rule declaring the end of a debate in the Senate.

SIGNIFICANCE: *By requiring 60 senators to vote to end debate on a bill, this promotes compromise and middle-of-the-road legislation.*

■ **Seniority:** Length of time served in a chamber of the legislature. Members with greater seniority have traditionally been granted greater power.

EXAMPLE: *The U.S. senator with the greatest seniority is Robert Byrd, Democrat from West Virginia. Byrd was first elected to the Senate in 1958.*

another, thereby postponing a vote. The goal is to tie things up until the other side backs down or decides to compromise. The tool used to cut off these debates is called **cloture**■. Here, three-fifths of the senators must vote to end the discussion of a bill—that is, "to invoke cloture." This rule can be used for general floor debate or to end a filibuster. Still another variation, often used these days, is called a **hold:** A senator signals to the rest of the chamber that it would be pointless to bring a piece of legislation to the floor, because he or she intends to use delaying tactics to stave off a final vote. A hold can be trumped, of course, with 60 votes for cloture.

Frustrated by what they perceived to be unreasonable delaying tactics by the Democrats in the Senate, particularly in regard to the confirmation of court nominees, Republicans responded by threatening the "nuclear option" in 2005. The plan was for the Senate president to rule that the U.S. Constitution prohibits filibusters against judicial nominations, and then a vote would be held on an appeal. If that happened, only 51 votes would be needed to uphold the ruling. Thus the Republicans would end the practice. So far, the Republicans have only threatened this change, but Democrats have taken notice. (Of course, some Republican senators worried that if they ended the right to filibuster, the tactic would be denied to them next time they were in the minority—which happened two years later.)

Unwritten Rules

You might think that informal rules or legislative norms and customs are less significant than the formal regulations. In fact, informal rules likely do *more* to structure the day-to-day legislative process than any other organizing mechanism. More than 40 years ago, a distinguished political scientist, Don Matthews, noted the power and importance of "folkways" in the legislature.[20] Much of what Matthews suggested still applies today.

> "Are there unwritten rules in the Senate? What are they?"
> —Student Question

Seniority■ stipulates that the longer a member of either chamber has served, the greater deference and the more power he or she should have. Such senior members usually deserve respect because of their long service and accumulated wisdom, but Senate traditions normally also grant them more power in the chamber. It is no longer a hard-and-fast rule that the longest-serving member of a committee becomes its chair (or, if in the minority party, its ranking minority member), but it still does occur. Senior members are often given a greater share of their appropriation requests than a novice, and they are more likely to have their bills at least considered by a committee. In recent years, junior members perceived to be vulnerable to an election defeat are helped by the party leadership, but generally speaking, seniority still matters.

Along with seniority, there is a powerful **apprenticeship norm.** In the past, green (novice) legislators were expected to work hard, get along, be deferential and polite, keep their mouths shut most of the time, and study the legislative process. They were to be "workhorses" instead of "show horses." This was true even when House members moved to the Senate; junior senators were expected to be seen and not heard. In recent years, this norm, like that of seniority, has been observed less and less. In fact, in some instances, party leaders have advised first-term senators to speak up and make a name for themselves, but the norm is not gone completely. Hillary Rodham Clinton, for example, who came to the Senate after being first lady, was careful to observe this tradition.

Civility is another powerful norm in both chambers. Regardless of party, ideology, or position on issues, it is expected that members accord each other respect and a high, even exaggerated level of courtesy. Even when tempers rise, politeness is to remain. "Political disagreements should not influence personal feelings,"[21] suggests Matthews. By tradition, a senator or a representative refers even to his or her bitter political rivals and personal enemies as "the distinguished gentleman [or lady] from" whatever the state might be. When members publicly lapse from this norm of civility, they are expected to apologize, which they very often do. In 2004, Vice President Dick Cheney, who as

Vice President Dick Cheney (center), flanked by Senate Minority Leader Mitch McConnell (R-KY) (left) and Senator Trent Lott (R-MS), speaks at the U.S. Capitol on April 24, 2007. ***—Does the decrease in civility in Congress reflect changes in culture, in politics, or both?***

■ **Specialization:** Extensive knowledge in a particular policy area.

SIGNIFICANCE: *This norm helps ensure that at least some members of the legislature are well versed in most policy areas. It is an individual action that serves a collective good.*

■ **Reciprocity/Logrolling:** Supporting a legislator's bill in exchange for support of one's own bill.

SIGNIFICANCE: *This norm allows individual legislators to provide specific assistance to constituents.*

president of the Senate was in the chamber for "picture day," turned to Vermont Democratic Senator Patrick Leahy and admonished him over the senator's criticism of the vice president. In response to Cheney, Leahy reminded Cheney that the vice president had once accused him of being a bad Catholic, to which Cheney replied with a vulgarity. "I think he was just having a bad day," said Leahy, "and I was kind of shocked to hear that kind of language on the floor."

PATHWAYS | of change from around the world

In 1997, a group of college-age students from around the world began looking for ways to stop crimes against humanity. They took a look at Rwanda, the former Yugoslavia, and other conflict zones and decided to create an organization with a goal of mobilizing the world's youth to prevent such atrocities from occurring in the first place. A committee of 15 youths from 10 different countries—including the former Yugoslavia, Guatemala, Cambodia, Nigeria, and the United States—spent 2 years building the organization. In August 1999, Global Youth Connect (GYC) was launched.

Since that time, GYC has developed dozens of innovative, successful programs. Their goal has been to support and inspire youth dedicated to human rights, community building, reconciliation, and peaceful resolution of conflicts. They believe that educated, compassionate, and empowered young people are the key to achieving tolerance, peace and justice throughout the world. "We want to be part of the solution and demonstrate to the world that there are alternatives that work, and work well," says GYC Executive Director Jennifer Kloes.

Recent initiatives include the Iraqi Refugee Solidarity Initiative (a program aimed at the Iraqi refugee crisis in Jordan); student winter break visits in Cambodia, Rwanda, and El Salvador to assist local organizations with hands-on field projects and to facilitate cross-cultural human rights workshops; and a study trip to Cambodia to explore the road to the Khmer Rouge Tribunal at the Extraordinary Chambers in the Court of Cambodia (ECCC) in Dangkao, Phnom Penh.

SOURCE: InterAction.Org: American Council for International Action Web Site, accessed March 13, 2009, at http://www.interaction.org/monday/11-20-06/youth_programs.html ■

Specialization■ is a norm that suggests members of both chambers are expected to become well versed in a small number of policy areas. Specialization allows members to defer to their colleagues on some policy matters rather than try to bone up on every issue that might come before the legislature. In this, there is an expectation of **reciprocity**■. That is, members are expected to support each other's initiatives on a "you scratch my back, and I'll scratch yours" basis. Wrote Don Matthews, "Every senator, at one time or another, is in the position to help out a colleague. The folkways of the Senate hold that a senator should provide this assistance and that he [or she] be repaid in kind."[22] This is often called **logrolling,** which means that members reciprocally exchange support, often on **earmarks**■, or what is sometimes termed **pork-barrel legislation.** *Pork* is slang for particularized assistance: federal money and programs that largely or wholly benefit just one state or congressional district. Every member wants to "bring home the bacon" to his or her district, and their constituents expect it. One way to get it is through logrolling. For instance, a House member from Tennessee might agree to support a New York City member's appropriation to build a commuter rail station in her district in return for her support for a new stretch of interstate through his part of Tennessee.

PATHWAYS | of action

Bridges to Nowhere?

Some of the highest-profile and most controversial earmarks in recent years have been for the state of Alaska. In 2005, the federal budget included funding for two massive bridges. Longer than the Golden Gate Bridge and higher than the Brooklyn Bridge, the new structure would connect Gravina Island (population 50) with Ketchikan (population 8,002). The price tag for its construction was $400 million. The budget also included several other massive, federally funded construction projects for Alaska. According to Taxpayers for Common Sense, a nonpartisan watchdog group in Washington, D.C., it broke down to $1,150 for every Alaskan,—or 25 times what the average American gets for his or her home state. This occurred at a time when most Americans, as well as members of Congress from both parties, had grown increasingly worried about the federal budget deficit. And it also took place at the same time residents of the Gulf Coast were struggling to rebuild after Hurricane Katrina.

So why would federal funds flow to Alaska and not, say, to Louisiana or Mississippi? Why the exceptional treatment for the forty-ninth state? The explanation lies in the clout of the Alaskan congressional delegation. At the time, Alaska's Republican Senator Ted Stevens was the powerful chair of the Appropriations Committee, the committee in charge of overseeing federal spending. And the state's lone member of the House was Republican Don Young, formerly chair of the House Transportation Committee, which oversees all federally funded construction projects across the nation. When Democrats and Republicans in both chambers voiced their opposition to the Alaskan earmarks, Stevens and Young let it be known that they would not take kindly to serious challenges. Few

Earmarks (Pork-Barrel Legislation): Legislation that benefits one state or district; also called *particularized legislation*.

EXAMPLE: *Ohio Representative Ralph Regula was able to provide his district federal funds for the creation of a Presidential First Ladies Museum.*

COMPARATIVE **Comparing Legislatures**

members of Congress wanted to get on the wrong side of these powerful chairs.

But then the national media got wind of the earmark. The conservative Heritage Foundation, for example, circulated a paper saying it was a "national embarrassment." Funding for the "Bridge to Nowhere" was eventually canceled. Most thought it would fade into the history books, but when John McCain selected Alaska Governor Sarah Palin as his running mate, it was once again a hot topic. While Palin claimed she'd said "thanks—but no thanks" to the project, Democrats dug up evidence suggesting she initially backed the endeavor.

SOURCE: Rebecca Clarren, "A Bridge to Nowhere," Salon.com, http://www.salon.com/news/feature/2005/08/09/bridges/index_np.html, August 9, 2005; Heritage Foundation, "The Bridge to Nowhere: A National Embarassment," http://www.heritage.org/Research/Budget/wm889.cfm, October 20, 2005; USA Today Online, "Alaska Thanks You," **http://** www.usatoday.com/news/opinion/editorials/2005-05-17-alaska-edit_x.htm, May 17, 2005. ■

So what might we conclude about the many mechanisms used to organize our national legislature? Many critics suggest that efforts to bring more efficiency into the legislative process have come at the expense of democracy. Not every member of the legislature is allowed the same input. Committee and subcommittee chairs preside over their policy domains, and little happens in their committees without their approval. Majority party members clearly have a leg up over minority party legislators, and of course, leaders on both sides of the aisle carry more weight than rank-and-file members do. Finally, there are a great many rules that stack the deck against certain members.

As a budding political activist, you must understand the importance of these organizing elements. Just as legislators must be strategic in negotiating the legislative maze, citizen travelers must carefully wend their way down any pathway that leads to trying to persuade legislators to act.

Organizing Congress: Rules and Norms

Practice Quiz

1. Which of the following can be said about official rules and norms of behavior in Congress?
   - **a.** Official rules can have a big impact on the fate of a piece of legislation, but only in the House.
   - **b.** Norms of behavior are an important organizing element in both the House and the Senate.
   - **c.** Filibusters are used more often in the House than in the Senate.
   - **d.** The Senate Rules committee sets clear guidelines on how long a bill can be debated.
2. Floor debate in the Senate and House rarely influences how an individual legislator votes; it is usually conducted for the benefit of the mass media.
   - **a.** true
   - **b.** false
3. What is a significant procedural difference between the Senate and the House?
   - **a.** The Senate needs a quorum (an established minimum number of senators present) to conduct the day's business, but the House does not.
   - **b.** Discussion on the floor of the House allows for spontaneous interruption from other representatives, whereas Senate discussion does not.
   - **c.** Discussion on a bill in the House is governed by rules created by a Rules Committee, whereas Senate discussion is not.
   - **d.** Discussion on a bill in the Senate is governed by parliamentary procedure, whereas House discussion is not.
4. What is one reason bills are introduced in Congress even though the sponsor knows they stand little chance of success?
   - **a.** because Article I of the Constitution obliges every member of Congress to sponsor at least one bill every 6 years
   - **b.** because most members of Congress have hired and are paying staffers for the primary purpose of drafting legislation
   - **c.** because representatives are then able to say, during a reelection campaign at home, that they are working hard to accomplish whatever the proposed bill suggests
   - **d.** because sponsoring such legislation takes a lot less work than sponsoring successful bills, yet it makes the representative look equally hardworking

Answers: 1-b, 2-a, 3-c, 4-c.

Discussion Questions

1. What are the advantages and disadvantages of a filibuster for the minority party—and for the majority party?
2. Does the Senate benefit or not from its more informal rules and procedures?

What **YOU** can do!

While rules of an organization or institution are easy to identify, norms of behavior are usually more difficult to recognize. Observe a group of which you are a member. It might be a formal group (for example, campus club, sorority or fraternity, sports team) or an informal group (for example, co-workers, dorm mates or room mates). What unwritten, unspoken norms guide your interactions?

■ **Bill Sponsor:** The member of Congress who introduces a bill.

EXAMPLE: *Not long after Janet Jackson exposed her breast during the Super Bowl Half-Time Show in 2005, Senator Tom Brownback of Kansas introduced the Broadcast Decency Enforcement Act. He was thus the bill sponsor.*

SIMULATION How a Bill Becomes a Law

How *a* Bill Becomes Law (pages 236–239)

How are laws made?

Once you begin to think about the many ways potential chaos gets channeled into constructive deliberation in Congress, you can begin to understand some of the many hurdles that bills must cross in order to become law. Here, we'll walk through this process in greater detail. Please keep in mind that this outline is a theoretical model and that in practice, things are rarely this neat. Also, the process is similar in both chambers, but it is not exactly the same. What follows is a general pattern (see Figure 6.4).

"Can anyone introduce a bill in Congress?"
—Student Question

Step 1. Introduction of a Bill. The idea (and frequently the language) of a bill can originate from many sources. Often, an administrative agency will draw up a bill. Interest groups also often have a hand, both in the broad outlines of a measure and in its exact wording. Yet to begin the actual process of legislating, a member of Congress must always introduce a bill in one chamber of that body. This person becomes the **bill sponsor**■, the official "parent" of the legislation. With the exception of tax bills, which under the Constitution can only be introduced in the House of Representatives, any member of the national legislature can introduce any measure he or she sees fit.

Step 2. Referral. Soon after a bill is introduced, it is referred to a committee, and from there, it is usually sent to the appropriate subcommittee.

Step 3. Committee Consideration. Most measures go no further than the subcommittee level. As we've seen, hearings are held, the language is sometimes modified (in the markup process), and if a bill is approved at this level, it is reported back to the full committee. Additional changes are sometimes made at the full-committee level, but the committee often will simply accept or reject the measure offered by the subcommittee.

Step 4. Rules for Floor Action. Any bill approved by a full committee is sent to the floor for full-chamber consideration. In the House of Representatives, however, a required stop is the Rules Committee. As already noted, here many procedural issues are set, such as the length of time the bill will be debated and the types of amendments, if any, that can be accepted. Once again, the majority party controls the Rules Committee. There is no similar procedure in the Senate.

Step 5. Floor Consideration. This is where every member of the chamber has an opportunity to express his or her support (or lack of support) for the bill. Most measures do not entail a lengthy floor debate. Indeed, robust, meaningful floor debate is rare even in the Senate, where rules allow each member more opportunity to speak. The reason for this is that most measures are low-profile, highly technical matters (such as adjustments to complex statutes) that draw little public interest. When the public becomes involved, however, floor debate can be intense. Few legislators are persuaded by floor debate, however; the fireworks are geared more to the constituents back home or to the national media than to persuading fellow legislators. By this time, just about every legislator's own mind will have been made up (whether or not the person says so in public).

Step 6. Conference Committee. For a bill to become a law, an identical version must be approved in both houses. Quite a few measures passed in one house will not have a counterpart in the other house. These are called **one-house bills.** If the other chamber has also passed an identical version of the bill, it is moved along to the president to be signed—or to face a veto (see step 7). Many times a similar (but not identical) bill is passed in the other chamber. To reconcile differences, a conference committee, created for that measure, sets to work. Three outcomes from conference deliberations are possible. First, one of the versions of the bills might be accepted as the final agreement (see Figure 6.4, for example). When this occurs, the chamber accepting changes has to vote on the measure again (for, as we have seen, each chamber must approve exactly the same wording). Second, some sort of compromise or middle-of-the-road position might be crafted, making it necessary for both houses to vote again on the compromise version. Finally, compromise might not be possible (this often happens when Congress is about to adjourn), and each measure remains a one-house bill.

Step 7. Presidential Action. Modern presidents and their staffs are involved with the goings-on in Congress and work closely with legislators. When the president is of the same party as the majority in both houses, it is rare that

FIGURE 6.4 | How a Bill Becomes a Law

The scheme to make each branch of government somewhat dependent on the others to perform their duties, and to be in certain ways checked by the other branches is well exemplified in "how a bill becomes a law." Some would say that the numerous steps and hurdles weed out unnecessary measures, but others argue that the system is too cumbersome and that it makes change too difficult. And when we add political parties to the mix, something that the framers did not envision, the process can become even more intricate. ***—What's your take on this important issue: Does this complex process serve the nation well, or does it inhibit needed change?***

Economic Stimulus Act of 2008

"To provide economic stimulus through rebates to individuals, incentives for business investment, and an increase in confirming and FHA loan limits."

Trigger

By early 2008, several indicators pointed to growing economic troubles and an increased risk of a recession. The subprime mortgage mess had become a crisis, the stock market seemed to be in freefall, and gas prices were at record levels. Federal Reserve Chairman Ben Bernanke testified before Congress that quick action was needed. Coupled with approaching congressional elections, these developments seemed to compel federal action.

Step 1. Introduction

HR 5140 is introduced by Speaker Nancy Pelosi (D–CA) on January 18, 2008.

Steps 2. Referral and 3. Committee Action

Bill is referred to Ways and Means, then to Subcommitte on Financial Services.

After considerable negotiation between Democrats and Republicans in the House as well as Bush administration officials, a bill was reported out of committee to the floor on January 24, 2008.

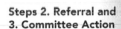

Step 4. Floor Action

The bill was approved by the House of Representatives in a vote of 385 to 35 on January 29, 2008.

Step 1. Introduction

Max Baucus (D–MT) introduced stimulus legislation on January 30, 2008. This bill is similar to the House version but not identical.

Steps 2. Referral and 3. Committee Action

The bill is referred to the Finance Committee, where Baucus is chair

A series of amendments are proposed, but most are rejected. However, a cloture vote is attempted on February 6, 2008, but this effort fails to net the 60–vote minimum.

Steps 4. Floor Action

One day later, on February 7, 2008 a deal is reached between parties, and a vote is taken on a measure that is similar but not identical to the House bill. It passess by a margin of 81 to 16.

Step 5. Resolving Differences

Rather than creating a Conference Committeee, the House takes up the Senate version and passess it on the floor later in the day on February 7, 2008, by a vote of 380 to 34. Now both chambers have passed identical bills.

Step 6. Presidential Signature
On February 13, 2008, President George W. Bush signed the $152 billion stimulus package into law. "We have come together on a single mission—and that is to put the people's interests first."

Tax rebate checks are mailed in late spring.

CONNECT THE LINK
(Chapter **7**, page **270**) Are vetoes more common when presidents of one party confront a Congress that is controlled by the other party?

Occasionally some members of Congress serve long enough to become masters at the lawmaking process. Pictured above (center, at the podium) is Democratic Senator Edward (Ted) Kennedy of Massachusetts who was first elected in 1962. Today he is known as the "Lion of the Senate" because of his legislative prowess and his ability to build consensus on important legislation. With him in this photo are Republican Senators Lindsay Graham of South Carolina (left) and Jon Kyl of Arizona (right).

important measures are approved without the president's blessing. (If they are, it is a sure sign that the president is in deep political trouble.) Even when there is a divided government, most bills approved by Congress do wind up winning presidential support. A bill becomes a law when the president signs it. If 10 days pass without the president having signed the bill—a rare occurrence that generally indicates the president does not like the bill but chooses not to cause an uproar by vetoing it—the bill becomes law. Or the president can veto the bill, sending it back to the Congress. As we'll discuss in LINK Chapter 7, page 270, vetoes have recently become quite rare, especially compared to the number of measures that win presidential approval. Given a president's grave concern about having his veto overridden, when the president does reject an important bill, it certainly makes news.

Step 8. Overriding a Presidential Veto. Presidential vetoes are always accompanied by a written message—a statement to Congress that says why the measure was rejected. The measure can still become a law if two-thirds of each house of Congress votes to override the veto.

Emergency Legislation

The process of passing legislation can be lengthy. The numerous steps—from markup to subcommittee hearings, full committee deliberation, floor action, and conference committee compromise—generally take months. Occasionally, however, emergencies arise during which the legislature is called upon to act quickly and to condense the process into a few days.

Such was the case with the Emergency Economic Stabilization Act of 2008, the so-called "Wall Street Bailout Bill." By mid-September of that year, the subprime mortgage crisis had reached a critical stage, with Secretary of the Treasury Henry Paulson openly concerned about an imminent crisis and the necessity for immediate action. Several massive investment banks and other financial institutions announced pending bankruptcy, leading the Treasury Department to take dramatic action to "bail out" a few of these institutions, such as American International Group (AIG), Fannie Mae, and Freddie Mac. Other businesses, such as Lehman Brothers, were allowed to collapse. It was a crisis of financial liquidity, meaning that because of momentous problems in lending practices, few banks were willing to lend money. And with credit gone, the economy would come to a halt and spiral downward. Americans were told this was the most serious economic crisis since the Great Depression. It was a time for decisive action.

Paulson, in close consultation with Federal Reserve Chairman Ben Bernanke, proposed a plan under which the U.S. Treasury would acquire up to $700 billion worth of mortgage-backed securities. By doing so, they argued, banks would again start lending money. The plan was backed by President George W. Bush, and negotiations began with leaders in Congress to draft the appropriate legislation. President Bush and Secretary Paulson told the public and members of Congress that a quick agreement was vital; it had to happen in the next few days.

Congress acted quickly, but not as fast as the Bush administration had hoped, because the issue was quite controversial. On the one hand, many legislators understood the urgency of the problem and that a massive governmental intervention was the only hope to stave off a financial collapse. On the other hand, many also knew that average citizens saw the proposed measure as helping the business elite. Why should *they* be saved from their own mistakes and greed? In short, the scheme was very unpopular back home.

Early measures passed in the Senate, but the House balked. The election was only weeks away: Every House member would be up for reelection, but only one-third of the Senate would face the voters. The process unfolded precisely as the framers of our system envisioned, with the Senate better able to rise above public opinion and the House seemingly beholden to it. Through a great deal of persuasion, negotiation, compromise, and added "sweeteners" (elements that aided particular districts), the measure passed on October 3, 2008.

A few lessons can be drawn from this issue. First, when emergencies arise, Congress can move quickly, but not nearly as rapidly as the executive branch can. This, too, is what the framers envisioned—immediate action from the executive branch, but greater deliberation in the legislature. Second, members of Congress face particularized constituencies. What is good for the nation might be unpopular in specific districts or states. The president, on the other hand, faces a national constituency. Third, the Senate, with six-year terms and rotation, seems better able than the House to confront important but unpopular measures. Finally, there is no easy answer to the age-old question of whether legislators should be delegates, trustees, or something in between.

Making Laws: Summary

The number varies somewhat from year to year, but roughly speaking, in the 2 years that any Congress sits, more than 10,000 measures are introduced. Of these, roughly 400 become law.[23] Most of these are low-profile, technical adjustments to existing laws; only a handful of truly significant measures gets passed each session. The road from introduction to presidential signature is long and difficult—deliberately so. Some measures are introduced in the full realization that they will not make the complete journey. This is done for many reasons, including attempts to satisfy special interest groups or draw attention to an issue for future political exploitation. But even proposals that seem popular in the legislature and are supported by most Americans can get bogged down. On the one hand, we might suggest that the difficulty of the process implies a shortcoming in the legislative process: The will of the people should be more easily and more quickly expressed through the national legislature. On the other hand, many people would agree that the process *should* be difficult, and that there *should* be many potholes, roadblocks, and detours along the pathway. They would argue that the federal government must act cautiously when deciding the laws citizens must obey. That, after all, was the intent of the framers of our Constitution.

How a Bill Becomes Law

Practice Quiz

1. Which of the following is a likely sequence for a bill that becomes law?
   a. It is drafted by a congressional staffer and an interest group, introduced by a member of Congress, signed by the president, amended in the appropriate subcommittee, and approved by a vote on the House floor.
   b. It is drafted by a congressional staffer with input from an interest group, introduced on the House floor by a sponsoring representative, referred to a standing committee, sent to the appropriate subcommittee where hearings about the measure are held and the markup is done, and sent back to the full committee and approved. Rules for its discussion on the House floor are then set by the Rules Committee. It passes by a majority vote in the House. Meanwhile, a nearly identical bill follows a nearly identical path in the Senate. A conference committee realizes there are no real differences between the two bills, and the president signs it into law.
   c. It is drafted in a Senate committee, discussed on the Senate floor, and passed by a majority vote. It is then referred to the House, where it goes into another committee and then to the appropriate subcommittee within that committee. Hearings are held, and language is agreed on. It is sponsored on the House floor, passed by a majority vote there, and then goes into a conference committee, where differences between the House and Senate versions of the bill are ironed out. The president then signs it into law.
   d. It is drafted by a group of staffers in the president's office. A conference committee consisting of powerful senators and members of Congress deliberates over the bill, drafting compromise language. It is then approved in subcommittees in both chambers. Next, the bill is voted for constitutionality by clerks for the Supreme Court and, if necessary, by the justices themselves. It is then signed into law by the president.
2. Most bills submitted by Congress are vetoed by the president as an element of political strategy by the White House.
   a. true **b.** false
3. Of the 10,000 bills introduced in Congress in each session, about how many pass into law?
   a. 5,000 **b.** 4,000
   c. 400 **d.** 100
4. The framers of the Constitution intended for the passage of bills into laws to be streamlined and fast; they would not approve of the slow pace of modern legislation.
   a. true **b.** false

Answers: 1-b, 2-b, 3-c, 4-b.

Discussion Questions

1. In what ways could partisanship by the majority party impact the management of bills by the conference committee?
2. Why are presidential vetoes so seldom overridden? Think in terms of the procedures in Congress as well as politics.

What **YOU** can do!

Thousands of bills are introduced in the House and Senate each year. One of the best online tracking sites is called Thomas, (**http://thomas.loc.gov**), sponsored by the Library of Congress. It is a powerful search engine that lets you look up legislation by key word or phrase. Check it out, and explore legislation that may be of interest to you.

Who Sits *in* Congress?

(pages 240–243)

How well does the membership of the House and Senate reflect average Americans? Why might this issue matter?

As we have emphasized in discussing representative democracy, *representation* means that someone speaks and works on behalf of others. Perhaps this process can be enhanced when the representative understands the issues and concerns that confront a district, and perhaps this is more likely to happen when he or she reflects the demographic makeup of the constituency of the district. Many people feel that at the very least, a legislative body should look like the nation as a whole. According to this viewpoint, race, ethnicity, gender, sexual orientation, occupation, age, and other demographics matter. This preference for *symbolic* or *descriptive representation* is the logic behind the drive, discussed earlier in this chapter, to create majority-minority districts.

> "Is Congress still mostly rich, white, and male?"
>
> —Student Question

Let's survey the range of types of Americans who have been members of Congress.

Gender

Let's start with the number of women in Congress. The first woman elected to the House of Representatives was Jeannette Rankin of Montana in 1916. She was elected even before women nationally got the right to vote under the Nineteenth Amendment. A peace activist, Rankin voted against declaring World War I. She was also in the House in 1941, where she cast the only vote against declaring war after Pearl Harbor. The first woman to serve in the Senate was Rebecca Felton from Georgia in 1922, who was appointed to fill a vacant seat. There were very few female members of either chamber during the following decades—about a dozen in the House and just two in the Senate. By the 1950s, there were 17 female national legislators in House and Senate combined, and that number actually dipped during the 1960s and 1970s. There has been a steady increase since the 1980s, with a big jump in both number and net worth coming after the 1992 election (called by journalists the "Year of the Woman" because of the large number of women who ran for office that year). In the 111th Congress, there are 17 women in the U.S. Senate—equal to the total number of women who had served in *all* the years before 1978, as noted in Figure 6.5. In the House of Representatives, there are 75 women in the 111th

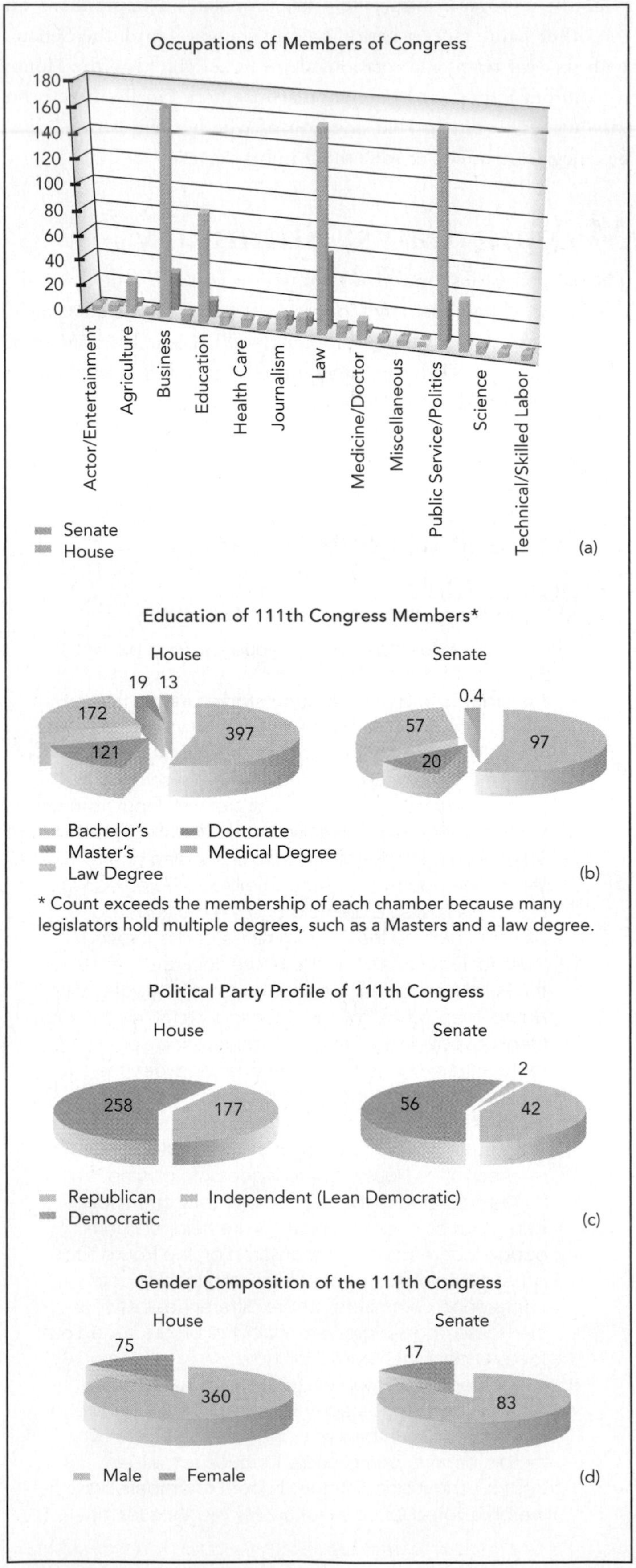

FIGURE 6.5 | Occupations, Education, Party Profile, and Gender Composition of the 111th Congress

What conclusions can you draw about the occupations, education and gender of Congress? How can it become more diversified and representative of the average citizen?

NOTE: Projected data as of November 10, 2008.

The late Congresswoman Barbara Jordan voted to impeach President Nixon during Watergate House Judiciary Committee meetings in 1974. ***—What forces have played a role in limiting the number of minorities and women in Congress?***

Congress. Most people would agree that things are moving in the right direction, with the change in the Senate being especially significant. Yet it would seem that parity between the genders is still a long way off.

Race and Ethnicity

The picture for African Americans in Congress in some ways resembles that for women, and in other ways, it is even more vexing. The first black elected to the House of Representatives was Joseph Hayne Rainey of South Carolina in 1870. Rainey was a slave as a child and was requisitioned for labor by the Confederacy during the Civil War. He escaped on a blockade-runner ship and made his way to Bermuda, a British colony where slavery had been abolished. After the Civil War, he returned to South Carolina and began working with the Republican Party. He was sent to the House after a special election in 1870, where he served for 8 years.[24] The first African American was also elected to the Senate in 1870: Hiram Rhodes Revels, representing Mississippi. Interestingly, he was elected by the "reconstructed" state legislature to complete Jefferson Davis's unfinished term. (Davis had left his place in the U.S. Senate to become president of the Confederacy.) After serving only 1 year, Revels left the Senate to become president of Alcorn State College.[25]

In all, only five African Americans have ever been elected to the Senate. In the House, just over 100 African Americans have served. These are discouraging statistics, especially in the Senate. As with women, however, the numbers seem to be improving since the 1980s. In recent years, about 37 members of the House have been black—roughly 8.5 percent of the chamber. Given that African Americans make up about 13 percent of the national population, we might say that the situation is improving, especially compared to that of women.

PATHWAYS | profile

Congresswoman Barbara Jordan of Texas

Barbara Jordan, the first black representative from Texas, was born in Houston on February 21, 1936. She was educated in the public schools of Houston and graduated from Phillis Wheatley High School in 1952. After receiving a B.A. in political science and history from Texas Southern University in 1956, she attended law school. In 1959, she was admitted to the Massachusetts and Texas bars, and she commenced practice in Houston in 1960.

In 1972, Jordan defeated Republican Paul Merritt to represent the 18th District of Texas in the U.S. House of Representatives. She was a member of the Judiciary Committee in the 93rd Congress and also joined the Committee on Government Operations during the 94th and 95th Congresses.

Shortly after the 93rd Congress convened in 1973, it began struggling with the Nixon administration over budgetary reform, a troubled economy, the war in Indochina, and other very serious issues. Jordan and other freshman representatives met with Speaker Carl Albert and arranged a meeting on the House floor in April to provide newly elected Democrats an opportunity to vent their frustration over the difficult relations between Congress and the executive branch. Jordan herself praised the House's capacity for self-reform. During the same Congress, she attached civil rights amendments to legislation authorizing cities to receive direct Law Enforcement Assistance Administration grants rather than apply to state governments for the money. Jordan questioned the civil rights record of House Republican leader Gerald Ford when President Nixon nominated him for the vice presidency. (This occurred after the previous vice president, Spiro Agnew, was forced to resign after he pleaded no contest to charges of having taken bribes.) Jordan joined seven other Judiciary Committee members in voting against Ford's confirmation.

Jordan won national acclaim during the Judiciary Committee's hearings into Nixon's possible impeachment in the summer of 1974. In a deep, resonant, and dignified voice that few who watched the televised proceedings could ever forget, she eloquently reaffirmed her faith in the Constitution while voting for all five articles of impeachment.

In December of 1977, Jordan announced that she would not be a candidate for reelection. In 1979, she became a professor at the Lyndon B. Johnson School of Public Affairs at the University of Texas in Austin. In August of 1994, President Bill Clinton awarded Jordan the Medal of Freedom, the nation's highest civilian honor. After suffering for years from a chronic illness, Jordan died on January 17, 1996, in Austin, Texas.

SOURCE: "Black Americans in Congress, 1870–1989," http://www.house.gov/jacksonlee/AllAboutHouston/barbara_charline_jordan.htm, March 2004. ■

Representative Loretta Sanchez (left), first elected in 1994, and her sister, Linda Sanchez, wave at supporters while waiting for election results from their congressional districts in 2002. Both won their races, making them the first sisters to serve in Congress. ***—Will Congress become more diverse in the years ahead?***

Hispanic Americans (Latinos) are the fastest-growing demographic group in America and have recently succeeded African Americans as the nation's largest minority group. It is estimated that by 2010, there will be roughly 45 million Hispanic Americans, making up some 15 percent of the population. (The U.S. Census Bureau estimates that Hispanics have accounted for 40 percent of the nation's population growth since 1990.) Their representation in Congress, however, has lagged far behind, but things have recently improved for Hispanics as well. Today, about 25 members of the national legislature, or about 5 percent, are of Hispanic descent.

Why are few women and minority citizens elected to Congress? One reason is that historically, fewer women and minorities have sought office, likely because of a wide range of factors, including biases in the campaign process, discriminatory voter attitudes, and lags in the number of these groups who entered professions—especially the law—that have typically led to a political career. For whatever reason, some Americans still find it difficult to vote for minority and female candidates. One prominent elections scholar has observed that one way "to achieve fairer and more equal representation for minorities is to eliminate the allegiances and attitudes (some consider them biases and prejudices) that favor the majority."[26] A related explanation lies in the nature of our electoral system and specifically in our reliance on single-member districts. There is no requirement in the Constitution that specific districts be drawn within each state, only (as noted earlier) that states receive an overall number of representatives relative to that state's population. We might consider an at-large system, under which states that have two or more representatives would have no distinct districts: Voters would vote for at-large candidates, and these candidates would get into the House in descending order according to the number of votes they won. (Alternatively, large states like California and New York could be divided into a number of large districts, each of which would elect a group of at-large representatives.) Under such a system, if a minority group makes up one-fifth of a state's population, which is often the case, and that state has been allotted 10 seats in the House of Representatives chosen at large, we might expect that more minority candidates—perhaps two—would be elected. When one candidate is selected from a single district, however, that same 20 percent minority group is simply drowned out by the majority. And if attitudes about supporting minority candidates do not change, the prospects of that group's gaining a voice in the legislature will be small.

"Why are there still so few women and minorities in Congress?"

—Student Question

Income and Occupation

What about income and occupation? Once again, we find that the national legislature does not reflect America very well. Members of Congress are far better educated and far wealthier than the average American (Table 6.4). (And that is what the framers of the Constitution—themselves drawn from the elite—expected.) The Senate is often called the "millionaires' club." According to a study conducted by CNN, about 40 of the 100 senators in the 108th Congress were millionaires.[27] During this same time, the average American household brought in $42,400, and only about 5 percent of Americans earned more than $150,000 per year. Less than 1 percent of Americans are worth a million dollars or more.[28]

And there have always been lawyers in Congress—lots and lots of lawyers. Roughly 40 percent of members of Congress serving at any given time are attorneys. Bankers and business professionals make up about the same percentage, and educators (schoolteachers and professors) account for roughly 15 percent.[29] All other occupational backgrounds, including clergy, farmers, and retired military personnel, have been represented by only 5 percent of the members. Laborers, small farmers, homemakers, service employees, and other blue-collar workers, who make up a vast majority of the American workforce,

"Can a legislature made up of elites really represent the average citizen?"

—Student Question

TABLE 6.4 | **Top Twenty Richest Members of Congress in 2006**

RANK	NAME	ESTIMATED NET WORTH
1	Jane Harman (D-CA)	$409,426,887
2	Darrell Issa (R-CA)	$337,440,028
3	John Kerry (D-MA)	$267,989,805
4	Vernon Buchanan (R-FL)	$191,695,634
5	Herb Kohl (D-WI)	$171,423,011
6	Edward M. Kennedy (D-MA)	$102,822,519
7	Jay Rockefeller (D-WV)	$ 91,713,012
8	Robin Hayes (R-NC)	$ 82,552,081
9	Dianne Feinstein (D-CA)	$ 79,555,657
10	Frank R. Lautenberg (D-NJ)	$ 79,051,090
11	Charles H. Taylor (R-NC)	$ 66,698,509
12	Rodney Frelinghuysen (R-NJ)	$ 49,515,595
13	Michael McCaul (R-TX)	$ 46,648,568
14	Elizabeth Dole (R-NC)	$ 43,867,072
15	Nita M. Lowey (D-NY)	$ 39,753,196
16	Nancy Pelosi (D-CA)	$ 38,539,554
17	John McCain (D-AZ)	$ 36,431,099
18	Tom Petri (R-WI)	$ 35,918,018
19	Carolyn B. Maloney (D-NY)	$ 34,069,544
20	John Campbell (R-CA)	$ 32,846,041

SOURCE: Opensecrets.org, "Net Worth, 2006," accessed at http://www.opensecrets.org/pfds/overview.php?type=W&year=2006

have never accounted for more than a tiny fraction of the members of Congress (see Figure 6.5).

Perhaps it makes sense that some occupations are overrepresented in Congress. Lawyers, after all, are trained to understand the nuances of the law; it is natural that they would take the lead in writing laws. We might hope that the best and the brightest would serve in the national legislature—perhaps the same kinds of individuals who have earned advanced degrees and succeeded at their profession (that is, made lots of money). This is precisely what the framers of our system hoped for Congress, especially the Senate. Of course, it is possible that such representatives can understand the concerns of diverse groups of people and work on their behalf. Some of the greatest legislative champions of women's rights have been male legislators, and some of Congress' most aggressive advocates for the poor have been rich. Many white legislators fought valiant battles against slavery and segregation. Moreover, given that all Americans have the right to vote and that most legislators do everything they can to stay in office, we can imagine that members of Congress would be very attentive to *all* their constituents—especially to large blocs of voters, many of whom are far from affluent. Yet those who feel underrepresented in the halls of Congress—women, African Americans, Asian Americans, Hispanics, blue-collar workers, farmers, gays and lesbians, persons with disabilities, and the poor—feel that their concerns would get more attention if more members of their group were players on the field rather than simply spectators from the sidelines or the bleachers.

Who Sits in Congress
Practice Quiz

1. Regarding gender representation in Congress, it's fair to say that
   - **a.** since the 1920s, the number of women in both chambers has steadily increased.
   - **b.** the percentage of women in Congress is finally close to the percentage in the general population.
   - **c.** the number of women in the federal legislature is higher now than in the 1920s, but still not close to reflecting the percentage of women in the general population.
   - **d.** women today make up only about 5 percent of the federal legislature.

2. Joseph Hayne Rainey was the first African American elected to the U.S. House of Representatives. When did that happen?
   - **a.** 1864
   - **b.** 1870
   - **c.** 1921
   - **d.** 1946

3. Barbara Jordan first claimed national attention
   - **a.** during her legislative work on civil rights in 1972.
   - **b.** by participating in nonviolent demonstrations in the South in the 1950s.
   - **c.** by arguing *Brown* v. *Board of Education* before the Supreme Court in 1954.
   - **d.** by her participation in the Judiciary Committee's hearings on President Nixon's impeachment in 1974.

4. Working-class Americans, service employees, small farmers, and ordinary housewives have always constituted a tiny fraction of the members of Congress.
   - **a.** true
   - **b.** false

Answers: 1-c, 2-b, 3-d, 4-a.

Discussion Questions

1. Describe and discuss the socioeconomic backgrounds of the members of Congress. What might this tell us about the respective legislative agendas of individual members?
2. How do you think the close 2008 Democratic primary contest between Barack Obama and Hillary Clinton affected diversity in Congress? Will more women and people of color consider running in the future?

What **YOU** can do!

Invite a diverse group of classmates for some coffee or lunch to talk about the policy issues that concern them the most. Talk about differences and similarities among your interests and opinions. Do any of you feel that your interests would be better represented by a congressperson who shares your demographic characteristics? Why or why not?

Congressional Ethics

(pages 244–245)

Are members of Congress more or less ethical than in the past?

"There have been so many scandals in Congress recently. Are things getting worse?"

—Student Question

One of the central players in Congress in the past decade was Tom DeLay, a Republican from Texas, first elected in 1984. When the Republicans captured control of the House in 1994, DeLay quickly emerged as a powerful player and was elected majority whip. He had a passion for politics and was bright, articulate, shrewd—and ruthless. His nickname, "The Hammer," seemed apt. He quickly rose in the Republican conference, and in 2002, he was elected majority leader and was one of the most powerful men in Washington.

By the spring of 2005, however, DeLay's fortunes had taken a dramatic downward turn: A grand jury in Austin, Texas, indicted him on criminal charges of conspiracy to violate election laws in 2002. In the spring of 2006, he was forced to relinquish his post as majority leader. Even though DeLay would stay in office while he fought the charges, everyone in Washington understood that the star had fallen. By summer, DeLay had withdrawn his name from the November ballot; he had decided to leave the House altogether.

About the same time that DeLay was stepping down from his leadership position, shivers were running through official Washington. An influential lobbyist named Jack Abramoff had been under investigation by federal law enforcement officials for some time, and they finally hit him with a string of indictments. Abramoff quickly agreed to cooperate with the prosecutors in exchange for a lighter sentence. In other words, Abramoff was ready to talk about the lobbying practices in Congress and to "name names." The case, replete with luxury skyboxes, politicians shilling for gambling interests, and lobbyists stealing from Indian tribes, seemed to symbolize Washington's extreme cash-for-policy culture. A year later, Idaho Senator Larry Craig was arrested for lewd behavior in a men's bathroom at the Minneapolis–St. Paul Airport, and Alaska Senator Ted Stevens came under investigation by the FBI and the IRS for possible corruption based on his close relationship with oil company executives who had pleaded guilty to bribing other legislators.

The DeLay, Abramoff, Craig, and Stevens scandals probably did not come as a surprise to most Americans. Ethical transgressions have periodically seemed an integral part of Congress. Mark Twain's oft-cited line that Congress is the only "distinctly native American criminal class" still seems accurate to most Americans. And there have certainly been enough high-profile scandals to buttress this cynical judgment. In 1875, during the corrupt administration of President Ulysses S. Grant, Americans were shocked by the bribes and kickbacks of the so-called Whisky Ring involving various prominent congressional crooks. In the 1920s, the Teapot Dome scandal implicated several prominent members of the Senate (as well as some of President Warren G. Harding's cabinet). More recently, the Abscam scandal of 1980 ensnared nearly 30 public officials, including a prominent senator; they were caught when federal law enforcement officers disguised as Arabian potentates proffered bribes. In 1989, five members of the Senate, including John McCain, were implicated in the Keating scandal, involving corrupt banking practices. In 1992, no fewer than 430 sitting and former members of the House were exposed in a scandal centered on the bank that the House maintains for the convenience of its members. And this dismal list does not include dozens of individual ethics violations that have occurred, many of them turning on money but others involving sex, alcohol, and drugs. In November of 2005, Randall "Duke" Cunningham resigned from the House and was sentenced to 6 years in prison after pleading guilty to federal charges of conspiracy to commit bribery, mail fraud, and tax evasion. He admitted receiving at least $2.4 million in bribes. Cunningham's tearful apology was touching, but few Americans were surprised to see another member of Congress led off in handcuffs. In one national survey, just 20 percent of Americans rate the ethics of members of Congress as "high" or "very high" (see Table 6.5).[30]

Social scientists and close observers suggest that members of Congress are more ethical today than at any point in our nation's history. Yet high-profile scandals continue to drive the perception that Congress is filled with scoundrels. Here influential lobbyist Jack Abramoff talks with his lawyers in the spring of 2006. ***—Do you agree that we have the "best Congress money can buy?"***

Recent Trends

Close observers of the legislative branch argue that in the past few decades, members of Congress have become more ethical and more upstanding than at any point in our nation's history. According to Fred Harris, a political scientist and former Democratic senator from Oklahoma, members of the national legislature are a good deal cleaner than the average American.[31] Another observer put it this way: "Most observers would suggest that real corruption on the Hill has in fact declined significantly over the past 20 or 30 years, whether the misbehavior is licentiousness or bribery or financial chicanery."[32]

What, then, might explain the gap between perceptions and reality? There are a number of plausible explanations. For one, there is

TABLE 6.5 | Public Opinion Poll on Congressional Ethics

"Would you rate the level of ethics and honesty of members of Congress as excellent, good, not so good, or poor?"	
Excellent	1%
Good	26%
Not so Good	36%
Poor	30%
Unsure	7%
"And would you rate the level of ethics and honesty of your own representative to the U.S. House of Representatives in Congress as excellent, good, not so good, or poor?"	
Excellent	9%
Good	45%
Not so Good	23%
Poor	13%
Unsure	10%
"When it comes to the level of ethics and honesty among politicians, do you think the Democrats are generally better than the Republicans, the Republicans are generally better than the Democrats, or isn't there much difference between them when it comes to ethics and honesty?	
Democrats Better	16%
Republicans Better	9%
Isn't Much Difference	72%
Unsure	3%

N = 1,044 adults nationwide. Margin of Error plus or minus 3. Fieldwork by ICR.
SOURCE: ABC News Poll, May 26-30, 2006.

simply much more reporting of ethical transgressions than in the past. Particularly after the Watergate scandal in the early 1970s, aggressive investigative journalism has become an omnipresent force in American politics. Reporters, thirsting—and driven by their media bosses—to find the next big scoop, scour public and private information for dirt. Second, this intense competition pushes news outlets to relentlessly pursue stories on what might once have been dismissed as minor infractions. Noted scholar Larry Sabato has called it "a spectacle without equal in modern American politics: the news media, print and broadcast, go after a wounded politician like sharks in a feeding frenzy."[33] Finally, because of a series of reforms, especially since the 1970s, members of Congress are subject to tougher rules and procedures and to far more public scrutiny than in the past.

In very important ways, however, it is the perception of the public that really matters. Numerous measures have been introduced to tighten ethical conduct, especially as it affects the relationship between legislators (and their staffers) and lobbyists. And of course, each party in Congress has attempted to portray itself as more ethical than the other party.

Corruption is almost inevitably entangled with power—especially *entrenched* power. The irony is that Republicans were implicated in the Abramoff scandal because they were the majority party and therefore the key decision makers—precisely the position that the Democrats coveted. (And that was precisely where, during the 1970s and 1980s, certain prominent members of the Democratic congressional majority were caught with their hands in the till.) By 2007, the tables had turned and the Democrats were in the majority—the very position in which lobbyists will want to shower them with favors.

Congressional Ethics
Practice Quiz

1. Who was the lobbyist ready to "name names" in 2006, sending shock waves across Washington?
   - **a.** "Tommy the Cork" Corcoran
   - **b.** Jack Abramoff
   - **c.** Heidi Fleiss
   - **d.** The K Street Gang
2. Most political scandals in the United States tend to occur in the executive branch.
   - **a.** true
   - **b.** false
3. Recent trends suggest that members of Congress have become *more* ethical than at any other time in our nation's history.
   - **a.** true
   - **b.** false
4. Why does the public think there have been more ethical violations in recent times?
   - **a.** The numbers graphically indicate that this is true.
   - **b.** The decline of religious belief among members of Congress contributes to this trend.
   - **c.** Society itself is simply more depraved and licentious.
   - **d.** There is simply much more reporting of ethical transgressions than in the past.

Answers: 1-b, 2-b, 3-a, 4-d.

Discussion Questions

1. Is there any connection between the strong ties that members of Congress have with special interest groups and problems with congressional ethics? Why or why not?
2. What impact does mass media coverage have on our perceptions of congressional ethics?

What YOU can do!

Make a short list of Congressional ethics violations discussed in the text. Visit the Bureau of Justice Statistics (**http://www.bjs.gov**), and look at nationwide statistics for similar crimes. How do the crime rates for average Americans compare to those of Congress as a whole? Let this lead you to a discussion of whether Americans expect their representatives to be "above average" when it comes to ethics and behavior.

Conclusion

Representation is the linchpin of our democracy. It is true that in some tiny communities, all citizens can participate directly in governmental decisions, but direct democracy is rare, is impracticable in all but the smallest settings, and presumes that all citizens *should* be involved in every decision. Our system relies on a small group to speak and act on behalf of the many. Ours is a representative republic, and few Americans would have it any other way.

Congress was established as the "first branch," because the framers believed it would be the part of our government closest to the people. Today, the real issues surrounding Congress have little to do with the value or legitimacy of legislative bodies or whether they should be seen as first among equals. Rather, what we worry about is how to make the system more efficient or more egalitarian. No one could realistically imagine getting rid of standing committees, leadership roles, or party structures, for instance, but at the same time, most people agree that these components do modify the character of the institution. Not every initiative that comes before Congress gets treated the same, and not every legislator has the same input in the process. What's more, for many Americans who are critical of Congress, the *kind* of person who gets to serve in our legislature raises deep questions about the breadth and quality of representation.

What does all this mean for individuals who want to change public policy by lobbying their representative or senator? For one thing, it means that many of Congress' organizational components create points of access. This also implies that the actors must be well versed in the nuances of legislative procedure—the precise route that measures travel from introduction to law, as well as the numerous pitfalls along the way. Insiders familiar with the complexity of the legislative process and having access to decision makers are in high demand. It is little wonder that former members of Congress are sought—and are very well paid—as lobbyists.

We might revel in the idea of a well-meaning, good-hearted "Mr. Smith" who goes to Washington, learns a few tricks, takes some bruises, and carries the day through grit and faith in the democratic process. (In 1939, the great actor James Stewart played this role in a famous film titled *Mr. Smith Goes to Washington* that you can watch on DVD or videotape. You will probably find the film rather naive and simplistic by today's standards.) We now know that Congress is a far more complex place than Mr. Smith could ever imagine. Still, average citizens *can* change the outcome of federal policy by lobbying members of Congress; it is a viable pathway of change today and will remain so in the future. A clear understanding of how legislatures work and where real power resides, however, is critical. Without this knowledge, the lobbying of decision makers pathway will give you no way out of the thick forest of legislative politics.

Key Objective Review, Apply, and Explore

The Nature and Style of Representation
(pages 212–215)

What is the job of a legislator? As simple as this question might seem, there are many approaches to "representation" and many ways a member of Congress might spend his or her time. Moreover, how members approach their work says a good deal about the way the entire legislature works and about the democratic character of our government.

KEY TERMS

Delegate Model of Representation 212
Trustee Model of Representation 212
Politico Model of Representation 212
Conscience Model of Representation 212
Constituent Service 214
Symbolic Representation 214

CRITICAL THINKING QUESTIONS

1. Is it possible that different groups of citizens will have different views about the appropriate model of representation? If so, what types of citizens would prefer each perspective?
2. A prominent scholar of the legislative process suggested that legislators have become individually responsive yet collectively irresponsible. What does this imply, and if true, does it bode poorly for the future of our system of government?

INTERNET RESOURCES

To learn more about the history of the U.S. Congress: **http://clerk.house.gov/histHigh/index.php**

ADDITIONAL READING

Fenno, Richard. *Homestyle: House Members in Their Districts.* Glenview, IL: Scott, Foresman, 1978.

Mayhew, David R. *Congress: The Electoral Connection.* New Haven, CT: Yale University Press, 1974.

Congress and the Constitution
(pages 216–223)

The framers of our system of government placed a great deal of faith in the legislative branch and provided it with clear, extensive powers. This section explores these powers and confronts their expansion over the last two centuries.

KEY TERMS

Bicameral Legislature 216
Seventeenth Amendment 217
Rotation 217
Pocket Veto 218
Elastic Clause (Necessary and Proper Clause) 218
At-Large District 219
Geographic Representation 219
Redistricting 219
Gerrymandering 219
Quorum 220
Majority-Minority District 221
***Baker* v. *Carr* (1961) 222**
Reapportionment 222

CRITICAL THINKING QUESTIONS

1. Why would the framers of our system provide the legislative branch with such sweeping powers? How is Congress different from the president or the courts?
2. Given the broad interpretation of the elastic clause, are there any limits to congressional policymaking? Put a bit differently, what are some of the checks on the legislature?

INTERNET RESOURCES

To read the specifics of Article I and to search for related court cases: **http://caselaw.lp.findlaw.com/data/constitution/article01**
To explore the Census Bureau's redistricting data: **http://www.census.gov/clo/www/redistricting.html**

ADDITIONAL READING

Devins, Neal, and Keith E. Whittington, eds., *Congress and the Constitution.* Durham, NC: Duke University Press, 2005.

Key Objective Review, Apply, and Explore

Organizing Congress: Committees

(pages 224–227)

Congress is comprised of 535 members, each with their own concerns and unique constituency. The forces promoting self-interest and individual action are great, but somehow, collective outcomes happen. One way this occurs is through committees, the workhorses of the legislature.

KEY TERMS

Subcommittees 224
Select Committees 224
Conference Committee 225
Joint Committees 225
Standing Joint Committees 225
Multiple Referrals 226
Hearings 226
Markup 226
Oversight 226

CRITICAL THINKING QUESTIONS

1. What are some of the disadvantages of relying upon a committee to decide the fate of a piece of legislation? Should a small group be able to "kill" a bill before other legislators get a chance to consider it?
2. If you were elected to Congress, on what sorts of committees would you wish to sit? Should this decision be based on your interests or on the concerns of your constituents?

INTERNET RESOURCES

Learn more about committees, specific pieces of legislation, roll call votes, and much more: **http://thomas.loc.gov**

ADDITIONAL READING

Davidson, Roger H., and Walter J. Oleszek. *Congress and Its Members* (10th ed.). Washington, D.C.: CQ Press, 2005.

Deering, Christopher J., and Steven S. Smith. *Committees in Congress* (3rd ed.). Washington, D.C.: CQ Press, 1997.

Organizing Congress: Political Parties and Leadership

(pages 228–231)

Americans often bemoan "partisanship" in Congress, but political parties and their leaders have served key organizing functions for over 200 years. And for all the talk of "nonpartisan" solutions and "independent-minded" legislators, the role of parties in Congress has actually increased in recent years.

KEY TERMS

Orientation Function 228
Voting Cues 228
Speaker 228
Majority Leader 228
Whip 229
President Pro Tempore 230
Minority Leader 230

CRITICAL THINKING QUESTIONS

1. Some would suggest that relying upon parties as a "voting cue" is a mistake—that legislators should weigh each issue on its own merits. Others suggest that party voting is a cost-saving, rational process. Who's right?
2. Does relying on powerful legislative leaders drastically limit the egalitarian nature of the national legislature?
3. Do you suppose there are common characteristics among successful legislative leaders? If so, what would those characteristics be?

INTERNET RESOURCES

Learn more about leadership in both chambers as well as party unity scores over time: **http://clerk.house.gov/histHigh/Congressional_History/index.php**

ADDITIONAL READING

Davidson, Roger H., Susan Webb Hammond, and Raymond W. Smock, eds. *Masters of the House.* Boulder, CO: Westview Press, 1998.

Key Objective Review, Apply, and Explore

Organizing Congress: Rules and Norms

(pages 232–235)

While there are important differences between the House and Senate, formal rules and informal norms of behavior help structure the legislative process in both chambers. Adherence to these modes of behavior streamlines the process, but they limit the democratic character of the process.

KEY TERMS

Unanimous Consent 232
Filibuster 232
Cloture 233
Hold 233
Seniority 233
Apprenticeship Norm 233
Specialization 234
Reciprocity/Logrolling 234
Earmarks/Pork-Barrel Legislation 234

CRITICAL THINKING QUESTIONS

1. Does it make sense that junior members of Congress should be deferential to more senior legislators? Shouldn't all legislators be on an equal footing? What purpose does seniority play?
2. How do rules like the filibuster sometimes stifle the will of the majority? What's the value of such rules anyway?

INTERNET RESOURCES

For an online directory of members of Congress and details of how to contact them: **http://www.visi.com/juan/congress**

ADDITIONAL READING

Matthews, Donald R. *U.S. Senators and Their World*. New York: Vintage Books, 1960.

Schroeder, Pat. *24 Years of House Work . . . and the Place Is Still a Mess: My Life in Politics.* Kansas City, MO: McMeel, 1998.

How a Bill Becomes a Law

(pages 236–239)

The process by which a bill becomes a law is complex, with numerous hurdles and pitfalls along the way. Some believe the process may be too difficult, but others argue that the bar should be high. Didn't the framers envision a slow, deliberate process, with numerous checks along the way?

KEY TERMS

Bill Sponsor 236
One-House Bill 236

CRITICAL THINKING QUESTIONS

1. Bills often die as a result of the lack of agreement between the House and Senate. Why do you suppose that happens? Do members from each chamber have different perspectives?
2. Are there any changes you would make to allow either easier or more difficult passage of legislation?

INTERNET RESOURCES

For an up-to-date look at what is happening on Capitol Hill: **http://www.rollcall.com**

Believe it or not, many students enjoy "Schoolhouse Rock" from their childhood. To view "How a Bill Becomes a Law," visit YouTube at: **http://www.youtube.com/watch?v=mEJL2Uuv-oQ**

ADDITIONAL READING

Hamilton, Lee. *How Congress Works and Why You Should Care*. Bloomington: Indiana University Press, 2004.

Rosenthal, Alan. *Heavy Lifting: The Job of the American Legislature*. Washington, D.C.: Congressional Quarterly, 2004.

Key Objective Review, Apply, and Explore

Who Sits in Congress

(pages 240–243)

Does the "people's branch" look like the rest of America? Does it matter that white males make up a vast majority of Congress? This section takes a look at the type of Americans called upon to represent the rest of us in Congress.

CRITICAL THINKING QUESTIONS

1. A former member of Congress, an outspoken feminist, once argued that we should amend the Constitution to ensure that each state send one woman and one man to the U.S. Senate. Does this make sense to you?
2. Do you suppose the outputs of the legislative process (new laws, appropriations) are shaped by the type of person who sits in Congress? Can you think of any problems that have been neglected by Congress because the white men that control the chamber "just don't get it"?

INTERNET RESOURCES

For an extensive look at the history of women in Congress: **http://womenincongress.house.gov/**

For a biographical database of all members of Congress, including your congressperson: **http://www.senate.gov/pagelayout/history/g_three_sections_with_teasers/people.htm**

ADDITIONAL READING

Bzdek, Vincent. *Woman of the House: The Rise of Nancy Pelosi.* New York: Palgrave Macmillan, 2008.

Congressional Ethics

(pages 244–245)

Long ago, a comedian once joked that our nation has "the best Congress money can buy." Today, many Americans share that sentiment, believing that most legislators are unethical and self-interested. But if Congress is filled with crooks, why are reelection rates generally above 95 percent?

CRITICAL THINKING QUESTIONS

1. If evidence suggests members of Congress are more ethical than in the past, why don't Americans feel better about the institution? Might high-profile scandals have an impact?
2. Do you think there would be less scandal in Congress if more women and minorities were elected?

INTERNET RESOURCES

For a detailed timeline of congressional scandals: **http://www.foxnews.com/story/0,2933,181733,00.html**

ADDITIONAL READING

Hilton, Stanley G., and Ann-Renee Testa. *Glass Houses: Shocking Profiles of Congressional Sex Scandals and Other Unofficial Misconduct.* New York: St. Martin's Press, 1998.

Stone, Peter. *Heist: Superlobbyist Jack Abramoff, His Republican Allies, and the Buying of Washington.* New York: Farrar, Straus and Giroux, 2006.

Chapter Review Critical Thinking Test

1. In recent years, Congress' mode of representation has shifted from a trustee to a delegate model. This has happened, in part, because
a. legislators no longer form strong political ideals of their own, so they follow the public's lead.
b. legislators are not as well educated as they used to be.
c. the public has become more capable of expressing their agendas to elected officials.
d. legislators care less about winning reelection and more about addressing the welfare of the public than in previous years.

2. Regarding representational style, members of Congress often decide to focus on either
a. national policy issues or the needs of their constituents.
b. the interests of lobbyists or the interests of their constituents.
c. the agenda of their own political party or a bipartisan agenda.
d. the dictates of their own conscience or the agenda of their senior colleagues.

3. How did the conflict between the Virginia Plan and the New Jersey Plan during the Constitutional Convention reflect two competing views of representation?
a. The former held that the states should be sovereign, and the latter held that individuals should be sovereign.
b. The former held that individuals should be sovereign, and the latter held that the states should be sovereign.
c. The former required legislators to be trustees of their constituents, and the latter required them to be delegates for their constituents.
d. The former required legislators to be delegates for their constituents, and the latter required them to be trustees of their constituents.

4. Legislative branch powers include
a. the power to veto legislation.
b. the power to declare legislation unconstitutional.
c. the power to regulate commerce.
d. the power to invoke executive privilege on behalf of the president.

5. What are majority-minority districts?
a. districts in which most minorities vote for a majority (usually white) candidate
b. districts in which most majority voters (usually white) vote for a minority candidate (usually African American or Latino)
c. districts designated by the Voting Rights Act as likely to produce the majority of the Congress' minority representatives
d. districts created through redistricting so that the majority of the voters in the district are minorities (African American, Latino, or Asian American, for example).

6. Reapportionment is the process whereby
a. members of Congress are required to represent more constituents per district because of population growth.
b. the number of seats granted each state is increased or decreased, depending on that state's population growth.
c. the total number of seats in the House is changed, depending on the national population growth.
d. districts within a state shift boundaries, depending on where most of the majority party's voters live.

7. In a 2006 case involving redistricting in Texas, the Supreme Court ruled that
a. states are free to draw redistricting lines as they want.
b. the Constitution does not prevent partisan redistricting.
c. redistricting in mid-decade (not just every 10 years) is legal.
d. a, b, and c

8. One of the advantages of the standing committee system in Congress is that
a. in a committee, seniority does not really matter.
b. committee membership changes frequently, so no small group of representatives possesses entrenched power over that committee.
c. committee deliberations slow the legislative process, which is what the framers of the Constitution intended.
d. Several issues can be considered simultaneously, thus improving efficiency.

9. The conference committee has been called
a. a "mini-legislature."
b. "the house of executive privilege."
c. "Congress's Congress."
d. "the third house of Congress."

10. About 90 percent of all proposed legislation stalls in committee and then dies, never reaching the chamber floor for a full vote.
a. true **b.** false

11. Markup happens in subcommittees, but what is it exactly?
a. a bill's sponsor's determination of the cost of enacting the legislature
b. the prime sponsor's working out of the language of the bill
c. adding amendments to a bill to make it more likely to pass the House or Senate
d. deciding which subcommittee considering the legislation will serve as the primary committee

12. Along with policymaking, congressional committees have what other crucial responsibility?
a. caucusing for partisan decision-making
b. adjusting a bill's language so that it is consistent with the bill in the other chamber
c. making sure that legislation gets properly implemented as federal law—that is, exercising congressional oversight
d. assessing the influence of special-interest groups on the committee's decision-making process

Chapter Review Critical Thinking Test

13. To investigate an issue or a matter of serious concern, the Senate or the House
- **a.** creates a committee for that particular investigation.
- **b.** uses the existing committee that best suits the circumstances.
- **c.** creates a joint Senate–House committee specifically for that investigation.
- **d.** either creates a special committee or uses an existing one that is appropriate for the circumstances.

14. Why should a student of congressional committees learn about Joseph McCarthy?
- **a.** He helped streamline committee work; the current efficiency of standing committees is due largely to his work.
- **b.** His anti-Communist crusade demonstrated, in a negative way, the high-profile committee investigations can attain.
- **c.** In 1924, he was the first senator on a judiciary committee to call into question the competence of a Supreme Court nominee.
- **d.** He was a Supreme Court nominee whose nomination notoriously failed in judiciary committee hearings.

15. Congressional committees are the principal decision-making structure of the legislative process.
- **a.** true
- **b.** false

16. When members of Congress need to vote on a measure in conference or on the chamber floor but have not had time to study the legislation in much depth,
- **a.** they invariably vote the way other representatives from their state vote.
- **b.** they often request a delay in the vote so they can bone up on the details.
- **c.** they vote the way they are told to vote by a memo from the national chairman of their party.
- **d.** they often infer and follow voting cues from the positions that senior members in their party have already staked out.

17. Rules in the Senate have the effect of giving individual senators, even when they are in the minority on an issue, much more leverage and freedom to express themselves than House rules grant individual representatives.
- **a.** true
- **b.** false

18. What is an example of a significant "folkway" in Congress?
- **a.** filibuster
- **b.** floor debate
- **c.** logrolling
- **d.** cloture

19. Because women's rights have been championed by male legislators and white legislators worked tirelessly against slavery and segregation,
- **a.** we can safely assume that Congress will always gradually move forward on civil rights issues.
- **b.** we should not automatically assume that the underrepresentation of women and minorities in Congress is a political problem for women and minorities nationwide.
- **c.** there is no reason for activists to try to improve the representation of women and minorities in Congress.
- **d.** no real progress is now needed in the area of civil rights.

20. On the whole, Congress is filled with well-to-do, white male lawyers.
- **a.** true
- **b.** false

Answers: 1-b, 2-a, 3-a, 4-c, 5-d, 6-b, 7-d, 8-c, 9-d, 10-a, 11-b, 12-c, 13-d, 14-b, 15-a, 16-d, 17-a, 18-c, 19-b, 20-a.

You decide!

Few Americans realize they can be directly involved in the legislative process. Anyone can write a bill and submit it to a member of Congress to be introduced in a legislative session. Identify a policy issue that has a direct impact on you and your peers. Then get the ball rolling by drafting a bill to address your concerns. Be sure to consider where the bill might fit into existing law, and be careful to use precise legislative language (visit the House or Senate Web sites for examples of legislative proposals). You might also get pointers from local interest groups who have drafted legislation. Find a potential sponsor by identifying members of Congress who also have an interest in your issue. Finally, visit with the legislators who might be potential sponsors. Be prepared to explain the importance of your proposal and the depth of support that it would have in the public.

Key Objective Outline

What are the forces that lead to presidential success or failure? How does one define presidential greatness?

Presidential Greatness
(page 276)

CHAPTER 7
THE PRESIDENCY

Have expanded presidential powers transformed the democratic nature of our system?

It is not unusual for presidents to hold "photo ops" events designed to capture the public's attention in order to sway policymakers. So it was not out of the ordinary when President George W. Bush decided to promote his education reform agenda by visiting the Emma E. Booker Elementary School in Sarasota, Florida, in early fall of 2001. The plan for the event was simple: The president was to talk to teachers and administrators and then sit with the children at a reading appreciation workshop.

This, however, was September 11, 2001. Shortly before President Bush sat down with the preschoolers, his staff informed him that a plane had just crashed into the North Tower of the World Trade Center in lower Manhattan at 8:45 A.M. Everyone, including the president, assumed that a horrible accident had occurred. Not wanting to disturb the children and break his schedule, the president continued his meeting with teachers and administrators and then sat down with the children to read *My Pet Goat*. Within a few minutes, the "horrible accident" turned into one of the most infamous events in America's history. At 9:03 A.M., a second plane crashed into the South Tower of the World Trade Center. This was no random mishap or accident; it was a strategic strike. The planes had been hijacked, and the United States had come under attack.

Within a blink of an eye, the role of the American president can be transformed from an actor at a public relations event to the most important person in the world. As commander in chief of the largest military in history, the American president is at the center of world affairs. As the events on September 11th unfolded, all thoughts turned to the victims of the horrific event—and to the whereabouts, safety, and actions of President George W. Bush.

STUDENT RESOURCE-CENTER
• Glossary
• Vocabulary Example
• LINK
• MyPoliSc Lab Connection

Prerogative Power: Extraordinary powers that the president may use under certain conditions.

EXAMPLE: *Lincoln jailed several northern newspaper editors who opposed Union Army efforts during the Civil War.*

CONNECT THE LINK (Chapter **2**, pages **58–59**) What did the framers of our system of government have in mind for the presidency?

The President and the Constitution (pages 256–257)

Why did the framers set aside concerns about the potential for abuse and bestow the executive branch with real powers?

The framers were ambivalent about the exact role that the executive branch would have under the Constitution. The history of strong executives with whom the framers were familiar was unsettling. From the very beginning of history, whenever human beings came together to form governments, the result was either autocracy (rule by one) or oligarchy (rule by a few).[1] Yet governing systems without executive power seemed inept, ripe for discord and anarchy. The framers were well versed in the philosophies of Hobbes, Montesquieu, and other theorists of the seventeenth and eighteenth centuries. These thinkers agreed that although we might wish for a political system without a powerful executive, governments that had none had proved ineffectual and short-lived. The English political philosopher John Locke, who was the thinker most admired by the framers of our Constitution, argued that legislative politics should be at the heart of a limited government—but also that it was necessary to give executives the powers to do "several things of their own free choice, where the law is silent, and sometimes, too, against the direct letter of the law, for the public good."[2] Locke called such action **prerogative power**.

Moreover, the experience under the Articles of Confederation suggested the need for a strong executive, for under the Articles, the national government lacked the power and the ability to respond quickly to emergencies. Advocates of an effective executive also had an ideal republican leader readily at hand: George Washington, the hero of the Revolution.[3]

At the Philadelphia Constitutional Convention in 1787 (see LINK Chapter 2, pages 58–59), the first scheme for a new government that the delegates discussed, the Virginia Plan, was vague about the executive branch. This plan was unclear on the basic questions of whether one person or a group of people would hold executive power, how long the term of office would be, whether the president could be reelected, and even what the precise powers of the presidency should be. The Virginia Plan's principal author, James Madison, was unsure about all these questions. The second scheme to emerge at the convention, the New Jersey Plan, was clearly more state centered, and although many of its provisions regarding the executive branch were also vague, it envisioned a relatively weak office. As months passed and few key questions about the executive were resolved, the weak model gained support. But then, concerned that the executive branch would be overwhelmed by the power of the legislature, some of the most prominent and most talented delegates pushed for a stronger model. James Wilson and Gouverneur Morris, both representing Pennsylvania, worked hard in the convention's sessions and in private meetings with other delegates to strengthen the executive office's constitutional powers. The "pro-executive" group grew and won victory after victory.[4] Shall the president have real powers—that is, shall presidents be authentic players in the system or merely administrators of what Congress decides? The answer was yes. The Constitutional Convention aimed to create a national government with real power. Therefore, argued the framers, the powers of the presidency should be real and significant. There would be no blank checks, wrote one scholar, and nearly all the presidential powers would be shared with Congress, but presidents were meant to be significant players in the system.[5] The principal powers granted by the Constitution to presidents allowed them to influence the judiciary by appointing judges to the bench, to have a modest say in making legislation, to conduct foreign policy, and to be the commander of the nation's armed forces during times of war. As we'll see in this chapter, these formal powers have proved to be merely the foundation of presidential authority.

Article II and Ratification of the Constitution

Previous chapters have noted that many of the fears about the new system were calmed by the central place that the legislature would have. But if Article I (the legislative branch) calmed citizens' fears, Article II raised their alarm. What was this "presidency," and what sorts of power would its occupants have? How long would this person serve? What would stop this person from gaining too much power and becoming another tyrant? Moreover, the scheme laid out in Article II was unfamiliar. As noted by a leading presidential scholar, "Not only was the presidency the most obvious innovation in the proposed plan of government, but its unitary nature and strong powers roused fears of the most horrifying political specter that most Americans could imagine: a powerful monarchy."[6]

Both proponents and opponents of the Constitution presented their arguments in the form of essays published in newspapers. Several essays in opposition were published under the pseudonym **Cato** in the *New York Journal*. One piece, appearing on September 27, 1787, only 10 days after conclusion of the Constitutional Convention, was a powerful assault on the executive branch:

> The deposit of vast trusts in the hands of a single magistrate, enables him in their exercise, to create a numerous train of dependents—this tempts his *ambition,* which in a republican magistrate is also remarked, *to be pernicious* and the duration of his office for any considerable time favors his views, gives him the means and time to perfect and execute his designs—*he therefore fancies that he may be great and glorious by oppressing his*

■ **Cato:** The pseudonym for a writer of a series of articles in opposition to the ratification of the Constitution.

SIGNIFICANCE: *This person, who many believe was George Clinton of New York, offered a thoughtful critique on the wisdom of broad executive powers. Many of his arguments resonate today.*

This picture by H. Brueckner is called *The Prayer at Valley Forge.* It is not possible to overstate the public's esteem for George Washington. In fact, much of the ambiguity in the Constitution regarding presidential powers springs from the near blind faith the framers had in Washington. ***—What was it about Washington that brought him this kind of trust?***

fellow citizens, and raising himself to permanent grandeur on the ruins of his country. [Emphasis in original.]

Cato seemed to hit the nail on the head: The scheme outlined by the framers would allow the president to use his long term of office to take such a firm hold of the reins of power that it would ruin the democratic experiment.

Alexander Hamilton had the difficult chore of countering Cato's argument. Simply put, he had to ease fears about the presidency, and he undertook that task in *The Federalist Papers,* particularly *Federalist No. 69*. There, Hamilton sought to "place in a strong light the unfairness of such representations" of the proposed executive branch. He notes that while the king gains his post through heredity and holds it throughout his life, the president is elected for only 4 years. The president can be impeached for treason, bribery, and other high crimes or misdemeanors, but the king can be subjected to no punishment—he is "sacred and inviolable." A president may be able to veto legislation, but this decision can be overridden by the legislature. A king's judgment, however, is absolute. Repeatedly, Hamilton works to underscore the differences between a king and a president, and with much effect. But it was not persuasive arguments that carried the day; rather, it was public sentiment toward one political leader. Everyone knew that George Washington would be the first president. He had not abused his authority as the commanding officer of the Continental Army, and many simply could not imagine such a great man amassing power and making himself a king. Faith in Washington allowed citizens to overcome their fears (for the moment) about a powerful executive.

> **"Did people really think they would end up with a monarch, after all they'd been through in the Revolution?"**
>
> —Student Question

The President and the Constitution
Practice Quiz

1. Although he asserted that legislative authority should be central to a limited government, John Locke also believed that an executive figure should be able to
   - **a.** exercise prerogative power in some circumstances, even if it runs counter to the law of the land.
   - **b.** execute the laws of the legislature when he believes them to be appropriate.
   - **c.** declare martial law if the country slips into chaos.
   - **d.** dissolve the legislature if it can no longer function effectively.
2. Among the principal powers granted to the president by the Constitution is the power to
   - **a.** conduct foreign policy
   - **b.** appoint judges
   - **c.** act as commander in chief of the armed forces
   - **d.** a, b, and c
3. During the formation of the Constitution, one strong argument for granting substantial authority to the executive branch was
   - **a.** the geographic breadth of the United States.
   - **b.** the precedent of strong monarchical rule in England.
   - **c.** George Washington's effective campaigning for such a position.
   - **d.** George Washington himself.
4. The experience under the Articles of Confederation mattered to the framers' discussion of the presidency because
   - **a.** that experience made it clear the national government needed a decisive commanding figure.
   - **b.** Washington, the acting president during that experience, had executed his duties very effectively.
   - **c.** that experience demonstrated how ineffective the new state governors were.
   - **d.** Washington, the nominal president during that experience, was not allowed to be an effective president.

Answers: 1-a, 2-d, 3-d, 4-a.

Discussion Questions

1. The framers of the Constitution intended that the president *share* powers with the other branches of federal government, especially Congress. Is this true today, or does the presidency seem the most powerful branch? Why or why not?
2. "Cato" worried the president "fancies that he may be great and glorious by oppressing his fellow citizens. . . ." Is this a legitimate worry for citizens today? Why or why not?

What **YOU** can do!

Visit the Web sites of the Republican (**http://www.gop.org**) ar cratic (**http://www.dnc.org**) parties to read about their appropriate scope of executive power, given a post-9/11

CONNECT THE LINK
(Chapter **6**, page **216**) Why did the framers of our system of government see the legislature as the core of the government?

Whig Model: A theory of restrained presidential powers; the idea that presidents should use only the powers explicitly granted in the Constitution.

SIGNIFICANCE: *Most nineteenth-century presidents held this view, leading to a legislative-centered government.*

The Evolution of the Presidency (pages 258–265)

What are the changes that have lead to the expansion of presidential powers?

The fact that the Constitution *allows* a powerful president is not the same as *mandating* a powerful executive. Article II is less clear than other parts of the Constitution. As such, the scope of presidential powers has been a function of the men who have served in the position and used those powers. Aggressive leaders have been able to use the vagueness of the Constitution to their advantage. In addition, the overall evolution of the presidency has been toward ever-greater powers, so much so that today few of us can imagine a time when the president was not the center of the federal government. But indeed, there have been such times in our history.

Models of Presidential Power

As we saw in LINK Chapter 6, page 216, the framers of our system believed that Congress would be the primary branch of government. And that was precisely what occurred during the first century of our nation's history. Presidents did not dominate the federal government for most of the nineteenth century; they seemed quite willing to follow Congress. There were, of course, strong presidents, such as George Washington, Thomas Jefferson, Andrew Jackson, and Abraham Lincoln. They were exceptions to the rule, however, and their powers sprang from extraordinary circumstances.

There were a number of reasons why it made sense that the presidency was not at the center of nineteenth-century American government.

First, the national economy still centered on agriculture. Aggressive supervision and guidance of economic matters was not as important during this time as it would be after industrialization and urbanization took hold, as they did by the 1890s.

Second, the United States was not a central player in world affairs. It was not until the twentieth century that the United States became a world power, involved in military, diplomatic, and economic activities across the globe.

Third, nineteenth-century political campaigning was party centered, with less emphasis on presidential candidates and more attention to party platforms and the entire "ticket"—the slate of party candidates, most of whom were running for legislative seats.

On top of this was the general belief among presidents themselves that they should not be at the center of government. Most nineteenth-century presidents—and a few twentieth-century ones—held closely to the idea that presidents are limited to the powers *explicitly* stated in the Constitution. This has been dubbed the **Whig model** of presidential powers. Presidents should not go beyond those constitutional powers or the additional powers explicitly granted to the executive branch by Congress in the years since the Constitution was written. This attitude ensured that presidents would take a passive approach to presidential powers, and it placed the executive branch in a more acquiescent position.

This view of executive power, however, had begun to erode by the end of the nineteenth century. This resulted in part from changing economic and geopolitical conditions. The nation's economy was shifting from farming to industry, and our position in global affairs was expanding. Moreover—and perhaps most significant—some of the men who occupied the White House after 1901 transformed the job of the president.

Most historians agree that the first truly assertive president who did not confront extraordinary circumstances was Theodore Roosevelt (1901–1909). Before becoming president, Roosevelt had been a vigorous, reform-minded governor of New York. There he learned the power of shaping public opinion and using public support to push his reform agenda through the state legislature. As president, he took the same route, transforming the office into a unique opportunity to preach to and inspire a "national congregation." It was becoming clear that by speaking out on controversial issues, the president could shape public opinion and direct the policy process. And TR, as the press called Roosevelt, was exceedingly good at it. According to one historian, "As a master of political theater with an instinctive understanding of how to dramatize himself and the policies he favored, TR was our first modern media president, and a brilliant huckster."[7]

Teddy Roosevelt held firmly to a new view of presidential powers, one with no restrictions on presidential authority except those that are strictly *forbidden* in the Constitution. This perspective, often referred to as the **stewardship model**, reversed the earlier approach: Instead of using only the powers expressly granted, Roosevelt believed that *all* was possible *except* what was prohibited. This was especially true, he argued, when the good of the nation was at stake. Looking back on his presidency, TR boasted, "I did not usurp power, but I did greatly broaden the use of executive power . . . I acted for the common well-being of our people . . . in whatever manner was necessary, unless prevented by direct constitutional or legislative prohibition."[8]

Not all the presidents who came after Roosevelt shared his activist views of presidential power. For example, his successor, William Howard Taft (1909–1913), took a more passive view of the

■ **Stewardship Model:** A theory of robust, broad presidential powers; the idea that the president is only limited by explicit restrictions in the Constitution.

EXAMPLE: *Theodore Roosevelt was a powerful, activist president.*

■ **Modern Presidency:** A political system in which the president is the central figure and participates actively in both foreign and domestic policy.

EXAMPLE: *Franklin D. Roosevlet, with his New Deal Program, ushered in an executive-centered system.*

Theodore Roosevelt believed that presidents should use their position to articulate values, offer policy alternatives, and challenge accepted wisdom. That is to say, presidents should lead public opinion rather than simply follow it. ***—But what if this "bullish" advocacy leads to a divided public? Should presidents be responsible for finding compromises and common ground?***

presidency. But activism returned to the White House with Woodrow Wilson, the twenty-eighth president (1913–1921). Wilson was very much a stewardship-model president. He believed that the president should lead not only in national politics but also in international relations. Following World War I, Wilson set his sights on creating an international body to settle disputes between nations, which he called the League of Nations and which he unsuccessfully tried to have the United States join. (The League was the predecessor of the United Nations, which the United States would help form at the end of World War II.) Wilson's efforts have not been lost on historians such as Robert Dallek, who wrote, "No vision in twentieth-century presidential politics has inspired greater hope of human advance or has done more to secure a president's reputation as a great leader than Wilson's peace program of 1918–1919."[9] Like Theodore Roosevelt, however, Wilson was followed in office

"How did FDR get people to accept his idea of a strong president?"

—Student Question

by successors who followed the Whig model by deferring to congressional leadership: Warren G. Harding (1921–1923), Calvin Coolidge (1923–1929), and to a lesser extent, Herbert Hoover (1929–1933).

The election to the presidency in 1932 of Franklin Delano Roosevelt shattered the restrained approach to the presidency and ushered in what many historians would describe as the **modern presidency**■. Roosevelt—a distant cousin of TR and, like him, a former governor of New York—ran for the White House at the depths of the Great Depression. He swept into the presidency on a wave of public anger, frustration, fear, and perceived weakness of his predecessor, Herbert Hoover. Within a day of being sworn in, FDR took charge of the federal government. With panicked depositors withdrawing their savings from bank accounts (which at the time were not insured) and thus threatening the country's banking system with collapse, his first move was to declare a national bank holiday—something that most people doubted he had the legal authority to do. Legally or not, Roosevelt ordered every bank in the country temporarily closed until federal inspectors could go through its books and declare it sound, thus reassuring depositors. Then, with equally dubious legality, he banned the buying and selling of gold and halted the practice of linking the value of the dollar to the price of gold. Next, he sent Congress an emergency banking reform bill, which the House passed in 38 minutes and the Senate accepted with very little debate that same night. This was just the beginning of a comprehensive package of measures designed to pull the nation out of the economic crisis. During the Hundred Days, as it was called, Roosevelt submitted to Congress a stream of proposed reform measures, all of which were quickly enacted into law. Roosevelt demanded "action—and action now." The New Deal, the name he gave to his series of programs and initiatives that transformed the national government, gave birth to the welfare state and shaped the modern presidency.[10]

Today, there no longer seems to be any question regarding the proactive role of the executive branch. Presidents are expected to lead the nation. They must come up with innovative solutions to our problems, give aid and comfort to American citizens in times of need, maintain a healthy and growing economy, and protect our nation from foreign and domestic threats. In times of peace and prosperity, we congratulate the president (who expects to be rewarded in the polls and at the ballot box), and in bad times, we place the blame squarely on the White House. This transformation has thus presented

COMPARATIVE
Comparing Executive Branches

■ **Cabinet:** A group of presidential advisers, primarily the secretaries of federal departments.

EXAMPLE: *As Secretary of State, Condoleezza Rice was an important member of George W. Bush's cabinet.*

presidents with a double-edged sword, but there is little question that the stewardship model, first articulated by Theodore Roosevelt, guides the contemporary presidency. Presidents have no choice but to lead—or else stand condemned as failures.

Institutional Changes

Along with changes regarding the role of the chief executive in the federal government have come changes within the institution of the presidency. We refer here to the support staff and the various offices and agencies designed to help the president succeed, as well as to the changing role of the vice president.

"The Constitution didn't even mention a cabinet, did it?"
—Student Question

THE CABINET Since the very beginning, presidents have relied on their staff. The framers of the Constitution rejected the idea of creating any type of council of presidential advisers, but once in office, Washington immediately realized that specific executive departments should handle the responsibilities of the federal government. The people who took charge of these departments became the president's **cabinet**■ (see Table 7.1). The cabinet consists of the secretaries of the major departments of the bureaucracy on whom the president relies heavily to carry out public policy. These officials are appointed by the president and are confirmed by the Senate. They can be removed at the president's will without the consent of the Senate. Unlike in parliamentary systems, members of the cabinet cannot also be members of Congress: The Constitution dictates that no one can hold more than one post in the federal government at the same time.

In Washington's administration, there were four cabinet members: secretary of state (Thomas Jefferson), to handle foreign affairs; secretary of the treasury (Alexander Hamilton); attorney general (John Marshall); and secretary of war (Henry Knox), in charge of the U.S. Army. In later administrations, a secretary of the navy was added, and after that, secretaries of the interior, commerce, agriculture, labor, and other departments. Some recent presidents expanded their cabinet by creating new departments. Jimmy Carter pushed Congress to create the Department of Education. Following the terrorist attacks

TABLE 7.1 | Departments of the United States Cabinet

Presidents have always surrounded themselves with policy advisers, especially as the powers and duties of the executive branch broadened with FDR's administration. One source of support comes from the cabinet. Why have the number of cabinet positions increased over time?

DEPARTMENT	CREATED	RESPONSIBILITIES
State	1789	Create foreign policies and treaties
Treasury	1789	Coin money, regulate national banks, and collect income taxes
War, Defense	1789, 1947	Security and defense
Interior	1849	Maintain national parks and natural resources
Agriculture	1862	Protect farmland, nature, and wildlife; provide resources to rural and low-income families; ensure agricultural products are safe for consumers
Justice	1789	Ensure justice and public safety by enforcing the law
Commerce	1903	Promote economic stability, growth, and international trade
Labor	1913	Protect the rights of working citizens and retirees; monitor changes in employment and economic settings
Health and Human Services	1953	Promote research; provide immunizations and health care to low-income families; ensure safety of food and drugs
Housing and Urban Development	1965	Guarantee everyone a right to affordable housing; enhance communities and increase the number of homeowners
Transportation	1966	Provide an efficient and safe transportation system that meets the needs of the American people
Energy	1977	Provide reliable energy and promote science while protecting the environment and national and economic securities
Education	1979	Ensure that all citizens can obtain a quality education
Veterans Affairs	1989	Provide support for the nation's veterans
Homeland Security	2002	Protect the United States from threats

SOURCES: http://www.whitehouse.gov; cabinet web sites.

Inner Cabinet: The advisers considered most important to the president—usually the secretaries of the departments of State, Defense, Treasury, and Justice.

EXAMPLE: *As Attorney General and brother to the president, Robert Kennedy was a key inner cabinet member in JFK's administration.*

Executive Office of the President (EOP): A group of presidential staff agencies created in 1939 that provides the president with help and advice.

SIGNIFICANCE: *These various offices provide presidents with massive amounts of information and advice, allowing him or her to remain at the center of domestic and foreign policy.*

of September 11, 2001, George W. Bush and Congress created a new cabinet-level agency, the Office of Homeland Security, soon transformed into the Department of Homeland Security.

Different presidents have used their cabinet in different ways. Some, such as Andrew Jackson, Dwight D. Eisenhower, Gerald Ford, and Jimmy Carter, staffed their cabinets with their closest advisers and allies. Other presidents have kept their cabinet at arm's length, consulting with members only for routine matters or for policy concerns within their particular area. John Kennedy once commented, "Cabinet meetings are simply useless . . . Why should the Postmaster General sit there and listen to a discussion of the problems of Laos?"[11] Bill Clinton rarely spoke directly with many of his cabinet officers, and Ronald Reagan once mistook his secretary of urban affairs for another official when they were later introduced. Furthermore, most presidents informally establish an "inner" and an "outer" cabinet, with the former being the most important secretaries, usually those representing the departments of State, Defense, Treasury, and Justice. Members of the **inner cabinet** have more access to the president and are considered closer advisers.

EXECUTIVE OFFICE OF THE PRESIDENT Before Franklin Roosevelt, all presidents had a handful of clerks and personal assistants. A few nineteenth-century presidents also relied on informal input from a trusted circle of advisers—for example, the political cronies whom Andrew Jackson named his "kitchen cabinet," who were not part of his official cabinet. As the role of the president in developing and carrying out federal programs expanded, however, so did the number of his personal advisers. FDR needed lots of experts, a great deal of information, and more staff, and he pushed hard for institutional changes. The greatest single leap in this direction was the creation of the **Executive Office of the President (EOP)** in 1939. An act of Congress established a number of groups of advisers under the broad heading of the EOP, including the White House staff, the Bureau of the Budget, and the Office of Personnel Management. Through the years, new divisions have been created, including the National Security Council, the Council of Economic Advisers, and the Office of Management and Budget. In George W. Bush's administration, the EOP consisted of many offices, each with a group of members and a large support staff (see Table 7.2).

> "So many offices and boards! Are they all necessary?"
> —Student Question

Each component of the EOP is important, but some have proved more significant than others. The **National Security Council (NSC)** was established in 1947, and although its membership varies from administration to administration, it always includes the vice president and the secretaries of defense and state. The job of the NSC is to provide the president with information and advice on all matters concerning national security, including foreign and domestic threats. One of the key players of this group is the **national security adviser.** This person is appointed by the president without confirmation and is not officially connected with the Department of State or the Department of Defense. As such, he or she is expected to give the president independent, unbiased advice on important national security matters. The **Office of Management and Budget (OMB)** has a number of sweeping responsibilities, including preparing the president's annual national budget proposal, monitoring the performance of federal agencies, and overseeing regulatory proposals. The **Council of Economic Advisers (CEA),** established in 1946, is led by three members—usually eminent economists—who are appointed by the president and confirmed by the Senate. Its duties include assisting

TABLE 7.2 | Executive Office of the President in 2008

- Council of Economic Advisers
- Council on Environmental Quality
- National Security Council
- Office of Administration
- Office of Management and Budget
- Office of National Drug Control Policy
- Office of Science and Technology Policy
- President's Foreign Intelligence Advisory Board
- United States Trade Representative
- White House Office
- Office of the Chief of Staff
- Office of Strategic Initiatives and External Affairs
- National Economic Council
- Domestic Policy Council
- Homeland Security Council
- Office of the White House Counsel
- Office of Legislative Affairs
- Office of the First Lady
- White House Management and Administration
- White House Office of Presidential Personnel
- Office of Presidential Advance
- White House Staff Secretary
- White House Office of Communications
- Other Presidential Staff
- Office of the Vice President

■ **Office of Management and Budget (OMB):** A Cabinet-level office that monitors federal agencies and provides the president with expert advice on policy-related topics.

SIGNIFICANCE: *The OMB is one of many offices that have broadened the scope of presidential power in recent decades.*

One of the best known national security advisors, and one who still advises presidents from time to time, is Henry Kissinger. Kissinger advised President Nixon during the Vietnam War, from 1969 until its end in 1974. ***—To what extent do you think presidents should depend on advisers like Kissinger, who aren't elected and don't answer to the people?***

the president in preparing an annual economic report to Congress, gathering timely information concerning economic developments and trends, evaluating the economic impact of various federal programs and activities, developing and recommending policies that boost the nation's economy, and making recommendations on economy-related policies and legislation.

PATHWAYS | of action

FDR Takes Charge!

When Franklin D. Roosevelt began his presidency in 1933, voters were looking for bold leadership and dramatic changes. Understanding his mandate, Roosevelt rolled up his sleeves and took the lead in redirecting the federal government. In doing so, he forever transformed the nature of the presidency. Many of the ideas for his New Deal programs came from a group of advisers, some of them college professors or other intellectuals, whom he called his "Brain Trust." Roosevelt's advisers and cabinet members did not always agree with one another—sometimes, in fact, their ideas were flatly contradictory—but in the crisis, FDR was willing to try anything that seemed as if it might work. In fact, his leadership style included always listening to advice from different viewpoints, always making the final decision himself, and always keeping his options open to try something else.

A partial list of Roosevelt's policy achievements included the Federal Deposit Insurance Corporation (FDIC), which insured savings deposits to prevent future banking crises; the Securities and Exchange Commission (SEC), which protects investors from fraudulent stock market practices; the Wagner Act of 1935, which strengthened the organizing power of labor unions; and several measures designed to help homeowners finance mortgages and keep their homes. Maximum work hours and minimum wages were also set for certain industries in 1938. The most far-reaching of all the New Deal programs, however, was **Social Security**■, enacted in 1935 and expanded in 1939, which provided old-age and widows' benefits, unemployment compensation, disability insurance, and welfare programs for mothers with dependent children. (Medicare and Medicaid were added to Social Security in 1964.) ■

Along with the expansion of presidential responsibilities has come a rapid growth in the president's personal staff. Today, the White House Office is a critical part of the Executive Office of the President. As you might expect, FDR expanded his personal staff significantly, to an average of 47. This number grew to 200 under Harry Truman and to 555 under Nixon. When Ronald Reagan left office, some 600 full-time employees had been working for him. These days, the number of White House staffers hovers around 500, scattered through numerous offices. The most important of the president's personal staff assistants is the *chief of staff*. Presidents have used their chiefs of staff differently; some have been granted more control and autonomy than others. Generally speaking, the chief of staff is especially close to the president and oversees all that the president might do on a typical workday, including who is allowed to meet the chief executive, what documents the president reads, and even what issues take up the president's time. Needless to say, this gatekeeping role makes the chief of staff one of the most important figures not only in the executive branch but also in the entire federal government.

RAMIFICATIONS OF STAFFING CHANGES Many observers of the American presidency have noted that the nature of the office has been transformed by the dramatic expansion of the presidential staff. The modern presidency is no longer what it originally was—a one-person job. Today, it is a massive network of

Social Security: A federal program started in 1935 that taxes wages and salaries to pay for retirement benefits, disability insurance, and hospital insurance. **SIGNIFICANCE:** *This federal "safety net" program, and many others, changed the relationship between citizens and the federal government.*

Institutional Presidency: The concept of the presidency as a working collectivity, a massive network of staff, analysts, and advisers with the president as its head. **SIGNIFICANCE:** *This term captures the meaning of an important shift in American politics—one where the president is placed at the center of both foreign and domestic politics.*

offices, staff, and advisers, requiring a complex organizational chart to keep track of duties and responsibilities. This change broadened presidential powers, because this massive network of staff has allowed presidents to be central to the policy process. Scholars now use the term **institutional presidency** to describe the burgeoning responsibilities and scope of presidential powers. Some suggest that the massive expansion of support staff has tipped the balance of power between the branches. It is little wonder, some would argue, that the president is now at the center of the federal government and that Congress has, in some respects, taken a back seat. The expansion of staff coincided with the changing perspective of presidential powers; some observers argue that this expansion played a key role in this change. It is true that over the years, congressional staffs have also increased, but not nearly at the pace of those in the executive branch. Others also point out that the duties and responsibilities of modern presidents have greatly expanded, making all this support necessary. And as you will see when we discuss the many jobs of the president, the list is, indeed, quite long. So perhaps, given these new obligations, the scales of power between the two branches have not been thrown drastically off-balance.

A second ramification has been growing internal conflict—that is, the balance of power *within* the executive branch seems to be shifting. It is true, as we've seen, that some recent presidents have relied on their cabinet officers more than others have. In the past, however, cabinet secretaries and other policy experts played a key role in the executive branch. The president could always reject their advice, but it was taken for granted that they would have the president's ear—that they would provide counsel on important issues. This has been changing in recent decades. As presidents have surrounded themselves with White House staff, who were essentially *political* experts—with the goal of helping their boss win reelection, boost his poll ratings, and build his historical legacy—policy advisers have been pushed to the side. That is to say, the battle for the president's ear has become intense, and most analysts agree that the political experts are winning over the "policy wonks."

Finally, when it comes to shaping the outcome of government, the explosion of executive branch staff has made citizen action a bit more complex. On the one hand, we might say that the number of people to talk to has increased, quite similar to what we saw in LINK Chapter 6, pages 224–227, in the case of Congress. Persuading a staffer close to the president can often be an effective means of shaping public policy. On the other hand, direct access to the president has become quite difficult. In an effort to protect their boss, White House aides may well be transforming the connection between the president and the people.

Riding a wave of popular support, Franklin D. Roosevelt transformed the nature of the presidency and the federal government. His New Deal program ushered in a series of programs and policies designed to pull the nation out of the Great Depression. In doing so, he forever placed the executive branch squarely at the center of American politics. ***—What would the framers think about the burgeoning powers of the executive?***

PATHWAYS | profile

Condoleezza Rice, Secretary of State and Political Scientist

Born in segregated Birmingham, Alabama, in 1954, Condoleezza Rice is the daughter of John Wesley Rice, who was a school guidance counselor and Presbyterian minister, and Angelena Rice, a schoolteacher. She excelled in her studies and became an outstanding pianist at an early age. She received a Bachelor of Arts degree in political science from the University of Denver in 1974 and, within a year, had received a Master of Arts degree from the University of Notre Dame. Rice then attended the University of Denver, where she received a Ph.D. in international studies in 1981—the same year she became a faculty member in the Political Science Department at Stanford University, where she became provost at the stunningly young age of 39.

Having worked briefly in George H.W. Bush's administration, Rice in 1999 became a key foreign policy adviser to his son, George W. Bush, as he prepared to run for the White House. After his election, she was named national security adviser, a key adviser to the president, and became a central figure in shaping the nation's foreign policy after the terrorist attacks on September 11, 2001.

Two of George Bush's closest advisors were Karl Rove (above) and Secretary of State Condoleezza Rice (below). Rove was a brilliant political strategist, and Rice an expert in foreign policy. One of the growing conflicts in the White House is access to the president. ***—In which situations might the interests of policy conflict with those of political advisors?***

This included, among other things, helping to craft the Iraqi war plan. On January 26, 2005, Rice was named secretary of state, becoming only the second woman—and the first African-American woman—in U.S. history to hold that post.

Rice's future is bright. Although she has suggested that she will return to academia after leaving the White House, there has been speculation about her prospects for a political career. Although she is a controversial figure because of her steadfast support of President George W. Bush's decision to invade Iraq, few people question Rice's qualifications or her intelligence. ■

CONNECT THE LINK

(Chapter **6**, pages **224–227**) How does the committee system afford citizens numerous points of access?

The Changing Role of the Vice President

Throughout most of American history, the vice presidency was considered an insignificant office. Benjamin Franklin once quipped that the vice president should be addressed as "your Superfluous Excellency."[12] Thomas Marshall, the vice president under Woodrow Wilson, once told a story of two brothers: "One ran away to sea; the other was elected vice president. And nothing was heard of either of them again."[13] In 1848, Senator Daniel Webster—who as one of his party's most influential figures had long hoped to gain the presidency—declined the vice presidential place on the Whig Party ticket. "I do not propose to be buried until I am dead," he snorted.[14] John Nance Garner, FDR's first vice president and a former speaker of the House, is quoted as saying that the vice presidency is "not worth a pitcher of warm spit."[15]

> "What does the vice president do? Does he just wait and see if the president gets sick or dies?"
>
> — Student Question

When Lyndon B. Johnson was asked by John Kennedy to be his running mate, the powerful Texas senator was reluctant to accept. Like Webster, LBJ worried about his political future. The job of vice president was mostly ceremonial—attending the funerals of dignitaries, dedicating bridges and parks, and sitting in the Senate on special occasions—and as majority leader of the Senate, Johnson stood at the hub of the federal government. But he was convinced by friends and colleagues to take the place on the ticket, because he would be a "heartbeat away from the presidency." And as fate would have it, Johnson did become president on November 22, 1963, upon the assassination of JFK. Indeed, the job of vice president has always been, first and foremost, to stand ready. Nine times in American history, a vice president has assumed the presidency: John Tyler, Millard Fillmore, Andrew Johnson, Chester Arthur, Theodore Roosevelt, Calvin Coolidge, Harry Truman, Lyndon Johnson, and Gerald Ford.

With the advent of the Cold War after 1945 and the proliferation of nuclear weapons, concerns grew about the vice president's readiness to take the helm at a moment's notice, fully abreast of world and military developments.[16] Truman, who became president on FDR's sudden death in April of 1945, had been kept in the dark about the American project to build an atomic bomb, and not been fully apprised of the rapidly mounting tension between the United States and its ally, the Soviet Union, as World War II drew to its close. Truman had to learn everything "on the job"; fortunately for him and for the nation, he was a man of intelligence and strong

The role of the vice president has evolved over the years, especially since Dick Cheney. Delaware Senator Joe Biden, pictured here, likely would not have agreed to run as Barack Obama's vice presidential candidate if he did not believe that he would be a "player" in the White House.

character who ranks as one of the country's near-great presidents. But it was a close call. Put a bit differently, by the 1950s, many Americans believed that there should be no learning curve for new presidents in an age of intercontinental ballistic nuclear missiles. Dwight Eisenhower remarked, "Even if Mr. Nixon (his vice president) and I were not good friends, I would still have him in every important conference of government, so that if the Grim Reaper [death] would find it time to remove me from the scene, he is ready to slip in without any interruption."[17] Thus began a move toward bringing vice presidents into the inner circle.

Consequently, in recent decades, the job of vice president has changed. Walter Mondale had full access to President Carter and became a trusted adviser on all important matters. Al Gore, Bill Clinton's vice president for 8 years, was given numerous important responsibilities and also had full access to the president, including weekly one-on-one lunch meetings. Gore was very much in the inner circle, "one of three or four people whose advice Clinton sought on virtually every important matter."[18] And Dick Cheney played a very powerful role; some have suggested that he was the most powerful vice president in American history. Along with this changing role of vice presidents has come an equally significant growth of personal staff and resources.

Ultimately, of course, the power of the vice president is only what the president chooses to allow the occupant of that office to have. But the role of the vice president has come a long way in recent years.

The Evolution of the Presidency
Practice Quiz

1. The first efforts to define presidential power and responsibility were vague.
   a. true **b.** false

2. What sort of role in legislative matters did the framers of the Constitution grant the president?
   a. none at all, because of worries about a president's tyrannical powers
   b. a substantial role, as a check on and balance to the powers of Congress
   c. a modest role, with veto power that Congress could override with a two-thirds majority vote
   d. a modest role, with veto power that Congress could override with a simple majority vote

3. We know that the framers of the Constitution thought that the legislative branch should be a check on presidential power in foreign affairs because
   a. they granted Congress the power to negotiate treaties.
   b. they granted Congress oversight of all foreign policy initiatives.
   c. they granted Congress the power to appoint ambassadors to foreign nations.
   d. they granted Congress the power to ratify treaties and confirm appointments of ambassadors.

4. What was Alexander Hamilton's role in the establishment of the presidency?
   a. He was the real author of the "Cato" argument against granting the president a 4-year term.
   b. He worked behind the scenes at the Constitutional Convention to be named the first president.
   c. He countered "Cato's" arguments by explaining in *The Federalist Papers* the differences between the U.S. presidency and a monarchy.
   d. He explained in *The Federalist Papers* why a limited executive branch was crucial to the endurance of democracy in this country.

Answers: 1-a, 2-c, 3-d, 4-c.

Discussion Questions

1. Discuss the strengths and weaknesses of the Whig model of presidential power versus the stewardship model.
2. During the ratification period, how did the founders try to reduce the fears of excessive executive power?

What **YOU** can do!

Find out about the backgrounds of some of the members of the president's cabinet. Go to the White House Web site at **http://www.whitehouse.gov/government/cabinet.html** and learn more.

Going Public: Appealing directly to the people to garner support for presidential initiatives. **EXAMPLE:** *When a president gives a series of speeches to build public support for this budget plan, he is "going public."*

The Informal Powers of the President (pages 266–267)

How might the "powers to persuade" extend beyond the Constitution and formal structures of government?

In 1960, the political scientist Richard Neustadt published an important book called *Presidential Power.* It suggested that the formal powers of the presidency, as outlined in the Constitution, were rather minor: They amounted to little more than a clerkship, by which the occupant of the White House is in the position to provide services to others in the federal government.[19] Yet if we look beyond the formal powers to the *informal* powers, there is a great deal at the president's disposal. Presidential power, Neustadt argued, is the power to persuade. The real powers of any president are to use a combination of personality and political skills to lobby members of Congress. A president who feels strongly about a program or a policy initiative can tap into the many informal tools that the office makes possible, including the office's prestige, charm, the fear of retribution, the need of a special favor, and bargaining skills. Neustadt's book was very much a prescription—a guide for presidents to understand the true breadth of their powers. Many took heed. Both John Kennedy and Bill Clinton, for example, were said to have kept *Presidential Power* next to their beds and to have read from it each night.

The ability (and necessity) to persuade has more or less always been central to a successful president. As president, Thomas Jefferson was a master of this tactic, holding dinner parties at which matters of state were informally discussed and decided by his cabinet and key members of Congress. A new route to persuasion opened up in the twentieth century and was used skillfully by Theodore Roosevelt, much to the benefit of presidential power; Instead of persuading lawmakers face to face, presidents could use the bully pulpit to sway public opinion. With the successive development of radio and television, presidents have had widening opportunities to use modern communications to speak directly to the public. In fact, the process is called **going public**. Presidents have always been keenly aware of public opinion and promoted themselves and their policies in a number of ways, including giving speeches, doing interviews with members of the press, writing articles, and distributing pamphlets. But with the dawn of mass communications technology, especially the advent of television, presidents began to realize the weight of personal appeals. Winning the public's hearts and minds was found to be even more potent than persuading a few members of Congress. Franklin D. Roosevelt, who broadcast "fireside chats" on the radio, first showed how a president could establish a deep personal bond with the American people. John F. Kennedy used television to build an image that was both glamorous and admired. Ronald Reagan, dubbed "The Great Communicator" by the press, was especially skillful at connecting with the public on television, due in no small measure to his years of training as an actor—and also to his admiration for FDR. Going public is clearly important, as it helps presidents advance their policy goals. As suggested by Figure 7.1, some presidents have been more successful at gathering support than others. Also, just because the president is supported by the public does not mean it will stay that way; events can make ratings drop quickly. Moreover, going public can be risky: Members of Congress often feel neglected when presidents ignore them and appeal directly to the public.

Presidents have learned that charisma can be used to advance their policy agenda, and one of the very best at this was John F. Kennedy. It is probably not a coincidence that Kennedy was also one of the first presidents to understand the power of television. ***—Are leaders who lack charisma destined to fail? Do you think a politician's television persona really matters?***

First Ladies

Another critically important source of presidential power has been first ladies. From Martha Washington to Laura Bush, these women have provided informal advice, advocated significant policy reform, undertaken a host of symbolic functions (such as attending public events), and lobbied lawmakers and foreign dignitaries to help promote their own agendas as well as those of their husbands.

> "What are the roles of first ladies?"
>
> —Student Question

During most of our nation's history, first ladies limited their political work

FIGURE 7.1 | The Ups and Downs of Presidential Approval Ratings

Presidents may benefit or suffer from the winds of public opinion. But on closer inspection, we see a pattern where most presidents begin their term of office with high approval ratings and end their stay with lagging support. ***—Are presidents bound to fail in the eyes of the public? What made Gerald Ford and Bill Clinton the exceptions?***

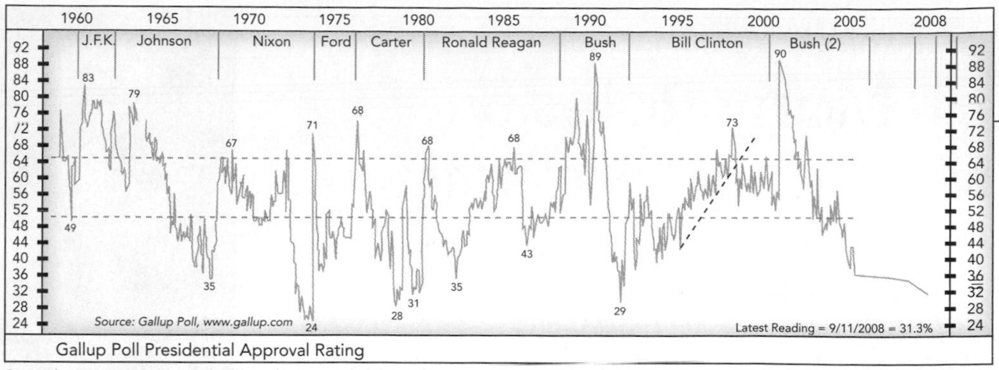

to informal, behind-the-scenes activities. For instance, the profound role played by Abigail Adams in helping her husband John maintain a cool head during his entire political career—and especially his presidency—is well documented. Among much else, Abigail Adams was an early feminist who reminded her husband to "remember the ladies." She was a central political figure during these early days of our nation, even though much of her work was never known to the larger public. Another critically important behind-the-scenes first lady was Edith Bolling Galt Wilson. Her husband, Woodrow, suffered a stroke and was left partly paralyzed in 1919. He was incapacitated for several months, during which time Edith spoke and acted on his behalf. She also handpicked the very few people who would have access to the ailing President Wilson. Her critics called her the "first lady president."

The activities of first ladies became much more public with Eleanor Roosevelt, the wife of Franklin D. Roosevelt. She traveled extensively and spoke on behalf of her husband's New Deal policies as well as her own concerns (centering mostly on the condition of poor children in America). She also wrote a newspaper column and worked tirelessly for Democratic candidates across the country. After her husband's death, Eleanor Roosevelt became a U.S. delegate to the United Nations, taking a lead on issues related to human rights and world poverty.

Perhaps the most dramatic change to the role of first ladies came about with Hillary Rodham Clinton. As a Yale-trained lawyer, Clinton had been a key policy adviser in her husband's administration when he was governor of Arkansas. Among much else, she spearheaded a successful education reform task force and in the process drew a good bit of national media attention. As she and her husband took up residence in the White House, her role as a powerful aide to her husband continued, and in a very public way. Upon leaving the White House in 2000, Hillary Rodham Clinton was elected U.S. senator from the state of New York, and of course, she nearly captured the Democratic nomination for the presidency in 2008.

Few people doubt that the role of presidential spouses will evolve in the coming years. As more and more women lead high-profile professional lives, the restricted role of merely providing behind-the-scenes advice and undertaking public ceremonial functions is probably a thing of the past. The real question is, what role will the "first gentleman" perform in the future?

The Informal Powers of the President
Practice Quiz

1. According to Richard Neustadt, the real power of the president is the power
   a. to manipulate. **b.** to threaten.
   c. to persuade. **d.** to communicate.

2. The president who used the "bully pulpit" to focus the public's attention on the White House was
   a. Theodore Roosevelt **b.** Franklin D. Roosevelt
   c. John F. Kennedy **d.** Ronald Reagan

3. According to Figure 7.1, which president (in the modern age) suffered the lowest approval rating?
   a. Lyndon Johnson **b.** Richard Nixon
   c. Jimmy Carter **d.** George H. W. Bush

4. Which first lady was the first to make her activities much more public?
   a. Dolley Madison **b.** Edith Bolling Galt Wilson
   c. Eleanor Roosevelt **d.** Hillary Rodham Clinton

Answers: 1-c, 2-a, 3-b, 4-c.

Discussion Questions

1. What are the advantages to "going public"? What are the risks?
2. What are the factors that contribute to a president's popularity? What factors could reduce a president's popularity?

What **YOU** can do!

New technologies allow students of the presidency to see and hear some of the earlier occupants of the White House. Listen to Franklin D. Roosevelt's inaugural address, and hear John F. Kennedy's call for America to land on the moon. How do these two speeches differ from what you hear today? Many great presidential speeches are only a click away at the American Presidency Project (**http://www.presidency.ucsb.edu**) or History and Politics Out Loud (**http://www.hpol.org**).

The Many Roles of Modern Presidents

(pages 268–275)

What are the duties, responsibilities, and functions of modern presidents?

Contemporary presidents are called on to perform a staggering number of duties and to play a dizzying variety of roles—and considering the awesome weaponry in the American military arsenal, it is not a mere figure of speech to say that the world's fate is at the president's fingertip. It has been said that no job can prepare you for the presidency, and no job is similar. Still, we can break down a modern president's task into several categories or functional roles.

The President as Chief of State

When George Washington took the helm of the federal government in April of 1789, his role in ceremonial events was unclear. On the one hand, everyone understood the importance of ritual and formal events. There would be occasions when the nation would need a leader to perform such functions—addressing Congress, greeting foreign dignitaries, speaking on the nation's behalf during times of celebration and grief, or even meeting ordinary citizens. If the president would not perform these functions, who would? In most political systems throughout the world, both then and now, a monarch or dictator undertakes chief-of-state functions. Would George Washington be king-like in this regard?

Washington rejected all titles. Vice President John Adams proposed to the Senate that the president be addressed with a dignified title, such as "His High Mightiness," but neither the senators nor Washington himself accepted such an idea, which would have been hated by most Americans of the time. Nor did Washington wear any sort of robe, crown, or military uniform. It was Washington who established two acceptable titles for all future chief executives: "Mr. President" or "Mr. [last name]." In many ways, presidents would be regular citizens.

Still, all presidents perform ceremonial functions. Washington held formal gatherings, called *levees,* at which citizens would line up and be greeted one by one with a grave presidential bow. That, in the late eighteenth century, was expected, as a way of investing the presidency with dignity. (But even that seemed too kingly to many Americans, and beginning with President Jefferson, a more informal tone permeated the presidency.) Today, we expect presidents to make a telephone call to the winning Super Bowl team, to throw out a baseball at the start of the World Series, and to pardon the White House turkey on Thanksgiving. We also look to presidents for stability, wisdom, and composure during times of crisis. When in 1995 the Murrah Federal Office Building in Oklahoma was bombed, killing 168 people, it was President Clinton who expressed the grief of all Americans at the memorial service. When the nation was shattered and shaken to its core by the terrorist attacks on September 11, 2001, we all turned to George W. Bush to steady the ship, to bring us together, and to help us move on.

At first glance, you might think the ceremonial duties of the president, such as throwing out the first pitch at a baseball game, are rather insignificant. Such events, however, are important in drawing us together as a nation. ***—Can you think of anyone else who could undertake these important acts? Would the Speaker of the House make sense, or perhaps the Chief Justice of the Supreme Court? Probably not.***

Some critics look down on the chief-of-state role, suggesting that these sorts of activities are all fluff. But they are wrong. Any nation our size, and surely any nation as diverse as ours, must come together in good times and in bad. Who else would perform such functions—the speaker of the House or the chief justice of the United States? Whether we live on a dairy farm in Vermont, in the suburbs of Los Angeles, or on a beach in North Carolina, we are all Americans. Ceremonial dinners and occasions to toss a baseball out at a special game might seem extraneous, but through these and many other unimportant events, our diverse nation becomes one. Moreover, when a president slips in his head-of-state role, the

FIGURE 7.2 | Congressional Support for Presidential Initiatives

This figure charts the percentage of presidential initiatives that are approved by Congress. Clearly, some presidents are more successful with the legislature than others. What makes this figure especially interesting is that presidents can be successful even when the other party controls Congress. ***—What force do you suppose leads to greater success with Congress, even when the president faces a "hostile" legislature?***

SOURCE: Harold Stanley and Richard Niemi, *Vital Statistics on American Politics, 2005-2006*, pp. 258-259. Copyright © 2006 CQ Press, a division of Congressional Quarterly, Inc. Reprinted by permission of CQ Press. www.cqpress.com

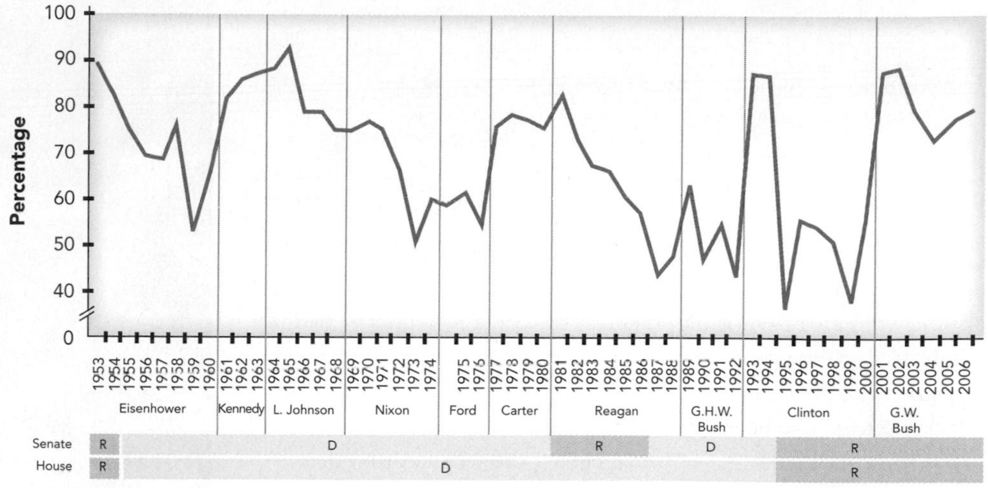

public reacts. When Hurricane Katrina slammed into New Orleans in September of 2005, George W. Bush was finishing the last days of his vacation on his ranch. It was only as the breadth of the disaster became obvious, 2 days later, that Bush traveled to the scene. Bush could have done little to ease the pain of the disaster in the early days, but the fact that he seemed aloof, indifferent to the plight of millions in the Gulf region, took many Americans aback. Where was our leader? Why did it take him days to address the nation? Bush's approval rating dropped sharply within a week.[20]

The President as Chief Legislator

Article I of the Constitution states that Congress will undertake legislative functions—the passing of laws and the collecting and distributing of funds. Article II makes the executive branch responsible for implementing the will of the legislative branch. At the same time, in keeping with the design of shared power, presidents are given some legislative authority: the power to veto bills, the ability to recommend measures for consideration, and the duty from time to time to inform Congress as to the "state of the union."

Consistent with the restrained view of presidential powers, occupants of the White House were reluctant to dig deeply into legislative matters during the first 140 years of our nation's history. Presidents believed it their role to wait for Congress to act. In the 8 years of his presidency, George Washington expressed an opinion on only five pieces of legislation.[21] Some presidents during this period—especially Andrew Jackson, Abraham Lincoln, Theodore Roosevelt, and Woodrow Wilson—were deeply immersed in legislative matters, but they were exceptions to the rule. A good estimate is that during this period, only about one-quarter of all significant policy initiatives originated with the executive branch.

This changed in 1933 with the inauguration of Franklin D. Roosevelt. Amid the crisis of the Great Depression, not only did FDR send a stream of measures to Congress for consideration, he and his aides also plunged into the legislative process with gusto, writing bills and twisting congressional arms to make sure that they passed. No one doubted that FDR was in charge of making policy during his first two terms, that he was very much the chief legislator.

All presidents since FDR have sought to lead the policymaking process, but some of them have been better at legislative matters than others. Lyndon Johnson was particularly good at "working the legislature." As a former member of the House, and especially as the Senate's majority leader, Johnson understood how the system worked, including the incentives that might be most effective with a legislative leader or a rank-and-file member. He was aggressive about getting his way, routinely giving reluctant members of Congress the "Johnson treatment." Jimmy Carter's story was altogether different. Having never worked in Washington or served as a state or local legislator before moving into the White House—his only prior office was one term as governor of Georgia—Carter was simply unfamiliar with how things worked in the national legislature. In the end, Carter got only modest support from Congress, even though his own party (the Democrats) controlled both chambers (see Figure 7.2).

"What happens when a president vetoes a bill?"
—Student Question

LEGISLATIVE TOOLS Presidents have at their disposal a number of tools and resources to aid their efforts with the legislature. The **veto** is critical. Presidents can shape legislation by rejecting measures passed by Congress. Sometimes presidents veto measures on principle, because they strongly disagree with the proposal (such as when George W. Bush vetoed a measure to increase funding for stem cell research) or think it unconstitutional; at other times, they may consider the goals laudable but the details wrong. There are two types of vetoes. One approach is to simply send the legislation back to Congress with a message as to why the president disapproves—this is called a *veto message*. The legislation can still become law if two-thirds of both houses of Congress vote to override it. Overrides are very rare; only about 3 percent of all vetoes have been overridden. This makes sense, given that the president's political party is often the majority party in Congress and that

■ **Veto:** Disapproval of a bill or resolution by the president.

SIGNIFICANCE: *This power allows presidents to play a significant role on shaping the outcome of legislation.*

The framers of our political system thought presidents would provide information to Congress, as the "state of the union," so that the legislative branch would be better informed. In recent decades, the State of the Union address, held every January, has become an important tool in building support for policy initiatives. ***—Do average Americans watch these speeches?***

presidents are very reluctant to lose face by vetoing bills that are likely to be overridden. If a president fails to act on a piece of legislation within 10 days, it becomes law. If Congress adjourns within those 10 days, however, the president can let the measure die through a *pocket veto*. Here, there is neither a signature nor a veto message. Pocket vetoes have been quite rare, especially on major legislation.

Some modern presidents have been more willing than others to veto bills, as Table 7.3 suggests. One of the most interesting things about the table is that presidents with a Congress controlled by the same party are not necessarily less prone to using their veto pen than are those with a hostile legislature controlled by the opposing party.

Table 7.3 is also misleading in a very important way: Actual vetoes are less significant in the legislative process than the *threat* of their use. That is, presidents will often send word to the legislature that if a piece of legislation comes before him, it will be vetoed. Not wanting to be embarrassed by the president or to waste everybody's time, the legislature responds either by not moving on the measure or by crafting a version of the bill that is acceptable to the president. Sometimes the threat is quite public. When Bill Clinton sought to reform the nation's health care system, he picked up a pen during a State of the Union address, waved it back and forth, and declared that if Congress did not send him a bill that covered all children, he would gladly use the pen to veto the bill. Many veto threats are delivered in private, either directly by the president or by presidential aides. It is difficult to know how often the threat of a veto is used, but observers of congressional and presidential dynamics agree on its significance.

The presidential duty to inform Congress regarding the state of the union each year has become another powerful legislative tool. Rather than considering this as a chore, presidents now understand it as a rare opportunity to set the legislative agenda for the coming year. It is an opportunity to lay out broad principles and to offer concrete measures. Even more important, it is an opportunity not only to speak to the legislature but also—ever since the invention of radio and television—to reach directly into people's living rooms. Many Americans watch the State of the Union address, and presidents use this rare occasion to shape public opinion, which of course goes a long way in persuading legislators.

TABLE 7.3 | Presidential Vetoes, 1901–2006

	REGULAR VETOES°	POCKET VETOES	TOTAL VETOES	VETOES OVERRIDDEN
T. Roosevelt	42	40	82	1
Taft	30	9	39	1
Wilson	33	11	44	6
Harding	5	1	6	—
Coolidge	20	30	50	4
Hoover	21	16	37	3
F. Roosevelt	372	263	635	9
Truman	180	70	250	12
Eisenhower	73	108	181	2
Kennedy	12	9	21	—
L. Johnson	16	14	30	—
Nixon	26	17	43	7
Ford	48	18	66	12
Carter	13	18	31	2
Reagan	39	39	78	9
G. H. W. Bush	29	17	46	1
Clinton	36	0	36	2
G. W. Bush	11	1	12	4

SOURCES: *Statistical Abstract of the United States*, 1986, p. 235; Senate Library, *Presidential Vetoes* (Washington, D.C.: Government Printing Office, 1960), p. 199; Thomas Cronin and Michael A. Genovese, *The Paradoxes of the American Presidency* (New York: Oxford University Press, 1998).

■ **Treaty:** A formal agreement between governments.

EXAMPLE: *The North America Free Trade Agreement, signed in 1992, eliminated most tariffs on products traded among the United States, Canada, and Mexico.*

■ **Executive Agreements:** Binding commitments between the United States and other countries agreed to by the president but, unlike treaties, not requiring approval by the Senate.

SIGNIFICANCE: *By not having to secure Senate approval, presidents have often used these "understandings" to craft foreign policy.*

STUDENT | PROFILE

One of the last things college students probably think about is retirement. After all, they have an entire career in front of them—and decades to save for it. Why should they worry, right? The snag, of course, is that Social Security, the core government program designed to assist elderly Americans, is in grave danger. By some estimates, the system is facing a $13.4 trillion shortfall, and there is an increasing likelihood that today's college-age students will confront a crisis when they want to retire.

So it's a big issue for young Americans—but can you really get young folks to care about the fate of Social Security? Apparently so. Students for Saving Social Security, also know as S4, is a new group that is spreading to campuses across the nation. It is a grassroots network that advocates for genuine Social Security reform. The foremost goals of the group are to help young Americans better understand the dangers that lie ahead and to push candidates for federal office to talk more about the issue. "This is not merely a distant crisis concerning retirement benefits. The immediacy of the problem for our generation is pressing," states the organization's Web site (**http://secureourfuture.org**). "Through honest, non-partisan debate we hope to represent the interests of young Americans." ■

The President as Chief Diplomat

Although presidential powers might be a bit cloudy in some areas of governance, when it comes to conducting foreign policy, the matter seems clear and long settled. Presidents are in charge of foreign affairs. This is what the framers had in mind, it is strengthened by 200 years of precedent, and it has been confirmed by several Supreme Court decisions. The president is the "sole organ" in conducting foreign affairs, stated the Court in *United States* v. *Curtiss-Wright* (1936), and his powers are "exclusive." Indeed, the president enjoys a freedom from congressional restrictions that "would not be admissible where domestic affairs alone are involved."[22] In other words, Congress should stay out of foreign affairs. Often, however, it refuses to do so.

There are a number of ways in which presidents can conduct foreign policy. Obviously, they can travel around the world, meeting with the leaders of other nations, forging ties and formal alliances. The Constitution states that they can appoint and receive ambassadors. In appointing ambassadors, which the Constitution requires them to do with the advice and consent of the Senate, presidents can choose officials who share their outlook toward a given nation or regarding foreign affairs more generally. Accepting ambassadors might seem a less significant act, but it can be used as a powerful tool. When presidents "accept" the emissary of another nation, it signifies that the United States recognizes that nation's existence and that its leaders hold power legitimately. For instance, neither Bill Clinton nor George W. Bush recognized the Taliban as the legitimate government of Afghanistan.

Another critically important foreign policy tool is the **treaty**■, a formal agreement between the United States and one or more other sovereign nations. The intent of the framers was that the Senate would work closely with the executive branch to negotiate and ratify treaties. This approach did not last long, as George Washington became frustrated with both the slow pace of the Senate and the difficulties of arriving at a consensus. From that point onward, presidents have negotiated treaties independently and then asked the Senate to ratify them by the two-thirds margin that the Constitution requires. Given that presidents have usually been of the same party as the majority in the Senate, it should come as no surprise that the Senate has rejected very few treaties. A good many, roughly 150, have been withdrawn because they seemed to lack support. Of the approximately 1,500 that have been sent to the Senate, however, only 15 have been voted down.

Sometimes more important than treaties are **executive agreements**■. The line between executive agreements and treaties is sometimes rather thin, but in general, these are less formal agreements, sometimes called "arrangements," between the United States and other nations. Whereas treaties are generally high-profile matters, usually attracting a great deal of media attention, executive agreements are often arranged in secret. They do not require Senate approval, which makes them especially appealing to presidents—particularly if the president confronts a hostile Congress—but the Case Act of 1972 requires the president to inform Congress of executive agreements within 60 days. Presidents may make executive agreements only in areas where they have the power to act, and they often deal with relatively minor concerns, such as tariffs, customs regulations, or postal matters. Yet some presidents have used executive agreements in very important ways. In 1973, President Nixon used an executive agreement to end the American conflict (never a declared war) with North Vietnam and to exchange prisoners of war. Such an agreement was also used in 1981 to form a strategic alliance with Israel. Perhaps not surprisingly, given the growing importance and complexity of world affairs as well as the potential roadblocks to winning Senate approval of treaties, the number of executive agreements made by presidents has increased greatly in the past few decades. Some observers speculate that such agreements, rather than formal treaties, have become the foreign policy tool of choice.

The Cold War with the Soviet Union and other communist powers was the primary focus of American foreign policy for all

Ronald Reagan understood that much of the power of the presidency comes from the ability to persuade. He used his impressive communication skills to transform both domestic and foreign policy. Here Reagan meets with Mikhail Gorbachev, leader of the former Soviet Union, during an arrival ceremony at the White House on December 8, 1987.

presidents between 1945 and the late 1980s, but that has now changed. Beginning in the 1980s, one of the most important transformations of the modern world has been the growth of global economic interdependence. Since the collapse of communism in the Soviet Union and Eastern Europe in 1989, and paralleling the rapid expansion of Asian economies (especially those of China and India), the management of America's trade relationships has been an expanding aspect of presidential foreign policy responsibilities. This change has created unique challenges for presidents. Opening foreign markets for American goods requires lowering or removing trade restrictions and tariffs on goods imported into the United States. Many imported products are cheaper because they are made by low-wage labor. Consumers want low-priced goods, but labor unions and manufacturers protest the importation of low-cost products, which threaten to close American factories and put Americans out of work.

To manage U.S. economic foreign policy, recent presidents have requested that Congress give them **fast-track trade authority**■. First used in 1974, fast-track authority allows presidents to negotiate new trade agreements with other nations, which they then submit to Congress for either approval or rejection. No amendments are allowed, and Congress has 90 legislative days to approve or reject the measure. Most observers agree that fast-track trade authority is a vital new presidential foreign policy power, but it is not without its critics. Some argue that it is yet another usurpation of legislative power—in other words, another example of how the executive branch has overstepped its bounds.

■ **Fast-Track Trade Authority:** The right of the president to negotiate trade agreements with other nations, which are then submitted to Congress for approval or rejection within a specified time.

SIGNIFICANCE: *While controversial, these agreements have become an important tool for presidents to craft economic policies with other nations.*

The President as Commander in Chief

Article II, Section 2, of the Constitution appoints the president commander in chief of all American military forces. When they take the oath of office, presidents swear that they will "preserve, protect, and defend" our nation. The framers of our system believed it essential that one person be responsible for decisive action during times of crisis—in the event of an invasion, for example, which was a real threat in the late eighteenth century. As for the oversight of an ongoing conflict or the direction of prolonged military engagements, however, the Constitution is a bit ambiguous. At the very least, this, too, is a shared power. That is, the president is commander in chief of the armed forces, but Congress is charged with declaring wars (in Article I, Section 8). Also, Congress has the responsibility to raise and support armies (that is, to raise and allocate funds for military matters).

During the first few decades of our nation, the decision to go to war was clearly shared with Congress. In 1803, for example, Thomas Jefferson sent the U.S. Navy to fight the Barbary pirates—North African rulers who were seizing American merchant vessels in the Mediterranean Sea and enslaving their crews unless the United States paid them tribute. But Congress had authorized this attack in advance.[23] Following the War of 1812 (which had been declared by Congress), presidential war powers began to expand. They took a leap forward during the Civil War. Congress was in recess when the southern states seceded at the end of 1860 and in early 1861, as well as when fighting began at Fort Sumter in April of 1861, only a few weeks after Lincoln's inauguration. Without congressional authorization, Lincoln called up the state militias, suspended the writ of habeas corpus, and slapped a naval blockade on the rebellious southern states. Critics claimed that Lincoln's acts were dictatorial, but he argued that they were necessary to preserve the Union. His defense of his "doctrine of necessity" is rather compelling:

> [My] oath to preserve the Constitution to the best of my ability imposed upon me the duty of preserving, by every indispensable means, that government . . . Was it possible to lose the nation and yet preserve the Constitution? By general law, the limb must be protected, yet often a limb must be amputated to save

War Powers Resolution: A measure passed by Congress in 1973 designed to limit presidential deployment of troops unless Congress grants approval for a longer period.

SIGNIFICANCE: *This act seems to compel compliance from Congress for military engagements, but all presidents have said their powers as commander in chief trump congressional control.*

> a life; but a life is never wisely given to save a limb. I felt the measures otherwise unconstitutional might become lawful by becoming indispensable to the preservation of the Constitution through the preservation of the nation.[24]

Essentially, Lincoln acted and left it to Congress either to accept or cancel his action later. Presidents since Lincoln have taken this "presidential prerogative" to heart, arguing that they are uniquely situated to protect the nation and should be given a free hand in all military emergencies.

In 1950, Harry Truman ordered troops to defend South Korea against a North Korean attack without requesting congressional authority (he said that the United States was engaging in a "police action" in support of a United Nations act). In the 1960s and early 1970s, both Lyndon Johnson and Richard Nixon waged the Vietnam War without a formal congressional declaration. Indeed, many observers think that the day of Congress actually declaring war—which last happened right after Japan's 1941 attack on Pearl Harbor—may now be over.

In 1973, after the United States and North Vietnam signed a peace agreement, Congress attempted to rein in presidential warmaking by passing the **War Powers Resolution**—and then overriding President Nixon's veto of it. This act requires that the president consult with Congress in "every possible instance" before sending troops to combat, that the president report to Congress in writing within 48 hours after ordering troops into harm's way, and that any military engagement must end within 60 days unless Congress either declares war or otherwise authorizes the use of force (provisions allowed for 90 days under certain circumstances). Since 1973, every president, Democratic or Republican, has claimed that the War Powers Resolution is unconstitutional. Nevertheless, rather than defy the act and test its constitutionality in the federal courts, and also in an effort to build broad public support (a critically important factor in waging successful long-term wars), all presidents who have sent American forces into battle have first sought congressional support for their action. For example, President George H. W. Bush asked for and received congressional authorization before launching the Persian Gulf War of 1991. So did President Clinton before leading NATO's military intervention in Kosovo in 1999, as did President George W. Bush before invading Afghanistan in 2001 and Iraq in 2003. But all these presidents have also made it clear that if Congress refused authorization, they would go ahead anyway.

> "What happens if Congress disagrees with the President on a military engagement?"
>
> —Student Question

ABOVE: **All presidents receive high levels of support** from the public and members of the military when hostile actions begin. But history has shown that this support often fades as wars drag on. George W. Bush has vowed to "stay the course" in Iraq, but election results in 2006 showed that the public was against staying in Iraq.

BELOW: **Some 58,000 American lives were lost** in Vietnam. While public support for our military efforts there was high in the early years, as the atrocities of the war and the number of casualties grew, Americans lost faith in Lyndon Johnson. ***—How does Congress have the right (and obligation) to step in and change the course of military engagements after a period of time? At what point should it take such action?***

It might seem, then, that modern presidents have unlimited foreign policy powers, but this is not exactly true. Congress still has the power to allocate or deny funds for military engagements. In 1974, Congress cut off further funding for the war in Vietnam. What if a situation arises in which the president sees military action

■ **Iran–Contra Affair:** The Reagan administration's unauthorized diversion of funds from the sale of arms to Iran to support the Contras, rebels fighting to overthrow the leftist government of Nicaragua.

SIGNIFICANCE: *While presidents boast commander in chief powers, Congress regulates federal spending—which can be a key factor in military engagements.*

■ **Executive Order:** A regulation made by the president that has the effect of law.

EXAMPLE: *Harry Truman ended segregation of the armed forces though an executive order in 1948.*

as being in our nation's interest but Congress disagrees and fails to appropriate the necessary resources? This issue came to a head in the 1980s in the **Iran–Contra Affair**■, when aides to Ronald Reagan channeled U.S. funds to rebels fighting the leftist government in Nicaragua—even though Congress had passed a measure forbidding it. The issue emerged late in Reagan's administration, drawing massive media attention, congressional ire, and an investigation by the Justice Department. To many people, this was a clear violation of the law: Congress had spoken, and Reagan, the executive, had thwarted its will. Supporters of the president answered that Reagan and his deputies were simply fulfilling their duty to protect the United States. The Justice Department moved forward and eventually secured a number of felony convictions. As for Reagan himself, the president claimed that he was unaware of these activities, and because his second term was ending, there was little enthusiasm for impeachment proceedings. Moreover, after losing reelection in 1992, George H.W. Bush pardoned everyone who had been convicted, and the scandal faded into the history books. The lesson from the Iran–Contra affair might be that although presidents see their commander-in-chief authority as sweeping, Congress still has one crucial power—the power of the purse.

The President as Chief Executive

We have already discussed several important elements of the president's chief executive function, including the assembling of staff and the cabinet. We know that the president is charged with carrying out the will of Congress: enforcing laws and spending the funds that are allocated and appropriated. The president is in many ways the nation's chief administrator and head bureaucrat. This role might suggest that the president's hands are tied by the will of Congress—that this function affords little leeway to shape policy—but this is only partially correct. At times, Congress makes its will clear with exact instructions to the executive branch. At other times, only vague outlines are provided, thereby leaving a great deal of ambiguity and leeway. This gives presidents and the federal bureaucracy (see LINK Chapter 8, pages 289–299) a chance to shape public policy.

Second, many authorities believe that nowadays, the very size of the federal bureaucracy has shifted the balance of power toward the executive branch. During the first few decades, our government had only about 1,000 federal employees (most of whom staffed local post offices). Even so, President Jefferson thought that there were too many officials and carried out a severe staff reduction! In recent years, the number of federal employees has climbed to roughly 2.6 million (excluding active duty members of the military). Although the vast majority of federal employees are civil service workers, the power to appoint certain high officials who lead the massive agencies and set their policies is an important executive function.

"So presidents don't have to depend on Congress to make policy?"
—Student Question

On top of this, presidents can issue **executive orders**■, which are essentially rules or regulations that have the effect of law. At times, executive orders are used to clarify existing legislation, but at other times, they have the effect of making new policy. There are three types of executive orders: *proclamations*, which serve the ceremonial purpose of declaring holidays and celebrations, and *national security directives* and *presidential decision directives*, both of which deal with national security and defense matters. Three of the most famous executive orders were used to ease some of the barriers to black men and women caused by generations of racial discrimination. Abraham Lincoln issued the Emancipation Proclamation, freeing the slaves of the South in 1863. Harry Truman issued an executive order in 1948 ending segregation in the armed forces, and Lyndon Johnson issued an executive order in 1966 making affirmative action a federal policy. Ronald Reagan issued an executive order to stop federal funding of fetal tissue research. Bill Clinton immediately rescinded this order when he became president, and one of George W. Bush's first acts was to reverse Clinton. George W. Bush also used an executive order to create the White House Office of Faith-Based and Community Initiatives in 2001. The goal of the new office is to help religious organizations compete for federal dollars to help fund social service programs.

Another tool that presidents can use to shape public policy is called **signing statements**■. Here, when a president signs a bill into law, he also issues a written proclamation of how the executive branch will interpret the measure, which is often different from what Congress intended. Controversy has arisen over the constitutionality of signing statements—especially the large number of statements issued by George W. Bush. During his tenure in office, Bush issued nearly 200 signing statements, challenging over 1,200 provisions in various laws.

Given the growing importance of the federal bureaucracy and the opportunity that bureaucratic regulations present to shape policy, interest groups have come to see the executive branch as an important pathway for change (see LINK Chapter 11, pages 404–413). A great deal of lobbying is directed at agency heads and other bureaucratic decision makers. Indeed, much can change in American government without the input of a single elected official. Even if an

CONNECT THE LINK
(Chapter **8**, pages **298–299**) How can presidents shape the policy process through appointments to the federal bureaucracy?

■ **Signing Statements:** Written proclamations issued by presidents regarding how they intend to interpret a new law.

SIGNIFICANCE: *Quite often, the president's interpretation differs from the intent of Congress, so signing statements have become quite controversial.*

SIMULATION **Presidential Leadership: Which Hat Do You Wear?**

President George W. Bush used signing statements to instruct federal agencies how to interpret new legislation. Quite often, however, these statements seemed to conflict with the intent of Congress. ***—Was Bush overstepping his bounds as chief executive?***

issue is taken up by the legislature, it is common for a federal agency to be brought into the mix. Political scientists have described a cozy, often secretive relationship in policymaking among interest groups (often representing a corporation, business, trade association, or labor union), legislative committees, and bureaucratic agencies. Scholars debate the extent to which these "policy communities" exist today, but the overarching point is that political actors can make a difference by directly lobbying nonelected bureaucrats.

Finally, presidents can shape public policy by working to secure funding for new or existing programs. While Congress has the ultimate authority to set federal budget policies, each year presidents offer their own budget plans. Developed by an extensive staff of experts with the Office of Management and Budget (OMB), the president's budget is generally considered the starting point for congressional negotiations. Because the president is "first off the mark" with a budget outline, and because of the expertise of the OMB, savy presidents often get a great deal of what they want. This is especially true when Congress is controlled by the same party as the president.

The Many Roles of Modern Presidents

Practice Quiz

1. In the long period from George Washington's presidency to Woodrow Wilson's, approximately how much significant legislation was initiated in the executive branch?
   a. 75 percent **b.** 50 percent
   c. 25 percent **d.** 5 percent

2. Which twentieth-century president was best known for his ability to cleverly and aggressively work his legislative agenda through Congress?
   a. Lyndon Johnson **b.** Jimmy Carter
   c. Gerald Ford **d.** Franklin D. Roosevelt

3. Why are presidential vetoes rarely overridden by Congress?
   a. because senators frequently filibuster to thwart such an action
   b. because presidents rarely exercise a veto that they think will be overridden
   c. because most legislators rarely object to presidential vetoes
   d. because the authority of the executive branch has become nearly overwhelming in the past 80 years

4. The president's status as commander in chief means, in part, that
   a. the president can declare war.
   b. the president is responsible for raising money for military matters.
   c. the president can send U.S. military forces into battle with congressional authorization.
   d. the president can control the size and nature of the country's military forces.

Answers: 1-c, 2-a, 3-b, 4-c.

Discussion Questions

1. In what way is the "Johnson treatment" an example of Neustadt's power to persuade?
2. Discuss the particulars of the president's role as commander in chief. In what ways is the president adequately checked by Congress in this important matter? In what ways is he more of an independent source of power?

What **YOU** can do!

In the United States, the president reports to Congress in the yearly State of the Union address. Compare this to the United Kingdom, where the prime minister takes questions every Wednesday from members of Parliament. These sessions are often grueling and raucous, and they require the prime minister to think on his or her feet. You can listen to the Prime Minister's questions from the BBC web site at **http://www.bbc.co.uk/fivelive/news/pmqs.shtml** or **http://www.parliament.uk/about/how/business/questions.cfm**

CONNECT THE LINK
Chapter **11**, pages **404–413**) How do interest groups lobby the executive branch?

Many Americans deemed Jimmy Carter inept because he couldn't do anything to secure the release of the 66 Americans held hostage for 444 days in Iran. ***—Perhaps we expect too much from presidents? What other actions may have obtained the hostages' release?***

Presidential Greatness

(pages 276–279)

What are the forces that lead to presidential success or failure? How does one define presidential greatness?

Many political scientists believe that an important development has occurred during the past few decades in the relationship between the president and the public. The term *personal presidency* describes the mounting expectations that the public places on the president—"expectations that have grown faster than the capacity of presidential government to meet them."[25] In short, we Americans have developed a personal connection, an emotional bond, with our president. A number of changes have led to this development, including the growing size and importance of the federal bureaucracy, the expansion of presidential powers, and the heavy use of television advertising during campaigns, which forces candidates to promise things they cannot deliver once in office. Americans put more and more faith in their presidents to solve their problems and meet all challenges, both foreign and domestic.

The problem, however, is that the executive branch is only one piece of the federal government and only one element of the world's economy. "For most Americans the president is the focal point of public life," write two experts on the presidency. "This person appears to be in charge, [which is] reassuring. But the reality of the presidency rests on a very different truth: Presidents are seldom in command and usually must negotiate with others to achieve their goals."[26] The outcome is dissatisfaction. Presidents often fail to meet our expectations, and we are left feeling disappointed and cynical. Some people would argue that this explains a string of "failed" presidencies. Harry Truman and Lyndon Johnson—both of them vice presidents who entered the White House upon their predecessors' deaths—were rejected by their own party after leading the nation into controversial military entanglements. Having won reelection in a landslide in 1972, Richard Nixon just 2 years later resigned in disgrace, facing impeachment and likely conviction, after his criminal misconduct in the Watergate affair was exposed. Jimmy Carter was perceived as bungling the nation's economy and being indecisive during the Iranian hostage crisis (which lasted for more than 12 months in 1979–1981), and the voters ejected him from office after just 4 years. Ronald Reagan faced a congressional inquiry into the Iran–Contra affair and may have escaped impeachment only because he was on the verge of retirement. George H. W. Bush was riding high early in his presidency and drew record high approval ratings after victory was won in the first Gulf War—but 1 year later, Bill Clinton defeated him, largely because the economy had turned bad. Clinton did serve for two full terms, but in some respects, he, too, had a failed presidency. Being just the second president in U.S. history to be impeached—on grounds stemming from personal conduct and despite acquittal by the Senate—was certainly no badge of honor. And George W. Bush left office with very low approval ratings. One might conclude that modern executives are destined to fail, that "presidential greatness" is a thing of the past.

What is presidential greatness, anyway? What is it that makes one chief executive better than another? Are there ingredients that can be combined to create a successful, distinguished presidency? Perhaps it is only when our nation confronts adversity that greatness can emerge. The three presidents who top nearly all scholarly lists of great chief executives—Washington, Lincoln, and Franklin D. Roosevelt—each confronted a major national crisis. Washington led the nation in its founding years, when the very success of the federal experiment hung in the balance; Lincoln had to preserve the Union and chose to abolish slavery during a civil war that cost 600,000 lives; and Roosevelt faced the gravest economic crisis in the nation's history and then fought World War II. No other presidents, even those who rank relatively high, had to surmount crises as dangerous as these.

George W. Bush has said that his presidency was shaped by the events of September 11, 2001. Some might conclude that he was a good president because he met the challenge of our new realities. Others will see his tenure in the White House as a failure because of the War in Iraq; they will argue he took the United States into the wrong war at the wrong time and against the wrong enemy.

Perhaps simple luck has much to do with successful or failed presidencies. But bad luck can only explain so much. Herbert Hoover—a man superbly qualified by education and early experience for the presidency—claimed to be the unluckiest president in

Comparing Chief Executives

Rate the Presidents

history, given the stock market's collapse on his watch in 1929. Yet Hoover was crippled by his rigid attempts to apply orthodox economic theories to a situation that required innovative thinking. He also projected a hard-hearted and uncaring image while millions of Americans lost their money, jobs, homes, and hope—an unfair judgment but also understandable given Hoover's dour personality. Lyndon Johnson inherited the probably unwinnable conflict in Vietnam from his White House predecessors, and despite his noble championing of the civil rights movement and his policies aimed at eradicating poverty, his presidency was plagued by riots in the black ghettos and by massive antiwar demonstrations on college campuses. Johnson's public image was also negative: After the glamorous and eloquent Kennedy, LBJ seemed an uncouth, untrustworthy, and ruthless wheeler-dealer who spoke with a widely mocked Texas drawl. Jimmy Carter's hands were tied when the Iranian militants who had seized the U.S. embassy in Tehran threatened to kill the American diplomats whom they had taken hostage. Like his predecessor Gerald Ford (who similarly rates as an unimpressive president), Carter also faced skyrocketing oil prices and a stagnating economy.

Lyndon Johnson was masterful at engineering compromises and pushing through important domestic policies. The war in Vietnam spun out of control during his administration, however, and his popularity plummeted. Modern presidents are powerful, but they are far from omnipotent.

"What determines a great president?"
—Student Question

It is worth remembering the words of the man always ranked as one of the greatest presidents, Abraham Lincoln, responding in 1864 to a newspaperman's question: "I claim not to have controlled events, but confess plainly that events have controlled me." How Lincoln *did* act when confronted with those events, however, is the measure of his greatness.

Circumstances matter. Yet even unlucky events can turn into triumphs of leadership if the president has the necessary character. And what defines great character in a political leader? Scholars and biographers have wrestled with this question for thousands of years, and there is no shortage of lists. The historian and presidential scholar Robert Dallek suggests that five qualities have been constants in the men who have most effectively fulfilled the presidential oath of office:[27]

Vision. All great presidents have had a clear understanding of where they wanted to lead the nation in its quest for a better future.

Pragmatism. All great presidents have been realists, leaders who understood that politics is the art of the possible and that flexible responses to changing conditions at home and abroad are essential.

Consensus building. Great presidents understood that their success depended on the consent of the governed. Moving government in a new direction, often down a difficult path, requires building a national consensus first.

Charisma. The personality of the president, along with his ability to capture and retain the affection and admiration of average citizens, has been a key ingredient of presidential greatness.

Trustworthiness. All truly successful presidents have credibility and have been able to earn the faith of their fellow citizens.

Many groups have attempted to measure presidential greatness. The conservative Federalist Society, joining forces with the

TIMELINE The Executive Order Over Time

SIMULATION You Are a President During a Nuclear Power Plant Meltdown

VISUAL LITERACY Presidential Success in Polls and Congress

TABLE 7.4 | Rankings of American Presidents

WALL STREET JOURNAL RANKING		C-SPAN RANKING	
RANK	NAME	RANK	NAME
1	George Washington	1	Abraham Lincoln
2	Abraham Lincoln	2	Franklin D. Roosevelt
3	Franklin D. Roosevelt	3	George Washington
4	Thomas Jefferson	4	Theodore Roosevelt
5	Theodore Roosevelt	5	Harry S Truman
6	Andrew Jackson	6	Woodrow Wilson
7	Harry S Truman	7	Thomas Jefferson
8	Ronald Reagan	8	John F. Kennedy
9	Dwight D. Eisenhower	9	Dwight D. Eisenhower
10	James K. Polk	10	Lyndon B. Johnson
11	Woodrow Wilson	11	Ronald Reagan
12	Grover Cleveland	12	James K. Polk
13	John Adams	13	Andrew Jackson
14	William McKinley	14	James Monroe
15	James Madison	15	William McKinley
16	James Monroe	16	John Adams
17	Lyndon B. Johnson	17	Grover Cleveland
18	John F. Kennedy	18	James Madison
19	William Howard Taft	19	John Quincy Adams
20	John Quincy Adams	20	George H. W. Bush
21	George H. W. Bush	21	Bill Clinton
22	Rutherford B. Hayes	22	Jimmy Carter
23	Martin Van Buren	23	Gerald R. Ford
24	Bill Clinton	24	William Howard Taft
25	Calvin Coolidge	25	Richard M. Nixon
26	Chester A. Arthur	26	Rutherford B. Hayes
27	Benjamin Harrison	27	Calvin Coolidge
28	Gerald R. Ford	28	Zachary Taylor
29	Herbert Hoover	29	James A. Garfield
30	Jimmy Carter	30	Martin Van Buren
31	Zachary Taylor	31	Benjamin Harrison
32	Ulysses S. Grant	32	Chester A. Arthur
33	Richard M. Nixon	33	Ulysses S. Grant
34	John Tyler	34	Herbert Hoover
35	Millard Fillmore	35	Millard Fillmore
36	Andrew Johnson	36	John Tyler
37	Franklin Pierce	37	William Henry Harrison
38	Warren G. Harding	38	Warren G. Harding
39	James Buchanan	39	Franklin Pierce
		40	Andrew Johnson
		41	James Buchanan

Note: William Henry Harrison, who died after just 30 days in office, and Garfield, who was mortally wounded 4 months after his inauguration and died 2 months later, are omitted from the *Wall Street Journal's* ranking.

Barack Obama, the nation's first African-American president, pictured here with his family before delivering his acceptance speech to a crowd of some 200,000 supporters in Grant Park in Chicago, comes into office with our nation facing historic challenges. ***—Will these difficulties draw out his greatness, or will they cripple his presidency from the beginning?***

Wall Street Journal in November of 2000, undertook one such effort. The study involved 78 randomly selected presidency scholars: historians, political scientists, and law professors. Another, conducted by C-SPAN, also surveyed scholars, whose responses seem to have been slightly weighted in favor of the more liberal or "progressive" presidents. Table 7.4 shows the results from both polls.

Although we might argue over the precise order of these rankings—whether one president should be ranked higher than another, whether Washington was better than Lincoln, or whether Harding, Buchanan, or Andrew Johnson was the worst of all—nearly all assessments of past presidents suggest similar groupings. Lincoln, Washington, both Roosevelts, and Jefferson were great leaders, and those at the bottom of this list, the presidents whose names seem the most obscure to us, are generally considered failures. The interesting part of this exercise is not the precise order but rather a consideration of the personal qualities and historical events that contributed to the success or failure of a given president. Why are James Madison and John Quincy Adams, who made enormous contributions to this country, not ranked among the greatest presidents? Why was Ulysses S. Grant at best only mediocre (as a president, not as a general), and why did Gerald Ford, such a fine American, fail as a president? What was it about Theodore Roosevelt that brings him near the top? Why is James K. Polk listed in the top tier in some rankings? And who *was* James K. Polk, anyway?

As for George W. Bush's place in this rankings, it is a bit early to tell. After his first 4 years in office, some began to speculate he would fall in the "average" range, but during his second term, the economy weakened, budget deficits grew, there were few legislative accomplishments, and the war in Iraq continued. His approval ratings languished in the 30 percent range for the last 3 years of his presidency. Moreover, many believe that Bush had extended the powers of the presidency beyond constitutional limits, such as with his unprecedented number of controversial signing statements. It seems likely that most historians will assess his tenure in office in an unfavorable light. By 2006, one commentator noted, "George W. Bush's presidency appears headed for colossal historical disgrace. Barring a cataclysmic event on the order of the terrorist attacks of September 11th, after which the public might rally around the White House once again, there seems to be little the administration can do to avoid being ranked on the lowest tier of U.S. presidents."[28]

Presidential Greatness

Practice Quiz

1. Which of the following acts best illustrates the notion of a "personal presidency"?
   - **a.** Ronald Reagan telling the president of the Soviet Union, "Mr. Gorbachev, tear down this wall!"
   - **b.** Bill Clinton telling the American people, "I feel your pain."
   - **c.** John F. Kennedy telling the country in his inaugural address, "Ask not what your country can do for you; ask what you can do for your country."
   - **d.** Abraham Lincoln's Emancipation Proclamation, which outlawed slavery in 1863 by executive order
2. U.S. presidents are less in charge of governmental actions than most Americans assume, because
   - **a.** presidents are trained to sound more sure of themselves than they really are.
   - **b.** no one can predict how circumstances will change after presidents have decided the course of governmental action.
   - **c.** the legislative branch in the American system is much stronger than the executive branch.
   - **d.** presidents must negotiate with other people to accomplish their goals.
3. Which president stated, "I claim not to have controlled events, but confess plainly that events have controlled me."
   - **a.** Andrew Jackson
   - **b.** Abraham Lincoln
   - **c.** Woodrow Wilson
   - **d.** Franklin D. Roosevelt
4. According to presidential scholar Robert Dallek, what is one of the qualities that effective presidents must possess?
   - **a.** great intelligence
   - **b.** eloquence
   - **c.** charisma
   - **d.** consistency

Answers: 1-b, 2-d, 3 b, 4-c.

Discussion Questions

1. Pick any two of Robert Dallek's criteria for a great president, and compare and contrast the importance of these qualifications to greatness.
2. Discuss the current status of George W. Bush in regard to presidential greatness. What incidents during his presidency would affect his ranking?

What **YOU** can do!

What qualities do you think should be used to determine presidential greatness? If you were commissioned to develop a ranking, whom would you consult?

Conclusion

The framers of our system might not have comprehended jet planes, skyscrapers, or suicide bombers. And they surely could not have imagined jets being flown into buildings, killing thousands of innocent people. They also could not have appreciated the speed at which the events of September 11, 2001, could be transmitted around the globe. Ours is a very different world than Franklin, Washington, Adams, Jefferson, and Madison could possibly have imagined.

If anything, however, the events of 9/11 have proved that the framers were visionaries and that they were right about the presidency. They anticipated grievous attacks against the United States and the necessity for an immediate response. They understood that after tragic events, citizens would look to a leader to calm, resolve, and console. They held that the heart of their new republic would be found in the legislature, but they also understood that a strong executive would keep the nation together during times of crisis. It is hard to imagine how our nation would have responded to any of the great challenges without the leadership of the president. Our first years under the Constitution were uncertain and turbulent, but to some extent, the steady hand and vision of George Washington helped keep the peace and ensure that the Union survived. Congress or state governments did not save the Union in 1861–1865, but the will, intellect, and political skill of Abraham Lincoln helped it to survive and be reborn. Congress and the Hoover White House were paralyzed by the strife and anguish of the Great Depression, so not until Franklin D. Roosevelt took the helm did the federal government respond. From his first inaugural address, FDR calmed the waters by reminding us that "the only thing we have to fear is fear itself," and he rallied a nation horrified by the Japanese attack on December 7, 1941—"a date," he said, "which will live in infamy." After the humiliations of the 1970s, Ronald Reagan made Americans once again feel proud of their nation, and it was through his unwavering mixture of determination and moderation that the Cold War was brought to a peaceful end. The will of the American people is best expressed through representatives, but our resolve, our spirit, and our sense of united purpose rests in the hands of the president. This is especially true during times of crisis.

Much as we may praise the advantages of a single leader, however, endowing this person with too much prerogative distorts the balance of power that the framers so carefully built into the constitutional system. Our nation has grown from fewer than 4 million people in 1790 to more than 300 million today, requiring the federal government to step into all aspects of American life—and the power of the chief executive has mushroomed along with that explosive growth. Dramatically different from what was envisioned by Madison and his colleagues in Philadelphia in 1787, modern presidents have three main tasks: first, to develop a legislative program and work to persuade Congress to enact it; second, to engage in direct policymaking through bureaucratic actions that do not require congressional approval; and third, to lead a massive network of staff with the singular goal of helping the occupant of the White House succeed in achieving these first two goals.[29] Presidents do not act in a vacuum. They must constantly respond to public opinion, interest groups, party activists, and the media. Many pathways of change run through the White House. Even so, when one person holds so much power in a political system, it is only sensible to wonder about the democratic character of that nation. The "imperial presidency," as scholars have branded what emerged under Richard Nixon,[30] which shows signs of revival today, is surely not what the framers had in mind.

Key Objective Review, Apply, and Explore

The President and the Constitution

(pages 256–257)

Unlike other branches of the new government, the framers of the U.S. Constitution were a bit unsure about the presidency. On the one hand, they wanted to vest the office with real powers—to afford "energy in the executive," as one noted. On the other hand, many worried that giving a president too much power would lead to corruption and perhaps even a new monarchy. This section explores that balance.

KEY TERMS

Prerogative Power 256
Cato 256
Alexander Hamilton 257

CRITICAL THINKING QUESTIONS

1. Did it make sense to allow future presidents to "fill in the blanks" regarding the ambiguity of presidential powers? Wasn't that a huge risk?
2. Do any of the worries of the Anti-Federalists regarding the presidency ring true today?

INTERNET RESOURCES

To explore a range of topics on the presidency, especially presidential elections, go to the American Presidency Web site at **http://ap.grolier.com**

ADDITIONAL READING

Ellis, Joseph J. *His Excellency: George Washington.* New York: Knopf, 2004.

The Evolution of the Presidency

(pages 258–265)

During much of the nineteenth century, most presidents held to the restrained model regarding their powers, meaning that they were limited to the powers expressly granted in the Constitution. Beginning with Teddy Roosevelt, and certainly later on, with his cousin Franklin D. Roosevelt, the activist model of presidential powers took hold. The omnipotent role that contemporary presidents play in American politics and international affairs would shock the framers.

KEY TERMS

Whig Model 258
Stewardship Model 258
Modern Presidency 259
Cabinet 260
Inner Cabinet 261
Executive Office of the President (EOP) 261
National Security Council (NSC) 261
National Security Adviser 261
Office of Management and Budget (OMB) 261
Council of Economic Advisers (CEA) 261
Social Security 262
Institutional Presidency 262

CRITICAL THINKING QUESTIONS

1. Other than the personalities of particular presidents, what are some of the forces that seemed to compel expanded presidential powers?
2. Given these new conditions, would the framers agree that stronger presidents are a necessity?
3. How has the system of shared powers/checks and balances been affected by burgeoning presidential powers? Have the scales tipped too far in the president's direction?

INTERNET RESOURCES

You can view some 52,000 documents at the American Presidency Project at **http://www.presidency.ucsb.edu/index.php.** This site also provides a number of important links.

ADDITIONAL READING

Greenstein, Fred I. *The Presidential Difference: Leadership Style from FDR to George W. Bush.* Princeton, NJ: Princeton University Press, 2004.

Key Objective Review, Apply, and Explore

The Informal Powers of the President

(pages 266–267)

Astute presidents have learned that much of their power comes from their own skills, the trappings of the office, and a steadfast spouse.

KEY TERM

Going Public 266

CRITICAL THINKING QUESTIONS

1. If "going public" has become a powerful tool in the arsenal of modern presidents, does that imply style is more important than substance?
2. What do you think will be the role of first ladies and first gentlemen in the decades to come? Has this position changed as society has changed?

INTERNET RESOURCES

Doing a research project on a president or a related topic? Check out the National Archives Web site at **http://www.archives.gov/research_room/getting_started/research_presidential_materials.html**. There is also a National First Ladies' Library: **http://www.firstladies.org/index.htm**

ADDITIONAL READING

Neustadt, Richard E. *Presidential Power: The Politics of Leadership.* New York: Free Press, 1991.

The Many Roles of Modern Presidents

(pages 268–275)

No job prepares a person for the presidency. Along with expanding powers comes a dizzying array of jobs and responsibilities. It is no wonder that many of the men who have taken up residence at the White House enter office full of energy, but end their stay seemingly exhausted.

KEY TERMS

Veto 269	**War Powers Resolution 273**
Treaty 271	**Iran–Contra Affair 274**
Executive Agreements 271	**Executive Orders 274**
Fast-Track Trade Authority 272	**Signing Statements 274**

CRITICAL THINKING QUESTIONS

1. Do we expect too much from modern presidents? If so, is there any way to shift some of the responsibilities to others or to other parts of the government? How would that work?
2. Can average citizens use presidents and their staff to shape the outcomes of the policy process? Put another way, does the pathway of change run through the White House?

INTERNET RESOURCES

The American Presidents Web site at **http://www.americanpresidents.org** contains a complete video archive of the C-SPAN television series *American Presidents: Life Portraits,* plus biographical facts, key events of each presidency, presidential places, and reference materials. You might also take a look at one of the presidential libraries. For links to them, try **http://www.archives.gov/research_room/getting_started/research_presidential_materials.html#faids**

ADDITIONAL READING

Schlesinger, Arthur M., Jr. *The Imperial Presidency.* Buena Vista, VA: Mariner Books (reprint ed)., 2004.

Key Objective Review, Apply, and Explore

Presidential Greatness

(pages 276–279)

While there is no formula for success, there are shared characteristics of great presidents. Truly successful presidents have vision but are also pragmatic. They understand the importance of public conscience, and they are trustworthy and charismatic. Perhaps because of growing demands and forces beyond their control, however, it seems that successful presidents are increasingly rare.

CRITICAL THINKING QUESTIONS

1. It has been argued that some Americans are increasingly disappointed with their presidents. Why might this be the case? Are there any changes you can think of that might ease some of the disappointment?
2. Of the characteristics of successful presdents, which seems most important? Might a charismatic president who lacks vision succeed? Would a trustworthy leader who lacks charisma get anything done in contemporary politics?

INTERNET RESOURCES

For a wealth of scholarly information on each of the presidents, visit the Miller Center of Public Affairs website at: **http://millercenter.org/academic/americanpresident**

The White House Web site at **http://www.whitehouse.gov** provides a wealth of information about the current presidency.

ADDITIONAL READING

Weisberg, Jacob. *The Bush Tragedy*. New York: Random House, 2008.

Chapter Review Critical Thinking Test

1. The responsibilities of the executive branch are spelled out in which article of the Constitution?
a. Article I **b.** Article II
c. Article III **d.** Article IV

2. One of the central tasks of a modern president is
a. developing a legislative agenda and persuading Congress to enact it.
b. declaring wars and ratifying peace treaties with foreign powers.
c. controlling the revenues and expenditures of the federal government.
d. interpreting and applying the laws of the land, as described in the Constitution.

3. All citizens of the United States select the president.
a. true **b.** false

4. Among the informal powers of the presidency are
a. the power to persuade.
b. going public.
c. appointing judges to the federal bench.
d. a and b.

5. A major component to presidential power in modern times is the personal connection, an emotional bond, that Americans form with the president.
a. true **b.** false

6. Over the centuries, the breadth of presidential authority has fluctuated, in part because
a. many amendments have been added to the Constitution that have widened and narrowed that authority.
b. some presidents have used the vagueness of the Constitution to maximize their power and some have not.
c. the American people's attitude toward presidential power has fluctuated as well.
d. modern society has experienced cultural and technological changes that affect how authority is implemented.

7. As the presidency has evolved, presidential authority has
a. remained steady.
b. steadily declined.
c. steadily increased.
d. fluctuated between increase and decline.

8. What is the "bully pulpit"?
a. the president's unique position to shape public opinion on important national issues
b. the lectern from which Franklin D. Roosevelt delivered his famous fireside chats
c. a position presidents adopt when they use their own religious convictions to address moral issues in American society
d. a metaphor for America's military superiority to other countries in the world

9. What president proudly claimed that he "did not usurp power but ... acted for the common well-being of our people ... in whatever manner was necessary, unless prevented by direct constitutional or legislative prohibition"?
a. Richard Nixon **b.** George Washington
c. Theodore Roosevelt **d.** Herbert Hoover

10. What three presidents make everyone's list in terms of presidential "greatness"?
a. George Washington, Theodore Roosevelt, Ronald Reagan
b. George Washington, Abraham Lincoln, Franklin D. Roosevelt
c. George Washington, Theodore Roosevelt, Franklin D. Roosevelt
d. George Washington, Abraham Lincoln, Theodore Roosevelt

11. Typically, a president's inner cabinet includes the heads of which departments?
a. Health, Education, and Labor
b. Transportation, Interior, and Homeland Security
c. Energy, Commerce, and Agriculture
d. Justice, Treasury, and Defense

12. The Executive Office of the President expanded most rapidly under which administration?
a. Gerald Ford's **b.** James Polk's
c. Bill Clinton's **d.** Franklin D. Roosevelt's

13. The expansion of the president's staff into an enormous network of individuals and offices has meant that
a. presidents themselves have become politically less significant.
b. presidents have had to make fewer decisions by themselves.
c. presidents have been able to play a central role in the policy process.
d. fewer persons have access to the executive branch.

14. Why have recent presidencies experienced conflict between policy and political advisers within the executive branch?
a. because presidents now retain advisers whose job is to make sure their boss remains politically popular, even if that means setting aside policy commitments
b. because presidents have become much more involved with the policy process, making conflict with the political agenda inevitable
c. because political advisers and policy advisers will inevitably be contentious
d. because presidents must now respond to the needs of more constituents, some of whom are bound to compete with one another

Chapter Review Critical Thinking Test

15. In the 1950s, what changed in the nature of the vice presidency, and why?

- **a.** Vice presidents no longer attended cabinet meetings, because the president's expanded staff could handle those responsibilities.
- **b.** Vice presidents began to be included in important presidential briefings so that they could quickly and competently assume the president's duties if necessary.
- **c.** Because television gave the office a much higher profile than it had before, vice presidents could take advantage of financial opportunities beyond the office.
- **d.** The vice president presided over the U.S. Senate much more often, because the president really needed an active representative in that forum.

16. What book touting the informal powers of the presidency did Presidents Kennedy and Clinton keep at hand throughout their time in the White House?

- **a.** *The Imperial Presidency*
- **b.** *Profiles in Courage*
- **c.** *Presidential Power*
- **d.** *Banging the Bully Pulpit*

17. What woman first demonstrated how substantial and public the role of first lady could be?

- **a.** Edith Bolling Galt Wilson
- **b.** Abigail Adams
- **c.** Hillary Rodham Clinton
- **d.** Eleanor Roosevelt

18. Modern presidents use the State of the Union address to set the legislative agenda for the coming year and try to shape public opinion in support of that agenda.

- **a.** true
- **b.** false

19. Despite their expanded authority, modern presidents still cannot initiate the deployment of American forces in foreign lands without the prior approval of Congress.

- **a.** true
- **b.** false

20. Given the substantial numbers and authority of bureaucratic decision makers within the executive branch, it is safe to say that

- **a.** there is not much an outsider can do to affect policy formation in the White House.
- **b.** a great deal can change in American government without the consent of an elected official.
- **c.** the president has little control over the policy direction of his own administration.
- **d.** the executive branch is not a promising pathway for change.

Answers: 1-b, 2-a, 3-b, 4-d, 5-a, 6-b, 7-c, 8-a, 9-c, 10-b, 11-d, 12-d, 13-c, 14-a, 15-b, 16-c, 17-d, 18-a, 19-b, 20-b.

You decide!

Imagine that you have decided to become a presidential candidate, and you are asked to complete a voter information questionnaire that asks following questions: Which past president will you try to emulate, and why? What is your view of presidential power in a post September 11th era? Which public figure would you ask to be your vice president? Why? How would you use your cabinet? As you answer these questions for yourself, consider how the current political and economic climate has shaped your perspective on these matters. Now imagine that you have been elected to office. Would your views about presidential power change if the country suddenly plunged into a depression? Do you think that the role of the president during an economic disaster should be the same as his or her role during a war? Why or why not?

Key Objective Outline

Is there a risk that the federal government will become too large and ineffective as new agencies are created to handle policy matters that attract the interest of Congress and the president?

Should the heads of federal agencies be the nation's top experts and managers, or should they be political appointees who will loyally follow the president's wishes?

Is there a better way to organize and run government agencies in order to reduce the undesirable aspects of bureaucracies?

How can the president and members of the president's cabinet make sure that workers within the government's many agencies are performing their duties properly?

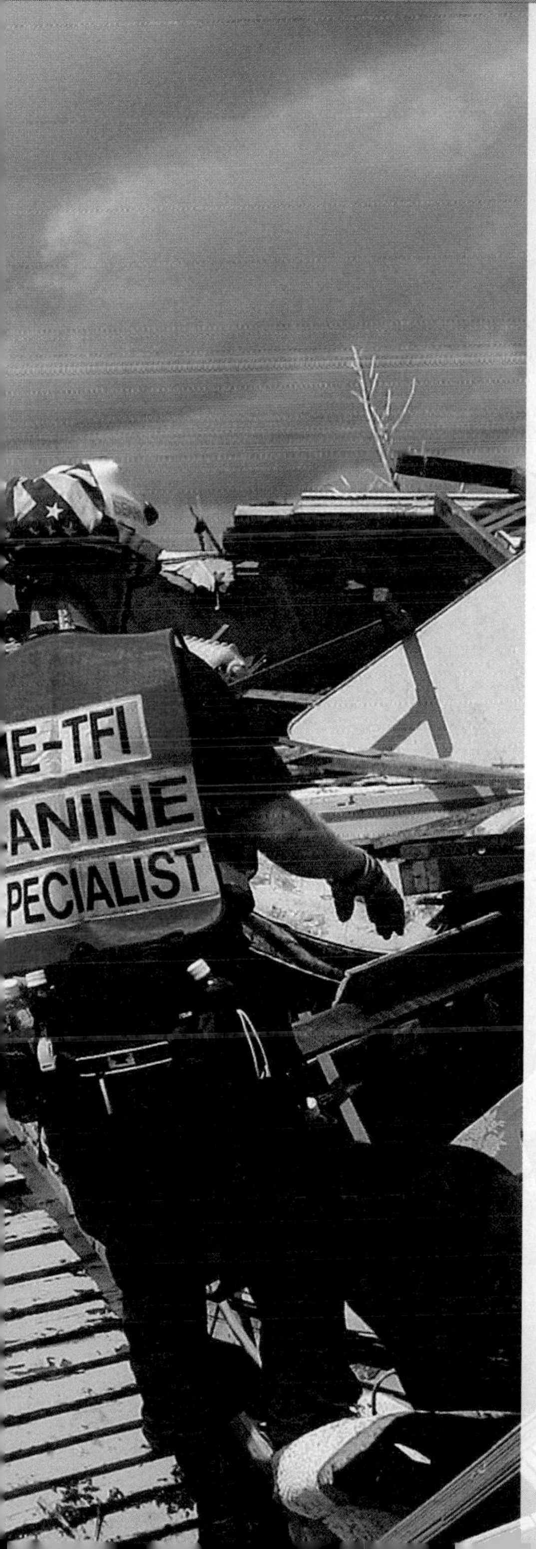

CHAPTER 8
BUREAUCRACY

Is the bureaucracy an essential contributor to the success of government or a barrier to effective government?

The residents of Greensburg, Kansas, went through their evening activities amid darkening skies on May 4, 2007. Suddenly, the air was pierced by the small town's tornado emergency siren. People hurried into their basements. Twenty minutes later, a powerful tornado roared through the town. The tornado was more than a mile wide, and its tremendous velocity made it especially destructive.[1] Minutes later, 95 percent of Greensburg's homes and businesses were gone. Tragically, 10 residents lost their lives. Moreover, nearly everyone in Greensburg was homeless, and their personal possessions were scattered.

How do Americans cope with such tragic circumstances? They look to the agencies of the government's bureaucracy to lend a helping hand. The Federal Emergency Management Agency (FEMA) sent 300 workers to Greensburg, provided millions of dollars for rebuilding, and delivered hundreds of trailers for temporary homes. FEMA received severe criticism for its slow response to the large-scale human tragedy after Hurricane Katrina's devastation of New Orleans in 2005. The agency sought to prove in Greensburg that it was capable of providing timely and meaningful assistance in the aftermath of disasters.[2]

In this chapter, we'll examine the agencies of the executive branch of the federal government that are collectively known as "the bureaucracy." When government agencies do their jobs well, Americans enjoy great benefits. For example, many lives have undoubtedly been saved by government systems for issuing tornado and hurricane warnings. On the other hand, much is expected of government agencies, and as flawed organizations composed of fallible human beings, they do not always fulfill their duties. Thus, for many Americans, memories of Hurricane Katrina continue to raise questions about whether government agencies can work effectively.

STUDENT RESOURCE-CENTER
• Glossary
• Vocabulary Example
• LINK
• MyPoliSciLab Connection

Bureaucracy: An organization with a hierarchical structure and specific responsibilities that operates on management principles intended to enhance efficiency and effectiveness. In government, it refers to departments and agencies in the executive branch.

EXAMPLE: *The Internal Revenue Service (IRS) is an agency in the federal bureaucracy that touches the lives of all Americans. It carries out the national tax laws through collection of income taxes and investigation of individuals and businesses that violate the legal obligation to pay the taxes required under the laws enacted by Congress.*

The Federal Bureaucracy (pages 288–295)

Is there a risk that the federal government will become too large and ineffective as new agencies are created to handle policy matters that attract the interest of Congress and the president?

The departments that comprise the executive branch of the federal government work under the direction of the president to carry out the nation's laws. For example, assistance provided to disaster victims by FEMA and other federal agencies is in accordance with laws enacted by Congress. These laws list the kinds of assistance to be provided by the federal government and authorize the spending of federal funds for disaster relief in specific locations. FEMA and other agencies do not simply decide for themselves when and where they will help. They must act within the guidelines set by Congress and the president. These guidelines typically leave room for agency officials to make specific decisions, but these officials cannot act beyond the scope of their authority as defined by law. For example, FEMA officials may decide that certain disaster-area counties need more money or other specific kinds of assistance than other disaster-affected counties. In essence, Congress and the president write laws to define public policy; the officials who work in federal agencies then act to carry out those laws and policies.

Ideally, the officials who work in federal agencies possess knowledge and experience concerning the policy matters that they handle. We want them to be expert professionals who are dedicated to public service for all Americans. We do not want them to be politicians who serve the interests of a particular political party. Despite this idealistic vision of government workers, these officials are not necessarily removed from the world of politics. In making their decisions, agency officials may be influenced by lobbying from legislators, state and local officials, and interest groups. Thus the bureaucracy becomes another arena of action for the policy-shaping pathway that relies on the lobbying of decision makers.

Americans depend on government agencies. Police and other emergency personnel must train in realistic scenarios in order to respond to a variety of possible disasters. Americans do not always think of emergency workers as part of the government bureaucracy. Yet, like others who work in government agencies, these public employees perform important tasks for society. Here a Seattle police officer trains in a simulated terrorist attack. ***—Which government agencies do you regard as most essential for society?***

The Bureaucracy and Public Policy

In this chapter, we'll examine the agencies of the executive branch of the federal government that are collectively known as "the bureaucracy." The word **bureaucracy** refers to an organization

Many Americans may take for granted that their drinking water is safe and clean, yet it is government agencies that set standards and inspections to ensure the safety of our water. ***—Do you trust government agencies to make sure that Americans enjoy a healthy, safe environment?***

"What do we mean by 'bureaucracy'? Is it a separate branch of government?"

—Student Question

with a hierarchical structure and specific responsibilities that operate on management principles intended to enhance efficiency and effectiveness. Bureaucracies exist in businesses, universities, and other organizational contexts; however, the general term *bureaucracy* is most frequently used to refer to government agencies. Action or inaction by these agencies determines whether and how policies are implemented and how these policies will affect the lives of Americans.

Agency officials can shape public policy through their authority to create rules for administering programs and for enforcing laws enacted by Congress and the president. They are also the source of information and ideas for members of Congress who wish to propose new statutes about various policy issues. The policy preferences of individual agency officials affect the day-to-day actions that these bureaucracies undertake, as do those officials' interactions with representatives from outside interest groups. And because the bureaucracy is part of the executive branch—and, thus, under the president's authority—policymaking decisions within government agencies can also be affected by partisan political considerations. Moreover, the president's political appointees assume the top positions in each agency.

Although the news media typically pay less attention to the bureaucracy than they do to the president, Congress, political parties, and interest groups, the agencies of the federal government are influential and important in determining the nature and impact of public policies. When an agency mishandles a situation for which it has responsibility, as FEMA did in the case of Hurricane Katrina, the repercussions may reverberate all the way to the White House.

PATHWAYS | of action

Arsenic Standards for Drinking Water

The Safe Drinking Water Act was passed by Congress in 1974 to protect the quality of drinking water in the United States. The act authorizes the Environmental Protection Agency (EPA) to create regulations that establish purity standards for drinking water systems. Exactly what those purity standards will be, however, can present a thorny issue affecting the safety and welfare of every person in the country. It's a good illustration of the politics of the federal bureaucracy.

A 1999 report by the National Academy of Sciences said that arsenic in drinking water can cause various kinds of cancer. In 2000, an environmentalist interest group, the Natural Resources Defense Council, sued the EPA over arsenic standards, seeking to have the regulations changed to mandate arsenic levels at only 3 parts per billion (ppb) rather than the existing standard of 50 ppb. As a result of the lawsuit, EPA officials in President Bill Clinton's administration proposed a new standard of 5 ppb.

Objections poured in from the mining and wood-preservative industries that use and produce arsenic. Local water systems also

■ **Department:** Any of the 15 major government agencies responsible for specific policy areas whose heads are usually called secretaries and serve in the president's cabinet.

EXAMPLE: *The U.S. Department of State is responsible for managing relationships with foreign governments, issuing passports to U.S. citizens, and providing assistance to Americans traveling in foreign countries. Dr. Condoleezza Rice, the secretary of state from 2005 to 2009, was appointed by President George W. Bush to be the head of the Department of State.*

raised concerns about the costs of meeting the proposed standard. As a result, the EPA adopted a standard of 10 ppb. This was in the waning days of the Clinton administration—but when President George W. Bush came into office in early 2001, his officials postponed the effective date of the new rule for 1 year. Critics complained that the Bush administration, which was perceived to be less concerned than the Clinton administration about water pollution and other environmental issues, was sacrificing public health in favor of the interests and profits of the manufacturing and mining industries.

Several months later, at the Bush administration's request, a committee of the National Academy of Sciences produced a new report that reconfirmed the health risks from arsenic in drinking water. So the Bush administration moved forward on the regulation limiting arsenic in drinking water to 10 ppb or less. The new rule angered the National Rural Water Association, an interest group representing small communities. It argued that the new standard would impose excessive costs on small towns that must upgrade their water systems. Nor did the rule satisfy the Natural Resources Defense Council and other environmentalist groups. They awaited new studies with the hope of convincing the EPA to amend the regulation and require an even lower level of arsenic. And there matters rest, with no party truly satisfied with the outcome.

This story is typical of today's regulatory politics. Officials in the bureaucracy make decisions about a policy rule that affects water systems throughout the country—but their rule is shaped by the officials' interactions with and responses to other actors involved with the issue of water quality. Scientists provide influential information for the bureaucracy, and interest groups apply pressure through lobbying and litigation.[3] ■

TABLE 8.1 | Cabinet Departments and Examples of Other Agencies

Departments	Independent Agencies
Agriculture	Environmental Protection Agency
Commerce	Peace Corps
Defense	Social Security Administration
Education	**Independent Regulatory Commissions**
Energy	Federal Communications Commission
Health and Human Services	Federal Trade Commission
Homeland Security	Nuclear Regulatory Commission
Housing and Urban Development	**Government Corporations**
Interior	National Railroad Passenger Corporation (Amtrak)
Justice	Overseas Private Investment Corporation
Labor	United States Postal Service
State	
Transportation	
Treasury	
Veterans Affairs	

SOURCE: LSU Libraries Federal Agencies Directory, http://www.lib.lsu.edu/gov/fedgov.html

Organization of the Federal Bureaucracy

The origins of the federal bureaucracy can be traced to the design of government presented in the U.S. Constitution of 1787. The federal bureaucracy changed over time in response to the changing problems facing the United States, moving toward greater governmental involvement in social issues and economic regulation. In addition, the bureaucracy experienced significant growth during the mid-twentieth century.

Today, the federal bureaucracy consists of four types of organizational entities: departments, independent agencies, independent regulatory commissions, and government corporations (see Table 8.1).

Departments■ typically are large organizations responsible for a broad policy realm, such as education, national defense, or transportation. **Independent agencies** have narrow responsibilities for a specific policy issue, such as the environment. They are independent in the sense that they are not subunits of a larger department, but like departments, their leaders are appointed by and under the control of the president. By contrast, **independent regulatory commissions** are not under the control of the president or a department. They have a focused policy mission governing a specific issue area, but they are run by a body of officials drawn from both political parties and appointed in staggered terms over the course of more than one presidential administration. **Government corporations** have independent boards and are intended to run like private corporations. They handle a specific function, such as the postal system or the passenger railroad, that Congress believes would not be handled effectively by private businesses, either because of the huge scope of the operation or because of issues of profitability. As you consider the role and operation of each of these components of the federal bureaucracy, ask yourself whether there might be a better way to organize the government. Alternatively, consider whether some of the bureaucracy's functions could be

PARTICIPATION The Evolution of the Federal Bureaucracy

handled effectively and appropriately by private businesses without the expenditure of taxpayers' money.

Development of the Federal Bureaucracy

The roots of the federal bureaucracy go back to the original U.S. Constitution of 1787. Article I, Section 8, gives Congress the power to enact laws for specified purposes. These include matters such as to "lay and collect taxes," to "coin Money," to "establish Post Offices," and to "provide and maintain a Navy." The president, as the head of the executive branch, is responsible for carrying out the nation's laws. It soon became apparent, however, that people working for the president must implement these laws and that agencies must be created to administer specific policies and programs. Post offices, tax agencies, and mints (where money is coined) handle tasks that require specialized personnel and facilities. They cannot be carried out inside the president's office in the White House. Indeed, Article I makes reference to congressional authority to "make all laws necessary and proper for carrying into Execution . . . all other Powers vested by this Constitution in the Government of the United States, or in any Department or Officer thereof." Thus the founding document explicitly acknowledged that government agencies, called "departments," would be established to carry out laws and programs.

> "Are all the bureaucratic agencies listed in the Constitution?"
>
> —Student Question

Article II of the Constitution, which discusses the president and executive power, provides further acknowledgment of the need to create governmental departments that will execute the laws under the president's supervision and control. For example, Article II says that the president "may require the Opinion, in writing, of the principal Officer in each of the executive Departments, upon any subject relating to the Duties of their respective Offices."

Although the Constitution thus clearly anticipated the existence of executive departments, the actual development and organization of those departments over the course of American history were shaped by social developments and the country's response to emerging policy issues and priorities.

THE FIRST DEPARTMENTS During the nation's first century, the federal government was involved in only a limited range of policy areas. The original departments of the federal government focused on policy matters related to specific powers granted by the Constitution to Congress and the president. Most policy issues came under the authority of state governments. This explains why the federal government after 1789 had only four departments:

Department of State—responsible for diplomacy and foreign affairs

Department of War (in 1947 consolidated, along with the Department of the Navy, a later creation, into the Department of Defense)—responsible for military matters and national defense

Department of Justice—responsible for legal matters under federal law

Department of the Treasury—responsible for tax revenues and government expenditures

These departments had very limited responsibilities, because there were few federal laws to carry out and the country was relatively small in terms of both geography and population. These early departments were also tiny compared to the gigantic departments that handle the same duties today.

Note how many of these agencies focused on matters that had motivated the Constitutional Convention to replace the Articles of Confederation with the new U.S. Constitution. Under the Articles, the national government lacked authority to handle taxation, the military, and interstate commerce; agencies to deal with these matters were clearly needed. Although the Department of Commerce was not created until the early twentieth century, the Constitution gave Congress the authority to enact laws regulating interstate commerce, and the Department of Justice could seek to enforce these laws.

As Congress and the president expanded the scope of federal activities in law and policy, departments were created to operate in new areas. First came the Department of the Navy. In the mid-nineteenth century, Congress created the Department of the Interior to manage federal lands and the Department of Agriculture to assist the nation's most important industry.

During the last decades of the nineteenth century, the United States began to undergo significant changes. Industrialization, urbanization, and immigration shaped a new economy in which people moved to cities to work in factories and service occupations. The corporations that dominated the nation's finance, transportation, energy, and manufacturing became national entities of vast wealth and size, acquiring and developing property, factories, and facilities across state borders. Issues arose about the corporations' influence over the economy and about the working conditions of employees in factories, railroads, coal mines, and other industrial settings.

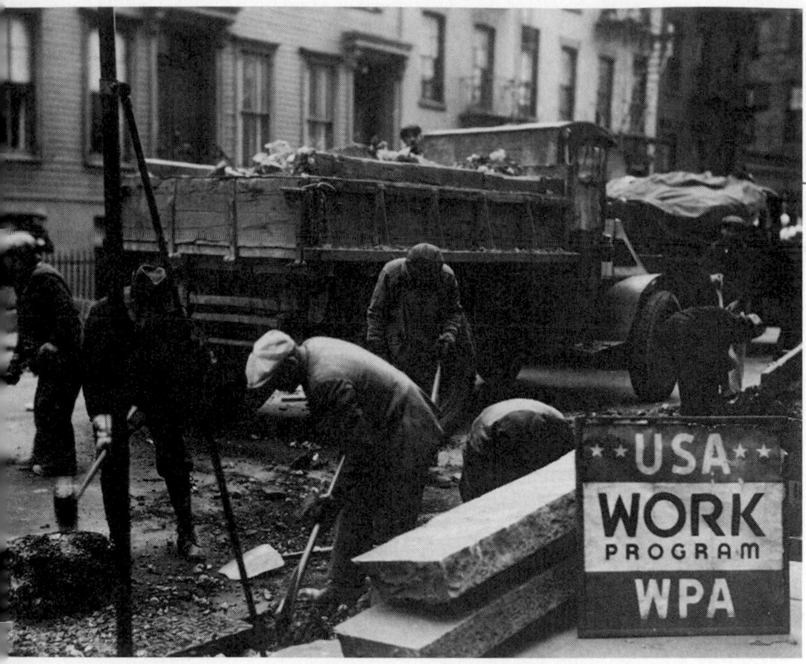

During the Depression, the Roosevelt administration expanded the size of government by creating programs to permit unemployed workers to earn money while repairing roads and undertaking other public service projects. ***—In light of economic difficulties in 2008, from the housing crisis to rising oil prices, should the federal government maintain permanent programs to employ people who cannot find jobs?***

Congress became increasingly assertive in using its constitutional authority to enact laws regulating interstate commerce to prevent business monopolies, control the exploitation of child labor, improve dangerous working conditions, and deal with other problems created by the new industrial economy. In the first decade of the twentieth century, Congress created the department of Commerce and the Department of Labor to address these emerging issues.

THE NEW DEAL AND ITS AFTERMATH The Great Depression, which began with the stock market crash of 1929, brought years of record-high unemployment and economic problems. At the depth of the Depression in 1932, Franklin D. Roosevelt was elected to the presidency. He strongly believed that the federal government had to take an active role in the economic and social welfare arenas in order to overcome the economic stagnation and correct the underlying causes of the Depression. He called his program the New Deal. The Roosevelt administration (1933–1945) contributed enormously to the growth in the federal bureaucracy by initiating various governmental programs, first in response to the Great Depression and later to wage World War II.

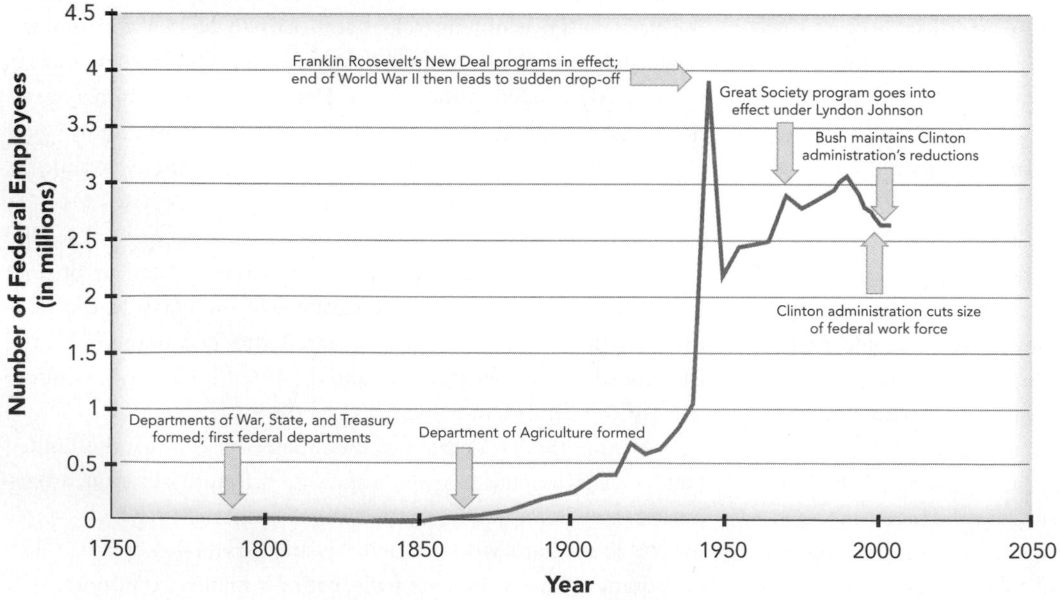

FIGURE 8.1 | **Growth in the Size of the Federal Bureaucracy**

The Roosevelt administration's programs to address the Depression and World War II dramatically increased the size of the federal bureaucracy. ***—After these crises had passed, why didn't the government shrink back to its size in the early years of the twentieth century?***

During the 1960s, President Lyndon B. Johnson tried to expand the activity and influence of federal governmental agencies in order to address poverty and racial discrimination. The Department of Housing and Urban Development (HUD) was created during his presidency. ***—Has expanded action by the federal government actually helped to solve social problems?***

For example, in 1935, Congress created Social Security to provide income for senior citizens and dependents of deceased workers. It later added coverage for disabled workers and their dependents. Other New Deal programs created jobs for the unemployed, such as the Works Progress Administration (WPA) and Civilian Conservation Corps (CCC), and regulated economic activity, such as the price supports and crop production limits introduced by the 1933 Agricultural Adjustment Act. The size and complexity of the federal government increased tremendously during the Roosevelt administration (see Figure 8.1). By the end of FDR's presidency in 1945, not only had the public accepted the federal government's involvement in a variety of policy issues, many Americans had come to *expect* federal action on important matters, eventually including such areas as education and criminal justice, which had traditionally been the exclusive preserve of state and local governments. Moreover, World War II had demonstrated the necessity of combining the War and Navy departments (as well as the newly created Air Force department) within a single structure, the Department of Defense.

In the 1950s, expanded public expectations of the federal government and the consequently broader range of legislative activity undertaken by Congress led to the creation of the Department of Health, Education and Welfare (HEW). The establishment of this department signaled the expansion of the federal bureaucracy's responsibilities into policy issues that the authors of the U.S. Constitution would never have envisioned as spheres of federal action. (In the 1970s, HEW was split into two agencies, the Department of Education and the Department of Health and Human Services.)

Heightened public awareness of urban decay, racial conflict, and poverty during the 1960s produced a new social welfare federal bureaucracy, the Department of Housing and Urban Development (HUD). Similarly, the Department of Transportation, created during the same decade, reflected concerns about urban mass transit as well as a recognition that air travel was expanding and continuing federal policy issues concerning ports and highways could be located in the new department.

Changes Since the 1960s

In 1973, the energy crisis struck. That year, the nation's ever-growing thirst for oil, natural gas, and other fossil fuels collided with the determination of the oil-producing countries comprising the Organization of Petroleum Exporting Countries (OPEC) to increase their profits. Many Americans found themselves waiting in long lines at gas stations and paying skyrocketing prices to fill up their gas-guzzling cars and heat their energy-inefficient homes. Responding to the crisis atmosphere, Congress created the Department of Energy to implement new laws and develop policies designed to encourage fuel efficiency, develop new sources of energy, and relieve the nation's dependence on foreign oil producers.

At the end of the 1980s, the Veterans Administration (created in 1930) was elevated to the status of a separate department called the Department of Veterans Affairs. Paying pensions and disability benefits to veterans had long been a federal responsibility in the aftermath of the Civil War, World Wars I and II, and the wars in Korea and Vietnam. By the 1980s, a huge cohort of World War II veterans had become senior citizens, and they looked to the federal government for health care and other benefits. Closely behind

CONNECT THE LINK
(Chapter **7**, page **260–261**) The members of the president's cabinet are the most visible and publicly recognizable individuals who work in the federal bureaucracy.

"Which Cabinet department was created most recently?"

—Student Question

followed a cohort of Korean War veterans, and the middle-aged Vietnam War veterans were increasingly in need of benefits and services. It was widely felt that veterans deserved greater attention from government and improved benefits and services. When an agency gets the status of an executive department, its head becomes a member of the president's cabinet and is literally "at the table" when the president's top executive appointees discuss policies and budgets. As you saw in LINK Chapter 7, pages 260–261, the cabinet plays an especially important and influential role in advising the president. Creation of the Department of Veterans Affairs implied a promise that veterans' interests would be taken into account in those discussions. By elevating to cabinet status the agency responsible for veterans, Congress symbolically demonstrated its concern about veterans and simultaneously sought the political benefits of granting increased attention and stature to an important constituency.

After terrorists attacked the World Trade Center and the Pentagon on September 11, 2001, public shock and congressional demands for action resulted in the creation of the federal government's newest department: the Department of Homeland Security (DHS). Like other departments, the DHS represented a response to a policy issue that had moved to the top of the nation's priorities. It consists of newly created agencies, such as the Transportation Safety Administration (TSA), as well as a consolidation of existing agencies moved from other departments.

The creation of the DHS involved the development of a new agency by pulling together various existing agencies in order to seek better coordination of government actions related to domestic security issues. President Bush initially resisted creating a new department. The principles of his Republican Party usually advocate efforts to reduce the size of government. Moreover, many observers recognized that creating a new department that included agencies from elsewhere in government would inevitably pose a variety of problems. Would agencies engage in "turf wars" over who should be in charge of specific tasks? Would employees resist a move to an unfamiliar department with unproven leadership and a still-developing mission? Could a new set of administrators provide guidance, supervision, and control over a gigantic and swiftly created department containing many employees who were accustomed to operating guidelines from a different department? Under pressure from Democrats and Republicans to take action in defense of national security, President Bush eventually moved forward with the creation of DHS, and inevitably, some of the feared problems materialized.

To give you an idea of the scope of the reorganization, this short list identifies a few of the agencies absorbed into the new department as well as their previous homes within the bureaucracy.

Federal Emergency Management Agency (FEMA)—previously an independent agency

Immigration and Naturalization Service (INS)—previously in the Department of Justice

Coast Guard—previously in the Department of Transportation

Secret Service—previously in the Department of the Treasury

The fact that these agencies had historical roots in very different departments, despite their need to coordinate homeland security efforts, raises questions about whether other related agencies scattered throughout the bureaucracy could be brought together to seek greater efficiency on issues such as commerce and the environment. The slow response and general ineffectiveness of FEMA during and after Hurricane Katrina, however, led many critics to complain that the DHS was too big. They claimed that individual agencies within the department had lost resources and suffered from diminished focus on their domestic mission in light of the department's broader concerns about preventing attacks by international terrorists. Calls were heard to consider whether some of these agencies—including FEMA—could better serve the public as freestanding entities.

The Federal Bureaucracy

Practice Quiz

1. The first departments of the federal bureaucracy were created as a result of
   - **a.** the requirements of the Declaration of Independence.
   - **b.** the original constitutional design of the federal government.
   - **c.** the Civil War.
   - **d.** President Franklin Roosevelt's New Deal program.
2. What kind of organizational entity in the federal bureaucracy is specifically mentioned in the U.S. Constitution?
   - **a.** government corporations
   - **b.** independent regulatory commissions
   - **c.** departments
   - **d.** independent agencies
3. What department was created in the 1980s in response to growing needs for medical care among a specific segment of the U.S. population?
   - **a.** Department of Disease Control and Prevention
   - **b.** Department of Health and Human Services
   - **c.** Department of Medicinal Arts
   - **d.** Department of Veterans Affairs
4. What department was created in response to the events of September 11, 2001?
   - **a.** Department of Homeland Security
   - **b.** Department of Defense
   - **c.** Department of Air Traffic Security
   - **d.** Department of Foreign Relations

Answers: 1-b, 2-c, 3-d, 4-a.

Discussion Questions

1. Based on the U.S. Constitution and the nature of the early federal government, what kind of bureaucracy did the founders intend to construct?
2. What societal changes and historic events led to the creation of new departments in the federal bureaucracy?

What **YOU** can do!

Using government Web sites, compare the number and kinds of agencies in the federal government with those in your state's government. Do you have ideas about agencies that ought to be created or eliminated? Why?

Departments and Independent Agencies (pages 296–301)

Should the heads of federal agencies be the nation's top experts and managers, or should they be political appointees who will loyally follow the president's wishes?

In order to understand how the bureaucracy operates, it is important to recognize which policy areas are under the authority of the governmental units, called *departments*, that work under the direction of the president's cabinet. By contrast, other kinds of agencies exert more independent influence over certain policy issues, because they are not directly under the supervision of the president and the cabinet.

Not all government employees are hidden away in office buildings. Some, like this national park ranger, interact directly with the public every day and provide valuable services, such as preserving natural resources and protecting public land. ***—Which agencies provide services directly to you?***

Departments

During every presidential administration, the president's cabinet consists of the heads of the executive departments. These department heads typically have the title of secretary, such as secretary of defense for the head of the Department of Defense. The head of the Department of Justice, however, is known as the attorney general of the United States. Because new departments have been created over time, the cabinet has grown to include 15 departments as well as the administrators of three agencies within the Executive Office of the President: the Office of Management and Budget (OMB), the Office of National Drug Control Policy, and the Office of the U.S. Trade Representative. The head of one independent agency, the EPA, also has cabinet rank. At earlier points in American history, the members of the cabinet would advise the president, debate policy options, and develop ideas to determine the president's agenda. In recent administrations, presidents have relied most heavily on their staffs and key cabinet members for advice. Cabinet meetings now serve the function of reporting to the president on the activities of each department. Cabinet members are expected to be loyal to the president to avoid any public indication that they question the president's agenda or actions.

The various departments are divided according to areas of policy responsibility. Within each department, various agencies are assigned to implement laws, keep detailed records, and make consistent decisions in accordance with established rules. Table 8.2 lists the 15 cabinet-level departments and some of the agencies housed in each. You'll notice many familiar agency names on the list, but you may be surprised within which department each agency operates. For example, many people don't realize that the National Weather Service is in the Department of Commerce and that the Financial Crimes Enforcement Network belongs to the Department of the Treasury rather than to the primary law enforcement department, the Department of Justice. The location of some agencies is a product of history and politics as much as of topical focus. For example, some people may believe that the Federal Bureau of Investigation (FBI) belongs in the new Department of Homeland Security, but it remains in its traditional home, the Department of Justice.

Table 8.2 also indicates the number of people employed in each executive department. The Office of Personnel Management reported in March 2004 that 2,640,212 civilians were employed in the executive branch of government. Nearly 1.7 million of these worked in the executive departments, and an additional 956,000 were employed in independent agencies that we'll discuss later in this chapter. Although people's perceptions of impersonal, impenetrable bureaucracies often lead them to believe that all federal government agencies are huge, the departments actually vary significantly in size. They range from the Department

"How many people work for the federal government?"

—Student Question

VISUAL LITERACY The Changing Face of the Federal Bureaucracy

PARTICIPATION Who Wants to Be a Bureaucrat?

TABLE 8.2 | **Departments in the Executive Branch of the Federal Government with Selected Subunits and Total Number of Employees, March 2004**

Department of Agriculture (98,803 employees)	**Department of Homeland Security (149,059 employees)**
Agricultural Research Service	Coast Guard
Animal and Plant Health Inspection Service	Customs and Border Protection
Cooperative State Research, Education, and Extension Service	Federal Emergency Management Agency
Economic Research Service	Secret Service
Farm Service Agency	**Department of Housing and Urban Development (10,330 employees)**
Forest Service	Government National Mortgage Association (Ginnie Mae)
Natural Resources Conservation Service	Office of Healthy Homes and Lead Hazard Control
Department of Commerce (37,126 employees)	Public and Indian Housing Agencies
Bureau of the Census	**Department of the Interior (70,240 employees)**
Bureau of Export Administration	Bureau of Indian Affairs
International Trade Administration	Bureau of Land Management
National Institute of Standards and Technology	Fish and Wildlife Service
National Oceanic and Atmospheric Administration	Geological Survey
National Weather Service	National Parks Service
Patent and Trademark Office Database	Office of Surface Mining
Department of Defense (667,192 civilian employees)	**Department of Justice (103,318 employees)**
Air Force	Bureau of Alcohol, Tobacco, Firearms, and Explosives
Army	Drug Enforcement Agency
Defense Contract and Audit Agency	Federal Bureau of Investigation
Defense Intelligence Agency	Federal Bureau of Prisons
Marine Corps	United States Marshals Service
National Guard	**Department of Labor (16,009 employees)**
National Security Agency	Mine Safety and Health Administration
Navy	Occupational Safety and Health Administration
Department of Education (4,448 employees)	**Department of State (32,977 employees)**
Educational Resources and Information Center	**Department of Transportation (57,668 employees)**
National Library of Education	Federal Aviation Administration
Department of Energy (15,140 employees)	**Department of the Treasury (126,408 employees)**
Federal Energy Regulatory Commission	Bureau of Engraving and Printing
Los Alamos Laboratory	Bureau of Public Debt
Southwestern Power Administration	Internal Revenue Service
Department of Health and Human Services (60,632 employees)	Office of the Comptroller of the Currency
Centers for Disease Control and Prevention	United States Mint
Food and Drug Administration	**Department of Veterans Affairs (232,818 employees)**
National Institutes of Health	

SOURCE: Office of Personnel Management, http://www.opm.gov, March 2004.

of Education, which has under 4,500 employees, to the Department of Defense, which has nearly 670,000 civilian employees in addition to 1.4 million active-duty military personnel and 1.2 million who serve in various reserve units.

There are also approximately 1,700 people who work directly for the president in the Executive Office of the President and its constituent agencies. Because they come under the direct control of the White House, these employees and agencies are typically considered an arm of the presidency rather than agencies within the federal bureaucracy.

The varying sizes of the bureaucracy's departments depend, in part, on whether they provide services at installations in

COMPARATIVE **Comparing Bureaucracies**

SIMULATION **You Are the Head of FEMA**

far-flung locations and employ agents who work in the field or primarily oversee the distribution of federal funds to state and local governments from a central office in Washington, D.C. For example, the Department of Housing and Urban Development, with only 10,000 employees, oversees the distribution of money, while the Department of Veterans Affairs, which runs veterans' hospitals and maintains other service offices, has 233,000 employees. Obviously, the large size of the Department of Defense is related to the number of bases and other facilities on which American military personnel serve throughout the United States and the world.

Political Appointees in the Bureaucracy

Presidential appointees who run federal executive departments are expected to be loyal members of the president's team. That means that they will defend the administration's policies and avoid public disagreements with the president. After being appointed by the president, they must be confirmed by the U.S. Senate. These appointees are usually not regarded as working within the bureaucracy; instead, they work directly for the president and try to guide and push the bureaucracy to act in accordance with the president's policy preferences. Secretaries and assistant secretaries who are appointed by the president do not necessarily possess expertise on the policy issues and laws administered by their departments. For example, a former member of Congress or former governor from the president's political party may be chosen to run an agency as a reward for political loyalty or because the president thinks this person will be an effective spokesperson or good administrator in a particular policy area. Other high-level appointments in the departments, such as assistant secretaries and inspector generals, may go to people with policy experience, but they may also go to party loyalists or to the children of prominent political figures. Critics have cited President George W. Bush's appointment of Michael Brown as the director of FEMA as an example of an appointment based on political connections and loyalty rather than on qualifications and experience. Brown's lack of experience in emergency management received widespread news attention amid the federal government's slow and ineffective response to the destruction, death, and human suffering in New Orleans when Hurricane Katrina struck the city in August of 2005. Before gaining a political appointment to a senior leadership position at FEMA in 2001, Brown had previously been a lawyer for the International Arabian Horse Association and had little, if any, training or experience in emergency management.[4]

> "What does the president look for in making appointments to federal offices?"
>
> —Student Question

PATHWAYS | of change from around the world

In December of 2005, students at the government dental college in Kozhikode, India, staged a protest against an order from the under secretary of the government's Department of Health and Family Welfare.[5] In the students' view, the order sought to change the existing procedures for placing dental students in residency programs as part of their training. Although residencies at government dental colleges were supposed to be reserved for students who studied at government colleges, the order sought to place a student from a private dental college in the government institution. Reportedly, the student in question was the daughter of an influential leader of a political organization.

Officials in government bureaucracies control valuable resources, and their decisions help to determine who gains benefits from government programs. Is there a risk that these benefits will be granted based on political connections, especially in a system like that of the United States, in which the heads of many government agencies are political appointees? Are there any decisions by officials in the government bureaucracy that could make you angry enough to protest? Think about policy issues of importance to you, such as the environment, education, or other matters. Can you think of decisions by federal officials with which you disagree? If not, do you think the decisions of such officials either have little impact or are not sufficiently visible to the public? ■

In the confirmation process, senators may expect that the secretaries and other appointed officials in specific departments possess relevant experience and expertise. This is most likely to be true for the departments of State, Defense, and the Treasury, owing to the overriding importance of foreign affairs, national security, and the economy. Because of the publicity and widespread perceptions about deficiencies in Michael Brown's performance as the director of FEMA during Hurricane Katrina, the list of appointed positions that receive close senatorial scrutiny may expand. For other positions, senators look less closely at the nominees' qualifications because they believe that presidents should generally be permitted to choose their own representatives to lead government agencies. Even the president's political opponents in the Senate may vote to

President George W. Bush meets with his cabinet in a private room at the White House. The news media can enter the room only for scheduled photo opportunities. ***—Should the president's cabinet meetings be televised so that all Americans can see the discussions among the leaders of the executive branch?***

PHOTO: Doug Mills/The New York Times

confirm nominees simply because they would like other senators to show the same deference for appointments by future presidents from a different political party.

Presidents do not merely reward loyalists in their appointments. They also use the upper-level appointed positions to place above the bureaucracy knowledgeable political figures who will vigorously enforce the laws and regulations with which the president agrees—or alternatively, will fail to enforce, enforce weakly, or attempt to change the laws and regulations with which the president disagrees. These elite actors influence the use of the bureaucracy's power and resources in shaping public policy.

Since the final decades of the twentieth century, presidents have used their appointment power to demonstrate a commitment to diversity as a means of pleasing their constituencies and attracting more voters. Women and members of minority groups increasingly receive appointments to highly visible positions at the top of executive departments. Presidents also seek geographic diversity so that the cabinet can be regarded as representing the nation. The composition of President George W. Bush's cabinet in 2004 illustrates this aspiration for diversity. Among the cabinet members were five former governors and members of Congress. There were three women, including Labor Secretary Elaine Chao, the first Asian-American woman to sit in a presidential cabinet. One Asian-American man was in the cabinet, Transportation Secretary Norman Mineta. The cabinet also included three African-American men: Colin Powell, secretary of state; Rod Paige, secretary of education; and Alphonso Jackson, secretary of housing and urban development. Powell was later replaced by Condoleezza Rice, the first African-American woman to serve as secretary of state. Just as Democratic President Bill Clinton had attempted to demonstrate bipartisanship through his appointment of former Republican Senator William Cohen as defense secretary, Republican President Bush sought to make the same point through the appointment of Transportation Secretary Mineta, a former Democratic congressman.

Only a half-dozen cabinet-level nominees have ever been rejected in the confirmation process by the U.S. Senate. The most recent instance was the Senate's vote against John Tower, President George H. W. Bush's nominee for defense secretary in the late 1980s, after allegations surfaced regarding Tower's excessive drinking and other aspects of his personal life. Generally, senators believe that the president ought to be able to choose the heads of government agencies. However, senators may oppose someone who is viewed as patently unqualified for a specific position or whose political views are regarded as too extreme.

Independent Agencies, Independent Regulatory Commissions, and Government Corporations

The executive branch includes nearly 100 independent agencies, independent regulatory commissions, and government corporations that operate outside the 15 executive departments. Table 8.3 on page 300 provides examples of some of the independent organizational entities in the federal government.

"What are 'independent agencies'?"
—Student Question

These agencies do not have identical functions. Some provide government grants or administer a specific government facility, such as a museum. Others are regulatory agencies that exert significant influence over public policy, because Congress has delegated to them

Joan Claybrook testifies at congressional hearings and uses press conferences to publicize issues of automotive safety and to educate government officials about health and safety problems. ***—Is it improper for such a policy advocate to be appointed to a leadership position in the federal bureaucracy?***

TABLE 8.3 | Examples of Independent Agencies, Independent Regulatory Commissions, and Government Corporations, by Type

Independent Agencies: Facility or Program Administration
General Services Administration
National Archives and Records Administration
National Aeronautics and Space Administration
Peace Corps
Selective Service System
Smithsonian Institution
Social Security Administration
Independent Agencies: Grants of Funds
Harry S Truman Scholarship Foundation
National Endowment for the Arts
National Endowment for the Humanities
National Science Foundation
Independent Regulatory Commissions
Consumer Product Safety Commission (toys, appliances, other products)
Federal Communications Commission (radio, television, cell phones)
Federal Elections Commission (campaign contributions, campaign advertising)
Federal Trade Commission (consumer credit, deceptive advertising)
National Labor Relations Board (labor unions, union voting, unfair practices)
National Transportation Safety Board (collisions involving aircraft, trains, trucks, other vehicles)
Nuclear Regulatory Commission (nuclear materials)
Securities and Exchange Commission (stock market, financial investments)
Government Corporations
Federal Deposit Insurance Corporation
National Railroad Passenger Corporation (Amtrak)
Overseas Private Investment Corporation
Pension Benefit Guaranty Corporation
United States Postal Service

broad authority to interpret statutes, create regulations, investigate violations of law, and impose sanctions on violators. The regulatory agencies are typically called *commissions* or *boards,* and as such names imply, they are led by a group of officials. The heads of these agencies often serve staggered terms so that no new president can replace the entire commission or board upon taking office. For example, the members of the Board of Governors of the Federal Reserve Board serve 14-year terms, with one new member appointed to the seven-member board every 2 years. The Federal Reserve Board acts independently to shape monetary policy by, for example, setting certain interest rates that affect the cost of borrowing money.

For some other commissions, the authorizing legislation requires that the appointees contain a mix of Republicans and Democrats. For example, the Federal Communications Commission (FCC) and the Federal Trade Commission (FTC) each have five members, but the law requires that no more than three members can be from one political party. The FCC regulates television, radio, cell phones, and other aspects of communications. It also investigates and imposes sanctions for violations of law and policy. For example, it slapped a $550,000 fine on Viacom, the parent company of CBS Television, for the "wardrobe malfunction" that led singer Janet Jackson's bare breast to be momentarily visible to a national audience during the half-time show at the 2004 Super Bowl. The FTC enforces consumer protection laws, such as fining companies that do not comply with rules concerning the fair treatment of applicants for credit or loans.

PATHWAYS | profile

Joan Claybrook

Joan Claybrook has spent her entire career advocating action by Congress and federal agencies to create and enforce regulations to protect the health and safety of consumers. After graduating from Goucher College and Georgetown University's Law School, Claybrook went to work for the National Traffic Safety Bureau. In 1966, she helped draft legislation to improve automobile safety and then left government service to work with Ralph Nader and others on automobile safety and other consumer issues. During the administration of President Jimmy Carter (1977–1981), she was appointed to serve as administrator of the National Highway Traffic Safety Administration, the successor agency to the one where she began her career. She later returned to Public Citizen, an advocacy organization that she had helped form in the 1970s, becoming its president and continuing her advocacy for government regulations

Scientists at NASA's Jet Propulsion Laboratory in Pasadena, California, show their excitement on seeing the first photos sent back from the Mars Rover. Many people believe that space exploration must be handled by government because it is too expensive and too important to be developed by private businesses. ***—What other activities and functions must be handled by government rather than by other kinds of organizations?***

concerning automobiles, the safety of medicines, fraudulent business practices, and other issues of concern to American consumers. Much of her career has been spent lobbying government agencies to create and enforce new kinds of safety regulations. ■

Some independent agencies are government corporations with their own boards of directors. For example, the National Railroad Passenger Corporation manages Amtrak, the nation's national system of passenger trains. These agencies generate their own revenue through the sale of products or services, fees, or insurance premiums. They need to convince Congress to provide them with whatever operating funds they need beyond what they can raise from customers. Some members of Congress see Amtrak, the U.S. Postal Service, and similar agencies as providing services that could be handled more efficiently by private businesses, which explains why arguments for cutting off government funding for such enterprises are often raised. Defenders of these agencies argue that these essential services must be maintained and that private businesses may cut back or eliminate unprofitable enterprises, such as national rail service, or charge unreasonable prices, as might occur under a completely private postal system. Thus they defend government control and subsidies for these agencies.

Independent agencies are responsible for government facilities, such as the national museums in Washington, D.C., administered by the Smithsonian Institution, or specific programs, such as the Peace Corps, which sends American volunteers to teach and provide community service around the world. Such facilities and programs are likely to be considered too unique and important to ever be subjected to privatization. Similarly, special agencies, such as the National Aeronautics and Space Administration (NASA), the space exploration agency, may do things that are so expensive and important that private organizations cannot match the federal government's ability to pursue the agency's goals.

Departments and Independent Agencies

Practice Quiz

1. Most members of the president's cabinet are heads of what kinds of organizational entities in the bureaucracy?
   a. departments
   b. independent agencies
   c. independent regulatory commissions
   d. government corporations

2. Members of the cabinet are
   a. elected by voters.
   b. appointed by the president and confirmed by Congress.
   c. appointed by the president and confirmed by the Senate.
   d. selected through civil service tests and interviews.

3. Amtrak, the agency that handles railroad passenger service, is currently a(n)
   a. department.
   b. independent agency.
   c. independent regulatory commission.
   d. government corporation.

4. The Federal Communications Commission is
   a. a department.
   b. an independent agency.
   c. an independent regulatory commission.
   d. a government corporation.

Answers: 1-a, 2-c, 3-d, 4-c.

Discussion Questions

1. What types of people are selected to be members of the president's cabinet? In your view, does this improve or detract from the quality of the executive branch?
2. Would the federal bureaucracy serve the public better if all departments were independent agencies?

What **YOU** can do!

Using the Internet, compare the backgrounds of cabinet appointees for the same position across several presidential administrations. What similarities and differences do you observe in comparing the appointees of different political parties? What about comparing only appointees from the same political party?

The Nature *of* Bureaucracy (pages 302–307)

Is there a better way to organize and run government agencies in order to reduce the undesirable aspects of bureaucracies?

Bureaucracies can be public entities, such as a state treasury department that collects taxes and enforces tax laws, or private entities, such as a bank with different departments for mortgages, commercial loans, and checking accounts. As you know very well, colleges and universities are also bureaucracies, with myriad offices responsible for admissions, financial aid, residential life, parking, and security. In a bureaucracy, workers typically have specific tasks and responsibilities, and there are clear lines of authority in the organization's pyramid of supervision and leadership. One person is responsible for leading and supervising the organization, and beneath the leader lie different levels of responsibility and supervisory authority. In a private organization, such as a business corporation, the leader might be called the president or the chief executive officer. In a government agency, the title of the head person may depend on the nature of the agency and the definition of the positions under relevant constitutional provisions or statutes. Departments are generally headed by a secretary, while independent regulatory commissions typically have a chairman.

People wait in line to mail income tax forms on the last day for filing taxes. U.S. Post Offices always expect long lines as the midnight deadline approaches.
—Have you had positive or negative experiences in dealing with government agencies?

The Image of Bureaucracy

In the minds of most Americans, the word *bureaucracy* does not conjure up idealistic notions of efficient organizations that carry out specialized responsibilities for the public's benefit. Instead, *bureaucracy* can convey an image of gargantuan organizations filled with employees who push paper around on their desks all day and worry only about collecting their paychecks and earning their pensions. In government service, because these employees have secure jobs, they may be perceived to feel no pressure to work industriously or efficiently.

A poll concerning the performance of five federal agencies conducted by the Pew Research Center for the People and the Press found that "the agencies get generally poor ratings for how well they carry out their administrative tasks." The groups that were polled "criticize the agencies for working too slowly and making their rules and forms too complicated."[6] The negative image of the bureaucracy may be enhanced by Americans' expectations that the government ought to operate for the benefit of the people in accordance with Abraham Lincoln's familiar words describing a "government of the people, by the people, and for the people." When people's anticipated Social Security checks are late or Medicare benefits are denied, citizens often feel frustrated and resentful about their treatment at the hands of bureaucrats who are paid by taxpayers yet do not seem responsive and obedient to the public. Perhaps you have felt such frustration in dealing with student loan applications or waiting for a tax refund.

"Why do Americans have such a negative image of bureaucracy?"
—Student Question

This negative image of bureaucracies obviously includes generalizations about large organizations and the frustrations that individuals may face in dealing with the officials who work there. What is your image of a bureaucracy? When we talk about the bureaucracy in terms of government agencies rather than banks, corporations, and universities, does your image of bureaucracy depend on which government officials come to mind? When a firefighter rushes into a blazing house and saves a child's life, few of us would associate this hero with the negative image of a bureaucracy. Yet the firefighter belongs to a bureaucracy: The fire department is a government agency, hierarchically organized and with specialized responsibilities for each rank, from the chief down through the captain and the individual firefighters.

As this example shows, our perceptions of government agencies may depend on actual experiences. When government officials respond quickly and provide expected services directly to us, there's no reason to associate these officials and their agency with the negative image of a bureaucracy. On the other hand, when responses to our requests are slow and we can't understand why we must fill out complicated forms or meet detailed requirements, the negative images come galloping back.

Because of their size and distance from many citizens, federal agencies may be especially susceptible to generating negative images. When citizens go to their local Social Security Administration office to apply for retirement or disability benefits, the office staff may need to seek approval from other officials back at Social Security headquarters. Meanwhile, we may have to fill out many forms and provide copies of various documents—and then wait weeks for an answer. "Red tape!" we mutter. Direct services from a local fire fighter or police officer put a human face on much-appreciated and immediate government services. But federal officials are often distant, faceless decision makers whose contacts with citizens are based on slow and frequently disappointing correspondence in response to questions and requests about important matters such as taxes, Social Security benefits, and medical assistance for veterans.

Unlike the equally faceless customer service representatives for online merchants and credit card companies, who nevertheless seem eager to respond to our phone calls and questions, the government officials with whom we communicate may appear detached and unresponsive—and (it seems) all too often, agents at the IRS, Social Security, or the Veterans Administration either insist that we pay more or tell us that we can't get some benefit. This does not necessarily mean that low-level government officials are cold-hearted by nature. They may need to fill out many forms and gain approvals from superiors before they can address our claims and questions in a slow-moving process. Whether or not individual government officials are uncaring, it is easy to understand why the bureaucracy often has a negative image in the minds of Americans.

According to Charles Goodsell, people expect too much from the bureaucracy. Says Goodsell, we have negative images in part because "we expect bureaucracies not merely to expend maximum possible effort in solving societal problems but to dispose of them entirely, whether solvable or not."[7] Do you agree that government agencies receive blame unfairly for falling short of perfection?

The Advantages of Bureaucracy

Officialdom does not exist by accident. Bureaucracies are created and evolve as a means to undertake the purposes and responsibilities of organizations. The German sociologist Max Weber (1864–1920) is known for describing an ideal bureaucracy involving competent, trained personnel with clearly defined job responsibilities under a central authority who keeps detailed records and makes consistent decisions in accordance with established rules. In theory, these are beneficial elements for running an organization efficiently. If you were in charge of distributing retirement benefits throughout the United States, how would you organize your system of distribution? Would you simply appoint one individual in each state to be the coordinator in charge of the retirees in that state and then send that individual all of the money each month for that state's retirees? This approach appears to eliminate the current centralized bureaucracy of the Social Security Administration, but it also may create many problems. How would you know whether each state coordinator was using the same criteria and rules for determining eligibility for retirement funds? How would you know whether the coordinators were sending out the appropriate amounts of money on time? By contrast, when agencies are organized in a hierarchical fashion with specialized responsibilities, the federal government can try to diminish the risks from these problems. In fact, bureaucracies, despite their flaws and problems, may provide a number of advantages for implementing laws and public policies.

- **Standardization.** By having a centralized administration and a common set of rules, benefits and services can be provided in a standard fashion that avoids treating similarly situated citizens differently. A retiree in Idaho can receive the same federal benefits and services as a retiree of the same age and employment history in Maine.
- **Expertise and Competence.** When people who work in an agency focus on specific areas of law and policy throughout their careers, they can develop expertise on those issues. This expertise will help them effectively carry out laws and policies and, moreover, permit them to advise Congress and the president on ways to improve law and policy. Presumably, their expertise will make them more competent than people who know little about the subject. Thus people who work for the EPA are typically hired because of their education and interest in environmental issues, and they develop greater expertise on this subject as they spend years working in this area.
- **Accountability.** Congress can authorize a specific budget for particular programs and then monitor results for the targeted policy area. If $50 million are earmarked to combat air pollution, the existence of an agency dedicated to environmental issues—the EPA—permits those funds to be directed to the targeted issues and not mixed together with funds destined for education, transportation, and defense, all of which are

Patronage System (Spoils System): Successful political candidates' and parties' rewarding their supporters with government jobs and firing supporters of the opposing party.

EXAMPLE: *An aspect of the patronage system continues to exist, as new presidents appoint supporters from their political party to top leadership positions in executive branch agencies. In earlier decades, such political appointments extended to even lower-level government jobs and created risks that government employees would be pressured to support a particular political candidate in order to keep their jobs.*

handled by separate agencies in the bureaucracy. After the money is spent, air pollution can be evaluated, and Congress and the president can assess whether the EPA spent the money effectively and whether their intended policies were carried out correctly.

- **Coordination.** Efforts of different agencies can be more effectively coordinated when each has clearly defined responsibilities and a hierarchical structure. Hierarchy enables the leaders in each agency to direct subordinates to work in cooperation with other agencies. For example, if officials in the Department of Education and the Department of Health and Human Services are instructed to cooperate in implementing an antidrug program or an education program aimed at preventing teen pregnancy, the leaders of the respective agencies can work together to delegate shared responsibilities. When individual officials throughout the country act independently on issues, it is much more difficult to coordinate efforts effectively.

In general, these advantages may be helpful in both government and business organizations. One additional advantage has special importance for government bureaucracy: merit systems for hiring. Merit, however, has not always been the criterion for hiring government workers.

Until a little over a century ago, government employees were hired and fired on the basis of their support for particular political parties and candidates for elective office. This was called the **patronage system**, or **spoils system**. Political parties rewarded their supporters by giving them government jobs. At the same time, supporters of the opposing party were fired as soon as an election placed new leaders in office. "To the victor belongs the spoils," said a prominent Jacksonian Era politician early in the nineteenth century, giving political patronage its alternative name, the *spoils system*. (By "spoils," he was referring to the practice of an army sacking a conquered city and soldiers carrying off whatever they could grab.)

Of course, the spoils system had many problems. There was an abrupt turnover in many government positions after elections in which a different political party gained power. Unqualified people got government jobs despite lacking the knowledge and interest to carry out their tasks properly. Government workers steered benefits and services to fellow partisans and sought to deprive their political opponents of government services. Officials spent too much time doing things that would help keep their party in power and themselves in their jobs. New roads, government contracts, and other benefits went to citizens who supported the elected officials who had hired the government workers. With self-interest unchecked, there were grave risks of corruption, as government workers and political leaders alike traded bribes for favoritism in distributing government services and benefits.

All these problems came to a head in the early 1880s. During the summer of 1881, a man claiming to be a disappointed office seeker (he was probably insane) shot President James Garfield. Garfield's assassination made him a martyr for the cause of "good government." This event helped push forward previous proposals to reform the employment system within the federal government. Congress and President Chester A. Arthur found themselves under irresistible public pressure to enact legislation establishing a **civil service system** based on merit.

"How does the civil service make bureaucracy less 'political'?"
—Student Question

In 1883, Congress passed and President Arthur signed the Pendleton Act, creating the first federal civil service system. Under this act, applicants for specified federal government jobs were supposed to be tested, demonstrate their qualifications, and keep their jobs based on competent performance rather than political affiliation. The new system reduced, but did not entirely eliminate, such problems as unqualified employees and bribery. Over time, more federal jobs were brought under civil service rules, and civil service systems eventually developed as well in state and local governments, especially during the Progressive Era in the first decades of the twentieth century.

The civil service system is still the framework for the federal bureaucracy. Today, the president can appoint the top officials who oversee most federal government agencies. In doing so, the president seeks to steer the bureaucracy in policy directions that reflect the voters' presidential choice in the most recent election. However, except for these high officials and the staff in the Executive Office of the President, the vast majority of other federal workers are civil service employees who remain at their jobs as presidential administrations come and go. Standardization, expertise, and competence would all be endangered—indeed, under today's conditions, they would collapse—if federal agencies experienced the kind of massive turnovers in personnel after each election that were typical of America in the mid-nineteenth century.

Civil service rules protect federal employees from being fired for failing to support a specific political party. Federal employees are further protected by the **Hatch Act,** a law that limits the participation of federal employees in political campaigns (see Table 8.4). They can vote and attend political rallies, but they cannot work on campaigns or endorse candidates. Although this law limits federal work-

Civil Service System: Government employment system in which employees are hired on the basis of their qualifications and cannot be fired merely for belonging to the wrong political party; originated with the federal Pendleton Act in 1883 and expanded at other levels of government in the half-century that followed.

EXAMPLE: *Federal employees in the Internal Revenue Service, National Park Service, U.S. Department of Transportation, and other agencies are hired based on their qualifications—education and experience—for a specific job, and they retain their positions over the years as new presidents win election, serve their terms, and are then replaced by new presidents.*

TABLE 8.4 | The Hatch Act

PERMITTED/PROHIBITED ACTIVITIES FOR EMPLOYEES WHO MAY NOT PARTICIPATE IN PARTISAN POLITICAL ACTIVITY

These federal employees *may*
- register and vote as they choose.
- assist in voter registration drives.
- express opinions about candidates and issues.
- participate in campaigns where none of the candidates represent a political party.
- contribute money to political organizations or attend political fund raising functions.
- attend political rallies and meetings.
- join political clubs or parties.
- sign nominating petitions.
- campaign for or against referendum questions, constitutional amendments, municipal ordinances.

These federal employees *may not*
- be candidates for public office in partisan elections.
- campaign for or against a candidate or slate of candidates in partisan elections.
- make campaign speeches.
- collect contributions or sell tickets to political fund raising functions.
- distribute campaign material in partisan elections.
- organize or manage political rallies or meetings.
- hold office in political clubs or parties.
- circulate nominating petitions.
- work to register voters for one party only.
- wear political buttons at work.

SOURCE: http://www.osc.gov/ha_fed.htm#regulations

ers' political participation, it is intended to prevent them from being pressured by elected officials to donate their money and time to political campaigns. Prior to the implementation of civil service systems, it was very common for government employees to be required to work on political campaigns in order to keep their jobs. The current system spares them from fearing that they will lose promotions, raises, and other benefits for failing to support the party in power.

The Problems of Government Bureaucracy

The advantages of a merit system do not mean, however, that government agencies necessarily fulfill their responsibilities efficiently and satisfy the expectations of citizens, the president, and Congress.

"Why is it so hard to make changes in a bureaucracy?"

—Student Question

Many practical problems tarnish the idealistic vision of civil service bureaucracies as effective, efficient organizations. For example, as organizations grow in size, decision-making layers proliferate between the employee whom the average citizen encounters and the policy-setting, upper-level managers with final authority. Higher-level decision makers may be far removed from the practical policy problems affecting citizens. When decisions must move through a chain of command, there are obvious risks of delay, including the chance that documents will be misplaced or lost so that new forms must be completed to start a decision-making process all over again.

Civil service protections can make it difficult for top officials to motivate government employees and spur them to take actions, especially when those actions require changing an agency's priorities or operating methods. Almost by nature, large organizations are resistant to change. People who have become accustomed to doing their jobs in a specific way may be reluctant to adopt new priorities and directives. Bureaucracies are not typically associated with innovation and bold ideas. They change slowly, and usually in incremental fashion. When the president or Congress wants law and policy to move in a new direction, getting the bureaucracy to reorder its priorities and operate in different ways can be akin to the familiar image of "turning a battleship at sea"—a slow, gradual, laborious process. If executive agencies are slow to implement new laws, they can hinder or even undermine the achievement of a president's policy goals.

For policy change to be effective, laws and programs must be designed by taking account of the resources, characteristics, experience, and organizational structure of the agencies that must implement those laws and programs. President George W. Bush, for example, touted his No Child Left Behind (NCLB) law, passed in 2002, as the key to improving education throughout the country. The NCLB law required the testing of all students and provided for punishing schools in which students perform poorly. Two years later, however, the federal government found that the law had been poorly implemented, because data about schools and students were not collected consistently and systematically throughout the nation. Implementation problems can be even more significant when, rather than just providing guidance and supervision for state and local governments, an agency bears responsibility for hiring staff, training personnel, and carrying out new tasks. When agencies are large bureaucracies, it can be exceptionally difficult to organize, implement, and monitor programs effectively. The federal bureaucracy bears responsibility for organizing initiatives nationwide, relying on

■ **Privatization:** Turning some responsibilities of government bureaucracy over to private organizations on the assumption that they can administer and deliver services more effectively and inexpensively.

EXAMPLE: *During the war in Iraq, the U.S. government hired private companies to handle food services, transportation of supplies, construction of facilities, and even personal protection (i.e., bodyguards) for American officials in Iraq. Problems arose, however, when some companies were accused of overcharging for services, bribing military officials for additional contracts, and violating the standards for behavior that are expected of American personnel.*

Transportation Security Administration (TSA) officers provide an essential service in attempting to protect public safety at airports. ***—How can we make sure that we have selected the best candidates to become TSA officers and have provided them with necessary training, equipment, and supervision?***

thousands of individuals spread throughout the country at hundreds of locations. Let's take an example: the Transportation Security Administration (TSA), which was created in November of 2001 in the aftermath of the 9/11 terrorist attacks. The TSA is now part of the Department of Homeland Security. Among other responsibilities, the TSA screens passengers and their baggage for weapons and explosives before they board commercial airliners. In its first few years, the new agency was plagued with problems. Eighteen-thousand screeners were hired and initially put to work without required background checks. Among the 1,200 screeners eventually fired after background checks revealed that they had lied on their applications or had criminal records, several with criminal pasts were permitted to remain on the job for weeks or even months before termination.[8] The federal government paid hundreds of thousands of dollars in claims after screeners were caught stealing from passengers' luggage while searching for weapons and explosives. Morale problems also developed as screeners complained of being required to work overtime without adequate compensation and of being assigned to use baggage-scanning equipment without receiving any training.[9] If the TSA had been given more time for planning, more opportunities to screen and train workers, and more resources to ensure adequate personnel and equipment at each airport, the implementation of the policy might have gone more smoothly. The bureaucracy, however, must work in a constrained environment in which limits on time, resources, and expertise often result in implementation problems.

Reform of the Bureaucracy

The gigantic size and nationwide responsibilities of modern federal agencies make it extremely difficult for the bureaucracy to live up to the ideals of efficient performance based on management principles in an organizational hierarchy. Some critics argue that alternative approaches to implementation could reduce the problems of government bureaucracy. One suggestion is to try **decentralization.** The federal government could give greater independence to regional offices that would be more closely connected to local issues and client populations. Alternatively, states could be given greater authority to handle their own affairs. For example, state inspection agencies could receive federal funds to enforce national air pollution or workplace safety laws. The argument for decentralization rests on a belief that smaller agencies, presumably more closely connected to local problems, can be more efficient and effective. There are risks, however, that decentralization would lead to inconsistent standards and treatment for people in different parts of the country. Officials in one state may vigorously enforce pollution laws, while those in another state may turn a blind eye to such problems because of the economic and political power of polluting industries.

Privatization■ has also been suggested as a cure for the problems of government bureaucracy. Critics argue that private businesses working under government contracts could deliver services and benefits to citizens with greater efficiency and less expense than when the bureaucracy handles such matters. All levels of government use private contracts in an effort to save money. Indeed, states have sent convicted offenders to prisons built and operated by private corporations, and governments pay private contractors to repair highways and build bridges.

In theory, businesses and nonprofit agencies are better than the government bureaucracy at finding ways to save money, developing innovations, and responding to feedback from client populations. One way that they save money is through compensation for low-level workers that is less generous than government pay and through flexible personnel policies that allow them to lay off or fire employees whose counterparts in government would have civil service job security protection. Privatization is controversial. In some circumstances, private contractors do not save money and do not deliver services more effectively than government agencies. In addition, it can be difficult to hold private companies accountable for their actions, because they are not necessarily subject to the same oversight laws that govern public agencies. Moreover, there are risks of favoritism and corruption as private companies use campaign contributions, personal contacts with government officials, and lobbying to encourage expenditures of government funds that add to their profits but do not necessarily address the public's needs.

Periodically, efforts are made to reform the bureaucracy in order to improve its effectiveness. For example, Congress established the **Senior Executive Service (SES)** in 1978. The SES consists of senior administrators with outstanding leadership and management skills who can be moved between jobs in different agencies in order to enhance the performance of the bureaucracy. The development of the SES was intended to add flexibility in shifting personnel resources within the federal bureaucracy.

The Nature of Bureaucracy
Practice Quiz

1. Which of the following is *not* assumed to be a beneficial aspect of bureaucracy?
   - **a.** employees' expertise on policy issues
   - **b.** citizens' direct access to high-level decision makers
   - **c.** vertical lines of authority for supervision and control
   - **d.** standardization of procedures and equal treatment of citizens
2. Civil service systems were developed in response to
   - **a.** the Great Depression.
   - **b.** Franklin Roosevelt's New Deal programs.
   - **c.** the spoils system.
   - **d.** the creation of independent regulatory commissions.
3. Decentralization of the federal bureaucracy would
   - **a.** give more authority to decision makers in regional and local offices.
   - **b.** eliminate the need for any government officials to work in Washington, D.C.
   - **c.** make the judiciary the most powerful branch of government.
   - **d.** permit the president to issue direct orders to the nation's governors.
4. Proposals for reform of the bureaucracy through privatization assume that
   - **a.** investors want to purchase the U.S. Capitol building.
   - **b.** government agencies should grow larger than they are today.
   - **c.** cabinet officers will be more highly motivated if they receive bonuses.
   - **d.** private businesses operate more efficiently than government agencies.

Answers: 1-b, 2-c, 3-a, 4-d.

Discussion Questions

1. How can the bureaucracy improve its image?
2. How can the public best be informed about important changes in the efficiency and cost-effectiveness of the federal bureaucracy?

What **YOU** can do!

Read about the history of the civil service at the Web site of the U.S. Office of Personnel Management at **http://www.opm.gov/biographyofanideal**. How would the bureaucracy be different today if these reforms had not taken place?

CONNECT THE LINK
(Chapter **6**, page **224–227**) Congressional committees each have responsibility for specific policy issues, and they interact frequently with officials in their counterpart agencies responsible for the same policy issues in the bureaucracy.

The Lobbying Pathway *and* Policymaking (pages 308–314)

How can the president and members of the president's cabinet make sure that workers within the government's many agencies are performing their duties properly?

From what you've read so far, you can see the bureaucracy's influence over policy through its responsibilities for implementation of laws enacted by Congress. As the examples of transportation safety and education have indicated, the effectiveness of agencies' implementation efforts can depend on their resources, information, and expertise.

The bureaucracy can affect policymaking in other ways, too. Its impact on the formulation of public policy comes primarily through the decisions and actions of elites—people with political connections, status, or expertise. This impact comes especially from the political appointees and policy experts at the upper levels of federal agencies. For example, officials in the bureaucracy formulate specific rules that provide precise details for how statutes should be implemented. In this section, we'll focus on these officials who influence the formulation of policies.

Lower-level personnel in the bureaucracy also affect policy outcomes through their influence over the day-to-day implementation of laws and regulations. These government employees include FBI agents, forest rangers, postal workers, water-quality inspectors, and many others who have direct contact with the public. If an FBI agent does not follow mandated procedures when investigating a case or arresting a suspect, the laws of Congress and the regulations of the Department of Justice have not been implemented properly. Full and proper implementation of many laws and policies can rest in the hands of relatively low-level officials who make discretionary decisions about how they will treat individuals and businesses when conducting investigations or administering the distribution of government services and benefits.

The Bureaucracy and Legislation

The ideal of the bureaucracy envisions employees with competence and expertise who work in a pyramid-shaped organizational structure with clear lines of authority and supervision. The lines of authority in a bureaucracy's organizational chart are meant to indicate that the downward flow of instructions guides the actions of personnel at each level of the agency. In reality, the decisions and actions of personnel within the bureaucracy are more complicated than that because of the influence of informal networks and relationships with organizations and actors outside the bureaucracy. In prior decades, political scientists often described the influence of these networks and relationships by focusing on the concept of the **iron triangle.**

The concept of the iron triangle described the tight relationship and power over policy issues possessed by three entities sharing joint interests concerning specific policy goals. These three entities were (1) interest groups concerned with a particular policy issue, (2) the key committee members in Congress and their staff with authority over that issue, and (3) the bureaucracy's leaders and the experts on that particular issue within a given department or subagency. Within their sphere of expertise and interest, these iron triangles could, through discussion, communication, and consensus among members, control the writing of laws and the development of policies. The linkages and power of the iron triangle were enhanced as interest groups provided campaign contributions to legislators on relevant congressional committees and rallied their own members to support or oppose legislative proposals emanating from the iron triangle. As you saw in LINK Chapter 6, pages 224–227, the committees in Congress are especially influential in shaping policy. The key committee members could draft legislation, block unwanted bills, and facilitate the passage of desired statutes through the legislative process. The bureaucracy's interested experts could provide needed information, help plan and facilitate implementation, and provide strategic opposition to counterproposals generated by those outside of the iron triangle. The concept of the iron triangle helped encourage recognition of the bureaucracy's role in shaping legislation through informal networks.

> "How does an iron triangle work?"
>
> —Student Question

Contemporary scholars view the iron triangle concept as limited and outdated. The governing system has changed. Growing numbers of interest groups are active in lobbying, and individual members of Congress today have less absolute power over committee processes. In the iron triangle process, legislation might have been controlled by lobbyists from a few interested corporations or advocacy groups, along with friendly members of Congress on the relevant committee and the top officials from a federal agency. With respect to some policy issues, many more interest groups have now become involved, and their strategies include advertising campaigns

Issue Networks (Policy Communities): Interest groups, scholars, and other experts that communicate about, debate, and interact regarding issues of interest and thus influence public policy when the legislature acts on those issues.

EXAMPLE: *The Bush administration's proposal to expand prescription drug benefits for senior citizens under the Medicare program developed with input from pharmaceutical companies, lobbying groups for senior citizens, and officials in the U.S. Department of Health and Human Services. Shortly after the proposal was passed into law, Representative Billy Tauzin, a key Republican leader who helped push the proposal through Congress, decided not run for reelection and became the highly paid president of the lobbying association for pharmaceutical companies.*

to arouse the public and calling the attention of the news media to issues that previously may have been decided largely behind the closed doors of a congressional committee room.

Realizing the inadequacies of the iron triangle framework for all policy issues, scholars now focus on concepts characterized as either **issue networks** or **policy communities**. Guy Peters describes these as "involving large numbers of interested parties, each with substantial expertise in the policy area.... They may contain competing ideas and types of interests to be served through public policy."[10] Both terms describe ongoing relationships and contacts between individuals interested in specific policy issues and areas. These individuals have expertise and remain in contact over time as their particular public policy concerns rise and fall on the nation's policy agenda. At government conferences presenting research on environmental issues, conference attendees who interact with each other are likely to include a variety of individuals representing different perspectives: scholars who study the environment, officials from the EPA, staff members from relevant congressional committees, representatives from interest groups concerned with such issues, and officials from businesses involved in waste disposal, manufacturing processes, and the cleanup of industrial sites.

Some of these individuals may change jobs over the years and move from universities and businesses into appointed positions in government or from congressional committees to interest groups. In 2004, it was reported that more than 90 former members of Congress were employed as lobbyists by businesses and interest groups, often with an emphasis on issue areas for which they were previously responsible on congressional committees.[11] High officials in the bureaucracy also move in and out of government. For example, Gale Norton, the Secretary of the Interior under George W. Bush from 2001 to 2006, had previously worked as an attorney for the Mountain States Legal Foundation, an interest group that challenged environmentalist groups in court by arguing against government restrictions on land use and by advocating the use of federal lands by ranchers, recreational vehicles, and oil exploration companies. She had moved in and out of government, holding positions in the departments of the Interior and Agriculture as well as working as a private attorney on related issues.

Even as these actors move between jobs, their interests and expertise keep them in contact with each other through conferences and individual communications as they develop working relationships. When bills are formally proposed, individuals from throughout the network are likely to use their contacts in seeking to amend the bill's wording, lobbying for its passage, or attempting to block its progress through the legislative process. The "revolving door" of employees moving between federal government service and interest groups or lobbying firms raises concerns that an agency may be "captured" or controlled by officials who have long alliances with and commitments to specific interest groups.

Gale Norton, the first Secretary of the Interior in the Bush Administration, shown here with President Bush, was a lawyer with experience as a policy advocate for businesses interested in economic development and energy exploration on federal lands. ***—Would the American public be better served by a Secretary of the Interior who is a scientist specializing in the forestry, wildlife, and water issues that are under the Department's authority?***

The Bureaucracy and Information

Officials appointed by the president to head executive agencies invariably advocate laws—at least in public—that reflect the president's policy agenda. This is especially true of the political appointees in each department, who were put in office precisely to create, revise, and implement laws that are consistent with the president's policy preferences.

Occasionally, long-time officials within the bureaucracy with experience and expertise may disagree with laws and policies sought by the president and presidential appointees. They may also disagree with new interpretations of existing laws or with presidential efforts to change current policies. These officials may get in

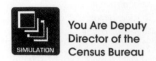

You Are Deputy Director of the Census Bureau
SIMULATION

touch with their contacts among personnel who work for congressional committees, thereby alerting sympathetic members of Congress to initiate investigations, publicize the president's actions, and oppose efforts to shape law and policy. They may also leak information to the news media in order to bring public attention to issues of concern to them.

An additional role played by officials in the bureaucracy is to provide information for Congress to use in crafting and approving statutes. They provide this information both formally and informally. Formally, some federal agencies, such as the U.S. Census Bureau, regularly send out a steady stream of information to all kinds of congressional committees that are interested in trends in the nation's population as well as in such demographic issues as home ownership, poverty, and education. Other agencies gather, analyze, and provide information about very specific policy issues, usually working only with those congressional committees that are specifically concerned with these issues. Informal communication between the bureaucracy and Congress occurs when legislative staffers or individual members of Congress contact agency officials with questions about policy issues and government programs. These informal contacts can help build relationships within issue networks that lead to cooperative working relationships as members of Congress rely on agency officials for advice when crafting new legislative proposals.

Congressional reliance on officials in the bureaucracy for information can create problems if presidential appointees use their authority to direct subordinates to withhold or distort information as a means of advancing the president's policy agenda. For example, in 2004, several conservative Republicans threatened to oppose President Bush's Medicare bill if it would cost more than $400 billion but had been reassured by the White House that it would not. The chief actuary for the Centers for Medicare and Medicaid Services conducted an analysis that indicated the legislation would cost at least $100 billion more, but his superior, the director of the Medicare office, threatened to fire him if he revealed this to members of Congress. Two months after Congress approved the legislation, the White House budget director revealed that the new law would actually cost more than $530 billion (see Figure 8.2).[12]

This risk of distorted information is one reason that Congress also seeks to gather its own information through legislative committees and through the Congressional Budget Office and Government Accountability Office, an investigative agency that reports to Congress. The range of policy issues is so vast, however, that Congress must inevitably rely on officials in the bureaucracy for important information about many public policies. Even though most employees in the federal bureaucracy are civil servants who are not formally affiliated with a political party, they may face pressure from presidential appointees to take actions that violate their own ideals of performing their jobs with neutrality and competence. If they disobey superiors, they may be passed over for promotion, transferred to undesirable positions or offices, or threatened with dismissal based on phony charges of incompetence.

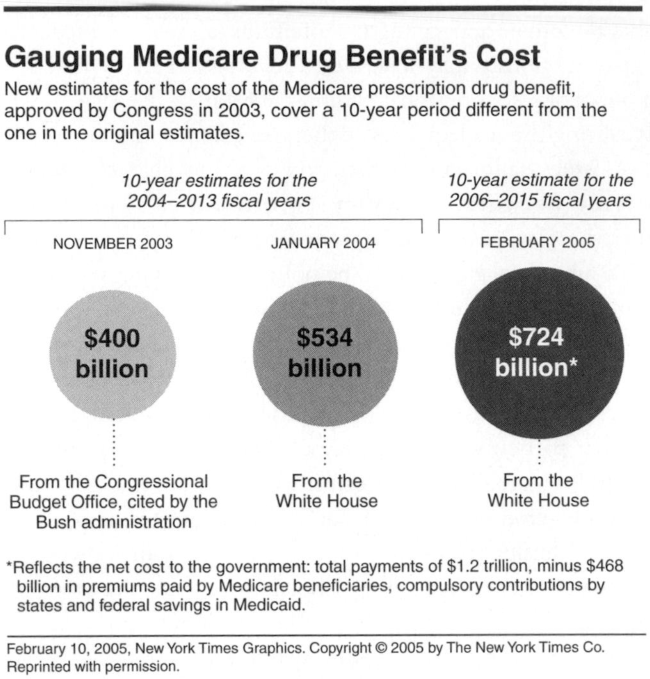
Gauging Medicare Drug Benefit's Cost
New estimates for the cost of the Medicare prescription drug benefit, approved by Congress in 2003, cover a 10-year period different from the one in the original estimates.
10-year estimates for the 2004–2013 fiscal years
10-year estimate for the 2006–2015 fiscal years
NOVEMBER 2003
JANUARY 2004
FEBRUARY 2005
$400 billion
$534 billion
$724 billion*
From the Congressional Budget Office, cited by the Bush administration
From the White House
From the White House
*Reflects the net cost to the government: total payments of $1.2 trillion, minus $468 billion in premiums paid by Medicare beneficiaries, compulsory contributions by states and federal savings in Medicaid.
February 10, 2005, New York Times Graphics. Copyright © 2005 by The New York Times Co. Reprinted with permission.

FIGURE 8.2 | **The Cost of Medicare Drug Benefits**

In seeking to gain congressional approval for its Medicare prescription drug plan, the Bush administration reportedly pressured an expert in the bureaucracy to keep quiet about cost projections that it knew would make the plan unacceptable to many Republican members of Congress. The figures showing significantly higher expected costs were only revealed after the program had been enacted into law. ***—Does the president have too much influence over the bureaucracy?***

SOURCE: The New York Times.

Some employees within the bureaucracy stand up against actions by executive branch superiors by providing information about misconduct by government officials. Individuals who are willing to provide such information are known as **whistleblowers,** and they often risk workplace retaliation in the form of dismissal, demotions, and other sanctions intended to punish them for their actions and to deter others from revealing politically damaging information. In 2004, for example, an issue emerged in the presidential campaign when a senior civilian contracting official in the

Regulations: Legal rules created by government agencies based on authority delegated by the legislature.

EXAMPLE: *In order to protect public safety, regulations issued by the U.S. Department of Transportation define how many hours each week truck drivers can be on the road and how many hours of rest they must have between driving shifts.*

SIMULATION You Are a Federal Administrator

SIMULATION You Are the President of MEDICORP

U.S. Army Corps of Engineers claimed that Halliburton Corporation, the business previously chaired by Vice President Dick Cheney, had received preferential treatment in the awarding of lucrative, no-bid contracts for reconstruction projects in Iraq.[13] Because the disclosure triggered investigative actions in Congress, the official's supporters feared that she would suffer retaliation. Her lawyer asserted that she should be shielded by the **Whistleblower Protection Act,** a federal law intended to prevent officials in the bureaucracy from being punished for their efforts to protect the country from governmental misconduct.

In theory, this statute should protect whistleblowers, but in individual cases, it may be difficult for affected individuals to refute their superiors' claims that they are being punished for poor performance rather than for providing well-intentioned, revealing information. For example, just as her attorney feared, the civilian whistleblower from the Army Corps of Engineers was removed from her position and demoted, with a reduction in salary, after she testified before a congressional committee about alleged improprieties in awarding no-bid contracts.[14]

Regulations

Depending on their responsibilities, federal agencies may receive rule-making authority from the statutes that Congress enacts. The rule-making process gives officials in the bureaucracy power over the development of public policy. In some cases, the legislation creating an agency will use general language to describe its mission. For example, as the political scientist Robert Katzmann concluded from his study of the FTC, "In the absence of clearly defined statutory objectives, the Federal Trade Commission apparently has wide discretion in determining the goal (or goals) that it should pursue."[15] General statutory language can become the basis for the bureaucracy's development of its own precise rules—agency-created laws called **regulations**, which govern the topics under a particular agency's jurisdiction. Commentators often describe regulations as filling in the precise details of rules for society based on the broader directives set forth in statutes. In other cases, Congress may enact statutes that specifically delegate to agencies the authority to formulate the precise rules to govern a particular subject. For example, Chapter VII of the Federal Food, Drug and Cosmetic Act, a statute intended to ensure the safety and effectiveness of these products, says that "the authority to promulgate regulations for the efficient enforcement of this Act . . . is vested in the Secretary [of Health and Human Services]."

Statutes written by Congress also specify the procedures that agencies must use in developing regulations. Normally, these procedures include publication of proposed regulations, a period during which the public may comment on the proposals, and a process for hearings about the desirability and potential effects of the proposed regulations. These procedures give interest groups the opportunity to encourage agencies to adopt new proposals, to work for change in proposals that originated with the government or other groups, or to block (if they can) proposed regulations adverse to their interests. For example, in 2004, food safety advocates pressed the government to issue regulations that would prevent the development and spread of mad cow disease in the United States. The National Cattlemen's Beef Association sought to halt the development of rules that would impose expensive new requirements on ranchers and meat processors.[16] The government ultimately issued more restrictive rules, but consumer advocates claimed that many slaughterhouses did not obey the regulations.

> "Who writes the actual rules? Congress or the federal agencies?"
>
> —Student Question

The rule-making process creates opportunities for influencing the results. Interested individuals' relationships with officialas in the bureaucracy come into play through issue networks. Interest groups that give campaign contributions and endorsements to the president's political party can also lobby overtly. Because some regulations are controversial, agencies are often instructed during election campaigns to slow down the processes by which rules are changed and created so that the political party opposing the president cannot use pending regulations as a campaign issue.[17]

Clearly, this rule-making process gives officials in the bureaucracy significant influence over the development of regulations affecting a wide range of policy issues, ranging from air pollution rules to workplace safety regulations to the approval of new drugs and medical treatments.

Although judgments about the desirability of specific regulatory changes always depend on the values of a particular observer, it is generally agreed that presidents have opportunities to exploit the rule-making process to advance their own policy agendas. For example, critics accused the Bush administration of using these tactics to advance policy goals that, if widely publicized, would be unpopular. Significant regulatory changes during Bush's first term included lengthening the hours that long-haul truckers could drive in one shift, despite evidence about the risk of car–truck collisions when drivers are tired; approving logging in federal forests without the usual environmental reviews; diluting rules intended to protect coal miners from black lung disease (see Figure 8.3); and relaxing air pollution regulations for factories and power plants.[18] The Bush

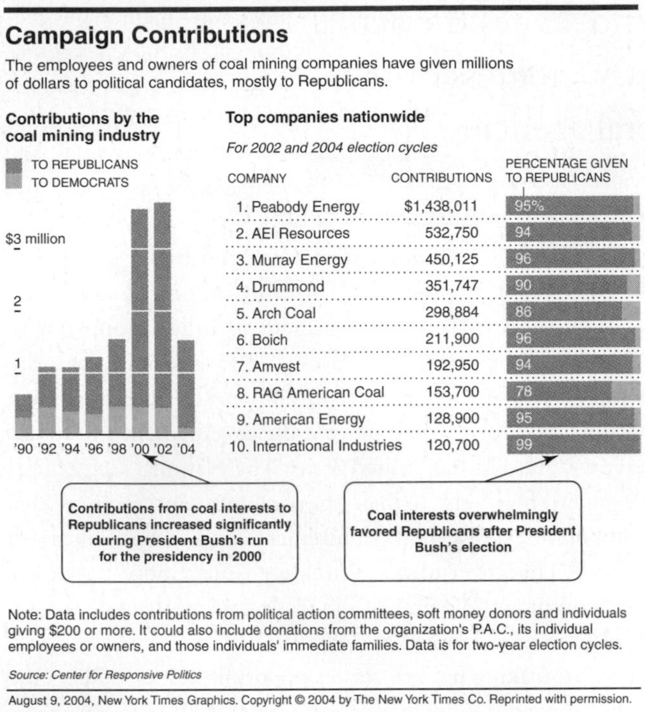
Campaign Contributions
The employees and owners of coal mining companies have given millions of dollars to political candidates, mostly to Republicans.
Contributions by the coal mining industry
TO REPUBLICANS
TO DEMOCRATS
$3 million
2
1
'90 '92 '94 '96 '98 '00 '02 '04
Top companies nationwide
For 2002 and 2004 election cycles
COMPANY
CONTRIBUTIONS
PERCENTAGE GIVEN TO REPUBLICANS
1. Peabody Energy $1,438,011 95%
2. AEI Resources 532,750 94
3. Murray Energy 450,125 96
4. Drummond 351,747 90
5. Arch Coal 298,884 86
6. Boich 211,900 96
7. Amvest 192,950 94
8. RAG American Coal 153,700 78
9. American Energy 128,900 95
10. International Industries 120,700 99
Contributions from coal interests to Republicans increased significantly during President Bush's run for the presidency in 2000
Coal interests overwhelmingly favored Republicans after President Bush's election
Note: Data includes contributions from political action committees, soft money donors and individuals giving $200 or more. It could also include donations from the organization's P.A.C., its individual employees or owners, and those individuals' immediate families. Data is for two-year election cycles.
Source: Center for Responsive Politics
August 9, 2004, New York Times Graphics. Copyright © 2004 by The New York Times Co. Reprinted with permission.

FIGURE 8.3 | **Coal Industry Campaign Contributions, 1990–2004**

The Mine Safety and Health Administration's efforts to rewrite coal regulations is part of a broader push by the Bush administration to help an industry that had been out of favor in Washington. Safety and environmental regulations often shift with control of the White House, but the Bush administration's approach to coal mining has been a particularly potent example of the blend of politics and policy.

SOURCE: The New York Times.

administration and its supporters responded to criticisms by claiming that the government hampers business productivity with too many needless regulations.

Quasi-Judicial Processes

The bureaucracy affects policy in some agencies through hearing processes that look similar to the duties of courts in examining evidence and issuing decisions. In the course of making these decisions, officials in the bureaucracy interpret statutes and regulations and thereby shape policy through their application of the law. Depending on the agency and the purpose of the adjudicative procedures, these processes can be formal or informal. There are also differences in the extent to which these processes are adversarial and thereby permit two sides to argue against each other in front of decision makers within the bureaucracy.

Officials in government agencies may use these processes when investigating whether individuals and corporations are obeying laws and regulations. For example, when the FCC receives a complaint about matters such as obscenity and profanity in radio or television broadcasts, its Enforcement Bureau investigates. When the Fox Network's reality show *Married by America* allegedly presented overtly sexual behavior and dialogue in a televised bachelor party, the Enforcement Bureau asked the network to provide information and respond to the charges. After the bureau concluded that the broadcast material had been indecent, it presented its findings to the five-member FCC, whose members, upon examining the evidence, voted to levy a $1.2 million fine against the network and its affiliates.[19] Much like judges in a court, the commissioners made their decision based on an examination of evidence and an interpretation of the law related to broadcast standards. Moreover, their interpretation of the law and their imposition of a strong sanction helped shape policy and provide guidance for other broadcasters about permissible program content.

Adjudicative processes also exist when citizens are denied requested benefits from the government. For example, if people believe that their physical or mental disabilities prevent them from working and that they qualify for disability payments from the Social Security Administration, they must file an application with their local Social Security office and provide medical evidence about their disability. If their local office deems them ineligible, they can appeal to an **administrative law judge (ALJ)** within the Social Security Administration. The ALJ holds a formal hearing, in which the claimant may be represented by an attorney, and medical evidence is presented to document the claimed disability[20] (see Table 8.5). Similar ALJ hearings and quasi-judicial decisions are made in other agencies concerning matters such as immigration and labor union disputes

STUDENT | PROFILE

In July of 2007, two law students at Cornell University, Kristen Echemendia and Heidi Craig, succeeded in persuading the Board of Immigration Appeals that an immigration judge had made mistakes in ordering the deportation of a Guatemalan man. The man had been tortured by military officials in Guatemala and had escaped to the United States, where he lived and worked quietly for 13 years. When he was arrested by American officials for entering the country illegally, he sought to gain asylum—in effect, special

TABLE 8.5 | **Applying for Social Security Disability Benefits**

APPLICANT	DECISION MAKERS
Step 1. *Submit application forms.* Records needed to demonstrate that applicant meets the criteria for 1) enough total years worked contributing money to the social security system to become eligible for consideration; 2) worked at least half the time in years preceding claimed disability; 3) contact information for doctors. *If disability claim is denied, then:*	*Decision makers:* After officials in Social Security Administration determine if applicant's work history makes individual qualified for benefits, medical personnel in state agency receive referral from Social Security Administration to obtain medical records and evaluate applicant's capacity to work.
Step 2. *Request reconsideration* *If disability claim is denied, then:*	*Decision makers:* Entire file reviewed by officials in Social Security Administration who did not take part in the original decision.
Step 3. *Appeal decision to quasi-judicial process in Social Security Administration* *If disability claim is denied, then:*	*Decision makers:* An administrative law judge (ALJ) within Social Security Administration will conduct a hearing at which the applicant and the applicant's attorney (if represented by counsel) can present evidence and witnesses before ALJ decides whether the original denial of benefits was improper.
Step 4. *Appeal decision to the Appeals Council within the Social Security Administration* *If disability claim is denied, then:*	*Decision makers:* Members of the Appeals Council within the Social Security Administration will review records and either deny the claim or refer the case back to the ALJ for further review.
Step 5. *File lawsuit in U.S. District Court.*	*Decision makers:* U.S. District Court judge considers evidence and determines whether the denial of benefits by the Social Security Administration was improper.

SOURCE: U.S. Social Security Administration, http://www.ssa.gov

permission to stay in the United States—because of the risk that he would be tortured and killed if he was sent back to Guatemala. He had no lawyer to represent him at his original immigration hearing, however, and he spoke little English. The Cornell students reviewed the records of the hearing and argued that he had been denied his constitutional right to a fair trial, because he had not been given adequate opportunity to present evidence about his physical scars and psychiatrists' reports on his depression and other problems resulting from the detention and torture in Guatemala.

As with other judicial-type processes within the bureaucracy, immigration hearings do not receive public attention, and large numbers of cases are processed with relatively little time spent on many of those individual cases. Thus the risks of error may be greater than in a regular criminal or civil court, in which each side is represented by a lawyer in public proceedings.

The Cornell students were able to help the man because they had specialized knowledge and advanced education in law. It would also be possible for undergraduate students to provide assistance for some people facing administrative proceedings. Simply by being aware of the nature and importance of Social Security disability processes, immigration hearings, and other matters within the bureaucracy, college students may be able to direct people to helpful resources. For example, they could inform people about law school programs to provide assistance to poor people on matters concerning immigration, Social Security, taxes, and other important matters handled by the federal bureaucracy. ■

Oversight and Accountability

As you've seen in the various ways by which agency officials shape policy, these bureaucrats can have significant influence. Yet their actions typically are not noticed by the public or the news media. Without public attention to the decisions of agency officials, it is

"Who holds bureaucrats accountable?"
—Student Question

difficult to know what they are doing and to make sure they do not exceed their authority or otherwise make improper decisions. However, oversight mechanisms do exist.

All three branches of government have the power to subject the bureaucracy to oversight and accountability. The president attempts to oversee, guide, and control the bureaucracy through the supervisory authority of political appointees at the top levels of each agency. These appointees are supposed to monitor the work of subordinates and ensure that officials in each agency, as they produce regulations and implement statutes, are working to advance the president's preferred interpretations of laws. The threat of sanctions exists, because even though it may be difficult to dismiss civil service employees for most of their actions, the superiors in each agency can affect promotions, bonuses, and job assignments through the performance evaluations that they conduct annually on each employee.

There is also legislative oversight. Christopher Foreman describes this as "two interlocking congressional processes: the efforts to *gather information* about what agencies are doing and to *dictate or signal* to agencies regarding the preferred behavior or policy."[21] Oversight by the legislative branch arises when congressional committees summon officials to testify. By pressing these bureaucrats with questions in a public hearing, members of Congress can attempt to discover whether laws are being implemented effectively and justly. If members are unhappy with the performance of officials in specific agencies, they can publicize these problems and thereby cast political blame on the president. This tactic puts pressure on the president and top appointees to ensure that agencies perform properly. Moreover, Congress controls each agency's budget. If agencies disappoint or clash with Congress, they risk losing needed resources. Congressional control over funding therefore creates incentives for cooperation and compliance by officials in the bureaucracy.[22]

Judicial oversight comes into play when individuals and interest groups file lawsuits claiming that agencies are not implementing laws properly or are not following proper procedures in creating regulations. The many quasi-judicial processes within the bureaucracy are also subject to oversight through appeals to the federal courts from adverse judgments by ALJs, agency commissions and boards, and other bureaucratic decision makers.

The Lobbying Pathway and Policymaking

Practice Quiz

1. What governmental entity creates regulations?
   - **a.** Congress
   - **b.** the president
   - **c.** the Supreme Court
   - **d.** U.S. Department of Health and Human Services
2. Someone inside the bureaucracy who reveals to Congress that an agency has violated its own rules or misused funds is generally called a
   - **a.** provocateur
   - **b.** whistleblower
   - **c.** administrative law judge
   - **d.** patron
3. What term has replaced *iron triangle* with reference to key factors affecting the development of policy by the bureaucracy?
   - **a.** regulatory process
   - **b.** *Federal Register*
   - **c.** issue network
   - **d.** Senior Executive Service
4. How many branches of the government possess the power to provide oversight and impose accountability on the bureaucracy?
   - **a.** three (Congress, president, judiciary)
   - **b.** two (Congress, president)
   - **c.** one (Congress)
   - **d.** none (the bureaucracy is independent)

Answers: 1-d, 2-b, 3-c, 4-a.

Discussion Questions

1. Briefly explain what a regulation is and how one is created in the federal bureaucracy.
2. List and briefly explain the quasi-judicial processes of the federal bureaucracy.

What **YOU** can do!

Go to the Federal Register online at **http://www.gpoaccess.gov/fr** and see whether there are any new or proposed regulations affecting issues of interest to you.

Conclusion

The size of the federal bureaucracy reflects the policy ambitions of the national government. If the government of the United States focused only on national defense, foreign relations, and taxation, as it did in the founding era and for most of the nineteenth century, the federal bureaucracy would be both smaller and narrowly focused on those limited areas. Today, however, Congress writes laws establishing rules and programs covering a host of policy issues, from agriculture to energy to health care. To implement these complex programs, create relevant regulations, and enforce the laws enacted by Congress, the bureaucracy needs sufficient resources and trained personnel. Despite the negative images the word *bureaucracy* calls to mind, the federal government needs large agencies to gather information, maintain records, educate the public, provide services, and enforce laws. As the national government enters new policy arenas or emphasizes new policy goals, such as homeland security in the aftermath of the terrorist attacks of September 11, 2001, the bureaucracy changes through reorganization and reallocations of money and personnel.

The bureaucracy plays a major role in public policy through a form of the lobbying decision makers pathway. Government agencies influence policy in several ways, none of which are clearly visible to the public or well covered by the media. Personnel in government agencies must implement the laws enacted by Congress and the policy initiatives developed by the president. If officials in the bureaucracy lack resources, knowledge, motivation, or supervision, the impact (or lack thereof) of policies on citizens' lives may differ from the outcomes intended by legislative policymakers and the executive branch.

Congress and the president rely on the bureaucracy for information and expertise about many policy issues. Officials in the bureaucracy may influence legislation through formal testimony to congressional committees as well as through informal contacts in the issue networks with committee staffers and interest groups. Officials in the bureaucracy also create law and policy through rule-making processes for developing, changing, and eliminating regulations. Modern presidents see the rule-making process as a means to advance their policy agendas without seeking the approval of Congress—and often without announcing to the public the precise implications of the changes that have been made. In light of the bureaucracy's daily involvement in the complete range of policy issues affecting the United States, this component of national government will remain extremely important and influential, despite the fact that the American public does not recognize or understand its actions and impact.

Key Objective Review, Apply, and Explore

The Federal Bureaucracy

(pages 288–295)

The bureaucracy in the executive branch of the federal government is composed of departments, independent agencies, independent regulatory commissions, and government corporations that have authority over specific topics across the vast array of policy issues facing the United States.

KEY TERMS

Bureaucracy 288
Department 290
Independent Agencies 290
Independent Regulatory Commissions 290
Government Corporations 290

CRITICAL THINKING QUESTIONS

1. Should any federal agencies be independent of presidential supervision and control? If so, why not make all agencies independent? How would you decide which agencies need to be independent?
2. Are there any new departments that should be created in the federal government (e.g., Department of Economic Development) or any agencies that should become cabinet-level departments?

INTERNET RESOURCES

Read about the organization and responsibilities of a federal department, such as the U.S. Department of Transportation at **http://www.dot.gov**, or the U.S. Department of Homeland Security at **http://www.dhs.gov**

Independent agencies have their own Web sites, such as the Federal Communcations Commission at **http://www.fcc.gov**, the Federal Trade Commission, at **http://www.ftc.gov**, and the National Labor Relations Board at **http://www.nlrb.gov**

ADDITIONAL READING

Goodsell, Charles T. *The Case for the Bureaucracy,* 4th ed. Washington, D.C.: CQ Press, 2003.

Departments and Independent Agencies

(pages 296–301)

The executive branch is organized into departments. The president appoints a secretary to head each department, as well as the attorney general to lead the Department of Justice. These appointees (plus the heads of a few other designated agencies) constitute the president's cabinet.

Political appointees may be politicians or individuals with policy expertise who share the president's policy goals.

Political appointees also have leadership positions in subcabinet positions, such as assistant secretaries, as well as in independent agencies. However, most personnel in the bureaucracy are civil service employees who remain on the job as presidents come and go.

CRITICAL THINKING QUESTIONS

1. Should there be minimum qualifications related to education and expertise in order to gain a presidential appointment to lead a department or other agency managed by a political appointee?
2. Is it important for Americans to see diversity in the president's cabinet? Why or why not?

INTERNET RESOURCES

Read about the individual appointees in the president's cabinet, and find links to the departments of the executive branch, at **http://www.whitehouse.gov/government/cabinet.html**

ADDITIONAL READING

Katzmann, Robert A. *Regulatory Bureaucracy*. Cambridge, MA: MIT Press, 1979.

Kettl, Donald F. *The Politics of the Administrative Process,* 3rd ed. Washington, D.C.: CQ Press, 2005.

Key Objective Review, Apply, and Explore

The Nature of Bureaucracy
(pages 302–307)

The popular image of the bureaucracy is of large, impersonal organizations that are inefficient and unresponsive.

The advantages of a bureaucracy stem from providing organizations with clear lines of authority in which each employee has specific responsibilities and expertise. Ideally, bureaucracies are useful for standardization and consistency in providing government services. However, bureaucracies often fall short of their intended performance goals.

In the late 1800s, the introduction of civil service systems emphasized the hiring of government employees based on qualifications rather than loyalty to specific politicians, as in the earlier, corruption-laden patronage or spoils system.

KEY TERMS

Patronage System (Spoils System) 304
Civil Service System 304
Hatch Act 304
Decentralization 306
Privatization 306
Senior Executive Service (SES) 307

CRITICAL THINKING QUESTIONS

1. Do the advantages of bureaucracy outweigh the disadvantages?
2. What are the advantages and disadvantages of privatization? Can you think of examples of the privatization of government functions that have worked well or worked poorly?

INTERNET RESOURCES

Learn about job opportunities and employment policies in the federal civil service at **http://www.usajobs.gov** and at the Web site for the U.S. Office of Personnel Management at **http://www.opm.gov**

Read a report by the Urban Institute on the privatization of government social services at **http://www.urban.org/publications/407023.html**

ADDITIONAL READING

Savas, E. S. *Privatization: The Key to Better Government*. Chatham, NJ: Chatham House, 1988.

Wilson, James Q. *Bureaucracy: What Government Agencies Do and Why They Do It*. New York: Basic Books, 1991.

The Lobbying Pathway and Policymaking
(pages 308–314)

The bureaucracy implements statutes and regulations, but its effectiveness is limited by its resources, information, and expertise.

Officials in the bureaucracy influence legislation through their communications with congressional committee staff and interest groups in their issue networks.

Whistleblowers in the bureaucracy provide information about misconduct within agencies. They are supposed to be protected from retaliation.

Presidents use the rule-making process to advance policy agendas through regulations. The rule-making process provides opportunities for interest groups to influence regulations.

The bureaucracy influences public policy through quasi-judicial processes.

No branch of government can completely control personnel within the bureaucracy.

KEY TERMS

Iron Triangle 308
Issue Networks (Policy Communities) 309
Whistleblower 310
Whistleblower Protection Act 311
Regulations 311
Administrative Law Judge (ALJ) 312

CRITICAL THINKING QUESTIONS

1. Do the unelected officials in government agencies possess too much power in the process for creating regulations?
2. Do adequate mechanisms exist to hold bureaucrats accountable for their decisions and actions?

INTERNET RESOURCES

A quasi-judicial process is described in the materials concerning hearings and appeals for Social Security disability claims at **http://www.ssa.gov/oha**

Read published proposed regulations awaiting public comments at **http://www.regulations.gov**

ADDITIONAL READING

Foreman, Christopher H., Jr. *Signals from the Hill: Congressional Oversight and the Challenge of Social Regulation*. New Haven, CT: Yale University Press, 1988.

Fritschler, A. Lee. *Smoking and Politics: Policymaking and the Federal Bureaucracy*, 3rd ed. Englewood Cliffs, NJ: Prentice Hall, 1983.

Chapter Review Critical Thinking Test

1. Why do bureaucracies exist?
 a. to impart greater authority to the organizations they represent
 b. to make sure the organizations they represent can cover a large geographic area
 c. to carry out the work of the organizations in an efficient and effective way
 d. to act as a buffer between the executive decision makers of the organizations and the constituents interacting with those organizations

2. The size of the federal bureaucracy reflects the policy objectives and commitments of the national government.
 a. true **b.** false

3. How does the bureaucracy share public policymaking with other governmental entities?
 a. The president shapes laws that help define public policy; Congress directs bureaucratic agencies to carry out those laws.
 b. Congress and the president create laws to define public policy; officials working in federal agencies carry out those laws and policies.
 c. experts in bureaucratic agencies enact statutes that are implemented by the president unless Congress vetoes the statutes.
 d. Working upward through a vertical hierarchy of authority, bureaucratic experts inform the president of laws that are necessary to conform to his political views; the president urges Congress to write and pass the appropriate legislation, which the judiciary then signs into law.

4. Which federal agency has primary responsibility for responding to natural disasters?
 a. None. It is the responsibility of state and local agencies.
 b. U.S. Coast Guard
 c. U.S. Department of Emergency Preparedness
 d. FEMA

5. A successful political candidate or party rewarding their supporters with government jobs and firing supporters of the opposing party is known as
 a. gerrymandering. **b.** logrolling.
 c. the merit system. **d.** the spoils system.

6. How many different organizational entities are in the federal bureaucracy?
 a. one (departments)
 b. two (departments and independent agencies)
 c. three (departments, independent agencies, and independent regulatory commissions)
 d. four (departments, independent agencies, independent regulatory commissions, and government corporations)

7. The creation of the Department of Health, Education, and Welfare (HEW) in the 1950s
 a. marked the expansion of the bureaucracy into policy areas that the Constitution did not anticipate.
 b. was a natural extension of the Constitution's original emphasis on federal responsibilities for public education.
 c. required a constitutional amendment, because it radically departed from the policy focus prescribed in the Constitution.
 d. shifted federal authority in policy matters from the legislative to the executive branch.

8. Approximately how many nonmilitary employees work in departments in the executive branch?
 a. 300,000 **b.** 850,000
 c. 1 million **d.** 2.6 million

9. What do the heads of federal executive departments do?
 a. work within their departments to make sure the officials and employees beneath them are content and well-compensated
 b. act as a liaison between the department and the economy
 c. work directly for the president in trying to make their department respond in accordance with the president's policy preferences
 d. act as a buffer between their own department and foreign governments

10. Regulatory entities are usually called
 a. councils. **b.** advisory boards.
 c. agencies. **d.** caucuses.

11. NASA is
 a. a governmental corporation.
 b. an independent agency.
 c. a department.
 d. an independent regulatory commission.

12. NASA's astronauts are part of the federal bureaucracy.
 a. true **b.** false

13. Why are people's negative perceptions of the federal bureaucracy often unfair?
 a. because federal employees are always working hard and in the best interests of the public at large
 b. because federal employees do not receive good wages or benefits
 c. because people often do not realize the challenges of administering government programs
 d. because "red tape" is an urban myth

14. Why was the civil service merit system enacted?
 a. to make federal employees more courteous on the job
 b. so that federal employees would get and retain their jobs based on their competence, not their political affiliation or personal connections
 c. so that federal employees could be legally bound to carry out their responsibilities effectively
 d. so that federal employees could be held to consistent performance standards and could be fired if their superiors disliked them

Chapter Review Critical Thinking Test

15. What is a significant practical problem with the federal bureaucracy?

a. Standards of competence are so high that it becomes difficult to find and retain suitable employees.

b. It contains so many departments that presidents often have a difficult time knowing which department should carry out a particular policy.

c. Its size makes it slow to change or respond to policy shifts signaled from the president or Congress.

d. People working in it always become lazy, knowing that they can never be fired.

16. In order to seek to save money, all levels of government use private contracts.

a. true **b.** false

17. Why are critics worried about the pattern of officials leaving the federal bureaucracy to join interest groups or lobbying firms in the same field of interest—and even returning to government service in that same field?

a. because they can often get cynical and burned out

b. because this pattern prevents a particular issue network from including a diverse group of participants

c. because such individuals might lack sufficient expertise

d. because the agencies might in effect become too heavily influenced by alliances in the private sector

18. Why do the Congressional Budget Office and the Government Accountability Office exist?

a. to gather and communicate to Congress information available only to Washington insiders

b. to communicate the results of congressional hearings to the public

c. to gather and provide to Congress information undistorted by the political agendas of the president or bureaucratic agencies

d. to monitor, in a nonpartisan way, the budgetary and policy actions of the federal courts—especially excise courts

19. What was President George W. Bush's typical approach to government regulation?

a. to add regulations or make them more stringent

b. to eliminate regulations or make them less stringent

c. to leave regulations unchanged

d. to defer to Congress on most issues related to regulation

20. When government agencies unduly influence policy, the public

a. usually finds out about it from the news media.

b. usually finds out about it from governmental publications.

c. almost never finds out about it.

d. really does not need to know about it.

Answers: 1-c, 2-a, 3-b, 4-d, 5-d, 6-d, 7-a, 8-d, 9-c, 10-c, 11-b, 12-a, 13-c, 14-b, 15-c, 16-a, 17-d, 18-c, 19-b, 20-c.

You decide!

Suppose you have been appointed to head the Federal Emergency Management Agency (FEMA). Using the FEMA Web site (**http://www.fema.gov**), click on "About Us," and read the agency's mission statement. How did its reassignment to the Department of Homeland Security affect its mission, goals, and administrative duties? What issue networks can you identify that may exist in connection with FEMA? Then, using the Federal Register online (**http://www.gpoaccess.gov/fr**), review some of the proposed rules and regulations that are currently open for comment. Who will be affected by these rules if they take effect? What comments would you expect citizens to make? What comments would you expect various private entities to make? How would you reconcile the two? Finally, review the FEMA Web site to obtain a sense of all its responsibilities. Which values seem to be most important in guiding decision-making in this agency: accountability, efficiency, equity, or technical expertise? How does this compare to other agencies within the Department of Homeland Security, such as the Transportation Safety Administration or the Office of Health Affairs?

Key Objective Outline

How influential should public opinion be in swaying policymakers and individuals in our society?

Public Opinion **(page 322)**

What factors promote stability, and why and how does public opinion change?

The Stability of Political Beliefs **(page 326)**

What is political ideology?

From Values to Ideology **(page 330)**

What factors influence how people acquire political values?

Political Socialization **(page 332)**

How does membership in different social groups impact political views and behavior?

Social Groups and Political Values **(page 336)**

What factors affect the quality and usefulness of poll data?

Measuring Public Opinion **(page 342)**

CHAPTER 9 POLITICAL SOCIALIZATION AND PUBLIC OPINION

How do people acquire their political values, and how stable is public opinion?

In 1969, there was growing concern over the health of our environment, prompting Senator Gaylord Nelson to call for a grassroots demonstration to raise environmental awareness the following spring. On April 22, 1970, the modern environmental movement was launched in the United States when 20 million people across the nation demonstrated their support for ensuring a healthy and sustainable environment—the first Earth Day. How successful has this movement been in changing public opinion about the importance of conservation and sound environmental practices? In some ways, the movement has been successful, but in other ways, their ability to get people to change their opinions and actions have been far from victorious.

In October of 2007, because of a severe drought and lack of conservation, it was feared that Atlanta and many communities in the Southeast would run out of water. Fortunately, rain eased the concerns for many cities (including Atlanta), but one Tennessee town (Orme) did run out of water. Orme had to truck water in from Alabama several times a week, and residents only had access to water in their homes and businesses for 3 hours a day. Imagine if you turned your water faucets on and no water emerged? How could you function? Despite these severe circumstances and potential disasters that could result from a lack of water, there is still not a great deal of general concern over creating national water and/or conservation policies. How can we change people's minds and show them how tangible environmental problems can be? More generally, by what processes do people acquire values, and how can these opinions be changed?

Although our culture and political values are relatively stable, change does occur—often gradually, but sometimes with dramatic speed. When our culture changes, our government responds. In the two chapters that follow, you will examine the power of opinion and culture to bring about change and influence our world.

STUDENT RESOURCE-CENTER
• Glossary
• Vocabulary Example
• LINK
• MyPoliSciLab Connection

■ **Public Opinion:** The attitudes of individuals regarding their political leaders and institutions as well as political and social issues.

EXAMPLE: *Public opinion tends to be grounded in political values and can impact political behavior.*

■ **Elitism:** The theory that a select few—better educated, more informed, and more interested—should have more influence than others in our governmental process.

EXAMPLE: *Many believe that the framers of our Constitution were elitists, because they were typically more wealthy and educated than the masses. Elites tend to view the world differently than those who are less advantaged.*

Public Opinion

(pages 322–325)

How influential should public opinion be in swaying policymakers and individuals in our society?

Our government, Abraham Lincoln reminded us in his Gettysburg Address, is "of the people, by the people, and for the people"—in short, a product and a reflection of the American public. So when you think about public opinion, the concept may at first seem quite straightforward—it's the opinion of the general public. In a society as large and diverse as ours, however, it is no easy job to determine *the* opinion of "the public." It is therefore helpful to think of **public opinion**■ as a mechanism that quantifies the various opinions held by the population or by subgroups of the population at a particular point in time. A complete picture of the opinions of more than 300 million Americans is difficult to estimate but nevertheless insightful.

Public opinion is grounded in political values, but it can be influenced by a number of sources and life experiences. Despite the fact that we are a highly educated society, this advanced level of education has not directly translated into a more politically informed citizenry. Seventy percent of Americans cannot name their senators or their members of Congress. Those who are politically knowledgeable, however, tend to have more stable political opinions. Many experts and political commentators believe that since most people don't base their opinions on specific knowledge, their opinions are neither rational nor reasonable.[1]

Other scholars have argued that a general sense of political understanding is enough to cast an informed ballot and to form reasonable political opinions.[2] Therefore, even though most citizens can't name the chief justice of the U.S. Supreme Court, they can nevertheless form rational and coherent opinions on issues of public policy and political preferences. It is important to note that research on public opinion most often focuses on the voting population rather than on the general population. This is an important distinction, because the voting population is generally more educated and more politically knowledgeable than the general population.

The Relationship Between Public Opinion and Public Policy

To what extent should public opinion drive public policy? There are many views on this, and they reflect assorted takes on the nature of democracy itself. Of central importance is the role of the public in the governing process. How influential should public opinion be? How much attention should our political leaders pay to the public's positions and attitudes? Some authorities believe (though they may not say this publicly) that public opinion should have little influence on the behavior and decision-making of our leaders. They argue that democracies need to limit the influence of the people, allowing the better-informed and more educated leaders to chart our path. Others argue that the views of the people should be given great weight, as a representative democracy needs to pay attention to the will of the people.

Those who believe that democracies need to limit the ability of the public to influence events argue that information must be controlled and narrowly shared. Leaders should do the thinking and the planning, and the masses should step up occasionally to select their leaders in periodic elections and spend the rest of their time as spectators.[3] Many analysts are concerned that public opinion can change easily and is too unstable, with little solid grounding, to be given much regard. In many ways, this line of thought makes sense, because most people are too busy to pay much attention to politics. They aren't lacking in intelligence, but they certainly are lacking interest. This fact is behind the argument that the public should defer to the few who have the skill, knowledge, and power to make wise decisions. Some researchers have found evidence to support the notion that it might be best for leaders to minimize the impact of public opinion and to allow citizens to influence policymakers primarily through elections.[4] This **elitism**■ was forthrightly expressed in the early days of our republic but is not widely acknowledged among political leaders and commentators today.

HISTORICAL VIEWS The founders, on the whole, thought that too much influence was given to the preferences of the people under the Articles of Confederation. As you've seen, the Articles created a system that was very responsive to the broad public but not very receptive to the elite. In the new constitutional system they created, the founders reacted by diminishing the relationship between the government and public opinion. The new system was designed to impose a sort of waiting period on the masses, reflecting the thought that officials should shape public opinion, not respond to it. For example, *Federalist No. 63* asserts that a "select and stable" Senate would serve as "an anchor against popular fluctuations," which would protect the people from their "temporary errors." In *Federalist No. 49,* Madison warns of the "danger of disturbing the public tranquility by interesting too strongly the public passions." Hamilton, in *Federalist No. 68,* argues for the indirect election of the president by a council of wise men (the Electoral College) who must not react too quickly to the passion of the people, and in *Federalist No. 71,* he further warns against following the "sudden breeze of passion" or listening to every "transient impulse" of the public. The founders saw the government as our guardian, protecting us from ourselves. They did believe that long-held views—those that lasted over the presidential term and the staggered Senate elections—should affect the course of government. They were more concerned with curbing *transient* ("here today, gone tomorrow") opinions, which they viewed as "common." Today, as we have become more educated and have adopted a political system with universal adult suffrage, people have come to expect their government to be open and responsive.

CONTEMPORARY CONSIDERATIONS In direct opposition to this elitist theory—and by far the more commonly held view of contemporary political leaders and political scientists—has been a position based on *pluralism*. Whereas elitists have argued that complex decisions need to be made free from public pressure, pluralists believe that citizens should be informed and should participate in democratic decision-making to ensure the health and vitality of the system. They argue that participation by the public gives legitimacy to the political process and governing officials. Pluralists urge that officials pay close attention to the desire of the people in charting their actions, because active participation is an essential part of a healthy democracy. Rational decision-making will occur when many active groups get informed about the issues and discuss the many arguments. This line of reasoning goes back to the ancient Greek philosopher Aristotle, who believed that collective judgments were more likely to be wise and sound than the judgments of a few.

Political scientist Sidney Verba makes a strong case that public opinion should be heeded because polls are a more egalitarian form of political expression than other forms of participation, which tend to benefit the more educated and affluent. Since each citizen has an equal (but tiny) chance of being selected in a poll, there is a greater chance that the opinion of the broad public will be accurately determined—that the data will not be skewed. Some theorists insist that other forms of political expression are better gauges of public opinion, because they require more effort from people. Verba, however, presents a strong argument that economic differences between the affluent and the less affluent make it difficult for the views of the general population to be heard, because the wealthy are better able to articulate and present their points of view. Hence, Verba says, it is a bit utopian to think that the concerns of all demographic groups could be fairly and accurately portrayed without public opinion polls.[5]

> "Do political decision makers pay attention to public opinion?"
> —Student Question

The reality of the situation probably lies somewhere between these two theories. There are times when officials respond to the views of the people—especially when the opinion is fairly popular and when an issue is presented that offers a chance to gain a political advantage. If the voting population is very interested in an issue and a dominant viewpoint seems to emerge, elected officials will be under great pressure to pay attention to the opinions and act accordingly. Even unelected officials, including judges, are often influenced by public opinion.

At other times, officials pay less attention to the views of the public, including the views of voters. This is likely to happen when the public has focused relatively little attention on an issue. Officials may also choose not to be responsive when their convictions come into conflict with the views of the people. Elected officials may take unpopular positions that they nevertheless believe in, risking their public support for their beliefs. Knowing when to follow public opinion and when to resist it is one of the marks of a truly great political leader.

One example of public opinion *not* swaying government policy is in the area of gun control. Imposing some form of gun control is popular among a large segment of the citizenry (especially in times following a publicized gun tragedy), but significant federal gun control legislation is rare. Passed in 1993, the Brady Bill, which mandated waiting periods when purchasing handguns, was

CONNECT THE LINK
(Chapter **11**, pages **414–415**) Do you think the power of interest groups is overestimated by most Americans?

the first major federal gun control law since 1968—and it was allowed to quietly die in 2004 despite its popularity among a large majority of Americans. Many critics cite this example to argue that public opinion is not influential in American politics.

Consider, however, a different example: drug policy. Following the highly publicized deaths of a few famous athletes, and with increased media coverage of drug abuse and the widespread availability of illicit drugs in the mid-1980s, the public became very concerned with drug abuse, citing it as the nation's most important problem. Congress and the White House struggled to catch up with public concern, each quickly presenting initiatives to address the country's "drug crisis." Significant legislation was passed, increasing the role of the federal government in a problem that historically had been regarded as primarily the responsibility of state governments. A major public service campaign was launched to persuade Americans to "just say no" to drugs. A federal "drug czar" was appointed, and a "War on Drugs" was declared.[6] Unlike gun control, this example demonstrates the power of the public in influencing government to respond to a problem—even though the War on Drugs has accomplished relatively little.

Why did the government respond to public concerns over drugs but fail to respond to the support for additional gun control provisions? In LINK Chapter 11, pages 414–415, will offer one explanation: Organized and powerful interest groups vehemently oppose gun control, whereas no organized interest groups opposed the War on Drugs. This, however, is the simple answer. The complete answer is far more complex. One reason why officials responded to the concern over drugs but not over guns is that people were more worried about the drug crisis than they were about assault weapons. In social science jargon, the drug crisis was simply more "salient" to the population. Moreover, the media reinforced the concern many felt about drug problems, but they did not focus much attention on concerns over the ready availability of military-style assault weapons. When public officials discuss issues and keep them in the limelight (as they did with drugs), public opinion can often be influenced.

Literacy is an issue close to Laura Bush's heart. First Ladies often participate in politics through initiatives to fight drugs, promote reading, and combat discrimination. Some believe that First Ladies should not engage in politics and instead remain involved only in traditional activities, keeping a low profile. ***—How active and in what sorts of things should First Ladies be involved? Do you think a First Gentleman would have similar roles, or would expectations of the president's husband vary from those we have for the president's wife?***

Fundamental Values

Most Americans are alike in many important ways and agree on a number of key political values. Most citizens can speak English and are proud to live in this country, and even though many see problems, they would rather live here than anywhere else. Most of us dream of a better future for our children and support our political institutions.

While we share many common values, we often disagree over their meaning and differ on specific policies related to these values. For example, one area of broad agreement is support for personal liberty. Our country was founded on the idea of protecting individual liberties and freedoms. As you saw in Chapter 5, our Constitution and Bill of Rights were written to protect individual freedoms "from" and "to." We are protected *from* unreasonable searches, *from* cruel and unjust punishments, and (with the Fourteenth Amendment) *from* discrimination. We are protected against infringement on our freedom *to* practice our religion freely, *to* express our minds, and *to* join with others in forming organizations. Most of us cherish these liberties, but the specific meaning of these freedoms can cause disagreement. Should hate groups have no limits on speech? Can the speech of the wealthy drown out the speech of the poor? When we move from the abstract to specific policies, there is often disagreement.

In addition to freedom, Americans highly value the idea of **individualism,** a belief that goes back to the earliest days of our republic. A reverence for individualism and individual rights is central to our democracy, because the government is expected to protect individuals and design policies that enhance the chances of reaching self-fulfillment. It is also central to our economic system: At the heart

Equality of Opportunity: The belief that all should have equal chances for success in education, employment, and political participation.

EXAMPLE: *Public schools were founded to allow all children equal opportunity to become educated and achieve success.*

Equality of Outcome: Egalitarian belief that government must work to diminish differences between individuals in society so that everyone is equal in status and value.

EXAMPLE: *Equality of outcome has produced calls to end discrimination in pay and was the theory that motivated the Equal Pay Act of 1963, which outlawed overt discrimination in pay between men and women.*

of capitalism lies a belief in individualism that in many cases permits individual interests to win out over community interests. (Socialism, by contrast, values community needs over individual wants.) The spirit of individualism also stresses the right of citizens to own property and to control their earnings (hence the conflict over tax policies). Comparing the general sense of individualism in the United States to that in Europe provides a vivid example of how varied opinions can be. Europeans generally have higher expectations of their government in addressing individual concerns, such as providing health care and alleviating poverty, than Americans do. Certainly, we Americans would like for everyone to have health insurance, but for the most part we do not believe it is the government's role to fund universal health insurance programs. Europeans believe that such programs are valuable and should be funded. The root of this markedly different set of attitudes is the difference of opinion between individual and community responsibility.

Americans also have high levels of support for their democratic government. We believe in majority rule, coupled with the need to protect minority rights. We see fair, free, and competitive elections as essential to our democracy. We feel strong national loyalty and patriotism, which together provide solid and crucial support for our governmental system, are very important.

Americans also strongly support the idea of equality. Equality is a very complex notion, involving both political and social aspects. There is near-universal support for political equality: The notion of one person, one vote is deeply embedded in our culture. But when we speak of equality in our society (meaning economic equality, educational attainment, social status, and power, for example), the issue becomes more complex. Most of us believe in the idea of **equality of opportunity** (the belief that everyone should have a chance of success), but many Americans find the idea of **equality of outcome** (using the government to ensure equality) more controversial. Examples of policies to grant equal opportunities for success are public schools and public defenders for people accused of crimes but who cannot afford their own lawyer. The Equal Pay Act of 1963, which required employers to pay men and women equal wages for equal work, was motivated by a belief in equality of outcome. Today, the idea of equal wages for both sexes is not controversial, but other policies to promote equality are. Affirmative action is another example of a public policy that tries to achieve equality of opportunity and equality of outcome, depending on how the policy is designed. Affirmative action in college admissions and scholarships provides equality of opportunity, as many well-qualified students might not otherwise have a chance to attend college. Affirmative action in granting governmental contracts to minority-owned construction firms, for example, is motivated by the goal of equality of outcome, ensuring that these firms are treated equally and without bias in business. Current controversies over affirmative action, however, provide a good example of how even though many people agree on the basic notion of equality, disagreement occurs when we put these values into action.

Public Opinion
Practice Quiz

1. Our highly educated society has resulted in a more politically informed citizenry.
   a. true b. false
2. *The Federalist Papers* warned about granting too much political authority to the unstable opinions of the general public.
   a. true b. false
3. Contemporary political leaders and political scientists view the participation of citizens in governmental decision-making
   a. from an intellectually elitist perspective.
   b. as a force that legitimizes our political process.
   c. as a problem, given how transient public opinion can be.
   d. b and c
4. Which of the following are fundamental values in America?
   a. personal liberty b. economic equality
   c. individualism d. a and c

Answers: 1-b, 2-a, 3-b, 4-d.

Discussion Questions

1. Are there times when political leaders need to oppose public opinion? What are some examples of instances in which leaders may need to act in a manner that is opposed by the majority?
2. What fundamental values do Americans support? Why do they support these values?

What **YOU** can do!

Research the debate between political commentator and journalist Walter Lippman and political philosopher John Dewey. What does the nature of their debate contribute to the discussion of elitism, pluralism, and public opinion in American politics?

DEBATE Civil Rights and Gay Adoption

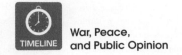

TIMELINE War, Peace, and Public Opinion

The Stability-*of*-Political Beliefs (pages 326–329)

What factors promote stability, and why and how does public opinion change?

Political culture is the set of economic, political, and governmental values and beliefs that support political institutions, processes and practices, and belief systems. Evidence shows that political culture is relatively stable over time, with party identification being the most stable.[7] Opinions can and do change over a lifetime, but major ways of thinking (partisanship, ideology, and economic and social values) tend to remain stable once a person reaches adulthood. Evidence also exists that adults often adjust their views to adapt to changing political environments and to changing life circumstances.[8]

One source of stability is the broad consensus on the key values we've just discussed. Because our political elites tend to be better educated, they are even more supportive of democratic ideals than typical individuals are. Elites perpetuate the system, aiding in its stability. Although we have experienced conflict, it has been more limited than in other societies. There have been few significant controversies over fundamental issues that have led individuals and groups desiring change to go beyond the established channels to promote their cause. A few exceptions exist: The Civil War is the foremost example of a fundamental conflict, but it ended in the decisive victory of one side, permanently settling the issues of slavery and secession. And a century later, U.S. society faced serious conflicts over the Vietnam War and civil rights. But on the whole, our society has been successful in avoiding violence by using political channels to promote change.

Another reason our system is stable is that in the United States, levels of political distrust, which can be very dangerous and lead to instability, are relatively low. Although trust goes up and down over the years, sufficient levels of trust remain to sustain our system. Well-known leaders can play important roles in influencing public opinion and are especially able to influence the less knowledgeable in society.

There have been periods in our history in which large shifts in opinion have occurred; often these shifts have reflected major transformations in American politics. Perhaps the greatest such shift was in the 1760s and 1770s, when overwhelmingly loyal British-American subjects turned into republican rebels against the Crown. More recently, there were large increases in support for civil liberties for communists, socialists, and atheists from the 1950s to the 1970s. From the end of World War II through the early 1970s, a national consensus emerged condemning racial segregation. Since the 1960s, opinion has become much more approving of interracial marriage and of equal employment rights for homosexuals. In 1958, only 4 percent of Americans approved of interracial marriages. The number has steadily increased since that time, rising from 20 percent in 1968 to 43 percent in 1983 and reaching 77 percent in 2007.[9] Support for equal employment opportunities for homosexuals has also risen steadily: 56 percent of American supported equal rights in 1977, 71 percent in 1989, and 89 percent in 2007.[10] Other dimensions of homosexual rights, however, remain hotly debated. These include same-sex marriage and the adoption of children by homosexuals. One of the largest changes in public opinion was the 48-percent increase between 1938 and 1975 in the number of people who agreed that it was appropriate for a married woman to work outside the home for wages even if she had a husband who could financially support her.[11]

Shifts in Public Opinion

Most of the significant changes in American public opinion have occurred gradually, over several decades. Rather than sharp changes, we more commonly find very slow changes in Americans' beliefs and life circumstances. Attitudes toward abortion, for example, provide a good illustration of the stability of public opinion (see Figure 9.1). Abortion has been a very controversial issue since the 1970s, but overall public opinion has remained consistent over the years. Most gradual change can be explained by **cohort replacement,** which simply means that younger people replace older people; and as each generation has experienced a different world, it is logical that each would have different opinions. It is estimated that 50 percent of the electorate is replaced every 20 years.[12] Demographic changes in society also help to explain gradual change, and so does changing technology. For example, computer usage clearly affects the way in which people become informed.

Sometimes, we do see rather abrupt changes in public opinion, particularly in the area of foreign policy. Political scientists Benjamin Page and Robert Shapiro found that shifts in opinions on foreign policy were three times as rapid as changes in domestic preferences, presumably because the landscape of international politics changed more quickly than that of domestic affairs.[13] Areas that saw abrupt changes were opinions regarding wars (World War II, Korea, Vietnam, the war in Iraq), foreign aid, defense spending, and the Middle East.[14] For example, before

> "What factors or events can lead to more sudden changes in political opinion?"
>
> —Student Question

Catalyst-for-Change Theory: The assertion that public opinion shapes and alters our political culture, thus allowing change.

EXAMPLE: *As public opinion became more accepting of less traditional roles for women in society, our political culture changed to support these less traditional roles.*

Barometer of Public Attitudes: The theory that the media reflect popular culture.

EXAMPLE: *Popular culture is reflected by the characters on network sitcoms, because the programs serve as barometers of public attitudes competing for acceptance.*

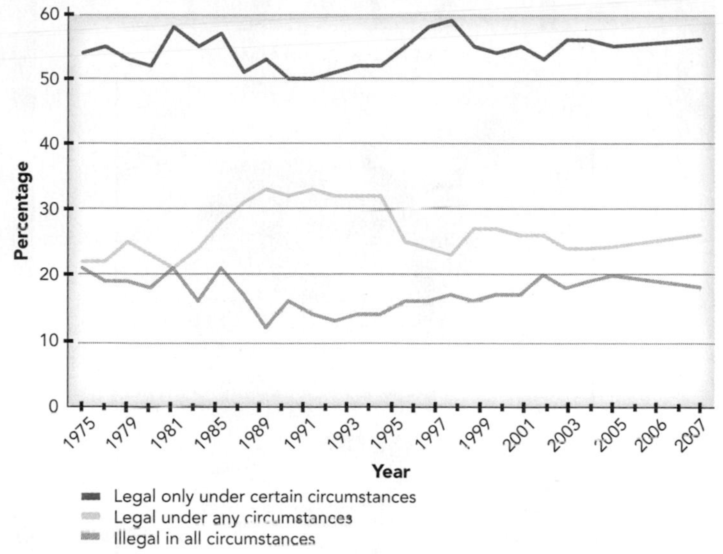

FIGURE 9.1 | **U.S. Public Opinion on Abortion, 1975–2007**

As you can see, opinion on this controversial issue has remained fairly stable. In 1975, 54 percent of Americans thought abortion should be legal under certain circumstances; today, that number is stable at 56 percent. Over the past three decades, the percentage in support of the idea that abortion should be legal under certain circumstances has ranged only between 50 and 59 percent.

SOURCE: 2005–2007 updates accessed from http://www.gallup.com/poll/27628/Public-Divided-ProChoice-vs-ProLife-Abortion-Labels.aspx on July 30, 2008. Copyright © 1975–2005 The Gallup Organization.

the attack on Pearl Harbor, public opinion overwhelmingly favored an isolationist foreign policy; those attitudes shifted with dramatic suddenness after December 7, 1941, the day of the attack on Pearl Harbor and the beginning of U.S. involvement in World War II.

The Impact of Popular Culture on Political Opinions and Values

Many people believe that our popular culture can influence our political values and culture. Politics and entertainment are becoming increasingly intertwined.[15] Celebrities often make political statements, ranging from open expressions of support for a particular candidate or party to organizing and articulating support for political issues or movements. When discussing the effect of popular culture on political culture, we discover several controversies, most notably focusing on the issue of cause and effect. Does popular culture affect values and beliefs, or do values and beliefs affect popular culture? For example, when in 1997 Ellen DeGeneres "came out" as a gay woman (both personally and as her character, Ellen Morgan, on the then-popular TV show *Ellen*), did she do so because the climate had changed, making it more acceptable to be gay? Or did her coming out lead to changed attitudes toward homosexuality? Was it both? It's difficult to determine what came first.

> "Can popular culture change political opinion, or do changes in political values influence popular culture?"
>
> —Student Question

Several theories have been advanced to explain the relationship between popular culture and political culture. One theory states that popular culture promotes change. According to this **catalyst-for-change theory**, popular culture shapes the independent attitudes and beliefs of the public. One example of the catalyst-for-change theory occurred in 1947, when Jackie Robinson became the first black player in Major League Baseball. Watching him display remarkable athletic ability as he played for the Brooklyn Dodgers, and his remarkable control and refusal to respond to the hail of racial slurs from fans that he faced in his first year, caused many people to rethink the common racial stereotypes of the time. In the same way, when Vanessa Williams was crowned the first black Miss America in 1983, many people in society began to think differently about issues of race and beauty. A second theory sees popular culture as a **barometer of public attitudes**, not as the shaper of those attitudes. According to this theory, Ellen DeGeneres was able to come out because our culture and beliefs had changed, permitting a more tolerant view of homosexuality. Furthermore, this theory explains the popularity of TV shows such as *Queer Eye for the Straight Guy* and *Will & Grace* and the Academy Award–winning film *Brokeback Mountain*—not because they caused us to see homosexuality differently, but because our attitudes had already begun to change. Still another explanation, **interactive theory**, asserts that popular culture both changes *and* reflects social values and beliefs. In a highly interactive process, popular culture serves as both a catalyst and as a barometer. This last theory seems most logical and dynamic.[16]

Consider how public opinion has changed regarding the status of women in our society. Opportunities for women have changed dramatically in recent decades. Because of a concerted effort to improve the position of women in our society, support for women's equality is higher today than ever in our history. Figure 9.2 shows the steady increase in the percentage of Americans who believe that women should have a role in society equal to that of men. Before the rise of the modern women's rights movement in the 1960s,

Interactive theory: The theory that popular culture both shapes and reflects popular opinion.

EXAMPLE: *When someone or something challenges the dominant views reflected in our popular culture, popular opinion often changes, and so does political culture. Changing views of homosexuality both reflect and lead to changes in political culture.*

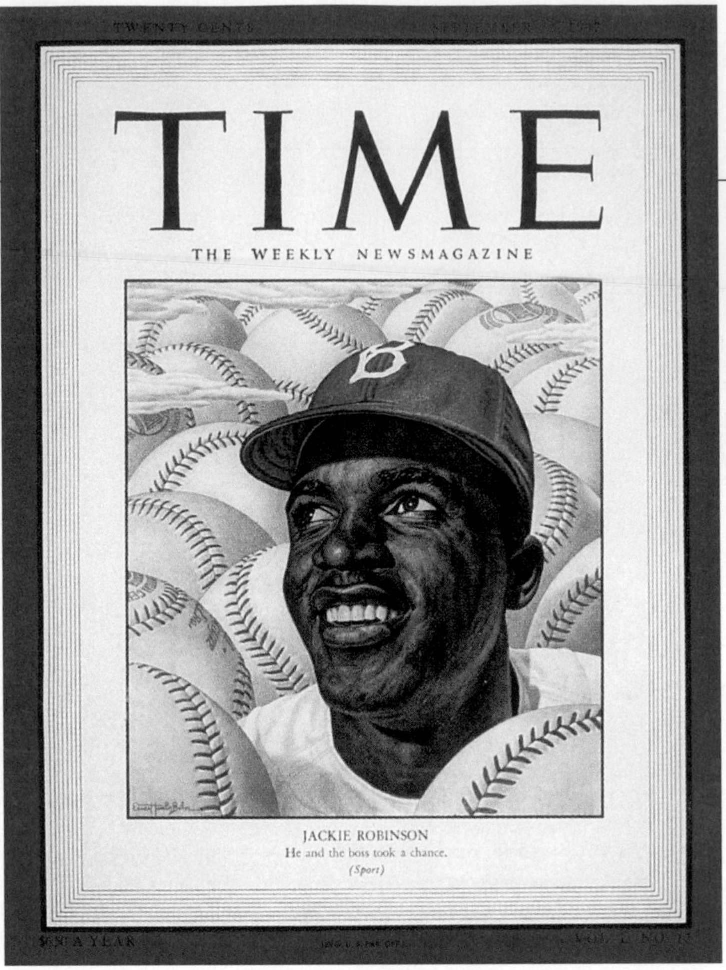

only 46 percent of Americans thought women should be equal with men in business, industry, and government; in 2004, the numbers had risen to 78 percent.[17] A number of consequences have emerged from this important cultural change. First, women are seeing a growth in opportunities, most notably in education and business. Today, there are more female-headed businesses than ever before. Nearly half of incoming business graduate students are women, and more than half of law students are women. Proportionately more women are now earning associate's and bachelor's degrees (though this is somewhat the result of declining male enrollment, which partly reflects the fact that men can earn high wages without the benefit of a college education in certain industries). Women now earn 42 percent of the doctoral degrees in the United States (though they disproportionately major in the lower-paid and less prestigious fields of education and the humanities). Although women have made progress, they are still significantly underrepresented in our government: Women make up 15 percent of Congress, 26 percent of statewide elective executive officials, and 23 percent of state legislators.[18] Women run fewer than 2 percent of Fortune 500 companies, and the number of female CEOs of these companies declined from nine to seven in 2005. The Department of Labor examined the "glass ceiling" and found it to be lower than many people thought, often keeping women from top corporate leadership positions. Recent class action lawsuits against Wal-Mart and Costco alleging sexual discrimination testify to the problem. The Wal-Mart case (*Dukes* v. *Wal-Mart Stores, Inc.*) is the largest civil rights class action ever certified. Both lawsuits charge that the companies discriminated against female employees in decisions involving pay and promotion. It is doubtful that such lawsuits would ever have been brought in the era before our culture changed to see women as equal participants in our society. Shifts in public opinion can result in tangible cultural change.

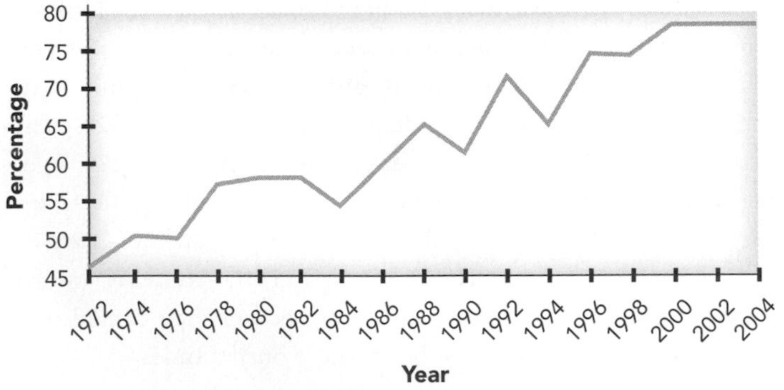

FIGURE 9.2 | **U.S. Public Opinion on the Proper Role of Women in American Society, 1972–2004**

The percentage of Americans who believe that women should have an equal role with men in business, industry, and government has increased steadily from 46 percent in 1972 to 78 percent in 2004. ***—What do you think is responsible for this dramatic increase? What does it mean that 8 percent of the public believes that women's primary role should be in the home? Are you surprised that roughly the same percentage of men and women held both sets of views? Why or why not?***

SOURCE: "The NES Guide to Public Opinion and Election Behavior," American National Election Studies. Accessed at http://www.uelectionstudies.org/nesguide/graphs/g4c_1_1.htm on July 29, 2008, graph 4c.1.1. Reprinted with permission.

The Power of Popular Culture

We can and should debate the ways in which popular culture influences our political culture and public opinion, and several historical examples demonstrate ways in which popular culture has had a significant effect. One early example occurred with the abolitionist movement, an antislavery movement that began in the North during the early 1800s but did not get onto the mainstream agenda until after the publication of Harriet Beecher Stowe's novel *Uncle Tom's Cabin* in 1851. The novel personalized the horror of

Pioneers in Sports: Jackie Robinson (page 328) broke the color barrier in Major League Baseball, and Danica Patrick (right) became the fourth woman to race in the Indy 500. In 2008, she became the first woman to win an Indy car race when she defeated her competitors in the Indy Japan race. ***—Since Patrick's accomplishment came after women were competitive, will it have the impact of Robinson's breakthrough? Do you think that these two individuals are role models for others? How important do you think role models are?***

slavery and mobilized people who had previously been unaware about the depth of the problem. The book sold more than 300,000 copies in the first year, and within 10 years, it had sold more than 2 million copies, becoming the all-time American best-seller in proportion to population. The film *Birth of a Nation* (released in 1916), which glorified the Ku Klux Klan and is arguably one of the most racist movies ever made in the United States, clearly harmed American race relations, especially after it was shown to children in many southern schools as a "history lesson." Betty Friedan's 1963 book *The Feminine Mystique* invigorated the feminist movement in the 1960s. During that same decade, folk and rock music powerfully influenced young people's perceptions of war and peace. Rap and hip-hop music today have both positive and negative aspects. On the one hand, its glorification of violence, its materialism, and degrading treatment of women can all be socially harmful. On the other hand, the music provides an important outlet through which African Americans can publicize the plight of poor urban residents.

The Stability of Political Beliefs

Practice Quiz

1. The theory that popular culture shapes the independent attitudes and beliefs of the public is known as
   - **a.** cohort replacement.
   - **b.** catalyst-for-change.
   - **c.** barometer of public attitudes.
   - **d.** elitism.
2. The fact that Americans tend to agree on fundamental values tends to
   - **a.** result in universal support of important public policies.
   - **b.** stabilize our political system.
   - **c.** cause noncompetitive elections.
   - **d.** allow challengers to win more often in elections.
3. Although women have made progress, they are still significantly underrepresented in
   - **a.** our government.
   - **b.** higher education.
   - **c.** corporate leadership.
   - **d.** a and c
4. The majority of Americans still do not believe that women should have a role in society equal to that of men.
   - **a.** true
   - **b.** false

Answers: 1-b, 2-b, 3-d, 4-b.

Discussion Questions

1. What aspects of society tend to stabilize public opinion?
2. Can you think of other examples that demonstrate the impact of popular culture on public opinion?

What **YOU** can do!

Sports history was made on April 20, 2008 when Danica Patrick became the first woman to win an Indy car race. Do an internet search on "Danica Patrick," and examine the press coverage. How does the coverage in official Indy Racing literature differ from coverage in popular media? Why do you think the coverage differs? Is her gender presented as relevant or irrelevant? Is it used in a way that makes her seem more or less professional or competent?

Political Ideology: A consistent set of beliefs that forms a general philosophy regarding the proper goals, purposes, functions, and size of government.

EXAMPLE: *Once people develop their ideology, barring major world events (such as a war or severe economic crisis), it is unlikely to change significantly throughout their lifetimes. Ideology guides an individual's worldviews and political behavior.*

CONNECT THE LINK (Chapter 11, pages 414–415) Many assert that Americans care less about politics than in the past. Do you agree?

VISUAL LITERACY **Who Are Liberals and Conservatives? What's the Difference?**

DEBATE **Are You a Liberal or a Conservative?**

From Values to Ideology (pages 330–331)

What is political ideology?

"What are the main differences between liberal beliefs and conservative beliefs?"

—Student Question

Political ideology is a consistent set of basic beliefs about the proper purpose and scope of government. Americans tend to fall into two camps: liberals and conservatives. In general terms, **liberals** tend to support social and cultural change (especially in connection with issues of equality) and want an activist government that encourages change. **Conservatives**, by contrast, tend to favor traditional views on social, cultural, and economic matters and demand a more limited role for government in most spheres. Although there is some ideological variation within each party, today's Republican Party is, generally speaking, the party of conservatives, whereas most liberals tend to identify with the Democratic Party.

Conservatives Versus Liberals

The conservative–liberal distinction holds true when looking at spending on public goods (entities that benefit many people, such as public parks, but are unlikely to emerge naturally in a market economy), but the distinction is less helpful in explaining other issues. Liberals favor government spending on environmental protection, education, public transportation, national parks, and social services. Conservatives want smaller governmental budgets and fewer governmental programs. In theory, liberals favor governmental activism, but they oppose governmental regulation of abortions. In theory, conservatives oppose governmental activism, but they support governmental restrictions on pornography and abortion.

STUDENT | PROFILE

One is Greater than None (1>0) is an organization started in 2007 by eight Long Island, New York, girls to help free forced child laborers in Ghana, Africa. The eight girls (then only 13 and 14 years old) became interested in the plight of enslaved child laborers following an emotional *Oprah Winfrey Show* (titled "The Little Boy That Oprah Couldn't Forget") aired on February 9, 2007, that depicted the horrific working conditions of enslaved children. The girls worked after school selling bracelets, necklaces, and clothes to raise money (as well as social awareness) to free the children. Rather than become discouraged to learn that it costs approximately $4,300 to free each child, they became determined to do what they could—deciding that saving one child is more than none (hence the name of the group). The girls have helped save eight children thus far and are now working on sponsoring 25 rescue missions in 2008. For more information, see their Web page (http://www.oneisgreaterthannone.org).

SOURCE: *Teen Vogue,* December/January 2008, p. 68.

Today, the critical difference between liberals and conservatives concerns not so much the *scope* of governmental activity as the *purpose* of governmental actions. Generally speaking, conservatives approve of using governmental power to promote order, including social order, though there are exceptions to these generalizations. Conservatives typically favor firm police action, swift and severe punishments for criminals, and more laws regulating behavior, such as teen curfews. As you will see in LINK Chapter 11, pages 414–415, such beliefs led many conservatives to support stringent anticommunist domestic and foreign policies in the 1940s and 1950s. Support for the USA PATRIOT Act, initially bipartisan and very popular as an immediate reaction to the September 11, 2001, terrorist attacks, now gets more conservative than liberal support. Conservatives want to preserve traditional patterns of social relations, including the importance of the domestic role of women in family life and the significance of religion in daily life and school. Conservatives today do not oppose equality, but they tend not to view securing equality as a prime objective of governmental action.

In general, liberals tend to worry more than conservatives do about the civil liberties implications of the USA PATRIOT Act and government surveillance of potential terrorists. Liberals are less

Getting accurate information from public opinion polls can be tricky business. Pollsters must carefully word questions to ensure accurate results.

Liberal: A person who generally supports governmental action to promote equality (such as welfare and public education), favors governmental intervention in the economy, and supports environmental issues.

EXAMPLE: *Liberals believe the promotion of equality is a prime governmental responsibility; as such, they support policies that allow for reproductive freedom, greater access to education for all, and legal protection for homosexuals.*

Conservative: A person who believes that government spending should be limited, that traditional patterns of relationships should be preserved, and that a large and powerful government is a threat to personal liberties.

EXAMPLE: *Conservatives argue that government ought to be concerned with promoting morality and traditional values; as such, they oppose pornography and prostitution along with same-sex marriages.*

TABLE 9.1 | **Percentage of Americans Identifying with a Particular Political Ideology, 1974–2004**

Why do you think the number of liberals declined to a low of 14 percent in 1994 but then returned in 2004 to levels similar to those seen in 1974? Why do you think the percentages identified with conservative ideology saw a steady increase from 1974 until 1994 and then a slight decline? How do the groups of people you come into contact with compare to this distribution?

SELF-CHARACTERIZATION	1974	1984	1994	2004
Extremely liberal, liberal, or slightly liberal	21	18	14	23
Moderate or middle-of-the-road	27	23	26	26
Extremely conservative, conservative, or slightly conservative	26	29	36	32
Don't know, or haven't thought about it	27	30	24	20

SOURCES: Data from "The ANES Guide to Public Opinion and Electoral Behavior," *American National Election Studies*, http://www.uelections.org/nesguide/toptable/tab3_1.htm, November 27, 2005, Table 3.1. Reprinted with permission.

likely to approve the use of governmental power to maintain order but are more willing to use governmental power to promote equality. Thus they tend to support laws to ensure that homosexuals receive equal treatment in employment, housing, and education. They favor policies that encourage businesses to hire and promote women and minorities, and they want to raise the minimum wage.

Table 9.1 shows how people have identified with ideology in the United States since 1974. There has been an increase in the percentage of people who consider themselves conservatives and a slight increase in the percentage of people who label themselves liberal. The growth of both groups has come at the expense of the "undecided" category (reflecting the manner in which society has become more polarized and has been growing more conservative).

In the 1970s and 1980s, the United States saw a revitalization of the conservative movement, as well as the emergence of a new conservative agenda. Several conservative groups came together, greatly increasing their visibility and power. Traditional conservatives, who focused on economic issues, merged with social conservatives, who focused on issues of traditional morality. Traditional conservatives had opposed many of the policies enacted during the civil rights movement of the 1960s, which often created social programs targeted to benefit minorities and the poor. Many of these programs were expensive and materially benefited only a small percentage of people. Many social conservatives resented policies that were designed to promote social change, feeling that they had to bear too much responsibility (including fiscal responsibility) for the change. They opposed the Equal Rights Amendment, busing to promote school integration, gun control, sex education in public schools, government poverty programs, abortion, welfare spending, and immigration. They wanted to preserve traditional cultural values, such as prayer in schools and traditional gender roles.[19] The unification of these two groups, fiscal conservatives and social conservatives, greatly expanded the appeal of the Republican Party.

From Values to Ideology
Practice Quiz

1. According to Table 9.1, most Americans characterize themselves as
   - **a.** liberal.
   - **b.** moderate.
   - **c.** conservative.
   - **d.** uncertain about their ideology.
2. If you favor using government resources to promote equality you are more
   - **a.** liberal.
   - **b.** conservative.
   - **c.** radical.
   - **d.** libertarian.
3. One clear distinction between liberals and conservatives in the United States is that the former always favor governmental regulation and the latter never do.
   - **a.** true
   - **b.** false
4. What explains the revitalization of the conservative movement in the 1970s and 1980s?
   - **a.** the unification of social and fiscal conservatives
   - **b.** increasing resentment of national policies that promoted social change, such as school desegregation, gun control, and the Equal Rights Amendment
   - **c.** Watergate
   - **d.** a and b

Answers: 1-c, 2-a, 3-b, 4-d.

Discussion Questions

1. What is political ideology? How do liberals differ from conservatives?
2. How has the distribution of political ideology changed in recent decades?

What **YOU** can do!

Explore libertarianism by reviewing policy and issue briefs published by the CATO Institute (**http://www.cato.org/**). Why do you think libertarianism holds a relatively strong ideological attraction for college students?

Agents of Political Socialization: Factors that influence how we acquire political facts and knowledge and develop political values.

EXAMPLE: *People who have similar experiences tend to have similar political views. Agents of socialization are especially important for young people and continue to shape political views throughout young adulthood.*

Political Socialization

(pages 332–335)

What factors influence how people acquire political values?

Political socialization is the conscious and unconscious transmission of political culture and values from one generation to another. It is the process by which people learn political information, organize political knowledge, and develop political values. Socialization is not a one-time event; it occurs continuously. The transmission of knowledge as a part of political socialization is a means of teaching one generation the lessons of its predecessors, ideally leading to social stability and better decision-making.

Research demonstrates that learning during childhood and adolescence affects adult political behavior[20]; we must therefore examine very carefully the process by which people learn about politics. Factors that influence the acquisition of political facts and the formation of values are called **agents of political socialization**■. Let's examine six such agents: family, school, peers and community, religion, the media, and events.

Schools are important agents of socialization, teaching children not only political facts but also a sense of patriotism and a belief in democratic practices. Children across the country begin their day by pledging allegiance to the American flag and reciting school rules. These practices help create a strong sense of loyalty and nationalism. ***—Do you think that schools focus too much on allegiance, failing to teach students to critically analyze our government, leaders, and policies? When, if at all, should one learn to question authority?***

Family

Children learn a wide range of social, moral, religious, economic, and political values from their family, and what they learn can dramatically shape their opinions. When parents are interested in politics, they tend to influence their children to become more politically interested and informed. Early studies found the family to be a very important agent of socialization, serving as an intermediary between children and society. Families are very successful at teaching political values, because children often try to copy the behavior of loved ones.[21] Observing how parents react to different situations can affect values that are learned and beliefs that are developed. For example, how parents react to the police can set the stage for how children will view authority. Parents' views of poverty can affect the attitudes of their children about welfare and social services. Parents are often most influential in transmitting party identification to their children, especially when both parents are of the same political party. If children do not adopt their parents' political party, they are more likely to define themselves as independents than to align with the opposite party.[22]

Researchers have shown that parents are especially influential in teaching gender roles and racial attitudes. Children who are raised by mothers who work outside the home for wages, for example, tend to have more progressive views of gender. Girls who are encouraged by a parent to be more assertive tend to be more independent and to have more independent careers.[23] Prejudiced parents are more likely to have prejudiced children. Children learn bigotry directly (from parental attitudes and comments) and indirectly (from watching parental interactions with others). Once children are exposed to different factors in adolescence, however, the relationship between parental intolerance and children's bigotry diminishes.[24] Parental influence wanes when children mature and other factors increase in importance.

Recent research concerning the influence of the family on political values has been mixed, finding that the actual levels of influence depend on a number of factors. Families with strong relationships and strong mutual ties tend to be the most likely to transmit values. As the nature of the family changes, we will need to continue examining its influence in shaping the development of children's values. Children today are more likely to be home alone and less likely to spend time with their parents, for example, and the number of families eating together has steadily declined. Moreover, the number of children living in single-parent homes has increased. The number of single mothers rose from 3 million in 1970 to 10.3 million in 2004, and during that same period, the number of single fathers from 393,000 to 2.3 million.[25] It's not hard to see that these changes in family structure and interaction may affect the role families will play in influencing children in the future.

School

Schools teach political knowledge, the value of political participation, and the acceptance of democratic principles. Their effectiveness in doing so, however, is debated. Schools seem to be more

■ **Efficacy:** The belief that one can influence government. *Internal political efficacy* is the belief that you have the knowledge and ability to influence government. *External political efficacy* refers to the belief that governmental officials will respond to the people.

EXAMPLE: *People with high levels of political efficacy tend to be better educated and politically active.*

effective in transmitting basic political knowledge than in creating politically engaged citizens.

Elementary schools introduce children to authority figures outside the family, such as the teacher, the principal, and police officers, while also teaching about the hierarchical nature of power. In doing so, the schools prepare children to accept social order, to follow rules, and to learn the importance of obedience. Children learn that good citizens obey the laws (just as good children obey the rules of the schools and of their parents). School elections for student council and mock presidential elections teach students important democratic principles and procedures, such as the notion of campaigning, voting, and majority rule. Most children emerge from elementary school with a strong sense of nationalism and an idealized notion of American government, thus building a general sense of good will for the political system that lays the foundation for future learning.[26] As they mature, children start to see their place in the political community and gain a sense of civic responsibility.

High schools continue building "good citizens" through activities and curriculum. Field trips to the state legislature and classes with explicit political content can result in a greater awareness of the political process and the people involved in it. The school curriculum teaches political facts, while the school atmosphere can affect political values. Students with positive experiences in school, who develop trust in school leaders, faith in the system, and a sense of efficacy, are more likely to show higher levels of support for the national political system. Students who feel they are treated fairly by school officials tend to have more trust in officials and feel less alienated from their government.[27] Civics classes in high school are a potentially good mechanism for encouraging student engagement in politics. Researchers have found that the simple existence of such classes is not enough to produce civically engaged students; the dynamic of the class is also important. Civics classes that are taught by people who generally like the subject matter and who themselves are politically engaged are far more successful in positively socializing students. On the whole, however, high school seniors are not very well informed about politics, are not very interested in politics, and have only moderate levels of support for democratic practices.[28]

Research consistently demonstrates that a college education has a liberalizing effect on noneconomic issues. Adults with college experience tend to be more liberal on social issues than adults with less education. Several theories have attempted to explain this. College tends to make individuals aware of differences between people and allows them to see the complexity of public policy issues. In classes such as the one you're now in, students are exposed to controversies in our society and learn that the issues are far more complicated than

"Does attending college make people more liberal?"
—Student Question

previously thought. Moreover, they learn that intelligent people can disagree. Hence, they tend to be more supportive of changing opinions and less supportive of the status quo. College students often meet a wider range of people than they had contact with in high school, giving them evidence to reject some social stereotypes and prejudices and to accept more diversity. Also, college faculty are significantly more liberal than their students—and than most people in society. Notwithstanding individual differences among faculty, those in the liberal arts and the sciences tend to be the most liberal.[29] This leads some conservatives to hypothesize that these liberal college faculty indoctrinate students, causing them to become more liberal. Whatever the explanation, people with a college education are generally more liberal on social issues than those who haven't been to college.

Peers and Community

Community and peers are also agents of political socialization. Your community consists of the people, of all ages, with whom you come in contact through work, school, or your neighborhood. Peers are friends, classmates, and coworkers who tend to be around the same age as you and who live in your community. Peer influence tends to be weaker than that of school and family, but our companions do affect us. Differences of opinions and preferences between generations are likely due to peer influence (especially regarding tastes in music, entertainment, clothing, hairstyle, and speech). Peers generally serve to reinforce one another, as people tend to socialize with those like themselves. Research shows that in heterogeneous communities, political participation tends to be higher, with more hotly contested and more competitive elections and more political debate, than in homogeneous environments. People are more likely to participate and pay attention to politics if they believe their vote counts, as is the case when there are a variety of views or disagreements and the election is closely contested.[30]

Politically diverse environments are also more likely to provide interesting stimuli and often result in a greater sense that one can have an effect on government.[31] Minorities living in racially diverse environments tend to have higher political **efficacy**■ than minorities living in segregated environments. Researchers found that African Americans living in predominantly black communities generally do not experience political socialization in a manner that encourages political participation and civic engagement.[32] Racial segregation tends to develop a sense of isolation and disinterest in the political system. Areas with high voter turnout, with politically engaged adult

CONNECT THE LINK
Chapter **10**, pages **376–377**) How important do you think the media are in influencing the values of young people?

role models, and with racial diversity appear to be the best environments to raise politically aware and knowledgeable children who have a sense that their voice can count.

Religion

Religions are important instructors, particularly when it comes to issues of morality, self-sacrifice, and altruism, and they are an important factor in the development of personal identity. Individuals raised in religious households tend to be socialized to contribute to society and to get involved in their communities.[33] Conservative denominations and religions tend to impart conservative attitudes (especially regarding abortion and other issues involving personal morality and sexuality) than more liberal churches do. People raised in Reform Judaism, more than in any other religious tradition, are often socialized to have the greatest involvement in their communities and the highest levels of civic engagement.[34] Those raised in religiously diverse communities are more likely to be engaged in politics and have higher levels of political participation.[35] Religion can act as a reinforcing mechanism of community and family values on a wide array of moral and political issues.

The Media

We will look more closely at the effect of the media in influencing values, politicians, and society in LINK, Chapter 10, pages 376–377. Here, it is appropriate to note that the media are an important agent of political socialization, with varied effects on public opinion. Many authorities believe that the effect of the media on political values and opinions has increased in the past several decades. Today, it is estimated that American children watch slightly over 1,000 hours of television a year (compared to 900 hours spent in school each year).[36] If we add to that the time spent listening to music, reading magazines, and watching movies and music videos, it's obvious that entertainment may have a big role in influencing values. Entertainment media often present behavior at odds with what is approved in the family, schools, and places of worship. Television and movies often show what appears to be the most pleasurable behavior with few consequences attached. Promiscuous sex, drug use, and materialism are common in contemporary programming, with little attention paid to potential consequences. By the time a typical child reaches eighteen, he or she will have seen 40,000 murders on television.[37] What can result is a competition for influence between media, parents, schools, and religion. Many analysts worry that this focus on negativity can adversely affect political efficacy and trust in government.[38]

"What political values and information do we get from the media?"
—Student Question

Recent research demonstrates that people do learn valid political information from the media. A poll by CNN found that viewers of late-night television programs were more politically informed than nonviewers. The best informed were the fans of *The Daily Show,* hosted by Jon Stewart on Comedy Central. In fact, viewers of

Nighttime talk-show hosts often joke about politics, governmental officials, and current affairs. Perhaps the best-known hosts today are Jon Stewart, host of *The Daily Show with Jon Stewart,* and Stephen Colbert, host of *The Colbert Report,* on Comedy Central. Watchers of these programs tend to be better informed than the general public on current affairs. ***—Do you think they are better informed because of the programs or because they tend to be better educated? Do you think that either comedian would be a viable candidate for political office? Why or why not?***

this program were more informed than those who read the newspaper regularly. On a test of political knowledge of current affairs, *Daily Show* viewers got 60 percent of the questions right, while Leno and Letterman fans answered 49 percent correctly. All of these scores are above the national average, although it should be noted that *Daily Show* viewers are more educated and more affluent than most, explaining some of the variation.[39]

Events

No event of recent decades has had a more dramatic impact on Americans than the terrorist attacks of September 11, 2001. Not enough time has passed to allow social scientists to assess the long-term effects of those attacks on youth socialization. In the short term, however, these events have altered public opinion in two ways. First, the public is more aware of the danger of terrorism and is consequently more afraid. Before the terrorist attacks, many Americans did not believe that our country was vulnerable to terrorist threats. Americans often viewed terrorism as a problem that occurred in other countries (with the clear exception of the Oklahoma City bombing). Following the 9/11 attacks, the number of Americans who expressed confidence that our government could keep us safe declined significantly. As time has passed, concerns over personal safety have diminished, but a general sense of fear remains high.[40] The second observed short-term change has been a surge in patriotism and a sense of uniting in battle. At least for a while after the attacks, we became a unified country, standing behind our government.

Long-term consequences are more difficult to ascertain. Research does show that important events can affect the socialization process, because significant events focus national attention. By examining other events in our nation's past that were of great political importance—the attack on Pearl Harbor, the Vietnam War, the assassination of President Kennedy, and the Watergate scandal are all examples—we can see how shocking events can alter politics. However, it is too early for researchers to assess with high confidence the long-term impact of 9/11. The attacks did focus public attention on political events and increased the amount of time and attention that younger people devote to following politics.[41] The attacks neither increased youth hostility toward immigrants nor diminished their support for diversity but, rather, served to bolster patriotism and national pride. Research that examined students before and after the attacks found they had higher levels of trust in government after the attacks than before. Once again, it is too soon to determine if this increase in trust will be sustained, but researchers did demonstrate that youth, like most other Americans, did "rally 'round the flag."[42]

Political Socialization

Practice Quiz

1. Political socialization refers to
   a. attending important social events involving politicians.
   b. the process whereby political systems become socialist in orientation.
   c. the process whereby each generation develops political consciousness, learns political information, organizes political knowledge, and forms political values.
   d. the process whereby people learn to accept the rules of government—the regulations, laws, and customs of their nation, state, and municipality.

2. Agents of political socialization include
   a. the community and the media.
   b. houses of worship.
   c. peers.
   d. a, b, and c

3. Heterogeneous environments tend to have higher levels of political participation.
   a. true **b.** false

4. Studies have shown that a college education has the effect of making most people *less* conservative about social issues than they used to be. Why is this so?
   a. Going to college often involves meeting a greater diversity of people, thus encouraging students to become more accepting of cultural differences.
   b. College prompts students to explore the complexities that often lie behind public policy issues.
   c. College education encourages an openness to change, both personally and culturally.
   d. a, b, and c

Answers: 1-c, 2-d, 3-a, 4-d.

Discussion Questions

1. Which agents of social change can negatively affect socialization? Which agents are reinforcing?
2. What impact does television have on socialization? How is the effect different among various age groups?

What **YOU** can do!

Partner with a classmate to identify the events that affected your political socialization. How did those events shape your opinions on government and politics? Go one step further by interviewing three or four people from different generations to find out about the defining events in their political socialization. How did those events influence their opinions? Note any clear generational differences in opinion that may be attributed to historical events.

Social Groups *and* Political Values (pages 336–341)

How does membership in different social groups impact political views and behavior?

People with similar backgrounds tend to develop similar political opinions. These group characteristics serve to divide Americans along lines of social class, education, religion, race and ethnicity, and gender. These factors tend to influence public opinion on a variety of domestic and foreign policies and must therefore be examined and understood.

We need to make several important points at the beginning of this section. First, we're going to be generalizing about how various factors influence political opinions, but many exceptions exist. For example, women as a whole tend to be more liberal than men on social issues, but there are many conservative women in our country. Whites tend to be more likely than African Americans to be members of the Republican Party, but many African Americans are Republicans. Second, most people are influenced by numerous factors. For some, religion may be the most important factor influencing their values and opinions. For others, it may be race or ethnicity; and for still others, it may be social class or gender. Moreover, the effects of specific factors may vary from issue to issue. Rarely do opinions on issues stem from one source—usually, opinions are influenced by many different factors.

We use the term **crosscutting cleavages** to explain how two or more factors work to influence an individual.[43] These cleavages (splits in the population) complicate the work of political scientists, for it is often difficult to say which factors are the most important in shaping particular attitudes. These cleavages can also moderate opinions and lead to stability over time. Take income as an example. There are many issues on which the poor agree; there are also many issues on which they disagree. As you will see, income has an important effect on opinions, but it is not the only factor. Race, gender, region, and religion (to name a few) also affect individuals.

Economic Bases of Partisanship and Public Opinion

Political socialization does not explain the distribution of party loyalties in the United States. Socialization is helpful in describing *how* rather than *why* an individual acquires party loyalty. One important factor in determining why an individual is a Democrat or a Republican is the person's economic standing and that of his or her parents. One principal generalization that you can make about loyalties to the parties in modern times is that they are often based on socioeconomic status.

Traditionally, Democrats have been regarded as the "party of the people" and Republicans as the "party of the rich." This characterization goes back to the 1800s, but it became more pronounced in the 1930s, when Democratic President Franklin D. Roosevelt launched his New Deal programs in the midst of the Great Depression. Labor legislation, Social Security, and minimum wage laws all reinforced the Democratic Party's image as the party of the have-nots. Even African Americans, who ever since the Civil War had aligned with the Republican Party, partly in loyalty to President Abraham Lincoln, abandoned it in the 1930s for the Democratic Party. Ironically, by aligning with the Democrats, African Americans found themselves in the same party with racist white southerners. Beginning in the late 1960s, southern whites who had opposed or remained lukewarm toward racial integration flocked into the Republican ranks.

Even today, many Americans who see themselves as middle and upper class tend to be Republicans, while those who identify themselves as working class tend to be Democrats. However, social class and party loyalties are not as closely linked in the United States as in other Western democracies. Both parties in the United States draw support from upper-, middle-, and lower-status groups. Thus it is difficult for either party to make overt appeals that reflect sharp class differences. When it comes to purely economic issues, the more affluent tend to be more conservative than the less affluent on fiscal issues such as taxation, *assuming that each group is defining its politics strictly on the basis of self-interest*. But when we add education to the equation, liberal views tend to increase along with rising income. In fact, the higher the level of education a person has received, the more liberal that individual tends to be on social and cultural issues. And because education is highly correlated with income, the relationship is complicated. For example, in 2004, the average annual earnings by highest level of education were

$116,514 for individuals holding advanced professional degrees
$56,788 for recipients of bachelor's degrees
$31,071 for high school graduates
$20,901 for adults with no high school diploma[44]

People with higher incomes tend to be more supportive of equal rights for women and minorities (including homosexuals) and more supportive of the rights of the criminally accused.[45] These policy stances are related to educational attainment rather than income. As you can see in Table 9.2, the more affluent you are, the more fiscally conservative you'll tend to be on issues relating to spending on the poor but the more liberal on social issues, such as gay rights and abortion rights.

TABLE 9.2 | **Percentage of Americans Favoring Particular Public Policies, by Family Income, 2004**

People of higher income tend to be more likely to oppose capital punishment and are more supportive of homosexual rights and reproductive freedoms. They are, however, less supportive of increased spending of tax dollars on the poor. Why do you think this is the case? (Pay attention to subsequent tables, and look at how self-interest affects public opinion. Also look to see if there are instances where self-interest doesn't seem to be as relevant as one might expect.)

PUBLIC POLICY STANCE	FAMILY INCOME			
	UNDER $25,000	$25,000 TO $50,000	$50,000 TO $80,000	MORE THAN $80,000
Oppose capital punishment	57	67	72	73
Favor making it harder to get guns	61	60	52	61
Favor allowing gays in the military	50	54	58	57
Favor allowing gays to adopt	43	45	53	54
Favor never allowing abortion	18	12	13	7
Favor increased spending on the poor	69	58	52	45

SOURCE: Center for Political Studies, *American National Election Study* (Ann Arbor: University of Michigan, 2004). Reprinted with permission.

Education

As we've discussed, education tends to increase citizens' awareness and understanding of political issues, often having a liberalizing effect on nonfiscal social issues. For example, a college-educated person will be more likely than a less educated person to choose personal freedom over social order (when they conflict). Thus the more educated groups are more likely to favor gun control and to want limits placed on police authority. There are also differences based on education in issues of foreign policy. The less educated tend to favor isolationist policies that would limit the role of the United States on the world scene, whereas the more educated favor greater U.S. engagement in international affairs.[46]

In Table 9.3, you can see rather significant differences in many areas of public debate. Better-educated people tend to be far more likely than the less educated to support homosexual rights (especially gays' right to adopt children) and far more supportive of abortion rights. Often, however, the more educated (and hence the more affluent) tend to be more fiscally conservative when it comes to economic issues like spending on the poor. The least economically secure people (as measured by income and education) tend to be the most supportive of increasing governmental spending on domestic social services, such as Social Security and the poor.[47] Whereas college-educated people generally favor governmental spending on social services, many of them are hesitant to support increased social spending, because it will result in higher taxes for them (the more affluent). The less educated overwhelmingly favor increased government spending on social programs. The more educated are also more likely to support gun control and, by a small margin, are less supportive of capital punishment.

Religion

Religion has always been extremely important in American life. Today, nearly 85 percent of Americans say that they belong to an organized religion; 75 percent say that religion is important to their lives, and 95 percent say that they believe in God.[48] From the beginning of the American Republic, there have always been religious differences on issues of public policy and party coalitions. Under the party system inaugurated by the New Deal, Catholics and Jews were among the most loyal supporters of the Democratic Party. Although the Democratic loyalty of Catholics has lessened in recent years, religion remains a significant indicator of political alignment today. Differences in ideology and support of political parties have more effect on voting than socioeconomic distinctions have. When income, education, and occupation are held constant, Catholics and Jews tend to be more liberal and support the Democratic Party, while nonsouthern Protestants tend to be more conservative and support the Republican Party. Jews have long been disposed to favor the Democratic Party because of their sense of internationalism and support for social and economic justice, central tenets of their faith. Catholics are traditionally tied to the Democratic Party because Catholic immigrants, especially in the Northeast, greatly benefited from the social services provided by urban Democratic Party machines in the late nineteenth and early twentieth centuries. (We'll say more about party machines in Chapter 13.) Like Jews, Catholics also felt themselves victimized by prejudice from Protestants, who were identified (in the North)

"Which religious denominations are most likely to vote Republican? Democratic?"

—Student Question

TABLE 9.3 | Percentage of Americans Favoring Particular Public Policies, by Education, 2004

Do the data presented here surprise you? Why do you think people with advanced degrees, and presumably high incomes, are more supportive of increased spending on the poor than those who attended or completed college? Considerable differences exist between the more educated and the less educated on issues of reproductive freedom, gun ownership, and homosexual rights. Why do you think this is the case?

PUBLIC POLICY STANCE	LEVEL OF EDUCATION				
	DID NOT COMPLETE HIGH SCHOOL	GRADUATED FROM HIGH SCHOOL	ATTENDED COLLEGE	OBTAINED A COLLEGE DEGREE	OBTAINED AN ADVANCED DEGREE
Favor capital punishment	61	70	71	68	53
Favor making it harder to get guns	58	53	51	64	72
Favor allowing gays in the military	47	48	56	58	66
Favor allowing gays to adopt	26	41	45	54	66
Favor never allowing abortion	28	13	12	11	8
Favor increased spending on the poor	66	63	52	48	58

SOURCE: Center for Political Studies, *American National Election Study* (Ann Arbor: University of Michigan, 2004). Reprinted with permission.

with the old Republican Party. The only three Catholics ever nominated for president (Al Smith in 1928, John F. Kennedy in 1960, and John Kerry in 2004) were all Democrats.

In recent decades, these fairly homogeneous alignments have been growing more complicated. Motivated by issues like abortion and gay rights, "traditional" Roman Catholics today tend to vote Republican, while other Catholics—especially those strongly committed to the reforms of Vatican Council II in the 1960s—have remained in the Democratic column out of concern over social justice and peace issues. Protestants from the so-called mainline denominations (Episcopalians, most Presbyterians, many Methodists, and some Lutherans, for example) tend to be more split between the political parties.[49] However, white (but not black) evangelicals, who once were mostly either Democrats or nonpolitical, constituted a record 51 percent of the GOP voters in the 2000 presidential election. Seventy-four percent of evangelical Christians voted in 2000 for George W. Bush, while a record 78 percent voted for him in 2004, representing the Republican Party's strongest constituency.[50] White evangelical Christians continue to give strong support to the Republican Party.

For example, early exit polling in the presidential election of 2008 indicates that 74 percent of white evangelical Christians voted for Senator John McCain, whereas 64 percent of white voters who were not evangelical voted for Senator Barack Obama.[51]

PATHWAYS | profile

Jim Wallis

Today, when most people think of evangelical leaders, they tend to think of them as conservative. While this would be true for most of the contemporary evangelical ministers (such as Jerry Falwell and Pat Robertson), more liberal evangelical leaders are also trying to mobilize voters, register nonvoters, and influence political leaders and party officials. One such leader is Jim Wallis.

Wallis is a founder and editor of the liberal evangelical magazine *Sojourners* and is the author of a number of books, the most recent of which is *God's Politics: Why the Right Is Wrong and the Left Doesn't Get It*. While he is critical of both the left and the right, he believes that liberals can come together with Christians to correct what he sees as social ills and to work for peace. He is frustrated with the Democratic Party, claiming that it is unable or unwilling to speak to the large group of Americans who have liberal ideological leanings but are also very spiritual. He asserts that the Democratic Party has lost the moral battle in politics because it shuns religion and allows the Republicans to define morality. He urges liberals, who traditionally believe in a strong separation of church and state, to avoid portraying themselves as "secular fundamentalists" and encourages them to speak in a manner that appeals to religious people and avoids being disrespectful of faith. He believes that the Democratic Party alienates religious voters because it does not speak their language and is dismissive of religion. He wants to unite liberal causes (fighting poverty, racism, and injustice) with spiritual guidance to improve society.

Jim Wallis has created a faith-based antipoverty organization, Call to Renewal, which is a federation of churches and faith-based organizations. He argues that the Bible demands we pay more direct attention to poverty and social justice. Challenging the liberal belief in separating faith from politics, he asserts that the church, the religious faithful, and religious communities need to be directly involved in politics, serving as the conscience of the state.

Many people believe that the Democratic Party should listen to Wallis' message. In the presidential elections of 2000 and 2004, its support declined among many religious communities. For example, in 2008, of those who attend church weekly, 67 percent voted for

Senator McCain, whereas 55 percent who never attend church voted for Senator Obama.[52] Only time will tell whether Wallis will be successful in encouraging liberals to embrace faith—and evangelicals to embrace liberalism. ■

When we examine the differences between religions on public policy issues, important trends emerge. On most every nonfiscal issue, Jews consistently take the most liberal policy stances, while Protestants take the most conservative. Catholics typically fall in between. Some of the most significant differences are found regarding gun control, homosexual rights, and abortion.

As you can see in Figure 9.3, there are important differences in the distribution of party loyalties based on religion. White Protestants, especially if they describe themselves as evangelicals, are more likely to be Republicans, while black Protestants (who are mostly evangelicals) are far more likely to be Democrats. The more religious Catholics (as measured by the regularity of their church attendance) have become more supportive of the Republican Party, whereas the less observant Catholics vote more heavily Democratic. Jews, on the other hand, have become even more supportive of the Democratic Party than previously. Americans who say that they are not members of organized religions are far more likely to be Democrats than Republicans.

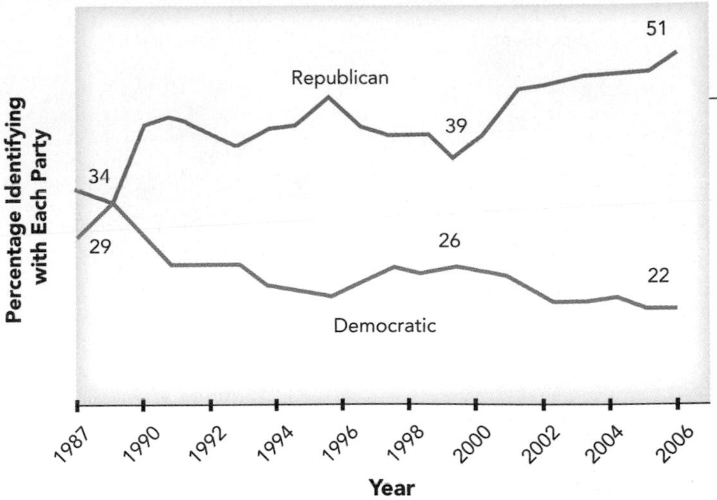

FIGURE 9.3 | **Party Identification among White Evangelical Protestants**

In 1988, white evangelical Protestants were evenly divided in their party identification between Democrats and Republicans. However, the division has since increased dramatically. ***—What consequences do you think this will have for both parties?***

SOURCE: The Pew Research Center for the People and the Press. "The 2004 Political Landscape Evenly Divided and Increasingly Polarized." 2004 updates accessed from http://people-press.org/commentary/?analysisid=95 on July 30, 2008.

Race and Ethnicity

At the beginning of the twentieth century, the major ethnic minorities in America were from Ireland, Germany, Scandinavia, Italy, Poland, and other European countries. They came or descended from those who came to the United States in waves from the 1840s to the early 1900s. These immigrants and their offspring concentrated in urban parts of the Northeast and Midwest. The religious backgrounds of these immigrants (mainly Catholic or Jewish, except for the Scandinavians) differed from the predominant Protestantism of those who had settled colonial America. They were politically energized during the Great Depression, becoming an integral component of the great coalition of Democratic voters that Franklin D. Roosevelt forged in the 1930s. For many years, immigrant groups had political preferences that were consistently different from those of "native" Anglo-Saxons. As these groups have assimilated into society and risen in economic standing, however, these differences have been disappearing.

Ever since black people were brought to North America as slaves, they have been at the bottom of the economic, political, and social totem poles. Their disadvantages still exist despite many important social and legal changes in our society.[53] Even today, African Americans and Hispanics in our society for the most part earn less than whites do.

Before the civil rights movement of the 1950s and 1960s, black participation in American politics was generally quite limited. It was not always so: African Americans gained not only freedom from slavery but also guarantees of civil rights and (for males) the right to vote after the Civil War, and at that time, the Republican Party had been associated with racial equality in the minds of both black and white Americans (largely because of the actions of President Lincoln). By the 1890s, though, blacks in the South (where most still lived) were often denied the right to vote through devious means and were subjected to harsh segregation laws. Blatant discrimination remained largely in place in the South until after World War II, but in the generation between about 1930 and 1960, racial politics began slowly to change direction. First, during these years, many black people moved from the South to northern cities, where they encountered very few obstacles to voting. Second, in the 1950s and 1960s, with the rise of black consciousness and the grassroots civil rights movement led by Martin Luther King, Jr., and others, African Americans emerged as a strong, national political force. Civil rights and social policies advanced by the Kennedy and Johnson administrations and the Democratic Congress in the 1960s brought most black people to see the national Democratic Party as the advocate of racial equality and integration. Ever since, black Americans have identified overwhelmingly with the Democratic Party.

Activism among other long-oppressed minority groups has also shaped modern political identity. As a result, Chicanos, Puerto Ricans, and Native Americans—but not Cuban Americans—also identify heavily with the Democratic Party.

Since the 1960s, white people and African Americans have evaluated civil rights issues differently. White people increasingly believe that "a lot" of positive change has occurred with regard to the life circumstances of African Americans, but fewer blacks feel

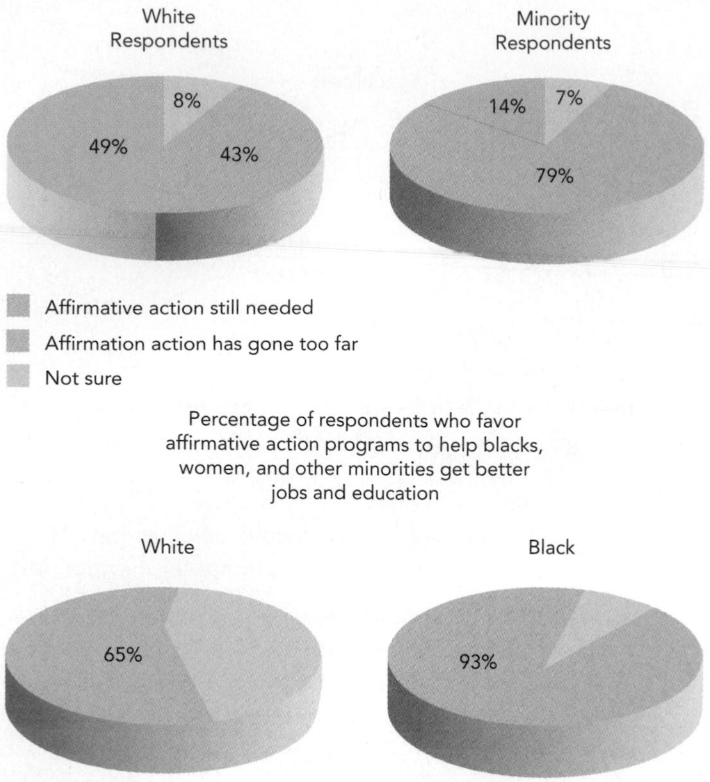

FIGURE 9.4 | **Differences in Views of Affirmative Action, by Race**

Dramatic differences exist between minorities and whites in our society. Forty-nine percent of white respondents think that affirmative action has gone too far, while 79 percent of minority respondents think that it is still needed. ***—What are some of the potential consequences of these polarized views?***

SOURCE: (Top) NBC News and the Wall Street Journal. Conducted by Hart and Tester Research Companies, January 16–21, 2003. Data provided by the Roper Center, University of Connecticut. (Bottom) Trends in Political Values and Core Attitudes: 1987–2007, Pew Research Center for the People & the Press, March 22, 2007. Accessed from http://people-press.org/reports/pdf/312.pdf on July 30, 2008.

similarly optimistic. Around 60 percent of African Americans say that black poverty is the result of social factors (discrimination, for example), while a plurality of whites (49 percent) attribute black poverty to its victims' personal characteristics, especially laziness.[54] Affirmative action, a policy designed to promote equality of opportunity for most racial and ethnic minorities, elicits considerably different reactions among white and minority respondents. Among whites, 49 percent believe that affirmative action has gone too far; only 14 percent of those belonging to minority groups (including self-identified Asians) feel this way (see Figure 9.4). Seventy-nine percent of minority Americans say that affirmative action is still needed; only 43 percent of whites agree.

Although they make up only about 13 percent of the general population—in southern states, California, the Southwest, and urban areas in northern states—Hispanics represent a sizable and a rapidly growing voting bloc. The Hispanic presence in key border states is very large: 25 percent in Arizona, 32 percent in Texas and California, and 42 percent in New Mexico. Although Hispanics are politically strong in some communities, they lag behind African Americans in organizing across the nation. In the last several election cycles, however, they have mounted important mobilization efforts.

African Americans and members of other minority groups display similar political attitudes, for several reasons. First, all racial minorities (excluding second-generation Asians and some Cuban Americans) tend to have low socioeconomic status—a direct result of racism. Substantial differences in earnings continue to exist. Moreover, individuals in all minority groups have been targets of racial prejudice and discrimination. African Americans and other minority members (mostly Hispanics) strongly favor governmental action to equalize incomes and provide extensive social services. Minorities are often concerned about issues of law and order, for they are more likely than white people to be victims of crime. There are consistent differences on public policy issues between white and African Americans, with a less clear pattern for Hispanic Americans. For example, significant differences separate white and African Americans on capital punishment, gun control, the right of gays to adopt, and spending on the poor. Given the size of some of these differences, we must be careful to be sensitive to issues of race when evaluating many public policies.

Gender Gap: Differences in voting and policy preferences between women and men.

SIGNIFICANCE: *The gender gap was coined in the early 1980s to explain the differences between men and women in voting, political party affiliation, and policy preferences. After controlling for other factors, women tend to be more liberal and Democratic than men.*

Gender

A **gender gap** separates American men and women in their patterns of voting behavior, party identification, ways of evaluating presidents, and attitudes toward various public policies. Some political scientists say that the difference in the way men and women vote first emerged in 1920, when newly enfranchised women registered overwhelmingly as Republicans. However, because women did not tend to vote in rates similar to those of men, it was not until the 1980 presidential election that the gender gap attracted much attention. In that election, when the Republican Ronald Reagan beat the Democratic incumbent Jimmy Carter, he did so with the votes of only 46 percent of the women—but he got the votes of 54 percent of the men. Substantial differences in policy preferences between men and women grew during the 1980s, with women considerably less approving of President Reagan than men were. On many issues, a majority of women embraced the Democratic (or anti-Reagan) position—including a much-publicized movement for declaring a nuclear freeze (a unilateral U.S. cessation in the production and deployment of nuclear weapons), a demand for spending more on social programs, and criticism of the administration's increased defense spending.

"Are there gender differences in political views?"

—Student Question

Gaps in public opinion continue to separate men and women. Since both parties are trying to recruit women officials and voters, the gender gap will probably continue shaping the political agenda for the foreseeable future. According to research from the Center for American Women in Politics at Rutgers University, consistent differences persist between men and women on key issues of public policy. In foreign affairs, women continue to oppose U.S. military intervention abroad and are more apt to favor diplomacy in settling foreign disputes. Domestically, women are more likely than men to support programs that protect health care and meet basic human needs, to support restrictions on the possession and use of firearms, and to favor affirmative action and other governmental efforts to achieve racial equality.[55] On the whole, women tend to be more liberal on all social issues, from capital punishment to gun ownership to gay rights. Perhaps surprisingly, however, men and women tend to have similar views on abortion.

The gender gap, coupled with the fact that more women than men vote, has changed the national agenda and the political landscape. Issues that were previously considered "women's issues" are now at center stage except in times of war or international crisis. Thus, during the 2000 presidential and congressional campaigns, when foreign tensions were relatively low, issues of education, Social Security, and health care dominated the agenda.

Several theories exist to explain the gender gap. The **attitude hypothesis** states that differences in voting preferences and issue stances between men and women result from the fact that men and women tend to have different opinions on issues of public policy. Women tend to favor more spending on social services and diplomacy, while men tend to want to spend less on social services and favor more aggressive foreign policy stances.

The **salience hypothesis** says that gender differences in party identification and voting result from the relative importance that men and women assign to issues. Abortion is a good example of gender differences in how important issues are perceived to be. Roughly equal percentages of men and women support legal access to abortions, but because women tend to rate the abortion issue as more important than men do, they may assign a higher priority to political decisions involving it. In this way, gender differences can show up even if there are no differences in the underlying attitudes.

A third potential explanation for the gender gap is the **situational hypothesis.** This states that the gender gap reflects the different situations men and women face in our society. According to this theory, women's position in American politics (such as their income, marital and parental status, and employment history) fuels gender differences in policy preferences and issue salience. Economics appears to be the most important issue, for women and female-headed households are far more likely to live in poverty. Given that the Democratic Party is more likely to advocate policies designed to promote economic equality, it is little wonder, according to the situational hypothesis, that women tend to be more supportive of Democrats.

Social Groups and Political Values
Practice Quiz

1. What factor tends to increase citizens' understanding of political issues and has a liberalizing affect on nonfiscal social issues?
   a. religion **b.** socioeconomic status
   c. education **d.** ethnicity

2. Studies suggest that within the same socioeconomic group,
   a. Catholics and Jews tend to be more conservative than Protestants.
   b. Catholics tend to be more conservative than Protestants.
   c. Jews tend to be more conservative than Catholics.
   d. Jews and Catholics tend to be more liberal than Protestants.

3. Since gaining the right to vote, most African Americans have consistently voted for Democratic Party candidates.
   a. true **b.** false

4. There is a clear and obvious gender gap in political views in the United States.
   a. true **b.** false

Answers: 1-c, 2-d, 3-a, 4-a.

Discussion Questions

1. What social factors do you think have an impact on why a gender gap exists in political views in the United States?
2. Why does education tend to have a liberalizing affect on political views?

What **YOU** can do!

Examine the demographic makeup of your college. How do you think demographics affect the atmosphere and student involvement in your school? Compare the results with a friend attending a different college that has different demographic patterns. How relevant do you think demographic patterns are in influencing your environment? Most universities publish demographic data; if not, you can obtain information for your community at **http://www.census.gov**

SIMULATION You Are a Polling Consultant

Measuring Public Opinion (pages 342–347)

What factors affect the quality and usefulness of poll data?

As a wise individual, often said to be Benjamin Disraeli, once tartly observed, "There are three kinds of lies: lies, damned lies, and statistics."

We ensure the accuracy of our measurements of public opinion through the use of polls.

Use of Polls

Political scientists and professional pollsters measure public opinion in a variety of ways. Polls are helpful in constructing a sense of what people want and think, but other means also exist to measure public opinion. In addition to polls, people can express themselves politically via protest demonstrations, news (such as people-in-the-street interviews), elections, initiatives or referendums, direct contact with officials, and letters to the editor. And of course, they can vote.

Polls represent an opportunity to view a snapshot of public opinion, and they allow officials a quick assessment of public policies. People who value citizen participation in a democracy are more likely to see the virtues of polling. Polls allow people to learn the collective preferences of their fellow citizens, but this has both positive and negative consequences. On the one hand, polls show people that others in their country may have different opinions, thus enabling citizens to grasp the complexity of many political issues. On the other hand, polls can also silence holders of minority opinions by convincing them that most people don't agree with them on a particular issue. Feeling isolated, such people may fail to voice their opinion, either abandoning their convictions or becoming deeply isolated. In examining the influence of polls on the public and on our leaders, Elizabeth Noelle-Neumann developed the theory of a "spiral of silence."[56] When the public learns about the dominant view on something or someone, dissenters come under pressure to remain silent and accept the majority viewpoint. One common way in which this phenomenon manifests itself is the "bandwagon" effect—the tendency for individuals to agree with the candidate or opinion that polls show to be attracting the most support or that receives the most media attention.

Many observers of contemporary politics are wary about using polls in our democracy. They argue that polls can be misleading, giving a false sense of the democratic process. Some critics assert that polls give the citizenry a false sense of power and influence, because in the critics' view, ultimately power is exercised by elites who may or may not follow the public's preferences.[57] As we noted at the beginning of this chapter, many believe that officials should not rely on public opinion and other poll data when making decisions but, rather, should analyze the information presented to them and make informed policy choices. As you will see, polls can be manipulated to advance a political agenda. Thus overreliance on poll data by our officials can be very dangerous.

The political scientist Benjamin Ginsberg thinks that polls weaken the influence of true public opinion.[58] Polls make it easy—perhaps too easy—for people to express their opinions. Often, polls give the impression that opinions are more strongly held than they really are and can create the impression that people actually have opinions on specific topics when in fact they may not. Other forms of political expression require more time and energy; people with deeply held opinions are therefore more likely to turn to them, giving a truer sense of public opinion. Polls rely on a passive form of expression (respondents do not volunteer to participate; they are solicited), hence you cannot be certain that poll results truly reflect the carefully considered opinion of members of the public who are interested in and care about politics. Polls may simply capture the fleeting thoughts of a group of people who are approached by the pollsters and agree to respond.

Other critics object that polls tend to measure bluntly what is sometimes a very complex entity—the opinions of the people. Reliance on poll data, say these critics, raises many concerns: Suggested opinions, sampling errors, the wording of questions, and the way poll questions are asked can all skew the responses that are obtained.

One thing that is certain, though: Public opinion polling is widespread in our society. Each major TV network has paired with a print media organization to conduct polls—CBS News with the *New York Times,* ABC News with the *Washington Post,* and NBC News with the *Wall Street Journal.* And many newsmagazines—*Newsweek, Time,* and *U.S. News and World Report,* for example—routinely commission polls. Research on these three newsmagazines' cover stories between 1995 and 2003 found that 30 percent of the articles cited polling data.[59] Every year, several million people are called on to participate in polls. Our government alone conducts over a million survey interviews every year.[60] To avoid being manipulated, it is very important for individuals to understand how polls are used, constructed, and interpreted.

Sample: A subset of the population under study; if selected correctly, it represents the population from which it was drawn with reliable and measurable accuracy.

SIGNIFICANCE: *Since it is nearly impossible to interview all people in a state, a sample is used to allow a large variety of research.*

Probability Sample: Selection procedure in which each member of the target population has a known or an equal chance of being selected.

EXAMPLE: *Probability samples are the most commonly employed by academic researchers, the media, and professional polling companies, because they have better results than other techniques.*

"Put me down for whoever comes out ahead in your poll."

People need to be cautious of public opinion data to be careful consumers: Be certain to examine who sponsored the poll, how accurate the poll is, and when it was conducted. ***—Why and when do you think that poll data are manipulated?***

Modern Polling Techniques

One of the major scientific breakthroughs of the twentieth century was the development of statistical sampling theory. This theory made possible scientific public opinion polling and survey research. Because opinion poll results are now reported so widely in the media, you must be knowledgeable about polling methods in order to make appropriate use of poll results. Moreover, you must avoid relying on a single poll as a definitive measure of public opinion; often, individual polls provide just a limited "snapshot" view of what the public is thinking. Informed consumers of public opinion polls must learn what can and cannot be correctly learned from them, as being knowledgeable about public opinion data is the best means of protection against being misled or manipulated.

SAMPLING: HOW MANY UNITS Once the unit of analysis is determined (for example, senior citizens in Florida or 18- to 24-year-olds nationally), the researcher must then decide how many of those units ought to be polled. Researchers almost never question every person in a unit; that would be prohibitively expensive and time-consuming. Instead, they take a **sample**—that is, they obtain a portion of the entire population. Sampling theory has grown with the polling industry and with survey research since the mid-1930s. The goal of sampling is to be able to make generalizations about a group by examining some of its members. Its basic assumption is that individuals can represent the groups out of which they are selected. Because people in similar situations in life are likely to hold similar opinions, it is not necessary to study all of them. On the other hand, because every person is somewhat different, it is necessary to talk to enough people from each major group so that individual uniqueness can be smoothed out and a typical response obtained.

One of the most important elements in a good sample is how *representative* it is of the major social groups that are apt to hold the opinions being researched. Choosing representative samples requires using the correct sampling technique and an appropriate sample size. The sampling technique most widely used today is the probability technique (discussed in the next paragraph). Good probability techniques should ensure a representative sample if the sample is sufficiently large. Commercial polling agencies, such as Gallup or Harris, normally use national samples of around 1,200 people. It is hard to imagine that so few could accurately represent the opinions of so many, especially in such a diverse society, but if proper techniques and protocols are followed, reliable data can be achieved.

TYPES OF SAMPLES Drawing a sample is usually a complex process. Several important decisions separate a good sample from a useless one. The first decision that needs to be made is how the sample will be chosen or drawn. Two basic methods of drawing samples are based on probability and nonprobability theories. A **probability sample** is one in which all potential respondents enter the sample with an equal or known probability of being selected. Professional pollsters rely almost exclusively on the probability method; it has been demonstrated to produce better results, with known levels of error and reliability. Nevertheless, nonprobability methods are sometimes used by nonprofessionals or for special situations. One of the most common nonprobability methods is the **accidental sample,** which is drawn by an unsystematic procedure, typically stopping and interviewing a specified number of people encountered in a public place. School newspapers often use this method to poll students. Reporters may go to the cafeteria and ask 20 people at random what they think of the food. (One commonplace example is the market research conducted in shopping malls, in which interviewers ask people who pass in front of them to participate in the survey.) Although this might be interesting, we have no evidence that those 20 people accurately reflect the entire population under study. For example, students in the cafeteria like the food well enough to be eating it; but what about the students who refuse to eat there? Journalists also use this technique when they solicit opinions by interviewing "people in the street." These types of samples are typically biased, because they depend on where the researcher goes to interview people. For example, you will get a different cross section of the public if you stand outside a high-end mall than you will outside a welfare office. Because of concerns over the reliability of nonprobability samples, professionals most often use probability techniques.

One of the simplest probability methods is a **simple random sample.** An easy demonstration of this technique is the way a lottery or raffle winner is selected. Each person who bought a ticket the receives a number that corresponds to a numbered ball. All the balls are put in a large container, which is mixed thoroughly. Then someone sticks a hand into the container and picks the winner. All potential winners have the same chance of victory. (Men used to be chosen for the military draft in the same way.) Similar procedures are followed in a simple random sample: The researchers keep "picking" until they have selected a predetermined number of respondents. If there is a large population—say, the voters in a state or the entire nation before a presidential election—computers can be used to select respondents randomly. Such a sample is quite easy to draw, and it produces reliable results. However, it can be used only when a comprehensive list of all members of the population is available, as well as a means for contacting them. If a list is not available, as is often the case, other techniques must be employed. Another frequently used probability sample is the **stratified sample,** which gets its name from the fact that the target population is broken into subgroups, or *strata* (plural of *stratum*), before the sample is drawn. Each stratum is further broken down until individual respondents can be selected at random, allowing researchers to draw a probability sample even if a comprehensive list of the target population does not exist.

Survey Research

Once the sample has been drawn, the researcher must turn to the art of developing a good questionnaire that accurately elicits respondents' opinions. The proper wording and phrasing of the questions are vitally important to producing reliable, objective data. How questions are worded can dramatically affect the responses people give, so great care must be put into developing questions that obtain true opinions. Several criteria exist to assist in the development of high-quality questions. First, researchers must use language and vocabulary appropriate for the population under study. For example, different vocabulary would be used in surveying new immigrants to the United States than would be used to poll corporate executives. Questions should also be worded to allow socially acceptable responses, thus minimizing the chance of false replies. If people are not given an acceptable way in which to respond to questions, they may lie.

A good example is voting. People are raised to believe that voting is an important right and responsibility and that a good citizen in our society exercises this right. However, not all people vote. So, when asking about whether a respondent has voted, the researcher will obtain more accurate data if the response options include a socially acceptable reason for nonvoting. If the researcher simply asks, "Did you vote in the last election?" a good percentage of nonvoters might lie to avoid looking bad. However, if respondents are asked, "Did you vote in the last election, or because of work or family responsibilities were you too busy?" nonvoters can say that they were too busy without looking bad. Such sensitivity to social acceptance is an important factor in producing superior questions and research.

Also, to get a person's true opinion, questions must be neutrally worded and should never suggest a response. Let's say you were interested in people's opinion of underage drinking. There are a number of ways in which you could phrase your question. You could ask, "What is your opinion of irresponsible underage people who consume alcohol?" You certainly would get an opinion, but would it be an objective one? Probably not, because you characterize the person as irresponsible and are thus leading the respondent to agree with your characterization. A more objectively worded question would be to simply ask, "What is your opinion of underage people consuming alcohol?" Poll results can vary dramatically depending on the manner in which the questions are worded and the alternative responses provided. Reliable polling agencies will provide a copy of the survey if asked.

Once the sample has been drawn and the questionnaire developed, it's time to administer the survey. Questionnaires can be administered in person, by mail, or by telephone. Each technique has advantages and disadvantages, once again requiring important choices. The researcher must choose the method that is most appropriate for the research and also fits the available budget.

TYPES OF QUESTIONNAIRES The **personal interview** presents the best opportunity for in-depth questioning. This type of survey is very useful for collecting a large amount of information and exploring the opinions of respondents in detail. Cost and the time required to complete the survey are the major disadvantages.

■ **Confidence Level:** The probability that the results found in the sample represent the true opinion of the entire public under study.

EXAMPLE: *The traditional standard confidence level is 95 percent, meaning that researchers are 95 percent sure that the sample accurately represents the views of the population under study.*

Telephone surveys, which have been increasing in popularity in recent decades, are attractive because they are quicker and cheaper than personal interviews. The media, for example, have turned to telephone surveys to obtain quick information about public opinion on current events. Researchers were critical of phone surveys in the past, when only fairly wealthy people had telephones, but today, nearly everyone has a phone.

Mail surveys are often used when the budget is limited; they are the cheapest way to survey the public. Low cost is the principal attraction of this type of survey, but there are several concerns. The main concern is low response rates. To some extent, the response rate depends on the socioeconomic status of the group to be sampled: Higher-status groups are more likely to complete and return the questionnaires than are lower-status groups, so this misrepresents the overall group being sampled. Given these limitations, mail surveys are far less desirable than other methods, but they may be the only affordable way for some groups to conduct research.

INTERPRETING PUBLIC OPINION POLLS A few additional points need to be made to ensure that you are an informed consumer of public opinion polls. First, political polls typically try to include only people who are likely to vote. This means that people who state they are unlikely to vote or are not registered to vote are often screened out and not interviewed. Second, not all polls are released to the general public. Some are conducted to provide politicians with campaign strategies or to determine likely responses to potential stands on an issue. Some groups commission polls but release the results only when they make them appear in a positive light. You must use caution when consuming public opinion data.

Furthermore, it is important that you understand how to interpret the information presented in a poll. Remember that polls rely on a sample of the target population. Even if all the issues identified earlier are accurately addressed, polls still have a chance of being inaccurate. This potential for inaccuracy is an unavoidable cost of using a sample rather than interviewing the entire population (which could never be done even if one had access to unlimited resources). Along with the poll results, the pollster should present two measures of accuracy: the margin of error and the confidence level. Let's provide an example and then explain each.

Say that a hypothetical national poll of likely voters shows that 35 percent of respondents have a favorable opinion of an individual who is considering running for president. How should you interpret this number? Thirty-five percent of the people who responded to the poll have a favorable view. However, we really aren't interested in the opinion of the poll respondents. We want to use the poll findings to figure out the likely feelings of the general population. To do this, we calculate the margin of error to establish a range in which we think that the actual percentage of favorable ratings will fall. The **confidence level**■ is the percentage of confidence that we have that the poll truly represents the feelings of everyone in the population.

Going back to the original example, let's say that the margin of error is plus or minus 3 percentage points and that the confidence level is 95 percent. This means that we are 95 percent sure that the actual percentage of people in the country who have favorable opinions of the potential candidate is between 32 and 38 percent.

Although the mathematics of calculating these numbers are complex (and not something that you need to understand), to be an informed consumer, it is important that you do understand how to interpret and apply both the margin of error and the confidence level. In many close elections, the numbers fall within the margin of error. When this happens, the media will say that the election is "too close to call."

Controversies Surrounding Polling

Call-in and Internet surveys, often called *pseudo-polls*, are controversial, because the results are often falsely presented to the public as scientific and reliable. These are nonprobability samples, so we can calculate neither the level of confidence in the results nor the likelihood of error. Only individuals watching a particular program on TV, tuning in to a particular radio talk show, or visiting certain Internet sites can participate in the poll. In addition, people who call in (especially if there is a cost in time or money) tend to hold more extreme positions than those who do not bother to participate. These surveys may be interesting, but they are statistically unreliable. Research done on the public perception of President George H.W. Bush's 1992 State of the Union address demonstrates how poor these call-in surveys can be. CBS encouraged viewers to call in with their opinion of whether they were better off than they were 4 years ago. At the same time, CBS conducted a scientific poll to compare the results. In the call-in poll, 54 percent of respondents stated that they were worse off, while in the scientific poll, only 32 percent claimed to be worse off.[61] Additional research has demonstrated similar problems with polls conducted on radio talk shows, whose listeners are unrepresentative of the population. They tend to be angrier, more conservative, more Republican, and mostly male.[62] Online surveys suffer many similar problems of self-selected and unrepresentative respondents.

Contemporary technology has made many people question how representative samples are. Caller ID and call-block have made it increasingly difficult for pollsters to reach many people and to

■ **Exit Polls:** Surveys of voters leaving polling places; used by news media to gauge how candidates are doing on election day.

SIGNIFICANCE: *Exit polls can be very helpful in providing immediate insight into who is voting for whom and why and in projecting the likely winner of an election.*

CONNECT THE LINK

(Chapter **12**, pages **430–435**) Do you think the controversies surrounding the 2000 presidential election have made people more or less interested in politics?

COMPARATIVE **Comparing Governments and Public Opinion**

select a random sample of the population. Moreover, refusal rates have been rising, with fewer and fewer of the people reached being willing to cooperate with the pollsters. In some surveys, less than 20 percent of calls result in a completed survey, raising the costs of surveys as well as the level of concern about their accuracy. In the 1960s, it was common for two-thirds of contacted people to participate. Today, cooperation rates hover around 38 percent for the national media surveys that take place over a few days, and overnight surveys often have much lower rates.[63] Research conducted in 2004, however, indicates that the low response rates are not too troubling, because "missing" respondents were found not to distort results.[64] Those who refused to participate were similar to those who agreed to participate in the survey, so the low response rates did not significantly alter the results.

Concerns have also arisen over the number of people who no longer use home phones but rely exclusively on cell phones. Currently, it is very costly (and in some cases illegal) for pollsters to call cell phones, so these people are excluded from samples. Once again, research has found that this may not be as large a problem as some have thought: Personal interviews with 2,000 randomly selected adults found that only 2.5 percent had cell phones but no home phones. This might, however, be a larger concern if the survey tries to include a large number of college-age individuals, who are more likely to rely exclusively on cell phones and who tend to move a lot.[65]

One area of public opinion polling that has recently come under much scrutiny is the media's reporting of polling data during campaigns and elections—and especially the use on election day of exit polls to predict outcomes before the votes are counted. **Exit polls**■ are taken at selected precincts while voting is in progress, with the pollsters typically asking every 10th voter how he or she has voted and why. In the past, exit polls have been helpful for news organizations as they raced to be the first to predict the winners of elections. But in 1980, having gotten bad news from exit polls in states in the Eastern and Central time zones, President Jimmy Carter conceded defeat to Ronald Reagan 3 hours before polls on the West Coast had closed. Democratic officials criticized Carter and the networks, claiming that prematurely publicizing adverse poll data had caused many western Democrats not to vote, affecting many congressional, state, and local elections. As a consequence, the networks agreed not to predict the presidential winner of a state until all polls in that state had closed. In the 2000 presidential election, the exit polls conducted by the Voter News Service (made up of the four major networks, CNN, and the Associated Press) were flawed by sampling errors. Faulty exit poll results in Florida—as well as forgetting that the state's western panhandle observes Central rather than Eastern time, so that voting there was still going on—led CBS to predict the incorrect winner not just once but twice. (This was not the only problem in the 2000 presidential elections; we discuss other issues in LINK Chapter 12, pages 430–435). As a consequence, the networks dropped the Voter News Service and, in 2004, used a new service. Exit polls in the 2004 presidential election were also criticized, however, especially those conducted in Ohio. In the future, as we see more and more people choosing early voting, the accuracy of exit polls for predicting winners and providing glimpses into the motivations of voters will be even more precarious.

Poll coverage in elections more generally is also troubling. The media often take the easy road and focus on "horse race" coverage (who's ahead in the polls, who is gaining, and so forth), to the detriment of discussing issues and other matters of substance. In 2004, several weeks before Canada's national election, the Canadian Broadcasting Corporation abruptly quit preelection polling, stating that constantly reporting poll results deflected public attention from issues and emphasized the superficial. Many critics call for the U.S. networks to follow suit.

Given all the concerns about public opinion polling that have been discussed in this chapter, many critics question the wisdom of the incessant reporting of polling to reflect public opinion and desires for social change. Some argue that we must rely on other forms of political expression to voice the views of the public; others believe that pollsters can adapt to these challenges and continue to provide important information about what the public is thinking.

PATHWAYS | of change from around the world

What do MySpace, Save Darfur Coalition, and Oxfam International have in common? They are working together to raise awareness of the horrific human rights violations and genocide in Sudan. On the Rock for Darfur 2007 MySpace page, several dozen bands announced they would donate proceeds from several scheduled engagements to the Save Darfur Coalition and Oxfam International (both groups work to raise awareness and minimize the devastation resulting from the genocide in the Sudan). Concerts from over 30 bands in countries ranging from the United States to Australia to South Africa raised much needed funds for these organizations. Maroon 5 and Fall Out Boy were just a few of the many artists who donated proceeds from their concerts to the Rock for Darfur 2007. So when some people criticize MySpace as being mindless and harmful, you can remind them that it can also be a powerful tool to mobilize people from around the world to fight injustice and violence. ■

Measuring Public Opinion

Practice Quiz

1. Why are polls sometimes problematic?
   - **a.** When their results are published, they sometimes have the effect of silencing members of the public who hold minority views.
   - **b.** As another voice of the people, they sometimes reflect the effectiveness of an elected official or governmental policy.
   - **c.** Increasing numbers of people, especially young people, rely exclusively upon cell phones, thereby excluding them from telephone samples.
   - **d.** a and c

2. In the polling process, the goal of sampling is to get
   - **a.** as diverse a set of responses as possible.
   - **b.** as random a set of responses as possible.
   - **c.** as representative a set of responses as possible.
   - **d.** as rapid a set of responses as possible.

3. If proper techniques and protocols are used, polls can reliably assess the opinions of the whole nation by gathering the responses of as few as 1,200 people.
   - **a.** true
   - **b.** false

4. Which is an example of an inappropriately worded polling question?
   - **a.** "Do you think abortion under all circumstances should be illegal?"
   - **b.** "Do you think that extremist antiabortion groups should be prohibited by law from protesting outside abortion clinics?"
   - **c.** "Have you ever witnessed a fellow student cheating on a test but been prevented by circumstances from reporting the infraction?"
   - **d.** "For whom did you just vote?"

Answers: 1-d, 2-c, 3-a, 4-b.

Discussion Questions

1. Can you think of any objections to exit polling? Does it violate the privacy of the voting booth? Can it affect the outcome of the actual voting? Some critics charge that the main advantage of exit polling is to help news organizations in their race to be first to predict the outcome on election night. Do you agree or disagree? Why?
2. What measures can be taken to ensure that polls are more accurate and reliable?

What **YOU** can do!

Consider the following forms of modern polling: personal interviews, telephone surveys, mail surveys, and Internet surveys. Make a list of the strengths and weaknesses of each technique. Pay special attention to the demographic groups that may be excluded with each technique. Which technique do you believe produces the most representative measure of public opinion? Why? Can you devise an alternative technique?

Conclusion

As you've seen, public opinion influences cultural change, but it can be hard to predict when public opinion will be influential. Examples exist that show how public opinion has influenced government, but other examples demonstrate that mass opinion has been largely ineffective in swaying people in authority. Politicians often use poll data to build support for policies and to avoid making unpopular decisions. Hence there is a reciprocal relationship in which public opinion can influence politicians *and* politicians can use public opinion to influence the people. Public opinion polling is an important device to gauge public sentiment and can influence change in our society. That explains why public opinion polling operations in the White House have become institutionalized. Each modern administration routinely polls the public.[66] Elites often use poll data to claim legitimacy for their positions. When elites disagree, they try to use poll data to claim the high road, thereby minimizing opposition and garnering additional support for their agenda. Polls become strategic tools by which political leaders seek to sell their views and positions to the public.[67] Politicians often act strategically by "rationally anticipating" shifts in public opinion and examining how these changes can affect future elections. In anticipating these changes, leaders can strategically modify their positions. Thus public opinion influences politicians directly, through elections, and also indirectly, because they tend to act rationally in anticipating change.[68]

Key Objective Review, Apply, and Explore

Public Opinion

(pages 322–325)

Public opinion is a far more complex phenomenon than many people appreciate. It is grounded in political values and tends to be very stable, but it can serve as a mechanism to promote cultural change.

Commentators disagree over the role that public opinion should play in influencing public officials. Some believe public opinion ought to have a limited role in American politics, arguing that people are too easily influenced and manipulated and that our elites need to have the freedom to make the important political decisions. The public can influence politics with the systematic review of elected officials that is permitted with free and competitive elections. Other political commentators believe that it is healthy in a democracy for public officials to track public opinion and act in accordance with it.

KEY TERMS

Public Opinion 322
Elitism 322
Individualism 324
Equality of Opportunity 325
Equality of Outcome 325

CRITICAL THINKING QUESTIONS

1. How is public opinion formed? How stable is it? What factors tend to stabilize public opinion, and what factors tend to lead to instability?
2. How do the elitist and pluralistic theories differ regarding the importance public officials ought to give public opinion when making decisions? What do you think?

INTERNET RESOURCES

American Association for Public Opinion Research (AAPOR): **http://www.aapor.org**

Pew Research Center for the People and the Press: **http://people-press.org**

ADDITIONAL READING

Bardes, Barbara, and Robert Oldendick. *Public Opinion: Measuring the American Mind,* 3rd ed. Florence, KY: Wadsworth, 2006.

Erickson, Robert, and Kent Tedin. *American Public Opinion: Its Origins, Content, and Impact,* 7th ed. New York: Longman, 2006.

Lewis, Justin. *Constructing Public Opinion: How Political Elites Do What They Like and Why We Seem to Go Along with It.* New York: Columbia University Press, 2001.

The Stability of Political Beliefs

(pages 326–329)

Americans largely agree on a number of fundamental values, including liberty, individualism, democratic institutions, basic principles, and equality. Disagreements occur when the government translates these rather abstract ideas into specific public policies.

Public opinion tends to be stable, though we do see substantial shifts during times of crisis or as a reaction to an important event. As we saw with such issues as gay rights, civil rights, and women's rights, gradual changes in public opinion also occur, reflecting and shaping our political and popular culture.

KEY TERMS

Cohort Replacement 326
Catalyst-for-Change Theory 327
Barometer of Public Attitudes 327
Interactive Theory 327

CRITICAL THINKING QUESTIONS

1. Do you think that Americans truly agree on basic issues? Is it important that we should agree?
2. How, if at all, does popular culture influence political culture?

INTERNET RESOURCES

EUROPA—Public Opinion Analysis of Europe, Eurobarometer Surveys: **http://europa.eu.int/comm/public_opinion/Index_en.htm**

Kinsey Institute for Research on Sex, Gender, and Reproduction, University of Indiana: **http://www.indiana.edu/~kinsey/resources/datasets.html**

National Gay and Lesbian Task Force: **http://www.ngltf.org**

ADDITIONAL READING

Rosenthal, Alan, Burdett A. Loomis, John R. Hibbing, and Karl T. Kurtz. *Republic on Trial: The Case for Representative Democracy.* Washington, D.C.: CQ Press, 2002.

Weissberg, Robert. *Polling, Policy, and Public Opinion: The Case Against Heeding the "Voice of the People."* New York: Palgrave-Macmillan, 2002.

Key Objective Review, Apply, and Explore

From Values to Ideology

(pages 330–331)

Political ideology is a consistent set of personal values and beliefs about the proper purpose and scope of government. Once formed, most people's political ideology remains rather stable (barring a critical world or domestic event). The range of political ideologies in the United States is narrower than in other societies; most Americans place themselves fairly close to the center of the political spectrum.

KEY TERMS

Political Ideology 330
Conservatives 330
Liberals 330

CRITICAL THINKING QUESTIONS

1. What is political ideology? What are the principal differences between liberals and conservatives today?
2. Do you a believe the differences between liberals and conservatives are more pronounced today than in past decades? Why or why not?

INTERNET RESOURCES

Polling Report **http://www.pollingreport.com/**

ADDITIONAL READING

Fiorina, Morris P., Samuel J. Abrams, and Jeremy C. Pope. *Culture War? The Myth of a Polarized America,* 2nd ed. New York: Longman, 2005.

Shea, Daniel. *Mass Politics: The Politics of Popular Culture.* New York: St. Martin's/Worth, 1999.

Political Socialization

(pages 332–335)

People acquire their political knowledge and beliefs through a process called political socialization. Family, schools, community and peers, religious groups, the media, and events all serve as agents of socialization, introducing individuals into the world of politics and influencing individuals' political values, beliefs, opinions, and ideologies.

KEY TERMS

Agents of Political Socialization 332
Efficacy 333

CRITICAL THINKING QUESTIONS

1. Why is the process of political socialization so important in our society?
2. What factors are the most important in political socialization, and what role do they play in the process?

INTERNET RESOURCES

National Opinion Research Center (NORC), University of Chicago: **http://www.norc.uchicago.edu**
Parents and Friends of Lesbians and Gays: **http://www.pflag.org**

ADDITIONAL READING

Gimpel, James G., J. Celeste Lay, and Jason E. Schuknecht. *Cultivating Democracy: Civic Environments and Political Socialization in America.* Washington, D.C.: Brookings Institution Press, 2003.

Jackson, David J. *Entertainment and Politics: The Influence of Pop Culture on Young Adult Political Socialization.* New York: Lang, 2002.

Key Objective Review, Apply, and Explore

Social Groups and Political Values

(pages 336–341)

People with similar life circumstances and experiences tend to develop similar opinions and values. We see many significant differences between groups based on their income, education, religion, race or ethnicity, and gender. Understanding the socialization process and the way in which demographic factors affect public opinion is important in fully appreciating the diversity of our country.

KEY TERMS

Crosscutting Cleavages 336
Gender Gap 340
Attitude Hypothesis 341
Salience Hypothesis 341
Situational Hypothesis 341

CRITICAL THINKING QUESTIONS

1. How does membership in relevant demographic groups affect public opinion?
2. What are some important differences between members of various groups on contemporary issues?

INTERNET RESOURCES

National Election Study, University of Michigan: **http://www.umich.edu/~nes**

Roper Center for Public Opinion Research: **http://www.ropercenter.uconn.edu**

ADDITIONAL READING

Althaus, Scott L. *Collective Preferences in Democratic Politics.* New York: Cambridge University Press, 2003.

Mattson, Kevin. *Engaging Youth: Combating the Apathy of Young Americans Toward Politics.* New York: Century Foundation Press, 2003.

Measuring Public Opinion

(pages 342–347)

Public opinion polls provide data on a plethora of issues that are important to Americans. We must be cautious, however, in using poll data to generalize about the population as a whole. Good public opinion polls are very useful for gauging public sentiment, but many factors can adversely affect the quality of the data obtained. Such factors include the representativeness of the sample, the wording of the questions posed and the issues explored, and the manner in which questionnaires are administered. Understanding the issues surrounding public opinion polling is an important part of being an informed consumer of political news and information.

KEY TERMS

Sample 343
Probability Sample 343
Accidental Sample 343
Simple Random Sample 344
Stratified Sample 344
Personal Interview 344
Telephone Surveys 345
Mail Surveys 345
Confidence Level 345
Exit Polls 346

CRITICAL THINKING QUESTIONS

1. What are the key considerations in determining the reliability of public opinion polls?
2. Why are many political commentators concerned with the contemporary use of public opinion polling? Do you share their concerns?

INTERNET RESOURCES

Gallup Organization: **http://www.gallup.com**

PollingReport.com: **http://www.pollingreport.com**

ADDITIONAL READING

Asher, Herbert. *Polling and the Public: What Every Citizen Should Know,* 7th ed. Washington, D.C.: CQ Press, 2007.

Rusk, Jerrold G. *Statistical History of the American Electorate.* Washington, D.C.: CQ Press, 2001.

Stanley, Harold W., and Richard G. Niemi. *Vital Statistics on American Politics, 2007–2008.* Washington, D.C.: CQ Press, 2007.

Chapter Review Critical Thinking Test

1. Truly great political leaders
   - **a.** never feel obliged to act in accordance with the popular opinions of their constituency.
   - **b.** usually act in accordance with the popular opinions of their constituency.
   - **c.** know when—and when *not*—to follow the popular opinions of their constituency.
   - **d.** will appear as if they care about popular opinion even when they really do not.
2. Most Americans believe it is appropriate for the government to ensure that every U.S. citizen has equal opportunities for success, but not to ensure equal outcomes.
   - **a.** true **b.** false
3. Most gradual change in public opinion happens through
   - **a.** cohort replacement.
   - **b.** dramatic events at the national level, such as Pearl Harbor and 9/11.
   - **c.** changes in technology.
   - **d.** a, b, and c
4. Although public opinion regarding the rights and status of women has become dramatically more favorable in the past 30 years,
   - **a.** women are still in the minority in many graduate and professional schools.
   - **b.** women still hit a "glass ceiling" when trying to gain promotions in the business world.
   - **c.** many women who are discriminated against in the workforce are still reluctant to challenge the discriminatory practices through legal or other means.
   - **d.** a, b, and c
5. Political scientist Sidney Verba suggested that
   - **a.** economic differences between rich and poor make it difficult for the views of the general population to be heard.
   - **b.** public opinion polls should be heeded, because they are a more egalitarian form of political expression.
   - **c.** education is not as important as social status in terms of public opinion formation.
   - **d.** b and c
6. The influence of popular culture on our political culture and public opinion has always been a positive feature of our democracy.
   - **a.** true **b.** false
7. In the past 20 years or so, Americans' political ideology has tended to become
   - **a.** more conservative. **b.** more inconsistent.
   - **c.** more polarized. **d.** a and c
8. International events can become important factors that impact political ideology in the United States.
   - **a.** true **b.** false
9. Some political scientists study the state of American families because
   - **a.** the nature of family life affects the family's role as an agent of socialization.
   - **b.** family life—how parents and children interact, how much money parents make, and other factors—helps us predict what values children will grow up to embrace.
   - **c.** parents' influence over their children becomes increasingly strong throughout adolescence.
   - **d.** a and b
10. As agents of socialization, elementary schools have the effect of
    - **a.** training children to value their own contributions to the decision-making process.
    - **b.** training children to think creatively.
    - **c.** training children to accept the hierarchical nature of power.
    - **d.** a, b, and c
11. Having people live in politically and racially diverse communities is good for our democracy, because
    - **a.** such communities cultivate higher political efficacy among individuals than homogeneous or segregated communities do.
    - **b.** such communities are more likely to produce uninformed children than homogeneous or segregated communities are.
    - **c.** living in such communities is the politically correct thing to do.
    - **d.** a and c
12. Viewing popular electronic media, such as late-night television comedy programs, is a way that people obtain political information.
    - **a.** true **b.** false
13. For most of the twentieth century, what demographic features characterized Republican Party loyalists?
    - **a.** white and well-to-do
    - **b.** ethnic minority and blue-collar
    - **c.** southern
    - **d.** a and c
14. What explains Jewish Americans' loyalty to the Democratic Party?
    - **a.** a concern for social and economic justice in the Jewish tradition
    - **b.** Jews' long-standing focus on international issues
    - **c.** the fact that Jewish-American immigrants benefited from social services instituted by Democratic administrations in the early twentieth century
    - **d.** a and b
15. For much of the twentieth century, the political preferences of immigrant groups in the United States were consistently different from those of Americans of Anglo-Saxon origin.
    - **a.** true **b.** false

Chapter Review Critical Thinking Test

16. What is the gender gap?

a. the inherent differences of ability between men and women

b. the difference between how women and men have tended to view political issues in this country

c. the difference between how many men and how few women become elected governmental officials

d. b and c

17. The media often take the easy road and focus on "horse race" coverage (who's ahead in the polls, who is gaining, and so forth) to the detriment of discussing issues and other matters of substance.

a. true **b.** false

18. Professional pollsters almost always use some form of probability sampling in their polling, because

a. it is the most convenient and least expensive method.

b. its use means that all potential respondents have a known or equal probability of being selected.

c. it produces more accurate results than other sampling techniques.

d. b and c

19. Anyone eager to influence American society should understand the nature of both public opinion and political socialization, because

a. both mechanisms can bring about social change by influencing elites in our country.

b. both reinforce conventional thinking—and therefore are worth resisting.

c. both are forces that politicians routinely ignore once they are in office.

d. a, b, and c

20. The political ideology of most Americans is relatively moderate compared to those of people from other countries, and it tends not to change much over the course of an individual's lifetime.

a. true **b.** false

Answers: 1-c, 2-a, 3-a, 4-d, 5-b, 6-b, 7-d, 8-a, 9-d, 10-c, 11-a, 12-a, 13-a, 14-d, 15-a, 16-b, 17-a, 18-d, 19-a, 20-a.

You decide!

Design and conduct a poll about attitudes on environmental issues (for example, global warming and alternative energy sources) on your campus. Be sure that the poll is demographically representative, and try to follow the standards for high-quality public opinion polling. Are their differences in opinion among people from different racial, ethnic, religious, and economic groups? What differences in opinion are there between men and women? Are certain people more or less concerned with different environmental issues? How knowledgeable are your colleagues regarding environmental issues?

Based on the information you gather, design an educational poster or pamphlet that can be used to educate your campus community. Be sure to dispel any misconceptions that you discovered among your colleagues. You may also want to write an editorial or an article for your campus newspaper describing what you found in the survey results. After a few weeks, do the survey again. Did knowledge and/or attitudes change? If so, how?

Key Objective Outline

How do the media shape and reflect our cultural values and struggles?

The Media and the Public in the Political Arena **(page 376)**

How can we negotiate the delicate balance between the need for governmental regulation and the desire for a vigorous and free press?

Governmental Regulations **(page 380)**

CHAPTER 10
THE POLITICS OF THE MEDIA

How powerful are the mass media in the United States?

On September 11, 2001, at 8:45 A.M. Eastern Daylight Time, a commercial airplane crashed into one of the World Trade Center towers in New York City, forever changing the world. Eighteen minutes later, a second airliner crashed into the other tower. Soon came the equally shocking news that a third airliner had hit the Pentagon and that a fourth hijacked plane, presumably bound for an attack on Washington, D.C., had gone down in a field in Shanksville, Pennsylvania.

The media's live coverage of the Twin Towers collapsing, vividly conveying the horror of the attack, dramatically altered history. Americans had shown relatively little concern over domestic terrorism before this attack. After the attack, terrorism dominated dinner conversations, news programs, the national consciousness, and the government's agenda.

Similarly, photos broadcast and printed in 2004 depicted the deplorable treatment of Iraqi prisoners at Abu Ghraib by U.S. military personnel, setting in motion an international debate regarding the definition of torture and the Bush administration's foreign policies. The domestic and international outrage was immediate, with many fearing that the scandal would further fuel anti-American sentiment through the Middle East.

Perhaps equally impressive were the images of raw emotion displayed by people across the country and worldwide on November 4, 2008, when Barack Obama was announced as the first African-American president-elect of the United States. Millions of people across the globe watched the new first family walk on stage in front of some 200,000 screaming supporters. His candidacy forever changed politics in the United States.

Impressions such as these can change the way people think about themselves, their government, and their world, making the media important actors in shaping and reflecting cultural change. As these experiences so powerfully demonstrated, the contemporary media allow us to see the world beyond our everyday lives, providing the opportunity to share experiences and events. This tremendous power of the media, however, comes with great responsibility. One of our aims in this chapter is to look at how important the media are in the cultural change pathway, paying attention not only to the media's potential to impact the political agenda but also to both reflect and shape popular culture.

■ **Marketplace of Ideas:** The concept that ideas and theories compete for acceptance among the public.

EXAMPLE: *When new issues arise, political parties, candidates, and interest groups will often present their position on the issues. The marketplace of ideas allows the public debate of issues, which ultimately makes the public better informed regarding complex matters.*

Mass Media

(pages 356-357)

How important are the media in American politics?

The importance of free media in a democratic society cannot be exaggerated. The success of our democracy depends on our being informed and aware about the policy issues facing our nation as well as the action—or inaction—of our government leaders in response to those issues. Your effective involvement as an actor in the country's democratic governing process, whether as a voter, an interest group member, or a political candidate, depends on your knowledge of current events. It is through the media that you see world events beyond those directly observed in your private life. The media show us the "big picture" worlds of politics, entertainment, sports, culture, and economics, as well as the lives of people living in other countries and other cultures.

The media's behavior has undergone intensive scrutiny, for it is widely asserted that the media are very powerful in socializing citizens' attitudes, beliefs, and behaviors. Furthermore, many people believe that the media are very influential in shaping the actions of government officials; some have even called the media the fourth branch of government. However, you should question how influential the mass media actually are. Rather than *shaping* our values and beliefs, do the media simply *reflect* them? Or do they do both—shape as well as reflect our cultural values and struggles? These are questions to keep in mind as you read this chapter.

Media and Democracy: An Interactive Relationship

There is a key link between public opinion, the media, and democracy—an interactive relationship in which each affects the others. All democratic governments must allow for a **marketplace of ideas**■, in which differing thoughts and beliefs are able to develop and thrive, and the media make possible, on a mass scale, the vitally important public debate over opposing opinions, ideas, and thoughts. This marketplace, in which ideas and values compete for acceptance, is crucial to a healthy democracy. Public discussions of important and often controversial issues are a fundamental component of a free society. Without free media, in which competing ideas can be discussed and debated openly, there can be no effective democratic decision-making. The two-way flow of information, from the government to the people and from the people to the government, is fundamental in a representative democracy. Obstructing the two-way information flow is a tactic dictators use to preserve their power. In this way, the media play an important role in our democracy, serving as a "communications bridge" between the governed and the governing. The importance of the media in linking government with the people has grown in recent times as the power, influence, and significance of the national government have grown and the clout of other institutions, notably political parties, has diminished.

Most Americans know that the media are very powerful. The media's news coverage can manipulate public opinion, influence policymaking, and affect elections and even the economy, and the entertainment component can also mold our political, social, and economic values. Today, the average American high school senior has spent more time watching TV than attending school. Even what is learned in school is often influenced by the media's portrayal of events. The average American adult spends nearly half of his or her leisure time watching TV, listening to the radio, and reading newspapers or magazines; the single greatest amount of time is spent watching television. Moreover, TV remains the primary source of news and entertainment in the United States.[1]

> "How much television does the typical American watch?"
>
> —Student Question

Television thus provides the unique opportunity for millions to share events and experiences, sometimes—as on September 11, 2001—with a dramatic power to alter the political climate and world events. The visual nature of television makes events seem more intimate and intense. It provides almost all of our political knowledge (for we do not observe firsthand most of the things that happen in the world) and thus mirrors a world much larger than any of us can ever know directly.

For example, Walter Cronkite, the CBS news anchor of the 1960s and 1970s, always ended his broadcast with the words "And that's the way it is." The influence of Cronkite, consistently cited as one of the most trusted men in America, was shown dramatically in 1968. During most of the 1960s, Cronkite had expressed support for the war in Vietnam, but that changed after he visited Southeast Asia in early 1968. Upon returning home, he took the unprecedented step of interjecting a personal opinion at the end of his February 27th broadcast: "For it seems more certain now than ever that the bloody experience of Vietnam is to end in a stalemate." President Johnson, after watching Cronkite's broadcast, is quoted as saying, "That's it. If I've lost Cronkite, I've lost Middle America." A month later, Johnson announced his decision not to seek reelection. Cronkite's words summed up the goal of his news program: his attempt to give Americans a glimpse into the larger world in which they lived.

The media's claim to be a mirror to the world raises many questions. Is this mirror an all-inclusive, unbiased, and neutral representation of world events? Or does the mirror reflect selective pictures, ideas, and opinions? Concerns over the objectivity of the media have caused a good deal of disagreement, which we will discuss throughout this chapter.

Given the impact of the media on public opinion and behavior, many people ask who should control the news. Governments? Superficially, it might seem to make sense for public officials to

For nearly 20 years, Walter Cronkite served as anchorman of the CBS Evening News (from 1962 to 1981), becoming one of the most trusted men in the country. His trademark exit line, "And that's the way it is," perfectly characterized his efforts to present fair, accurate, and reliable news to his viewers. He is best remembered for his coverage of the Cuban Missile Crisis, the assassination of President Kennedy, and the Vietnam War. ***—Do you think we will once again trust and admire journalists as the country did Cronkite? Why or why not?***

control the news, so that they can use the media to promote images and ideas that could strengthen our democracy. Historically, Americans have opposed censorship, believing that free and vigorous media are necessary to democracy. Authoritarian regimes assume that the government knows what's best for its citizens and thus seek to control all flows of information, thereby molding what their people think about and believe. Authoritarian governments believe that news and entertainment programs should not question government or its policies but, rather, should build support and loyalty. Conversely, democratic societies assume that government officials can and do make mistakes. This assumption is inherent in the American governing structure, with its checks and balances and its division of power. Democracies therefore insist that the public needs a free press to keep government in line. The citizens of a democracy need to challenge the officials' policies and, through public debate and discussion, build consensus and develop better policies. While it may be frustrating at times, especially when we don't agree with the media's portrayal, a free press is essential for democracy.

Mass Media
Practice Quiz

1. The media relate to cultural change by both
   - **a.** impeding and influencing it.
   - **b.** reflecting and impeding it.
   - **c.** reflecting and shaping it.
   - **d.** shaping and minimizing it.
2. The media serve as a "communication bridge" primarily between
   - **a.** the governed and the governing.
   - **b.** the advertisers and the consumers.
   - **c.** the United States and other countries.
   - **d.** the cultural present and the cultural future.
3. What prompted President Lyndon Johnson to say he had lost the support of Middle America?
   - **a.** the worsening situation for the United States in the Vietnam War.
   - **b.** the broadcasting of negative polling data on the nightly news.
   - **c.** a string of botched "pseudo-events" in the Chicago area.
   - **d.** Walter Cronkite's negative assessment of the Vietnam War on the news one night.
4. A perennial assumption about our political system is that government officials make mistakes and a free press is therefore needed to monitor them.
   - **a.** true
   - **b.** false

Answers: 1-c, 2-a, 3-d, 4-a.

Discussion Questions

1. Why is a free press vital in a democracy? What is the marketplace of ideas?
2. What would be the consequences of allowing government officials to control the media? Are there any circumstances under which you believe such control might at least temporarily be justified?

What **YOU** can do!

Compare stories published in the state-run paper, *China Daily,* with those published in the *South China Morning Post,* which is published in Hong Kong. (Both of these sources are published in English and can be found online at **http://www.chinadaily.com.cn** and **http://www.scmp.com**, respectively.) What differences do you see between the two sources in their coverage of the same events and issues? How does this highlight some of the advantages and disadvantages of government-controlled media for citizens, journalists, and government?

CONNECT THE LINK
(Chapter **2**, pages **56–58**) Do you think that the original intent of the founders is still a relevant consideration today?

The Growth of Mass Media (pages 358–363)

How have the media changed and developed?

Print media were the first form of mass communication. As technology has developed and changed, so, too, have the mass media. Today, electronic media are rapidly evolving, with more and more people looking to different sources for information and entertainment.

Print Media

The first newspaper published in what would become the United States was the *Boston News-Letter,* which began appearing in April of 1704. The paper was one page long and was published weekly. By 1725, Boston had three newspapers, and Philadelphia and New York City each had one. At the time of the Revolutionary War five decades later, 50 presses were operating in the 13 colonies.[2] The colonial authorities accepted these early newspapers in part because they generally tried to avoid controversial issues. Many of these early papers relied on government printing jobs as a key source to increase their revenue and could not afford to alienate local officials. The Revolutionary War changed all this: Newspapers became important tools in building public support for resistance to British policies and, by 1776, for independence. The historian Arthur Schlesinger, Sr., wrote that the war for independence "could hardly have succeeded without an ever alert and dedicated press."[3] By the late 1770s, most presses were actively promoting independence. This activity continued during the war, reporting Patriot successes (often with exaggeration) while downplaying losses.

Newspapers were also used to promote public support for ratifying the Constitution. Compared to the extreme partisanship of the Revolutionary War, their coverage was more balanced, giving opportunities for opponents to discuss their concerns. The best examples of the persuasive use of the press to advance a political agenda are the series of newspaper essays written (anonymously) by Alexander Hamilton, James Madison, and John Jay, later published as *The Federalist Papers.* As you saw in LINK Chapter 2, pages 56–58, these essays were powerful and persuasive testimonies in support of the Constitution and helped ensure its ratification in the crucial state of New York. To this day, *The Federalist Papers* remain one of the best expressions of the founders' original intent.

Following ratification of the Constitution, political leaders of the time thought it very important to promote newspapers, which informed citizens of major issues facing the new government. Sharing information was vital. Americans worried that the new federal government would prove too powerful and too remote for citizens to control. Using the press to report the actions of the new government kept people informed and eased their fears. The spread of political information through the press, declared the House of Representatives, is "among the surest means of preventing the degeneracy of a free government."[4] In view of the difficulties and expenses of publishing newspapers at the time, the federal government provided protection for newspapers by granting them special treatment—for example, by charging a reduced rate of postage for papers mailed to subscribers.

The number and circulation of newspapers in the early nineteenth century grew dramatically. For example, by the early 1830s, there were 12 daily newspapers published in Philadelphia and six in New York City. The number of newspapers published across the country soared, from around 200 in 1800 to around 1,200 in the mid-1830s.[5] These early newspapers were almost always created and funded to promote specific political and economic beliefs. For example, parties and political leaders normally encouraged and helped finance newspapers in important cities. Called **party presses,** these papers are best seen as arms of competing political factions. Most newspapers became unabashedly partisan, reaping rewards when their preferred party won an election and suffering when it lost. These papers were targeted to the elite, were relatively expensive, and did not have many subscribers. Ordinary citizens, however, often heard newspapers being read aloud and argued about in public gathering places, including taverns, inns, and coffeehouses.

NEWSPAPERS FOR THE COMMON PERSON The year 1833 saw an important change in the nature of journalism in the United States: the advent of the **penny press,** so called because these daily newspapers cost a penny, versus about 6 cents for the established newspapers of the day. These penny papers, the first of which was the *New York Sun,* were marketed to the "common man." (In the sexist thinking of the day, politics, like business, was assumed to be a masculine pursuit, something in which women should not participate.) They offered less political and business coverage but a more diverse range of material—crime and human interest stories, scandals, and sports. These newspapers quickly became very popular, changing the face of journalism by making it a true mass medium. Newspaper publishers covered the costs of publication and made a profit by selling advertising. Unlike earlier newspapers, which had relied on officials or travelers for their political and economic news, the penny presses relied more heavily on reporters who would ferret out stories. These presses were less partisan and were more financially independent of politicians, significantly affecting the way in which politics was covered.[6] This change in the nature of journalism encouraged the press to become freer and more vigorous.

By the mid-nineteenth century, newspapers had become somewhat more objective and fact-based. The invention of the telegraph in the 1840s helped this shift. The Associated Press (the world's largest and oldest news agency), created in 1848, inaugurated a new trend in journalism, marked by direct and simple writing designed to appeal to a wide range of readers.

So-called **yellow journalism,** featuring sensationalism, comics, and scandal to sell papers, became popular at the end of the nineteenth century. (The name came from the yellow-tinted newsprint that some of these papers used.) Papers that engaged in yellow journalism competed fiercely with one another and fought desperately to raise circulation. William Randolph Hearst, one of the earliest practitioners of yellow journalism, forthrightly said, "It is the [*New York*] *Journal's* policy to engage brains as well as to get news, for the public is even more fond of entertainment than it is of information."[7] The stories became increasingly outrageous and shocking. As the newspapers' extreme sensation mongering generated a public backlash, journalists responded by beginning to develop a code of professional ethics. Many newspapers, oriented toward a more "respectable" readership, rejected sensational journalism and still made profits by selling advertising. (The *New York Times* is a prime example.)

In the early twentieth century, the ownership of newspapers became more centralized, the result of competition that forced many papers to close or merge. We will discuss this centralization of ownership in more detail later in the chapter, but it is important to note the trend toward fewer and fewer independent sources of information. This trend was well under way by the 1930s, when the Hearst chain (consisting of 26 daily papers in 19 cities) controlled 13 percent of the nation's newspaper circulation. In 1933, six newspaper chains owned 81 daily papers, representing 26 percent of national circulation.[8] This trend has continued, paralleling a drastic shrinkage in the number of newspapers. In 2003, the Tribune Company owned 13 daily newspapers and 26 TV stations in 21 media markets. When it merged with the *Los Angeles Times* in 2000, the Tribune Company reached nearly 80 percent of U.S. households through one or more media outlets.[9] Currently, the Tribune Company is the only multimedia company that owns newspapers and television stations in all three of the largest media markets (New York, Los Angeles, and Chicago). As we'll discuss later in the chapter, many people are concerned with this trend toward concentration of ownership.

Electronic Media

The twentieth century witnessed an explosion in new means of mass communication, starting with radio.

RADIO In 1900, a professor of electrical engineering at the University of Pittsburgh named Reginald Fessenden made the first experimental radio transmission. His successful broadcast made radio communication a reality. During World War I, little was done to exploit this technology commercially, but after the war, there was a rush to set up private radio stations. Presidential election returns were broadcast for the first time in 1920. In 1923, the country had 566 radio stations. At first, radio was primarily an activity for hobbyists who built their own sets. By 1924, however, some 2.5 million Americans owned radio receivers, and the era of mass radio had begun.[10] When preassembled radios began to be sold in stores, a rapid and dramatic growth of radio audiences occurred. In 1930, for example, radio receivers—14 million of them—were in 45 percent of American households. One decade later, despite the Great Depression, 81 percent of households owned a total of 44 million receivers. By the late 1940s, when television started to become popular, 95 percent of households had radios.[11] Radio had become a source of information and entertainment for practically everyone.

The first radio stations had been strictly local, but the formation of radio networks with syndicated programming began in the late 1920s. This trend was encouraged when Congress passed the Radio Act of 1927, which regulated the rapidly growing industry. The Radio Act established the airwaves as a public good, subject to governmental oversight. Under the new federal policy, radio stations were privately owned, with the government regulating the technical aspects and issuing licenses to broadcast on specific frequencies. Freedom-of-speech concerns kept regulation from extending to content.

Not all liberal democracies have privately owned broadcast media. In the United Kingdom, for example, the government owns and controls the British Broadcasting Corporation, known as the BBC. Private stations do exist in Britain and are regulated by an independent regulatory agency, which is responsible to Parliament, but the BBC is the largest broadcasting corporation in the world, sending out programming on television, radio, and the Internet.

Mirroring the trend in American newspaper publishing, radio broadcasting consolidated as the twentieth century wore on. In 1934, one-third of all U.S. radio stations were affiliated with a network, and more than 60 percent were by 1940. Today, radio stations that are not affiliated with networks often have weaker signals and face financial problems. Consolidation helps defer costs, but it also concentrates power.

Technology Gap (Digital Divide): The differences in access to and mastery of information and communication technology between segments of the community (typically for socioeconomic, educational, or geographical reasons).

EXAMPLE: *Because more and more groups, organizations, and news outlets are relying on the Internet to reach their consumers and supporters, there is great concern that the technology gap is limiting the ability of some segments of the population to access important information.*

TELEVISION Like radio, once television was perfected, it grew at an astounding rate. Television became technically feasible in the late 1930s, but World War II delayed its commercial development. Commercial TV broadcasting began in the late 1940s. In 1950, there were 98 TV stations in the United States, with 9 percent of American households having TV sets. Four years later, the number of families owning sets had exploded, from less than 4 million to 28 million. By 1958, some 41 million families had TV sets. Today, more than 1,100 broadcast TV stations are licensed in the United States, 98 percent of households have televisions, and more than half of all households have two or more sets.[12] Television is unique in two ways—its immediacy (it can show events live) and its visual content, both of which convey a sense of legitimacy to viewers and increase emotional appeal.

> "Why does television have such a unique effect on public opinion?"
>
> —Student Question

Unlike newspapers and radio stations, which first were independently owned and only later consolidated into chains and networks, high costs dictated that almost from the beginning, TV stations were affiliated with networks, thus centralizing ownership. Today, however, unlike radio and newspapers, where concentration is intensifying, the ownership of television broadcasting is becoming more competitive and diverse. In the last 20 or 30 years, network television's audience has changed dramatically. Cable TV, satellite TV, and digital recorders have changed the nature of watching TV, reducing the audience for network programming. Meanwhile, the development of 'round-the-clock news networks, such as CNN, Fox News, CNBC, and MSNBC, coupled with the dramatic growth of news shows, such as *20/20, Dateline,* and *Primetime,* has altered the face of the broadcast media. The arrival of television marked a breakthrough in personalizing communication from officials to the masses, allowing intimate contact in a diverse and large society.

STUDENT | PROFILE

In 2004, Brittany and Robbie Bergquist of Norwell, Massachusetts, were appalled to learn that a soldier incurred an $8,000 telephone bill for calling his family from Iraq. Rather than sit back and do nothing, these two young people (then 12 and 13 years old) started Cell Phones for Soldiers, a nonprofit organization, with only $21. During the next 3 years, they collected enough used cell phones to raise over $1 million and donated 400,000 minutes for soldiers deployed overseas to call their families. Their goal is to collect enough used cell phones to donate 12 million prepaid calling-card minutes in 2008. It would have been easy for these two youngsters to ignore the problem, but they got involved and have helped many of our troops stay in desperate touch with their loved ones.[13] ■

THE INTERNET The Internet has revolutionized the way we communicate. Developed in the early 1980s, it was originally used to network Department of Defense computers, linking the Pentagon with far-flung military bases and defense contractors. Later, it was expanded to include large research universities; e-mail was its first main use. The growth of the Internet is tied directly to the explosive growth of personal computers and the development of graphics programming. (Early e-mail appeared on a blank screen, with no cute graphics or icons, and users had to rely on function keys to send messages manually.) As the technology rapidly developed, the public responded avidly. By the late 1980s, the Internet was coming into widespread public use. Recognizing the Internet's economic potential, companies introduced Web pages and developed marketing techniques for the new medium. Public officials also acted strategically, establishing Web sites through which citizens could contact them electronically. (Chapters 12 and Chapters 13 discuss the Internet as a tool for the public to mobilize and for groups to communicate.)

Richard Davis, a political scientist, has studied the political functions of the Internet. The Internet, he finds, serves as a link between government and the people, as virtually all elected officials and organizations maintain Web pages to provide information and a means for communication. Members of Congress, the president, governors, city councils, school boards, and mayors maintain Web pages that provide information and allow citizens to reach officials directly, facilitating communication and political engagement. The Internet can also serve as a forum for the discussion of political issues, though some experts are concerned the Internet can be used to fragment the public by framing issues very narrowly to appeal to a specialized group of people.[14]

It is important to note that a **technology gap**■ (also referred to as the **digital divide**) exists in the United States.[15] Class, race, and age all influence a person's access to personal computers and the Internet. The benefits made possible by the Internet are likely to be achieved by people who have basic computer skills and thus are already interested in and informed about politics—that is, the educated, the more affluent, and younger people.[16] Although most public libraries provide free Internet access, not all people are able to take advantage of this opportunity (for example, if they have no access to transportation, lack basic computer skills, or are not literate). Table 10.1 gives details on Internet access. Least likely to have Internet access are the elderly (who often find it difficult to learn how to use it), African Americans, Hispanics, and the less educated and less affluent. "The digital divide has turned into a 'racial ravine' when one looks at access among households of different races and ethnic origins."[17]

Furthermore, the very nature of the Internet makes it a potentially dangerous place to get *reliable* information. Anyone with basic computer skills and the interest can create a Web page and a blog—and there is no mechanism to differentiate irrelevant, biased, or intentionally manipulative information from reliable and accurate knowledge. You need to be an informed consumer, aware of the trustworthiness of each online source and careful not to be misled or swayed by imprecise or biased information.

The instantaneous nature of the Internet has dramatically changed news reporting today. For example, Internet users whose service provider offers instantly updated headline news can read the main stories featured in the newspaper many hours before they appear in print. Consequently, the way in which people get their news has changed, with people relying less on local news programs, cable news, nightly network news, newsmagazines, and daily newspaper for information and more on the Internet and news from their service providers (see Table 10.2). In addition to the issues of race and class with respect to access to the Internet, age also affects the manner in which people consume news. Those under 30 are far more likely to get their news online than from the newspaper or television, whereas people over 50 are far more likely to rely on television or the newspaper for their news information.[18] In 2004, 20% of people from the ages of 18 to 29 regularly learned something about the campaign from the Internet. Just 4 years later, that number increased to 42%, making the Internet the most common source of campaign information for young people.[19]

In addition to changing patterns of news consumption, a remarkable growth in the use of social networking Web pages (such as Facebook and MySpace) as a source of information on campaigns has occurred in the last few years. A remarkable 67 percent of people from 18 to 29 use social network sites, with 27% of them reporting that they get campaign information from these sites (with 37% of people between 18 and 24 using the sites to acquire campaign information). Only 1% of people over 40 reported using these networking sites to get campaign information. Given the success of Barack Obama's campaign in using these new technologies, we expect them to be regular elements used by all major candidates for the presidency, Congress, and many statewide elected offices during upcoming elections (see Table 10.3).

TABLE 10.1 | **Internet Access by Selected Characteristics, 2003**

The Census Bureau regularly conducts surveys of the American public, partly to provide the government with information but also to gauge the needs and status of the population (which then can influence public policies and resource allocations). In this survey, the government found that access to the Internet is not evenly divided across important demographic groups. People between the ages of 25 and 64 have more access, as do whites and Asians as well as those with higher educational attainment and family income. ***—How might the lack of access to the Internet become an issue in the future?***

	Internet Access
Age of Householder	
15–24 years	47.1%
25–34 years	60.4%
35–44 years	65.3%
45–54 years	65.1%
55–64 years	56.6%
65 years and older	29.4%
Race	
White, non-Hispanic	59.9%
African American	36.0%
Asian	66.7%
Hispanic	36.0%
Educational Attainment	
Less than high school graduate	20.2%
High school graduate/GED	43.1%
Some college or associate's degree	62.6%
Bachelor's degree	76.8%
Advanced degree	81.1%
Family Income (annual)	
Less than $25,000	30.7%
$25,000–$49,999	57.3%
$50,000–$74,999	77.9%
$75,000–$99,999	85.8%
$100,000 or more	92.2%

SOURCE: U.S. Census Bureau, Current Population Survey, October 2003.

COMPARATIVE Comparing News Media

VISUAL LITERACY Use of the Media by the American Public

TABLE 10.2 | **Where Americans Learn about Candidates and Campaigns**

A national survey of over 1,430 adults 18 and over, conducted from December 19 to 30, 2007, revealed that people are changing their pattern of news consumption compared to similar surveys conducted in 2000 and 2004. Adults in 2008 are relying less on local television news, TV news magazines, and daily newspapers for their information regarding candidates and campaigns than they did in 2000 and 2004. Today, they are relying substantially more on the Internet for such information. ***—Do you think this is a positive or a negative trend? Does it matter where people get their news from? Why or why not?***

REGULARLY LEARN SOMETHING FROM ...	2000	2004	2008
Local TV news	48%	42%	40%
Cable news networks	34%	38%	38%
Nightly network news	45%	35%	32%
Daily newspaper	40%	31%	31%
TV news magazines	29%	25%	22%
Morning TV shows	18%	20%	22%
Cable political talk	14%	14%	15%
Talk radio	15%	17%	16%
National Public Radio	12%	14%	18%
News magazines	15%	10%	11%
Late-night talk shows	9%	9%	9%
Religious radio	7%	5%	9%
Lou Dobbs Tonight	—	—	7%
Internet	9%	13%	24%

SOURCE: *Internet's Broader Role in Campaign 2008* (Washington, DC: The Pew Research Center for the People & the Press, January 1, 2008). http://people-press.org/report/384/internets-broader-role-in-campaign-2008. Reprinted with permission.

TABLE 10.3 | **Social Networking Sites and the Campaign, by Age**

	TOTAL	18–29	30–39	40+
Use social network sites	22%	67%	21%	6%
Get campaign information from sites	7%	27%	4%	1%
Signed up as a "friend" of candidate	3%	8%	3%	<1%

SOURCE: *Internet's Broader Role in Campaign 2008* (Washington, DC. The Pew Research Center for the People & the Press, January 1, 2008). http://people-press.org/report/384/internets-broader-role-in-campaign-2008. Reprinted with permission.

PATHWAYS | of change from around the world

In 1988, a pro-democracy uprising in Myanmar was quickly dispelled when the totalitarian government successfully shut the country's borders, expelled foreign journalists and dissidents, and controlled the flow of information. More than 3,000 people were killed in this Asian nation, with little world scrutiny. The government thought they could squash a similar uprising that began in 2007 by once again controlling the media and shielding themselves from the world (as they had successfully done a number of times in the past). This time, however, they did not anticipate the use of technology and how difficult it would be to control. Despite the fact that the country has one of the most repressed and censored media in the world and less than 1 percent of the country has access to the Internet, technology is certainly changing the nature of the conflict and the world's reaction.

The use of blogs (which are very popular with young Myanmarese), text messaging, and digital photos transmitted by cell phones have allowed the protests led by Buddhist monks to reach a global audience now able to watch the desperate call for democracy. Students throughout the country use text messaging to set up demonstrations and track the location of government soldiers. Exiled Myanmar students founded the Democratic Voice of Burma in Norway, which has become a leading voice to support the rebellion and transmit information to the world. The government has been trying to shut down Internet access and cut cell phone services but has been relatively unsuccessful—especially with students using satellite telephones. The students' and activists' use of technology makes it impossible for the government to isolate itself from global scrutiny. Currently, the protests continue with both sides deeply entrenched—but thanks to technology, transparency is becoming more commonplace. ■

The Growth of Mass Media

Practice Quiz

1. From the beginning, the press in colonial America featured scandal and controversy on the front page of newspapers and circulars.
   - **a.** true
   - **b.** false
2. When did owning and listening to radio first become popular in this country?
   - **a.** between 1880 and 1890
   - **b.** between 1900 and 1910
   - **c.** between 1920 and 1930
   - **d.** between 1940 and 1950
3. One disadvantage of the Internet as a site for political news and ideas is that
   - **a.** the information on it is not always reliable.
   - **b.** the news items are not covered in great depth.
   - **c.** only the best-informed individuals can post material on the Web.
   - **d.** most of the people who use the Internet are young and politically disconnected.
4. Remarkable growth has occured in the usage of social networking Web pages on the Internet. What percentage of 18- to 29-year-olds use them?
   - **a.** 75%
   - **b.** 67%
   - **c.** 50%
   - **d.** 27%

Answers: 1-b, 2-c, 3-a, 4-b.

Discussion Questions

1. How did the function of newspapers change when they became widely available to the public?
2. How have television and the Internet changed the reporting of news? Why must you be cautious about using the Internet as a source of political information?

What **YOU** can do!

Is there a digital divide in the town where you attend college? Develop a research design that you could use to determine whether such a divide exists. With whom would you speak? What data would you need to gather? To whom would you present your results? And what low-cost steps could be taken to bridge a gap if it exists?

Functions *of the* Media (pages 364–369)

What functions do the media perform in our society?

The media perform a multitude of functions in the United States, which can be summarized as entertaining, informing, and persuading the public. The media provide people with shared political experiences, which can in turn bring people together and affect public opinion. The media model appropriate behavior and reinforce cultural norms, but they also portray behavior that challenges cultural norms and expectations. And sometimes, they do both at the same time. Because the media (especially television) are increasingly national in scope, the presentation of some issues in one region to one group will reinforce cultural norms while the same material challenges cultural norms in another region. Consider same-sex marriage. In some regions, these unions are more accepted as normal expressions of love and commitment, while in other regions, most people consider them immoral. When the media portray such unions in the news or in sitcoms, the perspective they use can serve to frame the issue.

With its beginnings in 1975, *Saturday Night Live* has made a name for itself by spoofing famous people and politicians. Pictured above are Amy Poehler and Hillary Clinton. Showing her sense of humor, then-presidential candidate Clinton graciously embraced the comedian who impersonated her. ***—How relevant do you think comedy programs are in influencing public opinion of celebrities and politicians?***

Entertainment

Even as entertainment, the media can affect the image of officials and institutions. Consider late-night television, where being the frequent butt of jokes can undermine a leader's public image. The media's negative portrayal of governmental officials, even as entertainment, can have negative effects on public perception and attitudes. Research on media images of public officials from the mid-1950s through the 1990s has demonstrated that the way they were shown was more likely to be negative than positive. The only occupation with worse images was business. Before 1975, our political system itself was twice as likely to be portrayed positively on television than negatively, but by the 1980s, positive portrayals had become uncommon. This shift, the researchers claimed, reflected changes in public opinion in the aftermath of the Vietnam War and the Watergate scandal.[20]

The distinction between entertainment and news has become increasingly blurred as the news divisions of network media come under pressure to be entertaining in hopes of appealing to a broader audience and generating money for the network. A perfect example of this occurred when *Saturday Night Live's* Tina Fey began a remarkably successful parody of Republican vice presidential nominee Sarah Palin. Almost immediately upon Senator John McCain's nomination of Governor Palin for the Republican ticket, Ms. Fey put on her "power red suit and wig" and began a notable impersonation of the governor that dramatically escalated the ratings of *SNL*. Many critics of Governor Palin quickly seized Ms. Fey's characterizations, using them as evidence that the governor was unsuitable to be the vice president and, if the need arose, president. The clouding of entertainment and news media is not new, but given the popularity of YouTube, it may be the first time that such material was so widely accessible and available.

Social Effects of the Media

As noted, the distinctive nature of the news media in communicating makes them a unique and potentially powerful political actor. The news media have many functions in our society, with

In the summer of 2008, presidential candidate John McCain aired an ad depicting opponent Barack Obama as a celebrity, flashing pictures of Brittany Spears and Paris Hilton. Paris Hilton clearly took offense and aired her response ad generating a good deal of interest on You Tube and national talk programs. ***—Do you think that celebrities should use their fame to voice their political concerns?***

great political and social consequences. Harold Lasswell, a prominent political scientist who pioneered studying the effects of the media on American politics, identified three important societal functions of the media: surveillance, interpretation, and socialization.[21]

SURVEILLANCE TO REPORT WORLD EVENTS According to Lasswell, the media have a watchdog role as the "eyes and ears to the world." That is, the media report what's news, thus keeping us informed of significant events not only in our communities but also in our nation and around the globe. Their surveillance function draws attention to problems that need addressing. For example, news coverage on conditions at a local veterans' hospital could demonstrate the need for more oversight and better patient care. The story could then expand, looking at the quality of care in hospitals across the country, perhaps motivating Congress to examine the care our country provides to veterans, enhancing the quality of their lives. It is important to note, however, that not all surveillance reporting is positive. For example, research has shown that crime is often overreported, making people believe there is more criminal activity in their community than actually exists. Although it can be helpful for the media to probe into scandals and to uncover abuses, emphasizing negativity can also lead to public cynicism. Negative reporting on the economy has drawn much criticism, with some observers asserting stories that continually report economic downturns can spread fear among investors, causing them to act in ways that actually do worsen the economy.

PATHWAYS | profile

Dorothea Lange, Photojournalist

Dorothea Lange was one of America's first women photojournalists. Her work documented the plight of some of the most vulnerable groups in our society and recorded an important era in American history. Perhaps best known for documenting the terrible distress of migratory workers in California during the Great Depression, her photos gave poverty a face and personalized the issue for many who were far removed from the plight of the poor.

Lange later did powerful work recording images of World War II factory workers and the wartime internment camps for Japanese Americans. In retrospect, those camps were a serious blot on the United States. Beginning shortly after Pearl Harbor, 120,000 Japanese-American men, women, and children—more than two-thirds of them native-born U.S. citizens—were ordered relocated from the West Coast to the interior of the continent, even though no specific charges of disloyalty were made against any individuals. Lange took more than 700 photographs of Japanese internees as they were evicted from their homes, lost their businesses, and were forcibly relocated in what is now acknowledged as a gross violation of their civil rights. Though employed by the federal government, Lange quickly became sympathetic to the ethnic Japanese internees. As a government employee, all pictures she took were the property of the federal government, which censored her photos. Only after her death did the world get access to many of these important images.

Born in 1895, Lange worked hard to break down barriers facing women in American society who chose nontraditional careers. Throughout her life, she won many awards and was the first woman awarded a Guggenheim Fellowship, a prestigious prize given annually to individuals "who have demonstrated exceptional capacity for

ABOVE: **During the Great Depression,** many were desperately poor and in great need of assistance. The photograph shows migrant workers displaced by the severe drought and the Dust Bowl of the 1930s. The photograph is striking because it so intimately depicts the desperation these people felt.

BELOW: **Following the Japanese attack on Pearl Harbor,** many Japanese Americans were targeted with violence, intimidation, and isolation. In 1942, the U.S. government ordered that Japanese Americans be gathered up and moved away from the west coast of the country. Their internment lasted until 1945, resulting in significant property loss. The photo here shows a Japanese-owned grocery store shortly after the attack on Pearl Harbor.

■ **Investigative Reporting:** A type of journalism in which reporters thoroughly investigate a subject matter (often involving a scandal) to inform the public, correct an injustice, or expose an abuse.

EXAMPLE: *Some of the most important public scandals, such as Watergate, the Iran–Contra Affair, the collapse of Enron, and the torture of prisoners of war at Abu Ghraib have been made public through investigative reporting.*

productive scholarship or exceptional creative ability in the arts."[22] She worked as a photojournalist at *Life* magazine for nearly a decade, traveling extensively throughout the world. She died in 1965.

Lange is remembered for her realistic portrayal of people in their natural setting, for her commitment to documenting the lives of the most vulnerable individuals and groups, and for her pioneering efforts as a woman forging her place in the world. ■

One aspect of surveillance is **investigative reporting**■, in which reporters seek out stories and probe into various aspects of an issue in search of serious problems. Some of the earliest forms of investigative journalism, popular around 1900, were called **muckraking**—an expression that President Theodore Roosevelt coined in describing journalists who, he thought, tried to rake up too much sensational social filth. From the 1870s until World War I, there was a good deal of public interest in reforming government, politics, and business (see LINK Chapter 11, pages 394–395). To generate support for reform, journalists would investigate areas they believed needed to be changed and then present their findings to the public. One of the most famous examples is Upton Sinclair's examination of the Chicago stockyards. His resulting novel, *The Jungle,* published in 1906, was a scathing exposé of the meatpacking industry. It created a public outcry for reform during Theodore Roosevelt's administration, leading the federal government to regulate the industry and demand more sanitary conditions to make meat production safer. Muckraking lost public support around 1912, sending investigative journalism into a prolonged lull. The Watergate scandal of the early 1970s not only revived modern investigative journalism but also firmly entrenched it in the contemporary media.

Many Americans have welcomed the return of investigative journalism, pointing to the numerous abuses that reporters have recently uncovered. One excellent example is the *Chicago Tribune*'s investigation into the Illinois death penalty in 1999. The *Tribune* exposed serious flaws in the administration of the death penalty in that state. Its findings ultimately led Governor George Ryan to impose a moratorium on all executions in the state and to appoint a panel to recommend improving the public defender system, which provides lawyers for indigent persons accused of committing death-penalty offenses. Some critics, however, believe that investigative journalists often go too far, delving into matters that should be treated confidentially and privately—for example, the extramarital affairs of public officials or the behavior of these officials' children. Some areas, these critics say, should be considered off-limits out of respect for individuals' privacy.

CONNECT THE LINK
(Chapter **11**, pages **394–395**) When interest in reform is high, must the public rely upon the media to pressure government to institute changes? What other means are available?

DEBATE **Media Bias**

INTERPRETATION According to Lasswell, the second societal role of the media is to interpret the news, putting events into context and helping people to understand the complexities of the world. One example occurred upon the death of former president Ronald Reagan in 2004. Retrospective stories in the newspapers and on television put his presidency into context by focusing on his economic and social policies while typically ignoring the more controversial issues of his administration, such as the Iran–Contra scandal. The media drew historical parallels between Reagan and other presidents and compared his funeral to other presidential funerals. In essence, they put his life and death into context for the nation. The ability to set the context, frame the issue, interpret the facts, and potentially, provide legitimacy for people, issues, or groups gives the media enormous power. In framing how a story is told—in short, by creating heroes and villains—the media tell us, subtly or otherwise, who is "good" and who is "bad" in a way that is difficult to refute thereafter.

Take the civil rights movement as an example. Interpretive stories in the media about prominent figures and events in the movement have generally been framed to focus on the victims of racism rather than to show that civil rights activists challenged the status quo and broke laws doing it. In 1955, Rosa Parks intentionally and in full awareness broke the law of Montgomery, Alabama, by refusing to give up her seat on a city bus to a white man. Yes, she believed that the law was unjust, but it *was* the law at the time. Media accounts about her at the time of her death in 2005 portrayed her not as a lawbreaker but as a victim and a hero in the struggle for justice. Conversely, the media tended to portray the feminist activists of the late 1960s and early 1970s as extremist, man-hating, lesbian bra burners when they could have been depicted more sympathetically as women fighting gender oppression and patriarchy.

Interpretive journalism is very much in evidence in reporting on the war in Iraq. When the United States invaded Iraq in 2003, the American media framed the war primarily as a defensive measure, to rid the world of Saddam Hussein's weapons of mass destruction, and secondarily as a war to liberate the oppressed Iraqi people. Many Iraqis and others around the world, however, did not share America's announced goal of liberating the Iraqi population. Framing the invasion in terms of waging the post-9/11 War on Terror, rather than in terms of attacking another nation unprovoked certainly helped generate public support for the initial invasion, but events soon caused the war to be framed a bit differently. Neither the alleged stockpiles of weapons of mass destruction nor links between Saddam's Iraq and al-Qaeda were discovered, and a bitter Iraqi resistance to the American occupation developed. As U.S. military losses mounted and Iraq seemingly lurched toward sectarian civil conflict—and as the media repeatedly reported stories of poor planning for the invasion and of postinvasion chaos—the American public's support for the war and for President George W. Bush eroded. War critics became more outspoken, many of them preferring to see the war retroactively framed in terms of the United States having invaded a sovereign nation to impose our values and promote our economic self-interest. To what extent investigative journalists will eventually accept—and contribute to—this reframing of the war remains to be seen.

Consider another example in the United States: the images and controversies that emerged following the coverage of Hurricane Katrina. On August 30, 2005, two news sources—the Associated Press (AP) and Getty Images via Agence France-Presse (AFP)—published two similar pictures with very different captions. In the AP picture, an African-American man was shown "looting" a local grocery store, while in the AFP picture, two Caucasian people were depicted "finding" bread and soda at a local grocery store. Critics contended that the characterizations were based on racial stereotypes and were biased.[23] Others claimed that the captions may simply reflect stylistic differences associated with the two news agencies. As consumers, you need to be conscious of this sort of potential bias and seek numerous sources of news to ensure objectivity.

Many observers of all political stripes are concerned over what they see as bias in news coverage. Some perceive a liberal bias in the news, especially on public radio and television and in such newspapers as the *New York Times;* conservative political commentators such as Rush Limbaugh and Bill O'Reilly, as well as conservative politicians, make much of this alleged bias. Democrats and liberals counter by asserting that Fox News has a conservative bias (a belief echoed in the film *Outfoxed: Rupert Murdoch's War on Journalism*), that the mainstream media actually bend over backward to present conservative views, and that a good deal of reporting is, in fact, shaded in a conservative direction. Research on this volatile issue is mixed. In 1995, the Media Studies Center and the Roper Center for Public Opinion surveyed

> "Do the political leanings of reporters or editors lead to bias in news reporting?"
> —Student Question

CONNECT THE LINK
(Chapter **9**, pages **327–329**) Do you think the government should set standards for television shows requiring them to portray positive role models?

Washington-based reporters and national newspaper editors. It found that 50 percent of reporters identified themselves as Democrats, compared with 34 percent of the national public. Editors were more like the national public than reporters, with 31 percent claiming to be Democrats. Only 4 percent of reporters, however, said that they were Republicans, compared to 28 percent of the public and 14 percent of editors.[24] The research also probed political ideology, finding that reporters are far more likely to call themselves liberal than the general population. Editors were more conservative, dividing along the lines found in the population at large. In 2004, The Pew Center interviewed national and local reporters and found that 34% of national and 23% of local reporters considered themselves liberals (compared with 20% of the general public). Only 7% of national and 12% of local reporters self-identified as conservatives (compared with 33% of the public); the vast majority of each (54% and 61%, respectively) claimed they were moderates (compared with 41% of the public).[25] These data provide some evidence to bolster assertions that reporters are more likely to be liberals. Other research shows that historically, newspapers have been far more likely to endorse Republican presidential candidates, but the current trend is for papers to remain uncommitted at election time.[26] Research has failed to find empirical evidence that news reporting is biased in favor of either party.[27] So, even though reporters may be more liberal, their professional stance on the whole remains neutral. It is difficult to assess whether their neutrality is the result of the influence of editors and owners (both of whom are more conservative), of their ethical commitments, or of the competitiveness inherent in the modern journalistic environment.

If we expand the definition of the media to include talk radio, concerns over a liberal bias disappear. Unquestionably, conservative radio personalities and political commentators dominate talk radio, and self-described liberal or left-wing commentators have had difficulty finding a following in this environment. And as for Web sites and blogs, all shades of political opinion seem to have plentiful outlets (see Table 10.4).

TABLE 10.4 | The Typical Journalist

As you can see, journalists are not a cross-section of the U.S. population. They are more likely to be white, male, and politically liberal college graduates. Nonwhite journalists are more likely to be female. People question whether these disparities impact the fairness of news coverage. The research is mixed, with some concluding that the lack of diversity adversely impacts the manner in which news is framed and portrayed. Others argue that given the highly competitive nature of the news industry, coverage is generally fair and unbiased.

	1982	1992	2002
White	96.1%	91.8%	90.5%
Male	66.2%	66.0%	67.0%
College graduate	73.7%	82.1%	89.3%
Democrat	38.5%	44.1%	37.1%
Median age	32 years	36 years	41 years

SOURCE: David H. Weaver, Randal Beam, Bonnie Brownlee, Paul Voakes, and G. Cleve-lant Wilhoit, The American Journalist in the 21st Century (Mahwah, NJ: Erlbaum, 2006).

SOCIALIZATION The third effect of the media that Lasswell identified is to socialize people. As noted in LINK Chapter 9, pages 327–329, the media are an agent of socialization, teaching us political facts and opinions that help form our political belief structures and our political culture. Research since the 1970s has shown that the media are a crucial agent of socialization, teaching both facts and values. The media also reinforce economic and social values. Simply looking at MTV and VH1 provides testimony that the belief in capitalism is alive and well in the United States. Shows such as *The Fabulous Life, MTV Cribs,* and *My Super Sweet Sixteen,* which dwell on material acquisitions, reinforce the basic tenets of capitalism—the desire for more "bling-bling" drives our economic system.

In winter, young children spend an average of 31 hours a week watching TV. Eighty percent of the programming children watch is intended for adults and generally goes far beyond their life experiences, making the potential for molding their minds greater than that for adults.[28] Hence the concern in many areas of society is about programming content and the negative implications of the high levels of violence, sex, and materialism on television. The media can and do promote positive role models for children, celebrating national holidays and heroes, but there is no denying that negative images in the media far outweigh positive illustrations. For adults whose basic ideology and opinions are already formed, the media provide opportunities for reinforcement, especially with so many options available on TV, cable, the Internet, and in the immense variety of print publications. Adults can thus easily find programming to reinforce their ideology and political views; children are more susceptible to what they learn from TV.

Because the media today rely so heavily upon images, they, unlike many other political actors, have a greater ability to frame political messages. Republican vice presidential nominee Sarah Palin is pictured with Samuel "Joe the Plumber" Wurzelbacher. The image of "Joe" was invoked during the presidential campaign to demonstrate how well the Republican tax plan would serve the "common folk." ***—Do you think that the "common American" still looks like "Joe the Plumber"?***

Functions of the Media

Practice Quiz

1. What explains the increasingly negative portrayal of our political system on television after 1975?
   - **a.** consolidation of the networks
   - **b.** the rise of cable TV
   - **c.** the Vietnam War and the Watergate scandal
   - **d.** the Iran-Contra scandal
2. A series of articles in the *Chicago Tribune* in 1999 about the death penalty in Illinois is an example of investigative journalism that
   - **a.** goes too far, violating the privacy of noncelebrities.
   - **b.** is really more sensationalism than reporting of hard news.
   - **c.** does not go far enough, leaving social problems unaddressed.
   - **d.** discovers abuses in our system and leads to real change.
3. The personalities and political commentators on talk radio make it clear that this medium
   - **a.** is dominated by liberals.
   - **b.** is dominated by conservatives.
   - **c.** has succeeded in remaining politically neutral.
   - **d.** has shifted from a conservative to liberal bias.
4. According to the 2004 Pew Research Center data, most reporters considered themselves to be
   - **a.** liberals.
   - **b.** conservatives.
   - **c.** moderates.
   - **d.** without a definitive ideology.

Answers: 1-c, 2-d, 3-b, 4-c.

Discussion Questions

1. How do the entertainment media affect politics? How important do you think this effect is?
2. What are the positive and negative aspects of having the media serve as watchdogs? Why is the power of interpretation a powerful tool of the media?

What **YOU** can do!

If one function of the media is to socialize viewers, think about the television programs that may have played that role for you and your friends as you were growing up. Ask your parents what television programs they watched as they were growing up. Are there differences in the values and lessons taught? In the situations portrayed? In the kinds of characters that appeared?

SIMULATION You Are the News Editor

■ **Agenda Setting:** Featuring specific stories in the media to focus attention on particular issues.

EXAMPLE: *When the media cover a story and focus on a new issue, they raise public consciousness about it. The public then puts pressure on governmental authorities to address the issue, thereby setting the political agenda.*

Political Use *of the* Media (pages 370–375)

How influential are the media in interpreting and framing news stories?

Political parties, politicians, interest groups, and individuals use the media to manipulate the public and politics. Political elites have always used communication for political purposes. In 350 B.C., the ancient Greek philosopher Aristotle, in his *Rhetoric,* discussed the role of communication in keeping political communities intact. Today's modern mass media simply make the process easier. As you'll see, political leaders often directly appeal to the public (with a televised speech, for example) or indirectly (in advertisements designed to sway public opinion). It is important to realize that communication has always been used for political purposes, although today's technology has made it more sophisticated. In light of their exclusive focus on communication, the mass media in the United States should be considered an important political institution.

How Politicians Make the News

Politicians try very hard to get positive press coverage free of charge. Many of their actions are designed to increase the likelihood that the media will cover them. This is especially important for officials who are up for reelection. As you will see, people tend to put more credence in what they learn from news programs than in information presented during paid advertisements. Hence this so-called **earned media coverage** is very important for political officials and political candidates. It raises their visibility and exposes them to the public. Elected officials and other ambitious leaders use various means of getting attention. One popular tactic is to stage **pseudo-events** (a term coined by the historian Daniel J. Boorstin in 1961 to characterize events whose primary purpose is to generate public interest and news coverage).[29] For example, an incumbent may visit a successful drug rehabilitation center, discussing the treatment facility with a former drug addict who is now a productive citizen. The event gives the impression that the politician is sensitive and in control of the issue—but viewers should be aware that the entire event was staged with television and newspaper coverage in mind. The center was carefully selected, as was the "success story." Although the press does not like to cover these staged events, preferring to capture more realistic news, they will often show them for fear of getting scooped by rivals. Imagine if one network didn't send a crew and something interesting and unexpected happened, such as the "success story" addict's challenging the politician's good intentions! No media executive wants to be the one to make such an error, especially when the official makes a mistake or is put in an embarrassing situation. Politicians try to control the events, but sometimes, they are unsuccessful. President Bush was caught on camera once reading a children's book upside down, provoking much media ridicule. When announcing an elementary school spelling bee, Vice President Dan Quayle once misspelled *potato.* Innumerable jokes about his intelligence dogged him for the rest of his political career. Remembering these political goofs, politicians and their aides spend a great deal of time developing mechanisms to garner positive media attention.

There is often an adversarial relationship between public officials and the media. Officials want to control information about themselves and their policies, including the way such information is framed and presented, while the media reject such "spoon-feeding" and try to retain their independence. Government officials want to be seen in a positive light, whereas the media, perpetually seeking to boost ratings or circulation, always find controversies or conflicts more appealing. At the same time, however, reciprocal relationships bind the media, politicians, and the public together. Politicians need the media to communicate with their constituents and advance their agendas, the media need politicians to provide news and entertainment, and the public needs both to make informed voting decisions. The media influence the public with programming—but because the media are driven by the profit motive, the public (their source of revenue) influences them. Similarly, the public influences government through elections and by supporting or rejecting policies, and the government influences the public by making and enforcing policies. Research on the *New York Times, Washington Post,* and *Chicago Tribune* revealed that fully half the sources for front-page stories in these papers were government officials.[30]

How Journalists Report the News

Many people believe that the media's ability to select how and what they report is their greatest source of influence. This is called **agenda setting**■. It consists of determining which issues will be covered, in what detail, and in what context—and also deciding which stories are not newsworthy and therefore are not going to be covered. Agenda setting figures very prominently in the media's capacity to influence the public and politicians. As a consequence,

■ **Gatekeepers:** Group or individuals who determine which stories will receive attention in the media and from which perspective.

EXAMPLE: *When editors of major newspapers decide which stories will be covered and from what angle, they serve as gatekeepers of the news.*

much concern exists about how and by whom stories are decided to be newsworthy. In allowing certain stories to get on the public agenda and by sidelining others, the media are said to be acting as **gatekeepers**■. Concern stems from the fact that no one can check the media's selection of news: The media are their own guardians, open to no serious challenge. The media set the political agenda, choose how and when political issues get addressed, and decide which stories draw attention to a problem that is important and needs to be fixed. Thus they create a political climate that can frame subsequent discussions and shape public opinion. For instance, in June of 1998, the media publicized the gruesome death of a black man, James Byrd, Jr., by racist murderers who chained him to the back of a pickup truck and dragged him until he was dead, thus focusing public attention on racial tension and bigotry. In doing so, the media illustrated a problem, discussed its roots, and then demonstrated the need for change, helping set the public agenda. The amount of time and space such a story receives can dramatically affect whether it will make it onto the political agenda. These decisions, made by senior media managers, are often deliberative and conscious, leading some analysts to worry about potential media bias. There is only so much room for printing stories and so much time for broadcast; thus, the decision of what to cover confers great power.

President George W. Bush speaks with reporters in one of his relatively rare press conferences. President Bush prefers to have his interactions with the press more structured. ***—Do you think presidents can control the coverage of policies and programs? How effective do you think the president is in influencing press coverage?***

COVERING THE PRESIDENT The nature of the interactions and type of relationship with the media differ from president to president. Presidents use the media differently, depending on their personal style. President Clinton averaged 550 public talks each year (many very informal), while President Reagan, dubbed "the Great Communicator," averaged only 320. At the dawn of the television era, President Truman, who is today remembered for his vigorous and colorful ways of expressing himself in public, averaged a mere 88 talks a year.[31] Clinton's ability to communicate and relate to the public earned him a great deal of flexibility, allowing his candidacy and presidency to survive many scandals and even an impeachment trial. The relationship he was able to develop with the people, via the media, increased his popularity, providing some insulation against the serious charges of personal wrongdoing that he eventually faced.

As noted, there is an interesting dynamic between politicians and the media. Even if the relationship is uneasy, open warfare is rare. On the one hand, the relationship is by definition adversarial, because both sides want to control how information and events are framed. However, as you have seen, both sides need each other, too. Presidents put great effort into creating photo opportunities ("photo ops") and pseudo-events that are visually appealing and releasing to the press information that is favorable to the White House. News media with limited resources will often cooperate, but those with more resources can subject the material to greater scrutiny, often presenting information in a manner contrary to what the White House might prefer.

The office of the White House press secretary supplies the White House press corps and the Washington-based media with daily information about the administration. The president's press secretary customarily holds a daily press conference. In addition, each administration has an office of communications, which may be structured differently from administration to administration but is always used to oversee long-term public relations and presidential image-making.

Communication from the White House takes three general forms: **press releases, news briefings,** and **news conferences.** Press releases and news briefings are the routine ways to release news. Press releases are prepared text in which officials present information to reporters and are worded in hopes that they will be used just as they are, without rewriting. To allow the media to ask direct questions about press releases or current events, the presidential press secretary and other high officials regularly appear for news briefings. News conferences are direct opportunities for the president to speak to the press and the public. Theodore Roosevelt held the first news conference at the White House, but his and all later presidential news conferences until 1961 were conducted in private. In that year, John F. Kennedy was the first president to allow live, televised coverage. Some presidents are wary of conferences, as they can be difficult to control. Others, especially Kennedy, have been masters of the forum. The number of press conferences held each year has been in a decline in the age of investigative reporting; presidents today try to release information in a more cautious, controlled manner (see Figure 10.1).

Doris Graber has identified four major functions of media coverage of the executive branch.[32] First, the media serve to inform chief executives about current events, highlighting issues that need attention across the nation and the world. Second, the media inform the executive branch about the needs and concerns of the public, by reporting public opinion polls and by publishing letters to the editor and feature stories. Third, the media also allow presidents to express their positions and policy proposals directly to the people and other government officials by means of press conferences, televised speeches, and staged events, which always supply the administration in power with ample opportunity to explain its positions and garner support. Finally, the media keep the president in public view, reporting every scrap of available information about the first family's daily life. This reporting is generally framed from a human interest angle, but it also includes evaluations of presidential performance. All four of these functions allow the public to stay in touch with the actions and life of the president and allow the president to keep in touch with the American people. Presidents have used this relationship to their advantage, knowing that they can command a great amount of attention and interest in their words and actions. The first media-conscious president was Theodore Roosevelt, who used the White House as a platform to influence public opinion and pursue his political agenda. "I suppose my critics will call that preaching," Theodore Roosevelt said in 1909, "but I have got such a bully pulpit!"

PATHWAYS | of action

The Strategic Use of Leaks

It seems commonplace today to read a story in the newspaper or watch a report on the TV news in which important information is attributed to an unnamed "high-ranking source" or a "police insider." When this happens, you should ask yourself why these sources are not named and examine the implications of relying on information that is leaked.

There are many reasons why public officials leak information to the press. One is to gauge public reaction, sending up a "trial balloon" to see how a potential policy will be received and reported. For example, when Reagan administration officials were considering changing the guidelines for food programs for low-income children to allow ketchup to be considered a vegetable, they leaked this idea to the media. Public outcry was fast and negative, the guidelines remained unchanged, and ketchup was ruled out as a vegetable in federal food programs.[33]

Leaks can also be preemptive. Officials can strategically use leaked information to sway public opinion and pressure other officials. Consider a local school district's decision to eliminate all music classes. Someone on the board who opposes the proposal

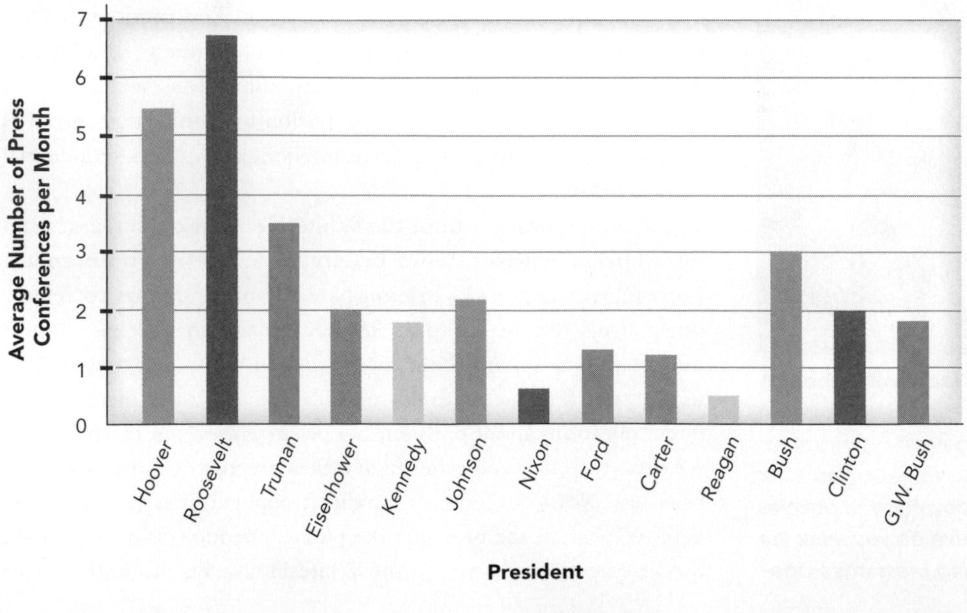

FIGURE 10.1 | Presidential Press Conferences

Over the last 80 or so years, the average number of presidential press conferences per month has decreased rather dramatically, from Franklin Roosevelt's high of 6.9 to Ronald Reagan's low of 0.5. ***—Why do you think this is the case? Why do you think presidents in the modern era of television are relying on other means to communicate with the country? Do you think this trend isolates the president too much from the press?***

SOURCE: Harold W. Stanley and Richard G. Niemi, Vital Statistics on American Politics, 2003–2004 (Washington, D.C.: CQ Press, 2003), p. 177.

might leak the material to the press in hopes of generating public pressure on the board to stop the cut. Preemptively leaking material can allow officials to change their minds before making a public vote, as it is often easier to pressure officials before they become publicly committed to a position. Unflattering or bad news can also be leaked a little at a time to lessen the damage it might cause. It is common knowledge that the best time to leak bad information is on weekends, when many full-time reporters are off and the public is too busy to watch the news. By Monday morning, the initial impact may have faded or been superseded by other news items.

Leaked information can also prompt change. A frustrated congressional committee staff member tipped off the *Philadelphia Inquirer* about bad treatment of kidney dialysis patients. When the *Inquirer* published a story about neglect of patients, immediate action was taken to reform the system.[34]

Leaks are also ways to get information from publicity shy groups or individuals. People involved with the court system or the police are typically reluctant to release sensitive information. Allowing them a chance to release information without being named could often serve as an important prompt for otherwise silent informants who are hesitant to go on record. It is long-established journalistic practice to grant leakers secrecy so that they are more willing to release information—even if it is illegal to do so. A contemporary example of an important political leak occurred on July 14, 2003, when the syndicated columnist Robert Novak published the name of Valerie Plame, a covert CIA officer—such a revelation is a felony if it is knowingly done. A subsequent special prosecutor's investigation into charges that officials in the Bush administration had leaked the name to media sources, including Novak, eventually led to the conviction of Vice President Cheney's chief of staff, I. Lewis "Scooter" Libby, for perjury and obstruction of justice. Plame is married to a former ambassador, Joseph Wilson IV, a strong public critic of the Bush administration's prewar claims about Iraq's developing and possessing weapons of mass destruction. Wilson suggested that the leak, which Novak printed 8 days after Wilson had criticized the Bush administration's rationale for the Iraq War in the *New York Times,* was made to discredit his critique and punish him for insubordination. The Bush administration strongly denied these charges and announced that it would cooperate with the investigation. At least six other journalists also knew Plame's identity before Novak revealed it; one was Judith Miller of the *New York Times.* Miller subsequently spent 85 days in jail for refusing to reveal to the special prosecutor's grand jury the name of her confidential source, citing her obligation as a journalist until, apparently, Libby released her from her pledge.

One needs to be careful, however, when analyzing material that is not attributed to a source. When informants are granted secrecy, they are often more willing to reveal information. The public should be skeptical of leaked information, however, because it is often released for self-serving reasons. Informants often get to influence how the story is told based on the information they provide, which might not be the full story or the objective truth. Since the name and agenda of the informant are withheld, the political dimensions of the story (and its self-serving motivations) are often hidden, with potentially devastating consequences. That is why reporters must exercise diligence in handling leaks.[35] ■

COVERING CONGRESS For several reasons, the media give far less attention to Congress than to the president. People tend to have more interest in the actions of the president, who is the country's highest-ranking official and has a nationwide constituency. No single member of Congress can make that claim or get that recognition. Furthermore, Congress is a much larger institution that requires coalition and consensus building, both of which take time and aren't particularly exciting. By contrast, the president is often seen as working alone, so it becomes easier for the press to focus on his actions. Also, as a deliberative body, Congress works slowly, even tediously, and without drama. Of course, interested people can turn to C-SPAN for gavel-to-gavel congressional coverage—but watching for several hours will reveal just how unexciting such deliberations can be. The local media often cover the actions and votes of members of Congress, with senators typically getting more attention. The preference for coverage of senators versus representatives is especially notable in large metropolitan areas that encompass several congressional districts, making it difficult to cover all members of the local congressional delegation in detail. To get mentioned in the local news or local papers, members of Congress often stage pseudo-events and attend local events—even lowly ones like the Watermelon Festival picnic, the Fourth of July parade, or a ribbon-cutting ceremony to celebrate opening a new town library can win visually appealing news coverage.

COVERING THE COURTS Of the three branches of government, the courts tend to get the least amount of coverage. Why? One reason is that federal judges rarely grant interviews lest their impartiality be questioned. Once appointed, judges normally do not receive much specific personal coverage; rather, attention is focused on their rulings and on the specific cases heard in their courts. The courts, moreover, deliberate and reach their decisions in secret, and very rarely do they allow televised or sound-recorded live coverage of cases as they are being argued.

Another area that receives considerable media attention is controversial confirmation hearings. The Senate must confirm all federal court judges, including Supreme Court justices, after the president has nominated them. Perhaps the most prominent example was the 1991 confirmation hearing for Supreme Court

While the media tend to focus less time and attention on the coverage of the courts, Supreme Court nominations typically receive a great deal of coverage today. In 1991, when it was revealed that law professor Anita Hill had accused Supreme Court nominee Clarence Thomas of sexually harassing her while they both worked at the U.S. Department of Education and at the Equal Employment Opportunity Commission, a storm of attention ensued. The attention was important for several reasons. Many thought the treatment of Hill by the all-white, all-male Senate Judiciary committee was unfair and disrespectful and may have stimulated some women to run for political office. Moreover, the coverage and analysis of the allegations focused national attention on the matter of sexual harassment, serving to raise awareness of this important issue.

A number of frustrated members of Congress charge up the steps of the Senate building. The women representatives were going to the Senate building to ensure that the charges of sexual harassment brought by Anita Hill against then-Supreme Court nominee Clarence Thomas be taken seriously and investigated. Their diligence was rewarded, and noted by other women concerned with the lack of female representation in government. These women served as role models for other women who became motivated to enter politics because of their actions. ***—How powerful do you think role modeling is? Can you think of a time that something you saw in the media stimulated you to take action?***

nominee Clarence Thomas. Testifying before the Senate Judiciary Committee, Anita Hill, a University of Oklahoma law professor, accused Thomas of sexual harassment when she was an employee at the U.S. Department of Education (ED), and the Equal Employment Opportunity Commission (EEOC), on which he served in the 1980s. A sharply divided national audience watched the Judiciary Committee's investigation into the charges. The hearings placed the issue of sexual harassment on the national agenda, resulting in many changes in laws, policies, and opinions. They also prompted many women, outraged by the confrontational manner in which Hill was treated by the all-white, all-male Senate Judiciary Committee, to enter politics and seek elected office.[36]

Under most other circumstances, national judges, including Supreme Court justices, rarely generate stories of a personal nature. However, the press does cover their rulings, especially Supreme Court decisions and controversial federal district and appellate court decisions. The media have been criticized for what some believe is poor coverage of the Supreme Court, but coverage may be improving. Reporting on the Supreme Court is difficult, because the Court tends to release several rulings at once, forcing reporters to cover numerous, often technical and difficult opinions. Typically, the press will select one or two main decisions and discuss them in more detail, while a summary box simply mentions the other Supreme Court decisions released that day. Several key decisions (for example, *Roe*

"Supreme Court decisions can have a powerful impact on our lives. Why do so few cases get major attention from the media?"

—Student Question

and *Brown,* both of which are discussed in other chapters) attracted enormous press coverage at the time they were released as well as retrospective stories on their anniversaries, follow-up analyses of their consequences, and even later revelations about how the decisions were reached. The media have ignored many important cases, however, and in other instances have presented information that had factual errors.[37]

How Groups Use the Media

Interest groups and outsiders use the media to promote their agendas, employing a variety of techniques. One popular technique is to stage events similar to politicians' pseudo-events. A child advocacy group might stage a rally to support a proposal for greater funding of a health insurance program for children, hoping that the news media will report it. Appearing on the news is very important, especially to groups that do not have large budgets, because positive coverage gives them exposure and often credibility. A second technique used by groups to get media coverage is to issue press releases and bulletins. The National Organization for Women (NOW), for example, routinely issues press releases on matters of importance to its members. Groups often issue video clips directly to news organizations in hopes that the clips will be aired with no editing to show the group in a positive light. So-called video news releases are designed to make it easy for television stations to use the videos. Groups also provide expert interviews and often have members (who do not necessarily identify themselves as members) write letters to the editor or contribute op-ed articles for local and national newspapers. Groups with sufficient means will also pay for issue advocacy advertising. One example of this is "Pork—the Other White Meat" commercials prompting consumers to consider including pork in a healthy diet. Because the media are such an important means for groups to raise visibility, win support, and influence both the public and officials, interest groups will continue to be creative in developing attention-grabbing tactics.

Political Use of the Media

Practice Quiz

1. Why are public officials and the media frequently adversarial?
- **a.** Each wants to control political news stories.
- **b.** Public officials resent how infrequently they get to use the media to reach voters.
- **c.** Public officials thrive on policy controversies, whereas the media boosts ratings by emphasizing what's right in the world.
- **d.** The media need politicians to provide news, yet politicians prefer to avoid the media spotlight.

2. Sometimes government officials intentionally leak news before official announcements in order to
- **a.** confuse the mass media, especially TV reporters.
- **b.** bypass First Amendment regulations.
- **c.** measure public reaction to policy changes before they are official.
- **d.** demonstrate their ideological purity to the public.

3. Why does Congress tend to get less attention from the media than the presidency?
- **a.** People seem to just be more interested in what the president is doing.
- **b.** Congress is a much larger institution and requires consensus, which is time-consuming and not very exciting.
- **c.** The work of Congress is not as important to the legislative process as the work of the president.
- **d.** a and b

4. Most Supreme Court decisions get substantial media coverage, especially on TV.
- **a.** true
- **b.** false

Answers: 1-a, 2-c, 3-d, 4-b.

Discussion Questions

1. Why is there an adversarial relationship between public officials and the media? In what ways do they need each other? What positive benefits emerge from this increased scrutiny? Can you think of any negative effects that such scrutiny might have?
2. What do we mean when we say that the media act as gatekeepers? How powerful is this role?

What **YOU** can do!

Compare how political candidates use their Web sites to communicate with voters and the media. Note where they publicize pseudo-events and press releases. Do they have a blog or a Facebook page? Do they try to respond to statements made by other candidates or information reported on political blogs?

SIMULATION You Are a Media Consultant to a Political Candidate

The Media and the Public in the Political Arena (pages 376–379)

How do the media shape and reflect our cultural values and struggles?

The print media—newspapers, magazines, and other periodicals—tend to cater to an upper-class, better-educated segment of society. Print media are very effective in translating facts, while TV is better at conveying emotion and feelings. Hence better-educated people are attracted to the print media, and their readers continue to be better informed about events, reinforcing their advantaged position in society. The fact that the more affluent have greater access to information than the general society gives them more opportunities to influence politics. For example, announcements of city council meetings or school redistricting plans are usually made in the local paper. Only individuals who routinely read the local paper will know about proposed changes, public meetings, and scheduled forums. Those who habitually do not read the paper remain uninformed about these events, which may have a significant impact on their lives. A cycle exists: Poorer people pay less attention to the print media, because print stories tend to cater to the interests of the more affluent. And because poor people don't subscribe in large numbers, newspapers continue to ignore the needs of the lower class, perpetuating biases in coverage, access to information, and lack of a diverse audience.

Media in Campaigns

It is a long-standing belief that the media are very powerful actors in elections in the United States; some people go so far as to claim that the media actually determine the outcomes of elections. Although this is certainly an overstatement, the media do have a great deal of power, especially in anointing the "front-running candidates" long before an election. Marking one or two candidates as front-runners usually has a snowball effect: The media and the public pay more attention to them, making it easier for them to get on the news and raise money. The more money they raise, the more prominent their campaign becomes, and the bigger the campaign, the more attention it gets from the media and the public.

Front-runner status develops its own cycle of success—though certainly, there is some liability in being declared the front-runner, too. (Front-runners get heightened media scrutiny, for example, which can be fatally damaging if they make gaffes or if skeletons lurk in their closet.) Many people are concerned about the power of the media in determining front-runners, because this tends to prematurely narrow the field of candidates, often very early in the nomination cycle. When the media focus on front-runners in polls and stories, lesser-known candidates often encounter many difficulties, especially with fundraising, and are often forced to withdraw early from the race. Moreover, the media often declare winners based not on the absolute vote total but on how well a candidate does compared to what had been expected. Bill Clinton, at the time governor of Arkansas, serves as a very good example. Massachusetts Senator Paul Tsongas won the most votes in the 1992 New Hampshire primary, but Clinton, simply because he did better than had been expected, was proclaimed "the winner" by the press. This accolade gave him increased media attention and public support. The "winner" designation sent Clinton's candidacy into high gear, and he went on to win the nomination and the election.

In the 2000 presidential primary cycle, only candidates who were perceived positively in public opinion polls received extensive media coverage. For the Democrats, the only candidate to receive media attention besides Vice President Al Gore (the "front-runner") was former New Jersey Senator Bill Bradley, who had been a star basketball player before turning to politics. The other candidates were felt to be uncompetitive and hence unworthy of attention. On the Republican side, Texas Governor George W. Bush, the former president's son, received one-third more coverage than all his competitors combined.[38]

NEGATIVE COVERAGE After the 2004 campaign season, a study by the Project for Excellence in Journalism, the Pew Research Center, and the University of Missouri School of Journalism, which analyzed newspaper, broadcast, and cable coverage from late March through early June in 2004, found that negative coverage of the two main presidential candidates was quite prevalent. Stories and images of President Bush were negative by more than a 3-to-1 margin. Media assessment of his Democratic opponent, Massachusetts Senator John F. Kerry, was more likely to be negative by a 5-to-1 margin. Moreover, the study found that the more people read the print media and watch TV coverage, the more they are likely to support the themes being emphasized by the media. The researchers found that the most common public perception about Bush was that "he is stubborn and arrogant," followed by "he lacks credibility." The most common themes reported about Kerry were that "he flip-flops on issues" and "he is very liberal." Both of these negative "definitions" of Kerry echoed the themes of Bush's campaign advertisements and speeches, and vice versa. It's hard to determine whether it was the press or the Bush campaign that influenced the public against Kerry; most likely, it was a combination of two reinforcing messages.[39]

PAID ADVERTISING One key aspect of media usage in campaigns is the need to purchase paid advertising, which is enormously expensive. Paid advertising is essential, however, because research consistently demonstrates that the news media increasingly portray candidates negatively, with fewer and fewer positive stories. Daniel Hallin found that 5 percent of news stories in the 1968 election were positive and 6 percent were negative. By 1988, however, only 1 percent of stories were positive but 16 percent were negative.[40] TV coverage of campaigns has also shrunk, coming to consist chiefly of tiny, frequently repeated visual snippets called **sound bites.** And even the length of the sound bites on network evening news programs shriveled, from an average of 42.3 seconds in 1968 to 7.2 seconds in 1996.[41] Given these circumstances, candidates desiring to get their message and vision out to the people must pay heavily for advertising.

The media are often criticized for their coverage of elections. —*Do you think they focus too much on the "horse race" and too little on the substance of the campaign? If they focused more attention on issues, do you think people would pay more or less attention?*

DEBATES Televised debates can also be important in affecting the public's perception of candidates. The most infamous example of this impact occurred in the very first televised presidential debate in 1960. John F. Kennedy's strong visual performance allayed the public's fears that he was too young and inexperienced compared to his well-known opponent, Vice President Richard M. Nixon. This debate underscored the importance of television's visual nature. TV viewers saw the physically attractive, tanned, and seemingly relaxed Kennedy verbally sparring with a sweaty, earnest, and less photogenic Nixon, and a majority of television viewers believed that Kennedy won the debate. Those listening to the debate on the radio, however, believed that Nixon had won on the substance of what was said. This stark contrast changed the way in which subsequent candidates have viewed the power of television and underscored the importance of cultivating visual images. Ronald Reagan's masterful performance in the 1980 and 1984 presidential debates showed that despite his advanced years, he was mentally alert and able. (His professional training as an actor helped him, too.) More recently, George W. Bush exceeded low initial expectations about his abilities when he used his performance in the 2000 debates against Al Gore to persuade many voters that he was sufficiently knowledgeable and capable to serve as president.[42]

The importance of television in campaigns and elections also has a powerful effect on the pool of eligible candidates and the types of people who are perceived to be "electable." Had TV existed in the 1930s, many believe Franklin D. Roosevelt could not have been elected, because having been crippled by polio, he was confined to a wheelchair. Indeed, Roosevelt worried that his disability would make him seem "weak," and newspaper and newsreel photographers of the day were careful not to show him in his chair or on crutches. Television puts charismatic, telegenic candidates at an advantage; hence candidates for high-profile positions usually hire coaches to teach them how to behave when appearing on television. For example, public opinion polls might show that a candidate is perceived to be "too stuffy." The campaign will then stage outdoor events to make him or her appear more informal, relaxed, and "ordinary." If a candidate is seen as not intellectual enough, events will be staged at a library or university. These coaches work on body language, speech presentations, clothing, and hairstyle. Although this seems superficial, television has made outward appearance crucial. You might wonder if such past presidents as George Washington and Abraham Lincoln could ever be elected today.

"Is a candidate's 'image' more important today than his or her ideas?"

— Student Question

Global Issues

CNN reaches every country in the world and has 85 million subscribers. A Russian edition of the *New York Times* is sold in Moscow. MTV is viewed on five continents, with an audience of 265 million.[43] Such availability of American culture raises concerns for many people, especially in other countries with very different cultures, who fear "McGlobalization." Foreigners worry that our culture and values, many of which they do not share, are "corrupting" citizens in their countries. This concern is especially significant in the Muslim world, where American and Western values are widely perceived as a mortal threat to Islam. Objections to "excessive" American cultural and political influence are heard around the globe, from Canada and France to China. If you consider the entertainment programs, fears abound over American cultural hegemony (dominance of one culture over others). Foreign programming is available in the United States, but given the fact that much of our programming is years ahead of many countries' (in technology and content alike), the trade is not equal. Because of concerns over American influence in China, for example, the Chinese government has banned all privately owned satellite dishes. Many historians attribute the fall of communism in the Soviet Union and Eastern Europe in part to exposure to Western thought and values on television. Countries proud of their culture, heritage, and values are greatly troubled by the trend of Americanization made possible by the global media.

Narrowcasting

Another area of concern for many is the trend of cable television and the Internet to appeal to narrower audiences. As television and other mass media have become more specialized, the targeting of specific audiences, known as **narrowcasting,** has become far more common. Some observers worry that specialized programming may cause groups to become more fragmented, as the media no longer cater to a mass audience. Consider the changes in print media (see Figure 10.2) and in programming for Spanish speakers in the United States. One study found that two-thirds of Hispanic Americans watch Spanish-language programming daily.[44] Telemundo and Univision both have nightly news programs, each with a slightly different focus in their stories than the English-language network news programs. Furthermore, because many Hispanic viewers are not watching national English-language news programs, these "mainstream" networks are less likely to offer programming that appeals to Latinos. As a result, the larger English-speaking audience is not sufficiently exposed to issues of concern primarily to Hispanic viewers. An endless cycle can develop that is troubling to many analysts, who worry that specialized programming with a narrow appeal will further fragment groups within American society.

Concentration and Centralization of Ownership

Concern also stems from the trend toward more concentrated media ownership, especially of the print media and in radio broadcasting. As media ownership becomes more centralized, a "nationalization" of the news is occurring, which tends to promote a sameness of opinion and experience. This trend has been under way ever since the rise of broadcast networks and of newspaper chains in the 1930s, but today, it is accelerating. Competition is generally believed to be healthy, because it makes possible a larger variety of opinions and points of view. There is concern today because much of the news comes from national news services and there is minimal or no competition between papers in major cities—especially between two or more morning or evening papers. Examine your local paper to see

Breaking News, Por Favor

The number of newspapers aimed at the growing Hispanic population in the United States has surged. In Texas, where Hispanics are estimated to become the state's majority in 20 years, several newspapers have been started in the last several years.

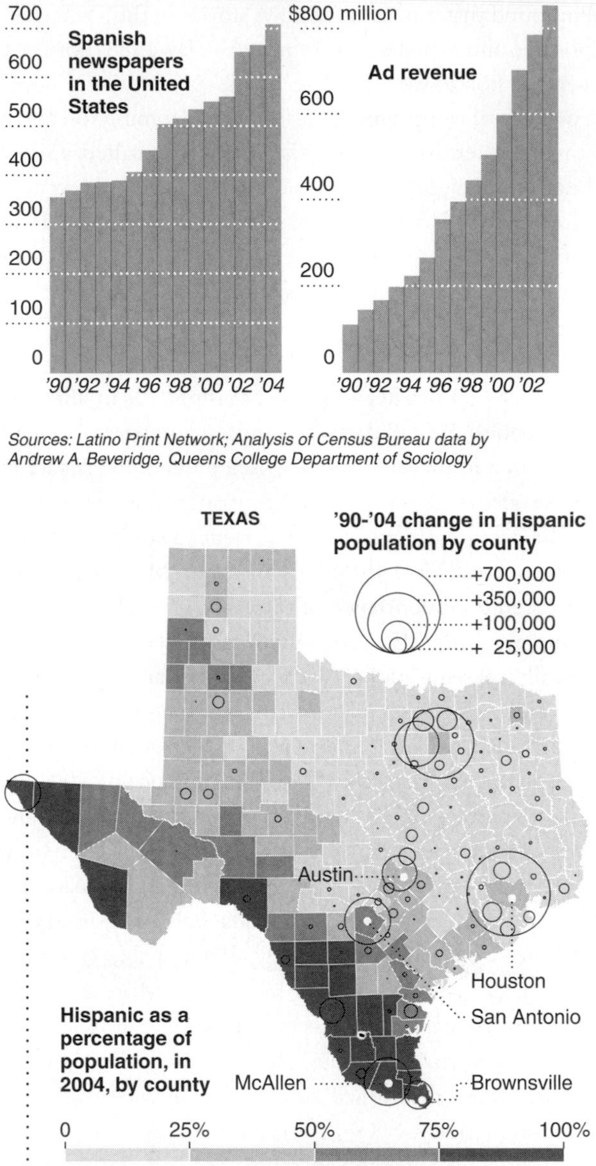

Sources: Latino Print Network; Analysis of Census Bureau data by Andrew A. Beveridge, Queens College Department of Sociology

FIGURE 10.2 | **Breaking News, Por Favor**

As the number of Hispanics in the United States increases, so does their purchasing power and the consumption of news. The last 15 years have seen dramatic expansion of Spanish newspapers and their profitability. In the 10-year period from 1993 to 2003, the ad revenue from Spanish newspapers increased from $200 million to over $800 million. As the numbers of Hispanics continue to grow, so, too, will these figures. Today, there are over 700 Spanish newspapers in the United States, helping inform these individuals. ***—What other areas do you think will be influenced by this large group and their purchasing power?***

■ **Competitive News Markets:** Locales with two or more news organizations that can check each other's accuracy and neutrality of reporting.

EXAMPLE: *While most cities only have one major paper, a number—including Boston, Chicago, Dallas/Fort Worth Metroplex, Denver, New York, the Twin Cities, Seattle, and Tampa Bay—have at least two newspapers, which makes for more competitive news markets.*

■ **News Monopolies:** Single news firms that controls all the media in a given market.

EXAMPLE: *Most locations in the United States are dependent on one print source for their local and national news, creating a news monopoloy.*

how many stories in the first section come from centralized news sources, such as the Associated Press, *New York Times,* or *Washington Post*. You will find that it is not uncommon for the entire first page to be from sources outside your community or state. This trend is evident even in college newspapers, where editorials and stories are often picked up from a news source and do not necessarily reflect the concerns of your particular campus community.

It is widely believed that competition results in the best product, an economic and political belief held by most theorists. Observers of the media enthusiastically approve of **competitive news markets**■ and regard **news monopolies**■ as potentially dangerous. Newspaper ownership in recent decades has tended toward monopolies and away from competitive markets. The changes in broadcasting are less clear. The influence of the networks has diminished thanks to the proliferation of cable and satellite alternatives, although ownership has become more centralized. In 1997, the media critic Ben Bagdikian noted that the number of major media corporations had decreased from more than 50 in the early 1980s to only 10 by the mid-1990s. By 2001, Bagdikian reported, six huge corporations—Time Warner, Disney, Viacom, News Corp., General Electric, and Bertelsmann—dominated the mass media.[45] Furthermore, as the media have become deregulated, cross-media ownership is rising, with corporations owning a variety of media outlets, including newspapers, TV and radio stations, newsmagazines, and production companies. In 1995, Capital Cities/ABC owned seven television stations, seven radio networks (with more than 3,000 affiliated stations), 18 radio stations, 75 weekly newspapers, as well as many magazines and trade publications. When it merged with Disney in 1995, this conglomerate grew even larger.[46]

The Media and the Public in the Political Arena

Practice Quiz

1. Why are so many people concerned about the media's ability to help determine the front-runners in a campaign?
   - **a.** because this determination happens so late in the nomination cycle that voters do not have enough time to assess these front-runners before election day
   - **b.** because the media's criteria for declaring favorites in a campaign is often different from voters' criteria
   - **c.** because the media historically have avoided playing such a political role
   - **d.** because the media declare front-runners so early in the nomination cycle, narrowing the field of candidates prematurely
2. Why has paid political advertising become increasingly important in presidential campaigns?
   - **a.** because voters value and expect it
   - **b.** in order to overcome negative coverage of candidates in the media
   - **c.** in order to comply with new FCC regulations
   - **d.** because media coverage is very thorough, and campaigns need to present more simplified images of their candidate
3. What is a potential downside to "narrowcasting"?
   - **a.** It may make mainstream networks less culturally diverse.
   - **b.** It may give minority viewers, such as Latinos, less access to Spanish-speaking shows.
   - **c.** It may create fewer choices for television and Internet users.
   - **d.** It may prevent third-party participation in presidential debates.
4. Why is the centralization of newspaper ownership troubling in a democracy?
   - **a.** because it makes news gathering less efficient
   - **b.** because it makes news gathering more expensive
   - **c.** because it gives readers fewer perspectives from which to see and understand the news
   - **d.** because it makes the newspaper business less profitable

Answers: 1-d, 2-b, 3-a, 4-c.

Discussion Questions

1. What do we mean when we say that the media cater to an upscale audience? What are the consequences of this tendency?
2. Why are many people troubled by the concentration of media ownership and the trend toward media cross-ownership?

What **YOU** can do!

Each day for a week, select two news stories and see how they are covered in different sources: the newspaper, radio, television, and the Internet. How does the coverage vary? How does the medium affect the way the story is told? Do you see patterns of differences in content or presentation? Do any sources seem biased in any way?

■ **Libel:** Publication of false and malicious material that defames an individual's reputation.

EXAMPLE: *Juries are very sensitive to the issue of libel and often rule in favor of the defendant. Media outlets that appeal to higher courts, however, usually have the lower court decision overturned in favor of the media. Libel suits against public officials are very difficult to win.*

Governmental Regulations (pages 380–383)

How can we negotiate the delicate balance between the need for governmental regulation and the desire for a vigorous and free press?

All societies have laws regulating the media, most commonly stemming from national security concerns. Laws that define and punish treason and sedition are always necessary to ensure national security; the dilemma is how much regulation is needed before it infringes on personal freedoms. There is a tension between the needs of the government to ensure national security and the desire of a people to be free, as guaranteed by the First Amendment to the Constitution. The 9/11 attacks and President George W. Bush's declaration of the War on Terror, which included enacting the USA PATRIOT Act, threw into high relief these concerns about balancing security and liberty.

Media and Government: A Tense Relationship

This tension is very evident in the relationship between the media and the government. The media want to be allowed to print what they think is newsworthy, while the government wants to limit disclosure in order to promote protection. This tension is most evident in wartime. Many people in government want to limit the amount of information shared, seeking to enhance national security. Ideally, from the government's perspective, only information it approves for dissemination would be shared with the public. For example, the government successfully structured the sharing of information during the Gulf War of 1991. Information and images passed through a tightly controlled, centralized governmental "feed," which released video to all the media; hence there was little variety in the information available. With limited information, however, it is difficult to ensure that the public knows how the war is being fought. Abuses in wartime are not common, but—as events at the Abu Ghraib prison in Iraq have shown—they do occur. Many people fear that in the absence of media scrutiny, abuse and cruelty could increase. For instance, does the public have the right to know if the Bush administration or high-ranking military officials approve the use of torture against enemy prisoners in the War on Terror? The tension between the public's right to know information to hold officials accountable versus the government's need to conduct war with secrecy to promote victory is very real. As we saw in the beginning of the chapter, revelations of the abuse of Iraqi prisoners at Abu Ghraib appear to have fanned anti-Americanism throughout the Middle East, putting the lives of American troops in greater danger. However, most citizens agree that the media should have been allowed to share this information to force reforms mandating the humane treatment of prisoners.

Even nonauthoritarian governments have laws to protect government secrets. For example, in the United States, laws make top-secret documents unavailable for public scrutiny until many years later, after they have been "declassified" (declared no longer secret). Questions of what is and is not "top secret" are often highly controversial. The government has a perspective very different from that of the press, often forcing the courts into the role of arbiter.

The Right to Privacy

Democratic societies also have laws that protect individual's privacy and society's morals—for example, bans against obscenity. The need for maintaining a careful balance in a free society continually raises challenges. This becomes evident when we examine privacy issues.

Regarding the right to privacy, two standards apply—those for public figures and those for private individuals. Courts have traditionally allowed a good deal of latitude in publishing personal information about people in the public eye, including celebrities, athletes, and politicians. Public "personalities" are assumed to have lower expectations for privacy and consequently have less protection. Controversy often stems from the right to privacy of *private* citizens, especially as it pertains to the victims of violent crimes. A 1975 rape and murder case in Georgia (*Cox Broadcasting Corporation* v. *Cohn*) provides a good example. The victim's family wanted her name withheld from news reports to protect her right to privacy, especially given the vicious sexual assault that preceded her murder. When newspapers nevertheless published her name and gave the specific details of her rape and murder, her family sued, claiming violation of the victim's privacy right. The court disagreed. Because her name was a matter of public record, newspapers were held to be within their rights to publish it. Papers often have policies not to publish the names of rape victims, but these rules are a matter of decency, not of law. One area where the right to privacy is protected is wherever providing a fair trial is in question. The right to privacy of the accused in order to ensure fair treatment in court is enforced, though less strongly today than in the past. Even in cases involving ordinary citizens—and certainly in cases involving celebrities—media coverage of crimes often reaches a saturation level, impelling some observers to question whether any potential jurors can be impartial. To help ensure a fair trial, gag orders can be issued, ordering all participants to refrain from discussing the case. In extreme circumstances, there can be a change of venue (holding the trial in

CONNECT THE LINK

(Chapter **5**, pages **156–159**) Should the government be allowed greater flexibility in censoring material that the press is allowed to publish to advance the acceptance of certain societal views?

■ **Prior Censorship:** Forbidding publication of material considered objectionable.

EXAMPLE: *Excluding times of war, the government has not been very successful in censoring material that is published or aired in the media. During times of war, the courts, in order to promote national security, are more likely to allow prior censorship than during times of peace.*

another city), or the judge might even sequester (put into seclusion) jurors to prevent them from consuming news reports and other media coverage of the trial. In the vast majority of criminal trials, however, these extraordinary measures are neither needed nor employed.

Rules Regarding Content and Ownership

The media are prohibited from publishing material that they know to be incorrect. **Libel**■ laws are designed to protect the reputations of individuals from negative and false reporting. In *New York Times v. Sullivan* (1964), the Supreme Court ruled that publishing a falsehood about a public official did not constitute libel unless that official could demonstrate "actual malice"—meaning that the media knew the published information was false or acted recklessly. Three years later, the *Sullivan* ruling was extended to cover celebrities and athletes. These rulings made it far more difficult for a public official or celebrity to sue for libel. It is easier for private citizens to sue for libel, because the standards of proof are lower. Therefore, private individuals are much more successful in bringing lawsuits.

The most controversial issues regarding content are concerns about **prior censorship**—the power of the government to prohibit in advance the publication or broadcast of certain material. Because we believe that a free press is the bedrock of a free society, the American courts are very hesitant to allow prior censorship. Instead, our system of government tends to rely on the threat of punishment after publication in order to keep the press in line. As you saw in LINK Chapter 5, pages 156–159, the courts have ruled that prior censorship is only allowed in the most extreme cases. Table 10.5 shows that while most of the American public believes the press is too free to publish material it deems appropriate, a large segment of the population also believes that too much governmental regulation currently exists.

Section 315 of the Communications Act of 1934 (and its many subsequent amendments) provides the central rules regarding censorship of the broadcast media. These rules do not apply to print media or the Internet. The act applied only to the broadcast media, because it was believed at the time that these media, perceived to be quasi-monopolies, needed more regulation. When the law was written, the print media seemed to be less monopolistic—and hence more open to ordinary people. Although this is no longer true today, the distinction still applies. Furthermore, as noted earlier, in 1934 the airwaves were considered part of the public domain, to be used for the public good—and hence in need of government regulation. Consequently, the print media do not have to comply with these regulations, whereas the broadcast media do.

TABLE 10.5 | Public Opinion on Censorship

A national survey of 1,000 adults aged 18 and older found that a plurality of Americans believe the media have too much freedom publishing material. This seems to (at least in the abstract) favor more governmental regulation. However, a large percentage also thinks that there is too much governmental censorship. ***—What do you think? Is there too much or too little governmental regulation of the media? What factors do you think might change public opinion either way?***

Agree that the media has too much freedom to publish anything it wants	43%
Believes there is too much government censorship	38%
Neither	10%
Both	4%
Don't know	5%

SOURCE: Survey by the Freedom Forum, American Journalism Review. *Methodology:* Conducted by Center for Survey Research and Analysis, University of Connecticut, June 3–15, 2003, and based on telephone interviews with a national adult sample of 1,000. Data provided by the Roper Center for Public Opinion Research, University of Connecticut. [USCSRA,03AMEND.R22]

"How does the government enforce regulations of the media?"

—Student Question

Regulation of the broadcast media falls to the Federal Communications Commission (FCC), an independent regulatory agency created by the Communications Act of 1934 to "serve the public interest, convenience, and necessity." The bipartisan FCC consists of five commissioners (there were originally seven, but the number was reduced for budgetary reasons). Appointed by the president and confirmed by the Senate, each commissioner serves for 5 years (formerly 7 years). Many observers want the FCC to be stronger and more independent, but the president and Congress continue to exert a good deal of influence on their decisions. Following Janet Jackson's "wardrobe malfunction" in 2004, the FCC has begun issuing large fines for infractions. In addition to privacy and censorship, two other rules exist with respect to television content issues in politics. If a station makes time available to one candidate running for political office, it must make similar time available under similar circumstances to other candidates running for the same office. This is the **equal time rule**■. Thus, if the Democratic candidate is allowed to purchase 30 seconds of prime-time television to run an advertisement, the Republican candidate for the same office must also be allowed to purchase 30 seconds of prime time at the same price. The station can refuse to sell time to any candidates from any political

■ **Equal Time Rule:** FCC rule that requires offering equal airtime in the broadcast media for all major candidates competing for a political office.

SIGNIFICANCE: *Without the equal time rule, lesser-known or less popular candidates would have a very difficult time communicating with voters, adversely impacting their chance for electoral success.*

party (including minor parties) for particular offices, but if it sells to one, it must sell to the others. A related and controversial issue regarding access is participation of minor party candidates in presidential debates. In 2004, the Presidential Commission on Presidential Debates ruled that for candidates to participate in the nationally televised presidential debates, they must be constitutionally eligible to hold the office of president, must be on enough state ballots to give them a mathematical chance of securing a majority vote in the Electoral College, and must have the support of 15 percent of the national electorate as measured by public opinion polls. Given the difficulty of meeting these tests, third-party and independent candidates are generally excluded from the nationally televised debates. The equal time rule does not apply to talk shows and regular newscasts. Hence David Letterman can invite one candidate on his show without inviting the others, and just because one candidate's speech is carried on the evening news does not require the network to carry a rival's speech as well.

A similar concept is the **fairness doctrine,** which was in effect from 1949 to 1985. The fairness doctrine was much broader than the equal time rule, which applies only to political candidates. Under the fairness doctrine, the broadcast media were required to allow "reasonable positions" to be presented on controversial issues of public interest. Hence we often see or hear news shows that have one person representing one side of an issue and another person speaking for the other side. Although this is not required any longer (partly at the urging of President Ronald Reagan), it is still a common practice.

In addition to regulating the content, the government also regulates the ownership of the media. Until recently, the federal government, attempting to keep the airwaves diverse, limited the number of TV or radio stations that one owner could possess in a single market. The Telecommunications Act of 1996 deregulated many previous ownership restrictions in an attempt to make broadcast media more competitive and responsive to audience concerns and interests, but this deregulation has been controversial. Opponents fear that the law has eliminated the consumer and diversity protections that were present in the Communications Act of 1934. As a result, we are seeing larger and larger mergers, such as Time Warner's acquisition of Turner Broadcasting Company.[47] Even so, one person or entity is still barred from controlling more than 35 percent of network market share and 30 percent of cable market share.[48]

The Role of Profits

The standards used for reporting news are controversial. Many critics attack the media's reliance on exploitative and sensational stories in an obsessive search for profits. The quest for profits, it is said, makes the media bloodthirsty hounds, exploiting the misfortune of others. The central question then becomes, "Who should control the media?" Some observers argue that they should police themselves, establishing their own standards of decency and ethics. Others argue that the media simply give us, the public, what we want—if we're displeased with what is being shown, we can use the power of the purse, including boycotts, to influence them. There are two theories regarding self-imposed control of the media. The **libertarian view** says that the media should show what they think the public wants, with no worry about the consequences. If viewers want violence, give them violence; if they want sex, give them sex. In contrast, the **social responsibility theory** (also called the **public advocate model** of news coverage) states that the media need to balance what the public wants with what is good for it. In essence, this theory asserts that the media should promote socially desirable behavior by providing information that advances people's ability to be good citizens, conveying information that allows clear and effective popular decision making.[49]

THE HUNT FOR RATINGS The need to make money often leads newspeople, especially in TV, to determine newsworthiness from the perspective of audience appeal rather than political, educational, or social significance. Historically, the networks did not expect to generate profits from news programs, which they believed were a public good, but in recent years, the networks have decided that news programs must not only cover their costs but also generate profits. Television is dependent on ratings to gauge how much it can charge advertisers. A mere 1 percent increase in the audience can mean millions of dollars in increased advertising revenue. Advertising rates in newspapers are also based on consumption, measured by paid circulation. Changes in programming that reflect profit-driven demands for audience appeal have prompted much criticism. News journalists increasingly believe that the quest for profits is harming coverage (see Table 10.6). For example, newspapers have made a variety of changes to increase circulation and profits: They now use more graphics, feature more but shorter stories, provide more news summaries (for example, bulleted lists of how a story relates directly to readers) and put more emphasis on soft news (such as travel, entertainment, weather, and gossip).[50] Similar changes have occurred on TV news shows, the most notable being the increased use of graphics, especially in reports on the weather. For example, to get a competitive edge in coverage of the 2008 presidential election, CNN used holograms as a visual tool to attract a larger share of the audience.

Some commentators on the state of the media believe that criticism of these developments is unfair and largely elitist. Critics often assert that the "ideal" citizen *should* want hard news—complex,

TABLE 10.6 | **Profits Pressures Hurting Coverage: Effect of Bottom-Line Pressure on News Coverage**

A survey of 547 national and local media reporters, producers, editors, and executives indicates that journalists believe the pressure to make a profit is harming both national and local news coverage. This trend goes back at least a decade. ***—Do you agree with the journalists? And if they feel this way, why do you think they can't resist that pressure?***

	NATIONAL			LOCAL		
	1995	1999	2004	1995	1999	2004
Hurting	41%	49%	66%	33%	46%	57%
Just changing	38%	40%	29%	50%	46%	35%
Other/don't know	21%	11%	5%	17%	8%	8%

SOURCE: The Pew Center for the People and the Press, "Bottom-Line Pressures Now Hurting Coverage, Say Journalists." Accessed at http://people-press.org/report/214/ on August 4, 2008. Reprinted with permission.

serious, and socially and politically relevant. But in fact, most people want soft news with light entertainment. Given the reality of their world of daily work, who can blame people for wanting to escape and relax in their leisure time? Hard stories and hard entertainment don't allow for diversion or reprieve. In a democracy, the antielitist critics argue, people should be free to choose their own entertainment and sources of information without being criticized for being lowbrow or anti-intellectual. Those who don't accept criticism of the media assert that if we want to make news more factual and intellectual, it nevertheless needs to be presented in a way that is appealing and interesting. This, they say, is the true challenge for reformers.

Governmental Regulations

Practice Quiz

1. It is against the law for a newspaper to publish the name of a rape victim.
   a. true **b.** false

2. Sometimes newspapers do not cover a criminal trial in much detail because
   a. few readers are interested in trial coverage.
   b. such coverage violates the First Amendment.
   c. in some cases, gag orders prevent participants from discussing the case.
   d. in some cases, gag orders prohibit journalists from covering a case.

3. Broadcasting regulations require that third-party candidates be included in nationally televised presidential debates if they are constitutionally eligible to be president, they are on enough state ballots to have a chance to win a majority of electoral college votes, and polls show that they have the support of at least
   a. 5 percent of the national electorate.
   b. 10 percent of the national electorate.
   c. 15 percent of the national electorate.
   d. 20 percent of the national electorate.

4. The theory that states the media need to balance what the public wants with what's good for it is the
   a. libertarian theory.
   b. social responsibility theory.
   c. market forces theory.
   d. ethical freedoms theory.

Answers: 1-b, 2-c, 3-c, 4-b.

Discussion Questions

1. Why is there tension between governmental regulation of the media and the desire for an independent and rigorous press?
2. How does the right to privacy differ for public officials and private individuals?

What **YOU** can do!

As more and more information about our personal lives becomes available on the Internet, do you think this should change the standards for libel? Go online, "google" yourself, and see what kinds of information appear. How much control should an individual have over information that is posted online about himself or herself? What opportunities should an individual have to correct false information posted online? Should the government be able to access a Facebook page to determine if the owner has information or photos that demonstrate he or she is breaking the law?

Conclusion

Although many researchers have examined the power of the media and their impact, the results are mixed. People certainly believe that the media are a powerful force in American politics. So do politicians. And because politicians believe the media are powerful, they may alter their behavior based on how that behavior might be portrayed in the media and received by the public. This belief is potentially a strong check on our leaders' actions. However, it is very hard to measure this potential impact of the media. Moreover, attempting to isolate how the media's portrayal of a candidate specifically influences voters is nearly impossible. Was it the image portrayed by the media or the candidate's qualifications or demeanor that registered in the minds of voters? The same quandary applies to the issues: Do people support an education bill because it was favorably reported in the news, or was it favorably reported because people support it? In light of these questions, establishing causal links is very hard. The complex task of decision-making simply has too many alternative variables. Clearly, the power of the media to influence the political agenda is important, because agenda setting affects what people see, think, and talk about. And the media's powers of agenda setting and issue framing also have great potential to influence public opinion.

Key Objective Review, Apply, and Explore

Mass Media
(pages 356–357)

The media are a powerful force in American politics, with the ability to influence what issues people think about and their response to them.

The need to balance a free press with government regulations raises many delicate issues. In times of war, we generally side with allowing more government regulations, but even then, tension exists.

The intimacy and immediacy of television make it exceptionally influential.

KEY TERM

Marketplace of Ideas 356

CRITICAL THINKING QUESTIONS

1. How powerful do you think the media are? Do they simply tell us what to think about, or are they able to influence and change our opinions?
2. Do you believe that all reasonable ideas have an equal opportunity to compete for acceptance? Or are the views of some groups or individuals given more attention and therefore are more likely to be adopted?

INTERNET RESOURCES

American Museum of Image: **http://livingroomcandidate.movingimage.us/index.php**

I Want Media: **http://www.iwantmedia.com/organizations/index.html**

ADDITIONAL READING

Graber, Doris A. *Mass Media and American Politics,* 7th ed. Washington, D.C: CQ Press, 2006.

Leighley, Jan E. *Mass Media and Politics: A Social Science Perspective.* Boston: Houghton Mifflin, 2004.

The Growth of Mass Media
(pages 358–363)

Newspapers were the first form of mass communication in the United States. When technological improvements allowed newspapers to be produced more cheaply, they became available to the masses, changing the way the news was reported as well as the ways in which governmental officials communicated with the people.

Once introduced, the electronic media quickly spread across the country. Radios were very popular, with ownership growing quickly upon their introduction. The ownership of television sets grew even quicker once technology was developed to allow mass production.

Since the 1980s, the Internet has witnessed remarkable growth. More and more people have access to the Internet, with its usage growing daily.

KEY TERMS

Party Presses 358
Penny Press 358
Yellow Journalism 359
Technology Gap (Digital Divide) 360

CRITICAL THINKING QUESTIONS

1. Do you think that printed versions of newspapers will become obselete? If so, what are some of the potential consequences (good and bad) of this change?
2. Do you believe there are reasons to be concerned about the technology gap, or do you think it is not that important?

INTERNET RESOURCES

Cell Phones for Soldiers: **http://www.cellphonesforsoldiers.com/**

CNN Young People Who Rock: **http://www.cnn.com/exchange/blogs/ypwr/**

Early Radio History: **http://earlyradiohistory.us/index.html**

The Museum of Broadcast Communications: **http://www.museum.tv**

ADDITIONAL READING

Briggs, Asa, and Peter Burke. *A Social History of the Media: From Gutenberg to the Internet.* Boston: Polity, 2005.

Starr, Paul. *The Creation of the Media.* New York: Basic Books, 2004.

Key Objective Review, Apply, and Explore

Functions of the Media

(pages 364–369)

As the distinction between news and entertainment has blurred, especially on television, programming has changed, causing concern among many observers.

The media perform many important social functions, from monitoring the government to interpreting the news to socializing citizens. These functions all come with the potential for a great degree of power and influence—and responsibility.

KEY TERMS

Investigative Reporting 366 **Muckraking 366**

CRITICAL THINKING QUESTIONS

1. Given the fact that the line between the entertainment and news functions of the media are increasingly being blurred, do you think that people are influenced by the public statements and behavior of celebrities? Do you think that celebrity endorsements of presidential candidates are helpful or simply entertaining?
2. Under what circumstances should readers be skeptical of investigative reporting? How and why can it be abused?

INTERNET RESOURCES

Black Entertainment Television: **http://www.bet.com**
British Broadcasting Company: **http://www.bbc.co.uk**
Freedom Forum: **http://www.freedomforum.org**
Univision: **http://www.univision.com**

ADDITIONAL READING

Entman, Robert M., and Andrew Rojecki. *The Black Image in the White Mind: Media and Race in America.* Chicago: University of Chicago Press, 2001.

Gillmor, Dan. *We the Media: Grassroots Journalism by the People, for the People.* Cambridge, MA: O'Reilly Press, 2006.

Political Use of the Media

(pages 370–375)

Candidates, officials, and groups use many tactics to get positive press coverage, which enhances their legitimacy and visibility and may help garner support.

One important aspect of the power of the media is in setting the political agenda by serving as gatekeepers. 'Round-the-clock news stations and the Internet have made it possible for a greater variety of stories to be explored in greater detail.

An uneasy relationship between the press and public officials exists. On the one hand, they need each other; on the other, they both want to control the manner in which the news is reported. Officials want to have the news framed supportively, while the media often look for controversy to generate audience interest.

KEY TERMS

Earned Media Coverage 370
Pseudo-Events 370
Agenda Setting 370
Gatekeepers 371
Press Releases 371
News Briefings 371
News Conferences 371

CRITICAL THINKING QUESTIONS

1. Given the multiple variety of news outlets today do you believe that the power of the media in gatekeeping is exaggerated?
2. How has the Internet impacted the power of the media elite to exert influence over the political agenda?

INTERNET RESOURCES

Accuracy in Media: **http://www.aim.org**
C-SPAN: **http://www.cspan.org/campaign2000/advertising.asp**
CNN: **http://www.cnn.com**
Fox News: **http://www.foxnews.com**
New York Times: **http://www.nytimes.com**

ADDITIONAL READING

Beasley, Maurine Hoffman. *First Ladies and the Press: The Unfinished Partnership of the Media Age.* Evanston, IL: Northwestern University Press, 2005.

Corner, John, and Dick Pels (eds.). *Media and the Restyling of Politics: Consumerism, Celebrity, and Cynicism.* Thousand Oaks, CA: Sage, 2003.

Farnsworth, Stephen, and S. Robert Lichter. *The Mediated Presidency: Television News and Presidential Governance.* Lanham, MD: Rowman & Littlefield, 2006.

Key Objective Review, Apply, and Explore

The Media and the Public in the Political Arena

(pages 376–379)

The media are very important in American elections. Earned media coverage (that obtained free of charge) is especially important, because Americans believe it to be more trustworthy and objective than paid advertisements. Paid ads are nevertheless important tools to reach the audience. They can be very effective, as they allow candidates to repeat controlled messages in attempts to sway public opinion.

Many are becoming increasingly concerned that the concentration of ownership of the media will stem the flow of communication, making the public reliant upon a relatively few sources for their news.

KEY TERMS

Sound Bites 377
Narrowcasting 378
Competitive News Markets 379
News Monopolies 379

CRITICAL THINKING QUESTIONS

1. Do you feel there is reason to be concerned over the centralization of news coverage? Why or why not?
2. Do you think that the public would tune in to longer advertisements, or are sound bites the best mechanism for politicians to communicate with the public?

INTERNET RESOURCES

Drudge Report: **http://www.drudgereport.com**
Pew Center for Civic Journalism: **http://www.pewcenter.org**

ADDITIONAL READING

Bagdikian, Ben H. *The New Media Monopoly.* Boston: Beacon Press, 2004.

Falk, Erika. *Woman for President: Media Bias in Eight Campaigns.* Urbana: University of Illinois Press, 2007.

Howard, Philip N. *New Media Campaigns and the Managed Citizen.* Cambridge, UK: Cambridge University Press, 2005.

Governmental Regulations

(pages 380–383)

The government exercises some regulation of the content and ownership of the media. The main concerns regarding regulation of the content stem from issues of prior restraint, privacy, and those related to accurate and fair reporting.

KEY TERMS

Libel 381
Prior Censorship 381
Equal Time Rule 381
Fairness Doctrine 382
Libertarian View 382
Social Responsilibity Theory (Public Advocate Model) 382

CRITICAL THINKING QUESTIONS

1. Do you think it should be easier for celebrities, public officials, and others in the public eye to sue for libel? Or is this type of scrutiny the "price of fame"?
2. Do you think the fairness doctrine should still be required today? Why or why not?

INTERNET RESOURCES

Take Back the Media: **http://www.takebackthemedia.com**
Youth Media Information Center: **http://www.freechild.org/youthmedia.htm**

ADDITIONAL READING

Cook, Timothy E. (ed.). *Freeing the Presses: The First Amendment in Action.* Baton Rouge: Louisiana State University Press, 2005.

Tumber, Howard. *Media at War: The Iraq Crisis.* Thousand Oaks, CA: Sage, 2004.

Chapter Review Critical Thinking Test

1. The media are a particularly significant force in which two pathways of political action?
- **a.** the grassroots mobilization and court pathways
- **b.** the lobbying decision makers and elections pathways
- **c.** the court and cultural change pathways
- **d.** the cultural change and election pathways

2. Free media are crucial for a democratic society, because
- **a.** citizens depend on the publication or broadcasting of polling data to know the majority opinions about policy issues.
- **b.** free media make possible national public debate on important political issues.
- **c.** without TV, voters would not know how charismatic their potential political leaders are.
- **d.** politicians' electoral success depends in part on their savvy use of the media.

3. Which statement best summarizes the functions of the media in the United States?
- **a.** The media entertain, inform, and persuade the public.
- **b.** The media divide the public and make reality less vivid.
- **c.** To reach the widest audience and make as much money as possible, the media strive only to entertain the public.
- **d.** The media primarily inform the public, with little concern for profit-making.

4. A recent survey of national and local media reporters, producers, editors, and executives indicates that journalists believe that the pressure to make a profit is harming both national and local news coverage.
- **a.** true **b.** false

5. In the early decades of the nineteenth century, newspapers in the United States were usually created to support a specific political party or set of economic beliefs.
- **a.** true **b.** false

6. As the American newspaper industry became more centralized, newspaper reporting became much more objective.
- **a.** true **b.** false

7. What makes televised news so powerful?
- **a.** the fact that it is not censored
- **b.** it makes clear distinctions between news and entertainment
- **c.** its objective, unbiased approach
- **d.** its intimacy and visual nature

8. The broadcast media in all liberal democracies are privately owned.
- **a.** true **b.** false

9. What do Murphy Brown's pregnancy and its political aftermath illustrate?
- **a.** that the series was amazingly realistic
- **b.** that single women should not get pregnant, especially if they want to have careers
- **c.** that the line between news and entertainment can become blurred
- **d.** that television programs can become trivial and boring

10. What would be an example of the surveillance function that the media can play in the realm of American politics?
- **a.** a television exposé about the mistreatment of undocumented workers at a few Wal-Mart stores
- **b.** television cameramen hiding outside a candidate's house and waiting to document an illicit affair
- **c.** a radio news program that makes use of secretly recorded phone calls between a criminal suspect and his or her lawyer
- **d.** a long newspaper article putting a politician's career in historical context after she has died

11. Rush Limbaugh is an example of
- **a.** a political liberal whose popularity suggests the left-leaning tendency of the media.
- **b.** someone who has been censored by the FCC.
- **c.** an enormously popular conservative commentator who has emphasized the liberal bias of mainstream media.
- **d.** someone who has moved from public office to broadcast journalism.

12. Only since about 1950 have politicians in this country used the media for political purposes.
- **a.** true **b.** false

13. What best describes the interrelationship of the public, the government, and the media?
- **a.** The government influences the media, which influence the public.
- **b.** The public influences the government, which influences the media.
- **c.** The media influence the government, which influences the public.
- **d.** Each of the three influences the others and is influenced by the others.

14. Who was the first president to discern and make effective use of the power of the media?
- **a.** Abraham Lincoln
- **b.** William McKinley
- **c.** Theodore Roosevelt
- **d.** John Kennedy

15. Why is it wise to regard news stories that are leaked with some skepticism?
- **a.** because they are usually not true
- **b.** because the leaker sometimes presents the information in an incomplete and self-serving way
- **c.** because leaking information is illegal
- **d.** because most people who leak secrets they are entrusted to keep are not trustworthy

16. Which branch of government gets covered least by the media?
- **a.** the judicial branch
- **b.** the legislative branch
- **c.** the executive branch
- **d.** All branches are covered about equally.

17. Issue advocacy advertising is an example of
- **a.** how work in the elections pathway uses the media.
- **b.** how interest groups use the media.
- **c.** the fairness doctrine in action.
- **d.** muckraking.

18. How do newspapers potentially worsen the political disengagement of poor people?
- **a.** by routinely endorsing candidates whose agendas disadvantage the poor
- **b.** by circulation policies that exclude poor neighborhoods, keeping poor residents ignorant about national affairs
- **c.** by using overly sophisticated language that only college-educated readers can easily understand
- **d.** by not covering many stories involving the poor, simply because most people with lower incomes cannot afford to subscribe to newspapers

19. What is cross-media ownership?
- **a.** owning one kind of media outlet, such as a radio station; selling it; and then buying another kind of media outlet, such as a newspaper
- **b.** owning all or nearly all of one kind of media outlet
- **c.** owning a variety of media outlets simultaneously
- **d.** the running of a media-owning corporation by a diverse group of individuals

20. Scholarly studies suggest that the effects of the media on American politics are clear and can be described statistically.
- **a.** true
- **b.** false

Answers: 1-d, 2-b, 3-a, 4-a, 5-a, 6-b, 7-d, 8-b, 9-c, 10-a, 11-c, 12-b, 13-d, 14-c, 15-b, 16-a, 17-b, 18-d, 19-c, 20-b.

You decide!

One criticism made of the mass media by political scientist Thomas Patterson relates to the media's important role in elections. In his book *Out of Order,* Patterson argues that as political parties have grown weaker, media outlets have filled gaps in providing information; however, because of biases in reporting that favor stories about conflict, for instance, the media is not able to present a reliable picture of political campaigns. Assuming this is the case, do you think this affects candidates' behavior and strategy? If so, in what ways? What other alternatives do we have for gathering reliable information about candidates? Patterson's book was written before the prevalence of more "democratic" forms of electronic media, such as blogs and wiki texts. Do you think these kinds of media can provide more reliable information about candidates and campaigns? What possible biases and problems can you see?

Key Objective Outline

How have activism and protest evolved in the United States? Why is it important to understand the roots of activism in order to understand contemporary issues?

What Constitutional foundations allow citizens to petition their government?

Why are interest groups important in the democratic process?

Why have we seen such a dramatic increase in the number and activity of interest groups during the last 40 years?

CHAPTER 11
INTEREST GROUPS, SOCIAL MOVEMENTS, AND CIVIC ENGAGEMENT

How do interest groups, social movements, and civic participation affect decision-making and public policy?

Rock the Vote seeks to politically motivate young adults. Founded in 1990, this nonpartisan, nonprofit group engages youth in the political process year-round. It encourages voter registration (in many states you can register to vote online from the organization's Web page at http://www.rockthevote.org), get-out-the vote drives, and voter education campaigns. In 1992, Rock the Vote and its partner organizations registered 350,000 young people and helped motivate more than 2 million new young voters, ending a two-decade decline in voter participation and achieving a 20-percent increase in youth turnout. Since then, the group has worked aggressively to make it easier to register to vote, provide voter guides to young voters, and teach youth to mentor activism in other youth to encourage year-round activism.

Rock the Vote has focused on discrimination and intolerance in recent years. In 2001, they partnered with MTV in a campaign called "Fight for Your Rights: Take a Stand Against Discrimination." In 2004, the group registered 1.4 million new voters (1.2 million online, and 200,000 by their Rock the Vote bus tour), marking a large surge in young-voter participation. In 2006, Rock the Vote continued their efforts to get young people engaged in politics and to vote by partnering with Facebook and Young Voter Strategies. Rock the Vote created a highly interactive Facebook group that focused first on registering young people to vote and then on promoting turnout. Within the first month, there were 14,620 members, with 62 different discussion topics.

Through their collaboration with many other organizations (most notably Young Voter Strategies), they exceeded their goal of registering 2 million new young voters in 2008, with the youth vote estimated to be nearly record-setting. In 2008, they launched a new program, Rock the Trail, to help aspiring young reporters across the country write and blog about the election for Rock the Vote 2008. Rock the Vote has helped this generation of young Americans find their voice and influence their world.

STUDENT RESOURCE-CENTER
- Glossary
- Vocabulary Example
- LINK
- MyPoliSciLab Connection

Activism *and* Protest *in the* United States (pages 392–393)

How have activism and protest evolved in the United States? Why is it important to understand the roots of activism in order to understand contemporary issues?

As renowned anthropologist Margaret Mead (right) said, "Never doubt that a small group of thoughtful committed citizens can change the world; indeed it's the only thing that ever has."

Americans claim as our birthright some of the most profound liberties and freedoms. Our Bill of Rights establishes many cherished liberties—freedom of speech, religion, press, and assembly, to name only a few. As a result, we have the unrivaled ability to influence our government and our fellow citizens. We have the freedom to speak our minds and to express our most controversial and complex thoughts—thoughts that might be unpopular or even unreasonable, but still ideas that can be presented in public and compete for acceptance. Furthermore, we have constitutionally guaranteed liberties that allow us to appeal to our government to address our concerns and issues. Using group action has a distinctive appeal to Americans, for whom the tradition is deeply ingrained in our national political culture. In this chapter, we will examine people and groups working to change our society, our laws, and our culture. Grassroots mobilization is an important pathway to influence our society, our government, and our social structures.

A Brief History

While traveling throughout the United States in 1831 and 1832 and studying its society, Alexis de Tocqueville, a young Frenchman, noted that group activities were essential for the development and maintenance of democracy. In his words, "I confess that in America I saw more than America; I sought the image of democracy itself, with its inclinations, its character, its prejudices, and its passions, in order to learn what we have to fear or to hope from its progress."[1] His journey resulted in the book *Democracy in America*, originally published in 1835. Tocqueville was only 25 years old when he came to America to observe our democracy, yet his account of our society is one of the most perceptive ever published.[2]

Tocqueville valued personal liberty, and he spent a good deal of time examining Americans' practice of freedom of association and political participation. Compared to Europeans of his time, he noted, Americans had a much stronger tendency to join together to solve problems, to articulate collective interests, and to form social relationships. He asserted that people living in democratic nations must join together to preserve their independence and freedoms. Coming together to help others is one of the binding factors in an otherwise complex and alien environment. Collective action is especially important for people who have little influence individually, as like-minded people can come together and act with greater strength. Tocqueville pointed out that the freedom of association allowed for "partisans of an opinion" to unite in the electoral arena:

> "Has freedom of association always been an important part of American political culture?"
> —Student Question

> The liberty of association has become a necessary guarantee against the tyranny of the majority. . . . There are no countries in which associations are more needed, to prevent the despotism of faction or the arbitrary power of the prince, than those which are democratically constituted. . . . The most natural privilege of man, next to the right of acting for himself, is that of combining his exertions with those of his fellow-creatures, and of acting in common with them. I am therefore led to conclude that the right of association is almost as inalienable as the right of personal liberty.[3]

As Tocqueville showed, the right to associate and to be active in public affairs is one of the most fundamental rights on which participatory democracy depends. To live in a free society, citizens must have the right of association to petition their government to address their grievances and concerns. Such an understanding of the functioning of collective action in democracies goes back to the infancy of our country. The importance of citizen participation is even greater today, because our society has grown far more complex, diverse, and technological, with intimate ties to the global community.

Activism is at the root of our "do something" political culture, and forming groups is essential for political action. Throughout our history, groups have emerged to challenge the status quo—and opposition groups have emerged to fight to preserve the status quo. Our main purpose in the following sections is to illustrate the validity of Tocqueville's observations about the importance of group action in the United States to promote change and enhance liberty as well as to provide a context for analyzing contemporary

DE TOCQUEVILLE.

Alexis Henry de Tocqueville (1805–1859), French writer and commentator, traveled across our country in 1831–1832. His account, *Democracy in America*, is still widely read and cited today. ***—Why do you think 25 year-old was so able to characterize the nature of our democracy? Do you think you must be an outsider to best understand a country?***

■ **Egalitarianism:**	**EXAMPLE:**
Doctrine of equality that ignores differences in social status, wealth, and privilege.	*Egalitarianism has led to laws that promote equality, such as equal pay for equal work for all people.*

CONNECT THE LINK (Chapter **2**, page **62**) Do you think that people still feel connected to their government?

group behavior. These activities are fundamentally important in shaping the very nature and definition of our democracy.

The Right to Revolt

"Where did the idea of a 'right to revolt' originate?"

—Student Question

One central idea underlying our political system is our belief in self-government and citizen action. At the end of the seventeenth century, the English philosopher John Locke argued that people have certain God-given, or natural, rights that are inalienable—meaning that they can neither be taken away by nor surrendered to a government (see LINK Chapter 2, page 62). Locke's social contract theory holds that people set up governments for the very specific purpose of protecting natural rights. All legitimate political authority, said Locke, exists to preserve these natural rights and rests on the consent of the governed. When a ruler acts against the purposes for which government exists, the people have the right to resist and remove the offending ruler. Thomas Jefferson relied on Locke's social contract theory of government when writing the Declaration of Independence: The central premise of the Declaration is that people have a right to revolt when they determine that their government has denied them their legitimate rights.

One consequence of the American Revolution was that faith in collective action, as well as in self-rule, became entrenched in the new United States. Rioting and mass mobilization had proved an effective tool to resist oppressive government. The Revolution also helped establish in the United States the sense of **egalitarianism**■—the belief that all people are equal. Our republican form of government, in which power rests in the hands of the people, reinforces this egalitarianism. A faith in the legitimacy of collective action, even violent action, in defense of liberty entered into our political culture.

Activism and Protest in the United States

Practice Quiz

1. According to Tocqueville, civic engagement serves all of the following purposes except
   a. promoting and transferring shared values and beliefs.
   b. strengthening the ability of isolated individuals and groups to come together for collective action.
   c. allowing like-minded individuals to unite to influence the electoral arena.
   d. allowing tyranny of the majority to develop and thrive.
2. Which political philosopher articulated the social contract theory?
   a. Plato **c.** Tocqueville
   c. Jefferson **d.** Locke
3. Group action has been deeply engrained in our political culture since the earliest days of our Confederation.
   a. true **b.** false
4. According to Tocqueville, the right of association is one of the most important freedoms to prevent tyranny of the majority.
   a. true **b.** false

Answers: 1-d, 2-d, 3-a, 4-a.

Discussion Questions

1. What do you think Jefferson meant when he commented that a little rebellion was necessary from time to time to preserve liberty?
2. What is meant by the expression "a nation of joiners"? Do you think we are still a nation of joiners? What impact does communications technology have on this question?

What **YOU** Can Do!

Think about an issue that is important to you. Using that issue as the key topic, do a search on the Web. How many organizations can you find that take a stand, one way or another, on your issue? Is there evidence that Tocqueville's observation that we are a nation of joiners still apt in describing America today?

CONNECT THE LINK (Chapter **1**, pages **20–23**) Under what circumstances do you think interest groups serve to heighten conflict in society?

CONNECT THE LINK (Chapter **5**, page **154**) Do you believe that our country is as committed to expression of speech, even if it is in the form of protests, as it was before 9/11?

Influencing *the* Government Through Mobilization *and* Participation (pages 394–395)

What Constitutional foundations allow citizens to petition their government?

Grassroots mobilization and interest group activities are very important for democracy. One key element in the democratic balance is the influence of the masses versus the influence of the elites in decision-making. For democracy to function and to thrive, there must be a collective sense of community: People must feel tied to each other and united with their government, whether or not they agree with its actions. The linkage of people and government is crucial for democratic rule, and organized groups and citizen engagement forge an important aspect of it.

Organized interests prompt leaders to "do something"—to address pressing problems in society, thus activating the "safety valve" that we discussed in LINK Chapter 1, pages 20-23. Without organized interests, many issues would be overlooked, and problems would grow. Race rioting in the 1960s, for example, showed anger bred from the frustration of African Americans at being marginalized and disregarded by white society. Years of discrimination and bigotry yielded frustration and rage—which had no structured outlet. By ignoring the racism that was evident in the United States, Americans created a situation that at last exploded violently.[4] Pressure from organized interests serves to hold governing officials accountable by forcing them to pay attention to issues that are important to the people. Involvement also fosters the acquisition of attributes important to democracy—tolerance, political efficacy, and political trust. Groups help teach citizens a sense of social integration and interaction. Joining with others outside our primary relationships (families) is fundamental to political activity. Being civically engaged allows people to develop associations and skills that are essential for healthy democratic communities.

Our founders were interested in making government function so that the people could control key elements of political power; hence there is an emphasis in our system on bargaining, compromise, and consensus building. We expect our government to listen to our preferences, and we expect to be influential. We acknowledge—or should acknowledge—that we can't always win, but we do expect government to allow us to be heard.

Organized groups provide one mechanism to petition our government. Groups are at the center of our democratic political system—and always have been. Imagine that a developer wanted to build a large factory just outside your neighborhood. You begin to worry about increased traffic, environmental impacts, and decreased property values. What would you do? Most likely, you would form an association to address your problem, gathering neighbors who share your concerns and petitioning your city council and zoning commission.

How do we allow citizens to pursue their self-interest while protecting society's interest as well? Balancing these often competing desires is difficult. The example of the neighborhood group organizing to prevent a factory from opening illustrates the dilemma. The neighborhood is probably rational in its concerns. Factories do alter traffic patterns, affect the local ecosystem, and lower property values. Factories also employ people who might desperately need the work, however, and they pay taxes that can benefit the entire community. How does the community navigate between the needs of local homeowners and the needs of the larger community? Who should win—homeowners or unemployed people in need of jobs? It is a difficult question, underscoring a central dilemma of government.

Constitutional Guarantees for Citizen Activism and Mobilization

The U.S. Constitution provides substantial guarantees that allow citizen participation, activism, and mass mobilization. For example, the Bill of Rights lists liberties that together ensure our right to petition the government. First Amendment freedoms are fundamental in our democracy, because they dramatically determine how we can influence our world, including our fellow citizens and leaders.

In totalitarian systems, lobbying, activism, protest, and other forms of political engagement among citizens are always severely limited—indeed, they are usually forbidden and harshly punished (see Figure 11.1). One vivid illustration of this occurred in June of 1989, in Beijing, China, when thousands of pro-democracy students gathered in Tiananmen Square to protest political oppression. The world watched in horror as the Chinese government massacred several thousand young pro-democracy protesters on live television. These students were demonstrating their desire for rights that all Americans enjoy but that many fail to appreciate. In the United States, we generally have vast freedom of expression, encompassing the freedoms of speech, religion, assembly, petition, and press. When we discuss freedom of expression (see LINK Chapter 5, page 154), we generally mean the broader concept of freedom to communicate. This freedom to communicate is the right of a citizen to convey his or her thoughts—verbally, visually, or in writing—without prior restraint.[5]

FIGURE 11.1 | Events in Tiananmen Square

To examine the 1989 crackdown on protestors in Beijing, American and Chinese researchers turned to Google to find images of what happened. They were shown two very different versions, due to the suppression of free speech on the Chinese version of Google.

One Search Subject, Two Results: Tiananmen Square

WHAT CHINESE SEARCHERS SEE The first five results on the Chinese version of Google Images, and dozens after them, largely concern tourism.

WHAT AMERICAN SEARCHERS SEE The first five results on Google Images in the United States show the solitary protester in the path of a tank column during the 1989 crackdown.

In theory, the majority of Americans support First Amendment freedoms of speech and assembly, but controversy erupts whenever these broad concepts are put into action. People generally see political participation and activism in positive terms, but they often wonder whether it is good for all groups. Should people be allowed to raise issues with which we disagree or that may offend us? Who should determine what types of activism are permissible and by whom? As a society, we tend to support rights and privileges for those with whom we agree but oppose the same rights for members of groups we do not support. As noted in Chapter 5, Americans generally rely on the judiciary to negotiate this fine balance. If we are to remain a strong participatory democracy, however, we as a society must come to grips with this controversy. Almost certainly, we will never see majority support for obscenity or violence-inducing behavior, but we also need to remember that in a free society, people can and do disagree. The question becomes, how do thoughtful citizens determine the boundaries for legitimate disagreement and allow reasonable access to free expression? Meanwhile, we must also be cautious, as the founders of our country were, to protect the rights of minorities, lest the majority silence their voices and trample their rights. ■

Influencing the Government Through Mobilization and Participation

Practice Quiz

1. What does it mean that our government was designed as a "how-to" system?
   - **a.** The Constitution makes clear which branch of government should do what and how it should do it.
   - **b.** The Constitution explains how the government should work and how it can be changed if it is not working.
   - **c.** With its emphasis on compromise and consensus building, the Constitution ensures that the people, not the elites, control key elements of political power.
   - **d.** The Constitution operates as a blueprint or owner's manual; any group of people can make our government work.
2. When an individual's self-interest is at odds with society's interest,
   - **a.** the Bill of Rights grants the individual the upper hand.
   - **b.** the interest most effectively lobbied for usually wins out—and should.
   - **c.** society's interest should usually win out, because it represents the greater good.
   - **d.** this conflict always presents a difficult balancing act for our society and government.
3. For democracy to work, people must feel tied to each other and united with their government, whether or not they agree with its actions.
   - **a.** true
   - **b.** false
4. Pressure from organized interest groups can help marginalized groups feel represented before their government.
   - **a.** true
   - **b.** false

Answers: 1-c, 2-d, 3-a, 4-b.

Discussion Questions

1. What role do Internet blogs play in an individual's ability and willingness to engage in political action?
2. What are the positive and negative aspects of popular participation in our country in modern times?

What **YOU** can do!

How difficult or easy would it be to plan a demonstration at your college? Examine the policy at your university regarding the rules that individuals or groups must follow to plan an organized protest. What factors do you think lead some universities to limit the ability of students to organize, petition, and protest while other universities in the same region allow broader access to these same rights?

■ **Interest Group:** A group of like-minded individuals who band together to influence public policy, public opinion, or governmental officials.

EXAMPLE: *Common Cause is an interest group that works to promote more effective government and advocates campaign finance reform. As such, they are highly critical of other interest groups that spend what they consider excessive amounts of money to influence elections.*

Interest Groups

(pages 396–399)

Why are interest groups important in the democratic process?

Interest groups■ are organizations outside the government that attempt to influence the government's behavior, decision-making, and allocation of resources. Ever since the nation's founding, Americans have formed groups to address their concerns and to influence their peers, their communities, and their government. We will examine why people join and remain in interest groups, and we will consider the impact that actions of interest groups have in the United States. You will also learn about the tools and tactics that these groups use as they *lobby*—that is, work to gain influence within the government and with the public at large in order to influence officials and win public support.

Many people look skeptically at interest groups and tend to see them in a very negative light. Although extremist members can heavily influence many groups, interest groups perform many valuable functions in our democracy. Often, there is tension between what is best for the group and its members and what is best for society. This tension can be healthy, however, because it focuses attention on issues that otherwise would not receive much notice and can promote constructive public debate.

Motivation to Join Interest Groups

In our diverse society, people join interest groups to find a place to belong, to articulate their point of view, and to promote their common goals. Three primary characteristics define interest groups. First, they are voluntary associations of joiners. Some interest groups are formal, including trade groups such as the American Medical Association (AMA); others are more informal, such as neighborhood groups that form to fight zoning changes. Second, the members of an interest group share common beliefs. Interest groups are collections of like-minded individuals who are drawn together because they have a common set of interests, beliefs, or values. Third, interest groups focus on influencing government. People join them because they want government policy to reflect their preferences, and consequently, interest groups spend time, energy, and money trying to influence public officials.

To highlight the impact that immigrants have in America, LULAC helped organize rallies across the country on May 1, 2006. Pictured above are Elba Castro and Saul Torres at the Dallas, Texas, rally at City Hall. ***—What challenges do you think LULAC will face when trying to mobilize immigrants? Why do you think that building coalitions is important for LULAC?***

PATHWAYS | of action

LULAC

The League of United Latin American Citizens (LULAC) is one of the oldest and most influential organizations representing Latinos in the United States. It was founded in 1929 in Corpus Christi, Texas, when three separate Hispanic groups banded together to demand equal rights and opportunities in education, government, law, business, and health care. Today, LULAC has 115,000 members in the United States and Puerto Rico, organized into 700 councils. LULAC provides its members with a number of important services, ranging from conducting citizenship and voter registration drives to pressuring localities into providing more low-income housing. It also strives to help Hispanic youth by providing training programs and educational counseling as well as by offering more than $1 million annually in scholarships.

Through its activism, LULAC has won a number of important successes that have advanced the civil rights and liberties of Hispanic Americans. In 1945, the California LULAC Council successfully sued to integrate the Orange County school system, which had justified segregation with the claim that Mexican children were "more poorly clothed and mentally inferior to white children."[6] LULAC also provided financial support and attorneys to challenge the practice of excluding Hispanics from juries (*Hernandez* v. *Texas*): in 1954, the U.S. Supreme Court ruled that such exclusion was unconstitutional. In 1966, LULAC marched with and financially supported the largely Spanish-speaking United Farm Workers union in its struggle for minimum wages. LULAC National Education Service Centers, Inc., created in 1973, today serves more than

SIMULATION You Are an Environmental Activist

VISUAL LITERACY Federal Election Rules, PACs, and the Money Trail

20,000 Hispanic students a year. The LULAC Institute was established in 1996 to provide model volunteer programs for Latino communities, and since 2004, the LULAC Leadership Initiative has been revitalizing Hispanic neighborhoods by creating grassroots programs in 700 Latino communities. ■

Functions of Interest Groups in a Democratic Society

Interest groups play an important role in our representative democracy. They serve as a vehicle for citizens to peacefully express their concerns to government officials—that is, to exercise their First Amendment right to petition their government. Without interest groups, Americans would be overwhelmed by the size of our government and by the fragmentation of our society. This chapter will show how interest groups both advance and hinder democracy.

"Why do so many people think interest groups are 'bad'?"

—Student Question

In the United States, interest groups serve five specific functions. First, interest groups *represent constituents* before the government. Without the organization and strength of interest groups, individual voices might drown in our complex society.

Second, interest groups provide an important *means of political participation*, often coupled with other forms of political activity. Volunteering time, taking part in a group, and contributing money are all important ways in which people can gain a sense of individual and collective power and thus a voice in our society. Such feelings of political efficacy promote other forms of political engagement.

A third function of interest groups is to *educate the public*. By sponsoring research, serving as advocates, testifying before congressional committees, conducting public relations campaigns, and engaging in similar activities, members of the public learn about various issues in more detail. Obviously, interest groups present only their viewpoint on an issue; they are not in the business of arguing their opponent's case. It should be noted, however, that on many controversial issues, interest groups emerge on both sides, leading to greater public awareness and knowledge.

Fourth, interest groups *influence policymaking* by agenda building—that is, simply by bringing an otherwise little-known issue to the forefront. By attempting to educate the public about certain issues or by running public relations campaigns, they focus the attention of both the public and officials on issues that might otherwise be ignored.

Finally, interest groups contribute to the governing process by serving as *government watchdogs*. They monitor government programs, examining their strengths and weaknesses and thereby assessing the effectiveness of programs that are important to their members. Of course, each individual group's verdict on the programs it monitors may be one-sided, but when we look at the activities of interest groups collectively, we can appreciate that their overall effect is to make our government serve its people more efficiently.

The Interest Group Explosion

Between the 1960s and the 1990s, the United States witnessed an explosion in the number and activity level of interest groups. In 1959, there were 5,843 organizations with a national scope. That number almost doubled by 1970, reaching 10,308; a decade later, 14,726 organizations had registered with the federal government. By the mid-1990s, the level of growth had tapered off to slightly over 22,200 national organizations, which is about the number that exist today.[7] Since 1960, there has been a dramatic surge in the number of citizen groups advocating civil rights and civil liberties as well as a sharp rise in the number of public interest groups that seek consumer and environmental protection. In the private sector, the number of groups representing businesses and trades has also risen, in part to counter the success of other public interest groups.

"How many interest groups are there in the United States?"

—Student Question

CAUSES AND CONSEQUENCES Before we discuss the specific types of groups, we need to examine the causes of this explosion of interest groups and some of its consequences. One of the many reasons why interest groups exist in the United States is to unify subgroups of people in our diverse and complex society. As the country grew in size and began to broaden the range of political power exercised by people of different religions, ethnicities, income levels, genders, and racial makeups, differences deepened to form social divisions or **cleavages.** The presence of these cleavages has been important in the development of various interest groups, because many of them strive to gather supporters across social cleavages, serving as a unifying factor in a fragmented society.

The nature of our governmental system itself is a second explanation for why interest groups have existed in our society since its earliest days. The American federal system provides many opportunities to influence government at different levels. Groups can appeal to the federal government, to state governments, to

TABLE 11.1 | Types of Interest Groups

TYPE	EXAMPLES	FOUNDED	MEMBERS	ISSUE	PAC	DONATIONS TO FEDERAL CANDIDATES IN 2004 AND 2006
Economic	U.S. Chamber of Commerce (http://www.uschamber.com)	1912	3 million businesses	Representation of businesses before the government	Yes	$173,150/ $170,500
	American Medical Association (http://www.ama-assn.org)	1847	13 million	Physician's cooperation on important issues	Yes	$2.04 million/ $2.0 million
Public interest	AARP (http://www.aarp.org)	1958	36 million	Quality of life for older citizens	No	
	Human Rights Campaign (http://www.hrc.org)	1980	700,000	Equal rights for gay, lesbian, bisexual, and transgender citizens	Yes	$1.17 million/ $741,287
	National Rifle Association (http://www.nra.org)	1871	4.3 million	Promote right to bear arms	Yes	$12.8 million/ $853,175
	MoveOn.org (http://www.moveon.org)	1998	3.3 million	Citizen participation in government	Yes	$203,422/ $784,186
Think tanks	Brookings Institution (http://www.brook.edu)	1916	140 resident/ nonresident scholars	Nonprofit research organization	No	
Governmental units	National Governors Association (http://www.nga.org)	1908	50	Bipartisan organization of the nation's governors	No	

SOURCE: http://www.fec.gov, http://www.opensecrets.org

county and municipal governments, and to special jurisdictions, such as school districts. Moreover, the division of power among the three branches of the federal government allows additional opportunities to petition.

What accounts for the large growth in interest groups during the past 40 years? Political scientist David Truman's **disturbance theory** has been well received as an explanation. Truman's theory states that groups form whenever other interests are perceived as threatening or the status quo is disturbed. Essentially, *social change* causes the growth of interest groups. As society becomes more complex, divisions emerge, which then become the basis for new groups. Not everyone agrees with this theory, however. Others argue that the development of groups depends crucially on the *quality of leadership* of the group.[8] If we modify the disturbance theory to include the role of leaders in causing social change, we can better explain the growth of groups in recent decades. A hybrid explanation would say that charismatic individuals come forward to lead the new groups that result from social change.

In addition to the fact that American society has been changing rapidly since 1960, the growth of interest groups in the United States can be attributed to the growth of government. As government takes on new responsibilities, interest groups arise to attempt to influence how those responsibilities are carried out. Interest groups also form as people try to get a "piece of the action"—that is, attempt to influence how government allocates resources in exercising its new responsibilities.

A third explanation for the rapid proliferation of interest groups lies in the changing social characteristics of the American population. Today, Americans are more educated and have more disposable income, making it easier for interest groups to target and activate them. As you will see, the more educated and wealthier citizens become, the more likely they are to participate in politics generally and to join interest groups. Thus interest groups have grown simply because the potential pool of likely members has also grown. In addition, groups have also benefited from new technology, which makes it easier to target potential members and contact interested people.

Types of Interest Groups

Interest groups span the political spectrum. To make sense of the variety, it's best to divide interest groups into four categories: economic groups, public interest groups, think tanks and universities, and governmental units (see Table 11.1). Each type of group exists to advance its goals, which may or may not be in the nation's best interest. We will discuss the specific tools that interest groups use to advance their cause, but first, it is important to understand the variety of groups as well as their commonalities and differences.

■ **Disturbance Theory:** The idea that interest groups form when resources become scarce in order to contest the influence of other interest groups.

EXAMPLE: *NARAL Pro-Choice America (an organization that supports reproductive freedom and choice) was formed in 1969 to work to repeal laws that prohibited abortion. When the Supreme Court decided in* Roe v. Wade *(1973) that prohibiting abortions was unconstitutional, many pro-life groups (such as National Right to Life) were created to fight to reverse the decision.*

CONNECT THE LINK
(Chapter **3**, pages **90–92**) How effective do you think local governments are in joining together to increase their influence?

ECONOMIC GROUPS Economic groups include trade associations, labor unions, and professional associations. **Trade associations** are organized commercial groups, ranging from industrial corporations to agricultural producers. One of the most prominent trade associations is the U.S. Chamber of Commerce. It presents the interests of member businesses to government officials and institutions. **Labor unions** are groups of workers who have joined together to negotiate collectively with employers and to inform the government and the public of their needs. **Professional associations** represent people—generally well-paid and highly educated ones—in a specific profession. Two prominent examples are the AMA for physicians and the American Bar Association (ABA) for attorneys.

PUBLIC INTEREST GROUPS Over the past 40 years, there has been a dramatic growth in **public interest groups,** which political scientist Jeffrey Berry defines as groups that form in the pursuit of "a collective good, the achievement of which will not selectively and materially benefit the membership or activists of the organization."[9] One of the earliest modern public interest groups was Common Cause, created in 1970 to advocate governmental reform. There is enormous variety in the goals of public interest groups, encompassing, for example, people either advocating or opposing gun control, abortion, and environmental protection. The National Association for the Advancement of Colored People (NAACP), the National Rifle Association (NRA), and the environmentalist Sierra Club are all public interest groups; so are the many right-to-life groups that oppose abortion.

THINK TANKS **Think tanks** are nonprofit institutions that conduct research on issues of public interest. One of the best-known think tanks is the Brookings Institution, which conducts relatively nonpartisan research on economic questions, foreign policy, and various other issues of governance. Think tanks often advocate a strong ideological viewpoint; examples include the conservative American Enterprise Institute and the Heritage Foundation.

GOVERNMENTAL UNITS Finally, state- and local-level **governmental units** form interest groups that petition federal authorities for help and to otherwise voice their concerns. As you saw in LINK Chapter 3, pages 90–92, when Congress cuts its financial support to the states and municipalities while at the same time piling more obligations on them, these government entities have to compete for scarce resources. So, naturally, they have formed interest groups, too. Two excellent examples of such groups are the National Governors Association (NGA) and the U.S. Conference of Mayors (USCM). The NGA is a bipartisan organization of the nations' governors that helps represent states before the federal government. Their reports share information about effective state programs, provide experts to help states address important issues, and create networking opportunities for governors and their staff. The USCM is a nonpartisan organization representing cities with populations larger than 300,000. It is an important tool for linking national and urban-suburban policy and strengthening federal and city relationships. The organization also helps mayors develop leadership and managerial skills and serves as an information-sharing forum.

Interest Groups
Practice Quiz

1. Some interest groups in this country bring together individuals from separate groups (as defined by race, religion, gender, or income); other interest groups reinforce the divisions among these subgroups.
   a. true **b.** false
2. Which of the following is a multi-issue interest group?
   a. the NRA **b.** LULAC
   c. the Sierra Club **d.** the UFW
3. Approximately how many interest groups are there in the United States?
   a. 1,500 **b.** 10,000
   c. 20,000 **d.** 250,000
4. Which of the following is *not* a factor that helps explain the rapid growth of interest groups since the 1960s?
   a. rapid social change
   b. increased awareness with more resources and education
   c. the growth of government itself
   d. voting

Answers: 1-a, 2-b, 3-c, 4-d.

Discussion Questions

1. Discuss how the influence of interest groups might conflict with the interest of the public at large.
2. What are some of the consequences of the increase in the number and type of interest groups?

What YOU can do!

Check out the Web site of LULAC, the League of United Latin American Citizens, at **http://www.lulac.org.** Click on the link for "Platform" to see this interest group's current legislative agenda.

Free-Rider Problem: The fact that public goods can be enjoyed by everyone, including people who do not pay their fair share of the cost for providing those goods.

EXAMPLE: *Public television relies on funding from viewers; however, people can watch programming without contributing. Programs such as* Sesame Street, Barney, Frontline, Eyes on the Prize, *and* The McLaughlin Group *are free to all even if no contributions are made.*

Public Goods (Collective Goods): Goods that are used or consumed by all individuals in society.

EXAMPLE: *Clean water, public roads, public parks, community libraries, and public pools are all forms of public goods that are available.*

Interest Group Mobilization (pages 400–403)

Why have we seen such a dramatic increase in the number and activity of interest groups during the last 40 years?

Before we examine how groups organize, it is important to discuss the barriers that affect organizing—the obstacles that any group must overcome before it can succeed. In this section, we will generalize about the experiences of all groups. It is important to stress, however, that specific subgroups in the American population may face additional barriers, and that some barriers may affect certain groups differently than others.

"Why is it harder to organize some groups than others?"

—Student Question

Take, for example, groups that seek to mobilize Latinos and Latinas. A good percentage of Spanish-heritage people, especially in border states, are not citizens, and many live in the United States illegally. Imagine that you are troubled by the economic exploitation of Latinos in the construction business in your state and want to organize the workers, but you learn that the majority of Spanish-speaking construction workers are not citizens or legal immigrants. You would certainly have trouble organizing them, because they may fear to speak up or even to identify themselves. This would be a major barrier to mobilizing them. Or take another example, perhaps closer to home: Imagine that you are a homosexual student on a conservative college campus where a number of hate-based crimes have been committed in recent months. You want to form a group of other homosexual, bisexual, and transgender students to pressure the university to protect your civil rights. Imagine the problems you would have in encouraging your peers to organize openly. They would be fearful, at worst, of violence against them and, at a minimum, of being ostracized.

In both examples, the pressure would be great to remain silent. Does this mean that neither type of group could be organized? Certainly not, but we must be clear about the barriers that may exist in order to overcome them. Moreover, we must look at barriers that are internalized in individuals and those that reflect the reality of collective action. For example, for you to join a group, you must have confidence in your own abilities to make an important contribution, and you also have to believe that your contribution will make a difference. As you will see, groups that are successful in recruiting and retaining members are sensitive to each concern and able to overcome these considerations.

The economist Mancur Olson described some of the key barriers facing people who share concerns and want to create formal problem-resolving organizations.[10] The first barrier is the tendency of individuals to allow others to do work on their behalf. (In essence, why should I spend my time and energy when others will do the work and I will benefit?) This is the **free-rider problem**. Olson notes that free riding is more likely to occur with groups that provide **public goods** or **collective goods**—things of value that cannot be given to one group exclusively but instead benefit society as a whole. Clean air is an example. Although one environmentalist group, or more likely a coalition of such groups, works to pass legislation to mandate cleaner automotive emissions, we all benefit from the clean air that legislation provides. The members of the group who gave their time, money, and energy are not the only beneficiaries—the entire community benefits, even though many people had not contributed to the group effort. Olson examined the incentives for joining groups from a rational perspective. A person will join a group when the benefits outweigh the costs, but if you can reap the benefits without incurring any costs, why join? As you will see, organized groups must be conscious of the free-rider problem so that they can provide other benefits to members to get them to join.

The second barrier that Olson identified in group formation is cost. This is a chief reason why many people who share common concerns do not organize. For one person to form a viable group that attracts many people and can be influential, money must be spent. It takes money to form and maintain a group, but it also takes a large commitment of time and energy. Some people and groups, of course, are better situated to bear the costs of organizing—most notably the affluent. Less affluent people frequently need to spend their time and energy earning money, including holding second jobs, and simply cannot volunteer or make large contributions to groups they may support.

The absence of a sense of political efficacy—the belief that one person can make a difference—is the third barrier to interest group formation that Olson identified. Even if you have confidence in your own abilities, you might fall into the pessimistic mind-set of "What can one person do?" Imagine that you are very concerned about changing the method of trash collection in your city (going from once to twice a week, for example). "But I'm only one person," you might think. "What can I do by myself?" Such pessimism affects not only people thinking of forming new groups but also those who might join or renew their membership in existing groups. Let's say that you're interested in promoting women's rights.

You investigate the National Organization for Women (NOW) and find that it advocates many positions with which you agree. You think about joining but then start to wonder: With 500,000 dues-paying members, what good will my $35 annual dues do? In truth, your dues alone won't do too much for the organization, but you might join once you understand the logic of collective action—that is, when you realize that the dues of 500,000 people come to $17.5 million, a sum that can make a large difference.

Overcoming Organizational Barriers

"What benefits do interest groups offer to attract members?"

—Student Question

Any group of people who hope to create and maintain an organization must understand these difficulties so that they can work to overcome them. Groups use many means to make membership attractive so that the benefits of membership outweigh the perceived costs. Organizations must also demonstrate to current and potential members that membership is important and that every member helps advance the collective goal. To overcome these barriers, **selective benefits** may be given to members—benefits that only group members receive, even if the collective good for which they strive remains available to everyone. For example, when the National Rifle Association (NRA) defeats a gun control bill, all citizens who believe in the rights of gun owners benefit, not just dues-paying NRA members. To encourage people to join, the NRA successfully recruits members by providing a variety of benefits. Because the organization works for a collective good—advances in protecting gun ownership apply not only to members of the organization but to all citizens—the NRA must fight the free-rider and efficacy problems and recruit dues-paying members to defer its maintenance costs. The following are some of the selective benefits the NRA provides to its members:

- **Material Benefits:** Insurance, training, and discounts. The group offers $25,000 life insurance policies to police officers who are members if they are killed in the line of duty. It also offers its members gun loss insurance, accidental death insurance at reduced rates, and discounts for eye care, car rentals, hotels, and airfares.
- **Solidary Benefits:** Its grassroots groups, Friends of the NRA, hosts dinners, national and state conventions, art contests, shooting competitions, safety and training classes and publishes magazines.
- **Purposive Benefits:** The feeling that one is doing something to advance one's view of the Second Amendment of the Constitution and to preserve access to shooting and hunting.

SOURCE: Adapted from National Rifle Association, http://www.nra.org

TYPES OF SELECTIVE BENEFITS As just mentioned in the NRA example, the first type of selective benefits is **material benefits**—tangible benefits that have value, such as magazines, discounts, and such paraphernalia as T-shirts and plaques. One of the first groups to offer material benefits was the American Farm Bureau. Many people, even nonfarmers, joined the organization in order to receive its insurance discounts. Today, the AARP uses a wider variety of material benefits to encourage membership, including discounts (on pharmacy services, airlines, automobiles, computers, vacations, insurance, restaurants, hotels, and cruises), tax information, magazine subscriptions, legal advice, and credit cards. In addition to material benefits, which are a major incentive for numerous individuals to join, many groups also offer **solidary benefits,** which are primarily social. Solidary benefits focus on providing activities and a sense of belonging—meetings, dinners, dances, and other such social activities that groups provide to give members a sense of belonging with other like-minded people. Finally, there are **purposive benefits** of group membership, "the intangible rewards that derive from the sense of satisfaction of having contributed to the attainment of a worthwhile cause."[11] Groups that organize blood drives often try to convey a purposive benefit. The sense of "helping people" and "doing good" are important motivators for many who give blood, encouraging them to endure a modest amount of discomfort and inconvenience. Many organizations rely on purposive benefits, typically in combination with other benefits, to attract members.

MEMBERSHIP REQUIRED Some organizations do not have to encourage membership; they can *demand* it. One prominent example of this is labor unions in many states. In accordance with the National Labor Relations Act of 1935, in some states unions can form agreements with employers that prevent non-union labor from being hired. In other states, "right to work" laws prohibit such contracts, but in nearly 30 states, people can be required, as a condition of employment, to join a union and pay dues. Unions, however, also provide many selective benefits (for example, insurance and employment security) as well as such solidary benefits as dinners, dances, and holiday parties.[12] Although these benefits are more important to recruit members in right-to-work states, they are still

■ **Equal Rights Amendment (ERA):** A proposed constitutional amendment that would have guaranteed equal rights for men and women. It was initially suggested following passage of the Nineteenth Amendment in 1920 but was not formally proposed by Congress until 1972 and failed to be ratified by the 1982 deadline.

EXAMPLE: *The fight for the ERA was bitter, with organized groups on each side. Even though it was never ratified, much of the overt discrimination it was designed to prevent has been eliminated from American society.*

used in states that compel membership in order to make the union more attractive and more popular among workers.

The Role of Interest Group Leaders

In addition to using incentives to mobilize support, interest groups have used inspirational leadership to build their membership. Charismatic and devoted leaders can entice potential members to join an organization. When people believe in the leaders of an organization, they are more supportive of its goals and more likely to support it financially. Effective leaders "sell" their issues to the public, thus attracting media attention and membership.

PATHWAYS | profile

Alice Stokes Paul

An instrumental actor in the fight for equal rights, Alice Stokes Paul lived to see remarkable changes for women in our society. Born in 1885 to Quaker parents in New Jersey, Paul's worldview was profoundly influenced by the central principle of the Quaker religion—equality of the sexes. She learned activism at the side of her mother, Tacie Paul, who brought young Alice with her to suffrage meetings.

Paul was highly educated, earning a bachelor's degree in biology from Swarthmore College in 1905, a master's in sociology from the University of Pennsylvania in 1907, a doctorate in economics from the University of Pennsylvania in 1912, and a law degree from Washington College of Law in 1922. Paul transformed from reserved young woman to militant leader when, on a visit to England in 1907, she met the "Pankhurst women," a mother and two daughters who were perhaps the most militant suffragists in England and whose motto was "Deeds, not words," the Pankhurst women took to criminal activities (such as breaking windows) to protest, often resulting in imprisonment. Paul was arrested three times in England. She returned to America determined to recharge the U.S. suffrage movement—and was arrested another three times.

To do so, she helped organize a publicity event to gain national attention—the first national suffrage parade in Washington, timed to coincide with Woodrow Wilson's presidential inauguration, on March 3, 1913. Onlookers attacked the women marchers, first verbally and then physically, while the police did little to intervene. In 1916, she founded the National Woman's Party to demand suffrage. The party organized individuals to stand outside the White House to protest the lack of suffrage for women. The protests continued even when the nation entered World War I, angering a large number of people who thought the women unpatriotic. The suffragists were arrested and sent to the filthy Occoquan Workhouse, a prison in Virginia, where the women, even the old and the frail, were beaten and brutalized. When the public learned of the prison's unsanitary conditions and the women's mistreatment, opinion toward the suffragists and their cause began to change. As a result, President Wilson reversed his previous opinion and embraced suffrage in 1917. Three years later, the Nineteenth Amendment was ratified, giving women the right to vote.

Paul's courageous behavior was important in changing the tides of opinion and winning women this key democratic right. After winning the vote, Paul continued fighting for equal rights for women, authoring the first **Equal Rights Amendment (ERA)**■, (which she called the "Lucretia Mott Amendment"). The amendment simply stated, "Men and women shall have equal rights throughout the United States and every place subject to its jurisdiction." The Equal Rights Amendment (ERA) failed to be ratified, but the legacy of this courageous woman still affects the rights of women today. On May 15, 2008, the House of Representatives passed legislation to award Alice Paul with the Congressional Gold Medal to honor her work for women's rights.

SOURCE: Alice Paul Institute, http://www.alicepaul.org ■

CHÁVEZ AND THE UFW César Chávez provides perhaps the best example of a leader's role in winning success for his organization in what appeared to be hopeless circumstances. Chávez grew up a poor migrant worker farming in states along the U.S.–Mexican border. Throughout his childhood, he was able to attend school only sporadically, because he had to move around with his family to work on farms. After serving in the U.S. Navy during World War II, Chávez returned to migratory farm work in Arizona and California. Seeing the desperate circumstances and gross exploitation of farm workers firsthand, Chávez dedicated his life to helping them organize and mobilize to demand fair treatment. In 1962, he organized the National Farm Workers Association, a labor union that later merged with other organizations to form the United Farm Workers of America (UFW). Chávez's UFW ultimately led a 5-year strike by California grape pickers and inspired a national boycott of California grapes. To draw national attention to the grape pickers' plight, Chávez headed a 340-mile march by farm workers across California in 1966 and went on a much-publicized, 25-day hunger strike in 1968. The UFW later led successful campaigns against lettuce growers and other agribusinesses (large, corporate farm industries), demanding fair treatment of farm workers. Chávez and his union gained crucial support from middle-class consumers who boycotted grapes and lettuce harvested by non-union labor, ultimately forcing the powerful agribusinesses to capitulate. What is perhaps most remarkable about the success of the

César Chávez was a dynamic leader who organized an unlikely group of activists—migrant farm workers (many of whom were not citizens). Pictured are César Chávez (third from the right) and Coretta Scott King (fourth from the right) leading a march in New York City to build support for a lettuce boycott in 1970. Through marches, protests and organized boycotts, Chávez was able to improve the working conditions and compensation for thousands of hard-working laborers. —***What characteristics do you think are the most important in distinguishing a truly great leader?***

DEBATE **Immigration**

groups that Chávez led is their ability to organize the most unlikely people—extremely poor, uneducated immigrants. By the early 1970s, the UFW had grown to 50,000 dues-paying members and had contracts with 300 growers. It succeeded not only in negotiating collective bargaining agreements but also in forcing the enactment of legislation to change migratory pickers' often deplorable working conditions. Activists and scholars alike agree that the success of the UFW owed much to Chávez's energy, appeal, and dedication to social justice. His charisma enabled Chávez to convince farm workers to unite and work with others—for example, California Governor Jerry Brown—to promote their collective interests. As a testimony to his commitment to social justice and nonviolent protest, Chávez was posthumously awarded the Presidential Medal of Freedom in 1994.

The UFW is a good example of a group of low-income people uniting to fight large corporations. By overcoming the barriers to organizing, having solid leadership, and providing benefits to members, groups of all kinds can successfully press for change. The challenges are often large, but the rewards can be profound.

Interest Group Mobilization

Practice Quiz

1. One of the strongest barriers to mobilizing potential members in socially vulnerable groups, such as gays or illegal immigrants, is
   a. the free-rider problem.
   b. the dangers to such individuals that might come with making their status public.
   c. the unlikelihood of government officials' listening to such individuals.
   d. the fact that their causes are not very strong.

2. Money is essential to the creation and ongoing support of an interest group.
   a. true **b.** false

3. If you are attending your labor union's holiday party, you are enjoying what sort of interest group benefit?
   a. material **b.** purposive
   c. solidary **d.** abstract

4. The unlikely success of the UFW in the early 1970s illustrates
   a. the power of a charismatic leader.
   b. the rising importance of technology in grassroots mobilization.
   c. the effectiveness of large-scale protest demonstrations.
   d. the efficacy of professional lobbyists.

Answers: 1-b, 2-a, 3-c, 4-a.

Discussion Questions

1. What would motivate a group of citizens to form an interest group? Consider this question from both a historical and a modern perspective.
2. What factors make some groups more successful and powerful than others? What role do leaders play in the formation, maintenance, and success of interest groups?

What YOU can do!

Go to the Sierra Club's Web page at **http://www.sierraclub.org**. What types of solidary, purposive, and material benefits does this organization provide to its members? Which benefits are likely to appeal to whom? Do you think any of the benefits would appeal to college students? Are the benefits likely to encourage the "typical" environmentalist to join the club?

Inside Lobbying: Appealing directly to lawmakers and legislative staff either in meetings, by providing research and information, or by testifying at committee hearings.

EXAMPLE: *Lobbyists often provide research and statistics to lawmakers and their aides during meetings on Capitol Hill in order to present the position of their clients.*

Gaining Access: Winning the opportunity to communicate directly with a legislator or a legislative staff member to present one's position on an issue of public policy.

EXAMPLE: *Interest groups often host parties or events to which elected officials and their staffs are invited with the hope that private conversations will occur.*

Inside Lobbying

(pages 404–407)

How have the tactics of appealing to public officials changed?

Politics is interactive. Successful political actors always pursue multiple ways to enhance their positions. The key to understanding influence in our governmental system is to realize that interest groups and individuals use different pathways, often at the same time, to advance their perspectives and petition their government. One pathway may prove a successful vehicle for a group at one point but fail at another time.

Outside lobbying, which we will discuss in the next section, aims primarily at influencing citizens rather than public officials; using the grassroots mobilization pathway, interest groups appeal indirectly to policymakers. By contrast, **inside lobbying** a tool used in the lobbying decision makers pathway, openly appeals to public officials in the legislature and the executive branch, which includes the bureaucracy. Because inside lobbying is a matter of personal contact with policymakers, it involves some form of direct interaction—often called **gaining access**—between a lobbyist and an agency official, a member of Congress, or a member of the legislator's staff. By having an opportunity to present the group's position directly to lawmakers, staffers, or officials, lobbyists have a greater chance of influencing the decision-making process. To be effective, however, lobbyists must be seen as trustworthy and must develop relationships with individuals who have influence in the relevant policy area.

Another inside lobbying tactic is to testify at congressional committee hearings. Such hearings normally occur when Congress is considering a bill for passage, when committees are investigating a problem or monitoring existing programs, or when a nominee for a high executive or judicial position is testifying before a confirmation vote. Testifying allows an interest group to present its views in public and "on the record," potentially raising its visibility and appealing to political actors. Although this is a more visible form of inside lobbying than privately meeting a policymaker in an office or a restaurant, it is often considered window dressing. Most people who follow politics seriously feel it is not a very effective tactic.

As you can see in Table 11.2, a great deal of money is spent by organizations to lobby the federal government. Such lavish spending, coupled with concern over corruption, has prompted legislation to regulate lobbying—although as you'll see shortly, the legislation was not strict enough to prevent the most distressing lobbying scandal in recent times.

TABLE 11.2 | **Spending on Inside Lobbying**

In addition to campaign contributions to elected officials and candidates, companies, labor unions, and other organizations spend billions of dollars each year to lobby Congress and federal agencies. Some special interests retain lobbying firms, many of them located along Washington's legendary K Street; others have lobbyists working in-house. A special interest's lobbying activity may go up or down over time, depending on how much attention the federal government is giving their issues. Particularly active clients often retain multiple lobbying firms, each with a team of lobbyists, to press their case for them.

CATEGORY	REPRESENTATIVE INTEREST GROUP	AMOUNT GROUP SPENT ON LOBBYING IN 2006
Corporations	AT&T	$23,160,220
Agriculture	American Farm Bureau Federation	$5,511,204
Trade associations	U.S. Chamber of Commerce	$45,740,000
Labor unions	Teamsters Union	$759,000
Professional associations	American Bar Association	$1,180,000
Citizen groups	Gun Owners of America	$600,278
	AARP	$23,160,000
Universities	University of Texas	$280,000
Governmental units	City of Los Angeles	$60,000

SOURCE: Center for Responsive Politics. http://www.opensecrets.org/lobbyists

You Are a Lobbyist

Two important parts of the Lobbying Disclosure Act of 1995 regulate direct lobbying. The first component of the law tries to provide "transparency" by requiring lobbyists to register with the federal government and report their activities. Many people believe that having full disclosure will raise public confidence in the system by minimizing the potential for abuse and corruption. The second set of provisions in the law bars certain types of informal lobbying activities that have been used in the past, such as giving expensive gifts, purchasing expensive meals, and paying for trips for members of Congress. Fees (called *honoraria*) for speaking engagements were outlawed in 1992. Even with this legislation, however, many people are concerned with the perception of impropriety and the potential for corruption; hence watchdog groups are valuable for increasing public trust.

"Doesn't inside lobbying sometimes become an attempt at bribery? How can we promote honest lobbying?"
—Student Question

This concern was proved well founded in 2006 when Jack Abramoff, a top political lobbyist, pleaded guilty to three felony accounts of tax evasion, fraud, and conspiracy to bribe a public official. In a deal that required him to cooperate with a broad investigation into public corruption, Abramoff admitted to corrupting governmental officials and defrauding his clients of $25 million. He spent money lavishly on lawmakers, their staffs, and executive branch officials, paying for luxury trips, expensive meals, entertainment, and tickets to sporting events. Moreover, he hired spouses of officials he was lobbying in efforts to manipulate their behavior. One charge Abramoff faced was that he arranged for a series of payments, adding up to $50,000, to the wife of a congressional staffer, who then helped defeat Internet gambling restrictions that were opposed by one of his clients.

The inquiry into Abramoff's activities began in 2004, when it became public that he and a partner had received $82 million from Indian tribes.[13] Thus far the investigation has led to the conviction of 12 individuals, including ex-Representative Bob Ney, former White House official David Safavian, and former Interior Secretary Steven Griles.

The largest lobbying scandal in contemporary times erupted when former high-powered lobbyist Jack Abramoff pled guilty to three felony counts on January 3, 2006. The guilty pleas followed months of intense investigations and will likely result in the indictment of others. Pictured above is Abramoff being sworn in before a U.S. Senate Committee hearing on Indian Affairs in 2004. ***—What do you think needs to be done to prevent this type of corruption?***

PHOTO: Carol T. Powers/The New York Times

STUDENT | PROFILE

In 2006, Alia Elnahas, a high school student at T. C. Williams High School in Alexandria, Virginia, founded United Student Activists (USA) to promote positive forms of student activism. USA is a student-based organization dedicated to promoting peace through political, environmental, and community activism. The group believes that peace can come through informed and nonviolent political action, the development of healthy energy sources, and a healthy environment free of toxins and pollution. In addition, they believe that volunteering in their community and helping to strengthen community ties between diverse groups will make the world a more peaceful place. ■

COMPARATIVE

Comparing Interest Groups

The presidential pardon of a Thanksgiving turkey provided a timely opportunity for political humorists to joke about the serious concern regarding political corruption and lobbying. ***—How widespread do you think such corruption is? Do you believe that media attention is proportionate to the problem?***

SOURCE: Mike Luckovich's Editorial Cartoons; © 2006 Mike Luckovich

PATHWAYS | of change from around the world

Kris Woodall had every reason to do nothing but complain. Instead, he took action. Being periodically homeless over a 2-year period motivated him to get active in his Hull, UK, community. In 2005, then 20 years old, he along with Richard Ellarby, then 16 years old, joined forces to found the Coalition of Hull's Young People (CHYP). The CHYP was created to challenge a local ordinance that allowed police to disperse outside gatherings of young people. Rather than simply sulk away, these young people came together to successfully challenge the ordinance by creating a petition, gathering signatures, and meeting with the police, city council, and other governmental officials. The group then turned their efforts toward helping a fellow volunteer, a young Afghani asylum seeker, receive permission to remain in the country. The CHYP continues to be successful in organizing and motivating young people to get involved in their community. Woodall's general motto, which is evident in his actions, is to get involved so that older people take you seriously. ■

Sheryl Crow, along with Don Henley, formed the Recording Artists Coalition (RAC) in 1998 to represent the interests of recording artists. Pictured above is Crow performing at a RAC benefit concert in 2002. ***—Do you think that musicians have legitimate concerns in trying to limit music sharing? Do you think that individuals have the right to share legally purchased music files with others? Can you think of a reasonable compromise that might be negotiated?***

Inside Lobbying

Practice Quiz

1. Inside lobbying involves a form of direct interaction to be effective, which is
   - **a.** gaining access.
   - **b.** insider trading.
   - **c.** working within the retired military officers corps.
   - **d.** bureaucratic infighting.
2. To be effective at inside lobbying, lobbyists must.
   - **a.** be seen as trustworthy.
   - **b.** develop relationships with influential individuals.
   - **c.** testify before congressional committees.
   - **d.** a, b, and c
3. Among those interest groups charted in Table 11.2, which group spent the most money on inside lobbying?
   - **a.** American Farm Bureau
   - **b.** A tie between AT&T and AARP
   - **c.** U.S. Chamber of Commerce
   - **d.** American Bar Association
4. Hosting a fundraiser for a political candidate is an example of what?
   - **a.** honoraria
   - **b.** gaining access
   - **c.** political corruption
   - **d.** new form of political fundraising

Answers: 1-a, 2-d, 3-d, 4-b.

Discussion Questions

1. Discuss at least two factors that are essential to be an effective inside lobbyist. Why are these factors so critical?
2. A lot of money is spent on inside lobbying by interest groups. What impact does this have on our electoral system? What does it tell us about the effectiveness of ordinary citizens?

What **YOU** can do!

Using LexisNexis, CQ, or the Thomas portal to the Library of Congress (**http://thomas.loc.gov/**), look up the Congressional record for hearings on a topic of your choosing. Can you identify any individuals we might consider to be engaging in inside lobbying? Are all sides of a particular issue represented?

Outside Lobbying (Grossroots Lobbying): Activities directed at the general public to raise awareness and interest and to pressure officials.

EXAMPLE: *E-mail alerts that groups send to members to notify them of political events are examples of ways in which interest groups try to mobilize their supporters and sympathizers.*

Outside Lobbying

(pages 408–413)

How do interest groups mobilize the masses?

Outside lobbying (or **grassroots lobbying**) is the attempt to influence decision makers indirectly, by influencing the public. In appealing directly to the public, interest groups are trying to build public sentiment in order to bring pressure to bear on the officials who will actually make the decisions. David Truman, in his classic analysis of interest groups, *The Governmental Process,* noted that organized interests engage in "programs of propaganda, though rarely so labeled, designed to affect opinions concerning interests" in hopes that concerned citizens will then lobby the government on behalf of whatever the group is trying to accomplish.[14]

"How do interest groups decide when to appeal directly to the public? Are some types of groups more successful using this tactic?"

—Student Question

There are several advantages in appealing to the public. First, an interest group can indirectly use the people through the elections pathway to directly affect the selection of officials. Citizens can also pressure officials to take action. Moreover, pressure from interest groups can influence which issues the government decides to address as well as the policies it adopts, modifies, or abandons. Appealing directly to the people can also be advantageous because citizens can take direct actions that can be used to further the group's agenda. By lobbying supporters and the general public, interest groups seek to demonstrate an issue's salience, showing public officials that the issue is important to the people. To succeed, interest groups often have to appeal to an audience beyond their supporters. Sometimes escalating conflict surrounding the issue can be a successful means of attracting public interest, in turn forcing elected officials to get involved.

Examining the activities of more than 90 interest group leaders, political scientist Ken Kollman found that 90 percent of interest groups engage in some kind of outside lobbying.[15] They do this because it can be very effective. Proportionately, more Americans than ever before are communicating—via letters, faxes, phone calls, and e-mails—with members of Congress, but this surge in communication is not spontaneous, however. Much of it is the direct result of coordinated efforts by organized interests.[16] This communication is intended to demonstrate to public officials that their constituents care about an issue—and that the public officials had better act.

Grassroots Mobilization

Interest groups increasingly are relying on grassroots mobilization as a form of outside lobbying to pressure policymakers. A trade association executive interviewed by Kenneth Goldstein gave a very good definition of grassroots mobilization: "The identification, recruitment, and mobilization of constituent-based political strength capable of influencing political decisions."[17]

Grassroots work is very difficult to measure, and its success is perhaps even more difficult to assess. Most experts, however, believe that grassroots mobilization is becoming far more common. Goldstein found that most Fortune 500 companies have full-time grassroots coordinators with solid plans to present their point of view by stirring up citizen interest, and that the media cover grassroots lobbying with greater frequency today.

While many believe that campaigning door-to-door is "old school," this can still be a very effective tactic. ***—For what types of groups do you think this tactic might be the most effective? Why?***

Direct Contact: Face-to-face meetings or telephone conversations between individuals.

EXAMPLE: *Personal interactions are seen as a very effective way to communicate and persuade others. As such, lobbyists try very hard to develop relationships with public officials in order to have opportunities for direct contact in either formal (for example, in their offices) or informal (social) settings.*

Direct Mail: Information sent by mail to a large number of people to advertise, market concepts, solicit orders, or, contributions.

EXAMPLE: *Political candidates often send mail to voters to present their issue stances and biographical information in order to persuade them to donate money to their campaign and/or vote for them in the upcoming election.*

Pictured is Cindy Sheehan, who became an antiwar activist after her son, Casey, was killed in the Iraq War on April 4, 2004. To raise public awareness of her concerns, Ms. Sheehan created "Camp Casey," a temporary camp a few miles from President Bush's Crawford, Texas, home. Her actions brought both criticism and praise.

Grassroots Lobbying Tactics

Many people believe that indirect lobbying is a new phenomenon. It is not. Indirect lobbying has been going on in our country since its earliest days, although the tools and tactics have evolved with the emergence of new technology.

TRADITIONAL TACTICS One of the earliest forms of grassroots mobilization, going back to the days of the antislavery movement and still used because it is so effective, is **direct contact**. Having committed supporters personally contact fellow citizens is a valuable tool for interest groups. Seeing others who care deeply enough to give of their time and energy can stimulate people to become involved with a cause. The civil rights movement effectively used direct contact to build grassroots support.

> "How do interest groups mobilize the masses, and is this effective?"
> —Student Question

Direct mail is another way for interest groups to contact potential supporters. Modern technology permits mailings to be personalized in ways that allow a group to frame its message narrowly so that it appeals to specific types of people. Such mailings have been shown to be effective in many cases, but they can be very expensive to produce. Knowing a good deal about the individuals targeted in its direct-mail campaign helps an interest group personalize its message and thus make it more efficient. Because modern technology collects and stores so much personal information, interest groups with substantial financial resources can acquire what they want to know about potential recipients, allowing them to exploit this form of propaganda more effectively.

"Getting members is about scaring the hell out of people,"[18] one interest group leader has said of direct mail. By playing on fear and predicting dire consequences if supporters don't unite, the direct-mail letter's tone is designed to elicit quick action—especially to raise money and stimulate an outpouring of letters and e-mails to legislators.

In their attempts to influence public opinion, interest groups often directly distribute information—including brochures and reprinted editorials—to potential supporters and policymakers. In fighting President Truman's plan for federal health insurance in the late 1940s, the American Medical Association (AMA) made one of the earliest and most successful uses of brochures and pamphlets. To bring public opinion to bear on policymakers, the AMA's literature, distributed through doctors' offices, made grim predictions about the potentially dire effects of "socialized medicine." The use of inflammatory language to exploit people's fears became a tactic that interest groups still commonly use today.

Historically, interest groups have also used the court pathway (litigation) to promote or resist change and to shape public opinion. Interest groups that are unsuccessful in bringing about change using other techniques often turn to litigation, with the most famous example being the NAACP's challenge to school segregation. Realizing that African Americans in the South were denied access to the elections pathway and were limited in their ability to use the lobbying decision makers pathway to pressure officials, the NAACP decided in

CONNECT THE LINK

(Chapter **5**, page **182–185**) Do you think this strategy could be used effectively for groups that are seeking greater protection of their civil rights today?

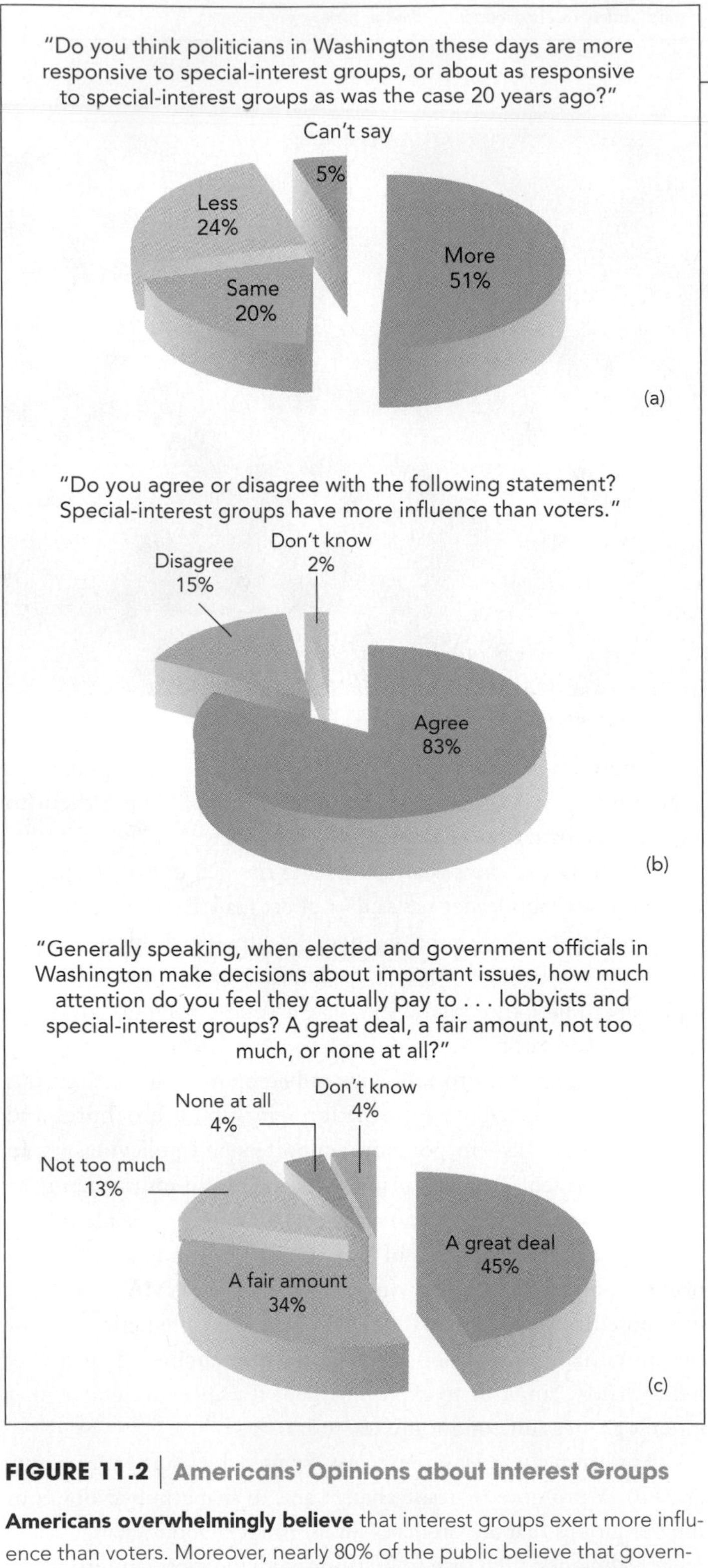
"Do you think politicians in Washington these days are more responsive to special-interest groups, or about as responsive to special-interest groups as was the case 20 years ago?"
Can't say
5%
Less
24%
Same
20%
More
51%
(a)
"Do you agree or disagree with the following statement? Special-interest groups have more influence than voters."
Don't know
2%
Disagree
15%
Agree
83%
(b)
"Generally speaking, when elected and government officials in Washington make decisions about important issues, how much attention do you feel they actually pay to . . . lobbyists and special-interest groups? A great deal, a fair amount, not too much, or none at all?"
Don't know
4%
None at all
4%
Not too much
13%
A great deal
45%
A fair amount
34%
(c)

FIGURE 11.2 | **Americans' Opinions about Interest Groups**

Americans overwhelmingly believe that interest groups exert more influence than voters. Moreover, nearly 80% of the public believe that government officials pay at least a fair amount of attention to interest groups when making important decisions. ***—Do you think that the public has legitimate concerns?***

SOURCE: Data Provided by The Roper Center for Publich Opinion Research, University of Connecticut.

the 1940s to rely on the courts to raise consciousness and force change. As discussed in LINK Chapter 5, pages 182–185, in 1954 its efforts resulted in the *Brown* v. *Board of Education* decision, which declared school segregation unconstitutional. Women have also been successful in using the court pathway in such areas as sexual harassment, employment discrimination, and domestic violence, as have disabled Americans and other marginalized groups.

Interest groups also use events and activities to influence the public and pressure policymakers. Many of these events are designed to provide members with solidary benefits (discussed earlier in the chapter), but they can also raise the organization's image in the community and demonstrate its importance. Labor unions and public interest groups are most likely to engage in this type of behavior, organizing rallies and marches to promote their cause. Groups that feel they are being ignored or marginalized often turn to other forms of political expression, including protests (the grassroots mobilization pathway). Peace groups in the United States and around the world have organized rallies to protest American wars from Vietnam to Iraq. Labor unions sometimes rely on marches and rallies to show the strength of their membership and thus remind policymakers of their potential to influence many people. Twentieth-century American civil rights organizations found a combination of boycotts, rallies, marches, and protests to be very effective tools in their fight to end segregation and racism. This route doesn't work for everyone: Trade associations, professional associations, and corporations have rarely, if ever, used protest demonstrations.

NEWER TOOLS OF INDIRECT LOBBYING The development in recent decades of more sophisticated means of communication has given interest groups far more options than they once had to motivate supporters, recruit new members, and mobilize the public. To sway public opinion, organized interest groups have aggressively and imaginatively used the media. As you can see in Figure 11.2, the public believes that interest groups are very effective in manipulating the media, though it is difficult to gauge how much manipulation actually occurs.

One way that organized groups try to exploit the media to advance their cause is by manipulating what gets reported and occasionally, they succeed. Pressured by deadlines, some reporters are willing to use in their stories information presented by interest groups. In this era of heightened expectations for investigative reporting, interest groups often try, sometimes covertly, to advance

> "How do interest groups manipulate the media?"
> —Student Question

Celebrities have the ability to garner media attention more easily than others do. Pictured above is Brad Pitt who has been very active and vocal about the need to rebuild New Orleans afer the vast devastation wrought by Hurricane Katrina. ***—Do you Pay more or less attention to an issue if a celebrity is involved? How influential do you think they are in altering public opinion and/or motivating activism?***

their views by prompting media exposés of controversial issues. Groups also like to stage visually appealing pseudo-events, such as schoolchildren marching in support of higher teacher pay, thus increasing the likelihood that the event will be shown on local TV and maybe even make the national news.

Many Americans believe there is an antibusiness bias in news coverage. Whether or not such a bias actually exists, citizen groups are often able to invoke sympathy in ways that large corporations cannot. For example, a news story about a local citizen group fighting some huge, impersonal corporation to protect a beautiful stream from pollution is very attractive. Such "David versus Goliath" stories have a human interest component that is quite appealing to media outlets, which know that people like to see the underdog win. To counter this perception of bias, many corporations and industrial groups spend large sums on public relations campaigns to soften their image. Well-heeled interest groups advertise in major newspapers and magazines as well as on TV to increase their visibility and improve their public image. Many of these ads are noncommercial—they aren't trying to sell anything or directly attract members but instead are designed to generate favorable public opinion. Groups also try to have their advocates appear as experts on talk shows. Having someone present the group's position on *Larry King Live*, for example, raises the group's visibility and credibility in important ways—because, as when using the lobbying decision makers pathway to influence public officials, groups must appear credible and trustworthy.

Over the past two decades, the Internet has offered interest groups some of the best possibilities for new tactics. Organized groups can use the Internet to advance their cause in many ways, including Web pages, e-mail campaigns, bulletin boards, and chat rooms. The Internet has great potential for mobilizing supporters and raising money, but not everyone can readily use it. Younger people who are more affluent and better educated have home access to the Internet at far greater rates than older, poorer, and less educated people. Interest groups should therefore be aware that certain portions of the public are hard to target with the Internet. Nevertheless, the Internet is a very appealing tool to communicate with the public.

Although the Internet has great potential for reaching people quickly, many analysts question whether it has a significant impact on public opinion and behavior. Most people who visit an environmentalist group's Web page, for example, probably are already committed environmentalists and are not necessarily being persuaded by what they read. Political supporters of a particular campaign are more likely to visit the candidate's Web page compared with people who are undecided or who support an opposing candidate. This does not mean that the Web page is irrelevant. Visiting a Web page may influence some people's opinions, and Web pages can certainly stir interested people to take action—and not just by sending money. Imagine someone who is interested in protecting a local lake that is threatened by pollution. That person might care a great deal about the issue but lack the tools to act. Visiting the Web pages of environmentalist groups might be very helpful to such a person, especially if the groups highlight the actions of individuals in local communities and provide specific organizational tips. The interested environmentalist might learn how to become an activist in the cause.

The Internet has the advantage of offering speed and convenience. Through e-mail campaigns and alerts, groups can communicate to their members instantaneously and virtually free of charge. Web pages communicate information, stimulate supporters to contact their representatives, and raise money for the group or its cause. Cliff Landesman of the Internet Nonprofit Center identifies eight purposes for which interest groups use the Internet: publicity, public education, communication, volunteer recruitment, research, advocacy, service provision, and fundraising.[19] Certainly, not all groups pursue all eight of these potential uses; many focus on just one or two. The Million Mom March against gun violence, held on Mother's Day in 2000, used the Internet quite effectively to mobilize support-

CONNECT THE LINK
(Chapter **12**, pages **442–449**) Many believe that interest groups have a corrupting influence in elections. Do you agree?

CONNECT THE LINK
(Chapter **12**, pages **446–449**) Do you think the latest round of campaign finance reform (the Bipartisan Campaign Finance Act of 2002) makes people more confident in our system of campaign finance?

The "Million Mom March" was a grassroots movement started by Donna Dees-Thomases and other mothers upset over gun violence. The first March was held on May 14, 2000, when thousands of supporters came together at the National Mall in Washington, D.C., to demand new gun control laws. The march received a good deal of national media attention. ***—Why do you think that organizations (such as Mothers Against Drunk Driving or MADD) and movements led by mothers gain more media attention?***

ers. This march of nearly 750,000 individuals started with a Web site created by one woman, Donna Dees-Thomases, whose idea quickly grew into a national movement. Supporters used Web pages to organize the march, create local chapters, provide logistics, attract media coverage, and raise money.[20]

Campaign Activities

As you will discover in LINK Chapter 12, pages 442–449, in the elections pathway, interest groups play a very active role in local, state, and national election campaigns. Organized groups obviously want to influence elections so that individuals who support their cause will get into office. Groups also want to influence the public during elections in order to influence incumbent policymakers. Groups get involved in elections in many different ways, their central motivation being to advance their own cause.

Most interest groups take part in electoral politics by rating and endorsing candidates. At every point on the political spectrum, special-interest groups rate the candidates to help influence their supporters and sympathizers. A typical example is the Christian Coalition, which provides voter guides (distributed in sympathetic churches across the nation) that examine candidates' voting records and note what percentage of the time they vote "correctly" on what the group considers key issues. In the same way, the AFL-CIO rates members of Congress on their votes regarding issues important to organized labor, likewise giving its supporters a voting cue. So, too, does the U.S. Chamber of Commerce, from the business perspective.

Today, many people worry about the influence that special-interest groups have on elections—and especially about the impact of interest group money on electoral outcomes and the subsequent actions of elected officials. It is important to note, however, that interest groups are simply associations of like-minded people. In a democracy, citizens *should* affect elections, even if those citizens are acting collectively. So, while we should certainly scrutinize interest groups' contributions to candidates and political parties, interest group involvement does not necessarily pollute the electoral system. Interest groups can serve as a political cue to their members, other interest groups, voters, and the media. When an interest group donates money to a candidate, it is making a public show of support that can be an important cue for others, either for or against that candidate.

Money has always been important in politics; today's requirement for limited campaign contributions and full disclosure (see LINK Chapter 12, pages 446–449) makes the system more transparent and honest. In the days when we did not know how much candidates received in contributions, or from whom they recieved contributions, we might have naively thought that there was less corruption; however, the opposite was probably true. Despite ready access to contributions, greater scrutiny today may in fact ensure that politicians have to be more honest.

Outside Lobbying

Practice Quiz

1. What is the primary difference between inside and outside lobbying?
   - **a.** Inside lobbying requires more money than outside lobbying.
   - **b.** Inside lobbying has faster results than outside lobbying.
   - **c.** Outside lobbying relies on mobilizing the public to influence decision makers while inside lobbying relies on more direct contact between lobbyists and decision makers.
   - **d.** Outside lobbying is largely considered less effective than inside lobbying.
2. What is the primary problem with direct-mail lobbying?
   - **a.** It is an indirect approach to legislators and thus is limited in effect.
   - **b.** "Junk" mail often alienates people.
   - **c.** It appeals to only one person at a time.
   - **d.** It is expensive.
3. What other types of events and activities can interest groups use to influence public opinion and pressure policymakers?
   - **a.** organizing rallies and marches
   - **b.** mass demonstrations
   - **c.** boycotts
   - **d.** a, b, and c
4. Outside lobbying can be helpful in increasing public interest toward issues that would otherwise be ignored.
   - **a.** true
   - **b.** false

Answers: 1-c, 2-d, 3-d, 4-a.

Discussion Questions

1. Much time is spent testifying before congressional committees. Is this an effective tactic for special interests? What are some alternatives to this tactic?
2. Select one type of event or activity an interest group can use to influence public opinion; discuss its merits and deficiencies.

What **YOU** can do!

Visit the Web site of any interest group engaged in grassroots mobilization. How are they using electronic media (such as blogs) to connect with potential and current members? Do they use any kind of rating system to evaluate how public officials have responded to their cause?

The Final Verdict: *The* Influence *of* Interest Groups (pages 414–415)

Are interest groups helpful for democracy?

One of the most troubling aspects for many when they consider interest groups is the perception that interest groups corrupt politics and politicians. As we have seen, there have been times when corruption does occur, but more often, it does not. Interest groups do raise and spend a good deal of money, but organizing a diverse society is expensive. Some interests—corporations and professions, for example—are better able to bear these than others, such as ordinary citizens. Despite this, as we have seen, citizen groups have thrived and brought about great change.

Bias in Representation: Who Participates?

At first glance, given the variety of groups, you might think that interest groups represent all Americans equally. They don't. Activists are not typical Americans—most of them are drawn from the elite strata of society. Activists are more politically sophisticated, more knowledgeable, and more involved in their communities. All Americans have the right to form groups, but the fact is that for many reasons, many categories of Americans do not.[21] Educational attainment, family income, and social class are among the largest factors in predicting participation in organized interest groups—and in politics more generally. There are many exceptions to this general pattern. The least biased form of political participation is voting; not surprisingly, the most skewed form of participation is making campaign contributions: People with more education and more income predominate. Participating in interest groups falls roughly between these two extremes. Moreover, whites and high-income people are encouraged by political leaders to participate in politics (from joining interest groups to being persuaded to run for elective office) far more often than people of color and those with low incomes.[22]

Because all American citizens can potentially participate in politics, many observers are not concerned that some Americans choose to remain politically uninvolved. Many other observers, however, are troubled by these patterns of unequal participation and mobilization when they look at the problem from an overall perspective. As Figure 11.3 shows, there is a profound difference among the races, and within races along gender lines, in the level of political participation in the United States. Participation allows voices to be heard, but people do wonder whether all voices are being heard equally effectively. When looking at politics in the aggregate, it is also clear that the immense economic resources of big business give it a disproportionate level of political influence. However, as the political scientist James Q. Wilson has noted, "One

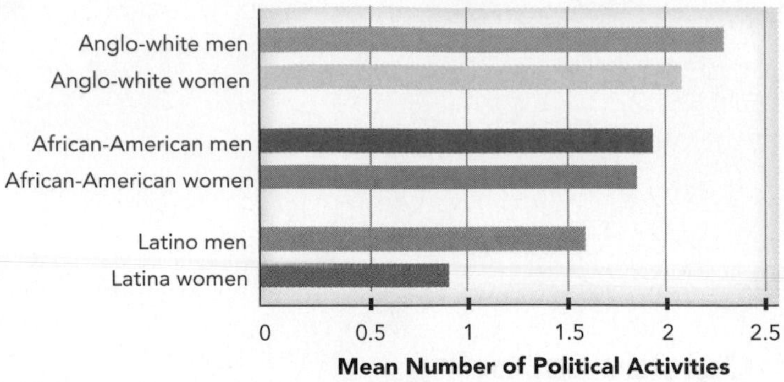

FIGURE 11.3 | **Mean Number of Political Activities**

On the whole, men participate more in politics than women do. Moreover, people of different races are more or less politically engaged. ***—Do you believe that these differences are important? Are you surprised by how few political activities the average person performs?***

SOURCE: Reprinted by permission of the publisher from *The Private Roots of Public Action: Gender, Equality, and Political Participation* by Nancy Burns, Kay Lehman Schlozman, and Sidney Verba, p. 93. (Cambridge: Harvard University Press, Copyright © 2001 by the President and Fellows of Harvard College.)

cannot assume that the disproportionate possession of certain resources leads to the disproportionate exercise of political power. Everything depends on whether a resource can be converted into power, and at what rate and at what price."[23]

The Age of Apathy?

The level of the American people's engagement with their society and government has caused concern for years and has received even more attention recently. As this book makes clear, to maintain a participatory democracy, it is of fundamental importance that citizens be engaged in politics and community action. Today, many observers of the American scene worry about what appears to be a heightened level of public disengagement from politics, and they dread the consequences in terms of diminished political trust, efficacy, and tolerance.

Nearly a century ago, L. Judson Hanifan became one of the first scholars to raise concerns about political disengagement in the United States. Hanifan is thought to have coined the phrase **social capital**■, which he defined as "good will, fellowship, sympathy, and social intercourse among the individuals and families who make up a social unit."[24] He argued that when citizens come together in social and personal interactions, they become accustomed to cooperating with one another and will often use this social capital to work together to improve community well-being.

Many scholars believe that social capital has been steadily declining since World War II and that for several generations, Americans have become too focused on their individual wants and needs at the expense of the collective good. This conclusion, however, is controversial. Some scholars suggest that the level of social engagement has not declined substantially but rather has changed in nature. Membership in traditional organizations (such as the PTA, bowling leagues, and the Girl Scouts and Boy Scouts) seems to be

Social Capital: Networks of relationships among individuals, groups, and institutions that foster trust and cooperation to solve societal problems and establish norms for appropriate behavior in pursuit of mutual benefits and shared interests.

EXAMPLE: *Many people are concerned that the Internet diminishes relationships between people and may harm social capital.*

in steady decline, but participation in other community organizations (such as youth sports leagues and neighborhood groups) appears to be growing.[25] A prominent social scientist, Theda Skocpol, has found a significant growth in membership in three types of organizations: advocacy groups, public interest groups, and business or professional associations.[26] By looking at the four aspects of social capital—associations, trust, civic participation, and volunteering—Robert Wuthnow has provided a good structure to analyze the issue of civic engagement.[27] As we have seen, membership levels in traditional organizations are decreasing, but this decline has been almost offset by increasing participation in other organizations. (Overall, there appears to have been a small decrease in associational membership.)

Volunteering has seen a dramatic increase: Wuthnow found that 46 percent of Americans volunteered in the early 1990s, compared to only 26 percent in the early 1970s.[28] As noted, volunteering is more common than ever today, especially among younger Americans. A recent international study found that the United States has the highest levels of volunteerism in the industrial world.[29] Moreover, concerted student-centered initiatives exist on many college campuses throughout the country to engage students in politics and in their communities.

The past decades, however, have witnessed a dramatic drop in levels of trust in government institutions and one's fellow citizens. In 1964, some 76 percent of Americans said that they could trust officials in Washington to do what was right most or all of the time; by 2004, that number had decreased to 47 percent.[30] Such a dramatic decline in trust is troubling, because the consequences can be vast and dramatic. Moreover, the disapproval ratings for the federal government continue to climb.

Thus we have no clear diagnosis regarding the health of civic engagement in the United States; however, nearly all observers agree that we are at a pivotal moment. As Theda Skocpol has noted, civic engagement is changing dramatically, and further technological changes are likely to continue this process.[31] The growth in advocacy groups raises concerns that political activity is increasingly becoming the sphere of paid professionals, offset by substantially less involvement by "common people." Some believe this new era of advocacy signals that we are entering an era of more and more leaders and fewer and fewer followers.

The Final Verdict: The Influence of Interest Groups

Practice Quiz

1. According to recent research, participating in organized interest groups usually makes people
   - **a.** more inclined to participate in other forms of political activity.
   - **b.** less inclined to participate in other forms of political activity.
   - **c.** less inclined to make financial contributions to a political campaign.
   - **d.** more likely to denigrate the political process in this country.
2. The scholar Theda Skocpol has found that membership has actually risen in three kinds of groups:
   - **a.** fraternal orders, unions, and political parties.
   - **b.** public interest groups, professional organizations, and advocacy groups.
   - **c.** alumni associations, recreational clubs (such as bridge and poker clubs), and religious-based coalitions.
   - **d.** philanthropic societies, Internet-based groups, and hobbyists' clubs.
3. Recent studies of the civic engagement patterns of young adults find that they are
   - **a.** volunteering in the community more but trusting people (including the government) less.
   - **b.** caring more about their own contentment and less about the feeling of others (especially the poor).
   - **c.** deepening their engagement in the political system as voters and joining advocacy groups in record numbers.
   - **d.** returning, in increasing numbers, to the activist habits of the young adults of the 1960s and 1970s.

Answers: 1-a, 2-b, 3-b, 4-a

Discussion Questions

1. Why do interest groups need money? How do they raise money? How is technology changing the patterns and tactics of fundraising?
2. How influential are interest groups in the United States? How influential does the public *think* interest groups are? What are some of the consequences of this public perception?

What **YOU** can do!

Survey your friends to see what kinds of involvement, if any, they have in their community. Based on your findings, you could prepare a resource guide to help your friends get more involved in their community. You could provide information about local volunteer opportunities, such as tutoring programs in local public schools, Big Brother/Big Sister programs, and local scouting organizations. Helping others get involved is a very rewarding form of political participation in itself.

CONNECT THE LINK
(Chapter **14,** page **494–496**) In your opinion, is the influence of interest groups in electoral politics greater or weaker than it was twenty years ago?

Conclusion

We have a "how-to" element in our government, focusing on bargaining and compromise that is public driven. Organized groups are among the most important actors in motivating the public, yet as a society, we have mixed feelings about interest groups.

On the one hand, we acknowledge the need for, and show our support for organized action. To help influence change, many of us join organized interests and readily form associations that range from parent organizations in schools and neighborhood improvement groups to larger, nationally oriented organizations. In fact, approximately 65 percent of Americans over the age of 18 belong to at least one politically active organization.[32] Even if we don't join organizations, many of us feel that an existing group is representing our interests. For example, many senior citizens are not dues-paying members of the AARP but nevertheless feel that the group represents them.

On the other hand, we also fear organized interests. Polls consistently show that Americans are wary about the influence of "special interests" and believe that the "common person" is not adequately represented. One lobbyist described others' perception of his profession thusly: "Being a lobbyist has long been synonymous in the minds of many Americans with being a glorified pimp."[33] Much of the public believes that interest groups have a great deal of influence with government officials and that their influence has been increasing. Moreover, fully 83 percent of Americans believe that interest groups have more influence than voters. Such feelings were a large reason the public supported the Bipartisan Campaign Reform Act of 2002, which we will discuss in LINK Chapter 12, pages 494–496.

Participating in groups affects individual citizens in several positive ways. Those who are members of organized interest groups are also more likely to participate in other forms of political activity, at least according to some researchers. Allan Cigler and Mark Joslyn found that people who participated in group activities had higher levels of political tolerance, more trust in elected officials, and a greater sense of political efficacy.[34]

Other research that focused on the impact of interest groups on social issues, however, paints a different picture. Although participation in interest groups may have positive effects on individuals, the growth of interest groups does correlate with the growth in distrust of government and fellow citizens, voter cynicism, and lower voting rates. Some hypothesize that when interest groups raise the level of conflict surrounding an issue, they simply alienate the public, thus raising the levels of citizen distrust, but a different interpretation is also possible. Just the reverse may be true: that interest groups are formed because citizens *do* distrust the government, *are* cynical, and *do* have low participation rates. It could be that people join interest groups in order to organize an otherwise chaotic world.

Even groups that seem to be advancing the best interest of the public may not be. Trade-offs are often inevitable. Consider environmentalist groups. They work to protect the environment so that all of us can benefit, but in the process, they sometimes create difficulties for a community or certain individuals. Forcing a mining company out of business, for example, might be very important for the local ecosystem but may also throw a large number of people out of work. Hence, it is debatable whether the behavior of the interest group is in the best interest of the mining community. In this example, the miners are certainly more interested in protecting their jobs than the environmentalists, who may live on the other side of the country. Such concerns and debates are important when we examine interest group behavior. To understand fully both the potentially positive and potentially negative impacts of interest group actions, a balanced analysis is essential.

Key Objective Review, Apply, and Explore

Activism and Protest in the United States

(pages 392–393)

Our constitutional guarantees of speech, religion, press, and assembly permit citizens to unite to petition the government about their concerns. These freedoms allow mass movements to develop, often changing our country and culture.

Organized interests provide a safety valve, especially in times of great social, economic, political, and cultural upheaval and change. In their absence, more violent forms of expression might be employed.

KEY TERM

Egalitarianism 393

CRITICAL THINKING QUESTIONS

1. Do you think collective action is more important today than in the past? Why or why not?
2. Do you think people still believe that we have a "right to revolt" if we disagree with the government? When, if ever, and under what circumstances do we lose this right?

INTERNET RESOURCES

Democracy Matters: **http://www.democracymatters.org**
Rock the Vote: **http://www.rockthevote.org**

ADDITIONAL READING

Baumgardner, Jennifer, and Amy Richards. *Grassroots: A Field Guide for Feminist Activism.* New York: Farrar, Straus and Giroux, 2005.

Milner, Henry. *Civic Literacy: How Informed Citizens Make Democracy Work.* Hanover, NH: University Press of New England, 2002.

Influencing the Government Through Mobilization and Participation

(pages 394–395)

Constitutional protections are very important in allowing us to petition our government and pursue collective action. Without these protections, we would have great difficulties in working with like-minded individuals and to influence our society.

The success of protests in colonial times left an important mark on our political culture, encouraging ordinary people to participate in civic affairs.

CRITICAL THINKING QUESTIONS

1. Do you think that constitutional protections should be suspended during times of war or conflict?
2. Which elements of the Bill of Rights do you believe should be most guarded and why?

INTERNET RESOURCES

Bill of Rights Institute: **http://billofrightsinstitute.org**
Constitution Society: **http://constitution.org**

ADDITIONAL READING

Gerston, Larry N. *Public Policy Making in a Democratic Society: A Guide to Civic Engagement.* New York: Sharpe, 2002.

Snow, Nancy. *Information War: American Propaganda, Free Speech and Opinion Control Since 9/11.* New York: Seven Stories Press, 2003.

Key Objective Review, Apply, and Explore

Interest Groups

(pages 396–399)

Interest groups serve many important purposes in democratic societies, from providing tools for participation to educating the public and governmental officials to influencing policymaking and governmental action.

The growth in the number of interest groups has both positive and negative effects. More groups provide additional outlets for participation, but more groups can also produce more conflict.

KEY TERMS

Interest Groups 396
Cleavages 397
Disturbance Theory 398
Trade Associations 399
Labor Unions 399
Professional Associations 399
Public Interest Groups 399
Think Tanks 399
Governmental Units 399

CRITICAL THINKING QUESTIONS

1. Do organized interest groups represent all people? If not, does this matter?
2. Why are there so many interest groups in the United States? What are some of the consequences of the growth that has occurred since 1960?

INTERNET RESOURCES

Brady Campaign to Prevent Gun Violence: **http://handguncontrol.org**
Center for Responsive Politics: **http://www.opensecrets.org**
Coalition to Stop Gun Violence: **http://www.csgv.org**
Feminist Majority Foundation: **http://www.feminist.org**
Gun Owners of America: **http://www.gunowners.org**
National Association for the Advancement of Colored People: **http://www.naacp.org**
National Organization for Women: **http://www.now.org**
U.S. Chamber of Commerce: **http://www.uschamber.com**
World Advocacy: **http://www.worldadvocacy.com/**

ADDITIONAL READING

Berry, Jeffrey, and Glyde Wilcox. *Interest Group Society,* 5th ed. New York: Longman, 2008.

Cigler, Allan J., and Burdett A. Loomis (eds.). *Interest Group Politics,* 7th ed. Washington, D.C.: CQ Press, 2007.

Interest Group Mobilization

(pages 400–403)

There are many costs associated with forming and maintaining organized groups. These costs include money, time, and overcoming the free-rider and political efficacy problems. To overcome these barriers, interest groups use a variety of tactics, from offering benefits to providing inducements.

Leadership is often a very important factor in group formation, maintenance, and success.

KEY TERMS

Free-Rider Problem 400
Public Goods (Collective Goods) 400
Selective Benefits 401
Material Benefits 401
Solidary Benefits 401
Purposive Benefits 401
Equal Rights Amendment (ERA) 402

CRITICAL THINKING QUESTIONS

1. What are the barriers to organizing interest groups? How do interest groups overcome these barriers?
2. What factors make some groups more successful and powerful than others? What role do leaders play in the formation, maintenance, and success of interest groups?

INTERNET RESOURCES

Commission for Environmental Cooperation (CEC): **http://cec.org**
Greenpeace: **http://www.greenpeace.org/usa/**
National Rifle Association: **http://nra.org**
Project Vote Smart: **http://www.vote-smart.org**

ADDITIONAL READING

Berry, Jeffrey M. *The New Liberalism: The Rising Power of Citizen Groups.* Washington, D.C.: Brookings Institution Press, 2000.

Key Objective Review, Apply, and Explore

Inside Lobbying

(pages 404–407)

Trying to gain access to present their positions, interest groups lobby directly by contacting officials, staffers and members of the bureaucracy.

Interest groups also testify at congressional hearings and spend a good deal of time and energy building long-term relationships, thus augmenting their credibility so that they can effectively communicate with policymakers.

KEY TERMS

Inside Lobbying 404 **Gaining Access 404**

CRITICAL THINKING QUESTIONS

1. Do you think inside lobbying corrupts politics, or does it provide much needed information to governmental officials? Are you bothered that some groups can afford to hire firms to provide expert information to members of Congress and their staffs?
2. Why do you think the public believes inside lobbying presents great opportunities for corruption? Do you deem it unethical and corrupt?

INTERNET RESOURCES

Center for Responsive Government: **http://www.opensecrets.org**
Center for Media and Democracy: **http://www.prwatch.org**
Federal Elections Commission: **http://www.fec/gov**

ADDITIONAL READING

DeKieffer, Donald E. *The Citizen's Guide to Lobbying Congress.* Chicago: Review Press, 1997.

Herrnson, Paul S., Ronald G. Shaiko, and Clyde Wilcox (eds.). *The Interest Group Connection: Electioneering, Lobbying, and Policymaking in Washington,* 2nd ed. Washington, D.C.: CQ Press, 2004.

Kamieniecki, Sheldon. *Corporate America and Environmental Policy: How Often Does Business Get Its Way?* Stanford, CA: Stanford University Press, 2006.

Outside Lobbying

(pages 408–413)

Indirect lobbying means trying to influence the government by mobilizing public support. Grassroots mobilization is one very effective tactic for indirect lobbying.

Traditional tactics of grassroots mobilization include direct contact, direct mail, and the creation of pamphlets to share information with supporters and the public. Newer tools include using the media to reach supporters and the general public. To get their message across, interest groups advertise, sponsor television shows, and appear as experts on news and entertainment programs.

KEY TERMS

Outside Lobbying (Grassroots Lobbying) 408 **Direct Contact 409**
Direct Mail 409

CRITICAL THINKING QUESTIONS

1. What is the difference between indirect and direct lobbying? Why and how is each used? To which practices do you think the public most objects? Why? What, if anything, should be done to reform lobbying practices?
2. What is grassroots mobilization? How have grassroots tactics changed? Do you think the more modern techniques are more effective than the tried-and-true methods? Why or why not?

INTERNET RESOURCES

Blog Search: **http://www.blogsearch.google.com**
Recording Artists Coalition: **http://www.recordingartistscoalition.com**
United Student Activists: **http://www.unitedstudentactivists.org/**

ADDITIONAL READING

Kollman, Ken. *Outside Lobbying: Public Opinion and Interest Group Strategies.* Princeton, NJ: Princeton University Press, 1998.

Nownes, Anthony J. *Total Lobbying: What Lobbyists Want (and How They Try to Get It).* New York: Cambridge University Press, 2006.

Key Objective Review, Apply, and Explore

The Final Verdict: The Influence of Interest Groups

(pages 414–415)

Debate exists over the actual influence of interest groups in the United States; however, the consensus among the public is that interest groups are very powerful—perhaps too powerful—relative to the influence of voters and other less organized citizens. The uneven growth pattern, with some groups increasing at much faster rates than others, has led some people to worry about potential bias in the articulation of the needs of some over the desires of individuals and groups with less representation.

KEY TERM

Social Capital 414

CRITICAL THINKING QUESTIONS

1. How influential are interest groups in the United States? How influential does the public *think* interest groups are? What are some of the consequences of this public perception?
2. Do you think that television and the Internet cause isolation, or do they promote engagement?

INTERNET RESOURCES

Center for Public Integrity: **http://www.publicintegrity.org**
Rock the Vote: **http://www.rockthevote.org**

ADDITIONAL READING

Barbour, Christine, and Gerald C. Wright, with Matthew J. Steb and Michael R. Wolf. *Keeping the Republic: Power and Citizenship in American Politics.* Washington, D.C.: CQ Press, 2006.

Kryzanek, Michael. *Angry, Bored, Confused: A Citizen Handbook of American Politics.* Boulder, CO: Westview Press, 1999.

Richan, Willard C. *Lobbying for Social Change,* 3rd ed. Binghamton, NY: Haworth Press, 2006.

Chapter Review Critical Thinking Test

1. A citizen's participation in an organized interest group is good for democracy, because it cultivates
- **a.** self-discipline, patience, and partisan fervor.
- **b.** wisdom, patriotism, and generosity.
- **c.** political connections, historical perspective, and political endurance.
- **d.** tolerance, political efficacy, and political trust.

2. What specifically prompted the modern American civil rights movement of 1955–1965?
- **a.** racism
- **b.** the assassination of Medgar Evers
- **c.** the revitalization of the Ku Klux Klan
- **d.** faltering civil rights progress after the *Brown* decision

3. What historical trend in this country triggered a reconsideration of forms of legal discrimination against women in the twentieth century?
- **a.** women's increased enrollment in universities after WWI
- **b.** the dramatic increase in numbers of women working outside the home after WWII
- **c.** the appointment of Sandra Day O'Connor to the Supreme Court in the 1980s
- **d.** the substantial increase, during the Clinton administration, in the number of women in the federal judiciary

4. Equal pay for equal work
- **a.** was a slogan begun by feminists in the 1980s as part of the ERA initiative.
- **b.** was the principle behind the Equal Pay Act of 1963.
- **c.** has finally been achieved in U.S. employment, no matter the sex of the employee.
- **d.** was a principle declared at the Seneca Falls convention of 1848.

5. Early social movements in this country, such as the abolition, suffrage, and temperance movements, helped make average citizens believe that they could attain political power through group action.
- **a.** true
- **b.** false

6. Which kind of interest group is the American Bar Association?
- **a.** a public interest group
- **b.** a governmental unit
- **c.** a think tank
- **d.** a professional association

7. Gun control advocates in this country
- **a.** represent a small minority viewpoint.
- **b.** have outspent their political opponents and triumphed legislatively.
- **c.** represent a majority viewpoint but have spent far less than their opponents.
- **d.** have no chance of succeeding politically.

8. Research indicates that current levels of civic engagement are now at their lowest level in American political history.
- **a.** true
- **b.** false

9. Grassroots mobilization via the Internet is particularly effective with
- **a.** older people who have limited incomes.
- **b.** people who are not already sympathetic to that particular cause.
- **c.** young, affluent, and well-educated people.
- **d.** migrant workers.

10. What is a major reason that interest groups need money?
- **a.** to pay congressional representatives to legislate in their favor
- **b.** to run advertisements that publicize their wealth and power over the government
- **c.** to raise additional money
- **d.** to testify before congressional committees

11. Being active in an interest group constitutes
- **a.** a shortcut around the democratic process.
- **b.** a legitimate form of political participation.
- **c.** a type of elite mobilization.
- **d.** a less hopeful means of participation—voting is better.

12. Interest groups contribute to the governing process by
- **a.** staffing polling agencies.
- **b.** monitoring government programs.
- **c.** representing the concerns of ordinary Americans.
- **d.** b and c

13. What are think tanks?
- **a.** Nonpolitical, unbiased research institutions
- **b.** public research institutions funded with federal tax dollars
- **c.** nonprofit public interest groups often operating from a partisan point of view
- **d.** public interest groups devoted to educational issues

14. Interest groups are inherently self-interested, nondemocratic organizations that tend to pollute the electoral system.
- **a.** true
- **b.** false

15. Most leaders of interest groups in this country
- **a.** come from the ranks of the socioeconomic elite.
- **b.** are Democrats.
- **c.** are middle class.
- **d.** are lawyers.

16. A friend refuses to join your fledgling interest group working to legalize the medical use of marijuana, saying "The 'War on Drugs' mentality is too powerful in this country." What barrier to interest group formation is in evidence here?
- **a.** the free-rider problem

Chapter Review Critical Thinking Test

b. the easy-rider problem
c. the cost problem
d. the absence of a sense of political efficacy

17. When a lobbyist for the American Medical Association (AMA) takes a congressional staff member out to an expensive lunch to discusses the limitations of HMOs, that's an example of
a. outside lobbying
b. inside lobbying
c. indirect lobbying
d. illegal lobbying

18. Interest groups use the Internet to recruit volunteers, raise funds, conduct research, and educate the public.
a. true
b. false

19. One way that the Christian Coalition participates in elections is by
a. distributing information in churches about the voting records of candidates, noting who voted "correctly" and who did not.
b. sponsoring debates among candidates for Congress.
c. organizing get-out-the-vote drives on college campuses across the country.
d. supporting candidates with a pro-labor union voting record.

20. In the minds of many Americans, which of the following professions is most analogous to that of the lobbyist?
a. gambler
b. thief
c. pimp
d. forger

Answers: 1-d, 2-d, 3-b, 4-b, 5-a, 6-d, 7-c, 8-b, 9-c, 10-c, 11-b, 12-d, 13-c, 14-b, 15-a, 16-d, 17-b, 18-a, 19-a, 20-b.

You decide!

Imagine you have been hired by a political consulting group to develop youth mobilization strategies for both the Democratic and Republican parties. Your first assignment is to catalog the ways in which college students participate in politics and civic life. Look across your campus. What behaviors and actions would you consider "measures" of civic engagement? What about volunteerism and participation in service learning opportunities? Do you think your campus is different from other schools on these measures? For a point of comparison, you might look at resources such as the University of Maryland's Center for Information and Research on Civic Learning and Engagement (CIRCLE), which promotes research on the civic and political engagement of Americans between the ages of 15 and 25 and has extensive resources on its Web site at **http://www.civicyouth.org**. Next, identify means for contacting and mobilizing college-age voters. Should both parties use the same communication tools? Why or why not? Which communication tools should they avoid? Finally, identify the issues that are most important for college-age student voters. What issues come up most frequently in the student newspaper and other student publications? Which issues are the most common sources of protest on campus? Are there issues that appear to matter a great deal for both Democratic and Republican students? Are there issues on which one party appears to have a clear advantage over the other in reaching college students? What might the other party do to counteract this advantage?

Key Objective Outline

Does money corrupt the election process, or is it simply a way for citizens to express their political views and support particular candidates?

The Role of Money in Elections **(page 442)**

How has the Internet changed the election process?

Campaigning Online **(page 450)**

Do average Americans, especially young Americans, take part in the election process?

Individual Participation in Elections **(page 454)**

CHAPTER 12
ELECTIONS AND PARTICIPATION IN AMERICA

We've grown accustomed to competitive, close elections in recent years. The 2000 presidential contest was settled when George W. Bush was announced the winner of Florida by a mere 539 votes. Several recent congressional races have also been exceedingly close, as have a number of senate contests and numerous state legislative races. In 2008, several U.S. Senate contests were extremely close, and they were settled only after lengthy recounts. But the smallest margin of victory in any statewide election in American history occurred in the Washington State gubernatorial contest in 2004. The winner was decided by only 129 votes.

The race pitted Republican Dino Rossi, a state senator and real estate agent from the Seattle suburbs, against Democrat Christine Gregoire, the State Attorney General. It was a hard-fought campaign and considered a toss-up throughout. Both candidates spent huge sums of money, more than doubling the total from the previous election. Television screens were filled with 30-second ads, mailboxes were stuffed with direct mail, and legions of activists hit the streets. Each side knew it would be close, and each side pulled out all the stops.

On Election Day, nearly 3 million voters came to the polls. The initial vote count gave Rossi a slim 261-vote lead. It seemed that the Republican had pulled it off. But a state law requires a recount when the margin of victory is narrow, and when the recount was completed, Rossi's lead had dropped to only 42 votes. A second recount—this time by hand—was ordered by the state courts, which gave Gregoire a victory by just 129 votes. Her margin of victory was 0.0045 percent. Now that's a close election!

A key lesson in American electoral politics, however, is that there is always another election around the corner. Rossi and Gregoire faced each other again in 2008, once more doubling fundraising records. This time, the outcome was again very close, with county-by-county results nearly identical to those of the 2004 contest. But with Barack Obama's wind at her back, Governor Gregoire was able to gather enough momentum to defeat her two-time rival with 52 percent of the vote, thereby winning reelection and another term as the chief executive of Washington State.

■ **Republican Form of Government:** A system of government in which the general public selects agents to represent it in political decision-making. **SIGNIFICANCE:** *Because we look to others to speak and act on our behalf, the process of selecting these agents is very important.*

■ **Plato (427–347 B.C.):** Greek philosopher often considered the first political scientist. **SIGNIFICANCE:** *Plato suggested rulers should not be voted into office but rather chosen based upon their intelligence.*

Elections *and* Democratic Theory (pages 426–429)

What are the theoretical strengths and limitations of elections?

We Americans put great faith in elections. We believe that they are a just means of resolving disputes and setting the course of government. Democracy means government by the people, and while there may be other ways of linking citizens to government, elections strike many people as the most efficient and most assured way to achieve this linkage. But is this actually so? Let's explore some theoretical issues regarding elections in a democracy.

Republicanism and Different Ways to Select Leaders

The United States boasts a **republican form of government**■. That is, ours is *not* a direct democracy, in which everyone has a say in what the government does, but is instead a system in which we select individuals—leaders—to work and speak on our behalf. This raises the question of how leaders are best chosen. There are many possibilities. We could randomly select members of the community—literally pick names out of a hat, much as we pick a trial jury. This would not guarantee a government run by experts, but so long as every citizen had the same chance of being selected, you could argue that it would be a fair system. (In fact, just such a system was used in an important city state in medieval Italy. It didn't work very well, because powerful families secretly decided whose names went into the hat!) **Plato (427–347 B.C.)**■, the first great political theorist, had something a bit different in mind. For Plato, some people are born to rule and some to be ruled. So another possibility would be to give an examination to citizens who are eager to serve and then fill government posts with those receiving the highest scores. Why not give the most qualified and most intelligent citizens the opportunity to serve? Still another option would be to allow public officials to handpick their own successors. Wanting to preserve their standing with the public and to ensure the continuity of their policies, these officials might be careful to choose citizens who would do a good job.

"I've heard our government called a republic *and* a democracy. Which is it?"
—Student Question

Plato was one of the first political theorists. Among many interesting ideas, he rejected the notion that average citizens should be allowed to select their leaders. ***—Most Americans would disagree, of course, but what are the significant downsides to the use of elections to pick public officials?***

Elections as an Expression of Popular Will

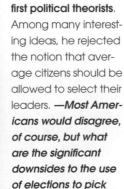

"Do elections just tell us who's the most popular candidate?"
—Student Question

In short, if choosing public officials were the *only* function of elections, an argument might be made that other options are available. Yet not everyone would agree that the only function of elections is to select leaders.

Another way to think about elections is to realize that they serve as an expression of popular will—as a means of telling government what is on the minds of citizens. This process can work in different ways. A **landslide election** (whereby the winners come to power with overwhelming public support) does more than send a person or group to office: It signals to all the leaders of the system (and, in the case of a national election, to the world at large) that the winning candidates' ideas are strongly favored by the voters.

Sometimes the expression of public sentiment in America is voiced through a minor party candidate. In 1992, independent candidate H. Ross Perot spent most of his time talking about the federal budget deficit. The main party candidates (Arkansas Governor Bill Clinton and President George H. W. Bush) were paying little attention to that issue, perhaps because doing so would force difficult choices on the nation and its leaders. Perot's hour-long political "infomercials," filled with graphs, charts, data, and statistics, seemed out of place and rather quirky. But on election day, Perot garnered close to the highest third-party vote in a century. Perot did not win, of course, but a clear message had been sent: The public cares about deficit reduction. And the issue was taken seriously by the administration of the winning candidate, Bill Clinton.

Legitimacy: The sense that the result of a decision-making process is a proper outcome in the minds of the people who must live with that outcome.

SIGNIFICANCE: *Because Americans believe that officials should be elected to office, the winners lack legitimacy if the mechanics of the election process are unfair.*

This famous shot of Abraham Lincoln was photographed the day after Lincoln arrived in Washington, D.C., for his inauguration. Lincoln faced a crisis of legitimacy from the very beginning. He had won the election with less than 40 percent of the popular vote, and he was vilified in the South.

Stability and Legitimacy

Although there may be other ways to select government leaders, a core consideration is **legitimacy**, the process of decision-making that is perceived to be proper by the people who must live with the outcome. Legitimacy requires that the mode of selecting leaders be both legal and, in the eyes of citizens, fair. When citizens accept the need for political representation and feel that the resulting selection of these leaders has been legitimate, they are most likely to accept—though they might not always agree with—the policies that follow.

That is precisely why the outcome of the 2000 presidential election between Democrat Al Gore and Republican George W. Bush was a bit worrisome. What happens when an election ends in a virtual tie, as it did that year? Worse yet, what happens when the candidate who receives fewer votes than the other nevertheless *legally* gets into office? Al Gore received about half a million more votes than George W. Bush in 2000, but because of the way state votes were distributed in the electoral college (discussed in detail later in this chapter), and after the U.S. Supreme Court had ruled on the dispute, Bush wound up with more electoral college votes and became the 43rd president of the United States. This raised two questions: Would the legitimacy of the federal government suffer? Would citizens lose faith in the entire electoral process?

A similar danger can arise when more than two candidates run for the same office. With only two candidates, the winner, by definition, has the support of a majority of voters (unless, perhaps, that choice has been filtered through a complex prism like the electoral college). But when a third or fourth relatively significant candidate enters the fray, the winner, at least in the American system, often winds up with the most votes (a plurality) but not with a majority of the votes cast. For example, because the 1860 presidential election was a three-person race, Abraham Lincoln was elected with just 39.8 percent of the popular vote—none of which came from southern states, where he wasn't even on the ballot! Did Lincoln have the legitimacy to lead the nation? Many southern whites thought that he did not, most of the southern states seceded, and the result was 4 years of civil war. Because minor-party or independent candidates have often joined presidential contests, and because the two major parties have been more or less balanced through the years, the United States has had plurality winners rather than majority winners 16 times since 1824. Bill Clinton won the White House in both 1992 and 1996 with a popular vote of less than 50 percent.

Given snafus of this sort, a question might arise: How does the American system maintain its postelection stability? First, faith in elections runs so deep in Americans that winners eventually are seen as legitimate, regardless of the potholes in the road. The aftermath of the 2000 election was not entirely placid, but very soon, the public accepted the outcome of the election as rightful. There was no rioting in the streets—just a few boos from the crowd as George W. Bush's inaugural parade made its way along Pennsylvania Avenue. Second, leaders in our system are bound by a powerful political culture that dictates a code of conduct for losing candidates. Ever since the election of 1800, when Thomas Jefferson and his Democratic-Republican followers defeated John Adams and his Federalist supporters, the losing candidates have accepted election results regardless of how close they were or how few citizens had turned out to vote. Losing candidates are gracious in our system, from the White House to the town council. (Adams, it must be said, did not set a particularly good precedent, sneaking out of Washington at dawn on the day of Jefferson's inauguration!) Most recently, Hillary Clinton waged a vigorous campaign against Barack Obama for the 2008 Democratic presidential nomination. The outcome was quite close but, accepting defeat, Clinton proved gracious and supportive of her party's choice.

PATHWAYS | of action

The Power of the Purple Finger

Just short of 2 years after the fall of Saddam Hussein's regime, citizens of Iraq took what many hoped would prove a historic step toward creating a democracy in their nation. On January 30, 2005, Iraqi citizens—both men and women—were granted the opportunity to cast a ballot for their leaders. It had been 50 years since the last competitive election in Iraq. Due to threats of violence, many thought that voters (especially those of a significant Muslim sect of Iraq, the Sunnis) would stay home. There was grave concern that the government would lack legitimacy.

Those projections proved mostly wrong, however, as massive numbers of Iraqis flooded polling places, forming lines that stretched around blocks. Some stood contentedly for hours, waiting to cast their first vote. "The people of Iraq have spoken to the world," said President George W. Bush, "and the world is hearing the voice of freedom from the center of the Middle East." To ensure that no one would be able to cast more than one ballot, each voter's right index finger was dipped in indelible purple ink. For days to follow, Iraqis would proudly raise their ink-stained finger.

Only time will tell whether this election was the beginning of a truly open government, but at least for a short time, the purple finger seemed to signify the inevitable triumph of democracy in the Middle East. Few claimed that voting alone would be enough to establish a

CONNECT THE LINK (Chapter **9**, pages **322–325**) Do average Americans follow public affairs closely?

■ **Civic Participation:** Citizen involvement in public matters.

EXAMPLE: *Joining clubs, voting, attending governmental meetings, or working on behalf of a candidate for public office are examples of civic particpation.*

SIMULATION **You Are a Campaign Manager: Countdown to 270!**

democracy, and in fact, the Sunnis actually boycotted the first election. But for many Iraqis, free elections—the chance for average citizens to cast a ballot to select public officials—seemed to be a sign that democracy might finally be arriving in their country. ■

Civic Education and Civic Duty

In a democracy, citizens must remain aware of the important issues, at least in a broad sense. As noted in LINK Chapter 9, pages 322–325, Americans pay only a limited amount of attention to public affairs. Things would be much worse were it not for the frequency of elections. Many studies have shown that voters actually learn a good deal from campaigns.[1] One study found that the more campaign ads a citizen sees, the more informed that person is. "The brevity of the advertising message may actually strengthen its informative value," the researchers reported. "The typical person's attention span for political information is notoriously short-lived . . . [and] the great majority of voters bypass or ignore information that entails more than minimal costs. . . . Campaign advertising meets the demand for both simplicity and access."[2] In other words, elections serve as a civics refresher course.

"How do elections help make us better citizens?"
—Student Question

Socialization is the means by which new members of society are introduced to the customs and beliefs of a political system. It is how a nation's values are spread from one generation to the next. A core element in our political culture is **civic participation**■. It is expected that each citizen occasionally leaves his or her private world to become involved in the affairs of state. Elections serve to introduce many Americans to their role as citizens. *Civic duty* means, at the very least, helping choose who will run the government. It is hoped that by giving citizens this basic opportunity, additional acts of civic participation will follow.

In January of 2005 an Iraqi woman flashes the victory sign with a purple finger, indicating she had just voted. Iraqis voted in their first free election in half a century despite a wave of suicide bombings and mortar attacks across the country. ***—Can democracy be brought to a nation simply by instituting elections?***

A Safety Valve

Americans sometimes take for granted that changes in the control of government are peaceful. We move from one administration to another and from control by one party to the other without violence, without sandbags being loaded into the White House windows or sentries being stationed at the entrance of the U.S. Capitol. Losing candidates and their supporters may not like the outcome, but they accept the "will of the voters" peacefully. For voters, elections become the safety valve for discontent; rather than picking up a gun or other weapon, Americans just vow to win the next election.

Elections as a Placebo?

Are there any downsides to using election to choose leaders? Indeed, there may well be. When we carefully explore the many avenues for changing the course of government—for modifying the outcome of the policy process—elections look like an imperfect choice. Elections do not guarantee that there will be any redirection in policy, only that the *people* running part of the government may change. Many aspects of government are beyond the immediate reach of elected officials, and even when they are not, dramatic change is rare. Some people have even begun to speculate that the distrust many Americans feel toward government is due to the frustration over this disconnect between elections and policy. "He told us that he would change things if he won the election," we might hear a citizen complain. "Well, he won, so why haven't things changed?"

An even bigger concern is that elections lead many citizens to believe voting is their *only* chance to make a difference. They may be frustrated with the way things are going but feel as though their only course of action is to vote or to help a candidate. This is called **episodic participation**■.

A Poor Measure of Public Sentiment

It is often said that elections direct the successful candidates to carry out a particular set of policy alternatives—in other words, the voters send them into office with a clear mandate—but this is not exactly what occurs. Instead, voters select a given candidate for many different reasons, a particular policy choice being just one possibility. Each voter has a slightly different motivation or mix of motivations for favoring one candidate over another. Assuming that the results of an election mean a particular thing can be a mistake.

COMPARATIVE **Comparing Voting and Elections**

■ **Episodic Participation:** Occasional citizen involvement in public matters, such as during elections.

SIGNIFICANCE: *Many believe that when Americans are only occasionally involved in politics, such as just at election time, the democratic character of our government suffers.*

Constricting the Pool of Public Officials

"Why do so many good people choose not to run for office?"

—Student Question

The tone and cost of contemporary elections in America limit the pool of candidates to individuals willing to undergo the rigors of campaigning. These days, campaigning requires a great deal of money and a tremendous amount of time and stamina. Running for statewide positions, and to some extent for congressional seats, has become a full-time job for more than a year before the election. And a trend in the press coverage of candidates is to disclose ever-more intimate information. A mudslinging campaign can subject a candidate and his or her family to stress that might well become unbearable. Many outstanding citizens, eager to serve their community, state, or nation, will never step forward because elections have become so grueling.

Michelle Obama shakes hands with supporters attending a rally in Noblesville, Indiana, in May of 2008. Running for office has never been easy, but many suggest the intense media attention on candidates and their spouses—and the fact that any gaffe will be replayed untold times on YouTube—make surviving the process unscathed nearly impossible. ***—Is this a good thing for our system, or is it destructive?***

A Broken Process?

Finally, perhaps the greatest limitation of the election process might be its vulnerability to malfunction. The heart of the election-democracy link is the idea that all citizens should have an equal opportunity to select leaders—that no candidate should have an unfair advantage—but what happens when some candidates have more campaign resources? What if laws limit which adults can vote and which cannot? Does it matter if a shrinking number of voters seem willing to make election decisions? Does it matter that today, most incumbent candidates in the House of Representatives—those who already occupy a seat—face no serious opposition? What if legal barriers aid certain political parties and limit the potency of others? Does poor, biased, or limited media coverage of the campaigns distort the process?

Elections and Democratic Theory

Practice Quiz

1. Elections are a process by which political leaders are chosen and
   - **a.** public policies are formulated.
   - **b.** the public indicates its thoughts about public policy.
   - **c.** the concerns of a new generation of citizens get clearly articulated.
   - **d.** the principles of the Constitution are reaffirmed.
2. In the 2000 presidential election, George W. Bush won the Electoral College vote
   - **a.** by 23 electoral votes.
   - **b.** only after a recount of electoral votes.
   - **c.** but lost the popular vote by about 64,000 votes.
   - **d.** but lost the popular vote by about 500,000 votes.
3. Studies indicate that voters learn a lot from campaigns.
   - **a.** true
   - **b.** false
4. It's fair to say that elections act as a "safety valve" for public discontent, because
   - **a.** if the elected officials are incompetent, there will always be another election to vote them out of office.
   - **b.** people believe that the authority of elected officials is legitimized by a popular vote.
   - **c.** voting is a safer way than violent rebellion to express the desire for change.
   - **d.** voting measures the political opinions of nearly every adult in the country.

Answers: 1-b, 2-d, 3-a, 4-c.

Discussion Questions

1. What are some ways in which citizens can avoid making irrational choices when voting?
2. What are some ways other than voting that citizens can exercise their civic duty?

What **YOU** can do!

Choose a recent presidential election. Using resources from your library and the Internet, list the three major issues that dominated each candidate's policy platform. Next, make a note of the percentage of vote each candidate garnered. Finally, investigate public opinion polls around the time of the election. Did the majority of public opinion on each issue match the position of the candidate who won the election? What could cause a discrepancy, if one exists? Discuss your findings with friends and classmates.

■ **Electoral College:** A device for selecting the president and vice president of the United States, defined in Article II of the Constitution, whereby the voters in each state choose electors to attend a gathering where the electors make the final decision.

SIGNIFICANCE: *This odd system shapes the way elections are conducted and can also determine the actual winner.*

VISUAL LITERACY The Electoral College: Campaign Consequences and Mapping the Results

DEBATE Democracy and the Internet

DEBATE Electoral College

The Electoral College

(pages 430–435)

What is the Electoral College, and is it really the best way to elect a president?

In August of 2004, former Vice President Al Gore opened the Democratic National Convention with the following:

> Friends, fellow Democrats, fellow Americans: I'll be candid with you. I had hoped to be back here this week under different circumstances, running for reelection. But you know the old saying: You win some, you lose some. And then there's that little-known third category.
>
> I didn't come here tonight to talk about the past. After all, I don't want you to think I lie awake at night counting and recounting sheep. I prefer to focus on the future because I know from my own experience that America is a land of opportunity, where every little boy and girl has a chance to grow up and win the popular vote.

The joke, of course, was that while Gore had won the popular vote, he did not win the presidency. All cheered, some laughed, and a few cried. Watching George W. Bush take over the White House in 2001, even though he had received half a million fewer popular votes than Gore, was a bitter pill to swallow for many Democrats. How different things might have been, they lamented, if the voice of the people had prevailed and Gore had become president. This breakdown in the election process was caused by the Electoral College—and it was not the first time it happened.

Former Vice President Al Gore, on stage in Boston's FleetCenter for opening night of the Democratic National Convention on Monday evening, July 26, 2004, declared that his heart is at peace, albeit with some longing for what might have been. ***—What is your opinion of the outcome of the 2000 presidential election?***

PHOTO: Richard Perry/The New York Times

Selection of the President

One of the most innovative and controversial aspects of American elections is outlined in the Constitution: use of the **Electoral College**■ to select the president and vice president. It would be hard to overstate the importance of the Electoral College in American politics. Occasionally, it shapes the "winner" of the election, as happened with George W. Bush, but in every election, this awkward procedure shapes the election *process*—from party nominations to the selection of running mates, overall strategy, fundraising activities, candidate events, distributing resources, media coverage, and much else. Depending on which state you live in, citizens will experience presidential campaigns in vastly different ways because of the Electoral College. Many argue that without this institution, elections would be much more democratic. On the other hand, others suggest that given our structure of government, the Electoral College is a necessary, albeit cumbersome, institution.

What Were the Framers Thinking?

> "Why would our founding fathers create such an unwieldy system for electing a president?"
>
> —Student Question

The framers of our system believed that only men of the highest caliber and intellect should become president. They worried about politicians with "talents for low intrigue, and the little arts of popularity," as noted by Alexander Hamilton in *Federalist No. 69.* So they worried about giving average citizens a direct voice in selecting the president. Instead, they decided that a group of wise citizens should be assembled for the sole purpose of picking the president. This would be an "electoral college." But who, exactly, should make up this group? One proposal, which had significant support at the Constitutional Convention, was to let Congress elect the president. Others suggested that this would blur the important separation between the branches. Also, many were concerned that average citizens should have

■ **Twelfth Amendment (1804):** A change to the Constitution that required a separate vote tally in the electoral college for president and vice president.	**SIGNIFICANCE:** *Presidential candidates now select their own vice presidential running mates.*

■ **Unit Rule:** The practice, employed by 48 states, of awarding all of a state's electoral college votes to the candidate for the presidency who receives the greatest number of popular votes in that state.	**EXAMPLE:** *Pennsylvania, often a "swing state" in presidential elections, allots all of its 21 electoral votes to the candidate that receives the most popular votes in the state.*

some say in the process. The compromise was to allow each state to select its electors by whatever method that state deemed appropriate.

The Electoral College was also a compromise that helped assuage a concern of delegates from small states. There were no political parties at the time, and it was assumed that each state would advance the candidacy of its "favorite son" meaning that each state's most popular politician would run for the presidency). If the selection of the president was based on popular vote, the largest states (the states with the most voters) would elect their favorite son every time.

So how does the Electoral College solve this problem? The Constitution states that in order to become president, a candidate must receive a majority of Electoral College votes. This does not mean the most votes (a plurality) but rather at least one-half of the overall number of electoral votes cast. When no candidate received at least 50 percent of the votes, the election is decided in the House of Representatives, where each state, regardless of its size, is given one vote. Because each state would advance a favorite son, and because there were no political parties, most assumed there would be few (if any) elections where a candidate netted a majority of Electoral College votes. Most elections would therefore be decided in the House, where the small states would have the same say as the largest states.

How the Electoral College Works

As you probably know, the Electoral College is a complex process. In brief, voters select electors to represent their state at a gathering that chooses the president. Figure 12.1, on page 432, provides some details of the Electoral College.

When Things Have Gone Wrong

Originally, each elector was given full independence to name any person he saw fit and would cast two votes, naming two different people. The candidate who got the most votes would become president, and the runner-up would become vice president. During the first decades, only a handful of states allowed voters to pick electors; most were chosen by state legislatures. This method worked smoothly during the first two elections, when Washington was unanimously selected as president, but it began to unravel as soon as Washington announced that he would not accept a third term.

For one thing, political parties—which the framers had neither foreseen emerging nor wanted—burst onto the scene in the 1790s, leading to partisan electors rather than enlightened statesmen doing the choosing. Also, the original design was to have the top vote getter become president and the second-place finisher become vice president, but this proved completely unworkable as soon as competing political parties arose. In the 1796 election, this arrangement meant that John Adams got the presidency and his archrival, the leader of the opposing party, Thomas Jefferson, became vice president. For the next 4 years, each tried to outmaneuver the other.

Finally, the year 1800 brought an electoral rematch between Adams and Jefferson. This time, it seemed that Jefferson had come in first. But, in fact, Jefferson and his running mate, Aaron Burr, were tied: *All* of Jefferson's supporters in the Electoral College had cast their second vote for Burr! The election had to be settled by the House of Representatives. Even though everyone knew that Jefferson was the "top of the ticket," Burr refused to back down, and it took dozens of votes in the House and much wrangling before Jefferson was finally named president and Burr had to settle for the vice presidency. As a result, the **Twelfth Amendment**■ was adopted, which says that in the Electoral College, the electors must indicate who they are voting for as president and who they are voting for as vice president.

> "How can a candidate who gets more votes lose the election?"
> —Student Question

There is yet another controversial part of the process: It is quite possible that the candidate who receives the most popular votes will not receive the most electoral votes. This can happen for two reasons. First, 48 of the 50 states use a winner-takes-all model, also called the **unit rule**■, under which the candidate who receives the most popular votes in that state gets all of that state's electoral votes. Second, the original scheme of allowing electors to use their own independent judgment was quickly replaced by partisan considerations. Today, partisan slates of electors compete against one another, meaning that if a Republican candidate wins that state, a Republican slate of electors are sent to the Electoral College. The same is true for Democratic candidates.

These two changes—the unit rule and partisan slates of electors—makes it *likely* that the most popular candidate (the highest vote getter) will become the president, but it does not *guarantee* it. In fact, the most popular candidate has been denied the presidency four times in American history:

- In 1824, four candidates were in the running, although one was felled by a stroke just before the election. (Despite being incapacitated, he finished in third place.) The second-place finisher was John Quincy Adams, who got 38,000 fewer popular votes than the top vote getter, Andrew Jackson. But no

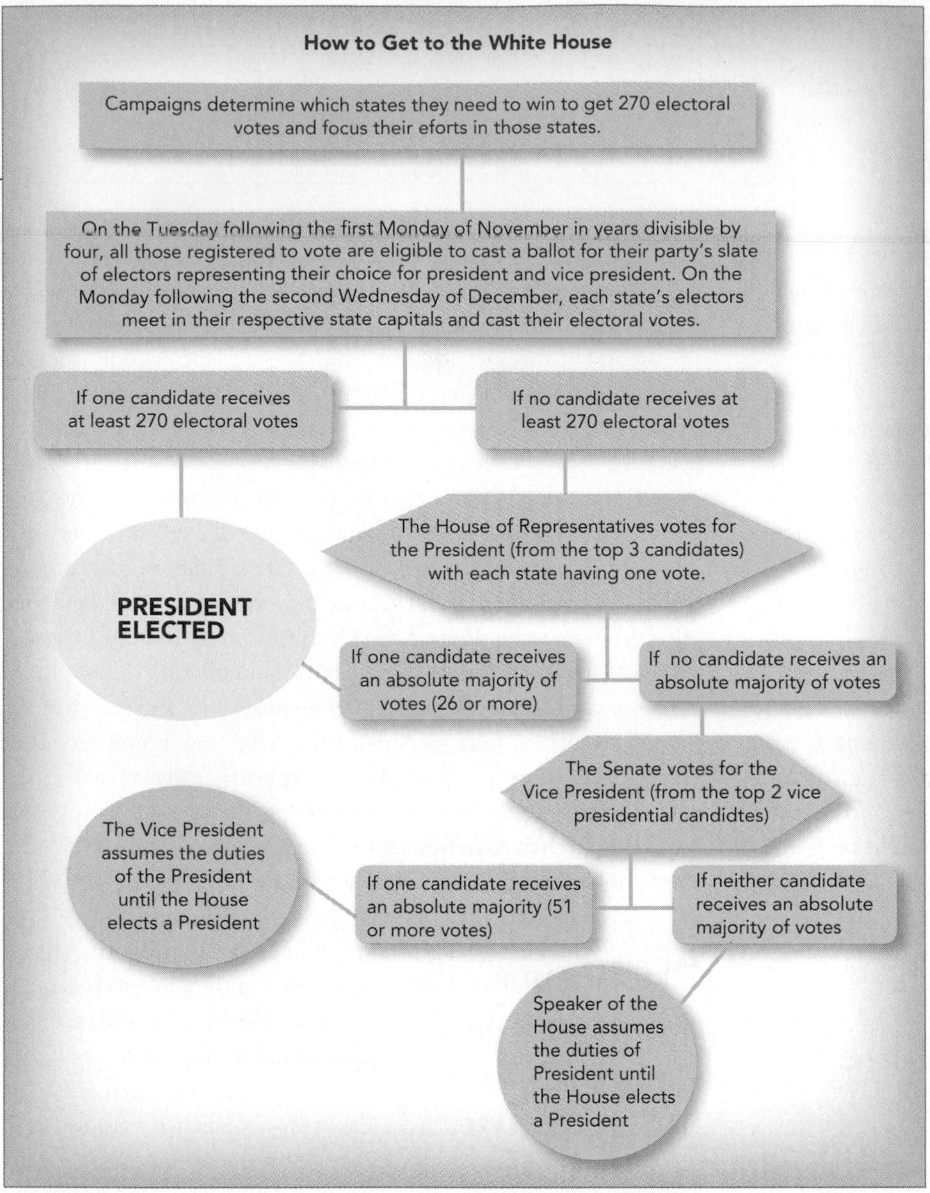

How to Get to the White House
Campaigns determine which states they need to win to get 270 electoral votes and focus their eforts in those states.
On the Tuesday following the first Monday of November in years divisible by four, all those registered to vote are eligible to cast a ballot for their party's slate of electors representing their choice for president and vice president. On the Monday following the second Wednesday of December, each state's electors meet in their respective state capitals and cast their electoral votes.
If one candidate receives at least 270 electoral votes
If no candidate receives at least 270 electoral votes
The House of Representatives votes for the President (from the top 3 candidates) with each state having one vote.
PRESIDENT ELECTED
If one candidate receives an absolute majority of votes (26 or more)
If no candidate receives an absolute majority of votes
The Senate votes for the Vice President (from the top 2 vice presidential candidtes)
The Vice President assumes the duties of the President until the House elects a President
If one candidate receives an absolute majority (51 or more votes)
If neither candidate receives an absolute majority of votes
Speaker of the House assumes the duties of President until the House elects a President

FIGURE 12.1 | **How to Get to the White House**

There are certainly drawbacks to the Electoral College—namely, that candidates that win more popular votes can be denied the presidency. For some, this alone is enough to jettison the scheme. Yet some argue there are problems with direct election process. ***—What were some of the reservations that the Framers had about direct elections?***

SOURCE: 2008 Election Preview, PM, ISBN 978013602544-3.

candidate won a majority of the Electoral College. Adams was awarded the presidency when the election was thrown to the House of Representatives, which under the Constitution had to choose among the *three* top Electoral College finishers. The fourth-place finisher, Speaker of the House Henry Clay, threw his support to Adams, who later named Clay as secretary of state. Jackson and his supporters howled that a "corrupt bargain" had deprived him of the White House, and Jackson ran again—this time successfully—in 1828.

- In 1876, nearly unanimous support from small states gave Republican Rutherford B. Hayes a one-vote margin in the Electoral College, despite the fact that he lost the popular vote to Democrat Samuel J. Tilden by 264,000 votes. There were also credible complaints of crooked vote counting in certain disputed states. The election was decided only when a commission of senators, representatives, and a Supreme Court justice declared Hayes the winner.
- In 1888, Republican candidate Benjamin Harrison lost the popular vote by 95,713 votes to the incumbent Democratic president, Grover Cleveland, but Harrison won by an Electoral College margin of 65 votes. In this instance, some say the Electoral College worked the way it is designed to work by preventing a candidate from winning an election based on support from one region of the country. The South overwhelmingly supported Cleveland, and he won by more than 425,000 votes in six southern states. In the rest of the country, however he lost by more than 300,000 votes. (Cleveland won a second term in a rematch election in 1892.)
- In 2000, Vice President Al Gore had over half a million votes more than George W. Bush (50,992,335 votes to Bush's 50,455,156). But after a recount controversy in Florida, and a U.S. Supreme Court ruling in the case of *Bush* v. *Gore* (2000), Bush was awarded the state by 537 popular votes. Like most states, Florida has a winner-takes-all rule. So the candidate who wins the state by popular vote, no matter how thin the margin, gets all of the state's electoral votes. Thus, Bush became president with 271 electoral votes—the barest possible majority.

How the Electoral College Shapes Campaign Activities

We can see that the mechanics of the Electoral College can have a direct bearing on the outcome of elections. It can also have an impact on the way campaigns are conducted. For instance, the unit rule, used in 48 states, puts a premium on winning the right combination of states to net at least 270 (out of 538) electoral votes (see Figure 12.2). Because of the partisan predisposition of voters, the election outcome in many states often is never really a question (see Figure 12.3 on page 434). For example, Republican candidates regularly win most southern states by large margins—as John McCain did in the 2008 election (see

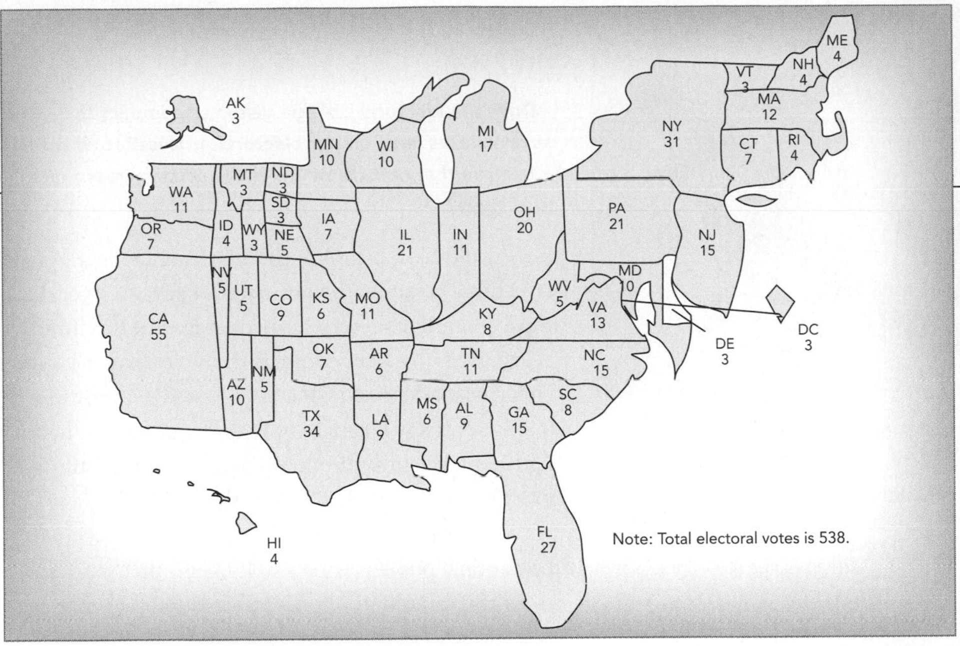

FIGURE 12.2 | **States to Proportion of Electoral Votes**

Some will look at a map after a presidential election and wonder why things are so competitive, given that Republicans seem to control so much of the nation. But, they would be referring to geography, not population. This map helps us to understand the importance of heavily populated states.

Swing States: States where the outcome of the presidential election is uncertain; states that are "up for grabs" in most presidential elections.

EXAMPLE: *In recent elections, Michigan, Ohio, and Florida have been "swing" states, as have roughly 10 other states.*

SIMULATION **You Are a Campaign Manager: Help McCain Win Swing States and Swing Voters**

SIMULATION **You Are a Campaign Manager: Lead Obama to Battleground State Victory**

Figure 12.4 on page 435). The Democrats, on the other hand, can count on West Coast states and most of the New England states. The number of "solidly Democratic" and "solidly Republican" states varies somewhat from year to year, but roughly speaking, there are about 35 to 40. Conversely, only about 10 to 15 states have been "in play" during elections. In 2008, candidates fought it out in just 15 states.

So what, in theory, should be a "national" campaign for the presidency boils down to dramatic, intense efforts in about a dozen states. Campaign operatives struggle to discern which states are solid and which are **swing states**■, and to put together a winning combination. Will Colorado be in play this time? What about Ohio or Michigan? What about any of the states in the Southwest? How will different candidates and vice presidential candidates shape which states are in play? Might a Republican from the Northeast put New Hampshire in play—or maybe even Maine? How about a southern Democrat on the ticket—might he or she help create a swing state in that region, or is the entire region a lost cause for Democrats? Is it worth trying to create a swing state by expending tons of resources, or should the campaign simply work to win those states already in play? These calculations—and many, many others—shape the nature of any presidential campaign and also the outcome of the election.

Moreover, residents living in swing states are bombarded with television ads, pamphlets, mailings, phone calls, rallies, media events and so forth. In the states that are not in play, however, the campaigns are relatively nonexistent. Another unfortunate by-product of the unit rule is that voters in solid states feel as if their votes and efforts are irrelevant. Why should a Democrat or Republican in New York or Wyoming, for example, bother to work for a candidate if the outcome of the election in their state seems a forgone conclusion? George Edwards, author of *Why the Electoral College Is Bad for America,* has noted, "At base, it violates political equality. . . . It favors some citizens over others depending solely on the state in which they cast their votes for president. So it's an institution that aggregates the popular vote in an inherently unjust manner and allows the candidate who is not preferred by the American public to win the election."[3]

The 2008 Election and Beyond

Given the outcome of the 2000 election, as well as the other problems, many had expected a popular uprising to abolish the Electoral College. Surely citizens would want to jettison this antiquated, undemocratic system. There was, indeed, a modest movement after the election, and it continues to simmer today. But in order to abolish the Electoral College, the Constitution would have to be amended—a complex, difficult process. (Setting aside the Bill of Rights and the Civil War Amendments, the Constitution has been altered only 14 times in our nation's history.) Surveys suggest that most Americans would like to have a direct vote for the presidency—in other words,

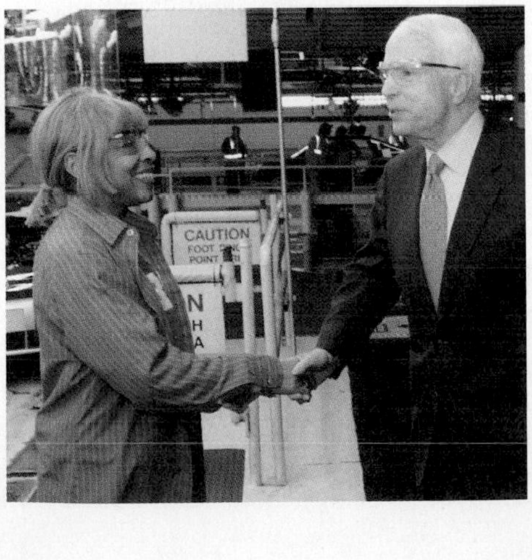

John McCain is greeted by an auto worker during a tour of Ford Motor Company's assembly plant in Wayne, Michigan, on February 21, 2008. Because of the Electoral College's winner-takes-all rule, used in 48 states, candidates focus their attention on roughly a dozen "swing" states.

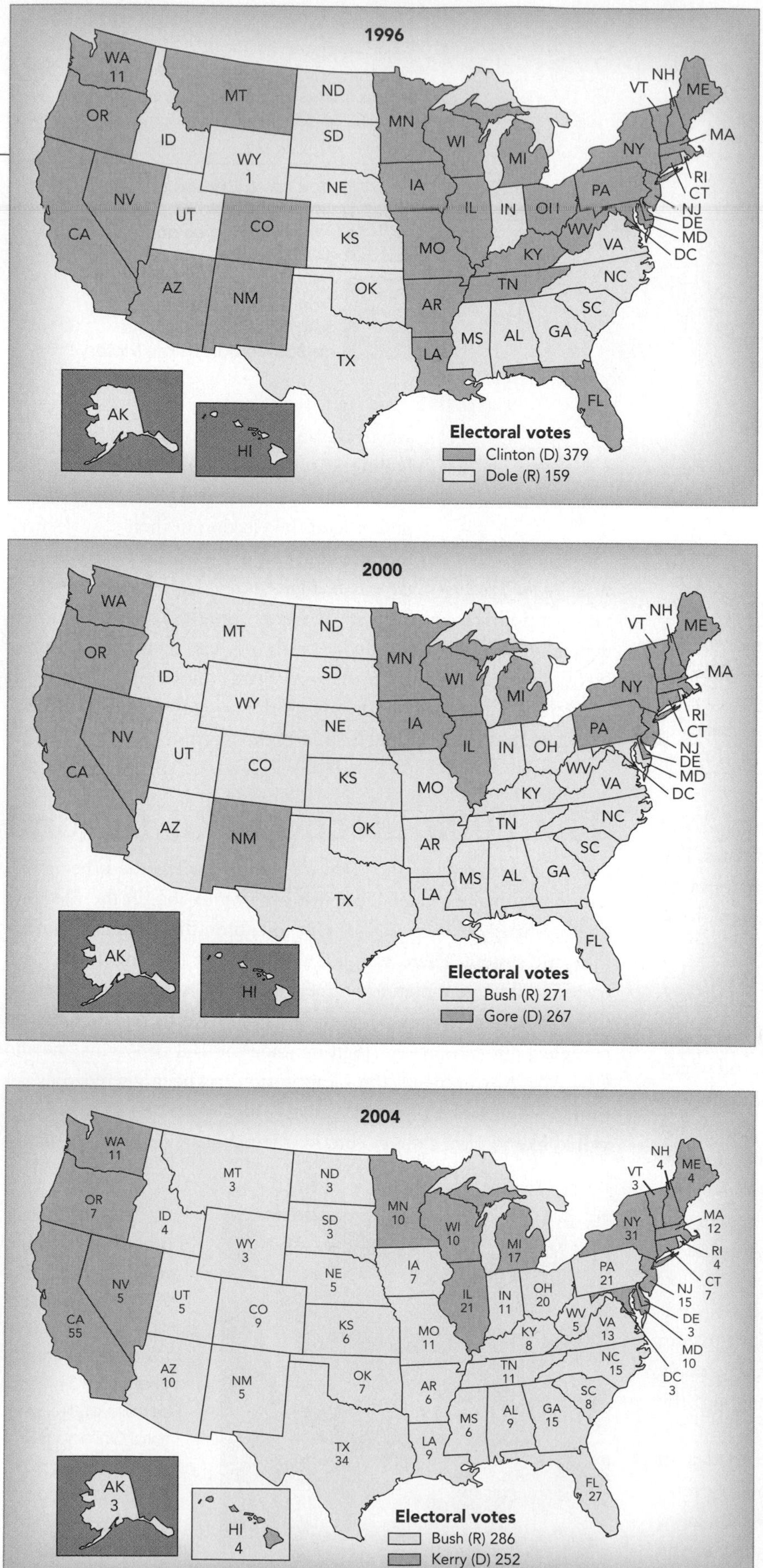

FIGURE 12.3 | **Electoral Votes for 1996, 2000, and 2004**

—Does the Electoral College distort the impact that certain states have on our electoral process? How would you argue that that distortion is the primary reason for scraping it?

they would like to abolish the Electoral College. At the same time, however, the prospects of passing a constitutional amendment seem limited (at least at this time).

Things are happening at the state level, however. The state of Maryland recently passed a measure that could eventually create a more direct process of choosing the president without amending the Constitution. Specifically, in April of 2007, they passed a law that would award the state's electoral votes to the winner of the national popular vote—so long as other states agree to do the same. The Constitution stipulates that each state can select electors as they see fit. So if every state agrees to appoint electors who would vote for the winner of the national popular vote, no matter who wins their state, the national popular vote would decide the winner. This would be a way to nullify the Electoral College without amending the Constitution.

One of the most significant changes that would result from Maryland's scheme would be the nationalization of presidential campaigns. Candidates would slug it out for votes throughout the nation, not just in particular states. Maryland State Senator Jamie Raskin, sponsor of the measure, said Maryland is largely ignored by presidential candidates during campaigns, because they assume it is a solid Democratic state. His hope is that Maryland's plan will start a national discussion and "kick off an insurrection among spectator states—the states that are completely bypassed and sidelined." Also, he argues, "going by the national popular vote will reawaken politics in every part of the country."[4]

Other states have considered similar measures. In 2006, legislation was introduced in Colorado, Illinois, Louisiana, Missouri, New York, and California. California actually passed a bill nearly identical to Maryland's, but it was vetoed by Governor Arnold Schwarzenegger. He argued that the allocation of Electoral College votes was an issue of state's rights, and that the law would make it possible that electors would vote for a candidate rejected by most their state's residents. In all, some 40 states have had measures introduced to modify the allocation of Electoral College votes. Hawaii was the only other state to actually pass a similar measure in 2007.

Not everyone agrees with these schemes. Defenders of the Electoral College argue that it adds to the popular support of winners. In other words, somehow we feel that the victor has more legitimacy if the Electoral

FIGURE 12.4 | 2008 Electoral Votes

Barack Obama's decisive win in the 2008 presidential election sprang from voter shifts that occurred across the county (discussed further in Chapter 15) and by flipping several key states, such as Virginia, Ohio, New Mexico, and Nevada.

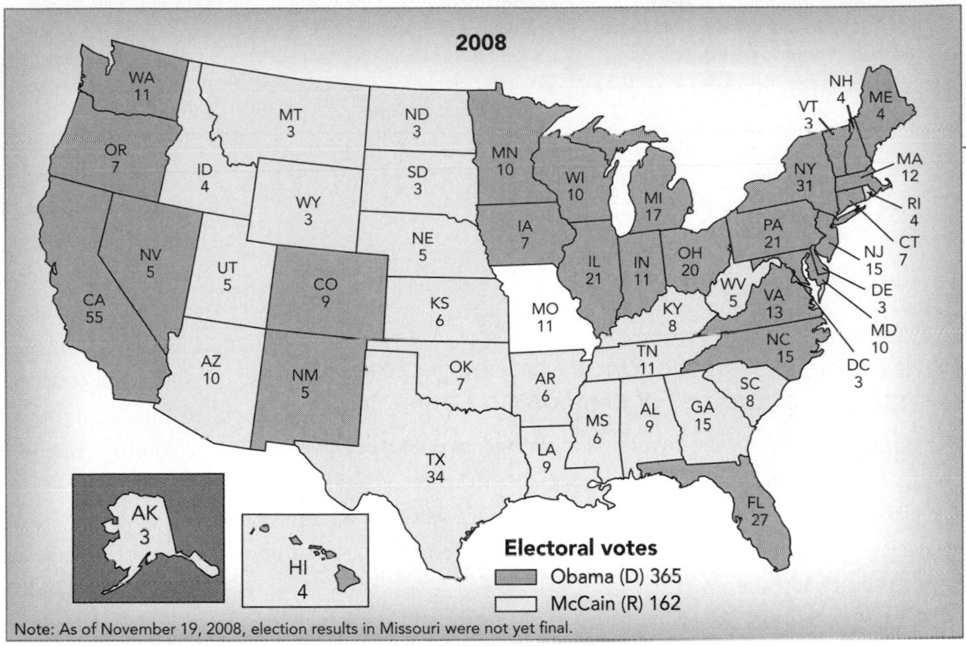

Note: As of November 19, 2008, election results in Missouri were not yet final.

College vote is won by a landslide, even if that candidate has won the popular vote by only a few percentage points. (In about one-half of presidential elections, the winner has actually netted less than 50 percent of the popular vote, given the closeness of elections and that minor party candidates often net a few percentage points of the vote.) The current system helps promote the legitimacy of the winners, an important part of elections. The Electoral College also forces candidates to strive for wide geographical appeal rather than concentrating all their efforts in a few large states. As noted by columnist George Will, "The system aims not just for majority rule but rule *by certain kinds of majorities.* It encourages candidates to form coalitions of states with various political interests and cultures."[5] Rural states worry that they would fall by the wayside in the pursuit of the largest national vote. Others worry that campaigns would focus almost exclusively on media and that the grassroots efforts, essential to win particular states, would vanish.

The Electoral College

Practice Quiz

1. Why did the founders establish the Electoral College?
   - **a.** They feared ordinary voters would elect a president who was popular rather than qualified.
   - **b.** They wanted smaller states to be more equally represented.
   - **c.** They wanted political parties to play a stronger role in the selection of presidential candidates.
   - **d.** a and b

2. Which constitutional amendment states that in the Electoral College, the electors must indicate who they are voting for as president and who they are voting for as vice president?
   - **a.** Tenth
   - **b.** Eleventh
   - **c.** Twelfth
   - **d.** Sixteenth

3. If no candidate receives a majority of the popular vote, who decides who wins the presidency?
   - **a.** The Senate
   - **b.** The House of Representatives
   - **c.** The Supreme Court
   - **d.** A constitutional convention

4. What was so unique about the Electoral College outcome in the 2000 presidential election?
   - **a.** For only the second time in history, the election was decided by the House of Representatives.
   - **b.** The State Election Commission in Florida actually awarded Florida's electoral votes to George W. Bush.
   - **c.** The Supreme Court made a ruling that allowed Florida's electoral votes be awarded to George W. Bush.
   - **d.** Al Gore never did concede the election.

Answers: 1-d, 2-c, 3-b, 4-c.

Discussion Questions

1. Describe and discuss how the Electoral College dictates campaign strategy. How does it impact smaller states? How does it determine television coverage?
2. Why do we still have an electoral college? Contrast the arguments given for retaining it with those for abolishing it.

What **YOU** can do!

One of the most controversial Supreme Court cases in recent years was *Bush* v. *Gore* (2000), in which it was decided that Florida could not conduct a manual recount, thus giving George W. Bush a narrow victory in the state and enough Electoral College votes to win the White House. To learn more—and to actually hear recordings of arguments in the case—visit the Oyez Web site at **http://www.oyez.org/oyez/resource/case/766/audioresource**

CONNECT THE LINK (Chapter **5**, pages **177–178**) How does the Fourteenth Amendment extend rights and privileges to all U.S. citizens?

■ **Fourteenth Amendment (1868):** A change to the Constitution that defines the meaning of U.S. citizenship and establishes that each state must guarantee equal protection of the laws to its citizens.

SIGNIFICANCE: *This change helped protect individual liberties, such as voting, from the infringement of states and the national government.*

■ **Fifteenth Amendment (1870):** A change to the Constitution that guarantees the right to vote shall not be denied to anyone on the basis of race.

SIGNIFICANCE: *This change began the voting enfranchisement of African Americans into the election process. Ironically, it did not speak to women's suffrage.*

Elections *and the* Law (pages 436–439)

Have numerous legal changes broadened the democratic character of elections in America?

For elections to be a viable avenue for change, two conditions must be present. First, there must be widespread faith in the system. Average citizens must believe that their efforts matter. Without a sense of efficacy, few will take the time to participate. The topic is taken up later in the chapter.

The second necessary condition is institutional guarantees for meaningful involvement. There must be laws affording all citizens the right to participate, and there must be a level playing field for candidates. As you will read, our system has taken many steps to broaden the right to vote. Whether or not there are additional steps to take is a debatable topic.

Constitutional Amendments

The first federal constitutional changes that broadened the scope of the electorate were the Fourteenth and Fifteenth Amendments. The **Fourteenth Amendment**■, ratified in 1868, deals with voting rights indirectly. Its first clause guarantees citizenship and the rights of citizenship to all persons born or naturalized in the United States (LINK Chapter 5, pages 177–178). While in modern times it might be assumed that this includes voting rights, it should be remembered that at the time, female citizens were denied the right to vote. If gender could be made a condition of suffrage despite citizenship, then so could race. In its second clause, the Fourteenth Amendment gave the states an incentive to grant minority citizens the right to vote, essentially basing representation in both Congress and the Electoral College not just on population but also on the percentage of its male citizens over age 21 who could vote. If states refused to give African Americans the vote, they would receive fewer seats in Congress and fewer electoral college votes, thus politically marginalizing these states at the national level.[6]

The Fourteenth Amendment did not work as well as its drafters had hoped in giving the vote to former slaves. Therefore, in 1870, the **Fifteenth Amendment**■ was adopted, stating (in its entirety) that "the right of citizens of the United States to vote shall not be denied or abridged by the United States or by any State on account of race, color, or previous condition of servitude."

The **Nineteenth Amendment**■, which gave the vote to women, was the product of a grassroots movement that began in 1848, but the amendment itself was not enacted until 1920. The feminist movement gained steam throughout the second half of the nineteenth century. (Advocates of women's suffrage had tried but failed to get Congress to add the word *sex* to the Fifteenth Amendment as grounds on which states could not deny the right to vote, but at the time, this was still considered too radical an idea.) Frontier life also helped fuel the movement for women's voting rights; on the frontier, women were considered equal partners in the family's fight for survival. It is not surprising that the first state to grant women the right to vote was Wyoming in 1890, followed by Utah and Idaho in 1896.

Pressure for amending the U.S. Constitution to grant women the vote came mainly from the western states, and opposition was mainly from the South and from eastern conservatives, who feared that women would support further Progressive changes, such as child labor restrictions.[7] Adopted in 1920, more than 70 years after the push for women's suffrage began, the Nineteenth Amendment initiated the most sweeping enlargement of the American electorate in a single act.

The **Twenty-Fourth Amendment**■ to the Constitution outlawed the poll tax in 1964. A fee imposed on voters, the poll tax had been one of the barriers to African American voting in the South. By 1962, however, when the amendment was proposed, it was used in only five states and generally amounted only to a dollar or two. Nevertheless, enactment of the Twenty-Fourth Amendment struck down one more symbol of the elitism and racism that had disfigured American democracy.

The Chrisman sisters are shown outside their house in 1886. These women were among the thousands of homesteaders who moved west in the late 1800s and set up housekeeping with the only natural resource the Great Plains had in abundance: sod. All settlers faced immense challenges on the frontier. Perhaps this is why many of the first states to grant women the right to vote were in the west.

Nineteenth Amendment (1920): A change to the Constitution that granted the right of women to vote. **SIGNIFICANCE:** *This change is a good example of how the grassroots mobilization pathway can bring about change in America.*	**Twenty-Fourth Amendment (1964):** A change to the Constitution that eliminated the poll tax. **SIGNIFICANCE:** *Prior to this change, states could limit certain populations of citizens from voting, including poor people and African Americans.*	**Twenty-Sixth Amendment (1971):** A change to the Constitution that granted 18-year-old citizens the right to vote. **SIGNIFICANCE:** *Most college students are allowed to participate in elections today because of this change.*

The **Twenty-Sixth Amendment**, giving 18-year-old citizens the right to vote, was the most recent change to the Constitution to extend the franchise. By the late 1960s, a growing proportion of Americans were in their late teens and had proved not only that they could be active in politics but also that they could be effective in promoting change. Images of young men going off to die in the Vietnam War but not being able to vote gave the movement its biting edge. On July 1, 1971, Congress passed the Twenty-Sixth Amendment, giving citizens 18 years and older the right to vote in all elections. It passed with little objection, and the state legislatures ratified it in only three and a half months.[8]

PATHWAYS | of change from around the world

A key Russian parliamentary election was held in December of 2007. Much to the surprise of many in the West, Vladimir Putin's United Russia party received roughly two-thirds of the youth vote (18–24 year olds) in that contest. Some had speculated that young voters would rebel against Putin and his hard-line positions on broadening democratic freedoms, but it seems that other forces came into play.

According to one account, the fact that Russia's economy had stabilized, stores were full of the latest Western products, and national pride had increased all contributed to strong support from young voters. "The high spirits, the propaganda about a great Russia and a growing economy [made] many young people come out and vote. And they voted for United Russia."

As noted Akhmad Dzhalolov, a 19-year-old Moscow resident, "The Kremlin has created an ideology for young people which is good. I voted for United Russia to make sure that Putin's course that stabilized the country over the past 7 years is continued."

On top of this, operatives in the United Russia party seemed to appreciate the importance of local youth organizations. They poured resources into these groups, allowing the local leaders to sponsor exciting, fun events.

SOURCE: Thomas Peter and James Kilner, "Putin a Winner with Russia's Young Voters," Reuters. November 27, 2007. Accessed at http://www.reuters.com/article/worldNews/idUSL27377396200711 27?sp=true

Voting and Legislative Acts

The Constitution says that as long as Congress remains silent, voting regulations and requirements are left to the states. There were many state-level restrictions on voting in the early days of the Republic. For roughly a decade after ratification of the Constitution, some states imposed religious qualifications, and most states had property ownership and tax-paying requirements. By the 1820s, the property owning requirements were generally abolished, and none of the states entering the Union after this time had property requirements for voting. Tax-paying requirements were not fully phased out until the Twenty-Fourth Amendment outlawed the poll tax. However, state laws were generally written so broadly that any citizen who paid a tax of any kind could vote—with the notable exception of the South's poll taxes.[9]

"Why didn't the Civil War Amendments make it possible for all African Americans to vote?"

—Student Question

Challenging Discriminatory Practices

In the late nineteenth century and well into the twentieth, southern states used their power to regulate elections to keep African Americans from the polls. Imposing a variety of restrictions—literacy tests, poll taxes, complicated registration and residency requirements, and the infamous "grandfather clause," which exempted a voter from all these requirements if his (free white) grandfather had voted before 1860—white-ruled southern states managed to

Long lines of African Americans wait to register to vote in a makeshift office in Alabama after the passage of the Voting Rights Act of 1965. ***—Do you believe that all racial barriers to voting in America have been removed?***

Voting Rights Act of 1965: Outlawed discriminatory voting practices responsible for the widespread disenfranchisement of African Americans.

SIGNIFICANCE: *Many consider this the centerpiece of civil rights legislation.*

Residency and Registration Laws: State laws that stipulate how long a person must reside in a community before being allowed to vote in that community.

SIGNIFICANCE: *Many Americans, especially young Americans, fail to vote because they do not register to vote well in advance of the election.*

disfranchise most blacks. In this, they had the tacit approval of Congress and the federal courts, which refused to stop these blatant violations of the Fourteenth and Fifteenth Amendments. A favorite exclusionary tool was the white primary. Because the Democratic Party dominated the South after the 1870s, the winner of the Democratic nomination was the de facto winner of the election. Southern election laws defined political parties as private organizations, with the right to decide their own membership. Thus, while blacks might enjoy the right to vote in the general election, as stipulated in the Fifteenth Amendment, they could not vote in the only election that really counted, the Democratic primary.[10] This practice remained in effect until the Supreme Court's decision in *Smith* v. *Allwright* (1944). The Court ruled that primaries were part of the electoral system, and therefore the exclusion of blacks from this process violated the Fifteenth Amendment.

"Do all states follow the same voter registration and election laws?"

—Student Question

The Civil Rights Act of 1957 created the U.S. Civil Rights Commission, an agency empowered to investigate voting rights violations and to suggest remedies. In 1964, a second and much more sweeping civil rights act was adopted. The most significant change that directly affected elections, however, came with the **Voting Rights Act of 1965**. Forcefully challenging the South's discriminatory practices, this law provided that for any congressional district in which fewer than 50 percent of adults went to the polls, a 5-year "emergency state" would be triggered. Affected districts could change their election regulations only with the approval of the civil rights division of the Justice Department, and the emergency could be ended only by appeal to a federal court with evidence that no discriminatory devices had been used during the past 5 years. In addition, the Justice Department could now send election examiners into the states to register voters and observe elections. Although the 1965 Voting Rights Act did not end discrimination, it became the most important tool in protecting the right to vote.[11] Election data reflect the act's importance: Overall, in 11 southern states in 1960, a meager 29.7 percent—and, in some states in the region, only a negligible number—of adult African Americans were registered to vote. By the end of the decade, this figure had more than doubled, to 63.4 percent.[12]

Reforms during the Progressive Era (roughly 1900–1917, a period that we'll discuss in greater detail in Chapter 13) were designed to clean up the all-too-common practice of fraudulent voting in general elections. Party bosses, for example, might pay people to travel around the city voting in numerous polling places. To this day, only half-jokingly, party operatives can be heard reminding supporters on election day to "vote early and vote often." Frequently, dead or nonexistent voters were discovered to have cast ballots. **Residency and registration laws** were the solution. Residency laws stipulate that a person can vote in a community only if that person has been a resident for a prescribed period. (The length of time varies from state to state, but the Voting Rights Act of 1970 established a maximum of 30 days.) Registration is the process of signing up to vote in advance of an upcoming election. In some states—Maine, Minnesota, New Hampshire, Oregon, Wisconsin, and Washington—a resident can register up to and including election day. In most other states, there is a stipulated, pre–election day cutoff.

The idea behind requiring residency and registration was to reduce corruption. In recent years, however, these laws have become controversial, and some people have even suggested that they are the main reason why many Americans do not vote. In their provocatively titled book *Why Americans Still Don't Vote: And Why Politicians Want It That Way,* Frances Fox Piven and Richard Cloward argue these laws have always been about keeping certain types of voters out of the process.[13] That is, these measures were not about corruption but about control. (And, indeed, middle-class Progressive reformers often wanted to keep "ignorant" immigrants away from the polls.) Perhaps trying to find a middle ground, Congress in 1993 required states to allow citizens to register to vote at numerous public facilities used by low-income people, such as state motor vehicle, welfare, and employment offices. This so-called **motor voter law** also stipulated that states must permit mail-in registration. Interestingly, data suggest that the motor voter law has increased the number of registered voters but has had a negligible impact on the number of Americans who actually show up at the polls.

In the wake of the confusion surrounding the 2000 presidential election, as discussed earlier, in 2002 Congress passed the **Help America Vote Act**. This measure was designed to create a more uniform voting system, replacing with more regularity and consistency the haphazard, state-by-state process that had existed for two centuries (see Figure 12.5). For example, some states were using punch cards and others old-fashioned voting machines, while still others were experimenting with touch screen machines. Some states kept up-to-date voter lists; others updated them only sporadically. The act set federal standards for all voting systems throughout the United States, provided $325 million to update voting systems, required states to create registered voter databases, and called for voter education and poll worker training.

Motor Voter Law: A law passed by Congress in 1993 designed to make it easier for Americans to register to vote.

EXAMPLE: *You can now register to vote in state motor vehicle offices.*

Help America Vote Act: A measure passed in 2002, in the wake of the controversy surrounding the 2000 election, designed to create a more uniform voting system throughout the 50 states.

SIGNIFICANCE: *This law afforded states resources to shift from older voting machines to the touch screen, computer-driven machines used in most states today.*

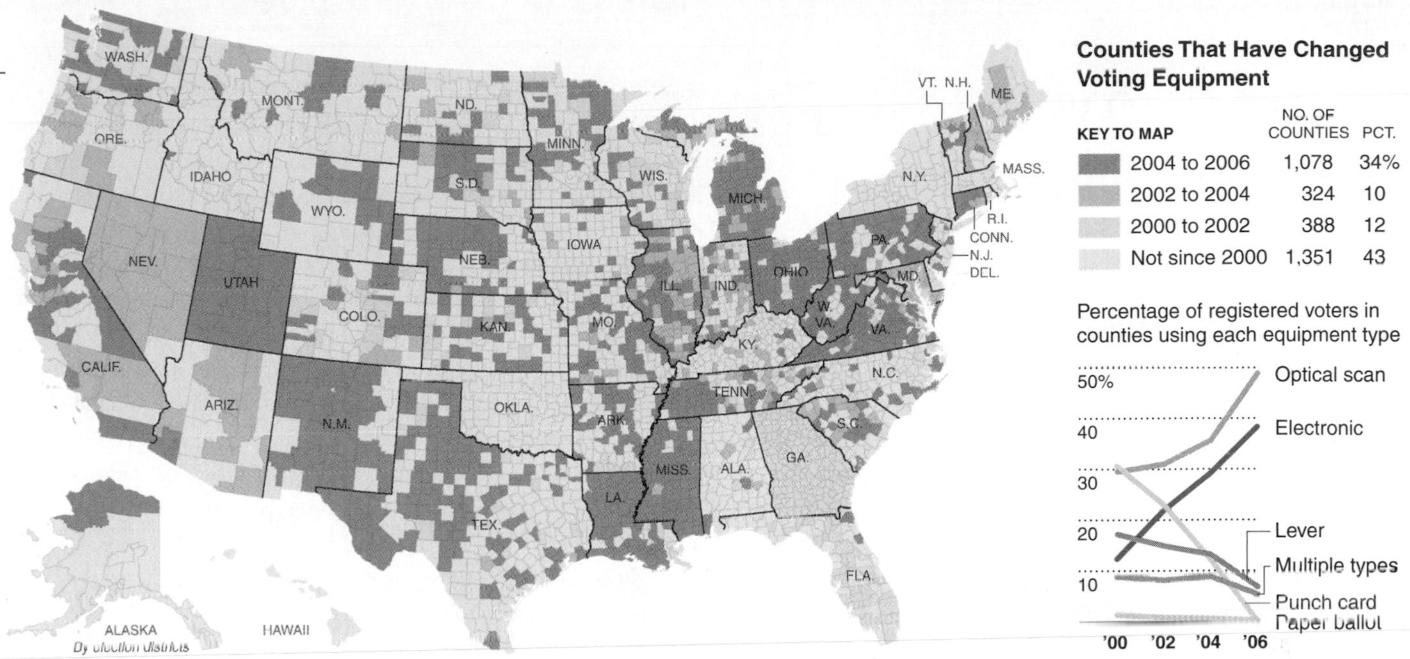

Source: Kimball W. Brace, Election Data Services

October 18, 2006, New York Times Graphics. Copyright © 2006 by the New York Times Co. Reprinted with permission.

FIGURE 12.5 | **The Mechanics of Voting in America**

Our faith in the voting process was shaken in the 2000 election, as the recount in Florida revealed numerous hidden problems. Some began to worry about the legitimacy of the process. In response, Congress passed the Help America Vote Act in 2002. Among much else, the measure pushed states to update their voting systems. This figure illustrates where changes in voting equipment have occurred through the 2006 election. ***—What factors might explain why some states have updated their machinery and others have not?***

Elections and the Law

Practice Quiz

1. The constitutional amendment granting voting rights to former (male) slaves was the
   a. Fourteenth Amendment **b.** Fifteenth Amendment
   c. Nineteeth Amendment **d.** Twenty-Fourth Amendment

2. The constitutional amendment granting rights of citizenship to all persons born or naturalized in the United States was the
   a. Fourteenth Amendment **b.** Fifteenth Amendment
   c. Nineteeth Amendment **d.** Twenty-Fourth Amendment

3. Women were granted the right to vote with passage of the
   a. Fifteenth Amendment
   b. Nineteeth Amendment
   c. Twenty-Fourth Amendment
   d. Twenty-Sixth Amendment

4. What legislation became the most important tool in protecting the right to vote?
   a. The Nineteeth Amendment
   b. The Civil Rights Act of 1957
   c. The Voting Rights Act of 1965
   d. The Voting Rights Act of 1968

Answers: 1-b, 2-a, 3-b, 4-c.

Discussion Questions

1. What role did southern state legislators play in voting rights?
2. What role did the Supreme Court play in voting rights?

What **YOU** can do!

The National Archives Web site includes an Electoral College calculator that allows you to predict which party will win the presidency based on different electoral strategies (**http://www.archives.gov/federal-register/electoral-college/calculator.html**). While you are at the site, investigate the history of the Electoral College, including criticisms and proposals for reform.

■ **Ballot Initiative:** A system whereby citizens decide policy matters through voting on election day. About half of the states allow this process.

EXAMPLE: *Several states have restricted gay marriages through ballot initiatives.*

■ **Recall:** Process whereby voters can remove from office an elected offical before the next regularly scheduled election.

EXAMPLE: *California Governor Gray Davis was recalled in 2003 by the voters and replaced by actor Arnold Schwarzenegger.*

Referendums, Initiatives, *and* Recalls (pages 440–441)

Should citizens be allowed to vote on policy matters?

"Do voters get to vote for specific issues rather than for candidates?"

—Student Question

Many Americans believe that elections are only used to select public officials. This is not the case, for about half the states also allow voters to use elections to have a direct say in making policy. (Such a process is not allowed at the federal level.) This is left over from the Progressive Era, when reformers were frustrated with the lack of change coming out of state legislatures. Progressive reformers thought up many ways to give voters a direct voice in writing new laws and regulations. These changes stuck, and in states where they are used today, they remain a key mechanism for allowing citizens to implement change.

Ballot initiatives■, now used in 24 states, allow voters the option of deciding policy matters (see Figures 12.6 and 12.7). To have a question or proposed law listed on the ballot, its advocates must gather a required number of valid voter signatures. Then, on election day, all citizens can vote either for or against the measure, and if a majority agrees, it becomes law. A referendum is a similar process that asks citizens on election day to reaffirm or reject an existing law. In actual practice, the terms *initiative* and *referendum* tend to be used interchangeably.

The questions that voters are asked to decide through initiative and referendum elections vary widely. A sampling from recent elections includes many "hot" issues, most of which elected politicians would prefer to ignore out of fear of offending some people—for example, allowing the medical use of marijuana, permitting doctor-assisted suicide, requiring English-only teaching in public schools, giving public school teachers pay raises, protecting wetlands and forests, outlawing the hunting of mountain lions, imposing legislative term limits, prohibiting the trapping of bobcats and bears, legalizing gambling, providing vouchers for students to attend private or parochial schools, and so on. In 2002, Oklahoma voters outlawed cockfighting, and Nevada voters refused to legalize the recreational use of marijuana. In 2006, Arizona voters put a ban on smoking in public places, Arkansas voters confronted whether to allow bingo to be played for charitable causes, and Michigan voters debated the legalization of dove hunting. In 2007, New Jersey voters reject a measure that would have lead to greater funding for stem cell research.

Yet another Progressive Era measure designed to give the policy process back to the will of the people is the **recall**■. In a recall, citizens can vote an officeholder out of office before the next regularly scheduled election. Petitions are circulated, and if enough signatures are collected, a special election date is set. The politician in office is ordinarily automatically listed on the ballot but goes back to private life if he or she gets fewer votes than another candidate.

Recall elections are rare. Most of the time, even if people become dissatisfied with elected officials, they simply bear with the situation until the next election. After all, it is the voters themselves who elected the person to office, and it has become part of our political culture to accept election outcomes and "wait till next time." Very few recall efforts have been successful in the states that allow them. The voters in California, however, shocked the nation in the fall of 2003 when they recalled Democrat Gray Davis, only the second governor ever to be recalled. In his place, they selected Austrian-born, Republican, film actor and former bodybuilder Arnold Schwarzenegger. The man who once ruled the movie box office stepped to the helm of the largest and in many ways most complex state in the Union.

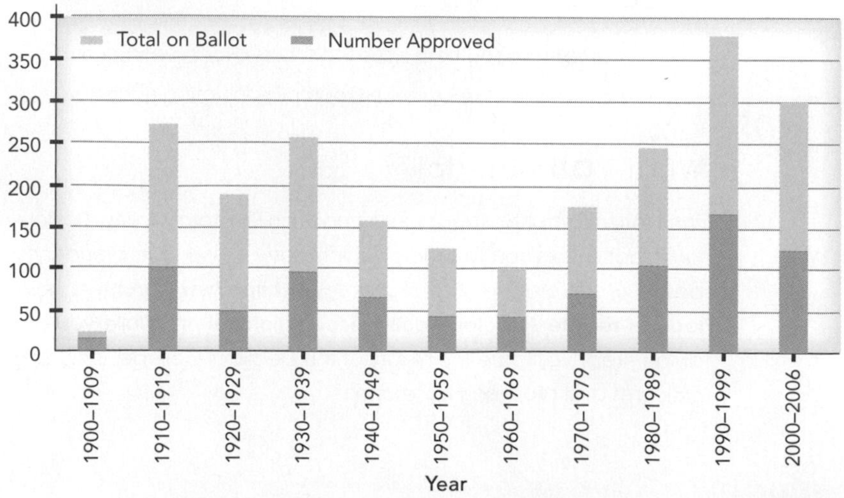

FIGURE 12.6 | **Number of Initiatives by Decade**

As this figure illustrates, the number of ballot initiatives has grown in recent years. ***—Do you think this is due to growing faith in the wisdom of average voters or concerns about legislators neglecting voters' concerns? Is it possible that issue advocates now see ballot initiatives as viable pathways for change?***

SOURCE: *Initiative Use* (Los Angeles, CA: Initiative & Referendum Institute, USC Law School, November 2006), p. 1. Reprinted with permission.

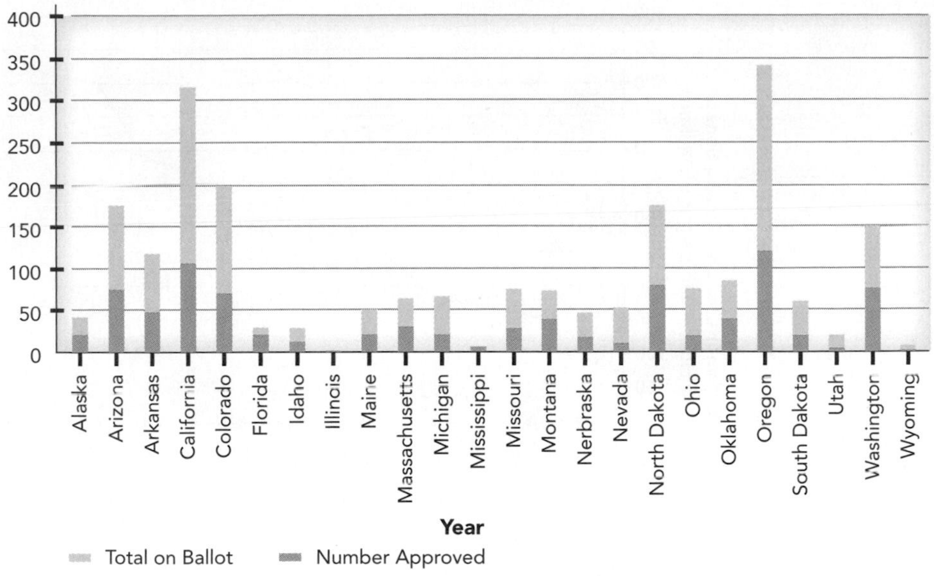

FIGURE 12.7 | Number of Initiatives by State, 1904–2007

Not every state allows for ballot initiatives. ***—Is it a random pattern or do you think there are state-based forces that push some states to referenda and others away from them?***

SOURCE: *Initiative Use* (Los Angeles, CA: Initiative & Referendum Institute, USC Law School, November 2006), p. 1. Reprinted with permission.

The Future of the Ballot Initiatives

To many people, initiatives, referendums, and recall elections represent democracy at its best—average citizens proposing changes in government, working to build support, and allowing the majority of the community to decide its fate. As the *Christian Science Monitor* editorialized, "Such grassroots efforts can help reenergize voters and preserve an outlet for direct democracy if entrenched interests control the legislature. Research shows that when there's an initiative on the ballot, voter turnout increases 3 to 7 percent."[14] Polls also suggest that roughly two-thirds of Americans believe that they should have some say in policy matters.[15] But direct democracy can be problematic, and the framers of our political system were rather fearful of such a process. (That is why ballot initiatives are permitted only at the state and local levels and not at the federal level.) Even more significant, many critics suggest that the initiative process has changed and no longer represents "democracy in action."

Arnold Schwarzenegger holds up a broom while announcing a "clean sweep" for the California recall election in 2003. Schwarzenegger won that race and was reelected in 2006. ***—Should voters have the option of recalling unpopular officials?***

Referendums, Initiatives, and Recalls
Practice Quiz

1. In order to have a question or proposed law listed on a ballot, advocates must gather a required number of valid voter signatures. Then, on election day, citizens can vote for or against the measure. This process is a
   a. voter initiative. **b.** referendum.
   c. straw poll. **d.** recall.
2. A process that asks citizens on election day to reaffirm or reject an existing law is a
   a. voter initiative. **b.** referendum.
   c. straw poll. **d.** recall.
3. A process whereby citizens can vote an office holder out of office before the next regularly scheduled election is a
   a. voter initiative. **b.** referendum.
   c. straw poll. **d.** recall.
4. Research shows that when an initiative is on the ballot, voter turnout increases 3 to 7 percent.
   a. true **b.** false

Answers: 1-a, 2-b, 3-d, 4-a.

Discussion Questions

1. What are the advantages to ordinary citizens of an initiative or referendum?
2. What are some of the procedural difficulties posed by a voter initiative or referendum?

What **YOU** can do!

Visit the Web site for the Initiative and Referendum Institute at the University of Southern California (**http://www.iandrinstitute.org/ballotwatch.htm**). Explore the results of initiatives from the last election. Are there similar initiatives across multiple states, or do most initiatives appear to be of local and regional interest only? Discuss the implications of your findings with your classmates.

CONNECT THE LINK (Chapter **13**, page **483**) Why have local party organizations become less important in recent decades?

The Role of Money in Elections (pages 442–449)

Does money corrupt the election process, or is it simply a way for citizens to express their political views and support particular candidates?

You might be surprised to hear that in the early days of the Republic, a common practice was to "treat" voters. This meant spending money to sponsor lavish picnics and barbecues. In Virginia, this was called "swilling the planters with bumbo." George Washington, for example, was said to have purchased a quart of rum, wine, beer, and hard cider for every voter in the district when he ran for the Virginia House of Burgesses in 1751 (there were only 391 voters).[16] In 1795, one would-be Delaware office holder roasted a steer and half a dozen sheep for his friends, and another candidate gave a "fish feast." Four decades later, Ferdinand Bayard, a Frenchman traveling in the United States, noticed that "candidates offer drunkenness openly to anyone who is willing to give them his vote."[17]

Another common means of spending campaign money during the nineteenth century was to purchase advertisements in newspapers and, more often, to actually purchase a newspaper completely. Some of the most heated campaigns of the century were conducted through "battling newspapers." Often, when a wealthy individual was anxious to aid a particular candidate, he would simply start a newspaper. It has been noted that "even Abraham Lincoln secretly purchased a small newspaper in Illinois in 1860."[18]

> "Why is money so important in elections?"
> —Student Question

As technology changed throughout the twentieth century, so did the cost of elections. By the late 1960s, money had become critical for four main reasons:

1. **Decline of Party Organizations.** Political parties went into decline (LINK Chapter 13, page 483). Given that party organizations were primarily responsible for connecting with voters, candidates needed new ways of reaching out. Many of these new means were extremely costly.
2. **More Voters Up for Grabs.** In 1790, there were fewer than 4 million Americans, almost a quarter of them slaves. In 1900, there were 75 million Americans, and in 1960, some 180 million. Today, the U.S. population is over 300 million. Reaching such a huge number of voters requires enormous amounts of money.

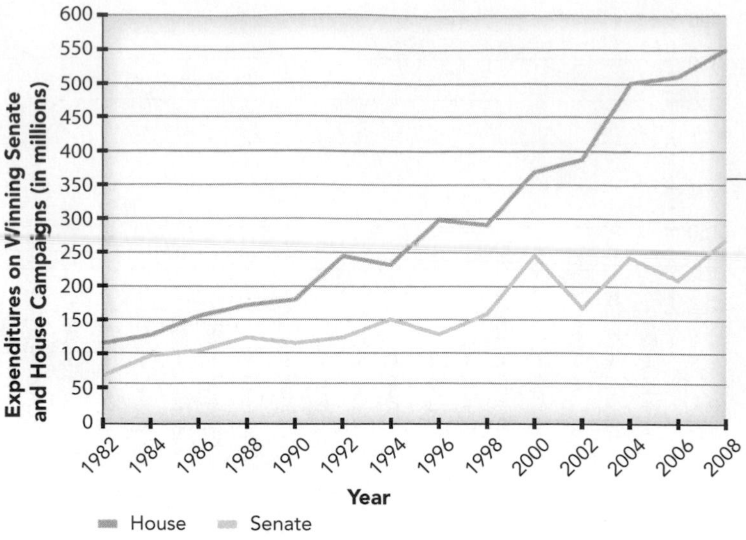

FIGURE 12.8 | Campaign Expenditures

This figure suggests that the cost of elections has grown dramatically, even when inflation is factored in. ***—What do you think is at the heart of rising elections costs? Does this suggest a serious flaw in the process or a sign of a robust exchange of ideas?***

3. **Television.** In the early 1950s, only a small percentage of homes boasted a television set; by the 1960s, TV was nearly universal. Television transformed much of American life and certainly changed the way political campaigns were run. And of course, buying advertising time requires huge sums of money.
4. **Campaign Consultants.** Coupled with the growing importance of political advertising on television were the professionals hired to create these commercials. Professional campaign consulting burst onto the scene in the 1960s, bringing such sophisticated techniques as direct mail and survey research. These methods proved effective, but they came with a hefty price tag.

One estimate is that in 1952, a presidential election year, *all* campaigns for political office, from president to dogcatcher, added up to $140 million.[19] By 2004, the equivalent figure had swelled to an estimated $4 *billion,* and in 2006, a midterm election year, a similar amount was spent. In the 1960s, it was common for a successful House candidate to spend less than $100,000, but by 2006, the average cost of winning a seat in the House of Representatives topped $1.3 million. An "expensive" U.S. Senate race in the 1960s was still under half a million dollars; in 2006, the *average* Senate race cost nearly $9 million.

The Rage for Reform

Efforts to control the flow of money in elections date from the Progressive Era, but these measures were largely symbolic. Real reform came in the early 1970s, when members of Congress began to worry about being thrown out of office by a wealthy candidate—

Federal Election Campaign Act (FECA): Law designed to limit the amount of money contributed to campaigns for Congress and the presidency and to broaden donation reporting requirements.	**SIGNIFICANCE:** *This was the first real attempt to limit the flow of big money into elections, but numerous loopholes, such as soft money, were found to circumvent parts of the law.*

Watergate: The "shorthand" name of a scandal that led to the resignation of President Richard M. Nixon in 1974.	**SIGNIFICANCE:** *A great deal was learned about the inner workings of the Nixon White House through this scandal, including the exceptional efforts used to raise huge sums of money for the 1972 reelection campaign.*

"So eventually the system was reformed?"

—Student Question

perhaps a political novice—who could simply outspend them. The **Federal Election Campaign Act (FECA)** was signed into law by President Richard Nixon in 1971. Three years later, after the **Watergate** scandal revealed a staggering level of corruption in presidential campaigns, a series of amendments made the law even more restrictive. In brief, the legislation limited how much money candidates could spend, how much an individual or group could give, and how much political parties might contribute. It also established voluntary public financing of presidential elections. Presidential candidates who choose to use this system are limited in the amount they can raise and spend.

Few politicians doubted that the provisions were real or that they would have a significant effect on the way elections were conducted. Yet shortly after the amendments took effect, James Buckley, a Conservative Party senator from New York, along with a group of politicians from both ends of the political spectrum, challenged the constitutionality of the law. Buckley argued that spending money was akin to free speech and that limiting it would abridge First Amendment protections. The case of ***Buckley v. Valeo*** (1976) was the most significant election centered court decision in American history. For the most part, the Supreme Court sided with Buckley by striking down provisions of the law that put limits on overall spending, on spending by the candidates, and on spending by independent groups. The justices also upheld the public funding of presidential elections so long as it is voluntary. Surprisingly, however, the Court also allowed limits on how much an individual or a group might *give* to a candidate.

"So did the reforms of the 1970s work?"

—Student Question

It is hard to overstate the effects of this decision. More than anything else, by suggesting campaign money is akin to free speech, *Buckley* shaped the nature of the election process for the next three decades. The restrictions on contributions seemed effective at first, but soon candidates and their consultants thought up new methods of stretching the legal system in each election. The most significant of the loopholes they found is called **soft money**. Although individuals and interest groups were limited in the amount they could contribute to a candidate, the law put no restrictions on giving money to a political party. "Fat cats" made immense contributions—often over $1 million—to the parties, which quickly filtered down to particular candidates. To many Americans, the soft-money loophole had become little more than a scam. "An illness that has plagued previous elections," wrote one observer, "has developed into an epidemic."[20]

Richard Nixon says goodbye to members of his staff outside the White House as he boards a helicopter for Andrews Air Force Base after resigning the presidency in August of 1974. As more information about the Nixon White House came to light, the push for campaign reform accelerated. ***—Should money in elections be regulated, or are campaign contributions akin to free speech?***

Political Action Committees

Another spinoff of FECA and *Buckley* has been the proliferation of political action committees (PACs). Earlier acts of Congress had barred labor unions and corporations from giving money to federal candidates. The idea of PACs was thought up in the 1940s to get around these restrictions. In PACs, none of the monies used to support a candidate came directly from the union or corporation but

■ ***Buckley* v. *Valeo* (1976):** The most significant Supreme Court case on campaign finance in American history.

SIGNIFICANCE: *The Court ruled that campaign expenditures are akin to free speech and are therefore protected by the First Amendment.*

■ **Soft Money:** Funds contributed through a loophole in federal campaign finance regulations that allowed individuals and groups to give unlimited sums of money to political parties.

SIGNIFICANCE: *This massive loophole fueled a public outcry for reform.*

instead from these groups' independent political units. Because FECA stipulates limits on how much candidates might raise from an individual, politicians were forced to solicit help from a broad range of sources. The contribution limit for PACs was originally five times higher than for individuals, so the number of groups exploded: In 1974, there were roughly 600 PACs, but by 2004, more than 4,000 were giving out contributions (see Figure 12.9).[21]

"Can PACs 'buy' politicians with contributions?"

—Student Question

Political action committees give money to candidates because the interest group that backs them wants a say in public policy. Businesses, for example, want policies that help them make a profit; environmentalists want policies that help protect the natural world; and labor seeks policies that help working men and women. But do these groups, through their PACs, "buy" policies with their contributions? This is a hotly debated issue. Some analysts suggest that the connection between contributions and policy is direct—that contributors are rational and not inclined to spend their money without a direct payback. The Center for Responsive Politics is a nonpartisan organization that tracks the flow of money in elections and the development of public policy. Its Web site (http://www.opensecrets.org) gives detailed information on who gives and who receives campaign money. On one of its pages, "Tracking the Payback," you can explore possible links between how a member of Congress votes on given policy issues and the source of his or her contributions in previous elections.[22] The organization's goal is to demonstrate that money may very well "buy" policies.

Precisely what PACs buy with their contribution is unclear, however, and political scientists have been unable to settle the matter. What is clear is that the public perceives a problem. An oft-heard remark is that we have "the best Congress money can buy!" Numerous public opinion polls confirm that regardless of what actually happens between contributors and public officials, average Americans regard the money flowing from PACs to candidates as a threat to the democratic process.

The Incumbent Fundraising Advantage

Candidates vying for office solicit funds from many sources: individuals (friends, spouses, associates, activists), political parties, PACs, and—believe it or not—other candidates (see Figure 12.10). Table 12.1 (and Figure 12.11) underscores important differences between the three types of candidates. *Incumbents* are candidates already holding the office and up for reelection, *challengers* are those opposing the incumbents, and *open-seat candidates* are running for seats for which no incumbent is seeking reelection. Political action committees hope that their money will somehow produce support for their policies, which means they hope their money will go to the eventual winner. (What can a losing candidate do to shape public policy?) Accordingly, they prefer to send their funds to incumbents, because those already in office have a head start—the so-called **incumbent advantage**■—when it comes to reelection. (See Table 12.1) And by sending their money to incumbents, PACs provide an even greater boost to incumbents' chances of reelection.

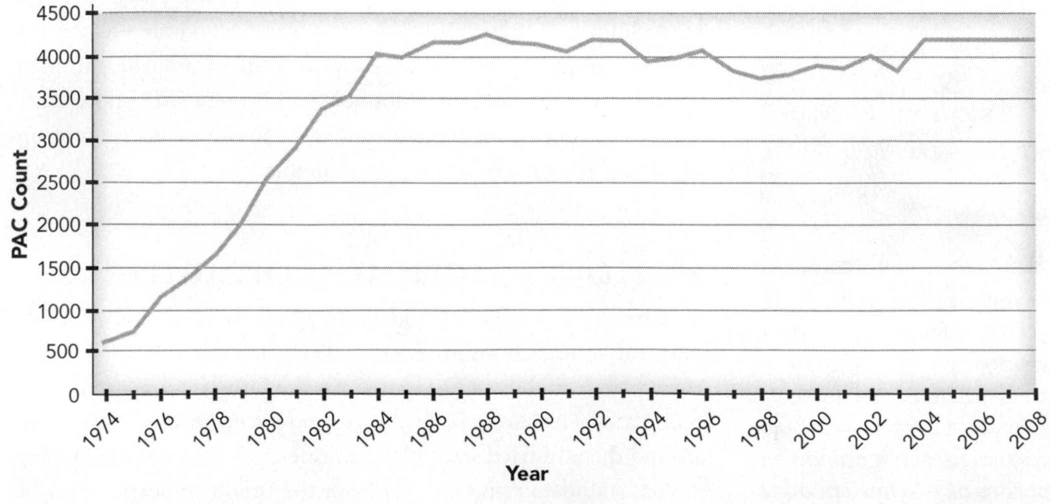

FIGURE 12.9 | Number of Registered Political Action Committees, 1974–2008

This figure shows a dramatic increase in the number of political action committees. In 2008, there were roughly 4,168 PACs. ***—What explains this increase, and what effect do you think this change will have on our electoral system?***

SOURCE: Federal Election Commission Online, http://www.fec.gov/press/press2008/20080117paccount.shtml

■ **Incumbent Advantage:** The various factors that favor office holders running for reelection over their challengers.

EXAMPLE: *Those in office seem to be able to raise much more money for their reelection campaigns than can their challengers.*

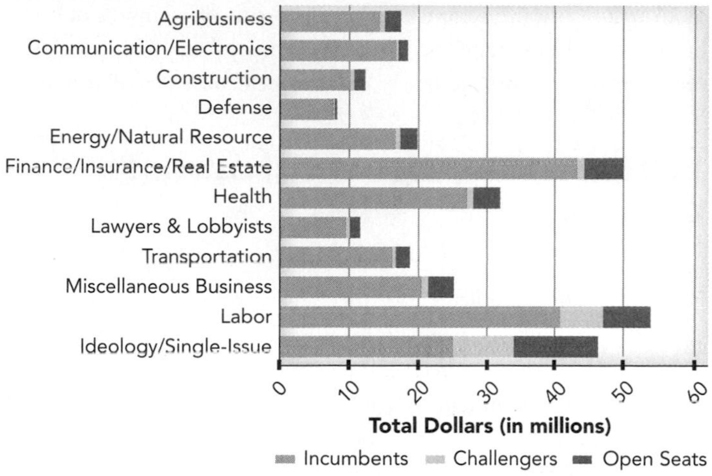

FIGURE 12.10 | **Contributions to Candidates**

There are several factors behind the incumbent advantage, and the ability to raise a great deal more money than their challengers—depicted in the figure—is at the center. ***—But if this is true, what can be done about it? Why would ideological groups be a bit of an exception?***

SOURCE: Reprinted by permission of the Center for Responsive Politics

TABLE 12.1 | **The Incumbent Fundraising Advantage in the 2006 Election**

Based on data released by the FEC on Monday, August 20, 2007. ***—Does this suggest a broken process?***

Type of Candidate	Total Raised	Number of Candidates	Average Raised
SENATE			
Incumbent	$350,827,780	31	$11,317,025
Challenger	$183,299,218	101	$1,814,844
Open seat	$99,942,000	35	$2,855,486
Total	$634,068,998	167	$3,796,820
HOUSE			
Incumbent	$538,842,476	424	$1,270,855
Challenger	$178,054,021	629	$283,075
Open seat	$154,779,515	265	$584,074
Total	$871,676,012	1,318	$661,363

SOURCE: http://www.opensecrets.org/bigpicture/incumbs.asp. Reprinted by permission of the Center for Responsive Politics.

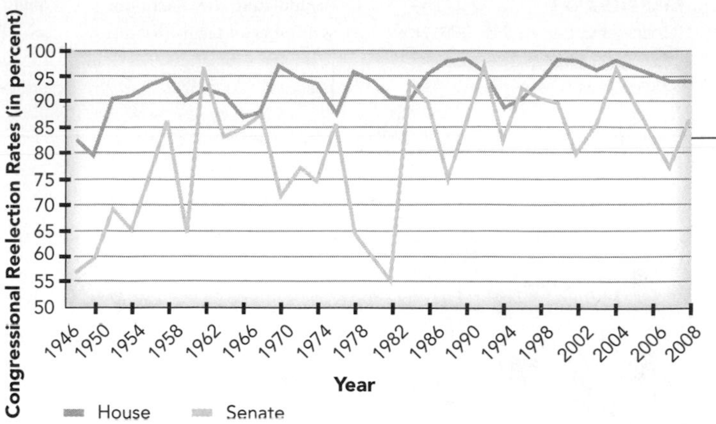

FIGURE 12.11 | **Congressional Reelection Rates, 1946-2008**

Since 1950, reelection rates in the House have fallen below 90 percent only five times. ***—Does this seem right, given the shrinking faith that many Americans have in elected officials? What do you think is driving this trend? In the Senate, reelection rates have risen above 90 percent only five times. Why do you suppose Senate races seem more competitive than House races?***

SOURCES: *Vital Statistics on Congress, 1999–2000* (Washington, DC: AEI Press, 2000); *Vital Statistics on American Politics, 2003 2004* (Washington, DC: CQ Press, 2004); *CQ Weekly*, November 6, 2004; Center for Responsive Politics, 2006 election stats, http://www.opensecrets.org

"Why do voters continue to reelect incumbents while complaining about 'Washington Politics'?"

—Student Question

In some recent elections (see Figure 12.11), more than 95 percent of incumbent House candidates won, even though many Americans are frustrated with "business-as-usual politics" and seem anxious to "throw the bums out." Incumbents have always had an advantage, but critics point to recent changes that have made matters worse. Yale University scholar David Mayhew was one of the first to draw attention to the problem.[23] In his seminal book *Congress: The Electoral Connection,* Mayhew argues that all legislative activity is now geared toward securing reelection. These efforts fall within three categories: *credit claiming,* which is receiving praise for bringing money and federal projects back to the district; *position taking,* or making sure to be on the popular side of issues; and *advertising,* which implies reaching out to constituents in many ways, especially through mailings (when paid for by the government, this is called "franking"). Others have pointed to additional sources of incumbent support, such as ongoing media attention, which challengers rarely get. The growing sophistication of drawing safe districts for members of Congress following every census (see LINK Chapter 6, pages 219–220) has also contributed to the problem. Many observers agree that things have gotten out of hand and that the democratic electoral process is threatened.

CONNECT THE LINK (Chapter **6**, pages **219–220**) How can the redistricting process help legislators win reelection?

Term Limits: Laws stipulating the maximum number of terms that an elected official may serve in a particular office.

SIGNIFICANCE: *Without term limits, it seems that many incumbents are able to stay in office for lengthy stretches—much longer than in previous eras.*

Bipartisan Campaign Reform Act (BCRA): Federal law passed in 2002 that outlawed soft-money contributions to party organizations.

SIGNIFICANCE: *This new law has pushed candidates to raise funds from a greater number of small donors.*

"Why would we need campaign finance legislation? I can't imagine public servants being so unpatriotic as to be influenced by money."

TERM LIMITS Many reforms have been suggested to reduce the incumbent advantage. One proposal is **term limits**. If we are worried about an unfair advantage given to politicians already in office, why not create more open-seat contests? Limiting legislative terms, as we do by allowing presidents just two terms, would guarantee turnover—a stream of new faces, energy, and ideas in the legislature. Representatives should know the concerns of average citizens, and what better way of ensuring that than by forcing entrenched legislators to step aside after a fixed period and make way for fresh blood? Opponents of term limits argue that the legislative process is complex, especially these days, and that it takes time to become familiar with the process. Term limits remove experienced legislators and replace them with green ones. Moreover, term limits deny voters a choice—the chance to reelect a legislator who may actually be doing a good job.

By the early 1990s, roughly half the states had adopted term limits for state legislators and candidates for federal office. Public opinion polls suggested that a majority of Americans favored these new restrictions, but many legal scholars wondered whether the states had the constitutional power to limit the terms of U.S. House and Senate members. The issue came to a head in the Supreme Court case of *U.S. Term Limits, Inc.* v. *Thornton* (1995). In a 5–4 decision, the Court majority stated that "allowing individual States to craft their own qualifications for Congress would . . . erode the structure envisioned by the Framers, a structure that was designed, in the words of the Preamble to our Constitution, to form a 'more perfect Union.'" With that decision, attempts to limit the terms of members of Congress ended. Many states do limit the terms of state legislators, but members of Congress are free to run for reelection year after year.

Reforming the Reforms: BCRA

By 2000, many Americans had once again come to the conclusion that the campaign finance system was out of whack. One survey found that 75 percent agreed (39 percent "strongly") that "our present system of government is democratic in name only. In fact, special interests run things."[24] Another poll, conducted in 2001, found that 80 percent of Americans felt that politicians often "did special favors for people or groups who gave them campaign contributions."[25] Clearly, the reforms of the early 1970s had done little to halt the flow of big money into elections and, if anything, had made matters worse by *seeming* to limit money. The loopholes were numerous and huge. The public was ripe for change, but reform measures stalled in the legislature. With much effort from Republican Senator John McCain and Democratic Senator Russ Feingold, the **Bipartisan Campaign Reform Act (BCRA)** was passed and signed into law by President George W. Bush in February of 2002.

The new law is sweeping: It outlaws soft-money contributions to the national political organizations and bans group-sponsored advertisements 30 days before primary elections and 60 days before general elections. Yet the law also raises the contribution limit to $2,300 for individuals (see Table 12.2), and it leaves open the ability

Arizona Senator John McCain, a Republican, and Wisconsin Senator Russ Feingold, a Democrat, worked together to push the Bipartisan Campaign Reform Act through Congress in 2002.

TABLE 12.2 | **Contribution Limits for 2007-2008**

Table 12.2 Lays out the restrictions on giving that have been established by a variety of election reforms. Critics of election reform often point out the "loopholes" that exist in the reformed system. ***—Looking at this table, what types of giving do you think a critic of reform would characterize as a loophole?***

	TO EACH CANDIDATE OR CANDIDATE COMMITTEE PER ELECTION	TO NATIONAL PARTY COMMITTEE PER CALENDAR YEAR	TO STATE, DISTRICT AND LOCAL PARTY COMMITTEE PER CALENDAR YEAR	TO ANY OTHER POLITICAL COMMITTEE PER CALENDAR YEAR[1]	SPECIAL LIMITS
Individual may give	$2,300*	$28,500*	$10,000 (combined limit)	$5,000	$108,200* overall biennial limit: • $42,700* to all candidates • $65,500* to all PACS and parties[2]
National Party Committee may give	$5,000	No limit	No limit	$5,000	$39,900* to Senate candidate per campaign[3]
State, District and Local Party Committee may give	$5,000 (combined limit)	No limit	No limit	$5,000 (combined limit)	No limit
PAC (multi-candidate)[4] may give	$5,000	$15,000	$5,000 (combined limit)	$5,000	No limit
PAC (not multi-candidate) may give	$2,300*	$28,500*	$10,000 (combined limit)	$5,000	No limit
Authorized Campaign Committee may give	$2,000[5]	No limit	No limit	$5,000	No limit

*These contribution limits are indexed for inflation.

[1]A contribution earmarked for a candidate through a political committee counts against the original contributor's limit for that candidate. In certain circumstances, the contribution may also count against the contributor's limit to the PACs. 11 CFR 110.6. See also CFR 110.1(h).

[2]No more than $42,700 of this amount may be contributed to state and local party committees and PACs.

[3]This limit is shared by the national committee and the national Senate campaign committee.

[4]A multicandidate committee is a political committee with more than 50 contributors which has been registered for at least 6 months and with the exception of state party committees, has made contributions to 5 or more candidates for federal office, 11 CFR 100.5(e)(3).

[5]A federal candidate's authorized committee(s) may contribute no more than $2,000 per election to another federal candidate's authorized committee(s) 11 CFR 102.12(c)(2).

SOURCE: Federal Election Commission. "How Much Can I Contribute," Accessed at: http://www.fee.gov/ans/answers_general.shtml#How_much_can_I_contribute

for wealthy individuals to donate soft money to state and local party organizations. The ban on soft money does not apply to political action committees, which are still free to raise unlimited cash.

The law was upheld in the Supreme Court in fall of 2003 in case of *McConnell* v. *Federal Election Commission*. In a 5–4 decision, the Court afirmed the law's most important elements. It was, according to a *New York Times* account, a "stunning victory for political reform."[26] There have been other cases, and a number of the law's provisions have been open to interpretation by the Federal Election Commission, leading to some controversy.

The Rise of 527 Groups

An important by-product of the latest reforms has been the growing number of groups not aligned with a political party but quite interested in certain policies. These groups have been named **527 Organizations**■ (after Section 527 of the Internal Revenue Code, which regulates their practices). They are allowed to raise unlimited sums of money. Most 527s are advocacy groups that try to influence the outcome of elections through voter mobilization efforts and television advertisements that praise or criticize a candidate's record. A great deal of the funds now flowing to 527s previously went to the parties in the form of soft money.

Two prominent examples of 527s in the 2004 election were the Swift Boat Veterans and POWs for Truth, and MoveOn.org. The Swift Boat Veterans were set up with the intention of portraying Democratic candidate John Kerry's past military service in a negative light. MoveOn.org, by contrast, was created by a group of Americans who were dissatisfied with George W. Bush. What is most impressive about this list is the massive sums that these organizations were able to raise. As one observer noted, "Although BCRA cracked down on soft money spending by the political parties, it did nothing to constrain spending by outside groups."[27] Indeed, one estimate is that 527 groups spent some $527 million on television ads alone in 2004.[28]

527 Organizations: Groups organized under Section 527 of the Internal Revenue Code, which allows the unlimited expenditure of campaign money. These organizations became important after the Bipartisan Campaign Reform Act outlawed soft money in 2002.

EXAMPLE: *In 2004, Americans Coming Together was a powerful group working on behalf of John Kerry.*

While pro-Republican groups, such as the Swift Boat 527, garnered a great deal of attention in 2004, four years later Democratic-leaning 527s were much more influential. In the 2008 election, Democratic-oriented 527s held a three-to-one financial advantage over Republican-oriented groups. At the top of the list were labor-based groups, such as AFSCME Special and the Service Employees International Union Political Action Fund. EMILY's List, a unit designed to support pro-choice women candidates, was also near the top. Combined, the top-five 527 groups in the 2008 election spent nearly $100 million.

Are 527s simply the latest loophole in campaign finance law, and do they corrupt the election process? Or are they simply a way for Americans to support candidates and to speak out during elections? If so, perhaps they are protected by the Constitution. The future of 527 Organizations remains unclear. The Federal Election Commission did move forward with rules regulating independent groups in 2007, but most observers agree that there remains enough leeway in the law for 527s to be key players for years to come.

TABLE 12.3 | 2008 Presidential Fundraising: Top Four Through October 15, 2008

DEMOCRATS	SPENDING (IN MILLIONS)
Barack Obama	$639
Hillary Clinton	$ 221
John Edwards	$ 48
Bill Richardson	$ 22
All Democrats (total)	$964
REPUBLICANS	**SPENDING (IN MILLIONS)**
John McCain	$335
Mitt Romney	$105
Rudy Giuliani	$ 59
Ron Paul	$ 34
All Republicans (total) $589	

SOURCE: Federal Elections Commission

Money in the 2008 Presidential Election

To say that the 2008 presidential election shattered fundraising records would be a vast understatement. In 1996, some $450 million was spent trying to take residency in the White House, a figure that jumped to $650 million four years later. By 2004, this amount had climbed to $720 million. In January of 2007, however, Federal Election Commission Chairman Michael Toner estimated that the 2008 race would be a "$1-billion election." He added, "The 2008 will be the longest and most expensive presidential election in American history. Candidates are going to have to raise $100 million by the end of 2007 to be a serious candidate."[29] Because the public funding system created after Watergate will provide just $150 million to candidates for both the primary and general elections, Toner and many others have suggested the system may be headed for extinction. Candidates can "opt-out" of the system if they prefer, but this was rarely done in the past. In the 2008 race, most of the major contenders had decided to reject public financing. As to whether the system can be resurrected for the next presidential election is yet to be seen.

Table 12.3 lists the spending by presidential candidates through October 15, 2008—about three weeks before the election. Barack Obama's dramatic advantage is immediately apparent. Obama, unlike McCain, decided against taking federal campaign funds. Obama's fundraising success was surprising for two reasons. First, Republican candidates have nearly always outraised Democratic candidates. Second, also unlike the past, a vast majority of Obama's funds came from small donations. In fact, roughly half of Obama's money was raised over the Internet, and it came in donations of less than $200.

Why did so much money flood into the 2008 election? There are several explanations: The frontloading of the primary calendar (discussed in Chapter 13) put a premium on early fundraising; in order to compete in 30 states by the middle of February, candidates needed cash. It was the first open-seat presidential contest in generations, and there was a great deal of excitement. Hot-button issues, such as the state of the economy and the war in Iraq, pushed folks to write checks, and several of the leading candidates, including Hillary Clinton and Barack Obama, were quite astute at raising funds. Senator Clinton, for example, harnessed the popularity of her husband Bill at many fundraising events, and Barack Obama's team skillfully used the Internet to raise record-breaking sums. Surely the prolonged nomination process had something to do with the shattered records, as did the close general election.

Still another reason for the unprecedented sums in 2008 was the broadening of contribution sources. In the past, a small number of wealthy individuals tended to provide the lion's share of campaign funds. Because of changes in campaign finance laws that eliminated massive soft-money contributions, and because of the growing use of the Internet to raise money, the number of citizens giving money to candidates has mushroomed. Some candidates have done better with smaller contributions than others have. To many, the gloomy picture of ever-increasing fundraising totals is somewhat offset by the widening pool of contributors.

TIMELINE Interest Groups and Campaign Finance

SIMULATION You Are a Campaign Manager: McCain Navigates Campaign Financing

Bill and Hillary Clinton make a campaign stop in Cedar Rapids, Iowa, in 2007. Most expected that Hillary Clinton would shatter all fundraising records—and she did. The real surprise, however, was that Barack Obama raised even more money than Clinton!

The Ironies of Money and Politics

In every election, a few candidates run for office on a shoestring budget, overcome the odds, and are sent into public life. We relish such stories: David-like candidates with guts, determination, and grassroots support bringing down overconfident, wealthy Goliaths. Maybe it is not money that wins elections, we think, but ideas and character. Unfortunately, elections of this sort are few and far between. Money plays a powerful role in today's electoral system; as Jesse Unruh, a retired California politician, once accurately but cynically said, "Money is the mother's milk of politics."[30] If we put an optimistic spin on the situation, perhaps we might conclude that fundraising is simply a measure of public sentiment: Some candidates raise more money than others because they are more popular and thus more likely to win on election day. We might applaud the flow of money into campaigns, seeing it as a form of free speech. In a democracy, we say, the more political speech, the better.

Most Americans are not so optimistic about money in politics and they regard the importance of big money in elections as troubling. They believe that it gives some candidates an unfair advantage and spills past the election into the policymaking process. It is one of the many ironies of an open political process: Individuals and interest groups are encouraged to back political candidates vigorously, but in doing so, their efforts distort the playing field. The freedom to participate creates a system with limited participation.

The Role of Money in Elections

Practice Quiz

1. One reason for the steep rise in campaign spending in this country is that
   - **a.** campaigns are now federally subsidized to "even the playing field" for all candidates.
   - **b.** blogs and mass e-mails are enormously expensive.
   - **c.** people are more inclined to vote for a candidate if they know he or she has spent a lot of money campaigning.
   - **d.** there are more potential voters to reach each year, making expensive broadcast advertising a higher priority

2. Advocacy groups that try to influence the outcome of elections through voter mobilization efforts as well as television advertisements that praise or criticize a candidate's record are known as
   - **a.** PACs.
   - **b.** 527 groups.
   - **c.** third parties.
   - **d.** pundits.

3. James Buckley challenged the constitutionality of the Federal Election Campaign Act by arguing that
   - **a.** limiting campaign contributions was a constraint of free speech.
   - **b.** the ability to raise campaign funds was a fair measure of a candidate's popularity.
   - **c.** limiting campaign contributions violated the principles of free market capitalism.
   - **d.** the Twelfth Amendment guaranteed citizens the right to participatory campaigning, which implicitly included monetary contributions.

4. Incumbents have a clear advantage in fund raising.
   - **a.** true
   - **b.** false

Answers: 1-d, 2-b, 3-a, 4-a.

Discussion Questions

1. What is the connection between money, politics, and television?
2. Given what we now know about the role of money, does *Buckley* v. *Valeo* (1976) still make sense?

What **YOU** can do!

Since the first modern national campaign finance reform, the Federal Election Campaign Act in 1971, subsequent reforms have been passed in order to close "loopholes" of previous reforms. For example, the Bipartisan Campaign Reform Act (BCRA) of 2000 closed loopholes left by the decision in *Buckley* v. *Valeo* (1976). What loopholes were created by the BCRA? Have all of them been closed? How? Brainstorm ways to close any remaining loopholes and prevent the need for future reform.

Campaigning Online
(pages 450–453)

How has the Internet changed the election process?

Constantly looking for a competitive edge, campaign strategists are often pushing the limits of new technology. The latest technology innovation is, of course, the Internet. Already a key tool in contemporary campaigns, use of Internet is evolving at a rapid pace.

Online Communications

The Internet and the applications built to take advantage of this network may constitute the most powerful communications tool known to humans. Through this medium, individuals can communicate with millions, and groups can organically emerge and facilitate complicated networks within the membership. The nature of these communications can take the shape of nearly all known media—text, video, graphics, audio, and so on. This potential alone makes the Internet a campaign manager's dream tool, yet figuring out how to use this resource effectively has been difficult.

WEB SITES One of the most important parts of Internet-based campaigning is a candidate's Web site. Web sites first appeared as presidential campaign communications tools in 1996 and since then have steadily increased in strategic importance. In the early iterations of campaign Web design, very few resources were devoted to developing and sustaining sites. In fact, it was common for candidates to ask a tech-savvy relative, friend, or college student to design and maintain the entire site. In a little more than a decade, the volunteer Web master has now been supplanted by professional Web design firms that specialize in online campaigning.

Running for president presents significant communications challenges, and a candidate's Web site has become essential to helping meet these challenges. It establishes 24-7 information resources for nearly all constituents of the campaign. Perspective voters browse for information in trying to make up their minds about the candidate; volunteers download critical information to help organize their work; news reporters find critical information and photos needed to help file candidate-related stories, and potential campaign contributors find answers to last-minute questions before they submit donations online. In addition to maintaining communications with core constituents, campaign Web sites typically provide a comprehensive calendar, endorsement-gathering tools, position papers on policies, tools for collecting public comments, assistance with organizing blogs, an online campaign store for purchasing paraphernalia, contact information for all campaign offices, and much more.

ONLINE NEWS Trends suggest voters are moving away from traditional newspapers to online news sources for campaign information. This started in the mid-1990s, when independent Web sites emerged to present campaign information. At the time, these sites were novel, because they were not developed and supported by traditional news providers, such as CNN, ABC, the CBC, and so forth. One of the most prominent early endeavors in this area was Web White and Blue (WWB), which was an online knowledge network that at one point had 17 charter sites at various colleges and universities contributing information to the network. It was similar in concept to a wiki environment, where independent writers submit content to a community or shared area. However, as general internet usage swelled in the United States to numbers that make the World Wide Web a common resource for many Americans, traditional news sources began repurposing their content to online sites. As CNN.com, MSNBC.com, CBSNews.com, and more began to establish their online resources, they soon overwhelmed the nonprofit and independent Web sites with their content and general information capacity.

The presence of comprehensive and immediate online news sources and the development of news aggregating engines (e.g., Google News) have caused a shift in the electorate. This was identified as early as 2000. In conducting a survey of WWB users, one scholar found that they had in general "*substituted* the Internet for newspapers as one of [their] two main election news sources."[31] He found that television news was the most common news source, followed by Internet news consumption. This supports more general findings from Pew's ongoing study, the Internet and American Life Project.[32] They find that U.S. citizens who note the Internet as a "main source of political campaign news" rose 18 percent between 2000 and 2004. The rise was 31 percent for U.S. citizens who cite the Internet as a source for "any election news." As noted in Table 12.4, by 2008, some 24 percent of Americans regularly use the Internet as their primary news source. Table 12.5 notes interesting generational differences.

BLOGGING An online information source that has attracted growing voter interest in recent elections is blogging (see Figure 12.12). **Blogs** (Web logs) are Web sites with information that is maintained by individuals (bloggers) and used to express opinions on particular topics (e.g., the 2008 campaign). Blogs are often referred to as *online journals* or *online diaries*. They usually contain personal observations and tend to be opinionated—often quite visceral. Many people like reading blogs about candidates, because they feel they can get an "honest" opinions. According to a recent Technorati Report,[33] the blogosphere (the collective network of all blogs) has been growing at a very rapid pace. The first blogs were reported in 1997, and it took a few years for them to become common enough to register any kind of campaign effect. In August of 2004, for example, there were approximately 3 million blogs online. One year later, the number had grown to 12 million. In August of 2006, Technorati indexed approximately 50 million blogs. In August of 2007 (only 10 years after they began), the Web hosted 94 million blogs.

While all 94 million blogs did not participate in the 2008 election, a substantial number did. For example, TechPresident (http://www.techpresident.com) reports that within a 1-month period (September 15–October 14, 2007), Hillary Clinton has been

TABLE 12.4 | Where the Public Learns About the Presidential Campaign

REGULARLY LEARN SOMETHING FROM ...	*CAMPAIGN YEAR 2000*		
	2000	2004	2008
Local TV news	48%	42%	40%
Cable news networks	34%	38%	38%
Nightly network news	45%	35%	32%
Daily newspaper	40%	31%	31%
Internet	9%	13%	24%
TV news magazines	29%	25%	22%
Morning TV shows	18%	20%	22%
National Public Radio	12%	14%	18%
Talk radio	15%	17%	16%
Cable political talk	14%	14%	15%
Sunday political TV	15%	13%	14%
Public TV shows	12%	11%	12%
News magazines	15%	10%	11%
Late-night talk shows	9%	9%	9%
Religious radio	7%	5%	9%
C-SPAN	9%	8%	8%
Comedy TV shows	6%	8%	8%
Lou Dobbs Tonight	—	—	7%

SOURCE: *Social Networking and Online Campaigns Take Off: Internet's Broader Role in Campaign 2008* (Washington, DC: The Pew Research Center for the People & the Press, January 11, 2008), p. 1. http://people-press.org/reports/pdf/384.pdf. Reprinted with permission.

mentioned in the blogosphere over 3,000 times on busy days and slightly under 1,000 times on light days. During the Fall of 2007, her name is mentioned, on average, approximately 1,400 times per day in the blogosphere.

Finally, and perhaps most importantly, a powerful connection has emerged between what happens on sites and blogs and the "established" media. Very often, campaign topics are raised first on blogs and later in mainstream media. Mark Halperin and John Harris write about this in their book *The Way to Win: Taking the White House in 2008*. Discussing the power of the Drudge Report (http://www.drudgereport.com), a popular political site and blog, they note:

TABLE 12.5 | Among the Young, TV Losing Ground to the Internet*

GET MOST ELECTION NEWS FROM ...†	2004	2007	CHANGE
Television	75%	60%	–15%
Newspapers	30%	24%	–6%
Internet	21%	46%	+25%
Radio	10%	10%	0%
Magazines	1%	4%	+3%
Other	4%	6%	+2%

*Based on 18– to 29-year-olds.
†First or second mentions.
SOURCE: *Social Networking and Online Campaigns Take Off: Internet's Broader Role in Campaign 2008* (Washington, DC: The Pew Research Center for the People & the Press, January 11, 2008), p. 4. http://people-press.org/reports/pdf/384.pdf. Reprinted with permission.

"Drudge's power derives only in part from the colossal number of people who visit his site . . . His power comes from his ability to shape the perceptions of other news media—Old and New alike."[34]

Online Fundraising

The Internet has been used as a fundraising tool since the development of e-commerce technology in the mid to late 1990s. John McCain surprised many by raising a modest sum in his 2000 bid for the White House, but it did not become a significant and widely recognized medium for collecting large sums until 2004, when Howard Dean's presidential campaign and groups like MoveOn.org demonstrated that the medium was capable of generating vast amounts of money.

The success in 2004 startled many observers, but as the 2008 election drew near, online fundraising systems were commonplace. All the presidential campaign sites displayed a prominent button encouraging visitors to make an online contribution. And while online contributions remain subject to all the campaign contribution guidelines enforced by the Federal Elections Commission (individuals can only contribute up to $2,300 per election, contributors must disclose basic contact information, and so on), they opened up new strategic territory for the ongoing fundraising needs of the 2008 presidential campaigns. The pace of collecting funds also stunned many observers. When the media reported that Hillary Clinton had won the Pennsylvania Democratic Primary, her online fundraising site started to hum. In the next 24 hours,

FIGURE 12.12 | Who Visits Blogs?

There are blogs out there for every political persuasion. But who is reading them? College graduates who are paying attention to the 2008 presidential campaign are the prime audience, according to a March 2007 New York Times/CBS News poll. Find a political blog that appeals to you. ***—What do you like about it?***

SOURCE: March 13, 2007, New York Times Graphics. Copyright © 2007 by the New York Times Co. Reprinted with permission.

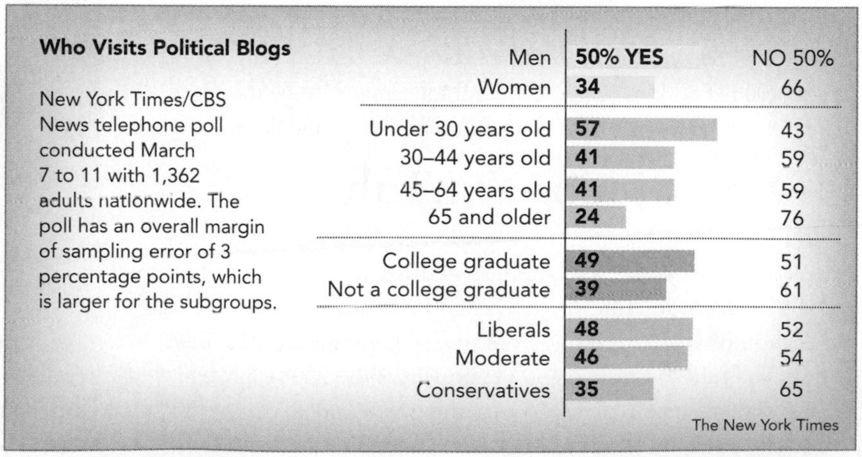

she raised over $3 million, a staggering sum in such a short period given that it came from relatively small donations.

Social Networks

In the 2008 campaign, online social networks emerged for the first time as a component of campaign strategies. Increasingly, candidates are leveraging social networks as a means to communicate with prospective voters. Online social networks have been around for a while; however, they have not been used in presidential campaign politics until recently. Online social networks bring individuals together in an environment with the explicit goal of connecting these individuals to form groups around common interests. Online tools used in this environment include chat, basic Web design, messaging, video and photo posting, blogging and vlogging (video blogging), discussion forums, file sharing, and more. Examples of existing social networks include:

- MySpace (http://www.myspace.com) is a general social network service for connecting friends. It has been reported as the sixth most popular Web site in any language. In September of 2007, MySpace reported to have more than 200 million accounts.
- Facebook (http://www.facebook.com) is a social networking site that is very similar to MySpace. It was started in 2004 by a student at Harvard College—and originally was only offered to Harvard students. Since then, Facebook networks have been initiated for high schools and large companies; however, the core of Facebook's business is still college students. In July of 2007, Facebook announced that it had over 34 million active members worldwide.
- Second Life (http://www.secondlife.com) is partly a social network and partly a virtual reality game. It started in 2003. In Second Life, residents (second life accounts) can interact with each other through several virtual or simulated realities.

All the 2008 presidential candidates had MySpace and Facebook accounts, with varying numbers of registered/networked "friends" (see Table 12.6). Through their accounts, candidates posted information similar to the content posted at their official campaign Web sites, but the collection of registered friends coming to the social network account was visible to the entire community, giving each individual a chance to meet and communicate with others. A few candidates established Second Life accounts with fully developed avatars (the virtual candidate in Second Life) and virtual campaign headquarters. Of the three social networking services, Second Life appears to be the service that received the least amount of attention from the candidates.

TABLE 12.6 | **MySpace Candidates (October 2007)**

DEMOCRATS	MYSPACE FRIENDS	REPUBLICANS	MYSPACE FRIENDS
Obama	181,497	Paul	69,624
Clinton	141,540	McCain	39,088
Edwards	48,649	Romney	30,945
Kucinich	32,395	F. Thompson	11,262
Richardson	20,563	Brownback	11,116
Biden	14,487	Giuliani	8,455
Gravel	10,480	Huckabee	7,842
Dodd	8,832	Hunter	6,797
		Tancredo	4,025

Online Video/YouTube

As you know from Chapter 11, television exploded onto the presidential campaign scene with the televised Kennedy–Nixon debates in 1960. In 2008, YouTube demonstrated a similar explosion with the publication of video streaming from nearly all campaigns. The mention of YouTube as a prominent component of the 2008 campaign is in itself rather remarkable, given that the online video-sharing Web site started in early 2005. As such, the 2008 presidential election was the first presidential election ever to be held with YouTube in existence—with some calling it the "YouTube Election."

While the 2008 campaign was the first *presidential* campaign to be influenced by YouTube, its impact was quite clear in the historic 2006 midterm elections. Several Republican seats were in jeopardy, with Democrats experiencing a general upswing in popularity in response to Bush's falling polling numbers. One of the races that Republicans lost in 2006 was a Virginia Senate seat. George Allen was running as the Republican candidate and had a very strong lead over Jim Webb, the Democratic candidate, well into the election. This lead held steady until one day on the campaign trail, when Allen called a rival campaign's worker "macaca" during a campaign event. The individual was Indian American, and the apparent racial slur was caught on tape. The clip was immediately posted to YouTube, receiving many views and sparking a larger national debate on the network news. Webb ended up closing the gap and

Senator George Allen of Virginia talks with the media in September of 2006 about recent allegations that he used a racial slur while on the football team at the University of Virginia. The issue of Allen's racial attitudes was raised after a video showing his use of a derogatory term was posted on YouTube. ***—Have YouTube and similar sites changed the nature of campaigns in America? If so, is this change for the better?***

ultimately defeated Allen in the 2006 election, and many attribute his success to the "macaca" incident. In previous elections, Allen's comment might have been missed, but in 2006, YouTube offered a video publication channel that altered the course of the campaign.

As 2008 strategies began to emerge early in the presidential election process, it became clear that candidates and their consultants were thinking formally about YouTube and how it might help the campaign process. A few individuals officially announced their candidacy on YouTube. This strategy was generally successful in 2008, because it heightened an otherwise dull story. For example, when Barack Obama announced he was running for President, the announcement in itself was newsworthy, as was the fact that he released his announcement over YouTube. The two newsworthy elements combined gave the story better legs and more exposure.

Several sermons by Rev. Jeremiah Wright, Jr., caused great controversy in the 2008 presidential campaign after being posted on YouTube. Did Obama share these views? In the end, Obama was forced to distance himself from his old friend. ***—Should politicians be judged by their friends and acquaintances?***

Beyond official candidacy announcements, several candidates routinely produced content for YouTube. For example, nearly all 2008 political ads were repurposed online. They were typically played to a specific television market via regional airwaves and then made available to everyone on YouTube. This allowed the campaigns to extend their reach, but it also gave journalists an easier way to monitor political advertisements.

One of the most extraordinary uses of YouTube came about on July 23, 2007. On that date, CNN sponsored a presidential debate in South Carolina in which questions were presented by "average" citizens over YouTube. The ground-up nature of the event, with citizens posing presidential questions, gave the debate a greater sense of democracy than many (maybe all) prior presidential debates.

The use of YouTube on the campaign trail underscores an important relationship that we have discussed already—the relationship between online information and the establishment media. As more and more citizens post videos of campaign events on YouTube, we learn new information about candidates, and often unflattering information. In the spring of 2008, as Barack Obama seemed to be sailing to the nomination, posts of Rev. Jeremiah Wright, the senator's pastor, began appearing on YouTube. These clips, containing portions of fiery, controversial sermons, were played and replayed by millions of Americans. What was Obama's precise relationship with this man? Did he share these controversial thoughts? The "Wright controversy" became Obama's greatest primary election obstacle, and it was perpetuated in no small measure due to YouTube.

Campaigning Online
Practice Quiz

1. According to recent research, television news is the most common news source, followed by Internet news consumption.
   a. true **b.** false
2. Web sites with information maintained by individuals and used in a manner to express opinions on particular topics are known as
   a. chat rooms. **b.** Internet cafes.
   c. punditocracies. **d.** blogs.
3. Very often, important campaign topics are first raised on blogs, then later in mainstream media.
   a. true **b.** false
4. The online development that seeks to bring individuals together with the explicit goal of forming groups around common interests using chat, basic Web design, messaging, and video and photo posting is known as
   a. a blog. **b.** a social network.
   c. a cybernetwork. **d.** a superblog.

Answers: 1-a, 2-d, 3-a, 4-b.

Discussion Questions

1. What advantages does the Internet bring to political campaigning?
2. What does the emphasis on the Internet do to traditional campaign techniques—and to the older audiences that traditional techniques appeal to?

What **YOU** can do!

While candidates can reach a new generation of voters online, some Web sites can present a problem for the campaign, because candidates have little to no control over what their supporters or opponents post online. Visit YouTube, MySpace, or other networking sites that allow individuals to post video. First, view several official videos posted by a candidate's campaign; next, view videos posted by individuals who support and oppose each candidate. Do you think these "unofficial" videos do any serious good or harm? Why or why not?

■ **Electoral Behavior:** Any activity broadly linked to the outcome of a political campaign.

EXAMPLE: *Sending a check to a candidate or attending a rally are forms of electoral behavior.*

■ **Turnout:** The percentage of citizens legally eligible to vote in an election who actually vote in that election.

EXAMPLE: *In the past three presidential elections, turnout was slightly above 50 percent.*

SIMULATION **You Are a Campaign Manager: Navigating Negativity**

Individual Participation *in* Elections (pages 454–459)

Do average Americans, especially young Americans, take part in the election process?

There are many ways average citizens can shape the course of government. The same is true of participation in the electoral process—there are many ways for citizens to become involved in campaigns and elections. Some people believe that voting is the foundation of all electoral participation, because very few get involved in other political activities without first being a voter. This is incorrect, however. For one thing, it is probably the case that many citizens are politically active but do not vote, and for some Americans, not voting is either a statement of contentment or a form of political protest. Also, even if there is some sort of "ladder of electoral participation," voting is probably not the bottom rung. Simply talking about different candidates with friends and family, for example, or reading news stories or watching television programs about election happenings are types of electoral participation. Any action that is broadly linked to the conduct or outcome of an election can be considered **electoral behavior**■. We might add to the list helping with a campaign; donating money; joining an election-focused interest group; attending election-centered rallies, dinners, or meetings; placing a yard sign in front of your house or a bumper sticker on your car; or even wearing a button. The point is that citizens can become involved in the election process in many ways. Voting is just one of them.

Another way to think about forms of political participation is to consider the difference between individualistic and collective participation. Individual participation occurs when a citizen engages in activity aimed at changing public policy without interacting with other citizens. Examples include voting, giving money to a candidate or party, watching political news on television, blogging about politics, or writing a letter to a candidate or an office holder. Collective participation occurs when a citizen takes action in collaboration with other like-minded citizens. Examples would be attending a rally, discussing politics with friends and family, working at a party or candidate's headquarters, or attending the local meeting of a political party (see Figure 12.13). Although both types of participation can be seen in the American setting, individualistic participation clearly occurs more often. Yet many see our individualistic tendencies as unfortunate and contrary to the ideals of democracy. Many of the most significant changes in public policy, such as worker rights, civil rights, and environmental legislation, stemmed from collective action—but for most Americans, politics is a private matter.

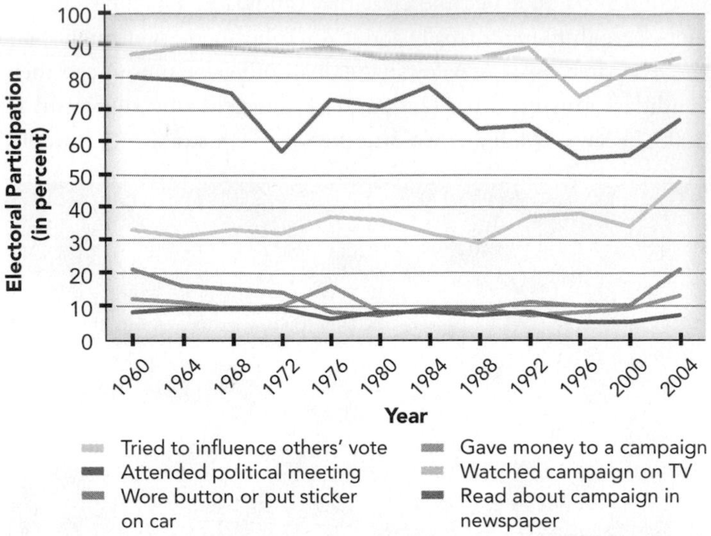

FIGURE 12.13 | **Forms of Electoral Participation**

As this figure suggests, there are many ways individuals can be active in electoral politics. Since the 1960s the trend has been less engagement—with the exception being 2004. ***—What do you think has caused this downward trend? What was it about the 2004 election that seemed to bring more Americans into the process?***

SOURCE: American National Election Studies, http://www.electionstudies.org/nesguide/gd-index.htm, Graphs 6.B and 6.D. Reprinted with permission.

Voter Turnout

"How do you measure voting turnout?"

—Student Question

In thinking about levels of political participation in any democratic system, we often look at **turnout**■. This is the number of citizens who actually vote on election day divided by the total number of citizens who are legally qualified to vote in that election—an easily quantifiable number. If 1 million residents are allowed to vote but only 600,000 do so, turnout is 0.6, or 60 percent. The number of citizens or residents of a nation does not factor into the turnout ratio; rather, it is the number of those who are legally eligible to vote.

As we noted in Chapter 2, there was not much interest in federal elections during the early days of our republic. Election turnout for presidential elections, measured by the percentage of eligible (male) voters, reached only into the teens until 1800, when it jumped to 31 percent. It slipped again during the so-called Era of Good Feelings (1816–1824), when there was relatively little partisan strife, falling to roughly 25 percent. After what Andrew Jackson called the "corrupt bargain" in the election of 1824, political participation shot up dramatically: In 1828, some 57 percent of eligible voters went to the polls, and by the 1860s, the voting rate had leveled off very high,

Hundreds of voters stand in line in the rain in Columbus, Ohio, on election day in 2004. ***—Are additional reforms needed to make voting easier? Would you favor mail-in ballots or even online voting?***

hovering around 80 percent for the rest of the nineteenth century. In the early twentieth century, however, election day turnouts began to slip. There were a number of likely causes. For one, during this period there was a flood of immigration, causing a population boom in urban areas. Although these new citizens would soon be assimilated into the political process, many of them did not immediately vote. Second, registration laws, residency requirements, and other restrictions during the Progressive Era made it harder for people in the lower socioeconomic class to participate in elections. Finally, the Nineteenth Amendment to the Constitution in 1920 granted women the right to vote, but at first, they were slow to exercise that right. The percentage of women voting improved with time, however, pushing the overall turnout up by the middle of the twentieth century.

When Vice President Richard Nixon and an upstart senator from Massachusetts by the name of John F. Kennedy squared off in the presidential election in 1960, some 61 percent of the electorate turned out to vote (see Figure 12.14). In the decades since, that figure has dropped more or less steadily. From 1980 until 2000, only about half of eligible voters turned out for presidential elections. Even worse is the participation in midterm congressional elections—the elections between presidential contest years: 1998, 2002, 2006, and so forth. In the 1960s, about 50 percent of Americans made it to the polls for these elections, but by the 1970s, the proportion had dropped to just over 40 percent—and it has shrunk to just over one-third in recent elections. The decline in many state and local elections has been even worse. Many cities have seen turnouts for elections to municipal posts, such as mayor and city council, drop into the teens.

One of the most surprising and encouraging bits of elections pathway news in recent years was the upsurge in turnout. In 2004, just over 55 percent of Americans came out to vote for either John Kerry, the Democrat, or George W. Bush, the incumbent Republican. Some observers speculate that the increased turnout was a reaction to the disputed outcome of the 2000 election, in which Al Gore got more popular votes but fewer electoral college votes than George W. Bush. Many Americans were motivated either to defeat the president or to keep him in the Oval Office. Other analysts point to the highly competitive nature of the 2004 election (the race was always close) and to the important issues of the day, not the least of which was terrorism in the wake of 9/11 and wars in Iraq and Afghanistan. Still others think that both campaign teams concentrated on get-out-the-vote efforts as never before. There is also the significant role that young voters played in the 2004 election, which we will discuss in greater detail shortly. But whatever the reason, the 2004 election suggested that Americans might once again be paying greater attention to elections.

The upward trend continued in 2008, with roughly 62 percent of eligible voters coming to the polls. This figure surpassed that in all previous elections since the 1960s. Voters in nearly every demographic groups flocked to the polls, but the greatest increases in turnout came from less affluent citizens, young voters, African Americans, and Hispanic Americans. Geographically, the largest increases in turnout were seen in the South and Rocky Mountain states. Dramatic candidates, a lengthy primary campaign, crosscutting issues, and massive get-out-the-vote efforts proved to be a "perfect storm" for voter mobilization in 2008.

FIGURE 12.14 | **Participation in Presidential Elections**

Most Americans believe we are one of the most democratic nations on earth. While that may be true in some respects, our participation in electoral politics is less than stellar. ***—What might explain the various fluctuations in turnout? Do you think 2004 marked a long-term reversal of the downward trend, or was it simply an exception?***

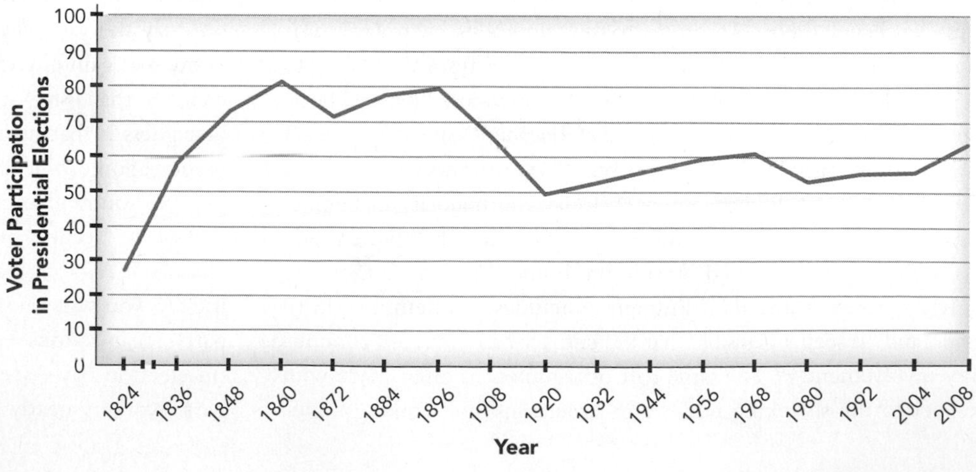

Explaining Modest Turnout

Most political observers agree that although turnout in 2004 and 2008 proved encouraging, it is confusing that nearly half of all Americans eligible to vote are sitting on the sidelines. One of the great questions of our day is the cause—or causes—of the post-1960 decline in electoral participation. Why was turnout so much higher 50 years ago? The decline has occurred during a period when we might expect *higher* levels of voting. More Americans than ever attend college, and higher education seems correlated with higher levels of voter turnout, as we will soon discuss. Registration barriers have been all but eliminated, and the civil rights movement has opened the door to far greater involvement by African Americans and other previously oppressed groups of citizens. With so many positive changes, why would levels of electoral participation be so modest?

"Isn't that a contradiction: Americans complain about their government, but don't bother to vote?"

—Student Question

There is no clear answer, but theories abound (see Figure 12.15). One possibility is attitudinal change. Increased cynicism, distrust, alienation, and the like are often identified as the root of the problem. Perhaps Americans are less sure about their own role in changing the course of government. Survey data seem to support the claim that negative attitudes about politics have increased over the decades. For instance, in the mid-1950s, about 75 percent of Americans might have been described as trusting their government to "do what is right all or at least most of the time." This number plummeted to just over 20 percent by the early 1990s but has since moved back up just a bit, to roughly the 47-percent range. About 22 percent of Americans in the 1950s thought "quite a few" politicians were crooked. That number jumped to 50 percent in the mid-1990s and today stands at about 35 percent. Many other indicators suggest that Americans are less confident about government and politics than in previous times.[35] However, can we link these attitudes to lower levels of electoral participation? Most scholars agree that these changes have had an impact on levels of participation, although they debate the degree of their importance.

Closely related to this perspective is what we might call the lifestyle-change theory. According to this hypothesis, life today is simply busier than in the past and offers more distractions. According to the sociologist Robert Putnam, author of the widely discussed book *Bowling Alone: The Collapse and Revival of American Community,* "I don't have enough time" and "I'm too busy" are the most often heard excuses for social disengagement.[36] Today, the majority of families have two wage earners, a massive shift from the 1950s, when relatively few women worked outside the home. "And since there are only 24 hours in the day," Putnam concludes, "something had to give," and "it seems plausible that the cutbacks also affected community involvement."[37] The same sort of argument is often made with respect to the shrinking number of Americans' nonworking hours.

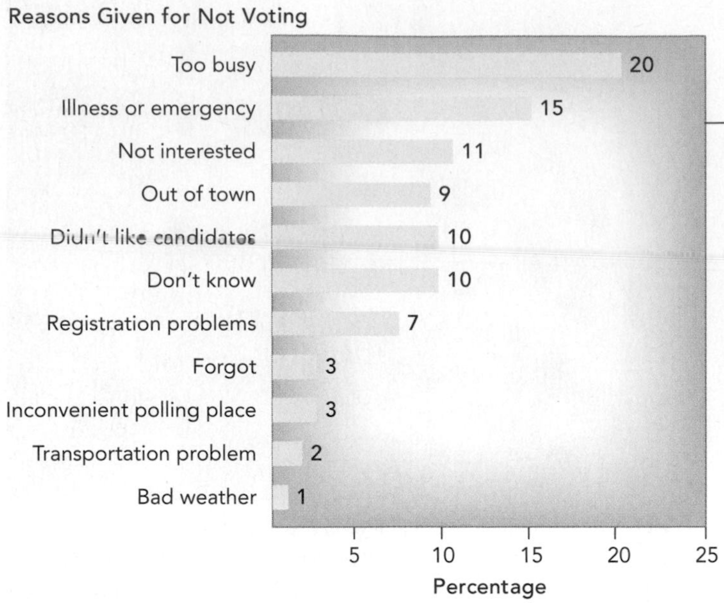

FIGURE 12.15 | Why People Don't Vote

One way to read this table is to consider the reasons for not voting, and explore changes that might help. For instance, if "too busy" explains about 20 percent of why people do not vote, perhaps we should consider making election day a national holiday. Another way to explore the data is with a keen eye toward differences in demographic groups. ***—Why would over twice as many respondents with less than a high school degree use "illness and disability" as an excuse for not voting, compared to those with some college? Are Asian Americans really healthier, but busier, than other demographic groups? Why are there so many registration problems for Hispanic Americans?***

SOURCE: U.S. Census Bureau Current Population Survey, November 2004.

This argument suggests that we are also more distracted by new technologies, especially television, and have to spend too many hours commuting long distances or putting in extra hours at our jobs to be heavily involved in politics. Above all, television competes for our scarce time: "TV watching comes at the expense of nearly every social activity outside the home," Putnam asserts.[38]

Putnam and others are quick to caution against overstating this argument, however. Although it may be true that more women are spending more time at a workplace and thus have less time to vote, these women also have more opportunity to vote because on election day they are *already* pulled out of the home by work, and we know that gainfully employed women are actually *more* involved in civic life than "stay-at-home" women.[39] As for television, Putnam's best guess is that no more than 15 percent of the decline in civic participation can be attributed to television.[40]

Although changes in attitudes and lifestyles may account for part of the decline, many analysts suggest that the deepest root lies elsewhere. A strong possibility would be changes in local party politics. As you will see in LINK Chapter 13, page 472 local-level party organizations—which historically pushed citizens to the polls on election day—seem to be withering. A generation ago, many party workers, nearly always volunteers, kept track of which known

CONNECT THE LINK
(Chapter **13**, page **472**) How do local parties engage average citizens in the electoral process?

TIMELINE **Close Calls in Presidential Elections**

VISUAL LITERACY **Voting Turnout: Who Votes in the United States?**

party members had voted and which had not yet showed up at the polling place. By dinner time on election day, those who had delayed voting would get a telephone call or even a visit from one of these workers and be "gently" reminded to vote. Political scientists have tested the relationship between local party vitality and levels of turnout, and the data are convincing: Turnout is much higher in communities that still have strong local parties.[41] But fewer and fewer communities have such organizations.

The nature of campaigns is also cited as a reason for voter alienation. Campaigns, especially for the presidency, have become much longer, conceivably leading to voter burnout. Negative campaigning *might* add to the burnout. The first scholarly take on the issue seemed to confirm this theory, but on closer inspection, things seem more complicated. Although some studies have found that negative ads do turn voters off, roughly an equal number of other studies have found that turnout actually increases in these negatively charged races.[42] One impressive study suggests that some voters—the less partisan ones—are turned off when the campaign gets nasty but that negative campaigning activates the most partisan voters.[43] Still another line of research suggests that the effects of negative ads depend on the voter's local political culture.[44] A citizen in Provo, Utah, might respond differently to attack ads than, say, a voter in Brooklyn, New York.

Finally, there is the role of the news media. Some social scientists have suggested that the recent turn toward what one scholar has called "attack journalism" or media "feeding frenzies" has repelled voters.[45] In the past, a politician's personal transgressions were kept out of the news. Journalists and average citizens alike drew a line between a politician's public and private lives. Probably due to the highly competitive nature of the news business, anything that draws the public's attention seems fair game to the media nowadays. Scholars have had difficulty directly linking these feeding frenzies with declining turnout, but most would agree that a connection seems likely.

PATHWAYS | profile

Mark Shields—"This I Believe"

Mark Shields has worked in politics for more than 40 years. He started as an assistant to Wisconsin Senator William Proxmire and then worked on four presidential campaigns and numerous other races. Shields is currently a political analyst for *The NewsHour with Jim Lehrer* on PBS. In March of 2006, Shields was asked by National Public Radio to comment on American politics and his career. Here is an excerpt from his remarks.

> I believe in politics. In addition to being great fun, politics is basically the peaceable resolution of conflict among legitimate competing interests. In a continental nation as big and brawling and diverse as ours, I don't know how else—except through politics—we can resolve our differences and live together. Compromise is the best alternative to brute muscle or money or raw numbers. Compromises that are both wise and just [and] are crafted through the dedication, the skill and, yes, the intelligence of our elected politicians.
>
> I like people who run for public office. For most of us, life is a series of quiet successes or setbacks. If you get the big promotion, the hometown paper announces your success. It doesn't add, "Shields was passed over because of unanswered questions about his expense account" or "his erratic behavior at the company picnic."
>
> But elections have been rightly described as a one-day sale. If you're a candidate, your fate is front-page news. By 8 o'clock on a Tuesday night, you will experience the ecstasy of victory or you will endure the agony of defeat. Everybody you ever sat next to in study hall, double-dated with or baby sat for knows whether you won or, much more likely, lost. Politicians boldly risk public rejection of the kind that the rest of us will go to any lengths to avoid

SOURCE: National Public Radio, March 13, 2006. Accessed at http://www.npr.org/templates/story/story.php?storyId=5256345 ■

Voting and Demographic Characteristics

Another closely related question is why certain groups of Americans participate less than others. Here, too, scholarly findings are inconclusive. One perspective centers on "community connectedness." This theory states that the more connected you are to your community, the more likely you are to vote. Demographic data suggest that poor people, for example, move more often than the affluent do, and they are certainly much less likely to own a home (which creates a strong connection to one's community). Every time you change your permanent address, of course, you also need to change your voter registration. Not surprisingly, the level of political participation for these highly mobile people is quite low. This perspective might explain why younger Americans seem less engaged; many young folks have little true connection to a particular community.

The "costs" of political participation seem to decline as people's level of formal education increases, as noted in Figure 12.16 on page 458. The Census Bureau has reported that less than 40 percent of registered voters without a high school diploma voted in 2004, as opposed to 78 percent of those with a college degree and 84 percent of those with a graduate degree. Not only does awareness of the mechanics of voting rise with formal education, so do the benefits of voting. People's sense of civic duty seems to build through education. As one pair of political behavior scholars have noted, "Length of education is one of the best predictors of an individual's likelihood of voting."[46]

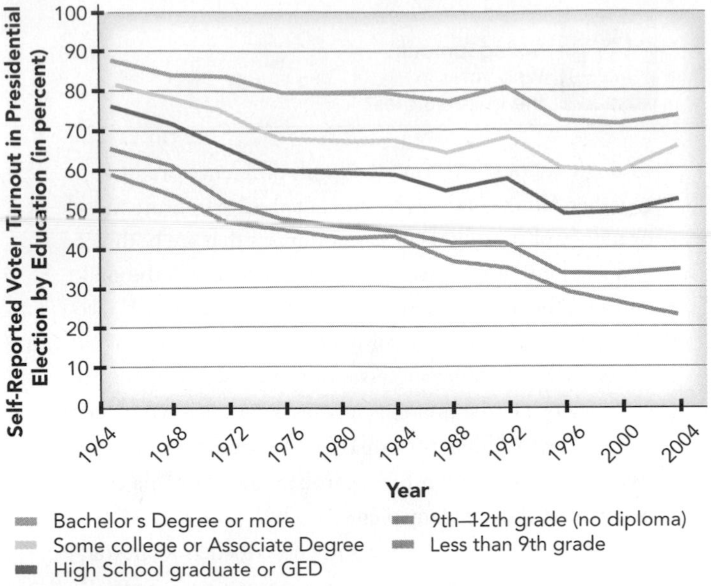

FIGURE 12.16 | **Presidential Election Voter Turnout by Education**

Level of education affects voter turnout, according to the Census Bureau. In 2004, only 40 percent of those without a high school degree voted, compared to the 78 percent with a college degree who voted. ***—Why has the rate of turnout for those with less education decreased faster than for those with higher levels of education? What might be the implications of this trend?***

Young Voters

Finally, there is the issue of age. Age has always been an excellent predictor of who participates in elections. Simply stated, young Americans have always voted at lower rates than older Americans have. This group has less *completed* education, is less affluent, and has much less likelihood of owning a home—all factors that seem related to participation, as you have seen. Younger citizens are also much more mobile, and they often get tripped up by residency requirements and voter registration issues. Yet survey data also suggest that young Americans are eager to contribute to the betterment of society; their rate of volunteering is just as high as that any other age group, as can be seen in Figure 12.17. The irony, of course, is that this willingness to become involved does not always seem to spread to political involvement.

Things might be changing, however. Much to the surprise of scholars, pundits, and older Americans, youth voting made a dramatic turnaround in 2004, and 2008 continued the trend. As you can see in Table 12.7, voter turnout in 2004 increased among all Americans by about 4 percent, but the increase was greatest among the youngest voters. Whereas just 36 percent of 18- to 24-year-olds voted in 2000, some 47 percent did in 2004. This represented an 11 percent increase—double the rate of increase in any other age group. In 2008, young voters flocked to the polls; about 52 percent of those under 25 came out to vote for either John McCain or Barack Obama—truly historic data. Fortunately for Obama, some 66 percent cast their vote for the senator from Illinois.

The robust youth turnout in the 2008 general election reflects a trend noticed in the presidential nomination process. In the winter and spring of 2008, record levels of young citizens participated in the primaries and caucuses. In Iowa, the first caucus of the season, turnout for those under 30 tripled from the 2004 and 2000 levels. Turnout in the primary elections held in Texas, Florida, Georgia, Missouri and several other states also tripled. In Tennessee, turnout for those under 30 quadrupled from 2004 levels.

As to why so many more young voters flocked to the polls in recent elections, there are a number of possible explanations. For one thing, the earlier decline in youth participation was so startling that many organizations and programs were initiated to bring young people back to the polls. Such activist groups included MTV's Rock the Vote and Choose or Lose, Justvotenow.org, the New Voters Project, Smack Down Your Vote! and Youth Vote Coalition, and Generation Engage. As it became apparent that the 2004 presidential election would be close, operatives on both sides sought out new groups of supporters, and young voters were a prime group targeted by both parties' campaigns. Several new elections pathway organizations tried bringing voters to the polls, including Americans Coming Together and MoveOn.org. Possibly the intensity of the campaign and the weight of the issues pulled young Americans into the electoral process. Issues such as the state of the economy, climate change, the war in Iraq, gay marriage, the future of Social Security, and stem cell research caught young voters' attention. "Young Americans turned out to vote at remarkable rates in the primaries. This reflects their deep concern about the critical issues at stake and the impact of this election on the country's future," notes one scholar. "The Millennials are beginning to make their distinctive and lasting mark on American politics."[47]

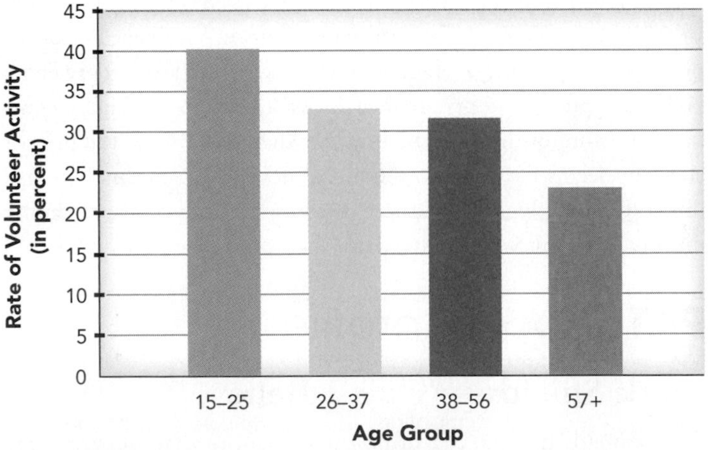

FIGURE 12.17 | **Volunteerism by Age Group**

Many older Americans believe that youngsters are apathetic, indifferent, and lazy. Yet this is not true. ***—Are you surprised by these figures? Why do you suppose young citizens are so ready to become engaged in numerous community programs and organizations but at the same time refrain from politics? What can be done to convince younger generations to join the political fray?***

SOURCE: Mark Hugo Lopez, "Volunteering among Young People," Center for Information and Research on Civic Learning and Engagement, http://www.civicyouth.org/PopUps/FactSheets/FS_Volunteering2.pdf, 2004. Reprinted by permission of CIRCLE School of Public Affairs, University of Maryland.

Clemson University students cheer as Barack Obama speaks during a campaign rally. ***—Have young Americans rediscovered the power of political action, or was their involvement in 2008 just a fad?***

TABLE 12.7 | Turnout by Age Groups in 2000, 2004, and 2008 Elections

The dramatic increase in young voter turnout in 2004 caught many by surprise. ***—What do you think caused this change?***

	18-24	25-44	45-64	65 AND OVER	OVERALL TURNOUT
2000	32.3%	49.8%	64.1%	67.6%	51.3%
2004	41.9%	52.2%	66.6%	68.9%	55.3%
2008	52%	56%	69%	69%	63%

SOURCE: U.S. Census Bureau. Current Population Survey. November 2004 and earlier reports. Released 26 May 2005. Accessed on 18 May 2006. Figures for 2008 are estimates based on data available on November 10, 2008.

STUDENT | PROFILE

Shortly after the 2004 election, Adrian and Devin Talbott, Justin Rockefeller, and Cate Edwards—each in their twenties and children of affluent, political families—decided to do something to get their generation involved in the political process. "The root of the problem," they argued, "lies in a self-perpetuating cycle. Young people do not have much money, so politicians don't seek their contributions. In turn, young people often feel ignored and don't see politics as relevant to their lives." Their organization, Generation Engage, or "GenGage," has moved in a rather unique direction. Their first step was to hire full-time local activists, who they call "Outreach Coordinators," and to have these young men and women set up satellite outreach programs. Second, the coordinators set up nonpartisan meetings on the topics most relevant to specific communities. Next, GenGage utilized technology, such as iChat videoconferencing tools, to hold massive meetings. "In this way," they argue, "GenGage connects disparate groups of members in communities across the country to lead interactive conversations with local, national, and international leaders." So far, GenGage iChats have been held with former President Bill Clinton; General Colin Powell; former Speaker of the House Newt Gingrich; former Vice President Al Gore; Supreme Court Justice Stephen Breyer; Speaker of the House Nancy Pelosi; Coretta Scott King; and Senators Hillary Clinton, Barack Obama, John Edwards, and Chuck Hagel, and many others. Bill Clinton seemed to hit the nail on the head during his GenGage iChat: "Whether you are Republican or Democrat, liberal or conservative, think government should or should not be more involved, you can't go on thinking, 'This is the way things are. There is nothing I can do.' It's not true," Clinton said. "You cannot for the rest of your life look in the mirror and say, 'I regret this, this, and this. I wish America were this, this, and this.' You know they're giving you a vehicle to do it. That's why I'm honored to be here to support the cause." For more information on this novel organization, visit their Web site at http://www.generationengage.com/ruralaccess.html.

SOURCE: Adrian Talbott, Devin Talbott, and Justin Rockfeller, *RL Magazine OnLine*. Accessed at http://entertainment.ralphlauren.com/magazine/editorial/wi07/generation_engage.asp, May 6, 2008. ■

Individual Participation in Elections
Practice Quiz

1. Attending a rally, discussing politics with friends and family, working at a party or candidate's headquarters, or attending the local meeting of a political party are all examples of
   a. individual participation. **b.** collective participation.
   c. positive campaigning. **d.** cohort campaigning.
2. Voter turnout was much stronger 50 years ago than it has been in modern times.
   a. true **b.** false
3. Voter turnout declined in the 2004 election, probably due to the unpopularity of both candidates.
   a. true **b.** false
4. What factor has contributed to negative attitudes about politics?
   a. attitudinal change **b.** lifestyle change
   c. role of the news media **d.** a, b, and c

Answers: 1-b, 2-a, 3-b, 4-d.

Discussion Questions

1. In your view, what factor has contributed the most to negative attitudes about politics? Why?
2. Make a case for individual participation being more useful than collective participation, and then argue the opposite case.

What **YOU** can do!

Discuss with a group of friends the emerging trend of increased levels of political participation among younger voters. Do you believe this is a true reversal of historical trends? If so, what do you think sparked the increase? How can individuals in your generation maintain this positive trend?

■ **Elite Democratic Model:** The view that a democracy is healthy if people acquire positions of power through competitive elections. The level of involvement by citizens in this process is unimportant so long as elections are fair.

SIGNIFICANCE: *Those who adhere to this view are less concerned about modest levels of individual electoral involvement.*

■ **Popular Democratic Model:** A view of democracy that stresses the ongoing involvement of average citizens in the political process.

SIGNIFICANCE: *From this vantage, low levels of electoral engagement signal a weakness in the democracy.*

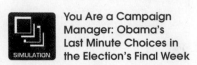

SIMULATION **You Are a Campaign Manager: Obama's Last Minute Choices in the Election's Final Week**

Conclusion

As you've read, Americans put a great deal of faith in the election process, and over the past two centuries, many changes have opened the system to more involvement. But at the same time, it seems that only a modest number are willing to get involved. What difference does it make if many Americans do not seem interested in politics and that Americans on the whole turn out to vote less often than citizens in other democracies? Is this really something to care about?

One way to answer such questions is to take a practical point of view. What policy difference would it make if nonvoters got into the act? Would the government head in a different direction if turnout were higher? Early studies suggested that on the whole, the policy preferences of nonvoters essentially paralleled those of voters. There would be little policy change if we had full election turnout. More recently, however, studies suggest that who votes *does* matter. The low turnout in the 1994 election allowed the Republicans to capture control of both houses of Congress and helped bring George W. Bush to the White House in 2000. In both cases, public policy shifts that followed these elections reflected a more conservative, more Republican agenda than overall public opinion would suggest.

Another way to answer such questions is to examine how you define *democracy*. For example, perhaps precise levels of participation are unimportant; so long as enough citizens are involved to make the process competitive, full participation is inconsequential. The people who refrain from involvement in politics are also likely the least well informed. Perhaps we do not want these folks involved in the process; is an uninformed vote really preferable to none at all? Along similar lines, some people speculate that less informed citizens (the nonvoters) are more prone to radical policy shifts, so their absence at the polls actually adds a degree of stability to public policy. The conservative columnist George Will, in a piece titled "In Defense of Nonvoting," argues that good government—not the right to vote—is the fundamental human right. He suggests that high voting rates in Germany's Weimar Republic (1919–1933) enabled the Nazis to take power in 1933.[48] Declining turnout in America, Will asserts, is no cause for worry. This perspective is often called the **elite democratic model**■. It insists that so long as fairness and political opportunity are guaranteed, the system is healthy.

The **popular democratic model**■, by contrast, suggests that the character of any political system is not simply the outcome of public policy but also the process by which it is reached (see *Pathways: The Struggle over Same-Sex Marriage* on Timeline pages T–9 and T–10 at the back of this book. This model puts a premium on electoral involvement. When this occurs, citizens develop an affinity for the system, because they are convinced that they have a stake in whatever policy results from political decisions. Put a bit differently, this theory says that systems of government designed to reflect the will of the people will do so better, and in the long run will be more prosperous and stable, if average citizens join the electoral process. Echoing this sentiment, the liberal political scientist and journalist E. J. Dionne, in his book *Why Americans Hate Politics,* has written that "a nation that hates politics will not long thrive as a democracy."[49] Which of these well-known commentators, Will or Dionne, in your opinion comes closer to the truth?

Key Objective Review, Apply, and Explore

Elections and Democratic Theory

(pages 426–429)

Americans put a great deal of faith in elections, believing that "the right to vote" is at the core of any democratic society. From a theoretical vantage, there seems to be several reasons to make such a claim. But there are also some downsides that most people rarely consider.

KEY TERMS

Republican Form of Government 426
Plato (427–347 B.C.) 426
Landslide Election 426
Legitimacy 427
Civic Participation 428
Episodic Participation 428

CRITICAL THINKING QUESTIONS

1. Which of the theoretical justifications for elections makes the most sense to you, and which of the arguments against elections seems most persuasive?
2. This section notes that elections push episodic and individualistic participation. But what's so wrong with keeping your politics private and engaging in politics only sporadically? Also, do you think the Internet has the potential to change this?

INTERNET RESOURCES

For information on electoral systems in other countries, visit the following sites: **http://www.electionguide.org/**, **http://www.electionworld.org/election/indexfrm.htm**, and **http://www.psr.keele.ac.uk/election.htm**

ADDITIONAL READING

Pomper, Gerald. *Voters, Elections and Parties: The Practice of Democratic Theory*. New York: Transaction Publishers, 1988.

Scher, Richard K. *The Modern Political Campaign: Mudslinging, Bombast, and the Vitality of American Politics.* New York: Sharpe, 1997.

The Electoral College

(pages 430–435)

Many forces shape the conduct of presidential elections, but none is more significant than the Electoral College. This complex, rather odd institution was yet another compromise at the Constitutional Convention, a means to moderate the "passions of the public" and to allow smaller states a greater say in the selection of the president. Today the Electoral College structures how and where campaigns are conducted and, occasionally, as in the 2000 presidential election, who takes up residence at the White House.

KEY TERMS

Electoral College 430
Twelfth Amendment 431
Unit Rule 431
Swing States 433

CRITICAL THINKING QUESTIONS

1. How, exactly, does the Electoral College benefit small states? Was this a fair compromise at the Constitutional Convention? Has the system worked as the framers intended?
2. What are some advantages of the Electoral College? Along similar lines, what would be some downsides to a direct presidential election? How can the Electoral College be made meaningless *without* amending the Constitution?

INTERNET RESOURCES

A number of Web sites feature the Electoral College. For a good one, see the U.S. National Archieves and Records Admission at **http://www.archives.gov/federal-register/electoral-college/index.html**

ADDITIONAL READING

Schumaker, Paul D. and Burdett A. Loomis (eds.). *Choosing a President: The Electoral College and Beyond*. Washington, D.C.: Congressional Quarterly, 2002.

Key Objective Review, Apply, and Explore

Elections and the Law

(pages 436–439)

On one level, elections take place outside the boundaries of government. As noted in the first chapter, elections are "processes," not institutions. In fact, some have thought it a bit strange that the framers of our system made little mention of how elections might be conducted. Yet there have been numerous constitutional and legal changes that have redefined the nature and practice of elections in America. This section explores several of these legal refinements.

KEY TERMS

Fourteenth Amendment 436
Fifteenth Amendment 436
Nineteenth Amendment 436
Twenty-Fourth Amendment 436
Twenty-Sixth Amendment 437
Voting Rights Act of 1965 438
Residency and Registration Laws 438
Motor Voter Law 438
Help America Vote Act 438

CRITICAL THINKING QUESTIONS

1. What, if any, additional legal changes do you think would enhance the democratic character of elections in America?
2. Some have speculated that younger Americans, perhaps beginning at age 16, should be given the right to vote. One proposal is to give these folks a partial vote, sort of like a "learner's permit." Does this make sense to you?

INTERNET RESOURCES

For information on a range of campaign-related issues, see the Federal Election Commission Web site at **http://www.fec.gov**

ADDITIONAL READING

Piven, Frances Fox, and Richard A. Cloward. *Why Americans Still Don't Vote: And Why Politicians Want It That Way.* Boston: Beacon Press, 2000.

Referendums, Initiatives, and Recalls

(pages 440–441)

When most of us think about elections, candidate selection comes to mind. But in about half the states, voters are allowed to cast ballots on policy questions. To many, ballot initiatives are a good way to insert the "will of the people" into the process. Others suggest these campaigns are about the manipulation of the public, and they are too often decided by financial resources.

KEY TERMS

Ballot Initiative 440
Recall 440

CRITICAL THINKING QUESTIONS

1. Why do you suppose the framers of our government chose not to allow ballot initiatives for federal policy?
2. Some have suggested that the public should not be given the chance to vote on policy questions, because they are uninformed and lack relevant information. Has the Internet changed things in this area? That is, given the volume of information on the Internet, perhaps average citizens should have greater opportunities to assess policy measures. Would you agree?

INTERNET RESOURCES

For information on ballot initiatives, recalls, and referendums, see the Ballot Initiative Institute's Web site at **http://www.iandrinstitute.org/ballotwatch.htp**

ADDITIONAL READING

Broder, David S. *Democracy Derailed: Initiative Campaigns and the Power of Money*. New York: Harvest Book, 2001.

Smith, Daniel A., and Caroline Tolbert. *Educated by Initiative: The Effects of Direct Democracy on Citizens and Political Organizations in the American States*. Ann Arbor; University of Michigan Press, 2004.

Key Objective Review, Apply, and Explore

The Role of Money in Elections

(pages 442–449)

For many Americans, money distorts the election process. Candidates awash in cash have a better chance than candidates strapped for resources. A number of laws have been passed to help level the playing field, most recently the Bipartisan Campaign Reform Act. Others argue that giving and collecting money is a form of political action, to be encouraged in a robust democracy. One thing is for sure, money will continue to be a critical part of the election process.

KEY TERMS

Federal Election Campaign Act (FECA) 443

Watergate 443

***Buckley* v. *Valeo* (1976) 443**

Soft Money 443

Incumbent Advantage 444

Term Limits 446

Bipartisan Campaign Reform Act (BCRA) 446

527 Organizations 447

CRITICAL THINKING QUESTIONS

1. What is your take on the central issue in *Buckley* v. *Valeo* (1976)? Is money a form of political speech, protected under the First Amendment? If so, would it make sense to regulate the size of campaign contributions?

2. One way to get around First Amendment protections is to create a voluntary public financing system for all elections—as is currently done at the presidential level. Candidates who chose to take public funds would be barred from additional fundraising. Does this make good sense? Are there downsides to this plan?

INTERNET RESOURCES

For a host of information on campaign finance, see two sites: the Center for Responsive Politics at **http://www.opensecrets.org**, and the Campaign Finance Institute at **http://www.cfinst.org/about/index.html**

ADDITIONAL READING

Farrar-Myers, Victoria A., and Diana Dwyre. *Limits and Loopholes: The Quest for Money, Free Speech, and Fair Elections*. Washington, D.C.: Congressional Quarterly, 2007.

Malbin, Michael J. (ed.). *Life after Reform: When the Bipartisan Campaign Reform Act Meets Politics.* Lanham, MD: Rowman & Littlefield, 2003.

Campaigning Online

(pages 450–453)

The history of campaigns in America is one of transformation and continual adjustment. The Internet is the latest development, and in many ways, it is altering the way candidates organize, raise funds, and reach voters. It is also shifting the way average citizens collect information and participate in the electoral process.

KEY TERM

Blog 450

CRITICAL THINKING QUESTIONS

1. Citizens surely benefit from the volume of political news on the Internet, but are there any downsides to these new technologies? In your opinion, have resources like YouTube and other recent innovations enhanced the electoral process?

2. Do you think the Internet helps level the playing field between affluent and poorly funded candidates, or is cash still "the mother's milk of politics"?

INTERNET RESOURCES

There are numerous political sites, as you know. For a link to many of the most prominent political blogs, see **http://www.time.com/time/specials/2007/article/0,28804,1725323_1727246,00.html**

ADDITIONAL READING

Teachout, Zephyr, and Thomas Streeter. *Mousepads, Shoe Leather, and Hope: Lessons from the Howard Dean Campaign for the Future of Internet Politics*. Denver: Paradigm Publishers, 2007.

Key Objective Review, Apply, and Explore

Individual Participation in Elections

(pages 454–459)

There are many ways that citizens can become involved in the election process—from voting or attending a rally to sending in a check to a candidate or talking about issues and candidates with friends. For many of us, elections are an important part of our civic lives. To others, electoral participation does not seem to be worth their time and effort. The 2004 and 2008 elections suggest growing interest in electoral politics, but many agree that we still have a way to go in terms of participation. This section explores these and other issues.

KEY TERMS

Electoral Behavior 454
Turnout 454
Elite Democratic Model 460
Popular Democratic Model 460

CRITICAL THINKING QUESTIONS

1. Most likely some of your friends and family do not participate in electoral politics. What do you think is at the root of their inactivity and/or indifference?
2. Data presented in this section suggest young Americans are paying greater attention to electoral politics. Why do you suppose this is true? What is different now than a few decades ago? Will it last?

INTERNET RESOURCES

For information on levels of political participation in America, see the Committee for the Study of the American Electorate Web page at **http://www.gspm.org/csae**

For information on youth political engagement, see the Center for Information and Research on Civic Learning and Engagement (CIRCLE) at **http://www.civicyouth.org**

ADDITIONAL READING

Patterson, Thomas E. *The Vanishing Voter: Public Involvement in an Age of Uncertainty.* New York: Knopf, 2002.

Shea, Daniel M., and John C. Green. *Fountain of Youth: Strategies and Tactics For Mobilizing America's Young Voters*. Lanham, MD: Rowman & Littlefield, 2007.

Chapter Review Critical Thinking Test

1. Elections serve as more than a measure of current opinions and preferences; they serve as a civics refresher course.
a. true **b.** false

2. Ironically, while fewer Americans have participated in elections in recent decades,
a. more people believe they are participating.
b. more people now have the opportunity to participate.
c. more people run for office.
d. more Americans vote from overseas.

3. Since 1824, how often have presidents been elected with a plurality—not a majority—of popular votes?
a. twice
b. seven times
c. sixteen times
d. twenty-six times

4. Regarding elections, the first priority of the framers of the Constitution was
a. governmental stability.
b. creating a truly democratic system.
c. making sure that everyone had equal access to the ballot box and public office.
d. making sure public policy represented the majority opinion of eligible voters.

5. A major reason for the creation of the Electoral College was to ensure that
a. the will of the majority of voters in each state would be accurately represented in presidential elections.
b. men of the best character and intellect would be deciding who the next president and vice president would be.
c. each state in the new Union would have equal representation in the election process.
d. England would not interfere with the election process.

6. Regarding the role of political parties in elections, the framers of the Constitution
a. reasoned that electors would rise above partisan preferences and vote for the candidates who would best serve the nation.
b. assumed that a two-party system would always present the electorate with a clear and fair choice between distinct political philosophies.
c. worried that partisan politics would compromise the electoral process.
d. said very little, because they never foresaw the emergence of parties in the first place.

7. Contributing funds through a loophole in federal campaign finance regulations that allow individuals and groups to give unlimited sums of money to political parties is known as
a. pork barrel spending.
b. vigorish.
c. money laundering.
d. soft money.

8. What federal law was enacted in 2002, following the vote-count chaos in the 2000 presidential election?
a. the 2002 Voting Rights Act
b. the Motor Voter Act
c. the Help America Vote Act
d. the Butterfly Ballot Abolition Act

9. Now used widely in presidential campaigns, MySpace, Facebook, and YouTube are all examples of
a. Internet blogs.
b. chat rooms.
c. pundit Web sites.
d. online social networks.

10. What prompted popular interest in the motor voter law?
a. the desire to help democracy and the domestic automobile industry
b. the desire to confine the pool of registered voters to responsible adults
c. the desire to counteract state registration laws that may have had the effect of unfairly limiting people's ability to register to vote
d. the desire to reinforce state registration laws requiring registered voters to be residents of their state and citizens in good legal standing

11. More and more voters—especially young voters—resort to online news sources as opposed to traditional sources such as television and newspapers.
a. true **b.** false

12. Which of the following is NOT a reason for the massive increase in the cost of political campaigns?
a. an increased dependence on television advertising
b. an increase in the number of voters that campaign advertising must reach
c. campaign consultants
d. the abolition of poll taxes

13. The unit rule and partisan slates of electors make it *likely* that the most popular candidate (the highest vote getter) will become the president but do not *guarantee* it.
a. true **b.** false

14. What did the Federal Election Campaign Act and its subsequent amendments prohibit?
a. limitless campaign spending on the part of candidates, and limitless contributions from individuals, groups, or political parties
b. warrantless wiretapping
c. making individual campaign contributions tax deductible
d. the use of soft money in campaigns

Chapter Review Critical Thinking Test

15. One result of the Supreme Court case *Buckley* v. *Valeo* (1976) was to lift most restrictions from the activities of political parties.

a. true **b.** false

16. Incumbency is a powerful advantage in elections. In recent House elections ________% of the incumbents won. One popular argument for why this happens is that ________

a. 65; incumbents always have more money to spend.
b. 75; incumbents are better, more seasoned leaders.
c. 85; incumbents have earned a greater degree of trust from most voters.
d. 95; nearly all legislative activity is now geared toward securing reelection.

17. What does BCRA stand for, and what, among other things, does it prohibit?

a. Bicameral Regulation Act; soft-money campaign contributions from political action committees
b. Bipartisan Campaign Reform Act; soft-money campaign contributions to national political organizations
c. Better Campaigns Regulation Act; individual campaign contributions over $500
d. Better Congressional Races Act; individual soft-money donations to state party organizations

18. One explanation for the decline in voter turnout during recent decades is that people's lifestyles have changed.

a. true **b.** false

19. What is so paradoxical about the low turnout of young voters?

a. The average age of political candidates themselves has steadily declined.
b. Young people keep up with the news more avidly than older voters do.
c. Young people are more inclined than ever before to volunteer to help their community.
d. Surveys indicate that young people are less disenchanted with the government than older people are.

20. The most notable change in turnout at primary elections has been the increase in the youth vote.

a. true **b.** false

Answers: 1-a, 2-b, 3-c, 4-a, 5-b, 6-d, 7-d, 8-c, 9-d, 10-c, 11-a, 12-d, 13-d, 14-a, 15-a, 16-d, 17-b, 18-a, 19-c, 20-a.

You decide!

While many scholars note the need for campaign reform, most also recognize that candidates for office face many pressures. Imagine you are a candidate in an extremely competitive election, such as the one described at the beginning of this chapter. Considering what you know about recent elections and voter turnout rates in the United States, what sort of campaign strategy would you employ? Which demographic groups (or what type of voter) would you rely on for your electoral victory? Why? What sort of message would you use to attract these voters? How would you organize your campaign, including advertisements, fundraising, and expenditures? Do you foresee any conflicts between your campaign strategy and organization? If so, how might you manage those?

Key Objective Outline

How are political parties different than other political organizations, and what functions do they serve in a democracy?

Party Functions
(page 470)

Are political parties important once a candidate gets in office?

Party-in-Government
(page 474)

What does "party identification" imply, and what bearing does this have on vote choice?

Party-in-the-Electorate
(page 478)

What are party "committees," and what do they seek to accomplish?

Party-as-Organization
(page 482)

CHAPTER 13
POLITICAL PARTIES

Do political parties enhance the democratic process?

The 2008 presidential nomination race began much earlier than most had expected. By the spring of 2007, candidates in both parties were making their official announcements, lining up staff, charting strategy, and raising funds. Arizona Senator John McCain threw his hat into the ring on April 25, 2007. He was a prominent figure in Washington politics, a tough campaigner, and a media darling. He would be a formidable opponent, surely one of the early frontrunners.

Things took an unexpected turn, however. McCain's fundraising dried up quickly, his staff took to bickering, and his message seemed flat. His polling numbers dropped.

Meanwhile, one of the Democratic candidates, John Edwards, was pulling together a "poverty tour" to underscore the plight of some Americans. The plan was to reach out to the poorest people, to the places where folks were down on their luck and in despair. Jay Leno made the joke on *The Tonight Show,* "Sen. John Edwards began what he's calling his poverty tour today. He's visiting people who have no money and no hope. His first stop: John McCain's campaign headquarters." By the start of the primary season, in January of 2008, things had gotten so bad for McCain's candidacy that *ABC News* commentator George Stephanopoulos raised the issue of whether McCain was a "dead man walking." It seemed like his political obituary was being written.

As the New Hampshire primary neared, McCain took a gamble. His $25 million war chest had dwindled to less than $500,000. Super Tuesday was around the corner, but McCain decided to pour everything into the Granite State contest. "When the pundits declared us finished, I told them, 'I'm going to New Hampshire, where the voters don't let you make their decision for them,'" McCain told a reporter.

McCain won the New Hampshire primary and went on to clobber his opponents in subsequent state contests. On March 4, 2008, he swept four Republican contests to become his party's presumptive nominee. Some have suggested it was due to his energy, ideas, and integrity, while others have speculated that his resurgence was due to lackluster opponents. Either way, John McCain's comeback is one of the great tales of the 2008 presidential election.

STUDENT RESOURCE-CENTER
• Glossary
• Vocabulary Example
• LINK
• MyPoliSciLab Connection

■ **Rational Party Model:** Where the goal is to win offices for material gain and to control the distribution of government jobs.

EXAMPLE: *Years ago, many local party "machines" were considered very pragmatic, very rational.*

■ **Responsible Party Model:** Where the goal is to shape public policy.

EXAMPLE: *A local party organization that is dedicated to lowering taxes in their community.*

SIMULATION **You Are a Campaign Manager: Voter Mobilization and Suppression: Political Dirty Tricks or Fair Games?**

Party Functions (pages 470–473)

How are political parties different than other political organizations, and what functions do they serve in a democracy?

One of the great ironies of American politics is that the very forces the framers of our Constitution most feared have proved to be the instruments that actually make elections work. We are speaking of political parties. One pair of scholars has called them the "institutions Americans love to hate."[1]

What Is a Political Party?

No single definition of political parties satisfies everyone. Any two observers of politics might define parties in different ways. The principal difference focuses on what we might expect from parties—that is, the goals of party activity.

One definition, often called the **rational party model**■, is that parties are organizations that sponsor candidates for political office under the organization's name in hopes of controlling the apparatus of government. The ends are the control of government, which has often meant the "perks" of control—patronage jobs, government contracts, and the like. A second definition comes from the other side of the spectrum. It is the **responsible party model**■. In this model, parties are organizations that run candidates to shape the outcomes of government—that is, to redirect public policy. Rational parties work to win elections in order to control government, whereas responsible parties work hard during elections in order to shape public policy.

> "What's the difference between a political party and an interest group?"
> —Student Question

Three factors distinguish political parties from other public organizations, such as interest groups, labor unions, trade associations, and political action committees:[2]

1. Political parties run candidates under their own label. Interest groups work hard to win elections—the Christian Coalition and the AFL-CIO both do all they can during each election cycle to win voter support for the candidates they endorse—but they do not nominate candidates to run under their label. Only political parties do this.
2. Political parties have a broad range of concerns, called a **platform**■. As umbrella organizations, they develop and put forward positions on an array of policy questions. In contrast, most interest groups limit their efforts to a narrow range of topics. The National Rifle Association, for instance, is concerned with gun regulation, and the Environmental Defense League focuses primarily on issues related to controlling pollution and protecting ecosystems.
3. Finally, ever since the Progressive Era, discussed in LINK Chapter 12, pages 436–441, political parties have been subject to numerous state and local laws. They are "quasi-public" institutions. Interest groups, on the other hand, are purely private and free of government regulations. Indeed, the extent to which parties are also private organizations has been recently debated in the federal courts.

What Parties Do

Just as there is disagreement over the precise definition of *party*, there are differences regarding what parties contribute to a democratic system. The following is a list of 10 key party functions. It contains numerous *overt* functions (activities that we can see and clearly measure) and also mentions many *latent* functions (theoretical activities that we hope parties provide).

1. **Organizing the Election Process.** Devising a system of elections to pick governmental leaders is much tougher than it sounds. Imagine dozens, perhaps even hundreds, of citizens vying for a single office. Parties serve an important organizing function, because they narrow the pool of office seekers to party **nominees**■ and establish a platform of issues for their candidates. Both functions help organize the process for voters.

Platform: The set of issues, principles, and goals that a party supports.

EXAMPLE: *Each of the national party committees created a platform at their conventions in the summer of 2008.*

CONNECT THE LINK (Chapter **12**, pages **436–441**) What changes to electoral politics were ushered in during the Progressive Era?

Nominees: The individuals selected by a party to run for office under that party's label.

EXAMPLE: *John McCain became the Republican nominee for the presidency.*

Both national party committees hold presidential nomination conventions every 4 years. Here Michael Reagan, at the podium, offers a tribute to his father, former President Ronald Reagan, at the Republican Convention in 2004.

2. **Facilitating Voter Choice.** Psychologists tell us that humans wish to make rational decisions with the least amount of information necessary. Given that we, as voters, need not know everything or even very much about a candidate other than his or her party affiliation, parties help us cast an informed, rational vote. If, for example, a voter prefers Republican policies and an election pits a Republican against a Democrat, the voter can make an informed choice with no additional information. (Notice that we are not saying that the voter is making the *best* choice—merely that knowing a candidate is supported by this or that party gives a voter who knows something about the parties *enough* information to make an *informed* choice among candidates.) Without party labels, the voter would have to study each candidate's positions in detail. Forced to undertake such a chore, many would simply sit on the sidelines or vote at random.
3. **Recruiting Candidates.** Anxious to win elections, parties often try to recruit good, qualified citizens to run for office. Of course, they don't always succeed. But when they do, they give voters excellent choices and a winner who is qualified to govern.
4. **Screening Candidates.** Parties also try to screen out unqualified or corrupt candidates. Receiving a party's nomination is a crucial step in winning a post in government. Parties deny endorsements to weak office seekers, not wishing to be tarnished by their shortcomings.
5. **Aiding Candidates.** Parties help candidates put their best foot forward to voters. In the past, assistance was primarily labor. Party workers would spread the word about their candidates and work on their behalf leading up to election day. More recently, parties have begun providing many high-technology campaign services, such as polling, computerized targeting, radio and television productions, and direct mail. Of course, fundraising has also become a huge part of how parties lend a hand.
6. **Organizing a Complex Government.** The complexity of our government can seem overwhelming, as discussed in several chapters in this book. There are three branches of the federal government, two houses in one of those branches, a massive bureaucracy, and state and local governments. This complexity was by design, part of the checks and balances envisioned by the framers, but in many ways, this structure makes united action difficult. Parties counteract this effect by helping bring the many pieces of our system into united action. For example, throughout American history, political parties have helped bridge the gap between executives

■ **Unified Party Control:** When the executive and a majority of members in both houses of the legislature are of the same political party.

EXAMPLE: *Franklin D. Roosevelt was able to move quickly on his New Deal legislation because his party also controlled both houses of Congress.*

■ **Divided Party Control:** When one party controls the White House and another party controls one or both branches of Congress.

EXAMPLE: *During George W. Bush's last 2 years, the federal government was divided, because he was a Republican and the Democrats controlled both the House and Senate.*

Party nomination contests have always been contentious "family affairs." That is, candidates of the same party will often slug it out for months, often leveling serious assaults on each other's qualifications, character, and issue positions. By the end of the process, the national party nomination conventions, the family feud is expected to be over. The convention is a time for the family—the party—to unite and celebrate the victor. Needless to say, it is also a time for the victor's actual family to breathe a bit easier. (Left photo) Pictured at the Democratic national convention with family members are President-elect Obama and Senator Biden. (Right photo) Pictured at the Republican national convention with family members are Senator McCain and Governor Palin, the first woman nominee for vice president on the Republican ticket.

(presidents, governors, or mayors) and legislatures as well as bring the two houses of the legislature into united action. (Strong parties are no guarantee of overcoming constitutional obstruction, as we have seen throughout American history, but you can imagine how much worse things would be without them.)

7. **Aggregating Interests.** In their efforts to win elections, parties try to build coalitions of groups. Just as our government is complex, so is our society. Parties want to win elections, and interest groups want a say in the policy process. The outcome of this mutually beneficial relationship is that individual and group interests are melded into a broad philosophy of governing.
8. **Educating Citizens.** As each party works to build support for its candidates, the by-product is voter education. Not only do the voters learn more about the candidates because of party activities, they also learn more about government policies and the workings of our system.
9. **Ensuring Accountability.** Because our political system is so complex, it is difficult for voters to make accountability judgments. Whom should we blame if the economy turns sour or medical costs skyrocket? Who should get credit if crime rates fall or inflation stays in check? Voters use parties to make these assessments. If the party in power has done a good job, its members tend to be voted back into office. If things get worse, voters often give the other party a chance. This process works best when one party controls all parts of the government, called **unified party control**■. In contrast, **divided party control**■ exists when each party controls at least one branch of the government but neither party controls all three branches. During much of our nation's history, control has been unified, but during the past 30 years, the norm has been a divided system, which makes accountability judgments more difficult.
10. **Promoting Civic Participation.** Either as part of their mission to build a more fully democratic system or simply

in an effort to win the current election, parties promote political participation. This has included the cultivation of candidates, donors, volunteers, and voters on election day through get-out-the-vote efforts. Many studies have found that communities with strong political parties have higher levels of voting and other modes of political participation.[3]

Party Functions

Practice Quiz

1. If you walked into a local Green Party headquarters and said, "Sign me up. We need better environmental policy coming out of the state house," you would be assuming what definition of political parties?
   a. the pragmatic party model
   b. the machine party model
   c. the responsible party model
   d. the long-range party model
2. One feature that distinguishes political parties from other public organizations, such as the Christian Coalition and the AFL-CIO, is that
   a. parties are private institutions.
   b. you have to pay to join a party.
   c. parties are not bound by federal or state regulation.
   d. parties nominate candidates and other public interest groups do not.
3. Parties perform all of these functions EXCEPT for
   a. focusing on one major issue at a time.
   b. organizing the election process.
   c. facilitating voter choice.
   d. recruiting candidates.
4. Unlike other public organizations that support candidates during an election, political parties run candidates under their own label.
   a. true **b.** false

Answers: 1-c, 2-d, 3-a, 4-a.

Discussion Questions

1. How would you describe the "educating the public" function of political parties?
2. How would you summarize the key differences between political parties and other politically active groups?

What **YOU** can do!

To find out more about how political parties serve two specific functions—organizing social functions and promoting civic participation—visit the Web sites for your state and local party organizations. Compare how the state, local, and even national parties accomplish these goals. Do you think that parties are doing enough in pursuit of these goals? If not, what else could they do?

CONNECT THE LINK
Chapter **6**, pages **228–231**)

CONNECT THE LINK
Chapter **6**, pages **229–231**) What role do leaders play in organizing the legislative process?

Party-*in*-Government

(pages 474–477)

Are political parties important once a candidate gets in office?

"When we say 'the Republican Party,' who are we talking about—the people who vote for Republicans, the Republican members of Congress, the people who raise money and work for the Republican Party, or all of these?"

—Student Question

One of the most confusing aspects of political parties is precisely what the term *party* implies. By the 1950s, political scientists developed what is called the **tripartite view of parties.** According to this model, political parties have three interrelated elements: party-in-government, party-in-the-electorate, and party-as-organization (see Figure 13.1).

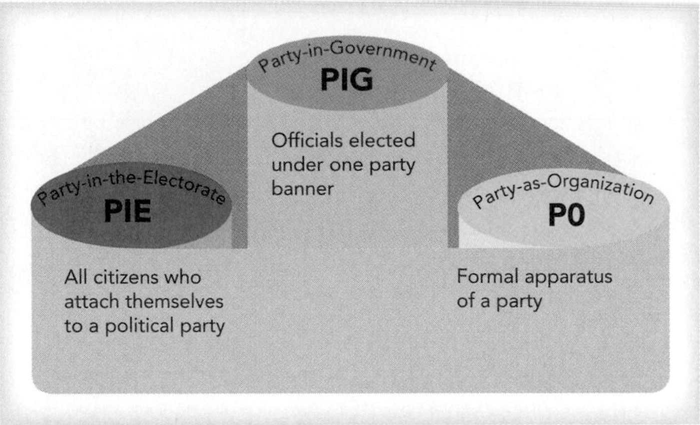

FIGURE 13.1 | **The Three Interrelated Elements of Political Parties**

This figure shows the three core pieces of American political parties: party-in-government (PIG), party-in-the-electorate (PIE), and party-as-organization (PO). While few would doubt that each exists, some believe that they should be seen as distinct elements rather than linked together. ***—When you think of "political party," which element comes to mind?***

Let's begin with party-in-government, which refers to the officials who were elected under a party banner. All the Republicans in the House of Representatives, for example, make up one piece of the GOP ("Grand Old Party," which is the nickname for Republicans) party-in-government. They call themselves the Republican Conference, and if they have a majority in the chamber, their leader is the speaker of the House; if not, he or she is the minority leader (see LINK Chapter 6, pages 228–231). Other segments of the Republican party-in-government include the Republicans in the Senate and the president when a member of the GOP. There are also sub-branches of the national party-in-government, such as governors, state-level elected officials, municipal officials, and so on. They, too, often form their own institution, such as the Republican Governors Association. Similarly, the House Democrats call themselves the Democratic Caucus, and all the Democrats in the Buffalo City Council consider themselves part of the same team.

"Do members of Congress always vote with their party?"

—Student Question

The American system is rather unique in that party-in-government structures are weak. In other democracies, it is expected that elected officials will vote with their party on most or all matters. Dissenters who vote with the opposition party are rare. If necessary, enormous pressure is exerted to force officials to "stay in line." In our system, however, party leaders *hope* that members will vote with the party, but the tradition is that elected officials can stray without serious repercussions. In fact, most voters in America look down on "party politics" and applaud their elected officials' independence. Still, you should keep in mind that the single best predictor of how legislators will vote on any given bill is their party affiliation. Most elected officials vote with their party most of the time, but in our political system, a degree of independence is both expected and accepted, as discussed in greater detail in LINK Chapter 6, pages 229–231.

One way to assess the extent to which legislators vote with their fellow partisans is through what are called **party unity scores.** There are different ways to measure party unity, but the concept is the same: a gauge of how often members of the same party stick together. Since 1954, there is a clear pattern of greater unity, echoing what many see as an increasingly polarized Congress. Whether this is a good thing for our political system has been the source of debate. Some analysts believe this polarization hinders

VISUAL LITERACY

State Control and National Platforms

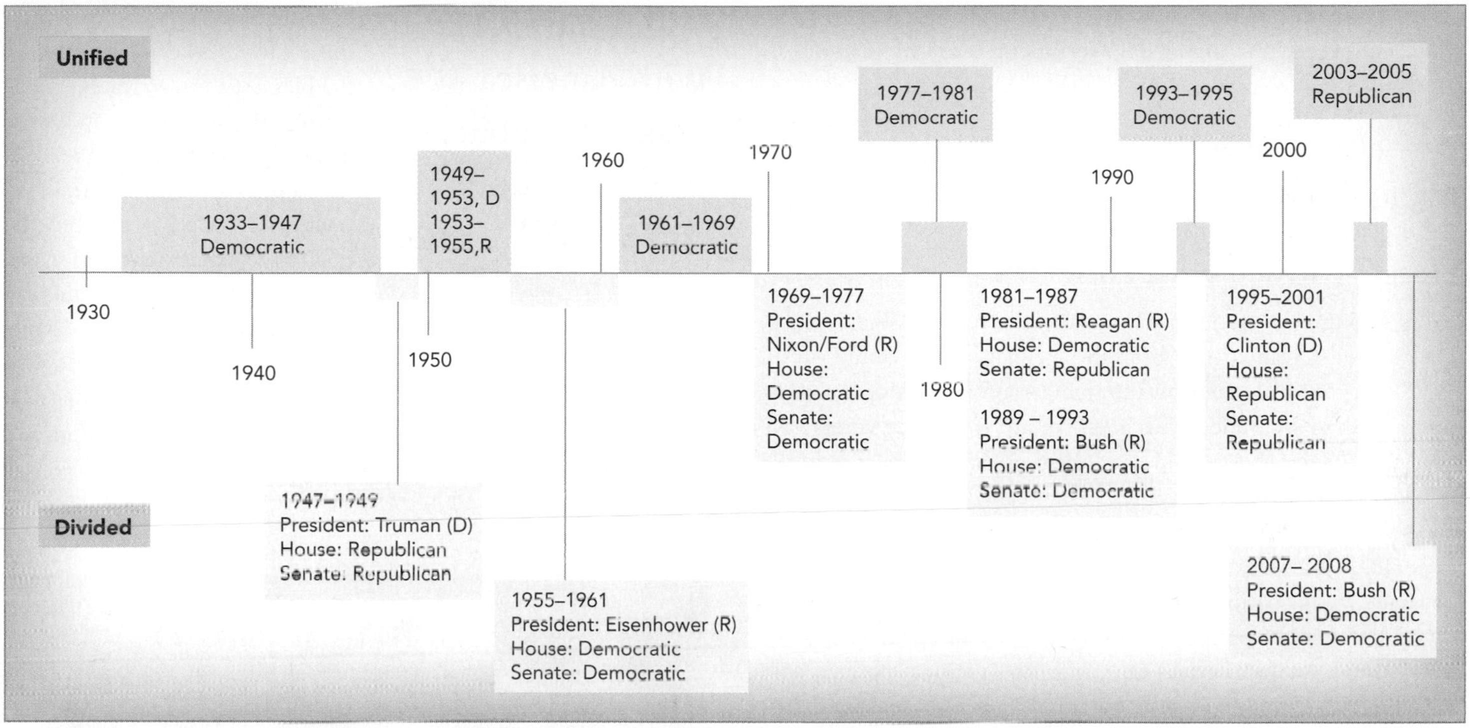

FIGURE 13.2 | **Party Control of Government 1933-2008**

As this figure suggests, our government has been divided most of the time since 1968. ***—What do you believe is the root of divided government? Why would voters split their vote between candidates of different parties? Perhaps most importantly, what are the differences between unified and divided governments? Do the pathways of change work the same when government is divided?***

SOURCE: http://www.laits.utexas.edu

the legislative process and makes moderate policies less likely, while others believe that sharp differences are good for the electorate, allowing voters a clear and meaningful choice on election day.

Related to this, as levels of party unity in Congress increase, the issue of divided versus unified party control takes on new importance. As we noted in the previous section, parties can help our disparate system of government move forward when one party controls both chambers of Congress and the presidency (dubbed a unified government). But when the government is divided and most members of Congress stick with their party-in-government, slow change seems to be the norm. Figure 13.2 notes the increased frequency of divided governments in recent decades. It should be

President Bush, a Republican, shakes hands with Speaker of the House Nancy Pelosi, a Democrat. Some suggest that divided government, where different parties control different parts of the system, leads to gridlock. Others argue that it slows down the process, leading to consensus and good public policy. ***—What is your take on this issue?***

noted that some believe slow, incremental change is preferable, while others believe divided government leads to gridlock, a government less able to respond to the needs of citizens.

PATHWAYS | of action

The Contract with America

In the spring of 1994, Republicans in the House of Representatives devised a plan to win back the majority. They would ask all GOP congressional candidates to sign a platform of popular positions and then announce, with great fanfare, that if the voters gave them the chance, they would vote on all of these items within the first 100 days of a new Congress. They called their platform the *Contract with America*. The principal architect of the strategy, Minority Whip Newt Gingrich of Georgia, reasoned that the Contract would nationalize local elections. That is, by suggesting to voters that all Republican candidates who had signed the agreement would vote as a group once in office, national policy could be changed dramatically and quickly. They also reasoned that Republican candidates would benefit from the plan, given that they would have something specific to offer voters.

The scheme worked. The Republican sweep in 1994 was hailed as a watershed event, a titanic shift in the political landscape. There was no shortage of metaphors; the media called the election an "earthquake," a "tidal wave," and a "meteor strike." Not only did the GOP take control of both chambers of Congress, many prominent Democrats were sent packing—including the sitting speaker, an upset that had not happened for 130 years.[4] Control in state legislatures across the country shifted to the Republicans, and Republican challengers defeated five sitting Democratic governors. It was a big event indeed.

The platform offered to voters in the Contract with America contained 10 popular policies, such as giving the president a line-item veto, a balanced-budget constitutional amendment, the death penalty for certain federal crimes, tax incentives for families wanting to adopt a child, and term limits on members of both the House and the Senate. True to the Contract's word, the House voted on each of these proposals in less than a 100 days—actually, 92 days—and all but the term-limit amendment were passed. Gingrich and his followers proudly boasted of "promises made, promises kept." Only two of the bills got through the Republican-controlled Senate and were finally signed into law by President Clinton. Nevertheless, the Contract with America changed the political dynamics in America, and perhaps more important, it changed the policy agenda. As one observer noted, "The Republicans had managed a sweeping change in the political agenda that would shape law and policy into the new century."[5] Gingrich and his colleagues made it clear that elections and party politics can merge on the pathway of change. ■

> "Did the Contract with America make Republicans more accountable to voters?"
> —Student Question

In the fall of 1994, Republicans, led by House Minority Whip Newt Gingrich (GA), spelled out their policy agenda in the Contract with America. Most scholars saw the move as a positive step in helping voters understand clear differences between the parties. ***—Do you think similar pledges would help restore confidence in the electoral process, or do you believe less partisanship and more compromise would help?***

Party-in-Government

Practice Quiz

1. How do political parties help organize the election process for voters?
   - **a.** by forcefully encouraging them to vote a certain way
   - **b.** by helping to get multiple candidates on the various ballots during an election so that voters have plenty of options from which to choose
   - **c.** by diminishing the number of nominees on a ballot so that voters do not have to choose from among dozens of candidates
   - **d.** by telling voters in which elections they should or should not participate

2. When the government is divided and most members of Congress stick with their party-in government, a slow rate of political change seems to be the norm.
   - **a.** true
   - **b.** false

3. Among other functions, political parties now provide which high-tech service?
   - **a.** touch-screen voting
   - **b.** computer voting
   - **c.** polling for candidates
   - **d.** cell-phone electioneering

4. Let's say Republican Party organizers call a meeting with Christian Coalition members and pro-Israel lobbyists to organize their support of a congressional candidate who strongly supports a pro-Israel U.S. foreign policy. Such a meeting would illustrate a political party's ability to
   - **a.** organize a complex government.
   - **b.** educate citizens.
   - **c.** ensure accountability.
   - **d.** work with aggregate interests.

Answers: 1-c, 2-a, 3-c, 4-d.

Discussion Questions

1. Which of the party functions that have been noted make our system of government *more* democratic?
2. Which of the party functions that have been noted make our system of government *less* democratic?

What **YOU** can do!

How often do your U.S. Representatives and Senators vote with their political parties? Visit the CQ Politics Web site (**http://www.cqpolitics.com/wmspage.cfm?parm1=53**) to find out. Remember to consider whether your representatives are aligned with the majority party or with the opposition.

Party Identification: A belief that one belongs to a certain party.

SIGNIFICANCE: *One's party identification shapes a great deal of a person's perceptions and behavior during elections—not the least of which is his or her choice on election day. That is, Democrats usually vote for Democrats, and Republicans for Republicans.*

Split-Ticket Voters (Swing Voters): Voters who cast ballots for candidates of different parties in a given election year or for candidates of different parties in different election years.

SIGNIFICANCE: *Split-ticket voters can help create divided governments.*

Party-*in-the*-Electorate

(pages 478–481)

What does "party identification" imply, and what bearing does this have on vote choice?

Party-in-the-electorate refers to every citizen who attaches himself or herself to that political party. An average citizen who says "I am a Democrat" or "a Republican" or "a Green" or "a Libertarian" is acknowledging membership in a party-in-the-electorate.[6] Another way of thinking about it is that the party consists of all the voters who consider themselves members of that party.

In many other countries, belonging to a political party can be a big deal. In dictatorships such as China, Cuba, or the old Soviet Union, being a member of the Communist Party—the only legal party—means joining the country's ruling class and gaining valuable career opportunities. It also requires proving political reliability and coming under strict discipline. In democratic countries such as Great Britain, citizens can choose among many parties and can change their affiliation any time they want, but they still have to join up officially, sign a membership card, pay dues, and attend local party meetings—and they get to vote directly for party leaders and the party platform. Identifying a British party-in-the-electorate is thus relatively straightforward.

Belonging to a party in the United States is very different. In this country, party-in-the-electorate is an ambiguous concept and the source of much scholarly debate. Some suggest that a person's attitude, or **party identification**, is enough to consider him or her a partisan. Party identification is the deep-seated feeling that a particular party best represents one's interests and outlook toward government and society. If a citizen tells a pollster, for example, that he thinks of himself as a "strong Republican," he would be considered part of the party-in-the-electorate.

As suggested in Figure 13.3, the percentage of Democratic and Republican identifiers has shifted a bit in the past two decades. In recent years, the number of Democrats seems to be gaining.

A number of factors can lead a citizen to choose an allegiance to one party or the other. Social scientists have noted both short- and long-term factors. Short-term factors include an affinity for a particular candidate or concern about a given issue. Clearly, in recent years, many Americans may have moved to the Democratic Party over concerns about the war in Iraq. Long-term factors, which can be quite powerful, include demographic factors, such as race, level of education, region of the country, and to some extent, even gender. Figure 13.5 notes the percentage of Democrats and Republicans, controlled by several demographic factors.

Zach Carper, 17, from Richlandtown, Pennsylvania, cheers at a political rally in 2008. ***—Are young Americans more interested in electoral politics today than in the past? If so, will they approach party politics the same way their parents did?***

"What does it mean to vote a 'split ticket'?"
—Student Question

Some suggest that an American's behavior is more important than attitude when it comes to determining partisanship. If a person votes for Democrats most of the time, then perhaps this person should be tagged a Democrat regardless of what he or she might tell a pollster. **Straight-ticket voters** are those who support candidates of the same party in every election. Voters who choose candidates from both parties on election day or who switch from one party to the other from election to election are called **split-ticket voters,** or **swing voters**. They might vote for the Republican gubernatorial candidate, the Democratic House candidate, and the Green Party candidate for mayor. Voting behavior of this sort would suggest that the citizen is a nonpartisan, or what we often call an **independent**. (There are many independents in the United States but no actual Independent Party.) The number of split-ticket voters has declined in recent years.

For people who consider themselves true partisans, the impact of this allegiance on their vote choice is significant. Overall, it seems that about 85 percent of voters choose candidates of their own party. Thus social scientists and pundits can make the claim that one's party identification is the best single predictor of how that person will vote on election day. Those who see themselves as "strong Republicans" or

Independent: A voter who is not registered or affiliated with any political party.

EXAMPLE: *If a friend suggests he does not belong to any political party, he would be an independent or nonpartisan voter.*

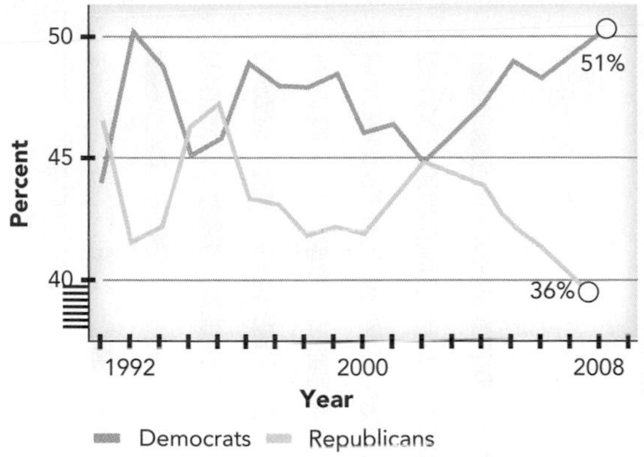

FIGURE 13.3 | **Party Affiliation (Percentage of registered voters who identified with or leaned toward each party)**

—Why do you think a growing number of Americans are siding with the Democratic Party in recent years?

SOURCE: Updated from *Trends in Political Values and Core Attitudes: 1987-2007, Political Landscape More Favorable to Democrats* (Washington, DC: The Pew Research Center for the People & the Press, March 22, 2007), p. 2. http://people-press.org/reports/pdf/312.pdf. Reprinted with permission..

"strong Democrats" nearly always vote with their party on election day. Very few true partisans defect, and when they do, it is usually for a compelling but temporary reason—a war, economic turmoil, or their party's nomination of a totally unacceptable candidate. Generally, they return to their old party in the next election.

Realignment Theory

Partisan realignment is a concept first advanced by the political scientist V. O. Key. It explains events in which the overall partisan balance of the electorate is transformed rapidly, often by a major event or crisis, resulting in a new party taking control of government for a significant length of time. In other words, occasionally there are "earthquake-like" elections that shift the partisan balance of the country and the policy agenda for a period. Most analysts regard the election of 1932 as "realigning," given that it occurred during the Great Depression and the Democrats took over the reins of government from the Republicans for the next several decades. Other commonly cited realigning elections are those of 1828, 1860, and 1896. Some experts have suggested that the elections of 1980, 1994, and perhaps 2006 or 2008 were realigning as well.

"What if voters don't return to their party in the next election?"

—Student Question

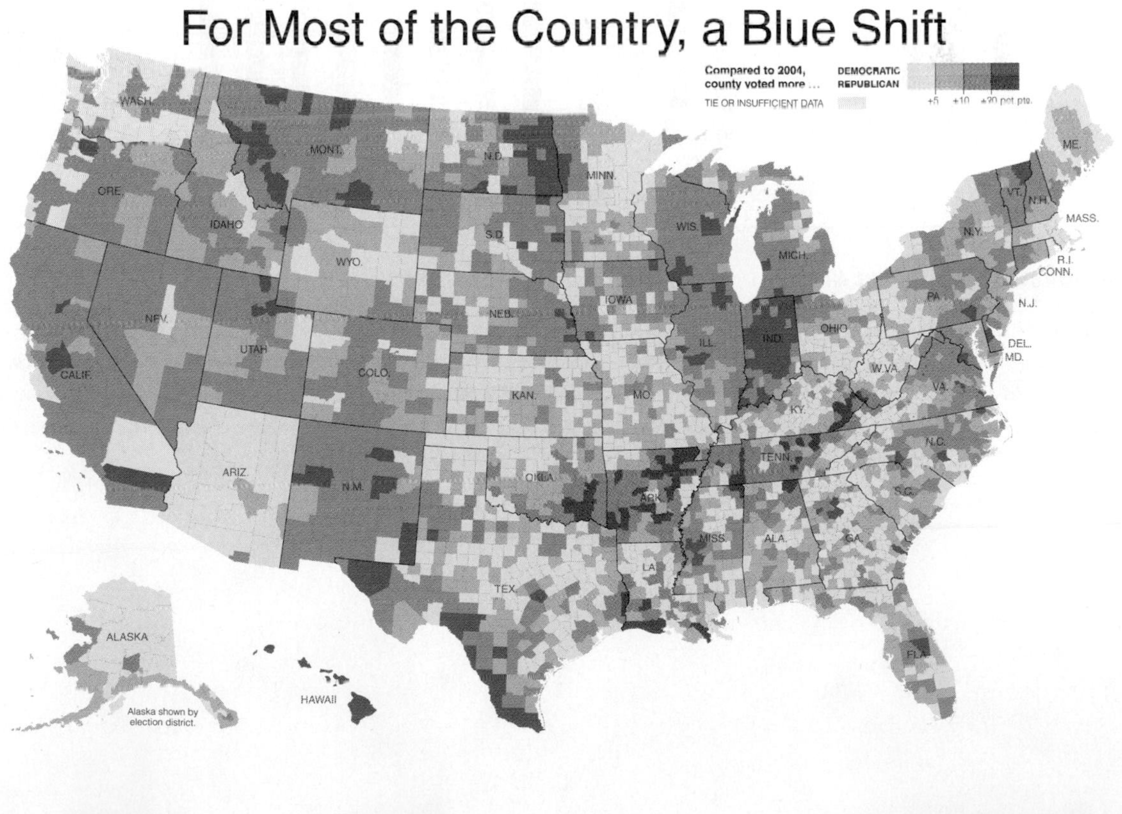

FIGURE 13.4 | **For Much of the Country, a Democratic Shift in the 2008 Election**

Some have suggested that 2008 was a realigning election, given the dramatic gains by the Democrats in so many parts of the country, as shown in this figure. But realignments imply a prolonged change, not simply big gains in a given contest. ***—Do you think we will look back at 2008 as a Democratic realignment?***

SOURCE: http://www.nytimes.com/interactive/2008/11/05/us/politics/20081104_ELECTION_RECAP.html. New York Times Graphics. Copyright © 2008 by the New York Times Co. Reprinted with permission.

COMPARATIVE

Comparing Political Parties

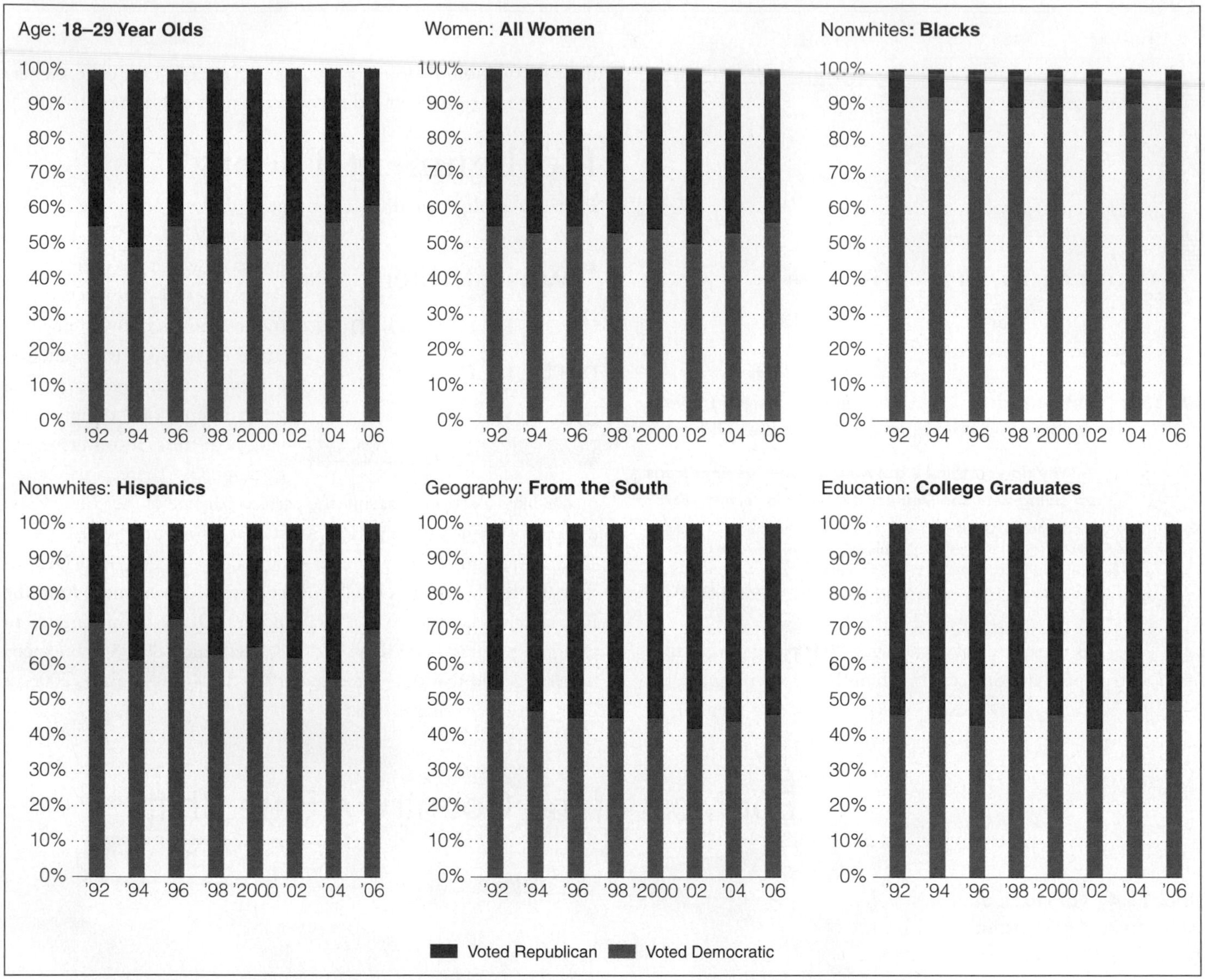

FIGURE 13.5 | **Support Among Different Groups over Time, 1992–2006**

This series of figures notes the level of support for the two major political parties among different demographic groups, several of which suggest rather significant changes. This data highlights interesting questions: ***—If long-term factors, such as demographics, shape partisan preferences, why would there be changes over time? What factors would influence how a group of Americans would view a political party?***

SOURCE: http://www.nytimes.com/2006/11/08/us/ politics/20061108_ELECTION_PORTRAIT_HOUSE.html. November 8, 2006, New York Times Graphics.

Partisan Realignment: Historic shifts of public opinion and voter concerns that generally lead to a different party's control of government and a new set of policies.

EXAMPLE: *The election of 1932 is often cited as a realigning election.*

Dealignment: The loss of affinity for party politics among voters who no longer consider themselves partisans.

SIGNIFICANCE: *There is a great deal more volatility between elections and more split-ticket voting in specific elections when dealignment is occurring.*

The idea of realignments and realigning periods is an attractive model for students of the electoral process. First, it does seem that some elections are more important, bigger, and more consequential than others. This label helps distinguish the truly big elections from others. Second, realignments seem to explain a number of interrelated phenomena. Before realignments, for instance, minor-party activity is especially pronounced, and during these events, turnout seems to rise and voter loyalties switch. Most young voters favor the newly dominant party. Immediately after these events, public policy moves in new directions, and the number of nonpartisan voters (independents) shrinks. Third, realignment theory helps break U.S. history into neat periods, which is handy for studying the past. We can talk of the "second" or "third party era," and most will understand what we are referring to.

Realignment theory has its problems, however. For example, although the theory holds that these events mark a prolonged period of one-party control, this has seldom been the case. For example, the decades following the 1896 election were considered part of a "Republican period," but Woodrow Wilson, a Democrat, served two terms as president during this time. Dwight Eisenhower, a Republican, was elected president during a "Democratic period." Realignment advocates will point to the reasons for these exceptions, but others suggest that with so many exceptions, the theory loses its power. Perhaps most important, elections in recent decades seem to confuse our understanding of realignment theory. When was our last true realignment? Some political scientists suggest 1968, given that Richard Nixon, a Republican, took control of the White House in that election and, except for Jimmy Carter from 1976 to 1980, other Republicans lived there until Bill Clinton in 1992. Yet Democrats maintained control of one or both houses of Congress during this period—and realignment implies comprehensive change, not simply a change in which party captures the presidency. Some experts point to 1994 as the last realigning election, given that the GOP swamped the Democrats and took control of both houses of Congress. Yet Bill Clinton was reelected just 2 years later, and although the Republicans controlled Congress for years thereafter, they lost seats in the next several elections. Moreover, until the 2004 election, it seemed that the system was undergoing a **dealignment**—meaning a movement away from party politics altogether—rather than any sort of realignment.

So where do scholars stand on realignment? Some continue to believe in the theory, some have never bought into it, and still others have sought to modify the model to explain some of its inconsistencies. Others have suggested that while the theory may have explained big elections in our past, realignments are no longer possible in American politics. One of your authors, Daniel M. Shea, argues that local parties were key players in past realignments, drawing average voters into the process. But as local party structures became less viable (a topic to be discussed shortly), the system has lost its base. Realignments, he argues, are a thing of the past.[6] Only time will tell if Shea is correct.

Party-in-the-Electorate
Practice Quiz

1. If voters do not return to their party in the next election, it is an example of
   - **a.** split-ticket voting.
   - **b.** realignment.
   - **c.** dealignment.
   - **d.** straight-ticket voting.
2. According to the theory of partisan realignment, which of the following historical events has provoked such a phenomenon?
   - **a.** World War I
   - **b.** the Great Depression
   - **c.** World War II
   - **d.** the Cold War
3. According to Shea, who were the key players in past party realignments?
   - **a.** party activists
   - **b.** pundits
   - **c.** strong candidates
   - **d.** local parties
4. Overall, it seems that about 85 percent of voters choose candidates of their own party.
   - **a.** true
   - **b.** false

Answers: 1-b, 2-b, 3-d, 4-a.

Discussion Questions

1. Why are most voters so loyal to one political party?
2. What are some of the factors that cause dealignment? Are any of them evident in today's politics?

What **YOU** can do!

Conduct an informal survey of your friends, classmates, and roommates. What political party, if any, do they identify with the most? Do the trends you discover match trends in national party identification? Report the results of your poll to your campus newspaper, or discuss them with your friends and classmates.

Richard Daley, Jr., is the current mayor of Chicago, and his father, pictured behind, was a powerful party boss in Cook County for decades. Most agree that party machines have mostly faded from the political landscape. ***—But is this something we should applaud or bemoan? What type of benefits did strong local party organizations provide?***

PHOTO: Peter Thompson/ The New York Time

Party-*as*-Organization

(pages 482–483)

What are party "committees," and what do they seek to accomplish?

The final piece of the tripod is party-as-organization, which means the formal apparatus of the party, including party headquarters, offices, and leaders. It is the official bureaucracy of the party, and it is found in the form of committees in every state and nearly every community in the nation. If you go to the telephone book and look up "Republican Party" or "Democratic Party," a phone number and address will be listed in most larger communities.

Party organizations exist at each layer of our political system (see Figure 13.6). At the national level are the Democratic National Committee (DNC) and the Republican National Committee (RNC). Each state has both a Republican and a Democratic party, as do most counties and cities across the nation. At the very bottom of the structure, you can still occasionally find ward or precinct organizations. The Chicago Democratic Committee, for example, is made up of a mass of different precinct organizations.

Many casual observers of party politics believe that a formal hierarchy connects the layers, with the national parties controlling the state parties and the state organizations dictating orders to the county or municipal committees. This is not the case. A somewhat unique aspect of the American parties is that while there is a good bit of interaction between layers of the system, most of it involving the sharing of resources, few commands find their way down to lower-level committees. For the most part, party organizations at all levels of the system operate as semi-independent units. The same is true with regard to horizontal linkages: County organizations in a state might touch base occasionally, but for the most part, they go it alone.

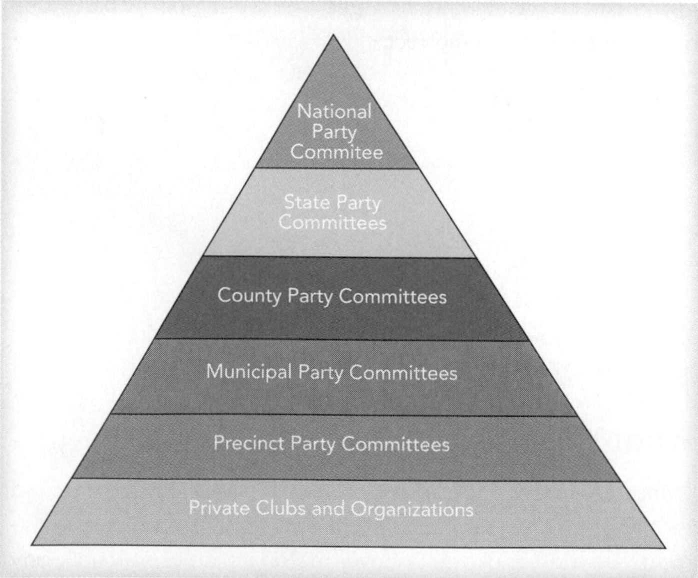

FIGURE 13.6 | Layers of the Party System

One should be careful in interpreting this figure. It is true that there are layers in the party system—that in some ways the national committee is "above" the state committees. But there is a strong tradition of autonomy in party politics in America, and many organizations would balk at the suggestion that a "higher" unit could send commands down the line.

Party activities and functions are conducted by the party organizations through activists. In most cases, these are volunteers, giving their time and efforts because they believe in the party's mission (its approach to government), see their efforts as somehow helping them down the line (perhaps with a job or a chance to run for office), or simply enjoy the social aspects of involvement. The national parties—and a growing number of the state party committees—use a mix of volunteers and paid staffers. Some of the larger county and city committees do much the same, but at the municipal level, most activists are amateurs—that is, unpaid. The foremost goal of state and national party committees is to build support for their slate of candidates.

Throughout much of our history, local party organizations had a rather distinctive, even aggressive face. These units, called **party machines**■, were especially strong around the turn of the twentieth century in large cities, such as New York City, Boston, Chicago, Philadelphia, and Kansas City. The leader of a machine was known as "the boss." Party machines wielded a double-edged sword: On the one hand, their strong desire to win elections and thereby control patronage jobs, city contracts, and enforcement of municipal regulations, as well as their efficient, "machine-like" organization, brought otherwise disfranchised citizens (those who could not vote) into the political process. This was particularly important for newly arrived immigrants, most of them poor, who flooded the cities during the

■ **Party Machines:** Local party organizations that influenced elections and operated on the basis of patronage and behind-the-scenes control.

EXAMPLE: *At the turn of the twentieth century in New York City, the Democratic machine was called Tammany Hall; it was written about in a classic work* Plunkitt of Tammany Hall.

CONNECT THE LINK (Chapter **12**, page **438**) How did Progressive Era reforms transform electoral politics in America?

second half of the nineteenth century. In exchange for their help on election day, party bosses and their machines provided poor people with a kind of social safety net. (This, remember, was long before Social Security, welfare, and unemployment insurance existed.) If a man needed a job, if a family was evicted from its apartment and needed another place to live, if a widow needed a loan to pay for a funeral or some cash to post bond for her wayward son—the party machine would lend a hand. In exchange, voters would support the party's slate of candidates on election day. There was also an accountability mechanism: If the machine failed to take care of the citizens of the community, it could be voted out of office and a new group given a chance. Few machines, however, were ever voted out of office.

A great deal of corruption was thrown into the mix of machine politics. Election fraud was rampant. One of the last of the real big-city bosses, Chicago's Richard Daley (the father of today's Chicago mayor of the same name), would urge his workers on election day, with only a hint of a smile, to "vote early and vote often." Because the machines controlled the reins of government, they also rigged the workings of the government (including the enforcement or nonenforcement of local ordinances) to suit their political needs. For example, in many cities, public employees were required to kick back a portion of their pay—generally about 2 or 3 percent—to the machine, which had gotten them their job. The machine's humanitarian efforts extended only to supporters and potential voters. Some racial minorities, especially African Americans, did not get machine assistance because they were of no use, given that most either could not vote or did not vote "correctly."

For these and other reasons, a series of reforms were passed at the end of the nineteenth century, collectively called the Progressive movement (see LINK Chapter 12, page 438). Change sometimes took decades to have a real effect, but gradually, big changes occurred in the workings of party machines. Civil service reforms deprived the machines of some of their power over patronage (jobs handed out to loyal supporters), the secret ballot lessened the machine's control of people's votes on election day, and the direct primary undermined their ability to control nominations. Local party organizations survived these changes, but the machines faced overwhelming challenges and slowly faded away.

> "Why are local party organizations becoming weaker? Is this bad?"
> —Student Question

The fate of party organizations at the dawn of the twenty-first century is unclear. State and national party organizations seem to be doing well; they have benefited from a massive influx of campaign contributions and have more equipment and staff as well as better facilities than at any point in American history. But the picture is much different at the local level. Local party organizations—what have been called the "mom and pop shops of the party system"[8]—are finding it difficult to survive. This is mostly because they rely on volunteers. Whereas a few decades ago many local committees were vibrant, dynamic organizations, today this would be the exception. Do you suspect that this change has altered the relationship between parties and average citizens?

Party-as-Organization
Practice Quiz

1. A local party organization that influences elections and operates on the basis of patronage and behind-the-scenes control is known as
   - **a.** a pressure group.
   - **b.** a ward-heeler.
   - **c.** a syndicate.
   - **d.** a political machine.
2. The foremost goal of state and national party committees is to build support for their slate of candidates.
   - **a.** true
   - **b.** false
3. For the most part, party organizations at all levels of the system operate as semi-independent units.
   - **a.** true
   - **b.** false
4. What was one factor in the demise of political machines?
   - **a.** civil service reforms
   - **b.** the dominance of the Democratic Party in the middle decades of the twentieth century
   - **c.** the presidency of Dwight D. Eisenhower
   - **d.** the Great Depression

Answers: 1-d, 2-a, 3-a, 4-a.

Discussion Questions

1. Political machines are a relic of the past—or are they? What evidence is there that they may still exist?
2. What are the advantages of semi-independent party organizations? Are there advantages to more centralized control of a party's platform? Why or why not?

What **YOU** can do!

Recent studies suggest that the U.S. has entered an era of "baseless" parties, with weak community organizations but strong state and national party organizations. Do an online search for local party committees in your community and surrounding communities. What do these sites suggest about the strength of party organizations in your area?

■ **Democratic-Republicans:** The first American political party, formed by believers in states' rights and followers of Thomas Jefferson. **SIGNIFICANCE:** *This party challenged the Federalists in the election of 1800, which ushered in the party system.*

■ **Federalist Party:** A party, founded by Alexander Hamilton, whose members believed in a strong, centralized government and were supporters of the Washington and Adams administrations. **SIGNIFICANCE:** *This party challenged the Democratic-Republicans in the election of 1800.*

Party Eras *in* American History (pages 484–487)

How have political parties shifted and changed throughout our nation's history?

Like nearly every other aspect of American government, the nature of the party system has changed over time. In reviewing the history of American political parties, two points emerge. First, from nearly the beginning, political parties have been at the center of the American electoral process. Second, the story of parties in the United States continues to unfold.

Phase 1: The Emergence of Parties in America (1790s–1828)

James Madison warned his fellow Americans about the dangers of party-like organizations, which he called "factions," in *Federalist No. 10.* A few years later, George Washington, in his famous Farewell Address, suggested much the same: "Let me...warn you in the most solemn manner against the baneful effects of the spirit of party....It is truly [our] worst enemy." Many other statesmen and early political thinkers uttered similar words of caution: Political parties were the bane of democratic systems.

What drove these apprehensions? Before this, political systems that had allowed ordinary citizens the opportunity to speak up and organize invariably degenerated into rival groups, each vying for its own interests. Consideration of the whole came second to consideration of the self. This was particularly likely in our early Republic, given that a national identity—and, indeed, a national citizenship—would not develop until much later. (Many historians have suggested that this national identity was forged only by the Civil War.) The freedom to speak out and join up with like-minded citizens made it even more likely that factions, or parties, would emerge.

Within a decade after the adoption of the Constitution, parties had burst onto the scene. Wishing to fill his cabinet with the best and brightest minds of the day, President Washington selected Thomas Jefferson for secretary of state and Alexander Hamilton for secretary of the treasury. Both men were distinguished and intelligent, and each had impressive Revolutionary War credentials (important for the legitimacy of the new government). The problem was that Hamilton and Jefferson passionately disagreed about the future of the nation. Jefferson believed that America's hope lay in small, agriculture-based communities. Hamilton, on the other hand, believed that the future of the nation lay in the development of vibrant cities, based on a strong manufacturing sector. He was a capitalist through and through and was convinced that a strong central government was the best mechanism to ensure long-term economic growth. An additional issue that helped solidify the partisans behind Jefferson and Hamilton was the French Revolution, which had begun in 1789 and turned very radical by 1793. Jefferson felt that the U.S. government should back the French revolutionaries in the war that had broken out with Great Britain. The French, after all, had helped America in its own revolution. But to Hamilton and his supporters, the French Revolution meant "anarchy" and mob rule. Washington sought to keep America out of the conflict—to remain neutral.

Partisan animosity got even worse during the presidency of John Adams. Opponents of the administration (led by Jefferson and his "antiparty" friend James Madison) called themselves **Democratic-Republicans**■. Supporters of Adams and Hamilton organized the **Federalist Party**■. (The Federalist Party was unrelated to the supporters of the Constitution in 1787–1788, who also called themselves Federalists.) One prominent historian described this period as the "great consolidation," when parties finally emerged in America.[9]

The dispute over the legitimacy of political parties was mostly settled with the election of 1800. Even James Madison, who had attacked factions in *The Federalist Papers,* had been an ardent Democratic-Republican (he was elected president as Jefferson's successor in 1808) and in his old age embraced the party system.[10] The Federalists, lacking a large base of support outside New England, gradually faded from the scene.

Phase 2: The Heyday of Parties (1828–1900)

A backlash against the **Corrupt Bargain of 1824**■, discussed in LINK Chapter 2, page 61, was felt across America, which showed itself in two ways. First, the National Republican Party was torn apart, and by the mid-1830s, another major party, the Whig Party, had arisen. Second, what was left of the National Republicans regrouped as the Democratic Party. Like their Whig rivals, the Democrats also represented many different interests, from urban workers and immigrants to southern slave owners, but in the main, the Democrats were the party of small government, states' rights, and personal freedom (except for slaves, of course). The leaders of the Democrats were Andrew Jackson (the colorful general who, at the Battle of New Orleans in 1815, had brought the War of 1812 to a victorious conclusion) and a wily New York politician named

CONNECT THE LINK
(Chapter **2**, page **61**) What was Jacksonian democracy?

TIMELINE **The Evolution of Political Parties in the United States**

Corrupt Bargain of 1824: The alleged secret agreement in the disputed election of 1824 that led the House of Representatives to select John Quincy Adams, who had come in second in the popular vote, as president if he would make Speaker of the House Henry Clay his secretary of state.

SIGNIFICANCE: *This event sparked the birth of popular participation in American elections.*

Martin Van Buren. Jackson, on Van Buren's advice, used local party organizations to rally opposition to Adams. These organizations helped Jackson unseat Adams in 1828, to reelect Jackson in 1832, and to elect Van Buren as his successor in 1836. By that time, Van Buren faced the organized opposition of the Whig Party.

"What was 'democratic' about Jacksonian democracy?"
—Student Question

This period was a rebirth of party politics, this time down at the community level. Party operatives spread the word that unless average citizens became involved, the nation would be ruled through elite deals like the Corrupt Bargain. Both of the new national parties called on the average citizen to stand up and exert his role in the political process. (Politics at this time was supposed to be for men—white men—only.) This emphasis on individual involvement ushered in a new era in electoral politics, which historians have called *Jacksonian democracy* (see LINK Chapter 2, page 61). Simply put, this was a move toward egalitarian politics and a more democratic social life.

THE CIVIL WAR AND THE RECONSTRUCTION OF THE PARTY SYSTEM Although local party politics was cemented in American political and social life, the lines of division between the parties shifted in the mid-nineteenth century. Slavery caused the most significant disruption, and both the Whigs and the Democrats were desperate to avoid the question. Competition between the two was fierce, and neither party wanted to alienate its southern or northern supporters. It was better to dodge the issue of slavery altogether. "Northern abolitionists were often uncomfortably seated next to slave holders in presidential cabinets and in the halls of Congress."[11] As new states sought admission to the Union, however, the slavery question was thrust to the fore, and the delicate sectional balance was tested. Democratic Senator Stephen Douglas from Illinois in 1854 offered the **Kansas–Nebraska Bill** in an attempt to strike a sectional compromise. Under what Douglas called popular sovereignty, the voters in proposed new states would decide for themselves whether to allow slavery. But far from satisfying each side, opening up the West to even the *possibility* of slavery poured fuel on the fire. By 1854, a group of antislavery politicians from all the major parties met in Ripon, Wisconsin, to create a new political party, the modern Republican Party. One participant observed, "We came into the little meeting held in a schoolhouse. Whigs, Free Soilers, and Democrats. We came out of it Republicans."[12]

The sectional split only worsened in the late 1850s. In the election of 1856, the Republicans failed to win the presidency by a slim margin, and clashes between northerners and southerners grew increasingly violent. Things came to a head in the election of 1860. Abraham Lincoln, the Republican nominee, won an Electoral College victory with a majority of votes in the more populous Northeast and the Midwest. He was not even on the ballot in the South, however, and his nationwide popular vote total fell well short of a majority. His election was the last straw for many white southerners. Between December of 1860 and April of 1861, most of the slave states seceded from the Union and organized a new nation, the Confederate States of America. When Lincoln sent federal troops to suppress the "insurrection," the Civil War began. It would last until 1865, cost nearly 1 million lives (3 percent of the population), and consume most of the South's wealth. But when the North won and reabsorbed the Confederacy, it had also preserved the Union and put an end to slavery.

The Civil War, the North's victory, and the postwar Reconstruction period reordered the party system. By 1877, when the last federal troops were withdrawn from the old Confederacy and all the southern states resumed self-government, the system had once again settled into two camps. The Republican Party was essentially the party supported by industrial interests in the Northeast. The Democratic Party was the party of the white South. The two parties battled it out for the votes of the agricultural Midwest and West. During the so-called Gilded Age, from 1877 through 1896, the two parties were very closely matched. Elections were always hard-fought and close, and the battling parties mobilized the average (male) citizens in huge numbers to vote. Most Americans took their party allegiances very seriously, because such allegiances reflected a mixture of religious affiliation, economic interest, social class, ethnic heritage, and regional loyalties forged in the Civil War.

Phase 3: Party Decline (1900–1970s)

Politics in the post–Civil War era were notoriously corrupt. Graft—the bribes, kickbacks, and other "perks" that politicians took in—was rampant. Responding to public outrage, a number of important changes were gradually made. To strip political machines of their ability to use the patronage jobs by which they controlled government, the **merit system** (also called the **civil service**) was introduced in 1883 and later expanded, making many office holders career bureaucrats rather than temporary political appointees. To reduce the ability of bosses to control what happened in polling places, the **Australian ballot** (or "secret ballot") was instituted; now voters no longer had to either orally announce their vote or publicly deposit their ballot in the box of one party or the other. And to reduce the chance that bosses would simply handpick nominees who faithfully toed the

■ **Kansas–Nebraska Bill:** An act of Congress in 1854 that allowed residents of the new territories in the West to decide whether slavery would be permitted in their state.

SIGNIFICANCE: *Its passage exacerbated the rift between northern and southern states.*

■ **Australian Ballot:** The secret ballot, which keeps voters' choices confidential.

SIGNIFICANCE: *This change, along with many other reforms, weakened the role of party machines in local elections.*

Many wonder how progressive reforms were successful, given that party machines and large corporations controlled public policy. The key was muckraking journalists, such as Ida Tarbell, who brought the depth of the corruption to light for average Americans. In the end, it was middle class citizens who demanded change. The Progressive Movement underscores the power of different pathways of change in a democratic political system. ***—Do you think a similar reform movement is possible in the years ahead?***

party line, the direct primary was established. In this system, the rank-and-file would choose the party nominee by casting a secret ballot on primary-election day. All told, these and many other reforms greatly reduced the power of party machines.

These new laws and the flurry of media coverage did away with most party machines. So did the prosecutions of corrupt political bosses that district attorneys were empowered to launch after 1900—anticorruption crusades that on occasion brought a triumphant prosecutor into a governor's chair or a Senate seat. The reins of government were slipping from machine hands, and the public's trust in party politics was shaken. The Progressive Era marked a sea change in the place of party organizations in American politics. The heyday period was over.

The Great Depression dealt another blow, although sometimes a slow-moving one, to machine politics. The economic crisis of the 1930s tore to shreds the "safety net" that political machines had provided to help out-of-luck citizens get through tough times. To replace these tattered safety nets, President Franklin D. Roosevelt's New Deal established federal Social Security, unemployment insurance, public works projects, and social welfare programs, all of which undermined ordinary people's dependence on political bosses.

THE RISE OF CANDIDATE-CENTERED POLITICS

By the 1960s, public attitudes about political parties had grown especially sour. On top of this—and, perhaps, partly fueling this change—candidates came to realize that parties were no longer necessary or even desirable. Historically, party workers were needed to bring the candidate's message to the voter, but by the 1960s, television and direct mail could reach more voters in a single day than party operatives could contact in weeks. Party assistance also came with a price tag, as it suggested that the candidate was not "independent-minded." Moreover, new-style campaign consultants burst on the scene in the 1960s. These professionals could be hired (for a lot of money), and their allegiance would be solely to the candidate.

What we might call the post-1960 **Candidate-Centered Era**■ sent repercussions throughout the political system. With candidates pitching themselves as independent, voters saw little reason to hold to any notion of partisanship. Party organizations lost even more sway. As more citizens became independent, voting cues were lost, leading to lower election day turnouts. Once in office, elected officials saw little reason to stick to the party caucus, leading to less policy coherence and a less efficient legislative process.

Phase 4: Organizational Resurgence (1970s–Present)

By the 1970s, many observers came to believe that parties were fading permanently from the scene. But if anything is true about political parties, it is that they are adaptive creatures, eager to adjust whenever confronted with adverse conditions. National party operatives, at first mostly at the Republican National Committee, realized that they were quickly becoming irrelevant and that changes were essential. Instead of improving their relations with voters, however, the parties chose to expand their services to candidates. Parties became service-oriented, meaning that they broadened their activities to include a host of high-tech services to candidates. They developed, for example, computerized direct-mail operations, in-house television and radio production studios, and sophisticated polling operations. This also meant hiring new professionals—their own new-style campaign consultants—and

■ **Candidate-Centered Era:** After 1960, a period when candidates began to portray themselves as independent from party politics, even though they often ran under a party banner.

EXAMPLE: *When a candidate boasts about working equally well with both parties, and runs for office without the aid of either party.*

The "Daisy Girl" advertisement from the 1964 election marked a sea change in the use and power of television in elections. Candidates could now reach voters directly, without the aid of party organizations. ***—Are electronic communications quite different than interpersonal messages? And is face-to-face politics better for our system than 30-second "spots?"***

greatly expanding their facilities. Of course, all this cost a great deal of money.

This change has had significant ramifications. For one thing, the parties have seemed to get back on their feet in recent years, again becoming central players in elections. But there have been negative effects, too. Sophisticated services require ever-increasing resources. In their never-ending efforts to get around campaign finance laws, politicians and their consultants discover new loopholes each year, breeding voter cynicism. At precisely the same time that party organizations are regaining their footing, a growing number of Americans see parties as corrupt, and while the national parties have done well during this period, revitalization has not yet reached the grass roots—that is, local party committees. Finally, while many candidates appreciate the help they receive, the parties know that they can get more mileage out of targeting only a handful of races. In short, the revitalization of the national party *committees* has been significant, but some believe it has also transformed the nature of the party *system*.

Party Eras in American History

Practice Quiz

1. What best characterizes the disagreement between Thomas Jefferson and Alexander Hamilton that led to the creation of separate political parties?
   - **a.** Hamilton called for the creation of a national bank, and Jefferson abhorred the idea.
   - **b.** Jefferson called for a national investment in infrastructure (roads, bridges, canals, and so on), and Hamilton distrusted big government and the raising of taxes.
   - **c.** Hamilton thought that level-headed landowners should influence democracy, but Jefferson thought cities and city dwellers should dictate policy.
   - **d.** Jefferson trusted the average (usually landowning) citizen to dictate policy in the Republic, but Hamilton believed in a more centralized government run by elites.
2. Which leaders first inspired the Federalist Party?
   - **a.** George Washington and Thomas Jefferson
   - **b.** John Adams and Alexander Hamilton
   - **c.** Aaron Burr and James Madison
   - **d.** James Madison and Thomas Jefferson
3. The political philosophy of Democrats in the 1830s was
   - **a.** that the federal government should help the less fortunate and avoid entanglements abroad.
   - **b.** that the federal government should be small, states' rights robust, and personal freedom (for whites) forever preserved.
   - **c.** that the government should help nurture industrial development and individual morality.
   - **d.** that slavery is evil and the union of states sacred.
4. What were elections like in the Gilded Age?
   - **a.** corrupt
   - **b.** one-sided, with low voter turnout
   - **c.** close, with high voter turnout
   - **d.** close, with little party allegiance on the part of voters

Answers: 1-a, 2-b, 3-b, 4-c.

Discussion Questions

1. Some people have suggested that regardless of the framers' concerns, parties were inevitable. Why would that be the case?
2. What are some differences and similarities between the politics of the Gilded Age and the politics of today?

What **YOU** can do!

How do the two major political parties view their own historical evolution? To find out, visit the Web site of each party (**http://www.dnc.org** and **http://www.rnc.org**), and access the "Party History" page. Pay special attention to whether each party's self-described history reflects the changes in party eras that have been described by scholars.

■ **Institutional Barriers:** Legal impediments, such as laws, court decisions, and constitutional provisions, that limit the possibilities of minor parties in the United States.

EXAMPLE: *Many states have laws that make it difficult for minor-party candidates to get on the general election ballot.*

CONNECT THE LINK (Chapter **12**, pages **430–435**) What is the Electoral College and how does it work?

PARTICIPATION **Third Parties in American History**

Minor Parties *in* American Politics (pages 488–489)

What role do minor parties play in our political system?

The barriers to minor-party success in the United States can be divided into two categories (see Figure 13.7). Let's consider first the **institutional barriers**■—the legal impediments created by statutes, by court decisions, or by the Constitution itself. The most significant of these is the single-member district or first-past-the-post system that is used in legislative elections. In the American model, legislative districts have only one legislator, who gets into office simply by getting more votes than any other candidate. Imagine that candidates from *three* parties are competing for a congressional seat. One candidate winds up with 45 percent of the vote, and the others get about 27 percent each. Because the first candidate received more votes than the others—was "the first past the post"—and because only one person can represent the district, that candidate is sent to Washington. The losing parties get nothing for their efforts. Eventually, operatives of the losing parties will consider joining forces if they are not too far apart ideologically. The outcome is a two-party system.

Another institutional barrier to third parties is the Electoral College. Because 48 states rely on a winner-take-all system (see LINK Chapter 12, pages 430–435), to have a chance at winning the presidency, a candidate has to win states outright; he or she gains nothing by running a strong second. Many states also have **ballot access laws,** which help sustain the two-party system. Beginning at the turn of the twentieth century, states created schemes to limit the number of candidates on the general election ballot—while at the same time make things easy for the major parties. (After all, members of the two major parties were writing the regulations!)

The second category of barriers to minor-party success is **attitudinal barriers**■. Perhaps the greatest attitudinal hurdle is the wasted-vote syndrome. Because minor-party candidates usually stand little chance of victory, most Americans are reluctant to support such candidates on election day, "wasting" (they say) their vote. It is revealing that support for minor-party candidates often peaks several weeks before the election. But as election day approaches, voters abandon the minor-party candidate, hoping to add their voice to the contest between the "real" candidates, one of whom everyone knows is going to win. This would also explain why so many Americans tell pollsters that they want more parties in the election process but at the same time minor-party candidates languish on election day. A second attitudinal barrier is widespread support for centrist policies. That is, most Americans consider themselves ideologically moderate and in the middle class. This leads them to support middle-of-the-road parties; such as the two major parties. Whereas "extremist" parties can do well in other countries, they have languished in our system.

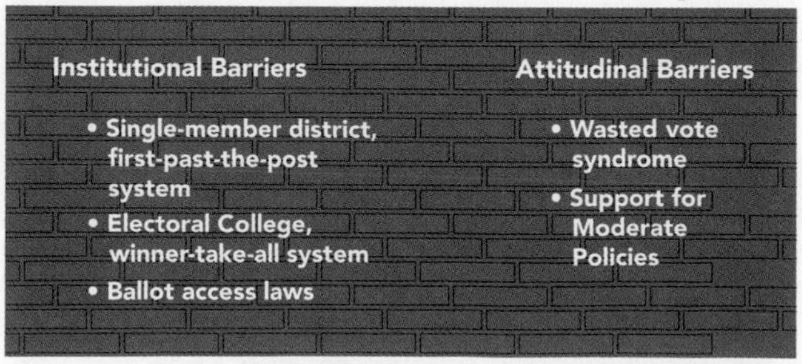

Institutional Barriers
Attitudinal Barriers
• Single-member district, first-past-the-post system
• Electoral College, winner-take-all system
• Ballot access laws
• Wasted vote syndrome
• Support for Moderate Policies

FIGURE 13.7 | **Barriers to Minor Party Success** It is clearly difficult for minor parties in American politics. ***—But do we really want a viable multiparty system, especially given the structure of our government (federalism, separation of powers, etc.)?***

TABLE 13.1 | **Third Parties in American History**

As this figure suggests, there have been many minor parties in American history—although their success at the polls has been limited. ***—Do these organizations play a important role in our political system as most social scientists suggest? What functions would these minor parties afford the system?***

THIRD PARTY	YEAR	PERCENTAGE OF POPULAR VOTE	ELECTORAL VOTES	FATE IN NEXT ELECTION
Anti-Masons	1832	7.8	7	Endorsed Whig candidate
Free Soil	1848	10.1	0	Received 5% of the vote
Whig-American	1856	21.5	8	Party dissolved
Southern Democrat	1860	18.1	72	Party dissolved
Peoples' Populist	1892	8.5	22	Endorsed Democratic candidate
Progressive (T. Roosevelt)	1912	27.5	88	Returned to Republican Party
Socialist	1912	6	0	Received 3.2% of vote
Progressive (R. LaFollette)	1924	16.6	13	Returned to Republican Party
States' Rights Democrats	1948	2.4	39	Party dissolved
American Independent (G. Wallace)	1968	13.5	46	Received 1.4% of vote
H. Ross Perot	1992	18.9	0	Formed Reform Party and ran again 1996
Green (R. Nader)	2000	2.7	0	

SOURCE: Adapted from *Two Parties – or More? The American Party System*, 2nd edition, by John F. Bibby and L. Sandy Maisel, p. 23. Copyright © 2003, 1998 by Westview Press, a member of the Perseus Books Group. Reprinted by permission of Westview Press, a member of Perseus Books Group.

H. Ross Perot was unsuccessful in his 1992 bid for the presidency, but he did have a significant impact on public policy: He drew attention to mounting federal deficits. ***—How is the "voice of the people" expressed through elections—even when a candidate loses?***

■ **Attitudinal Barriers:** Those perceptions and beliefs that help maintain the two-party system in America.

EXAMPLE: *Many appear willing to support minor party candidates before an election, but when the day rolls around, they support one of the major party candidates, not wanting to "waste" their vote.*

History of Minor Parties

This is not to suggest that minor parties play *no* role in our system. Quite the contrary. Minor parties have sprouted up throughout American political history and have changed the political landscape. They fall into two categories. First have been the fledgling parties that appeared on the rare occasions when one or both of the major parties were actually collapsing. Second have been the true third parties that periodically challenged the established two-party system and provoked changes in both parties. Table 13.1 lists many of the significant minor parties throughout American history.

The strongest minor-party presidential candidate in recent years was H. Ross Perot. He netted a huge 19 percent of the popular vote—which did not translate into a single Electoral College vote. Perot's political star kept a bit of its luster after the 1992 election. He tried to mobilize the public against NAFTA, the free-trade agreement with Mexico and Canada, but failed. He also decided to put his efforts into creating the Reform Party. Its platform focused on two issues: cleaning up the electoral system by removing big money from the process, and cutting the soaring national deficit. Emphasizing these issues, Perot entered the 1996 presidential contest and, of course, received his own party's nomination. This time, he got a still respectable 12 percent of the popular vote but, again, not a single Electoral Collage vote. The Reform Party struggled after the 1996 election, due in large measure to the absorption of its issues by the two major parties—a common fate of third parties.

Role of Minor Parties

Given the challenges that minor parties face in the American system as well as their limited success at the polls throughout our history, you might be tempted to conclude that they are a waste of time—that they play no role in changing the course of government. Nothing could be further from the truth. Minor parties have played a significant role in shaping public policy by drawing attention to particular issues and by threatening to drain support from the major parties. In fact, it has often been the initial success of minor parties that has led to their downfall: Once a new party dramatizes an issue and shows that there are votes at stake, one (or even both) of the major parties will pick up the issue, and the voters will fall back in line. The major parties are reinvigorated precisely because minor parties nip at the edges of the process. History also shows that minor parties have played a significant role in bringing more citizens into the political process. Voters often begin to feel distrustful of the major parties—or at the very least not represented by them. They slowly withdraw, only to be drawn back into the process by the energy and excitement of minor-party activity.

Minor Parties in American Politics

Practice Quiz

1. How do single-member districts discourage the continuation of minor parties?
   - **a.** because such districts require a particularly high number of petitions for any third-party candidate to get on the ballot
   - **b.** because such districts usually bar third-party candidates
   - **c.** because parties whose candidates repeatedly place in second or third place (and therefore lose elections in such districts) usually dissolve, or combine forces into one party
   - **d.** because one of the two dominant parties usually adopts the policy position that brought the third party into existence in the first place
2. What is the "wasted vote" syndrome?
   - **a.** voters' tendency to vote for candidates they know will lose—just to "send a message"
   - **b.** voters' tendency not to vote for a minor-party candidate, even if they significantly prefer him or her, because they are sure that candidate will not win
   - **c.** legislators' tendency to vote for a measure they know will be defeated or vetoed—just to demonstrate their own commitment to a certain policy
   - **d.** votes that, because of some technical malfunction, cannot be read and tabulated by election officials and so must be literally discarded
3. Which of the following is true about ballot access laws?
   - **a.** They vary from state to state.
   - **b.** They make it difficult for minor party candidates, but easy for the major party candidates.
   - **c.** They first appeared during the Progressive Era, around the turn of the 20th Century.
   - **d.** All of the above.

Answers: 1-b, 2-b, 3-c.

Discussion Questions

1. Would our system be more democratic if additional parties competed for power? Is our system undemocratic because usually only two parties have a chance of victory?
2. What issue in today's politics would be most likely to ignite a third party movement?

What **YOU** can do!

Check out the Web sites of a few minor parties in the United States. You might start with the Green Party (**http://www.gp.org**), the Libertarian Party (**http://www.lp.org**), and the Constitution Party (**http://www.constitutionparty.com**). Gauge the activity level of the parties as well as the breadth of their party platforms.

CONNECT THE LINK
(Chapter **9**, pages **330–331**) What is the difference between a conservative and liberal ideology?

Political Parties *and* Ideology (pages 490–491)

Are there real differences between the two major parties?

When Alabama Governor George Wallace threw his hat into the ring for the presidency in 1968 as an American Independent, he summed up his rationale for not running as a Democrat—or as a Republican, for that matter: "There isn't a dime's worth of difference between the two parties." In other words, Wallace claimed that voters deserved a true choice, something not provided by the two major parties.

Is this true? Are the two major parties in the United States really two sides of the same coin? On one hand, there would seem to be a bit of truth to this contention, especially from a comparative perspective. As noted in the previous section, major political parties in America tend to be centrist, meaning that they adhere to policies at the middle of the political spectrum and seek incremental change rather than sweeping reform. In most democracies, numerous parties are viable, each representing different points on the ideological spectrum. In the American setting, Republicans are thought to be "conservative" and Democrats "liberal." We covered this topic in greater detail in LINK Chapter 9, pages 330–331, but we should reiterate here that in general, conservatives believe in the least possible government (except in national security matters) and in "traditional family values." They tend to favor, for instance, state over federal action, fiscal responsibility, limited government spending, following a supply-side economic strategy, restricting or outlawing abortion, ensuring more efficient crime control, eliminating gun control, defending traditional marriage structures, and cutting taxes.[13] Liberals, who sometimes prefer to call themselves progressives, believe that government can be used to help cure some of society's ills—especially economic inequality. They back policies designed to ensure a healthy environment; are tolerant toward different lifestyle choices; want to protect women's reproductive rights; advocate wider access to health care, education, and housing; demand caution about using the military and want to cut military spending; hope to increase the minimum wage; and propose paying for all these "positive" government programs with higher taxes on the wealthiest Americans.

It is true that many of the most involved members of the two major parties in the United States, the party activists, are quite ideological. Most Republican activists are very conservative, and most Democratic activists are quite liberal. Table 13.2 takes a look at the differing views of the 2008 convention delegates in both parties. As you will note, there are clear differences between party *activists*. The problem with relying on this information to suggest that parties in America are ideological is the relatively small size of the activist wing in both parties. It is likely that they constitute less than 20 percent of the overall population. A solid majority of Americans are far less ideological. That is, they are much more centrist, as we noted in Chapter 9.

This does not mean that Wallace was right—that "there isn't a dime's worth of difference" between the parties. Table 13.2 compares the platforms of the Democratic and Republican parties at the time of the 2008 presidential elections.

Both major parties approve platforms at their presidential nominating conventions, held every 4 years. These statements do not formally bind the parties to any specific positions, nor do they require that every member of the party hold the same outlook. But they do lay out in general terms the principles and policies that appeal to most members of the party. If you read the "planks"—the specific provisions—in the Democratic and Republican platforms over the years, you'll be struck by elements of consistency and difference (for a complete list of the platforms for the two major parties since 1840, visit the American Presidency Project at http://www.presidency.ucsb.edu/platforms.php). Both parties firmly endorse our approach to governance and our capitalist economic system, as well as the many elements of the democratic creed summarized in the Introduction to this book. With regard to specific policies, however, the two parties differ dramatically, especially when it comes to such contemporary issues as reproductive rights, stem cell research, gun control, private school vouchers, the legal rights of gay couples, and the war in Iraq.

> "Do the parties soften their positions to try to attract the large group of 'in-between' voters?"
> —Student Question

So is there really a "dime's worth of difference between the parties"? The answer probably depends on your perspective. Visitors from other nations have a difficult time seeing big differences between the major American parties. Nor can hard-core activists in this nation at either end of the political spectrum. Many academics also complain of the centrist policies advanced by the two major parties.[14] But for average Americans, who themselves are rather centrist, these middle-of-the-road parties suit them very well. Most citizens do see differences between the parties. They see a big difference in policies when the Republicans control Congress or when the Democrats run city hall. And they tend to feel strongly about whatever they see.

TABLE 13.2 | Party Positions in the 2008 Election

DEMOCRATIC PARTY POSITION	REPUBLICAN PARTY POSITION
Taxes Implement tax relief to middle and working classes; repeal the Bush tax cuts for households earning more than $250,000.	**Taxes** Make the Bush tax cuts permanent; cut the corporate tax rate from 35 to 25 percent.
The War in Iraq End America's involvement in Iraq quickly but responsibly; begin withdrawing troops by spring of 2009.	**The War in Iraq** Maintain troop levels until the Iraq Government is capable of governing itself and safeguarding its people.
Climate Change Support a mandatory cap-and-trade system to reduce carbon emissions 80 percent below 1990 levels by 2050; require all transportation fuels in the United States to contain 5 percent less carbon by 2015 and 10 percent less carbon by 2020.	**Climate Change** Advocate a global effort that would include developing countries to reduce greenhouse gases; establish a market-based system to curb greenhouse gas (GHG) emissions, mobilize innovative technologies.
Energy Oppose gas-tax holiday; support taxing windfall profits; oppose drilling in the Arctic and offshore; support ethanol subsidies; reluctant to expand nuclear power.	**Energy** Support gas-tax holiday; oppose taxing windfall profits; support drilling in "new oilfields" in Alaska and elsewhere, as well as developing nuclear power and clean coal.
Health Care Require that all children have health insurance; pay for it by rolling back Bush tax cuts for households earning over $250,000; aim for universal coverage.	**Health Care** Support a free-market, consumer-based system to create affordable health care for every American without mandates.
Abortion Support reproductive rights and uphold the Supreme Court decision of *Roe* v. *Wade*.	**Abortion** Overturn *Roe* v. *Wade*; support a human-life amendment to the Constitution.
Education Propose $18 billion a year in new federal spending on early childhood classes, teacher recruitment, performance pay, and other initiatives.	**Education** Maintain core belief that the federal government should play a limited role in public education.
Immigration Support a path to legalization for illegal immigrants that includes learning English and paying fines; toughen penalties for employers who hire illegal immigrants.	**Immigration** Finish securing our borders; implement a secure, accurate, and reliable electronic employment verification system; undocumented individuals will be required to enroll in a program to resolve their status.

Political Parties and Ideology

Practice Quiz

1. Which of the following policy positions does NOT typically get advocated by current members of the Republican Party?
   - **a.** cutting taxes
   - **b.** state action over federal action
   - **c.** more efficient crime control
   - **d.** gun control
2. Which of the following policy positions does NOT typically get advocated by current members of the Democratic Party?
   - **a.** using government to compensate for the consequences of economic inequality
   - **b.** environment-friendly legislation
   - **c.** lowering taxes on the wealthiest Americans
   - **d.** advocating wider access to health care
3. Why do visitors from other countries have a difficult time discerning genuine political differences between the Republican and Democratic parties?
   - **a.** because of the centrist political tendencies in the American electorate and, thus, in our two major parties
   - **b.** because people from other countries do not really understand how our electoral process works
   - **c.** because during most of the presidential election season (when foreigners are most interested in American politics), the two major parties appear quite similar; it's when the primaries are over that the differences emerge
   - **d.** because what used to be the Republican Party's platform in the nineteenth century has become the Democrats', and vice versa
4. About what percentage of the American electorate are activists in their political parties?
   - **a.** 5 percent
   - **b.** 10 percent
   - **c.** 20 percent
   - **d.** 25 percent

Answers: 1-d, 2-c, 3-a, 4-c.

Discussion Questions

1. What is a "liberal" in today's politics? How is this different from previous eras?
2. Throughout our history, it has often been difficult to discern the ideological differences between the two major political parties. Is the same true of today's politics? What are the key differences between the parties today?

What **YOU** can do!

Where do you fall on the ideological spectrum? One way to find out is to take a political personality test. Visit George Mason University's *Politopia* Web site (**http://www.politopia.com/**), and answer a series of questions to know more about your political ideology.

TIMELINE Nominating Process

■ **Closed Primary System:** Primary election process in which only registered members of the party are allowed to cast ballots. Roughly half the states use this system.

EXAMPLE: *In order to vote in a Republican primary in New York, you must be registered as a Republican.*

Parties *and the* Nomination Process

(pages 492–497)

How do political parties select their candidates?

As you have seen in this chapter, political parties serve many functions. Here, we'll outline one of the most important: the process of choosing candidates to appear on the general election ballot under the party's banner—a procedure called *nomination*. For voters, nominations limit their choices on election day. On the one hand, we might applaud this process, given that without nominations we might find dozens or even hundreds of candidates on each ballot. On the other hand, perhaps voters want more choices than they usually get, and the winnowing down by the parties limits the types of candidates on the ballot. Write-in candidates, allowed to run but without party backing, stand very little chance of winning.

Even if we accept the usefulness of party nomination, how might the parties go about this process? In the early years, a handful of party leaders did the choosing. The party was a private organization, they argued, and nominating was simply their own business. At first, few people objected; if the voters did not like the candidates they chose, they could simply vote for someone else. The nomination process changed during the Progressive Era, when laws were passed mandating that the parties get widespread voter input in selecting nominees. We call this process *direct primary elections*. Today, both major parties choose their candidates by letting rank-and-file members (average citizens) vote.

Different Primary Systems

"What's the difference between an open primary and a closed primary?"
—Student Question

Not every state uses the same primary system (see Figure 13.8). Roughly half the states have what is called a **closed primary system**■. In these states, only registered members of the party are allowed to vote in the primary. In some states, the voter must declare his or her party registration in advance of the primary election—often 30 days or so—while in other states, the registration can be done (or changed) on primary day. Either way, the states that rely on this system allow only registered members of the party

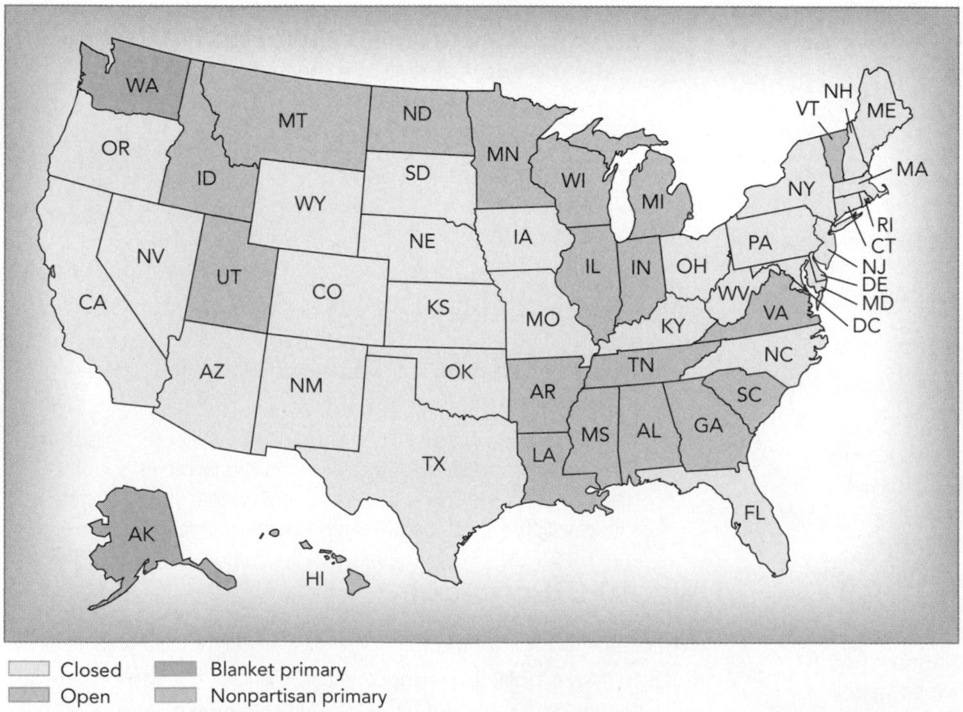

FIGURE 13.8 | **Primary Systems in the United States**

As this figure suggests, the split between open and closed primary states is about even. But this does not mean that they are randomly distributed across the United States. ***—Can you see any geographic patterns? If so, what might explain the configuration?***

SOURCE: http://www.csulb.edu

Open Primary System: Primary election process in which voters are allowed to cast ballots in the primary election without declaring which party they are voting for.

EXAMPLE: *In South Carolina, a voter can cast a vote in either Democratic or Republican primaries.*

National Nominating Convention: A meeting of delegates from communities across the nation to discuss candidates' qualifications, choose their party's nominee, and adopt a party platform.

SIGNIFICANCE: *In the past, these gatherings selected the party's nominee, but in recent years, the selection is done through binding primaries and caucuses.*

to vote on prospective nominees. If you're registered as a Democrat or are an independent, you cannot vote in the Republican primary. Most other states use an **open primary system**. Under it, voters are allowed to participate in the primary election without declaring membership in a party. On primary day, the voter can choose to vote in the Republican primary or the Democratic primary, and no record is kept. (Of course, one cannot vote in both parties' primaries.) Some people have criticized the open primary system because activists in one party can vote for the *weaker* candidates in the other party's primary election. Others suggest this sort of "strategic primary voting" is quite rare.

Presidential Nominations

Our political system began without political parties and with great hopes that parties ("factions") would not arise. Thus the framers of the Constitution saw no reason to specify a procedure for nominating presidential candidates. They assumed that the local notables who would gather in each state to cast its Electoral College votes would select the most qualified men. That was how George Washington was unanimously chosen as the first president. When the early party system of Democratic-Republicans and Federalists nevertheless emerged, each party's representatives in Congress named its presidential (and, beginning in 1804, its vice presidential) candidates. The caucus-based nomination system became so important in selecting the eventual president that it became known as King Caucus. The Corrupt Bargain of 1824, however, suggested that the reign of King Caucus should end and that something less elitist—something that better reflected the will of average voters—should be substituted. The outcome was the **national nominating convention**. The idea was that delegates should be sent from communities across the nation to discuss the strengths and weaknesses of potential candidates and thus produce the best choice. The convention would also be an opportunity to hammer together a party platform as well as rules for conducting party business. It would be a gathering of local party representatives every 4 years. The major parties held their first national conventions in 1832 and have done so every 4 years since. More will be said about these events below.

One of the sticking points in the convention system was how delegates would be chosen from their communities and what role they might play at the convention. A few states developed mechanisms to allow rank-and-file party members to select delegates, but most simply allowed state and local party bosses to handpick who went to the national convention. Once there, these delegates were obliged to follow the orders of their party leader. This often led to high drama at party conventions. Party bosses used their delegates as negotiating chips, looking to play a key role in nominating the candidate—for what could be better than to be perceived as the party's "kingmaker"?

> "What used to happen at the early conventions?"
>
> —Student Question

Conventions were about selecting the presidential nominee and about cutting deals in "smoke-filled rooms." There were florid speeches, tumultuous floor fights, protracted voting (the Democratic convention of 1924 took 103 ballots before nominating a colorless compromise candidate). This system lasted nearly 140 years, through the 1960s.

The strain between party bosses and average party followers came to a head in a fight over the 1968 Democratic presidential nomination. As 1968 began, everyone assumed that President Lyndon B. Johnson would accept his party's renomination. But there arose a groundswell of opposition to Johnson within the Democratic Party over his waging of the Vietnam War. When Johnson failed to win decisively in the March New Hampshire primary, he announced that he was withdrawing from the race. A sharp division emerged between the party leaders, who backed Vice President Hubert Humphrey, and the "antiwar Democrats," who supported either Minnesota Senator Eugene McCarthy (not to be confused with Senator Joseph McCarthy of Wisconsin, the anticommunist demagogue of the 1950s) and New York Senator Robert F. Kennedy (the late President John F. Kennedy's younger brother and his former attorney general). Kennedy gradually outpaced McCarthy in the primary elections, yet the party bosses continued to back Humphrey, who was staying out of the primaries. (At that time, many states did not have presidential primaries.) Robert Kennedy's assassination in 1968 on the night he won the California primary created a crisis for the antiwar Democrats. Faithful to their bosses, the majority of delegates at the Democratic National Convention in Chicago nominated Humphrey, while thousands of antiwar young people filled the streets in protest outside the convention hall and were beaten and bloodied by Mayor Daley's police. Humphrey went on to lose the general election to Richard Nixon. The Democratic Party seemed in shambles.

After this disastrous election, Democrats implemented a series of changes designed to create a more "open, timely, and representative" nomination processs. Most notably, **binding primaries** were established in most states, where voters picked delegates who pledged their support for a particular presidential candidate. The winners in each state are sent to the convention, where they vote to nominate that candidate. Another way to pick delegates, used in about 15 states, is a **nomination caucus.** Here, rank-and-file party members attend

Binding Primaries: Process established in most states whereby voters in primary elections choose delegates who have pledged their support to a particular presidential candidate. The delegates then vote for this candidate at the nominating convention.

SIGNIFICANCE: *These events have stripped the power of local party bosses in the nomination process.*

Invisible Primary: Raising money and attracting media attention early in the election process, usually before the primary election year.

SIGNIFICANCE: *The candidate that jumps out quickly in the invisible primary stands a good chance of winning the party's nomination.*

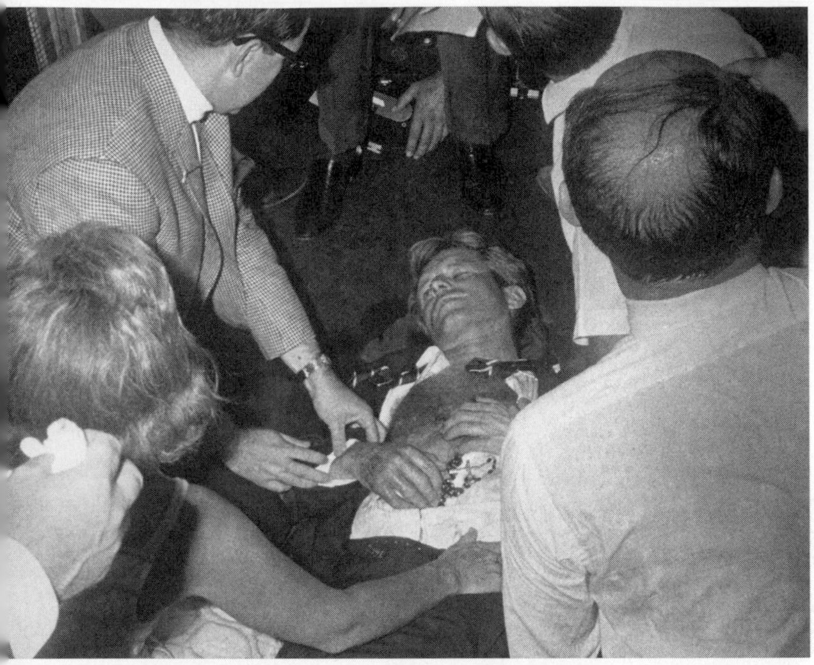

Many agree that 1968 was one of the most turbulent years in American history. Here, Robert Kennedy lies dying after being shot on the evening of the California Democratic presidential primary, which he had won. Hubert Humphrey was later given the nomination, even though many "regulars" in the party wanted a true anti-Vietnam War candidate. Four years later, the party had transformed its nomination rules—leading to binding primaries and caucuses. ***—But have these changes made the system truly more democratic?***

a neighborhood meeting, share ideas and concerns about particular candidates, and cast a ballot for pledged delegates to attend a statewide meeting. There, the same process takes place, and the delegates who win at the state level go to the national party convention. The key difference between primaries and caucuses is that the former is an election and the latter a series of "town hall–like" meetings.

The Republican Party was not bound by the new Democratic Party rules. As the notion of binding primaries and caucuses spread, however, they felt compelled to abandon the boss-centered model. Put a bit differently, as the Democrats moved to what was perceived to be a more open system, the older model lost legitimacy, and the Republicans were obliged to make similar changes.

A Better Process?

The nomination reforms of the early 1970s dramatically transformed the way Americans select presidents. It is hard to overstate the importance of the shift from party boss to voter control. Many have applauded the change; the process, they argue, better reflects the will of the electorate and therefore is more democratic. Perhaps more important, it is a process that most Americans believe is fair. It conveys legitimacy, which is essential for any political system.

Critics, however, point to a number of problems with the new process, and in recent years, the alarm bell has grown louder and louder. Is the process really more representative? Are there no downsides to the new process? Consider the following items:

- The nomination process may *not* reflect the will of the average party member, let alone the average American, because relatively few people participate in the primaries and caucuses—and the ones who do are much more ideological, more "extremist," than the typical citizen. Turnout in presidential primaries is generally less than 20 percent of eligible voters, and attendance at caucuses rarely gets beyond 10 percent.
- Because candidates win or lose based on how citizens feel about them, the nomination process has become very expensive, time-consuming, and negative. Candidates who can raise the most money—and raise it the fastest—have every advantage. This money can be used to attack the other candidates, who are all part of the same party. Some of the hardest attacks against presidential candidates come during the primaries, not the general election. The bitterness of the primaries leaves many Americans distrustful about the electoral process. Many argue that it turns off voters—especially young voters.
- Those candidates who are able to grab media attention before the primary and caucus season do much better, which gives an unfair advantage to the best-known and best-funded candidates. Together, the ability to raise early money and to draw media attention has been called the **invisible primary**.
- The nomination process puts a premium on winning early primary and caucus contests—and winning there, of course, helps raise more money and draw more media hype. Many critics have argued that small and perhaps atypical New Hampshire and Iowa, which hold their events at the very start of the process, exert grossly disproportionate weight in selecting the eventual nominee.

The 2008 Leapfrog Contest

Perhaps the greatest issue prior to the 2008 contest was the rapid pace at which the nomination process ended. The Iowa Caucus comes first, followed by the New Hampshire Primary. Both states have passed legislation protecting their first-in-the-nation status, and the Democratic National Committee supports these states.

Candidates who win these early races are often crowned the nominee even though the vast majority of primaries and caucuses have not taken place. They are perceived to be invincible, and the other candidates drop from the contest.

By 2007, mounting frustration over this truncated process had lead one state after another to move its primary or caucus earlier in the election calender. If the process is over by March, why not move your state's event to the February? As noted by political analyst Karen Tumulty of *Time Magazine;*

> For a number of years, the larger states—places like California, New Jersey—have essentially been afterthoughts in the nominating process. And they've looked at themselves and they've thought, "You know, here we are, big, diverse states where a lot of voters live, where a lot of politicians come to raise money, and yet by the time our states get around to voting, the nominations are essentially a lock." And so this was the year when a lot of those states decided that was the end of that, and they moved their primary dates up.[15]

Thus began a rapid succession of changes, where one state moved its nominating contest earlier, only to be leapfrogged by another state. In response, that first state again moved up its date.

Several problems seemed to spring from this turbulent process. It put even more pressure on the early stages of the nomination process, creating an unprecedented early campaign season for the 2008 election. Nearly all candidates in both parties had declaired their intentions to run a full 18 months before the general election. Indeed, Republican Fred Thompson was criticized for his late entry into the race—in early September of 2007. In past presidential elections, few candidates formally declared their intentions until after Labor Day. Another implication seemed to be the importance of early and successful fundraising. Finally, and of no little consequence, many speculated that the early campaign season will lead to record levels of "voter fatigue." How long can we expect voters to pay attention to electoral politics?

We now know that many, but not all, of these concerns proved correct. Early money proved critical, as did success in initial primary and caucus states. Yet the process shut down quickly in only one party: John McCain was annointed the winner by late January, well before voters in most states had their say. For the Democrats, the unprecedented and dramatic battle between Barack Obama and Hillary Clinton extended throughout the spring and summer and included important contests in all 50 states. Early contests proved critical, but so did later states. In fact, Obama did not really have the nomination buttoned down until the primaries in Indiana and North Carolina on May 6, 2008. Concerns shifted to whether the protracted contest would invigorate the Democratic party or would tear the party apart. Given Obama's success in the general election, it seems that the rough-and-tumble nomination process did not hurt his candidacy. In fact, many commentators have suggested that this battle with Hillary Clinton made him an even more formidable candidate against John McCain.

Barack Obama gestures for time as Hillary Rodham Clinton responds to a question during a Democratic presidential debate in Los Angeles in 2008. Some of the sharpest criticism leveled at presidential candidates comes from members of their own party during the nomination process. ***—Is intraparty fighting of this sort good for our political system?***

STUDENT | PROFILE

In the early 1980s, the Democratic National Committee was anxious to bring their elected officials and prominent figures into the party fold, so they created a special category of participants at the presidential nomination conventions: superdelegates. Instead of being elected like other delegates, these men and women would be appointed, and they would have the flexibility to vote for whichever candidate they deemed fitting. Yet because they made up less than 20 percent of the overall delegate pool, and because none of the nomination races since the 1980s were protracted, the role of superdelegates in the process drew little attention. Most Americans had never even heard of them until 2008, when all that changed.

Not very long into the battle between Barack Obama and Hillary Clinton, it became apparent that neither one would garner enough regular delegates to secure the nomination—and that the superdelegates would decide the outcome. All eyes turned to who these folks were and how they would vote. Many were familiar names, such as governors, members of Congress, and prominent Democratic activists.

But not all. A 21-year-old junior at Marquette University in Wisconsin by the name of Jason Rae went from being a U.S. Senate page to the youngest elected representative of the Democratic National Committee. He actually couldn't vote when he was first elected, because he was 6 months shy of 18. But he wanted to represent what he calls "America's next generation." So he and his friends hand-painted posters with the slogan "A ray of hope for the future." It worked.

Throughout the spring of 2008, Rae was wooed by both sides for his coveted vote. He dined with Hillary Clinton's daughter, Chelsea; had a meeting with Barack Obama; and received dozens of calls from some of the highest-profile politicians from across the country. He also appeared on numerous television programs, including CNN, MSNBC, *Good Morning America,* and *The Early Show* on CBS. "I have gotten very comfortable with the camera and even more comfortable with that little earpiece I get all the time," said Rae. "Now I can put it in with my eyes closed."

As to who Rae eventually voted for? Barack Obama.

SOURCE: "Young People Who Rock," CNN.com, February 16, 2006. Accessed at http://ypwr.blogs.cnn.com/category/political-activists/ on May 10, 2008. ■

Believe it or not, as a Democratic Party superdelegate, Jason Rae, just 18 years old, was courted by both Hillary Clinton and Barack Obama. ***—Have you ever considered becoming a participant in local party politics?***

"Reforming the reforms" is on everyone's mind these days, and few expect the current process to last beyond 2008. What will the system look like in the years ahead? One approach that is often raised would be to have regional primaries and caucuses. The South might start the process during one election, and the Midwest the next. The problem with this process is that large, multistate events will likely reduce the importance of interpersonal campaigning—what many dub "retail politics." In its place will be ever-more television commercials. And of course, the push for enough money to compete in multistate events will be powerful. Another model, often dubbed the "American Plan," is to start with nomination contests in the smallest states and move to progressively larger states throughout the primary season, ending with Texas and California. Retail politics is preserved, but so is the invisible primary and the momentum of early states.

Party Conventions

Each of the major parties holds these massive, week-long events at the end of the summer during presidential election years. In previous eras, these "gatherings of the faithful" from across the country were designed to build unity, create a party platform, review party rules and procedures, and most of all, select the party's general election nominee. One candidate or another might come to the convention with strong support from certain party leaders, but things were up in the air until the wrangling and backroom deals were complete. There were also rules that stipulated the successful candidate needed a majority, not simply a plurality, of delegates. This often led to multiple "ballots," meaning any number of votes until one candidate received at least 50 percent plus one delegate vote. It was common for a nominating convention to hold dozens of ballots (and, at times, up to 100), with high drama and intrigue drawing the nation's attention along the way. News coverage of these conventions was "gavel to gavel" (that is, inclusive).

Things have changed since the rise of binding primaries and caucuses. We now know the nominees for both parties well in advance of the conventions, and party bosses no longer control delegates anyway. Occasionally, there is drama surrounding the nominees' selection of a vice presidential running mate, but this is often decided in advance as well. Sometimes there is tension over the wording of the party's platform, and once in a while, a group within the party will protest one issue or another. For the most part, Americans only "tune in" to the conventions to hear a few speeches, the most important being the candidate's acceptance speech and the keynote address. Some 40 million Americans tuned in to hear both Barak Obama and John McCain give their acceptance speeches. The keynote address has taken on importance in recent years, as each party uses this opportunity to showcase an up-and-coming politician. Barack Obama gave the keynote address 4 years before receiving his party's nomination, and Bill Clinton did the same in 1988. (Clinton's story is, however, a bit different than Obama's, as noted in the *Pathways Profile*.)

News coverage of conventions is no longer "gavel to gavel," and in fact, it has shrunk dramatically in recent years. Some have suggested that conventions are increasingly meaningless—simply a week-long commercial for the candidate. Where party conventions are headed in the future is anyone's guess, but the chance of returning to the smoke-filled rooms and the backroom deals are probably rather slim.

PATHWAYS | profile

Bill Clinton

There was a great deal of excitement and anticipation at the Democratic National Convention in 1988 over the keynote speaker. Keynote addresses are always important, always rousing, and this time would surely be no different. A young, little-known governor from a small, southern state was chosen for the task. He was smart, attractive, and articulate—surely a rising star in the party. And with a northeastern liberal as the party's presidential nominee (Michael Dukakis of Massachusetts), it made good strategic sense to give a southern moderate the stage when so many Americans would be watching. As for the governor, it was a chance of a lifetime—an opportunity to make his mark in history and set the stage for the future.

To say the speech was a disaster would be an understatement. It failed to arouse the delegates and was long—way, way too long. In fact, 40 minutes into the address, boredom had set in, and there were even jeers from the crowd. When the governor finally said, "In conclusion," the delegates cheered! By all counts, it was a catastrophe, and the governor's future in national politics seemed shattered. Few, if any, could bounce back from such a fiasco.

The governor's name was Bill Clinton—and, within 4 years, he would become President of the United States. ■

Parties and the Nomination Process

Practice Quiz

1. In the first years of our country, a small group of congressional leaders nominated presidential candidates.
   a. true
   b. false

2. When were direct primary elections first instituted?
   a. during the "Era of Good Feelings"
   b. after the Corrupt Bargain of 1824
   c. in the first election after the Civil War
   d. in the Progressive Era

3. What replaced national conventions as the actual mechanisms for establishing presidential nominees?
   a. binding primaries and nomination caucuses
   b. national primary elections
   c. indirect primaries
   d. national polls

4. In the current nomination process, who has the greatest advantage among candidates?
   a. the candidate who has the most appealing personality
   b. the candidate who is most favored by the media
   c. the candidate who represents the largest minority population
   d. the candidate with the most money

Answers: 1-a, 2-d, 3-a, 4-d.

Discussion Questions

1. If the primaries tend to determine the party's nominee well in advance of the party convention, why are conventions still held?

2. Why is money so important in electoral politics in our time? Is this democratic?

What **YOU** can do!

Using Internet and library resources, explore voter turnout in each state during the most recent presidential primary season. Choose five states with open primary systems and five with closed primary systems. Do you detect any informal patterns in voter turnout based on the type of primary system?

Conclusion

At the dawn of the American experiment, the founders assumed that any organization designed to capture control of government would be adverse to the public interest. But what these great men—and many others—failed to recognize is that political parties, or similar electoral organizations, are inevitable in a free society. Whether they emerge in response to a desire to change public policy or simply to grab control of the reins of office is unclear. What seems elementary, nevertheless, is that they *will* emerge. They can also enhance the democratic process: Parties can educate voters, aggregate interests, check the ambitions and abuses of those in power, mobilize opposition, and in short, turn private citizens into public actors. There is more to party politics than mere "partisan wrangling."

There is not a modern democracy that does not have political parties. A prominent political scientist is very emphatic: "It should be flatly stated that political parties created democracy and that modern democracy is unthinkable save in terms of political parties."[16] This might be an overstatement, but few people would dispute that parties have been and will continue to be an integral part of the election process for years to come. What these structures will look like, what they will seek to accomplish, and how they will aid average citizens in their struggle to keep government responsive by using the elections pathway in the twenty-first century is, however, anyone's guess.

A related issue is what role political parties play in shaping public policy. Do parties help the average American use the elections pathway to mold the outcomes of the policy process? Or do parties perhaps get in the way, distorting the will of the people? Many of the functions discussed in this chapter imply that parties have made a big difference in the past—that they have been a key link in our democratic system. Yet a transformation is under way—a dramatic change in the party system. Party-line voting in Congress is approaching record levels, as are levels of individual party identification. Will these adjustments enhance the democratic process or strain the system, alienating new groups of citizens? Local parties seem to be on the endangered species list, while state and national organizations, flush with cash, technology, and expertise, are filling the void. Many people applaud this "renewal," but it is also fair to ask whether the role of citizens will be enhanced or reduced in the years ahead. Historically, local party organizations have been the access point into the election process. If these structures disappear, will the election pathway continue to be a viable route for change? And if so, for whom?

Key Objective Review, Apply, and Explore

Party Functions

(pages 470–473)

While the framers of our political system thought organizations like political parties would be harmful, and perhaps even destructive, to the fledgling democracy, we now understand that they served numerous important functions, not the least of which is helping to organize the election process.

KEY TERMS

Rational Party Model 470
Nominees 470
Responsible Party Model 470
Unified Party Control 472
Platform 470
Divided Party Control 472

CRITICAL THINKING QUESTIONS

1. Parties aid candidates in many ways, but if paid consultants can do the same, why are parties necessary in a democracy? What's so special about parties?

2. A prominent scholar once noted, "Democracy is unthinkable save in terms of the parties." Wasn't he overstating things a bit?

INTERNET RESOURCES

For a look at the role of parties in our system, visit MSNBC at **http://encarta.msn.com/encyclopedia 761580668/political_parties.html**

ADDITIONAL READING

Aldrich, John. *Why Parties? The Origin and Transformation of Political Parties in America*. Chicago: University of Chicago Press, 1995.

Party-in-Government

(pages 474–477)

We often think of political parties when it comes to the election pathway. Yet parties have also been key elements of the operation of government since the dawn of the nineteenth century. Parties help structure an otherwise disparate, chaotic system.

KEY TERMS

Tripartite View of Parties 474
Party Unity Scores 474

CRITICAL THINKING QUESTIONS

1. Does it really make sense for legislators to adhere rather closely to the party's agenda, or should they evaluate every issue independent of partisan concerns?

2. It has been said that parties and party leaders help structure the legislative process, but at what cost? That is, are legislatures less democratic when party pressures are significant?

INTERNET RESOURCES

To explore party unity scores in Congress, visit CQ.com at **http://public.cq.com/public/senate_unity_state.html**

ADDITIONAL READING

Brown, Sherrod. *Congress from the Inside: Observations from the Majority and the Minority*. Kent, OH: Kent State Press, 1999.

Key Objective Review, Apply, and Explore

Party-in-the-Electorate

(pages 478–481)

The number of Americans who consider themselves a member of a political party has shifted over the years. Exactly how one's partisanship is established and how it is used during election periods are important elements of American politics.

KEY TERMS

Party Identification 478
Straight-Ticket Voters 478
Split-Ticket Voters (Swing Voters) 478
Independent 479
Partisan Realignment 479
Dealignment 481

CRITICAL THINKING QUESTIONS

1. Some have suggested party identification serves as a rational shortcut when picking candidates. How might this be true?
2. What would happen to levels of turnout in the United States if fewer and fewer citizens developed a party identification?

INTERNET RESOURCES

For all kinds of information on levels of partisanship in America, visit the American National Election Study at **http://www.electionstudies.org/**

ADDITIONAL READING

White, John K., and Daniel M. Shea. *New Party Politics: From Jefferson and Hamilton to the Information Age,* 2nd ed. Belmont, CA: Wadsworth, 2004.

Party-as-Organization

(pages 482–483)

In every state and nearly every community in the country, Democratic and Republican organizations vie for voter support. While national and state committees have strengthened in recent decades, local units have waned. Will our democracy suffer if local party committees vanish?

KEY TERM

Party Machines 482

CRITICAL THINKING QUESTIONS

1. What do you think is the relationship between high levels of party identification in a community and the weight of local party organizations in that same community? Could it be that party organizations are strongest where party identification is weakest?
2. Why would democratic theorists fret about the fate of local party committees?

INTERNET RESOURCES

To find your local party committee, simply search under the name of your city or county, such as "Cook County Democratic Committee" or "Chicago Republicans."

ADDITIONAL READING

Riordon, William L. *Plunkett of Tammany Hall.* New York: Signet, 1995.

Key Objective Review, Apply, and Explore

Party Eras in American History

(pages 484–487)

Even though parties have been with us from nearly the beginning, their weight in our system of government has fluctuated. Few speculate that they will regain the prominence they had in the second half of the nineteenth century, but there has been a modest resurgence in recent decades.

KEY TERMS

Democratic-Republicans 484
Federalist Party 484
Corrupt Bargain of 1824 484
Kansas–Nebraska Bill 485
Merit System (Civil Service) 485
Australian Ballot 485
Candidate-Centered Era 486

CRITICAL THINKING QUESTIONS

1. What external forces likely shape party dynamics? Are parties weaker or stronger when certain things are happening in society?
2. What's your take on realignment? Does it help to explain transformations in party eras?

INTERNET RESOURCES

To explore party history in America, visit NewsVOA.com at **http://www.voanews.com/specialenglish/2008-04-23-voa1.cfm**

ADDITIONAL READING

Reichley, A. James. *The Life of the Parties: A History of American Political Parties.* Lanham, MD: Rowman & Littlefield, 2000.

Minor Parties in American Politics

(pages 488–489)

Politics in the United States has always centered on the two-party model, but at the same time, minor parties have served important democratic functions. Moreover, the number of Americans anxious for more choices on election day seems to be on the rise.

KEY TERMS

Institutional Barriers 488
Ballot Access Laws 488
Attitudinal Barriers 488

CRITICAL THINKING QUESTIONS

1. Why do you suppose the chips seem stacked against minor parties in the United States? In most other democracies, numerous parties vie for power, so why just two in our country?
2. What is the most important role played by minor parties in American politics?

INTERNET RESOURCES

For a look at the many, many minor parties in the United States, visit **http://www.dcpoliticalreport.com/PartyLink.htm**

ADDITIONAL READING

Bibby, John F., and L. Sandy Maisel. *Two Parties or More? The American Party System,* 2nd ed. Boulder, CO: Westview Press, 2003.

Key Objective Review, Apply, and Explore

Political Parties and Ideology
(pages 490–491)

It has been said that the two major parties in the United State are quite similar—that they both adhere to centrist policies. While that might be true, it is also true that there are real differences between what Democrats and Republicans believe. At the very least, activists on both sides passionately disagree about a host of public policy questions.

CRITICAL THINKING QUESTIONS

1. Why would radical parties—ones on the far liberal or far conservative side of the spectrum—not do well in American politics?
2. Do you agree that there are significant differences between the two major parties? If so, do you think these differences will increase or decrease in the years ahead?

INTERNET RESOURCES

For the 2008 platforms of the two major parties, visit **http://www.democrats.org/index.html** and **http://www.rnc.org/**

ADDITIONAL READING

Hershey, Marjory. *Party Politics in America,* 13th ed. New York: Longman, 2008.

Parties and the Nomination Process
(pages 492–497)

One of the core functions of political parties is to select their candidates for the general election. This has always been a contentious process, especially at the presidential level and in recent years.

KEY TERMS

Closed Primary System 492
Open Primary System 493
National Nominating Convention 493
Binding Primaries 493
Nomination Caucus 493
Invisible Primary 494

CRITICAL THINKING QUESTIONS

1. Should party nomination contests be limited to only those registered as members of the party (closed primaries), or should all citizens have a say in picking party nominees of either party (open primaries)?
2. Is the current presidential nomination system broken? If so, what reforms would you suggest?

INTERNET RESOURCES

For more information on the presidential nomination process, visit the *Online NewsHour* at **http://www.pbs.org/newshour/extra/teachers/lessonplans/history/primaries_12-19.html**

ADDITIONAL READING

Mayer, William G. and Andrew E. Busch. *The Frontloading Problem in Presidential Nominations*. Washington, D.C.: Brookings Institution Press, 2003.

Chapter Review Critical Thinking Test

1. Political parties educate voters, aggregate interests, and help turn private citizens into public actors.
a. true **b.** false

2. What would the framers of our Constitution have thought of the political successes of the Christian Coalition?
a. They would have applauded it.
b. They would have predicted its success—as spelled out in *The Federalist Papers.*
c. They would have been outraged by its combination of religion and party politics.
d. It is impossible to tell, since they never addressed the idea of political parties or religion in politics.

3. What strategic change in campaigning do both major parties often make when the election season shifts from the primaries to the general election?
a. They use much more negative campaigning.
b. They become less centrist in their appeals.
c. They become more centrist in their appeals.
d. They abandon negative campaigning.

4. Which of the following is NOT a *long-term* factor that influences a voter's party allegiance?
a. race
b. popularity of a particular candidate
c. level of education
d. region of the country

5. What phenomenon seems to be a key reason for the decline of the average citizen's participation in the election process?
a. how unimportant the issues seem these days
b. how uninspiring or incompetent most candidates seem these days
c. the decline in the parties' attempts to communicate with average citizens
d. the decline of local party organizations

6. Studies indicate that communities with vital political party operations
a. have higher levels of voting.
b. have more negative campaigning.
c. have lower levels of voting.
d. are becoming more common.

7. What is a party's "platform"?
a. its positions on a broad range of issues
b. its mission or founding principle, articulated when the party was first formed (for example, abolition is the platform of the modern Republican Party)
c. the financial base by which a party pays its expenses
d. the software by which a party connects with its members electronically

8. In the United States, legislators vote along party lines
a. all of the time.
b. almost all of the time.
c. just a little more than half the time—party loyalty is not really expected.
d. most of the time.

9. A semiformal hierarchy or "chain of command" exists among national, state, and local party committees, in descending order of authority.
a. true **b.** false

10. Which political party dominated national politics in the early nineteenth century?
a. the Federalist Party
b. the Whig Party
c. the Democratic-Republican Party
d. the Liberty Party

11. What was one characteristic of Jacksonian democracy?
a. an antielite sentiment
b. a dependence in campaigns on special interests
c. low voter turnout
d. a rejection of advertising presidential candidates in a certain image

12. What prompted the creation of the modern Republican Party in 1854?
a. the Gold Rush **b.** slavery
c. prohibition **d.** anti-immigration sentiment

13. In recent years, at the same time that party organizations are regaining their footing nationally, a growing number of Americans see parties as corrupt.
a. true **b.** false

14. Regarding minor parties, it is fair to say that
a. they have all come and gone and made little difference in how electoral politics and governing have unfolded in this two-party country.
b. there have been a handful of cases in which minor parties have triumphed, but these cases are the exception.
c. they have all come and gone, but a number of them have significantly affected the political landscape of their time.
d. in a few instances, minor parties have become major parties, evolving into the two parties that now dominate the political landscape.

15. Major political parties in America tend to be centrist: They adhere to policies at the middle of the political spectrum and seek incremental change rather than sweeping reform.
a. true **b.** false

Chapter Review Critical Thinking Test

16. Ralph Nader ran for President in 2000 as a member of which third party?
- **a.** the Socialist Party
- **b.** the Green Party
- **c.** the Progressive Party
- **d.** the Reform Party

17. Recent surveys indicate that Americans would view the emergence of a third party with
- **a.** increasing skepticism.
- **b.** approval.
- **c.** disapproval.
- **d.** outrage.

18. How is an open primary different from a closed primary?
- **a.** In an open primary, voters from one party can vote in the primary election of the other party.
- **b.** In an open primary, candidates in one party can run in the primary election of the other party.
- **c.** In an open primary, voters from either party can cast one vote in *both* parties' primary elections.
- **d.** In an open primary, a third-party candidate can be on the ballot of either of the two main parties.

19. According to some, one problem with the voter-controlled primary system is that
- **a.** it has made the nomination a popularity contest.
- **b.** it has made the nomination process too short.
- **c.** it grants a disproportionate significance to voters and caucus members in two states with few electoral votes, New Hampshire and Iowa.
- **d.** it has exaggerated candidates' need to appeal to big-city voters.

20. Does the withering of local party organizations mean that the role of citizens in the electoral process has been reduced?
- **a.** Definitely so.
- **b.** Definitely not.
- **c.** There's a good chance it will be, but we don't know yet.
- **d.** It's unlikely, but it's too soon to tell.

Answers: 1-a, 2-c, 3-c, 4-b, 5-c, 6-a, 7-a, 8-d, 9-b, 10-c, 11-a, 12-b, 13-a, 14-c, 15-a, 16-b, 17-b, 18-a, 19-c, 20-c.

You decide!

Imagine you are a political consultant who has been hired by one of the major political parties. Your job is to help party leaders reverse the trend of dealignment and bring voters back into party politics. How would you go about this task? Would you focus on strengthening the party organization? Why or why not? What sort of party platform might you suggest to attract voters? Would you suggest the party alter its processes or rules? If so, how?

Key Objective Outline

How do values shape the nature of policies and solutions?

Why are there three main types of public policies?

Are all parts of the policy process equally open to political influence?

How is economic policy regulated in the United States?

What are some of the numerous factors that shape foreign policy development in the United States?

The Basics of Foreign Policy **(page 524)**

CHAPTER 14
The Policy Process

Why is public policy political?

In the fall of 2003, President Bush asked for congressional action on the nation's energy policy, and the U.S. House of Representatives responded by introducing a bill that provided tax incentives for companies involved in energy production, conservation incentives for consumers, and changes in energy regulation. The bill was controversial, because it contained what some people saw as unwise rollbacks of federal regulations on the energy industry that could potentially damage air and water quality. Environmentalists and their champions in the House—mostly Democrats—blasted the bill as a gift to the energy industry and a threat to the environment.[1]

One other small detail caught the attention of Congress watchers. Some members of the House had inserted language into the bill that would allow localities to issue tax-free bonds to fund local development projects. One of the businesses that stood to benefit from this part of the bill was Hooters, a chain of eateries in which minimally dressed young women wait on customers. Democrats and their allies jumped at this poetic opportunity to claim the bill was a legislative giveaway to "Hooters and polluters."

Because the Senate did not pass the version of the bill containing the "Hooters" provision, this legislative effort never became law. However, the attempt gave many people, both inside and outside of government, the feeling that the nation's policies were at the mercy of special interests who used their influence—in the form of campaign contributions and other possible rewards—to get more than their fair share.

This cynicism has more than a grain of truth in it, but just how does our government make policy? So far, you have learned how a bill becomes a law (in Chapter 7) and how the laws get administered (in Chapter 9), but public policy is more than simply passing and enforcing laws. As the political scientist Harold Lasswell noted, politics is the study of who gets what, when, and how.[2] If we apply this deceptively simple formula of questions to public policy, a rich picture emerges of a complex government with many sources of influence over what it does and does not do.

STUDENT RESOURCE-CENTER
- Glossary
- Vocabulary Example
- LINK
- MyPoliSciLab Connection

Ideas *and* Values *in* Public Policy

(pages 508–509)

How do values shape the nature of policies and solutions?

The very existence of a problem often creates a highly charged political atmosphere even before any discussion of potential solutions occurs. Take global warming, for example. Opponents have had many heated debates over whether the earth is really heating up and what role, if any, human activity may play in this process. Each part of the process of policy formation has the potential to be influenced by and, in turn, to influence the multiple pathways we have discussed throughout this text. Think about public policy as what comes after the equal sign in a mathematical equation. The structure of the government plus the political process forms the elements on the left side of the equation. The sum of these interactions equals the policies that affect each citizen. Any change caused by the effects of the policies (the right side of the equation) influences the structure of the government and the political process (the left side of the equation), and vice versa.

You probably see the point by now: Public policy is more than just a law, the action of an agency, or a court decision. For a complete understanding of public policy, you must know why these tangible outputs of government exist in the first place and anticipate how they may change in the future.

> "What is the difference between *politics* and *policy?*"
> —Student Question

Politicians, members of the media, and everyday citizens often draw a distinction between politics and policy. This difference rests on the notion that politics is like a game—or even a war, in which strategies are used to gain advantages over opponents and win battles. (The very word *campaign* is borrowed from the vocabulary of warfare.)

Policy is the output of politics and, to some people, is not political in itself. You may have heard commentators praising presidential debates as a time for "setting politics aside," forcing the candidates to deal with *policy* issues. This common notion of an either-or relationship, however, is an artificial way of thinking about these two concepts.

As defined, public policy is what you get after the equal sign in the equation of politics plus government. Elections, social movements, interest group activity, and the actions of political institutions such as Congress or the federal courts all go into the equation *before* this equal sign. Using this metaphor, public policy is inherently political. It reflects the exercise of power in our system of government, our economic system, and our society in general.

Very often, however, social scientists and other policy specialists think about public policy as a collection of phases in a process, as though the intricacies of the process were somehow disconnected from the political world. There is a well-worn approach to the study of the process of policy formation, usually called the **policy process model**■, which begins with the identification of a problem and concludes with the analysis of the effectiveness of the solutions applied to that problem.[3] This model forms the core of this chapter, but we will also help you see the pathways that connect politics with public policy and the effect of these variables on the public as well as other segments of our society and political world.

> ■ **Policy Process Model:** A way of thinking about how policy is made in terms of steps in a progression.
> **EXAMPLE:** *Most bills passed by Congress go through phases that mirror the early parts of the policy process model.*

As you read this chapter, keep in mind that theories about policy and the process of public policymaking are not just abstract stabs at ideas motivated by academic curiosity. Rather, the need to theorize comes from the desire to make sense of what seems, at first, like a tangled mess of motivations, actors, and actions.

The Steps of Policymaking

The policy process model describes policymaking in five or six steps: (1) identifying the policy problem, (2) setting an agenda, (3) formulating a solution, (4) legitimizing the solution, (5) implementing the solution, and in some versions, (6) evaluating the solution. Deborah Stone is one of several political scientists who believes the policy process model lacks connections to the ways that real people and their governments make decisions about policy. She uses slightly different terms to describe a major shortcoming of this model, but her point is clear:

> The production [process] model fails to capture what I see as the essence of policy making in political communities: the struggle over ideas. Ideas are a medium of exchange and a mode of influence even more powerful than money and votes and guns . . . . Ideas are at the center of all political conflict. Policymaking, in turn, is a constant struggle over the criteria for classification, the boundaries of categories, and the definition of ideals that guide the way people behave.[4]

For Stone, the heart of policymaking is how people interpret values such as equity, efficiency, security, and liberty as well as how they use these values in the identification of problems and possible solutions. For example, most people would agree that equality is a highly desirable goal for our society. Should we therefore guarantee an equal level of health care for all citizens? Or should the government simply offer the *opportunity* for health care through policies that help businesses hire more workers, who might then receive some health care coverage through their employers? Our answers to such questions reflect our preferences about the role of government in our lives. They also reflect the influence exerted on us by the government, the media, and other organized interests.

Many often point to the overt policy actors, such as lobbyists, legislators, executives, and members of the bureaucracy, to help understand the fate of a given policy initiative. A focus on core values and political ideology, however, helps bring the grassroots mobilization and cultural change pathways into sharper focus. In the 1970s, the environmentalist movement scored major legislative victories with the passage of laws such as the Clean Air Act and the Clean Water Act. This movement also helped mold the mind-set of today's more ecologically aware public, which takes for granted the recycling of glass and plastic bottles and many other formerly discarded items. The changes we have seen since that time are a powerful use of the cultural change pathway.

PATHWAYS | profile

Rachel Carson

Rachel Carson (1907–1964) was notable for many reasons. She was a woman who became a leading voice in the male-dominated scientific community of the 1950s and 1960s, and she won renown as the author of *Silent Spring*, a 1962 book laying out the science behind species destruction that became a best-seller among the general public. She was also a highly articulate and committed policy entrepreneur whose actions had a direct role in the founding of the modern environmental movement, in formulating major parts of government policy regulating air and water quality, and in the creation of the federal Environmental Protection Agency (EPA).

A marine biologist, Carson first achieved public recognition with her beautifully written book on the ocean and sea life, *The Sea Around Us*, published in 1951. In the late 1950s, she became aware of the deaths of large populations of songbirds and began researching possible causes. At that time, the federal government regulated pesticides and other potentially hazardous chemicals only casually, and pesticides were often misused and overused. Carson's findings pointed out that one chemical in particular, DDT, a highly effective pesticide and disinfecting agent, was responsible for a sizable decline in the songbird population. She argued that if the use of DDT continued to be unregulated, it would cause a massive decrease in—or even the extinction of—many bird species. The consequence would be unthinkable: a springtime without the sound of bird songs. When the nation's chemical companies, determined to head off federal regulation, attacked her findings and tried to discredit her ideas, Carson fought back. Shortly before her death in 1964, she testified before Congress as an expert on the effects of regulatory policy on the environment.

Rachel Carson's ability to shape public opinion and mobilize legislative and administrative action makes her a prime example of someone who mastered key aspects of the pathways of political action. ■

Ideas and Values in Public Policy

Practice Quiz

1. For political scientist Deborah Stone, the key to how public policy is formed is
   - **a.** the sequence that begins with political actors identifying a problem and ends with the implementation and assessment of a solution.
   - **b.** how people interpret principles such as liberty, equality, and efficiency.
   - **c.** who has political power and what their relation to the perceived problem is.
   - **d.** when, in the policy process cycle, political actors converge to address the perceived problem.
2. Which of the following is not a step in the policy formation process?
   - **a.** identifying the problem
   - **b.** setting the agenda
   - **c.** soliciting support from interest groups
   - **d.** implementing the solution
3. According to your text, which of the following underscores the importance of grassroots movements and the cultural change pathway?
   - **a.** success of the dramatic health care reform movement in the 1990s
   - **b.** increased environmental protection policies in recent years
   - **c.** the policy to end federal funding for embryonic stem cell research
   - **d.** Nothing. These pathways are never important in the policy process.
4. According to the authors, many struggle to find real differences between the terms *policy* and *politics* when in reality they both mean about the same thing.
   - **a.** true **b.** false

Answers: 1-b, 2-c, 3-b, 4-b.

Discussion Questions

1. Take a position on taxpayer-funded higher education and defend it; then, defend the opposite position. What did you learn from this exercise?
2. Can you think of any growing issue that is likely to draw the attention of policy makers in the near future?

What **YOU** can do!

The core American values of equality and freedom each have multiple definitions. Your preferences for public policy likely depend on your choice of definition for these values. Consider two other core "values" of American politics: individualism and democracy. Do these terms have multiple definitions? How might your definition of each of these terms affect your policy preferences?

■ **Policy Categories:** A way of classifying policies by their intended goal and means of carrying out that goal.

EXAMPLE: *Social welfare programs, such as Medicaid, can be categorized as redistributive, because they use tax dollars to provide benefits to a wide segment of the population.*

Types *of* Public Policy

(pages 510–511)

Why are there three main types of public policies?

So far, we've discussed public policy as a process that is influenced by many factors, especially the basic underlying beliefs people hold about politics and government. We've also seen where each of the five pathways of action can lead in both the substance and the process of public policy. Moving beyond these rather theoretical and somewhat philosophical ideas, how can we study public policy in order to compare one policy choice with another in a meaningful way? How can we find better solutions to ongoing problems?

For answers, we can look at all the attempts to solve problems in a particular issue area, a broad category such as the environment, which contains the problems of preserving old-growth forests and of reducing air pollution. Organizing policies by issue areas helps us make sense of the broad contours of both the problems and their possible solutions, but it is a rather blunt instrument for studying existing policies and figuring out how to devise new ones.

The Basic Functions of Government

A more sophisticated approach to studying public policy involves creating **policy categories**■ that classify what policies do and how they do it. To accomplish this, political scientists break down the basic functions of government into **distribution, regulation,** and **redistribution.**[5]

DISTRIBUTION A government *distributes* a society's resources, such as wealth, services, or other things of value, when it gives benefits to specific groups in that society. (When undertaken by a legislature, such distribution is often given the negative label "pork barrel" spending, because it seems designed to bring credit to the congressperson who proposed it.)

REGULATION *Regulation* takes place when a government uses legislative, military, or judicial power to stop an action by a person, organization, or group or when it mandates other behaviors or actions. For example, because of the actions of citizens like Rachel Carson, today's energy producers must meet federal regulations designed to limit air pollution. If an electric plant does not meet these requirements, its owners can be fined or punished in other ways.

Water and ice being distributed in Saucier, Mississippi, following Hurricane Katrina in 2005. ***—Do you think tangible benefits are the responsibility of federal, state or local government? Why or why not?***

REDISTRIBUTION *Redistribution* resembles distribution in many ways, but instead of a specific group benefiting from the actions of government, a much larger segment of society receives goods or services. Of course, redistributive policies mean that resources are taken from one part of society and then given to another. An example of a redistributive policy is taxing workers to fund social welfare programs for the poor. Because redistributive policies usually pit one social class against another, they are generally the most difficult policies to enact and implement.

Because all government policies can be placed in one of these three categories, this approach allows us to see the way governments operate and, with a bit more thought, how each of the pathways of political action can influence each of these government functions.

TANGIBLE OR SYMBOLIC BENEFITS Categorizing policies by the nature of their benefits is also useful. Policies themselves can produce either tangible benefits for the public or merely symbolic benefits.[6] A tangible benefit, like the federal government's policy of assistance for victims of hurricanes and other natural disasters, is something the recipients will experience in a material way—say, truckloads of clean drinking water and dry ice to preserve food. A symbolic benefit does not offer concrete, material results; it provides a theoretical solution to a problem. For example, the independent commission that investigated the intelligence failures leading up to the 9/11 terrorist attacks could not directly change the U.S. government's antiterrorism policy, nor could it restore life to the almost 3,000 people who perished in the attacks. And although a number of its suggestions have not been adopted by the federal government, the actions of the commission did communicate to the public that the government was working to solve this very difficult problem. The benefit—the feeling of security we may get from knowing that intelligent and dedicated people are trying to make us safer—may not help put food on the table, but it is still a benefit.

PATHWAYS | of change from around the world

In Scotland, the government has embarked on a strategy to help young people gain employment and help them to avoid or get past some of the more difficult problems that beset young people in any nation, including drug abuse and crime. The programs aimed at addressing these problems are collectively know as "youth work," and they have strong support among Scotland's young people. Some policymakers and educators are pushing to make these programs a part of the curricula for Scotland's schools; however, a number of organizations representing young people have been working to keep participation in these youth work programs voluntary. Their argument is that when the programs are compulsory and part of a structured educational setting, the most at-risk young people—school dropouts—will be left out of the benefits that youth work can offer. The executive branch of the Scottish government, the Scottish Executive, has asked for a review of the programs and wants to create a more structured relationship between schools and those who administer youth-based programs. The debate over the future of youth work is ongoing, and part of the discussion is coming from young people themselves, who are represented by the Scottish Youth Parliament, an organization supported in part by the Scottish Executive and designed as a way to have ongoing input from Scotland's younger citizens about a wide range of policy issues.

SOURCE: http://www.scottishyouthparliament.org.uk/Home.htm and http://www.cypnow.co.uk/Archive/login/760181/ ■

Types of Public Policy

Practice Quiz

1. When the government uses legislative, military, or judicial power to stop an action or when it mandates other behaviors or actions, it is engaged in
   a. distribution. **b.** regulation.
   c. redistribution. **d.** a and c

2. The independent commission that investigated the intelligence failures leading up to the 9/11 terrorist attacks is an example of
   a. a nontaxable benefit. **b.** a material benefit.
   c. a symbolic benefit. **d.** a tangible benefit.

3. Redistribution policies tend to pit one social class against another.
   a. true **b.** false

4. Distribution policies implemented by legislatures often are given the negative label of
   a. logrolling. **b.** nest-building.
   c. bundling. **d.** pork barrel spending.

Answers: 1-b, 2-c, 3-a, 4-d.

Discussion Questions

1. Taxation is one form of redistribution policy; what are some others? What objections could be raised about them?
2. Is military service a tangible benefit, a symbolic benefit, or both? Discuss the reasons for your response.

What **YOU** can do!

Consider the three functions of public policy: distribution, regulation, and redistribution. List one policy from each area that impacts your daily life in a tangible or symbolic manner. Think about whether the impact is the same for individuals of a different race, ethnicity, geographic region, age, gender, occupation, and socioeconomic status. How might this affect the types of policies that are made in the United States?

The Policy Formation Process

(pages 512–517)

Are all parts of the policy process equally open to political influence?

Much of what we know about public policy and how it is made can be related to the policy process model, which we discussed earlier in the chapter. Like all models, it is a generalization—a simplified representation of reality. It must exclude some complexities in order to make a very intricate process easier to understand.

Although scholars in the field of public policy disagree over some details, the major parts of the policy process model are generally thought to consist of the following five steps: (1) identifying the problem, (2) setting an agenda, (3) formulating policy, (4) legitimizing policy, and (5) implementing policy (see Figure 14.1). (Some versions of this model also include evaluating policy—analyzing how well a policy works to solve the problem it was intended to solve. Other versions of the model omit policy evaluation, regarding it as an administrative or academic pursuit and therefore too disconnected from politics to have a place in the model.)

Process implies separate actions that lead to a final goal. The process of making dinner might consist of peeling and chopping vegetables and slicing meat for a main course, then cooking the raw ingredients so that they come together in a way that produces a pleasing meal. The order of the steps is important in cooking, and doing things out of order may produce disastrous results. The process model offers a recipe for creating public policy.

This analogy between cooking and policymaking is faulty, however, because in many cases, the steps in the process do not directly flow one from the other. (Because of this, we can say that the policy process model is not truly *linear,* with all parts flowing in one direction. Nor is it truly *cyclical,* with each part necessarily following from the preceding part.)

Imagine, for example, a chef cooking the vegetables for a stew and then peeling them. In the policy process, such disjunctures are not necessarily the disasters they are in the kitchen. They may not be the best way to make policy, but what the policy process model does well is to tell us how policy was made—well, poorly, or indifferently. The fact that making public policy is a highly political endeavor—open to and resulting from the activity of political actors moving along the pathways of politics—helps explain why the model does not always reveal a nice, neat set of predictable

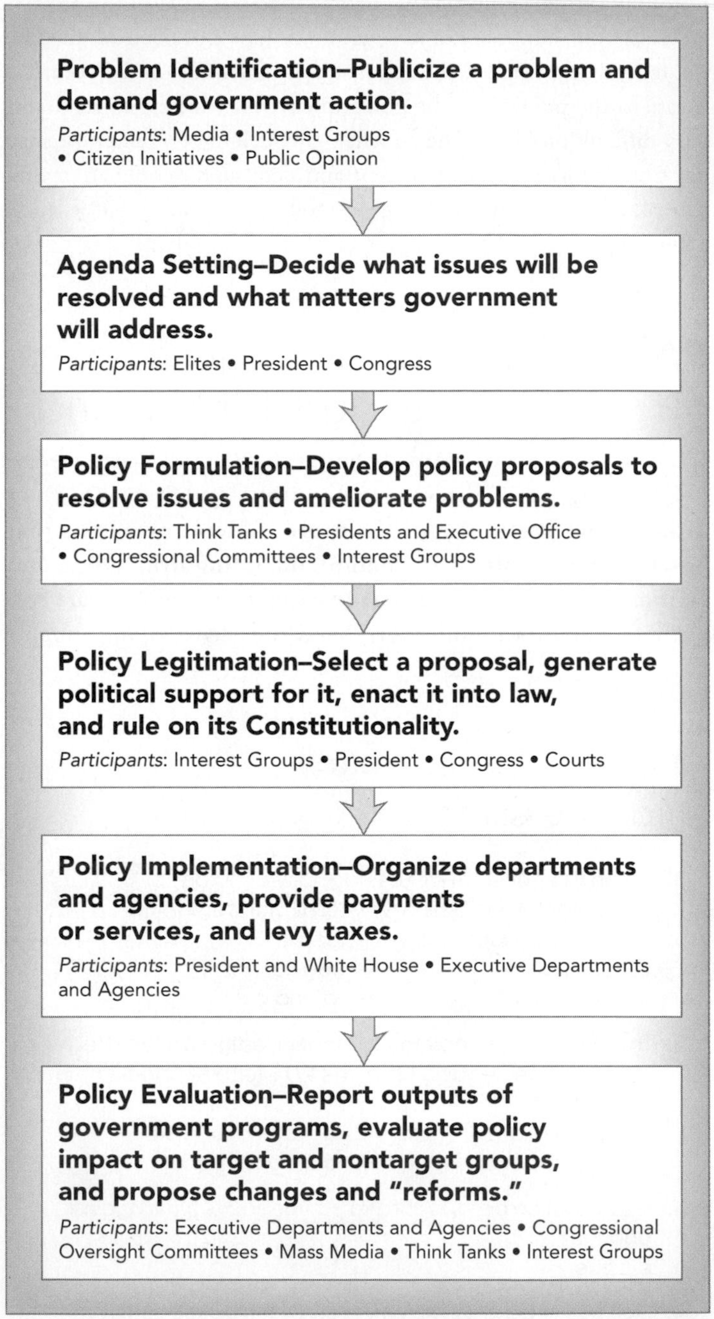
Problem Identification–Publicize a problem and demand government action.
Participants: Media • Interest Groups • Citizen Initiatives • Public Opinion
Agenda Setting–Decide what issues will be resolved and what matters government will address.
Participants: Elites • President • Congress
Policy Formulation–Develop policy proposals to resolve issues and ameliorate problems.
Participants: Think Tanks • Presidents and Executive Office • Congressional Committees • Interest Groups
Policy Legitimation–Select a proposal, generate political support for it, enact it into law, and rule on its Constitutionality.
Participants: Interest Groups • President • Congress • Courts
Policy Implementation–Organize departments and agencies, provide payments or services, and levy taxes.
Participants: President and White House • Executive Departments and Agencies
Policy Evaluation–Report outputs of government programs, evaluate policy impact on target and nontarget groups, and propose changes and "reforms."
Participants: Executive Departments and Agencies • Congressional Oversight Committees • Mass Media • Think Tanks • Interest Groups

FIGURE 14.1 | **The Policymaking Process**

The process model presents a picture of policymaking that begins with the identification of a problem and eventually moves to reexamination of the solution or solutions to that problem. Real-world policymaking is not always so orderly. It may begin at some point other than the identification of a problem.

President Reagan signs legislation that forced states to either impose a 21-year-old drinking age or lose federal aid. ***—Do you think policymakers should reconsider these views?***

■ **Institutional Agenda:** The set of problems that governmental decision makers are actively working to solve.

EXAMPLE: *Bills introduced into Congress are part of the federal government's institutional agenda.*

steps. Political actors can affect the process at every stage, and sometimes, they cause an unexpected progression of phases or the elimination of phases. This is a point worth keeping in mind as you read about each of the five major parts of the policy process model.

Identifying the Problem

Just how do we know that a problem exists? There is no easy answer, which is true of many of the issues that confront policymakers. Scholars of public policy have supplied few guidelines for identifying problems. Determining whether an issue is a problem depends for the most part on who is advocating each position. Well-organized groups with the resources of money, larger memberships, and connections are more likely to gain access to decision makers to persuade them to see things their way. Disorganized collections of people, even those representing very large segments of the population, may not sway decision makers simply because their message is not as well focused. There is a major debate within the social sciences about this question: To whom do the policymakers listen? Social scientists calling themselves **pluralists** argue that our system of open government, with its multiple points of access to policymakers, allows people without resources like money and connections to still have their voices heard.[7] Others argue that policymaking is really driven by elitism—that only people with power and money will get access to the decision makers.[8]

Without a doubt, some problems simply cry out for action. Terrorism on American soil crystallized in an unforgettable display of violence and brutality on September 11, 2001. Such events, including many of far lesser magnitude, are known as **focusing events,** because they bring a problem to the attention of both the public and policymakers. At least at first, there is no debate about the existence of a problem, and the event serves as a **trigger mechanism**—a means of propelling an established problem on to the next stage of the policy process, setting an agenda.[9]

Setting an Agenda

At some point in your life, you have probably attended at least one meeting of a school club, a town planning board, or some other formal gathering. To make good use of time and provide structure, well-organized meetings are always planned around an *agenda*—a list of issues and ideas up for discussion or actions to be undertaken. Of course, this is probably old news to you, but what you may not have thought about is the power available to the individuals who set the agenda. Many groups and organizations use rules that exclude or severely limit any action on—or even discussion of—items not listed on the agenda. The ability to exclude an item from the agenda, for whatever reason, is a powerful way to control what government does.[10]

Let's take an example from American politics. In the 1950s and 1960s, one of the Senate's most powerful members, Georgia's Richard Russell, was instrumental in keeping civil rights policy off the nation's agenda by declaring there was no problem with racial segregation, because segregation worked![11]

The process of crafting a solution—even to shockingly obvious problems, such as the racial segregation of the 1950s—cannot begin until formal decision makers, generally those who hold positions of governmental authority, actually place the problem on the nation's formal or **institutional agenda**■.[12] For example, the flood of legislation introduced in Congress after 9/11 gave tangible proof that our national legislators now believed the problem of terrorism to be urgent enough to require an immediate solution. There had been terrorism on U.S. soil before 9/11, of course. The underground parking garage of the World Trade Center had been bombed in 1993 (luckily with little loss of life). Yet awareness and concern do not always transport a problem onto the institutional agenda. Often, a focusing event is needed to provide this push. Think of the issue of global warming today. Many scientists and citizens are deeply concerned about it, yet no focusing event seems to have occurred—so far. (Although it's too early to know for sure, some suspect that Al Gore's book and movie, *An Inconvenient Truth,* may prove to be a focusing event.)

Like problem identification, agenda setting in the absence of a major crisis is largely determined by the organization and resources of individuals and coordinated interests. People and groups who can best articulate their position or who have what it takes to gain access to policymakers (such as money for reelection campaigns, the support of group members, or well-connected lobbyists) will usually succeed in getting their problem on the agenda.

Once a problem is on the agenda, how do you keep it there? There is no guarantee that policymakers will consistently treat an issue as a high priority, year in and year out. Anthony Downs has created a valuable way of thinking about the nature of agenda items that he calls the **issue-attention cycle.**[13] Downs argues that some issues are more likely to remain on the formal agenda, just as others are doomed to fade away. Even issues that affect small slices of the population, which lack political, economic, or social clout, or that are difficult to address may first grab lots of attention. Usually, however, they fall off the agenda because of the cost and inconvenience associated with solving them or the inability of the affected parties to keep the decision makers' attention. For example, a series of highly publicized events in the 1960s, including a badly polluted river actually catching fire, propelled the state of our environment onto the nation's policy agenda. Although pollution and other environmental issues have not completely disappeared from that agenda, they did get bumped down the list of priorities once people learned of the difficulties associated with the proposed solutions to overconsumption of fossil fuels—such as giving up their big, gas-guzzling cars. Downs's thoughts about agenda setting remind us that multiple pathways shape this and all phases of the policy process.

Formulating and Legitimizing Policy

Clearly, many actors both inside and outside government can affect the agenda-setting process. Once a problem makes it onto the agenda, however, the political pathways haven't reached their end. In fact, the next phase of the policymaking process, formulation, is as politically driven as agenda setting—if not more so.

Formulating policy means crafting solutions to identified problems. Of course, how you define the problem will frame the acceptable solutions. Was the terrorist attack on 9/11 a crime against U.S. citizens and property, or was it an act of war? If your answer, like that of the Bush administration, is that 9/11 was an act of war, then legal actions (such as capturing those who planned and funded the attacks, trying them in court, and possibly, sentencing them to death) won't do. If your answer is that 9/11 was a crime, then the solution is simply to track down the "bad guys" and bring them to justice.

Solutions can come in many forms. Clearly, the **laws** passed by legislatures, like those passed by Congress, are attempts to solve problems. (The legislative process itself, including the introduction of bills, hearings, and floor debates, are all parts of formulating public policy: At each of these stages, the solution can change and evolve.) When presidents issue executive orders directing the federal government to do—or to stop doing—various things, they are also engaging in problem solving. The decisions made by courts, especially the U.S. Supreme Court, are policies, because other branches of government and the nation's citizens are bound by these decisions as though they were laws passed by Congress. When Congress passes legislation that delegates congressional lawmaking authority for specific problem-solving purposes, the actions of the federal government's departments and agencies are also considered laws.

Citizens' ability to affect the formulation of policy is also crucial to the legitimacy and stability of any system of government. Openness and rules may be meaningless if the public does not believe it can influence the solutions that are being crafted to solve problems. If the public beats its fists on the doors of the Congress by lobbying and mobilizing grassroots public relations campaigns only to have the House and Senate ignore these concerns, the final result will likely be a law that is mocked as illegitimate. This is why most policymakers take great pains to follow the rules of their institutions and, where practical, make room for public involvement. Back in the late seventeenth century, the great political thinker John Locke, who had a major influence on the framers of our Constitution, argued that the people enter into a contract with government by giving their consent to be governed. Locke's argument is still valid: On that consent rests our belief in the legitimacy of the entire process of governing, including the formulation of policy.

Implementing Policy

Once policies have been created, someone actually has to do something with them. As its name implies, the executive branch of government is charged with executing or implementing the policies made by a legislature, the courts, or the executive branch itself—as in the executive orders issued by presidents and the rules crafted by departments and agencies. The framers of our system divided the functions of government in order to lessen the chance it might take away the people's liberty. The result is that policy implementation is largely done by the executive branch; however, the other two branches also influence how the policies they make are carried out. Add to this the openness of the government to citizen activity, and a picture emerges of implementation as a highly political process.

Discretion: The power to apply policy in ways that fit particular circumstances.

SIGNIFICANCE: *Along with rule-making authority, discretion is one of the major sources of power for the executive branch.*

Garbage Can Model: A way of thinking about policymaking as an unordered mix of problems and solutions.

SIGNIFICANCE: *Because solutions can exist without problems, the garbage can model underscores how powerful political actors may be waiting to apply their preferred resolution to as-yet-unidentified problems.*

This may seem like simple common sense, but for a long time, political scientists and other scholars of public policy did not see the links between politics and implementation. In fact, one branch of political science focuses on *public administration* as distinct from *public policy*. This view of a policy-administration divide may have been based on a desire to separate the executers of policy from outside pressure so that good policy would not be subverted by biased implementation. This sounds like a reasonable goal, and if we take this idea to a more everyday level, its worth becomes even more apparent.

Many of us, when driving above the speed limit, have passed a police officer yet received no ticket. Clearly, the law—a policy setting a maximum speed limit—was broken. What explains the lack of a ticket in this case is the **discretion** given to the individuals who implement policy. Perhaps going a few miles over the speed limit is acceptable for that stretch of road at that time of the day with that level of traffic and that weather. A change in one of these circumstances might mean getting a ticket. Because formulating a law for each stretch of highway, while factoring in things such as road conditions and weather, would be nearly impossible, legislatures often write laws with the presumption that the executive branch will use reasonable discretion in applying them. The key word in this presumption is *reasonable*. What if a police officer pulled over all drivers exceeding the speed limit by *any* amount, but only if they sported a "McCain" bumper sticker? Or what if this officer gave speeding tickets only to African Americans? We would rightfully argue that this kind of law enforcement was unjust and an unreasonable exercise of discretion. These are dramatic examples of prejudice (which, unfortunately, sometimes do occur), but there are other, more subtle ways in which discretion is used that are out of step with the intent of policy and demonstrate the political aspect of implementation. Knowing this, legislators must be especially attuned to the implementation process.

Because all democratic legislatures, including the U.S. Congress, are bodies in which majorities are needed to pass laws, legislation is often written in ways designed to attract wide support among the diverse membership. One way to do this is to write a vaguely worded policy that allows legislators to read their own interests as well as the interests of their constituents into the proposal. Another reason for the lack of specificity in legislative proposals is the highly scientific and technical expertise required. Members of Congress are often generalists, knowing a little about many things but lacking deep knowledge about most things. It therefore makes a lot of sense for Congress to give general directions to an executive agency or department and not go into specific details.

"So who checks to see that laws are well written and carried out?"

—Student Question

As a result of the need for vaguely worded policy and the need to rely on the executive branch for expert formulation of the details and implementation, legislators cannot simply walk away from a policy once it is in the implementation phase. Legislatures typically review policy implementation through oversight. Legislative oversight takes two forms, reauthorization and investigation. Often, measures passed by Congress expire after a certain amount of time. **Reauthorization** gives legislators feedback about how—and how effectively—the policy is being carried out. If the results are unsatisfactory, Congress can influence the executive branch to implement the policy more effectively by threatening to cut off or reduce funding. **Investigation** is where Congress calls officials of the executive branch before its committees to answer questions about alleged problems with implementation. Like reauthorization, investigations can result in measures designed to change the executive branch's implementation of policy. Sometimes, as Table 14.1 on page 516 demonstrates, congressional investigations can be dramatic and far-reaching.

Alternative Views of the Policy Formation Process

So far, we have traced the policy process model from identifying the problem to setting the agenda to formulating and implementing the policy designed to fix the problem. Yet people who study public policy have documented considerable variations. Some scholars think of policymaking by using the so-called **garbage can model**, which depicts problems, solutions, actors, and other parts of the policymaking universe jumbled together, much as trash builds up in a garbage can.[14] In this model, no clear order of steps dictates what happens first or next. Solutions can exist without problems, just as easily as problems can exist without solutions.

For example, in the 1990s, when the nation seemed flush with oil and gasoline prices were low, there were people (whom some called **policy entrepreneurs**)[15] pushing for policies that would support the development of hybrid cars. The entrepreneurs were advocating a solution to a problem that did not yet exist or could only be glimpsed on the horizon. In the

Policy Entrepreneurs: Advocates of particular solutions to problems.

EXAMPLE: *As recently as 2001, average gasoline prices were around $1.50, and there was little discussion of the need for alternative fuels, such as bio-diesel or ethanol. However, advocates for these fuels were making their case for the development and funding of programs to promote the use of gasoline alternatives.*

TABLE 14.1 | Major Senate Investigations in Recent Decades

1973–1974: Select Committee on Presidential Campaign Activities (Watergate Committee) Investigation of possible corruption in the 1972 presidential election campaign
1987–1989: Select Committee on Secret Military Assistance to Iran and the Nicaraguan Opposition (Iran–Contra Hearings) Investigation into alleged covert sales of military equipment to Iran and diversion of the proceeds to aid the Nicaraguan Contra rebels
1991–1993: Select Committee on POW/MIA Affairs Investigation into the possibility that some unaccounted-for American servicemen might have survived in captivity even after POW repatriations at the conclusion of World War II, the Korean War, Cold War incidents, and particularly, the war in Vietnam
1995–1996: Special Committee to Investigate Whitewater Development Corporation and Related Matters (Whitewater Committee) Investigation into the way White House officials handled documents in the office of White House Deputy Counsel Vincent Foster after his death; matters related to actions by the White House or the Resolution Trust Corporation in handling the Madison Guarantee Savings and Loan Association or Whitewater Development Corporation; and other related matters
1997–1998: Committee on Governmental Affairs Investigation of 1996 Election Campaign Investigation into illegal or improper activities in connection with the 1996 federal election campaign
2002: Joint Inquiry into Intelligence Community Activities Before and After the Terrorist Attacks of September 11, 2001 Investigation into the intelligence community's activities before and after the terrorist attacks of September 11, 2001, by the U.S. Senate Select Committee on Intelligence and U.S. House Permanent Select Committee on Intelligence
SOURCE: http://www.senate.gov/reference/reference_index_subjects/Investigations_vrd.htm

garbage can model, all the elements of public policy float together, and the solving of problems—if it happens at all—is often based on the unintended mix of ideas and players, not on a set of linear steps.

A refinement of the garbage can approach involves what the political scientist John Kingdon describes as policy windows and streams. He envisions problems, solutions, and political factors (such as elections and interest group campaigns) as three separate streams that flow at the same time but often do not merge with one another. Like the garbage can model, these streams are not linear steps or cyclical phases but rather factors that exist at the same time. When the three streams can be brought together in the proper combination, the policy process goes to work. To bring the streams together, however, an opportunity or "policy window" must open.[16] A national crisis is one such policy window. The 9/11 terrorist attacks opened the window for Congress to pass a sweeping set of measures, known as the USA PATRIOT Act, which raised the permissible level of government surveillance of the public considerably (see Figure 14.2). Without the events of 9/11, it is highly unlikely that Congress would have considered such a dramatic policy shift.

These alternative approaches do not attempt to supplant the process model and its phases. Rather, they offer a way to use the process model more realistically and give us a better sense of how the pathways of political action link up with real-world policymaking.

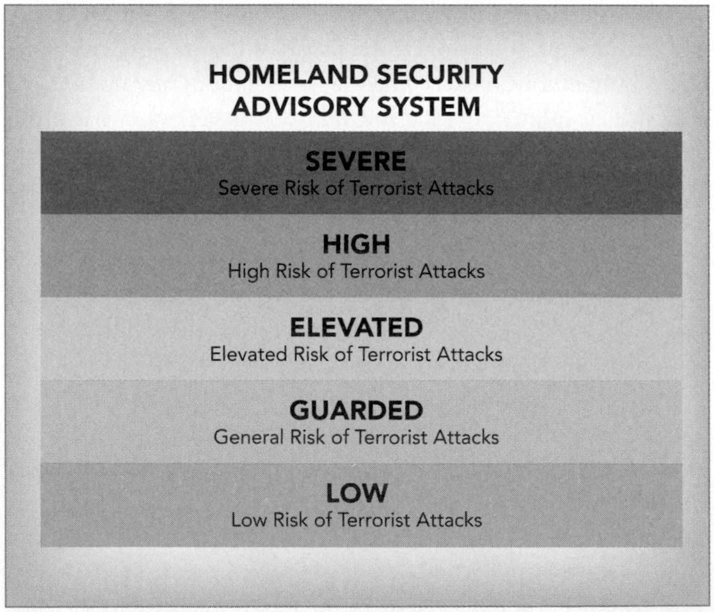

FIGURE 14.2 | The Homeland Security Advisory System

The Department of Homeland Security (DHS) is one of many parts of the federal government tasked with implementing the USA PATRIOT Act. One of the more well-known actions taken by DHS in the wake of 9/11 has been to issue advisories about the level of terrorist threat by way of a color-coded graph. ***—Should the DHS create a terrorism warning system along the lines of the "Amber Alert" systems that many states and localities now have in place for abducted or missing children?***

STUDENT | PROFILE

Jonathan Fantini Porter's political activism stems from his disagreement with the foreign policy of the United States in Iraq. The 22-year-old Georgetown University student is the founder of the Collegiate Forum, a group that champions progressive political causes and shares information and viewpoints among students across the globe. Jonathan comes from a politically active family and notes that the mode of political participation has changed a great deal from his parents' early activist years. Today, technological advances have created a new set of opportunities for mobilization and organization of activists. The proliferation of social networking sites, such as Facebook and MySpace, have changed the way students think about activism. These advances have also changed their access to information and eased the barriers to participation. Jonathan speaks a truism for any generation when he encourages students to take a break from their studies, see what is going on in the world around them, and take action on those issues they feel need attention.

SOURCE: http://www.24-7pressrelease.com/press-release-rss/wall-street-journal-profiles-student-activistrun-policy-think-tank-the-collegiate-forum-25643.php ■

The Policy Formation Process

Practice Quiz

1. The policy process model is
   - **a.** linear.
   - **b.** not always linear.
   - **c.** cyclical.
   - **d.** never cyclical.
2. Which of the following would be the most likely example of a focusing event?
   - **a.** finding illegal immigrants working at a restaurant in California
   - **b.** a 5-percent increase in handgun fatalities in this country in 2007
   - **c.** the federal response to Hurricane Katrina
   - **d.** 100-degree weather on the same day in all 48 states in the continental United States
3. Which of the following is NOT a policy formulation?
   - **a.** the independent, bipartisan 9/11 commission
   - **b.** the No Child Left Behind law
   - **c.** any executive order
   - **d.** *Roe* v. *Wade*
4. The courts exercise a form of oversight of policy implementation.
   - **a.** true
   - **b.** false

Answers: 1-b, 2-c, 3-a, 4-b.

Discussion Questions

1. What sort of focusing events would be likely trigger mechanisms for the general public? What sort would only attract the attention of activist groups?
2. Why is Hurricane Katrina a good example of Downs's issue-attention cycle?

What **YOU** can do!

How long do policy problems/debates stay on the policy agenda? Using newspapers, Web sites, magazines, and television news, follow a policy issue that is currently under debate. Be sure to note how many times the policy is mentioned each day. How long did the issue stay in the public's attention? Did the issue leave the public agenda because it had been resolved or for some other reason?

The Basics *of* Economic Policy (pages 518–523)

How is economic policy regulated in the United States?

It can be argued that government economic policy has a more profound impact on the quality of our democracy and personal well-being than any other type of government action. In general, policies either regulate economic processes and institutions, such as loans and the mortgage industry, or they distribute or redistribute the wealth of our society, usually by taxation. The degree of power that is exerted on us by a government is an obvious measure of how much freedom exists in a society. Indeed, a major divide in our nation concerns different notions of freedom: Some people view most actions by government as a loss of freedom for the citizens, whereas others see government action creating the ability for citizens to enhance their well-being. Another divide focuses on equality. One perspective focuses on the outcomes each citizen reaches in the quest for fundamental objectives, such as a good education, quality health care, and social and political rights; others would perceive equality when the opportunity to reach these goals is in place. When government regulates or fails to regulate the mortgage industry, when it drafts legislation to use tax dollars to bail out lenders who made unwise loans, or when it considers using a federal program to help those who are buried in debt because of easy credit, government affects all of us. We are often consumers of or investors in the things that are made and sold, and we are always citizens who pay taxes and live in a nation that has its democracy shaped by the expectations that drive policy decisions.

The Big Five: Measuring Economic Performance

When economists gauge the economy's performance, they usually focus on five figures: (1) inflation, (2) unemployment, (3) gross domestic product, (4) the balance of trade, and (5) the budget deficit or surplus. These measures matter to politicians as well. A healthy economy helps incumbents stay in office. In fact, politicians are often more willing to make potentially painful economic decisions early in the political cycle—right after an election—in hopes the actions will produce long-term benefits that will show up before the next election. (As the first President Bush and President Carter will tell you, however, your timing has to be right.) The first two measures in particular seem to resonate with the voting public. Let's examine all of them in turn.

INFLATION **Inflation** measures the rate at which prices increase. The classic definition of inflation is "too many dollars chasing too few goods." Inflation is bad. High inflation rates can undermine and distort all other aspects of the economy. When inflation is out of control, it can wipe out the middle class' savings, devalue the dollar, and cause immense social and political unrest. The inflation rate is measured by the **Consumer Price Index (CPI),** a figure computed by the Department of Labor. The CPI is calculated at regular intervals and is based on the changing costs of a specified "market basket" of goods and services. The Federal Reserve Board, or the Fed, must also guard against **deflation**—dropping prices. Deflation might sound good, but falling prices discourage spending: If prices are going down, consumers refuse to spend today in hopes of paying less tomorrow. Consumers who sit on their wallets are not engaging in the kind of economic activity that creates jobs and a vibrant economy. Eroding prices mean eroding jobs. The last significant episode of deflation in American history occurred during the Great Depression.

One of the most significant issues that our nation has confronted in over a century is the home foreclosure crisis. This issue, along with the "Wall Street Bailout Plan," dominated the 2008 presidential election.

UNEMPLOYMENT The **unemployment rate** measures the percentage of Americans who are out of work. It is not a perfect measure, both because it accounts only for people who identify themselves as actively seeking work and because sampling techniques are used in calculating it. Those who have given up looking for jobs are not counted, either as employed or unemployed—they are simply regarded as outside the workforce. The several million "undocumented" workers and those involved in the illegal or "underground" economy are also left out. Unemployment therefore is often understated in particular geographic areas or during periods of great poverty. A "good" unemployment rate is thought to be around 5 percent. (One-hundred percent employment would be impossible, because a certain number of people are always between jobs or just entering the workforce.) In the 1980s, many economists considered 5 percent to be full employment, only to have unemployment drop below that figure in the late 1990s and again in 2005 and 2006.

GROSS DOMESTIC PRODUCT The **gross domestic product (GDP)** is the value of all the goods and services produced in the United States. GDP measures the size of the American economy. Generally, economic growth is good. Overly rapid economic growth, however, can be harmful, because it can feed inflation. Here is where the Fed steps in to try to curb runaway growth before inflation can gain a foothold. A good growth target for GDP is between 3 and 4 percent. The growth rate commonly reported in the media is the "real GDP" rate—that is GDP adjusted to account for the effects of the CPI so that actual economic growth does not falsely include the rate of inflation.

BALANCE OF TRADE The **balance of trade** measures the difference between imports and exports. A positive balance means that a nation has a trade surplus—it exports more goods than it imports. A negative balance of trade means a trade deficit—the country imports more goods than it exports. The United States has been running a significant trade deficit for years. The same American consumers who express their concerns about the outsourcing of American jobs also love to buy cheap imported goods. We'll talk more about trade later, because it is a complex political and economic issue.

THE BUDGET DEFICIT A major concern for the U.S. economy has been the budget deficit and the rising national debt. The **budget deficit** is the amount by which, in a given year, government spending exceeds government revenue. (The rare circumstance when revenue outstrips expenditures is called a **budget surplus;** see Figure 14.3.) The net sum of the budget deficit minus the surplus is the **national debt,** or the amount that the government owes. With the exception of the 4 years between 1998 and 2001, the United States has run a budget deficit every year since 1970. That's added up to a national debt of about $10.6 trillion. When the nation went into an economic crisis in the fall of 2008, the Congress and President Bush got together a $700 billion bailout program to shore up our financial institutions. The spending for the bailout package also moved Congress and the President to increase the amount the nation can legally borrow to cover our debts from $10.4 billion to $11.3 billion. The national debt must be financed through money that is

FIGURE 14.3 | **Federal Deficits and Surpluses**

The federal government has operated with budget deficits for most of the past 25 years. The few years of budget surpluses were caused by a thriving economy in the late 1990s. The return to budget deficits came after 9/11, when the federal government cut taxes and then soon initiated expensive military actions in Afghanistan and Iraq and also experienced rising costs in entitlement programs.
Source: 2006 Statistical Abstract of the U.S. http://www.census.gov/compendia/statab/tables/0650459. Updated to 2007.

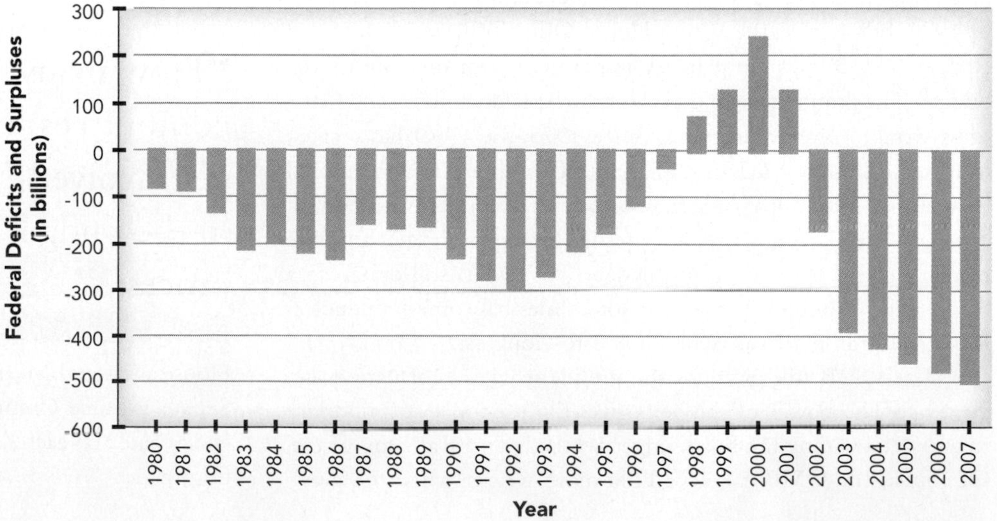

COMPARATIVE **Comparing Economic Policy**

CONNECT THE LINK
(Chapter **6**, pages **224–227**) Because it has the constitutional prerogative to start all tax legislation, the House Ways and Means Committee has an institutional policymaking advantage over its counterpart in the Senate.

borrowed—with interest—both at home and abroad, which makes balancing the budget that much harder with each passing year. With Republicans no longer controlling both Congress and the White House, the politics of deficit financing have taken an interesting turn. With the budget shortfalls of recent years, many Republicans, long-time deficit hawks (opponents of increasing the deficit), have turned into deficit doves (supporters of increasing the deficit), even as an increasingly vocal faction of the Republican Party has sounded the alarm.

U.S. Senate Finance Committee Chairman Max Baucus (left) and Ranking Member Chuck Grassley (right) share a private comment. The Senate Finance Committee has a great deal of jurisdiction over tax policy and other issues at the core of the nation's economy.

Types of Economic Policy

There are two primary types of economic policy: fiscal and monetary. Fiscal policy is the taxing and spending decisions enacted by Congress in cooperation with the president. Monetary policy concerns the money supply and is managed by the independent Federal Reserve Board ("the Fed"). Both fiscal and monetary policy can affect growth, employment, and inflation. Often, the goals of fiscal and monetary policy clash because the Fed, the president, and Congress do not always share the same objectives.

FISCAL POLICY The game of politics is all about deciding who gets what. Part of the answer to that question involves deciding who pays for what. That is what **fiscal policy**—the politics of taxing and spending—is all about. With the federal budget now at $3.1 trillion, there is a lot of money up for grabs.

Budgets are created through interactions between Congress and the president, but there are several other major actors in the realm of fiscal policy, the most significant of which is the **Congressional Budget Office (CBO).** A research arm of Congress, the CBO was created by the Budget and Impoundment Act of 1974. Before this, the White House Office of Management and Budget (OMB) had the primary responsibility for drawing up the budget. The president would present the basic document, and Congress would make adjustments. Since 1975, the CBO has created long-term budget outlooks, analyses of the president's proposed budget, and fiscal impact statements for every bill that comes out of a congressional committee. As a result, Congress has become the primary player in creating the budget. The OMB still draws up a budget, and although that budget sometimes has some influence, it is often "dead on arrival" when it gets to Congress.

The OMB still provides the president with information and guidance. The power of the veto gives the president an important role in determining the final budget, which is always a compromise. Of course, the OMB carries a little more weight when the presidency and Congress are both controlled by the same party. Since 1946, the president has also had the "help" of the Council of Economic Advisers (CEA), which was created by Congress back when the initial budget document was primarily the chief executive's responsibility in order to help the White House make budget decisions. The CEA's three members are usually leading academic economists who are appointed by the president. Some presidents, notably John F. Kennedy, have relied heavily on the CEA; others, such as Ronald Reagan, have all but ignored it.

As you saw earlier (LINK Chapter 6, pages 224–227), committees do the real work of Congress. Although the Constitution requires that all revenue bills originate in the House, the 436 House members sitting together could never write a budget. Instead, appropriations and tax bills are products of committees in the Senate and the House. Each chamber has an appropriations committee, which has primary responsibility for deciding where federal money should be spent. The House Ways and Means Committee is responsible for tax bills; the Senate Finance Committee serves as its counterpart. The House and Senate also each have budget committees, which review the fiscal process.

> "How many committees get involved in the budget process?"
> —Student Question

SIMULATION Making Economic Policy

VISUAL LITERACY Evaluating Federal Spending and Economic Policy

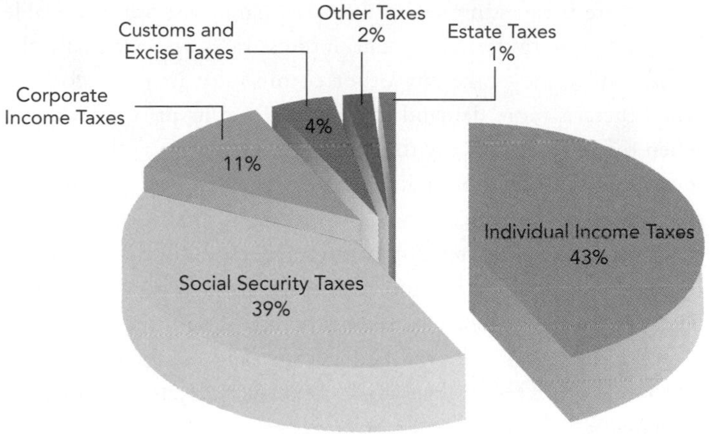

FIGURE 14.4 | **The Federal Revenue Budget**

Federal government revenue comes primarily from individual income tax and payroll taxes for Social Security and Medicare. How can an increase in the unemployment rate affect tax revenues?

Figuring out how to spend federal money is an immensely important task, as you can imagine. A second big question confronts revenue—how the government raises money (see Figure 14.4). No one likes paying taxes, but the government needs a source of revenue to fund even the most minimal services. Should the wealthy be taxed at a higher rate—a more progressive rate—in order to provide more services for the poor? Critics argue that the current economic system is unfair. They say that the disparity between rich and poor is too wide. Despite significant gains in real GDP (GDP after factoring out inflation), most real-wage increases have gone to the wealthiest Americans. Would a more progressive tax system help reverse that trend, or would it discourage the wealthy from putting forth the extra effort and productive investments that lead to gains in productivity? A related question is this: Does fairness matter as much as efficiency? Should the government try to foster an economic system that generates revenue while boosting the overall economy, or is it preferable to sacrifice growth for equity? Many Americans disagree about the answers.

MONETARY POLICY In the simplest terms, **monetary policy** involves managing the supply of money in circulation within the United States. It is essential to strike a balance. Too much money coursing through the economy will be inflationary—remember the definition of inflation as "too much money chasing too few goods." Too little money will stifle economic growth. Keeping the balance right by managing monetary policy is the job of the Federal Reserve Board of Governors and its Federal Open Market Committee.

Created in 1913 by an act of Congress, the **Federal Reserve System (the Fed)** is our nation's independent central bank. (In most other Western nations, the central bank is controlled by the national government.) Although it is accountable to

The tools used by the Secretary of the Treasury and the Chairman of the Federal Reserve to regulate and influence the nation's economy are often difficult to employ with precision. In the wake of the credit crisis that started in the fall of 2008, Secretary Paulson was given discretion over a large pool of money for propping up the nation's lending institutions. The Fed's lowering of interest rates was an additional action designed to free up credit and forestall a more serious economic decline.

CONNECT THE LINK
(Chapter **6**, pages **238–239**) The Emergency Economic Stabilization Act of 2008, the so-called "Wall Street Bailout Bill," is discussed. Do you agree with the way the government responded to the financial crisis that boiled over in the fall of 2008?

Former Federal Reserve Chairman Alan Greenspan was very effective in communicating with the business community in ways that generally helped to avoid inflation and other problems. Thus he was appointed and reappointed by both Republican and Democratic presidents. Appearing before the House Oversight and Reform Committee in October 2008, Greenspan said, "We are in the midst of a once-in-a century credit tsunami." When asked if he had made any mistakes during his tenure as Federal Reserve chairman that may have contributed to the mortgage crisis, Greenspan admitted it was a mistake to presume that lenders themselves were more capable than regulators of protecting their finances.

Congress, the Fed is free from political pressure because of the way it is structured. The seven members of its Board of Governors are appointed by the president of the United States, but they hold staggered 14-year terms. This makes it difficult for any president or for Congress to exert too much influence over its policies. Moreover, there are 12 regional federal reserve banks within the Fed, each of which selects its own president, subject to approval by the Board of Governors. Although the presidents' terms are 5 years, most are reappointed. This further shields the Fed from political pressure.

The Fed, along with the U.S. Treasury, faced a huge challenge in the fall of 2008 as they attempted to deal with the fallout of the financial crisis that froze credit markets and sent stocks on a wild up and down ride. The tools used by the Federal Reserve to regulate and influence the nation's economy are often difficult to employ with precision. Any actions taken to address the crisis may not yeild immediate results or may produce unintended consequences. (LINK Chapter 6, pages 238–239).

The Fed has several tools to manipulate monetary policy. The federal funds rate is a market-driven interest rate that banks charge one another for short-term (often overnight) loans. Rates drop when there is excess money in the system; they rise when available loan money is restricted. In fact, interest rates are essentially the "price" of money. Like any other commodity, its price goes up when there is more demand than supply, and its price goes down when there is more supply than demand. Another way the Fed can intervene is through the discount rate. This is the interest rate that the Fed charges its member banks for loans. The discount rate is generally about 0.1 percent above the federal funds rate. Although the discount rate does not directly set the prime rate, the rate that banks charge their best customers, there is significant correlation between the two. Finally, the Fed can buy and sell foreign currencies in an effort to stabilize world financial markets and currency exchange rates. Although this instrument is generally not used to affect the U.S. money supply, it is sometimes used to adjust the value of the dollar relative to other currencies.

The most significant of these tools are open-market operations and the discount rate. True monetarists favor creating a target money supply and manipulating policy to achieve that goal. Other economists, with less strictly monetarist views, choose different targets to keep inflation under control.

Monetary and fiscal policies don't always work together. Fiscal actions, taken by politicians, tend to inflate the economy. Elected officials are continually trying to serve their constituents and get through the next election cycle; their goal is to keep the economy going until their jobs are secured. The monetary policies of the Fed, by contrast, are focused on long-term economic interests. Former Fed Chairman Greenspan voiced concerns about rising budget deficits, and Congress, for its part, has often criticized the Fed for keeping too tight a rein on the money supply. Some members of Congress have occasionally gone so far as to threaten the Fed's independence.

When push comes to shove, however, the Fed has more weapons in its arsenal than Congress does. By tightening the money supply sufficiently, it can significantly reduce the inflationary aspects of tax cuts or increased government spending. A concerted effort by the Fed could even put pressure on Congress to bring the debt problem under control. By tightening the money supply and driving up interest rates, the Fed could make deficit financing so expensive that it becomes a big issue sooner rather than later.

Economic Policy and Democracy

The underpinnings of our democracy both shape and are shaped by the making and implementation of economic policy. When some groups of people or institutions gain wealth, they often gain political influence as a result. At the same time, other groups or institutions may have to give up or miss out on benefits that come with the loss of favorable policy decisions, and they may have diminished political clout, too. Who gets what, when, and how are questions we have asked before in this book, because they speak to the essential characteristic of our democracy. The choices made by policymakers about financial and monetary matters clearly reflect the value choices that form the answers to these questions.

The Basics of Economic Policy

Practice Quiz

1. What are the five figures that economists use to measure economic performance?
   - **a.** inflation, interest rate, income tax rate, unemployment, and gross domestic product
   - **b.** gross domestic product, balance of trade, annual percentage rate, federal funds rate, and the budget deficit or surplus
   - **c.** inflation, unemployment, gross domestic product, the balance of trade, and the budget deficit or surplus
   - **d.** prime rate, sales tax rate, inflation, gross domestic product, and unemployment
2. Monetary policy is the taxing and spending decisions enacted by Congress in cooperation with the President.
   - **a.** true
   - **b.** false
3. It is accurate to state that in terms of partisan politics, the Federal Reserve Board is
   - **a.** liberal
   - **b.** independent
   - **c.** conservative
   - **d.** aligned with the sitting president's politics
4. Congress has more power to influence fiscal and monetary realities in the United States than the Fed does.
   - **a.** true
   - **b.** false

Answers: 1-c, 2-b, 3-b, 4-b.

Discussion Questions

1. Which of the five economic factors can be influenced by political action? Give some recent examples.
2. Describe some ways in which the Federal Reserve Board can manipulate economic performance using the policies discussed in this section.

What **YOU** can do!

Review the Federal Reserve Board's monetary policy (**http://www.federalreserve.gov**) by finding the current and historical reserve ratio, federal funds rate, discount rate, and prime rate. Compare and contrast trends for these rates. Pay special attention to whether some rates undergo more radical changes than others.

TIMELINE The Evolution of Foreign Policy

The Basics *of* Foreign Policy (pages 524–529)

What are some of the numerous factors that shape foreign policy development in the United States?

We commonly talk of American foreign policy and domestic policy as two separate areas, but it is important to realize that the boundary separating domestic and foreign policy is not—and never has been—watertight. First, let's consider the impact of domestic policies on American foreign policy by looking at how the United States approaches human rights and environmental issues at the global level.[17] Three guiding principles lie at the heart of our country's human rights foreign policy. First, American policy, both domestic and foreign, emphasizes individual legal rights and civil liberties; it pays less attention to economic and social rights. Second, Washington usually regards hostile, overly strong governments as the primary threat to human rights; rarely does American policy see a need to strengthen foreign governments in order to promote human rights. Third, American foreign policy generally rejects violence as a means for promoting human rights. Attempts to advance workers' rights or civil rights through violence have never been received favorably in the United States; instead, we generally look to legal and electoral means of promoting rights. Because this historical experience is not shared by many other countries, American calls for rejecting violence as a means of change are often met with skepticism.

The influence of American domestic policy on American foreign policy is also evident in U.S. environmental policy. By and large, international environmental proposals put forward by the United States have not imposed new costs on Americans; they have instead sought to persuade other countries to adopt American standards. For example, the United States was one of the strongest advocates of a 10-year ban on commercial whaling, an area in which the United States has few economic interests but many citizens who worry about the fate of the world's whale population. However, the United States has also vigorously opposed efforts to establish an international register of toxic chemicals, and it has refused to ratify the 1993 **Kyoto Protocol** on reducing greenhouse gases—in both cases citing the costs to American firms and the threat to American living standards.

Nelson Mandela, the revered former president of South Africa (1994–1999), visits President Bush at the White House. Mandela served nearly three decades in prison for seeking to overthrow the previous white-supremacist government of South Africa. When Mandela was released from prison in 1990, he lobbied American officials to impose sanctions on his country as part of the effort that eventually led to the creation of a multiracial democracy in 1994.
—How do foreigners use the lobbying pathway in an effort to influence American policy?

International Influence on U.S. Political Activity

You should know that foreign lobbying has become big business in Washington. Between 1998 and 2004, companies with headquarters in 78 foreign nations spent more than $620 million lobbying the U.S. government. These companies employed 550 lobbying firms and a total of 3,800 lobbyists, more than 100 of them former members of Congress. In 2003, Bob Livingstone, a former Republican representative from Louisiana and the one-time chair of the House Appropriations Committee, helped Turkey defeat an attempt by the Republican-controlled Congress to take away $1 billion worth of foreign aid because of that nation's failure to help the United States in the Iraq War

Many foreign governments are deeply concerned about American foreign aid legislation and arms sales. To secure their objectives in these areas, they pursue a two-step lobbying campaign. First, they try to gain leverage by lobbying the executive branch,

Globalization: The expansion of economic interactions between countries.

EXAMPLE: *The North American Free Trade Act (NAFTA) encourages globalization by lowering or eliminating trade barriers between the United States, Mexico, and Canada.*

usually the White House, the State Department, and the Defense Department. Second, they also lobby Congress.

The primary concern of foreign firms that operate in the United States is the ability of their affiliates to conduct business profitably and without hindrance. Between 1998 and 2004, for example, 22 foreign companies operating in the United States actively lobbied the EPA over issues connected with the agency's Superfund cleanup policies. At the state and local levels, taxation, zoning, education, and labor laws and policies are all of considerable concern to foreign firms. In one well-known case, Sony threatened to stop planned construction of new plants in California and Florida unless those states repealed portions of their tax codes that would have taxed Sony on its worldwide sales rather than on sales of items produced in that particular state. After both states changed their tax laws, Sony went ahead and built the new plants. In 2005, Toyota was planning the location of a new automotive plant in either the United States or Canada. Although several U.S. states offered more lucrative tax packages, both the national government and several provincial governments in Canada offered money for worker training; in addition, the Canadian system of universal health care allowed Toyota to save on the cost of health care benefits. Canada ended up getting the plant.

"So the United States allows foreign governments and businesses to lobby *our* government in support of *their* interests?"

—Student Question

The scale of foreign political activity in the United States has repeatedly raised two concerns. The first is that the more our representatives listen to foreign lobbyists, the less they will hear from the American public. The second is that foreign interests and American interests may not be compatible. By listening to and responding to foreign voices, policymakers may ignore or, worse, harm American national interests. This concern is reinforced by periodic revelations of foreign attempts at bribery and espionage. For example, in 2002, it was revealed that Taiwan kept a secret $100 million fund to buy influence in this country, and in 2005, two former employees of a pro-Israeli lobbying firm were indicted for disclosing U.S. defense information.

The ever-increasing pace of **globalization** has added a third concern. Foreign governments and firms might not stop at seeking to influence American political decisions; they might also seek to influence American economic decisions in ways that harm the United States. In 2005, it was announced that CNOOC Ltd., a Chinese government–controlled oil company, was attempting to buy Unocal Corporation, the third-largest U.S. oil company. When the news broke, many American lawmakers raised economic and security issues and threatened to block the takeover. In their view, China was a major competitor with the United States for global influence and power. Faced with this opposition, CNOOC withdrew its $18.4 billion offer—clearing the way for Chevron, the second-largest American oil company, to acquire Unocal, even though its offer was $700 million less. In 2006, domestic and

Analysts debate whether food assistance provided to foreign countries actually promotes the interests of American farmers and the U.S. government more than it helps impoverished people in foreign lands. ***—Should the United States be more generous in providing assistance to foreign countries?***

DEBATE **Farm Subsidies**

foreign policy again collided in the controversy about turning over the operation of American ports to a company with ties to the government of the United Arab Emirates. Would this be a national security risk or a prudent economic move?

Foreign Aid

"Who really benefits from foreign aid?"

—Student Question

One obvious answer to this question might be the country receiving the assistance, but there are other answers. For example, one of the best-known and best-supported foreign aid programs is Food for Peace. It allows countries to buy American farm products in local currency. This is important because it means they can reserve their limited amounts of "hard currency," such as dollars, euros, and pounds sterling, to buy other products from countries (including the United States) that will not accept their local currencies as payment.

Where does this food come from, however? U.S. government warehouses, filled with American farm products purchased under price support programs. Without these programs, many farm products would sell at such low prices farmers would be driven out of business. (Agricultural price supports were introduced in the New Deal era and have been maintained ever since.) The peasant farmers in the countries buying the food are undersold by relatively cheap American imports, which depresses local markets. Some critics argue that the Food for Peace program really amounts to foreign aid for American farmers. In fact, one of the major stumbling blocks to reaching a new international trade agreement today is the insistence of Third World countries on an end to U.S. price support programs for agricultural products. Prospects for ending these subsidies—which today go mainly to agribusinesses and the wealthiest farmers—are very small, however, because of the power of agricultural lobbies in the U.S. Congress.

As the cost of foreign policy increases, requiring that domestic programs be canceled, cut back, or delayed because of economic pressures, support for foreign policy decreases.[18] The Democrats used to be the low-tariff party, going back to its days as an agrarian party based in the South and West. The GOP has always been more protectionist, because it appealed to manufacturers and (often) workers who feared "cheap foreign competition." But protectionism was widely, and rightly, blamed for intensifying the Great Depression, so in the post–World War II world, U.S. foreign policy favored trade liberalization and the expansion of American exports. Globalization, however, has complicated matters. Today, the Democrats are becoming increasingly protectionist to appeal to workers threatened with job loss and to environmentalists worried about the environmental impact of industrializing the Third World. And the Republicans have become the party of free trade, because they represent the interests of export-oriented American business and emphasize the benefits of international trade to American consumers.

"What else affects Americans' support of foreign policy?"

—Student Question

Although the evidence is not as clear-cut as once thought, Americans also weigh the cost of foreign policy by counting the number of battlefield deaths. This grim equation first contributed to the erosion of the American public's support of the Vietnam War—which ultimately cost the lives of more than 55,000 U.S. troops—in the late 1960s and early 1970s. The conventional wisdom is that the greater the number of American deaths in a foreign war, the less support Americans give to the president waging that war. To some extent, this happened to President George W. Bush. In 2006, as casualties mounted and Iraq showed little sign of ending its insurgency and establishing a viable government, Bush's standing in public opinion polls (overall job rating, handling of the war, and honesty) plummeted to record lows. A decline in presidential popularity does not appear to be automatic, however. Even as battlefield deaths mount, solidarity among political elites and a widely accepted military mission may keep a president's standing in the opinion polls high.[19] But the U.S. experience in Vietnam suggests that such public support cannot be maintained indefinitely in the absence of visible military success. The Republican's loss of both houses of Congress in 2006 was an indication that while President Bush had counted on this type of solidarity, it had substantial limits with the voting public. Moreover, the President's public opinion approval poll numbers continued to remain historically low throughout the remainder of his term.

Public concerns about the benefits and costs of American foreign policy today run high in two areas: international trade policy and protection of civil liberties. In 2005, the Bush administration battled in the House of Representatives for passage of the Central American Free Trade Agreement (CAFTA), which passed by a vote of 217–215. Supporters argued that CAFTA was vital to the overall economic health of the U.S. economy in an era of globalization, because it fostered competition from abroad and provided consumers with more choices at competitive prices. They argued that CAFTA would also help long-impoverished countries develop

TIMELINE Comparing Foreign and Security Policy

SIMULATION You Are the President of the United States

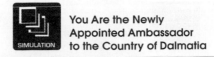

SIMULATION You Are the Newly Appointed Ambassador to the Country of Dalmatia

and diversify their economies. Opponents cited the potential loss of American jobs as firms moved overseas to produce goods and then sell them in the American market. The U.S. sugar lobby also fought CAFTA, because it slightly increased the amount of sugar Central American countries could export to the United States, cutting into the profits of wealthy American sugar producers.

The second area of public concern is how to safeguard civil liberties while fighting the War on Terror. Particularly worrisome to some are provisions of the USA PATRIOT Act, which was passed after the 9/11 attacks and renewed in 2006. These provisions give law enforcement officials access to an individual's private information without his or her knowledge. New federal laws also curtail the rights of foreigners who are detained on suspicion of being or aiding terrorists. Suspects can be detained for indefinite periods without being charged with a crime or having access to legal representation. Revelations that the Bush administration, on its own authority, approved electronic eavesdropping inside the United States were equally controversial.

The U.S. invasion of Iraq was the nation's first use of preemptive war. The ongoing rebuilding of that nation requires a substantial commitment of money and the presence of U.S. troops, like these soldiers on patrol in an Iraqi city.

Conflicting Evaluations of the Iraq War

On March 19, 2003, following much public debate in the United States, political maneuvering at the United Nations, and presentation of a 48-hour ultimatum to Iraq's dictator, Saddam Hussein, the Iraq War began. President George W. Bush had branded Iraq part of an "axis of evil," along with North Korea and Iran, in his 2002 State of the Union address. The Bush administration argued that Iraq's possession of **weapons of mass destruction** required preemptive military action on the part of the United States. (That claim was later recognized as incorrect.) The military operation was a spectacular success. On April 9, Baghdad fell, and on May 1, President Bush declared an end to major combat operations.

Violent opposition continued throughout the region, however, and the American occupation of Iraq proved far more difficult than expected. In July of 2003, deaths among U.S. combat forces in Iraq reached the level of the 1991 Persian Gulf War. In September of 2004, they passed the 1,000 mark. In October of 2005, they surpassed 2,000, and by the end of George W. Bush's term they had reach beyond 4000 (about 1,000 more than were killed in the terrorist attacks on September 11, 2001).

Political and economic setbacks, unforeseen by the war's planners, have also been numerous. Iraq's oil production has been slow to recover, and U.S. funds aimed at economic recovery have had to be diverted to improve security. Amid seemingly endless sectarian and ethnic strife, including a major insurgency supported by the once-dominant Sunni Arab minority, Iraqi political leaders repeatedly failed to meet reestablished deadlines to lay the foundation for a new democratic political order. And the American security presence in Iraq became the source of added controversy when, in April of 2004, photos were published around the world graphically depicting the torture and mistreatment of Iraqi prisoners by U.S. personnel at Abu Ghraib prison. Many Americans have come to doubt the wisdom of the war, yet there are several different perspectives

Neoconservatives view the Iraq War as essential to the future security of the United States. It is the second military operation in the War on Terror (the invasion of Afghanistan was the first). In their view, removing Saddam Hussein from power was necessary even if he did not have weapons of mass destruction, because his was a dangerous and aggressive government that had once tried to obtain these weapons and, if permitted, would do so again. Removing him from power was also necessary in order to build democracy in Iraq and set the stage for the democratization of the Middle East. In the neoconservative view, the United States cannot leave Iraq until democracy and economic recovery are assured, just as they were in post–World War II West Germany and Japan.

Neoliberals shed no tears over Saddam Hussein's downfall, recognizing that he was a ruthless dictator with a record of foreign aggression and domestic genocide. Before the war, however, neoliberals had asserted that nonmilitary means, such as economic

DEBATE Economic Sanctions and Cuba

SIMULATION You Are President John F. Kennedy

General David Petraeus testifies to Congress about the progress being made in Iraq. There has been some speculation that he may seek elected office, maybe even the presidency. ***—How important is it to you for members of Congress or the president to have a background in the military?***

sanctions, were a preferable line of action for removing Saddam from power. They had also cautioned that occupying and reconstructing Iraq would be difficult and that democracy could not be imposed from outside. Neoliberals also maintain that if the reconstruction of Iraq is to succeed, the United Nations must play a larger role so that the stigma of a largely American occupation is removed and concern for respecting human rights, meeting basic human needs, and establishing the rule of law will replace the emphasis on counterterrorism.

Foreign policy conservatives make two general points about the Iraq War. First, to wage it, they would have favored creating a true international alliance to reduce the political and economic costs to the United States, both in the actual fighting of the war and during the subsequent occupation. Second, conservatives see the Iraq War as having distracted the United States from pursuing the true enemy: Osama bin Laden and his terrorists. In fact, this group argues the Iraq War gave anti-American terrorism new life and that Iraq became a magnet for international terrorist groups. Related to this is the conservatives' concern that by acting unilaterally, the United States disrupted the balance of global politics, in the end leaving our country less secure. Conservatives believe that other countries—especially those we defined as enemies—drew the conclusion that unchecked American power is dangerous and must be countered.

Finally, the **isolationists** mostly supported the war in Afghanistan, because it was a direct response to the 9/11 terrorist attack. They see little value added in the Iraq War, however, and regard attempts at building democracy in Iraq and the Middle East as a "fool's errand." Isolationists prefer to focus on more rigorous efforts to promote homeland security.

The Years Ahead

The terrorist attacks on the World Trade Center and the Pentagon on September 11, 2001, marked a turning point in American foreign policy. For more than a decade, foreign policy had seemed adrift, and the American public seemed uninterested in world affairs.

Despite this apathy, American foreign policy has never really been separate from domestic policy. Ideas used to guide American foreign policy have their roots in domestic policy, and American foreign policy provides an avenue for foreign governments and firms to participate in the American political process. Most important, American foreign policy has created winners and losers among domestic groups. The terrorist attacks of 9/11 represent a turning point, not as America's reentry into world affairs but as a new point of reference for an ongoing debate over the content and conduct of American foreign policy.

The making of American foreign policy is the product of interaction between people and institutions. The American public expresses its voice through public opinion, elections, interest group activity, and political protest. Policymakers often have difficulty understanding what they hear from the public. They also have a desire to use the American public to help achieve their goals, which often reduces their willingness to listen. Presidents face a similar dilemma in reaching out for advice, whether to their White House staff or to the foreign policy bureaucracies. They want and need information but often hear unwelcome news. Competition among offices in the White House and within the foreign affairs bureaucracy provides the president with many choices of information sources and sets the stage for controversy. This controversy is often played out in public, especially when it involves conflict between the president and Congress.

Finally, it is important to remember that terrorism is not the only foreign policy issue facing the United States today. A wide range of military security, economic, and human welfare issues are on the national agenda. Failure to address them adequately today may hold dire consequences for the future.

The Basics of Foreign Policy
Practice Quiz

1. Which of the following is a key principle of neoconservative foreign policy?
   - **a.** Global crusades, such as building democracies abroad, divert the U.S. from real and more immediate dangers.
   - **b.** The United States' unparalleled military power in the world is the central instrument of American foreign policy.
   - **c.** It is better to take military action through alliances and coalitions than to act alone.
   - **d.** The major threats to U.S. security come from an overactive foreign policy.
2. Although there are important differences between neoliberal and neoconservative approaches to foreign policy, one belief they share is that
   - **a.** the United States should never hesitate to use its military force to achieve foreign policy ends.
   - **b.** the United States should routinely solicit the support of coalition governments and international institutions, such as the United Nations, to help achieve its foreign policy ends.
   - **c.** the United States should include in its foreign policy objectives for the spreading of democracy throughout the world.
   - **d.** world politics is a realm defined by conflict and struggle.
3. Historically, how has U.S. foreign policy responded to the violation of human rights abroad?
   - **a.** through military intervention
   - **b.** through clandestine attempts to foster revolt
   - **c.** through legal and electoral means to promote rights
   - **d.** through inaction
4. Invariably, a president's popularity drops during a high-casualty war.
   - **a.** true
   - **b.** false

Answers: 1-b, 2-c, 3-c, 4-b.

Discussion Questions

1. To what extent does the United States prioritize human rights in its foreign policy? How does this change depending on cultural and political factors?
2. Review U.S. foreign policy highlights over the last few years, then consider: To what extent do the two major political parties differ on foreign policy? To what extent are they similar?

What **YOU** can do!

Search the Internet for public opinion polls regarding the views of the U.S. public on foreign policy. You might start with the Pew Center (**http://www.pewtrusts.org/our_work_detail.aspx?id=298**) or World Public Opinion (**http://www.worldpublicopinion.org/?nid=&id=&lb=hmpg**). How well does current foreign policy represent public opinion?

Conclusion

Now that you have learned more about public policy, let's go back to the discussion at the beginning of the chapter of what people want from the American version of democracy. Should any government be able to swiftly change public policy on a grand scale? You might assume that modern liberals, with their greater faith in the positive power of government, would answer yes to this question but that modern conservatives, with their desire for a reduced role of government, would answer no.

Comprehensive domestic or foreign policy change is unusual in the United States for a number of reasons. Our fragmented branches of government, the existence of political parties, the power of interest groups and social movements that are often in competition with one another—these are a few of the main factors that fulfill what James Madison sought in his plan for the Constitution. No single interest or faction, even one comprising a majority of the population, can easily take control of such a system and use it to its own advantage. This plan for society and government often sounds strange to Americans because of our deep belief in the fairness of majority rule. The low popularity of Congress today (and in the past) offers a good example. The negative view of Congress arises in part because of the assumption that there is one public good, or general set of values, that most of us share. It is widely felt that if only Congress would stop catering to the needs of special interests and follow the will of the people, we would have much better government and much better public policy![20]

No one disputes the influence of so-called special interests, but congressional policymaking is often a reflection of an increasing diversity of interests in our nation of 300 million people. For many (if not most) policy issues, there is no one public good but rather a wide range of solutions for the many different people in a single congressional district or state.

Because of the structure of our government and the diversity of our wants and needs, much of our policymaking is best described as incremental in its impact.[21] These small modifications to existing policy make sense in a government as open to the pathways of political action as our own, in which citizens, groups, corporations, the mass media, and other actors have multiple ways to influence outcomes. The pathways can be used to hinder or block the actions of others as well as to open access to the policy process. Large, comprehensive policy changes are often hard to come by unless there is a crisis, such as 9/11, or an unusual political change, such as a dramatic realigning election.

In their plan for our government and society, the founders sought stability, not flexibility. If the incremental policymaking that we see in the contemporary United States is any indication, they succeeded. Small changes keep political, economic, and social arrangements in relatively the same relationship to one another. People who are happy with the status quo may applaud our incremental policymaking system; others might be willing to trade a degree of stability for a more responsive and responsible policymaking system. How do you feel? In either case, the pathways of political action offer you opportunities to participate in the policymaking process.

Key Objective Review, Apply, and Explore

Ideas and Values in Public Policy
(pages 508–509)

Public policy can be thought of as what comes after the "equal sign" in the equation of the structure of government plus the political process. Public policy is both what the government does and does not do.

The nature of public policy rests on the values of the public and policy decision makers. Freedom and equality are values that are especially important in determining what government ought to do and the way it should go about it. These two concepts are the basis for a model of political ideology that contrasts the liberal and conservative approaches to politics and government.

KEY TERM

Policy Process Model 508

CRITICAL THINKING QUESTIONS

1. How might a society's values shape both the outcome of policy debates and the policy process?
2. Can you think of an example of public policy in the United States that springs from our political culture?

INTERNET RESOURCES

Learn about policy issues from the liberal or progressive viewpoint: **http://www.movingideas.org**

Learn about policy issues from the conservative viewpoint: **http://www.heritage.org**

ADDITIONAL READING

Stone, Deborah. *Policy Paradox: The Art of Political Decision Making.* New York: Norton, 1997.

Types of Public Policy
(pages 510–511)

Public policies can be categorized by issue area (such as the environment, education, and agriculture) or by the functions of government necessary to carry out the policy. The three basic policy functions are distribution, regulation, and redistribution. It is also possible to categorize policy outputs as either tangible or symbolic.

KEY TERMS

Policy Categories 510
Distribution 510
Regulation 510
Redistribution 510

CRITICAL THINKING QUESTIONS

1. Why do redistributive polices cause so much political conflict? Are there distributive and regulatory policies that can cause as much conflict?
2. What are the best ways for a government to collect taxes?

INTERNET RESOURCES

Learn about the roles of the departments and agencies of the federal government in formulating distributive, regulatory, and redistributive public policies: **http://www.firstgov.gov/Agencies/Federal/Executive.shtml**

ADDITIONAL READING

Theodoulou, Stella Z., and Chris Kofinis. *The Art of the Game: Understanding American Public Policy Making.* Belmont, CA: Wadsworth, 2004.

Key Objective Review, Apply, and Explore

The Policy Formation Process

(pages 512–517)

The policy process model shapes much of our thinking about public policy. The model's limitations are that policymaking is not always a linear or cyclical process and that policymaking is more than the functioning of formal political institutions.

KEY TERMS

Pluralists 513
Focusing Events 513
Trigger Mechanisms 513
Institutional Agenda 513
Issue-Attention Cycle 514
Laws 514
Discretion 515
Reauthorization 515
Investigation 515
Garbage Can Model 515
Policy Entrepreneurs 515

CRITICAL THINKING QUESTIONS

1. The process model of policymaking says a great deal about how the institutions of government function but not much about our role as citizens in any of the phases of the process. At which phases in the process does citizen action have an impact on the final result? Why?
2. Explain how oversight works. Is oversight a necessary part of policymaking? Why or why not?

INTERNET RESOURCES

The House of Representatives is a policymaker with oversight functions. Find out what it is doing in both these areas: **http://www.house.gov**

The Senate is also a policymaker with oversight functions: **http://www.senate.gov**

Presidents are powerful policy players. See what issues President Obama supports: **http://www.whitehouse.gov**. To see what former President George W. Bush supported: **http://www.gpoaccess.gov/pubpapers/gwbush.html**

Learn about the federal courts and their roles as policymakers: **http://www.firstgov.gov/Agencies/Federal/Judicial.shtml**

ADDITIONAL READING

Derthick, Martha A. *Up in Smoke*. Washington, D.C.: CQ Press, 2002.

Lindblom, Charles E., and Edward J. Woodhouse. *The Policy-Making Process*, 3rd ed. Englewood Cliffs, NJ: Prentice Hall, 1993.

Spitzer, Robert J. *The Politics of Gun Control*. Washington, D.C.: CQ Press, 2004.

The Basics of Economic Policy

(pages 518–523)

Property rights and capitalism are at the heart of the American economic system. Americans have a greater degree of economic freedom than most of the world's population.

The most important measures of the health of the U.S. economy are inflation, employment, gross domestic product, the budget deficit or surplus, and the balance of trade.

KEY TERMS

Inflation 518
Consumer Price Index (CPI) 518
Deflation 518
Unemployment Rate 519
Gross Domestic Product (GDP) 519
Balance of Trade 519
Budget Deficit 519
Budget Surplus 519
National Debt 519
Fiscal Policy 520
Congressional Budget Office (CBO) 520
Monetary Policy 521
Federal Reserve System (the Fed) 521

CRITICAL THINKING QUESTIONS

1. What is the difference between the deficit and the national debt? How is inflation measured?
2. How does the Congressional Budget Office exercise budgetary power?
3. Do you think corporations pay their fair share of taxes? Why or why not? What are the consequences of raising corporate taxes?

INTERNET RESOURCES

Concord Coalition, a nonpartisan group lobbying for sound fiscal policy: **http://www.concordcoalition.org**

ADDITIONAL READING

Greider, William. *Secrets of the Temple: How the Federal Reserve Runs the Country*. New York: Touchstone, 1987.

Levitt, Steven D. *Freakonomics: A Rogue Economist Explores the Hidden Side of Everything*. New York: William Morrow, 2005.

Woodward, Bob. *Maestro: Greenspan's Fed and the American Boom*. New York: Simon & Schuster, 2000.

Key Objective Review, Apply, and Explore

The Basics of Foreign Policy

(pages 524–529)

Three different types of linkages exist between American foreign policy and domestic policy. First, American policy, both domestic and foreign, emphasizes individual legal rights and civil liberties. Second, Washington usually sees hostile, overly strong governments as the primary threat to human rights. Third, American foreign policy generally rejects violence as a means for promoting human rights.

KEY TERMS

Kyoto Protocol 524
Globalization 525
Weapons of Mass Destruction 527
Neoconservatives 527
Neoliberals 528
Foreign Policy Conservatives 528
Isolationists 528

CRITICAL THINKING QUESTIONS

1. How does American domestic policy influence American foreign policy? Does it affect participation in politics here at home?
2. In what ways does American foreign policy create winners and losers in domestic politics?

INTERNET RESOURCES

For more information on globalization, see the United Nations Environmental Program Web page: **http://www.unep.org/**

ADDITIONAL READING

Friedman, Thomas L. *The World Is Flat: A Brief History of the Twenty-First Century*. New York: Farrar, Straus and Giroux, 2005.

Chapter Review Critical Thinking Test

1. What is public policy?
  a. another word for the laws that Congress creates and the president signs
  b. laws and policies pertaining to public spaces, such as highways, parks, and public schools
  c. the action or inaction of the government on an issue of concern to the public
  d. governmental decisions that come from public input

2. Policy is the product of political processes, but some consider it not political in itself.
  a. true **b.** false

3. What are all the phases and their chronological order in the classic policy process model?
  a. a focusing event, setting an agenda, formulating policy, and implementing policy
  b. identification of the problem, setting an agenda, legitimizing policy, formulating policy, and implementing policy
  c. identification of the problem, setting an agenda, formulating policy, legitimizing policy, and implementing policy
  d. a focusing event, setting an agenda, identifying the problem, formulating policy, implementing and assessing policy

4. What is one common reason why certain issues on the country's "institutional agenda" fade away and are never acted on?
  a. The issue only serves one geographic segment of the country.
  b. The would-be policy only possesses symbolic value.
  c. The would-be policy excites the emotions of the public, and legislators resist such a coercive context.
  d. The would-be policy would be too costly or inconvenient to enact and enforce.

5. In the absence of a major crisis, what force is crucial to keeping certain problems on the institutional agenda?
  a. the continuation of the problem
  b. effective lobbyists
  c. elections
  d. legislators' patience

6. Where can average citizens most easily enter into the policy formation process?
  a. through the executive branch
  b. through the judicial branch
  c. through the Senate
  d. through the House of Representatives

7. Why is discretion so essential to the implementation of a law or policy?
  a. Policies are sometimes worded vaguely enough to attract keen interest in Congress, so those doing the actual implementation must decide on the details.
  b. The ambiguous nature of language itself always leaves a lot of room for interpreting policy.
  c. Legislators are often quite proficient in technical matters, but executive agencies or departments that implement policy usually are not. Thus laws are written in language that the implementers can understand.
  d. Article II of the Constitution grants those agencies or departments that implement policy the authority to shift the emphasis or focus of any law or policy provided they do not violate the "spirit of the law."

8. What is congressional oversight?
  a. when high-ranking members of the executive branch monitor the actions of Congress during policy formation
  b. when Congress monitors what is and is not on its 2-year policy agenda
  c. when Congress makes sure the policies it helped create are being carried out appropriately
  d. when the House or Senate neglects some segments of legislation the other legislative body has included in a bill

9. Unlike Congress, the courts do exercise oversight of policy implementation.
  a. true **b.** false

10. The negative view that many people hold of Congress' policymaking is probably unfair, because
  a. people do not realize Congress usually *does* create policies that serve the public good.
  b. the media routinely distorts what Congress does, and does not report the problematic policies that Congress almost always rejects.
  c. people forget there is not one public good; Congress' policymaking often reflects the vast diversity of interests in this country.
  d. people do not realize the Constitution prevents Congress from making policy on a great many issues.

11. What is the difference between fiscal policy and monetary policy?
  a. Fiscal policy concerns the national money supply; monetary policy is focused on taxing and spending decisions.
  b. Monetary policy is focused on budget deficits and surpluses; fiscal policy is concerned with interest rates and employment rates.
  c. Fiscal policy concerns taxing and spending decisions; monetary policy focuses on the national money supply.
  d. Fiscal policy is economic policy formulated by the Federal Reserve Board; monetary policy is economic policy formulated by the Congress and the president.

12. What exactly is the national debt?
  a. how much the U.S. government owes private investors and other countries in a given year
  b. the budget deficit plus the trade deficit in a given year
  c. the net sum of the budget deficit, minus the surplus
  d. the budget deficit plus the trade deficit, minus the Social Security Trust Fund

Chapter Review Critical Thinking Test

13. America's gross domestic product continues to grow,

- **a.** yet when you factor in inflation, it has actually shrunk.
- **b.** yet most real-wage increases have gone to the wealthiest Americans.
- **c.** and middle-class Americans have prospered the most.
- **d.** and everyone has enjoyed proportionally equivalent real-wage increase (a rising tide raises all boats).

14. The U.S. government has run budget deficits for about how long?

- **a.** 5 years
- **b.** 15 years
- **c.** 25 years
- **d.** 35 years

15. The primary aim of the Federal Reserve Board is to

- **a.** make sure the president's economic policy is working well.
- **b.** make sure Congress' economic policy is working well.
- **c.** regulate the national banking system.
- **d.** try to control inflation and keep the economy stable and growing.

16. Which of the following approaches dominated the foreign policy of George W. Bush's administration?

- **a.** neoliberal
- **b.** isolationist
- **c.** foreign policy conservative
- **d.** neoconservative

17. Neoliberals probably would have handled Saddam Hussein and the regime change in Iraq

- **a.** by extending the economic sanctions against Iraq and, if fighting broke out, trying to enable the Iraqis to create a democratic government from within.
- **b.** by defeating Hussein militarily and installing an interim, U.S.-controlled Iraqi government.
- **c.** by not doing anything—such regime change would not be a foreign policy priority.
- **d.** by extending the economic sanctions against Iraq and, if that did not work, bombing all Iraqi locations where weapons of mass destruction were thought to exist.

18. American policy—both domestic and foreign—pays much more attention to individual legal rights and civil liberties than it does to economic and social rights.

- **a.** true
- **b.** false

19. What best characterizes current U.S. global environmental policy?

- **a.** more environmentally progressive than almost any other country
- **b.** not environmentally progressive at all
- **c.** environmentally progressive when such progress does not come at the expense of American economic interests
- **d.** forward thinking about global climate change but not in some other areas

20. What is CAFTA, and who was one of its opponents?

- **a.** a trade agreement ratified during the Clinton administration; H. Ross Perot strongly opposed it, citing the loss of U.S. jobs as its result
- **b.** a trade agreement ratified during the George W. Bush administration; wealthy U.S. sugar producers opposed it, because it would cut into their profits
- **c.** a trade agreement ratified during the Reagan administration; the airline industry opposed it, because it would tighten competition for them
- **d.** an organization within the United Nations created during the Carter administration; American libertarians opposed it, because it required funding from industrialized countries, such as U.S. taxpayer money

Answers: 1-c, 2-a, 3-c, 4-d, 5-b, 6-d, 7-a, 8-c, 9-b, 10-c, 11-c, 12-c, 13-b, 14-d, 15-d, 16-d, 17-a, 18-a, 19-c, 20-b.

You decide!

Policy entrepreneurs are individuals who advocate particular solutions to public policy problems. Which public policy problem would you address as a policy entrepreneur? What solution would you advocate? How would you get your policy onto the agenda? Develop a plan to keep your policy problem and solution in the public eye. How would you go about moving your policy through the next stages of the traditional public policy process (formulating/legitimizing and implementing)? Be sure to anticipate any resistance you may encounter, and develop a plan to address any concerns from other players in the policymaking process.

Appendices

APPENDIX I

The Declaration of Independence of the Thirteen Colonies

In CONGRESS, July 4, 1776

By the early 1770s, relations between Great Britain and 13 colonies in North American had become strained. Actual hostilities broke out in 1775 at Lexington and Concord, marking the beginning of the Revolutionary War. But the "patriot cause" was not universally accepted thoughout the colonies. A second Continental Congress was called, and on May 10, 1775, representatives appointed by state legislatures from all of the colonies except Georgia convened in Philadelphia. A committee consisting of John Adams, Benjamin Franklin, Robert R. Livingston, Roger Sherman, and a slim, quiet delegate from Virginia named Thomas Jefferson (the "Committee of Five") was formed to draft a statement that would justify a war for independence. Adams suggested that Jefferson take the first stab at writing a draft document. With a few minor edits from Adams and Franklin, Jefferson presented his "Declaration" to the Continental Congress on June 28, 1776. Many agree that it is one of the most eloquent political statements ever written.

THE UNANIMOUS DECLARATION OF THE THIRTEEN UNITED STATES OF AMERICA

The Preamble of the Declaration is influenced by Enlightenment philosophy, a seventeenth-century European intellectual movement that held that all questions of math, science, and government could be solved through clear logic and careful experimentation. As such, it rejected superstition and religious "truths."

These words also clearly reflect the writings of English philosopher John Locke (1632–1704), particularly his *Second Treatise on Government*. Jefferson also seemed to be "borrowing" from the Virginia Declaration of Rights, which had been adopted about a month earlier.

When in the Course of human events, it becomes necessary for one people to dissolve the political bands which have connected them with another, and to assume among the powers of the earth, the separate and equal station to which the Laws of Nature and of Nature's God entitle them, a decent respect to the opinions of mankind requires that they should declare the causes which impel them to the separation.

Jefferson presents a notion of natural rights. That is, individuals possess certain privileges—certain guarantees by virtue of being human. These rights are *not* granted by government, but instead by God, or what Jefferson calls the "Creator". They cannot be given, nor can they be taken away.

We hold these truths to be self-evident, that all men are created equal, that they are endowed by their Creator with certain unalienable Rights, that among these are Life, Liberty and the pursuit of Happiness. That to secure these rights, Governments are instituted among Men, deriving their just powers from the consent of the governed, that whenever any Form of Government becomes destructive of these ends, it is the Right of the People to alter or to abolish it, and to institute new Government, laying its foundation on such principles and organizing its powers in such form, as to them shall seem most likely to effect their Safety and Happiness.

Here Jefferson introduces the social contract theory, drawn in large measure from the writings of John Locke. Humans have the option of living alone in what he called "the state of nature." According to this theory, humans originally lived without government or laws, enjoying complete personal freedom. Yet the state of nature meant "a war of all against all," in which—in the words of another philosopher, Thomas Hobbes—life was "solitary, poor, nasty, brutish, and short." To end this perpetual conflict and insecurity, people created governments, thereby giving up some of their freedoms in order to protect their lives and their property.

Jefferson also agreed with Locke that governments, having been created by the people to protect their rights, are limited; they get their powers from the will of the people and no one else. (In arguing this, Locke was attacking the traditional claim that kings ruled by the will of God.)

When a government fails to respect the will of the people—that is, when it appears no longer to be limited—it becomes the right, indeed the obligation, of citizens to change the government. This passage is Jefferson's call for revolution.

Prudence, indeed, will dictate that Governments long established should not be changed for light and transient causes; and accordingly all experience hath shewn, that mankind are more disposed to suffer, while evils are sufferable, than to right themselves by abolishing the forms to which they are accustomed. But when a long train of abuses and usurpations, pursuing invariably the same Object evinces a design to reduce them under absolute Despotism, it is their right, it is their duty, to throw off such Government, and to provide new Guards for their future security. —Such has been the patient sufferance of these Colonies; and such is now the necessity which constrains them to alter their former Systems of Government. The history of the present King of Great Britain [George III] is a history of repeated injuries and usurpations, all having in direct object the establishment of an absolute Tyranny over these States. To prove this, let Facts be submitted to a candid world.

Here Jefferson seems to provide a caution: Governments should be responsive to the will of the people, but just because the public is upset with government does not imply the need for revolution. Yes, governments can be changed, but not for "light and transient causes."

This next section is called the List of Grievances, which is essentially a laundry list of all the bad things that the British Government has done to the colonies. The idea here was to create such a long and powerful list that few would disagree with the need for a change.

He has refused his Assent to Laws, the most wholesome and necessary for the public good. He has forbidden his Governors to pass Laws of immediate and pressing importance, unless suspended in their operation till his Assent should be obtained; and when so suspended, he has utterly neglected to attend to them.

In all these passages, "He" refers to King George III.

He has refused to pass other Laws for the accommodation of large districts of people, unless those people would relinquish the right of Representation in the Legislature, a right inestimable to them and formidable to tyrants only.

He has called together legislative bodies at places unusual, uncomfortable, and distant from the depository of their public Records, for the sole purpose of fatiguing them into compliance with his measures.

He has dissolved Representative Houses repeatedly, for opposing with manly firmness his invasions on the rights of the people.

Precisely what defined a "government by the people" was still a bit vague at this time, but many suspected that representative assemblies were a necessary ingredient. So when the King dissolved these legislatures it seemed that he was striking a direct blow against self-rule.

He has refused for a long time, after such dissolutions, to cause others to be elected; whereby the Legislative powers, incapable of Annihilation, have returned to the People at large for their exercise; the State remaining in the mean time exposed to all the dangers of invasion from without, and convulsions within.

He has endeavoured to prevent the population of these States; for that purpose obstructing the Laws for Naturalization of Foreigners; refusing to pass others to encourage their migrations hither, and raising the conditions of new Appropriations of Lands.

He has obstructed the Administration of Justice, by refusing his Assent to Laws for establishing Judiciary powers.

An independent judiciary was also an element deemed essential for democratic governance, and the King's control of the courts seems a clear illustration of tryany.

He has made Judges dependent on his Will alone, for the tenure of their offices, and the amount and payment of their salaries.

He has erected a multitude of New Offices, and sent hither swarms of Officers to harass our people, and eat out their substance.

While most countries keep "standing armies" these days, in the eighteenth-century armies were assembled only when war was at hand. Many colonists saw the King's army as an instrument of aggression and control.

He has kept among us, in times of peace, Standing Armies without the consent of our legislatures.

He has affected to render the Military independent of and superior to the Civil power.

What is interesting about the list of grievances is that many of the items refer to more theoretical matters pertaining to just governance and the rights of citizens. But other items point to pragmatic issues, such as improperly taking money from colonists. Make no mistake, the Revolution was about creating a democratic system of government, a government responsive to "the people," but it was also about creating a system where average citizens could prosper financially.

He has combined with others to subject us to a jurisdiction foreign to our constitution and unacknowledged by our laws; giving his Assent to their Acts of pretended Legislation:

For Quartering large bodies of armed troops among us:

For protecting them, by a mock Trial, from punishment for any Murders which they should commit on the Inhabitants of these States:

Many colonists were anxious to pursue independence because they believed in self-rule, but many others were mostly interested in commercial issues (economic gain). So the "open trade" issue was critical for building broad public support for independence.

For cutting off our Trade with all parts of the world:

For imposing Taxes on us without our Consent:

For depriving us, in many cases, of the benefits of Trial by Jury:

For transporting us beyond Seas to be tried for pretended offences:

For abolishing the free System of English Laws in a neighbouring Province, establishing therein an Arbitrary government, and enlarging its Boundaries so as to render it at once an example and fit instrument for introducing the same absolute rule into these Colonies:

For taking away our Charters, abolishing our most valuable Laws, and altering fundamentally the Forms of our Governments:

For suspending our own Legislatures, and declaring themselves invested with power to legislate for us in all cases whatsoever.

He has abdicated Government here, by declaring us out of his Protection and waging War against us.

He has plundered our seas, ravaged our Coasts, burnt our towns, and destroyed the lives of our people.

He is at this time transporting large Armies of foreign Mercenaries to compleat the works of death, desolation and tyranny, already begun with circumstances of Cruelty and perfidy scarcely paralleled in the most barbarous ages, and totally unworthy the Head of a civilized nation.

He has constrained our fellow Citizens taken Captive on the high Seas to bear Arms against their Country, to become the executioners of their friends and Brethren, or to fall themselves by their Hands.

He has excited domestic insurrections amongst us, and has endeavoured to bring on the inhabitants of our frontiers, the merciless Indian Savages, whose known rule of warfare, is an undistinguished destruction of all ages, sexes and conditions.

In every stage of these Oppressions We have Petitioned for Redress in the most humble terms: Our repeated Petitions have been answered only by repeated injury. A Prince whose character is thus marked by every act which may define a Tyrant, is unfit to be the ruler of a free people.

Nor have We been wanting in attentions to our British brethren. We have warned them from time to time of attempts by their legislature to extend an unwarrantable jurisdiction over us. We have reminded them of the circumstances of our emigration and settlement here. We have appealed to their native justice and magnanimity, and we have conjured them by the ties of our common kindred to disavow these usurpations, which would inevitably interrupt our connections and correspondence. They too have been deaf to the voice of justice and of consanguinity. We must, therefore, acquiesce in the necessity, which denounces our Separation, and hold them, as we hold the rest of mankind, Enemies in War, in Peace Friends.

Again, many saw colonial assemblies as the foundation of a free society, so the King's suspension of their laws suggested tyrannical rule.

With the French and Indian War only a few years distant, many of the colonists continued to have grave fears about hostilities with Native Americans. So to suggest that the King was inflaming conflict was no small matter.

This was perceived as especially harsh language. To call the King "a Tyrant" was considered an act of treason.

Was the Declaration of Independence effective in rallying support behind the revolutionary cause? We do know that many New Yorkers were so inspired upon hearing these words that they toppled a statue of King George and had it melted down to make 42,000 bullets for war. Still, many balked at joining the revolution and even enlisted in the British Army. We also know that public support for the Continental Army, headed by George Washington, lagged considerably throughout the Revolution.

We, therefore, the Representatives of the united States of America, in General Congress, Assembled, appealing to the Supreme Judge of the world for the rectitude of our intentions, do, in the Name, and by the Authority of the good People of these Colonies, solemnly publish and declare, That these United Colonies are, and of Right ought to be Free and Independent States; that they are Absolved from all Allegiance to the British Crown, and that all political connection between them and the State of Great Britain, is and ought to be totally dissolved; and that as Free and Independent States, they have full Power to levy War, conclude Peace, contract Alliances, establish Commerce, and to do all other Acts and Things which Independent States may of right do. And for the support of this Declaration, with a firm reliance on the protection of divine Providence, we mutually pledge to each other our Lives, our Fortunes and our sacred Honor.

All the signers assumed that they were, in effect, signing their own death warrant if indeed the Revolution were to fail. The above paragraph, about absolving allegiances to the British Crown and creating independent states, would surely be interpreted as treason in England. Signing the Declaration was an act of true courage.

On July 19, 1776, Congress ordered a copy be handwritten for the delegates to sign, which most did on August 2, 1776. Two delegates never signed at all. As new delegates joined the Congress, they were also allowed to sign. A total of 56 delegates eventually signed.

The signers of the Declaration represented the new states as follows:

NEW HAMPSHIRE
Josiah Bartlett, William Whipple, Matthew Thornton

MASSACHUSETTS
John Hancock, Samuel Adams, John Adams, Robert Treat Paine, Elbridge Gerry

The first and most famous signature on the embossed copy was that of John Hancock, President of the Continental Congress.

RHODE ISLAND
Stephen Hopkins, William Ellery

CONNECTICUT
Roger Sherman, Samuel Huntington, William Williams, Oliver Wolcott

NEW YORK
William Floyd, Philip Livingston, Francis Lewis, Lewis Morris

NEW JERSEY
Richard Stockton, John Witherspoon, Francis Hopkinson, John Hart, Abraham Clark

PENNSYLVANIA
Robert Morris, Benjamin Rush, Benjamin Franklin, John Morton, George Clymer, James Smith, George Taylor, James Wilson, George Ross

Franklin was the oldest signer, at 70.

DELAWARE
Caesar Rodney, George Read, Thomas McKean

MARYLAND
Samuel Chase, William Paca, Thomas Stone, Charles Carroll of Carrollton

VIRGINIA
George Wythe, Richard Henry Lee, Thomas Jefferson, Benjamin Harrison, Thomas Nelson, Jr., Francis Lightfoot Lee, Carter Braxton

Two future presidents signed the Declaration—Thomas Jefferson and John Adams.

NORTH CAROLINA
William Hooper, Joseph Hewes, John Penn

SOUTH CAROLINA
Edward Rutledge, Thomas Heyward, Jr., Thomas Lynch, Jr., Arthur Middleton

Edward Rutledge, at age 26, was the youngest signer of the Declaration.

GEORGIA
Button Gwinnett, Lyman Hall, George Walton

After its adoption by the Congress, a handwritten draft was then sent a few blocks away to the printing shop of John Dunlap. Through the night between 150 and 200 copies were made, now known as "Dunlap broadsides." One was sent to George Washington on July 6, who had it read to his troops in New York on July 9. The 25 Dunlap broadsides still known to exist are the oldest surviving copies of the document. The original handwritten copy has not survived.

The signed copy of the Declaration of Independence is on display at the National Archives.

APPENDIX 2

The Constitution of the United States

THE PREAMBLE

We, the People of the United States, in Order to form a more perfect Union, establish Justice, insure domestic Tranquility, provide for the common defence, promote the general Welfare, and secure the Blessings of Liberty to ourselves and our Posterity, do ordain and establish this Constitution for the United States of America.

"We, the people." Three simple words are of profound importance and contentious origin. Every government in the world at the time of the Constitutional Convention was some type of monarchy, wherein sovereign power flowed from the top. The Founders of our new country rejected monarchy as a form of government and proposed instead a republic, which would draw its sovereignty from the people.

It is this very sense of empowerment that allows the "people" to influence our government and shape the world in which we live. We are among the freest people in the world largely because of this document. We are presented with multiple pathways to influence our government and better our lives.

Article I

THE LEGISLATIVE ARTICLE

Article I. The very first article in the Constitution established the legislative branch of the new national government. Why did the framers start with the legislative power instead of the executive branch? The framers truly believed it was the most important component of the new government.

It was also something that calmed the anxieties of average citizens. That is, they had experience with "legislative-centered governance" under the Articles and even during the colonial period. It was not perfect, but the legislative process seems to work.

Legislative Power

SECTION 1. All legislative Powers herein granted shall be vested in a Congress of the United States, which shall consist of a Senate and House of Representatives.

Section 1. Section 1 established a bicameral (two-chamber) legislature, or an upper (Senate) and lower (House of Representatives) organization of the legislative branch.

A bicameral legislature offers more opportunities to influence the policy process, as you can appeal to both your Senators and your representatives through the lobbying decision makers pathway, or indirectly through the elections pathway, the grassroots mobilization pathway, or the cultural change pathway. If you do not like a law passed by Congress, you can appeal to the courts to invalidate it or to change its meaning.

House of Representatives: Composition; Qualifications; Apportionment; Impeachment Power

SECTION 2 CLAUSE 1. The House of Representatives shall be composed of Members chosen every second Year by the People of the several States, and the Electors in each State shall have the Qualifications requisite for Electors of the most numerous Branch of the State Legislature.

Section 2 Clause 1. This section sets the term of office for House members (2 years) and indicates that those voting for Congress will have the same qualifications as those voting for the state legislatures. Originally, states limited voters to white property owners. Some states even had religious disqualifications, such as Catholic or Jewish.

There was a great deal of discussion about how long a legislator should sit in office before appealing to constituents for reelection. Short terms of office, such as the 2 years used in the House of Representatives, help force members to pay attention to the needs of their constituents.

CLAUSE 2. No Person shall be a Representative who shall not have attained to the Age of twenty five Years, and been seven Years a Citizen of the United States, and who shall not, when elected, be an Inhabitant of that State in which he shall be chosen.

Clause 2. This section sets forth the basic qualifications of a representative: at least 25 years of age, a U.S. citizen for at least 7 years, and a resident of the state in which the district is located. Note that the Constitution does not require a person to be a resident of the district he or she represents.

Clause 2 does not specify how many terms a representative can serve in Congress, but some critics support limiting the number of terms members can serve in order to make Congress more in touch with the citizenry—and to overcome some of the advantages incumbents have created to help win elections. Currently the average length of service in the House is 9 years (4.6 terms).

CLAUSE 3. Representatives and direct Taxes[1] shall be apportioned among the several States which may be included within this Union, according to their respective Numbers, which shall be determined by adding to the whole Number of free Persons, including those bound to Service for a Term of Years, and excluding Indians not taxed, three fifths of all other Persons.[2] The actual Enumeration shall be made within three Years after the first Meeting of the Congress of the United States, and within every subsequent Term of ten Years, in such Manner as they shall by Law direct. The Number of Representatives shall not exceed one for every thirty Thousand, but each State shall have at Least one Representative; and until such enumeration shall be made, the State of New Hampshire shall be entitled to chuse three, Massachusetts eight, Rhode-Island and Providence Plantations one, Connecticut five, New-York six, New Jersey four, Pennsylvania eight, Delaware one, Maryland six, Virginia ten, North Carolina five, South Carolina five, and Georgia three.

Clause 3. This clause contains the Three-Fifths Compromise, in which American Indians and blacks were only counted as 3/5 of a person for congressional representation purposes. This clause also addresses the question of congressional reapportionment every 10 years, which requires a census. Since the 1911 Reapportionment Act, the size of the House of Representatives has been set at 435. This is the designated size that is reapportioned every 10 years. Based on changes of population, some states gain and some states lose representatives.

While the Constitution never directly addresses the issue of slavery, this clause and others clearly condone its existence. It ultimately took the Civil War (1861–1865) to resolve the issue of slavery.

CLAUSE 4. When vacancies happen in the Representation from any State, the Executive Authority thereof shall issue Writs of Election to fill such Vacancies.

Clause 4. This clause provides a procedure for replacing a U.S. representative in the case of death, resignation, or expulsion from the House. Essentially, the governor of the representative's state will determine the selection of a successor. Generally, if less than half a term is left, the governor will appoint a successor. If more than half a term is remaining, most states require a special election to fill the vacancy.

CLAUSE 5. The House of Representatives shall chuse their Speaker and other Officers; and shall have the sole Power of Impeachment.

Clause 5. Only one officer of the House is specified, the Speaker. The House decides all other officers. This clause also gives the House authority for impeachments—the determination of formal charges—against officials of the executive and judicial branches.

Interestingly, this clause does not stipulate that the Speaker be a member of Congress. The House might choose an outsider to run their chamber, but this has never happened—and will likely not happen in the future.

Senate Composition: Qualifications, Impeachment Trials

SECTION 3 CLAUSE 1. The Senate of the United States shall be composed of two Senators from each State, chosen by the Legislature thereof,[3] for six Years; and each Senator shall have one Vote.

Section 3 Clause 1. This clause treats each state equally—all have two senators. Originally, state legislators chose senators, but since passage and ratification of the 17th Amendment, they are now elected by popular vote. This clause also establishes the term of a senator—6 years, three times that of a House member.

This clause is very important when thinking about pathways of change. For one, it creates a mechanism by which the minority, through their Senators, can thwart the will of the majority. Each state has the same number of Senators. A majority of Senators, representing states with small populations, have the ability to control the process—or at least stall things. In our system "majority will" does not always prevail.

Also, 6-year terms give Senators the chance to worry only periodically about an approaching reelection. Unlike members of the House, who come up for reelection so frequently that their actions may be constantly guided by a concern for pleasing the voters, this extended term in office offers Senators some leeway to do what they think is best for their state and the nation, rather than what might be seen as popular.

CLAUSE 2. Immediately after they shall be assembled in Consequence of the first Election, they shall be divided as equally as may be into three Classes. The Seats of the Senators of the first Class shall be vacated at the Expiration of the second Year, of the second Class at the Expiration of the fourth Year, and of the third Class at the Expiration of the sixth Year, so that one third may be chosen every second Year; and if Vacancies happen by Resignation, or otherwise, during the Recess of the Legislature of any State, the Executive thereof may make temporary Appointments until the next Meeting of the Legislature, which shall then fill such Vacancies.[4]

Clause 2. To prevent a wholesale replacement of senators every 6 years, this clause provides that one-third of the Senate will be elected every 2 years. In other words, in order to remove at least one-half of the Senators from office, two elections are needed.

Senate vacancies are filled in the same way as the House—either appointment by the governor or by special election. Currently the average length of service in the Senate is 11.3 years (slightly less than two terms).

CLAUSE 3. No Person shall be a Senator who shall not have attained to the Age of thirty Years, and been nine Years a Citizen of the United States, and who shall not, when elected, be an Inhabitant of that State for which he shall be chosen.

Clause 3. This clause sets forth the qualifications for U.S. senator: at least 30 years old, a U.S. citizen for at least nine years, and a citizen of a state. The equivalent age of 30 today would be 54 years old. The average age of a U.S. senator at present is 59.5 years.

Clause 4. The only constitutional duty of the vice president is specified in this clause—president of the Senate. This official only has a vote if there is a tie vote in the Senate; then the vice president's vote breaks the tie.

The split between Democrats and Republicans in Congress has been tiny in recent years. Not surprisingly, the Vice President has been called upon to cast several deciding votes.

CLAUSE 4. The Vice President of the United States shall be President of the Senate, but shall have no Vote, unless they be equally divided.

Clause 5. One official office in the U.S. Senate is specified—temporary president, who fills in during the vice president's absence (which is normally the case). All other Senate officers are designated and selected by the Senate.

CLAUSE 5. The Senate shall chuse their other Officers, and also a President pro tempore, in the Absence of the Vice President, or when he shall exercise the Office of President of the United States.

Clause 6, 7. The Senate acts as a trial court for impeached federal officials. If the accused is the president, the Chief Justice of the U.S. Supreme Court presides. Otherwise, the vice president normally presides. Conviction of the charges requires a two-thirds majority vote of those senators present at the time of the vote. Conviction results in the federal official's removal from office and disqualification to hold any other federal appointed office.

CLAUSE 6. The Senate shall have the sole Power to try all Impeachments. When sitting for that Purpose, they shall be on Oath or Affirmation. When the President of the United States is tried, the Chief Justice shall preside: And no Person shall be convicted without the Concurrence of two thirds of the Members present.

CLAUSE 7. Judgment in Cases of Impeachment shall not extend further than to removal from Office, and disqualification to hold and enjoy any Office of honor, Trust or Profit under the United States: but the Party convicted shall nevertheless be liable and subject to Indictment, Trial, Judgment and Punishment, according to Law.

Congressional Elections: Times, Places, Manner

Section 4 Clause 1. Through the years this clause has proven to be a critical aspect of the elections pathway. By allowing states to regulate elections procedures (that is, until Congress acts), the types of citizens able to participate in the process have been limited. First, religious and property qualifications were common, and many southern states used this provision to discriminate against black voters until the 1960s. Many states barred women from voting in election until the ratification of the 19th Amendment, and still others kept 18-year-olds out until the 25th Amendment.

Lingering issues include residency and registration requirements. In some states citizens can register to vote on Election Day, but in many others they have to take this step 30 days in advance. Indeed, many argue that residency and registration requirements unnecessarily inhibit voting, especially for young folks who tend to be more mobile. Others argue that such laws help to reduce voter fraud.

SECTION 4 CLAUSE 1. The Times, Places and Manner of holding Elections for Senators and Representatives, shall be prescribed in each State by the Legislature thereof; but the Congress may at any time by Law make or alter such Regulations, except as to the Places of chusing Senators.

Clause 2. The states determine the place and manner of electing representatives and senators, but Congress has the right to make or change these laws or regulations, except for the election sites. Congress is required to meet annually, and now, by law, annual meetings begin in January.

CLAUSE 2. The Congress shall assemble at least once in every Year, and such Meeting shall be on the first Monday in December, unless they shall by Law appoint a different Day.[5]

Powers and Duties of the Houses

Section 5 Clause 1. This clause enables each legislative branch to essentially make its own rules. Normally, to take a vote, a quorum is necessary. But if no votes are scheduled, fewer than a quorum can convene a session.

SECTION 5 CLAUSE 1. Each House shall be the Judge of the Elections, Returns and Qualifications of its own Members, and a Majority of each shall constitute a Quorum to do Business; but a smaller Number may adjourn from day to day, and may be authorized to compel the Attendance of absent Members, in such Manner, and under the Penalties as each House may provide.

CLAUSE 2. Each House may determine the Rules of its Proceedings, punish its Members for disorderly Behaviour, and, with the Concurrence of two thirds, expel a Member.

Clause 2. Essentially, each branch promulgates its own rules and punishes its own members. Knowing exactly how each chamber of the legislature conducts its proceedings is essential for political activists. The lobbying decision makers pathway can be a potent means of shifting public policy, but only when internal rules are well understood. Perhaps this is one of the reasons why former members of Congress make such good lobbyists.

CLAUSE 3. Each House shall keep a Journal of its Proceedings, and from time to time publish the same, excepting such Parts as may in their Judgment require Secrecy; and the Yeas and Nays of the Members of either House on any question shall, at the Desire of one fifth of those Present, be entered on the Journal.

Clause 3. An official record called the Congressional Record, House Journal, etc., is kept for all sessions. It is a daily account of House and Senate floor debates, votes, and members' remarks. However, a record is not printed if a proceeding is closed to the public for security reasons. Many votes are by voice vote, and if at least one-fifth of the members request, a recorded vote of Yeas and Nays will be conducted and documented. This procedure permits analysis of congressional role-call votes.

CLAUSE 4. Neither House, during the Session of Congress, shall, without the Consent of the other, adjourn for more than three days, nor to any other Place than that in which the two Houses shall be sitting.

Clause 4. This clause prevents one house from adjourning for a long period of time or to some other location without the consent of the other house.

Rights of Members

SECTION 6 CLAUSE 1. The Senators and Representatives shall receive a Compensation for their Services, to be ascertained by Law, and paid out of the Treasury of the United States. They shall in all Cases, except Treason, Felony and Breach of the Peace, be privileged from Arrest during their Attendance at the Session of their respective Houses, and in going to and returning from the same; and for any Speech or Debate in either House, they shall not be questioned in any other Place.

Section 6 Clause 1. This section refers to a salary paid to senators and members of the House from the U.S. Treasury. This clearly states that federal legislators work for the entire nation, and not for their respective states.

Currently, the salary for members of congress is $165,200; some leadership positions, like Speaker of the House, receive a higher salary. The Speaker receives a salary of $212,100. Members of Congress receive many other benefits: free health care, fully funded retirement system, free round trips to their home state or district, etc. This section also provides immunity from arrest or prosecution for congressional actions on the floor or in travel to and from the Congress. For example, few members of Congress have ever been charged with drunk driving.

CLAUSE 2. No Senator or Representative shall, during the Time for which he was elected, be appointed to any civil Office under the Authority of the United States, which shall have been created, or the Emoluments whereof shall have been encreased during such time; and no Person holding any Office under the United States, shall be a Member of either House during his Continuance in Office.

Clause 2. This section prevents the U.S. from adopting a parliamentary democracy, since congressional members cannot hold executive offices and members of the executive branch cannot be members of Congress.

Legislative Powers: Bills and Resolutions

SECTION 7 CLAUSE 1. All Bills for raising Revenue shall originate in the House of Representatives; but the Senate may propose or concur with Amendments as on other Bills.

Section 7 Clause 1. This clause specifies one of the few powers specific to the U.S. House—revenue bills. Since the House was intended to be more closely tied to the people (since members are elected more frequently and they represent fewer people than the Senate), the founders wanted to grant them the power of the purse.

Given that much of politics centers on the allocation of scarce resources (the distribution of money), this provision is a key piece of information for would-be political activists.

CLAUSE 2. Every Bill which shall have passed the House of Representatives and the Senate, shall, before it becomes a Law, be presented to the President of the United States; If he approve he shall sign it, but if not he shall return it, with his Objections to that House in which it shall have originated, who shall enter the Objections at large on their Journal, and proceed to reconsider it. If after such Reconsideration two thirds of that House shall agree to pass the Bill, it shall be sent, together with the Objections, to the other House, by which it shall likewise be reconsidered, and if approved by two thirds of that House, it shall become a Law. But in all such Cases the Votes of both Houses shall be determined by yeas and Nays, and the Names of the Persons voting for and against the Bill shall be entered on the Journal of each House respectively. If any Bill shall not be returned by the President within ten Days (Sundays excepted) after it shall have been presented to him, the Same shall be a Law, in like Manner as if he had signed it, unless the Congress by their Adjournment prevent its Return, in which Case it shall not be a Law.

Clause 2. The heart of the checks and balances system is contained in this clause. Both the House and Senate must pass an identical bill and present it to the president. If the president fails to act on the bill within 10 days (not including Sundays), the bill will automatically become law if Congress is in session. If the president signs the bill, it becomes law. If the president vetoes the bill and sends it back to Congress, this body may override the veto by a two-thirds vote in each branch. This vote must be a recorded vote.

The systems of checks and balances, as well as a division of power at the federal level, allow many ways to pursue change by a variety of pathways.

CLAUSE 3. Every Order, Resolution, or Vote to which the Concurrence of the Senate and House of Representatives may be necessary (except on a question of Adjournment) shall be presented to the President of the United States; and before the Same shall take Effect, shall be approved by him, or being disapproved by him, shall be repassed by two thirds of the Senate and House of Representatives, according to the Rules and Limitations prescribed in the Case of a Bill.

Clause 3. This clause covers every other type of legislative action other than a bill. Essentially, the same procedures apply in most cases. There are a few exceptions. For example, a joint resolution proposing a new congressional amendment is not subject to presidential veto.

Powers of Congress

SECTION 8 CLAUSE 1. The Congress shall have Power To lay and collect Taxes, Duties, Imposts and Excises, to pay the Debts and provide for the common Defence and general Welfare of the United States; but all Duties, Imposts and Excises shall be uniform throughout the United States.

CLAUSE 2. To borrow Money on the credit of the United States;

Section 8 Clause 1, 2. This power allows the federal government to deficit-spend (which most states are not allowed to do). Thus, when times of economic difficulty arise, individuals and groups can petition government for financial aid and relief with job shortages.

CLAUSE 3. To regulate Commerce with foreign Nations, and among the several States, and with the Indian Tribes;

Clause 3. This is one of the most sweeping powers granted Congress, because so much can be linked to interstate "commerce." Since the early twentieth century, the U.S. Supreme Court has defined interstate commerce broadly and thereby enabled Congress to use this power to pass antidiscrimination laws, criminal justice laws, and other statutes.

CLAUSE 4. To establish an uniform Rule of Naturalization; and uniform Laws on the subject of Bankruptcies throughout the United States;

Clause 4. This provision helps us understand why Congress, rather than state legislatures, has been at the center of the recent immigration reform debate.

CLAUSE 5. To coin Money, regulate the Value thereof, and of foreign Coin, and fix the Standard of Weights and Measures;

CLAUSE 6. To provide for the Punishment of counterfeiting the Securities and current Coin of the United States;

CLAUSE 7. To establish Post Offices and post Roads;

> **Clause 5, 6, 7.** Congressional power over coining money, counterfeiting, and post offices provides the justification for the creation of many criminal laws that are handled by federal law enforcement agencies such as the Federal Bureau of Investigation (FBI) and Secret Service. Because these matters are specified as under federal authority in the Constitution, it is a federal crime—rather than a state crime—to counterfeit money and engage in mail fraud. Most other kinds of crimes, such as murders, robberies, and burglaries victimizing ordinary citizens, are governed by state law.

CLAUSE 8. To promote the Progress of Science and useful Arts, by securing for limited Times to Authors and Inventors the exclusive Right to their respective Writings and Discoveries;

CLAUSE 9. To constitute Tribunals inferior to the supreme Court;

> **Clause 9.** Congress is responsible for the design of and procedures used in the federal court system. The U.S. Supreme Court is the only court created by the Constitution (see Article III). The lower federal courts are created by—and can be changed by—laws enacted by Congress. When there are changes in the design of the federal court system, such as the creation of a new court, these matters are under the power of Congress rather than under the control of the Supreme Court.

CLAUSE 10. To define and punish Piracies and Felonies committed on the high Seas, and Offences against the Law of Nations;

CLAUSE 11. To declare War, grant Letters of Marque and Reprisal, and make Rules concerning Captures on Land and Water;

> **Clause 10, 11.** Although Congress possesses the exclusive authority to declare war, presidents use their powers as commander-in-chief (see Article II) to initiate military actions even when there is no formal congressional declaration of war. There have been periodic disputes about whether presidents have exceeded their authority and ignored the Constitution's explicit grant of war-declaring power to Congress.

CLAUSE 12. To raise and support Armies, but no Appropriation of Money to that Use shall be for a longer Term than two Years;

CLAUSE 13. To provide and maintain a Navy;

> **Clause 11, 12, 13.** These three clauses, clauses 11, 12, and 13, ensure that Congress is involved in foreign policy decisions; thus citizens and groups can appeal to Congress if they do not like the president's foreign policy decisions or actions. Giving Congress the power to make appropriations to fund the military is potentially a significant power they have in rivaling the president for influence.

CLAUSE 14. To make Rules for the Government and Regulation of the land and naval Forces;

CLAUSE 15. To provide for calling forth the Militia to execute the Laws of the Union, suppress Insurrections and repel Invasions;

CLAUSE 16. To provide for organizing, arming, and disciplining, the Militia, and for governing such Part of them as may be employed in the Service of the United States, reserving to the States respectively, the Appointment of the Officers, and the Authority of training the Militia according to the discipline prescribed by Congress;

> **Clause 14, 15, 16.** These clauses establish what are known as the "expressed" or "specified" powers of Congress.

CLAUSE 17. To exercise exclusive Legislation in all Cases whatsoever, over such District (not exceeding ten Miles square) as may, by Cession of particular States, and the Acceptance of Congress, become the Seat of the Government of the United States, and to exercise like Authority over all Places purchased by the Consent of the Legislature of the State in which the Same shall be, for the Erection of Forts, Magazines, Arsenals, dockYards, and other needful Buildings;

> **Clause 17.** This clause establishes the seat of the federal government, which was first located in New York. It eventually was moved to Washington, D.C., when both Maryland and Virginia ceded land to the new national government, which then established the District of Columbia.

Clause 18. This clause, known as the "Elastic Clause," provides the basis for the doctrine of "implied" congressional powers, which was first introduced in the U.S. Supreme Court case of *McCulloch* v. *Maryland* (1819). It greatly expanded the power of Congress to pass legislation and make regulations.

The "necessary and proper" clause increases the powers of Congress, granting the legislature a great deal more authority and influence in our system of government. It has proven essential in creating a stong national government and in placing Congress at the center of the policy process.

CLAUSE 18. To make all Laws which shall be necessary and proper for carrying into Execution the foregoing Powers, and all other Powers vested by this Constitution in the Government of the United States, or in any Department or Officer thereof.

Powers Denied to Congress

Section 9 Clause 1. This clause was part of the Three-Fifths Compromise. Essentially, the new Congress was prohibited from stopping the importation of slaves until 1808, but it could impose a head tax not to exceed $10 for each slave.

Condoning slavery, from today's perspective, clearly clashed with the Declaration of Independence's assertion that all men are created equal. It is hard to understand the hypocrisy of a free society with slaves. Without this provision, however, southern delegates would have left the Constitutional Convention, and southern states would not have voted to ratify the new Constitution.

SECTION 9 CLAUSE 1. The Migration or Importation of such Persons as any of the States now existing shall think proper to admit, shall not be prohibited by the Congress prior to the Year one thousand eight hundred and eight, but a Tax or duty may be imposed on such Importation, not exceeding ten dollars for each Person.

Clause 2. Habeas Corpus is a judicial order forcing law enforcement authorities to produce a prisoner they are holding, and to justify the prisoner's continued confinement. Congress cannot suspend the writ of habeas corpus except in cases of rebellion or invasion. The writ of habeas corpus permits a judge to inquire about the legality of detention or deprivation of liberty of any citizen. This is one of the few legal protections for individuals enshrined in the Constitution before the Bill of Rights.

CLAUSE 2. The Privilege of the Writ of Habeas Corpus shall not be suspended, unless when in Cases of Rebellion or Invasion the public Safety may require it.

Clause 3. This provision prohibits Congress from passing either bills of attainder (an act of legislature declaring a person or group of persons guilty of some crime, and punishing them, without benefit of a trial) or ex post facto laws (retroactive crimes after passage of legislation). Similar restrictions were put in many state constitutions. These protections were among the few specifically provided for individuals in the body of the Constitution before the creation of amendments.

CLAUSE 3. No Bill of Attainder or ex post facto Law shall be passed.

Clause 4. This clause was interpreted to prevent Congress from passing an income tax. When the Supreme Court struck down congressional efforts to impose an income tax, passage of the 16th Amendment in 1913 counteracted the Supreme Court decision and gave Congress this power.

CLAUSE 4. No Capitation, or other direct, Tax shall be laid, unless in Proportion to the Census or Enumeration herein before directed to be taken.[6]

Clause 5. This section establishes free trade within the U.S. That is, one state cannot tax the importation of domestic goods, and the federal government cannot tax state exports.

CLAUSE 5. No Tax or Duty shall be laid on Articles exported from any State.

Clause 6. This clause also applies to free trade within the U.S. The national government cannot show any preference to any state or maritime movements among the states.

CLAUSE 6. No Preference shall be given by any Regulation of Commerce or Revenue to the Ports of one State over those of another; nor shall Vessels bound to, or from, one State, be obliged to enter, clear, or pay Duties in another.

Clause 7. This clause prevents any expenditure unless it has been provided for in an appropriations bill enacted by Congress. At the beginning of most fiscal years, Congress has not completed the budget. Technically, the government cannot then spend any money, and would have to shut down. So Congress usually passes a Continuing Resolution Authority providing temporary authority to continue to spend money until the final budget is approved and signed into law.

CLAUSE 7. No Money shall be drawn from the Treasury, but in Consequence of Appropriations made by Law; and a regular Statement and Account of the Receipts and Expenditures of all public Money shall be published from time to time.

CLAUSE 8. No Title of Nobility shall be granted by the United States: And no Person holding any Office of Profit or Trust under them, shall, without the Consent of Congress, accept of any present, Emolument, Office, or Title, of any kind whatever, from any King, Prince, or foreign State.

Clause 8. Feudalism would not be established in the new country. We would have no nobles. No federal official can accept a title of nobility (even honorary) without permission of Congress.

Powers Denied to the States

This section sets out the prohibitions on state actions.

SECTION 10 CLAUSE 1. No State shall enter into any Treaty, Alliance, or Confederation; grant Letters of Marque and Reprisal; coin Money; emit Bills of Credit; make any Thing but gold and silver; Coin a Tender in Payment of Debts; pass any Bill of Attainder, ex post facto Law, or Law impairing the Obligation of Contracts, or grant any Title of Nobility.

Section 10 Clause 1. This clause is a laundry list of denied powers. These restrictions cannot be waived by Congress. States cannot engage in foreign relations or acts of war. Letters of marque and reprisal were used to provide legal cover for privateers. The federal government's currency monopoly is established. The sanctity of contracts is specified, and similar state prohibitions are specified for bills of attainder, ex post facto, etc.

CLAUSE 2. No State shall, without the Consent of the Congress, lay any Imposts or Duties on Imports or Exports, except what may be absolutely necessary for executing its inspection Laws: and the net Produce of all Duties and Imposts, laid by any State on Imports or Exports, shall be for the Use of the Treasury of the United States; and all such Laws shall be subject to the Revision and Controul of the Congress.

Clause 2. This section establishes the monopoly control of the national government in matters of both national and international trade. The only concession to states is health and safety inspections.

CLAUSE 3. No State shall, without the Consent of Congress, lay any Duty of Tonnage, keep Troops, or Ships of War in time of Peace, enter into any Agreement or Compact with another State, or with a foreign Power, or engage in War, unless actually invaded, or in such imminent Danger as will not admit of delay.

Clause 3. This final section of the Legislative article establishes the war monopoly power of the national government. The only exception to state action is actual invasion or threat of imminent danger.

Article II

THE EXECUTIVE ARTICLE

Article II. This article establishes an entirely new concept in government—an elected executive power. This was a touchy topic in 1787. On one hand, there was great worry about executive power—it was seen as the root of tyranny. On the other hand, many believed that a powerful executive was necessary for long-term stability for the new nation. The right balance was a system with a strong executive, where the executive's power could be limited.

Nature and Scope of Presidential Power

SECTION 1 CLAUSE 1. The executive Power shall be vested in a President of the United States of America. He shall hold his Office during the Term of four Years, and, together with the Vice President, chosen for the same Term, be elected as follows:

Section 1 Clause 1. This clause establishes the executive power in the office of the president of the United States of America. It also establishes a second office—vice president. A 4-year term was established, but not a limit on the number of terms. A limit was later established by the 22nd Amendment.

CLAUSE 2. Each State shall appoint, in such Manner as the Legislature thereof may direct, a Number of Electors, equal to the whole Number of Senators and Representatives to which the State may be entitled in the Congress: but no Senator or Representative, or Person holding an Office of Trust or Profit under the United States, shall be appointed an Elector.

Clause 2. This paragraph establishes the electoral college to choose the president and vice president. Each state can determine how electors will be allotted to different candidates. For instance, today 48 states give the candidate who receives the most votes from citizens all of its electoral votes. This "winner take all" system puts an important twist on presidential election strategy. The trick for the candidates is to amass 270 electoral votes from different combinations of states.

Another implication of this system of choosing an executive is that it is possible for one candidate to receive more votes from citizens than other candidates, but still not become president. This has occurred four times in American history, most recently in 2000, when Al Gore received roughly 500,000 votes more than George W. Bush but fewer Electoral College votes.

CLAUSE 3. The Electors shall meet in their respective States, and vote by Ballot for two Persons, of whom one at least shall not be an Inhabitant of the same State with themselves. And they shall make a List of all the Persons voted for, and of the Number of Votes for each; which List they shall sign and certify, and transmit sealed to the Seat of the Government of the United States, directed to the President of the Senate. The President of the Senate shall, in the Presence of the Senate and House of Representatives, open all the Certificates, and the Votes shall then be counted. The Person having the greatest Number of Votes shall be the President, if such Number be a Majority of the whole Number of Electors appointed; and if there be more than one who have such Majority and have an equal Number of Votes, then the House of Representatives shall immediately chuse by Ballot one of them for President; and if no Person have a Majority, then from the five highest on the List the said House shall in like Manner chuse the President. But in chusing the President, the Votes shall be taken by States, the Representation from each State having one Vote; A quorum for this Purpose shall consist of a Member or Members from two thirds of the States, and a Majority of all the States shall be necessary to a Choice. In every Case, after the Choice of the President, the Person having the greatest Number of Votes of the Electors shall be the Vice President. But if there should remain two or more who have equal Votes, the Senate shall chuse from them by Ballot the Vice President.[7]

Clause 3. This paragraph has been superseded by the 12th Amendment. The original language provided for a House election in the case of no majority vote or a tie vote among the top five candidates. Now the number of candidates is three. The Senate is to select the vice president if a candidate does not have an electoral majority or in the case of a tie vote. The Senate considers only the top two candidates. The amendment also clarifies that the qualifications of the vice president are the same as those for president.

CLAUSE 4. The Congress may determine the Time of chusing the Electors, and the Day on which they shall give their Votes; which Day shall be the same throughout the United States.

Clause 4. Congress is given the power to establish a uniform day and time for the state selection of electors.

CLAUSE 5. No Person except a natural born Citizen, or a Citizen of the United States, at the time of the Adoption of this Constitution, shall be eligible to the Office of President; neither shall any Person be eligible to that Office who shall not have attained to the Age of thirty five Years, and been fourteen Years a Resident within the United States.

Clause 5. The qualifications for the offices of president and vice president are specified here—at least 35 years old, 14 years' resident in the U.S., and a natural-born citizen. The 14th Amendment clarified who is a citizen of the U.S., a person born or naturalized in the U.S. and subject to its jurisdiction. But the term "natural-born citizen" is unclear and has never been further defined by the judicial branch. Does it mean born in the U.S. or born of U.S. citizens in the U.S. or somewhere else in the world? Unfortunately, there is no definitive answer.

CLAUSE 6. In Case of the Removal of the President from Office, or of his Death, Resignation, or Inability to discharge the Powers and Duties of the said Office, the Same shall devolve on the Vice President, and the Congress may by Law provide for the Case of Removal, Death, Resignation or Inability, both of the

Clause 6. This clause concerns presidential succession and has been modified by the 25th Amendment. Upon the death, resignation, or impeachment conviction of the president, the vice president becomes president. The new president nominates a new vice president, who assumes the office if approved by a majority vote in both congressional branches. The president is also now able to notify the Congress of his or her inability to perform the duties of office.

President and Vice President, declaring what Officer shall then act as President, and such Officer shall act accordingly, until the Disability be removed, or a President shall be elected.[8]

Clause 7. This section covers the compensation of the president, which cannot be increased or decreased during his/her office. The current salary is $400,000/year. The prohibition against decreasing the president's salary was considered an important part of the separation of powers. If Congress were at odds with the president and also able to decrease his pay, then it could drive him from office or punish him by reducing his salary.

CLAUSE 7. The President shall, at stated Times, receive for his Services, a Compensation, which shall neither be encreased nor diminished during the Period for which he shall have been elected, and he shall not receive within that Period any other Emolument from the United States, or any of them.

Clause 8. This final clause in Section 1 is the oath of office administered to the new president. Interestingly, the phrase "so help me God," is not part of this oath, but has become customary in recent years.

CLAUSE 8. Before he enter on the Execution of his Office, he shall take the following Oath or Affirmation:—"I do solemnly swear (or affirm) that I will faithfully execute the Office of President of the United States, and will to the best of my Ability, preserve, protect and defend the Constitution of the United States."

Powers and Duties of the President

Section 2 Clause 1. This clause establishes the president as commander-in-chief of the U.S. armed forces. George Washington was the only U.S. president to actually lead U.S. armed forces, during the Whiskey Rebellion.

The second provision is the basis for cabinet meetings that are used to hear the opinions of executive department heads. The last provision grants an absolute pardon or reprieve power for the president.

Since the president is commander-in-chief, citizens and groups concerned with U.S. foreign policy (especially armed military conflicts) can hold the president accountable for policy decisions. Litigation, protests, marches, and electoral battles have all been used by citizens dissatisfied with presidential foreign policy decisions.

SECTION 2 CLAUSE 1. The President shall be Commander in Chief of the Army and Navy of the United States, and of the Militia of the several States, when called into the actual Service of the United States; he may require the Opinion, in writing, of the principal Officer in each of the executive Departments, upon any Subject relating to the Duties of their respective Offices, and he shall have Power to grant Reprieves and Pardons for Offences against the United States, except in Cases of Impeachment.

Clause 2. This clause covers two important presidential powers: treaty making and appointments. The president (through the State Department) can negotiate treaties with other nations, but these do not become official until ratified by a two-thirds vote of the U.S. Senate.

The president is empowered to appoint judges, ambassadors, and other U.S. officials (cabinet officers, military officers, agency heads, etc.) subject to Senate approval.

These powers are important to ensure the division of power between the three branches of our national government as well as the system of checks and balances. Sharing these powers allows for input by the people and organized groups. The Senate approves most treaties and most presidential appointments, especially if it is controlled by members of the same party as the president. But this is not always true; many treaties and appointments have been rejected, often because the Senate was responding to strong public opinion.

CLAUSE 2. He shall have Power, by and with the Advice and Consent of the Senate, to make Treaties, provided two thirds of the Senators present concur; and he shall nominate, and by and with the Advice and Consent of the Senate, shall appoint Ambassadors, other public Ministers and Consuls, Judges of the supreme Court, and all other Officers of the United States, whose Appointments are not herein otherwise provided for, and which shall be established by Law: but the Congress may by Law vest the Appointment of such inferior Officers, as they think proper, in the President alone, in the Courts of Law, or in the Heads of Departments.

Clause 3. This allows recess appointments of the officials listed in Clause 2 above. These commissions automatically expire unless approved by the Senate by the end of the next session. Presidents have used this provision to fill jobs when the nomination process is stalled.

CLAUSE 3. The President shall have Power to fill up all Vacancies that may happen during the Recess of the Senate, by granting Commissions which shall expire at the End of their next Session.

Section 3. This section provides for the annual State of the Union address to a joint session of Congress. Presidents have learned that the ability to reach out to the public can be the source of tremendous power. The State of the Union address is thus an important opportunity to speak directly to the American public, build support for initiatives, and shape the policy agenda. The president is also authorized to call special meetings of either the House or Senate. If there is disagreement between the House and Senate regarding adjournment, the president may adjourn them. This would be extremely rare. The next-to-last provision, to faithfully execute laws, provides the basis for the whole administrative apparatus of the executive branch.

SECTION 3 He shall from time to time give to the Congress Information of the State of the Union, and recommend to their Consideration such Measures as he shall judge necessary and expedient; he may, on extraordinary Occasions, convene both Houses, or either of them, and in Case of Disagreement between them, with Respect to the Time of Adjournment, he may adjourn them to such Time as he shall think proper; he shall receive Ambassadors and other public Ministers; he shall take Care that the Laws be faithfully executed, and shall Commission all the Officers of the United States.

Section 4. This section provides the constitutional authority for the impeachment and trial of the president, vice president, and all civil officers of the U.S. for treason, bribery, or other high crimes and misdemeanors (the exact meaning of this phrase is unclear and is often more political than judicial). Impeachment proceedings have been undertaken against two presidents in American history: Andrew Johnson, in 1868, and Bill Clinton in 1998. In both cases the Senate failed to convict the president, and both were allowed to stay in office. Richard Nixon would have also confronted impeachment proceedings in 1974 for his involvement in the Watergate scandal, but he resigned from office and avoided the process.

SECTION 4 The President, Vice President and all civil Officers of the United States, shall be removed from Office on Impeachment for, and Conviction of, Treason, Bribery, or other high Crimes and Misdemeanors.

Article III Section 1. This section establishes the judicial branch in very general terms. It only provides for the Supreme Court; Congress must create the court system. It first did so in the Judiciary Act of 1789, when it established 13 district courts (one for each state) and 3 appellate courts. All federal judges hold their offices for life and can only be removed for breaches of good behavior—a very ambiguous term. Federal judges have been removed for drunkenness, accepting bribes, and other misdemeanors. To date, no justice of the U.S. Supreme Court has ever been removed.

The tenure of judges in office, which can be for life, is meant to give judges the ability to make decisions according to their best judgments without facing the prospect of removal from office for issuing an unpopular judgment. While this protected tenure is an undemocratic aspect of the Constitution in the sense that it removes federal judges from direct electoral accountability, it has been an important aspect of the judiciary's ability to enforce civil rights and liberties on behalf of minority groups and unpopular individuals.

This protected tenure is one aspect of government that makes the court pathway especially attractive to individuals, small groups, and others who lack political power. For example, federal judges acted against racial discrimination in the 1950s at a time when most white Americans accepted the existence of such discrimination when applied to African Americans.The salary of federal judges is set by congressional act but can never be reduced.

Article III

THE JUDICIAL ARTICLE

Judicial Power, Courts, Judges

SECTION 1 The judicial Power of the United States, shall be vested in one supreme Court, and in such inferior Courts as the Congress may from time to time ordain and establish. The Judges, both of the supreme and inferior Courts, shall hold their Offices during good Behaviour, and shall, at stated Times, receive for their Services, a Compensation, which shall not be diminished during their Continuance in Office.

Section 2 Clause 1, 2, 3. This section establishes the original and appellate jurisdiction of the U.S. Supreme Court. Original jurisdiction cases are essentially limited to disputes between states. The 11th Amendment limited the ability of individuals to sue states. Even in these cases involving states, the Supreme Court now typically appoints a special judge to hear the evidence and make a recommendation to the justices rather than hold an actual trial at the Supreme Court. Since 1925, the Supreme Court no longer hears every case on appeal but can select which cases it will accept, which is now only about 75–85 cases per year. Although this provision mentions trial by jury in all cases, the Supreme Court's interpretations of the jury trial right, also contained in the 6th Amendment, limits the right to criminal cases involving serious crimes with punishments of 6 months of more of imprisonment.

Jurisdiction

SECTION 2 CLAUSE 1. The judicial Power shall extend to all Cases, in Law and Equity, arising under this Constitution, the Laws of the United States, and Treaties made, or which shall be made, under their Authority;—to all Cases affecting Ambassadors, other public Ministers and Consuls;—to all Cases of admiralty and maritime Jurisdiction;—to Controversies to which the United States shall be a Party;—to Controversies between two or more States—between a State and Citizens of another State;[9]—between Citizens of different States;—between Citizens of the same State claiming Lands under Grants of different States, and between a State, or the Citizens thereof, and foreign States, Citizens, or Subjects.

CLAUSE 2. In all Cases affecting Ambassadors, other public Ministers and Consuls, and those in which a State shall be Party, the supreme Court shall have original Jurisdiction. In all the other Cases before mentioned, the supreme Court shall have appellate Jurisdiction, both as to Law and Fact, with such Exceptions, and under such Regulations as Congress shall make.

Clause 1, 2, 3. This section establishes the original and appellate jurisdiction of the U.S. Supreme Court. Original jurisdiction cases are essentially limited to disputes between states. The 11th Amendment limited the ability of individuals to sue states. Even in these cases involving states, the Supreme Court now typically appoints a special judge to hear the evidence and make a recommendation to the justices rather than hold an actual trial at the Supreme Court. Since 1925, the Supreme Court no longer hears every case on appeal but can select which cases it will accept, which is now only about 75–85 cases per year. Although this provision mentions trial by jury in all cases, the Supreme Court's interpretations of the jury trial right, also contained in the 6th Amendment, limits the right to criminal cases involving serious crimes with punishments of 6 months of more of imprisonment.

CLAUSE 3. The Trial of all Crimes, except in Cases of Impeachment, shall be by Jury; and such Trial shall be held in the State where the said Crimes shall have been committed; but when not committed within any State, the Trial shall be at such Place or Places as the Congress may by Law have directed.

Treason

SECTION 3 CLAUSE 1. Treason against the United States, shall consist only in levying War against them, or in adhering to their Enemies, giving them Aid and Comfort. No Person shall be convicted of Treason unless on the Testimony of two Witnesses to the same overt Act, or on Confession in open Court.

Section 3 Clause 1, 2 Treason is the only crime defined in the U.S. Constitution. Congress established the penalty of death for treason convictions. Note that two witnesses are required to convict anyone of treason.

CLAUSE 2. The Congress shall have Power to declare the Punishment of Treason, but no Attainder of Treason shall work Corruption of Blood, or Forfeiture except during the Life of the Person attainted.

Article IV

INTERSTATE RELATIONS

Full Faith and Credit Clause

Article IV Section 1. This section provides that the official acts and records (for example, marriages and divorces) of one state will be recognized and given credence by other states. It is one of several clauses that were designed to create a strong national government. Concerns about this clause have taken on new importance in recent years, as the gay marriage issue has heated up in most state legislatures.

SECTION 1 Full Faith and Credit shall be given in each State to the public Acts, Records, and judicial Proceedings of every other State. And the Congress may by general Laws prescribe the Manner in which such Acts, Records and Proceedings shall be proved, and the Effect thereof.

Privileges and Immunities; Interstate Extradition

SECTION 2 CLAUSE 1. The Citizens of each State shall be entitled to all Privileges and Immunities of Citizens in the several States.

Section 2 Clause 1 This clause requires states to treat citizens of other states equally. For example, when driving in another state, a driver's license is recognized.

CLAUSE 2. A person charged in any State with Treason, Felony or other Crime, who shall flee from Justice, and be found in another State, shall on Demand of the executive Authority of the State from which he fled, be delivered up, to be removed to the State having Jurisdiction of the Crime.

Clause 2. *Extradition* is the name of this clause. A criminal fleeing to another state, if captured, can be returned to the state where the crime was committed. But this is not an absolute. A state's governor can refuse, for good reason, to extradite someone to another state.

Clause 3. This clause was included to cover runaway slaves. It has been made inoperable by the thirteenth Amendment, which abolished slavery.

CLAUSE 3. No person held to Service or Labour in one State, under the Laws thereof, escaping into another, shall, in Consequence of any Law or Regulation therein, be discharged from such Service or Labour, but shall be delivered up on Claim of the Party to whom such Service or Labour may be due.[10]

Admission of States

Section 3 Clauses 1, 2. This section concerns the admission of new states to the Union. In theory, no state can be created from part of another state without permission of the state legislature. But West Virginia was formed from Virginia during the Civil War without the permission of Virginia, which was part of the Confederacy. With 50 states now part of the Union, this section has not been used for many decades. The only foreseeable future use may be in the case of Puerto Rico or perhaps Washington, D.C.

SECTION 3 CLAUSE 1. New States may be admitted by the Congress into this Union; but no new State shall be formed or erected within the Jurisdiction of any other State; nor any State be formed by the Junction of two or more States, or Parts of States, without the Consent of the Legislatures of the States concerned as well as of the Congress.

CLAUSE 2. The Congress shall have Power to dispose of and make all needful Rules and Regulations respecting the Territory or other Property belonging to the United States; and nothing in this Constitution shall be so construed as to Prejudice any Claims of the United States, or of any particular State.

Republican Form of Government

Section 4. This section commits the federal government to guarantee a republican form of government to each state and to protect the states against foreign invasion or domestic insurrection.

By mandating a republican form of government, the Constitution guarantees that power rests in the hands of the citizens and is exercised by their elected representatives. As such, citizens are able to appeal directly to their governing officials through several pathways, such as through the courts, via elections, or by lobbying.

SECTION 4. The United States shall guarantee to every State in this Union a Republican Form of Government, and shall protect each of them against Invasion; and on Application of the Legislature, or of the Executive (when the Legislature cannot be convened) against domestic Violence.

Article V

THE AMENDING POWER

Article V. Amendments to the U.S. Constitution can be originated by a two-thirds vote in both the U.S. House and Senate or by two-thirds of the state legislatures asking for a convention to propose amendments. Proposed amendments, by either route, must be approved by three-fourths of state legislatures or by three-fourths of conventions convened in the states for purposes of ratification. Only one amendment has been ratified by the convention method—Amendment the twenty-first, to repeal the 18th Amendment establishing Prohibition.

Thousands of amendments have been proposed; few have been passed by two-thirds vote in each branch of Congress. The Equal Rights Amendment was one such case, but it was not ratified by three-fourths of state legislatures. There have only been 27 successful amendments to the U.S. Constitution.

Since both the federal and state levels of government are involved in amending the Constitution, interested parties have several strategies to pursue to increase the likelihood that a proposed amendment is successful or is defeated.

The Congress, whenever two thirds of both Houses shall deem it necessary, shall propose Amendments to this Constitution, or, on the Application of the Legislatures of two thirds of the several States, shall call a Convention for proposing Amendments, which, in either Case, shall be valid to all Intents and Purposes, as Part of this Constitution, when ratified by the Legislatures of three fourths of the several States, or by Conventions in three fourths thereof, as the one or the other Mode of Ratification may be proposed by the Congress; Provided that no Amendment which may be made prior to the Year One thousand eight hundred and eight shall in any Manner affect the first and fourth Clauses in the Ninth Section of the first Article; and that no State, without its Consent, shall be deprived of its equal Suffrage in the Senate.

Article VI

THE SUPREMACY ACT

CLAUSE 1. All Debts contracted and Engagements entered into, before the Adoption of this Constitution, shall be as valid against the United States under this Constitution, as under the Confederation.

Clause 1. This clause made the new national government responsible for all debts incurred during the Revolutionary War. This was very important to banking and commercial interests.

CLAUSE 2. This Constitution, and the Laws of the United States which shall be made in Pursuance thereof; and all Treaties made, or which shall be made, under the Authority of the United States, shall be the supreme Law of the Land; and the Judges in every State shall be bound thereby, any Thing in the Constitution or Laws of any State to the Contrary notwithstanding.

Clause 2. This is the National Supremacy Clause, which provides the basis for the supremacy of the national government. This seems to be a rather straightforward issue these days, but until the conclusion of the Civil War, "national supremacy" was not a settled concept.

CLAUSE 3. The Senators and Representatives before mentioned, and the Members of the several State Legislatures, and all executive and judicial Officers, both of the United States and of the several States, shall be bound by Oath or Affirmation, to support this Constitution; but no religious Test shall ever be required as a Qualification to any Office or public Trust under the United States.

Clause 3. This clause requires essentially all federal and state officials to swear or affirm their allegiance to and support of the U.S. Constitution. Note that a religious test was prohibited for federal office. However, some states used religious tests for voting and office qualification until the 1830s.

Article VII

Article VII. In the end, all 13 states ratified the Constitution. But it was a close call in several states.

RATIFICATION

The Ratification of the Conventions of nine States, shall be sufficient for the Establishment of this Constitution between the States so ratifying the Same.

Done in Convention by the Unanimous Consent of the States present the Seventeenth Day of September in the Year of our Lord one thousand seven hundred and Eighty seven and of the Independence of the United States of America the Twelfth. In Witness whereof We have hereunto subscribed our Names.

Realizing the unanimous ratification of the new Constitution by the 13 states might never have occurred, the framers wisely specified that only 9 states would be needed for ratification. Even this proved to be a test of wills between Federalists and Anti-Federalists, leading to publication of the great political work *The Federalist Papers.*

Amendments

The Bill of Rights

[The first ten amendments were ratified on December 15, 1791, and form what is known as the "Bill of Rights."]

The Bill of Rights applied at first only to the federal government and not to state or local governments. Beginning in 1925 in the case of *Gitlow* v. *New York,* the U.S. Supreme Court began to selectively incorporate the Bill of Rights, making its provisions applicable to state and local governments, with some exceptions, which will be discussed at the appropriate amendment.

Until the Supreme Court incorporated the Bill of Rights to include protections from state governments, citizens had to look to state constitutions for protections of civil liberties.

AMENDMENT 1

RELIGION, SPEECH, ASSEMBLY, AND PETITION

Congress shall make no law respecting an establishment of religion, or prohibiting the free exercise thereof; or abridging the freedom of speech, or of the press; or the right of the people peaceably to assemble, and to petition the Government for a redress of grievances.

Amendment 1. This amendment protects five fundamental freedoms: religion, speech, press, assembly, and petition. The press is the only business that is specifically protected by the U.S. Constitution. Freedom of religion and speech are two of the most contentious issues and generate a multitude of Supreme Court cases.

These freedoms are crucial for nearly every pathway of change; without each fundamental right, individuals and groups could not pursue change without fear of reprisal. This amendment is perhaps the most crucial to guarantee a free society.

Amendment 2. Those who favor gun ownership, either for protection, hunting or sport, cite this amendment. This amendment has not been incorporated for state/local governments; that is, state and local governments are free to regulate arms, provided such regulation is not barred by their own state constitutions.

There is controversy as to the meaning of this amendment. Some believe that it specifically refers to citizen militias, which were common at the time of the Constitution but now have been replaced by permanent armed forces (state national guard units), thereby allowing the federal government to regulate gun ownership. Others believe that the amendment refers to individuals directly, therefore guaranteeing private citizens the right to own guns. The Supreme Court's decisions have never declared that this amendment guarantees to individuals the right to own or carry firearms.

AMENDMENT 2
MILITIA AND THE RIGHT TO BEAR ARMS

A well-regulated Militia, being necessary to the security of a free State, the right of the people to keep and bear Arms, shall not be infringed.

Amendment 3. It was the practice of the British government to insist that colonists provide room or board to British troops. This amendment was designed to prohibit this practice. Today, military and naval bases provide the necessary quarters and this issue does not arise. This amendment has not been incorporated and applies only against the federal government.

AMENDMENT 3
QUARTERING OF SOLDIERS

No Soldier shall, in time of peace be quartered in any house, without the consent of the Owner, nor in time of war, but in manner to be prescribed by law.

Amendment 4. This extremely important amendment is designed to prevent the abuse of police powers. Essentially, unreasonable searches or seizures of homes, persons, or property cannot be undertaken without probable cause or a warrant that specifically describes the place to be searched, the person involved, and the suspicious things to be seized.

People who believe that these rights have been violated have successfully used the court-centered pathway for protection, either by seeking to have improperly obtained evidence excluded from use in court or by seeking money damages from police officials to compensate for the invasion of a home or an improper search of an individual's body.

Many people feel that the rights of the accused are often given more precedence than the rights of victims. The Constitution does not contain rights for victims, but a constitutional amendment has been proposed to protect victims' rights. This does not mean that victims are unprotected by the law. States and the federal government have statutes that provide protections and services for crime victims.

AMENDMENT 4
SEARCHES AND SEIZURES

The right of the people to be secure in their persons, houses, papers, and effects, against unreasonable searches and seizures, shall not be violated, and no Warrants shall issue, but upon probable cause, supported by Oath or affirmation, and particularly describing the place to be searched, and the persons or things to be seized.

Amendment 5. Only a grand jury can indict a person for a federal crime. (This provision does not apply to state/local governments because it has not been incorporated by the Supreme Court.) This amendment also covers double jeopardy, or being tried twice for the same crime in the same jurisdiction. This amendment also covers the prohibition of compelled self-incrimination. The deprivation of life, liberty, or property is prohibited unless due process of law is applied. This provision applies to the federal government, and there is a parallel provision that applies to state and local governments in the 14th Amendment. Finally, private property may not be taken under the doctrine of "eminent domain" unless the government provides just compensation.

AMENDMENT 5
GRAND JURIES, SELF-INCRIMINATION, DOUBLE JEOPARDY, DUE PROCESS, AND EMINENT DOMAIN

No person shall be held to answer for a capital, or otherwise infamous crime, unless on a presentment or indictment of a Grand jury, except in cases arising in the land or naval forces, or in the Militia, when in actual service in time of War or public danger; nor shall any person be subject for the same offence to be twice put in jeopardy of life or limb; nor shall be compelled in any criminal case to be a witness against himself, nor be deprived of life, liberty, or property, without due process of law; nor shall private property be taken for public use, without just compensation.

AMENDMENT 6

CRIMINAL COURT PROCEDURES

In all criminal prosecutions, the accused shall enjoy the right to a speedy and public trial, by an impartial jury of the State and district wherein the crime shall have been committed, which district shall have been previously ascertained by law, and to be informed of the nature and cause of the accusation; to be confronted with the witnesses against him; to have compulsory process for obtaining witnesses in his favor, and to have the Assistance of Counsel for his defence.

Amendment 6. This amendment requires public trials by jury for criminal prosecutions. However, the Supreme Court only applies the right to trial by jury to serious offenses, not petty offenses. Anyone accused of a crime is guaranteed the rights to be informed of the charges; to confront witnesses; to subpoena witnesses for their defense; and to have a lawyer for their defense. The government must provide a lawyer for a defendant unable to afford one for any case in which the defendant faces the possibility of a jail or prison sentence.

There are serious questions about the adequacy of attorney performance and resources for criminal defense. In some jurisdictions, there are not enough defense attorneys for poor defendants, so that the attorneys spend little time on each case. In addition, the Supreme Court does not have strict standards for attorney performance, so some defendants have been represented by attorneys who know very little about criminal law.

AMENDMENT 7

TRIAL BY JURY IN COMMON LAW CASES

In Suits at common law, where the value in controversy shall exceed twenty dollars, the right of trial by jury shall be preserved, and no fact tried by a jury shall be otherwise reexamined in any Court of the United States, than according to the rules of the common law.

Amendment 7. The right to trial by jury in civil cases will never be incorporated by the Supreme Court for application against state and local governments, because it would impose a huge financial burden (jury trials are very expensive).

AMENDMENT 8

BAIL, CRUEL AND UNUSUAL PUNISHMENT

Excessive bail shall not be required, nor excessive fines imposed, nor cruel and unusual punishments inflicted.

Amendment 8. The Supreme Court has not clearly defined the limits imposed by prohibition of excessive bail or excessive fines. Thus these rights rarely arise in legal cases, and bail amounts in excessive of $1 million will periodically be imposed for serious crimes or wealthy defendants. The prohibition on cruel and unusual punishments focuses on criminal punishments, not other contexts (such as the punishment of children in public schools or civil fines against businesses). Cruel and unusual punishments are defined according to current societal values and thus the definition of what is "cruel and unusual" can change over time. This provision bars punishments that are either excessive or torturous.

Capital punishment is covered by this amendment, as well as the treatment of prisoners inside prisons. Court cases challenging the constitutionality of capital punishment cite this amendment's language prohibiting cruel and unusual punishment. For a period of 4 years (1973–1976), the Supreme Court banned capital punishment as it was then being applied by the states. When states modified their statutes to provide a two-part judicial process of guilt determination and punishment, the Supreme Court allowed the reinstitution of capital punishment by the states.

AMENDMENT 9

RIGHTS RETAINED BY THE PEOPLE

The enumeration in the Constitution, of certain rights, shall not be construed to deny or disparage others retained by the people.

Amendment 9. This amendment implies that there may be other rights of the people not specified by the previous amendments, but the wording gives no guidance about what those rights might be. Instead, when the Supreme Court has identified rights not specifically mentioned in the Bill of Rights, it has tended to claim that these rights, such as privacy and the right to travel between states, are connected to the right to "due process" found in the 5th and 14th Amendments.

AMENDMENT 10

RESERVED POWERS OF THE STATES

The powers not delegated to the United States by the Constitution, nor prohibited by it to the States, are reserved to the States respectively, or to the people.

Amendment 10. The 10th Amendment was seen as the reservoir of reserved powers for state governments. But the doctrine of implied national government powers, which was established by the U.S. Supreme Court in *McCulloch* v. *Maryland* (1819), undercut the words and apparent intent of this amendment. With the exception of a few decisions, the Supreme Court has generally deferred to assertions of federal power since the 1930s.

AMENDMENT 11
SUITS AGAINST THE STATES

[Ratified February 7, 1795]

The Judicial power of the United States shall not be construed to extend to any suit in law or equity, commenced or prosecuted against one of the United States by Citizens of another State, or by Citizens or Subjects of any Foreign State.

Amendment 11. Article III of the U.S. Constitution originally allowed federal jurisdiction in cases of one state citizen against another state citizen or state. This amendment removes federal jurisdiction in this area. In essence, states may not be sued in federal court by citizens of another state or country.

AMENDMENT 12
ELECTION OF THE PRESIDENT

[Ratified June 15, 1804]

The Electors shall meet in their respective states, and vote by ballot for President and Vice-President, one of whom, at least, shall not be an inhabitant of the same state with themselves; they shall name in their ballots the person voted for as President, and in distinct ballots the person voted for as Vice-President, and they shall make distinct lists of all persons voted for as President, and of all persons voted for as Vice-President, and of the number of votes for each, which lists they shall sign and certify, and transmit sealed to the seat of the government of the United States, directed to the President of the Senate;—The President of the Senate shall, in the presence of the Senate and House of Representatives, open all the certificates and the votes shall then be counted;—The person having the greatest number of votes for President, shall be the President, if such number be a majority of the whole number of Electors appointed; and if no person have such majority, then from the persons having the highest numbers not exceeding three on the list of those voted for as President, the House of Representatives shall choose immediately, by ballot, the President. But in choosing the President, the votes shall be taken by states, the representation from each state having one vote; a quorum for this purpose shall consist of a member or members from two-thirds of the states, and a majority of all the states shall be necessary to a choice. And if the House of Representatives shall not choose a President whenever the right of choice shall devolve upon them, before the fourth day of March next following, then the Vice-President shall act as President, as in the case of the death or other constitutional disability of the President.[11] The person having the greatest number of votes as Vice-President, shall be the Vice-President, if such a number be a majority of the whole numbers of Electors appointed, and if no person have a majority, then from the two highest numbers on the list, the

Amendment 12. This was a necessary amendment to correct a flaw in the Constitution covering operations of the Electoral College. In the election of 1800, Thomas Jefferson and Aaron Burr, both of the same Democratic-Republican Party, received the same number of electoral votes, 73, for president. Article II of the original Constitution specified that each elector would cast two ballots. It did not specify for whom. This amendment clarifies that the electoral vote must be specific for president and vice president. The original Constitution provided that if no candidate received a majority of electoral votes, the House would decide from the candidates with the top five vote totals. This amendment reduces the candidate field to the top three vote totals. If the House delays in this selection past the fourth day of March, the elected vice president will act as president until the House selects the president. The original Constitution provided that the candidate with the second highest number of electoral votes would become vice president.

This amendment, which requires a separate vote tally for vice president, provides for selection by the U.S. Senate if no vice presidential candidate receives an electoral vote majority.

Senate shall choose the Vice-President; a quorum for the purpose shall consist of two-thirds of the whole number of Senators, and a majority of the whole number shall be necessary to a choice. But no person constitutionally ineligible to the office of President shall be eligible to that of Vice-President of the United States.

AMENDMENT 13
PROHIBITION OF SLAVERY

[Ratified December 6, 1865]

SECTION 1 Neither slavery nor involuntary servitude, except as a punishment for crime whereof the party shall have been duly convicted, shall exist within the United States, or any place subject to their jurisdiction.

SECTION 2 Congress shall have power to enforce this article by appropriate legislation.

Amendment 13. This is the first of the three Civil War amendments. Slavery is prohibited under all circumstances. Involuntary servitude is also prohibited unless it is a punishment for a convicted crime.

AMENDMENT 14
CITIZENSHIP, DUE PROCESS, AND EQUAL PROTECTION OF THE LAWS

[Ratified July 9, 1868]

SECTION 1 All persons born or naturalized in the United States, and subject to the jurisdiction thereof, are citizens of the United States and of the State wherein they reside. No State shall make or enforce any law which shall abridge the privileges or immunities of citizens of the United States; nor shall any State deprive any person of life, liberty, or property, without due process of law; nor deny to any person within its jurisdiction the equal protection of the laws.

Amendment 14 Section 1. This section defines the meaning of U.S. citizenship and protection of these citizenship rights. It also establishes the Equal Protection Clause, meaning that each state must guarantee fundamental rights and liberties to all of its citizens. It extended the provisions of the 5th Amendment of due process and protection of life, liberty, and property and made these applicable to the states. The due process clause has been especially important for the expansion of civil rights and liberties as the Supreme Court interpreted it in a flexible manner to recognize new rights (e.g., privacy, right of choice for abortion, etc.) and to apply the Bill of Rights against the states.

SECTION 2 Representatives shall be apportioned among the several States according to their respective numbers, counting the whole number of persons in each State, excluding Indians not taxed. But when the right to vote at any election for the choice of electors for President and Vice President of the United States, Representatives in Congress, the Executive and Judicial officers of a State, or the members of the Legislature thereof, is denied to any of the male inhabitants of such State, being twenty-one years of age, and citizens of the United States, or in any way abridged, except for participation in rebellion, or other crime, the basis of representation therein shall be reduced in the proportion which the number of such male citizens shall bear to the whole number of male citizens twenty-one years of age in such State.

Section 2. This section changed the Three-Fifths Clause of the original Constitution. At the time of ratification of this amendment, all male citizens, 21 or older, were used to calculate representation in the House of Representatives. If a state denied the right to vote to any male 21 or older, the number of denied citizens would be deducted from the overall state total to determine representation.

This is the first time that gender was entered into the Constitution. It was not until 50 years later (in 1920 with the 19th Amendment) that women were granted the right to vote.

Section 3. This section disqualifies from federal office or elector for president or vice president anyone who rebelled or participated in an insurrection (that is, the Confederate Army after the Civil War) against the Constitution. This was specifically directed against citizens of Southern states. Congress by a two-thirds vote could override this provision.

SECTION 3 No person shall be a Senator or Representative in Congress, or elector of President and Vice President, or hold any office, civil or military, under the United States, or under any State, who, having previously taken an oath, as a member of Congress, or as an officer of the United States, or as a member of any State legislature, or as an executive or judicial officer of any State, to support the Constitution of the United States, shall have engaged in insurrection or rebellion against the same, or given aid or comfort to the enemies thereof. But Congress may by a vote of two-thirds of each House, remove such disability.

Section 4, 5. Section 4 covers the Civil War debts; Section 5 grants to Congress the very specific authority to create legislation that will implement and enforce the provisions of the 14th Amendment.

Unlike the Bill of Rights, which is intended to protect individuals by limiting the power of the federal government, including Congress, Section 5 intends to empower Congress to create laws that will protect individuals from actions by states that violate their rights.

Although the 13th and 14th Amendments were designed to end slavery, and provide citizenship, due process, and equal protection rights for freed slaves and their offspring, they were interpreted very narrowly until the 1960s. Civil rights activists had to use the court-centered, cultural change, and grassroots mobilization pathways to force legal, political, and social change to allow all individuals, regardless of color or race, to enjoy full civil rights.

SECTION 4 The validity of the public debt of the United States, authorized by law, including debts incurred for payment of pensions and bounties for services in suppressing insurrection or rebellion, shall not be questioned. But neither the United States nor any State shall assume or pay any debt or obligation incurred in aid of insurrection or rebellion against the United States, or any claim for the loss or emancipation of any slave; but all such debts, obligations and claims shall be held illegal and void.

SECTION 5 The Congress shall have power to enforce, by appropriate legislation, the provisions of this article.

Amendment 15 Section 1, 2. This final Civil War amendment states that voting rights could not be denied by any states on account of race, color, or previous servitude. It did not mention gender. Accordingly, only male citizens 21 or over were guaranteed the right to vote by this amendment. Some states sought to defeat the intent of the amendment by adopting additional restrictions to voting rights (such as poll taxes, whites-only primaries and literacy tests) in order to block the participation of African-American voters. These restrictions were eliminated in the 1960s as civil rights activists effectively used several pathways for change: court, lobbying decision makers, and grassroots mobilization.

AMENDMENT 15
THE RIGHT TO VOTE

[Ratified February 3, 1870]

SECTION 1 The right of citizens of the United States to vote shall not be denied or abridged by the United States or by any State on account of race, color, or previous condition of servitude.

SECTION 2 The Congress shall have power to enforce this article by appropriate legislation.

Amendment 16. Article I, Section 9 of the original Constitution prohibited Congress from enacting a direct tax unless in proportion to a census. Congress in 1894 passed an income tax law, levying a 2 percent tax on incomes over $4,000. In 1895, the U.S. Supreme Court in a split decision (5–4) found that the income tax was a direct tax not apportioned among the states and was thus unconstitutional. Thus, Congress proposed an amendment allowing it to enact an income tax. Once this amendment was ratified, the flow of tax money to Washington increased tremendously.

AMENDMENT 16
INCOME TAXES

[Ratified February 3, 1913]

The Congress shall have power to lay and collect taxes on incomes, from whatever source derived, without apportionment among the several States, and without regard to any census or enumeration.

AMENDMENT 17
DIRECT ELECTION OF SENATORS

[Ratified April 8, 1913]

The Senate of the United States shall be composed of two Senators from each State, elected by the people thereof, for six years; and each Senator shall have one vote. The electors in each State shall have the qualifications requisite for electors of the most numerous branch of the State legislatures.

When vacancies happen in the representation of any State in the Senate, the executive authority of such State shall issue writs of election to fill such vacancies: Provided, That the legislature of any State may empower the executive thereof to make temporary appointments until the people fill the vacancies by election as the legislature may direct.

This amendment shall not be so construed as to affect the election or term of any Senator chosen before it becomes valid as part of the Constitution.

Amendment 17. Before this amendment, U.S. senators were selected by state legislatures. Now U.S. senators would be selected by popular vote in each state. Further, the governor of each state may fill vacancies, subject to state laws.

AMENDMENT 18
PROHIBITION

[Ratified January 16, 1919. Repealed December 5, 1933 by Amendment 21]

SECTION 1 After one year from the ratification of this article the manufacture, sale, or transportation of intoxicating liquors within, the importation thereof into, or the exportation thereof from the United States and all territory subject to the jurisdiction thereof for beverage purposes is hereby prohibited.

SECTION 2 The Congress and the several States shall have concurrent power to enforce this article by appropriate legislation.

SECTION 3 This article shall be inoperative unless it shall have been ratified as an amendment to the Constitution by the legislatures of the several States, as provided in the Constitution, within seven years from the date of the submission hereof to the States by the Congress.[13]

Amendment 18. This amendment was largely the work of the Women's Christian Temperance Union and essentially banned the manufacture, sale, or transportation of alcoholic beverages. Unintended consequences of this attempt to legislate morality were the brewing of "bathtub gin" and moonshine liquor and the involvement of organized crime in importing liquor from Canada. The 21st Amendment repealed this provision. This is also the first amendment where Congress fixed a period for ratification—7 years.

AMENDMENT 19
FOR WOMEN'S SUFFRAGE

[Ratified August 18, 1920]

The right of the citizens of the United States to vote shall not be denied or abridged by the United States or by any State on account of sex.

Congress shall have power to enforce this article.

Amendment 19. Women achieved voting parity with men. It took enormous efforts by a large number of women and men to win this right, spanning over 70 years (from the call for the right to vote at the first women's rights convention in Seneca Falls, New York, in 1848). Suffragists protested, sued, marched, lobbied, and were imprisoned in their battle to win equal voting rights for men and women.

Amendment 20. Called the Lame Duck amendment, this amendment fixes the dates for the end of presidential and legislative terms. A new president is elected in November, but the current president remains in office until January 20th of the following year, thus the term "lame duck." Legislative terms begin earlier, on January 3rd.

AMENDMENT 20
THE LAME DUCK AMENDMENT

[Ratified January 23, 1933]

SECTION 1. The terms of the President and Vice President shall end at noon on the 20th day of January, and the terms of the Senators and Representatives at noon on the 3d day of January, of the years in which such terms would have ended if this article had not been ratified; and the terms of their successors shall then begin.

SECTION 2 The Congress shall assemble at least once in every year, and such meeting shall begin at noon on the 3d day of January, unless they shall by law appoint a different day.

SECTION 3 If, at the time fixed for the beginning of the term of the President, the President elect shall have died, the Vice President elect shall become President. If a President shall not have been chosen before the time fixed for the beginning of his term, or if the President elect shall have failed to qualify, then the Vice President elect shall act as President until a President shall have qualified; and the Congress may by law provide for the case wherein neither a President elect nor a Vice President elect shall have qualified, declaring who shall then act as President, or the manner in which one who is to act shall be selected, and such person shall act accordingly until a President or Vice President shall have qualified.

SECTION 4 The Congress may by law provide for the case of the death of any of the persons from whom the House of Representatives may choose a President whenever the right of choice shall have devolved upon them, and for the case of the death of any of the persons from whom the Senate may choose a Vice President whenever the right of choice shall have devolved upon them.

SECTION 5 Sections 1 and 2 shall take effect on the 15th day of October following the ratification of this article.

SECTION 6 This article shall be inoperative unless it shall have been ratified as an amendment to the Constitution by the legislatures of three-fourths of the several States within seven years from the date of its submission.

AMENDMENT 21
REPEAL OF PROHIBITION

[Ratified December 5, 1933]

SECTION 1 The eighteenth article of amendment to the Constitution of the United States is hereby repealed.

SECTION 2 The transportation or importation into any State, Territory, or possession of the United States for delivery or use therein of intoxicating liquors, in violation of the laws thereof, is hereby prohibited.

SECTION 3 This article shall be inoperative unless it shall have been ratified as an amendment to the Constitution by conventions in the several States, as provided in the Constitution, within seven years from the date of the submission hereof to the States by the Congress.

Amendment 21. This unusual amendment nullified the 18th Amendment. The amendment called for the end of Prohibition unless prohibited by state laws.

This is the only instance of one amendment nullifying another. Here, governmental actions reflected the will of the majority. Initially, there was concern that the production and consumption of alcohol was detrimental to society, but as time passed, public opinion shifted. The public became less concerned about consumption and more worried about the illegal manufacture of alcohol and the subsequent growth of illegal markets and urban violence.

AMENDMENT 22
NUMBER OF PRESIDENTIAL TERMS

[Ratified February 27, 1951]

SECTION 1 No person shall be elected to the office of the President more than twice, and no person who has held the office of President, or acted as President, for more than two years of a term to which some other person was elected President shall be elected to the office of the President more than once. But this article shall not apply to any person holding the office of President when this article was proposed by the Congress, and shall not prevent any person who may be holding the office of President, or acting as President, during the term within which this article becomes operative from holding the office of President or acting as President during the remainder of such term.

SECTION 2 This article shall be inoperative unless it shall have been ratified as an amendment to the Constitution by the legislatures of three-fourths of the several states within seven years from the date of its submission to the states by the Congress.

Amendment 22. This amendment could be called the Franklin D. Roosevelt amendment. It was FDR who broke the previously unwritten rule, established by George Washington, of serving no more than two terms as president. Democrat Roosevelt won election to an unprecedented four terms as president (although he died before completing his fourth term). When the Republicans took control of the Congress in 1948, they pushed through the 22nd Amendment, limiting the U.S. president to a lifetime of two full 4-year terms of office.

AMENDMENT 23
PRESIDENTIAL ELECTORS FOR THE DISTRICT OF COLUMBIA

[Ratified March 29, 1961]

SECTION 1 The District constituting the seat of government of the United States shall appoint in such manner as the Congress may direct:

A number of electors of President and Vice President equal to the whole number of Senators and Representatives in Congress to which the District would

Amendment 23. This amendment gave electoral votes to the residents of Washington, D.C., which is not a state and thus not included in the original scheme of state electoral votes. Currently, Washington, D.C., has 3 electoral votes, bringing the total of presidential electoral votes to 538. Residents of Washington, D.C., do not, however, have voting representation in Congress. Puerto Ricans are citizens of the U.S. but have no electoral votes. Both Washington, D.C., and Puerto Rico are represented in Congress by non-voting delegates.

be entitled if it were a state, but in no event more than the least populous state; they shall be in addition to those appointed by the states, but they shall be considered, for the purposes of the election of President and Vice President, to be electors appointed by a state; and they shall meet in the District and perform such duties as provided by the twelfth article of amendment.

SECTION 2 The Congress shall have power to enforce this article by appropriate legislation.

Amendment 24. The poll tax was a procedure used mostly in southern states to discourage poor white and black voters from registering to vote. Essentially, one would have to pay a tax to register to vote. The tax was around $34/year (sometimes retroactive), which amounted to a great deal of money to the poor, serving to disenfranchise a great proportion of the poor. As part of the fight for universal voting rights for all, the poll tax was abolished. Literacy tests, another device to disqualify voters, were abolished by the Voting Rights Act of 1965.

By banning this tax (coupled with other civil rights reforms), the United States delivered what the civil rights amendments promised — full voting rights for all citizens regardless of race.

AMENDMENT 24

THE ANTI-POLL TAX AMENDMENT

[Ratified January 23, 1964]

SECTION 1 The right of citizens of the United States to vote in any primary or other election for President or Vice President, for electors for President or Vice President, or for Senator or Representative in Congress, shall not be denied or abridged by the United States or any state by reason of failure to pay any poll tax or other tax.

SECTION 2 The Congress shall have power to enforce this article by appropriate legislation.

Amendment 25. President Woodrow Wilson's final year in office was marked by serious illness. It is rumored that his wife acted as president. There was no constitutional provision to cover an incapacitating illness of a president. This amendment provides a procedure for this eventuality. The president can inform congressional leaders of his/her incapacitation, and the vice president then takes over. When the president recovers, he/she can inform congressional leaders and resume office.

The amendment also recognizes that the president may not be able or wish to indicate this lack of capacity. In this case, the vice president and a majority of cabinet members can inform congressional leaders, and the vice president takes over. When the president informs congressional leadership that he/she is back in form, he/she resumes the presidency unless the vice president and a majority of the cabinet members disagree. Then Congress must decide who is to be president. The likelihood that this procedure will ever be used is relatively small.

The most immediate importance of this amendment concerns the office of vice president. The original Constitution did not address the issue of a vacancy in this office. This amendment was ratified in 1967, only a few years before it was needed. In 1973, the sitting vice president, Spiro Agnew, resigned his office. Under the provisions of this amendment, President Nixon nominated Gerald Ford as vice president. As a former member of the House, Ford was quickly approved by the Congress. But a year later, President Nixon also resigned. Now Vice President Ford became President Ford, and he in turn appointed Nelson Rockefeller as the new vice president. For the first time in our history, neither the president nor the vice president were selected by the electoral college after a national election.

AMENDMENT 25

PRESIDENTIAL DISABILITY, VICE PRESIDENTIAL VACANCIES

[Ratified February 10, 1967]

SECTION 1 In case of the removal of the President from office or of his death or resignation, the Vice President shall become President.

SECTION 2 Whenever there is a vacancy in the office of the Vice President, the President shall nominate a Vice President who shall take the office upon confirmation by a majority vote of both Houses of Congress.

SECTION 3 Whenever the President transmits to the President pro tempore of the Senate and the Speaker of the House of Representatives his written declaration that he is unable to discharge the powers and duties of his office, and until he transmits to them a written declaration to the contrary, such powers and duties shall be discharged by the Vice President as Acting President.

SECTION 4 Whenever the Vice President and a majority of either the principal officers of the executive departments, or of such other body as Congress may by law provide, transmit to the President pro tempore of the Senate and the Speaker of the House of Representatives their written declaration that the President is unable to discharge the powers and duties of his office, the Vice President shall immediately assume the powers and duties of the office as Acting President.

Thereafter, when the President transmits to the President pro tempore of the Senate and the Speaker of the House of Representatives his written declaration that no inability exists, he shall resume the powers and duties of his office unless the Vice President and a majority of either the principal officers of the executive department, or of such other body as Congress may by law provide, transmit within four days to the President pro tempore of the Senate and the Speaker of the House of Representatives their written declaration that the President is unable to discharge the powers and duties of his office. Thereupon Congress shall decide the issue, assembling within forty-eight hours for that purpose if not in session. If the Congress, within twenty-one days after receipt of the latter written declaration, or, if Congress is not in session, within twenty-one days after Congress is required to assemble, determines by two-thirds vote of both Houses that the President is unable to discharge the powers and duties of his office, the Vice President shall continue to discharge the same as Acting President; otherwise, the President shall resume the powers and duties of his office.

AMENDMENT 26

EIGHTEEN-YEAR-OLD VOTE

[Ratified July 1, 1971]

SECTION 1 The right of citizens of the United States, who are 18 years of age or older, to vote, shall not be denied or abridged by the United States or by any state on account of age.

SECTION 2 The Congress shall have power to enforce this article by appropriate legislation.

AMENDMENT 27

CONGRESSIONAL SALARIES

[Ratified May 7, 1992]

No law varying the compensation for the services of the Senators and Representatives shall take effect until an election of Representatives shall have intervened.

Amendment 26 Section 1, 2. During the Vietnam War, 18-year-olds were being drafted and sent out to possibly die in the service of their country. Yet they did not even have the right to vote. This incongruity led to the 26th Amendment, which lowered the legal voting age from 21 to 18.

Before the passage of this amendment, young people, being denied the ability to express themselves peacefully with the vote, often felt frustrated with their inability to express their concerns and influence public policy. With the passage of this amendment, those citizens over the age of 18 could pursue the election-centered pathway (and others) to instigate change.

Amendment 27. This is a "sleeper" amendment that was part of 12 amendments originally submitted by the first Congress to the states for ratification. The states only ratified 10 of the 12, which collectively became known as the Bill of Rights. But since Congress did not set a time limit for ratification, the other two amendments remained on the table. Much to the shock of the body politic, in 1992, three-fourths of the states ratified original amendment 12 of 12. This reflected the disgust of seeing Congress continuing to increase its salary and benefits. The amendment delays any increase of compensation for at least one election cycle.

1 Modified by the 16th Amendment
2 Replaced by Section 2, 14th Amendment
3 Repealed by the 17th Amendment
4 Modified by the 17th Amendment
5 Changed by the 20th Amendment
6 Modified by the 16th Amendment
7 Changed by the 12th and 20th Amendments
8 Modified by the 25th Amendment
9 Modified by the 11th Amendment
10 Repealed by the 13th Amendment
11 Changed by the 20th Amendment
12 Changed by the 26th Amendment
13 Repealed by the 21st Amendment

APPENDIX 3

The Federalist, No. 10, James Madison

To the People of the State of New York: Among the numerous advantages promised by a well-constructed union, none deserves to be more accurately developed than its tendency to break and control the violence of faction. The friend of popular governments, never finds himself so much alarmed for their character and fate, as when he contemplates their propensity of this dangerous vice. He will not fail, therefore, to set a due value on any plan which, without violating the principles to which he is attached, provides a proper cure for it. The instability, injustice, and confusion introduced into the public councils, have, in truth, been the mortal diseases under which popular governments have every-where perished; as they continue to be the favorite and fruitful topics from which the adversaries to liberty derive their most specious declamations. The valuable improvements made by the American constitutions on the popular models, both ancient and modern, cannot certainly be too much admired; but it would be an unwarrantable partiality, to contend that they have as effectually obviated the danger on this side, as was wished and expected. Complaints are everywhere heard from our most considerate and virtuous citizens, equally the friends of public and private faith, and of public and personal liberty, that our governments are too unstable; that the public good is disregarded in the conflicts of rival parties; and that measures are too often decided, not according to the rules of justice, and the rights of the minor party, but by the superior force of an interested and overbearing majority. However anxiously we may wish that these complaints had no foundation, the evidence of known facts will not permit us to deny that they are in some degree true. It will be found, indeed, on a candid review of our situation, that some of the distresses under which we labor have been erroneously charged on the operations of our governments; but it will be found, at the same time, that other causes will not alone account for many of our heaviest misfortunes; and, particularly, for that prevailing and increasing distrust of public engagements, and alarm for private rights, which are echoed from one end of the continent to the other. These must be chiefly, if not wholly, effects of the unsteadiness and injustice, with which a factious spirit has tainted our public administrations.

By a faction, I understand a number of citizens, whether amounting to a majority of the whole, who are united and actuated by some common impulse of passion, or of interest, adverse to the rights of other citizens, or to the permanent and aggregate interests of the community.

There are two methods of curing the mischiefs of faction: the one, by removing its causes; the other, by controlling its effects.

There are again two methods of removing the causes of faction: the one, by destroying the liberty which is essential to its existence; the other, by giving to every citizen the same opinions, the same passions, and the same interests.

It could never be more truly said, than of the first remedy, that it was worse than the disease. Liberty is to faction what air is to fire, an aliment without which it instantly expires. But it could not be a less folly to abolish liberty, which is essential to political life, because it nourishes faction, than it would be to wish the annihilation of air, which is essential to animal life, because it imparts to fire its destructive agency.

The second expedient is as impracticable, as the first would be unwise. As long as the reason of man continues fallible, and he is at liberty to exercise it, different opinions will be formed. As long as the connection subsists between his reason and his self-love, his opinions and his passions will have a reciprocal influence on each other; and the former will be objects to which the latter will attach themselves. The diversity in the faculties of men, from which the rights of property originate, is not less an insuperable obstacle to an uniformity of interests. The protection of these faculties is the first object of government. From the protection of different and unequal faculties of acquiring property, the possession of different degrees and kinds of property immediately results; and from the influence of these on the sentiments and views of the respective proprietors, ensues a division of the society into different interests and parties.

The latent causes of faction are thus sown in the nature of man; and we see them everywhere brought into different degrees of activity, according to the different circumstances of civil society. A zeal for different opinions concerning religion, concerning government, and many other points, as well of speculation as of practice; an attachment to different leaders ambitiously contending for preeminence and power; or to persons of other descriptions whose fortunes have been interesting to the human passions, have, in turn, divided mankind into parties, inflamed them with mutual animosity, and rendered them much more disposed to vex and oppress each other, than to cooperate for their common good. So strong is this propensity of mankind, to fall into mutual animosities, that where no substantial occasion presents itself, the most frivolous and fanciful distinctions have been sufficient to kindle their unfriendly passions and excite their most violent conflicts. But the most common and durable source of factions, has been the various and unequal distribution of property. Those who hold, and those who are without property, have ever formed distinct interests in society. Those who are creditors, and those who are debtors, fall under a like discrimination. A landed interest, a manufacturing interest, a mercantile interest, a moneyed interest, with many lesser interests, grow up of necessity in civilized nations, and divide them into different classes, actuated by different sentiments and views. The regulation of these various and interfering interests forms the principal task of modern legislation, and involves the spirit of the party and faction in the necessary and ordinary operations of the government.

No man is allowed to be a judge in his own cause; because his interest will certainly bias his judgment, and, not improbably, corrupt his integrity. With equal, nay, with greater reason, a body of men are unfit to be both judges and parties at the same time; yet what are many of the most important acts of legislation, but so many judicial determinations, not indeed concerning the right of single persons, but concerning the rights of large bodies of citizens? And what are the different classes of legislators, but advocates and parties to the causes which they determine? Is a law proposed concerning private debts? It is a question to which the creditors are parties on one side, and the debtors on the other. Justice ought to hold the balance between them. Yet the parties are, and must be, themselves the judges; and the most numerous party, or, in other words, the most powerful faction, must be expected to prevail. Shall domestic manufacturers be encouraged, and in what degree, by restrictions on foreign manufacturers? Are questions which would be differently decided by the landed and the manufacturing classes; and probably by neither with a sole regard to justice and the public good. The apportionment of taxes, on the various descriptions of property, is an act which seems to require the most exact impartiality; yet there is, perhaps, no legislative act, in which greater opportunity and temptation are given to a predominant party to trample on the rules of justice. Every shilling, with which they overburden the inferior number, is a shilling saved to their own pockets.

It is in vain to say, that enlightened statesmen will be able to adjust these clashing interests, and render them all subservient to the public good. Enlightened statesmen will not always be at the helm, nor, in many cases, can such an adjustment be made at all, without taking into view indirect and remote considerations, which will rarely prevail over the immediate interest which one party may find in disregarding the rights of another, or the good of the whole.

The inference to which we are brought is, that the causes of faction cannot be removed; and that relief is only to be sought in the means of controlling its effects.

If a faction consists of less than a majority, relief is supplied by the republican principle, which enables the majority to defeat its sinister views, by regular vote. It may clog the administration, it may convulse the society; but it will be unable to execute and mask its violence under the forms of the Constitution. When a majority is included in a faction, the form of popular government, on the other hand, enables it to sacrifice to its ruling passion or interest, both the public good and the rights of other citizens. To secure the public good, and private rights, against the danger of such a faction, and at the same time to preserve the spirit and the form of popular government, is then the great object to which our inquiries are directed. Let me add, that it is the great desideratum, by which alone this form of government can be rescued from the opprobrium under which it has so long laboured, and be recommended to the esteem and adoption of mankind.

By what means is this object attainable? Evidently by one of two only. Either the existence of the same passion or interest in a majority, at the same time, must be prevented; or the majority, having such coexistent passion or interest, must be rendered, by their number and local situation, unable to concert and carry into effect schemes of oppression. If the impulse and the opportunity be suffered to coincide, we well know that neither moral nor religious motives can be relied on as an adequate control. They are not found to be such on the injustice and violence of individuals, and lose their efficacy in proportion to the number combined together; that is, in proportion as their efficacy becomes needful.

From this view of the subject, it may be concluded, that a pure democracy, by which I mean a society consisting of a small number of citizens, who assemble and administer the government in person, can admit of no cure for the mischiefs of faction. A common passion or interest will, in almost every case, be felt by a majority of the whole; a communication and concert, results from the form of government itself; and there is nothing to check the inducements to sacrifice the weaker party, or an obnoxious individual. Hence, it is, that such democracies have ever been spectacles of turbulence and contention; have ever been found incompatible with personal security, or the rights of property; and have in general been as short in their lives, as they have been violent in their deaths. Theoretic politicians, who have patronized this species of government, have erroneously supposed, that by reducing mankind to a perfect equality in their political rights, they would, at the same time be perfectly equalized and assimilated in their possessions, their opinions, and their passions.

A republic, by which I mean a government in which the scheme of representation takes place, opens a different prospect, and promises the cure for which we are seeking. Let us examine the points in which it varies from pure democracy, and we shall comprehend both the nature of the cure and the efficacy which it must derive from the union.

The two great points of difference, between a democracy and a republic, are, first, the delegation of the government, in the latter, to a small number of citizens, elected by the rest; secondly, the greater number of citizens, and greater sphere of country, over which the latter may be extended.

The effect of the first difference is, on the one hand, to refine and enlarge the public views, by passing them through the medium of a chosen body of citizens, whose wisdom may best discern the true interest of their country, and whose patriotism and love of justice, will be least likely to sacrifice it to temporary or partial considerations. Under such a regulation, it may well happen, that the public voice, pronounced by the representatives of the people, will be more consonant to the public good, than if pronounced by the people themselves, convened for the purpose. On the other hand the effect may be inverted. Men of factious tempers, of local prejudices, or of sinister designs, may by intrigue, by corruption, or by other means, first obtain the suffrages, and then betray the interest of the people. The question resulting is, whether small or extensive republics are most favourable to the election of proper guardians of the public weal; and it is clearly decided in favour of the latter by two obvious considerations.

In the first place, it is to be remarked that, however small the republic may be, the representatives must be raised to a certain number, in order to guard against the cabals of a few; and that however large it may be, they must be limited to a certain number, in order to guard against the confusion of a multitude. Hence, the number of representatives in the two cases not being in proportion to that of the constituents, and being proportionally greatest in the small republic, it follows, that if the proportion of fit characters be not less in the large than in the small republic, the former will present a greater option, and consequently a greater probability of a fit choice.

In the next place, as each representative will be chosen by a greater number of citizens in the large than in the small republic, it will be more difficult for unworthy candidates to practice with success the vicious arts, by which elections are too often carried; and the suffrages of the people being more free, will be more likely to centre in men who possess the most attractive merit, and the most diffusive and established characters.

It must be confessed, that in this, as in most other cases, there is a mean, on both sides of which inconveniences will be found to lie. By enlarging too much the number of electors, you render the representatives too little acquainted with all their local circumstances and lesser interests; as by reducing it too much, you render him unduly attached to these, and too little fit to comprehend and pursue great and national objects. The federal constitution forms a happy combination in this respect; the great and aggregate interests being referred to the national, the local and particular to the state legislatures.

The other point of difference is, the greater number of citizens, and extent of territory, which may be brought within the compass of republican, than of democratic government; and it is this circumstance principally which renders factious combinations less to be dreaded in the former, than in the latter. The smaller the society, the fewer probably will be the distinct parties and interests composing it; the fewer the distinct parties and interests, the more frequently will a majority be found of the same party; and the smaller the number of individuals composing a majority, and the smaller the compass within which they are placed, the more easily will they concert and execute their plans of oppression. Extend the sphere, and you take in a greater variety of parties and interests; you make it less probable that a majority of the whole will have a common motive to invade the rights of other citizens; or if such a common motive exists, it will be more difficult for all who feel it to discover their own strength, and to act in unison with each other. Besides other impediments, it may be remarked, that where there is a consciousness of unjust or dishonourable purposes, communication is always checked by distrust, in proportion to the number whose concurrence is necessary.

Hence, it clearly appears, that the same advantage, which a republic has over a democracy, in controlling the effects of faction, is enjoyed by a large over a small republic—is enjoyed by the union over the states composing it. Does this advantage consist in the substitution of representatives, whose enlightened views and virtuous sentiments render them superior to local prejudices, and to schemes of injustice? It will not be denied that the representation of the union will be most likely to possess these requisite endowments. Does it consist in the greater security afforded by a greater variety of parties, against the event of any one party being able to outnumber and oppress the rest? In an equal degree does the increased variety of parties, comprised within the union, increase the security? Does it, in fine, consist in the greater obstacles opposed to the concert and accomplishment of the secret wishes of an unjust and interested majority? Here, again, the extent of the union gives it the most palpable advantage.

The influence of factious leaders may kindle a flame within their particular states, but will be unable to spread a general conflagration through the other states; a religious sect may degenerate into a political faction in a part of the confederacy; but the variety of sects dispersed over the entire face of it, must secure the national councils against any danger from that source: a rage for paper money, for an abolition of debts, for an equal division of property, or for any other improper or wicked project, will be less apt to pervade the whole body of the union than a particular member of it; in the same proportion as such a malady is more likely to taint a particular county or district, than an entire state.

In the extent and proper structure of the union, therefore, we behold a republican remedy for the diseases most incident to republican government. And according to the degree of pleasure and pride we feel in being republicans, ought to be our zeal in cherishing the spirit, and supporting the character of federalists. ■

APPENDIX 4

The Federalist, No. 51, James Madison

To what expedient, then, shall we finally resort, for maintaining in practice the necessary partition of power among the several departments as laid down in the Constitution? The only answer that can be given is that as all these exterior provisions are found to be inadequate the defect must be supplied, by so contriving the interior structure of the government as that its several constituent parts may, by their mutual relations, be the means of keeping each other in their proper places. Without presuming to undertake a full development of this important idea I will hazard a few general observations which may perhaps place it in a clearer light, and enable us to form a more correct judgment of the principles and structure of the government planned by the convention.

In order to lay a due foundation for that separate and distinct exercise of the different powers of government, which to a certain extent is admitted on all hands to be essential to the preservation of liberty, it is evident that each department should have a will of its own; and consequently should be so constituted that the members of each should have as little agency as possible in the appointment of the members of the others. Were this principle rigorously adhered to, it would require that all the appointments for the supreme executive, legislative, and judiciary magistracies should be drawn from the same fountain of authority, the people, through channels having no communication whatever with one another. Perhaps such a plan of constructing the several departments would be less difficult in practice than it may in contemplation appear. Some difficulties, however, and some additional expense would attend the execution of it. Some deviations, therefore, from the principle must be admitted. In the constitution of the judiciary department in particular, it might be inexpedient to insist rigorously on the principle: first, because peculiar qualifications being essential in the members, the primary consideration ought to be to select that mode of choice which best secures these qualifications; second, because the permanent tenure by which the appointments are held in that department must soon destroy all sense of dependence on the authority conferring them.

It is equally evident that the members of each department should be as little dependent as possible on those of the others for the emoluments annexed to their offices. Were the executive magistrate, or the judges, not independent of the legislature in this particular, their independence in every other would be merely nominal.

But the great security against a gradual concentration of the several powers in the same department consists in giving to those who administer each department the necessary constitutional means and personal motives to resist encroachments of the others. The provision for defense must in this, as in all other cases, be made commensurate to the danger of attack. Ambition must be made to counteract ambition. The interest of the man must be connected with the constitutional rights of the place. It may be a reflection on human nature that such devices should be necessary to control the abuses of government. But what is government itself but the greatest of all reflections on human nature? If men were angels, no government would be necessary. If angels were to govern men, neither external nor internal controls on government would be necessary. In framing a government which is to be administered by men over men, the great difficulty lies in this: you must first enable the government to control the governed; and in the next place oblige it to control itself. A dependence on the people is, no doubt, the primary control on the government; but experience has taught mankind the necessity of auxiliary precautions.

This policy of supplying, by opposite and rival interests, the defect of better motives, might be traced through the whole system of human affairs, private as well as public. We see it particularly displayed in all the subordinate distributions of power, where the constant aim is to divide and arrange the several offices in such a manner as that each may be a check on the other—that the private interest of every individual may be a sentinel over the public rights. These inventions of prudence cannot be less requisite in the distribution of the supreme powers of the State.

But it is not possible to give to each department an equal power of self-defense. In republican government, the legislative authority necessarily predominates. The remedy for this inconveniency is to divide the legislature into different branches; and to render them, by modes of election and different principles of action, as little connected with each other as the nature of their common functions and their common dependence on the society will admit. It may even be necessary to guard against dangerous encroachments by still further precautions. As the weight of the legislative authority requires that it should be thus divided, the weakness of the executive may require, on the other hand, that it should be fortified. An absolute negative on the legislature appears, at first view, to be the natural defense with which the executive magistrate should be armed. But perhaps it would be neither altogether safe nor alone sufficient. On ordinary occasions it might not be exerted with the requisite firmness, and on extraordinary occasions it might be perfidiously abused. May not this defect of an absolute negative be supplied by some qualified connection between this weaker department and the weaker branch of the stronger department, by which the latter may be led to support the constitutional rights of the former, without being too much detached from the rights of its own department?

If the principles on which these observations are founded be just, as I persuade myself they are, and they be applied as a criterion to the several State constitutions, and to the federal Constitution, it will be found that if the latter does not perfectly correspond with them, the former are infinitely less able to bear such a test.

There are, moreover, two considerations particularly applicable to the federal system of America, which place that system in a very interesting point of view.

First. In a single republic, all the power surrendered by the people is submitted to the administration of a single government; and the usurpations are guarded against by a division of the government into distinct and separate departments. In the compound republic of America, the power surrendered by the people is first divided between two distinct governments, and then the portion allotted to each subdivided among distinct and separate departments. Hence a double security arises to the rights of the people. The different governments will control each other, at the same time that each will be controlled by itself.

Second. It is of great importance in a republic not only to guard the society against the oppression of its rulers, but to guard one part of the society against the injustice of the other part. Different interests necessarily exist in different classes of citizens. If a majority be united by a common interest, the rights of the minority will be insecure. There are but two methods of providing against this evil: the one by creating a will in the community independent of the majority—that is, of the society itself; the other, by comprehending in the society so many separate descriptions of citizens as will render an unjust combination of a majority of the whole very improbable, if not impracticable. The first method prevails in all governments possessing an hereditary or self-appointed authority. This, at best, is but a precarious security; because a power independent of the society may as well espouse the unjust views of the major as the rightful interests of the minor party, and may possibly be turned against both parties. The second method will be exemplified in the federal republic of the United States. Whilst all authority in it will be derived from and dependent on the society, the society itself will be broken into so many parts, interests and classes of citizens, that the rights of individuals, or of the minority, will be in little danger from interested combinations of the majority. In a free government the security for civil rights must be the same as that for religious rights. It consists in the one case in the multiplicity of interests, and in the other in the multiplicity of sects. The degree of security in both cases will depend on the number of interests and sects; and this may be presumed to depend on the extent of country and number of people comprehended under the same government. This view of the subject must particularly recommend a proper federal system to all the sincere and considerate friends of republican government, since it shows that in exact proportion as the territory of the Union may be formed into more circumscribed Confederacies, or States, oppressive combinations of a majority will be facilitated; the best security, under the republican forms, for the rights of every class of citizen, will be diminished; and consequently the stability and independence of some member of the government, the only other security, must be proportionally increased. Justice is the end of government. It is the end of civil society. It ever has been and ever will be pursued until it be obtained, or until liberty be lost in the pursuit. In a society under the forms of which the stronger faction can readily unite and oppress the weaker, anarchy may as truly be said to reign as in a state of nature, where the weaker individual is not secured against the violence of the stronger; and as, in the latter state, even the stronger individuals are prompted, by the uncertainty of their condition, to submit to a government which may protect the weak as well as themselves; so, in the former state, will the more powerful factions or parties be gradually induced, by a like motive, to wish for a government which will protect all parties, the weaker as well as the more powerful. It can be little doubted that if the State of Rhode Island was separated from the Confederacy and left to itself, the insecurity of rights under the popular form of government within such narrow limits would be displayed by such reiterated oppressions of factious majorities that some power altogether independent of the people would soon be called for by the voice of the very factions whose misrule had proved the necessity to it. In the extended republic of the United States, and among the great variety of interests, parties, and sects which it embraces, a coalition of a majority of the whole society could seldom take place on any other principles than those of justice and the general good; whilst there being thus less danger to a minor from the will of a major party, there must be less pretext, also, to provide for the security of the former, by introducing into the government a will not dependent on the latter, or, in other words, a will independent of the society itself. It is no less certain that it is important, notwithstanding the contrary opinions which have been entertained that the larger the society, provided it lie within a practicable sphere, the more duly capable it will be of self-government. And happily for the republican cause, the practicable sphere may be carried to a very great extent by a judicious modification and mixture of the federal principle. ■

APPENDIX 5

The Gettysburg Address, Abraham Lincoln

Gettysburg, Pennsylvania
November 19, 1863

Four score and seven years ago our fathers brought forth on this continent, a new nation, conceived in Liberty, and dedicated to the proposition that all men are created equal.

Now we are engaged in a great civil war, testing whether that nation, or any nation so conceived and so dedicated, can long endure. We are met on a great battlefield of that war. We have come to dedicate a portion of that field, as a final resting place for those who here gave their lives that that nation might live. It is altogether fitting and proper that we should do this.

But, in a larger sense, we can not dedicate—we can not consecrate—we can not hallow—this ground. The brave men, living and dead, who struggled here, have consecrated it, far above our poor power to add or detract. The world will little note, nor long remember what we say here, but it can never forget what they did here. It is for us the living, rather, to be dedicated here to the unfinished work which they who fought here have thus far so nobly advanced. It is rather for us to be here dedicated to the great task remaining before us—that from these honored dead we take increased devotion to that cause for which they gave the last full measure of devotion—that we here highly resolve that these dead shall not have died in vain—that this nation, under God, shall have a new birth of freedom—and that government of the people, by the people, for the people, shall not perish from the earth. ■

SOURCE: *Collected Works of Abraham Lincoln*, edited by Roy P. Basler. The text above is from the so-called "Bliss Copy," one of several versions which Lincoln wrote, and believed to be the final version. For additional versions, you may search *The Collected Works of Abraham Lincoln* through the courtesy of the Abraham Lincoln Association.

Related Links

Battlefield Map (Library of Congress)
Civil War Institute (Gettysburg College)
Gettysburg Address Essay Contest (Lincoln Fellowship of Pennsylvania)
Gettysburg Address Exhibit (Library of Congress)
Gettysburg Address Eyewitness (National Public Radio)
Gettysburg Address News Article (New York Times)
Gettysburg Address Teacher Resource (C-SPAN)
Gettysburg Civil War Photographs (Library of Congress)
Gettysburg Discussion Group (Bob & Dennis Lawrence)
Gettysburg Events (NPS)
Gettysburg National Military Park (NPS)
Letter of Invitation to Lincoln (Library of Congress)
Lincoln at Gettysburg
Lincoln at Gettysburg Photo Tour
Lincoln Fellowship of Pennsylvania
Lincoln's Invitation to Stay Overnight (Library of Congress)
Lincoln's Letter from Edward Everett (Library of Congress)
Photograph of Lincoln at Gettysburg (Library of Congress)
Reading of the Gettysburg Address (NPR)
Recollections of Lincoln at Gettysburg (Bob Cooke)
Response to a Serenade
Seminary Ridge Historic Preservation Foundation
The Gettysburg Powerpoint Presentation (Peter Norvig)
Wills House

Related Books

Graham, Kent. *November: Lincoln's Elegy at Gettysburg.* Indiana University Press, 2001.
Hoch, Bradley R. and Boritt, Gabor S. *The Lincoln Trail in Pennsylvania.* Pennsylvania State University Press, 2001.
Kunhardt, Philip B., Jr. *A New Birth of Freedom—Lincoln at Gettysburg.* Boston: Little, Brown, 1983.
Wills, Garry. *Lincoln at Gettysburg: The Words That Remade America.* Touchstone Books, 1993.

APPENDIX 6

"I Have a Dream," Martin Luther King, Jr.

In 1950s America, the equality of man envisioned by the Declaration of Independence was far from a reality. People of color, blacks, Hispanics, Orientals, were discriminated against in many ways, both overt and covert. The 1950s were a turbulent time in America, when racial barriers began to come down due to Supreme Court decisions, like *Brown* v. *Board of Education*; and due to an increase in the activism of blacks, fighting for equal rights.

Martin Luther King, Jr., a Baptist minister, was a driving force in the push for racial equality in the 1950s and the 1960s. In 1963, King and his staff focused on Birmingham, Alabama. They marched and protested nonviolently, raising the ire of local officials who sicced water cannon and police dogs on the marchers, whose ranks included teenagers and children. The bad publicity and breakdown of business forced the white leaders of Birmingham to concede to some antisegregation demands.

Thrust into the national spotlight in Birmingham, where he was arrested and jailed, King organized a massive march on Washington, D.C., on August 28, 1963. On the steps of the Lincoln Memorial, he evoked the name of Lincoln in his "I Have a Dream" speech, which is credited with mobilizing supporters of desegregation and prompted the 1964 Civil Rights Act. The next year, King was awarded the Nobel Peace Prize.

The following is the exact text of the spoken speech, transcribed from recordings.

I am happy to join with you today in what will go down in history as the greatest demonstration for freedom in the history of our nation.

Five score years ago, a great American, in whose symbolic shadow we stand today, signed the Emancipation Proclamation. This momentous decree came as a great beacon light of hope to millions of Negro slaves who had been seared in the flames of withering injustice. It came as a joyous daybreak to end the long night of their captivity.

But one hundred years later, the Negro still is not free. One hundred years later, the life of the Negro is still sadly crippled by the manacles of segregation and the chains of discrimination. One hundred years later, the Negro lives on a lonely island of poverty in the midst of a vast ocean of material prosperity. One hundred years later, the Negro is still languishing in the corners of American society and finds himself an exile in his own land. So we have come here today to dramatize a shameful condition.

In a sense we have come to our nation's capital to cash a check. When the architects of our republic wrote the magnificent words of the Constitution and the Declaration of Independence, they were signing a promissory note to which every American was to fall heir. This note was a promise that all men, yes, black men as well as white men, would be guaranteed the unalienable rights of life, liberty, and the pursuit of happiness.

It is obvious today that America has defaulted on this promissory note insofar as her citizens of color are concerned. Instead of honoring this sacred obligation, America has given the Negro people a bad check, a check which has come back marked "insufficient funds." But we refuse to believe that the bank of justice is bankrupt. We refuse to believe that there are insufficient funds in the great vaults of opportunity of this nation. So we have come to cash this check—a check that will give us upon demand the riches of freedom and the security of justice. We have also come to this hallowed spot to remind America of the fierce urgency of now. This is no time to engage in the luxury of cooling off or to take the tranquilizing drug of gradualism. Now is the time to make real the promises of democracy. Now is the time to rise from the dark and desolate valley of segregation to the sunlit path of racial justice. Now is the time to lift our nation from the quicksands of racial injustice to the solid rock of brotherhood. Now is the time to make justice a reality for all of God's children.

It would be fatal for the nation to overlook the urgency of the moment. This sweltering summer of the Negro's legitimate discontent will not pass until there is an invigorating autumn of freedom and equality. Nineteen sixty-three is not an end, but a beginning. Those who hope that the Negro needed to blow off steam and will now be content will have a rude awakening if the nation returns to business as usual. There will be neither rest nor tranquility in America until the Negro is granted his citizenship rights. The whirlwinds of revolt will continue to shake the foundations of our nation until the bright day of justice emerges.

But there is something that I must say to my people who stand on the warm threshold which leads into the palace of justice. In the process of gaining our rightful place we must not be guilty of wrongful deeds. Let us not seek to satisfy our thirst for freedom by drinking from the cup of bitterness and hatred.

We must forever conduct our struggle on the high plane of dignity and discipline. We must not allow our creative protest to degenerate into physical violence. Again and again we must rise to the majestic heights of meeting physical force with soul force. The marvelous new militancy which has engulfed the Negro community must not lead us to distrust of all white people, for many of our white brothers, as evidenced by their presence here today, have come to realize that their destiny is tied up with our destiny and their freedom is inextricably bound to our freedom. We cannot walk alone.

As we walk, we must make the pledge that we shall march ahead. We cannot turn back. There are those who are asking the devotees of civil rights, "When will you be satisfied?" We can never be satisfied as long as the Negro is the victim of the unspeakable horrors of police brutality. We can never be satisfied, as long as our bodies, heavy with the fatigue of travel, cannot gain lodging in the motels of the highways and the hotels of the cities. We can never be satisfied as long as a Negro in Mississippi cannot vote and a Negro in New York believes he has nothing for which to vote. No, no, we are not satisfied, and we will not be satisfied until justice rolls down like waters and righteousness like a mighty stream.

I am not unmindful that some of you have come here out of great trials and tribulations. Some of you have come fresh from narrow jail cells. Some of you have come from areas where your quest for freedom left you battered by the storms of persecution and staggered by the winds of police brutality. You have been the veterans of creative suffering. Continue to work with the faith that unearned suffering is redemptive.

Go back to Mississippi, go back to Alabama, go back to South Carolina, go back to Georgia, go back to Louisiana, go back to the slums and ghettos of our northern cities, knowing that somehow this situation can and will be changed. Let us not wallow in the valley of despair.

I say to you today, my friends, even though we face the difficulties of today and tomorrow, I still have a dream. It is a dream deeply rooted in the American dream.

I have a dream that one day this nation will rise up and live out the true meaning of its creed: "We hold these truths to be selfevident: that all men are created equal."

I have a dream that one day on the red hills of Georgia the sons of former slaves and the sons of former slave owners will be able to sit down together at the table of brotherhood.

I have a dream that one day even the state of Mississippi, a state sweltering with the heat of injustice, sweltering with the heat of oppression, will be transformed into an oasis of freedom and justice.

I have a dream that my four little children will one day live in a nation where they will not be judged by the color of their skin but by the content of their character.

I have a dream today.

I have a dream that one day, down in Alabama, with its vicious racists, with its governor having his lips dripping with the words of interposition and nullification; one day right there in Alabama, little black boys and black girls will be able to join hands with little white boys and white girls as sisters and brothers.

I have a dream today.

I have a dream that one day every valley shall be exalted, every hill and mountain shall be made low, the rough places will be made plain, and the crooked places will be made straight, and the glory of the Lord shall be revealed, and all flesh shall see it together.

This is our hope. This is the faith that I go back to the South with. With this faith we will be able to hew out of the mountain of despair a stone of hope. With this faith we will be able to transform the jangling discords of our nation into a beautiful symphony of brotherhood. With this faith we will be able to work together, to pray together, to struggle together, to go to jail together, to stand up for freedom together, knowing that we will be free one day.

This will be the day when all of God's children will be able to sing with a new meaning, "My country, 'tis of thee, sweet land of liberty, of thee I sing. Land where my fathers died, land of the pilgrim's pride, from every mountainside, let freedom ring."

And if America is to be a great nation this must become true. So let freedom ring from the prodigious hilltops of New Hampshire. Let freedom ring from the mighty mountains of New York. Let freedom ring from the heightening Alleghenies of Pennsylvania!

Let freedom ring from the snowcapped Rockies of Colorado!

Let freedom ring from the curvaceous slopes of California!

But not only that; let freedom ring from Stone Mountain of Georgia!

Let freedom ring from Lookout Mountain of Tennessee!

Let freedom ring from every hill and molehill of Mississippi. From every mountainside, let freedom ring.

And when this happens, when we allow freedom to ring, when we let it ring from every village and every hamlet, from every state and every city, we will be able to speed up that day when all of God's children, black men and white men, Jews and Gentiles, Protestants and Catholics, will be able to join hands and sing in the words of the old Negro spiritual, "Free at last! free at last! thank God Almighty, we are free at last!" ■

APPENDIX 7 Presidents and Congresses, 1789–2008

Term	President and Vice President	Party of President	Congress	Majority Party	
				House	Senate
1789–97	**George Washington**	None	1st	N/A	N/A
	John Adams		2d	N/A	N/A
			3d	N/A	N/A
			4th	N/A	N/A
1797–1801	**John Adams**	Fed	5th	N/A	N/A
	Thomas Jefferson		6th	Fed	Fed
1801–09	**Thomas Jefferson**	Dem Rep	7th	Dem Rep	Dem Rep
	Aaron Burr (1801–5)		8th	Dem Rep	Dem Rep
	George Clinton (1805–9)		9th	Dem Rep	Dem Rep
			10th	Dem Rep	Dem Rep
1809–17	**James Madison**	Dem Rep	11th	Dem Rep	Dem Rep
	George Clinton (1809–12)[1]		12th	Dem Rep	Dem Rep
	Elbridge Gerry (1813–14)[1]		13th	Dem Rep	Dem Rep
			14th	Dem Rep	Dem Rep
1817–25	**James Monroe**	Dem Rep	15th	Dem Rep	Dem Rep
	Daniel D. Tompkins		16th	Dem Rep	Dem Rep
			17th	Dem Rep	Dem Rep
			18th	Dem Rep	Dem Rep
1825–29	**John Quincy Adams**	Nat'l Rep	19th	Nat'l Rep	Nat'l Rep
	John C. Calhoun		20th	Dem	Dem
1829–37	**Andrew Jackson**	Dem	21st	Dem	Dem
	John C. Calhoun (1829–32)[2]		22d	Dem	Dem
	Martin Van Buren (1833–37)		23d	Dem	Dem
			24th	Dem	Dem
1837–41	**Martin Van Buren**	Dem	25th	Dem	Dem
	Richard M. Johnson		26th	Dem	Dem
1841	**William H. Harrison**[1]	Whig	27th	Whig	Whig
	John Tyler (1841)				
1841–45	**John Tyler**	Whig	28th	Dem	Whig
	(VP vacant)				
1845–49	**James K. Polk**	Dem	29th	Dem	Dem
	George M. Dallas		30th	Whig	Dem
1849–50	**Zachary Taylor**[1]	Whig	31st	Dem	Dem
	Millard Fillmore				
1850–53	**Millard Fillmore**	Whig	32d	Dem	Dem
	(VP vacant)				
1853–57	**Franklin Pierce**	Dem	33d	Dem	Dem
	William R. D. King (1853)[1]		34th	Rep	Dem
1857–61	**James Buchanan**	Dem	35th	Dem	Dem
	John C. Breckinridge		36th	Rep	Dem
1861–65	**Abraham Lincoln**[1]	Rep	37th	Rep	Rep
	Hannibal Hamlin (1861–65)		38th	Rep	Rep
	Andrew Johnson (1865)				
1865–69	**Andrew Johnson**	Rep	39th	Union	Union
	(VP vacant)		40th	Rep	Rep
1869–77	**Ulysses S. Grant**	Rep	41st	Rep	Rep
	Schuyler Colfax (1869–73)		42d	Rep	Rep
	Henry Wilson (1873–75)[1]		43d	Rep	Rep
			44th	Dem	Rep
1877–81	**Rutherford B. Hayes**	Rep	45th	Dem	Rep
	William A. Wheeler		46th	Dem	Dem
1881	**James A. Garfield**[1]	Rep	47th	Rep	Rep
	Chester A. Arthur				
1881–85	**Chester A. Arthur**	Rep	48th	Dem	Rep
	(VP vacant)				
1885–89	**Grover Cleveland**	Dem	49th	Dem	Rep
	Thomas A. Hendricks (1885)[1]		50th	Dem	Rep
1889–93	**Benjamin Harrison**	Rep	51st	Rep	Rep
	Levi P. Morton		52d	Dem	Rep
1893–97	**Grover Cleveland**	Dem	53d	Dem	Dem
	Adlai E. Stevenson		54th	Rep	Rep

Term	President and Vice President	Party of President	Congress	Majority Party: House	Majority Party: Senate
1897–1901	**William McKinley**[1] Garret A. Hobart (1897–99)[1] Theodore Roosevelt (1901)	Rep	55th 56th	Rep Rep	Rep Rep
1901–09	**Theodore Roosevelt** (VP vacant, 1901–05) Charles W. Fairbanks (1905–09)	Rep	57th 58th 59th 60th	Rep Rep Rep Rep	Rep Rep Rep Rep
1909–13	**William Howard Taft** James S. Sherman (1909–12)[1]	Rep	61st 62d	Rep Dem	Rep Rep
1913–21	**Woodrow Wilson** Thomas R. Marshall	Dem	63d 64th 65th 66th	Dem Dem Dem Rep	Dem Dem Dem Rep
1921–23	**Warren G. Harding**[1] Calvin Coolidge	Rep	67th	Rep	Rep
1923–29	**Calvin Coolidge** (VP vacant, 1923–25) Charles G. Dawes (1925–29)	Rep	68th 69th 70th	Rep Rep Rep	Rep Rep Rep
1929–33	**Herbert Hoover** Charles Curtis	Rep	71st 72d	Rep Dem	Rep Rep
1933–45	**Franklin D. Roosevelt**[1] John N. Garner (1933–41) Henry A. Wallace (1941–45) Harry S Truman (1945)	Dem	73d 74th 75th 76th 77th 78th	Dem Dem Dem Dem Dem Dem	Dem Dem Dem Dem Dem Dem
1945–53	**Harry S Truman** (VP vacant, 1945–49) Alben W. Barkley (1949–53)	Dem	79th 80th 81st 82d	Dem Rep Dem Dem	Dem Rep Dem Dem
1953–61	**Dwight D. Eisenhower** Richard M. Nixon	Rep	83d 84th 85th 86th	Rep Dem Dem Dem	Rep Dem Dem Dem
1961–63	**John F. Kennedy**[1] Lyndon B. Johnson (1961–63)	Dem	87th	Dem	Dem
1963–69	**Lyndon B. Johnson** (VP vacant, 1963–65) Hubert H. Humphrey (1965–69)	Dem	88th 89th 90th	Dem Dem Dem	Dem Dem Dem
1969–74	**Richard M. Nixon**[3] Spiro T. Agnew (1969–73)[2] Gerald R. Ford (1973–74)[4]	Rep	91st 92d	Dem Dem	Dem Dem
1974–77	**Gerald R. Ford** Nelson A. Rockefeller[4]	Rep	93d 94th	Dem Dem	Dem Dem
1977–81	**Jimmy Carter** Walter Mondale	Dem	95th 96th	Dem Dem	Dem Dem
1981–89	**Ronald Reagan** George Bush	Rep	97th 98th 99th 100th	Dem Dem Dem Dem	Rep Rep Rep Dem
1989–93	**George Bush** J. Danforth Quayle	Rep	101st 102d	Dem Dem	Dem Dem
1993–2001	**William J. Clinton** Albert Gore, Jr.	Dem	103d 104th 105th 106th	Dem Rep Rep Rep	Dem Rep Rep Rep
2001–2009	**George W. Bush** Richard Cheney	Rep	107th 108th 109th 110th	Rep Rep Rep Dem	Dem Rep Rep Dem
2009–	**Barack H. Obama** Joseph R. Biden, Jr.	Dem	111th	Dem	Dem

[1] Died in office. [2] Resigned from the vice presidency. [3] Resigned from the presidency. [4] Appointed vice president.

APPENDIX 8 Supreme Court Justices

Name[1]	Years on Court	Appointing President
JOHN JAY	1789–1795	Washington
James Wilson	1789–1798	Washington
John Rutledge	1790–1791	Washington
William Cushing	1790–1810	Washington
John Blair	1790–1796	Washington
James Iredell	1790–1799	Washington
Thomas Johnson	1792–1793	Washington
William Paterson	1793–1806	Washington
JOHN RUTLEDGE[2]	1795	Washington
Samuel Chase	1796–1811	Washington
OLIVER ELLSWORTH	1796–1800	Washington
Bushrod Washington	1799–1829	J. Adams
Alfred Moore	1800–1804	J. Adams
JOHN MARSHALL	1801–1835	J. Adams
William Johnson	1804–1834	Jefferson
Brockholst Livingston	1807–1823	Jefferson
Thomas Todd	1807–1826	Jefferson
Gabriel Duvall	1811–1835	Madison
Joseph Story	1812–1845	Madison
Smith Thompson	1823–1843	Monroe
Robert Trimble	1826–1828	J. Q. Adams
John McLean	1830–1861	Jackson
Henry Baldwin	1830–1844	Jackson
James M. Wayne	1835–1867	Jackson
ROGER B. TANEY	1836–1864	Jackson
Philip P. Barbour	1836–1841	Jackson
John Cartron	1837–1865	Van Buren
John McKinley	1838–1852	Van Buren
Peter V. Daniel	1842–1860	Van Buren
Samuel Nelson	1845–1872	Tyler
Levi Woodbury	1845–1851	Polk
Robert C. Grier	1846–1870	Polk
Benjamin R. Curtis	1851–1857	Fillmore
John A. Campbell	1853–1861	Pierce
Nathan Clifford	1858–1881	Buchanan
Noah H. Swayne	1862–1881	Lincoln
Samuel F. Miller	1862–1890	Lincoln
David Davis	1862–1877	Lincoln
Stephen J. Field	1863–1897	Lincoln
SALMON P. CHASE	1864–1873	Lincoln
William Strong	1870–1880	Grant
Joseph P. Bradley	1870–1892	Grant
Ward Hunt	1873–1882	Grant
MORRISON R. WAITE	1874–1888	Grant
John M. Harlan	1877–1911	Haves
William B. Woods	1881–1887	Haves
Stanley Matthews	1881–1889	Garfield
Horace Gray	1882–1902	Arthur
Samuel Blatchford	1882–1893	Arthur
Lucious Q. C. Lamar	1888–1893	Cleveland
MELVILLE W. FULLER	1888–1910	Cleveland
David J. Brewer	1890–1910	B. Harrison
Henry B. Brown	1891–1906	B. Harrison
George Shiras, Jr.	1892–1903	B. Harrison
Howel E. Jackson	1893–1895	B. Harrison
Edward D. White	1894–1910	Cleveland
Rufus W. Peckman	1896–1909	Cleveland
Joseph McKenna	1898–1925	McKinley
Oliver W. Holmes	1902–1932	T. Roosevelt
William R. Day	1903–1922	T. Roosevelt
William H. Moody	1906–1910	T. Roosevelt
Horace H. Lurton	1910–1914	Taft
Charles E. Hughes	1910–1916	Taft
EDWARD D. WHITE	1910–1921	Taft
Willis Van Devanter	1911–1937	Taft
Joseph R. Lamar	1911–1916	Taft
Mahlon Pitney	1912–1922	Taft
James C. McReynolds	1914–1941	Wilson
Louis D. Brandeis	1916–1939	Wilson
John H. Clarke	1916–1922	Wilson
WILLIAM H. TAFT	1921–1930	Harding
George Sutherland	1922–1938	Harding
Pierce Butler	1923–1939	Harding
Edward T. Sanford	1923–1930	Harding
Harlan F. Stone	1925–1941	Coolidge
CHARLES E. HUGHES	1930–1941	Hoover
Owen J. Roberts	1930–1945	Hoover
Benjamin N. Cardozo	1932–1938	Hoover

Name[1]	Years on Court	Appointing President
Hugo L. Black	1937–1971	F. Roosevelt
Stanley F. Reed	1938–1957	F. Roosevelt
Felix Frankfurter	1939–1962	F. Roosevelt
William O. Douglas	1939–1975	F. Roosevelt
Frank Murphy	1940–1949	F. Roosevelt
HARLAN F. STONE	1941–1946	F. Roosevelt
James F. Brynes	1941–1942	F. Roosevelt
Robert H. Jackson	1941–1954	F. Roosevelt
Wiley B. Rutledge	1943–1949	F. Roosevelt
Harold H. Burton	1945–1958	Truman
FREDERICK M. VINSON	1946–1953	Truman
Tom C. Clark	1949–1967	Truman
Sherman Minton	1949–1956	Truman
EARL WARREN	1953–1969	Eisenhower
John Marshall Harlan	1955–1971	Eisenhower
William J. Brennan, Jr.	1956–1990	Eisenhower
Charles E. Whittaker	1957–1962	Eisenhower
Potter Stewart	1958–1981	Eisenhower
Byron R. White	1962–1993	Kennedy
Arthur J. Goldberg	1962–1965	Kennedy
Abe Fortas	1965–1970	L. Johnson
Thurgood Marshall	1967–1991	L. Johnson
WARREN E. BURGER	1969–1986	Nixon
Harry A. Blackmun	1970–1994	Nixon
Lewis F. Powell, Jr.	1971–1987	Nixon
William H. Rehnquist	1971–1986	Nixon
John Paul Stevens	1975–	Ford
Sandra Day O'Connor	1981–2006	Reagan
WILLIAM H. REHNQUIST	1986–2005	Reagan
Antonin Scalia	1986–	Reagan
Anthony Kennedy	1988–	Reagan
David Souter	1990–	G. H. W. Bush
Clarence Thomas	1991–	G. H. W. Bush
Ruth Bader Ginsburg	1993–	Clinton
Stephen Breyer	1994–	Clinton
JOHN G. ROBERTS, JR.	2005–	G. W. Bush
Samuel A. Alito, Jr.	2006–	G. W. Bush

[1]Capital letters designate Chief Justices

[2]Never confirmed by the Senate as Chief Justice

pathways | Capital Punishment and the Courts

COURTS · ELECTIONS · GRASSROOTS MOBILIZATION · LOBBYING DECISION-MAKERS

PRO-DEATH PENALTY

1976

Gregg* v. *Georgia

The death penalty is reactivated after approving Georgia's revised procedures for trying and sentencing accused murderers. The new procedures include a trial to determine guilt and then a separate hearing to consider the death penalty. Six justices conclude that the new procedures resolve the previous problems with inconsistent and arbitrary application of capital punishment.

1988

Anti-Drug Abuse Act

Congress makes capital punishment a penalty for murders committed as part of drug trafficking.

1989

Stanford* v. *Kentucky

Supreme Court upholds capital punishment for juveniles who are 16 or 17 at the time that they commit murders.

1987

McCleskey* v. *Kemp

The court rules that statistics cannot be used to prove that the death penalty violates the equal protection clause of the Fourteenth Amendment.

1989

Penry* v. *Lynaugh

Supreme Court upholds capital punishment for mentally retarded murderers.

1970 — 1980 — 1990

ANTI-DEATH PENALTY

1989

Fierro* v. *Gomez

U.S. Court of Appeals declares the gas chamber a violation of the Eighth Amendment.

1986

Ford* v. *Wainwright

The Supreme Court rules that the death penalty cannot be applied to insane people.

1972

Furman* v. *Georgia

The Supreme Court hears three capital punishment cases as a group. These cases are pursued by interest group lawyers for the NAACP Legal Defense Fund. Two cases concern interracial rapes in Georgia and Texas and the other concerns a murder in Georgia. The death penalty is temporarily halted when five of the Court's nine justices agree that the punishment is applied inconsistently and arbitrarily.

1976

Roberts* v. *Louisiana

State laws making the death penalty mandatory for first-degree murder are declared unconstitutional by the U.S. Supreme Court. Each case must be decided on an individual basis.

Capital Punishment, Courts, and Reactions to Court Decisions: The Varied Pathways of Policy Change

Debates about capital punishment continue to rage, just as they have since the 1960s. Opponents of capital punishment have had limited success using the election pathway. Instead, they have focused their efforts on the court pathway. Beginning in 1972, anti-capital punishment interest groups succeeded in persuading some justices on the Supreme Court that the death penalty can violate the Constitution's requirements concerning due process and the prohibition on cruel and unusual punishment. Supporters of the death penalty used the elections and lobbying pathways to push revisions of state capital punishment laws that would satisfy the concerns of most Supreme Court justices, and thus the death penalty was reinstated in 1976. Since the 1970s, the court pathway has brought mixed results for capital punishment opponents. Although they failed to win a major case on racial discrimination in 1987, their litigation efforts eliminated the punishment for mentally retarded (2002) and juvenile offenders (2005). At the same time, highly publicized cases of innocent people being convicted and later released from death row helped spur grassroots mobilization and indications of cultural change, as well as pardons and moratoriums announced by governors. However, the fear of crime and attacks of 9/11 may have solidified public support for the death penalty in specific cases, such as convicted terrorists and serial killers.

essay questions

1. Many observers expect the Supreme Court to turn its attention to the question of whether it is "cruel and unusual" to execute murderers suffering from mental illnesses. Imagine that you are a lawyer. Choose a side—for or against—and create arguments concerning this issue.
2. Several states are attempting to create more careful processes that will guard against the risk that innocent people will be convicted of murders and sentenced to death. Create three suggestions for ways to reduce the risk of mistakes in murder trials. Explain how your suggestions will improve the process.

2000

1997
The American Bar Association passes a resolution requesting all death penalty jurisdictions to place a moratorium on executions until they confirm their systems are not flawed.

2000
New Hampshire state legislature votes to abolish the death penalty but the bill is vetoed by the governor.

2000
Governor George Ryan of Illinois places a moratorium on capital punishment when a media investigation discovered more than a dozen men on death row to be innocent. Opponents of the death penalty lobby Ryan for the moratorium.

PHOTO: Jim Wilson/The New York Times

2002
Atkins* v. *Virginia
Supreme Court prohibits the execution of mentally retarded individuals violates the Eighth Amendment.

2005
Stanley "Tookie" Williams is put to death by lethal injection in California. Grassroots organizations on both sides of the divide agitate strenuously prior to Williams' death.

PHOTO: Jim Wilson/The New York Times

2005
Roper* v. *Simmons
Supreme Court rules the execution of murderers who committed the crime while they were under the age of 18 is "cruel and unusual punishment."

2007
New Jersey legislature bans the use of capital punishment.

2008
Baze* v. *Rees
Supreme Court refuses to ban lethal injection as a means of execution

2008
Advances in DNA testing and reinvestigation of cases since the mid-1970s lead to the release of 129 prisoners who had been wrongly convicted of murder and sentenced to death.

2008
Kennedy* v. *Louisiana
Supreme Court prohibits the death penalty for the crime of child rape.

pathways | The Stem Cell Research Battle

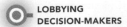

COURTS · CULTURAL CHANGE · ELECTIONS · GRASSROOTS MOBILIZATION · LOBBYING DECISION-MAKERS

PRO-STEM CELL RESEARCH

2001

February 22
Eighty Nobel Prize winners sign a letter to President Bush lobbying him to allow government funded researchers to experiment with stem cells.

March 26
A letter from University Presidents (including Yale, Stanford, Harvard and Princeton) and three higher education associations is sent to President Bush lobbying him to continue federal funding of embryonic stem cell research.

2002

May 2
The Christopher and Dana Reeve Paralysis Research Center opens. Much of their work is focused on advocating additional funding for stem cell research.

2004

October 10
Christopher Reeve dies. In many of the news reports of his death this president's opposition to federal funding is discussed. Public opinion in favor of greater funding seems to be mounting.

2004

November 2
California voters pass Proposition 71, a ballot measure to allocate $3 billion over 10 years to stem cell research, becoming the first state to fund stem cell research.

2005

January 11
Due to behind-the-scenes efforts by interest groups and mounting public pressure, New Jersey's governor announces the state will fund a $150 million stem cell research center and promises to champion a ballot initiative to allocate another $230 million.

2001 · 2002 · 2004 · 2005

ANTI-STEM CELL RESEARCH

2001 February
The month after taking office, and after much lobbying from conservative religious organizations, President George W. Bush requests a review of the NIH funding guidelines and puts a hold on federal funds for stem-cell research.

2001 July 29
Due, in part, to pressure from their conservative base, Senate and House Republican leaders come out in opposition to federal funding for research even though public opinion polls suggest most Americans disagree.

2001 August 9
The pressure from religious groups continues and President Bush announces his decision to limit funding to a few dozen lines of embryonic stem cells already in existence at that date.

Federal Funding for Stem Cell Research and the Lobbying Process

Who could have imagined a few decades ago that medical researchers would unlock the life-saving potential of the human embryo? Medical researchers now hold that embryonic stem cell research has the possibility of transforming the very nature of medicine. But this work is controversial because it often entails the destruction of a human embryo, leading some to view it immoral.

The public policy question in recent years has been over the federal funding of stem cell research. The government spends a great deal of resources on all kinds of medical research, generally through the National Institute of Health. But is stem cell research something with which the Federal government should be involved? This pathways figure illustrates the importance of pressure groups, high profile individuals, and the lobbying decision-makers pathway—especially when it comes to narrow policy questions such as funding for a particular type of research.

essayquestions

1. Pennsylvania Senator Arlen Specter once remarked, "Quite candidly, when Hollywood speaks, the world listens. Sometimes when Washington speaks, the world snoozes." How might this apply to the story of federal funding for stem cell research, noted above. Also, what does this figure (and Specter's comment) suggest about the relationship between direct lobbying and public opinion?

January 31
Michael J. Fox foundation for Parkinson's Research announced that it awarded nearly one million dollars in grants to four stem cell researchers. This move draws public attention to need for additional research funding.

2005

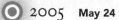

2005 **May 24**
Public pressure, patient advocacy groups, and medical research advocates push the House of Representatives to reverse course. It approves H.R. 810 to loosen Bush's restrictions on federal funding for stem cell research. In voting in favor of the bill, 50 Republicans break with Bush.

2005 **May 31**
Biotech industry leaders and voters push Connecticut lawmakers to earmark $100 million for stem cell research over 10 years in an effort to compete with California and New Jersey.

July 13
Responding to lobbying efforts and public opinion polls, Illinois Gov. Rod Blagojevich circumvents the legislature using an executive order to dedicate $10 million for stem cell studies after bills allocating funds for the research were voted down or shelved without a vote.

2005 **August 9**
Coalition for the Advancement of Medical Research held "Call the White House" Day, urging President Bush to support the bi-partisan bill.

2006
March 21
The First Annual Stem Cell Summit held in Chicago with much attention to increase federal funding.

May 5
Poll results say 72% of Americans support stem cell research. The public is now solidly behind more federal funding.

2006 **July 18**
Public pressure and direct lobbying Congress to pass the Stem Cell Enhancement Act; many Republicans break ranks and support the measure.

2006

2006 **July 19**
Sticking to his guns and responding to pressure from Christian conservative groups, George W. Bush vetoes the Stem Cell Enhancement Act.

2007 **June 7**
Congress approves legislation to ease restrictions on federally funded embryonic stem cell research.

2007

2007 **June 20**
President Bush once again vetoes the legislation. He also issues an executive order encouraging scientists to derive new methods to obtain stem cells without harming humans.

2008 **November 4**
Michigan voters pass referendum removing restriction on stem cell research.

2008

2. In many respects, the story of federal funding for stem cell research speaks to the complexities of federalism. Although the national government might limit its support for a project or policy, state governments can often move forward on their own. Write an essay on how you believe state governments can influence whether or not the federal government will increase funding for embryonic stem cell research.

pathways | Environmental Movement

COURTS | CULTURAL CHANGE | ELECTIONS | GRASSROOTS MOBILIZATION | LOBBYING DECISION-MAKERS

PRO-ENVIRONMENTAL MOVEMENT

1962
Rachel Carson writes *Silent Spring*, a book that alerted the country to the dangers, especially for humans, of pesticides.

1969
National Environmental Policy Act, first major environmental legislation, created the Environmental Protection Agency.

1969
Santa Barbara oil spill fouls Southern California beaches and arouses public anger against pollution.

1970
April 22
Earth Day! Millions protest for air and water cleanup and the preservation of nature.

1972
Life Magazine publishes a photo essay about the effects of mercury pollution on the children of Minemata, Japan.

1973
Endangered Species Act passes—a powerful tool in protecting the environment.

1977
Supreme Court upholds the 1973 Endangered Species Act and stops construction of the Tellico Dam (*Tennessee Valley Authority* v. *Hill* et al). Rules that the extinction of a species is to be prevented no matter the cost (Congress amends law to allow dam construction in 1982).

1960 | 1970

ANTI-ENVIRONMENTAL MOVEMENT

1973
July 29
Congress approves the Alaska pipeline.

The Delicate Balance between Environmental and Economic Concerns As scientific evidence shows that there is increased global warming, a reduction in rain forests, and higher levels of pollution, the international community struggles to cope. Governments today must strike a delicate balance between economic growth and development and environmental protections. If there is too much regulation of business to protect the environment, businesses may relocate to other countries or regions, harming the U.S. economy. If there is too little regulation, the environment suffers, because businesses don't want to risk the higher costs that go along with environmentally friendly practices.

When countries go through the complex process of industrialization, concerns for the environment typically take a back seat to concerns for economic growth; countries usually only become concerned with protecting the environment once they are completely industrialized. Environmental protection will enter national consciousness only when the culture of a society changes sufficiently to see this as a priority. Until then, countries usually focus on economic development with little regard for environmental concerns. What do you think? How far should the government go to protect our environment?

essayquestions

1. It is often very hard to balance the need to protect the environment and regulate business. Since most regulations to promote clean air and water cost businesses extra money, some believe that they can unduly harm our economy as businesses have less operating funds to expand and invest. Do you think that these concerns are reasonable? Or do you think that environmental protection is worth the costs?
2. Do you think that public opinion ought to influence our environmental policy or should we rely upon the recommendations of the scientific community? How large of a role do you think business leaders ought to play? How should we as a society balance these competing needs?

1978
Love Canal scandal—neighborhood finds out that they are living on a major toxic waste dump in Niagara Falls, NY. Alerts the government and society to the dangers of pollution.

1979
Three Mile Island nuclear power facility loses coolant and nearly has a meltdown.

1980
Congress passes the "Superfund" legislation (CERCLA: The Comprehensive Environmental Response, Compensation and Liability Act), directing the EPA to clean up abandoned toxic waste dumps.

1986
April 26
The worst nuclear disaster to date—Reactor Number Four at Chernobyl suffers a fire and explosion. Raises public awareness of environmental threats.

1989
March 24
Exxon-Valdez disaster. 11 million gallons of oil spilled in Prince William Sound, Alaska. Raises public awareness of destruction of environment.

2006
January 24
Al Gore's documentary on global warming, "An Inconvenient Truth," premieres at the Sundance Film Festival.

July
Newsweek issue on " The Greening of America."

2008 **June 27**
Prime Minister Tony Blair urged the G8 nations to agree to a global goal of halving greenhouse gas emissions by 2050.

2008 **November 5**
Moshe Rubashkin of Brooklyn, NY sentenced to 16 months in federal prison and ordered to pay over $450,000 in restitution for illegally storing hazardous waste which caused several suspicious fires in Allentown, Pennsylvania.

1980 1990 2000

1980
James Watt appointed Secretary of the Interior under President Reagan. Proposes many anti-environmental acts and resolutions.

1980s
Joseph Coors organizes the Sagebrush Rebellion and The Heritage Foundation, both anti-environmental groups that attack the rights gained to date by the environmental movement.

1995
Loggers win fight to resume logging of old-growth forests in the Pacific Northwest despite environmental concerns.

Tom Delay invites group of 350 lobbyists for the energy industries to draft legislation to dismantle federal health, safety, and environmental laws.

1997
Kyoto Protocol (international treaty designed to reduce carbon dioxide and other greenhouse gases) adopted by 121 nations, but not ratified by U.S. American businesses warn of economic disasters if treaty enforced.

2003
The Bush administration proposes limiting the authority of states to object to offshore-drilling decisions and proposes removing environmental protections for most American wetlands and streams.

2008
June 18
Presidential nominee John McCain proposes to increase offshore oil drilling, which is becoming more popular with voters as gas prices approach $5 per gallon.

pathways | Immigration Debate

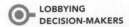

COURTS — CULTURAL CHANGE — ELECTIONS — GRASSROOTS MOBILIZATION — LOBBYING DECISION-MAKERS

PRO-IMMIGRATION

The Struggle over Immigration Policy Before 1882, anyone wishing to live in the United States could. Things have changed dramatically since that time. One of the more controversial issues facing our government today is the determination of who should be allowed to immigrate to our country, what we should do to secure our borders, and what should be done with immigrants illegally residing in the country today. Both sides in this debate have taken to the streets to appeal to others to join them and have increasingly turned to mass protest to express their positions. The Pew Hispanic Center estimates the number of illegal immigrants in the United States to be as many as 12 million, or about 1 in 20 workers.

essayquestions

1. Many proposals for immigration reform have been debated in recent years. Write an essay in which you critically examine the various proposals presented, being certain to indicate which proposal(s) you think would be most effective in addressing illegal immigration.
2. Why do you think that immigration has become such a hotly contested issue? Why do you think that we are more worried about immigration from Mexico than from other countries? Do you think that Hispanic immigrants are changing our culture? If so, how and in what ways?

1986 — **Immigration Reform and Control Act** allows illegal aliens living in America continuously since January 1, 1982 to apply for legal status; the act also forbids the hiring of illegal aliens, outlines penalties for lack of compliance, and raises annual immigration ceiling to 540,000.

1990 — **Immigration Act** sets immigration quotas at 700,000 annually for the next 3 years and 675,000 for every year thereafter; and eliminates denial of admittance to the U.S. on the basis of individual's beliefs, statements, or associations.

1960 — 1980 — 2000

1965 — **Immigration Act of 1965** Major reform in immigration policy. Sets overall limit of 170,000 immigrants from the Eastern Hemisphere and 120,000 from the Western Hemisphere. Touches off current illegal immigration problem by limiting the number of legal immigrants from neighboring countries.

1977 — New act repeals 1965 law; limits immigration to 290,000 worldwide with no more than 20,000 coming from any one country.

1978 — John H. Tanton founds the Federation for American Immigration Reform, an anti-immigration group.

1980 — **Refugees Act** distinguishes refugees from other immigrants and limits the worldwide immigration quota to 270,000.

1996 — **Immigration Act** doubles Border Patrol to 10,000 agents over 5 years; also calls for fences to be built at key points on the America-Mexico border; and approves a program to check job applicants' immigration status.

1996 — President Clinton signs a bill into law cutting numerous social programs for both legal and illegal immigrants in the interest of welfare reform.

1997 — Craig Nelson founds ProjectUSA, an anti-immigration group.

ANTI-IMMIGRATION

2004 2005 2006 2007 2008

2001

Zadvydas* v. *Davis

Supreme Court rules that when a detainee's deportation cannot be carried out within a reasonable time period (usually 6 months), the government cannot continue to detain the person.

2001

INS* v. *St. Cyr

Supreme Court rules that the government cannot deport aliens without judicial review and cannot apply deportation standards retroactively.

2002

The Homeland Security Act places the Immigration and Naturalization Service under the Department of Homeland Security. Immigration responsibilities are then divided into Citizenship and Immigration Services, Customs and Border Protection, and U.S. Immigration and Customs Enforcement.

2004

Leocal* v. *Ashcroft

Supreme Court rules that a drunk driving conviction does not allow for mandatory deportationof legal immigrants.

2004

Kerry's campaign spends $1 million on Spanish-language ads, largest amount ever spent by a presidential candidate.

2004

Bush announces new plan allowing 8 million illegal immigrants to obtain temporary worker status.

2004

Benitez* v. *Mata

Supreme Court rules that any previously deported immigrant can be prohibited re-entry and can face future deportation.

2005

The Minuteman Project is launched on the America–Mexico border. Minutemen were civilians who volunteered to monitor 23 miles of the border, claiming that the U.S. Border Patrol was spread too thin to adequately perform its duties.

2006

March 11

Around 300,000 people march in Chicago to protest the Border Protection, Antiterrorism, and Illegal Immigration Control Act of 2005.

2006

May 1 Boycott Day

About a million immigrants join in a nationwide protest against immigration reform.

2006 July 9

Anti-Immigration protest held in Los Angeles involving the Minuteman Project and other groups.

2006

October 26

President Bush signs into law a plan to enhance border security.

2007 April 9

President Bush unveils a plan for immigration reform including sending 6,000 more national guard troops to the Mexican border.

2007 June

Section of new barrier between United States and Mexico must be moved at a cost of over $3 million because it was mistakenly built on Mexican soil.

2008

Department of Homeland Security announces plans to waive over 25 environmental and cultural laws to speed construction of the border barrier, worrying many environmentalists who fear the move will harm many delicate ecosystems.

2008 November

Jose Ledesma was at least the fifth U.S. citizen to be detained and ordered deported since 2007 because authorities incorrectly refused to accept his California birth as proof of citizenship.

pathways | The Struggle over Same-Sex Marriage

COURTS · CULTURAL CHANGE · ELECTIONS · GRASSROOTS MOBILIZATION · LOBBYING DECISION-MAKERS

PRO-SAME-SEX MARRIAGE

1999
Dec. 20
A Vermont Supreme Court rules that same-sex partners must be eligible for the same benefits as spouses.

2001
March 2001
Responding to constituents, the Vermont State Legislature legalizes civil unions.

2003
Nov. 18
By a 4–3 vote, the Massachusetts Supreme Court rules that there is no "constitutionally adequate reason" to prevent same-sex couples from marrying.

2004
Feb. 12
In San Francisco, city officials respond to pressure from constituents and a strong lobbying effort and perform the first same-sex civil marriage in the United States.

2004
July 14
After much debate and a heated lobbying campaign on both sides of the issue, a constitutional amendment banning same-sex marriages fails in the U.S. Senate.

1999 — 2001 — 2003 — 2004

ANTI-SAME-SEX MARRIAGE

2004
Feb. 24
Pressured by conservative organizations, President George W. Bush announces his support for a constitutional amendment banning same-sex marriage. He claims that the "sanctity of marriage" must be protected. He reiterates this stand throughout his reelection campaign in November.

2004
March 2
Mayor Jason West of New Paltz, NY is charged with 19 counts of solemnizing marriages without a license; these were same-sex marriages.

2004
March 11
California Supreme Court orders San Francisco officials to immediately cease the issuing of marriage licenses to same-sex couples.

2004
March
Pressure from voters and organized interest groups push the Wisconsin State Legislature to overwhelmingly approve an amendment to the state constitution banning civil unions and same-sex marriages.

The Battle Over Gay Marriage and the Election Process Throughout American history, citizens have turned to the election pathway to express concerns and vent frustrations. Most of this activity is focused on bringing certain politicians into office, but it's also been directed at the ballot initiative process. As we have said, ballot initiatives, also called referendums, are policy issues on which citizens vote. Twenty-three states allow them. Another possibility for using the election pathway to bring about change is to amend state constitutions.

All of these election pathway routes—the selection of certain officials, ballot initiatives, and amendments to state constitutions—have come into play over the issue of same-sex marriage. The trigger for this activity was court cases suggesting that gay marriage was a protected right. The public reacted to these decisions by using elections.

essayquestions

1. We sometimes hear that court decisions are the last word in policy disputes; that once the courts speak, the issue is resolved. But the battle over gay marriage in America suggests that in many instances voters can overrule court decisions. First, explain how this can happen. Second, discuss whether or not voters should be able to overturn court decisions in a democracy.
2. Many suggest that the gay marriage issue is rooted in generational differences—that young Americans are more tolerant of homosexual lifestyles and more open to providing gay couples full rights than are older Americans. First, does your experience confirm this perspective? Second, if it were true, how do you think generational differences will shape the gay marriage controversy in the years ahead?

2004
Aug. 3
Missouri voters pass a constitutional amendment specifying marriage to be between a man and a woman.

2004
Sept. 18
A constitutional amendment that bans same-sex marriages is passed by Louisiana voters.

2004
Nov. 2
Turning to the elections pathway, constitutional amendments banning same-sex marriage are passed by voters in Arkansas, Georgia, Kentucky, Michigan, Mississippi, Montana, North Dakota, Ohio, Oklahoma, Oregon, and Utah.

Nov. 2
George W. Bush is sent back to the White House, and the Republicans maintain control of both houses of Congress, seemingly due, in part, to their opposition to gay marriage.

2005

2005
Feb. 2
A New York Supreme Court judge rules that denying same-sex couples the right to marry violates rights to liberty and privacy and is therefore unconstitutional.

2005
March 14
A California Superior Court judge rules that same-sex marriage bans are unconstitutional.

2005
April 5
A constitutional amendment banning same-sex marriages is approved by voters in Kansas.

2005
April 20
Connecticut legislature passes a bill allowing same-sex civil unions. This is the first bill not passed as a direct result of a court case.

2005
November
Voters in Texas pass a constitutional amendment banning same-sex marriages.

2006

2006
January
Maryland's legislature passes a bill to allow same-sex civil unions, but it is vetoed by Governor Robert Ehlrich after pressure from conservative groups.

2006
June 7
A proposed constitutional amendment to ban same-sex marriages fails in the U.S. Senate by 11 votes. Once again, groups on both sides push hard through lobbying operations.

2006
July 18
A same-sex marriage amendment is blocked in the House of Representatives.

2006
November
Colorado, South Carolina, South Dakota, Tennessee, Virginia, and Wisconsin all vote to approve a ban on gay marriage.

2007
June 14
Massachusetts legislature defeats constitutional amendment to ban same-sex marriage.

2008
May 15
Supreme Court of California overturns the state ban on same-sex marriage; by early June, gay men and women are being wed in the state.

2008
June 9
Anna Quindlen of *Newsweek* writes article dubbed "The Same People," where she argues the struggle for same-sex marriage is nearly won.

2008
November 4
Voters in three states (Arizona, Flordia, and California) pass measures to ban same-sex marriages.

GLOSSARY

A

Accidental Sample A nonprobability sample in which the researcher randomly invites respondents to participate in the survey; not a statistically valid sampling technique. (Ch. 9)

Accommodationist Interpretive approach to the establishment clause of the First Amendment that would permit the government to provide financial support for certain religious institutions and programs or sponsor specific religious practices, such as prayer in public schools. (Ch. 5)

Acts for Trade A series of moves by Parliament to channel money from the American colonies back to the commercial class in Great Britain during the mid-1700s. (Ch. 2)

Adams, John (1735–1826) One of the founders of the American political system. He served as vice president under George Washington and as president from 1797 to 1801. (Ch. 2)

Administrative Law Judge (ALJ) Official who presides over quasi-judicial proceedings within government agencies and renders decisions about disputes governed by statutes, such as appeals from denials of Social Security disability benefits. (Ch. 8)

Adversarial System Legal system used by the United States and other countries in which a judge plays a relatively passive role as attorneys battle to protect each side's interests. (Ch. 4)

Affirmative Action Measures taken in hiring, recruitment, employment, and education to remedy past and present discrimination against members of specific groups. (Chs. 5, 12)

Agenda Setting Featuring specific stories in the media to focus attention on particular issues. (Ch. 10)

Agents of Political Socialization Factors that influence how we acquire political facts and knowledge and develop political values. (Ch. 9)

Amicus Briefs Written arguments submitted to an appellate court by those who are interested in the issue being examined but are not representing either party in the case; often submitted by interest groups' lawyers to advance a specific policy position. (Ch. 4)

Anti-Federalists Opponents of ratification of the U.S. Constitution in 1787 and 1788. (Ch. 2)

Appellate Briefs Written arguments submitted by lawyers in appellate court cases. (Ch. 4)

Appellate Jurisdiction Authority of specific courts to hear appeals concerning allegations of specific errors in cases previously decided in trial courts. (Ch. 4)

Apprenticeship Norm The norm that new members of Congress are expected to work hard and quietly learn the legislative process. (Ch. 6)

At-Large Districts Districts encompassing an entire state, or large parts of a state, in which House members are elected to represent the entire state. (Ch. 6)

Attitude Hypothesis The theory that distinctive male and female attitudes and voting preferences arise from gender differences in political perceptions and issue preferences. (Ch. 9)

Attitudinal Barriers Those perceptions and beliefs that help maintain the two party system in America. (Ch. 13)

Attitudinal Model An approach to analyzing judicial decision making that looks at individual judges' decision patterns to identify the values and attitudes that guide their decisions. (Ch. 4)

Australian Ballot The secret ballot, which keeps voters' choices confidential. (Ch. 13)

Authoritarian Regime A system of government in which leaders face few formal or legal restrictions but are checked by noninstitutional forces such as political parties, religious groups, and business leaders. (Ch. 2)

Authority The recognized right of a particular individual, group, or institution to make binding decisions for society. (Ch. 2)

B

***Baker* v. *Carr* (1961)** Supreme Court case that set the standard that House districts must contain equal numbers of constituents, thus establishing the principle of "one person, one vote." (Ch. 6)

Balance of Trade The net difference between a nation's imports and its exports. (Ch. 14)

Ballot Access Laws Laws in each state that determine how a third-party candidate can get on the general election ballot. (Ch. 13)

Ballot Initiative A system whereby citizens decide policy matters through voting on election day. About half of the states allow this process. (Ch. 12)

Barometer of Public Attitudes The theory that the media reflect popular culture. (Ch. 9)

***Barron* v. *Baltimore* (1833)** Early Supreme Court interpretation of the Fifth Amendment declaring that the Bill of Rights provided legal protections only against actions by the federal government. (Ch. 5)

Bench Trials Trials in which a judge presides and makes determinations of fact and law, including decisions about guilt, without a jury. (Ch. 5)

Bicameral Legislature A legislature composed of two houses. (Ch. 6)

Bill of Rights The first 10 amendments to the U.S. Constitution, ratified in 1791, protecting civil liberties. (Ch. 2)

Bill Sponsor The member of Congress who introduces a bill. (Ch. 6)

Binding Primaries Process established in most states whereby voters in primary elections choose delegates who have pledged their support to a particular presidential candidate. The delegates then vote for this candidate at the nominating convention. (Ch. 13)

Bipartisan Campaign Reform Act (BCRA) Federal law passed in 2002 that outlawed soft-money contributions to party organizations. (Ch. 12)

Block Grants (sometimes called *revenue-sharing grants*) Grants of money to states, which are given substantial discretion to spend the money with minimal federal restrictions. (Ch. 3)

Blog A Web log or online journal. (Ch. 12)

Boycott A coordinated action by many people who agree not to buy a specific product, use a specific service, or shop at a specific store until a policy is changed. (Ch. 1)

***Brown* v. *Board of Education of Topeka* (1954)** U.S. Supreme Court decision that overturned *Plessy* v. *Ferguson* (1896) and declared that government-mandated racial segregation in schools and other facilities and programs violates the equal protection clause of the Fourteenth Amendment. (Ch. 5)

***Buckley* v. *Valeo* (1976)** The most significant Supreme Court case on campaign finance in American history. (Ch. 12)

Budget Deficit The amount by which a government's expenditures exceed its revenues. (Ch. 14)

Budget Surplus The amount by which a government's revenues exceed its expenditures. (Ch. 14)

Bureaucracy An organization with a hierarchical structure and specific responsibilities that operates on management principles intended to enhance efficiency and effectiveness. In government, it refers to departments and agencies in the executive branch. (Ch. 8)

Burke, Edmond (1729–1797) A member of Great Britain's House of Commons during the American Revolution, of which he was a strong supporter. (Ch. 2)

C

Cabinet A group of presidential advisers, primarily the secretaries of federal departments. (Ch. 7)

Candidate-Centered Era After 1960, a period when candidates began to portray themselves as independent from party politics, even though they often ran under a party banner. (Ch. 13)

Capitalism An economic system where business and industry are privately owned and there is little governmental interference. (Ch. 1)

Capital Punishment A criminal punishment, otherwise known as the *death penalty*, in which a person is subject to execution after conviction. Reserved for the most serious offenses. (Ch. 5)

Case Precedent A legal rule established by a judicial decision that guides subsequent decisions. The use of case precedent is drawn from the common law system brought from Great Britain to the United States. (Ch. 4)

Catalyst-for-Change Theory The assertion that public opinion shapes and alters our political culture, thus allowing change. (Ch. 9)

Categorical Grants Grants of money from the federal government to state or local governments for very specific purposes. These grants often require that funds be matched by the receiving entity. (Ch. 3)

Cato The pseudonym for a writer of a series of articles in opposition to the ratification of the Constitution. (Ch. 7)

Census A precise count of the population. (Ch. 2)

Chávez, César (1927–1993) Latino civil rights leader who founded the United Farm Workers and used nonviolent, grassroots mobilization to seek civil rights for Latinos and improved working conditions for agricultural workers. (Ch. 5)

Checks and Balances A system in our government where each branch (legislative, executive, judicial) has the power to limit the actions of others. (Ch. 1)

Civic Participation Citizen involvement in public matters. (Ch. 12)

Civil Law A body of law that applies to private rights, such as the ownership of property or the ability to enter into contracts. (Ch. 2)

Civil Lawsuits Legal actions filed by individuals, corporations, or governments seeking remedies from private parties for contract violations, personal injuries, or other noncriminal matters. (Ch. 4)

Civil Liberties Individual freedoms and legal protections guaranteed by the Bill of Rights that cannot be denied or hindered by government. (Ch. 5)

Civil Rights Public policies and legal protections concerning equal status and treatment in American society to advance the goals of equal opportunity, fair and open political participation, and equal treatment under the law without regard to race, gender, disability status, and other demographic characteristics. (Ch. 5)

Civil Rights Act of 1964 Federal statute that prohibited racial discrimination in public accommodations (hotels, restaurants, theaters), employment, and programs receiving federal funding. (Ch. 5)

Civil Service System Government employment system in which employees are hired on the basis of their qualifications and cannot be fired merely for belonging to the wrong political party; originated with the federal Pendleton Act in 1883 and expanded at other levels of government in the half-century that followed. (Ch. 8)

Clear and Present Danger Test A test for permissible speech articulated by Justice Oliver Wendell Holmes in *Schenck* v. *United States* (1919) that allows government regulation of some expressions. (Ch. 5)

Cleavages Divisions of people based on at least one social characteristic, such as educational attainment or race. (Ch. 11)

Closed Primary System Primary election process in which only registered members of the party are allowed to cast ballots. Roughly half the states use this system. (Ch. 13)

Cloture Rule declaring the end of a debate in the Senate. (Ch. 6)

Coercive Acts/Intolerable Acts A series of laws passed by the British Parliament in 1774 in response to growing unrest in the American colonies. Enforcement of these laws played a major role in precipitating the outbreak of the American Revolutionary War. The colonists called them the **Intolerable Acts.** (Ch. 2)

Cohort Replacement Natural phenomenon of generational replacement due to death. (Ch. 9)

Commercial Speech Texts such as advertising, promoting business ventures. Such speech is subject to government regulation to ensure truthfulness and to protect the public from unsafe products. (Ch. 5)

Compelled Self-Incrimination Being forced through physical abuse or other coercion to provide testimony against oneself in a criminal case, a practice that is prohibited by the Fifth Amendment. (Ch. 5)

Competitive News Markets Locales with two or more news organizations that can check each other's accuracy and neutrality of reporting. (Ch. 10)

Concurring Opinion Appellate court opinion by judge who endorses the outcome decided by the majority of judges, but wants to express different reasons to justify that outcome. (Ch. 4)

Conference Committee A committee of members of the House and Senate that irons out differences in similar measures that have passed both houses to create a single bill. (Ch. 6)

Confidence Level The probability that the results found in the sample represent the true opinion of the entire public under study. (Ch. 9)

Congressional Budget Office (CBO) The research arm of Congress, a major player in budget creation. (Ch. 14)

Connecticut Compromise See *Great Compromise.* (Ch. 2)

Conscience Model of Representation The philosophy that legislators should follow the will of the people (that is, act like a delegate) until they truly believe it is in the best interests of the nation to act differently. (Ch. 6)

Conservative A person who believes that government spending should be limited, that traditional patterns of relationships should be preserved, and that a large and powerful government is a threat to personal liberties. (Ch. 9)

Constituent Service A legislator's responsiveness to the questions and concerns of the people he or she represents. (Ch. 6)

Constitutional Convention A meeting in Philadelphia in 1787 at which delegates from the colonies drew up a new system of government. The finished product was the Constitution of the United States. (Ch. 2)

Constitutional Government A political system in which leaders are subject to both procedural checks and institutional limits. The United States has a constitutional government. (Ch. 2)

Constitutional Monarchy A political system in which the king or queen performs ceremonial duties but plays little or no role in actually governing the country. (Ch. 2)

Consumer Price Index (CPI) Figure representing the cost of a specific set of goods and services tracked at regular intervals by the Department of Labor. (Ch. 14)

Cooperative Federalism The powers of the federal and state government are intertwined and shared. Each level of government shares overlapping power, authority, and responsibility. (Ch. 3)

Corrupt Bargain of 1824 The alleged secret agreement in the disputed election of 1824 that led the House of Representatives to select John Quincy Adams, who had come in second in the popular vote, as president if he would make Speaker of the House Henry Clay his secretary of state. (Ch. 13)

Council of Economic Advisers (CEA) A group of economists within the Executive Office of the President, appointed by the president to provide advice on economic policy. (Ch. 7)

Court-Packing Plan President Franklin D. Roosevelt's unsuccessful proposal in 1937 to permit the appointment of additional justices to the U.S. Supreme Court. (Chs. 3, 4)

Courts of Last Resort The highest courts in each American court system, typically called supreme courts, that hear selected appeals from the lower courts. (Ch. 4)

Criminal Law A body of law that applies to violations against rules and regulations defined by the government. (Ch. 2)

Criminal Prosecutions Legal processes in which the government seeks to prove that an individual is guilty of a crime and deserving of punishment for it. (Ch. 4)

Crosscutting Cleavages Divisions in society that separate people into groups. (Ch. 9)

D

Dealignment The loss of affinity for party politics among voters who no longer consider themselves partisans. (Ch. 13)

Decentralization Proposed reform for government agencies intended to increase efficiency in administration and create closer contacts with the local public; permits regional and local offices to manage their own performances without close supervision from headquarters. (Ch. 8)

De Facto Segregation Racial segregation in housing and schools that was presumed to occur through people's voluntary choices about where they wanted to live but was actually facilitated by the discriminatory actions of landlords, real estate agents, and banks. (Ch. 5)

Defamation In law, false, harmful statements either through spoken words (*slander*) or through written words (*libel*). (Ch. 5)

Deflation A decrease in prices over time. (Ch. 14)

De Jure Segregation Racial segregation mandated by laws and policies created by government officials. (Ch. 5)

Delegate Model of Representation The philosophy that legislators should adhere to the will of their constituents. (Ch. 6)

Democracy A political system in which all citizens have a chance to play a role in shaping government action and are afforded basic rights and liberties. (Ch. 2)

Democratic-Republicans The first American political party, formed by believers in states' rights and followers of Thomas Jefferson. (Ch. 13)

Department Any of the 15 major government agencies responsible for specific policy areas whose heads are usually called secretaries and who serve in the president's cabinet. (Ch. 8)

Devolution Transfer of jurisdiction and fiscal responsibility for particular programs from the federal government to state or local governments. (Ch. 3)

Dictator The sole ruler of a political system with the power to control most or all actions of government. (Ch. 2)

Digital Divide See *Technology Gap*. (Ch. 10)

Dillon's Rule Iowa state court decision in 1868 that narrowly defined the power of local governments and established the supremacy of state governments when conflict exists with localities. Subsequently upheld by the Supreme Court. (Ch. 3)

Direct Mail Information sent by mail to a large number of people to advertise, market concepts, or solicit orders. (Ch. 11)

Discretion The power to apply policy in ways that fit particular circumstances. (Ch. 14)

Dissenting Opinion Appellate court opinion explaining the views of one or more judges who disagree with the outcome of the case as decided by the majority of judges. (Ch. 4)

Distribution Government providing things of value to specific groups. (Ch. 14)

Disturbance Theory The idea that interest groups form when resources become scarce in order to contest the influence of other interest groups. (Ch. 11)

Divided Party Control When one party controls the White House and another party controls one or both branches of Congress. (Ch. 13)

Doctrine of Nullification Theory that state governments had a right to rule any federal law unconstitutional and therefore null and void in that state. The doctrine was ruled unconstitutional but served as a source of southern rebellion, contributing to the secession of southern states from the Union and ultimately the Civil War. (Ch. 3)

Doctrine of Secession Theory that state governments had a right to declare their independence and create their own form of government. Eleven southern states seceded from the Union in 1860–1861, created their own government (the Confederate States of America), and thereby precipitated the Civil War. (Ch. 3)

Double Jeopardy Being tried twice for the same crime, a practice prohibited by the Fifth Amendment. (Ch. 5)

Dual Court System Separate systems of state and federal courts throughout the United States, each with responsibilities for its own laws and constitutions. (Ch. 4)

Dual Federalism The powers of the federal and state governments are strictly separate, with interaction often marked by tension rather than cooperation. (Ch. 3)

Due Process Clause A statement of rights in the Fifth Amendment (aimed at the federal government) and the Fourteenth Amendment (aimed at state and local governments) that protects against arbitrary deprivations of life, liberty, or property. The Fourteenth Amendment phrase is also interpreted by the Supreme Court to expand a variety of rights. (Ch. 5)

E

Earmarks/Pork-Barrel Legislation Legislation that benefits one state or district; also called *particularized legislation*. (Ch. 6)

Earned Media Coverage Airtime provided free of charge to candidates for political office. (Ch. 10)

Efficacy The belief that one can influence government. *Internal political efficacy* is the belief that you have the knowledge and ability to influence government. *External political efficacy* refers to the belief that governmental officials will respond to the people. (Ch. 9)

Egalitarianism Doctrine of equality that ignores differences in social status, wealth, and privilege. (Ch. 11)

Elastic Clause/Necessary and Proper Clause A statement in Article I, Section 8, of the U.S. Constitution that grants Congress the power to pass all laws "necessary and proper" for carrying out the list of expressed powers. (Ch. 6)

Electoral Behavior Any activity broadly linked to the outcome of a political campaign. (Ch. 12)

Electoral College A device for selecting the president and vice president of the United States, defined in Article II of the Constitution, whereby the voters in each state choose electors to attend a gathering where the electors make the final decision. (Ch. 12)

Elite Democratic Model The view that a democracy is healthy if people acquire positions of power through competitive elections. The level of involvement by citizens in this process is unimportant so long as elections are fair. (Ch. 12)

Elitism The theory that a select few—better educated, more informed, and more interested—should have more influence than others in our governmental process. (Ch. 9)

Entitlements Government expenditures required by law. (Ch. 17)

Episodic Participation Occasional citizen involvement in public matters, such as during elections. (Ch. 12)

Equality of Condition Conception of equality that exists in some countries that value equal economic status as well as equal access to housing, health care, education, and government services. (Ch. 5)

Equality of Opportunity Conception of equality that seeks to provide all citizens with opportunities for participation in the economic system and public life but accepts unequal results in income, political power, and property ownership. (Chs. 5, 9)

Equality of Outcome Egalitarian belief that government must work to diminish differences between individuals in society so that everyone is equal in status and value. (Ch. 9)

Equal Rights Amendment (ERA) A proposed constitutional amendment that would have guaranteed equal rights for men and women. It was initially suggested following passage of the Nineteenth Amendment in 1920 but was not formally proposed by Congress until 1972 and failed to be ratified by the 1982 deadline. (Ch. 11)

Equal Time Rule FCC rule that requires offering equal airtime in the broadcast media for all major candidates competing for a political office. (Ch. 10)

Establishment Clause Clause in the First Amendment guaranteeing freedom from religion by providing a basis for Supreme Court decisions limiting government support for and endorsement of particular religions. (Ch. 5)

Exclusionary Rule General principle that evidence obtained illegally, including through the violation of Fourth Amendment rights, cannot be used against a defendant in a criminal prosecution. The Supreme Court has allowed certain exceptions to the rule that permit the use of improperly obtained evidence in particular circumstances. (Ch. 5)

Executive Agreements Binding commitments between the United States and other countries agreed to by the president but, unlike treaties, not requiring approval by the Senate. (Ch. 7)

Executive Office of the President (EOP) A group of presidential staff agencies created in 1939 that provide the president with help and advice. (Ch. 7)

Executive Order A regulation made by the president that has the effect of law. (Ch. 7)

Exit Polls Surveys of voters leaving polling places; used by news media to gauge how candidates are doing on election day. (Ch. 9)

Expressed Powers The powers explicitly granted to the national government in the U.S. Constitution. (Ch. 2)

F

Fairness Doctrine Policy that required television and radio broadcasters to provide time for opposing viewpoints on controversial issues so as to ensure fair and balanced reporting; formally abolished in 1987. (Ch. 10)

Fast-Track Trade Authority The right of the president to negotiate trade agreements with other nations, which are then submitted to Congress for approval or rejection within a specified time. (Ch. 7)

Federal Election Campaign Act (FECA) Law designed to limit the amount of money contributed to campaigns for Congress and the presidency and to broaden donation reporting requirements. (Ch. 12)

The *Federalist Papers* A series of 85 essays in support of ratification of the U.S. Constitution that were written by James Madison, Alexander Hamilton, and John Jay and published under the byline Publius in New York City newspapers between October 27, 1787, and May 28, 1788. (Ch. 2)

Federalist Party A party, founded by Alexander Hamilton, whose members believed in a strong, centralized government and were supporters of the Washington and Adams administrations. (Ch. 13)

Federalists Supporters of the ratification of the U.S. Constitution. (Ch. 2)

Federal Reserve System (the Fed) The independent central bank of the United States. (Ch. 14)

Federal System A system of government in which power and authority is divided between a central government and regional subunits. (Ch. 3)

Fifteenth Amendment (1870) A change to the Constitution that guarantees the right to vote shall not be denied to anyone on the basis of race. (Ch. 12)

Filibuster Process in the U.S. Senate used to block or delay voting on proposed legislation or on an appointment of a judge or other official by talking continuously. Sixty senators must vote to end a filibuster. (Ch. 4, 6)

Fiscal Policy Taxation and spending decisions made by the government. (Ch. 14)

527 Organizations Groups organized under Section 527 of the Internal Revenue Code, which allows the unlimited expenditure of campaign money. These organizations became important after the Bipartisan Campaign Reform Act outlawed soft money in 2002. (Ch. 12)

Flexible interpretation An approach to interpreting the U.S. Constitution that permits the meaning of the document to change with evolving values, social conditions, and problems. (Ch. 4)

Focusing Events Moments that capture attention and highlight the existence of a problem. (Ch. 14)

Foreign Policy Conservatives People who believe that the United States is currently threatened by the desires of other international actors and that it must be prepared to use military power to preserve its current global status based on its own best interests. (Ch. 14)

Formula Grants Specific type of categorical grant in which money is allocated and distributed based upon a prescribed formula. (Ch. 3)

Fourteenth Amendment (1868) A change to the Constitution that defines the meaning of U.S. citizenship and establishes that each state must guarantee equal protection of the laws to its citizens. (Ch. 12)

Free Exercise Clause Clause in the First Amendment guaranteeing freedom to practice one's religion without government interference as long as those practices do not harm other individuals or society. (Ch. 5)

Free-Rider Problem The fact that public goods can be enjoyed by everyone, including people who do not pay their fair share of the cost of providing those public goods. (Ch. 11)

French and Indian War The nine-year conflict (1754–1763) in North America that pitted Great Britain and its North American colonies against France. France lost, and the British maintained control of much of North America. (Ch. 2)

G

Gaining Access Winning the opportunity to communicate directly with a legislator or a legislative staff member to present one's position on an issue of public policy. (Ch. 11)

Garbage Can Model A way of thinking about policymaking as an unordered mix of problems and solutions. (Ch. 14)

Gatekeepers Group or individuals who determine which stories will receive attention in the media and from which perspective. (Ch. 10)

Gender Gap Differences in voting and policy preferences between women and men. (Ch. 9)

Geographic Representation The idea that a legislator should represent the interests of the people living in a specific geographic location. (Ch. 6)

Gerrymandering Drawing legislative district boundaries in such a way as to gain political advantage. (Ch. 6)

***Gitlow* v. *New York* (1925)** The case in which the U.S. Supreme Court applied the First Amendment right of free speech against the states. It was the first case to incorporate a personal right from the Bill of Rights into the due process clause of the Fourteenth Amendment. (Ch. 5)

Globalization The expansion of economic interactions between countries. (Ch. 14)

Going Public Appealing directly to the people to garner support for presidential initiatives. (Ch. 7)

Governmental Units Associations of state-and/or local-level governments that are created to petition the federal government to address their particular concerns. (One prominent example is the National Governors' Association). (Ch. 11)

Government Corporations Agencies with independent boards and the means to generate revenue through sales of products and services, fees, or insurance premiums, and which are intended to run like private corporations. (Ch. 8)

Grants-in-Aid Funds given from one governmental unit to another governmental unit for specific purposes. (Ch. 3)

Great Compromise/Connecticut Compromise An agreement at the Constitutional Convention that the new national government would have a House of Representatives, in which the number of members would be based on each state's population, and a Senate, in which each state would have the same number of representatives. (Ch. 2)

Great Squeeze A period prior to the American Revolution when the British Parliament sought to recoup some of the costs associated with the French and Indian War by levying new taxes and fees on colonists. (Ch. 2)

Gross Domestic Product (GDP) The value of all goods and services produced in a nation. (Ch. 14)

H

Hamilton, Alexander (1755–1804) One of the framers of the Constitution and secretary of the treasury in George Washington's administration. (Ch. 7)

Hatch Act (1939) A law that limits the participation of federal employees in political campaigns. (Ch. 8)

Hearings Committee sessions for taking testimony from witnesses and for collecting information on legislation under consideration or for the development of new legislation. (Ch. 6)

Help America Vote Act A measure passed in 2002, in the wake of the controversy surrounding the 2000 election, designed to create a more uniform voting system throughout the 50 states. (Ch. 12)

Hobbes, Thomas (1588–1679) An English philosopher who argued that humans are selfish by nature and live lives that are "nasty, brutish, and short." For safety, people form governments but give up certain rights. His most influential book was *Leviathan,* published in 1651. (Ch. 2)

Hold Rule that allows a senator to announce the intention to use delaying tactics if a particular piece of legislation moves to a vote. (Ch. 6)

Home Rule In contrast to Dillon's Rule, this view asserts that local governments should be granted greater authority. According to this view, local government may exercise all authority not specifically denied to it by state constitution or state law. (Ch. 3)

I

Impeachment Process in Congress for removal of the president, federal judges, and other high officials. (Ch. 4)

Incorporation Process used by the Supreme Court to protect individuals from actions by state and local governments by interpreting the due process clause of the Fourteenth Amendment as containing selected provisions of the Bill of Rights. (Ch. 5)

Incumbent Advantage The various factors that favor office holders running for reelection over their challengers. (Ch. 12)

Independent A voter who is not registered or affiliated with any political party. (Ch. 13)

Independent Agencies Federal agencies with narrow responsibilities for a specific policy issue, such as the environment, not covered by one of the fifteen departments. (Ch. 8)

Independent Regulatory Commissions Organizational entities in the federal government that are not under the control of the president or a department. (Ch. 8)

Individualism A social theory that stresses the importance of guaranteeing freedoms, rights, self-expression, and independent actions of human beings. (Ch. 9)

Inflation An increase in prices over time. (Ch. 14)

Inner Cabinet The advisers considered most important to the president—usually the secretaries of the departments of State, Defense, Treasury, and Justice. (Ch. 7)

Inquisitorial System Legal system in most of Europe in which a judge takes an active role in questioning witnesses and seeking to discover the truth. (Ch. 4)

Inside Lobbying Appealing directly to lawmakers and legislative staff either in meetings, by providing research and information, or by testifying at committee hearings. (Ch. 11)

Institutional Agenda The set of problems that governmental decision makers are actively working to solve. (Ch. 14)

Institutional Barriers Legal impediments, such as laws, court decisions, and constitutional provisions, that limit the possibilities of minor parties in the United States. (Ch. 13)

Institutional Presidency The concept of the presidency as a working collectivity, a massive network of staff, analysts, and advisers with the president as its head. (Ch. 7)

Interactive Theory The theory that political culture both shapes and reflects popular opinion. (Ch. 9)

Interest Group A group of like-minded individuals who band together to influence public policy, public opinion, or governmental officials. (Ch. 11)

Intermediate Appellate Courts Courts that examine allegations concerning uncorrected errors that occurred during trials; such courts exist in the federal court system (circuit courts of appeals) and in most state court systems (usually called courts of appeals). (Ch. 4)

Intolerable Acts See *Coercive Acts.* (Ch. 2)

Investigation A form of congressional oversight in which committees scrutinize the actions of the executive branch and other political actors by calling witnesses and holding hearings to gain information about problems with programs and policies. (Ch. 14)

Investigative Reporting A type of journalism in which reporters thoroughly investigate a subject matter (often involving a scandal) to inform the public, correct an injustice, or expose an abuse. (Ch. 10)

Invisible Primary Raising money and attracting media attention early in the election process, usually before the primary election year. (Ch. 13)

Iran–Contra Affair The Reagan administration's unauthorized diversion of funds from the sale of arms to Iran to support the Contras, rebels fighting to overthrow the leftist government of Nicaragua. (Ch. 7)

Iron Triangle The tight relationships between employees in government agencies, interest groups, and legislators and their staff members, all of whom share an interest in specific policy issues and work together behind the scenes to shape laws and public policy. (Ch. 8)

Isolationists People who feel that the United States is overly involved in world affairs and believe that military power should be used only for self-defense. (Ch. 14)

Issue-Attention Cycle The pattern of problems quickly gathering attention but then failing to remain in the spotlight. (Ch. 14)

Issue Networks (Policy Communities) Interest groups, scholars, and other experts that communicate about, debate, and interact regarding issues of interest and thus influence public policy when the legislature acts on those issues. (Ch. 8)

J

Jacksonian Democracy A political and social movement that rejected political aristocracy and emphasized the role of the average citizen in public life. It began in 1828 with the election of Andrew Jackson to the presidency and lasted several decades. (Ch. 2)

Jim Crow Laws Laws enacted by southern state legislatures after the Civil War that mandated rigid racial segregation. The laws were named after a minstrel song that ridiculed African Americans. (Ch. 5)

Joint Committee Units that conduct oversight or issue research, but do not have legislative power. (Ch. 6)

Judicial Review The power of American judges to nullify decisions and actions by other branches of government if the judges decide those actions violate the U.S. Constitution or the relevant state constitution. (Ch. 4)

Judiciary Act of 1789 Early statute in which Congress provided the initial design of the federal court system. (Ch. 4)

Jury Trials Trials in which factual determinations, decisions about guilt (criminal cases), and imposition of liability (civil cases) are made by a body of citizens drawn from the community. (Ch. 4)

K

Kansas–Nebraska Bill An act of Congress in 1854 that allowed residents of the new territories in the West to decide whether slavery would be permitted in their state. (Ch. 13)

King, Martin Luther, Jr. (1929–1968) Civil rights leader who emerged from the Montgomery bus boycott to become a national leader of the civil rights movement and a recipient of the Nobel Peace Prize. (Ch. 5)

Kyoto Protocol An international agreement to address the problem of global warming. The United States was involved in its negotiation but has refused to ratify the agreement, citing excessive economic costs. (Ch. 14)

L

Labor Union An association of workers formed to promote collective interests, such as fair pay and working conditions. (Ch. 11)

Landslide Election An election in which the winners come to power with overwhelming public support. (Ch. 12)

***Lawrence* v. *Texas* (2003)** U.S. Supreme Court decision invalidating state laws regulating consenting noncommercial, private sexual conduct between adults as violations of the constitutional right to privacy. Many such laws had been enforced against gays and lesbians. (Ch. 5)

Laws Rules created or recognized by government. (Ch. 14)

Legal Model An approach to analyzing judicial decision making that focuses on the analysis of case precedent and theories of interpretation. (Ch. 4)

Legitimacy The sense that the result of a decision-making process is a proper outcome in the minds of the people who must live with that outcome. (Ch. 12)

***Lemon* Test** A three-part test for establishment clause violations deriving from the U.S. Supreme Court's decision in *Lemon* v. *Kurtzman* (1971), which examines whether government policies or practices provide support for religion or cause an excessive entanglement between government and religion. (Ch. 5)

Libel Publication of false and malicious material that defames an individual's reputation. (Ch. 10)

Liberal A person who generally supports governmental action to promote equality (such as welfare and public education), favors governmental intervention in the economy, and supports environmental issues. (Ch. 9)

Libertarian View The idea that the media should be allowed to publish information that they deem newsworthy or of interest to the public without regard to the social consequences of doing so. (Ch. 10)

Locke, John (1632–1704) An English political theorist who introduced the notion of a "social contract" under which all just governments derive their powers from the consent of the governed. Locke's writings provided the theoretical framework of Thomas Jefferson's Declaration of Independence and the entire Revolutionary movement in America. (Ch. 2)

Logrolling See *Reciprocity*. (Ch. 6)

M

Mail Surveys A public opinion survey conducted by mail. Response rates tend to be low, making the reliability of the results questionable. (Ch. 9)

Majority Leader The head of the majority party in the Senate; the second-highest-ranking member of the majority party in the House. (Ch. 6)

Majority-Minority District Voting districts in which members of a minority group make up the majority of the population. (Ch. 6)

Majority Opinion Appellate court opinion that explains the reasons for the case outcome as determined by a majority of judges. (Ch. 4)

***Mapp* v. *Ohio* (1961)** U.S. Supreme Court decision that applied the exclusionary rule to state criminal justice cases. (Ch. 5)

***Marbury* v. *Madison* (1803)** Case in which the U.S. Supreme Court asserted the power of judicial review despite the fact that this is not explicitly mentioned in the U.S. Constitution. (Ch. 4)

Marketplace of Ideas The concept that ideas and theories compete for acceptance among the public. (Ch. 10)

Markup The section-by-section review and revision of a bill by committee members; the actual writing of a piece of legislation. (Ch. 6)

Marshall, John (1755–1835) Important chief justice of the early U.S. Supreme Court (1801–1835) who wrote many opinions establishing the power of the federal government and the authority of the Court. (Ch. 5)

Material Benefits Benefits that have concrete value or worth. (Ch. 11)

Mayflower Compact An agreement made by the male pilgrims aboard the Mayflower in 1620 that provided for the temporary government of the Plymouth Colony. The document created a government that was designed to promote the general good of the colony. (Ch. 2)

***McCulloch* v. *Maryland* (1819)** U.S. Supreme Court decision that defined the respective powers of the state and federal governments. Written by Chief Justice John Marshall, the opinion established that the Constitution grants to Congress implied powers for implementing the Constitution's express powers in order to create a functional national government, and that state action may not impede valid constitutional exercises of power by the Federal government. (Ch. 3)

Merit Selection A method for selecting judges used in some states that seek to reduce the role of politics by having the governor select new judges from lists of candidates presented by a selection committee. (Chs. 4, 13)

***Miller* v. *California* (1973)** U.S. Supreme Court decision that provided the primary test for obscenity to determine what materials, especially pornography, can be regulated as outside of the protection of the First Amendment. (Ch. 5)

Minority Leader The leading spokesperson and legislative strategist for the minority party in either the House or the Senate. (Ch. 6)

***Miranda* v. *Arizona* (1966)** U.S. Supreme Court decision that requires police officers, before questioning a suspect in custody, to inform that suspect about the right to remain silent and the right to have a lawyer present during custodial questioning. (Ch. 5)

Modern Presidency A political system in which the president is the central figure and participates actively in both foreign and domestic policy. (Ch. 7)

Monarchy A system of hereditary rule in which one person, a king or queen, has absolute authority over the government. (Ch. 2)

Monetary Policy Money supply management conducted by the Federal Reserve. (Ch. 14)

Monopoly Exclusive control by one group or individual over specified services or commodities. (Ch. 3)

Motor Voter Law A law passed by Congress in 1993 designed to make it easier for Americans to register to vote. (Ch. 12)

Muckraking Investigating and exposing societal ills such as corruption in politics or abuses in business. (Ch. 10)

N

Narrowcasting Creating and broadcasting highly specialized programming that is designed to appeal to a specified subgroup rather than to the general population. (Ch. 10)

National Association for the Advancement of Colored People (NAACP) Civil rights advocacy group founded by African Americans and their white supporters in 1909; used the court pathway to fight racial discrimination in the 1930s through the 1950s and later emphasized the election and lobbying pathways. (Ch. 5)

National Debt The nation's cumulative deficits. (Ch. 14)

National Nominating Convention A meeting of delegates from communities across the nation to discuss candidates' qualifications, choose their party's nominee, and adopt a party platform. (Ch. 13)

National Sales Tax A flat tax collected on all purchases. (Ch. 17)

National Security Adviser The chief adviser to the president on national security matters; a lead member of the National Security Council. (Ch. 7)

National Security Council (NSC) An organization within the Executive Office of the President to advise the president on foreign and domestic military policies related to national security. (Ch. 7)

Natural Rights Basic rights that no government can deny. (Ch. 2)

Necessary and Proper Clause See *elastic clause.* (Ch. 3)

Neoconservatives People who believe that the United States has a special role to play in world politics; they advocate the unilateral use of force and the pursuit of a values-based foreign policy. (Ch. 14)

Neoliberals People who strongly support international law and organizations and are skeptical about the use of military force because they attribute many of the world's problems to economic, political, and social conditions. (Ch. 14)

New Deal Programs designed by President Franklin D. Roosevelt to bring economic recovery from the Great Depression by expanding the role of the federal government in providing employment opportunities and social services; advanced social reforms to serve the needs of the people, greatly expanding the budget and activity of the federal government. (Ch. 3)

New Institutionalism An approach to understanding judicial decision making that emphasizes the importance of courts' structures and processes as well as courts' roles within the governing system. (Ch. 4)

New Jersey Plan A scheme for government advanced at the Constitutional Convention that was supported by delegates from smaller states. It called for equal representation of states in a unicameral legislature. (Ch. 2)

News Briefings A public appearance by a governmental official for the purpose of releasing information to the press. (Ch. 10)

News Conferences A media event, often staged, where reporters ask questions of politicians or other celebrities. (Ch. 10)

News Monopolies Single news firms that control all the media in a given market. (Ch. 10)

***New York Times Company* v. *United States* (1971)** U.S. Supreme Court decision prohibiting prior restraint of the Pentagon Papers, thus permitting major newspapers to publish information on the Vietnam War that the government had sought to keep secret. (Ch. 5)

Nineteenth Amendment (1920) A change to the Constitution that granted the right of women to vote. (Ch. 12)

Nomination Caucus A meeting of party activists to choose delegates to support candidates at their party's presidential nominating convention. (Ch. 13)

Nominees The individuals selected by a party to run for office under that party's label. (Ch. 13)

O

Office of Management and Budget (OMB) A Cabinet-level office that monitors federal agencies and provides the president with expert advice on policy-related topics. (Ch. 7)

Oligarchy A government run by a small group of people. (Ch. 2)

One-House Bill A bill that is passed in only one house of Congress. (Ch. 6)

Open Primary System Primary election process in which voters are allowed to cast ballots in the primary election without declaring which party they are voting for. (Ch. 13)

Orientation Function The job of familiarizing a new member of Congress with the procedures, norms, and customs of the chamber. (Ch. 6)

Original Jurisdiction A court's authority to hear a case in the first instance; authority typically possessed by trial courts but also to a limited extent by the U.S. Supreme Court in certain cases, primarily lawsuits filed by one state against another. (Ch. 4)

Outside Lobbying (Grassroots Lobbying) Activities directed at the general public to raise awareness and interest and to pressure officials; also known as *grassroots lobbying.* (Ch. 11)

Oversight Congress' responsibility to keep an eye on agencies in the federal bureaucracy to ensure that their behavior conforms to its wishes. (Ch. 6)

P

Paine, Thomas (1737–1809) An American revolutionary writer and a democratic philosopher whose pamphlet *Common Sense* (1776) argued for complete independence from Britain. (Ch. 2)

Partisan Realignment Historic shifts of public opinion and voter concerns that generally lead to a different party's control of government and a new set of policies. (Ch. 13)

Party Identification A belief that one belongs to a certain party. (Ch. 13)

Party Machines Local party organizations in major cities that influenced elections and operated on the basis of patronage and behind-the-scenes control. (Ch. 13)

Party Presses Newspapers popular in the early nineteenth century that were highly partisan and often influenced by political party machines. (Ch. 10)

Party Unity Score Various ways to measure the extent to which legislators of the same party vote together on policy matters. (Ch. 13)

Pathways of Action The activities of citizens of American politics that affect the creation, alteration, and preservation of laws and policies. (Ch. 1)

Patronage System (Spoils System) Successful political candidates' and parties' rewarding their supporters with government jobs and firing supporters of the opposing party. (Ch. 8)

Penny Press Cheap newspapers containing sensationalized stories sold to members of the working class in the late nineteenth and early twentieth centuries. (Ch. 10)

Personal Interview Administration of a survey questionnaire verbally, face to face. (Ch. 9)

Prerogative Power Extraordinary powers that the president may use under certain conditions. (Ch. 7)

Pilgrims The name commonly applied to the early settlers of the Plymouth Colony who had left England in 1620 aboard the Mayflower. (Ch. 2)

Platform The set of issues, principles, and goals that a party supports. (Ch. 13)

Plato (427–347 B.C.) Greek philosopher often considered the first political scientist. (Ch. 12)

Plea Bargains Negotiated resolution of a criminal case in which the defendant enters a guilty plea in exchange for a reduction in the nature or number of charges or for a less-than-maximum sentence. (Ch. 4, 5)

***Plessy* v. *Ferguson* (1896)** U.S. Supreme Court decision that endorsed the legality of racial segregation laws by permitting "separate but equal" services and facilities for African Americans even though the services and facilities were actually inferior. (Ch. 5)

Pluralism A system of government in which multiple competing and responsive groups vie for power. (Ch. 2)

Pluralists People who believe that power is widely distributed in a society. (Ch. 14)

Pocket Veto The president's killing of a bill that has been passed by both houses of Congress, simply by not signing it; occurs only if Congress has adjourned within 10 days of the bill's passage. (Ch. 6)

Police Powers The powers reserved to state governments related to the health, safety, and well-being of citizens. (Ch. 2)

Policy Categories A way of classifying policies by their intended goal and means of carrying out that goal. (Ch. 14)

Policy Entrepreneurs Advocates of particular solutions to problems. (Ch. 14)

Policy Process Model A way of thinking about how policy is made in terms of steps in a progression. (Ch. 14)

Political Equality Fundamental value underlying the governing system of the United States that emphasizes all citizens' opportunities to vote, run for public office, own property, and enjoy civil liberties protections under the Constitution. (Ch. 5)

Political Ideology A consistent set of beliefs that forms a general philosophy regarding the proper goals, purposes, functions, and size of government. (Ch. 9)

Political Speech Expressions concerning politics, government, public figures, and issues of public concern—the form of expression that contemporary commentators view as most deserving of First Amendment protection. (Ch. 5)

Politico Model of Representation The philosophy that legislators should follow their own judgment (that is, act like a trustee) until the public becomes vocal about a particular matter, at which point they should follow the dictates of constituents. (Ch. 6)

Politics The process by which the actions of government are determined. (Ch. 1)

Popular Democratic Model A view of democracy that stresses the ongoing involvement of average citizens in the political process. (Ch. 12)

Pork-Barrel Legislation See *Earmarks.* (Ch. 6)

Powell Doctrine A view that cautions against the use of military force, especially where public support is limited, but states that once the decision to use force has been made, military power should be applied quickly and decisively. (Ch. 18)

Power The ability to exercise control over others and to get individuals, groups, and institutions to comply. (Ch. 2)

President Pro Tempore The chief presiding officer of the Senate in the absence of the vice president. (Ch. 6)

Press Releases Written statements that are given to the press to circulate information or an announcement. (Ch. 10)

Press Shield Law Statute enacted by legislatures establishing a reporter's privilege to protect the confidentiality of sources. (Ch. 5)

Prior Censorship Forbidding publication of material considered objectionable. (Ch. 10)

Prior Restraint Government prohibition or prevention of the publication of information or viewpoints. Since its decision in *Near* v. *Minnesota* (1931), the U.S. Supreme Court has generally forbidden prior restraint as a violation of the First Amendment freedom of the press. (Ch. 5)

Privatization Turning some responsibilities of government bureaucracy over to private organizations on the assumption that they can administer and deliver services more effectively and inexpensively. (Ch. 8)

Probability Sample Selection procedure in which each member of the target population has a known or an equal chance of being selected. (Ch. 9)

Pro Bono Short for the Latin phrase *pro bono publico,* meaning "for the benefit of the public" and describing lawyers' representing clients without compensation as a service to society. (Ch. 4)

Professional Associations Organizations that represent individuals, largely educated and affluent, in one particular occupational category. (Ch. 11)

Project Grants A type of categorical grant in which a competitive application process is required for a specific project (often scientific or technical research or social services). (Ch. 3)

Pseudo-Events Events that appear spontaneous but are in fact staged and scripted by public relations experts to appeal to the news media or the public. (Ch. 10)

Public Advocate Model See *Social Responsibility Theory.* (Ch. 10)

Public Goods (Collective Goods) Goods that are used or consumed by all individuals in society. (Ch. 11)

Public Interest Groups Citizen organizations that advocate issues of public good, such as protection of the environment. (Ch. 11)

Public Opinion The attitudes of individuals regarding their political leaders and institutions as well as political and social issues. (Ch. 9)

Public Policy What government decides to do or not do; government laws, rules, or expenditures. (Ch. 1)

Purposive Benefits Intangible rewards people obtain from joining a group they support and working to advance an issue in which they believe. (Ch. 11)

Q

Quorum The minimum number of members that must be present at a meeting to make proceedings valid. (Ch. 6)

R

Rational Choice Model An approach to analyzing judicial decision making that identifies strategic decisions by judges in order to advance their preferred case outcomes. (Ch. 4)

Rational Party Model Where the goal is to win offices for material gain, to control the distribution of government jobs. (Ch. 13)

Reapportionment The process by which seats in the House of Representatives are reassigned among the states to reflect population changes following the census (every 10 years). (Ch. 6)

Reasonable Time, Place, and Manner Restrictions Permissible government regulations on freedom of speech that seek to prevent disruptions or threats to public safety in the manner in which expressions are presented. Such regulations cannot be used to control the content of political speech. (Ch. 5)

Reauthorization A process undertaken by Congress to decide if an existing program or policy will continue and to indicate a level of funding for the appropriation of money for ongoing programs and policies. (Ch. 14)

Recall Process whereby voters can remove from office an elected official before the next regularly scheduled election. (Ch. 12)

Reciprocity/Logrolling Supporting a legislator's bill in exchange for support of one's own bill. (Ch. 6)

Redistribution Government providing a broad segment of the society with something of value. (Ch. 14)

Redistricting The process of redrawing legislative district boundaries within a state to reflect population changes. (Ch. 6)

Regressive Tax A tax structured such that higher-income individuals pay a lower percentage of their income in taxes. (Ch. 17)

Regulation Government prohibiting or requiring certain actions of organizations and businesses. (Ch. 14)

Regulations Legal rules created by government agencies based on authority delegated by the legislature. (Ch. 8)

Reporter's Privilege The asserted right of news reporters to promise confidentiality to their sources and to keep information obtained from sources, including evidence of criminal activity, secret. The U.S. Supreme Court has held that reporter's privilege does *not* fall within the First Amendment right to freedom of the press. (Ch. 5)

Representative Democracy A republic in which the selection of elected officials is conducted through a free and open process. (Ch. 2)

Republic A system of government in which members of the general public select agents to represent them in political decision-making. (Ch. 2)

Republican Form of Government A system of government in which the general public selects agents to represent it in political decision-making. (Ch. 12)

Residency and Registration Laws State laws that stipulate how long a person must reside in a community before being allowed to vote in that community. (Ch. 12)

Responsible Party Model Where the goal is to shape public policy. (Ch. 13)

Restrictive Covenant A clause added to a deed restricting real estate sales for a reason. (Ch. 5)

Retention Elections Elections held in merit selection systems in which voters choose whether to keep a particular judge on the bench after that judge has completed a term in office. (Ch. 4)

Right to Privacy A constitutional right created and expanded in U.S. Supreme Court decisions concerning access to contraceptives, abortion, private sexual behavior, and other matters, although the word *privacy* does not appear in the Constitution. (Ch. 5)

***Roe* v. *Wade* (1973)** Controversial U.S. Supreme Court decision that declared women have a constitutional right to choose to terminate a pregnancy in the first 6 months following conception. (Ch. 5)

Rotation The staggering of senatorial terms such that one-third of the Senate comes up for election every 2 years. (Ch. 6)

S

Salience Hypothesis The theory that the gender gap is largely a function of the fact that men and women put different priorities on different issues, thereby impacting their voting behavior and their political party affiliations. (Ch. 9)

Sample A subset of the population under study; if selected correctly, it represents the population from which it was drawn with reliable and measurable accuracy. (Ch. 9)

Select Committee A temporary committee created to deal with a specific issue. (Ch. 6)

Selective Benefits Benefits provided only to members of an organization or group. (Ch. 11)

Senatorial Courtesy Traditional deference by U.S. senators to the wishes of their colleagues concerning the appointment of individuals to federal judgeships in that state. (Ch. 4)

Senior Executive Service (SES) Program within the federal executive branch, established by Congress in 1978 to enable senior administrators with outstanding leadership and management skills to be moved between jobs in different agencies to enhance the performance of the bureaucracy. (Ch. 8)

Seniority Length of time served in a chamber of the legislature. Members with greater seniority have traditionally been granted greater power. (Ch. 6)

Separationist Interpretive approach to the establishment clause of the First Amendment that requires the clause saying a "wall of separation" exists between church and state. (Ch. 5)

Settlements Negotiated resolutions of civil lawsuits prior to trial. (Ch. 4)

Seventeenth Amendment Change to the U.S. Constitution, ratified in 1913, that provides for the direct election of senators. (Ch. 6)

Sharing of Powers The U.S. Constitution's granting of specific powers to each branch of government while making each branch also partly dependent on the others for carrying out its duties. (Ch. 2)

Shays's Rebellion An armed uprising in western Massachusetts in 1786 and 1787 by small farmers angered over high debt and tax burdens. (Ch. 2)

Signing Statements Written proclamations issued by presidents regarding how they intend to interpret a new law. (Ch. 7)

Simple Random Sample A probability sample in which each person in the population under study has an equal chance of being selected. (Ch. 9)

Situational Hypothesis The assertion that the gender gap is largely a function of the differences in living conditions between men and women (most notably differentials in income and living standards). (Ch. 9)

Smith, Adam (1723–1790) A Scottish political and economic philosopher whose views on free trade and capitalism were admired in colonial America. (Ch. 2)

Social Capital Networks of relationships among individuals, groups, and institutions that foster trust and cooperation to solve societal problems and establish norms for appropriate behavior in pursuit of mutual benefits and shared interests. (Ch. 11)

Social Contract Theory A political theory that holds individuals give up certain rights in return for securing certain freedoms. If the government breaks the social contract, grounds for revolution exist. This notion was at the core of the Declaration of Independence. (Ch. 2)

Socialism An economic system in which the government owns and controls most factories and much or all of the nation's land. (Ch. 1)

Social Responsibility Theory/Public Advocate Model The idea that the media should consider the overall needs of society when making decisions about what stories to cover and in what manner. (Ch. 10)

Social Security A federal program started in 1935 that taxes wages and salaries to pay for retirement benefits, disability insurance, and hospital insurance. (Ch. 7)

Soft Money Funds contributed through a loophole in federal campaign finance regulations that allowed individuals and groups to give unlimited sums of money to political parties. (Ch. 12)

Solidary Benefits Benefits derived from fellowship and camaraderie with other members. (Ch. 11)

Sound Bites A short outtake from a longer film, speech, or interview. (Ch. 10)

Sovereignty The exclusive right of an independent state to reign supreme and base absolute power over a geographic region and its people. (Ch. 3)

Speaker The presiding officer of the House of Representatives, who is also the leader of the majority party in the House. (Ch. 6)

Special Governments Local governmental units established for very specific purposes, such as the regulation of water and school districts, airports, and transportation services. (Ch. 3)

Specialization Extensive knowledge in a particular policy area. (Ch. 6)

Speedy and Public Trial A right contained in the Sixth Amendment to prevent indefinite pretrial detention and secret trials. (Ch. 5)

Split-Ticket Voters (Swing Voters) Voters who cast ballots for candidates of different parties in a given election year or for candidates of different parties in different election years. (Ch. 13)

Stamp Act Congress A meeting in October 1765 of delegates from Britain's American colonies to discuss the recently passed Stamp Act. The Congress adopted a declaration of rights and wrote letters to the King and both houses of Parliament. Many historians view this gathering as a precursor of the American Revolution. (Ch. 2)

Standing Joint Committee A congressional committee composed of members from both legislative chambers. Most of its work involves investigation, research, or oversight of agencies that are closely related to Congress. (Ch. 6)

Statutes Laws written by state legislatures and by Congress. (Ch. 4)

Stewardship Model A theory of robust, broad presidential powers; the idea that the president is only limited by explicit restrictions in the Constitution. (Ch. 7)

Straight-Ticket Voters Voters who cast ballots only for candidates of the same party in a given election year. (Ch. 13)

Stratified Sample A probability sample in which the population under study is divided into categories (strata) that are thought to be important in influencing opinions. Then a random sample is drawn from each stratum. (Ch. 9)

Strict Scrutiny An exacting test for violations of fundamental rights by requiring the government to demonstrate a compelling interest when policies and practices clash with certain constitutional rights. (Ch. 5)

Subcommittees Specialized groups within standing committees. (Ch. 6)

Swing States States where the outcome of the presidential election is uncertain; states that are "up for grabs" in most presidential elections. (Ch. 12)

Symbolic Representation The assumption that a legislator will represent or favor his or her own ethnic group or gender among the constituency, as opposed to the entire population; also known as *descriptive representation.* (Ch. 6)

Symbolic Speech The expression of an idea or viewpoint through an action, such as wearing an armband or burning an object. Symbolic speech can enjoy First Amendment protections. (Ch. 5)

T

Technology Gap/Digital Divide The differences in access to and mastery of information and communication technology between segments of the community (typically for socioeconomic, educational, or geographical reasons). (Ch. 10)

Telephone Surveys Administration of a survey questionnaire over the telephone. (Ch. 9)

Term Limits Laws stipulating the maximum number of terms that an elected official may serve in a particular office. (Ch. 12)

Test Case A case sponsored or presented by an interest group in the court pathway with the intention of influencing public policy. (Ch. 4)

Think Tank A group of individuals who conduct research in a particular subject or a particular area of public policy. (Ch. 11)

de Tocqueville, Alexis A French scholar who traveled throughout the United States in the early 1830s. Significance: His published notes, *Democracy in America,* offers a telling account of our nation's formative years—a book that is still widely read. (Ch. 1)

Totalitarian Regime A system of government in which the ruling elite holds all power and controls all aspects of society. (Ch. 2)

Trade Association A professional organization that represents the interests of members of a particular industry. (Ch. 11)

Treaty A formal agreement between governments. (Ch. 7)

Trial by Jury A right contained in the Sixth Amendment to have criminal guilt decided by a body of citizens drawn from the community. (Ch. 5)

Trigger Mechanism The means, often tied to focusing events, to push a recognized problem further along in the policy cycle. (Ch. 14)

Tripartite View of Parties A model based on the theory that parties have three related elements: party-in-government, party-in-the-electorate, and party-as-organization. (Ch. 13)

Trustee Model of Representation The philosophy that legislators should consider the will of the people but act in ways they believe best for the long-term interests of the nation. (Ch. 6)

Turnout The percentage of citizens legally eligible to vote in an election who actually vote in that election. (Ch. 12)

Twelfth Amendment (1804) A change to the Constitution that required a separate vote tally in the electoral college for president and vice president. (Ch. 12)

Twenty-Fourth Amendment (1964) A change to the Constitution that eliminated the poll tax. (Ch. 12)

Twenty-Sixth Amendment (1971) A change to the Constitution that granted 18-year-old citizens the right to vote. (Ch. 12)

U

Unanimous Consent Agreement of all senators on the terms of debate, required before a bill goes to the floor. (Ch. 6)

Unemployment Rate The percentage of Americans who are currently not working but are seeking jobs. (Ch. 14)

Unified Party Control When the executive and a majority of members in both houses of the legislature are of the same political party. (Ch. 13)

Unitary System A system of government in which political power and authority is located in one central government that runs the country and that may or may not share power with regional subunits. (Ch. 3)

Unit Rule The practice, employed by 48 states, of awarding all of a state's electoral college votes to the candidate for the presidency who receives the greatest number of popular votes in that state. (Ch. 12)

U.S. Commission on Civil Rights Federal commission created in 1957 to study issues of discrimination and inequality in order for the federal government to consider whether additional laws and policies are needed to address civil rights matters. (Ch. 5)

U.S. Equal Employment Opportunity Commission Federal commission created in 1964 to handle complaints about employment discrimination and file lawsuits on behalf of employment discrimination victims. (Ch. 5)

Universal Suffrage The right to vote for all adult citizens. (Ch. 5)

V

Veto Disapproval of a bill or resolution by the president. (Ch. 7)

Virginia Plan A plan made by delegates to the Constitutional Convention from several of the larger states, calling for a strong national government with a bicameral legislature, a national executive, a national judiciary, and legislative representation based on population. (Ch. 2)

Voting Cues Summaries encapsulating the informed judgment of others in the legislature; members of Congress rely on these to streamline the decision-making process. (Ch. 6)

Voting Rights Act of 1965 Federal statute that outlawed discriminatory voting practices, such as literacy tests, responsible for the widespread disenfranchisement of African Americans. (Chs. 5, 12)

W

War Powers Resolution A measure passed by Congress in 1973 designed to limit presidential deployment of troops unless Congress grants approval for a longer period. (Ch. 7)

Warrant A judicial order authorizing a search or an arrest. Under the Fourth Amendment, police and prosecutors must present sufficient evidence to constitute "probable cause" in order to obtain a warrant from a judge. (Ch. 5)

Warren, Earl (1891–1974) Chief Justice of the Supreme Court (1953–1969) who led the Court to its unanimous decision in *Brown* v. *Board of Education of Topeka* (1954) and also took a leading role in many decisions expanding civil liberties and promoting civil rights. (Ch. 5)

Watergate The "shorthand" name of a scandal that led to the resignation of President Richard M. Nixon in 1974. (Ch. 12)

Weapons of Mass Destruction Weapons capable of inflicting widespread devastation on civilian populations. (Ch. 14)

Whig Model A theory of restrained presidential powers; the idea that presidents should use only the powers explicitly granted in the Constitution. (Ch. 7)

Whips Assistants to House and Senate leaders, responsible for drumming up support for legislation and for keeping count of how members plan to vote on different pieces of legislation. (Ch. 6)

Whistleblower An employee who reports or reveals misconduct by government officials or others. (Ch. 8)

Whistleblower Protection Act A federal law intended to prevent employees in the bureaucracy from being punished for reporting or revealing governmental misconduct. (Ch. 8)

Writ of Certiorari A legal action that asks a higher court to call up a case from a lower court; the legal action used to ask the U.S. Supreme Court to accept a case for hearing. (Ch. 4)

Writ of Mandamus A legal action that asks a judge to order a government official to take a specific action. (Ch. 4)

Y

Yellow Journalism Sensationalistic stories featured in the daily press around the turn of the twentieth century. (Ch. 10)

NOTES

Chapter 1

1. Virginia Gray and David Lowery, "Where Do Policy Ideas Come From? A Study of Minnesota Legislators and Staffers," *Journal of Public Administration Research and Theory 10* (2000): 573–595.
2. George F. Cole and Christopher E. Smith, *The American System of Criminal Justice,* 9th ed. (Belmont, CA: Wadsworth, 2001), pp. 83–84.
3. Quoted in John K. White and Daniel M. Shea, *New Party Politics: From Jefferson and Hamilton to the Information Age,* 2d ed. (Belmont, CA: Wadsworth, 2004), p. 13.
4. Thomas Dye, *Politics in America,* 4th ed. (Upper Saddle River, NJ: Prentice Hall, 2001), p. 25.
5. For an interesting discussion of the link between political culture and system stability, see Oliver H. Woshinsky, *Culture and Politics* (Upper Saddle River, NJ: Prentice Hall, 1995).
6. Ibid., pp. 117–118.
7. Gunnar Myrdal, *An American Dilemma: The Negro Problem and Modern Democracy* (New York: Harper Bros., 1944), p. 27.
8. Ibid.
9. Arthur M. Schlesinger, Jr., *The Disuniting of America: Reflections on a Multicultural Society* (New York: Norton, 1992), p. 27.
10. Robert A. Dahl, *Who Governs? Democracy and Power in an American City* (New Haven, CT: Yale University Press, 1961), pp. 316–317.

Chapter 2

1. Ray Raphael, *Founding Myths: Stories That Hide Our Patriotic Past* (New York: The Free Press, 2004), p. 177.
2. Max Weber, "Politics as a Vocation" (1918), in *From Max Weber: Essays in Sociology,* ed. H. H. Gerth and C. Wright Mills (New York: Oxford University Press, 1946), p. 128.
3. Theodore J. Lowi and Benjamin Ginsberg, *American Government: Freedom and Power,* 2nd ed. (New York: Norton, 1992), p. 10.
4. Ibid.
5. David McCullough, *John Adams* (New York: Simon & Schuster, 2001), p. 60.
6. McCullough, *John Adams.*
7. Audrey Williamson, *Thomas Paine: His Life, Work, and Times* (London: Allen & Unwin, 1973), p. 122.
8. Ibid., pp. 60–61.
9. Howard Bement, ed., *Burke's Speech on Conciliation with America* (Norwood, MA: Ambrose, 1922), pp. 45, 54–55, 61.
10. Barbara Ehrenreich, "Their George and Ours," *New York Times,* July 4, 2004, sec. 4, p. 9.
11. Ibid.
12. "Thomas Paine: Life in America," Encyclopaedia Britannica Online, http://search.eb.com, 2004.
13. Ehrenreich, "Their George and Ours," sec. 4, p. 9.
14. Thomas Jefferson, letter to William Stephens Smith, November 13, 1787.
15. "Articles of Confederation," Encyclopaedia Britannica Online, http://search.eb.com, 2004.
16. See Robert A. Feer, *Shays's Rebellion* (New York: Garland, 1988), pp. 504–529, cited in Larry Berman and Bruce Allen Murphy, *Approaching Democracy,* 3rd ed. (Upper Saddle River, NJ: Prentice Hall, 2001), pp. 38–39.
17. George Washington, quoted in Samuel E. Morrison, Henry Steele Commager, and William Leuchtenberg, *The Growth of the American Republic,* vol. 1 (New York: Oxford University Press, 1969), p. 244.
18. Bruce Miroff, Raymond Seidelman, and Todd Swanstrom, *The Democratic Debate: An Introduction to American Politics,* 4th ed. (Boston: Houghton Mifflin, 2007), p. 26.
19. James Madison, *Federalist No. 10.*
20. Ray Raphael, *Founding Myths: Stories That Hide Our Patriotic Past* (New York: New Press, 2004), p. 87.
21. Ibid.
22. ushistory.org. "Selections from the Diary of Private Joseph Plumb Martin." www.ushistory.org/march/other/Martiandiary.htm, ushistory.org. Accessed 7/5/08.
23. Theodore J. Lowi and Benjamin Ginsberg, *American Government: Freedom and Power* (New York: Norton, 1990), p. 41.
24. Ibid., p. 42.
25. Joseph J. Ellis, *Founding Brothers: The Revolutionary Generation* (New York: Vintage Books, 2002), p. 94.
26. Ibid., p. 91.
27. Alexander Hamilton, James Madison, and John Jay, *Federalist No. 57.*
28. "Essays of Brutus, No. 1," in *The Complete Anti-Federalist,* ed. Herbert Storing (Chicago: University of Chicago Press, 1981).
29. George Mason, quoted in Berman and Murphy, *Approaching Democracy,* p. 67.
30. Ibid.
31. Ibid.

Chapter 3

1. Morris P. Fiorina, Paul E. Peterson, Bertram Johnson, and D. Stephen Voss, *The New American Democracy,* 4th ed. (Upper Saddle River, NJ: Prentice Hall, 2005), p. 57.
2. "Era of Colonization," Encyclopaedia Britannica Online, http://search.eb.com, 2006.
3. M. Judd Harmon, *Political Thought: From Plato to the Present* (New York: McGraw Hill, 1964), p. 289.
4. Charles F. Hobson, *The Great Chief Justice: John Marshall and the Rule of Law* (Lawrence: University Press of Kansas, 1996), p. 206.
5. James W. Loewen, *Lies My Teacher Told Me: Everything Your American History Textbook Got Wrong* (New York: Simon & Schuster, 1995), p. 141.
6. See Howard Gillman, *The Constitution Besieged: The Rise and Demise of* Lochner *Era Police Powers Jurisprudence* (Durham, NC: Duke University Press, 1993).
7. Gerald Gunther, *Constitutional Law,* 11th ed. (Mineola, NY: Foundation Press, 1985), p. 129.
8. Morton Grozdins, *The American System,* ed. Daniel J. Elazar (Chicago: Rand McNally, 1966).
9. U.S. Office of Management and Budget, 2008.
10. For a succinct discussion of the crises faced across the nation, see David Osborne and Peter Hutchinson, *The Price of Government* (New York: Basic Books, 2004).

Chapter 4

1. Tamar Lewin, "Schools Across U.S. Await Ruling on Drug Tests," *New York Times,* March 20, 2002. http://www.nytimes.com
2. Linda Greenhouse, "Justices Allow Schools Wider Use of Random Drug Tests," *New York Times,* June 28, 2002. http://www.nytimes.com
3. Christopher E. Smith, *Courts, Politics, and the Judicial Process,* 2nd ed. (Chicago: Nelson-Hall, 1997), p. 37.
4. Stephen L. Wasby, *The Supreme Court in the Federal Judicial System,* 4th ed. (Chicago: Nelson-Hall, 1993), pp. 56–57, 238–244.
5. See Doris Marie Provine, "Courts in the Political Process in France," in *Courts, Law, and Politics in Comparative Perspective,* ed. Herbert Jacob et al. (New Haven, CT: Yale University Press, 1996), pp. 181–185.
6. Henry J. Abraham, *The Judicial Process,* 6th ed. (New York: Oxford University Press, 1993), pp. 96–97.
7. Michael McCall, Madhavi McCall, and Christopher E. Smith, "Criminal Justice and the U.S. Supreme Court's 2006–2007 Term," *University of Missouri-Kansas City Law Review* (Vol. 76 forthcoming 2008).
8. Jeffrey A. Segal and Harold J. Spaeth, *The Supreme Court and the Attitudinal Model* (New York: Cambridge University Press, 1993), pp. 64-73.

9. Lawrence Baum, *The Puzzle of Judicial Behavior* (Ann Arbor: University of Michigan Press, 1997), pp. 89-124.
10. Herbert Kritzer, "Martin Shapiro: Anticipating the New Institutionalism," in *The Pioneers of Judicial Behavior*, ed. Nancy Maveety (Ann Arbor: University of Michigan Press, 2003), p. 387.
11. Wasby, *The Supreme Court,* p. 155.
12. Joseph D. Kearney and Thomas W. Merrill, "The Influence of Amicus Curiae Briefs on the Supreme Court," *University of Pennsylvania Law Review* 148 (2000): 753.
13. Jeff Yates, *Popular Justice: Presidential Prestige and Executive Success in the Supreme Court* (Albany: State University of New York Press, 2002), p. 2.
14. Gerald Rosenberg, *The Hollow Hope: Can Courts Bring About Social Change?* (Chicago: University of Chicago Press, 1991).
15. Bradley C. Canon, "The Supreme Court and Policy Reform: The Hollow Hope Revisited," in *Leveraging the Law: Using the Courts to Achieve Social Change*, ed. David A. Schultz (New York: Lang, 1998), pp. 215–249.
16. See Richard E. Morgan, *Disabling America: The "Rights Industry" in Our Time* (New York: Basic Books, 1984); Jeremy Rabkin, *Judicial Compulsions: How Public Law Distorts Public Policy* (New York: Basic Books, 1989).
17. Gallup Poll, "Civil Liberties," national opinion poll conducted September 14–15, 2001, http://www.galluppoll.com
18. Tariq Ali, "Pakistan's people want an end to the nightmare," *Guardian Unlimited* (U.K.), August 10, 2007. Accessed on September 15, 2007 at http://www.guardian.co.uk/commentisfree/2007/aug/10/pakistan.comment1

Chapter 5

1. Henry J. Abraham, *Freedom and the Court: Civil Rights and Liberties in the United States,* 5th ed. (New York: Oxford University Press, 1988), p. 41.
2. Ibid., p. 206.
3. Thomas R. Hensley, Christopher E. Smith, and Joyce A. Baugh, *The Changing Supreme Court: Constitutional Rights and Liberties* (St. Paul, MN: West, 1997), p. 131.
4. Linda Greenhouse, "Documents Reveal the Evolution of a Justice," *New York Times,* March 4, 2004, p. A16.
5. Thomas R. Hensley, Christopher E. Smith, and Joyce A. Baugh, *The Changing Supreme Court: Constitutional Rights and Liberties* (St. Paul, MN: West, 1997), p. 329.
6. Joshua Lipton, "Vanessa Leggett: Why She Wouldn't Give Up Her Notes," *Columbia Journalism Review,* March–April 2002. Accessed at http://www.cjr.org/issues/2002/2/qa-leggett.asp on August 23, 2008.
7. Frances Harrison, "'Mass Purges' at Iran Universities," BBC News, December 20, 2006. Accessed at http://news.bbc.co.ut/1/hi/world/middle_east/6196069.stm on August 23, 2008.
8. Frances Harrison, "Student Editor Detained in Tehran," BBC News, May 7, 2007. Accessed at http://news.bbc.co.uk/1/hi/world/middle_east/6631715.stm on August 23, 2008.
9. George F. Cole and Christopher E. Smith, *Criminal Justice in America,* 4th ed. (Belmont, CA: Wadsworth, 2004), p. 10.
10. See Lee Epstein and Joseph Kobylka, *The Supreme Court and Legal Change* (Chapel Hill: University of North Carolina Press, 1992).
11. Mark Costanza, *Just Revenge: Costs and Consequences of the Death Penalty* (New York: St. Martin's Press, 1997), pp. 95–111.
12. Stanley Cohen, *The Wrong Men* (New York: Carroll & Graf, 2003), pp. 298–322; Death Penalty Information Center, http://www.deathpenaltyinfo.org
13. Christopher E. Smith, *Courts and the Poor* (Chicago: Nelson-Hall, 1991), p. 118.
14. See, for example, Peter Kolchin, *American Slavery, 1619–1877* (New York: Hill & Wang, 1993); Walter Johnson, *Soul by Soul: Life Inside the Antebellum Slave Market* (Cambridge, MA: Harvard University Press, 1999); Ira Berlin, Marc Favreau, and Steven F. Miller, eds., *Remembering Slavery* (New York: New Press, 1998); John Hope Franklin and Loren Schweninger, *Runaway Slaves: Rebels on the Plantation* (New York: Oxford University Press, 1999).
15. See, for example, Andrew Hacker, *Two Nations: Black and White, Separate, Hostile, Unequal* (New York: Scribner, 1992); Tom Wicker, *Tragic Failure: Racial Integration in America* (New York: Morrow, 1996).
16. Eric Foner, *The Story of American Freedom* (New York: Norton, 1998), p. 104.
17. Kolchin, *American Slavery,* p. 215.
18. Ibid., pp. 220–224.
19. David E. Kyvig, *Explicit and Authentic Acts: Amending the U.S. Constitution, 1776–1995* (Lawrence: University Press of Kansas, 1996), pp. 182–183.
20. Foner, *Story of American Freedom,* p. 105.
21. William Gillette, *Retreat from Reconstruction, 1869–1879* (Baton Rouge: Louisiana State University Press, 1979), pp. 335–347.
22. Ronald Takaki, *A Different Mirror: A History of Multicultural America* (Boston: Little, Brown, 1993), pp. 191–221.
23. James W. Loewen, *Lies My Teacher Told Me: Everything Your American History Textbook Got Wrong* (New York: Simon & Schuster, 1995) p. 165.
24. Ibid., pp. 164–166.
25. See Richard Kluger, *Simple Justice* (New York: Random House, 1975), pp. 657–747.
26. Summary drawn from Peter H. Irons, *The Courage of Their Convictions* (New York: Penguin Books, 1990), pp. 65–79.
27. Adrianne Deweese, "BSU to Have Panel, Demonstration About Hate Crimes, Discrimination," Kansas State Collegian Online, October 19, 2007. Accessed at http://media.kstatecollegian.com
28. See Gunnar Myrdal, *An American Dilemma: The Negro Problem and Modern Democracy* (New York: Harper Bros., 1994)
29. Taylor Branch, *Parting the Waters: America in the King Years, 1954–1963* (New York: Simon & Schuster, 1988), pp. 128–205.
30. Williams, *Eyes on the Prize,* pp. 59–89.
31. Ibid., pp. 99–113.
32. Branch, *Parting the Waters,* p. 891.
33. Williams, *Eyes on the Prize,* p. 197–200.
34. Ibid., pp. 276–277.
35. Gerald Gunther, *Constitutional Law,* 11th ed. (Mineola, NY: Foundation Press, 1985), p. 932.
36. Eleanor Flexner, *Century of Struggle: The Women's Rights Movement in the United States,* rev. ed. (Cambridge, MA: Harvard University Press, 1975), pp. 154–158.
37. Ibid., pp. 167–171, 295.
38. Ibid., p. 228.
39. Ibid., p. 300.
40. Oscar J. Martinez, "A History of Chicanos/Mexicanos along the U.S.–Mexico Border," in *Handbook of Hispanic Cultures in the United States: History,* ed. Alfredo Jimenez (Houston: Arte Publico Press, 1994), pp. 261–280.
41. Pedro Caban, Jose Carrasco, Barbara Cruz, and Juan Garcia, *The Latino Experience in U.S. History* (Paramus, NJ: Globe Fearon, 1994), pp. 208–220.
42. Ibid., pp. 282–287.
43. "Tamil Law Students Protest Discrimination In Admissions," TamilNet, December 28, 2006. Accessed at http://www.tamilnet.com

Chapter 6

1. Kelly D. Patterson and Daniel M. Shea, eds., *Contemplating the People's Branch* (Upper Saddle River, NJ: Prentice Hall, 2000), p. 6.
2. Patterson and Shea, *Contemplating the People's Branch,* p. 7.

3. Roger H. Davidson and Walter Oleszek, *Congress and Its Members,* 10th ed. (Washington, D.C.: CQ Press, 2004), p. 122.
4. Gary W. Cox and Jonathan N. Katz, *Elbridge Gerry's Salamander* (Cambridge: Cambridge University Press, 2002), p. 3.
5. See, for example, Ralph Blumenthal, "GOP Is Victorious in Remapping," *New York Times,* January 7, 2004, p. A12.
6. Adam Clymer, "Why Iowa Has So Many Hot Seats," *New York Times,* October 27, 2002, p. A22.
7. L. Sandy Maisel, *Parties and Elections in America: The Electoral Process,* 3rd ed (Lanham, MD: Rowman & Littlefield, 1999), p. 207.
8. Cox and Katz, *Elbridge Gerry's Salamander,* pp. 12–13.
9. Ibid., pp. 25–28.
10. Davidson and Oleszek, *Congress and Its Members,* 10th ed., 2004, pp. 193–194.
11. Ibid., p. 199.
12. Opening remarks of Senator Arlen Specter before the Senate Subcommittee on Labor, Health and Human Services, Education, and Related Agencies, Committee on Appropriations, June, 5, 1997.
13. Ibid., p. 337.
14. David J. Vogler, *The Politics of Congress* (Madison, WI: Brown & Benchmark, 1993), p. 76.
15. Michael J. Malbin, *Unelected Representatives: Congressional Staff and the Future of Representative Government* (New York: Basic Books, 1979).
16. Charles Peters, *How Washington Really Works* (Reading, MA: Addison-Wesley, 1992), p. 133; Fred Harris, *In Defense of Congress* (New York: St. Martin's Press, 1995), pp. 40–41.
17. Patterson and Shea, *Contemplating the People's Branch,* pp. 133–134.
18. Ibid., p. 136.
19. Michele Cottle, "House Broker," *New Republic,* June 11, 2008, accessed on line at: http://tnr.com/politics/story/html?id=869a5b6c-b4db-4205-8e88-63e0e02e2543&p=2
20. Donald R. Matthews, *U.S. Senators and Their World* (New York: Vintage Books, 1960).
21. Ibid., p. 97.
22. Ibid., p. 99.
23. Davidson and Oleszek, *Congress and Its Members,* p. 234.
24. Congressional Black Caucus, http://www.congressionalblackcaucus.net, accessed February 2004.
25. Ibid.
26. Stephen J. Wayne, *Is This Any Way to Run a Democratic Election?* 2nd ed. (Boston: Houghton Mifflin, 2003), p. 54.
27. Sean Loughlin and Robert Yoon, "Millionaires Populate U.S. Senate," CNN.com/Inside Politics, June 13, 2003, http://www.cnn.com
28. "Income," U.S. Census Bureau, http://www.census.gov/hhes/www/income.html, February 2004.
29. Roger H. Davidson and Walter Oleszek, *Congress and Its Members,* 7th ed. (Washington, D.C.: CQ Press, 2000), pp. 128–129.
30. Roger H. Davidson and Walter Oleszek, *Congress and Its Members,* 10th ed. (Washington, D.C.: CQ Press, 2006), p. 479.
31. Harris, *In Defense of Congress,* p. 59.
32. Norman J. Ornstein, "Prosecutors Must Stop Their Big Game Hunt of Politicians," *Roll Call,* April 26, 1993, p. 6.
33. Larry J. Sabato, *Feeding Frenzy: How Attack Journalism Has Transformed American Politics* (New York: Free Press, 1993), p. 1.

Chapter 7

1. Theodore J. Lowi and Benjamin Ginsberg, *American Government: Freedom and Power* (New York: Norton, 1990), p. 241.
2. John Locke, *The Second Treatise on Government,* cited in ibid., p. 241.
3. Sidney M. Milkis and Michael Nelson, *The American Presidency: Origins and Development, 1776–1998* (Washington, D.C.: CQ Press, 1999), p. 26.
4. Milkis and Nelson, *American Presidency, 1776–1998,* p. 28.
5. David Mervin, *The President of the United States* (New York: Harvester Press, 1993), p. 22.
6. Michael Nelson, ed., *The Evolving Presidency,* 2d ed. (Washington, D.C.: CQ Press, 2004), p. 10.
7. Robert Dallek, *Hail to the Chief: The Making and Unmaking of American Presidents* (New York: Hyperion, 1996), p. 14.
8. Theodore Roosevelt, "The Stewardship Doctrine," in *Classics of the American Presidency,* ed. Harry Bailey (Oak Park, IL: Moore, 1980), pp. 35–36.
9. Dallek, *Hail to the Chief,* p. 18.
10. Michael A. Genovese, *The Power of the American Presidency, 1789–2000* (New York: Oxford University Press, 2001), p. 132.
11. Ibid, p. 143.
12. Sidney M. Milkis and Michael Nelson, *The American Presidency: Origins and Development, 1776–2002* (Washington, D.C.: CQ Press, 2003), p. 424.
13. Ibid.
14. Ibid., p. 428.
15. Nathan Miller, *FDR: An Intimate History* (Lanham, MD: Madison Books, 1983), p. 276.
16. Edward S. Greenberg and Benjamin I. Page, *The Struggle for Democracy,* 5th ed. (New York: Longman, 2002), p. 361.
17. Milkis and Nelson, *American Presidency, 1776–2002,* p. 438.
18. Ibid., p. 440.
19. Richard Neustadt, *Presidential Power* (New York: John Wiley and Sons, 1960), p. 193.
20. "Poll: Bush Ratings Hit New Low," CBS News.com, October 6, 2005. http://www.cbsnews.com/stories/2005/106/opinion/polls/main924485
21. Gary King and Lyn Ragsdale, *The Elusive Executive: Discovering Statistical Patterns in the Presidency* (Washington, D.C.: CQ Press, 1988), p. 35.
22. The Supreme Court case was *United States* v. *Curtis Wright Corp.,* 299 U.S. 304 (1936).
23. Louis Fisher, "Invitation to Struggle: The President, Congress, and National Security," in James P. Pfiffner and Roger Davidson, eds. *Understanding the Presidency* (New York: Longman, 1996), p. 269.
24. Abraham Lincoln, "A Special Session Message, July 4, 1861," cited in Genovese, *Power of the American Presidency,* p. 81.
25. Theodore J. Lowi, *The Personal President: Power Invested, Promise Unfulfilled* (Ithaca, NY: Cornell University Press, 1985), p. xii.
26. Ibid., p. 1.
27. Dallek, *Hail to the Chief,* p. xx.
28. Sean Wilentz, "The Worst President Ever?" *Rolling Stone,* April 21, 2006.
29. These points are made by political scientist Fred I. Greenstein, "A Change and Continuity in Modern Presidency," in *The New American Political System,* ed. Anthony King (Washington, D.C.: American Enterprise Institute, 1978), pp. 45–46.
30. Arthur M. Schlesinger, Jr., *The Imperial Presidency,* 2nd ed. (Boston: Houghton Mifflin, 1989).

Chapter 8

1. "Tornado Toll Rises in Splintered Remains of a Kansas Town," *New York Times,* May 8, 2007. Accessed at http://www.nytimes.com/2007/05/08/us/08tornado.html?_r=1&oref=slogin on July 20, 2008.
2. Roxana Hegeman, "FEMA Repairing Its Reputation in Greensburg," *Lawrence Journal-World,* September 7, 2007. Accessed at http://www2.ljworld.com/news/2007/sep/07/fema_repairing_its_reputation_greensburg/ on July 20, 2008.
3. "Arsenic in Drinking Water," Environmental Protection Agency. Accessed at http://www.epa.gov/safewater/arsenic/ on July 20, 2008. "Bush Administration's Belated Arsenic Decision Doesn't Imply Insensitivity, Expert Says," Alabama Cooperative Extension Service. Accessed at http://www.aces.edu/dept/extcomm/newspaper/nov8a01.html on July 20, 2008. "EPA Delays Lower Arsenic Standards for

Water," CNN.com. Accessed at http://archives.cnn.com/2001/HEALTH/03/20/epa.arsenic/index.html on July 20, 2008.

4. Eric Lipton and Scott Shane, "Leader of Federal Effort Feels the Heat," *New York Times*, September 3, 2005. Accessed at http://www.nytimes.com/2005/09/03/national/nationalspecial/03fema.html?_r=1&oref=slogin on July 21, 2008. Daren Fonda and Rita Healy, "How Reliable Is Brown's Resume?" *Time*, September 8, 2005. Accessed at http://www.time.com/time/nation/article/0,8599,1103003,00.html on July 21, 2008.
5. "Dental Students Protest Against 'Illegal' Order," *The Hindu*, online edition, December 15, 2005. Accessed at http://www.hindu.com/2005/12/15/stories/2005121507180300.htm on March 20, 2008.
6. Pew Research Center for the People and the Press, "Performance and Purpose: Constituents Rate Government Agencies." Accessed at http://people-press.org/report/41/ on July 21, 2008.
7. Charles T. Goodsell, *The Case for Bureaucracy* (Chatham, NJ: Chatham House, 1983), p. 15.
8. "TSA Takes Heat for Background Check Miscues," Government Security. Accessed at http://govtsecurity.securitysolutions.com/ar/security_tsa_takes_heat_index.htm on July 21, 2008.
9. Jeff Johnson, "TSA Screeners Claim They're 'Being Used for Cannon Fodder,'" CNSNews.com. Accessed at www.cnsnews.com/ViewPrint.asp?Page=%5CPolitics%5Carchive%5C200303%5CPOL20030304b.html on March 20, 2008.
10. B. Guy Peters, *American Public Policy: Promise and Performance,* 5th ed. (Chatham, NJ: Chatham House, 1999), p. 33.
11. Elizabeth Gettelman, "The K(a-ching!) Street Congressman," *Mother Jones,* November–December 2004, p. 24.
12. Tony Pugh, "Medicare Cost Estimates Concealed, Expert Says," *San Diego Union-Tribune.* Accessed at www.cnsnews.com/ViewPrint.asp?Page=%5CPolitics%5Carchive%5C200303%5CPOL20030304b.html on July 21, 2008.
13. "General: Army Leaned on Whistleblower," CBSNews.com. Accessed at http://www.cbsnews.com/stories/2004/10/28/national/main652183.shtml on July 21, 2008.
14. Neely Tucker, "A Web of Truth," *Washington Post,* October 19, 2005, p. C1.
15. Robert A. Katzmann, *Regulatory Bureaucracy* (Cambridge, MA: MIT Press, 1980), p. 180.
16. Stephen Labaton, "Agencies Postpone Issuing New Rules until after Election," *New York Times,* September 27, 2004. Accessed at http://www.nytimes.com/2004/09/27/business/27regs.html on July 21, 2008.
17. Ibid.
18. Joel Brinkley, "Out of Spotlight, Bush Overhauls U.S. Regulations," *New York Times,* August 14, 2004. Accessed at http://www.nytimes.com/2004/08/14/politics/14bush.html?ex=1250136000&en=1bf32d7574b25b2b&ei=5090 on July 21, 2008.
19. Paul Davidson, "FCC Seeks $1.2 Million Fine for FOX Marriage Show," USATODAY.com, October 12, 2004. Accessed at http://www.usatoday.com/life/televison/news/2004-10-12-fox-fcc_x.htm on July 21, 2008.
20. See Donna Price Cofer, *Judges, Bureaucrats, and the Question of Independence* (Westport, CT: Greenwood Press, 1985).
21. Christopher H. Foreman, Jr., *Signals from the Hill: Congressional Oversight and the Challenge of Social Regulation* (New Haven, CT: Yale University Press, 1988), p. 13.
22. See Lawrence C. Dodd and Richard L. Schott, *Congress and the Administrative State* (New York: Wiley, 1979).

Chapter 9

1. See, for instance, the seminal work by Angus Campbell, Philip Converse, Warren Miller, and Donald Stokes, *The American Voter* (Chicago: University of Chicago Press, 1960).
2. See, for instance, V. O. Key, Jr., *The Responsible Electorate* (Cambridge, MA: Belknap Press, 1966); see also Warren E. Miller and J. Merrill Shanks, *The New American Voter* (Cambridge, MA: Harvard University Press, 1996).
3. Walter Lippmann, *Public Opinion* (New York: Macmillan, 1922).
4. Robert Weissberg, *Polling, Policy, and Public Opinion: The Case Against Heeding the "Voice of the People"* (New York: Palgrave-Macmillan, 2002).
5. Sidney Verba, *Participation in America: Political Democracy and Social Equality* (Chicago: University of Chicago Press, 1972).
6. Herbert Asher, *Polling and the Public: What Every Citizen Should Know,* 6th ed. (Washington, D.C.: CQ Press, 2004), p. 195.
7. Starting with the seminal research of Philip E. Converse, "The Nature of Belief Systems in Mass Publics," in *Ideology and Discontent,* ed. David E. Apter (New York: Free Press, 1964), pp. 206–261.
8. Robert S. Erikson and Kent L. Tedin, *American Public Opinion,* 5th ed. (Boston: Allyn & Bacon, 1995), p. 144.
9. Joseph Carroll, "Most Americans Approve of Interracial Marriages," Gallup Poll. Accessed at http://www.gallup.com/poll/28417/Most-Americans-Approve-Interracial-Marriages.aspx on August 16, 2007.
10. Lydia Saad, "Tolerance for Gay Rights at High-Water Mark," Gallup Poll. Accessed at http://www.gallup.com/poll/27694/Tolerance-Gay-Rights-HighWater-Mark.aspx on May 29, 2007.
11. http://poll.gallup.com/content/default.aspx?ci=1651. Accessed on January 9, 2006.
12. Paul Abramson, *Political Attitudes in America* (San Francisco: Freeman, 1983).
13. Benjamin I. Page and Robert Y. Shapiro, *The Rational Public* (Chicago: University of Chicago Press, 1992), p. 178.
14. Ibid., 179.
15. See David J. Jackson, *Entertainment and Politics: The Influence of Pop Culture on Young Adult Political Socialization* (New York: Lang, 2002), ch. 1.
16. See Daniel Shea, "Introduction: Popular Culture—The Trojan Horse of American Politics?" in *Mass Politics: The Politics of Popular Culture,* ed. Daniel Shea (New York: St. Martin's/Worth, 1999).
17. "The NES Guide to Public Opinion and Electoral Behavior," *American National Election Studies.* Accessed at http://www.umich.edu/~nes/nesguide/graphs/g4c_1_1.htm on November 30, 2005, graph 4C.1.1.
18. "Women in Elective Office, 2006," Center for American Women in Politics. Accessed at http://www.rci.rutgers.edu/~cawp/Facts/Officeholders/elective.pdf, 2006, on March 15, 2008.
19. Kul B. Rai, David F. Walsh, and Paul J. Best, eds. *America in the 21st Century: Challenges and Opportunities in Domestic Politics* (Upper Saddle River, NJ: Prentice Hall, 1998).
20. Jackson, *Entertainment and Politics,* p. 9.
21. M. Kent Jennings and Richard G. Niemi, *Generations and Politics: A Panel Study of Young Adults and Their Parents* (Princeton, NJ: Princeton University Press, 1981).
22. Stuart Oskamp, *Attitudes and Opinions,* 2nd ed. (Englewood Cliffs, NJ: Prentice Hall, 1991), p. 160.
23. Ibid., ch. 15.
24. U.S. Census Bureau, *America's Families and Living Arrangements, 2004* (Washington, D.C.: Government Printing Office, 2004).
25. David Easton, *A Systems Analysis of Political Life* (New York: Wiley, 1965).
26. James G. Gimpel, J. Celeste Lay, and Jason E. Schuknecht, *Cultivating Democracy: Civic Environments and Political Socialization in America* (Washington, D.C.: Brookings Institution Press, 2003), p. 147.
27. Lee Anderson, *The Civics Report Card* (Princeton, NJ: Educational Testing Service, 1990).
28. U.S. Census Bureau, *Educational Attainment in the United States, 2003* (Washington, D.C.: Government Printing Office, 2003).
29. Earnest Boyer and Mary Jean Whitelaw, *The Condition of the Professorate* (New York: Harper & Row, 1989).

30. Gimpel, Lay, and Schuknecht, *Cultivating Democracy,* p. 63.
31. Ibid.
32. Ibid., p. 92.
33. See, for instance, Penny Edgell Becker and Pawan H. Dhingra, "Religious Involvement and Volunteering: Implications for Civil Society," *Sociology of Religion 62* (2001): 315–335; Corwin Smidt, "Religion and Civic Engagement: A Comparative Analysis," *Annals of the American Academy of Political and Social Sciences 565* (1999): 176–192.
34. Gimpel, Lay, and Schuknecht, *Cultivating Democracy,* p. 142.
35. Ibid., p. 143.
36. Landrea Wells, "Viewing," Children and Television. Accessed at http://iml.jou.ufl.edu/projects/Spring03/Wells/viewing.htm, 2003.
37. http://www.truceteachers.org, on July 30, 2008.
38. See, for instance, Gimpel, Lay, and Schuknecht, *Cultivating Democracy,* p. 35.
39. Brian Long, "Daily Show Viewers Ace Political Quiz." Accessed at http://www.cnn.com/2004/SHOWBIZ/TV/09/28/comedy.politics/index.html on September 29, 2004.
40. Gimpel, Lay, and Schuknecht, *Cultivating Democracy,* ch. 7.
41. Ibid., p. 182.
42. Ibid., p. 191.
43. Paul Lazarfeld, Bernard Berelson, and Hazel Gaudet, *The People's Choice* (New York: Columbia University Press, 1944).
44. U.S. Census Bureau, *Current Population Survey, 2007: Annual Social and Economic Supplement* (Washington, D.C.: Government Printing Office, 2005). Accessed at http://pubdb3.census.gov/macro/032007/perinc/new04_001.htm on July 30, 2008.
45. Erikson and Tedin, *American Public Opinion,* p. 181.
46. Ibid., p. 183.
47. William H. Flanigan and Nancy H. Zingale, *Political Behavior of the American Electorate,* 11th ed. (Washington, D.C.: CQ Press, 2006), p. 132.
48. Pew Research Center for the People and the Press, "Religion in American Life." Accessed at http://people-press.org on April 10, 2001.
49. Flanigan and Zingale, *Political Behavior,* p. 106.
50. James L. Guth, Lyman A. Delestedt, John C. Green, and Corwin E. Smidt, "A Distant Thunder? Religious Mobilization in the 2000 Elections," in *Interest Group Politics,* 6th ed., ed. Allen J. Cigler and Burdett A. Loomis (Washington, D.C.: CQ Press, 2002), pp. 161–184.
51. Accessed at http://www.cnn.com/ELECTIONS/2008/results/polls/#val=USP00p2 on November 6, 2008.
52. Accessed at http://www.cnn.com/ELECTIONS/2008/results/polls/#val=USP00p2 on November 6, 2008.
53. Oskamp, *Attitudes and Opinions,* p. 390.
54. Ibid., p. 391.
55. Center for American Women and Politics, *The Gender Gap: Attitudes on Public Policy Issues* (New Brunswick, NJ: Eagleton Institute of Politics, Rutgers University, 1997); Susan J. Carroll and Richard F. Fox, eds., *Gender and Elections* (New York: Cambridge University Press, 2006).
56. Reported in Justin Lewis, *Constructing Public Opinion: How Political Elites Do What They Like and Why We Seem to Go Along with It* (New York: Columbia University Press, 2001), p. 34.
57. Asher, *Polling and the Public,* p. 23.
58. Benjamin Ginsberg, *The Captive Public: How Mass Opinion Promotes State Power* (New York: Basic Books, 1986).
59. Asher, *Polling and the Public,* p. 3.
60. Lewis, *Constructing Public Opinion,* p. 41.
61. Asher, *Polling and the Public,* p. 10.
62. Andrew Kohut, "The Vocal Minority in American Politics," Times Mirror Center for the People and the Press, Washington, D.C., July 16, 1993.
63. Richard Morin, "Don't Ask Me: As Fewer Cooperate on Polls, Criticism and Questions Mount," *Washington Post,* October 25, 2004, p. C1.
64. Ibid.
65. Ibid.
66. Ibid., p. C25.
67. See, for instance, Lewis, *Constructing Public Opinion,* p. 37.
68. James A. Stimson, *Public Opinion in America,* 2nd ed. (Boulder, CO: Westview Press, 1999), p. 122.

Chapter 10

1. W. Lance Bennett, *News: The Politics of Illusion,* 6th ed. (New York: Longman, 2005), p. 6.
2. Alfred McClung Lee, *The Daily Newspaper in America,* (New York: Macmillian, 1937), p. 21.
3. Quoted in Philip Davidson, *Propaganda and the American Revolution, 1763–1783* (Chapel Hill: University of North Carolina Press, 1941), p. 285.
4. *Messages and Papers of the Presidents 1789–1908,* vol. 1 (Washington, D.C.: Bureau of National Literature and Art, 1909), p. 132.
5. Lee, *The Daily Newspaper in America,* pp. 716–717.
6. See Jan E. Leighley, *Mass Media and Politics: A Social Science Perspective* (Boston: Houghton Mifflin Company, 2004) ch. 1.
7. Quoted in W.W. Swanberg, *Citizen Hurst* (New York: Scribner, 1961), p. 90.
8. Lee, *The Daily Newspaper in America,* pp. 215–216.
9. Doris A. Graber, *Mass Media and American Politics,* 7th ed. (Washington, D.C.: CQ Press, 2006), p. 38.
10. Edwin Emery and Michael Emery, *The Press and America* (Englewood Cliffs, NJ: Prentice Hall, 1984), pp. 372–379.
11. Frank Luther Mott, *American Journalism, A History: 1690–1960* (New York: Macmillian, 1962), pp. 679.
12. Richard Davis, *The Press and American Politics* (Upper Saddle River, NJ: Prentice Hall, 2001) p. 2.
13. CNN, Young People Who Rock. Accessed at http://www.cnn.com/exchange/blogs/ypwr/archive/2007_12_01_index.html
14. See, for instance, Bennet, *News: The Politics of Illusion.*
15. See, for instance, Christopher P. Latimer, "The Digital Divide: Understanding and Addressing." Accessed at http://www.nysfirm.org/documents/html/whitepapers/nysfirm digital_divide.htm on May 15, 2008.
16. Kathy Koch, "The Digital Divide," in *The CQ Researcher Online 10.3* (2000). 10 July 2004. Document ID: cqresrre2000012800.
17. "Falling Through the Net, III: Defining the Digital Divide," National Telecommunications and Information Administration, July 1999, p. 8.
18. The Pew Research Center for the People and the Press, "Internet Sapping Broadcast News Audience." Accessed at http://people-press.org/reports/display.php3?ReportID=36 on June 11, 2000.
19. "Internet's Broader Role in Campaign 2008," Pew Research Center for the People and the Press, January 1, 2008. Accessed at http://www.people-press.org/report/384/internets-broader-role-in-campaign-2008 on August 1, 2008.
20. Robert S. Lichter, Linda S. Lichter, and Daniel Amundson, "Government Goes Down the Tube: Images of Government in TV Entertainment, 1955–1998," *The Harvard International Journal of Press/Politics 5* (2000): 96–103.
21. Harold D. Lasswell, "The Structure and Function of Communication in Society," in *Mass Communications,* ed. Wilbur Schramm (Urbana: University of Illinois Press, 1969), p. 103.
22. Accessed at http://www.gf.org/broch.html# top on Auguest 4, 2008.
23. For a good analysis of the issue of race and media coverage, see Robert M. Entman and Andrew Rojecki's *The Black Image in the White Mind: Media and Race in America* (Chicago: University of Chicago Press, 2001).
24. Reported in Jerry L. Yeric, *Mass Media and the Politics of Change* (Itasca, IL: Peacock Publishers, 2001), ch. 6.

25. "Bottom-Line Pressure Now Hurting Coverage, Say Journalists," Pew Research Center for the People and the Press. Accessed at http://people-press.org/reports/display.php3?PageID=825 on May 23, 2004.
26. Harold W. Stanley and Richard G. Niemi, *Vital Statistics on American Politics, 2003–2004,* 6th ed. (Washington, D.C.: CQ Press, 2003).
27. See Yeric, *Mass Media and the Politics of Change,* and Graber, *Mass Media and American Politics.*
28. Graber, *Mass Media and American Politics,* p. 198.
29. Daniel Boorstin, *The Image: A Guide to Pseudo-Events in America* (New York: Vintage, 1961).
30. Ibid., p. 102.
31. Ibid., p. 271.
32. Garber, *Mass Media & American Politics,* p. 185.
33. David L. Protess, Fay Lomax Cook, Jack C. Doppelt, James S. Ettema, Margaret T. Gordon, Donna R. Leff, and Peter Miller, *The Journalism of Outrage: Investigative Reporting and Agenda Setting* (New York: Builford Press, 1991), p. 180.
34. See, for instance, Bennett, *News: The Politics of Illusion.*
35. Ibid.
36. For a good discussion of the impact the Thomas hearings had in mobilizing women voters and candidates, see Linda Witt, Karen M. Paget, Glenna Matthews, *Running as a Woman: Gender and Power in American Politics* (New York: Free Press, 1994).
37. See, for instance, Graber, *Mass Media and American Politics,* p. 311; see also Vincent James Strickler and Richard Davis, "The Supreme Court and the Press," in *Media Power, Media Politics,* ed. Mark J. Roxell (Lanham, MD: Rowman & Littlefield), 2003.
38. Graber, *Mass Media and American Politics,* p. 311.
39. Howard Kurtz, "Paint by Numbers: How Repeated Reportage Colors Perceptions," *Washington Post,* Monday, July 12, 2004, p. C1.
40. Daniel C. Hallin, "Sound Bite News: Television Coverage of Elections, 1968–1988," *Journal of Communication 42* (1992) 15.
41. Robert S. Lichter and Richard E. Noyes, "There They Go Again: Media Coverage of Campaign '96," in *Political Parties, Campaigns, and Elections,* ed. Robert E. DeClerico (Upper Saddle River, NJ: Prentice Hall, 2000), p. 98.
42. For a good discussion of debates, see Graber, *Mass Media and American Politics,* ch. 8.
43. Davis, *The Press and American Politics,* p. 93.
44. Ana Vecina-Suarez, *Hispanic Media USA: A Narrative Guide to Print and Electronic Media in the United States* (Washington, D.C.: Media Institute, 1987).
45. Ben H. Bagdikian, *The Media Monopoloy,* 5th ed. (Boston: Beacon Press), p. x.
46. Graber, *Mass Media and American Politics,* p. 41; see also Yeric, *Mass Media and the Politics of Change,* ch. 1.
47. For a good discussion of deregulation, see Leighley, *Mass Media and Politics,* ch. 2.
48. Graber, *Mass Media and American Politics,* p. 49.
49. Ibid., pp. 19–21.
50. Leighley, *Mass Media and Politics,* p. 80.

CHAPTER 11

1. Alexis de Tocqueville, *Democracy in America,* ed. Richard Heffner (New York: New American Library, 1956), vol. 1, p. 16. (Originally published 1835.)
2. His actual charge was to examine our penal system, but his true interest was to examine our democracy so that he could take lessons back to France.
3. Tocqueville, *Democracy in America,* vol. 1, p. 220.
4. For a good discussion of the importance of organized groups in democratic theory, see Jane Mansbridge, "A Deliberative Theory of Interest Representation," in *The Politics of Interests: Interest Groups Transformed,* ed. Mark P. Petracca (Boulder, CO: Westview Press, 1992).
5. Ibid., p. 38.
6. League of United Latin American Citizens. Accessed at http://www.lulac.org on June 1, 2008.
7. Frank R. Baumgartner and Beth L. Leech, *Basic Interests: The Importance of Groups in Politics and in Political Science* (Princeton, NJ: Princeton University Press, 1998), p. 103.
8. Robert Salisbury, "An Exchange Theory of Interest Groups," *Midwest Journal of Political Science* (February 1969): pp. 1–32.
9. Jeffrey M. Berry, *Lobbying for the People: The Political Behavior of Public Interest Groups* (Princeton, NJ: Princeton University Press, 1977), p. 7.
10. Mancur Olson, *The Logic of Collective Action* (Cambridge, MA: Harvard University Press, 1971).
11. James Q. Wilson, *Political Organizations* (New York: Basic Books, 1974), p. 34.
12. Anthony Nownes, *Pressure and Power: Organized Interests in American Politics* (Boston: Houghton Mifflin, 2001), p. 50.
13. Susan Schmidt and James V. Brimald, "Abramoff Pleads Guilty to 3 Counts," *Washington Post,* January 4, 2006, p. A1.
14. David B. Truman, *The Governmental Process: Political Interests and Public Opinion,* 2nd ed. (New York: Knopf, 1971), p. 213.
15. Ken Kollman, *Outside Lobbying: Public Opinion and Interest Group Strategies* (Princeton, NJ: Princeton University Press, 1998), p. 58.
16. Kenneth M. Goldstein, *Interest Groups, Lobbying, and Participation in America* (Cambridge, UK: Cambridge University Press, 1999) p. 125; see also Nownes, *Pressure and Power.*
17. Ibid., p. 3.
18. William P. Browne, *Groups, Interests, and U.S. Public Policy* (Washington, D.C.: Georgetown University Press, 1998), p. 23.
19. Cliff Landesman, "Nonprofits and the World Wide Web," Internet Nonprofit Center. Accessed at http://www.nonprofits.org/website.htm on June 5, 2008.
20. Christopher J. Bosso and Michael Thomas Collins, "Just Another Tool? How Environmental Groups Use the Internet," in *Interest Group Politics,* 7th ed., ed. Allan J. Ciglar and Burdett A. Loomis (Washington, D.C.: CQ Press, 2007), p. 101.
21. D. Truman, *Governmental Process.*
22. Sidney Verba, Kay Lehman Schlozman, and Hendry E. Brady, *Voice of Equality: Civic Voluntarism in American Politics* (Cambridge, MA: Harvard University Press, 1995). pp. 150–154.
23. James Q. Wilson, "Democracy and the Corporation," in *Does Big Business Rule America?* ed. Ronald Hessen (Washington, DC: Ethics and Public Policy Center, 1981), p. 37.
24. Quoted in Robert D. Putnam and Kristin A. Gross, "Introduction," in *Democracies in Flux,* ed. Robert D. Putnam, (New York: Oxford University Press, 2002), pp. 5–6.
25. See Robert D. Putnam, *Bowling Alone: The Collapse and Revival of American Community* (New York: Simon & Schuster, 2000), and Theda Skocpol and Morris P. Fiorina, *Civic Engagement in American Democracy* (Washington, D.C.: Brookings Institution Press, 1999), for a good discussion of the controversy in assessing community engagement.
26. See Skocpol and Fiorina, *Civic Engagement in American Democracy,* for a good discussion of the alternative methods used to examine civic engagement.
27. Robert Wuthnow, "United States: Bridging the Privileged and the Marginalized," in *Democracies in Flux,* ed. Robert D. Putnam (New York: Oxford University Press, 2002), p. 74.
28. Ibid.
29. Ibid., p. 88.
30. Michael Kryzanek, *Angry, Bored, Confused: A Citizen Handbook of American Politics* (Boulder, CO: Westview Press, 1999), p. 60.

31. Theda Skopol "U.S.: From Membership to Advocacy" in the above text.
32. Verba, Schlozman, and Brady, *Voice of Equality,* pp. 81–82.
33. Jeffrey H. Birnbaum, *The Lobbyists* (New York: Times Books, 1992), p. 7.
34. Allan J. Ciglar and Mark Joslyn, "Group Involvement and Social Capital Development," in *Interest Group Politics,* 6th ed., ed. Allan J. Ciglar and Burdett A. Loomis (Washington, D.C.: CQ Press, 2002).

CHAPTER 12

1. See, for example, Stephen Ansolabehere and Shanto Iyengar, *Going Negative: How Political Advertisements Shrink and Polarize the Electorate* (New York: Free Press, 1997), ch. 3.
2. Ibid., p. 60.
3. As stated on National Public Radio, *Morning Edition,* October 19, 2004. Accessed at http://www.npr.org/templates/story/story.php?storyId=4115994
4. Associate Press, "Maryland Sidesteps Electroral College," MSNBC, April 11, 2007. Accessed at http://www.msnbc.msn.com/id/18053715/ on September 19, 2007.
5. George Will, "From Schwarzenegger, a Veto for Voters' Good," *Washington Post,* October 12, 2006, p. A27.
6. Alan P. Grimes, *Democracy and the Amendments to the Constitution* (Lexington, MA: Lexington Books, 1978), pp. 44, 45.
7. Ibid., pp. 94, 95.
8. Ibid., pp. 131, 142–147.
9. Alexander Keyssar, *The Right to Vote: The Contested History of Democracy in the United States* (New York: Basic Books, 2000).
10. Ibid., p. 111.
11. Ibid., pp. 264–265.
12. L. Sandy, Maisel, *Parties and Elections in America: The Electoral Process,* 3rd ed. (Lanham, CT: Rowman and Littlefield, 1999), p. 97.
13. Frances Fox Piven and Richard A. Cloward, *Why Americans Still Don't Vote: And Why Politicians Want It That Way* (Boston, Beacon Press, 2000).
14. "Bubble-Up Democracy" [editorial], *Christian Science Monitor,* November 8, 2002, p. 10.
15. Jack Citrin, "Who's the Boss? Direct Democracy and Popular Control of Government," in *Broken Contract?* ed. Stephen C. Craig (Boulder, CO: Westview Press, 1996), p. 271.
16. John K. White and Daniel M. Shea, *New Party Politics: From Jefferson and Hamilton to the Information Age* (New York: Bedford St. Martin's, 2000), p. 210.
17. Quoted in Robert Dinkin, *Campaigning in America: A History of Election Practices* (Westport, CT: Greenwood Press, 1989), p. 8.
18. White and Shea, *New Party Politics,* 1st ed., p. 210.
19. Howard L. Reiter, *Parties and Elections in Corporate America* (New York: St. Martin's Press, 1987), p. 171.
20. Anthony Corrado, "Financing the 1996 Elections," in *The Election of 1996: Reports and Interpretations,* ed. Gerald M. Pomper (Chatham, NJ: Chatham House, 1997), p. 151.
21. White and Shea, *New Party Politics,* 1st ed., p. 220.
22. "Tracking the Payback," Center for Responsive Politics, http://www.opensecrets.org/payback/index.asp, April 23, 2003.
23. David Mayhew, *Congress: The Electoral Connection* (New Haven, CT: Yale University Press, 1974).
24. Roper Center for Public Opinion Research, 1994, cited in Center for Responsive Politics, *The Myths About Money in Politics* (Washington, D.C.: Center for Responsive Politics, 1995), p. 19.
25. Bloomberg News Poll, conducted by Princeton Survey Research Associates, July 31–August 5, 2001.
26. "A Campaign Finance Triumph" [editorial], *New York Times,* December 11, 2003, p. 42A.
27. Marian Currinder, "Campaign Finance: Funding the Presidential and Congressional Elections," in *The Election of 2004,* ed. Michael Nelson (Washington, D.C.. CQ Press, 2005), p. 122.
28. Ibid.
29. David D. Kirkpatrick, "Death Knell May Be Near for Public Election Funds," New York Times, January 23, 2007. Accessed at: http://www.nytimes.com/2007/01/23/us/politics/23donate.html?_r=1&ref=todayspaper&oref=slogin on April 20, 2008.
30. This remark was made by California State Treasurer Jesse Unruh. See White and Shea, *New Party Politics,* p. 95.
31. Arthur Lupia and Zoë Baird PS, "Can Web Sites Change Citizens? Implications of Web, White, and Blue 2000. *Political Science and Politics,* Vol. 36, No. 1 (Jan., 2003), pp. 77–82.
32. The Pew Research Center funds The Pew Internet & American Life Project. The Project "produces reports that explore the impact of the Internet on families, communities, work and home, daily life, education, health care, and civic and political life." Reports can be found at http://www.pewinternet.org.
33. Technorati (http://www.technorati.com) is a search engine similar to Google; however, it is exclusively devoted to blogs. They produce a regular industry report (State of the Blogosphere) based on their total indexed blogs.
34. Mark Halperin and John F. Harris, *The Way to Win: Taking the White House in 2008* (New York: Random House, 2006), p. 54.
35. These data, and much else, can be found at the National Election Study Cumulative Data File, 1952–2000, at http://www.umich.edu/~nes/nesguide/nesguide.htm
36. Robert Putnam, *Bowling Alone: The Collapse and Revival of American Community* (New York: Simon & Schuster, 2000), p. 189.
37. Ibid., p. 194.
38. Ibid., p. 237.
39. Ibid., p. 196.
40. Ibid., p. 284.
41. John P. Frendreis, James L. Gibson, and Laura L. Vertz, "Electoral Relevance of Local Party Organizations," *American Political Science Review 84* (1990): 225–235; Stephen Brooks, Rick Farmer, and Kyriakos Pagonis, "The Effects of Grassroots Campaigning on Political Participation," paper presented at the annual meeting of the Southern Political Science Association, November 8–10, 2001, Atlanta.
42. For details of these studies, see Richard Lau, Lee Sigelman, Caroline Heldman, and Paul Babbit, "The Effects of Negative Political Advertising: A Meta-Analytic Assessment," *American Political Science Review 93* (1999): 851–875.
43. Ansolabehere and Iyenger, *Going Negative,* ch. 5.
44. Kelly D. Patterson and Daniel M. Shea, "Local Political Context and Negative Campaigns: A Test of Negative Effects across State Party Systems," *Journal of Political Marketing 3* (2004): 1–20.
45. Larry J. Sabato, *Feeding Frenzy: How Attack Journalism Has Transformed American Politics* (New York: Free Press, 1993).
46. William H. Flanigan and Nancy H. Zingal, *Political Behavior and the American Electorate,* (Washington, D.C.: CQ Press, 1998), p. 40.
47. Peter Levine, Center for Information and Research on Civic Learning and Engagement, press release: "Over 3 Million Citizens Under the Age of 30 Participate in Super Tuesday," February 6, 2008, accessed at http://www.civicyouth.org/PopUps/PR_08_Super%20Tuesday.pdf
48. George F. Will, "In Defense of Nonvoting," *Newsweek,* October 10, 1983, p. 96.
49. E. J. Dionne, *Why Americans Hate Politics* (New York: Simon & Schuster, 1991), p. 355.

CHAPTER 13

1. Colin Campbell and Bert A. Rockman, "Introduction," in *The Clinton Presidency: First Appraisals,* ed. Colin Campbell and Bert A. Rockman (Chatham, NJ: Chatham House, 1996), p. 14.
2. John K. White and Daniel M. Shea, *New Party Politics: From Jefferson and Hamilton to the Information Age* (New York: Bedford St. Martin's, 2000), p. 19.

3. See, for example, John P. Frendreis, James L. Gibson, and Laura L. Vertz, "Electoral Relevance of Local Party Organizations," *American Political Science Review 84* (1990): 225–235.
4. Clyde Wilcox, *The Latest American Revolution: The 1994 Elections and Their Implications for Governance* (New York: St. Martin's Press, 1995), p. 1.
5. James G. Gimple, *Fulfilling the Contract: The First 100 Days* (Needham Heights, MA: Allan & Bacon, 1996), p. 95.
6. White and Shea, *New Party Politics,* p. 20.
7. Daniel M. Shea, "The Passing of Realignment and the Advent of the 'Base-Less' Party System," *American Politics Quarterly 27* (1999): 33–57.
8. White and Shea, *New Party Politics,* p. 174.
9. William Nisbet Chambers, *Political Parties in a New Nation: The American Experience, 1776–1809* (New York: Oxford University Press, 1963).
10. E. E. Schattschneider, *Party Government* (New York: Rinehart, 1942), p. 1.
11. White and Shea, *New Party Politics,* p. 45.
12. George H. Mayer, *The Republican Party, 1954–1964.* (New York: Oxford University Press, 1964), p. 26.
13. Jack Plan and Milton Greenbert, *The American Political Dictionary,* 10th ed. (Orlando, FL: Harcourt Brace, 1997), p. 7.
14. Theodore J. Lowi, "Toward a Responsible Three-Party System: Plan or Obituary?" in *The State of the Parties,* 3rd ed., ed. John C. Green and Daniel M. Shea (Lanham, MD: Rowman & Littlefield, 1999), pp. 171–189.
15. As noted on *The NewsHour with Jim Lehrer,* August 9, 2007. Accessed at http://www.pbs.org/newshour/bb/politics/july-dec07/primary_08-09.html on September 12, 2007.
16. Schattschneider, *Party Government,* p. 1.

CHAPTER 14

1. "Congratulations" [editorial], *Washington Post,* November 23, 2003, p. B6.
2. Harole Lasswell, *Politics: Who Gets What, When, and How* (New York: Smith, 1950).
3. For a well-known example, see Charles E. Lindblom and Edward J. Woodhouse, *The Policy-Making Process,* 3d ed. (Englewood Cliffs, NJ: Prentice Hall, 1993).
4. Deborah Stone, *Policy Paradox: The Art of Political Decision Making* (New York: Norton, 1997), p. 11.
5. Theodore J. Lowi, "American Business, Public Policy Case Studies, and Political Theory," *World Politics 16* (1965): 677–715.
6. Murray Edelman, *The Symbolic Uses of Politics* (Urbana: University of Illinois Press, 1967), ch. 2.
7. See Robert A. Dahl, *Who Governs? Democracy and Power in an American City* (New Haven, CT: Yale University Press, 1961).
8. See C. Wright Mills, *The Power Elite* (Oxford: Oxford University Press, 1956).
9. Roger W. Cobb and Charles D. Elder, *Participation in American Politics: The Dynamics of Agenda Building* (Baltimore: Johns Hopkins University Press, 1983), pp. 82–93.
10. For a fascinating discussion of how power is exercised by controlling the agenda, see Peter Bachrach and Morton S. Baratz, "Two Faces of Power," *American Political Science Review 56* (1962): 947–952.
11. Robert A. Caro, *Master of the Senate: The Years of Lyndon Johnson* (New York: Knopf, 2002), ch. 7.
12. Cobb and Elder, *Participation in American Politics,* p. 86.
13. Anthony Downs, "Up and Down with Ecology: The 'Issue-Attention Cycle,'" *Public Interest,* Summer 1972, pp. 38–50.
14. Michael D. Cohen, James G. March, and Johan P. Olsen, "A Garbage Can Model of Organizational Choice," *Administrative Science Quarterly 17* (1972): 1–25.
15. John W. Kingdon, *Agendas, Alternatives, and Public Policies* (New York: Harper & Row, 1984), pp. 129–130.
16. Ibid., ch. 8.
17. Glenn Hastedt, ed., *One World, Many Voices* (Englewood Cliffs, NJ: Prentice Hall, 1995), pp. 240–250, 288–300.
18. Peter Trubowitz, *Defining the National Interest* (Chicago: University of Chicago Press, 1998).
19. Miroslav Nincic, "Domestic Costs, the U.S. Public and the Isolationist Calculus," *International Studies Quarterly 41* (1997): 593–610; Bruce Jentleson, "The Pretty Prudent Public: Post-Vietnam American Opinion on the Use of Force," *International Studies Quarterly 36* (1990): 49–74.
20. John R. Hibbing and Elizabeth Theiss-Morse, *Congress as Public Enemy* (New York: Cambridge University Press, 1995).
21. For a through discussion of the incremental approach, see Charles E. Lindblom, "The Science of Muddling Through," *Public Administration Review 19* (1959): 79–88.

CREDITS

COVER: Copyright © Photographer's Choice Photography/Veer

CHAPTER 1: *2–3* Scott Olson/Getty Images; *6* UPI Photo/David Yee/Landov; *8* Joshua Roberts/Reuters/Landov; *12* (above) Barrie Fanton/Omni-Photo Communications, Inc.; (below) Dirck Halstead/Time Life Pictures/Getty Images; *13* (above) Stephen Ferry/Getty Images; (below) Michael Smith/Getty Images; *15* Kevin Dietsch/UPI/Landov; *18* (left) Carol T. Powers/The New York Times/Redux Pictures; (right) Carmel Zucker/The New York Times/Redux Pictures; *21* Joseph Sohm/Visions of America/Corbis; *22* Micah Walters/Reuters/Corbis; *23* H. Darr Beiser/USA Today

CHAPTER 2: *30–31* Bettmann/Corbis; *36* Courtesy of the Plymouth Hall Museum, Plymouth, MA; *39* Michael Nicholson/Corbis; *40* Bettmann/Corbis; *42* (above) The Granger Collection; (below) Craig Nelson/Cox Newspapers, Inc.; *45* The Granger Collection; *49* Bettmann/Corbis; *52* The Granger Collection; *54* (above) Joseph Sohm/Visions of America/Corbis; (below) Kenneth Garrett/National Geographic Image Collection; *59* The Granger Collection; *60* The Granger Collection; *62* Library of Congress

CHAPTER 3: *70–71* Corbis; *73* AP Images/Greg Gibson; *76* Architect of the Capitol; 79 Bettmann/Corbis (2); *80* AP Image; *81* Lewis Hine (American, 1874-1940), "A Carolina Spinner," 1908. Gelatin silver print, 4 3/4 x 7 in. Milwaukee Art Museum, Gift of the Sheldon M. Barnett Family. M1973.83; *82* Library of Congress; *87* Bettmann/Corbis; *92* Larry Downing/Reuters/Corbis

CHAPTER 4: *100–101* AP Images/J. Scott Applewhite; *103* Ben Curtis/Pool/Reuters/Corbis; *106* Mark Wilson/Getty Images (4); *107* (left to right) Matthew Cavanaugh/epa/Corbis; Mark Wilson/Getty Images; Paul J. Richards/AFP/Getty Images; Mark Wilson/Getty Images; Mark Wilson/Getty Images; *108* The Granger Collection; 111 John Marshall by Chester Harding (1792 1886), Oil on canvas, 1830. U.R. 106.1830. Collection of the Boston Athenaeum.; *118* Sharkpixs/Zuma Press; *119* Doug Mills/The New York Times/Redux Pictures; *122* Stephen Crowley/The New York Times/Redux Pictures; *128* Doug Mills/The New York Times/Redux Pictures; *130* Akhtar Soomro/The New York Times/Redux Pictures

CHAPTER 5: *138–139* AP Images/Missouri Department of Corrections; *140* North Wind Pictures Archives; *142* Bettmann/Corbis; *144* (left) NARA; (right) Bettmann/Corbis; *145* (above) David Leeson/Time Life Pictures/Getty Images; (below) Carol T. Powers/The New York Times/Getty Images; *146* (above) Scott Gries/Getty Images; (middle) Bettmann/Corbis; (below) Oleg Volk/Volk Studios; *147* John Nordell/The Christian Science Monitor/Getty Images, Inc.; *148* (above) William F. Campbell/Time Life Pictures/Getty Images; (below) Michael Stravato/The New York Times/Redux Pictures; *151* (left) Alex Wong/Getty Images; (right) Used by permission of Sentinel, an imprint of Penguin Group (USA) Inc.; *152* Bettmann/Corbis; *154* AP Images/David J. Phillip; *157* AP Images; *158* Scott Gries/Getty Images; *160* Oleg Volk/Volk Studio; *162* (left) AP Images/John Marshall Mantel; (right) AP Images/Susan Walsh; *164* AP Images/Don Ryan; *165* William F. Campbell/Time Life Pictures/Getty Images; *167* AP Images/Mark Foley; *168* Bettmann/Corbis; *170* (above) Chip Somodevilla/Getty Images; (below) Robert Kusel Photography, Inc.; *172* William Thomas Cain/Getty Images; *174* (left) Doug Mills/The New York Times Redux Pictures; (right) Bettmann/Corbis; *176* Karen Kasmauski/Corbis; *177* The Museum of the Confederacy Richmond, Virginia. Copy Photography by Katherine Wetzel.; *179* (left) Hulton Archive/Getty Images; (right) Flip Schulke/Corbis; *180* Bettmann/Corbis (2); *183* Bettmann/Corbis; *184* (above) Paul J. Richards/AFP/Getty Images; (below) Corbis; *190* Bettmann/Corbis; *191* MPI/Getty Images; *192* Bob Gomel/Time Life Pictures/Getty Images; *194* Bettmann/Corbis; *196* Monica Almeida/The New York Times/Redux Pictures; *198* Stephen Crowley/The New York Times/Redux Pictures

CHAPTER 6: *210-211* Matthew Cavanaugh/epa/Corbis; *213* (clockwise from top left) The Marblehead Historical Museum and Historical Society; Bettmann/Corbis; Bettmann/Corbis; AP Images/Kevin Rivoli; *214* AP Images/Pablo Martinez Monsivais; *217* AP Images/Seth Perlman; *221* Bob Daemmrich/Corbis; *229* Alex Wong/Getty Images; *230* Kevin Dietsch/UPI/Landov; *232* Strom Thurmond Photograph Collection, Special Collections, Clemson University Libraries, Clemson, South Carolina; *233* Mark Wilson/Getty Images; *237* (clockwise from top right) AFP/Getty Images; UPI/Newscom; AP Images/Dennis Cook; AP Images/Manuel Balce Ceneta; Alex Wong/Getty Images; Jim Watson/AFP/Getty Images; Roll Call Pix/Newscom; *238* Jonathan Ernst/Getty Images; *241* Bettmann/Corbis; *242* Adrees Latif/Reuters/Landov; *244* AP Images/Dennis Cook

CHAPTER 7: *254–255* Reuters/Corbis; *257* Library of Congress; *259* Bettmann/Corbis; *262* Keystone/Getty Images; *263* Hulton Archive/Getty Images; *264* (above) Alex Wong/Getty Images; (below) Pablo Martinez Monsivais/Getty Images; *265* Jim Young/Reuters/Landov; *266* AP Images; *268* AP Images/Lawrence Jackson; *270* AP Images/Ron Edmonds; *272* AFP/Getty Images; *273* (above) Attila Kisbenedek/epa/Corbis; (below) AP Images/Pfc. L. Paul Epley; *275* Reuters/Corbis; *276* AP Images; *277* AP Images/Jack Kightlinger; *278* AP Images/Kyodo

CHAPTER 8: *286–287* Joshua Lott/Bloomberg News/Landov; *288* Dan Levine/AFP/Getty Images; *289* TongRo/Beateworks/Corbis; *292* Bettmann/Corbis; *293* Cecil Stoughton/Bettmann/Corbis; *296* AP Images/Jakum Moser; *299* Doug Mills/The New York Times/Redux Pictures; *300* Mike Temchine/AFP/Getty Images; *301* Bill Ingalls/NASA/Getty Images; *302* Mario Tama/Getty Images; *306* Paul J. Richards/AFP/Getty Images; *309* Luke Frazza/AFP/Getty Images

CHAPTER 9: *320–321* Jason Laure/Woodfin Camp; *324* AP Images/Al Behrman; *328* Time Inc./TimeLife Pictures/Getty Images; *329* Chad Buchanan/Getty Images; *330* Dave Carpenter/Cartoon Stock; *332* Robyn Beck/AFP/Getty Images; *334* (above) AP Images/Jason DeCrow; (below) AP Images/C. Aluka Berry, The State; *343* Joseph Farris/Cartoon Stock

CHAPTER 10: *354–355* National Security Archive; *357* Bettmann/Corbis; *364* AP Images/Dana Edelson/NBCU Photo Bank; *366* Dorothea Lange/Bettmann/Corbis (2); *371* Mark Wilson/Getty Images; *374* (left) Bettmann/Corbis; (right) Paul Hosefros/The New York Times/Redux Pictures; *377* AP Images/Mary Ann Chastain

CHAPTER 11: *390–391* Rock the Vote; *392* Bettmann/Corbis; *393* Bettmann/Corbis; *396* Brandon Thibodeaux/Dallas Morning News/Corbis; *403* Bob Parent/Hulton Archive/Getty Images; *405* Carol T. Powers/The New York Times/Redux Pictures; *406* (above) © 2006 Mike Luckovich. All rights reserved. Used with the permission of Mike Luckovich and Creators Syndicate.; (below) Tim Mosenfelder/ImageDirect/Getty Images; *408* David Young-Wolff/PhotoEdit Inc.; *409* AP Images/LM Otero; *410* AP Images/Alex Brandon; *412* Larry Downing/Reuters/Corbis

CHAPTER 12: *424–425* AP Images/Elaine Thompson; *426* The Art Archive/Corbis; *427* The Granger Collection; *428* Andrew Parsons/AFP/Getty Images; *429* Mark Wilson/Getty Images; *430* Richard Perry/The New York Times/Redux Pictures; *433* Sam VarnHagen/Ford Motor HO/Reuters/Landov; *436* AP Images; *437* Flip Schulke/Bettmann/Corbis; *441* Blake Sell/Corbis; *443* AP Images; *446* (left) Joseph Farris/Cartoon

Stock; (right) Chip Somodevilla/Getty Images; *449* AP Images/Laura Schmitt/The Gazette; *452* AP Images/Alexa Welch Edlund/Richmond Times Dispatch; *453* AP Images/Paul Sancya; *455* AP Images/Mark Duncan; *459* Keith Bedford/Bloomberg News/Landov;

CHAPTER 13: *468–469* AP Images/Alan Diaz; *471* Vincent Laforet/The New York Times/Redux Pictures; *472* (left) Dennis Brack/Landov; (right) Roger L. Wollenberg/Landov; *475* AP Images/Pablo Martinez Monsivais; *476* Erik Freeland/Corbis; *478* AP Images/Alex Brandon; *482* Peter Thompson/The New York Times/Redux Pictures; *486* Picture History/Newscom; *487* Lyndon Baines Johnson Library Collection; *489* James Glen/Corbis; *494* Bettmann/Corbis; *495* AP Images/Chris Carlson; *496* Journal Sentinel/Jeffrey Phelps

CHAPTER 14: *506–607* William Manning/Corbis; *510* Robert Sullivan/AFP/Getty Images; *513* Bettmann/Corbis; *518* Justin Sullivan/Getty Images; *520* Win McNamee/Getty Images; *521* Chip Somodevilla/Getty Images; *522* Mark Wilson/Getty Images; *524* Brooks Kraft/Corbis; *525* Howard Burditt/Reuters/Corbis; *527* Michael Kamber/The New York Times/Redux Pictures; *528* Chuck Kennedy/MCT/Landov

INDEX

Q

R